Federal Rules of Evidence at a Glance

FOURTH EDITION

LAW OF EVIDENCE FOR CRIMINAL JUSTICE PROFESSIONALS

IRVING J. KLEIN, B.S. in S.S., J.D.

Professor Emeritus of Law and Police Science
John Jay College of Criminal Justice
The City University of New York

West / Wadsworth

I(T)P®an International Thomson Publishing Company

Belmont, CA • Albany, NY • Bonn • Boston • Cincinnati • Detroit • Johannesburg
London • Los Angeles • Madrid • Melbourne • Mexico City • Minneapolis / St. Paul
New York • Paris • Singapore • Tokyo • Toronto • Washington

Library of Congress Cataloging-in-Publication Data

Klein, Irving J.
    Law of evidence for criminal justice professionals / Irving J. Klein. — 4th ed.
        p.   cm.
    Includes index.
    ISBN 0-314-20077-0 (alk. paper)
        1. Evidence, Criminal—United States.   2. Evidence (Law)—United States.   I. Title.
KF9660.K55   1997
345.73'.6—dc20
[347.3056]   96-26937

I dedicate this book to my dear wife and confidante,
Dr. Marta Arias Klein, for her forbearance, encouragement, and wise counsel
during the many days and hours that I spent away from her company
while gathering information and writing this work.

PREFACE

The third edition of *Law of Evidence for Criminal Justice Professionals* was published in 1989. The first two editions of this work were titled *Law of Evidence for Police*. As the work was enlarged to include more topics and the professionalism of the police function became more recognized, it was decided that the contents of the book were well suited for the use of other law enforcement personnel in addition to police officers. Hence, the title was changed to indicate inclusion of topics of interest to all criminal justice professionals. In its present form, it is very well suited as a classroom text, as well as a reference source when a problem arises as to the admissibility of evidence in a trial or as to the procedural aspects of police activity.

The previous edition omitted the exclusionary rules regarding the admissibility of evidence based on constitutional grounds. This was intentionally done because this area of law has been changing so rapidly that it was decided to relegate this material to another book and another course of study concerned exclusively to this topic. However, because of the requests of several professors, the publisher and I have decided to include a chapter dealing with an overview of this subject.

We have always been very interested in obtaining suggestions from professors who teach this subject and use this book. Many professors and readers have cooperated by giving us ideas on how they would like the book improved. We are thankful to them because we are constantly searching for excellence and this helps us reach as close as we can to perfection.

To comply with their suggestions, this book contains the following additions:

1. Each topic is assigned a dual-number designation. The first number is the chapter number, and the second number is the sequential topic number within that chapter. Thus topic 22 of Chapter 2 is indicated as §2.22.
2. An overview of the constitutional basis for excluded evidence is provided in Chapter 19.
3. A glossary is included so that students who are not familiar with some legal words used in the text portion or in the court decisions will have the definitions of these words available.
4. A reasonable number of the edited cases that were included in the third edition have been retained in the fourth edition. However, some have been deleted to make room for recent cases. The overall number of edited cases is substantially the same as in the prior edition. Some professors may prefer not to cover all of the cases because of time limitations. On the other hand, others find that they cover these cases more rapidly in their classes and like to cover all of them.
5. An introduction to each of the edited cases will help students observe relevant information in the decision that relates to the subject studied in that chapter.

6. In Chapter 3, a difficult factual pattern in one of the edited cases is worked out in the introduction to acquaint students with a methodology that I have used successfully many times when the facts of the decision are difficult to understand.
7. The Federal Rules of Evidence have been updated.
8. The index of topics is now keyed to topic numbers instead of page numbers.
9. The table of contents is also keyed to topic numbers.
10. A series of short questions has been added at the end of each chapter, taken from material included in that chapter.
11. A separate appendix titled "Answers to Practice Questions" is included.
12. A table of contents titled "Federal Rules of Evidence at a Glance" appears on the endpapers of this book. This has been adopted from *Courtroom Handbook on Federal Evidence 1995*, by Steven Goode and Olin Guy Wellborn III, © West Publishing Company, with permission of West Publishing Company.
13. A section in Chapter 1 gives instructions to students on how to find the law on a specific topic of interest.
14. Interested students can use the cross-reference source material at the end of Chapter 3 through 19 for future study.
15. In addition to the above, discussions now include
    (a) eye-witness identification—reliability
    (b) the insanity defense
    (c) presumptions—court records
    (d) privilege—informant, government sources
    (e) executive privilege
    (f) the neutron activation test
    (g) the chain of custody of evidence
    (h) the preservation of the stability of evidence
    (i) reasons for the use of legalese language
    (j) the latest information on DNA reliability and laboratory standards

As we all know, English language usage has changed in that the use of the word "he" to indicate both "he and she" is no longer favored. While I believe the females of our society are entitled to a specific reference to their gender, it was not the practice of judges to refer to both genders in decisions prior to the early 1980s. Some judges, to this day, refuse to use the "he or she" designation. I first used the designation s/he in a book that I wrote dealing with constitutional law in 1986, and, for a while, I was severely criticized by some professors for doing this. We know that change comes about very slowly in the discipline of law.

In this book, you will find that when I am writing about a principle of law or a situation, I invariably refer to a person or to he or she. However, when I am referring to what a judge has written, whether it be a quotation or a summary, I use the judge's method of expression. This is also true when a judge uses the word "which" instead of "that." I believe that historically I should continue with the judge's language to keep the contents of the book authentic.

In publishing a book of this nature, one must always remember that it is not the sole work of the author. Many people behind the scenes support the author and are indispensable to the completion of the project. I am deeply indebted to many persons, some of whom are unknown to me. Those I know who deserve mention are my wife, Dr. Marta A. Klein, whose encouragement and forbearance during the many hours that I spent writing this offering were greatly appreciated; and my secretary, Maria L. Marin, B.A., who patiently typed and retyped, as well as edited, material, without complaint, until we were both satisfied with the results. Special thanks are extended to professors who have been very loyal to me in using my books in their classes. There are too many to mention, and if I omitted someone's name, he or she would have a justifiable complaint. I therefore thank each and every one of them collectively.

However, I feel it necessary to particularly thank the following persons who have identified themselves and have given me suggestions for the improvement of books that I have written: Professors T. Kenneth Moran, Henry Morse, Christopher Morse, and Nilsa Santiago, all of John Jay College of Criminal Justice in New York City; Professor Michael R. Klein of Nassau Community College in Garden City, New York; President Jay Sexter of Mercy College in Dobbs Ferry, New York; Professor William Osborne of Mountain Empire Community College in Big Stone Gap, Virginia; and Professor Brian Felmet of St. Leo College in St. Leo, Florida, and Ft. McPhearson, Georgia.

I must also thank the people at West Educational Publishing and West Publishing Corp., including, but not limited to, Joan Gill, editor; Angela Barnhart, editorial assistant; and Lisa R. Gunderman, assistant production editor; Sheralyn Goldbecker for her excellent copyediting; Elaine Fleming of Lachina Publishing Services; Sabre Horne, Editor of Wadsworth Publishing Company; and others whose names are not known to me who created the printed pages—the typists, the typesetters, the printers, the binders, the shipping clerks, the office staff, and the truckers.

As always, the publisher and I welcome comments from professors and/or readers of the book. These comments may be sent to me as follows:

Professor Emeritus Irving J. Klein
John Jay College of Criminal Justice, C.U.N.Y.
Law, Police Science, and Criminal Justice
Administration Department—4th Floor
899 10th Avenue
New York, NY 10019

Irving J. Klein
Miami, FL
May 31, 1996

Summary of Contents

CONTENTS

TABLE OF EDITED DECISIONS

CHAPTER 1

Introduction

§ 1.1 EVOLUTION OF EVIDENCE LAW

The discipline now known as dispute resolution is an outgrowth of conflicts that have developed between members of the human race. In the early history of this discipline, many cultures developed various methods to resolve disputes between individuals and also between tribes and nations. This resolution usually involved the use of violence. The strongest person, the strongest tribe, or the strongest nation would win the dispute regardless of the equity of the victor's assertion.

Later, the religions that developed adopted certain codes of ethics, like the Judeo-Christian religions' Ten Commandments. Eventually, codes of laws were developed around this basic concept. Other religions added affirmative and negative commandments. I have read that even Neolithic people had conflicts among themselves that were resolved the same way as we resolve problems today. I refer you to an article by Gerhard O.W. Mueller and Freda Adler, entitled "The Emergence of Criminal Justice: Tracing the Route to Neolithic Times,"[1] where the authors present a comprehensive history of early criminal justice, giving their own and other authorities for their findings.

In more modern times, the member of a community who was usually the roughest of the ruffians became the chief or king. He or she (yes, there are reports that females assumed this status, sometimes disguised as men) would provide a set of laws. However, in the beginning, the chief could do no wrong and was above these laws. Later, the powers of many monarchs were limited, and still later republics and democracies developed.

The various nations adopted codes of laws, and eventually, they fashioned trial procedures, either codified in statutes or established by the common law. Through evolution, we have arrived at modern procedures for the adjudication of disputes and the determination of the guilt or innocence of a person accused of an offense against society.

For example, criminal justice professionals and others frequently believe that grave injustices have been done when they are not permitted to testify to certain parts of the facts of a given situation because the defense attorney has objected to the introduction of such evidence and the objection is sustained by the judge.

When a judge sustains an objection by opposing counsel, the evidence is not permitted into the record of the case, and the trier of the facts, be it the judge or the jury, depending on the nature of the case, does not consider this testimony in the deliberation of the issue.

---

[1] Joan McCord and John H. Laub (eds.), *Contemporary Masters in Criminology* (New York: Plenum Press, 1995), pp. 59–79. Referred to by permission of Doctors Gerhard O. W. Mueller and Freda Adler, the copyright holders.

However, a ruling by a judge excluding evidence from the trial record may be the basis of a reversal when the case is heard on appeal. In order to make the point appealable, the trial counsel is required, in most instances, to voice his or her exception to the judge's ruling on the record. Some jurisdictions have taken the position that when a judge overrules an objection, there is no further necessity for the objecting counsel to record the exception on the record in order to have the issue considered on appeal.

Another method to preserve alleged error in the record for purposes of appeal is by a device known as an "offer of proof." If the judge in a jury trial excludes, for example, certain witness testimony, the trial counsel will ask for a side bar conference to make an offer of proof. The judge should then request counsel for all sides and the court stenographer to approach the bench, and in a tone of voice not audible to the jury, the attorney will place on the record the offer of proof by indicating that his or her purpose in asking the question of the witness is to show the court and jury some facet of the case that he or she believes to be material to the litigated issues and admissible in evidence pursuant to some rule of law. The judge at that time may reverse the previous ruling or, in the alternative, either indicate the reasons for the ruling or stand by the previous ruling without comment. In any case, the jury is never privy to the conversations taking place at the side bar conference. It is, however, advised before the commencement of the trial that such conferences may take place and that the rules of evidence developed over the centuries as a means of ascertaining truth dictate that such conferences be conducted out of the hearing of the jury.

An incorrect ruling from the bench may be revised by an appellate court if there is a plain error that affects a substantial right. Even though the error was not brought to the attention of the court, the appellate court may reverse on its own discovery of the error. See Federal Rule of Evidence 102.

With the establishment of a jury system, England formulated a complete set of rules for determining the admissibility of evidence. This law of evidence was not developed overnight; it was based on trial and experience.

The United States adopted the rules of evidence of the English courts, but over the years, the rules in the United States courts and English courts have been changed by the courts and legislative bodies. Today the rules of evidence are more strict in the United States than in England.

The American rules of evidence vary from one state to another but are substantially the same in all states. Since the passage of the Federal Rules of Evidence, effective July 1, 1975, there has been a trend toward even greater uniformity.

The law of evidence is an ever-changing law. As our society and government seek better methods for determining guilt or innocence, so, too, will our rules of evidence change to protect the weak from the strong and the strong from the weak.

The rules of evidence are not perfect and probably never will be, as Justice Sutherland stated in Funk v. United States, 290 U.S. 371, 381, 54 S.Ct. 212, 78 L.Ed. 369, 93 A.L.R. 1136 (1933). "The fundamental basis upon which all rules of evidence must rest—if they are to rest upon reason—is their adaptation to the successful development of the truth. And since experience is of all teachers the most dependable, and since experience also is a continuous process, it follows that a rule of evidence at one time thought necessary to the ascertainment of the truth should yield to the experience of a succeeding generation whenever that experience has clearly demonstrated the fallacy or unwisdom of the old rule."

The study of law of evidence is fascinating if you keep in mind that it is similar to a puzzle or a game. Just as you try one method or another to reach a desired goal in a puzzle, so, too, in the law of evidence, the goal an attorney strives to reach is to have the evidence admitted into the record of the case. There may be many roadblocks but often if the road to admissibility is blocked by one obstruction, the possibility exists that by clever maneuvering, the obstruction may be circumvented and the evidence is admitted.

§ 1.2 "LEGALESE LANGUAGE"

Some words used in this book may not be initially familiar to you. If you obtain a legal dictionary and consult it as soon as an unfamiliar word or phrase is used, you will have no difficulty understanding the thought expressed. In a short time, you will find that you have little need for the legal dictionary. For the convenience of readers who have no legal dictionary available, a glossary of legal terms has been included in this book. You should refer to this glossary whenever you encounter unfamiliar words.

Students have frequently questioned why lawyers use words not ordinarily used in conversation in the community. I usually reply by saying that in many cases the law has to be certain as to the meaning of words; if it were otherwise, lawmakers or contracting people, for example, may arrive at different conclusions as to what the meaning of a sentence is. This would cause great confusion in the interpretation of agreements, or the prohibitions of a penal statute, or the statutes requiring compliance with a particular code of conduct, or many other similar writings. For that reason, it is necessary in written law to be as precise as possible. This is commonly referred to as "legalese language." It is jargon.

§ 1.3 FINDING THE LAW

Finding the law is known as legal research. There are courses given in law school that devote a full semester's study to legal research. While several professors have requested that I include information in this book about how a student can find a legal point applicable to a given situation, it would be impractical for me to include an extensive discourse on legal research. However, I believe I can help students in a peripheral way to find the law that is applicable in the states that they are interested in. The procedure is as follows:

1. Search the index of this book for the topics that you are interested in.
2. Turn to the page in this book where the topic is covered.
3. Seek out a case citation that includes a West Publishing Corp. reporter. This is usually the second reference after the case title: e.g., People v. Picciotti, 4 N.Y.2d 340, 175 N.Y.S.2d 32, 151 N.E.2d 191 (1958). Here, the citation indicates that West Publishing Corp. published this decision in volume 175 of the New York Supplement, 2d Series, at page 32.
4. Visit a legal library, usually found in the courthouse of the county seat, or a law school library, or a well-stocked college or university library, and find the New York Supplement, 2d Series. Then find volume 175 and turn to page 32.

On that page, you will find a description of the facts, the legal history of what happened to the case in the lower court, and a synopsis of the court's decision.

Beneath this material, you will find, in boldface type, a number and a category. In this case, it reads **1. Criminal law** ⚷ **997.(9).** This is a reference to the West Key Number classification system.

After this, you will find a headnote, which is a description of something mentioned in the decision.

After this, you will find three other Key Numbers and descriptions of items that are mentioned in the decision.

5. If you find a topic that you are interested in, and its West Key Number, you can then look for West's most recent state digest, or regional digest, covering the state you are interested in. Select the volume where criminal law is indicated on the spine, and use the West Key Number to locate the court cases on the topic you are researching.

6. Always remember to look at the pocket part inside the back cover of this book. It may include the latest cases and changed West Key Numbers.

7. When you find the citation of a case that interests you, read the full case in the state or regional reporter.

8. When you have completed this work and taken notes on the case, it is best to consult the appropriate volumes of Shepard's Citations to learn if the decision has been reversed or followed in later cases. The instructions on how to use these citations are included in the beginning of each volume. Be sure to consult all the volumes in which the case is cited, and especially the latest volumes available in order to get the most recent law on the subject.

As I indicated when I began this topic, the foregoing is a peripheral legal research method. I have not covered Westlaw, which is a very comprehensive and up-to-the-minute computer database, nor have I covered the works of other publishers that may be consulted.

Another facet of legal research involves statutory law. In order to determine statutory law in the area of criminal justice, you must consult the statutes enacted by legislative bodies. These include the definitions of crimes, the sanctions applied to each crime or offense, the limitation of time during which the perpetrator is liable for arrest, the procedures used to bring this person to justice, etc.

You may obtain this information by consulting the state statutes, which are available in many public libraries. When consulting these books, seek out volumes with such titles as Penal Law, Criminal Procedural Law, or Crimes in the statutes of each state. There is no uniformity with regard to these titles in the statutes of each state.

In any event, when you take the volume off the shelf, consult the index, usually in the back of the volume. Generally, there is a table of contents in the front of the volume, which you may also consult. Always be sure to look in the pocket part, if any, inside the back cover of the book to find the most recent law.

In federal law, Title 18 of the United States Code contains many, but not all, federal criminal statutes.

For both state and federal statutes, it is a good practice to consult the annotated volumes. This means that after the statute is presented, the publisher of that book provides references to court decisions that have interpreted that section of the law.

§ 1.4 COMMON LAW AND STATUTORY LAW

"The law of evidence is based on both common law and statutory law. The common law concept is Anglo-Saxon in origin. It is distinguished from the Roman law, the modern civil law, the canon law, and other systems. The common law is that body of law and juristic theory which was originated, developed, and formulated and is administered in England, and has obtained among most of the states and peoples of Anglo-Saxon stock." Lux v. Haggin, 69 Cal. 255, 10 P. 674 (1886).

As I have previously explained, in the preceding paragraph I have expressed a definition of common law, and immediately after the definition, the name of a case appears with numbers and abbreviations after it. This is known in law to be a citation. Therefore, Lux v. Haggin, 69 Cal. 255, 10 P. 674 (1886), means that the statement immediately preceding the citation was derived from a decision of the court in the case of Lux against Haggin and the full decision may be read by looking at volume 69 of the California Reports beginning on page 255; it may also be found in volume 10 of the Pacific Reporter beginning on page 674. In New York State, many students have difficulty in their first encounter with the abbreviation for New York Supplement, which is cited as N.Y.S. Frequently, a reciting student will incorrectly read this as New York State. For example, the case often cited as a good illustration of the manner in which incompetent evidence should be objected to is Bell v. Bumstead, 60 Hun. 580, 14 N.Y.S. 697 (1891). This citation means that the decision of the case of Bell v. Bumstead may be found in volume 14, New York Supplement, page 697; it may also be found in volume 60, Hun's New York Reports, page 580.

Sometimes the citation indicates that a second series has been published beginning with volume number 1 and continuing: e.g., 10 N.Y.S.2d 457. In addition to the above, you may find the following as a citation: Michelson v. United States, 335 U.S. 469, 69 S.Ct. 213, 93 L.Ed. 168 (1948). This means that the case may be read in volume 335 of the United States Reports on page 469; in volume 69, Supreme Court Reporter, page 213; and in volume 93, United States Supreme Court Reports, Lawyers' Edition, page 168.

A further refinement may sometimes be found in the following citation, wherein proper evidence is described as something capable of being weighted in scales of reason and compared and estimated with other matter of the probative sort: Pa.—Neely v. Provident Life & Accident Ins. Co. of Chattanooga, Tenn., 322 Pa. 417, 185 A. 784, 788 (1936).

You now can see that the case may be read in volume 322 of the Pennsylvania State Reports on page 417. You may also find it in volume 185 of the Atlantic Reporter, wherein the case begins on page 784, but the exact phrase quoted may be seen on page 788.

The number encased in the half-circle brackets, thus (1936), indicates the year the case was decided.

In law, all of us, as professionals, want to be letter-perfect in what we write. But we are not immune to errors. If we find an error, we usually try to correct it. In reading a judge's decision, you may find that critical words have been omitted. If it is obvious what the judge had in mind, the reporter of the decision will insert what is generally believed to be the proper word. This is done by surrounding the new word with cornered brackets thus: [word]. The reader knows that this word was not included by the judge, but was inserted by the reporter so that the judge's decision is clear.

§ 1.5 COMMON LAW

A further examination of the theory of common law becomes necessary in order for the student to have a knowledge of the fundamental concepts of the law of evidence. Common law, then, is a body of law built up over centuries by the decisions of learned judges in Anglo-Saxon and American courts. The process is very much like building a house, and each succeeding judicial decision may be compared to the foundation of the building. It is seldom that a dispute arising between parties in one case is exactly the same as a dispute arising between other parties at a different time and place. However, points of similarity often may be seen, and the judge will rely on these points of similarity in coming to a judicial decision.

Inasmuch as there are seldom two cases that have the same factual pattern, the decisions are constantly changing. In aid of the changing decisions are the change in the personnel of the judiciary and the change in their thinking, their mores, and their customs. Figure 1 will help you to understand the concept of gradual change in our law, in which the factual pattern of each case that comes before the court is slightly different and the case is said in law "not to stand on all fours with the previous case." Our law is capable of changing through ordinary legal means in a slow, evolutionary manner.

The basic foundation of the law of evidence in the United States is the common law, based on court decisions. This is described by the Latin phrase "stare decisis," which means to abide by, or adhere to, decided cases. It is further defined as the policy of courts to stand by precedent and not to disturb a settled point. Ill.— Neff v. George, 364 Ill. 306, 4 N.E.2d 388, 390, 391 (1936).

Mention has been made of the connection of statutory law to the law of evidence, but statutory law has not been explained.

§ 1.6 STATUTORY LAW

Statutory law is the law that has been reduced to writing and has been passed by the legislative branch of the government and acceded to in one form or another by the executive branch of the government. Another way of describing it is as an act of the legislature declaring, commanding, or prohibiting something; a particular law enacted and established by the will of the legislative branch of government;

Figure 1
The Changing Law

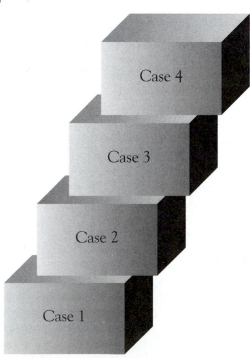

the written will of the legislature, solemnly expressed according to the forms necessary to make it the law of the state. Federal Trust Co. v. East Hartford Fire Dist., 283 Fed. 95, 98 (2d Cir. 1922). In the case of federal law, any action that is legislative in character must be performed by passage in both houses and presentment to the President. EEOC v. Ingersoll Johnson Steel Co., 583 F.Supp. 983 (S.D.Ind. 1984). You can therefore understand that a faster way to change the law is by statutory enactment rather than by the slower process of stare decisis.

Accordingly, legislatures have often taken this fiat and changed the rules of evidence when, in their opinion, such change was necessary.

The basic concept of the rules of evidence is that they are established in aid of the search for the truth. They are the aggregate of rules and principles that regulate the admissibility, relevancy, weight, and sufficiency of evidence in legal proceedings.

§ 1.7   STATE RULES OF EVIDENCE

The Tenth Amendment to the United States Constitution, commonly referred to as the reserved powers amendment, provided that the powers not delegated to the United States by the Constitution or prohibited by it to the states are reserved to the states respectively, or to the people. The United States government being a government of delegated powers, and no delegation having been made in the Constitution as to the police powers governing the health, welfare, and morals of the people, the states were free to set up their own courts and their own judicial and evidentiary procedures.

The federal government has not interfered with the administration of the state court system except when a substantial right of a citizen of the United States has been interfered with. Mapp v. Ohio, 367 U.S. 643, 81 S.Ct. 1684, 6 L.Ed.2d 1081 (1961). Accordingly, each state may have its own rules of evidence, but the rules tend to be substantially the same in each state that bases its rules on the common law.

§ 1.8   THE FEDERAL RULES OF EVIDENCE

The law of evidence in many state jurisdictions is based on both common law and statutory law. The trend in recent years has been toward the statutory codification of the rules of evidence, leading to a hopeful uniformity in the courts of the United States. Before July 1, 1975, a federal court sitting in California might have been operating under a different rule of evidence from the same type of court sitting in North Carolina. Up to that time, each federal court would operate under the rules of evidence in effect in the state in which the court convened. This led to unequal justice in many cases and some confusion, notwithstanding the fact that the basic concepts of the law of evidence applied throughout the United States were substantially the same.

To avoid this possible confusion, a thirteen-year study was made, beginning in 1961, by distinguished jurists, Congress, lawyers, and others interested in the administration of justice in federal courts.[2]

Unlike most legislation, this was a joint effort by Congress and the United States Supreme Court. During March 1969, the Judicial Conference printed and

---

[2] U.S. Congress. House. Federal Rules of Evidence. Report No. 93–1277 to accompany H.R. 5463, 93rd Cong., 2nd Sess., 1974.

widely circulated a preliminary draft of a proposed Federal Rules of Evidence, accompanied by notes. Revisions were made and a final draft forwarded to the Supreme Court in October 1971. In 1972, the Supreme Court promulgated the Federal Rules of Evidence pursuant to various enabling acts in the United States Code. These rules became P.L. 93–12, enacted by Congress in 1974 to become effective July 1, 1975. The rules govern proceedings in the courts of the United States and before United States bankruptcy judges and United States magistrates to the extent, and with the exceptions, stated in Rule 1101 of the Federal Rules of Evidence. For a more detailed explanation, refer to Rule 1101 in the Appendix.

As with most statutory enactments, the courts have construed the meaning and applicability of many of the sections in the Federal Rules of Evidence. Furthermore, amendments were made in 1975, 1978, 1982, and 1984. The basic rules appear in the Appendix and were current at the time of publication. For a comprehensive and up-to-date version of the Federal Rules of Evidence, along with many court decisions construing the respective rules, the reader should refer to Title 28 of the United States Code Annotated, later indicated as U.S.C.A. This two-volume, comprehensive treatment of the Federal Rules of Evidence is brought up to date annually.

One by one the states are adopting codified rules of evidence, primarily based on the Federal Rules of Evidence. It is anticipated that changes will be made from time to time in accordance with the principle of law expounded by Justice Sutherland in Funk v. United States, 290 U.S. 371, 54 S.Ct. 212, 78 L.Ed. 369 (1933). When writing of the rules of evidence, he indicated: "Those rules being founded in reason, one of the oldest maxims is, that where the reason of the rule ceased the rule also ceased."

§ 1.9 DEFINITIONS

In order for a student of the law of evidence to communicate with others on the rules of evidence, he or she must learn a new language. The language is based on the English language, but the vocabulary is enlarged, and some words may have several meanings, depending on the way they are used. For example, the word "issue," which you will frequently see in this book, has several meanings, depending on the context in which it is used. It may mean the children of a man and woman. They may be referred to in the law as the issue of Mary and John. On the other hand, if we say that the issue on trial is whether a defendant entered a premises to commit a crime therein or to get shelter from inclement weather, the word "issue" here is used to indicate a disagreement between two versions of what occurred. Another application of the word "issue" is when there is a disagreement between litigants as to the meaning of a statute or a court decision.

In the law of evidence, the word "issue" means a single certain and material point, deduced by the pleadings of the parties, which is affirmed on the one side and denied on the other. Pa.—Whitney v. Borough of Jersey Shore, 266 Pa. 537, 109 A. 767,769 (1920).

If there was a dispute between you and a contractor of building siding with respect to the square footage of aluminum siding that he installed on your home, resulting in a court action, a witness who might be called to testify as to the square footage of your plot of land would not be testifying relating to facts in issue between you and the contractor. Therefore, all testimony relating to the square footage of your plot of land is incompetent because it is immaterial and irrelevant to the issue between you and the contractor (i.e., the square footage of the outside of your home covered with aluminum siding). The word "evidence" has been defined to include all the means by which any alleged matter of fact, the truth of which is submitted to investigation, is established or disproved. N.Y.—Dibble v. Dimick, 143 N.Y. 549, 38 N.E. 724, 725 (1894).

§ 1.10 ADMISSIBLE EVIDENCE

It is the goal of an attorney to get evidence favorable to the party he or she is representing admitted into the trial record within the rules of the law of evidence. On the other hand, it is the goal of the opposing attorney, representing the party against whom this evidence would be damaging, to prevent its admission into the trial record, also within the rules of the law of evidence. All evidence, to be admissible, must withstand certain tests. If these tests are passed, then the evidence is admissible.

There are two basic concepts in the common law of evidence that were enunciated by Thayer in his Preliminary Treatise on Evidence (1898). He wrote

1. that nothing is to be received which is not logically probative of some matter requiring to be proved; and
2. that everything which is thus probative should come in, unless a clear ground of policy or law excludes it.

To explain this another way, one might say

1. that no evidence is admissible unless it is logically relevant and
2. that all logically relevant evidence is admissible unless it is barred by an exclusionary rule.

Another way to describe admissible evidence is to consider all evidence as liquid. This liquid is to pass through a funnel (see Figure 2). At the top of the funnel, there is an opening through which we pour the liquid evidence. In the funnel are obstacles that prevent the evidence from going to the bottom of the funnel. If the evidence is not filtered out by the obstacles, then it goes to the bottom and is admissible.

The first and foremost obstacle is relevancy. If the evidence is not relevant, or is irrelevant, as it is sometimes called, then the evidence will not be admitted.

To understand the concept of relevancy I return to the issue of the amount of aluminum siding needed to cover the walls of your home. If the witness were to testify as to the square footage of your plot of land, it would not be relevant to what we are looking for. We are looking for the size of the area that was covered by aluminum siding, not the size of the plot.

Other obstacles in the funnel are discussed in later chapters. To mention just a few that are indicated in Figure 2, they are

1. immaterial and irrelevant evidence,
2. opinion evidence by lay witness,
3. dying declaration improperly given,
4. hearsay statement—not subject to exception,
5. self-serving declaration,
6. character evidence improperly solicited,
7. privileged communications,
8. self-incriminatory statements,
9. best evidence rule,
10. parol evidence rule,
11. unconstitutionally obtained evidence.

Figure 2
The Funnel of Admissibility

Evidence based on improper search –
Parol evidence –
Unconstitutionally obtained evidence –
Not best evidence –
Self-serving declaration –

– Self-incriminatory statement
– Immaterial evidence
– Irrelevant evidence
– Opinion by layman
– Hearsay not subject to exception
– Privileged communication
– Dying declaration improperly given
– Character evidence improperly solicited

§ 1.11   EXCLUSIONARY RULES

As discussed earlier in this chapter, certain rules of evidence have been developed over the centuries to ferret out the truth. Specific types of testimony have been found to be less reliable than others. Thus, rules were developed by court decision and by statute to exclude those types of testimony where experience has shown that untruths may be testified to, even if there is no motive or intent on the part of the witness to testify falsely. These types of evidence are then kept out of the record and are not to be considered by the triers of the facts in their deliberations.

There are other reasons why evidence may be excluded from the record. For example, it may confuse the jury; cause undue surprise; be unduly prejudicial; unduly prolong the trial; be remote, uncertain, conjectural, or speculative; or be in violation of constitutional safeguards of the Fourth, Fifth, or Sixth Amendment to the United States Constitution, as interpreted by the Supreme Court of the United States. Other reasons will be developed later in the book. Therefore, we say that a body of evidence rules has evolved that excludes certain types of testimony because they are subject to an exclusionary rule and are not admissible. Sometimes we refer to these types of testimony as inadmissible. I will discuss each of the exclusionary rules referred to in much greater detail in subsequent chapters.

§ 1.12   EVIDENCE ADMISSIBLE FOR A PARTICULAR PURPOSE ONLY

Some evidence may be admissible for a particular purpose only and not for any other purpose. Evidence may be admitted merely to show that a particular statement was made, without regard for the truth of the statement; for instance, in a will probate contest in which the issue is the testamentary capacity of a testator, a witness may be permitted to testify that the testator had said to the witness, "Did you know that I abdicated the throne of England so that I could marry?"

This, from a person who never set foot in England and who never was offered the job, is admissible to show the state of mind of the testator.

§ 1.13   FUNCTION OF JUDGE AND JURY

The parties to a court action are called the litigants. Their respective attorneys are characterized as adversaries. The judge is referred to as the court. If more than one judge is sitting at a trial, one judge is designated as the presiding judge, and the other judge or judges are called associate judges. Each jurisdiction designates its judge as either a judge or a justice. Therefore, the judge of a United States Circuit Court is designated as a judge, whereas a justice of the United States Supreme Court is designated as a justice. Whether the person conducting the trial is given the title judge or justice, his or her function remains the same: to conduct an impartial trial adhering to the law of evidence and the rules of the court, to rule on the admissibility of evidence, and to decide issues of law.

Sometimes the presiding judge or justice is given the authority by the litigants to decide both questions of law and questions of fact. This occurs when the parties waive a jury trial. In effect, they are saying to the judge that they will rely on his or her decision with respect to the facts as well as the law of this case. If either litigant demands a jury trial, he or she is entitled to it in most jurisdictions in both criminal and civil trials. The jury determines questions of fact only and applies the law as explained to it by the judge. An illustration of this concept follows.

"A" is arrested and tried for the offense of burglary. The facts are that "A" was an alcoholic and was intoxicated on the date of the alleged offense. In order to get out of the inclement weather, he entered the premises of a cleaning store whose proprietor had closed at the end of the day and had mistakenly left the front door ajar. "A," seeing this, entered the premises and promptly fell asleep. "O," the officer on foot patrol in the area, made his rounds and tried doors on his post. When he arrived at the cleaning store, he found the door opened and entered the store in the company of a fellow officer. Both officers came upon "A," who was found asleep on the pressing table of the store. "A" was arrested and charged with burglary. The prosecution contended that "A" had entered the premises with intent to steal clothing but upon seeing the two officers acted as if asleep. If this statement of the facts is true, "A" would be chargeable with a higher degree of crime than the one he contends he is guilty of (trespass). The jury hears the evidence presented by both sides and then comes to a conclusion as to what the facts of this incident are. If the jury finds that "A" did not enter the premises with intent to steal, the judge will then apply the law of the crime of trespass in rendering the sentence.

§ 1.14   EVIDENCE—DEFINITION

Before discussing the types of evidence, it is best that we know what evidence is. It has been defined as any species of proof, or probative matter, legally presented at the trial of an issue, by the act of the parties through the medium of witnesses, records, documents, concrete objects, etc., for the purpose of inducing belief in the minds of the court or jury as to their contention.

Evidence includes all means by which an alleged matter of fact is submitted to investigation and is established or disproved. N.Y.—Dibble v. Dimick, 143 N.Y. 549, 554, 38 N.E. 724, 725 (1894). Proof is the belief or conclusion arrived at by a consideration of the evidence. Evidence is further subdivided into legal evidence, direct evidence, circumstantial evidence, real evidence, testimonial evidence, documentary evidence, relevant evidence, irrelevant evidence, competent evidence, incompetent evidence, corroborative evidence, prima facie evidence, and hearsay evidence. Each of these will be more thoroughly discussed in later chapters, but you should familiarize yourself with the general meaning of these terms at this time to enable you to understand the concepts and examples explained in the later chapters.

§ 1.15   REAL EVIDENCE

Real evidence is that evidence furnished by things themselves on view or inspection, as distinguished from a description of them by the mouth of a witness. Black's Law Dictionary (Rev. 6th Ed. 1979).

§ 1.16   LEGAL EVIDENCE

Legal evidence is defined in Black's Law Dictionary (Rev. 6th Ed. 1979) as a broad general term meaning all admissible evidence, including both oral and documentary evidence, but with a further implication that it must be of such a character as tends reasonably and substantially to prove the point, not to raise a mere suspicion or conjecture. Conn.—Curtis v. Bradley, 65 Conn. 99, 31 A. 591, 594, 28 L.R.A. 143 (1895). Legal evidence is also defined as that which is used or is intended to be used at trial or at hearings before courts, judges, commissioners, referees, arbitrators, hearing officers, etc.

§ 1.17   RELEVANT EVIDENCE

Relevant evidence is evidence that logically tends to prove or to disprove one or more of the principal facts in issue. N.Y.—People v. Nitzberg, 287 N.Y. 183, 187, 38 N.E.2d 490 (1941). Material evidence is that measure of proof that affects a fact or issue of the case in an important way. To be competent, evidence must be legally adequate and sufficient. It is an omnibus term used for all of the exclusionary rules.

An example of a relevant, competent, and material evidence problem follows.

Let us assume that there is a contractual dispute with respect to the floor measurements of your living room. The carpet dealer from whom you just purchased wall-to-wall carpeting tells you that your room was 18 feet wide by 18 feet long and that he used 36 square yards to carpet your living room and that the carpet was from an 18-foot roll. Your contention is that he used only 25 square yards, in that your living room is 15 feet by 15 feet, and you refuse to pay him for the 36 square yards. He sues you, and a trial of the issue between both of you (the size of the room) results. You have someone measure the width of your home, and this witness takes the stand. You ask the witness, "What, if any, is your means of earning a living?" He answers that he is a carpet salesman and measures the size of the rooms for the purpose of furnishing carpeting to prospective customers. After showing the court that he has been so employed for five years, the court accepts him as an expert in measuring for the purpose of furnishing carpet. You now ask him whether or not he measured the size of your home. There is an instant objection from your adversary because he tells the judge that the size of your home is not relevant, competent, or material to the issue (i.e., the size of your living room). You argue that it is relevant, competent, and material and ask the judge to accept this testimony "subject to connection." The judge answers that he will accept it "subject to connection," but if it is not connected later, he will direct the jury to disregard the testimony in its deliberations. The expert then testifies that the width of your house is 16 feet and the house is rectangular. Inasmuch as the carpet vendor had already testified in his direct case that he sold you carpeting for an 18-foot-wide room, you have now introduced testimony that is relevant, material, and competent and is proof that the room could not be 18 feet by 18 feet. It is therefore connected to the issue of the case.

Another way of describing relevant evidence is such evidence as relates to, or bears directly upon, the point in issue and proves, or has a tendency to prove, the proposition alleged.

Still another way of describing material evidence is evidence that has an effective influence or bearing on the question in issue.

The terms "material" and "relevant" are generally used interchangeably, although it is possible that evidence may be logically relevant but immaterial. Evidence that is so remote as to be of no practical value in determining the issues is immaterial, even though it may have some logical relevancy to the issues involved.

In actual practice, the distinction between the relevancy and materiality is obscure, and in most cases, whether it is characterized as irrelevant or immaterial makes little practical difference.

§ 1.18   DIRECT EVIDENCE

Direct evidence is that method of proof that tends to show the existence or nonexistence of a disputed fact without the intervention of proof of another fact. Ky.—Stark's Adm'x v. Herndon's Adm'r, 292 Ky. 469, 166 S.W.2d 828 (1943). Another court held that "direct evidence," when strictly defined, means that which immediately points to the question at issue, or is evidence of the precise fact at issue and on trial, by witnesses who can testify that they saw the act done or heard the words spoken that constituted the facts to be proved. Mo.—Stern v. Employers' Liability Assur. Corp., Limited, of London, England, 249 S.W. 739 (Mo.App. 1923).

I like to think of direct evidence as something the witness can testify to, something he or she saw, smelled, tasted, heard, or felt that is directly related to the issue between the litigants.

Let us hypothesize that a police officer was on routine motor patrol when she received a report of a stolen vehicle of a particular make, model, and color and bearing a particular licenses plate. Shortly after she received this alarm, she observed "D" and "B" seated in the wanted vehicle. "D" was in the driver's seat, and "B" was in the front passenger seat. The vehicle was standing in a "no standing" zone in front of the entrance to a national bank that was located on a street that had considerable pedestrian traffic. The bank was open for business. The officer observed "B" walking into the bank while "D" remained in the driver's seat with the motor running.

After signaling for assistance, the officer parked her police vehicle to the rear of the stolen vehicle and remained in her car, waiting for reinforcements.

"D" and "B" had planned to perpetrate a robbery of the national bank. As part of the plan, if something went wrong on the outside, "D" was to honk the vehicle's horn twice and try to get away from the scene on foot. While "B" was waiting in line to reach a teller, he heard two honks on the horn of the stolen vehicle.

The perpetrators further arranged beforehand that if the horn was sounded before "B" had made his demands known, he was to ask the teller for change of ten dollars and disappear into the crowd.

"B," having heard the horn, followed the scheduled procedure.

Shortly after the horn was sounded, another officer arrived at the scene just in time to see "D" emerging from the vehicle.

The second officer on the scene apprehended "D" and frisked him, only to find no contraband. This officer charged "D" with larceny of the motor vehicle and possession of stolen property. The officer did not see "D" steal the vehicle. He could not testify that he saw him commit larceny. He did, however, observe him in the driver's seat with the motor running. This is direct evidence that he saw, heard, and possibly smelled (exhaust fumes). These observations could be testified to by the officer to satisfy some of the elements of the offense "possession of stolen property." Most jurisdictions require such a defendant to go forward with the evidence when he is found with the recent and exclusive possession of stolen property. N.Y.—Knickerbocker v. People, 57 Barb. 365, *aff'd*, 43 N.Y. 177 (1870). In this hypothetical, one may find several inferences that other crimes were about to be committed. We will discuss them in the next section.

§ 1.19   CIRCUMSTANTIAL EVIDENCE

Circumstantial evidence is evidence that does not directly prove the existence of a fact but merely gives rise to a logical inference that it exists; such evidence is admissible if it affords a basis for a reasonable inference of the existence of the fact. N.C.—Wilkerson v. Clark, 264 N.C. 439, 141 S.E.2d 884, 887 (1965). "Circumstantial evidence" is the proof of facts that have a legitimate tendency from the laws of nature, the usual connection of things, and ordinary transactions of business, etc., to show the reasonable mind that the disputed fact was or was not in existence. Del.—Fahey v. Niles, 7 Boyce 454, 108 A. 135 (1918).

Let us return now to our hypothetical attempted bank robbery. Let us suppose that the first officer on the scene knew that "D" and "B" were acquainted and observed "B" coming out of the bank. By prearrangement, each officer was to apprehend one of the participants. When "B" was apprehended and frisked, he was found to possess a fully loaded revolver. When "D" was frisked, he was "clean" (had no contraband on his person).

When the prosecutor heard the full information, he decided to charge both "D" and "B" with (1) attempted robbery, (2) possession of stolen property, (3) unauthorized use of a motor vehicle, (4) possession of a revolver in violation of law, (5) conspiracy, and (6) standing a motor vehicle in a "no standing" zone. In short, he decided to "throw the book" at the defendants.

The officers could testify what they directly observed and leave the inferences to be drawn by the fact finder to ascertain whether or not the defendants committed the crimes for which they were charged. The inference that will be drawn from the presence of the stolen vehicle in a "no standing" area, with motor running, with "D" in the driver's seat, with "B" in the bank with a fully loaded revolver, with "B" having arrived at the bank in the vehicle with "D," with the signal on the vehicle's horn, with the dispersal plan executed, is that a bank robbery was being attempted.

Taken together, the enumerated acts circumstantially tend to prove the commission of the attempted robbery and the conspiracy.

§ 1.20   RELATIVE WEIGHT OF CREDIBILITY

We have all seen the symbol of justice as a blindfolded woman holding a weight scale in her hand. It is to be presumed that she does not see who or what is being placed on either side of the scale, but eventually one side of the scale should be heavier than the other. It is also to be presumed that the side that has the heavier weight is the side that prevails in a lawsuit. A more detailed discussion of the quantum of proof required to prevail is undertaken in the next chapter.

For our purposes at this juncture, we should know that when witnesses testify, some of their testimony will be believed more by the trier of the facts than will other testimony. We refer to this concept as the weight of testimony. When a witness testifies to a material fact at issue and the trier of the facts believes the testimony of the witness, we say in law, "The testimony of that witness was heavy."

The greater number of witnesses that testify for a particular side in a lawsuit does not necessarily tip the scale in favor of the litigant for whom they are testifying. There is always the issue of credibility of the testimony.

Frequently, a witness who is aged may be, but need not necessarily be, regarded as untrustworthy. In weighing testimony, the old age of a witness may support a presumption that his memory is to a considerable extent, untrustworthy with respect to recent events. U.S.—Bentley v. Phelps, 3 F.Cas. 244 No. 1331 (C.C.Mass. 1847). A witness of mature age may well remember facts that occurred in his childhood, but his testimony should be received with caution. Ill.—Moffett v. South Park Commissioners, 138 Ill. 620, 28 N.E. 975 (1891).

Confidence in the testimony is greatly reduced if the witness was of extremely tender years. La.—Flettrich v. State Farm Mutual Ins. Co., 238 So.2d 220 (La.App. 1970).

The witness may not be believed because he might be biased toward one of the litigants. U.S.—Pritchett v. United States, 185 F.2d 438 (D.C.Cir. 1950), *cert. denied*, 340 U.S. 905, 71 S.Ct. 608, 95 L.Ed. 1344. Or the weight to be given to evidence of character depends largely on the facts involved in a particular case and is a question for the jury to determine. Fla.—Mitchell v. State, 43 Fla. 188, 30 So. 803 (1901).

There are many factors that cause a jury to disbelieve a witness. Some additional reasons may be that the witness has a bad reputation for veracity, or has testified to inconsistent statements, or is intoxicated or under the influence of narcotics while testifying or while at the scene of the occurrence, or has poor perceptive ability, or is a paid expert who earns the bulk of his or her income by testifying for a particular type of litigant, or has a demeanor on the witness stand that does not favorably impress the trier of the facts; a variety of other reasons could produce a "gut" reaction in the mind of the trier of the facts.

§ 1.21   TESTIMONIAL EVIDENCE

All forms of evidence admitted in a trial are frequently referred to as testimony. This is an inaccurate use of the term "testimony." Testimony is more accurately defined to designate only a particular kind or species of evidence, namely that which comes to the tribunal through living witnesses speaking under oath or affirmation in the presence of the tribunal. Ark.—Poe v. State, 95 Ark. 172, 129 S.W. 292 (1910); Neb.—Meyers v. State, 112 Neb. 149, 198 N.W. 871 (1924); Tex.—*Ex parte* Jackson, 470 S.W.2d 679 (Tex.Crim.App. 1971). However, testimony need not be made to a judicial tribunal. Police departments frequently have disciplinary trials wherein a superior officer brings charges against a subordinate for a violation of department rules and regulations. This is not a judicial tribunal, but it is an administrative hearing. When the superior officer or any other complainant is sworn and begins to testify, his or her presentation to the administrative hearing officer constitutes testimony and hence is testimonial evidence.

There are other situations of a nonjudicial character that result in the same type of testimonial evidence being presented.

It has been said that what witnesses say under oath is testimony, but only so much of it as impresses the mind of the court trying the facts is "evidence." N.J.—Mick v. Mart, 65 A. 851 (Ch. 1907).

Now that we know what testimonial evidence is, we should differentiate as to what it is not. In Fine v. Kolodny, 263 Md. 647, 284 A.2d 409 (1971), *cert. denied*, 406 U.S. 928, 92 S.Ct. 1803, 32 L.Ed.2d 129 (1972), a former patient at a private psychiatric clinic sued the clinic and others for false imprisonment. She acted as her own attorney in the trial of the action. In so doing, she did not testify in her own behalf but indulged in colloquies with the bench and posed improper questions to witnesses. The court held, inter alia, that statements made by plaintiff were not subject to cross-examination and impeachment.

§ 1.22   COMPETENT EVIDENCE

Competent evidence means evidence which tends to establish the fact in issue and does not rest on mere surmise or guess. La.—Clifton v. Arnold, 87 So.2d 386 (La.App. 1956). One must develop a logical feel for the competency or incompetency of evidence. The evidence must be logically probative of the fact in issue, but sometimes we find that competent evidence is not admissible because it is not the character of proof which the law permits in a particular case. See N.Y.—Porter v. Valentine, 18 Misc. 213, 41 N.Y.S. 507 (1896), for a discussion of this point. Evidence is incompetent if not fit for the purpose for which it is offered. Me.—Torrey v. Congress Square Hotel Co., 145 Me. 234, 75 A.2d 451 (1950).

We often hear the standard hoop skirt (covers all but touches nothing) objection of "I object on the grounds that the testimony is incompetent, immaterial, and irrelevant." This is a standard objection and sometimes works to the advantage of the objector to exclude certain evidence that he or she feels might be damaging to the case or that might raise collateral issues not before the court.

§ 1.23   DOCUMENTARY EVIDENCE

Documentary evidence is that furnished by written instruments, inscriptions, and documents of all kinds. N.Y.—Ticknor v. Ticknor, 23 Misc.2d 257, 200 N.Y.S.2d 661 (1960). The term includes every form of writing and applies to both public and private documents. R.I.—Arnold v. Pawtuxet Valley Water Co., 18 R.I. 189, 26 A. 55, 19 L.R.A. 602 (1893). In the private document sector, we might find deeds, wills, agreements, etc. In the public document area, we might find public records; birth, marriage, and death certificates; election registers; motor vehicle accident reports; and licenses. N.Y.—Woltin v. Metropolitan Life Ins. Co., 167 Misc. 382, 4 N.Y.S.2d 296 (1938).

When a portion of an article of documentary evidence is put in evidence by a plaintiff on direct examination of a witness, a defendant, after cross-examining the witness on the documentary evidence, is entitled to have the whole article placed in evidence. Del.—Chavin v. Cope, 243 A.2d 694 (1968).

The usual way to present a document into evidence is to have the lawyer who is interested in getting the document admitted ask the court to direct the stenographer to mark the document for identification. After it has been so marked, reference is then made to the identification number in phrasing a question to the witness:

> Mr. (witness's name), when, if ever, have you seen People's exhibit "A" for identification before?

After the witness indicates that he has seen the exhibit previously, he is asked the circumstances under which he saw the exhibit. If the exhibit is established to be competent, material, and relevant to the issue at trial, the attorney then offers "People's exhibit 'A' for identification in evidence as People's exhibit 'A' in evidence."

The exhibit is then shown to his adversary, who has an opportunity to object to the introduction in evidence of this particular exhibit. If the objection is sustained, the exhibit is not introduced into evidence, and the triers of the facts shall not consider the exhibit as part of the evidence in their deliberations, notwithstanding the fact that certain testimony was elicited while it was introduced as People's exhibit "A" for identification.

The procedure outlined above might be used for all types of inanimate objects that the trier of the facts must consider in the deliberations of the issues between the litigants.

§ 1.24 VIDEOTAPE—DEPOSITION (DEPOVISION)

One of the more recent innovations in the law of evidence has been the use of videotape in the courtroom. It is no secret that court calendars are overcrowded and that much delay is experienced in the trial of cases, both criminal and civil. In an effort to remedy this problem and to make the best use of available resources, experiments have been conducted that introduce the use of videotape in the courtroom.

Historically, our rules of law and, more particularly, our rules of evidence change very slowly. Many roadblocks are placed in the way of change. Practitioners are set in their ways whether they are judges or trial counsel, but more and more the organized bar is accepting the challenge to make changes. In all fairness, it must be said that change comes slowly in the law also to ensure that justice is done and that changes are not made merely for the sake of change itself.

Many jurisdictions now allow the use of depovision of expert witnesses. Frequently, a litigant is unable to obtain a fair trial because the cost of having an expert appear in the courtroom has been too expensive. Accordingly, provision has been made for an expert to be examined in a place other than the courtroom, with the opportunity being given to all litigants for direct, cross-, redirect, and recross-examination. Objections to testimony are recorded, and the witness is permitted to answer. The judge views the testimony in chambers before the jury sees the videotape, and the judge makes rulings on the objections at that time. The tape is then edited to omit the testimony that the judge has ruled inadmissible, and at the proper time in the trial, the videotape is shown to the jury.

Some states are admitting videotapes into evidence for other uses. Naturally, videotapes were unknown in the early common law. Accordingly, the states are enacting statutes to permit videotapes into evidence. An example of such a statute is Section 92.53 of the Florida Statutes, enacted in 1984 as Section 90.90 but redesignated in 1985 as Section 92.53. It authorizes the in-camera videotaping of the testimony of a victim or a witness in a sexual abuse or child abuse case who is under the age of sixteen, whether civil or criminal in nature, to be used at trial in lieu of trial testimony in open court, on a finding that there is substantial likelihood that such victim or witness would suffer severe emotional or mental distress if required to testify in open court.

§ 1.25   HYPNOTICALLY INDUCED TESTIMONY— TRUTH SERUM

As indicated previously, the rules of evidence are founded on the search for truth. Surely a person who is testifying and who is under the hypnotic influence of another cannot be thought to be testifying to the truth. Some effort has been made to gain a certain modicum of respectability for the use of truth serums or narcoanalysis, as well as the use of hypnosis. No court known to me has permitted the use of these methods. For an extended review, see Teitlebaum, Admissibility of Hypnotically Adduced Evidence and The Arthur Nebb Case, 8 St. Louis U.L.J. 205 (1963), and Polen, The Admissibility of Truth Serum Tests in Court, 35 Temp.L.Q. 401 (1962).

§ 1.26   PRIMA FACIE EVIDENCE

The police officer often hears that he or she has the responsibility of providing the evidence to prove a prima facie case in order to be free of a possible judgment against him or her for false imprisonment. The prosecutor might be heard to say that all the police officer needs to hold the defendant is a prima facie case. The question now is, what is a prima facie case?

Naturally, we know that "prima facie" has a Latin derivation. A literal definition might be "at first view" or "on its face." When we combine "prima facie" with "case," we mean one which, in the absence of explanation or contradiction, constitutes an apparent case sufficient in the eyes of the law to establish the fact and, if not rebutted, remains sufficient for that purpose. Idaho—Miller v. Belknap, 75 Idaho 46, 266 P.2d 662 (1954).

When the prosecution "puts in" the prima facie case in the initial hearing, it is not an acceptable practice to buttress the case with additional testimony. The reason for this is that the prosecution does not require the additional testimony at the initial hearing and does not have to give the adversary all the evidence that the government has against the defendant at this time.

However, the trend is for the prosecution to be required to disclose whatever information the government has, whether exculpatory or inculpatory, as the case progresses toward trial.

§ 1.27   CORROBORATIVE EVIDENCE

Evidence that strengthens, confirms, or makes certain other evidence is corroborative evidence. It is additional evidence of a different character about some point that will support, strengthen, or confirm evidence already received. Many jurisdictions require corroboration of a female's testimony for a rape conviction. It was much too easy for a female to disarray her clothing or injure herself before reporting the rape. However, the pendulum swung too much in favor of the male population, in that it became almost impossible to convict a defendant of rape because most rapes are not conducted under the watchful eye of disinterested witnesses. Accordingly, many jurisdictions have removed the necessity of corroboration for conviction in the crime of rape. If the trier of the facts believes the victim in these states, the defendant can be convicted on the victim's testimony alone. For a more detailed analysis of the use of corroboration, the reader is referred to 45 A.L.R.2d 1316, 7 Wigmore Evidence 2056–2060 (3rd Ed. 1940), 60 A.L.R. 1124, 100 A.L.R.2d 612, and 21 A.L.R.2d 1013.

§ 1.28 PRELIMINARY QUESTIONS OF ADMISSIBILITY

Sometimes there is a question as to whether or not certain evidence will be permitted in a trial. Often a defendant wants to know this before he or she takes the witness stand. The reason for this is that if certain evidence may be introduced in the impeachment or cross-examination phase of this witness, the defendant may elect not to take the witness stand. In this way, the defendant may be able to keep the knowledge of this evidence away from the trier of the facts. Each jurisdiction has a procedure to get a ruling from the court on this issue before the trial or, at the very least, before the defendant takes the stand. A motion may be made by the defendant to obtain all the information that the prosecution has in its possession of any criminal conviction of the defendant and to be told whether the prosecution intends to introduce this information at trial if the defendant should take the stand. Many jurisdictions have adopted the procedure of the prosecution's advising the defendant of all the evidence that it has and can use in the trial. This is usually done on the premise that if the defendant knows in advance of the trial that the government has a solid case, the defendant may be more amenable to plea bargain and thus avoid the expense and the usual nerve-wracking experience of all adversaries before and during trial. However, as indicated in Rule 609 of the Federal Rules of Evidence, not every prior conviction can be introduced into evidence at the trial. When there is a question as to the admissibility of this evidence, the defendant usually will make a motion to the trial judge to conduct a preliminary hearing as to the admissibility of this type of evidence. After the trial judge makes a ruling, the defendant may then decide whether to proceed to trial or make a bargain with the prosecutor as to a mutually agreeable plea. See the section in Chapter 6 entitled "Offers to Plead and Withdrawal."

§ 1.29 LIMITED ADMISSIBILITY OF EVIDENCE

In many criminal trials, more than one defendant is tried at the same time. Sometimes, on motion, or sua sponte, by the presiding judge, the trial of one or more of the defendants is severed, to be tried separately at a later date. When this is done, there is no need for the judge to permit evidence in the trial that would be applicable to some of the defendants but not all the defendants. However, the courts usually do not grant a motion for severance because it is felt that the whole trial would have to be conducted time and time again for each defendant. To avoid the problem of an unfair trial, which might of itself create a reversal on appeal, many states provide by rule, and the United States provides by Rule 105 of the Federal Rules of Evidence, that "when evidence which is admissible as to one party or for one purpose but not admissible as to another party or for another purpose is admitted, the court, upon request, shall restrict the evidence to its proper scope and instruct the jury accordingly." United States v. Rodriguez, 765 F.2d 1546 (11th Cir. 1985).

§ 1.30 EXCLUSION OF RELEVANT EVIDENCE ON GROUNDS OF PREJUDICE, CONFUSION, OR WASTE OF TIME

You will read many times in this book that appellate courts give a trial court wide discretion as to what to admit, or what not to admit, as evidence in a trial. However, if the appellate court concludes that the trial court abused its discretion in this area so as to have committed a substantial (sometimes called prejudicial) error, the appellate court will reverse the judgment and most times, if it is thought that sufficient evidence is available, will remand the case for a new trial.

A trial court may invoke a state rule similar to Rule 403 of the Federal Rules of Evidence, which reads as follows: "Although relevant, evidence may be excluded if its probative value is substantially outweighed by the danger of unfair prejudice, confusion of the issues, or misleading the jury, or by considerations of undue delay, waste of time, or needless presentation of cumulative evidence."

It is easy to understand, after reading Rule 403, that there may be different opinions by various judges as to what each of the exclusionary items might mean. Accordingly, the usual rule is that even though the appellate court would not have excluded a relevant item of evidence, if a reasonable person might have excluded the item based on one or more of the categories indicated in Rule 403, the appellate court will affirm the trial court's ruling. Situations in this area call for balancing the probative value of and the need for the evidence against the harm likely to result from its admission. For a thorough discussion of these points, the reader is referred to Slough, Relevancy Unraveled, 5 Kan.L.Rev. 1, 12–15 (1956), and United States v. Falcon, 766 F.2d 1469 (10th Cir. 1985).

§ 1.31   EXCLUSION OF CONSTITUTIONALLY PROTECTED EVIDENCE

This book is not designed to fully acquaint you with evidence that is not admissible in a trial because if it were admitted, it would violate a constitutional right afforded to every defendant in a criminal trial. Undergraduate colleges and universities, as well as law schools, usually conduct at least a full-semester course dealing with this topic.

With the popularization of live presentations of trials, television broadcasts of trials that now come into our living rooms, and home movies, as well as commercial movies, depicting criminal trials, most attentive persons are now acquainted with the Fourth, Fifth, Sixth, Eighth, and Fourteenth Amendments as they relate to a criminal trial or, in some cases, even a civil trial.

When reference is made to any of these amendments, it means that because of the particular amendment to the United States Constitution, certain evidence is not permitted in the trial.

The amendments to the United States Constitution are formally designated in the said Constitution as

ARTICLES IN ADDITION TO, AND AMENDMENT OF THE CONSTITUTION OF THE UNITED STATES OF AMERICA, PROPOSED BY CONGRESS, AND RATIFIED BY THE LEGISLATURES OF THE SEVERAL STATES, PURSUANT TO THE FIFTH ARTICLE OF THE ORIGINAL CONSTITUTION.
ARTICLE [I.] . . . .
ARTICLE [II.] . . . .
ARTICLE [III.] . . . .
ARTICLE [IV.] . . . .

The right of the people to be secure in their persons, houses, papers, and effects, against unreasonable searches and seizures, shall not be violated, and no Warrants shall issue, but upon probable cause, supported by Oath, or affirmation, and particularly describing the place to be searched, and the persons or things to be seized.

The Fourth Amendment requires the issuance of a search warrant by a court of law and prohibits all unreasonable searches and seizures. There are "mountains" of litigation where the United States Supreme Court has interpreted this amendment in different factual situations.

Many states refused to ratify the Constitution unless a bill of rights was included. Accordingly, in compliance with a promise made to these states, James Madison arose in the First Congress to introduce the proposal of the first ten amendments. They were quickly passed by Congress on September 25, 1789, and ratified by three-fourths of the states by December 15, 1791. They became known as the Bill of Rights.

The fear of many people at that time was that without this protection the new government might be a replication of the authoritarian regime then operating in England.

According to the United States Constitution, a three-branch system was created: the legislative branch, to enact the laws; the executive branch, to enforce the laws; and the judicial branch, to interpret the laws. Hence, the judiciary was called on to interpret the provisions of the United States Constitution. At first, the judiciary was the weakest branch of the government, but through the leadership of Chief Justice John Marshall in the case of Marbury v. Madison, 5 U.S. 137, 2 L.Ed. 60 (1803), the Court was elevated to be an important organ of government.

In that case, the Court found that a specific section of the Judiciary Act of 1789 was a violation of Article III of the United States Constitution, making the said constitution the supreme law of the land. Accordingly, Section 13 of the said Judiciary Act, which stated that the Supreme Court could issue warrants of mandamus in "cases warranted by the principles and usages of law, to any courts appointed or holding office under authority of the United States," was held to be an enlargement of the original jurisdiction of the Court, as stated in Article III of the Constitution. Thus, it was an unconstitutional grant of authority to the Court.

Article X of the amendment (the Tenth Amendment) reads as follows:

The powers not delegated to the United States by the Constitution, nor prohibited by it to the States, are reserved to the States respectively, or to the people.

One of the powers not delegated to the United States was the police power. Thus, the police power was reserved to the states.

Many court decisions have attempted to define the term "police power." These decisions vary slightly from one another, but generally police power has been interpreted to include

the authority conferred by the American constitutional system upon individual states, through which they are entitled to establish a special department of police, adopt such regulations as tend to prevent the commission of fraud, violence, or other offenses against the state; aid in the arrest of criminals; and secure generally the comfort, health, and prosperity of the state, by preserving the public order, preventing a conflict of rights in the common intercourse of the citizens, and insuring to each an uninterrupted enjoyment of all the privileges conferred upon him by the laws of his country. [Lalor, Pol. Enc. s.v., found also in Black's Law Dictionary, 6th Edition.]

The state law enforcement agencies and the city, county, village, park, transportation, and other entities get their authority from state legislatures, who have the responsibility for law enforcement at the local level.

As we all know, the federal government also has authority to exercise law enforcement powers. These powers are derived initially from the executive branch of the government, as contained in Article II of the United States Constitution, where the president takes an oath or affirmation before he or she enters on the execution of the office by stating:

> I do solemnly swear (or affirm) that I will faithfully execute the Office of President of the United States, and will to the best of my ability, preserve, protect, and defend the Constitution of the United States.

To put it another way, he or she is entrusted with enforcing compliance with the United States Constitution and all laws created under the authority of the United States Constitution.

Many such laws are enacted by Congress that apply to crimes against the good order and efficiency of the United States government and the rights of persons within the jurisdiction of the United States, as enunciated in the United States Constitution and the decisions of the United States Supreme Court defining these rights. Therefore, we arrive at laws that designate federal crimes and that are found primarily in the United States Code and other codes and in the laws of the federal government. While a great many of these laws may be found in Title 18 of the United States Code, this title is not the only location where federal offenses are found.

A person may commit an offense that is designated as a state crime and may also be charged with a similar offense, sometimes slightly different in wording, found in a federal statute. This has been held not to constitute the much publicized prohibition against double jeopardy, found in the Fifth Amendment of the United States Constitution. A decision upholding this concept is United States v. Lanza, 260 U.S. 377, 382, 43 S.Ct. 141, 142, 67 L.Ed. 314 (1922), where the Court held: "An act denounced as a crime by both the state and federal government is an offense against the peace and dignity of each, and may be separately punished by each."

After discussing the foundations for our law, we can now treat violations of the rights that the United States Constitution gives persons because state or federal law enforcement agencies might cause trial evidence to be excluded from admission in the record of a trial.

Some of these that come to mind are as follows:

1. depriving a suspect of legal counsel while he is in law enforcement custody.
2. failing to arraign a suspect before a judicial officer promptly after arrest.
3. failing to warn a suspect of his or her so-called Miranda rights before being questioned by law enforcement personnel.
4. depriving a person of the right of free speech within the limits provided by court decisions.
5. conducting an unreasonable search and seizure of wrongfully possessed contraband.
6. unlawfully depriving persons of the right to congregate for public meetings in streets, parks, and public buildings.

The list goes on almost ad infinitum.

I again remind you that this book is not intended to include a course on constitutional law, and I leave it to other courses to enrich your mind on this subject.

Suffice it to say that in certain instances when evidence is obtained in violation of a defendant's constitutional right, it may be excluded by the court from consideration by the trier of the facts when the defendant or the defendant's attorney makes a motion to the court. This motion takes the form of an objection that the evidence is tainted because of the constitutional violation and should be excluded from the trial record. This may also be done by the trial judge sua sponte (on the judge's own will). A more usual procedure is known as a motion to suppress evidence. When the defendant's attorney becomes aware of allegedly unconstitutional acts by the law enforcement personnel before the trial commences, the attorney will prepare a motion for the suppression of any evidence obtained by allegedly unconstitutional means. This is usually implemented by the aforesaid motion accompanied by affidavits or affirmations by witnesses to the acts. A further discussion of this topic appears in Chapter 19.

§ 1.32   HEARSAY EVIDENCE

A good portion of this text will cover exceptions to the hearsay exclusionary rule. The rule basically states that if the testimony is hearsay, it should not be admissible at trial. However, as with most legal rules, there are exceptions founded on reason and logic. The most frequently met exceptions are delineated in the pages that follow.

Funk v. United States

Supreme Court of the United States, 1933. 290 U.S. 371, 54 S.Ct. 212, 78 L.Ed. 369.

James S. Funk was convicted of conspiracy to violate the National Prohibition Act. This act was enacted by Congress as a result of passage of the Eighteenth Amendment to the United States Constitution, which reads in part:

> Section 1. After one year from the ratification of this article the manufacture, sale, or transportation of intoxicating liquors within, the importation thereof into, or the exportation thereof from the United States and all territory subject to the jurisdiction thereof for beverage purposes is hereby prohibited.
> Section 2. The Congress and the several States shall have concurrent power to enforce this article by appropriate legislation.

This was known as the "Prohibition Amendment." The term "bootlegger" was used to describe those persons who were violating this act. Many leaders in this business acquired notoriety and were called "gangsters." It serves no useful purpose to memorialize their names in this text, and I therefore intentionally omit some of the most infamous.

In the Funk v. United States decision that follows, John S. Funk was allegedly one of those persons who conspired to violate this act.

He was convicted at the trial level, but he raised an objection through his attorney that his wife should have been permitted to testify in his favor. The trial judge denied his request based on the law at the time of the trial.

This case went to the United States Supreme Court, and the Court changed the law of the case, so that in a federal trial a wife may now testify in favor of her husband, and reversed his conviction.

The numbers appearing after the case title have been explained in detail in Section 1.4 of this book. Meanwhile, permit me to further explain that this case was decided by the United States Supreme Court in 1933. The primary evidentiary issue in this case was whether in a criminal case, in a federal court, a wife is competent to testify in favor of her husband. Her competency to testify against him was not involved.

The Court reviewed the history of the common law rule making the wife incompetent to testify in federal court in favor of her husband in a criminal matter. It found that the courts were considering her incompetent to testify in favor of her husband in such a trial based on the Judiciary Act of 1789. This act of Congress established the federal courts, and by omitting any specific reference to the issue of a wife's right to testify in favor of her husband, the Congress relied on the common law rule in force in the respective states at that time that prohibited her testifying in favor of her husband.

The Court also touched on two other acts of Congress. In 1864, Congress enacted a law that no witness should be excluded from testifying in any civil action, with certain exceptions, because he or she was a party to or interested in the issue to be tried, and in 1878, in 28 U.S.C.A. § 632, Congress made a defendant in any criminal case a competent witness in his or her own defense.

With reference to the wife's competence to testify in favor of her husband, the Court said, "The public policy of one generation may not, under changed conditions, be the public policy of another." Patton v. United States, 281 U.S. 276, 306, 50 S.Ct. 253, 74 L.Ed. 854, 70 A.L.R. 263 (1930).

Another hurdle that the Court had to overcome was whether the Court had the power to change rules of evidence of the common law. To overcome this hurdle, the Court stated that

> . . . the common law is not immutable but flexible, and by its own principles adapts itself to varying conditions. . . . ". . . One of its oldest maxims was that where the reason of a rule ceased the rule also ceased. . . . No rule of the common law could survive the reason on which

it was founded. It needed no statute to change it but abrogated itself." . . . "Since courts have had an existence in America, . . . they have never hesitated to take upon themselves the responsibility of saying what are the proper rules of the common law." . . . "Congress has the power [to change the law]; but, if Congress fail to act, as it has failed in respect of the matter now under review, and the court be called upon to decide the question, is it not the duty of the court, if it possesses the power, to decide it in accordance with present day standards of wisdom and justice rather than in accordance with some outworn rule of the past?

Author: →
Should "fail"
be "fails"?

For those who are reading a court decision for the first time, I will synthesize the decision of the Court further:

1. The federal trial court would not permit the wife of the defendant in a criminal matter to testify in behalf of her husband.
2. The issue found its way to the United States Supreme Court.
3. The United States Supreme Court, now and hereafter referred to in this book as "the Court," reviewed the history of this evidentiary rule and found that it was a common law rule; i.e., it was part of the system of jurisprudence derived from Anglo-Saxon law and comprised of principles and rules based on justice, reason, and common sense that were judicially originated. The principles change with the needs of the community.
4. The Court found that as late as 1864 a defendant in a civil case could not testify in his or her own defense. That is, if you were sued for nonpayment of rent on an apartment, you could not testify in your own defense.
5. The Court found that as late as 1878 a defendant in a criminal case could not testify in his or her own defense. That is, if you were tried for an assault on someone, you could not testify that you were in class studying evidence law at the time of the alleged assault.
6. The law on the competency of the defendant to testify has changed with changing conditions, and the law on the competency of the wife to testify in favor of her husband should change also.

7. It is the duty of the Court to make the change if Congress has failed to make the change by statute.
8. A wife is now permitted to testify in favor of her husband in a federal criminal trial.

Therefore, you can see that the law of evidence is an ever-changing law. As our society and government seek better methods for determining guilt or innocence, so, too, will our rules of evidence change to protect the weak from the strong and the strong from the weak.

The edited decision containing the reasoning of the majority of the justices follows:

* * *

On Writ of Certiorari to the United States Circuit Court of Appeals for the Fourth Circuit.

John S. Funk was convicted of conspiracy to violate the National Prohibition Act, and to review a judgment of the Circuit Court of Appeals [66 F.2d 70], affirming the judgment of conviction, he brings certiorari.

* * *

Mr. Justice SUTHERLAND delivered the opinion of the Court.

The sole inquiry to be made in this case is whether in a federal court the wife of the defendant on trial for a criminal offense is a competent witness in his behalf. Her competency to testify against him is not involved.

The petitioner was twice tried and convicted in a federal District Court upon an indictment for conspiracy to violate the prohibition law. His conviction on the first trial was reversed by the Circuit Court of Appeals upon a ground not material here. 46 F.2d 417. Upon the second trial, as upon the first, defendant called his wife to testify in his behalf. At both trials she was excluded upon the ground of incompetency. The Circuit Court of Appeals sustained this ruling upon the first appeal, and also upon the appeal which followed the second trial. 66 F.2d 70. We granted certiorari, limited to the question as to what law is applicable to the determination of the competency of the wife of the petitioner as a witness.

Both the petitioner and the government, in presenting the case here, put their chief reliance on prior decisions of this court. The government relies on United States v. Reid, 12 How. 361, 13 L.Ed. 1023 (1851); Logan v.

United States, 144 U.S. 263, 12 S.Ct. 617, 36 L.Ed. 429 (1892); Hendrix v. United States, 219 U.S. 79, 31 S.Ct. 193, 196, 55 L.Ed. 102 (1911); and Jin Fuey Moy v. United States, 254 U.S. 189, 41 S.Ct. 98, 65 L.Ed. 214 (1921). Petitioner contends that the cases, if not directly contrary to the decisions in Benson v. United States, 146 U.S. 325, 13 S.Ct. 60, 36 L.Ed. 991 (1892), and Rosen v. United States, 245 U.S. 467, 38 S.Ct. 148, 150, 62 L.Ed. 406 (1918), are so in principle. We shall first briefly review these cases, with the exception of the Hendrix Case and the Jin Fuey Moy Case, which we leave for consideration until a later point in this opinion.

In the Reid Case, two persons had been jointly indicated for a murder committed upon the high seas. They were tried separately, and it was held that one of them was not a competent witness in behalf of the other who was first tried. The trial was had in Virginia; and by a statute of that state passed in 1849, if applicable in a federal court, the evidence would have been competent. Section 34 of the Judiciary Act of 1789 (28 U.S.C.A. § 725) declares that the laws of the several states, except where the Constitution, treaties, or statutes of the United States otherwise provide, shall be regarded as rules of decision in trials at common law in the courts of the United States in cases where they apply; but the court said that this referred only to civil cases, and did not apply in the trial of criminal offenses against the United States. It was conceded that there was no act of Congress prescribing in express words the rule by which the federal courts would be governed in the admission of testimony in criminal cases. "But," the court said (page 363 of 12 How.), "we think it may be found with sufficient certainty, not indeed in direct terms, but by necessary implication, in the acts of 1789 and 1790, establishing the courts of the United States, and providing for the punishment of certain offences."

The court pointed out that the Judiciary Act regulated certain proceedings to be had prior to impaneling the jury, but contained no express provision concerning the mode of conducting the trial after the jury was sworn, and prescribed no rule in respect of the testimony to be taken. Obviously, however, it was said, some certain and established rule upon the subject was necessary to enable the courts to administer the criminal jurisprudence of the United States, and Congress must have intended to refer them to some known and established rule "which was supposed to be so familiar and well understood in the trial by jury that legislation upon the subject would be deemed superfluous. This is necessarily to be implied from what these acts of Congress omit, as well as from what they contain." Page 365 of 12 How. The court concluded that this could not be the common law as it existed at the time of the emigration of the colonists or the rule which then prevailed in England, and [therefore] the only known rule which could be supposed to have been in the mind of Congress was that which was in force in the respective states when the federal courts were established by the Judiciary Act of 1789. Applying this rule, it was decided that the witness was incompetent.

In the Logan Case it was held that the competency of a witness to testify in a federal court sitting in one state was not affected by his conviction and sentence for felony in another state; and that the competency of another witness was not affected by his conviction of felony in a Texas state court, where the witness had since been pardoned. The indictment was for an offense committed in Texas and there tried. The decision was based, not upon any statute of the United States, but upon the ground that the subject "is governed by the common law, which, as has been seen, was the law of Texas . . . at the time of the admission of Texas into the Union as a state." Page 303 of 144 U.S., 12 S.Ct. 617, 630.

We next consider the two cases upon which petitioner relies. In the Benson Case two persons were jointly indicted for murder. On motion of the government there was a severance, and Benson was first tried. His codefendant was called as a witness on behalf of the government. The Reid Case had been cited as practically decisive of the question. But the court, after pointing out what it conceived to be distinguishing features in that case, said (page 335 of 146 U.S., 13 S.Ct. 60, 63): "We do not feel ourselves, therefore, precluded by that case from examining this question in the light of general authority and sound reason." The alleged incompetency of the codefendant was rested upon two reasons, first, that he was interested, and second, that he was a party to the record, the basis for the exclusion at common law being fear of perjury. "Nor," the court said, "were those named the only grounds of exclusion from the witness stand. Conviction of crime, want of religious belief, and other matters were held sufficient. Indeed, the theory of the common law was to admit to the witness stand only those presumably honest, appreciating the sanctity of an oath, unaffected as a party by the result, and free from any of the temptations of interest. The courts were afraid to trust the intelligence of jurors. But the last 50 years have wrought a great change in these respects, and today the tendency is to enlarge the domain of competency, and to submit to the jury for their consideration as to the credibility of the witness those matters which heretofore were ruled sufficient to justify his exclusion. This change has been wrought partially by legislation and partially by judicial construction." Attention then is called to the fact that Congress in 1864 had enacted that no witness should be excluded from testifying in any civil action, with certain exceptions, because he was a party to or interested in the issue tried; and that in 1878 (c. 37, 20 Stat. 30 [28 U.S.C.A. § 632]) Congress made the defendant in any criminal case a competent witness at his own request. The opinion then continues (page 337 of 146 U.S., 13 S.Ct. 60, 64):

"Legislation of similar import prevails in most of the states. The spirit of this legislation has controlled the decisions of the courts, and steadily, one by one, the merely technical barriers which excluded witnesses from the stand have been removed, till now it is generally, though perhaps not universally, true that no one is excluded therefrom unless the lips of the originally adverse party are closed by death, or unless some one of those peculiarly confidential relations, like that of husband and wife, forbids the breaking of silence.

". . . If interest and being party to the record do not exclude a defendant on trial from the witness stand, upon what reasoning can a codefendant, not on trial, be adjudged incompetent?"

That case was decided December 5, 1892. Twenty-five years later this court had before it for consideration the case of Rosen v. United States, *supra*. Rosen had been tried and convicted in a federal District Court for conspiracy. A person jointly indicted with Rosen, who had been convicted upon his plea of guilty, was called as a witness by the government and allowed to testify over Rosen's objection. This court sustained the competency of the witness. After saying that, while the decision in the Reid Case had not been specifically overruled, its authority was seriously shaken by the decisions in both the Logan and Benson Cases, the court proceeded to dispose of the question, as it had been disposed of in the Benson Case, "in the light of general authority and of sound reason."

"In the almost twenty [twenty-five] years," the court said, "which have elapsed since the decision of the Benson Case, the disposition of courts and of legislative bodies to remove disabilities from witnesses has continued, as that decision shows it had been going forward before, under dominance of the conviction of our time that the truth is more likely to be arrived at by hearing the testimony of all persons of competent understanding who may seem to have knowledge of the facts involved in a case, leaving the credit and weight of such testimony to be determined by the jury or by the court, rather than by rejecting witnesses as incompetent, with the result that this principle has come to be widely, almost universally, accepted in this country and in Great Britain.

"Since the decision in the Benson Case we have significant evidence of the trend of congressional opinion upon this subject in the removal of the disability of witnesses convicted of perjury. Rev.St. § 5392, by the enactment of the federal Criminal Code in 1909 with this provision omitted and section 5392 repealed. This is significant, because the disability to testify, of persons convicted of perjury, survived in some jurisdictions much longer than many of the other common-law disabilities, for the reason that the offense concerns directly the giving of testimony in a court of justice, and conviction of it was accepted as showing a greater disregard for the truth than it was thought should be implied from a conviction of other crime.

"Satisfied as we are that the legislation and the very great weight of judicial authority which have developed in support of this modern rule, especially as applied to the competency of witnesses convicted of crime, proceed upon sound principle, we conclude that the dead hand of the common-law rule of 1789 should no longer be applied to such cases as we have here, and that the ruling of the lower courts on this first claim of error should be approved."

* * *

The rules of the common law which disqualified as witnesses persons having an interest long since in the main have been abolished both in England and in this country; and what was once regarded as a sufficient ground for excluding the testimony of such persons altogether has come to be uniformly and more sensibly regarded as affecting the credit of the witness only. Whatever was the danger that an interested witness would not speak the truth—and the danger never was as great as claimed—its effect has been minimized almost to the vanishing point by the test of cross-examination, the increased intelligence of jurors, and perhaps other circumstances. The modern rule which has removed the disqualification from persons accused of crime gradually came into force after the middle of the last century, and is today universally accepted. The exclusion of the husband or wife is said by this court to be based upon his or her interest in the event. Jin Fuey Moy v. United States, *supra.* And whether by this is meant a practical interest in the result of the prosecution or merely a sentimental interest because of the marital relationship makes little difference. In either case, a refusal to permit the wife upon the ground of interest to testify in behalf of her husband, while permitting him, who has the greater interest, to testify for himself, presents a manifest incongruity.

Nor can the exclusion of the wife's testimony, in the face of the broad and liberal extension of the rules in respect of the competency of witnesses generally, be any longer justified, if it ever was justified, on any ground of public policy. It has been said that to admit such testimony is against public policy because it would endanger the harmony and confidence of marital relations, and, moreover, would subject the witness to the temptation to commit perjury. Modern legislation, in making either spouse competent to testify in behalf of the other in criminal cases, has definitely rejected these notions, and in the light of such legislation and of modern thought they seem to be altogether fanciful. The public policy of one generation may not, under changed conditions, be the public policy of another. Patton v. United States, 281 U.S. 276, 306, 50 S.Ct. 253, 74 L.Ed. 854, 70 A.L.R. 263 (1930).

The fundamental basis upon which all rules of evidence must rest—if they are to rest upon reason—is their adaptation to the successful development of the truth. And, since experience is of all teachers the most dependable, and since experience also is a continuous process, it follows that a rule of evidence at one time thought necessary to the ascertainment of truth should yield to the experience of a succeeding generation whenever that experience has clearly demonstrated the fallacy or unwisdom of the old rule.

It may be said that the court should continue to enforce the old rule, however contrary to modern experience and thought, and however opposed, in principle, to the general current of legislation and of judicial opinion it may have become, leaving to Congress the responsibility of changing it. Of course, Congress has that power; but, if Congress fail to act, as it has failed in respect of the matter now under review, and the court be called upon to decide the question, is it not the duty of the court, if it possess the power, to decide it in accordance with present-day standards of wisdom and justice rather than in accordance with some outworn and antiquated rule of the past? That this court has the power to do so is necessarily implicit in the opinions delivered in deciding the Benson and Rosen Cases. And that implication, we think, rests upon substantial ground. The rule of the common law which denies the competency of one spouse to testify in behalf of the other in a criminal prosecution has not been modified by congressional legislation; nor has Congress directed the federal courts to follow state law upon that subject, as it has in respect of some other subjects. That this court and the other federal courts, in this situation and by right of their own powers, may decline to enforce the ancient rule of the common law under conditions as they now exist, we think is not fairly open to doubt.

In Hurtado v. California, 110 U.S. 516, 530, 4 S.Ct. 111, 118, 28 L.Ed. 232 (1884), this court, after suggesting that it was better not to go too far back into antiquity for the best securities of our liberties, said:

"It is more consonant to the true philosophy of our historical legal institutions to say that the spirit of personal liberty and individual right, which they embodied, was preserved and developed by a progressive growth and wise adaptation to new circumstances and situations of the forms and processes found fit to give, from time to time, new expression and greater effect to modern ideas of self-government.

"This flexibility and capacity for growth and adaptation is the peculiar boast and excellence of the common law. . . . And as it was the characteristic principle of the common law to draw its inspiration from every fountain of justice, we are not to assume that the sources of its supply have been exhausted. On the contrary, we should expect that the new and various experiences of our own situation and system will mould and shape it into new and not less useful forms."

Compare Holden v. Hardy, 169 U.S. 366, 385–387, 18 S.Ct. 383, 42 L.Ed. 780 (1898).

To concede this capacity for growth and change in the common law by drawing "its inspiration from every fountain of justice," and at the same time to say that the courts of this country are forever bound to perpetuate such of its rules as, by every reasonable test, are found to be neither wise nor just, because we have once adopted them as suited to our situation and institutions at a particular time, is to deny to the common law in the place of its adoption a "flexibility and capacity for growth and adaptation" which was "the peculiar boast and excellence" of the system in the place of its origin.

The final question to which we are thus brought is not that of the power of the federal courts to amend or repeal any given rule or principle of the common law, for they neither have nor claim that power, but it is the question of the power of these courts, in the complete absence of congressional legislation on the subject, to declare and effectuate, upon common-law principles, what is the present rule upon a given subject in the light of fundamentally altered conditions, without regard to what has previously been declared and practiced. It has been said so often as to have become axiomatic that the common law is not immutable but flexible, and by its own principles adapts itself to varying conditions. In Ketelsen v. Stilz, 184 Ind. 702, 111 N.E. 423, L.R.A. 1918D, 303, Ann. Cas. 1918A, 965 (1916), the Supreme Court of that state, after pointing out that the common law of England was based upon usages, customs, and institutions of the English people as declared from time to time by the courts, said (page 707, of 184 Ind., 111 N.E. 423, 425):

"The rules so deduced from this system, however, were continually changing and expanding with the progress of society in the application of this system to more diversified circumstances and under more advanced periods. The common law by its own principles adapted itself to varying conditions and modified its own rules so as to serve the ends of justice as prompted by a course of reasoning which was guided by these generally accepted truths. One of its oldest maxims was that where the reason of a rule ceased the rule also ceased, and it logically followed that when it occurred to the courts that a particular rule had never been founded upon reason, and that no reason existed in support thereof, that rule likewise ceased, and perhaps another sprang up in its place which was based upon reason and justice as then conceived. No rule of the common law could survive the reason on which it was founded. It needed no statute to change it but abrogated itself."

That court then refers to the settled doctrine that an adoption of the common law in general terms does not require, without regard to local circumstances, an unqualified application of all its rules; that the rules, as declared by the English courts at one period or another, have been controlling in this country only so far as they were suited to and in harmony with the genius, spirit, and objects of American institutions; and that the rules of the common law considered proper in the eighteenth century are not necessarily so considered in the twentieth. "Since courts have had an existence in America," that court said (page 708 of 184 Ind., 111 N.E. 423, 425), "they have never hesitated to take upon themselves the responsibility of saying what are the proper rules of the common law."

* * *

The Supreme Court of Connecticut, in Beardsley v. City of Hartford, 50 Conn. 529, 542, 47 Am.Rep. 677 (1883), after quoting the maxim of the common law, cessante ratione legis, cessat ipsa lex, said:

"This means that no law can survive the reasons on which it is founded. It needs no statute to change it; it abrogates itself. If the reasons on which a law rests are overborne by opposing reasons, which in the progress of society gain a controlling force, the old law, though still good as an abstract principle, and good in its application to some circumstances, must cease to apply as a controlling principle to the new circumstances."

The same thought is expressed in People v. Randolph, 2 Parker, Cr.R. 174, 177 (N.Y. 1855): "Its rules [the rules of the common law] are modified upon its own principles and not in violation of them. Those rules being founded in reason, one of its oldest maxims is, that where the reason of the rule ceases the rule also ceases."

It was in virtue of this maxim of the common law that the Supreme Court of Nevada, in Reno Smelting Works v. Stevenson, 20 Nev. 269, 21 Pac. 317, 4 L.R.A. 60, 19 Am.St.Rep. 364 (1889), in a well-reasoned opinion, held that the common-law doctrine of riparian rights was unsuited to conditions prevailing in the arid land states and territories of the West, and therefore was without force in Nevada; and that, in respect of the use of water, the applicable rule was based upon the doctrine of prior appropriation for a beneficial use.

In Illinois it was held at an early day that the rule of the common law which required an owner of cattle to keep them upon his own land was not in force in that state, notwithstanding its adoption of the common law of England, being unsuited to conditions there in view of the extensive areas of land which had been left open and unfenced and devoted to grazing purposes. Seeley v. Peters, 5 Gilman 130 (Ill. 1848).

Numerous additional state decisions to the same effect might be cited; but it seems unnecessary to pursue the matter at greater length.

It results from the foregoing that the decision of the court below, in holding the wife incompetent, is erroneous. But that decision was based primarily upon Hendrix v. United States and Jin Fuey Moy v. United States, *supra*, and in fairness to the lower court it should be said that its decision was fully supported by those cases.

In the Hendrix Case the opinion does not discuss the point; it simply recites the assignment of error to the effect that the wife of Hendrix had not been allowed to testify in his behalf, and dismisses the matter by the laconic statement, "The ruling was not error." In the Jin Fuey Moy Case it was conceded at the bar that the wife was not a competent witness for all purposes, but it was contended that her testimony was admissible in that instance because she was offered, not in behalf of her husband, that is, not to prove his innocence, but simply to contradict the testimony of government witnesses who had testified to certain matters as having transpired in her presence. The court held the distinction to be without substance, as clearly it was, and thereupon disposed of the question by saying that the rule which excludes a wife from testifying for her husband is based upon her interest in the event, and applies without regard to the kind of testimony she might give. The point does not seem to have been considered by the lower court to which the writ of error was addressed ([D.C.] 253 F. 213); nor, as plainly appears, was the real point as it is here involved presented in this court. The matter was disposed of as one "hardly requiring mention." Evidently the point most in the mind of the court was the distinction relied upon, and not the basic rule which was not contested. Both the Hendrix and Jin Fuey Moy Cases are out of harmony with the Rosen and Benson Cases and with the views which we have here expressed. In respect of the question here under review, both are now overruled.

Judgment reversed.

Mr. Justice CARDOZO concurs in the result.

Mr. Justice McREYNOLDS and Mr. Justice BUTLER are of opinion that the judgment of the court below is right and should be affirmed.

Federal Trust Co. v. East Hartford Fire District

United States Circuit Court of Appeals, Second Circuit, 1922. 283 Fed. 95.

This is an old case, but the rules of law explained in the decision of the United States Circuit Court of Appeals, Second Circuit are still in effect today.

In reading the beginning of this case, you may wonder what is meant by the statement "In Error to the District Court of the United States for the District of Connecticut." This means that a petition for a writ of error was made to the next higher court to the District Court of the United States for the District of Connecticut, where the case was heard initially.

In this lower court, the defendant won the case merely by submitting a demurrer to the court, and the court ruled in favor of the defendant. A demurrer is a pleading that is an answer to a complaint and that declares that even if all the facts stated in the complaint are true, it does not state a cause of action. The court ruling on a demurrer may grant summary judgment for the prevailing party, thus terminating the case. No summary judgment should be granted by the court if there is a dispute between the litigants as to the facts.

In this case, there was no dispute as to the facts, and thus the lower court granted a summary judgment. The plaintiff then petitioned for a writ of error, and the United States Circuit Court of Appeals granted the writ of error.

Each United States Circuit Court of Appeals had its name changed in 1948 to the United States Court of Appeals for a particular circuit. The older Circuit Courts of Appeals entertained petitions for writs of error made by losing parties in the United States District Courts. The newer procedure is that when a review of a decision of the United States District Court is desired, the losing party in that court makes an appeal to the United States Court of Appeals for the circuit in which the United States District Court is located. Now an appeal from the United States District Court is made as a matter of right, but there are strict time limitations in which this must be done. Again, it is not the intention of this book to explain the method

that is to be taken by a prospective appellant, but suffice it to say that there are rules of appellate procedure that are promulgated, amended, and adopted by orders of the United States Supreme Court and the respective United States Court of Appeals for its own procedures.

However, if the losing party in a decision by an administrative agency, board, commission, or officer wants a review of the decision, that party must file within the time prescribed by law either a petition to enjoin, set aside, suspend, modify, or otherwise review or a notice of appeal, whichever form is indicated by the applicable statute or rule.

The decision in Federal Trust Co. v. East Hartford Fire District explains what a statute is and compares a private act and a special act. It further explains that a legislature may affect or modify special acts by general statutes.

The edited decision follows:

* * *

In Error to the District Court of the United States for the District of Connecticut.

Action by the Federal Trust Company against the East Hartford Fire District. Judgment for defendant on demurrer, and plaintiff brings error. Reversed and remanded, with directions.

> The defendant fire district is a minor municipal corporation of Connecticut, created in 1889 (10 Sp.Laws Conn. p. 1316). This act of incorporation was amended from time to time, always by "special laws" duly passed by the Connecticut Legislature, until in 1899 (13 Sp.Laws, p. 492, § 14) the district was given the power and authority to make and maintain waterworks, and to do so by lawfully obtaining "the same rights, powers, and duties as were conferred and imposed upon the East Hartford Water Company by its charter approved May 10, 1887, and the amendments thereto."

Defendant thus became entitled to procure by eminent domain the watersheds necessary for its waterworks in like manner as the East Hartford Water Company had been entitled so to do. That water company had, by virtue of certain "special laws," "full power . . . to take water from any brook in [certain enumerated towns including Glastonbury] or from any other source as said company may desire."

The method of exercising this right of taking water is prescribed by special law (10 Sp.Laws, p. 729, § 8) thus: "Said corporation [district] shall pay all damages, that shall be sustained by any person or persons or corporation in their property or estate by the taking of any real estate or easement, or by the taking the water from any brook," etc.

The statute then declares that, if the damages shall not be agreed upon, they shall be assessed under the supervision of the superior court, upon an application made to that court either by the condemning corporation or by the person sustaining damages, "which application shall be accompanied by a summons served upon the owner of the property as in the case of civil process before said court."

Another proviso of this series of special laws declares: "Said court may make any order necessary for the protection of the rights of all persons or corporations interested in said property or sustaining such damages: but said property shall not be taken or interfered with by said corporation until the amount of said judgment shall be paid to the person to whom it is due, or deposited for his use with the treasurer of Hartford county." Section 10.

By virtue of this conference of the power of eminent domain the fire district in December, 1916, began proceedings in the superior court against the Glastonbury Power company et al. to condemn "the waters of Cold brook" in the town of Glastonbury. After appeal to the Supreme Court of the state (East Hartford Fire District v. Glastonbury Power Co., 92 Conn. 217, 102 Atl. 592), the proceeding succeeded, and on December 12, 1918, judgment was entered in said superior court awarding to the Glastonbury Power Company damages for the taking of Cold brook in the sum of $7,500.

In 1904 said power company had duly made a mortgage, affecting all its property including the Cold brook lands. Plaintiff, Federal Trust Company, is the mortgagee as trustee for bondholders. The mortgage was duly recorded and was in full force during the whole of the above referred to condemnation proceeding; but (as averred in the complaint) plaintiff had "no notice of said condemnation proceedings, nor was it cited as a party defendant in" the same. The amount of plaintiff's mortgage was $57,000. The complaint does not aver that it had matured when complaint was filed (December 1920), or that the mortgagor was down to that date in default. But (continues the complaint) "as such mortgagee plaintiff was entitled to payment of said award to the extent of the amount due upon the mortgage before any sum was paid to he owner of the property. No payment of any amount has been made to the plaintiff on account of said award of damages, although plaintiff requested defendant to pay said sum over to the plaintiff." Complaint concludes with a prayer for general damages, viz. $100,000.

To this complaint defendant demurred, assigning for cause of demurrer that at the time of action begun no "sum of money was due and payable from defendant to plaintiff," and that it was not alleged that "defendant is indebted to plaintiff." This in substance was a general demurrer.

At all times during the pendency of the condemnation proceeding above referred to, and since 1895, there had been and was in force in Connecticut a general statute (Gen. Stat. Conn. Revision of 1918, § 5192), reading as follows: "Whenever any real estate, or any interest in real estate, is taken by right of eminent domain under any statute, notice shall be given to all persons appearing of record to hold any mortgage, lien or other incumbrance on the property to be taken, and the amount due to such mortgagee, lienor or other incumbrancer, not exceeding the amount to be paid for the property taken, shall be paid to them in the order of their respective rights before any sum is paid to the owners of the property."

The trial court sustained the demurrer and gave judgment absolute for defendant, whereupon plaintiff brought this writ.

* * *

Before HOUGH, MANTON, and MAYER, Circuit Judges.

HOUGH, Circuit Judge (after stating the facts as above). Plaintiff certainly had an interest in the lands condemned, and its action is for damages to that interest. It rests on the alleged unlawful act of defendant in failing to give notice or opportunity to assert its right to the plaintiff pursuant to the statute. The judgment below is in effect a holding that under the allegations made it is impossible, on benevolent reading of the complaint, to discover any recoverable damage.

Yet it is equally plain that, if defendant was bound by the provisions of Gen.Stat. § 5192, it failed in a duty imposed by law, and plaintiff should have opportunity to show a jury that damage to it—i.e., to its interest in the Glastonbury property—was thereby proximately caused. On demurrer we cannot speculate as to whether damages are likely to be provable.

The judgment complained of is sought to be justified by the assertion that the act imposing obligation on one exercising eminent domain to give notice to the mortgagors and lienors of record is a general statute, whereas the defendant possessed and exercised its power of condemning the Cold brook lands wholly by virtue of "special acts," and therefore the general statute has no application.

It is not and cannot be asserted that the Legislature may not affect or modify special acts by general statutes; but this, it is said, requires specific reference to them. The language of the general statute in force when condemnation began is that whoever takes by eminent domain "under any statute of this state" shall do the thing which this defendant did not do; and we are of opinion that the phrase "any statute of this state" covers and includes all statutes of Connecticut, whether denominated general or special, public or private.

A statute or statute law is by long-accepted definition the express written will of the Legislature, rendered authentic by certain prescribed forms and solemnities. Potter's Dwarris, 37. Cf. Lewis' Sutherland on Statutory Construction, § 321 et seq.; Bishop on the Written Law, § 42a et seq., and Bouvier, tit. "Statutes."

A "statute of a state" is any law directly passed by the Legislature of that state (Cumberland, etc., Co. v. Memphis, 198 F. 955, 957 (D.C.Tenn. 1912)); and any enactment to which a state gives the force of law is a statute of the state (Atlantic, etc., Co. v. Goldsboro, 232 U.S. 548, 34 S.Ct. 364, 58 L.Ed. 721 (1914)).

Historically the phrases "special act" and "private act" mean the same thing; and in Unity v. Burrage, 103 U.S. 447, 455 (26 L.Ed. 405 [1880]) it was pointed out that such acts or statutes as those incorporating counties, establishing courthouses and the like "all operate upon local subjects, [but] they are not for that reason special or private acts. In this country the disposition has been, on the whole to enlarge the limits of this class of public acts, and to bring within it all enactments of a general character, or which in any way affect the community at large."

Nor does the fact that a given statute affects only a portion of the territory under the Legislature's dominion influence the matter at all, if the statute affects all of the population within the limited area. Lewis' Sutherland, supra, and cases cited. Finally, whether a law be local, or otherwise entitled to some peculiar appellation, is a question of fact, and not of form. Gray v. Taylor, 227 U.S. 51, 33 S.Ct. 199, 57 L.Ed. 413 (1913).

For these reasons, while inclined to think that the special acts giving to defendant the power of eminent domain are public acts in fact, we hold that they are plainly statutes of Connecticut, and therefore within the phrase "any statute of this state."

It appears to have been held below as another reason for sustaining demurrer that there was nothing "due" to this plaintiff at the time of condemnation. But the word "due," as applied to debts, is sometimes used to express the mere state of indebtedness, and it is then equivalent to "owed" or "owing" (United States v. State Bank, 6 Pet. 29, 8 L.Ed. 308 [1803]); and the word in its larger and general sense signifies that which is owed, that which one contracts to pay to or perform to another (Wyman v. Kimberly-Clark Co., 93 Wis. 554, 556, 67 N.W. 932 [1896], with full citation of authorities).

We are clear that the word "due," as used in this statute, imports existing obligations or indebtednesses of records, without regard to maturity; if it were otherwise, the statute would wholly fail of its obvious purpose, which is to prevent exactly the condition of affairs that here exists. For these reasons, the judgment must be reversed, and the defendant required to answer over on payment of costs and within a time to be fixed by the lower court.

For the sake of accuracy it should be pointed out that, while defendant's whole case has hitherto rested upon the assertion of rights under private acts or special acts, the case has been treated as though the acts in question were general and public, for the court has taken cognizance of them on demurrer without pleading or proof. Observance of the fundamental rule that acts, if really private, must be pleaded, would have prevented a journey to this court on general demurrer.

As trial before a jury would be the natural result of this decision, we point out again that the action is for damages to the plaintiff's estate or interest by the appropriation of certain mortgaged lands without compensation to it. Like all damages, they must be proved, and not presumed. This is not an action for debt. Non constat but that the remaining lands are amply sufficient to satisfy plaintiff's mortgage lien.

Judgment reversed, with costs, and case remanded, with directions to proceed in a manner not inconsistent with this opinion.

People v. Nitzberg
Court of Appeals of New York, 1941. 287 N.Y. 183, 38 N.E.2d 490.

This case was ultimately decided in New York State's highest court. In New York State, felony cases are usually tried in what is designated as a Supreme Court of the State of New York for a designated county of the state. Actually, this is not a supreme court as the name implies, but a trial court that may have a criminal part and a civil part. The criminal part tries cases of a felony grade. The Appellate Court of the Supreme Court is known as the Appellate Division of the Supreme Court of a particular department. There are four designated departments, each having an Appellate Division. Appeals may be entertained by the Appellate Division, as of right, but a further appeal to the Court of Appeals is done by a motion for leave to appeal in most cases. There are also strict limitations of time in which to serve the necessary papers.

The characterization of "People" in the case name means "The People of the State of New York." It may be interesting to know that Abraham Reles, the chief witness for the people, was in the protective custody of the New York City Police Department and was kept on a very high floor of a hotel located in Coney Island, Brooklyn, New York, called The Half Moon Hotel. While in police custody, he is alleged to have jumped to the street below, and he was mortally wounded. To this day, so far as I know, there has never been an absolute determination whether he voluntarily jumped to his death or was thrown to his death by an unknown person or persons.

The group to which he belonged was named "Murder Incorporated." Its members were, as Reles testified, in the business of murder in Brooklyn.

The decision stands for the principle, among other principles, that anything irrelevant or not logically probative is not admissible in the trial as a rational principle of evidence.

The edited decision follows:

LOUGHRAN, Judge. The defendant stands convicted of murder in the first degree. One Shuman was the victim of the homicide. On January 10, 1939, his slain body was found in an automobile that was parked on a street in Brooklyn.

(1) Abraham Reles—a self-confessed accomplice in the crime—was the chief witness for the People. Put into direct discourse his story in substance was this: My business was murder in Brooklyn. Lepke was one of my bosses. In December 1938, Mendy Weiss and I visited Lepke at his hideout apartment where Mendy "told Lep that Pug Shuman was speaking to Inspector McDermott, giving him information against him." Lepke said, "If he is giving information against me go out and take him." After that, I got from the defendant— who knew the man—a promise to lure Shuman into the hallway of a building near the intersection of Eastern parkway and Buffalo avenue in Brooklyn so that we could kill him there. Later on I thought less of that plan when I recalled that a traffic policeman was usually on duty at that street intersection. I told this to the defendant and gave him another plan which was carried out on the night of January 9, 1939. The defendant at that time got Shuman to go riding with him in a stolen automobile I had supplied and shot him to death while I followed in another automobile in which the defendant and I drove away.

Reles having given this testimony, the prosecution in its direct case brought Dorothy Walker, Philip J. Bang, Herman Breitman, Michael F. McDermott, Bernard Moskowitz and Bernard Freundlich to the witness stand. Walker—the housekeeper for Lepke at his so-called hideout apartment—testified that Reles and others (of whom the defendant was not one) had visited Lepke there in the latter part of 1938. Bang testified that, as a member of the police department assigned to traffic patrol on Eastern parkway throughout December, 1938, he had during that month spent some time at the corner of Eastern parkway and Buffalo avenue, because accidents frequently happened at that spot. McDermott is the police inspector to whom Reles referred in his testimony. McDermott's evidence was that from time to time in December, 1938, he had had conversations with Shuman at police headquarters in Brooklyn and at the office of the District Attorney of the county of New York. Breitman was the owner of the automobile in which Shuman's body was found. He testified that the vehicle had been stolen from a garage in Long Island City in September, 1938. Moskowitz was the keeper of that garage. He gave similar testimony. Freundlich testified that the license plates that were on the car in which Shuman's body was found had been stolen in December, 1938, from another automobile owned by himself.

For convenience we shall here and there refer to Walker, Bang, McDermott, Breitman, Moskowitz and Freundlich as the non-accomplice witnesses.

After the trial judge had delivered his charge to the jury he was requested by counsel for the defendant to instruct them that the facts sworn to by the non-accomplice witnesses were "insufficient evidence to corroborate the accomplice." The judge responded: "That is right, and I so charge, that those facts which you have just stated are not intended to connect the defendant with the commission of the crime, but they are intended to corroborate the witness as to whether or not he is telling the truth as to credibility." Counsel for the defendant thereupon made this protest: "I say that that evidence cannot tend to connect the defendant with the commission of the

crime." Again the judge rejoined: "I so charge, but it does tend to show, or prove or disprove the credibility of a witness." To these rulings, and to the refusal of the trial judge to strike out the testimony of some of the non-accomplice witnesses, counsel for the defendant took exceptions which are now pressed upon us.

Each and every of the matters sworn to by the non-accomplice witnesses was undisputed by the defendant. Not a single item of the testimony of any of them had any applicability whatsoever to his identity as a participator in this crime. So, indeed, the trial judge ruled. In that state of the case the question is whether we can sustain the further ruling that such independent testimony was nonetheless to be used by the jury in constructing for the accomplice-witness Reles a general credibility that would perhaps amount to a sanction for his narration of the vital and controverted particulars of his story against the defendant.

Was the fact that Walker (in the defendant's absence) saw Reles in Lepke's apartment relevant to show that Reles was truthful in his testimony that he and the defendant planned this crime? Was the fact that Officer Bang patrolled Eastern parkway relevant to show that Reles was truthful in his testimony that he told the defendant an officer was on duty there? Was the fact that Shuman was in communication with Inspector McDermott relevant to show that Reles was truthful in his testimony that he had prevailed on the defendant to kill Shuman? Was the fact of the theft of the automobile in which Shuman's body was found relevant to show that Reles was truthful in his testimony that he procured that stolen vehicle for the defendant? There is no element of novelty in any of these queries, save as they bring to the top of our minds one or two rules of ordinary human thought that have seldom called for explicit statement in the case law.

"There is a principle—not so much a rule of evidence as a presupposition involved in the very conception of a rational system of evidence . . . —which forbids receiving anything irrelevant, not logically probative." Thayer, Preliminary Treatise on Evidence, 264, 265. "It is not the law which furnishes the test of relevancy, but logic. Probative value, or capability of supporting an inference, is a matter of reasoning . . . and the rules of relevancy aim only to determine whether a given fact is of sufficient probative value to be admissible at all." 1 Greenleaf on The Law of Evidence, Wigmore's 16th Ed., § 14. For the purposes of the present case it is enough in the way of a definition of relevancy to say that a fact is relevant to another fact when the existence of the one renders the existence of the other highly probable, according to the common course of events. See Sir James Stephen, Digest of the Law of Evidence, Chase's 2d Ed., Introduction XVIII. Cf. Platner v. Platner, 78 N.Y. 90, 94 (1879).

The fact sworn to by Walker—the presence of Reles in the Lepke apartment—was a criminal fact. On the say-so of Reles that fact initiated the killing of Shuman. The fact sworn to by Breitman, Moskowitz and Freundlich—the theft of the vehicle in which Shuman's body was found—was on the face of it a criminal fact. On his own say-so, too, Reles was closely tied to that fact. Now it was precisely because he was attainted in that way that Reles as a witness stood in need of support from a purer source to show that he was not doing a bad turn by putting the defendant in his place in the disputed accusatory parts of his story. In other words, Reles' self-confessed connection with those criminal facts put him outside the limit of the presumption that witnesses ordinarily are honest up to their lights. In the face of all this the trial judge, nevertheless, told the jury in respect of Reles that the independent evidence of those very criminal facts "does tend to show, or prove or disprove the credibility of a witness."

We think it unnecessary to probe this idea that a strong implication of the non-credibility of a witness may be rebutted by independent evidence which confirms him in his confession of the very criminality which gives rise to that implication. Whatever its merits, such a process, we believe, is not fit for the trial of issues on which life and liberty depend. To our minds it appears safe enough to say at once that the testimony of Walker, Breitman, Moskowitz and Freundlich did not indicate with any fair degree of probability that Reles might here be taken in the light of common

experience to have been over all a truthful witness. We do not mean, however, that their testimony was not receivable as evidence of a part of the principal occurrence in issue. Cf. People v. Sherman, 103 N.Y. 513, 9 N.E. 178 (1886).

The testimony of Officer Bang has a somewhat different aspect. The location of his post of duty was a fact that had no necessary connection with Reles. Indeed, it was a fact that was known to everybody. But if an accomplice-witness could be supported at large by independent evidence that he told the truth in matters of that sort, then every accomplice (not incompetent for want of understanding) could always rake into his story materials for such confirmation of it. See Commonwealth v. Bosworth, 22 Mass (Pick.) 397, 399 (1839). It has been a long time since an accomplice-witness has been suffered so to lift himself by his own bootstraps. Cf. People v. Katz, 209 N.Y. 311, 342, 103 N.E. 305 (1913). We are not persuaded that the location of the post of Officer Bang on Eastern parkway made it highly probable in point of reason that Reles was truthful in his testimony that he told the defendant an officer was usually on duty there.

So with the testimony of Inspector McDermott that Shuman (the victim of this crime) had been in communication with him. We will make the good-sized assumption that this testimony was well enough as evidence that Reles had reported the same fact to Lepke. This report of Reles (as he said) had been made in a secret conference among him, Lepke and Weiss when they were privately assembled for the sake of their common protection from interference by the police. To us it seems that the results of ordinary human experience do not countenance the notion that the testimony of Inspector McDermott was proximately probative of the fact that the truth was in Reles once more when (after his arrest and with the promise that the District Attorney "would speak to the court for me") he testified that the major part in the commission of this crime had been taken over by this defendant.

In a word, all the testimony of the non-accomplice witnesses was, in our judgment, inadmissible as evidence of the credibility of the accomplice witness Reles, because it was of merely slight, remote or conjectural significance in respect of that issue—to say nothing for the moment of the fact that such a use of that testimony inevitably tended unnecessarily to confuse the real issues and unfairly to surprise the defendant to his prejudice. See People v. Harris, 209 N.Y. 70, 102 N.E. 546 (1913).

Perhaps it should be added at this point that there was in this case no question of restoring the credit of Reles after his impeachment as a witness. The facts that discredited him came out on his direct examination and, as we have noticed, the non-accomplice witnesses were called by the prosecution in its direct case. See People v. Edwards, 282 N.Y. 413, 26 N.E.2d 957 (1940).

* * *

(4) We come now to an often burdensome question. May the error be regarded as technical and insufficient to require a reversal? See People v. Marendi, 213 N.Y. 600, 618, 620,

107 N.E. 1058 (1915). This defendant took the stand. His guilt is far from being clearly exhibited by the record. Of the three witnesses for the People who gave evidence sufficient to satisfy the statutory requirement of corroboration of Reles two had been prisoners in a jail where the defendant had been confined. Their testimony was that the defendant admitted his guilt to them or in their hearing to persons who visited him there. The third of these witnesses was a thrice-convicted criminal.

In that state of the record we cannot say that the inadmissible use made of the testimony of the non-accomplice witnesses did not affect the result. It is quite manifest that their testimony was adduced in the apprehension that without such use thereof it was not unlikely that the verdict would be not guilty.

The judgment of conviction should be reversed and a new trial ordered.

RELATED DECISIONS
Testimony and Evidence

Ex Parte Jackson
Court of Criminal Appeals of Texas, 1971.
470 S.W.2d 679.

When the words "Ex Parte" appear in the name of a case, it means literally "on one side only; by or for one party; done for, in behalf of, or on the application of, one party only." Black's Law Dictionary (6th Ed. 1990).

As used in connection with this case, it means that an application for extradition of Martin Arnold Jackson a/k/a Jack Alvin Cage was made by the state of Arizona directed to the state of Texas for a crime of robbery committed in Arizona. Texas was the state where the subject was residing, and thus Texas was known as the "asylum state." The governor of Texas issued an executive warrant authorizing the arrest of the suspect in Texas. The suspect contested the extradition proceedings, claiming that he was not in the state of Arizona at the time of the alleged incident.

This case presents judicial definitions of the words "testimony" and "evidence" and distinguishes the meanings of these words.

The edited decision of the court follows:

OPINION

ONION. Presiding Judge. This is an appeal from an order entered in a habeas corpus proceeding in the 59th District Court of Grayson County remanding appellant to custody for extradition to the State of Arizona to answer the charge of robbery.

* * *

A formal order of the court entered later reflects the court had heard "evidence and argument of counsel" and the order concludes: "It is ordered, adjudged and decreed that extradition be granted and relator be placed in custody of Jack Bowen for removal to the State of Arizona *ad* directed in Governor's Warrant."

The Executive Warrant of the Governor of Texas and the supporting papers from the demanding state are in the record before us. The Executive Warrant appears regular on its face. Appellant's brief acknowledges that he received copies of the same on the date of the hearing, and that he was responsible for filing the same with the clerk on November 26, 1970.

There does appear in the record two agreed "statement of facts." One filed on January 14, 1971, bearing the approval of both counsel and the Judge, reads as follows.

"The State of Texas called Jack Bowen to the stand as a witness, and he testified as follows:

"That he was a deputy sheriff in Tucson, Arizona. That he had seen Martin Arnold Jackson one time in his life and that was at a barbeque party, and this was a week or so before the alleged offense occurred in 1968. That he had not seen him since and that he had not seen him on the date the alleged offense was committed. He identified Martin Arnold Jackson as being the same person wanted by the State of Arizona. There was no other testimony presented by the State.

"Martin Arnold Jackson testified that he was not in Arizona at the time of the alleged offense, but that he was living in New Orleans, Louisiana, at the time of the alleged offense. He denied being at any barbeque party or ever having seen Deputy Jack Bowen. There was no other testimony presented on behalf of Martin Arnold Jackson.

"This, in substance, truly and accurately sets out all the testimony at said hearing."

Another instrument (entitled "Statements of Facts") bearing the date of January 21, 1971, but reflecting no file mark is found in the record. Such statement shows the following:

"On behalf of the State of Texas Jack Bowen testified as follows:

"that he is a deputy sheriff in and for Pima County, Arizona and is acquainted with Martin Arnold Jackson who is also known as Jack Alvin Cage. That he was acquainted with the said Martin Arnold Jackson on and before the 27th day of November, 1968. That he did not see Martin Arnold Jackson in Tucson, Arizona on the 27th day of November, 1968, but that he did see him about a week prior to that time in Tucson which is in Pima County.

"Martin Arnold Jackson testified on behalf of himself that on the 27th day of November, 1968, he was in New Orleans, Louisiana which was his residence. He testified that he had lived in Pima County, Arizona prior to November 27, 1968, but that he had not been in such county for several weeks prior to the date of the alleged offense.

"The foregoing represents in substance the testimony adduced at said hearing."

It is appellant's contention the evidence offered was insufficient to justify extradition.

"In proceedings to challenge the legality of the arrest and detention of an accused under an executive warrant for his extradition, the state has the initial burden of showing that the arrest and detention are lawful." 25 Tex.Jur.2d, Extradition, Sec. 3, p. 180, citing Ex parte Hagler [161 Tex.Cr.R. 387], 278 S.W.2d 143.

The Executive Warrant of the Governor of the asylum state would appear to be an indispensable part of the evidence in any such proceeding. *Ex parte* Hagler, *supra*. If such warrant is in the courtroom at the habeas corpus hearing, it should be introduced in evidence by the State. If it is not introduced, it must be presumed that it does not authorize extradition. *Ex parte* Hagler, *supra*.

It is well established that when the Executive Warrant, regular on its face, is introduced into evidence, a prima facie case authorizing extradition is made out. By the same token, such prima facie case is not established until the Executive Warrant is introduced. *Ex parte* Hagler, *supra*.

In *Ex parte* Sykes, 400 S.W.2d 568 (Tex.Cr.App. 1966), the order remanding Sykes for extradition was reversed. There the court said:

"The statement of facts agreed to be a true and correct statement of all the evidence introduced in the case consists only of the testimony of appellant elicited by his counsel.

"The Executive Warrant of the Governor of Texas is not found in the record, though the order appealed from recites that it was considered. The same is true as to the Requisition of the Governor of Arizona, and supporting documents.

"In the absence of the Executive Warrant or other evidence offered by the state, there was no showing that appellant was lawfully restrained."

Sykes is distinguished from the instant case in two respects. First, the Executive Warrant, regular on its face, is in the record before us. Second, the agreed "Statement or Statements of Facts" relate only to the testimony given and do not purport to include all the evidence presented as in Sykes.

"Testimony" is evidence given by a competent witness under oath or affirmation as distinguished from evidence derived from writing and other sources. See Black's Law Dictionary, DeLuxe Fourth Ed.; Cauble v. Key, 256 S.W. 654, 655 (Tex.Cir.App. 1924). Although "testimony" and "evidence" are frequently used synonymously, Superior Lloyds of America v. Foxworth, 178 S.W.2d 724, 726 (Tex.Civ.App. 1944), the terms are not synonymous. Bednarik v. Bednarik, 18 N.J.Misc. 633, 16 A.2d 80, 89 (1940). Evidence is the broader term and includes all testimony which is one species of evidence. Bednarik v. Bednarik, *supra*. It is clear that the "agreed Statement or Statements of Facts" applied only to the testimony found in the spoken words of the witnesses and did not attempt to encompass all the evidence introduced at the habeas hearing.

Since the Texas Governor's Warrant, regular on its face, is in the record before us, and the trial judge's order clearly indicated it was before him when he entered his order, we deem the record sufficient to reflect its introduction and to establish a prima facie case authorizing extradition.

Once the Executive or Governor's Warrant is in evidence, then the burden is upon the person named therein to overcome the prima facie proof of the existence of every fact which the Texas Governor was obliged to determine before issuing the extradition warrant, including the fact that the person named in the warrant was in the demanding state at the time of the commission of the offense charged. See *Ex parte* Mach, 448 S.W.2d 126 (Tex.Cr.App. 1970). See also 25 Tex.Jur.2d, Extradition, Sec. 31, pp. 182–183.

In addition to the warrant, the State offered the testimony of an Arizona deputy sheriff that the petitioner had been in Arizona "about a week prior" to the date of the alleged offense. Appellant admitted he had lived in Arizona prior to the date in question but had not been in the county where alleged offense occurred for several weeks prior to the date of the alleged offense, claiming he was living in New Orleans, Louisiana on that date.

It should be noted that testimony of the appellant standing alone is insufficient to require a finding that he was not in the demanding state at the time the offense was alleged to have been committed. *Ex parte* Martin, 374 S.W.2d 436 (Tex.Cr.App. 1964); *Ex parte* Overaker, 404 S.W.2d 595 (Tex.Cr.App. 1966); *Ex parte* Gibson, 149 Tex.Cr.App. 543, 197 S.W.2d 109 (1946); *Ex parte* Moore, 436 S.W.2d 901 (Tex.Cr.App. 1969). See also 25 Tex.Jur.2d, Extradition, Sec. 12, p. 140.

The judgment is affirmed.

RELATED DECISIONS
Documentary Evidence

Ticknor v. Ticknor
Supreme Court, Special Term, Nassau County, Part I, 1960. 23 Misc.2d 257, 200 N.Y.S.2d 661.

This case is a motion (application) for alimony pendente lite and counsel fees in an action for separation. In nonlegal language, this means that the wife is seeking to be paid support and to have her counsel fees paid to her attorney during the course of the action for separation from her husband. Many times marital actions such as this could take months, or years, to be finally disposed of either by a court decision or by a settlement agreement. She had no other means of support.

This decision presents a discussion of the nature of documentary evidence. The edited decision follows:

FRANK A. GULOTTA, Justice. This is a motion for alimony pendente lite and counsel fee in a separation action which includes general allegations of cruel and inhuman treatment, conduct on the part of the defendant which has made it unsafe for plaintiff to cohabit with him, abandonment, refusal and neglect of the defendant to provide for plaintiff, and adultery.

The defendant has made a cross-motion for summary judgment, pursuant to Rule 113 of the Rules of Civil Practice, asking that the complaint be dismissed on the ground that the parties were divorced in the State of Alabama by decree dated June 16, 1958, issued by the Circuit Court of that State in the Tenth Judicial District. In support of his contention defendant has submitted documentary evidence consisting of a power of attorney executed by the plaintiff on May 31, 1958, authorizing one William L. Allison to appear for her in the action commenced by this defendant against her in the State of Alabama, an Answer and Waiver signed by her and the Final Decree of Divorce.

Plaintiff counters by saying she did not know what she was signing and that defendant "(threatened) the plaintiff with bodily harm unless she executed some documents which were thrust under her nose."

It appears that the parties were married on July 18, 1952. There is no issue of this union although plaintiff has a daughter by a prior marriage. On April 18, 1958, the parties separated, plaintiff returning with her daughter to the family home in Sunbury, Pennsylvania, and the defendant remaining in Mount Vernon, New York, where they then lived.

Plaintiff contends that the reason for the separation was that defendant no longer desired to live with her. On the other hand, defendant says that plaintiff just packed her belongings and with her daughter went to reside in Sunbury, Pennsylvania, because she couldn't live in New York and got too homesick and lonesome. Defendant's version seems to be substantiated by a letter postmarked May 8, 1958, sent by plaintiff from Sunbury, Pennsylvania, to defendant at Mount Vernon, New York, wherein she says, in part:

> ". . . as I told you don't think I'll ever live in N.Y. again. I get too homesick & lonesome. . . . Maybe it is best we call it quits as I don't feel you could settle here ever & you have a good job so please keep it. In time I feel you will probably find a nice girl. There is no one else I want & probably never will marry again. If I ever do it will be a surprise to me. So if you want to go out go. Also in time you can get a divorce if you want as I won't stop you."

The letter is very solicitous and written in a very friendly and understanding tone. It ends as follows: "Be good & take care of yourself. May God Bless You. Love, Loretta."

The Alabama documents above referred to were signed by her on May 31, 1958, some three weeks later, when defendant visited her in Pennsylvania. The power of attorney was executed before a Notary Public in Sunbury and her signature to the Answer and Waiver was witnessed by the same Notary.

Apparently both parties felt that a divorce was the only solution because on May 20, 1958, defendant wrote to plaintiff: "If you feel that divorce is our solution, why don't you see about obtaining one in Sunbury there. You have established a residence there and know a great many people. I would be more than willing to shoulder whatever expense would be incurred in such action." Plaintiff could not have been surprised by being given the Alabama papers to sign for the correspondence on both sides was leading to just that. On May 26, 1958, she received a letter from defendant stating:

> I cannot see much practical sense in us being married when you are out there in Sunbury and I am working and trying to get along up here alone. My lawyer is a very nice man and he feels that a clean break is the best thing for both of us under the circumstances.
>
> "I do want you and Phyllis to have all your personal belongings and things that you might want. That is why I am coming out and I can bring the papers for you to sign in order to make the necessary preparations for divorce."

For two years plaintiff did nothing and has now suddenly brought this action on very tenuous allegations, with no facts.

There is no need to discuss the lack of probability of success in the plaintiff's matrimonial action, since the only point involved is the validity of the Alabama decree. Concededly the defendant has not supported the plaintiff since it was obtained and that decree must be the justification for not having done so, or there is none.

Insofar as the foreign decree is attacked because the plaintiff was not a bona fide resident, that avenue is no longer open, since it cannot now be questioned in Alabama on that ground, neither can it be collaterally attacked in New York, and it must be accorded full faith and credit here. Boxer v. Boxer, 7 A.D.2d 1001, 184 N.Y.S.2d 303 (1959); Sherrer v. Sherrer, 334 U.S. 343, 68 S.Ct. 1087, 1097, 92 L.Ed. 1429 (1948).

The question of alleged duress presents a different problem. Were we to have a case of true duress, i.e., coercion in forcing defendant to sign an authorization of appearance so overwhelming that the act would not represent a voluntary act of the defendant at all, it may be assumed that such facts could form the basis for a direct attack in the forum of the decree or for an oblique attack here. Finan v. Finan, 47 N.Y.S.2d 429 (Sup. 1944).

The facts here do not support such a conclusion; in fact they point the opposite way.

However, to bring this case within the new Rule 113 which permits a defendant in a matrimonial action to move for summary judgment when his defense is based on documentary evidence or official records it is necessary to consider whether the plaintiff's letter of May 8, 1958, fits into the first category.

The divorce decree is undoubtedly an official record, but the letter is needed to prove the absence of duress. I think a letter may properly be considered a document Richardson on Evidence, 8th Edition, § 2, states:

"Documentary evidence is evidence in the form of a writing or writings. White v. Merchants Despatch Co., 256 App.Div. 1044, 10 N.Y.S.[2d] 962; Schusterman v. C. & F. Caters, 192 Misc. 564, 566, 77 N.Y.S.[2d] 718. It has been more elaborately defined as follows: a document is 'any substance having any matter expressed or described upon it by marks capable of being read,' and when 'produced for the inspection of the court . . . such documents are called documentary evidence.' Chase's Stephen's Digest of the Law of Evidence, pp. 3, 4."

Tripps' Guide to Motion Practice, cp. 289, states:

"The documentary proof contemplated by the rule is not defined or limited. Any document which meets a dictionary definition of that term is a document within the meaning of Rule 113, R.C.P., as it need not 'completely and conclusively establish the defense, without resort to extrinsic or fragmentary connecting links of proof supplied by affidavit or scattered entries or memoranda.' (Chance v. Guaranty Trust Co. of New York, 173 Misc. 754, 20 N.Y.S.[2d] 635, *aff'd,* 257 App.Div. 1006, 13 N.Y.S.[2d] 785, 285 N.Y. 802)."

Black's Law Dictionary defines documentary evidence as:

"Evidence supplied by writings and documents of every kind in the widest sense of the term; evidence derived from conventional symbols (such as letters) by which ideas are represented on material substances. Such evidence as is furnished by written instruments, inscriptions, documents of all kinds, and also any inanimate objects admissible for the purpose, as distinguished from 'oral' evidence, or that delivered by human beings viva voce. People v. Purcell, 22 Cal.App.2d 126, 70 P.2d 706, 709."

The doctrine of "divisible divorce" does not obtain where there was in personam jurisdiction to support the foreign decree and thus the determination of the duress issue likewise disposes of the applicability of § 1170–b of the Civil Practice Act.

The plaintiff's motion is denied and the defendant's cross-motion is granted.

Short form order signed.

RELATED DECISIONS
Quantum of Proof Required

Fine v. Kolodny
Court of Appeals of Maryland, 1971.
263 Md. 647, 284 A.2d 409.

The plaintiff in this case was a mentally deranged person who represented herself (pro se) instead of hiring an attorney to represent her at trial. In so doing, she was unable to get testimony admitted into evidence because her statements were rhetorical and were conversations between her and the witnesses. As a result, her statements were not subject to cross-examination, and no opportunity to question her capacity to testify was afforded to the defendants.

The edited decision follows:

* * *

FINAN, Judge.

Mrs. Margaret B. Fine, plaintiff-appellant, filed suit in the Circuit Court for Baltimore County against Dr. A. Lewis Kolodny and Mildred Kolodny, his wife; Paul C. Wolman, Jr., Esq.; Taylor Manor Hospital; and Isaac H. Taylor and Dr. Irving J. Taylor, licensees of Taylor Manor Hospital, defendants and appellees, for false imprisonment. The case was tried before a jury with Maguire, J., presiding and upon conclusion of the appellant's case, the court directed verdicts in favor of the defendants. Mrs. Fine has appealed from these judgments.

The court below in entering the directed verdicts ruled that the plaintiff's evidence showed that she voluntarily consented to her own admission and treatment at the Taylor Manor Hospital (hospital), a private psychiatric clinic in Howard County, and submitted to confinement in that institution.

Unfortunately, Mrs. Fine acted as her own counsel in the court below and her case was not enhanced by her lack of knowledge of court procedure and the rules of evidence. On appeal her counsel contend that there was evidence in the record from which the jury could have found that Mrs. Fine did not voluntarily submit to admission and treatment at the hospital and hence the lower court erred in granting the directed verdicts in favor of the defendants. Tully v. Dasher, 250 Md. 424, 440, 244 A.2d 207 (1968); Trionfo v. R.J. Hellman, Inc., 250 Md. 12, 15, 241 A.2d 554 (1968). After reviewing the record we are of the opinion that the undisputed evidence compels the conclusion that she did voluntarily enter the hospital for treatment. It would serve no useful purpose to relate in detail the sequence of bizarre and sad events which led to Mrs. Fine's confinement, since her act of voluntarily submitting herself to admission and treatment at the hospital rendered her previous actions and those of the defendants only tangentially relevant. However, in fairness to the defendants, we would characterize their roles as that of "good Samaritans."

The evidence discloses that close to midnight of September 25, 1965, Dr. Kolodny, a family friend and neighbor of the Fines, was aroused by the sound of firearms being discharged in the vicinity of the Fine residence.

Knowing that Mrs. Fine was at that time separated from her husband and probably alone, Dr. Kolodny, fearing for her safety, summoned the police and accompanied a police officer in an unmarked car to the Fine home. The house was in darkness. The police officer placed a portable red light behind the windshield of the police vehicle and they attempted to locate Mrs. Fine, calling her by name. A bullet narrowly missed the police officer as he proceeded, flashlight in hand, around the corner of the house. Shortly thereafter, Mrs. Fine emerged from a wooded area near the home carrying a rifle and a revolver. Strung between the trees and the house was a trip-wire with bells attached. The trio then entered the house where it appeared that several windows had been shot out from within the home. Mrs. Fine appeared to be in a highly emotional state. A police lieutenant, another policeman and the Fines' family attorney, Paul Wolman, Jr., Esq., shortly arrived on the scene.

Mrs. Fine was eventually persuaded to go to the hospital. Efforts were made to reach Mr. Fine but to no avail and Dr. Kolodny made arrangements for her admission. Dr. Kolodny, Mrs. Kolodny and Paul Wolman, Jr. accompanied Mrs. Fine in an automobile to the hospital. One of the police officers followed in the unmarked police car. The testimony of the police officers who were present at the Fine home and that of the officer who followed the car transporting Mrs. Fine was that she went voluntarily to the hospital and no threats or restraints were employed. This was uncontroverted. The evidence reveals that upon arrival at the hospital Mrs. Fine was at first reluctant to sign a voluntary admission form but several hours thereafter, around 9 a.m. she did. The execution of this form was witnessed by Dr. Henry Klark, a reputable psychiatrist, who testified that he spent most of the night trying to relieve Mrs. Fine's overwrought condition. Dr. Klark's psychiatric impression of Mrs. Fine was "schizophrenic reaction paranoid, probably long time latent." The Taylor Manor Hospital records also contain certificates of two independent physicians, Dr. McGrath and Dr. Herbert, dated October 2nd and 7th respectively, certifying her to be mentally incompetent. On October 8, 1965, at her husband's request she was transferred to Seton Institute.

Dr. James Miller and Dr. Charles Williams also examined Mrs. Fine the day after she entered Seton Institute and certified her as mentally incompetent. Doctors Hyman S. Rubenstein, Jonas Rappaport and George Lasson, all witnesses called by Mrs. Fine, testified as to her mental instability. The record reveals that she left Seton Institute on October 21, 1965, against medical advice.

In any action for false imprisonment it is necessary for the plaintiff to prove by a preponderance of evidence that he was deprived of his liberty by another without his consent and without legal justification. Great Atlantic & Pacific Tea Company v. Paul, 256 Md. 643, 654, 261 A.2d 731 (1970). The witnesses called by Mrs. Fine supported the opposite conclusion. Recognizing the weakness of her case, Judge Maguire gratuitously inquired several times of Mrs. Fine as to whether she wished to testify on her own behalf and she failed to avail herself of these opportunities. Judge Maguire very clearly and patiently explained to her the effect of the motion for a directed verdict and, without expressly so stating, implied to her, before so ruling, that unless she took the witness stand to testify or produce additional testimony, she had not presented sufficient evidence to warrant the case going to the jury.

In argument on appeal, her counsel ingeniously now posit that she did testify. They contend that the rhetorical questions which Mrs. Fine posed to the witnesses, her argumentative questions to them and the many colloquies between her and the bench should be considered as evidence. In these exchanges she stoutly disclaimed that she voluntarily submitted herself to admission and confinement at the Taylor Manor Hospital, denied her signature on the admission form and stated that she was taken from her home against her will. Unfortunately for her, she did not testify to these material facts as a witness.

The appellant's counsel in oral argument emphasized that the mere fact that the statements made by Mrs. Fine in the courtroom during the progress of the trial were not conditioned by an oath, pursuant to the provisions of the Maryland Code (1968 Repl.Vol.), Art. 1, § §9, 10 and 11 or given in an orthodox manner from the witness stand, should not have barred them from being considered as testimony. Counsel further argues that, were these statements to have been considered as testimony, the issue of the voluntariness of her admission to the hospital would have been controverted and accordingly, the case should have gone to the jury.

Assuming, *arguendo*, that the fact that the statements made by Mrs. Fine were not under oath or by affirmation should not have prevented her statements from being considered testimony, there is yet a more significant reason as to why her statements should not be equated with testimony, namely, because these statements were not subject to cross-examination by the defendants' counsel or subject to impeachment. Indeed, the defendants did not even have the opportunity to question her capacity to testify, were they so disposed. Wigmore on Evidence, Vol. II, § 477, 3rd ed. This in our opinion would constitute a violation of the "due process" clause of the Constitution of the United States (Article XIV, Section 1) and Article 23 of the Declaration of Rights of the Constitution of Maryland. In Ridgeway Shopping Center, Inc. v. Seidman, 243 Md. 358, 364, 221 A.2d 393, 396 (1966), Prescott, C.J., speaking for the Court stated:

> "Of course, cross-examination plays a most important part in the administration of justice in this country. It has been stated that it is one of the most efficacious tests for the discovery of the truth. Regester v. Regester, 104 Md. 1 [64 A. 286]. And, when it relates to the facts in issue or to the issues themselves, it may, within reasonable limits, be pursued as a matter of right. 98 C.J.S. Witnesses § 368. . . ." (243 Md. at 364, 221 A.2d at 396).

Additionally, were such a procedure, as urged upon us by the appellant, to be condoned in those cases where a litigant appears *pro se*, there would be no line of demarcation between statements made by the litigant in his capacity as his own counsel and those intended as his testimony as a witness. Indeed, under such a procedural format the opening and closing statement might well be construed as narrative testimony. Obviously, such an amorphous procedure would lead to forensic chaos.

The appellant also challenges the rulings of the lower court regarding its refusal to issue subpoenas for certain witnesses and to continue the case until the witnesses were available. A review of the record reveals that these objections are without merit. There was no proffer made as to what the substance of the testimony of the witnesses might be, nor was there compliance with Maryland Rule 527 c. We likewise find no merit to Mrs. Fine's contention regarding questions asked by the court of witnesses, one of which covered the recapitulation of officer Krauch's testimony on both direct and cross-examination, and the other being in the nature of a summation of the testimony of Dr. Klark. Judge Maguire demonstrated commendable restraint throughout this trial and endeavored to assist Mrs. Fine in every legitimate way to try her case. He did attempt on two occasions to sum up rather disjointed testimony by asking a question of the witnesses which summarized and explained their testimony; however, we hold that under the circumstances this action would have proved helpful to the jury, should the case have gone to the jury, and was within permissible limits of interrogation by the court. Cumberland and Allegheny Gas Company v. Caler, 157 Md. 596, 601, 146 A. 750 (1929).

Finally, appellant complains that the court stenographer did not make available to her for the purpose of impeachment of witnesses the transcript of testimony in a former divorce case. The record reveals that her request for this transcribed testimony was not timely made, that no proffer was made concerning its relevance to the present case, nor were the witnesses whose testimony she wished to impeach by the transcript called by her. Furthermore, it would appear that Judge Maguire made every effort to obtain for her the requested portions of the transcript and apparently was successful in obtaining some of it. In short, we fail to see how Mrs. Fine's case was prejudiced by the unavailability of the transcript.

Judgments affirmed, appellant to pay costs.

✔ PRACTICE QUESTIONS

Indicate whether each statement is true or false.

1. The common law is law that is applicable to the common people, while the nobility had other laws applicable to their conduct.

2. The common law may be changed by court decision if the court determines that a change is in order because of changed customs or mores.

3. When a person wants to find what the law is on a designated question, that person should consult a dictionary of the English language.

4. Statutory law is law that is changed by courts through the theory of stare decisis.

5. Stare decisis is a method by which courts may gradually change the common law.

Select the best answer to complete each statement.

6. Each state is free to codify rules of evidence to be used in trials, provided
   (a) the rule is exactly the same as has been used in that state for more than 100 years.
   (b) the rule has been judged to be equitable by the highest court of that state.
   (c) the rule does not violate a constitutional right that the United States Supreme Court has decided should be afforded to a person within the jurisdiction of the United States.
   (d) (a) and (b) above.

7. The term "legalese language" is
    (a) a formal legal description.
    (b) jargon used to describe a method of expression or form of speech used by lawyers, but not often used in informal conversation by law people.
    (c) a slang expression used by persons who have not become accustomed to the technical language frequently used between attorneys.
    (d) none of the above.

CHAPTER 2

Examination of Witnesses and Trial Procedures

§ 2.1 INTRODUCTION

In the trial of a lawsuit, whether it is of a criminal nature or of a civil nature, one party is arguing against the other. This is known as an adversary proceeding. In such a proceeding, the party who is making the charge has the burden of proving his or her case before the trier of the facts. In law, it is said that the moving party has the burden of proof. There are various degrees of proof, which can best be shown by looking at Figure 3. The scale is supposed to be the scale of justice, and at the beginning of a trial the scale is balanced. As the trial progresses, one side or the other begins to drop, with the corresponding rise on the other side of the scale. Sometimes the evidence will be very heavy on one side, causing that side of the scale to momentarily drop. Then a barrage of excellent cross-examination of the witness may cause the weight to shift toward the other side. The trier of the facts theoretically has a scale of justice in his or her or their minds (depending on whether or not the trial is a jury trial), and when the trial is finally over, the trier makes a determination in favor of one side or the other. If a jury makes this determination, we refer to it as a jury's verdict. If a judge makes the determination, we refer to it as a judgment.

Whether it is a criminal trial, an administrative hearing, or a civil trial, we have what is known as the quantum of proof. This basically means the weight of the evidence sufficient to get a determination of the case for one side or the other. Different quanta of proof are required for the three types of trials. A defendant in a criminal trial must be proved guilty beyond any reasonable doubt. All that is necessary is that a reasonable or average person would have no reasonable doubt that the defendant is guilty. If the prosecution cannot prove this, then the defendant is entitled to have the charge or indictment dismissed and will be permitted to go free. This is shown on the scale of justice in Figure 4.

If it would be necessary to prove the defendant guilty beyond all doubt, the scale would appear as in Figure 5.

In a criminal case, the burden of proof does not shift, but when the government establishes a prima facie case, it is then for the defendant to overcome inferences reasonably to be drawn from the proven facts. U.S.—Wallace v. United States, 281 F.2d 656 (4th Cir. 1960).

Even when the state establishes a prima facie case, the burden of proof in a criminal case does not shift, but the accused is required only to overcome the in-

Figure 3
Criminal Trials: The Scale of Justice

Figure 4
Criminal Trials: Proof Beyond Any Reasonable Doubt

ference the state has established. S.C.—State v. Attardo, 263 S.C. 546, 211 S.E.2d 868 (1975).

Reasonable doubt is not mere guess or surmise that a person may not be guilty; it is such a doubt as a reasonable person may entertain after a fair review and consideration of the evidence, a doubt for which some good reason arising from the evidence can be given. N.Y.—People v. Friedland, 2 App.Div. 332, 37 N.Y.S. 974 (1896). Another case held that a reasonable doubt exists if the doubt is of such a

Figure 5
Criminal Trials: Proof Beyond All Doubt

substance as to cause the prudent person to hesitate and pause in matters of importance in his or her own affairs.

Probable cause is a term used in criminal law to indicate when an officer, acting and thinking as a reasonable person, might have cause to make an arrest. It is more than mere suspicion but less than beyond a reasonable doubt. "Thus a police officer might have probable cause to make an arrest which would make a prima facie case, yet he may not be able to prove the defendant guilty beyond a reasonable doubt." U.S.—United States v. Leaphart, 513 F.2d 747 (10th Cir. 1975).

A defendant charged with a capital offense (one wherein a death penalty may be imposed upon conviction) can be convicted in every state and federal jurisdiction known to me by a determination by the trier of the facts that the defendant is guilty beyond a reasonable doubt. In some cases, the wrong person has been convicted of a crime; sometimes, many years later, the convicted person has been vindicated and set free. The government has usually compensated the wronged person for the mistake by the payment of money and sometimes by public recognition of the wrong inflicted on that person. However, when a person has wrongfully been put to death by the government, no form of compensation can properly repay the dead person or his or her relatives for the wrong incurred. For this and other reasons, many people abhor the imposition of a death penalty. The author suggests that equity demands that laws be changed to require the trier of the facts to find a defendant guilty beyond *all* doubt, instead of beyond any reasonable doubt, before a death penalty may be imposed.

Figure 6
Administrative Hearings: Substantial Evidence

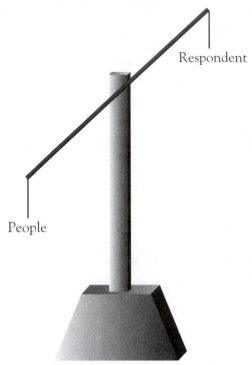

Respondent

People

§ 2.2   SUBSTANTIAL EVIDENCE

What is substantial evidence? The answer of Chief Justice Hughes is this: "Substantial evidence is more than a mere scintilla. It means such relevant evidence as a reasonable man might accept as adequate to support a conclusion."[1] Mere uncorroborated hearsay or rumor does not constitute substantial evidence. The evidence must be such as a reasonable mind would accept,[2] although other like minds would not do so. Substantial evidence is the quantum of proof required for a prosecution to prevail in an administrative hearing (see Figure 6).

Civil trials require still another quantum of proof. This is known as the preponderance of evidence theory. All the successful party must do at the close of the case is to tip the scale in his or her favor, as shown in Figure 7.

The right side of the scale in the diagrams is indicated by different nomenclature. In the criminal and civil cases, the person against whom the action is directed is called the defendant. In the administrative hearing or trial, this person is called the respondent. The left side of the scale also has different appellation. In the criminal trial, the word "People" represents the moving party. This means that the district or county attorney, the attorney general of the state, or the United States attorney of the federal government is the moving party. The non-law

---

[1] U.S.—Consolidated Edison Co. v. N.L.R.B., 305 U.S. 197, 229–230, 59 S.Ct. 206, 216–217, 83 L.Ed. 126 (1938).

[2] U.S.—International Ass'n of Machinists v. N.L.R.B., 110 F.2d 29, 35 (D.C.Cir. 1939), *aff'd*, 311 U.S. 72, 61 S.Ct. 83, 85 L.Ed. 50 (1940).

Figure 7
Civil Cases: Preponderance of Evidence

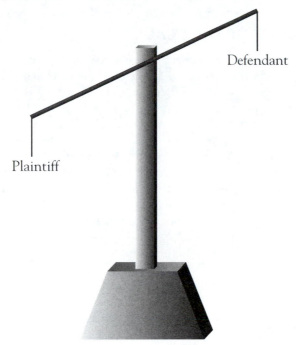

enforcement person who is making the charge against the defendant is called the complainant.

Similarly in an administrative proceeding, the word "People" is used to represent an agent of the government that is prosecuting the respondent. The nongovernmental person making this charge is called the complainant. In some administrative hearings, an officer of the government becomes the complainant. This is the situation that prevails in police department disciplinary trials when a superior officer makes a charge of a violation of a departmental rule against a subordinate. The superior officer is the complainant, and the subordinate is the respondent.

An administrative hearing is not a trial in a court of law, and the participants in such a hearing are not required to adhere to the legal rules of evidence. All evidence, however, should be material and relevant to the issues, and a determination must be based on some legal evidence. The hearing officer is given great latitude in deciding what may be introduced into the hearing. Some hearings in this category are police department disciplinary trials (hearings), traffic adjudication hearings (some jurisdictions use this noncriminal procedure for trying traffic offenses), professional disciplinary hearings (disciplinary hearings for attorneys and physicians), and arbitration hearings.

The civil case deserves our attention. This is an action between two or more persons, natural or corporate, to determine their respective rights to property. These actions may be tort actions (dealing with private wrongs), breach of contract actions, equitable actions (seeking, e.g., injunctions), probate proceedings, or other actions to determine the rights and privileges of parties. In tort and breach of contract actions, the moving party is called the plaintiff, and the other party is called the defendant. In equitable actions, the moving party is designated as petitioner, and the adverse party is designated as respondent. In probate proceedings, one party is designated as proponent, and the other is designated as contestant.

§ 2.3   THE ORDER OF THE TRIAL

The order of the trial usually proceeds by the party having the burden of proof putting its side of the controversy before the trier of the facts first. This may be done in several ways, depending on whether the trier of the facts is a judge or a jury. If the trier of the facts is a jury, the attorney representing the plaintiff, in a civil action, or the people or government, in a criminal action, will "open to the jury." This means that the attorney will introduce himself or herself and the parties and their counsel to the jury and briefly explain the factual situation surrounding the causes of action and what his or her side intends to prove. Local court procedures vary, but usually the side that has the burden of proof may not waive the opening to the jury.

The defendant's attorney also has an opportunity to open to the jury after his or her adversary has finished. He or she will espouse his or her client's cause in this opening statement. In some jurisdictions, the defendant alone may waive the right to open to the jury.

The side that has the burden of proof (the people in a criminal action, the plaintiff in a civil action) then must place its first witness on the stand and, in question-and-answer form, must elicit proof to substantiate the claim if it is to prevail in the case. The attorney is required to ask questions in a particular form, which will be explained later. If the attorney deviates from the prescribed form, and if the adversary objects, the court may sustain the objection, and the witness would be directed by the court not to answer the question.

After the attorney who has the burden of proof completes the questioning of the witness, he or she may say to the adversary, "You may inquire." This means that he or she has completed the direct questioning of the witness and now gives the adversary an opportunity at cross-examination.

Cross-examination questions may be phrased differently from direct examination questions. The manner in which these questions may be asked is more fully explained in later sections.

After the cross-examination of the witness is concluded, the attorney who initially called the witness to the stand may attempt to rehabilitate the witness by asking further questions. This is known as redirect. Then the other attorney may ask questions of the witness, which is known as recross. This procedure may continue according to the needs of the attorneys and the discretion of the presiding judge.

The trial continues with the side having the burden of proof calling other witnesses for direct examination, then cross, then redirect, then recross, and so on.

When the attorney for the side that has the burden of proof thinks that he or she has proved the case, he or she will call no further witness. If the case is a criminal case, the prosecutor will announce to the court, "Your honor, that is the people's case," or similar language may be used to the same import.

In a criminal case, the defendant's attorney will then move to dismiss the charges on the ground that the people have failed to prove a prima facie case. This means that on the testimony adduced at the trial, as a matter of law (as opposed to as a matter of fact), the people have failed to prove that the defendant is guilty of the crime charged. This motion is seldom granted because the prosecutor usually has carefully caused testimony to be elicited that covers the elements of the crime charged.

Assuming that the defendant's motion for dismissal is denied, the defendant may remain mute, may take the stand in his or her own defense, may bring witnesses to testify in his or her favor, or need not bring witnesses to testify in his or her behalf.

If the defendant decides not to have witnesses testify in his or her behalf and to remain mute, his or her attorney may move the court to dismiss on the ground that the people have failed to prove the defendant guilty beyond any reasonable doubt. This motion is sometimes granted at the end of the people's case.

If the defendant decides to take the stand and testify in his or her own defense, or if the defendant has witnesses in his or her behalf take the stand and testify, he or she and his or her witnesses will be subjected to direct examination by defense counsel, then cross-examination by the prosecutor, then redirect, then re-cross, etc., in the same manner as the prosecutor's witnesses were questioned. The only difference is that each of the defendant's witnesses will first be questioned by the defense attorney and later by the prosecutor.

At the conclusion of the parade of witnesses for the defense, the defense attorney will say to the court, "The defendant rests." Thereupon the prosecutor may ask the court for permission to reopen his or her direct case with newly found evidence, and the court, in its discretion, may permit this to occur.

There is also a procedural device known as prosecution's rebuttal. The prosecution is limited to testimony that might refute the evidence presented by the defendant. New witnesses may be called, but these may only be witnesses whose testimony might negate the testimony of the defendant's witnesses. If, for example, the defense raises the issue of insanity or infancy, the prosecution may offer evidence to show that the defendant was not insane or was not an infant, respectively. Even these witnesses may be cross-examined by the defendant or his or her counsel.

If the prosecution uses a rebuttal, the defendant may have the opportunity to introduce evidence contrary to that introduced by the prosecution as rebuttal. This is known as a rejoinder. This give-and-take is subject to the discretion of the trial judge.

If both sides rest, the court will finally determine this and so indicate on the record of the case. Motions will then be entertained by the court. This is usually done outside of the presence of the jury but in open court. The jury is normally excused while these arguments of counsel are placed before the court.

Sometimes it is good practice for the defendant's attorney to renew his or her motion to dismiss because of failure of the prosecutor to prove a prima facie case even though it was previously denied. The judge may reverse the prior decision based on new testimony heard at the trial. In any event, the judge may ask the attorney for the grounds of his or her motion, and the attorney will explain the reasons for asking for the dismissal and may cite court decisions to support these contentions. The judge may then ask the other attorney what he or she has to say to counter these arguments.

This same procedure is followed with respect to the next motion, that is, the motion to dismiss on the grounds that the people have failed to meet their burden of proof.

Assuming that the judge denies these motions, the attorneys will then give their summation to the jury. In most jurisdictions, the defendant's attorney will "sum up" first, followed by the prosecutor. The summation consists of a speech to the jury recalling parts of the testimony of the trial and placing special emphasis on the testimony that favors the position of his or her client.

The next step in the order of trial is the judge's charge to the jury. This usually occurs when the courtroom doors are locked to prevent spectators from moving in and out of the courtroom. The judge usually reads from a prepared text that explains the law of the case but leaves the determination of the facts to the jury. If the criminal charge is one of intentional murder, the judge may charge that if the jury finds that the defendant intentionally killed the victim, then it is to come back with a verdict of guilty of murder, but if the jury finds that the defendant killed the victim in the heat of passion, it is to return to the court with a verdict of manslaughter.

After the charge is over, the jury exits the courtroom and enters the deliberation room. When the jurors have made their decision (in a criminal case, some jurisdictions require a unanimous decision; others now require five jurors in agreement in a six-person jury or ten jurors in agreement in a twelve-person jury), they return, and the foreman of the jury is asked by the court clerk as to whether the jury has reached a verdict. The jury foreman, who is standing, will say, "We have." The court clerk will ask, "What is your verdict?" The jury foreman will reply guilty of murder first degree, guilty or manslaughter, not guilty, or whatever the jury may have decided.

After the initial shock has worn off, the losing attorney may make what are known as posttrial motions. The only one that should interest the reader is the motion to poll the jury. The judge will ask the court clerk to poll the jury. The court clerk will ask each juror by name how he or she voted, and each juror will reply. The jurors are then discharged by the judge, who will usually thank them for their services.

The procedure described varies slightly in different jurisdictions, but generally this is the order of a trial. The order of trial has been included in this book so that you might be more aware of the safeguards that are included in an orderly trial in which the ultimate goal is equal justice under law.

§ 2.4 OATH OR AFFIRMATION REQUIRED FROM EACH WITNESS

Every witness is asked, on entry into the witness box, to swear or affirm that he or she will testify truthfully. This is done to impress on his or her mind the duty to do so. The procedure is designed to provide flexibility in dealing with religious cults, atheists, mental defectives, children, and conscientious objectors.

§ 2.5 INFANT AS A WITNESS

When an infant (i.e., a minor) is a necessary witness, a special problem arises as to the question of whether the infant is capable of understanding the nature of an oath or affirmation. This problem is often resolved by the judge in camera. The child is taken into the judge's chambers or robing room, and testimony is taken in the presence of the litigants, their attorneys, and a court reporter. The situation is informal, and the judge usually sits at his or her desk and may or may not be clothed in his or her robe. The judge conducts what is known as a voir dire (oral examination) of the prospective infant witness.

The usual procedure is for the judge to introduce himself or herself to the infant in a kindly manner and proceed to ask questions relative to the child's school; his or her accomplishments in school; whether the child attends a church or synagogue; if so, how often; whether he or she has ever told a lie; if so, how often. If the infant admits to having told a lie, the judge may ask him or her what lies he or she has told. The judge may ask the child who would punish him or her if he or she told a lie. Sometimes the child will say that God will punish him or that her mother or father will punish her. The judge may then ask how God or the parent would punish him or her. The judge usually gives all trial counsel an opportunity to examine the infant before determining whether he or she will take the child's testimony under oath or affirmation or merely permit the child to testify not under oath or affirmation. In United States v. Spoonhunter, 476 F.2d 1050 (10th Cir. 1973) the voir dire of the trial judge was as follows:

The Court: *I'll ask her a few questions. Donna, how old are you?*
Donna: *Seven.*
The Court: *You are seven?*
Donna: *Uh-huh.*
The Court: *What grade are you in school?*
Donna: *Second.*
The Court: *Do you think you remember what occurred on the night of July 13, 1971?*
Donna: *Yes.*
The Court: *Do you know what it is to tell the truth when you raise your hand and are sworn?*
Donna: *Yes.*
The Court: *And if I administer the oath to you, you will swear to tell the truth and you know that you can be punished if you don't tell the truth? You understand that?*
Donna: *Yes.*
The Court: *I think she is qualified. You raise your right hand then (Sworn).*
The Court: *Do you so swear, do you?*
Donna: *Yes.*
The Court: *Very well.*

It has been held that a child's unsworn testimony is inadmissible in a civil action. N.Y.—Stoppick v. Goldstein, 174 App.Div. 306, 160 N.Y.S. 947 (1916); People *ex rel.* Niebuhr v. McAdoo, 184 N.Y. 304, 77 N.E. 260 (1906); People v. Oyola, 6 N.Y.2d 259, 189 N.Y.S.2d 203, 160 N.E.2d 494 (1959).

In criminal prosecutions, most jurisdictions permit a child who does not understand the nature of an oath to testify without being sworn if the child appears to be of sufficient intelligence to justify the reception of evidence. However, in New York, a conviction cannot be had on such testimony given by a child less than twelve years of age that is not supported by other evidence.

New York Criminal Procedure Law, cited hereafter as N.Y.—CPL § 60.20, reads as follows:

§ 60.20 Rules of evidence; testimonial capacity; evidence given by children

1. Any person may be a witness in a criminal proceeding unless the court finds that, by reason of infancy or mental disease or defect, he does not possess sufficient intelligence or capacity to justify the reception of his evidence.
2. Every witness more than twelve years old may testify only under oath unless the court is satisfied that such witness cannot, as a result of mental disease or defect, understand the nature of an oath. A child less than twelve years old may not testify under oath unless the court is satisfied that he understands the nature of an oath. If the court is not so satisfied, such child or such witness over twelve years old who cannot as a result of mental disease or defect, understand the nature of an oath may nevertheless be permitted to give unsworn evidence if the court is satisfied that the

witness possesses sufficient intelligence and capacity to justify the reception thereof.

3. A defendant may not be convicted of an offense solely upon unsworn evidence given pursuant to subdivision two.

There is a rebuttable presumption that a child over fourteen is competent to be sworn in a civil case, but, in fact, there is no rule of law that qualifies an infant to be sworn at any particular age. U.S.—Wheeler v. United States, 159 U.S. 523, 16 S.Ct. 93, 40 L.Ed. 244 (1895).

Anyone who has had experience with the testimony of children can understand that one must be overly careful if one accepts their testimony as the truth. This is not to say that their testimony is not to be accepted, but that children frequently have great imaginations, which may color their testimony, particularly in the area of sex offenses, when their testimony should be carefully weighed. The courts have held that in sexual offense cases the evidence must be "more than usually clear and convincing." N.Y.—People v. Oyola, 6 N.Y.2d 259, 189 N.Y.S.2d 203, 160 N.E.2d 494 (1959).

§ 2.6   IDENTITY OF WITNESS

When a witness takes the stand, the trier of the facts is looking for an introduction. The judge or jury, as the case may be, may want to know who the witness is, where he or she lives, how long the witness has lived there, the employment history, marital status, school and grade achieved in that school, if applicable. If the witness is a police officer, it might be useful to inquire how long the witness has been so employed and what assignments he or she had with that police department, or other police departments where he or she was so employed, and so on. These questions are frequently asked by the attorney who summoned the witness to the stand to testify. The extent to which the attorney may go is limited by his or her adversary's sustained objections or by the discretion of the presiding judge. The ostensible intent of the attorney who summons a witness to testify is to give the impression that the witness is a responsible member of society who is worthy of belief.

Many times a complaining witness does not want to divulge where she lives because of fear of reprisal from the defendant or his or her cohorts. For this reason, the prosecution may attempt to have a witness testify without stating where she lives. This practice is permissible, but when the witness is asked on cross-examination "Where do you live?" she is under a duty to tell where she lives, or in the alternative all of her direct examination may be struck from the record. "The question 'Where do you live?' was not only an appropriate question preliminary to the cross-examination of the witness but on its face, without any such declaration of purpose as was made by counsel here, was an essential step in identifying the witness with his environment, to which cross-examination may always be directed."[3] A witness's prior address must also be disclosed.

Sometimes divulging the location of the residence of the witness might endanger the life of the witness or members of his or her family. When this issue is raised, the court may conduct a preliminary examination out of the hearing of the jury and the defendant.

The threat, however, must be actual and not the result of conjecture. U.S.—Shaw v. Illinois, 394 U.S. 214, 89 S.Ct. 1016, 22 L.Ed. 2d 211 (1969). If the court

---

[3] U.S.—Alford v. United States, 282 U.S. 687, 51 S.Ct. 218, 75 L.Ed. 624 (1931)

determines that the true name, address, and place of employment of the witness are not critical enough to deny effective cross-examination, the witness will not be required to reveal this information. However, if the judge concludes that the defendant is not entitled to this information, the defendant is entitled to ask any other relevant question that may aid the jury in weighing the witness's credibility. U.S.—United States v. Palermo, 410 F.2d 468 (7th Cir. 1969).

§ 2.7   COMPETENCY OF WITNESS

It is presumed that every person who is called to the witness stand to testify in a trial is competent, except as indicated earlier in the situation in which a young child might be testifying and there is a question as to whether the child understands the nature of an oath. This is a rebuttable presumption, and during or after the testimony of the witness the trier of the facts, whether it is the jury or the judge, will soon discover whether the subject witness is mentally incompetent, and a determination will be made as to the witness's credibility. The Federal Rules of Evidence treat this matter in both criminal and civil cases in Rule 601, General Rule of Competency: "Every person is competent to be a witness except as otherwise provided in these rules. However, in civil actions and proceedings, with respect to an element of a claim or defense as to which State law supplies the rule of decision, the competency of a witness shall be determined in accordance with State law." Therefore, no mental or moral qualifications for testifying as a witness are specified.

§ 2.8   DEAD MAN'S STATUTE AND RELIGIOUS BELIEFS

Some states will not permit a witness in a civil action to testify to a personal transaction or communication with a deceased or lunatic if the witness is interested in the outcome of the trial or if his or her predecessor in interest is incompetent to testify about the personal transaction or communication. An example of this might be in a will contest in which a person not named as a legatee in the will would like to testify about conversation with the decedent wherein the decedent is alleged to have indicated to the witness that the decedent had made a will in which everything the decedent owned would be given to the witness when the decedent died. The will offered for probate contained no such legacy, and the witness is objecting to the admission of the will on various grounds (i.e., undue influence; decedent did not understand, speak, or read the English language; etc.).

In this case, if this litigation took place in a state that had a statutory "Dead Man's Statute," the witness would not be permitted to testify to this conversation with the deceased. However, any other person present at the time of the conversation who heard the decedent say this could testify as to what the decedent said, providing the second person was not interested in any way in the outcome of the trial.

Many states are removing this statutory restriction in the same way as they removed the restriction that a defendant was unable to testify in his own behalf or that a spouse was unable to testify in behalf of the other spouse (Funk v. United States, 290 U.S. 371, 54 S.Ct. 212, 78 L.Ed. 369 [1933]), or any provisions that would enhance or impair a person's credibility based on his religious beliefs or lack of religious beliefs (Federal Rule of Evidence 610).

The court may also ask questions of a witness on either direct examination or cross-examination. Furthermore, the court may call witnesses to the stand to testify.

§ 2.9   UNDERCOVER INFORMER AS A WITNESS

The situation respecting the use of undercover informers is very tricky. The prosecution may not need the testimony of the informer in order to spell out a prima facie case against a defendant. However, this is not always the situation. In such a case, the prosecutor is faced with a dilemma. In some cases, if he or she exposes the informer or undercover police officer to the defendant, the witness may not live to testify at the trial, his or her death being brought about by unnatural causes. In other cases, the witness himself or herself may be fearful about testifying. In still others, the usefulness of the informer or undercover police officer in future arrests is nullified by the prosecutor's divulging his or her identity to the defense. A prosecutor is therefore not compelled to reveal the identity of the informer or undercover police officer. He or she is not compelled to identify the informer, but if the judge determines that the identification is necessary for a fair trial, and the prosecutor refuses to identify the informer, the case may be dismissed on motion by defendant, or sua sponte by judge.

In McCray v. Illinois, 386 U.S. 300, 87 S.Ct. 1056, 18 L.Ed.2d 62 (1967), and in Spinelli v. United States, 393 U.S. 410, 89 S.Ct. 584, 21 L.Ed.2d 637 (1969), it was held that the revelation of the identity of the informer was not required on the facts of those cases if the trial judge is convinced by evidence submitted in open court that the officers did rely in good faith on creditable information supplied by a reliable informant. The court indicated, however, that there might be some circumstances in which such a revelation might be required.

If the informer is a material witness at the trial of the action, and if the prosecution wishes to prevail, the informer must be produced to give the defendant an opportunity of cross-examination as is guaranteed to every defendant by the Sixth Amendment of the United States Constitution, which was made applicable to state and federal trials by virtue of the Fourteenth Amendment. U.S.—Pointer v. Texas, 380 U.S. 400, 85 S.Ct. 1065, 13 L.Ed.2d 923 (1965).

The Supreme Court has granted this right only to trials and not to preliminary hearings, grand jury proceedings, or sentencing hearings. Because these proceedings are not to determine guilt or innocence, the Supreme Court has held that the Sixth Amendment is not applicable. The Court said in Pointer v. Texas (*supra*), "We must remember also that we are not dealing with the trial of the criminal charge itself. There the need for a truthful verdict outweighs society's need for an informer privilege."

However, where there is a threat to the life of a witness, the right of the defendant to have the witness's true name, address, and place of employment is not absolute. The threat must be actual and not the result of conjecture. U.S.—Shaw v. Illinois, 394 U.S. 214, 89 S.Ct. 1016, 22 L.Ed.2d 211 (1969). The government bears the burden of proving to the district judge the existence of such a threat. The trial judge can then ascertain the interest of the defendant in the answer and exercise an informed discretion in making the ruling. U.S.—United States v. Palermo, 410 F.2d 468 (7th Cir. 1969).

In McCray v. Illinois, 386 U.S. 300, 87 S.Ct. 1056, 18 L.Ed.2d 62 (1967), it was held that an Illinois statute that gave discretion to the presiding judge at a preliminary (motion to suppress) hearing as to whether or not an informer's identity need be disclosed was constitutional. In Nutter v. State of Maryland, 8 Md.App. 635, 262 A.2d 80,86 (1970), the court said:

> The State has the privilege to withhold from disclosure the identity of persons who furnish information to police officers concerning the commission of crimes. However, the privilege is not absolute. On the issue of guilt or innocence (not on Fourth

Amendment issues) and only upon demand by the defendant, the trial court may, in the exercise of its judicial discretion compel such disclosure upon determination that it is necessary and relevant to a fair defense. Factors to be considered in ascertaining whether such disclosure is necessary and relevant to a fair defense include the nature of the crime charged; the importance of the informer's identity to determination of innocence, as for example, whether the informer was an integral part of the illegal transaction and the possible significance of his testimony; and the possible defenses. Whether the privilege must yield depends upon the facts and circumstances of the particular case. But if the informer testifies for the State the privilege may not be invoked by it.

As a practical matter, then, the prosecutor has the alternative of concealing the identity of the informer or undercover police officer when the prosecutor believes that his or her usefulness would be wasted on a small offender. It is hoped that the undercover officer or informer will give information leading to the "big fish" in the operation. If the prosecutor fails to continue the prosecution at this point, there is always the specter of civil liability hanging over the government as well as the prosecutor individually. However, when no malice is proved, the probability of the defendant's recovering under such a situation is nil.

It is interesting to note that the one who has most to lose under this problem—the informer or undercover officer—has little input as to whether he or she will have to testify. The privilege of not divulging the identity is that of governmental authority, not that of the informant. The government alone may waive the privilege. U.S.—United States v. Reynolds, 345 U.S. 1, 73 S.Ct. 528, 97 L.Ed. 727 (1953).

It is probably most difficult for anyone not directly involved in the problem to fully appreciate the feelings that an undercover police officer has when he or she is confronted with the requirement that he or she testify in open court. I have had experience in such a problem, but no amount of writing about it will fully place the reader in the shoes of such a person. As a change in the popular phrase goes, "Try it, you won't like it."

§ 2.10 EXCLUSION OF WITNESSES FROM COURTROOM

Often an astute attorney will move the court to exclude from the courtroom all those who will be called as witnesses in the instant case. It should be quite evident to the reader that this is an effective means of preventing collusion among the various witnesses as to how the facts of the case occurred. In most jurisdictions, this motion is addressed to the court's discretion. If the request is made in good faith, however, there is ordinarily no reason it should be denied.[4] In many jurisdictions, statutes now provide for the exclusion of witnesses on examination of the accused before committing magistrates. In New York, however, a party to the action is entitled to be present during trial, and his or her counsel may not be excluded (N.Y. Const. Art. I, Section 6).

The courts of New York have not permitted this constitutional provision to negate the proper administration of justice. A defendant cannot be disorderly in court to an extent that warrants removal of the defendant from the courtroom and then, after conviction, be successful in an appeal based on a violation of that section of the constitution. This was the situation in New York (People v. Crown, 51 A.D.2d 588, 378 N.Y.S.2d 775 [1976]), in which the Appellate Division of the

---

[4] N.Y.—Philpot v. Fifth Avenue Coach Co., 142 App.Div. 811, 128 N.Y.S. 35 (1911).

New York Supreme Court held that the defendant's removal from the courtroom after he continually disrupted the trial and refused to aid his court-appointed attorney, with whom he was given every opportunity to speak, did not constitute denial of effective assistance of counsel.

A further extension of this concept is to be found in N.Y.—CPL § 260.20, wherein it is provided that "a defendant must be personally present during the trial of an indictment, provided, however, that a defendant who conducts himself in so disorderly and disruptive a manner that his trial cannot be carried on with him in the courtroom may be removed from the courtroom if, after he has been warned by the court that he will be removed if he continues such conduct, he continues to engage in such conduct." The notice requirement of the court was construed in People v. Sanchez, 65 N.Y.2d 436, 482 N.E.2d 56, 492 N.Y.S.2d 577 (1985), in which the defendant voluntarily absented himself from the trial after being told that the trial was about to begin or after the trial had begun.

It is reasonable to assume that a reader located in a state other than New York has a similar constitutional provision and a like statute. If none is found, however, the New York court decisions might be persuasive argument against a defendant who is absent from the trial either because of courtroom behavior or because of voluntary absence. If a witness fails to leave the courtroom on direction by a judge, he or she may be punished for contempt of court (interference with the business of the court).

§ 2.11   USE OF MEMORANDA

Many times a witness, particularly a police officer witness, has no independent recollection of the facts that are involved in the instant case. The common law and the statutory law of some states provide that his or her memory may be refreshed by the use of memoranda. In the case of the police officer witness, it is proper, on application to the presiding judge, that the officer look at departmental forms such as reports that he or she prepared at the time of the instant case, and after reading this material, he or she may answer the questions put to him or her by counsel. When, however, a witness has so far forgotten the facts that he or she cannot recall them, even after looking at the memorandum of them, and testifies that he or she once knew them and made a memorandum of them at the time or soon after they transpired, that he or she intended to make the memorandum correctly, and that he or she believes it to be correct, such memorandum in his or her own handwriting may be received as evidence of the facts therein contained, although the witness has no present recollection of them.[5] It is not necessary to the use of the memorandum that it should have been made by the witness himself or herself, since it is not the memorandum that is the evidence, but the recollection of the witness.[6] A witness may refresh his or her recollection from a memorandum made by others. Conn.—Neff v. Neff, 96 Conn. 273, 114 A. 126, 128 (1921).

§ 2.12   PAST RECOLLECTION RECORDED ADOPTED BY WITNESS AS HIS OR HER TESTIMONY

A memorandum of a past recollection is not, of itself, independent evidence of the facts contained therein. However, it may be received in evidence, provided it is connected to the testimony of the witness. The witness swears to the facts con-

---

[5] Conn.—State v. Masse, 1 Conn.Cir. 381, 186 A.2d 553 (1962); N.Y.—McCarthy v. Meaney, 183 N.Y. 190, 76 N.E. 36 (1902).

[6] N.Y.—Taft v. Little, 178 N.Y. 127, 70 N.E. 211 (1904).

tained in the memorandum because of his or her confidence in the accuracy of the written memorandum. The writing therefore becomes a present evidentiary statement of the witness verified by the oath of the witness. Now the contents may be read to the trier of the facts and taken together as equal to a present positive statement of the witness as he or she affirms the truth of the facts stated in the memorandum.[7]

§ 2.13   USE OF MEMORANDA FOR CROSS-EXAMINATION

If the witness uses a memorandum to refresh his or her recollection, even though it may not be shown to the jury evidentially, it may be used by opposing counsel in that he or she has a right to inspect it and use it to test the credibility of the witness.[8]

The reader will recall that a police officer frequently is required by departmental rules and regulations to make a memorandum of the nature of police business that he or she has attended to. The trial of the issues of this police business may not take place until a considerable time after the event, thereby dulling the police officer's recollection of the happening. With the permission of the presiding jurist, the officer may refresh his or her recollection by reading to himself or herself the entries contained in the memorandum. However, once he or she uses the memorandum in this way, he or she opens the door for the opposing counsel to inspect the memorandum for the purpose of cross-examination.

The prosecutor should carefully look at the memorandum first to see that no information not relevant to the issues of the case and not testified to by the police officer on his or her direct examination is made available to defense counsel. This irrelevant material may be blocked out with adhesive tape, providing application is made to the court and the application is granted. Care should be taken that no injury is done to the blocked out portions so that they are available for an appellate court to inspect, should conditions warrant.

§ 2.14   USE OF PRETRIAL STATEMENTS MADE BY PROSECUTION WITNESS

Sometimes the prosecution in a criminal action will ask its witness to sign statements during the investigatory stage of the proceeding. In both federal courts and state courts, the defendant has a right to inspect and use for purposes of impeachment on cross-examination any pretrial statement given by the witness to the authorities, provided that the statement relates to the witness's testimony and provided "that the necessities of effective law enforcement do not require the statement be kept secret or confidential."[9]

Congress, as a result of the Jencks v. United States decision, enacted Section 3500 of Title 18 of the U.S. Code, which reads as follows:

> § 3500. **Demands for production of statements and reports of witnesses**
>
> (a) In any criminal prosecution brought by the United States, no statement or report in the possession of the United States which was made by a government witness or prospective Government witness (other than the defendant) to an agent of the Government shall be the subject of subpoena, discovery, or inspection until said witness has testified on direct examination in the trial of the case.

---

[7] Wis.—Manning v. School District No. 6, 124 Wis. 84, 102 N.W. 356 (1905).

[8] N.Y.—People v. Gezzo, 307 N.Y. 385, 121 N.E.2d 380 (1954).

[9] U.S.—Jencks v. United States, 353 U.S. 657, 77 S.Ct. 1007, 1 L.Ed.2d 1103 (1957).

(b) After a witness called by the United States has testified on direct examination, the court shall, on motion of the defendant, order the United States to produce any statement (as hereinafter defined) of the witness in the possession of the United States which relates to the subject matter as to which the witness has testified. If the entire contents of any such statement relate to the subject matter of the testimony of the witness, the court shall order it to be delivered directly to the defendant for his examination and use.

(c) If the United States claims that any statement ordered to be produced under this section contains matter which does not relate to the subject matter of the testimony of the witness, the court shall order the United States to deliver such statement for the inspection of the court in camera. Upon such delivery the court shall excise the portions of such statement which do not relate to the subject matter of the testimony of the witness. With such material excised, the court shall then direct delivery of such statement to the defendant for his use. If, pursuant to such procedure, any portion of such statement is withheld from the defendant and the defendant objects to such withholding, and the trial is continued to an adjudication of the guilt of the defendant, the entire text of such statement shall be preserved by the United States and, in the event the defendant appeals, shall be made available to the appellate court for the purpose of determining the correctness of the ruling of the trial judge. Whenever any statement is delivered to a defendant pursuant to this section, the court in its discretion, upon application of said defendant, may recess proceedings in the trial for such time as it may determine to be reasonably required for the examination of such statement by said defendant and his preparation for its use in the trial.

(d) If the United States elects not to comply with an order of the court under paragraph (b) or (c) hereof to deliver to the defendant any such statement, or such portion thereof as the court may direct, the court shall strike from the record the testimony of the witness, and the trial shall proceed unless the court in its discretion shall determine that the interests of justice require that a mistrial be declared.

(e) The term "statement," as used in subsections (b), (c) and (d) of this section in relation to any witness called by the United States, means—

(1) a written statement made by said witness and signed or otherwise adopted or approved by him; or

(2) a stenographic, mechanical, electrical, or other recording, or a transcription thereof, which is a substantially verbatim recital of an oral statement made by said witness to an agent of the Government and recorded contemporaneously with the making of such oral statement. [Added Pub.L. 85–269, Sept. 2, 1957, 71 Stat. 595.]

As a practical matter, however, the United States attorney often makes this information available to defense counsel at least one day before the anticipated date on which the witness is scheduled to testify. In this way, defense counsel has no valid grounds to ask the court for a continuance in order to have sufficient time to study the statements or report. The lawyers refer to this as 3500 material.

§ 2.15   INTERPRETERS

The usual procedure is to require witnesses to answer questions directed at them in English and to respond in the English language. Those who are unable to speak the English language, who do not have a good command of the English language, or who are deaf and dumb may testify through court-appointed interpreters. If the witness is a deaf mute, the interpreter must be familiar with the code signs used by the witness. An interpreter must be sworn to interpret properly and truly. Testimony repeated on the witness stand of what an interpreter, not on the witness stand, said when the police examined the accused is hearsay, and hence inadmissible.[10]

The student should have some understanding of what procedures exist in foreign countries with respect to this problem in order to fully appreciate the fundamental fairness that American courts provide in this area of the law. It is urged on the student if he or she has occasion to visit a foreign non-English-speaking jurisdiction, that the student go to a court and observe what transpires when an English-speaking defendant is brought before the court. I was shocked at what I observed in a Canadian court in Quebec Province. Fortunately, I was not the defendant in the case that was observed, but it certainly made me appreciate more fully the American system of providing interpreters when necessary.

§ 2.16 MODELS, DIAGRAMS, AND MAPS

The parties have a right to introduce properly authenticated models, diagrams, and maps to illustrate and explain the testimony of witnesses.[11]

However, if the models, diagrams, and maps are not essential to an understanding of the testimony and are merely cumulative in effect, the judge has discretion as to whether or not to permit them.

There is a distinction between the use of a map or drawing for purposes of illustration and its admission in evidence. If it is used for the purpose of illustration alone, it is said that the testimony of the witness is the evidence. On the other hand, if it is used with intent to have it admitted as evidence, then it possesses within itself evidentiary characteristics tending to establish a particular fact. Ala.—Crocker v. Lee, 261 Ala. 439, 74 So.2d 429 (1954).

The use of a blackboard for illustration purposes or to aid trial counsel in his or her arguments is within the discretion of the trial judge. However, it is improper to photograph the blackboard in the presence of the jury for purpose of the record on appeal. Fla.—Ratner v. Arrington, 111 So.2d 82 (Fla.App. 1959).

Generally, a map, diagram, or sketch must be accurate in order to warrant its admission. The paper must correctly represent the situation as it existed at the time under consideration. Ark.—Arkansas Louisiana Gas Co. v. Lawrence, 239 Ark. 365, 389 S.W.2d 431 (1965); Va.—Cowles v. Zahn, 206 Va. 743, 146 S.E.2d 200 (1966).

It has been held that it is not essential that the person making the map, diagram, or the like testify to its correctness, but any person acquainted with the facts may do so. Miss.—Crawford v. City of Meridian, 186 So.2d 250 (Miss. 1966).

Therefore, as a practical matter, the cartography section of a law enforcement agency could make the diagram or map, and any officer or representative familiar with the facts could refer to it and/or testify to its accuracy for purposes of its admission.

§ 2.17 LEADING QUESTIONS

A witness may testify in a narrative response to a general question, explaining what he or she saw or heard at a particular time and place. He or she may also respond to a series of specific questions. The former type of questioning is inherently

---

[10] N.Y.—People v. Sing, 242 N.Y. 419, 152 N.E. 248 (1926).
[11] U.S.—Grayson v. Williams, 256 F.2d 61 (10th Cir. 1958); Calif.—Smith v. Addiego, 54 Cal.App.2d 230, 129 P.2d 953 (1942).

more dangerous because the witness may testify to facts that are wholly incompetent, immaterial, and irrelevant. The latter method is far more suitable for trial purposes because only necessary testimony will be included in the trial. The questions and the method used to ask the questions are within the discretion of the trial judge. Like all other discretionary acts of a governmental official, it is subject to review by a higher tribunal and may be overturned if the discretion used was arbitrary, discriminatory, or prejudicial.

When a question is asked in such a manner as to suggest an answer, the question is called a "leading question." Whether a leading question may be put to the witness rests in the trial judge's discretion. However, generally, subject to well-defined exceptions, leading questions may not be used in the direct examination of a witness, although they may be used in cross-examination.

Even though the question may call for a yes or no answer, it may not necessarily be leading unless it is so worded that, by permitting the witness to answer yes or no, the witness would be testifying in the language of the interrogator rather than his or her own.

A question is a leading one when it indicates to the witness the real or supposed fact that the examiner expects and desires to have confirmed by the answer; for example, "Do you live at 360 Park Avenue South, in the City of New York?" "Have you not lived there for ten years?"

It is not apparent on every occasion whether or not a question is a leading question. Many times it may become a leading question by the intonation of the questioner's voice.

In Steer v. Little, 44 N.H. 613 (1944), the court divided leading questions as follows:

1. questions that call for no answers other than yes or no
2. questions that are framed so as to suggest to the witness the answer desired
3. questions that assume facts in controversy

The test of whether a question is leading is one not of form, but of whether the question does, in fact, suggest the answer.

A question framed to suggest an answer to the witness is illustrated in the following: "Did you not hear the defendant say, 'I'll kill John when I see him'?" However, the alternative form, "Did you or did you not hear the defendant say, 'I'll kill John when I see him'?" is an acceptable question because it does not suggest a yes answer to the witness.

A question that assumes a controverted fact is also a leading question; for example, "What did the defendant do when he was driving the car to the scene of the homicide?" This is leading and objectionable when there is a question as to whether or not the defendant was driving the car at the scene of the homicide.

For an extensive discussion on the probative value of leading questions, the reader is referred to Pa.—Arey v. Arey, 7 Adams L.J. 86 (1965).

§ 2.18   Leading Questions on Introductory Matters

Leading questions are permissible under certain controlled conditions. They are permissible when they relate to introductory matter and tend to carry the witness quickly to matters material to the issue. Accordingly, a witness may be asked, "Were you in the vicinity of 10th Avenue and 59th Street in the County of New York on a specified time and date?" (yes) "Did you make any observations at that time and place with respect to the defendant?" (yes)

Both of these questions are clearly leading questions but are allowed because they lead the witness up to the facts of the time at issue, and this facilitates the movement of the trial without any corresponding reduction in the veracity of the witness's testimony.

§ 2.19 Hostile Witnesses

A leading question is permitted, even in direct examination, when the witness appears to be hostile, biased, or unwilling to testify. A hostile witness conceals much and reveals as little of the truth as skill and intellect will permit, and it is therefore concluded that there is no danger of coloring the witness's testimony by suggesting desired answers.

If a witness is unwilling to testify, he or she may also be led by the question. This often occurs in the prosecution of sex crimes when the witness is embarrassed. U.S.—Antelope v. United States, 185 F.2d 174 (10th Cir. 1950). In a prosecution for statutory rape, permitting the district attorney to ask the prosecutrix leading questions was not reversible error when the prosecutrix was a young, timid Indian girl and was in strange surroundings. The questions were embarrassing to her, and she testified in a timid, halting manner. U.S.—United States v. Spoonhunter, 476 F.2d 1050 (10th Cir. 1973). In the final analysis, the judge makes the decision as to who is biased, hostile, or unwilling to testify; the judge alone decides whether or not to permit leading questions.

§ 2.20 Elderly, Infant, or Mentally Deficient Witnesses

In its quest for the truth, the court, in its discretion, will permit trial counsel to assist an elderly person, a child, or a mentally deficient person who may be nervous when testifying or who may have a fleeting recollection of the facts in issue to testify by means of responses to leading questions on direct examination. N.Y.—Nicoletti v. Dieckmann, 89 Misc. 131, 151 N.Y.S. 520 (1956). It should be noted, however, that if a person is so mentally retarded as to make him an incompetent witness, his testimony should not be admitted unless his testimony was merely cumulative. N.Y.—People v. Rensing, 14 N.Y.2d 210, 250 N.Y.S.2d 401, 199 N.E.2d 489 (1964).

§ 2.21 Patently Erroneous Statements

When it is apparent that a witness has inadvertently answered a question incorrectly or that he did not understand the question, a leading question may be used on direct examination to give the witness an opportunity to correct the mistake. Va.— Hargrow v. Watson, 200 Va. 30, 104 S.E.2d 37 (1958).

§ 2.22 Facts Not Remembered

When the witness has exhausted his or her recollection, suggestions of the interrogator are allowed to assist the witness's memory. Suggestions with respect to name, date, or itemized lists are permitted. For example, it is unrealistic to expect a police officer to remember dates and what took place in a complicated police occurrence. For the purpose of assisting the officer to testify, the questioner may say something like this: "You made a written report of this occurrence at the scene shortly after the time of the occurrence, didn't you?" After an affirmative answer, the next question might be "You have this report on your person now?" Both of these questions call for a yes or no answer, and if asked on direct examination, both suggest an affirmative answer. They are usually permitted by the court in its discretion.

The questions are not critical questions going to the gravamen of the main issue, and no harm can be done to the adversary by their inclusion in the trial record.

§ 2.23   Memorandum

If a memorandum is used to refresh the recollection of the witness, a leading question with respect to this memorandum is admissible; for example, "Did you make a memorandum of this event in the normal course of your business?" "Was it a normal course of your business to make such a memorandum?" "Was this memorandum that you made of this event in the normal course of your business?"

§ 2.24   Cross-Examination

The witness to be cross-examined is a hostile witness, and therefore the interrogator may use leading questions. N.Y.—People v. Sexton, 187 N.Y. 495, 80 N.E. 396 (1907). If, however, the witness who is to be cross-examined is, in fact, biased in favor of the cross-examiner, leading questions may not be permitted. A situation such as this might occur when a plaintiff calls the defendant to the stand as his or her witness and the witness is then cross-examined by his or her own counsel.

A cross-examiner who elicits new matter from the witness, however, is placed in the same position as one who is directly examining, and therefore he or she cannot use leading questions.

§ 2.25   The Court

The court may, in its discretion, ask leading questions of a witness, provided the trial judge does not impress the jury with his opinion as to which of the parties is entitled to judgment. Tenn.—Parker v. State, 132 Tenn. 327, 178 S.W. 438 (1915).

§ 2.26   Discretion of Trial Court

The trial court has great discretion whether or not to permit leading questions, and the appellate courts are reluctant to interfere with this discretion.

Some cases state the rule to be that the discretion of the court in this matter is subject to being reviewed but that the determination of the trial court will not be regarded as error unless the discretion is abused. N.Y.—Budlong v. Van Nostrand, 24 Barb. 25 (1857). Other cases have stated that if an established rule of law has been violated, the party injured has an undoubted right to relief and the court should feel no reluctance in such a case to grant it.

The New York Court of Appeals has gone so far as to indicate that the trial court's discretion to determine whether a question is leading, and whether it should be permitted even though leading, is not subject to review or appeal. N.Y.—Walker v. Dunspaugh, 20 N.Y. 170, 7 N.Y.S. 781 (1890). However, if the judge shows his own opinion on the factual issue when he asks the leading question, the case may be reversed. N.Y.—People v. Mendes, 3 N.Y.2d 120, 164 N.Y.S.2d 401, 143 N.E.2d 806 (1957).

§ 2.27   The Federal Rule

The Federal Rules of Evidence have prescribed for the use of leading questions as follows:

> **Rule 611(c): Leading questions.** Leading questions should not be used on the direct examination of a witness except as may be necessary to develop the witness's testimony. Ordinarily leading questions should be permitted on cross-examination. When

a party calls a hostile witness, an adverse party, or a witness identified with an adverse party, interrogation may be by leading questions.

§ 2.28 CROSS-EXAMINATION

The purpose of direct examination is to get the witness to tell the court whatever relevant and competent knowledge he or she may know respecting the issue of the trial. Leading questions are not generally permitted on direct examination except under certain exceptional conditions as heretofore explained. On cross-examination, however, we find that there are reasons for permitting leading questions.

The reason we have rules of evidence is that over the centuries these rules have proved most reliable in eliciting the truth. If we have a rule and then an exception to the rule, the exception is permitted because there is necessity and a high probability of reliability.

Therefore, in the exceptions to the leading question exclusionary rule, a necessity and a high degree of reliability are present.

In cross-examination, we are attempting to do three things:

1. challenge the credibility of the direct examination;
2. bring out additional facts relating to those elicited as direct examination in addition to the facts that were favorable to the opposing party;
3. give the trier of the facts an opportunity to observe the witness under stress.

In such a climate, the witness becomes a hostile witness, and as stated previously a hostile witness may be asked leading questions.

The right of cross-examination is so fundamental to our law that it is included in the Sixth Amendment to the U.S. Constitution. If the opposing party is denied the right of cross-examination, all of the direct examination is to be expunged from the record. Ala.—Wray v. State, 154 Ala. 36, 45 So. 697 (1908).

This right also is given to the prosecution in a criminal trial to cross-examine defense witnesses.

§ 2.29 Extent

The extent to which the cross-examiner may go rests within the discretion of the trial judge. Only if the judge's rulings are arbitrary, capricious, unreasonable, or prejudicial will an appeal court overrule him or her. This is seldom done. It is therefore apparent that the trial court has great authority in conducting a trial.

See United States v. Darwin, 757 F.2d 1193 (11th Cir.), *reh'g denied*, 767 F.2d 938 (11th Cir. 1985), *cert. denied*, 474 U.S. 110, 106 S.Ct. 896, 88 L.Ed.2d 930 (1986), and People v. Sandoval, 34 N.Y.2d 371, 314 N.E.2d 413, 357 N.Y.S.2d 849 (1974); as to a limited and restricted inquiry only as to defendant, see People v. Ocasio, 47 N.Y.2d 55, 389 N.E.2d 1101, 416 N.Y.S.2d 581 (1979).

If a cross-examiner asks questions that were not brought out on direct examination, he or she makes the witness his or her own witness, and the witness is bound by his or her answers.

A trial judge has been held not to abuse the judge's discretion when he or she shuts off a continuation of cross-examination into collateral and immaterial matters. U.S.—United States v. Hall, 342 F.2d 849(4th Cir. 1965).

Answers to certain collateral cross-examination questions need not be adopted by the interrogator, even though they may introduce new matter. For example, a witness may be asked whether or not he or she has ever been convicted of a crime. If he or she answers negatively, the statutes of many jurisdictions provide that a judgment of conviction is admissible to affect his or her credibility. N.Y.—Civil Practice Law and Rules (CPLR) 4513, N.Y.—CPL § 60:40. See also Harris v. United States, 371 F.2d 365 (9th Cir. 1967), for further qualifications, and Federal Rule of Evidence 609.

§ 2.30   IMPEACHMENT OF WITNESSES

Impeachment is a term used when attempting to attack the credibility of a witness by convincing the trier of the facts that the testimony may not be truthful.

There are various methods of impeachment, some of which are as follows:

1. showing that the witness has been convicted of a crime after his or her denial of such conviction (Recent law limits this method; see Federal Rule of Evidence 609.)
2. surprising the witness—showing that the witness had made other statements to the interrogator on previous occasion
3. interrogating the witness regarding an immoral, vicious, or criminal act by the witness that may affect his or her character and tend to show that he or she is not worthy of belief
4. introducing extrinsic evidence
5. showing the witness's bias against the cross-examiner or the party he or she represents
6. showing that either at the time of the occurrence to which the witness has testified or at the time of giving the testimony, he or she was under the influence of drugs or alcohol, or was sick, or was mentally incompetent, or was incompetent to testify because of a lack of appreciation of the solemnity of an oath or because of other physical or mental incapacity
7. showing the witness's general bad reputation with respect to truth and veracity
8. showing that the witness was in an improper position or location to make the observation that he or she testified to
9. impeaching experts using literature in the field of knowledge
10. impeaching experts by questioning their qualifications
11. showing specific instances of misconduct
12. showing a defect in perception
13. showing other, similar acts that the witness has done to negate the defense of mistake or accident, to infer motive, to show intent, to prove identity, or to show a common scheme or plan.

§ 2.31   Witness Had Been Convicted of a Crime

A witness may be asked in direct or cross-examination whether or not he or she has ever been convicted of a crime. When this is asked in direct examination, it may be for the following reasons:

1. to show the jury that this person has never been convicted of a crime and therefore is worthy of belief
2. to show the jury that the witness has previously been convicted of a crime but that this does not mean he or she committed the instant crime
3. to lessen the blow that might be expected on cross-examination when the adversary asks the question

For impeachment purposes, as indicated previously, a witness may also be asked this question to attack his or her credibility. If he or she answers falsely in the negative, statutory authority in most jurisdictions permits the questioner to put into evidence a properly certified copy of a conviction of the witness. This then affects his or her credibility.

When this occurs, his or her own lawyer may, with court permission, engage in redirect examination to attempt to rehabilitate the witness. The witness may testify that he or she pleaded guilty but did not believe that this was a conviction. He or she thought that a conviction occurred only after a trial.

There has been a movement away from this theory of questions. People v. Mallard, 78 Misc.2d 858, 358 N.Y.S.2d 913 (1974), adopted the concept of People v. Sandoval, 34 N.Y.2d 371, 314 N.E.2d 413, 357 N.Y.S.2d 849 (1974), in not permitting cross-examination of a defendant's prior criminal record unless its purpose is to directly relate it to the crime charged.

Federal Rule of Evidence 609 pertains to previous criminal convictions of a witness and reads as follows:

Rule 609. Impeachment by Evidence of Conviction of Crime

(a) General Rule. For the purpose of attacking the credibility of a witness,
   (1) evidence that a witness other than an accused has been convicted of a crime shall be admitted, subject to Rule 403, if the crime was punishable by death or imprisonment in excess of one year under the law under which the witness was convicted, and evidence that an accused has been convicted of such a crime shall be admitted if the court determines that the probative value of admitting this evidence outweighs its prejudicial effect on the accused; and
   (2) evidence that any witness has been convicted of a crime shall be admitted if it involved dishonesty or false statement, regardless of the punishment.

(b) Time Limit. Evidence of a conviction under this rule is not admissible if a period of more than ten years has elapsed since the date of the conviction or of the release of the witness from the confinement imposed for that conviction, whichever is the later date, unless the court determines, in the interests of justice, that the probative value of the conviction supported by specific facts and circumstances substantially outweighs its prejudicial effect. However, evidence of a conviction more than 10 years old as calculated herein, is not admissible unless the proponent gives to the adverse party sufficient advance written notice of intent to use such evidence to provide the adverse party with a fair opportunity to contest the use of such evidence.

(c) Effect of Pardon, Annulment, or Certificate of Rehabilitation. Evidence of a conviction is not admissible under this rule if (1) the conviction has been the subject of a pardon, annulment, certificate of rehabilitation, or other equivalent procedure based on a finding of the rehabilitation of the person convicted, and that person has not been convicted of a subsequent crime which was punishable by death or imprisonment in excess of one year, or (2) the conviction has been the subject of a pardon, annulment, or other equivalent procedure based on a finding of innocence.

(d) Juvenile Adjudications. Evidence of juvenile adjudications is generally not admissible under this rule. The court may, however, in a criminal case allow evidence of a juvenile adjudication of a witness other than the accused if conviction of the offense would be admissible to attack the credibility of an adult and the court is satisfied that admission in evidence is necessary for a fair determination of the issue of guilt or innocence.

(e) Pendency of Appeal. The pendency of an appeal therefrom does not render evidence of a conviction inadmissible. Evidence of the pendency of an appeal is admissible.

§ 2.32 Showing That Witness Had Made Prior Statements to Interrogator

After a proper foundation is laid, a witness who has made a prior inconsistent statement may be asked questions relating to what he or she had stated or written on a previous occasion.

Laying a proper foundation means that the witness must just be asked

1. whether he or she made such as statement,
2. whether he or she made it to a specified person, and
3. whether he or she made it at a particular time and place.

The purpose of the foundation is to furnish the witness with specific enough information about the former statement that he or she can recall it.

If the witness admits having made the statement, the impeaching attorney cannot adduce any extrinsic evidence of the prior inconsistent statement. If the witness admits having made the statement but offers an explanation for the apparent inconsistency—for example, "the former statement was signed by him unread"—the explanation will be permitted for what the jury thinks it is worth.

The Federal Rules of Evidence treat this problem in Rule 613.

Rule 613. Prior statements of witnesses

(a) Examining witness concerning prior statement—in examining a witness concerning a prior statement made by him, whether written or not, the statement need not be shown nor its contents disclosed to him at that time, but on request the same shall be shown or disclosed to opposing counsel.

(b) Extrinsic evidence of prior inconsistent statement of witness—Extrinsic evidence of a prior inconsistent statement by a witness is not admissible unless the witness is afforded an opportunity to explain or deny the same and the opposite party is afforded an opportunity to interrogate the witness thereon, or the interests of justice otherwise require. This provision does not apply to admissions of a party-opponent as defined in rule 801(d)(2).

§ 2.33 Introducing Extrinsic Evidence

Extrinsic evidence is elicited not on cross-examination (from the witness's own mouth or suggested by the cross-examiner), but through the introduction of the testimony of independent witnesses or perhaps tangible evidence directed at attacking the credibility of the witness who is being impeached. This type of impeachment is usually introduced when it is the impeacher's turn to put on his or her case. Sometimes the intent is to discredit a particular statement made by the witness rather than to discredit the person generally; for example, to show that a clergyman of great reputation in the community made an error in his testimony, yet the impeacher does not want to discredit this clergyman's total person.

However, according to Federal Rule of Evidence 613(b), extrinsic evidence of a prior inconsistent statement by a witness is not admissible unless the witness is afforded an opportunity to explain or deny the same and the opposite party is afforded an opportunity to interrogate him or her thereon, or the interests of justice otherwise require. This provision does not apply to admissions of a party-opponent as defined in Rule 801(d)(2).

§ 2.34 Showing Witness Bias Against Cross-Examiner or Party Represented

In New York, the Court of Appeals stated in Schultz v. Third Avenue R.R. Co., 89 N.Y. 242, 250 (1882), that the evidence to show hostile feelings of a witness "should be direct and positive, and not very remote and uncertain, for the reason that the trial of the main issues in the case cannot be properly suspended to make out the case of hostile feeling by mere circumstantial evidence from which such hostility or malice may or may not be inferred." In other cases, it has been held that the extent to which a cross-examiner may go to show bias or hostility rests with the trial judge, but a trial judge abuses his or her discretion if he or she rules out all questions to show hostility or bias.

The party cross-examining a witness has the same right to show bias or hostility that the party who called the witness to the stand has in calling him.

Many techniques and reasons may be demonstrated to show bias or hostility. A previous quarrel, jealousy, an overzealous police officer, prejudice against a particular race or religion, being a close friend of one of the parties, political publicity, a sexual desire for the mate of the defendant, a breach of a commercial agreement by one of the adversaries, a higher insurance premium for the witness if the other party is successful, and a loss of money if the other party is successful, are only a few of the types of motivation that might lead to bias or hostility.

§ 2.35 Showing That Either at the Time of the Occurrence or at the Time of Testifying Witness Was Under the Influence of Drugs or Alcohol, Was Ill Mentally and/or Physically, Did Not Understand the Nature of an Oath, or Was Under Other Physical or Mental Incapacity

Assuming that the witness is an honest witness, we may impeach the witness on his or her ability to perceive what she has observed. Many of us will look at a person and fail to remember what color tie he wore or what color dress she wore. When we look at a situation and perceive all of the details of that situation to the extent that we can turn our heads away and look in another direction and verbalize what we have previously observed, we can say we have perceived what we have seen.

This area of testimony is particularly well suited to impeachment procedure in healthy individuals. It is also particularly well suited to people whose perceptive ability is impaired because of the use of drugs or alcohol or because of illness. If it can be shown that the witness's perception was incapacitated because of the use of drugs, narcotics, or alcohol or that the witness was physically incapacitated (e.g., by color blindness, poor eyesight, poor hearing, lack of proper illumination) or mentally defective, the weight of the witness's testimony is reduced in the eyes of the jury. 28 U.S.C.A. § 2904.

Often a child or mentally retarded adult is permitted to testify. If this witness is shown not to understand the seriousness of an oath or affirmation, this, too, may affect the weight of the witness's testimony.

§ 2.36 Showing Witness's Bad Reputation for Truth and Veracity

A witness may have a reputation in the community for being a congenital liar. If this is so, his or her testimony may be refuted by other witnesses who may testify that they have heard rumors or reports in the community that the witness cannot be believed.

All authorities agree, however, that testimony as to the reputation of a witness with respect to any specific trait of character other than veracity is not admissible for the purpose of impeaching the creditability of the witness; for example, a complaining witness in an assault may not be impeached by testimony of his or her general bad reputation for not paying just debts.

The time that the reputation is flooding the community need not be very recent, nor should it be too remote. See N.Y.—Sturmwald v. Schreiber, 69 App.Div.

476, 74 N.Y.S. 995 (1948). A witness may give an opinion of another witness's untruthfulness; U.S.—United States v. Dotson, 799 F.2d 189 (5th Cir. 1986).

Specific examples of misconduct may not be introduced in the direct examination of the character witness, but it may be asked of the witness on cross-examination.

§ 2.37   Showing That Witness Was in an Improper Position to Observe What Was Testified To

Frequently, a witness will testify that he or she observed a gun in the right hand of the defendant or that he or she observed the traffic light to be green for a particular party. A cross-examiner might be able to show that the witness was in such a location at the time of the incident as to only hear the noise of the gun shooting or the collision of the vehicles. The witness then ran to the location of the incident and concluded that the facts were as he or she had testified without actually seeing them occur because he or she was out of the line of sight of the situs of the instant case.

§ 2.38   Showing Entrapment of Defendant

Frequently, a defendant's attorney will raise the defense of entrapment to save his or her client from being convicted. There is a popular misconception as to what the word "entrapment" means. Black's Law Dictionary (Rev. 6th Ed. 1979) defines entrapment as "the act of officers or agents of government in inducing a person to commit a crime not contemplated by him for the purpose of instituting a criminal prosecution against him." Va.—Falden v. Commonwealth, 167 Va. 549, 189 S.E. 329 (1937). The mere act of an officer in furnishing the accused an opportunity to commit a crime, where the criminal intent was already present in the accused's mind, is not ordinarily entrapment. Wash.—State v. Cowling, 161 Wash. 519, 297 P. 172 (1931).

Many statutory laws exist prohibiting law enforcement officers from entrapping defendants. They are an outgrowth of the federal standards as set forth in Sorrells v. United States, 287 U.S. 435, 53 S.Ct. 210, 77 L.Ed. 413 (1932), and Sherman v. United States, 356 U.S. 369, 78 S.Ct. 819, 2 L.Ed.2d 848 (1958). In essence, a law enforcement officer cannot successfully encourage a person to commit a crime unless that person was previously disposed to commit that crime. An illustration may make this concept clearer.

Let us assume that because of a rash of auto burglaries in the vicinity of a hospital where out-of-town visitors were accustomed to park their cars, leaving valuables within the vehicle, the local police set up a "stake-out." They parked a vehicle in the street near the hospital with a camera and a woman's pocketbook plainly visible on the front seat. Officers in jeans and sport shirts were stationed near the car and played a game of cards on a stoop of a building located near the subject vehicle. "C" and "D" were seen walking along the street, looking into parked vehicles as they walked. As they came to the designated car, they stopped, they had a short conversation, and then "D" took instruments from his right coat pocket and proceeded to pick the lock. "C" assisted by taking one of the instruments from "D" and inserting it into the lock to keep the dust cover of the lock open while "D" did his picking. After a time, the door was opened, and entry was made. "D" picked up the camera, and "C" picked up the woman's handbag. At this point, the officers sprang to action, and the arrests were made.

One may think that this was a clear case of entrapment. This, however, was not entrapment because the defendants had an apparent previous disposition to commit the crime. Accordingly, if the defense of entrapment is raised, the prosecutor would have to elicit testimony as to what the defendants were doing prior to the burglary as they walked down the street looking at cars. This could be brought out on redirect examination, or the prosecutor could have the officers testify to it on direct examination. In United States v. Russell, 411 U.S. 423, 93 S.Ct. 1637, 36 L.Ed. 2d 366 (1973), the United States Supreme Court held that there is no defense of entrapment available to a defendant previously disposed to commit the crime when the government agent supplies a necessary ingredient to manufacture a controlled substance. In its 1976 Term, the Court decided Hampton v. United States, 425 U.S. 484, 96 S.Ct 1646, 48 L.Ed.2d 113 (1976), by a 5–4 decision, which held that when a defendant had a predisposition to commit a crime, the defense of entrapment may still be available if there was "outrageous police conduct." There was no definition of what outrageous police conduct might be. In the *Hampton* case, the defendant was accused of distribution of heroin, and both the suppliers and the purchasers were government agents or informers.

§ 2.39   Expert Witness Testimony—Not Always Accepted by Court

You have no doubt heard of expert witnesses who testify in both civil and criminal trials. An expert is usually paid a fee by one of the litigants to testify, presumably in favor of the party who has called him or her to the witness stand. It is not objectionable for the opposing party to request the witness to testify with respect to the amount of the fee that he or she is getting for the service. The very fact that the expert witnesses is getting a fee does not mean that the trier of the facts should disbelieve his or her testimony. This is how expert witnesses earn their living.

Before an expert witness is permitted to testify, the court should make a decision as to whether his or her testimony could be presented by lay witnesses. If this can be done, no expert opinion evidence should be admitted. A voir dire is conducted as to this issue, as well as to the witness's qualifications to testify as an expert.

If a fact in issue is within the ken of the average lay juror, expert opinion testimony is not necessary. Mott v. Sun Country Garden Products, Inc., 120 N.M. 261, 901 P.2d 192 (App. 1995).

Law enforcement officials who based their opinion testimony on various hearsay sources, rather than on personal perceptions, were not testifying as "lay witnesses." Neb.—State v. Simants, 248 Neb. 581, 537 N.W.2d 346 (1995).

§ 2.40   Impeaching Experts Using the Literature in the Field

Certain disciplines have books that are recognized authorities in the area of the alleged expertise of the expert witness. Frequently, the witness will make statements that are at variance with the theories or practices expressed in the works of the recognized authorities in the discipline. The expert witness may be confronted with these statements if he or she recognized them as authoritative in the field in which he or she claims expertise. Embarrassing encounters result when the witness's statements are at variance with some statement he or she has made in a publication. This lessens the weight of his or her testimony in the minds of the jury.

However, a medical book or treatise must be shown to be a recognized authority before it can be used in cross-examination of an expert medical witness. N.J.—Ruth v. Fenchel, 37 N.J.Super. 295, 117 A.2d 284 (1955), *aff'd*, 21 N.J. 171, 121 A.2d 373 (1956). The cross-examination must be confined to legitimate impeachment of what the witness has testified to, to showing such deficiency in the knowledge of the expert as to the science about which he is testifying as is calculated to impair the weight of his testimony. Tex.—Gulf, C. & S.F.R. Co. v. Farmer, 102 Tex. 235, 115 S.W. 260 (1909).

§ 2.41 Impeaching Experts by Questioning Qualifications

The trial court has wide discretion in determining who may be qualified to testify as an expert witness, and its decision on that question will not be reversed unless it abused that discretion. Ala.—CSX Transportation Inc. v. George E. Dansby, 659 So.2d 35 (Ala. 1995).

An expert witness is first required to establish his or her credentials to the satisfaction of the trial judge before he or she may be called on to answer a question that requires a conclusion. When the judge is satisfied that the witness is an expert, the witness may then testify on direct examination with respect to conclusions in the area of his or her expertise.

On cross-examination in a voir dire examination, the interrogator may delve more thoroughly into the witness's qualifications to testify as an expert and may elicit information that the witness's experience in the discipline is not sufficiently extensive to warrant that he or she testify as an expert.

It may be timely to note that a voir dire examination is conducted on application to the judge by the adversary before the expert witness is permitted to testify as an expert and is almost like a cross-examination but is different in that the adversary inquires only into the fitness of the witness to testify as an expert and at that juncture does not inquire into the facts of the instant case. Calif.—Eble v. Peluso, 80 Cal.App.2d 154, 181 P.2d 680 (1947); N.J.—Carbone v. Warburton, 11 N.J. 418, 94 A.2d 680 (1953); Pa.—Hoffman v. Berwind-White Coal Mining Co., 265 Pa. 476, 109 A. 234 (1920).

§ 2.42 Showing Specific Instances of Misconduct

In New York, a specific act of misconduct relevant only as tending to impair the witness's credibility can be elicited only on his or her cross-examination; it may not be proved by extrinsic evidence. If the witness denies committing the act, the cross-examiner cannot refute the answer by calling other witnesses or producing other evidence. N.Y.—People v. McCormick, 303 N.Y. 403, 103 N.E.2d 529 (1952). However, the cross-examiner may, if in good faith, continue the cross-examination of the witness on the chance that the witness may change his or her answer. N.Y.—People v. Sorge, 301 N.Y. 198, 93 N.E.2d 637 (1950). The specific act of misconduct must have some relevancy to show that the witness is a person of moral turpitude. N.H.—Curtice v. Dixon, 74 N.H. 386, 68 A. 587 (1908); N.Y.—People v. Montlake, 184 A.D. 578, 172 N.Y.S. 102 (1918).

§ 2.43 Showing Defect in Perception

As indicated previously, a person may see something occur, but he or she may be unable to verbalize the occurrence because he or she did not perceive it. Perception has been defined as a mental impression or the act or ability to become aware of something. It is therefore possible for a witness to see something with his or her eyes and yet not become mentally aware of what he or she sees. I have used the following method with some success in cross-examination. I would turn my back on the witness and ask the witness to describe what color shirt and tie I was wearing and what distinctive characteristics could be found in my face. If the witness was unable to identify these objects or characteristics after having been questioned by me for a lengthy period of time before the perception test, this fact would be brought out to the jury in summation to discredit the witness's perceptive ability.

§ 2.44   One's Own Witness

In common law, a party calling a witness to the stand in effect vouched for the truth and veracity of his or her testimony and could not impeach his testimony. Colo.—Scott v. Shook, 80 Colo. 40, 249 P.259, 47 A.L.R. 1108 (1926); N.Y.—Bulkley v. Kaolin Products Co., 187 App.Div. 103, 175 N.Y.S. 219 (1919).

This has been modified by statute in some jurisdictions; see, for example, N.Y.—CPLR 3117, 4514, N.Y.—CPL § 60:35(i), where a witness who makes a contradictory statement on the witness stand may be impeached by the party who called him or her to testify, providing the witness previously made either a written statement signed by him or her or an oral statement under oath, said statement being contrary to his or her testimony from the stand at the present time.

However, a party whose witness has testified to contradictory information and who has not made a prior statement under oath or a written prior statement signed by the witness available to him may prove his claim by other evidence and is not bound to his witness's testimony. Conn.—Nicholson Realty, Inc. v. Libby, 144 Conn. 555, 135 A.2d 738 (1957); Ill.—Wisniewski v. Shimashus, 22 Ill.2d 451, 176 N.E.2d 781 (1961); N.Y.—Quick v. American Can Co., 205 N.Y. 330, 98 N.E. 480 (1912); Pa.—Frew v. Barto, 345 Pa. 217, 26 A.2d 905 (1942).

Federal Rule of Evidence 607 spells out this deviation from the common law practice very clearly. Rule 607 provides that "the credibility of a witness may be attacked by any party, including the party calling him." The same result is found in California Evidence Code § 785, Kansas Code of Civil Practice § 60–420, and New Jersey Evidence Rule 20.

§ 2.45   Showing Other, Similar Acts

A defendant may be prone to do certain acts that, standing alone, may not demonstrate criminal behavior but, if considered collectively, may logically imply that the intent of the subject was to violate the law. In this category of behavioral patterns, we may find an implication

1. to show motive,
2. to show intent,
3. to show absence of mistake,
4. to show common scheme or plan, or
5. to show identity of person charged.

§ 2.46   Motive—Intent

A motive is an inner reason for doing a given act. Intent is having the mind closely fixed on a subject. A person may have a reason to steal to support his or her family without resorting to public assistance. Therefore, his or her motive is to support his or her family; his or her intention is to steal. If it can be demonstrated that he or she desperately needed money, this fact would be admissible in a larceny trial.

Another example of this principle might occur if shortly after the homicide of a husband the defendant married the wife of the deceased. The fact of the marriage could be introduced to show motive on the part of the defendant to commit the homicide. In order for this type of testimony to be admissible, it must have a logical relation to the commission of the crime charged. Conn.—Lomartira v. Lomartira, 159 Conn. 558, 271 A.2d 91 (1970); Fla.—River Hills, Inc. v. Edwards, 190 So.2d 415 (Fla.App. 1966); Ky.—Flynn v. Songer, 399 S.W.2d 491 (1966); N.Y.—People v. Namer, 309 N.Y. 458, 131 N.E.2d 734 (1956).

However, subsequent acts may not be considered as showing previous fraudulent intent. Mich.—Sachs v. Karos, 310 Mich. 577, 17 N.W.2d 759 (1945), *cert. denied*, 326 U.S. 794, 66 S.Ct. 483, 90 L.Ed. 482 (1946).

§ 2.47   Absence of Mistake

A defendant may have made a mistake, and the wrongdoing that he or she committed is excusable. However, if this alleged "mistake" occurred with some frequency, it might be admissible to introduce other, similar acts, which would negate the defense of mistake.

For example, a defendant was charged with the homicide of his mother, and his defense was that he was awakened in the middle of the night by his mother requesting medicine for a heart palpitation attack. He went to the medicine cabinet in the bathroom and returned with a brown medicine, which his mother had told him was in the medicine cabinet. He administered the medicine to his mother and immediately both he and she realized that it was the wrong medicine. He had given her a preparation to be used to remove warts. When he realized his mistake, he called the police to get a stomach pump to his mother immediately. His mother died within a short time after he gave her the medicine. The medicine that he should have given her was in a similar bottle and was similar in appearance to the wart remover. If there was a similar type of occurrence previously with this same defendant, it could have been introduced into evidence to show that it was not a mistake. It may interest the reader to know that such a situation as this occurred and that the author was the police officer who responded to the call.

The overriding reason for admission of other, similar acts—absence of mistake—is based on the following two theories:

1. Probability theory—the greater the repetition, the less probable that it was a mistake
2. Knowledge theory—as the number of acts increase, there is a greater opportunity to gain knowledge.

§ 2.48   Common Scheme or Plan

Other, similar acts may be introduced into evidence to show a common scheme or plan. There are two types of situations that should be considered. In the first type, there will be at least two crimes committed, but there will be only one objective. The second type envisages the commission of several crimes with the relation of time and space being very close.

An example of more than one crime with one objective may occur if three persons are coconspirators and rob a bank. The agreement among them was that they would divide the proceeds of the robbery equally. After the successful completion of the robbery, two of the participants agree to murder the third in order to divide his portion among them. They murder the third person, and then the defendant felt that his was an easy way to get rich, so he murdered the second participant. At the trial of the defendant for either of the murders, evidence may be introduced that his objective was to get all the proceeds for his own use, and therefore testimony of the first murder could be introduced. This is very close to motive and almost indistinguishable.

An example of the commission of several crimes with the relation of time and space being very close might be the apprehension of a burglar in an apartment of an apartment house containing forty apartments, two of which reported burglaries having taken place on the same evening that the defendant was apprehended and the defendant having been caught with the proceeds of the other burglaries on his person. In order to grasp this concept clearly, the student should ask the following questions:

1. Is it relevant?
2. Does it have substantial relevancy?
3. If it does, will the substantial relevancy outweigh the undue prejudice?

§ 2.49   Identity of Person Charged

The Federal Rules of Evidence have codified the principles of Rule 404(b), which reads as follows:

> **(b) Other Crimes, Wrongs, or Acts.** Evidence of other crimes, wrongs, or acts is not admissible to prove the character of a person in order to show action in conformity therewith. It may, however, be admissible for other purposes, such as proof of motive, opportunity, intent, preparation, plan, knowledge, identity, or absence of mistake or accident, provided that upon request by the accused, the prosecution in a criminal case shall provide reasonable notice in advance of trial, or during trial if the court excuses pretrial notice on good cause shown, of the general nature of any such evidence it intends to introduce at trial.

Other similar acts may be introduced to show the identity of the person charged. An example of this concept might be if a burglar has been leaving his trademark by defecating on top of the bedspread that is on the bed in the master bedroom of the burglarized premises. The burglar is later apprehended coming out of the rear window of a burglarized home. Inspection by the police officers revealed that there was fresh feces on the bedspread in the master bedroom. Evidence might be introduced in the trial of this defendant for the other burglaries that he defecated in each of the burglaries in a peculiar manner. This would tend to logically imply that the same person committed all of the burglaries and that the defendant was that person.

For a thorough discussion of these principles, the reader is referred to U.S.—Drew v. United States, 331 F.2d 85 (D.C. Cir. 1964); N.Y.—People v. Molineaux, 168 N.Y. 264, 61 N.E. 286, 62 L.R.A. 193 (1901).

RELATED DECISIONS
Examination of Witness and Trial Procedures

Alford v. United States

Supreme Court of the United States, 1931.
282 U.S. 687, 51 S.Ct. 218, 75 L.Ed 624.

This case involved a prosecution of the petitioner on a charge of using the mail to defraud. The case had come to the United States Supreme Court on a writ of certiorari. A writ of certiorari is a common law writ (court order) issued from a higher court to an inferior court. It commands the inferior court to certify and send the record of a particular case previously decided by the inferior court to the higher court for review of the inferior court's actions in the case.

At the trial, the defendant's attorney, at cross-examination, asked a prosecution witness where he lived. The prosecutor objected to the question on the grounds that it was not proper cross-examination. The trial court agreed with the prosecution by sustaining the objection. However, even after the trial court's ruling was affirmed by the Circuit Court of Appeals, the United States Supreme Court reversed. The Court stated that cross-examination is a matter of right and that the extent of cross-examination is within the sound discretion of the trial court, but no obligation is imposed on the trial court to protect a witness from being discredited on cross-examination, short of an attempted invasion of his constitutional protection from self-incrimination, properly invoked.

There are many more facts and principles expressed in this decision, and I leave these for you to extract. The edited decision follows:

* * *

On Writ of Certiorari to the United States Circuit Court of Appeals for the Ninth Circuit.

J.W. Alford was convicted of using the mails to defraud, the conviction being affirmed by the Circuit Court of Appeals [41 F.2d 157], and he brings certiorari.

* * *

Mr. Justice STONE delivered the opinion of the Court.

Petitioner was convicted in the District Court for southern California of using the mails to defraud in violation of section 215 of the Criminal Code (18 U.S.C.A. § 338). This court granted certiorari, 282 U.S. 826, 51 S.Ct. 77, 75 L.Ed. 624, October 20, 1930, to review a judgment of affirmance by the Court of Appeals for the Ninth Circuit, which upheld certain rulings of the trial court upon the evidence. 41 F.2d 157.

In the course of the trial the government called as a witness a former employee of petitioner. On direct examination he gave damaging testimony with respect to various transactions of accused, including conversations with the witness when others were not present, and statements of accused to salesmen under his direction, whom the witness did not identify. Upon cross-examination questions seeking to elicit the witness's place of residence were excluded on the government's objection that they were immaterial and not proper cross-examination. Counsel for the defense insisted that the questions were proper cross-examination, and that the jury was entitled to know "who the witness is, where he lives and what his business is." Relevant excerpts of the record are printed in the margin.

Later, the jury having been excused, counsel for the defense urged, as an "additional" ground for asking the excluded questions, that he had been informed that the witness was then in the custody of the federal authorities, and that such fact might be brought out on cross-examination "for the purpose of showing whatever bias or prejudice he may have." But the court adhered to its previous rulings, saying that if the witness had been convicted of a felony that fact might be proved, but not that he was detained in custody.

The Court of Appeals, after stating that it is customary to allow cross-examination of a witness with reference to his place of residence, upheld the trial court, saying, page 160 of 41 F.2d:

> The purpose of such evidence is to identify the witness and to some extent give proper background for the interpretation of his testimony. In this case, however, the counsel indicated his purpose to use the information for the purpose of discrediting the witness. It is part of the obligation of a trial judge to protect witnesses against evidence tending to discredit the witness unless such evidence is reasonably called for by exigencies of the case. A witness is not on trial and has no means of protecting himself. Here it was evidence that the counsel for the appellant desired to discredit the witness, without, so far as is shown, in any way connecting the expected answer with a matter on trial. If it had been contended that the witness was in custody because of his participation in the transaction with which the appellant was charged, and if it was sought to show that he was testifying under some promise of immunity, it would undoubtedly have been prejudicial error to have excluded such testimony; but counsel avowed no such purpose, and indicated that the proposed question was merely in pursuit of a fishing expedition by which he hoped to discredit the witness. The witness was examined at great length concerning his relation to the appellant and great latitude was accorded in that examination.

Cross-examination of a witness is a matter of right. The Ottawa, 3 Wall. 268, 271, 18 L.Ed. 165 (1859). Its permissible purposes, among others, are that the witness may be identified with his community so that independent testimony may be sought and offered of his reputation for veracity in his own neighborhood, cf. Khan v. Zemansky, 59 Cal.App. 324, 327ff., 210 Pac. 529 (1923); 3 Wigmore, Evidence (2d Ed.) § 1368, I. (1)(b); that the jury may interpret his testimony in the light reflected upon it by knowledge of his environment, Kirschner v. State, 9 Wis. 140 (1859); Wilbur v. Flood, 16 Mich. 40, 93 Am. Dec. 203 (1867); Hollingsworth v. State, 53 Ark. 387, 14 S.W. 41 (1890); People v. White, 251 Ill. 67, 72ff., 95 N.E. 1036 (1911); Wallace v. State, 41 Fla. 547, 574ff., 26 So. 713 (1900); and that facts may be brought out tending to discredit the witness by showing that his testimony in chief was untrue or biased. Tla-koo-yel-lee v. United States, 167 U.S. 274, 17 S.Ct. 855, 42 L.Ed. 166 (1897); King v. United States, 112 F. 988 (C.C.A. 1902); Farkas v. United States, 2 F.2d 644 (C.C.A. 1925); see Furlong v. United States, 10 F.2d 492, 494 (C.C.A. 1926).

Counsel often cannot know in advance what pertinent facts may be elicited on cross-examination. For that reason it is necessarily exploratory; and the rule that the examiner must indicate the purpose of his inquiry does not, in general, apply. Knapp v. Wing, 72 Vt. 334, 340, 47 A. 1075 (1901); Martin v. Elden, 32 Ohio St. 282, 289 (1877). It is the essence of a fair trial that reasonable latitude be given the cross-examiner, even though he is unable to state to the court what facts a reasonable cross-examination might develop. Prejudice ensues from a denial of the opportunity to place the witness in his proper setting and put the weight of his testimony and his credibility to a test, without which the jury cannot fairly appraise them. Tla-koo-yel-lee v. United States, supra; King v. United States, supra; People v. Moore, 96 App.Div. 56, 89 N.Y.S. 83 (1949), affirmed without opinion, 181 N.Y. 524, 73 N.E. 1129 (1905); cf. People v. Becker, 210 N.Y. 274, 104 N.E. 396 (1914). To say that prejudice can be established only by showing that the cross-examination, if pursued, would necessarily have brought out facts tending to discredit the testimony in chief, is to deny substantial right and withdraw one of the safeguards essential to a fair trial. Nailor v. Williams, 8 Wall. 107, 109, 19 L.Ed. 348 (1868); see People v. Stevenson, 284 P. 491 (Cal.Sup. 1930); cf. Brasfield v. United States, 272 U.S. 448, 47 S.Ct. 135, 71 L.Ed. 345 (1926). In this respect a summary denial of the right of cross-examination is indistinguishable from the erroneous admission of harmless testimony. Nailor v. Williams, supra.

Q. Where do you live, Mr. Bradley?

Mr. Armstrong: That is objected to as immaterial and not proper cross-examination.

The Court: I cannot see the materiality.

Mr. Friedman: Why, I think the jury has a perfect right to know who the witness is, where he lives and what his business is, and we have the right to elicit that on cross-examination. I may say that this is the first witness the Government had called that they have not elicited the address from.

The Court: I will sustain the objection.

Q. By Mr. Friedman: What is your business, Mr. Bradley? **A.** My profession is an accountant, public accountant.

Q. What is your occupation now? **A.** I am not doing anything at the present time on account of this case.

Q. On account of this case? **A.** Yes.

Q. Do you live in Los Angeles?

Mr. Armstrong: That is objected to as immaterial and invading the Court's ruling.

The Court: I have ruled on that question.

Mr. Friedman: I will temporarily pass on to something else. I would like leave to submit authorities on my right to develop that on cross-examination. I haven't them with me.

The Court: All right. . . .

The Jury were thereupon excused by the court until 9:30 o'clock on the morning of July 24, 1929, whereupon the jury retired after which the following proceedings were had relative to the materiality of the testimony, as to the residence and place thereof of Cameron Bradley.

The Court: So ordered. In what particular do you think that evidence is material?

Mr. Friedman: I think it is material for this purpose, first, not only on the general grounds I urged in asking the question, but on the additional grounds that I have been informed and caused to believe that this witness himself is now in the custody of the Federal authorities.

Mr. Armstrong: You mean Mr. Bradley? You mean by the Federal authorities here?

Mr. Friedman: I don't know by what authorities, but that is my impression, that he is here in the custody of the Federal authorities. If that is so, I have a right to show that for the purpose of showing whatever bias or prejudice he may have.

The Court: No; I don't think so. If you can prove he has ever been convicted of a felony, that is a different thing.

Mr. Friedman: I realize that is the rule. I may impeach him if he has been convicted of a felony.

The Court: No. You may prove that fact as going to his credibility, but you can't merely show that he is detained or in charge of somebody. Everybody is presumed to be innocent until proven guilty.

Mr. Friedman: It is a violent presumption sometimes, I know.

The Court: Your defendant is certainly to be given the benefit of that presumption.

Mr. Friedman: I have no doubt of that.

The Court: If that is all you have, I will have to stand on the ruling. . . .

Mr. Friedman: I would like, if the Court please, our exception noted to the Court's ruling made yesterday after the jury retired to the effect that we could not inquire as to the present address and residence of the witness.

The Court: Very well.

The present case, after the witness for the prosecution had testified to uncorroborated conversations of the defendant of a damaging character, was a proper one for searching cross-examination. The question "Where do you live?" was not only an appropriate preliminary to the cross-examination of the witness, but on its face, without any such declaration of purpose as was made by counsel here, was an essential step in identifying the witness with his environment, to which cross-examination may always be directed. State v. Pugsley, 75 Iowa 742, 38 N.W. 498 (1888); State v. Fong Loon, 29 Idaho 248, 255ff., 158 Pac. 233, L.R.A. 1916F, 1198 (1916); Wallace v. State, supra; Wilbur v. Flood, supra; 5 Jones, Evidence (2d Ed.) § 2366.

But counsel for the defense went further, and in the ensuing colloquy with the court urged, as an additional reason why the question should be allowed, not a substitute reason, as the court below assumed, that he was informed that the witness was then in court in custody of the federal authorities, and that that fact could be brought out on cross-examination to show whatever bias or prejudice the witness might have. The purpose obviously was not, as the trial court seemed to think, to discredit the witness by showing that he was charged with crime, but to show by such facts as proper cross-examination might develop, that his testimony was biased because given under promise or expectation of immunity, or under the coercive effect of his detention by officers of the United States, which was conducting the present prosecution. King v. United States, supra; Farkas v. United States, supra, and cases cited; People v. Becker, supra; State v. Ritz, 65 Mont. 180, 211 P. 298 (1923), and cases cited on page 188, 211 Pac. 298; Rex v. Watson, 32 How.St.Tr. 284. Nor is it material, as the Court of Appeals said, whether the witness was in custody because of his participation in the transactions for which petitioner was indicted. Even if the witness were charged with some other offense by the prosecuting authorities, petitioner was entitled to show by cross-examination that his testimony was affected by fear or favor growing out of his detention. See Farkas v. United States, supra; People v. Dillwood, 4 Cal.Unrep. 973, 39 Pac. 438 (1895).

The extent of cross-examination with respect to an appropriate subject of inquiry is within the sound discretion of the trial court. It may exercise a reasonable judgment in determining when the subject is exhausted. Storm v. United States, 94 U.S. 76, 85, 24 L.Ed. 42 (1876); Rea v. Missouri, 17 Wall. 532, 542–543, 21 L.Ed. 707 (1873); Blitz v. United States, 153 U.S. 308, 312, 14 S.Ct. 924, 38 L.Ed. 725 (1894). But no obligation is imposed on the court, such as that suggested below, to protect a witness from being discredited on cross-examination, short of an attempted invasion of his constitutional protection from self-incrimination, properly invoked. There is a duty to protect him from questions which go beyond the bounds of proper cross-examination merely to harass, annoy or humiliate him. President, etc., of Third Great Western Turnpike Road Co. v. Loomis, 32 N.Y. 127, 132, 88 Am.Dec. 311 (1865); Wallace v. State, supra; 5 Jones, Evidence (2nd Ed.) § 2316. But no such case is presented here. The trial court cut off in limine all inquiry on a subject with respect to which the defense was entitled to a reasonable cross-examination. This was an abuse of discretion and prejudicial error. Tla-koo-yel-lee v. United States, supra; Nailor v. Williams, supra; King v. United States, supra; People v. Moore, supra; cf. People v. Becker, supra. Other grounds for reversal were set up in the petition for certiorari, but we do not find it necessary to pass upon them.

Reversed.

RELATED DECISIONS
Cross-Examination

United States v. Palermo
United States Court of Appeals, Seventh Circuit, 1969. 410 F.2d 468.

This case expands on the principles of law expressed in Alford v. United States, *supra*.

In this case, there was a real threat to the life of the witness, which was told to the trial judge in camera. The prosecution did not want to reveal the true name, address, and place of employment of the witness. This case was remanded to the trial court to reconsider the issue of whether the witness has to give his true name, address, and place of employment pursuant to the guidelines expressed in the opinion because the decision cannot be made in a vacuum. The trial judge must investigate the reasons for the prosecution's and the defense attorney's positions and arrive at an informed decision. You may amplify this analysis by reading the decision.

KERNER, Circuit Judge. Defendants were indicted for conspiring to violate the Hobbs Act, 18 U.S.C.A. § 1951, by interfering with commerce by extorting money from a builder and in so doing, interfering with interstate shipments of construction materials. The jury found all defendants guilty and from these convictions they appeal.

From 1962 to 1965 Riley Management Company, with William G. Riley as president, was building various apartment building complexes in suburbs surrounding Chicago. Melrose Park Plumbing was a subcontractor on Riley's first construction project in Addison, Illinois, in 1962. Nick Palermo, a defendant and the owner of Melrose Park Plumbing, wanted to be sure that Riley would use his company on all of Riley's building projects. To accomplish this, Palermo and defendant Joseph Amabile, also known as Joe Shine, conspired together with others to force Riley into using Melrose Park Plumbing as a subcontractor and at the same time having Riley pay them extra money for their work. See United States v. Battaglia, 394 F.2d 304 (7th Cir. 1968). In essence, Amabile, Palermo and others agreed to obtain as much money as possible from Riley by threatening him with work stoppages and physical violence.

Early in 1962, Riley became interested in building another apartment complex in Northlake, Illinois. In April of 1962, defendant Henry Ed Neri, Mayor of Northlake, and Wayne Seidler, an unindicted co-conspirator, met with Riley's attorney at which time Mayor Neri told him it would cost $100 per unit or $70,000 in order to build the project in Northlake. Without this money, required zoning changes would not be made nor would building permits be issued. A few days later Amabile told Neri that he and Nick Palermo were taking over the project in Northlake and could obtain at least $40,000 for Neri's people. Neri then asked Amabile for $10,000 before the next meeting of the Zoning Board.

Defendants Leo Shababy and Joseph Drozd were aldermen in Northlake. They and some members of the Zoning Board received various monies from Amabile for rezoning the area. When the money demanded was not being paid on time, Shababy, Drozd, Seidler and Neri put pressures on Amabile including withholding approval of the zoning change and refusing to issue building permits. In turn, Amabile and Palermo pressured Riley into paying them $64,000 by threatening him both with work stoppage at the Addison project and physical violence to himself and his family. Riley testified that Palermo hit him in the face and threatened to make him understand with a baseball bat. See United States v. Battaglia, 394 F.2d 304, 308 (7th Cir. 1968).

* * *

CROSS-EXAMINATION

Alford v. United States, 282 U.S. 687, 51 S.Ct. 218, 75 L.Ed. 624 (1931), and Smith v. Illinois, 390 U.S. 129, 88 S.Ct. 748, 19 L.Ed.2d 956 (1968), require reversal where the district judge refuses to allow questions as to a witness' address and present employment since they are threshold questions of cross-examination. "The purpose of the inquiry is to make known to the jury the setting in which to judge the character, veracity or bias of the witness. . . . Since there is no requirement of materiality, it is not necessary to show the possibility of the witness being in custody in order to make such inquiry." United States v. Varelli, 407 F.2d 735, p. 749 (7th Cir. 1969).

However, the decision to disclose a witness' address or place of employment cannot be made in a vacuum. This Court is not unaware of the problem that the government has in obtaining witnesses in cases where a witness' life may be in jeopardy if he testifies. As Justice White said in his concurrence in Smith v. Illinois, 390 U.S. 129, 133–134, 88 S.Ct. 748, 751 (1968), "In Alford v. United States, 282 U.S. 687, 694, 51 S.Ct. 218, 220, 75 L.Ed. 624 (1931), the Court recognized that questions which tend merely to harass, annoy, or humiliate a witness may go beyond the bounds of proper cross-examination. I would place in the same category those inquiries which tend to endanger the personal safety of the witness."

This Court agrees with Justice White that where there is a threat to the life of the witness, the right of the defendant to have the witness' true name, address and place of employment is not absolute. United States v. Varelli, 407 F.2d 735 (7th Cir. 1969). However, the threat to the witness must be actual and not a result of conjecture. Shaw v. Illinois, 394 U.S. 214, 89 S.Ct. 1016, 22 L.Ed.2d 211 (1969). The government bears the burden of proving to the district judge the existence of such a threat.

An actual threat being shown, the government must also disclose to the district judge *in camera* the relevant information. United States v. Varelli, 407 F.2d 735 (7th Cir. 1969). Knowing of the existence of an actual threat and the witness' location, the district judge must determine whether the information must be disclosed in order not to deny effective cross-examination. "The trial judge can then ascertain the interest of the defendant in the answer and exercise an informed discretion in making his ruling." (White, J. concurring) Smith v. Illinois, 390 U.S. 129, 134, 88 S.Ct. 751 (1968). Such decision is reviewable on appeal. Under almost all circumstances, the true name of the witness must be disclosed. Smith v. Illinois, 390 U.S. 129, 88 S.Ct. 74 (1968). If the witness is located in a penal institution, this, too, must be disclosed. Alford v. United States, 282 U.S. 687, 51 S.Ct. 218 (1931). A witness' prior address must also be disclosed if the witness does not intend to return to this location. United States v. Varelli, 407 F.2d 735 (7th Cir. 1969). If the trial judge concludes that the defendant does not have a right to the exact address of the witness and his place of employment, the defendant is entitled to ask any other relevant questions which may aid the jury in weighing the witness' credibility.

Here, the trial judge, having been requested to order Seidler and Riley to disclose their addresses and present employment, refused to order them to answer. While there was an adequate showing of a threat to the life of Riley, there was no showing as to Seidler. In neither case was the relevant information disclosed to the trial judge in order that he could make an informed decision. On remand the government must comply with the standards set out above.

Remanded with directions.

Pointer v. State of Texas
Supreme Court of the United States, 1965.
380 U.S. 400, 85 S.Ct. 1065, 13 L.Ed.2d 923.

This case revolves around a conviction based on a transcript taken at a preliminary hearing where the witness against the petitioner was a defendant at the time of the hearing, having been accused of robbery and other crimes in Texas. In Texas, this hearing is called an "examining trial." This hearing is nothing more than a prima facie hearing, which determines if the complaint on its face and not explained could result in a conviction.

The witness was never cross-examined by the petitioner, although the trial judge noted that the petitioner was present and had been "accorded the opportunity of cross examining the witness there against him." The petitioner had no lawyer representing him at the hearing.

The court accepted the reading of the transcript into the trial record over the objection of Pointer's trial attorney.

It is suggested that you read this decision to ascertain whether the United States Supreme

Court decided that the trial court had ruled properly.

Mr. Justice BLACK delivered the opinion of the Court.

The Sixth Amendment provides in part that:

"In all criminal prosecutions, the accused shall enjoy the right . . . to be confronted with the witnesses against him . . . and to have the Assistance of Counsel for his defence."

Two years ago in Gideon v. Wainwright, 372 U.S. 335, 83 S.Ct. 792, 9 L.Ed.2d 799 (1963), we held that the Fourteenth Amendment makes the Sixth Amendment's guarantee of right to counsel obligatory upon the States. The question we find necessary to decide in this case is whether the Amendment's guarantee of a defendant's right "to be confronted with the witness against him," which has been held to include the right to cross-examine those witnesses, is also made applicable to the States by the Fourteenth Amendment.

The petitioner Pointer and one Dillard were arrested in Texas and taken before a state judge for a preliminary hearing (in Texas called the "examining trial") on a charge of having robbed Kenneth W. Phillips of $375 "by assault, or violence, or by putting in fear of life or bodily injury," in violation of Texas Penal Code Art. 1408. At this hearing an Assistant District Attorney conducted the prosecution and examined witnesses, but neither of the defendants, both of whom were laymen, had a lawyer. Phillips as chief witness for the State gave his version of the alleged robbery in detail, identifying petitioner as the man who had robbed him at gunpoint. Apparently Dillard tried to cross-examine Phillips but Pointer did not, although Pointer was said to have tried to cross-examine some other witnesses at the hearing. Petitioner was subsequently indicted on a charge of having committed the robbery. Some time before the trial was held, Phillips moved to California. After putting in evidence to show that Phillips had moved and did not intend to return to Texas, the State at the trial offered the transcript of Phillips' testimony given at the preliminary hearing as evidence against petitioner. Petitioner's counsel immediately objected to introduction of the transcript, stating, "Your

Honor, we will object to that, as it is a denial of the confrontment of the witnesses against the Defendant." Similar objections were repeatedly made by petitioner's counsel but were overruled by the trial judge, apparently in part because, as the judge viewed it, petitioner had been present at the preliminary hearing and therefore had been "accorded the opportunity of cross-examining the witness there against him." The Texas Court of Criminal Appeals, the highest state court to which the case could be taken, affirmed petitioner's conviction, rejecting his contention that use of the transcript to convict him denied him rights guaranteed by the Sixth and Fourteenth Amendments. 375 S.W.2d 293: We granted certiorari to consider the important constitutional question the case involves. 379 U.S. 815, 85 S.Ct. 88, 13 L.Ed.2d 28.

* * *

. . . In this case the objections and arguments in the trial court as well as the arguments in the Court of Criminal Appeals and before us make it clear that petitioner's objection is based not so much on the fact that he had no lawyer when Phillips made his statement at the preliminary hearing, as on the fact that use of the transcript of that statement at the trial denied petitioner any opportunity to have the benefit of counsel's cross-examination of the principal witness against him. It is that latter question which we decide here.

I.

The Sixth Amendment is a part of what is called our Bill of Rights. In Gideon v. Wainwright, supra, in which this Court held that the Sixth Amendment's right to the assistance of counsel is obligatory upon the States, we did so on the ground that "a provision of the Bill of Rights which is 'fundamental and essential to a fair trial' is made obligatory upon the States by the Fourteenth Amendment." 372 U.S., at 342, 83 S.Ct., at 795. And last Term in Malloy v. Hogan, 378 U.S. 1, 84 S.Ct. 1489, 12 L.Ed.2d 653 (1964), in holding that the Fifth Amendment's guarantee against self-incrimination was made applicable to the States by the Fourteenth, we reiterated the holding of Gideon that the Sixth Amendment's right-to-counsel guarantee is

"'a fundamental right, essential to a fair trial,'" and "thus was made obligatory on the States by the Fourteenth Amendment." 378 U.S., at 6, 84 S.Ct., at 1492. See also Murphy v. Waterfront Comm'n, 378 U.S. 52, 84 S.Ct. 1594, 12 L.Ed.2d 678 (1964). We hold today that the Sixth Amendment's right of an accused to confront the witnesses against him is likewise a fundamental right and is made obligatory on the States by the Fourteenth Amendment.

It cannot seriously be doubted at this late date that the right of cross-examination is included in the right of an accused in a criminal case to confront the witnesses against him. And probably no one, certainly no one experienced in the trial of lawsuits, would deny the value of cross-examination in exposing falsehood and bringing out the truth in the trial of a criminal case. See, e.g., 5 Wigmore, Evidence § 1367 (3d ed. 1940). The fact that this right appears in the Sixth Amendment of our Bill of Rights reflects the belief of the Framers of those liberties and safeguards that confrontation was a fundamental right essential to a fair trial in a criminal prosecution. Moreover, the decisions of this Court and other courts throughout the years have constantly emphasized the necessity for cross-examination as a protection for defendants in criminal cases. This Court in Kirby v. United States, 174 U.S. 47, 55, 56, 19 S.Ct. 574, 43 L.Ed. 890 (1899), referred to the right of confrontation as "[o]ne of the fundamental guaranties of life and liberty," and "a right long deemed so essential for the due protection of life and liberty that it is guarded against legislative and judicial action by provisions in the constitution of the United States and in the constitutions of most, if not of all, the states composing the Union." Mr. Justice Stone, writing for the Court in Alford v. United States, 282 U.S. 687, 692, 51 S.Ct. 218, 219, 75 L.Ed. 624 (1931), declared that the right of cross-examination is "one of the safeguards essential to a fair trial." And in speaking of confrontation and cross-examination this Court said in Greene v. McElroy, 360 U.S. 474, 79 S.Ct. 1400, 3 L.Ed.2d 1377 (1959):

"They have ancient roots. They find expression in the Sixth Amendment which provides that in all criminal cases the accused shall enjoy the right 'to be confronted with the witnesses against him.' This Court has been zealous to protect these rights from erosion." 360 U.S. at 496–497, 79 S.Ct., at 1413 (footnote omitted).

There are few subjects, perhaps, upon which this Court and other courts have been more nearly unanimous than in their expressions of belief that the right of confrontation and cross-examination is an essential and fundamental requirement for the kind of fair trial which is this country's constitutional goal. Indeed, we have expressly declared that to deprive an accused of the right to cross-examine the witnesses against him is a denial of the Fourteenth Amendment's guarantee of due process of law. In In re Oliver, 333 U.S. 257, 68 S.Ct. 499, 92 L.Ed. 682 (1948), this Court said:

> A person's right to reasonable notice of a charge against him, and an opportunity to be heard in his defense—a right to his day in court—are basic in our system of jurisprudence; and these rights include, as a minimum, a right to examine the witnesses against him, to offer testimony, and to be represented by counsel. 333 U.S., at 273, 68 S.Ct., at 507 (footnote omitted).

And earlier this Term in Turner v. State of Louisiana, 379 U.S. 466, 472–473, 85 S.Ct. 546, 550, 13 L.Ed.2d 424 (1965), we held:

> In the constitutional sense, trial by jury in a criminal case necessarily implies at the very least that the 'evidence developed' against a defendant shall come from the witness stand in a public courtroom where there is full judicial protection of the defendant's right of confrontation, of cross-examination, and of counsel.

Compare Willner v. Committee on Character & Fitness, 373 U.S. 96, 103–104, 83 S.Ct. 1175, 1180–1181, 10 L.Ed.2d 224 (1963).

We are aware that some cases, particularly West v. State of Louisiana, 194 U.S. 258, 264, 24 S.Ct. 650, 652, 48 L.Ed. 965 (1904), have stated that the Sixth Amendment's right of confrontation does not apply to trials in state courts, on the ground that the entire Sixth Amendment does not so apply. See also Stein v. People of State of New York, 346 U.S. 156, 195–196, 73 S.Ct. 1077, 1098–1099, 97 L.Ed. 1522 (1953). But of course since Gideon v. Wainwright, supra, it no longer can broadly be said that the Sixth Amendment does not apply to state courts. And as this Court said in Malloy v. Hogan, supra, "The Court has not hesitated to re-examine past decisions according the Fourteenth Amendment a less central role in the preservation of basic liberties than that which was contemplated by its Framers when they added the Amendment to our constitutional scheme." 378 U.S., at 5, 84 S.Ct., at 1492. In the light of Gideon, Malloy, and other cases cited in those opinions holding various provisions of the Bill of Rights applicable to the States by virtue of the Fourteenth Amendment, the statements made in West and similar cases generally declaring that the Sixth Amendment does not apply to the States can no longer be regarded as the law. We hold that petitioner was entitled to be tried in accordance with the protection of the confrontation guarantee of the Sixth Amendment, and that that guarantee, like the right against compelled self-incrimination, is "to be enforced against the States under the Fourteenth Amendment according to the same standards that protect those personal rights against federal encroachment." Malloy v. Hogan, supra, 378 U.S., at 10, 84 S.Ct., at 1495.

II.

Under this Court's prior decisions, the Sixth Amendment's guarantee of confrontation and cross-examination was unquestionably denied petitioner in this case. As has been pointed out, a major reason underlying the constitutional confrontation rule is to give a defendant charged with crime an opportunity to cross-examine the witnesses against him. See, e.g., Dowdell v. United States, 221 U.S. 325, 330, 31 S.Ct. 590, 592, 55 L.Ed. 753 (1911); Motes v. United States, 178 U.S. 458, 474, 20 S.Ct. 993, 999, 44 L.Ed. 1150 (1900); Kirby v. United States, 174 U.S. 47, 55–56, 19 S.Ct. 574, 577, 43 L.Ed. 890 (1899); . . . Nothing we hold here is to the contrary. The case before us would be quite a different one had Phillips' statement been taken at a full-fledged hearing at which petitioner had been represented by counsel who had been given a complete and adequate opportunity to cross-examine. Compare Motes v. United States, supra, 178 U.S., at 474, 20 S.Ct., at 999. There are other analogous situations which might not fall within the scope of the constitutional rule requiring confrontation of witnesses. The case before us, however, does not present any situation like those mentioned above or others analogous to them. Because the transcript of Phillips' statement offered against petitioner at his trial had not been taken at a time and under circumstances affording petitioner through counsel an adequate opportunity to cross-examine Phillips, its introduction in a federal court in a criminal case against Pointer would have amounted to denial of the privilege of confrontation guaranteed by the Sixth Amendment. Since we hold that the right of an accused to be confronted with the witnesses against him must be determined by the same standards whether the right is denied in a federal or state proceeding, it follows that use of the transcript to convict petitioner denied him a constitutional right, and that his conviction must be reversed.

Reversed and remanded.

People of the State of New York v. Benjamin Oyola

Court of Appeals of New York, 1959.
6 N.Y.2d 259, 189 N.Y.S.2d 203, 160 N.E.2d 494.

This decision was handed down by the highest court in the state of New York. Unlike most states, New York does not have a New York Supreme Court as its highest court. The state does have a court designated as a supreme court, but this court is a trial court or a court where motions may be heard, that is, a supreme court of a county. It may be designated, for example, Supreme Court, Nassau County. This means that its jurisdiction only applies to Nassau County and its appellate jurisdiction is limited in certain matters, such as appeals to bail conditions set in lower courts of that county.

In this case, the issue presented is the admissibility of sworn testimony of a ten-year-old child that she became morally depraved after being assaulted in the third degree, a misdemeanor, by her father. The allegations testified to by the child were against her father, who was undergoing marital problems with her mother around the time of the alleged incident.

There was a presumption in New York State that in criminal proceedings a child under twelve years of age does not in the opinion of the court or magistrate understand the nature of an oath, although the unsworn statement of the child may be received. "But no person shall be held or convicted of an offence [sic] upon such testimony unsupported by other evidence." A presumption determines from whom the proof must come. Therefore, if the subject child had not been sworn, corroboration would have been required of every material fact essential to constitute the crime.

It is suggested that you read the decision that follows to ascertain how the Court of Appeals decided whether or not the defendant's conviction was affirmed.

*   *   *

VAN VOORHIS, Judge. Appellant has been convicted in the New York City Court of Special Sessions of causing the morals of a child under 16 years of age to become depraved in violation of subdivision 1 of section 483 of the Penal law, and of assault in the third degree in violation of subdivision 1 of section 244. Both of these misdemeanors are claimed to have been perpetrated on the daughter of appellant and his wife. Matrimonial differences had arisen which culminated in appellant's removal from the home when his wife had him arrested following the alleged incident on which these criminal charges depend. The evidence against him consists of testimony by Nancy, their 10-year-old daughter, and an admission which his wife testified that he subsequently made to her on the telephone. We are satisfied that this conversation was erroneously admitted into evidence for reasons hereinafter stated.

The police were in the Oyola home within four hours and Mrs. Oyola was there within two hours of the earliest possible happening of this alleged sexual assault. The child testified to all the particulars of a completed act of intercourse upon her by her father, soon after she had retired for the night. She said that she had on her nightgown, and that he was clothed. In spite of the early arrival of both mother and the police, no evidence was offered by the People of any examination of the child's body, nor the finding of any residual evidence of a seminal emission in or about the child's sex organs, adjacent area nor on any other portion of her body, bedclothes or nightgown nor upon appellant's clothing or anywhere else. No evidence was introduced of any cutaneous, structural or tissue injury or disturbance of this girl's private parts, such as abrasions, lacerations, discoloration, redness, swelling or the like. No circumstantial evidence supports the child's version of what occurred, all of which appellant has denied. In answer to questions from the Presiding Judge at Special Sessions, Nancy said that her mother had rehearsed her story privately with her five times before the daughter told it to anyone else. Appellant had no previous criminal record. His good character was attested by his employer and another witness and was recognized by Special Sessions when he was sentenced to an indefinite term in the New York City Penitentiary. Nancy testified that he had done the same thing to her and to her playmate each on one prior occasion, but that this was the first time when she told her mother. This disclosure coincided in time with her mother's lawyers' instruction to Nancy to remember that she would have to repeat the same testimony in a matrimonial action against her father.

The question is whether this evidence against appellant was sufficient to prove him guilty beyond a reasonable doubt. In People v. Ledwon, 153 N.Y. 10, 46 N.E. 1046 (1897), it was held that the burden being upon the People of establishing the guilt of the accused beyond a reasonable doubt, a mere scintilla or even some proof is not enough to create an issue of fact. In the exercise of their judicial function, courts have often held that in certain situations as a matter of law the evidence must be more than usually clear and convincing. The degree of proof required may be affected by whether the testimony is contradicted by other evidence, whether it is consistent, credible or contains elements of suspicion. Moreover all evidence is to be weighed according to the proof which it was in the power of the party to have produced, as Lord Mansfield observed (2 Wigmore, Evidence, § 285, p. 163). Upon the record in this case including the omission of any circumstantial evidence lending credibility to the testimony of this child, we have concluded that appellant has not been proved guilty beyond a reasonable doubt.

Our attention has been directed to the circumstance that in the instance of this and certain other sexual offenses no statute specifically requires corroboration of the testimony of the complainant, like the statutes in the cases of abduction (Penal Law, § 71), adultery (id., § 103), compulsory prostitution (id., §§ 1091, 2460), compulsory marriage (id., § 1455), rape (id., § 2013), and until the crime was abolished, seduction under promise of marriage (id., § 2177). It is not altogether clear on what principle the Legislature adopted separate statutes in regard to these crimes. If appellant had been indicted under section 483–a of the Penal Law (carnal abuse of a child) he would have been charged with a felony punishable on conviction by imprisonment for not more than 10 years. That is exactly the same punishment prescribed for rape in the second degree (Penal Law, § 2010), yet in the latter instance there is a statute expressly requiring corroboration of the testimony of the complainant (§ 2013) whereas in the case of the former there is no such statute. The absence of legislation requiring other evidence to support the testimony of the complainant extending to every material fact essential to constitute the crime, as in case of rape (People v. Downs, 236 N.Y. 306, 140 N.E. 706 (1923); People v. Page, 162 N.Y. 272, 274, 56 N.E. 750, 751 (1900)), does not signify that courts fail to scrutinize with special care the same type of testimony in view of the case with which crimes of this nature are charged and the difficulty of disproving them, and in view of the instinctive horror with which they are regarded by mankind (People v. Friedman, 139 App.Div. 795, 124 N.Y.S. 521 (1910); People v. Donohue, 114 App.Div. 830, 100 N.Y.S. 202 (1906)).

Attention is called to the provision in Section 392 of the Code of Criminal Procedure that when in criminal proceedings a child under 12 years of age does not in the opinion of the court or magistrate understand the nature of an oath, the unsworn statement of the child may be received "But no person shall be held or convicted of an offence upon such testimony unsupported by other evidence." Corroboration would have been required of every material fact essential to constitute the crime if Nancy Oyola had not been sworn (People v. Meeks, 283 N.Y. 694, 28 N.E.2d 413 [1940]; People v. Dutton, 305 N.Y. 632, 111 N.E.2d 889 [1953]). In a series of decisions, however, where the infant complainant was sworn, this court has reversed convictions on charges of this nature and dismissed the indictments or informations as not proved beyond a reasonable doubt on the records before the court which depended upon the testimony of the complaining witness alone (People v. Churgin, 261 N.Y. 661, 185 N.E. 782 [1933] [9 years old]; People v. Slaughter, 278 N.Y. 479, 15 N.E.2d 70 [1938] [15 years old]; People v. Derner, 288 N.Y. 599, 42 N.E.2d 605 [1942] [10 years old and 12 years old]; People v. Rosen, 293 N.Y. 683, 56 N.E.2d 297 [1944] [8 years old]; People v. Meyers, 309 N.Y. 837, 130 N.E.2d 622 [1956] [9 years old]). A child under 12 years of age is presumed to be incompetent to be sworn as a witness in a criminal trial, and this presumption must be overcome by proper preliminary examination (People v. Klein, 266 N.Y. 188, 194 N.E. 402 [1935]). Olshansky v. Prensky, 185 App.Div. 469, 172 N.Y.S. 856 (1919), indicates the nature of such preliminary examination. The records of the preliminary examinations in the cases cited lead to the conclusion that the application of this test is necessarily superficial and inconclusive in most instances. Some children were sworn who were younger than in other cases where unsworn statements were taken. The difficulty in applying the test of the understanding of an oath is illustrated by the preliminary examination of the 10-year-old girl upon whose testimony appellant's fate depends, in which she repeated five times to the Presiding Judge of Special Sessions that she had never told a lie, but added, on reconsideration, that she had lied about 20 times during the previous year. She stated that she believed that, although one may sin by lying, nobody can do anything to you if you do lie. Can it be, in cases of this nature, that the need to have some verification of the testimony of the child depends altogether upon

such collateral factors as whether, for example, this child had said in her preliminary examination that she had told 30 lies instead of 20 lies during the year before, or to whom she told the lies, or when she stopped lying? Mention of this is not frivolous, since this is the kind of thing in preliminary examinations of children under Section 392 of the Code of Criminal Procedure which would determine the guilt or innocence of defendants unless the courts required some objective earmarks of truth even in cases where the child witness has been sworn. Where the witness has been sworn, it may not be necessary to have supporting evidence of every material fact essential to constitute the crime but the courts are not automatons of the Legislature to such a degree as to make patchwork of the law by being obliged to require full corroboration in instances where the trial court has taken the unsworn statement of the witness, but at the same time being compelled to dispense with all objective verification where an oath has been administered. To draw this sharp distinction would be as unreal today as the older law preventing atheists from testifying in court on the basis that they do not appreciate the nature of an oath (Jackson ex dem. Tuttle v. Gridley, 18 Johns. 98, 104 (1920)). This can hardly have been intended by the Legislature. Whether a child eight years old is sworn as in People v. Rosen, supra, or a child of nine years has an unsworn statement taken as in People v. Dutton, supra, is largely fortuitous. Causing the criminal liability of a defendant to depend entirely upon this collateral and largely accidental circumstance would have almost as little to do with deliberative justice as trial by ordeal where, under a practice now happily extinct, the guilt or innocence of a defendant was determined by whether his hand was burned when he thrust it into boiling water or fire.

It is said that the acts charged against this appellant are usually performed in secret, out of the view of corroborating witnesses. That does not signify that some circumstantial evidence cannot be obtained lending veracity to the complainant's narrative where the charge is true. Moreover the same criticism would be applicable to the other sexual offenses to which reference has been made where specific statutes require corroborative evidence. Our liberties are based upon the idea that it is better for some of the guilty to go free than for any who are innocent to be convicted. In the extensive discussion of this subject by Professor Wigmore, to which the dissenting opinion in People v. Porcaro, 6 N.Y.2d 248, 253, 189 N.Y.S.2d 194 (1959), refers, it is recognized that the general rule is to require corroboration of charges of all offenses against the chastity of women (Vol. III, p. 467; Vol. VII, p. 342 et seq.). His recommendation of changes in the law relate to the extension of existing rules to require in addition the psychiatric examination of complaining witnesses. It is noteworthy that a recommendation of such examinations was contained in the 1937–1938 Report of the American Bar Association's Committee on the Improvement of the Law of Evidence (3 Wigmore, Evidence, p. 466), and that out of the fullness of his experience Professor Wigmore distrusted testimony by complainants in these cases advising the retention of whatever rules of corroboration exist under statute or case law, and reminded the bench and bar that errant young girls and women are given to "contriving false charges of sexual offenses by men" (p. 459) concerning which he observed (p. 460) that "It is time that the Courts awakened to the sinister possibilities of injustice that lurk in believing such a witness without careful psychiatric scrutiny." Psychiatric scrutiny goes beyond anything at issue on this appeal. The subject is mentioned only on account of the attention which has been given to it in the dissenting opinion in People v. Porcaro, supra, decided herewith.

The alleged admission against interest which appellant's wife testified that he made to her consisted in a telephone call to her about two weeks after she had brought about his arrest, during which interval they had been separated. She testified that he said over the telephone "that it was true what he done" and that "he was sorry for what he did to his daughter, and then I told him that I couldn't forgive him for what he had done to her" and "that he violated his rights as a father, and then he told me about this other woman that he had." If this statement, which appellant denied having made, could amount to an admission of a sexual assault upon his daughter,

which is not altogether clear, we consider the objection to its introduction into evidence should have been sustained on the ground that it was a confidential communication between husband and wife induced by the marriage relation. It is true that they had been living separately for a short time after appellant's arrest, but the circumstances indicate that (if spoken at all) this statement was part of an attempted reconciliation between husband and wife (People v. Daghita, 299 N.Y. 194, 198–199, 86 N.E.2d 172, 173–174, 10 A.L.R.2d 1385 [1908]; Warner v. Press Pub. Co., 132 N.Y. 181, 185–186, 30 N.E. 393, 394–395 [1892]; Parkhurst v. Berdell, 110 N.Y. 386, 393, 18 N.E. 123, 126 [1888]). The presumption of confidentiality has not been rebutted as was held in Poppe v. Poppe, 3 N.Y.2d 312, 165 N.Y.S.2d 99 [1957]). The Appellate Division held that this conversation was erroneously admitted.

The conviction appealed from should be reversed upon the ground that appellant has not been proved guilty of the offenses charged beyond a reasonable doubt.

* * *

CONWAY, C.J., and FROESSEL, J., concur with VAN VORHISS, J.

FULD, J., concurs in his separate concurring opinion in People v. Porcaro, 6 N.Y.2d 248, 252, 189 N.Y.S.2d 194 (1959), decided herewith.

BURKE, J., dissents in an opinion in which DYE, J., concurs and in which DESMOND, J., concurs in a separate opinion.

Judgments reversed and information dismissed.

State of Nebraska v. Erwin Charles Simants

Supreme Court of Nebraska, 1995.
248 Neb. 581, 537 N.W.2d 346.

This case is presented at this point in the text to acquaint you with the procedure of the annual review hearing, used to determine privileges given or withheld in a mental health custodial facility. Furthermore, the rules of legal evidence are practiced in these hearings. In the decision that follows, the inmate was seeking an enlargement of his privileges and contested various aspects of the mental health commitment proceeding. One of the objections he made was to the admissibility of conclusions made from hearsay evidence by law enforcement personnel.

The decision follows:

WHITE, C.J., and CAPORALE, FAHRN-BRUCH, LANPHIER, WRIGHT, CONNOLLY, and GERRARD, JJ.

CONNOLLY, Justice.

Erwin Charles Simants appeals from an order entered by the district court for Lincoln County following the 1994 annual review of his commitment to the Lincoln Regional Center (LRC). At the hearing, appellant sought release from the LRC or, in the alternative, to have his status at the LRC upgraded to include less restrictive monitoring. The district court found there was clear and convincing proof appellant remained both mentally ill and dangerous to others by reason of his mental illness. The district court further found that appellant's status at the LRC should not be upgraded due to public safety concerns. Finding the district court's determinations were not clearly erroneous, we affirm.

FACTUAL BACKGROUND

On January 17, 1976, appellant was convicted on six counts of first degree murder for the October 18, 1975, deaths of a Sutherland, Nebraska, family and was sentenced to death. This court affirmed those convictions and sentences. State v. Simants, 197 Neb. 549, 250 N.W.2d 881 (1977). Appellant's convictions were subsequently vacated, and the cause was remanded for retrial due to irregularities and misconduct in connection with the sequestration and deliberations of the jury during the original trial. Simants v. State, 202 Neb. 828, 277 N.W.2d 217 (1979). After his second trial, appellant was found not guilty by reason of insanity. He was civilly committed by the Lincoln County Mental Health Board and was admitted to the LRC on October 29, 1979.

On August 23, 1994, the district court for Lincoln County conducted an annual review hearing on appellant's status, pursuant to Neb.Rev.Stat. § 29–3703 (Cum.Supp. 1994), which provides in pertinent part:

(1) The court which tried a person who is found not responsible by reason of insanity shall annually . . . review the records of such person and conduct an evidentiary hearing on the status of the person. . . .

(2) If as a result of such hearing the court finds that such person is no longer dangerous to himself, herself, or others by reason of mental illness or defect and will not be so dangerous in the foreseeable future, the court shall order such person unconditionally released from court-ordered treatment. If the court does not so find, the court shall order that such person participate in an appropriate treatment program specifying conditions of liberty and monitoring consistent with the treatment needs of the person and the safety of the public. The treatment program may involve any public or private facility or program which offers treatment for mental illness and may include an inpatient, residential, day, or outpatient setting. The court shall place the person in the least restrictive available treatment program that is consistent with the treatment needs of the person and the safety of the public.

At the hearing, the State introduced the following evidence: (1) three exhibits of prior Lincoln County proceedings involving appellant; (2) the testimony of Nebraska State Patrol Superintendent Ronald Tussing, Lancaster County Attorney Gary Lacey, and Lincoln Police Chief Tom Casady; (3) the testimony of the LRC's medical records manager; (4) the deposition testimony of expert witness Dr. Jack Anderson; (5) a "1994 Annual Report to Lincoln County District Court on Erwin Charles Simants" prepared by Dr. Louis Martin; and (6) a report containing the LRC's records and statistics on recent escapes from the LRC.

Appellant introduced the following evidence: (1) the testimony of two expert witnesses, Dr. Beverly Mead and Dr. Martin; (2) the testimony of four employees of the LRC; and (3) a "Report of Psychiatric Clinical Interview with Erwin 'Herb' C. Simants" prepared by Dr. Mead.

In its order, the district court stated that it found clear and convincing evidence that appellant is and continues to be mentally ill and dangerous to others by reason of his mental illness and will continue to be dangerous in the foreseeable future, as demonstrated by the overt acts of October 18, 1975. As a result, the district court ordered appellant to remain in the care and custody of the LRC. The court further found that appellant's request to have his status at the LRC upgraded should be denied due to public safety concerns.

ASSIGNMENTS OF ERROR

Appellant assigns four errors: (1) that the district court violated the appellant's right to confrontation as guaranteed by the Sixth Amendment to the U.S. Constitution and article 1, § 11, of the Nebraska Constitution when it allowed the State to introduce evidence of previous Lincoln County proceedings involving the appellant; (2) that the district court erred in permitting three members of local law enforcement to testify regarding public safety concerns in connection with a proposed upgrade in appellant's status at the LRC, in violation of the rules of evidence and appellant's rights to due process and treatment; (3) that the State did not prove by clear and convincing evidence that appellant was mentally ill and dangerous; and (4) that the district court violated appellant's "right to treatment" by not ordering the LRC to administer a specific treatment plan.

* * *

Testimony of Law Enforcement Officials

Appellant next argues that the district court erred in permitting three members of local law enforcement to testify about public safety concerns in connection with a proposed upgrade in appellant's status at the LRC. Appellant's contention is that none of these law enforcement officials were qualified to give their opinions, as lay witnesses or as expert witnesses, and that the admission of such testimony violated the Nebraska rules of evidence and appellant's right to due process and treatment.

The district court denied the request of appellant and the recommendations of the LRC to change appellant's status at the LRC from modified code 2 to code 3. A code 2 patient is permitted on the LRC's grounds under supervision where the staff/patient ratio is at least 2:10. A code 2 patient is not permitted to go

on therapeutic outings off the LRC's grounds. Code 3 status allows a patient to go on therapeutic outings off the LRC's grounds under supervision where the staff/patient ratio is at least 2:10. These outings include trips to the circus, basketball games, swimming at available facilities, and attending picnics or movies in the Lincoln community. Appellant's code 2 status has been judicially modified to permit appellant to go on therapeutic outings off the LRC's grounds under at least one-on-one supervision of a staff member. However, the LRC must notify local law enforcement agencies before taking appellant on these outings.

At the hearing, the State called as witnesses the heads of three law enforcement agencies covering the jurisdiction of Lancaster County, where the LRC is located. These witnesses were Tussing, the superintendent of the State Patrol; Lacey, the Lancaster County Attorney; and Casady, the chief of the Lincoln Police Department. Each of these law enforcement officials testified, over the relevance, foundation, and lack of personal knowledge objections of appellant's counsel, that in his opinion appellant's request to be upgraded from modified code 2 to code 3 should be denied due to public safety concerns.

The State also called as a witness the LRC's medical records manager. She testified to the number and categories of recent escapes from the LRC. Her testimony is not challenged by appellant. Appellant's two expert witnesses, and four employees of the LRC, testified in favor of upgrading appellant's status.

The three law enforcement officials testified that they do not have day-to-day contact with appellant and do not have access to his treatment records. Thus, these witnesses based their opinion testimony upon various hearsay sources, rather than personal perceptions as required by Neb.Evid.R. 701, and therefore were not testifying as lay witnesses.

If scientific, technical, or other specialized knowledge will assist the trier of fact to understand the evidence or to determine a fact in issue, a witness qualified as an expert by knowledge, skill, experience, training, or education may testify thereto in the form of an opinion or otherwise. Neb.Evid.R. 702. As previously discussed, if the facts or data upon which an expert bases an opinion are of a type reasonably relied upon by experts in the particular field in forming such opinions, the facts or data need not be admissible in evidence. Rule 703.

No attempt was made to qualify these law enforcement officials as experts in the fields of psychology or psychiatry or to have these officials testify in terms of appellant's mental illness or dangerousness. Their testimony was confined to terms of public safety in response to appellant's request to have his status at the LRC upgraded. The duties of all three witnesses deal with coordinating and protecting public safety. Because the record reflects that all three witnesses are experienced, educated, and trained in the area of public safety, they clearly possess specialized knowledge and are qualified as expert witnesses on the subject.

Having determined these witnesses qualify as experts on public safety pursuant to evidence rule 702, we turn to three other issues which must be resolved before ultimately determining whether such expert testimony was admissible evidence: (1) whether the experts' testimony was relevant; (2) whether the experts' testimony assisted the trier of fact to understand the evidence or determine a controverted factual issue; and (3) whether the experts' testimony, even though relevant and admissible, should have been excluded in light of Neb.Evid.R. 403. See, State v. Chambers, 241 Neb. 66, 486 N.W.2d 481 (1992); State v. Reynolds, 235 Neb. 662, 457 N.W.2d 405 (1990).

Relevant evidence is evidence having a tendency to make the existence of any fact that is of consequence to the determination of the action more probable or less probable than it would be without the evidence. Neb.Evid.R. 401.

The express wording of § 29-3703 makes clear that courts are to consider public safety when determining what conditions of liberty and monitoring to place upon a person found to be mentally ill and dangerous. Thus, the opinion testimony of the State's experts concerning the impact an upgrade in appellant's

status from modified code 2 to code 3 could have upon public safety was relevant evidence.

Furthermore, such testimony assisted the trier of fact in understanding the evidence and determining the outcome of this controverted status issue raised by appellant. Moreover, it cannot be said that the probative value of this relevant evidence is substantially outweighed by the danger of unfair prejudice, confusion of the issues, misleading of the fact finder, or needless presentation of cumulative evidence. See rule 403. This testimony was probative on the issue of public safety. There is no indication that the testimony was applied by the district court, as the trier of fact, outside the public safety context. Thus, the district court did not err by permitting these three law enforcement officials to testify concerning public safety in relation to a proposed upgrade in appellant's status at the LRC.

Mentally Ill and Dangerous

Appellant next contends that the district court erred in finding that there was clear and convincing evidence that he is still mentally ill and dangerous. The trial court's findings have the effect of a verdict and will not be set aside unless clearly erroneous. RaDec Constr. v. School Dist. No. 17, 248 Neb. 338, 535 N.W.2d 408 (1995); State v. Masters, 246 Neb. 1018, 524 N.W.2d 342 (1994). More specifically, an appellate court will not interfere on appeal with a final order made by the district court in a mental health commitment proceeding unless the court can say as a matter of law that the order is not supported by clear and convincing proof. State v. Simants, 245 Neb. 925, 517 N.W.2d 361 (1994); Hayden I.

* * *

CONCLUSION

We affirm the district court's order because

(1) there was clear and convincing proof appellant remains both mentally ill and dangerous and

(2) his status at the LRC should not be upgraded due to public safety concerns.

Affirmed.

RELATED DECISIONS
Expert Witness Testimony

CSX Transportation, Inc. v. George E. Dansby

Supreme Court of Alabama, 1995.
659 So.2d 35.

The case concerns a Federal Employer's Liability Act claim wherein a former employee is seeking monetary redress from CSX Transportation, Inc., an owner and operator of a railroad. One of the issues was that the claimant challenged the trial court's right to have an audiologist testify as to the cause of plaintiff's hearing loss. This involved the testimony of an expert witness and the acceptance by the trial judge of the qualifications of the witness to testify as to conclusions. The edited decision follows:

* * *

ON APPLICATION FOR REHEARING
PER CURIAM.

This Court's order of affirmance entered on August 19, 1994, without opinion, is withdrawn, and the following is substituted therefor.

George E. Dansby, a retired employee of CSX Transportation, Inc. ("CSX"), sued CSX for damages under the Federal Employer's Liability Act ("FELA"), alleging negligence.[1] Dansby alleged that he had sustained a hearing loss due to exposure to air horns and locomotive noise during his employment as a locomotive engineer with CSX. The jury returned a verdict in favor of Dansby for $105,000 in compensatory damages. The trial court denied CSX's motion for a judgment notwithstanding the verdict or for a new trial and entered a judgment on the verdict. CSX appeals.

A jury's verdict is presumed correct and will not be disturbed unless it is plainly erroneous or manifestly unjust. Alpine Bay Resorts, Inc. v. Wyatt, 539 So.2d 160, 162 (Ala. 1988). A judgment based upon a jury verdict and sustained by the denial of a motion for a new trial will not be reversed unless it is plainly and palpably wrong. Ashbee v. Brock, 510 So.2d 214 (Ala. 1987). Because the jury returned a verdict for Dansby, any disputed

questions of fact must be resolved in his favor, and we must presume that the jury drew from the facts any reasonable inferences necessary to support its verdict. State Farm Auto. Ins. Co. v. Morris, 612 So.2d 440, 443 (Ala. 1993). In short, in reviewing a judgment based upon a jury verdict, this Court must review the record in a light most favorable to the appellee. Continental Cas. Ins. Co. v. McDonald, 567 So.2d 1208, 1211 (Ala. 1990).

Congress enacted the FELA in 1906 to establish "a tort remedy for railroad workers injured on the job." Lancaster v. Norfolk & Western Ry., 773 F.2d 807, 812 (7th Cir. 1985), *cert. denied,* 480 U.S. 945, 107 S.Ct. 1602, 94 L.Ed.2d 788 (1987). It was enacted in response to the special needs of railroad workers, Sinkler v. Missouri Pacific R.R., 356 U.S. 326, 329, 78 S.Ct. 758, 761–62, 2 L.Ed.2d 799 (1958), and it is construed liberally for their protection. To prevail on an FELA negligence claim, the plaintiff must prove the traditional common law elements of negligence: duty, breach of that duty, foreseeability, and causation. Adams v. CSX Transportation, Inc., 899 F.2d 536 (6th Cir. 1990). Pursuant to the FELA, a railroad company has the duty to provide its employees with a reasonably safe work environment; it must use reasonable care in fulfilling this duty. Shenker v. Baltimore & Ohio R.R., 374 U.S. 1, 7, 83 S.Ct. 1667, 1671–72, 10 L.Ed.2d 709 (1963); Carlew v. Burlington Northern R.R., 514 So.2d 899, 901 (Ala. 1987).

* * *

CSX next contends that the trial court erred in failing to submit its requested special interrogatories to the jury. Those interrogatories would have required the jury to make a specific finding as to whether Dansby discovered his hearing loss within the time specified by the statute of limitations.

Rule 49(a), Ala.R.Civ.P., provides that the jury's determination should be by a general verdict "in simple cases where the general verdict will serve the ends of justice." This Court has approved the use of special interrogatories in complicated cases such as "crashworthiness" cases tried pursuant to the Alabama Extended Manufacturer's Liability Doctrine (AEMLD). See General Motors Corp. v. Edwards, 482 So.2d 1176 (Ala. 1985). However, in this relatively uncomplicated case, we cannot hold that the trial court abused its discretion in not submitting the interrogatories to the jury.

Last, CSX contends that the trial court erred in denying its Rule 60(b)(6), Ala.R.Civ.P., motion, which sought relief from the judgment because of statements made by certain jurors in affidavits obtained after the trial.

Generally, affidavits are inadmissible to impeach a jury's verdict. Wiberg v. Sadoughian, 514 So.2d 940 (Ala. 1987). An affidavit showing that extraneous facts influenced the jury's deliberations is admissible; however, affidavits concerning "the debates and discussions of the case by the jury while deliberating thereon" do not fall within this exception. Alabama Power Co. v. Turner, 575 So.2d 551,

557 (Ala. 1991). We have thoroughly reviewed the affidavits obtained from the jurors in this case. We conclude that these affidavits concern the "debates and discussions" involved in the jury's deliberations, and are therefore not admissible to impeach the jury's verdict. Alabama Power Co., supra. Therefore, the trial court did not err in denying CSX's Rule 60(b)(6) motion.

For the foregoing reasons, the judgment of the trial court is affirmed.

APPLICATION GRANTED; ORDER OF AFFIRMANCE WITHDRAWN; JUDGMENT AFFIRMED.

ALMON, SHORES, HOUSTON AND INGRAM, JJ., concur.

MADDOX, J., concurs specially in part and concurs in the result in part.

* * *

---

[1] Dansby also alleged a violation of the Locomotive Boiler Inspection Act, 45 U.S.C. §§ 22–34, but he voluntarily dismissed that claim at trial.

✔ PRACTICE QUESTIONS

Indicate whether each statement is true or false.

1. In a criminal action, the defendant has the responsibility of proving his or her innocence of the crime(s) charged beyond a reasonable doubt.

2. Reasonable doubt may be defined as such a doubt as a reasonable person may entertain after a fair review and consideration of the evidence.

3. Even if there is a threat to the life of a witness in a trial, the defendant has an absolute right to have the witness's true name, address, and place of employment.

4. Leading questions have been defined as questions that call for answers of yes or no, questions that are framed so as to suggest to the witness the answer desired, and questions that assume facts in controversy.

5. Leading questions are not admissible if used by a party for introductory matters to be asked of that party's witness.

Select the most correct answer to complete each statement.

6. In a trial, interpreters may be used if a party or witness does not understand the English language.
   (a) An interpreter need not be sworn or affirmed in order to interpret properly and truly.
   (b) If the witness is deaf and/or mute, the interpreter must be familiar with the code signs used by the witness.

(c) Testimony repeated on the witness stand of what an interpreter, not on the witness stand, said when the police examined the accused is admissible.

(d) All countries supply interpreters to criminal defendants if the defendants do not speak the language of the realm.

7. In a trial,
    (a) a hostile witness may be asked leading questions.
    (b) a hostile witness may not be asked leading questions.
    (c) the attorney asking the questions of the witness makes the final determination as to whether the witness is hostile.
    (d) none of the above.

8. In a trial,
    (a) cross-examination is a matter of right.
    (b) an opportunity for cross-examination is not a mandatory component.
    (c) the purpose of cross-examination is to cause the witness to be embarrassed.
    (d) one may never be permitted to impeach a witness by cross-examination.

9. Quantum of proof means
    (a) evidence presented to the court in a civil trial.
    (b) evidence presented to the court in a criminal trial.
    (c) the weight of evidence sufficient to get a determination of the case in favor of one side or the other in the controversy.
    (d) that a defendant in a criminal trial must be proved guilty by substantial evidence.

10. An administrative hearing
    (a) takes place in a court of law.
    (b) requires adherence to the legal rules of evidence.
    (c) requires substantial evidence as to the quantum of proof for a prosecution to prevail in the hearing.
    (d) is similar to a mediation conference.

CHAPTER 3

Circumstantial Evidence

§ 3.1 DEFINITION

Perhaps the best way to understand the concept of circumstantial evidence is to contrast it with direct evidence. Direct evidence is that which immediately points to the question at issue or is evidence of the precise facts at issue and on trial, by witnesses who can testify that they saw the act done or heard the words spoken which constitute the facts to be proved. Mo.—Stern v. Employers' Liab. Assurance Corp., Ltd. of London, England, 249 S.W. 739 (Mo. App. 1923). Another definition of direct evidence is a recital of facts testified to by eyewitnesses. Ohio—Rio Bar, Inc. v. State, 117 N.E.2d 522 (Comm.Pl. 1954). Circumstantial evidence is evidence that, without going directly to prove the existence of a fact, gives rise to a logical inference that such fact does exist. N.C.—Wilkerson v. Clark, 264 N.C. 439, 141 S.E.2d 884 (1965); Or.—La Barge v. United Ins. Co., 221 Or. 480, 349 P.2d 822 (1960).

Let us hypothesize that a witness heard screams coming from a room in a house other than the room the witness was currently in. The witness ran to the room from which the noises emanated and saw the defendant standing over the body of the deceased, holding a bloody nine-inch knife in his right hand. The deceased, although then still alive, was unable to talk because of a preexisting organic problem. The deceased was bleeding profusely from his stomach and head, and his body was surrounded by a pool of thick blood. When the witness entered the room, he almost slipped and fell because he had stepped into the blood, and the soles of his shoes had lost traction. The defendant denied that he had committed the homicide. The witness testified as to the gory facts as I have related them. The jury could logically infer that the defendant committed this crime, even though he was not seen to directly plunge the knife into the deceased.

§ 3.2 ULTIMATE FACT

An ultimate fact may be established by circumstantial evidence, but the circumstances relied on must have probative force sufficient to constitute a basis of legal inference. It is not enough that the facts raise a mere surmise or suspicion of the existence of the fact or permit a purely speculative conclusion. The circumstances relied on must be reasonably satisfactory and convincing and must not be equally consistent with the nonexistence of the ultimate fact. Tex.—Summers v. Fort Crockett Hotel, Ltd., 902 S.W.2d 20 (Tex.App. 1995). Another way that I would state the rule is that when no one can testify as to what happened, testimony as to what could have happened is not admissible as circumstantial evidence if there is a great probability that it could have happened another way.

§ 3.3 ADMISSIBILITY

The admissibility of circumstantial evidence is within the wide discretion of the trial court. Great latitude generally is allowed in admitting it. Fla.—Baugher v. Boley, 63 Fla. 75, 58 So. 980 (1912); Or.—Byrd v. Lord Bros. Contractors, Inc., 256 Or. 421, 473 P.2d 1018 (1970). However, the facts offered as circumstantial evidence must afford a reasonable inference of the existence or nonexistence of the fact sought to be proved. N.Y.—*In re* Dale's Will, 159 Misc. 578, 288 N.Y.S. 564 (1936).

§ 3.4 EXCLUSIONARY RULES

Throughout the study of the law of evidence, you will encounter exclusionary rules. These rules exclude certain types of evidence in the interest of justice. The courts, in their search for truth, have found it desirable to exclude evidence that, although relevant and competent, may tend to be too slight, remote, or conjectural to have any legitimate influence in determining the issues between the parties. N.Y.—People v. Feldman, 299 N.Y. 153, 85 N.E.2d 913 (1949). A decision may not be rested on remote inference. Tenn.—Quaker Oaks Co. v. Davis, 33 Tenn.App. 373, 232 S.W.2d 282 (1949). Sometimes the trial judge will refuse to permit the introduction of evidence when the danger of its admission would prolong the trial to an unreasonable extent without any corresponding advantage, or would confuse the issues and mislead the jury, or unfairly surprise a party or create substantial danger of undue prejudice to one of the parties. N.Y.—People v. Harris, 209 N.Y. 70, 102 N.E. 546 (1913); Thayer, Preliminary Treatise on Evidence at the Common Law (1898), p. 516.

§ 3.5 INFERENCE

An inference is a deduction from the facts given which is usually less than certainty but may be sufficient to support a finding of fact; by this process, a fact or proposition sought to be established is deduced as a logical consequence from other facts by virtue of common experience that will support but not compel such deduction.

§ 3.6 REMOTENESS

As explained *supra*, evidence that is too remote will not be admitted. So, too, with inferences which are too remote. An inference must be reasonably drawn from and supported by the facts on which it purports to rest. Tex.—Dotson v. Royal Indem. Co., 427 S.W.2d 150 (Tex.Ct.App. 1968); Va.—Virginia Transit Co. v. Schain, 205 Va. 373, 137 S.E.2d 22 (1964).

§ 3.7 PREJUDICE

The fact that evidence may prejudice the adverse party in the minds of the jury will in itself be insufficient grounds to exclude the evidence. A party cannot be deprived of the benefit of evidence which is relevant and material because it may also have a tendency to prejudice the adverse party in the eyes of the jury. Ga.—Fuller v. Fuller, 107 Ga.App. 429, 130 S.E.2d 520 (1963); Kan.—Harmon v. Electric Theater Co., 111 Kan. 252, 206 P. 875 (1922). However, where there is a possibility of unfair prejudice, the court may exclude such evidence. N.H.—Bunten v. Davis, 82 N.H. 304, 133 A. 16 (1926); N.Y.—People v. Harris, 209 N.Y. 70, 102 N.E. 546 (1913).

§ 3.8 CONJECTURE

If evidence is too conjectural so that many different deductions may be drawn, it should be excluded. It cannot be based on surmise, speculation, conjecture, or guess. Ark.—Glidewell v. Arkhola Sand & Gravel Co., 212 Ark. 838, 208 S.W.2d 4 (1948); N.J.—Rivera v. Columbus Cadet Corps. of America, 59 N.J.Super. 445, 158 A.2d 62 (1960). However, whenever the evidence is such that fair-minded people may draw inferences, a measure of speculation and conjecture is required on the part of those whose duty it is to choose the most reasonable of inferences. N.Y.—Rocco v. N.Y. Cent. Sys., 6 A.D.2d 828, 176 N.Y.S.2d 234 (1958). Therefore, the trial court must exercise discretion in weighing whether the conjecture to be drawn would cover too many logical deductions to be reliable.

§ 3.9 CONFUSION OF JURY

The jury usually is composed of laypeople with average intelligence. When speaking of average intelligence, one might analogize it to the height of the average man. Let us assume that the average American male is five feet, ten inches. Many American males are six feet, two inches, and many are five feet, five inches. So, too, with the intelligence of the person who is called on to perform jury duty. It is hoped that the collective intelligence of the jury is that of the person with average intelligence. Because the attorneys who select the jury are limited to the array that is before them, they are not always fortunate enough to get an intelligent body of jurors. Accordingly, the evidence that is introduced should not be of such a nature as to confuse the jury to the extent that it may erroneously apply the evidence. N.J.—Gindin v. Baron, 16 N.J.Super. 1, 83 A.2d 790 (1951).

§ 3.10 UNDUE PROLONGATION OF TRIAL

The history of calendar delay in the trial of lawsuits in the federal and state courts is well known. Although it is important to our system of government to afford every litigant his or her day in court, for all practical purposes it is impossible to give a fair trial to all if the trials that are to be tried go on and on and include evidence that, although relevant, will on balance be outweighed by the danger that its admission would prolong the trial to an unreasonable extent without any corresponding advantage. Md.—Huber v. State, 2 Md.App. 245, 234 A.2d 264 (1967); Pa.—Sunshine Packing Corp. v. Commonwealth, 45 Erie 231 (1961), *motion denied*, 45 Erie 237.

§ 3.11 UNFAIR SURPRISE

The concept of unfair surprise is a nebulous one. We cannot expect an adversary to tell the other side in advance of trial exactly what his or her offense or defense will be. However, court rules in various jurisdictions are requiring extensive disclosures on the part of all litigants. It is presumed that if each side of a controversy exposes its cases before trial, there will be a greater disposition to settle the case and thus avoid the time and expense of a trial and subsequent appellate processes. When a litigant is required by law or court rule to disclose a certain evidentiary item and fails to do so, a subsequent attempt to introduce that item at trial is subject to a successful objection. However, when counsel for the proponents of a will had ample opportunity to inspect hospital records at the trial in county court that admitted the will to probate, admission of hospital records in evidence in subsequent trial in district court was not objectionable on ground that proponents had been unfairly surprised by failure of contestants to deliver a copy of the records a reasonable time before trial in district court. Tex.—Greene v. Watts, 332 S.W.2d 419 (Tex.Ct.App. 1960).

§ 3.12 DEFENDANT'S CHARACTER

In a criminal prosecution, a defendant may introduce reputation evidence as to his own good character for the purpose of raising an inference that he would not be likely to commit the offense charged. N.Y.—People v. Van Gaasbeck, 189 N.Y. 408, 82 N.E. 718, 22 L.R.A. (N.S.) 650 (1907). Defendant, whom the law does not invest with the presumption of good character, is accorded the privilege or option of initially introducing evidence of his good character on the theory that such circumstantial evidence as may bear on probability that he did not commit the crime charged. U.S.—Brown v. Haynes, 385 F.Supp. 285 (D.Mo. 1974). An accused has the right to offer evidence of his good character, inferred from reputation testimony, to show that he was unlikely to have acted in the manner and with the intent charged in the indictment. U.S.—United States v. Lewin, 467 F.2d 1132 (7th Cir. 1972).

In Strader v. State, 208 Tenn. 192, 344 S.W.2d 546 (1961), a trial judge would not permit a defendant to introduce character evidence in his behalf because, although he had lived in the community for thirty-five years, he had absented himself for five years and had returned for two months prior to trial. The Supreme Court of Tennessee reversed and ordered a new trial, indicating that there is a presumption of continuance of good character applicable within reasonable limits until the contrary is shown. Also see Federal Rule of Evidence 404(a)(1).

From a reading of the cases cited, you can understand how circumstantial evidence of good character may be introduced into a trial to raise an inference that the defendant did not commit the crime for which he or she is charged. This is not to say that character traits wholly unrelated to the crime charged may be introduced. Evidence may be introduced only if it relates to the trait of character that makes it probable or improbable that the accused would have done the kind of fact that is alleged to have constituted a crime. U.S.—Springer v. United States, 148 F.2d 411 (9th Cir. 1945). A further treatment of character evidence appears in Chapter 6.

§ 3.13 SKILL

If a defendant is found to be in possession of stolen articles that had been unlawfully taken from the locked trunk of an automobile, the fact that the defendant has completed a course of study as a locksmith is relevant to show that he or she possesses the necessary skill to open the trunk and therefore is inferentially guilty not only of receiving stolen property, but also of committing the actual burglary and larceny. In this way, the fact that the defendant possesses the necessary skill, considered together with other factors, is relevant. Existence of a skill may be shown by prior acts indicative of its possession. Ky.—Paducah First Nat'l Bank v. Wisdom, 111 Ky. 135, 63 S.W. 461 (1901).

§ 3.14 PHYSICAL CAPACITY

If a man has a history of sexual impotence, it is logical to infer that the possibility of him committing a rape of a female is unlikely. Likewise, if a woman is crippled to the extent that she is unable to walk and must move only with the aid of a wheelchair, the likelihood of her running 1/20th of a mile in eighteen seconds is improbable. This type of evidence is therefore admissible to prove that the defendant may have been incapable of committing the crime with which she is charged. N.Y.—People v. Messina, 278 A.D. 592, 102 N.Y.S.2d 262 (1951).

§ 3.15 MENTAL CAPACITY

One is presumed to know those things which are matters of common knowledge. Ill.—Schaefer v. Stamm, 68 Ill.App.2d 42, 215 N.E.2d 9 (1966). A party is presumed to know, or is chargeable with knowledge of, matters which he had an opportunity to know. Fla.—Kennedy v. Vandine, 185 So.2d 693 (Fla. 1966). It therefore may be inferred that a defendant knew matters of common knowledge and is thus obliged in his defense to go forward with the evidence to show that he did not have the knowledge requisite to make him or her liable for the commission of the offense.

§ 3.16 THREATS

On the issue of whether a defendant acted in self-defense in inflicting a mortal wound on the deceased, it is permissible to introduce evidence which indicates that the deceased had made threats on the life of the defendant. Declarations are admissible to prove the inference of a particular motive on the mind of the declarant. Ga.—Conoly v. Imperial Tobacco Co., 63 Ga.App. 880, 12 S.E.2d 398 (1940); Mass—Leach v. Wilbur, 91 Mass. (9 Allen) 212 (1864).

§ 3.17 MEANS TO ACCOMPLISH ACT

When a defendant has the means to perform an act, this fact may be introduced as circumstantial evidence tending to prove that he did commit the act. In the case of People v. Molineux, 168 N.Y. 264, 61 N.E. 286, 62 L.R.A. 193 (1901), the defendant was a pharmacist who had chemicals at his disposal. Evidence was introduced to show this fact in a homicide case where the decedent had been poisoned. Also see People v. Soper, 243 N.Y. 320, 153 N.E. 433 (1926).

§ 3.18 TECHNICAL KNOWLEDGE

The fact that a defendant had the technical knowledge to commit a crime may also be shown to prove that the defendant did, in fact, perpetrate the offense. People v. Molineux (*supra*). Knowledge may be established by circumstantial evidence, even if the defendant claims ignorance. Ala.—Liberty Nat'l Life Ins. Co. v. Weldon, 267 Ala. 171, 100 So.2d 696, 61 A.L.R.2d 1346 (1957); Mo.—Fireman's Fund Ins. Co. v. Trippe, 402 S.W.2d 577 (1966).

§ 3.19 CONDUCT AS EVIDENCE OF GUILT

Most police officers develop a sixth sense. The officer might say, when speaking of the defendant, "He just didn't look right to me." What the officer means is that the defendant participated in some course of conduct that aroused the officer's suspicion. Suspicion alone, however, is insufficient to cause an arrest.

In some situations, however, conduct could be circumstantial cause for an arrest. Let us suppose that an officer on patrol hears the crash of an auto accident but does not see the crash. As the officer proceeds to the location of the collision, he observes a youth running away from the scene. Instead of directly going to the scene, he stops the youth and questions him. The officer handcuffs the youth after the suspect cannot give a satisfactory explanation of why he is running from the scene. The operator of one of the vehicles cannot be found. The passenger in the other vehicle was ejected from the vehicle after hitting his head on the windshield, subsequently resulting in his death. Witnesses saw one unidentified youth run from the vehicle that had no driver but cannot positively identify the apprehended youth as the one who fled the scene. The fact that the apprehended youth was running away from the scene of the collision may be introduced in evidence to circumstantially prove that he was the driver of the now driverless vehicle. Accordingly, the identity of a person is a fact to be proved like any other fact and may be proved by circumstantial evidence. Conn.—State v. Couture, 2 Conn. Cir.Ct. 683, 205 A.2d 387 (1964); Fla.—Stettler v. Huggins, 134 So.2d 534 (Fla.App. 1961); Pa—*In re* Lupenski's Estate, 57 Berks 204, 15 Fiduciary 548 (1965).

§ 3.20 EVIDENCE OF OTHER CRIMES

A prosecutor must be particularly careful when introducing evidence of other crimes alleged to have been committed by a defendant. It is axiomatic that every defendant is entitled to a fresh start at the bar of justice. The fact of his or her previous criminal behavior may be so prejudicial as to result in a reversal when the case goes on appeal. In some situations, however, the courts have permitted the introduction into evidence of the commission by the defendant of other, similar crimes to circumstantially prove that the defendant committed the crime for which he or she is being tried in the instant case. Cases in which this is allowed are usually cases in which the other, similar crimes have an inherently unique quality to them. Such a situation occurred in People v. Seaman, 107 Mich. 348, 65 N.W. 203 (1895), in which in a prosecution for manslaughter in committing an abortion it was proper to receive evidence that the defendant had performed other abortions in the same house to negate the defense of abortion due to accidental causes.

The trial judge must balance all of the relevant factors in order to decide whether the prejudicial character of the introduction of other crimes outweighs the probative value of the evidence.

§ 3.21 OTHER FALSE REPRESENTATION

Frequently, a defendant falsely represents a certain fact in order to cause an unsuspecting victim to part with his or her money. Let us suppose that a defendant is charged with larceny of the sum of $50.00. His modus operandi was to frequent a location in a large city where there was a high concentration of bars and bawdy houses. He would size up a likely prospect, usually a visiting stranger looking for some extracurricular fun. He would accost the victim and furtively give him a glimpse of what appeared to be a diamond ring and ask the victim if he would like to buy it for $100.00. Sometimes the defendant would indicate in some manner that it was "hot" (recently stolen) and that he wanted some quick cash for it. The victim, having a little larceny in his soul, offers him $50.00 for it, and the defendant gives the ring to the victim in exchange for the $50.00. After having the ring appraised and finding that he was swindled, the stranger makes it his lifework to bring the defendant to the bar of justice. Instead of watching the neighborhood for the defendant to put him in the arms of the law, the victim changes his appearance and "cases" (follows) the defendant for several days. He sees the defendant make several sales of similar merchandise to others. The initial victim introduces himself to the other victims and explains to them that they, too, have been swindled. They exchange identification and agree that they will not report the theft to the police immediately but will wait until ten persons who are victimized agree to prosecute. Then the defendant will be arrested, and all will cooperate in the prosecution. When the tenth victim agrees to this scheme, the first victim points out the defendant to the police, who assist in arresting the defendant initially on the complaint of the first victim.

At the trial, the other victims could testify as to what had happened to them to circumstantially prove that the false representation happened to the victim in the case on trial.

The preceding case is hypothetical but could conceivably take place. In an actual case, the defendant charged with interstate transportation of a stolen vehicle, who rented automobiles approximately one month prior to committing the offense in the cases at bar by identifying himself with a stolen credit card, was prosecuted by the admission into evidence of the prior transaction involving substantially the same method as alleged in the instant case. U.S.—United States v. Coleman, 410 F.2d 1133 (10th Cir. 1969).

§ 3.22 POSSESSION OF THE FRUITS OF THE CRIME

An expression among law enforcement people goes like this: "The prisoner was caught with his hand in the till." This means that the person was caught either with his hands in the cash register or with the "goods" (stolen property) on his person or in a location under his control. When this occurs, the defendant is required to go forward with the evidence to overcome the presumption of guilt. N.Y.—People v. Langan, 303 N.Y. 474, 104 N.E.2d 861 (1952). Note that the prosecution continues to have the burden to prove the defendant guilty beyond a reasonable doubt. Further treatment of this topic is found in Chapter 17.

§ 3.23 CRIME OF CONSPIRACY

The least serious type of crime of conspiracy is defined in the New York Penal Law, which reads as follows:

> 105.00   **Conspiracy in the sixth degree**—A person is guilty of conspiracy in the sixth degree when, with intent that conduct constituting a crime be performed, he agrees with one or more persons to engage in or cause the performance of such conduct.
>
> Conspiracy in the sixth degree is a class B misdemeanor.

Like so many criminal statutes, if one looks to its practical application, successful prosecution of this statute might be difficult unless the prosecutor invokes the aid of circumstantial evidence. There is little likelihood that direct evidence can be obtained of two or more defendants agreeing to commit a crime. With the exception perhaps of a legal wiretap or an electronic device, or an officer with the ability to read lips or with a vivid enough "imagination" to overhear conversations, direct evidence of the agreement to commit a crime is almost nonexistent.

Circumstantial evidence, however, wherein a course of criminal conduct is observed that is entered into by two or more persons acting together, or independently as part of an overall scheme, can be used to prove a conspiracy. The individual members of the conspiracy need not know the others who are involved in order to spell out the commission of this offense. It is a jury question to determine the intent of the parties. N.Y.—People v. Flack, 125 N.Y. 324, 26 N.E. 267, 11 L.R.A. 807 (1891). The conspiracy itself could be established by evidence of particular acts which taken together furnish a basis for a finding that a conspiracy existed. N.Y.—People v. Connolly, 253 N.Y. 330, 171 N.E. 393 (1930).

The test as to its [circumstantial evidence] sufficiency is whether common human experience would lead a reasonable person, putting his mind to it, to reject or accept the inferences asserted for the established facts. State v. Saksniit, 69 Misc.2d 554, 332 N.Y.S. 2d 343 (1972).

§ 3.24 SEX CRIMES

The question often arises in the prosecution of crimes of rape or sodomy whether the victim is making the complaint for a nefarious reason. Often there is a long-standing relationship between the parties wherein they frequently have indulged in sexual contact with each other, but because of a disagreement, a complaint is made by the alleged wronged party. In such a case, circumstantial evidence may be introduced to show the prior sexual contact between them when such evidence has a legitimate tendency to show the disposition between the parties at or about the time of the offense charged in the indictment. Evidence of such acts, whether prior to or subsequent to the act in question, is admissible where they are so related by brevity of time or continuity of disposition or otherwise to the principal act as to indicate the mutual disposition of the parties. N.Y.—People v. Thompson, 212 N.Y. 249, 106 N.E. 78 (1914).

It should be noted, however, that a forceful sodomy could take place notwithstanding the existence of prior or subsequent sexual contact between the parties. This should be brought to the attention of the jury in presenting the factual conditions of the case at bar.

§ 3.25 REPETITION IN DEFAMATION ACTION

There are actions in civil law known as actions for libel and actions for slander. The person who brings the action complains that because of the acts of the defendant in spreading certain knowledge about the plaintiff, the plaintiff was injured in a monetary way. If the defendant is alleged to have placed this information in writing for others to read, it is called an action in libel. If the defendant is alleged to have disseminated this information by word of mouth, it is called slander. Both libel and slander have been characterized as actions for defamation. There are defenses against these actions such as truth of the declaration or fair comment with respect to public officials. As law enforcement people are particularly subject to such an accusation, you should be careful in your contacts with members of the public to avoid spreading false information that might injure people in a financial way. In one such case, a potentially aggrieved person brought an action for damages and declaratory relief against city and county police officials under 42 U.S.C.A. § 1983, which creates a right of action against a person who, under color of state law, subjects another to the deprivation of any right secured by the United States Constitution. The plaintiff had been arrested for shoplifting, and his picture was included in a police flyer of "active shoplifters," distributed to merchants. The petitioner could have brought his action for defamation in Kentucky courts but chose instead to invoke the aid of the federal courts pursuant to the aforementioned statute. The United States District Court permitted the "flyer" evidence into the trial but dismissed the action on other grounds.

This case found its way to the United States Supreme Court, which held that the words "liberty" and "property" as used in the Fourteenth Amendment do not single out reputation as a candidate for special protection over and above other instruments that may be protected by state law. U.S.—Paul v. Davis, 424 U.S. 693, 96 S.Ct. 1155, 47 L.Ed.2d 405 (1976). This is not to say that Davis did not have a remedy in state court that he did not avail himself of. In any event, the evidence was relevant and was admissible in the district court, and there was no question as to repetition, as the photos were shown to many shopkeepers.

§ 3.26 VALUE OF PERSONAL PROPERTY STOLEN

The value of personal property at a given time is a nebulous concept. When we speak about the monetary value of personal property, we really mean the amount of money that an average bona fide purchaser would pay for this property if it were put up for sale. Anyone who has ever tried to sell an automobile has a good insight into this problem. Therefore, when we speak about the value of personal property, we are speaking about an approximate amount of money.

Let us imagine that you own a motor vehicle for which you just paid $17,300.00. You take it out of the dealer's showroom and drive it for one day, traveling about sixty miles. The second day you decide to take the new vehicle for a ride, and as you proceed through a cross street near your home, a vehicle traveling at an excessive rate of speed approaches the intersection from the right, goes through a stop sign, and demolishes your vehicle. You were wearing a seat belt, which prevented your ejection from the vehicle and major personal injury. However, your car is totally destroyed. While you are being treated in the emergency room of the local hospital, a tow truck unlawfully hoists the remains of your vehicle on its crane and removes it from the scene.

Three miles from the scene a police officer stops the tow truck to determine if the driver of the truck has proper authority to tow your vehicle. On learning that the operator of the tow truck has no authority to remove your vehicle, he is arrested and charged with grand larceny. In this jurisdiction, the threshold between grand larceny and petty larceny is $500.00.

At the trial, the prosecutor is obliged to demonstrate that the value of this wreck was over $500.00. The defense contends that this was junk and had a salvage value of less than $100.00.

In this hypothetical case, for the purpose of proving your damages in a civil action against the owner and driver of the other vehicle who caused the damage, the value of the automobile and the value of its remains that the tow truck took from the scene are different. Each side in both court actions will attempt to prove its position by testimony of experts, who will testify what they believe the auto could have been sold for at the particular point of time involved in each case. They will base their opinions on what price other vehicles with similar virtues or disabilities were sold for in that locality in the recent past, before the time of the occurrence. This type of evidence is admissible as circumstantial evidence. Mo.—Bader v. Hylarides, 374 S.W.2d 616 (1963); R.I.—Anderson v. Friendship Body & Radiator Works, Inc., 112 R.I. 445, 311 A.2d 288 (1973). In an action on a burglary policy, a witness may be permitted to testify as to the value of perfect diamonds of a similar size to those which were burglarized. Fla.—New Amsterdam Casualty Co. v. James, 122 Fla. 710, 166 So. 813 (1935).

§ 3.27 REPUTATION OF THE VICTIM OF THE CRIME

The reputation of the victim in certain crimes might tend to prove or disprove that the crime was committed. If a deceased in a violent homicide case had a reputation for being involved in street muggings and the accused contends that he or she killed the deceased in the course of being mugged by the decedent, it is relevant to prove the issue of self-defense or justifiable homicide by showing that the deceased had perpetrated an attempted mugging on the defendant. The defendant may have been acting lawfully in killing the deceased. This is circumstantial evidence, introduced to tend to prove that the occurrence took place as the defendant argues. When the issue is self-defense in a murder trial, one court has said that "the accused, after giving evidence to show that he acted in self-defense, may prove that the general reputation of the deceased was that of a quarrelsome, vindictive or violent man and that such reputation had come to his knowledge prior to the homicide." N.Y.—People v. Rodawald, 177 N.Y. 408, 70 N.E. 1 (1904). The reputation of the deceased is admissible only to show the state of mind of the defendant. It therefore is necessary that the reputation of the deceased is known to the defendant at the time of the homicide. A different rule prevails, however, if threats were made to others that the deceased was going to kill the defendant. This is not reputation evidence but tends to prove circumstantially that the deceased was the aggressor. N.Y.—People v. Taylor, 177 N.Y. 237, 69 N.E. 534 (1904).

§ 3.28 EFFECT ON OTHER OCCASIONS

It frequently becomes necessary to determine the cause of a situation without anyone having observed it. For example, it is generally known that if people are sleeping in a room that is airtight, the heating of this room by a gas range will eventually use up all of the oxygen in the room, and the occupants are likely to die. We therefore can infer as an initial presumption, subject to later forensic examinations, that people found dead in such a setting died of asphyxiation caused by the flame's using all of the oxygen in the room.

Where a poison is administered which produces distinctive symptoms in the victims, it may circumstantially be inferred that the second victim ingested the same poison as the first. N.Y.—People v. Molineux, 168 N.Y. 264, 61 N.E. 286, 62 L.R.A. 193 (1901); People v. Feldman, 296 N.Y. 127, 71 N.E.2d 433 (1947). Motive and intent may be proved by circumstances from which intent may be reasonably inferred. U.S.—United States v. Brettholz, 485 F.2d 483 (2d Cir. 1973); N.Y.—Kramer v. Skiatron of America, Inc., 32 Misc.2d 1022, 223 N.Y.S.2d 283 (1961).

§ 3.29 TRACKING WITH DOGS

Dogs have been taking on a more important role in apprehension of criminals. The keen olfactory sense possessed by certain dogs, combined with great intelligence, has made them a useful tool in law enforcement. For many years, dogs have been used to follow the path of a malefactor as he or she fled from the scene of a crime. Such dogs were characterized as bloodhounds. In recent years, dogs have been trained to detect drugs and explosives. The problem arises, however, when the prosecutor attempts to get the dog's findings into evidence. For this purpose, the courts have required that a proper foundation be laid. The dog's handler must first testify as to his or her own qualifications and experience. He or she must testify with respect to the dog's ability to do the task that is relevant to the case at bar. He or she also must testify as to the training that the dog received and, if it is a tracking case, that the trail was fresh and had not been interfered with by others before the tracking. If it is a tracking case, the dog must be placed at an initial position where it is definitely known that the perpetrator of the crime was previously present. When this foundation is laid, evidence may then be introduced with respect to the actions of the dog that inferentially lead to the conclusion that that defendant is the perpetrator. This evidence must be corroborated by other evidence tending toward identification. Such tracking evidence has been held to be admissible in both civil and criminal cases, providing the proper foundation has been laid. Md.—Terrell v. State, 3 Md.App. 340, 239 A.2d 128 (1968); Minn.—Crosby v. Moriarity, 148 Minn. 201, 181 N.W. 199 (1921).

§ 3.30 SUFFICIENCY

For many years, a criminal conviction could not be based wholly on circumstantial evidence unless the trier of the facts was convinced that the circumstances must be so clearly proven that they point not merely to the possibility of guilt, but to a moral certainty of guilt and inference which may reasonably be drawn from the facts proved as a whole; must not only be consistent with guilt, but inconsistent with every reasonable hypothesis of innocence. U.S.—Ah Ming Cheng v. United States, 300 F.2d 202 (5th Cir. 1962). In recent years, however, there has been a noticeable but slow change in this rule of law, as was found in United States v. Moore, 505 F.2d 620 (5th Cir. 1974), *cert. denied,* 421 U.S. 918, 95 S.Ct. 1581, 43 L.Ed.2d 785 (1975), in which the court said that the proper test of sufficiency of evidence in all cases, including those involving circumstantial evidence, is not whether the trial court or appellate court is able to find evidence inconsistent with every hypothesis of innocence, but whether a reasonably minded jury could so conclude. Another case held that the "rule" that the facts must exclude every other hypothesis than that of guilt is simply another form of the rule that the jury must be convinced beyond a reasonable doubt of the guilt of the defendant. U.S.—United States v. Lewin, 467 F.2d 1132 (7th Cir. 1972). Some states steadfastly adhere to the old rule, but their number is diminishing.

§ 3.31   CIRCUMSTANTIAL AND DIRECT EVIDENCE CREDIBILITY COMPARISON

You have now been exposed to the difference between direct and circumstantial evidence. Sometimes the question arises as to which is more credible. It is my belief that it depends on the circumstances of each case and on who was testifying. Many people viewing a factual situation will verbalize different recollections of that fact pattern, and this would be an example of direct evidence. In a circumstantial evidence problem, we sometimes encounter similar variances as to the inference to be drawn from designated conduct.

§ 3.32   FEDERAL RULE

The Federal Rules of Evidence do not specifically indicate that circumstantial evidence is admissible, but Rule 402 reads:

§ Rule 402. Relevant evidence generally admissible: irrelevant evidence inadmissible

All relevant evidence is admissible, except as otherwise provided by the Constitution of the United States, by Act of Congress, by these rules, or by other rules prescribed by the Supreme Court pursuant to statutory authority. Evidence which is not relevant is not admissible.

Furthermore, Rule 404(b) reads:

> **Other crimes, wrongs, or acts.** Evidence of other crimes, wrongs, or acts is not admissible to prove the character of a person in order to show that he acted in conformity therewith. It may, however, be admissible for other purposes, such as proof of motive, opportunity, intent, preparation, plan, knowledge, identity, or absence of mistake or accident, provided that upon request by the accused, the prosecution in a criminal case shall provide reasonable notice in advance of trial, or during trial if the court excuses pretrial notice on good cause shown, of the general nature of any such evidence it intends to introduce at trial.

The circumstantial relevance of habit is referred to in Rule 406, where it reads:

> **§ Rule 406. Habit; routine practice**
>
> Evidence of the habit of a person or of the routine practice of an organization, whether corroborated or not and regardless of the presence of eyewitnesses, is relevant to prove that the conduct of the person or organization on a particular occasion was in conformity with the habit or routine practice.

Therefore, we see that the Federal Rules of Evidence do permit the introduction of all evidence, whether direct or circumstantial, that is relevant to a determination of the issues of the case at bar.

CROSS REFERENCES

Federal Civil Judicial Procedure and Rules (West 1996) (Rules 402 and 406).
Goode & Wellborn, Courtroom Handbook on Federal Evidence (West 1995) (Rules 402 and 406).
McCormick, Evidence § 184 (4th ed. 1992)

RELATED   DECISIONS
Circumstantial Evidence

Wilkerson v. Clark

Supreme Court of North Carolina, 1965.
264 N.C. 439, 141 S.E.2d 884.

This case involves observations made by a witness who did not actually see an automobile accident occur but did observe the manner in which the vehicle involved in the crash was proceeding prior to the crash.

There was a question as to the admissibility of his testimony about how the vehicle was proceeding. The trial judge admitted the testimony, but during the trial, he told the jury that he was sustaining the objection of the defendant. The issue of whether this testimony was admissible and the court's reasons for its determination are presented in the decision of the case. You are encouraged to read it and discover how the court decided this issue.

BOBBITT, Justice. Clark, 34 or 35, and Wilkerson, 29, were frequent associates and close friends. Clark was the manager of Clark Chevrolet Company of Apex, N.C., a business owned solely by his father, defendant David Judson Clark. On occasion, Wilkerson did part time work for Clark Chevrolet Company.

Clark Chevrolet Company sold Corvairs. The Corvair involved in the wreck on March 31, 1962, "was a brand new Corvair demonstrator." On March 31, 1962, the "Beltline," now U.S. 1, was under construction. It had not been "opened for traffic." However, certain lanes thereof had been paved. It was not "opened for traffic" until September 19, 1962.

U.S. 1, a primary north-south highway, runs generally east-west in the area where the wreck occurred. However, the lanes for traffic from Raleigh toward Apex are referred to as lanes for southbound traffic and those for traffic toward Raleigh as lanes for northbound traffic.

U.S. 1, between where it overpasses Western Boulevard and where it underpasses the Cary-Macedonia Road, is a four-lane highway, the two 12-foot lanes for southbound traffic being separated by a median strip from the two lanes for northbound traffic. Southbound traffic, before reaching the Cary-Macedonia underpass, comes to an exit ramp which extends obliquely to the right from U.S. 1 and provides access to the Cary-Macedonia Road. An additional traffic lane is provided for approaching motorists who plan to leave U.S. 1 and enter said exit ramp. Where the highway lanes and the ramp converge, the total width of the pavement is 56 feet. The exit ramp itself is 20 feet wide at said point of convergence and 16 feet wide beyond that point.

The portions of highway referred to above had been paved. The shoulders, consisting of red clay, were under construction.

There was evidence tending to show the following facts: The Clark Corvair, although the "Beltline" had not been "opened for traffic," was proceeding thereon from Raleigh toward Apex. Approaching the Cary-Macedonia exit ramp, it did not travel in the additional lane providing access thereto but traveled in the right lane of said two 12-foot lanes for southbound traffic. It passed a short distance beyond the point of entry to the exit ramp, cut to its right across the "V" dirt median between said lane and said ramp, crossed the ramp and the dirt shoulder thereof, went down the shoulder embankment into a 40-foot-deep ravine and finally stopped some sixty feet beyond said embankment. The wrecked Corvair, with Wilkerson's body and Clark *therein*, was discovered prior to 2:45 A.M.

There was sufficient admitted evidence to support a finding that Clark was the driver and that his actionable negligence proximately caused the wreck and Wilkerson's death. A review of this evidence is unnecessary to decision on this appeal. The court properly overruled defendant's motion(s) for judgment of nonsuit.

There was evidence tending to show the "Beltline," then under construction, underpassed the Jones-Franklin Road; and that the Jones-Franklin Road is "almost parallel" with the Cary-Macedonia Road and is "about a half a mile towards Raleigh from the Cary-Macedonia Road."

Freeman, plaintiff's witness, testified in substance, except when quoted, as follows: On Friday night, March 30, 1962, he was visiting on Dillard Drive. He left "around 12:00, five minutes after or something like that," to go to Mebane, where he then lived. Traveling along the Jones-Franklin Road, he stopped his car on the bridge over the "Beltline" to determine whether the "Beltline" was then open for traffic. While stopped there, he saw only one car. This car approached on the "Beltline" from his right (from the direction of Raleigh) and traveled to his left after passing under the Jones-Franklin bridge. He saw this car as it traveled three-tenths of a mile approaching the underpass and as it traveled three-tenths of a mile beyond the underpass. When he last saw it, this car was headed toward and lacked "approximately two-tenths of a mile" of reaching "the Cary-Macedonia exit." He saw only the headlights, taillights and top of this car. He is familiar with Corvair cars and could and did identify this car as a Corvair. During the time he saw it, this Corvair, in his opinion, "was traveling in excess of 80 miles an hour."

Freeman testified he told Cecil Wilkerson, brother of plaintiff's intestate, substantially what he had testified at the trial, and Cecil Wilkerson so testified.

After plaintiff had offered his evidence and rested, the judge instructed the jury he had come to the conclusion that said testimony of Freeman and of Cecil Wilkerson had been improperly admitted in evidence, and that defendants' objections thereto should have been and were now sustained. Thereupon, the court instructed the jury "not to consider that testimony at all in the trial of this case," and to dismiss it from their minds completely "just as if it were never spoken in this court by anybody." Plaintiff excepted and assigns as error the exclusion of said testimony and the court's said instructions in relation thereto.

If Freeman saw the Clark Corvair, and if the wreck occurred after its uninterrupted travel from where it was when Freeman last saw it to the scene of the wreck, the testimony of Freeman is not inadmissible on account of

remoteness or otherwise. Under the facts here, the distance between the point when last observed by Freeman and the scene of the wreck would bear on the weight rather than the competency of Freeman's testimony. Honeycutt v. Strube, 261 N.C. 59, 64, 134 S.E.2d 110 (1964), and cases cited.

"Circumstantial evidence is evidence which, without going directly to prove the existence of a fact, gives rise to a logical inference that such fact does exist." C.J.S. Evidence § 161.

Under our decisions, actionable negligence may be established by circumstantial evidence; and where there is evidence of the facts and circumstances from which it may be inferred that actionable negligence is the more reasonable probability, the issue is for jury determination. Frazier v. Gas Company, 247 N.C. 256, 100 S.E.2d 501 (1957); Drum v. Bisaner, 252 N.C. 305, 113 S.E.2d 560 (1960); Patton v. Dail, 252 N.C. 425, 114 S.E.2d 87 (1960).

In State v. Johnson, 199 N.C. 429, 154 S.E. 730 (1930), Stacy, C.J., referring to circumstantial evidence in criminal cases, said: "The general rule is that if there be any evidence tending to prove the fact in issue, or which reasonably conduces to its conclusion as a fairly logical and legitimate deduction, and not merely such as raises a suspicion or conjecture in regard to it, the case should be submitted to the jury." Since State v. Stephens, 244 N.C. 380, 93 S.E.2d 431 (1956), to which reference is made for a full discussion by Higgins, J., this Court has approved the quoted statement as the established rule in this jurisdiction.

The question here is whether there was evidence of facts and circumstances from which *it may be* inferred as the more reasonable probability (1) that Freeman saw the Clark Corvair *and* (2) that the wreck occurred after its uninterrupted travel from where it was when Freeman last saw it to the scene of the wreck. If so, it was for the jury to determine whether the evidence is sufficient to establish such facts and circumstances *and* to warrant findings in plaintiff's favor as to both propositions. In this connection, see Morgan v. Bell Bakeries, Inc., 426 N.C. 429, 98 S.E.2d 464 (1957), where circumstantial evidence was held admissible and sufficient to support a finding that a particular bread truck was in fact the motor vehicle involved in the accident; also, see Annotation, "Proof, in absence of direct testimony, of identity of motor vehicle involved in accident." 81 A.L.R.2d 861–888.

There was evidence tending to show the following facts: In the late afternoon of Friday, May 30, 1962, Clark asked Wilkerson to come by the place of business of Clark Chevrolet Company at or about 9:00 P.M., closing time, just to ride around with him. The car in which they were riding was "a brand new Corvair demonstrator." Clark and Wilkerson "left Raleigh about midnight," Clark driving. They traveled "out of Raleigh on the Western Boulevard and onto the new Beltline," headed back toward Apex. The paved roadway on which they traveled had not been "opened for traffic." At 2:45 A.M., when a Cary police officer arrived, Wilkerson was dead. His neck was broken and his body "felt clammy, cold, or cool." Clark was seriously injured. The Corvair was on its right side. Clark's back was against the top. His feet and legs extended over the legs of Wilkerson. Clark did not know what occurred after the wreck until he heard a car stop and voices of investigating officers.

In addition to the foregoing: When and by whom the wrecked Corvair was discovered does not appear. There is no evidence the "Beltline," then under construction and not "opened for traffic," had been or was being used by unauthorized persons other than Clark. Testimony as to tire marks, course of travel, damage to the Corvair and tragic consequences to the occupants, are consistent with Freeman's testimony as to speed.

Delay in the discovery of the wrecked Corvair, notwithstanding evidence the lights thereon were burning, is consistent with non-use of the "Beltline" by the traveling public. If Clark "left Raleigh about midnight," it may be reasonably inferred that he passed under the Jones-Franklin bridge approximately at the time referred to in Freeman's testimony; and, then headed for Apex, it would seem reasonable to infer it would be improbable he would be traveling the same course at a later hour.

Further discussion of the evidence is deemed inappropriate. In our view, the circumstantial evidence was sufficient *to permit* the jury to find that Freeman saw the Clark Corvair and that the wreck occurred after its uninterrupted travel from where it was when Freeman last saw it to the scene of the collision. If the jury should so find by the greater weight of the evidence, Freeman's testimony as to speed was competent. Hence, Freeman's testimony should have been admitted and the jury should have been instructed as indicated with reference to the findings prerequisite to its consideration as evidence relating to the speed of the Clark Corvair.

Defendants contend the court's exclusion of Freeman's testimony and of said portion of Cecil Wilkerson's testimony, if error, was not prejudicial to plaintiff. They contend this evidence was first admitted and was before the jury "over a day" before excluded by the court's ruling. However, the court, in substance, instructed the jury there was no evidence Freeman saw the Clark Corvair. We must assume the jury acted in compliance with the court's ruling and positive direction. Thereafter, the evidence for jury consideration as to what occurred in respect of speed and other alleged negligence prior to and at the time of the wreck related solely to physical facts observed at the scene after the wreck occurred. Under the circumstances, we cannot say the erroneous ruling did not substantially prejudice plaintiff.

For the error indicated, a new trial is awarded. Discussion of other assignments of error, relating to matters which may not recur at the next trial, is deemed unnecessary.

New trial.

Byrd v. Lord Brothers Contractors, Inc.

Supreme Court of Oregon, 1970.
256 Or. 421, 473 P.2d 1018.

The following case presents an issue of whether a set of circumstances would be admissible to lead a trier of the facts to determine who caused an accident involving a motor vehicle. The prime issue involved was whether what had been observed by a witness was too remote to be admissible to determine the cause of the end result of smashing the windshield of an auto and injuring the driver. The decision of the court follows:

HOLMAN, Justice. Plaintiff brought an action to recover damages for personal injuries occasioned when he was hit by a piece of concrete. Plaintiff appealed from a judgment entered on a jury verdict for defendant. The only issues relate to the admissibility of evidence.

At about ten o'clock in the evening, plaintiff was operating his motor vehicle on Lombard Street under the 33rd Street overpass in the city of Portland, when a piece of concrete came through the windshield and injured him. Defendant was engaged in the remodeling of the overpass, which involved removing a concrete walk and railing along one side. A bulkhead had been constructed for the purpose of confining debris. The testimony was in dispute as to its efficiency. Concrete had previously been broken away below the bulkhead for the purpose of inserting beams for its support. No work was being done at the time of the accident, but work had been performed that day. The overpass was open to pedestrians and vehicular traffic at the time of the accident. There was no direct evidence concerning the cause of the falling concrete.

Defendant introduced evidence, to which plaintiff objected, that at approximately the time of the accident, four or five boys around junior high school age were seen running west on Columbia Boulevard at its intersection with 27th Street. The intersection where the boys were seen is six blocks west and one block north of where the accident occurred. However, the north end of the overpass is approximately at the intersection of 33rd Street and Columbia Boulevard, six blocks from where the boys were seen. There was no other evidence to connect the boys to the chunk of concrete which struck plaintiff.

The problem is one of relevancy. The conclusion sought to be drawn is that the boys threw the concrete from the overpass. The fact from which this conclusion is to be inferred is that they were seen six blocks away running in a direction away from the north end of the overpass at about the time of the accident. The question is whether this fact has sufficient probative bearing on the issue to make it relevant and thus admissible. McCormick says as follows:

"What is the standard of relevance or probative quality which evidence must meet if it is to be admitted? We have said that it must 'tend to establish' the inference for which it is offered. How strong must this tendency be? Some courts have announced tests, variously phrased, which seem to require that the evidence offered must render the inference for which it is offered more probable than the other possible inferences or hypotheses, that is, the chances must appear to preponderate that the inference claimed is the true one. It is believed, however, that while this might be a reasonable standard by which to judge the sufficiency of all of a party's proof to enable him to get to the jury on the issue, it makes too heavy a demand upon a given item of proof at the admissibility stage, when we are gathering our bits of information piece by piece. And, in fact, much circumstantial evidence is commonly received which does not meet so stringent a test. . . . It is believed that a more modest standard would better reflect the actual practice of the courts, and that the most acceptable test of relevancy is the question, does the evidence offered render the desired inference *more probable than it would be without the evidence?* . . ." (footnotes omitted; emphasis his.) McCormick, Evidence 317–18 § 152 (1954).

The jury, of course, realized that there was the possibility that the concrete was thrown from the overpass by someone, because the public had access to the overpass. From the jury's knowledge of everyday life, it could have legitimately concluded that boys are inclined to run away from the scene of a wrong. From the same knowledge, they could believe that children are more likely to throw things from an overpass than are adults. Under these circumstances, we cannot say that the admitted testimony had no probative value.

Admittedly, the boys could have come from numerous other places than the overpass and could have been running for any one of the various reasons that boys run. The relation between the boys and the overpass six blocks away is an attenuated one, but we believe that, after the introduction of the evidence in question, there was a greater possibility that the concrete was thrown from the overpass than would have so appeared in the absence of such evidence. Had the boys been seen running from the end of the overpass, no one would have any difficulty in concluding that the evidence was highly relevant. When the same thing occurs six blocks away, its probative value is very greatly lessened. However, we cannot say it has none. We do not mean that it was probable that the boys threw the concrete or that the evidence would justify the submission of a case to the jury if they were being sued for having caused the injury. Wigmore has the following to say:

"On the other hand, the judges constantly find it necessary to warn us that their function, in determining Relevancy, is not that of final arbiters, but merely of preliminary testers, i.e., that the evidentiary fact offered does not need to have strong, full, superlative, probative value, *does not need to involve demonstration* or to produce persuasion by its sole and intrinsic force, but merely to be *worth consideration by the jury.* It is for the jury to give it the appropriate weight in effecting persuasion. The rule of law which the judge employs is concerned merely with admitting the fact through the evidentiary portal. The judge thus warns the opponent of the evidence that he is not entitled to complain of its lack of absolute demonstrative power; a mere capacity to help in demonstration is enough for its admission" (footnote omitted; emphasis his). 1 Wigmore on Evidence 411, § 29 (3d ed. 1940).

The plaintiff had the burden of persuading the jury that the defendant was negligent. The defendant is entitled to make this burden as heavy as possible by calling to the jury's attention any fact which would raise a not completely unreasonable *possibility* that the untoward occurrence happened in a manner inconsistent with its negligence.

When the offered testimony gets to the outer fringes of relevancy, courts allow the trial judge a certain amount of leeway in evaluating its admissibility. 1 Conrad, Modern Trial Evidence 53, § 37 (1956) expresses it this way:

". . . Before evidence can be excluded on the ground of irrelevancy, it is essential that it appear so beyond doubt. If the question is doubtful, the settled rule is that the evidence should go to the jury for evaluation by it . . ." (footnote omitted).

Plaintiff also contends that the trial court erred in admitting the following testimony over objection because it called for a conclusion which was the ultimate question to be decided by the jury:

"Q. State whether or not, Mr. Percival, there was any way for debris to come down, and if so, explain how it could come down.
". . .
"A. The only way it would have to come over the top of the bulkhead."

Even if the evidence was conclusory and therefore not admissible, no prejudicial error was involved. Substantially, the same evidence came in without objection from another witness.

"Q. Were there in fact any breaks in that bulkhead or holes in it that would have permitted debris to pass through?
"A. No."

The judgment of the trial court is affirmed.

People v. Feldman
Court of Appeals of New York, 1949.
299 N.Y. 153, 85 N.E.2d 913.

While the following case is an old one, the law of the case remains the same today as it was in 1949.

This case involves a pharmacist who stood accused of administering strychnine, a deadly poison, to his wife, causing her death. There was no direct evidence to conclude that he had done this, but circumstantial evidence that he was a pharmacist and had the means available to him to do such a heinous act and that he brought medicine to her bedside that he had assisted in preparing caused his conviction. The prosecution's expert on toxicology testified on direct examination, and his cross-examination was limited by the trial court. This is one of many interesting cases in this book, and no doubt you would like to find out what the court's decision was. I urge you to read this decision.

CONWAY, Judge. Proof of guilt of administering poison to another, resulting in death, is always difficult and the instant case constitutes no exception. Unless there be a confession or direct testimony by observers of the act, dependence must be upon circumstances attending the event and then the question, in a capital case, which is presented to us for our consideration is whether the guilt of the accused has been established to a moral certainty by circumstances which not only point to the guilt of the accused but are inconsistent with his innocence. People v. Fitzgerald, 156 N.Y. 253, 258, 50 N.E. 846, 849 (1898); People v. Razezicz, 206 N.Y. 249, 99 N.E. 557, 556 (1919); People v. May, 290 N.Y. 369, 49 N.E.2d 486 (1898).

One of the difficulties here is that there is no direct proof that the defendant had anything to do with the strychnine which it is alleged was administered to his wife, the deceased. There was no proof that he ever purchased or possessed any. As a substitute for such proof it is pointed out that the defendant was a licensed employed pharmacist and thus had access to the poison. The bottle alleged to have contained it was discarded as refuse in the hospital (contrary to good practice) by the nurse in attendance on the deceased after her death. Thus no one can say with certainty that the bottle contained strychnine. The toxicologist, who was not a physician, testified to the presence of strychnine in the organs of the deceased, other than intestines, when he performed an autopsy and analyses some five months after burial. He also testified that in discovering it, all of the organs supplied him consisting of the brain, lungs, liver, spleen, heart, kidneys, blood, empty stomach, two pieces of rib and a male foetus, were used up and that no material is left. There is thus in existence no tangible evidence which others may check and test which would show the presence or amount of strychnine at any time in the body of the deceased. The "very few notes" made on pieces of paper from time to time during the tests which took about a week, were destroyed after being typed by the toxicologist personally, after he had completed his examination and tests. We must proceed, of course, upon the assumption, for the purpose of this opinion, that the toxicologist made no error in *estimate of quantity* of strychnine in the body of deceased and the matter is adverted to only for the purpose of indicating that the entire proof of guilt here depends on oral testimony and not upon articles or objects which can now be touched or viewed. To put it succinctly, the opinion testimony revolved about the estimate of "the total amount of strychnine in the entire body, exclusive of the gastrointestinal tract and exclusive of the urine" and was calculated upon a body weight of 132 pounds or approximately "60 kilos." Moreover, the stomach showed too small a trace of strychnine to estimate it. The case against the defendant hung upon the correctness of the estimate and calculation plus the opinion testimony. It is rare when a charge in a capital case may depend upon such an "estimate" and conviction should follow only upon the clearest and unconfused proof.

In addition to the toxicologist, four experts or opinion witnesses were called upon to give testimony. No one of the five had seen Mrs. Feldman in life. The doctors who had seen and attended her at home on December 7th and in the hospital on December 8th, before her death in the early morning hours of December 9th, diagnosed her case as one of tetany accompanying pregnancy. That indicated a calcium deficiency. The five opinion witnesses called upon the trial all agreed that on December 7th, the deceased had ingested strychnine. There is no contention by the People that the accused had anything to do with that. The two opinion witnesses for the defendant gave it as their opinion that the deceased died from the December 7th ingestion. The three opinion witnesses called by the People gave it as their opinion that she did not, but died from the ingestion of strychnine in the early hours of December 9th at the hospital. There was no strychnine found at either hospital or home. If the deceased died from the ingestion of strychnine in her home on December 7th, the accused was entitled to acquittal of the charge made. If she died from the ingestion of strychnine in the hospital on December 9th, the guilt of the accused depended on whether he had put strychnine in one of the bottles which he brought to the hospital and delivered to the nurse in attendance upon his wife and no part of the contents of which was analyzed because of the conduct of the nurse in disposing of it, to which reference has already been made.

In a case as close as this one, it is clear that it was essential for the trial court to make certain that no error in the admission or exclusion of evidence occurred and that there was no confusion as to facts. Concededly that was not an easy task. It is against the background outlined that we consider some of the facts and some of the rulings made.

* * *

On the night of December 7, 1943, the deceased was visited by her sister about 9 o'clock. She was alone while her husband, the defendant, was on duty at the drugstore in which he was employed. Following her sister's visit, she became ill and suffered convulsions. Her condition was diagnosed as a calcium deficiency by two physicians and she was removed before midnight to a hospital. The defendant had requested the first doctor called to engage a consultant. At the hospital Mrs. Feldman had a convulsion at 9 o'clock in the morning of December 8th, and then improved. Shortly after noon of that day a third physician, a specialist in "tetany and calcium metabolism" was engaged at defendant's insistence. The defendant on December 8th had suggested that it might be well to get a doctor from Johns Hopkins Hospital but was told that the first two doctors consulted had selected for further consultation the specialist in tetany to whom reference has been made. That specialist reached the hospital at 6 o'clock in the evening and found Mrs. Feldman comfortable. The only troublesome symptom was that Mrs. Feldman complained of some tenderness in her feet. The doctor thought her condition was "strongly suggestive of hypocalcemic tetany of pregnancy" and finding the prognosis good he dictated a prescription consisting of "60 grains of calcium chloride in 150 cc. of elixir lactate of pepsin" to be administered every four hours. That prescription would be contained in six bottles. It was designed to build up calcium content of the blood. He also prescribed a patented medicine known as Hytakerol to be given once a day. That consisted of highly concentrated vitamin D.

One of the doctors met defendant in the corridor, told him his wife might be suffering from tetany "and if so the patient would be very much better by tomorrow, and from all indications she ought to do very well." Defendant was then given the two prescriptions which had been written on a prescription pad. He was told that he could get the Hytakerol at the pharmacy of one Jacoff and while there he might as well have the other prescription filled.

The defendant went to Jacoff's pharmacy and obtained the Hytakerol. He was driven there by the husband of his wife's sister, one Kushner. Then Kushner drove him to the drugstore of Ruvinsky where the defendant was employed. There defendant asked one Rothbaum to help him make up the prescription. The defendant prepared the bottles individually, weighing out each quantity prescribed separately and putting it into the bottle then under preparation. Ruvinsky and Rothbaum said that there was nothing unusual about the method of preparation. The largest graduate measure used in the store held but thirty-two ounces. To put thirty ounces as required by the prescription for the five-ounce bottles into the quart measure would render it difficult to stir the compound without spilling it. Rothbaum helped defendant get out the calcium chloride and lactate of pepsin. After the preparation of the first two bottles was completed, Rothbaum left for his home. Ruvinsky was busy waiting on customers but could see the defendant if he looked toward him. There was a cabinet of poisonous drugs near the defendant but no proof that he opened it. After preparing the six bottles containing the medicine he was driven with them, again by Kushner, at about 10:30 in the evening to the hospital where he knocked on his wife's door and placed them and the bottle of Hytakerol in the hands of nurse Bierle. Shortly thereafter contents of one of the six bottles was administered to Mrs. Feldman. At 2:30 on the morning of December 9th, nurse Worrell, who had succeeded as the attending special nurse, administered the second bottle. One-half hour later the deceased was seized with a convulsion. She died one hour later at 4 o'clock. The nurse thereafter threw out all of the six bottles. The cause of death certified was "tetany with convulsions; cause unknown, associated with pregnancy."

* * *

Moreover, we think the judgment of conviction must be reversed because of the ruling of the court upon the right of the defendant to cross-examine the expert or opinion witnesses. When the toxicologist was being cross-examined, the following questions were asked of him:

"Q. Now, you said that you got part of your information or knowledge about toxicology from literature; is that right? A. That's right.

"Q. Did you ever read 'Textbook of Physiology' by Howell? A. I've glanced at it."

The court, without more, then ruled that if counsel wished to refer to any textbook or literature he must show it to the witness and that if the witness agreed with it and adopted it, the witness might then be questioned about it. The court said, " . . . I shall not permit you to read from that book or any other book. If you wish to question this witness regarding any material, any writing, any dissertation or questions or statements contained in that book, you will first refer to the witness; let him read it and if the witness replies that he is in agreement with it or that he adopts that argument as his own, then I will allow you to make reference to it. Otherwise, not."

During the same discussion the court repeated the ruling as follows: " . . . you will first refer the book to this witness and if the witness tells the Court that he is in agreement with that statement or that writing and adopts that argument as his own, you may then question him regarding such statement or such argument. Otherwise I shall exclude it."

In this State when an expert witness has given opinion testimony and on cross-examination has testified that a book called to his attention is recognized by him as an authority upon the subject as to which he has given an opinion, he may be confronted with a passage from the book which conflicts with the opinion he has expressed. This is permitted for the purpose of discrediting or weakening his testimony. Egan v. Dry Dock, East Broadway & Battery R. Co., 12 App.Div. 556, 42 N.Y.S. 188 (1897); Hastings v. Chrysler Corp., 273 App.Div. 292, 77 N.Y.S.2d 524 (1902). In the Egan case, supra, it was said: ". . . it has been the custom, in this state at least, to call the attention of expert witnesses, upon cross-examination, to books upon the subject, and ask whether or not authors whom he admitted to be good authority had not expressed opinions different from that which was given by him upon the stand. The reference to books in such cases is not made for the purpose of making the statements in the books evidence before a jury, but solely for the purpose of ascertaining the weight to be given to the testimony of the witness." 12 App.Div. at page 571, 42 N.Y.S. at page 200.

* * *

The judgment of conviction should be reversed and a new trial ordered.

RELATED DECISIONS
Hearsay—Other, Similar Acts

United States v. Brettholz
United States Court of Appeals, Second Circuit, 1973.
485 F.2d 483.

The following case relates the tale of some very conscientious federal narcotics agents making a drug "bust" (arrest) with the aid of a government informer. Since I have had the privilege of participating in similar situations as a plainclothes police officer, I believe the situation described herein is very realistic, and an exciting one in which to participate. Needless to say, it is also a very dangerous part of law enforcement.

The defendants were convicted at trial and appealed on the basis that the trial court should not have permitted testimony in which a codefendant, turning government witness, said that he purchased cocaine from another defendant ten times within a year prior to the transaction in question.

To find out what the court said about this question, I urge you to read the decision.

MOORE, Circuit Judge. James Brettholz and Milton Santiago appeal from judgments of conviction entered after trial by jury in the United States District Court for the Eastern District of New York. The indictment charged appellants and three other persons, Jerry A. Rosenblum, Jory Ira Prince, and Lon M. Posner, in three counts with violations of the federal narcotics laws: Count I charged defendants with knowingly and unlawfully possessing with intent to distribute one quarter kilo-gram of cocaine, in violation of 21 U.S.C.A. § 841(a)(1); Count II charged defendants with attempted distribution of cocaine, in violation of 21 U.S.C.A. §§ 841(a)(1), 846; Count III charged defendants with conspir-ing to conceal, possess, and distribute cocaine, in violation of 21 U.S.C.A. § 841 (a)(1). A fourth count, naming appellant Santiago only, charged him with forcibly assaulting, imped-ing, and intimidating a federal narcotics agent engaged in the performance of his official du-ties, in violation of 18 U.S.C.A. §§ 111 and 1114.

Prior to trial, defendants Rosenblum, Prince, and Posner pleaded guilty to Count III, the conspiracy count, and appeared as government witnesses against appellants Brettholz and Santiago. Both appellants were found guilty as charged on the first three counts of the indictment; Santiago was also found guilty on Count IV. Brettholz was sen-tenced to a term of five years on each of the first three counts, the sentences to run con-currently, plus a parole term of three years, plus a fine of $1,000 on each count, for a total of $3,000. Santiago was sentenced to a term of five years on each of the first three counts, the sentences to run concurrently, plus a special parole term of three years; he was sentenced on Count IV to a term of imprisonment of three years, the sentence to run concurrently with those imposed under the first three counts of the indictment.

On appeal appellants raise no material is-sues of fact but argue (1) that reversible error occurred when the trial court permitted the introduction of testimony by co-defendant Posner that Brettholz had sold cocaine to Pos-ner on ten prior occasions; . . .

A brief recital of the facts concerning this attempted sale of cocaine is necessary to a de-termination of the issues raised by appellants.

At trial the government's evidence estab-lished that during the last week of July, 1972, after he had been contacted by government informer Gary Kaplan, co-defendant Jerry Rosenblum telephoned co-defendant Jory Prince for the purpose of securing one-half pound of cocaine. Prince in turn telephoned co-defendant Posner, who indicated that he would see whether he could find a source for

the narcotic. Several days thereafter Posner contacted appellant Brettholz, informed the latter that he had a prospective purchaser of cocaine, and asked whether Brettholz could supply the drug. Brettholz told Posner to call back later that week; Posner did so and on that occasion Brettholz indicated that he could supply the half-pound of cocaine, and that he would meet with Posner the following day, August 5, 1972. (Trial Transcript, herein-after "Tr.," at 326–27).

The next day Brettholz met with Posner at the latter's place of business, a car wash lo-cated in Far Rockaway, New York, which was co-managed by co-defendant Prince. Brett-holz gave Posner a small sample of cocaine for the latter's customer to "taste", indicating that he would be able to supply only seven, and not eight, ounces of the drug. (Tr. 328–31). Posner then gave Brettholz the telephone number at co-defendant Prince's home in Far Rockaway, instructing Brettholz to telephone him there at 7:30 that evening. (Tr. 331–32). After Prince himself had "tasted" the cocaine sample, he and Posner telephoned Rosen-blum, who in turn contacted government in-former Kaplan, with the information that the deal would be consummated that evening at the home of Jory Prince. (Tr. 152, 332). Kap-lan quickly contacted the federal narcotics agent to whom he informed, Agent Hall, who made plans to be present with other agents and Kaplan in the vicinity of Prince's home that evening.

At approximately 7:30 that night, the vari-ous characters in this narrative began to arrive at Prince's house. First to arrive were Posner and Rosenblum, who went up to Prince's up-stairs bedroom for conversation. Posner had brought with him a brown shopping bag con-taining a scale with which to weigh the co-caine to be brought to the house by appellants Brettholz and Santiago; at trial Posner testi-fied that the shopping bag had contained nothing but the scale. (Tr. 400, 433). In addi-tion to the scale, Posner had brought the co-caine sample supplied earlier that day at the car wash by appellant Brettholz. (Tr. 336–37). Next to arrive at the house was government informer Kaplan, who secretly had been wait-ing in a parked auto with two federal under-cover narcotics agents; Rosenblum went to the parked auto and accompanied Kaplan to the Prince house. All persons again convened in Prince's upstairs bedroom. Kaplan "tasted" the cocaine, expressed approval, and was told to go back to his auto until the full supply of the drug had arrived. (Tr. 165, 178–79). At this same time the pre-arranged telephone call from Brettholz was received at the Prince residence. (Tr. 179, 340). Posner told Brettholz that "everything seemed to be all right, everything looked cool and he should come by." (Tr. 340). Brettholz announced that he would do so after finishing his dinner.

At approximately 9:00 P.M. that evening appellants Brettholz and Santiago arrived at the house. The two men immediately went to the upstairs bedroom to confer with co-defendants Rosenblum, Posner, and Prince. (Tr. 341–43). After expressing concern at the number of autos parked outside, announcing that the cocaine was still in their auto, and looking around the house to chart an escape route just in case something went wrong (Tr. 185, 189), Brettholz, accompanied by Santiago, went back to their auto, to return to the house a few minutes later with the cocaine. Upon their return, Santiago positioned himself downstairs at the front door while Brettholz took the cocaine to the upstairs bedroom. (Tr. 190–91). Brettholz asked Rosenblum if he was the buyer; answering in the negative, Rosenblum then went outside to get the "purchaser," government informer Kaplan. Rosenblum and Kaplan re-entered the house and were promptly searched for weapons by appellant Santiago, who was still keeping his vigil at the front door. (Tr. 127–28). Once upstairs Kaplan "snorted" or sampled the cocaine which Brettholz had brought, expressed satisfaction with the deal, and left the house, ostensibly to go to his auto for the purchase money. (Tr. 464).

Back at the auto, Kaplan informed the agents that the cocaine had arrived. At this point Kaplan and agents Hall and Lightcap went to the house. Lightcap waited outside. Santiago, still standing watch at the front door, latched the door after Kaplan and Agent Hall had entered, and admonished Kaplan for bringing others to the house against orders. (Tr. 467). Santiago, using colorful expletives to make his point, further warned Kaplan and

Hall that nothing had better go wrong because "We f___ people that f___ us." (Tr. 467). While Santiago was searching Hall for weapons, the latter unlatched the door to allow Agent Lightcap to enter; thereupon, Hall took out his badge, identified himself to Santiago as a federal agent (a fact which appellant Santiago disputes), and announced an arrest. (Tr. 469–70). Santiago responded by throwing a punch at Agent Hall and screaming, "Jimmy, Jimmy," appellant Brettholz's nickname (Tr. 505). Other agents quickly entered the house and ran to the upstairs bedroom. Having heard all the commotion, defendants Prince, Posner, Rosenblum, and Brettholz went into action upstairs; Brettholz grabbed the cocaine and was seen by Agent Hall to be leaving out of a bathroom window. In the ensuing chaos, Brettholz escaped, only to turn himself in several days later. The other defendants were arrested on the spot.

After the arrests the agents conducted a search of the premises and the surrounding vicinity. A small plastic bag containing seven ounces of cocaine was found on the roof of a garage located directly behind the Prince house. (Tr. 528). The agents also found three small bags of marijuana in a shopping bag stuffed into a drawer of a bureau in Prince's bedroom. (Tr. 537).

At trial both Brettholz and Santiago testified in their own defense, and each supported the other's testimony. In essence, their defense was that they had gone to the Prince house not with the intention of selling cocaine, but for the purpose of buying marijuana from Posner for their personal use. The jury returned a guilty verdict on all counts of the indictment.

Appellants' first argument on appeal is that the trial court committed reversible error by permitting a government witness, co-defendant Posner, to testify that he had bought cocaine from appellant Brettholz on ten occasions within a year prior to the transaction in question. Prior to Posner's testimony the Assistant United States Attorney made an offer of proof to the trial court as to what Posner would testify, i.e., that Brettholz had sold cocaine to him on ten prior occasions. The prosecutor asked that the testimony be admitted on the theory that the ten prior sales "show[ed] that there was intent to distribute on the part of defendant [Brettholz] as opposed to being used for his own personal use." (Tr. 136). The trial court ruled that the offered testimony would be admitted, as it later was over defense objection, on the ground that:

> [I]t is pretty well established that proof of each commission of acts of a similar nature previously and not too remotely, of course, is some evidence of intent in a crime where intent is a necessary factor as it is in this case. (Tr. 137).

> * * *

> I think the testimony would be admissible for the purpose I have stated a moment ago, that is, to show intent on the part of the defendant Brettholz. (Tr. 138).

Appellants contend that the admission of Posner's testimony was reversible error since, they argue, "there was not and could not be any real issue of intent in the case." (Brief, hereinafter "Br.," at 13). We disagree.

The law in this Circuit is that evidence of prior similar acts is admissible "for all purposes except to show the criminal character or disposition of the defendant." United States v. Warren, 453 F.2d 738, 745 (2d Cir. 1972), certiorari denied, 406 U.S. 944, 92 S.Ct. 2040, 32 L.Ed.2d 331. See also, United States v. Deaton, 381 F.2d 114, 117 (2d Cir. 1967); United States v. Knohl, 379 F.2d 427, 438 (2d Cir. 1967); United States v. Bozza, 365 F.2d 206, 213 (2d Cir. 1966); McCormick, Evidence § 190, at 447 et seq. (2d ed. 1972). The case law and the legal scholars uniformly indicate that such evidence is admissible if offered to prove knowledge, intent, or design on the part of the defendant; 2 Wigmore, Evidence § 300, at 192–93 (3d ed. 1940); McCormick, supra, Evidence § 190 at 449; United States v. DeCicco, 435 F.2d 478, 483 (2d Cir. 1970). In ruling on the admissibility of such evidence, the trial judge is required to balance all of the relevant factors to determine whether the probative value of the evidence outweighs its prejudicial character. Spencer v. State of Texas, 385 U.S. 554, 561, 87 S.Ct. 648, 17 L.Ed.2d 606 (1967); United States v. Deaton, supra, 381 F.2d at 117. As summarized by one scholar,

> the problem is not merely one of pigeonholing, but one of balancing, on the one side, the actual need for the other-crimes evidence in the light of the issues and the other evidence available to the prosecution, the convincingness of the evidence that the other crimes were committed and that the accused was the actor, and the strength or weakness of the other-crimes evidence in supporting the issue, and on the other, the degree to which the jury will probably be roused by the evidence to overmastering hostility.

McCormick, supra, Evidence § 190 at 453. See United States v. Byrd, 352 F.2d 570, 574 (2d Cir. 1965).

Appellants place great reliance upon the concurring opinion of Judge Lumbard in United States v. DeCicco, supra, and upon opinions from other circuits, for the proposition that evidence of similar prior acts is not admissible unless the defendant himself has first raised the issues of motive or intent. See 435 F.2d at 486. Appellants' reliance is misplaced, however, since the cases in this Circuit provide otherwise. See, e.g., United States v. Freedman, 445 F.2d 1220, 1224 (2d Cir. 1971), where we held:

> Evidence of similar acts by a defendant is admissible to prove his knowledge, intent, or design if knowledge, intent, or design "is placed in issue in the case at trial, either by the nature of the facts sought to be proved by the prosecution or the nature of the facts sought to be established by the defense." United States v. DeCicco, 435 F.2d 478, 483 (2 Cir. 1970).

See also, United States v. Birrell, 447 F.2d 1168, 1172 (2d Cir. 1971), certiorari denied 404 U.S. 1025, 92 S.Ct. 675, 30 L.Ed.2d 675 (1972); United States v. Egenberg, 441 F.2d 441, 443–44 (2d Cir.), certiorari denied 404 U.S. 994, 92 S.Ct. 530, 30 L.Ed.2d 546 (1971); United States v. Klein, 340 F.2d 547, 549 (2d Cir.), certiorari denied 382 U.S. 850, 86 S.Ct. 97, 15 L.Ed.2d 89 (1965).

In the case before us, intent was placed in issue by the defendants themselves in maintaining that they had gone to the Prince house not with the intention of selling cocaine (although the proof overwhelmingly showed otherwise), but with the intention of purchasing marijuana for their own use. Under the circumstances, it cannot be said that the trial court abused its discretion in determining that the probative value of Posner's testimony as to the ten prior cocaine transactions outweighed its prejudicial effect. Inasmuch as the prior acts of Brettholz involved a situation virtually identical to the transaction for which appellants were indicted, and inasmuch as intent was an element of the defense case, there was no error in the admission of Posner's testimony.

The judgments of conviction are affirmed.

State v. Saksniit

Supreme Court, Special Term, New York County, Part I, 1972.
69 Misc.2d 554, 332 N.Y.S.2d 343.

The facts in the following case should act as a caveat to any student who believes that he or she can outsmart the system by using someone else to do required school assignments and passing the other person's work as his or her own work. It is a violation of several laws to conspire to do this, and if the recipient student is apprehended, it might affect that student's lifework. With this admonition in mind, I believe you will be very interested in reading the decision of this case.

ABRAHAM J. GELLINOFF, Justice:

The Attorney General has brought an action to dissolve the corporate defendant and to enjoin all defendants from engaging in certain allegedly fraudulent acts [Exec.Law, § 63(12); Bus.Corp.Law, § 1101]. Pending trial of the action, the Attorney General makes this application for a preliminary injunction and the appointment of a temporary receiver [Bus.Corp.Law, §§ 1113, 1115].

The documents obtained by the Attorney General through a subpoena *duces tecum* [Exec.Law, § 63(12)], demonstrate that the only business actually conducted by defendants is the preparation and sale of term papers to high school and college students. Indeed the word "termpapers" are featured in the name under which each of the defendant companies does business—*Termpapers*, Inc.; New York City *Termpapers*, Inc.; *Termpapers* Unlimited of New York, Inc.; and *Termpapers* Unlimited of New York.

The words "term paper" mean "a major written assignment in a school or college course representative of a student's achievement during a term" [Webster's Third New International Dictionary]. A termpaper measures a student's ability to research and write upon a particular subject, and the grade he receives on a termpaper is a substantial factor in determining the grade he receives in the course. The satisfactory completion of the termpaper is generally a requirement for obtaining course credit for the particular course involved; and a certain number and type of course credits are necessary in order to obtain a diploma, degree or certificate.

Almost all of defendant's customers are students who have been attracted either through advertising in college newspapers, or by "fliers" given to passersby at college campuses. The advertisements, with the motto, "We give results," proclaim: "Great savings, 10,000 papers at $1.90 a page." More recently, the advertisements have added the statement, "Twice as many papers as last semester with summaries and grade levels on every one."

The "flier" states:

> "Do you have a termpaper assignment that's a little too much work? Are you cramped for time with a nightmarish deadline closing in? Let us help you. We have a team of professional writers who can handle any subject. Our papers are custom made, and professionally typed. We offer the most economical work anywhere, at no sacrifice in quality or service to you."

At the bottom of the "flier" is the statement, "This material is intended to be used for research and reference purposes only."

The student may respond to defendants' advertising in person or by mail. If he comes to their office, he sees three signs on the wall, reading: "We don't guarantee grades," "We don't condone plagiarism" and "No refunds." The student receives a form to fill out, which requests, besides the student's name and address, the name of his school, course and instructor. Although the form bears the statement, "For research and reference purposes only," it also provides a large blank space in which the student is requested to state the number of pages the termpaper should have, to give a "detailed description of desired paper," and to list "references left behind"—textbooks and other data for use in preparing the termpaper. The student pays the required fee in advance; $1.90 per page for a termpaper defendants have in stock, or $3.85 per page for a custom written termpaper ($4.85 for a "rush" job). About a week later, he receives a fully written termpaper.

The termpapers are produced for defendants by free-lance writers who are college graduates with some expertise in the subject involved in the particular paper. The writers have signed a contract with defendants, promising "to submit research and writing that is commencerate [sic] in quality with *work sufficient to be accepted in a Graduate Program at an accredited University*." [Emphasis added.] Additionally—and ironically—each writer promises "that all work he produces and submits will be original and the products of his own research and writing, and the final product will not be work prepared for him by others."

The Attorney General, pursuant to his statutory authority to "take proof and make a determination of the relevant facts and to issue subpoenas in accordance with the civil practice law and rules" [Exec.Law, § 63(12)], has taken the testimony of various customers of defendants. These students, constituting a fairly representative sample of defendants' customers, testified that they submitted the defendants' product, either in whole or in substantial part, as their own work, and received grade credit for it (or, if they did not, it was only because the paper was delivered too late to be submitted).

Section 224, subdivision 2 of the Education Law, so far as here pertinent, provides:

> "No person shall . . . attempt to obtain by fraudulent means any diploma, certificate, or other instrument purporting to confer any literary, scientific, professional or other degree . . ."

A violation of the section is a misdemeanor and "any person who aids or abets another . . . to violate the provisions of this section" is "liable to the same penalties" [Educ.Law, § 224(3)].

Any student who submits a "ghost-written" termpaper as his own, cheats. There is, conceptually, little difference between the "ghost-written" termpaper and the copied examination paper or the hiring of another to take an examination in place of a student. Any student, therefore, who submits as his own work a termpaper bought from defendants, gets

credit for a course through fraud, and thereby attempts to obtain his diploma or degree by "fraudulent means" [Educ.Law, § 224(2); see, also, Educ.Law, § 225]. And if defendants sell termpapers to students, with reason to believe that the students intend to submit them as the students' own work, then defendants are aiding and abetting the students to attempt to obtain their diplomas or degrees by "fraudulent means" [Educ.Law, § 224(3)].

The court has before it many samples of the order forms filled out by defendants' customers. In the blank space where the customer is requested to furnish a "Detailed Description of Desired Paper . . . ," one student, after a lengthy analysis of the subject matter, informs defendants:

> "Footnotes and bibliography are required. Plagiarism must be carefully avoided, as the professor knows the criticism of Donne exceedingly well. The paper should be well planned, well organized and should indicate serious thought. The paper must be able to withstand aggressive and hostile examination. It will be carefully read and evaluated."

Another students says he "needed 15 references. Bibliography in alphabetical order." Another, informing defendants that the paper must be written "in Spanish," also adds, "Accents may be written in pencil." Still another, apparently leaving nothing to chance, instructs defendants to "leave name on paper blank," while another emphasizes that the "footnotes must be on a separate page at the end of the paper . . . not at bottom of page."

Other order forms contain similar instructions:

> "The paper must be at least 2000 words and at least 10 pages plus an additional page for bibliography. Footnotes are required. *This paper is for a graduate English course and must develop a thesis.* Both primary and secondary sources must be used." [Emphasis added.]

> "Please use many *recent* references." [Emphasis in original.]

> "I need code number 1281. It is an 8 page Shakespeare paper relating to two tragic characters. I need the paper for Prof. [name omitted], English [title omitted] class at Queens College.

Please let me know if anyone had used this paper for him before." [Emphasis added.]

"If possible, try to make it as evaluative and interpretive as possible. This is an advanced course, so led [sic] the writer not be afraid that [sic] it to [sic] fancy. *Make it as best [sic] and as fancy as you possibly can."* [Emphasis added.]

"Do not make the language too flowery."

"Must be backed up with actual case problems listed in any set of law books. If you cannot back up with actual noted case problems—void and return money."

"Paper being written for male college junior."

"I will supply cover sheets and the bibliography. . . . Do the paper in Outline form—It must be good *as you can see by her* [the instructor's] *remarks."* [Emphasis added.]

"Paper should be broad and simple for undergraduate course."

"Any topic, but I would most prefer a paper on human nature in 'The Discourses.'" [Emphasis added.]

"Not to be too general. *Specific area up to writer.* Research required—footnotes please. No bibliography. Margins—1-1/2" each side, 2" top, 1" bottom, double spaced." [Emphasis added.]

These instructions show that the student is plainly telling defendants that he intends to palm off the termpaper he receives from the defendants as his own. And these instructions—furnished in response to defendant's request on its order form for a "Detailed Description of Desired Paper"—also show that defendants recognize the student's avowed purpose to palm off defendants' termpaper as his own. Indeed, John Frederick Magee, formerly defendants' administrative assistant, testified before the Attorney General that defendants' purpose in requesting the students to list their school, course and instructor on the order form, is to enable the student to "use the paper verbatim" without fear that someone else in the same course will submit an identical paper to the same instructor. Defendants' termpapers are not mere outlines (unless that is what the student requests), nor are they in the form of reference guides; they are fully written termpapers. The custom made

papers, prepared according to the "detailed description," are typed on plain white paper, without any indication of their source or authorship. All a student has to do with the custom made paper is append his name and submit it. Any doubt that defendants know the students buy their termpapers in order to submit them as the student's own scholastic achievement, is dispelled by the agreement defendants exact from their writers, to submit "work sufficient to be accepted in a Graduate Program at an accredited university."

Defendants' advertising actively encourages the submission of their product as the students' own work. Their "flier"—advertising "custom made, and professionally typed" termpapers by "professional writers who can handle any subject," for students who are "cramped for time" with an "assignment that's a little too much work," and a "nightmarish deadline"—urges a student to have his scholastic work done for him instead of doing it himself. In their recent newspaper advertising, defendants claim to be able to provide "twice as many papers as last semester with summaries and *grade levels* on every one." [Emphasis added.] This obviously conveys the impression that students who have submitted defendants' papers in the past have received good grades. It lures students into believing that, by purchasing defendants' termpapers rather than doing the work themselves, they can be assured of creditable grades.

Defendants protest they did not know they were encouraging fraud. They point to their various disclaimers—"This material is intended to be used for research and reference purposes only"; "We don't condone plagiarism." Yet in the very same breath they boast of the grades their former termpapers have received. Their warning, "We don't guarantee grades," only accentuates their awareness that some students could be relying on defendants' termpapers for their grades.

The defendants liken themselves to the *Encyclopedia Britannica Library Research Service.* Each of the *Britannica* pages is on stationery bearing the *Encyclopedia Britannica* letterhead. Their reports consist exclusively of quoted excerpts from source materials, at the conclusion of which the author and the title of the quoted source are documented. Their reports do not contain any original writing whatsoever. The average length of their reports is four to six pages, the length being determined by themselves. Their research service is available only to purchasers of their encyclopedia, not to the general public through sale or otherwise. *Britannica* has on occasion received written requests for termpapers, with detailed instructions down to the type of paper to be used and the size of the margins. Requests of this nature are uniformly rejected. The function of their report is to furnish the subscriber with excerpts from documented source materials which he may then use as a basis for his own original research and writing.

The defendant Saksniit, president and office manager of defendant organizations, states in a reply affidavit that

> "students were informed that [specific] requests could not be complied with, that the research and reference report would be prepared in the normal manner regardless of specific instructions. If, in the normal procedure entertained by our staff and/or writers, the research and reference report delivered did comply with some of the numerous requests, it was purely coincidental."

In light of the other indisputable evidence, this unsupported assertion is rejected by the court as unbelievable.

The evidence as to the nature and conduct of defendants' business is both direct and circumstantial. The test as to its sufficiency is "whether common human experience would lead a reasonable man, putting his mind to it, to reject or accept the inferences asserted for the established facts" (People v. Borrero, 26 N.Y.2d 430, 435, 311 N.Y.S.2d 475, 479, 259 N.E.2d 902, 905 [1970]). Applying that test, the court is convinced that defendants are engaged in the business of selling termpapers to students, thereby knowingly aiding and abetting them to attempt to obtain by fraudulent means a diploma, degree or certificate, in violation of Education Law, § 224, subdivisions 2 and 3.

The complaint seeks a dissolution of the corporate defendant on the ground that the "business activities of defendants," have the "direct capacity and tendency of subvert-

ing the process of learning and encouraging intellectual dishonesty and cheating," and are therefore contrary to the "public policy of this State in maintaining and preserving the integrity of the educational process."

"Education," wrote James Madison, "is the true foundation of civil liberty." Assisting and promoting plagiarism—the most serious academic offense—strikes at the core of the educational process, and thus at the very heart of a free society. Doing a student's work for him not only deprives him of the valuable disciplines of the learning process, but tends to destroy his moral fibre by lending credence to the all too prevalent notion that anything, including a college degree, can be bought for a price.

The damage which defendants' business does to the fabric of the scholastic community is dramatically made clear in a plea from a young college student who writes to the Attorney General urging action:

> "I am in competition with many students for entrance into a medical school. Spaces are few and the many students make the competition fierce. Only one student will occupy a seat desired by many, and he will be the student with the best grades.
>
> "The situation is tight enough as is, but what chance do I stand if my independent work (term papers) must compete not with those of my peers but with those of professionals—people with Masters and even Doctorates in the areas in which they write? *I am subtly being blackmailed into using their immoral services*.
>
> "An ironic development is the distrust my instructors have developed toward any above-average term paper I submit.
>
> "Sir—can your office do anything to relieve this injustice? I do not believe I am exaggerating if I claim that my future *and my integrity* are at stake." [Emphasis added.]

The legislature of our state has enacted laws to prevent fraud in obtaining degrees or diplomas (Educ.Law, § 224), and to guard the sanctity of the scholastic examinations (id., § 225). It has thus declared it to be the public policy of this state that the integrity of the educational process should be protected and preserved. Whenever "our courts are called upon to scrutinize a [business] . . . which is clearly repugnant to sound morality and civic honesty, they need not look for a well fitting definition of public policy. . . ." (Veazey v. Allen, 173 N.Y. 359, 368, 66 N.E. 103 [1903]).

The business defendants are conducting is morally wrong. It subverts the learning process and encourages intellectual dishonesty and cheating. It is directly opposed to the declared public policy of our State. It exceeds the purposes for which the corporate defendant was formed as set forth in its certificates of incorporation and is *ultra vires* [see State v. Abortion Information Agency, Inc., 37 A.D.2d 142, 330 N.Y.S.2d 927 (First Dept. 1971)].

The defendant Saksniit and defendant Termpapers, Inc. appear to be doing business under the purported corporate or assumed names of New York City Termpapers, Inc., Termpapers Unlimited of New York, Inc., and Termpapers Unlimited of New York. These latter companies are without authority to do business in New York. The use of those names is a fraud [Bus.Corp.Law, § 109(a)(2), (a)(3); Gen.Bus.Law, § 130(9)].

In light of the foregoing, the Attorney General's motion is granted in all respects. [See State v. Abortion Information Agency, Inc., 323 N.Y.S.2d 597 (Sup.Ct.N.Y.Co. 1971), aff'd, 37 A.D.2d 142, 330 N.Y.S.2d 927 (1st Dept. 1971); State v. Remedial Education, Inc., N.Y.L.J., February 15, 1972, p. 16, col. 7 (Sup.Ct.N.Y.Co. 1972)]. All defendants are enjoined, during the pendency of this action, from carrying on, conducting or transacting business as sellers of essays, theses, termpapers or other school assignments. They are enjoined from advertising, soliciting, accepting, delivering and contracting for the production and sale of termpapers or other research material to students. Except with the permission of and under the further order of this court, the defendants and the officers and directors of the defendant companies (if there be any purporting to act), are enjoined from and may not pay out or cause to be paid out any of the money of the corporate defendant Termpapers, Inc., nor any money of the other companies under which it or defendant Saksniit operates, to wit, New York City Termpapers, Inc., Termpapers Unlimited of New York, Inc. and Termpapers Unlimited of New York; and Termpapers, Inc. and said other companies and its officers and directors (if there by any

purporting to act), and defendant Saksniit may not sell, transfer, assign or deliver, or cause to be sold, transferred, assigned or delivered the property of Termpapers, Inc. or of the other aforementioned defendant companies under which names Termpapers, Inc. or defendant Saksniit operates [Exec.Law, § 63(12); Bus.Corp.Law, §§ 109, 1115; Gen.Bus.Law, § 130].

A temporary receiver will be appointed to preserve the assets of the corporation Termpapers, Inc. and of the other aforementioned companies, with the usual powers and duties of temporary receivers [Bus.Corp.Law, § 1113, Article 12].

Settle order on one day's notice, with provision for an early trial as the parties may agree, furnishing the court with suggestions as to the bond of the receiver.

Matthew A. Summers, B/T His Guardian Mary Alice Summers and Suzanne Summers, Appellants, v. The Fort Crockett Hotel, Ltd., Mitchell Energy & Development Corporation, Corporation of the Southwest, and Morris & Aubrey, Appellees.

Court of Appeals of Texas, Houston (1st Dist.), 1995.
902 S.W.2d 20.

This case is a civil action against a hotel for alleged negligence in not providing a sufficient guardrail on the balcony of a hotel room and not warning persons of the possibility of falling off the balcony to their injury or death.

The facts are simple and interesting and should be read to fully appreciate the issues in this case, which involves, among other items, the admissibility of expert testimony and circumstantial evidence. Suffice it to say that a person fell, and at the time of this appeal, and since the incident, he has been in a persistent vegetative state, by falling from the balcony of a hotel guest room. His guardian sued for $12 million and his estranged wife for $1 million. The decision follows:

Before O'CONNOR, HUTSON–DUNN and WILSON, J.J.

* * *
OPINION

O'CONNOR, Justice

The issue in this case is whether a defendant is entitled to a summary judgment when there is no direct proof of causation and the circumstantial evidence is susceptible to conflicting inferences. We hold he is.

The appellant, Matthew Summers, through his guardian Mary Alice Summers (Mrs. Summers), appeals from a summary judgment granted the appellees, Fort Crockett Hotel and Mitchell Development Corporation (collectively, the hotel).[1] Mrs. Summers sued the hotel for negligence after her son fell four stories from the balcony of a hotel room. We affirm.

Fact Summary

In the afternoon of July 12, 1986, Matthew Summers (Matthew), joined his mother and his brother, Michael Summers, at the San Luis Hotel in Galveston for a family party in celebration of Matthew's 25th birthday. Only Mrs. Summers and Michael were booked in the room; they slept on the two double beds. Matthew decided to stay over and sleep on the floor. The room was on the eighth floor.

Matthew and his family spent the afternoon around the pool. Michael Summers stated in his deposition that his brother had about four beers at the poolside. Later, Matthew went to a liquor store and purchased a bottle of Jack Daniels. The three of them took the bottle with them when they went to Gaido's for a late dinner. In her deposition, Mrs. Summers said Matthew had one drink at Gaido's, purchased from the restaurant. After dinner, the three of them went to a country and western dance club where they shared the bottle of Jack Daniels. They each had about three drinks. Around midnight, they left the club and went back to the hotel. Michael went up to the room but Matthew and his mother then went to the lounge at the San Luis where they each had one drink and danced. After about an hour, Matthew and his mother went to the hotel room. Mrs. Summers went to sleep.

Matthew went back downstairs to the hotel's hot tub. About an hour later, he returned to the hotel room, which was located on the eighth floor. He knocked on the door and his mother let him in. They talked briefly and then Matthew told his mother he was going to go out onto the balcony to look at the water. Mrs. Summers said she heard the sliding glass door to the balcony shut and she went to sleep.

About 5:30 A.M., Mrs. Summers awoke to flashing lights on the sliding glass door. When she went to the balcony, police asked her if anyone was missing from the room—that someone had been found on the roof of the building four flights below. She realized Matthew was not in the room. No one witnessed the fall. Matthew has been in a persistent vegetative state since the accident.

The Hotel's Arguments

No one knows what caused Matthew to fall from the balcony and any theory that his fall was caused by a defect in the balcony or the use of the hot tub can only be speculation.

The height, diameter, and design of the balcony railing were not unreasonably dangerous because they complied with all building standards. Nothing about the balcony, including its railing, posed an unreasonable risk of harm.

The railing was a sufficient warning itself. Because the hazards were open and obvious, there was no duty to warn.

The hotel was not negligent in failing to warn Matthew about the use of hot tubs and alcohol. The use of the hot tub, two hours before the accident, was not a proximate cause.

The hotel was not negligent because it had no notice of defects in the premises.

The hotel did not control the hotel beverage service.

Mrs. Summers sued the hotel for negligence, alleging the hotel knew of the unreasonably dangerous condition of the railing—the low height and large width. In her petition, Mrs. Summers also alleged the hotel did not warn that the use of the hot tub in connection with alcohol could cause changes in blood pressure, pulse rate, or problems with balance. Mrs. Summers also alleged that employees and agents of the hotel were negligent in serving Matthew alcohol. Mrs. Summers pled damages of $12 million. Matthew's wife, also a plaintiff in the suit, sought damages of $1 million.[2]

The Hotel's Motion for Summary Judgment

The hotel moved for summary judgment on eight grounds, and the plaintiffs responded to each ground. Below is a summary of their arguments.

The Plaintiff's Response

> There are only three possibilities why Matthew fell—he jumped, he was pushed, or he fell. Mrs. Summers contends she presented evidence that eliminated the possibility her son jumped or was pushed; thus, he must have fallen accidentally. If he fell, it must be because of the balcony's height and design.
>
> Even though the railing met the minimum standards of the building code, it does not mean the hotel is not liable. Compliance with a statute does not preclude a finding that the railing was unreasonably dangerous.
>
> The hotel should have posted a warning on the balcony that the railing met the minimum standards but was of too great a diameter to afford a grip.
>
> There are fact issues with regard to the effect of the use of the hot tub and consumption of alcohol.
>
> The design and height of the balcony handrails was a permanent condition of which the defendants had more than adequate notice.
>
> The alcohol in question was served on the hotel premises.

The Hotel's Summary Judgment Evidence

Attached to the hotel's motion for summary judgment are: (1) the affidavit of James M. Davis, an architect, (2) excerpts from the building code, (3) excerpts from the depositions of Mrs. Summers and Michael Summers, the brother, (4) the affidavit of Ron Vuy, the hotel manager, (5) the affidavit of David Mollendor, another hotel manager, (6) a copy of the hotel bill, (7) a copy of the hotel incident report, (8) excerpts from the deposition of Dr. David E. Clement, an engineer, (9) the affidavit of Burt Cabanas, senior vice president for the Woodlands Corporation, who supervised the management of the hotel at the time of the incident, and (10) the affidavit of Lee D. Tracy, an engineer.

In his affidavit, Davis stated that in his opinion a 42-inch high balcony railing—the height of the one in question in this case—is not unreasonably dangerous for a person.[4] He also stated that the height, diameter, and design of the balcony railing complied with all applicable building codes and the design is one that is typical in the industry. The hotel also included excerpts from the Southern Standard Building Code (1960–61) that states that guard rails for dwellings and within individual dwelling units or rooms may be 36 inches high. In the excerpts from Mrs. Summers deposition, she states that Matthew was not a registered guest at the hotel, and that he did not appear intoxicated at any point during the evening. In the excerpt from Michael Summers, he states that his brother did not show any signs of intoxication, and had full control of his faculties.

In the affidavits of both Vuy and Mollendor, the two managers at the San Luis Hotel stated there had not been any other incidents involving the balcony railings, balcony door sills, or the hot tub. The hotel bill lists three times purchases were made from the hotel bar the night of the incident, totaling $66.99. The hotel incident report stated that the guests in the fourth floor room heard a loud crash about 5:30 A.M. and then saw a man unconscious outside their window. The report stated that an empty beer bottle and a quart of Jack Daniels two-thirds empty were found in Matthew's hotel room. In his deposition, Clement stated that no one knows how Matthew got over the balcony.

In his affidavit, Cabanas stated that there were never any other incidents or complaints involving the balcony railing, balcony door sills, or the hot tub brought to his attention. In his affidavit, Tracy, a loss prevention manager, stated that the handrails on the balconies were installed according to design and that he conducted regular visual site surveys of the balconies and had not observed any deterioration.

Summers' Summary Judgment Evidence

Attached to the response are: (1) the deposition of Mrs. Summers, (2) the deposition of

Michael Summers, (3) the deposition of Dr. Harold Bursztajn, a psychiatrist, and (4) the deposition of David E. Clement, an engineer.

In his deposition, Dr. Bursztajn stated Matthew showed no signs of depression and there was no evidence of a suicide attempt. Bursztajn stated that Matthew had a blood alcohol level of "170" or .17 at the time of the incident[5] and had two driving-while-intoxicated convictions. In his deposition, Clement stated that the top rail of the balcony was 42 inches high.

* * *

Standard of Review

For summary judgment to be proper, the movant must prove it is entitled to judgment as a matter of law, and there are no issues of material fact. Lear Siegler, Inc. v. Perez, 819 S.W.2d 470, 471 (Tex. 1991); Mayer v. State Farm Mut. Auto. Ins. Co., 870 S.W.2d 623, 624 (Tex.App.—Houston [1st Dist.] 1994, no writ). For a defendant to be entitled to summary judgment, the defendant must disprove, as a matter of law, one of the essential elements of the plaintiff's cause of action. Lear Siegler, 819 S.W.2d at 471. On review, we view the evidence in the light most favorable to the non-movant. See id. When a summary judgment does not specify the ground upon which the trial court granted it, the reviewing court will affirm the judgment if any one of the theories advanced in the motion is meritorious. Carr v. Brasher, 776 S.W.2d 567, 569 (Tex. 1989).

In its judgment, the trial court did not specify the ground on which the summary judgment was granted. We note that before issuing the judgment, the trial judge wrote a letter to the parties explaining he planned to grant the summary judgment and giving his reasons. We consider only the judgment. The court denied a motion for new trial.

Proximate Cause

In point of error one, Mrs. Summers contends the court erred in granting the hotel's motion for summary judgment by holding as a matter of law that she cannot recover without direct evidence of the cause of the incident in question, thus imposing an improper burden upon her.

* * *

The hotel contends that Mrs. Summers did not meet her burden of proving causation and that there is no evidence that the hotel's negligence caused the fall. The hotel asserts that once it provided evidence to support its right to summary judgment, it was Mrs. Summers' burden to raise an issue of material fact. The hotel contends that Mrs. Summers' claims are based only on speculation, not direct or circumstantial evidence.

We agree with the hotel. We have held before that causation cannot be established by surmise or suspicion.

> An ultimate fact may be established by circumstantial evidence, but the circumstances relied upon must have probative force sufficient to constitute a basis of legal inference. It is not enough that the facts raise a mere surmise or suspicion of the existence of the fact or permit a purely speculative conclusion. The circumstances relied on must be of such a character as to be reasonably satisfactory and convincing, and must not be equally consistent with the non-existence of the ultimate fact.

Texas Dep't of Corrections v. Jackson, 661 S.W.2d 154, 157 (Tex.App.—Houston [1st Dist.] 1983, writ ref'd n.r.e.).

To prove negligence, the plaintiff must show (1) the defendant owed the plaintiff a duty, (2) the defendant breached that duty, and (3) the defendant's negligence was the proximate cause of the plaintiff's injuries. St. James Transp. Co., Inc. v. Porter, 840 S.W.2d 658, 664 (Tex.App.—Houston [1st Dist.] 1992, writ denied). Proximate cause in Texas consists of two elements: (1) cause in fact and (2) foreseeability. Farley v. M M Cattle Co., 529 S.W.2d 751, 755 (Tex. 1975). Both of these elements must be present. Id. Although proximate cause may be established by circumstantial evidence, it cannot be established by mere conjecture or guess, but rather must be proved by evidence of probative force. Id.

In this case, we find there was no evidence, circumstantial or direct, to show how Matthew got over the balcony railing. Nothing indicates the balcony had anything to do with Matthew's fall and we are left to speculate as to how he fell. We find Mrs. Summers did not present any material fact to show the hotel proximately caused her son's fall.

* * *

Res Ipsa Loquitur

We note that in her brief, Mrs. Summers asserts the doctrine of res ipsa loquitur. In a reply point, the hotel contends Mrs. Summers waived this point because this was not a ground asserted in her response to the motion for summary judgment. We agree and find Mrs. Summers waived this point. Issues not expressly presented to the trial court by written motion, answer, or other response cannot be considered on appeal as grounds for reversal. TEX.R.CIV.P. 166a(c); City of Houston v. Clear Creek Basin Auth., 589 S.W.2d 671, 676 (Tex. 1979); Dickey v. Jansen, 731 S.W.2d 581, 583 (Tex.App.—Houston [1st Dist.] 1987, writ ref'd n.r.e.).

We overrule point of error one.

Balcony Railing Design and Product Liability

In point of error two, Mrs. Summers asserts the trial court erred in granting the hotel's motion for summary judgment by finding that the design of the balcony was not unreasonably dangerous as a matter of law because it complied with all applicable standards. In point of error three, Mrs. Summers asserts that the trial court erred in granting the hotel's motion for summary judgment by holding that a warning was not necessary as a matter of law. We analyze these points of error together as a products liability claim because Mrs. Summers cites Liability 72 C.J.S.Supp. § 2–3. A fundamental principle of the law of products liability is that the plaintiff must prove that the defendants supplied the product that caused the injury. Gaulding v. Celotex Corp., 772 S.W.2d 66, 68 (Tex. 1989). In this case, the hotel did not sell or manufacture the balcony railing and is not liable under a products liability action as a matter of law. We overrule points of error two and three.

Premises Liability

In point of error four, Mrs. Summers contends the trial court erred in granting the hotel's motion for summary judgment on the issue of notice. In point of error five, Mrs. Summers argues that the trial court erred in granting the hotel's motion for summary judgment because there was a question of fact about Mat-

thew's status and the duty owed him. We address these points together.

Mrs. Summers contends the hotel did have notice of the condition of the balcony even though there were no previous incidents or claims involving the railing. Mrs. Summers asserts the hotel was aware of the large diameter of the railing and that it was difficult for someone to grasp it.

The hotel contends that summary judgment was proper because Mrs. Summers did not raise an issue of fact in response to the evidence regarding notice. The hotel contends that its expert, James Davis, an architect, testified that the railing was typical of that used in the industry for the applicable design environment, and was not unreasonably dangerous considering the height, diameter, and design. In this situation, the hotel contends, the danger of falling off a balcony is well known and there is no duty to warn. The hotel argues that the railing itself is a sufficient warning of the danger.

* * *

The Supreme Court also stated that if there are dangers that are open and obvious of which an invitee knows or of which it is charged with knowledge, then the occupier owes the invitee no duty to warn or to protect the invitee. Halepeska v. Callihan Interests, Inc., 371 S.W.2d 368, 378 (Tex. 1963). When there is no duty to warn a person of things he already knows, or of dangerous conditions or activities that are so open and obvious, as a matter of law he will be charged with knowledge and appreciation thereof. Id. In this case, the fact that a person can fall from an eighth story balcony is an open and obvious condition that we find Matthew knew. Even Mrs. Summers stated in her deposition that her son would know he would fall if he went over a balcony railing.

* * *

We affirm the summary judgment granted for the hotel.

---

[1] The Fort Crockett Hotel, Ltd., owns the San Luis Hotel.
[2] Suzanne Summers and Matthew had separated about a year before the accident.
[4] Matthew Summers stood about 5 feet 9 inches tall.
[5] For purposes of most intoxication offenses, a person is considered legally intoxicated with a blood alcohol level of .10 or higher in Texas. TEX.PENAL CODE ANN. § 49.01(2)(B) (Vernon Pamph. 1995).

✔ PRACTICE QUESTIONS

Select the most correct answer to complete each statement.

1. A decision may _____ be based on remote inferences.
   (a) never
   (b) always
   (c) none of the above

2. The admission of circumstantial evidence is
   (a) an inalienable right of a litigant.
   (b) subject to the wide discretion of the trial judge.
   (c) never possible in criminal actions.
   (d) never possible in civil actions.

3. A defendant in a criminal trial may _____ offer evidence as to his or her good character.
   (a) never
   (b) not
   (c) always
   (d) none of the above

4. Reputation of a victim may _____ be relevant when a defendant is charged with homicide of the victim.
   (a) in some cases
   (b) never
   (c) always
   (d) none of the above

5. Circumstantial evidence is evidence that
   (a) goes directly to prove the existence of a fact.
   (b) does not go directly to prove the existence of a fact.
   (c) does not go directly to prove the existence of a fact but gives rise to a logical inference that such fact exists.
   (d) none of the above.

Indicate whether each statement is true or false.

6. A trial judge may never prevent an attorney from asking a question of a witness.

7. Evidence that is relevant may be admitted, even if it is based on surmise, speculation, conjecture, or guess.

CHAPTER 4

Opinion Evidence

§ 4.1 OPINION TESTIMONY

Generally, witnesses may testify as to what they heard, saw, smelled, tasted, or touched. In other words, they may testify as to facts, but they may not testify generally as to a conclusion that they made as a result of the experience of using any one of the five senses. Necessity, however, has dictated that there be exceptions to this general rule.

Two characterizations are given to witnesses with respect to this problem. One type of witness is designated an "expert witness," and the other is a "lay witness."

An expert witness is permitted to testify to conclusions that he or she arrived at as a result of using one or more of his or her five senses. In some situations, a lay witness may also testify to a conclusion. Another way to state this principle is to say that the general rule excluding opinion evidence has many important exceptions, which may be classified into two divisions:

1. opinions of expert witnesses
2. opinions of lay witnesses

§ 4.2 REASON FOR OPINION RULE

The opinion evidence rule is intended to protect against the danger of invasion of the province of the jury. "Opinion testimony in its broadest sense encroaches upon the province of the jury to determine for themselves the ultimate facts of the case." Neb.—McNaught v. New York Life Ins. Co., 143 Neb. 213, 12 N.W.2d 108 (1943).

However, if found by the trial court to be of aid to the jury, an opinion may be admitted notwithstanding it bears directly on the main issue. Ala.—Glover v. City of Birmingham, 255 Ala. 596, 52 So.2d 521, 522 (1951); Neb.—Drahota v. Wieser, 183 Neb. 66, 157 N.W.2d 857, 859 (1968).

§ 4.3 SKILLED OR EXPERT WITNESSES

Many old decisions have held that an inference opinion or conclusion of a skilled or expert witness ordinarily is excluded. However, modern tendency clearly seems to be away from that rule. Ill.—Wawryszyn v. Illinois Cent. Railroad Co., 10 Ill.App.2d 394, 135 N.E.2d 154, 61 A.L.R.2d 801 (1956). It therefore has been held that where the matter under inquiry is properly the subject of expert testimony, it is no objection that the opinion sought to be elicited is on the issue to be decided. U.S.—Miller's Nat'l Ins. Co., Chicago, Ill. v. Wichita Flour Mills Co., 257 F.2d 93 (10th Cir. 1958); Pa.—Whigham v. Metropolitan Life Ins. Co., 35 Berks 457, *modified on other grounds*, 343 Pa. 149, 22 A.2d 704 (1941). Therefore, expert witnesses may be permitted to testify, in the discretion of the trial judge, when issues to be determined by the jury could not be intelligently determined by them without the aid of expert advice. Tenn.—Phillips v. Newport, 28 Tenn.App. 187, 187 S.W.2d 965 (1945).

§ 4.4 EXPERT OPINIONS

§ 4.5 Criminal Cases

In criminal law, an expert opinion is often needed. The advances made in the study of criminology, police science, forensic science, and related disciplines have increased the certainty of solving many crimes. Accordingly, there is need to draw on the expertise of those trained in these disciplines to enlighten the triers of the facts to conclusions that they might not otherwise be able to arrive at. The necessary requirements before an expert may testify, however, remain similar to those found in civil actions. These are as follows:

1. Is the subject on which he or she is to testify one on which the opinion of an expert can be received (i.e., beyond the knowledge of the average person)?
2. What qualifications should an expert possess to qualify to give his or her opinion?
3. Does the witness have these qualifications?
4. Will his or her testimony aid the jury in its search for the truth?

It must be stated at this juncture that the jury may accept or reject the conclusion of the expert witness.

§ 4.6 Probability—Not Sufficient When Standing Alone

The issues that require expert opinions are often those involving variable conclusions. An expert in mathematics would not be needed to explain that, in his opinion, if one adds ten bushels of wheat to a truck that already has ten bushels of wheat in it, the resultant number of bushels would be twenty. There is no probability that the final count of bushels of wheat in the truck would be nineteen or twenty-one. However, when uncertainties are involved in a conclusion, the court, in its search for the truth, may draw on the expertise, experience, and reasoning powers of the expert. The expert, however, does not have to be certain in his or her conclusion. He or she may testify, for example, that it is his or her considered opinion that to a reasonable medical certainty or based on medical probabilities the patient will sustain pain in the future. Wis.—Peterson v. Western Casualty & Sur. Co., 5 Wis.2d 535, 93 N.W.2d 433 (1958).

In most jurisdictions, testimony that a certain cause or effect is possible, conceivable, or reasonable does not constitute substantial evidence or is of little or no probative value. Ill.—Manion v. Brant Oil Co., 85 Ill.App.2d 129, 229 N.E.2d 171 (1967); Pa.—Marushock v. Associated Transport, Inc., 65 Lack.Jur. 145 (1963). The weight that a jury should give to the testimony of an expert witness who testifies that a certain result is probable presents a serious question. In the case of a blood test to establish paternity, when medical science has definitely determined negative results—that it is not possible for a particular person to have fathered the child—an expert may not testify that it is possible that the respondent fathered the child, but he may testify that it is impossible for the respondent to have fathered the child. N.Y.—J. v. J., 35 Misc.2d 243, 228 N.Y.S.2d 950 (1962). It must be kept in mind that mere possibility is not a basis for a finding of fact; it must be more than mere possibility. In the case of the blood test for paternity, it must be established

1. that the blood and the person from whom it was taken are clearly identified and
2. that the test is performed by competent and qualified medical technicians.

The defendant/respondent, however, must be given an opportunity to examine the witness who made the tests as to his competency, the means employed by him, and all other factors having to do with the reliability of the tests. Tenn.—Nicks v. Nicks, 51 Tenn.App. 520, 369 S.W.2d 909 (1962). As is the situation in all expert opinion evidence, the expert should not be permitted to testify based on facts considered by him and statements made to him which were not placed in evidence at the trial. Mo.—Bledsoe v. Northside Supply & Dev., 429 S.W.2d 727, 35 A.L.R.3d 599 (Mo. 1968).

§ 4.7 Weighed Like Other Evidence

Expert opinion is ordinarily to be considered or weighed like other evidence and may not be arbitrarily disregarded; but it is to be disregarded when it is contrary to common sense or knowledge, to undisputed facts, or to physical laws. Ind.—*In re* Meyer's Estate, 138 Ind.App. 649, 215 N.E.2d 556 (1966); Vt.—Kerr v. Rollins, 128 Vt. 507, 266 A.2d 804 (1970).

§ 4.8 EXPERT WITNESS

§ 4.9 Determination of Competency

Whether a particular witness has the necessary qualifications to testify as an expert, and hence to testify as to his or her opinions, is a question to be determined by the court (judge) and not by the jury or a witness. Cal.—Applegate v. Wilson, 156 Cal.App.2d 330, 319 P.2d 401 (1957). This is determined by a preliminary examination of the witness by the proponent's lawyer and the presiding judge. The adversary, through his or her attorney, has this opportunity at an examination known as a voir dire (see Section 2.3, supra).

The adversary may try to cut the proponent's preliminary examination short by saying that "to save the time of the court, the defendant will accept Mr. X as an expert." Make no mistake about it—he or she is not trying to save the time of the court but is trying to hide the expert's unusually high qualifications from the trier of the facts. Cases have held that when the party calling the expert as a witness insists, he or she has a right to have the expert testify regarding his or her qualifications so that the jury might better evaluate the weight of the expert's testimony.

The court has reasonably wide discretion to accept or reject a witness as an expert. It has been held that a witness may qualify as an expert on the basis of study alone. This situation occurs where a qualified person, such as a physician, may study a particular area of medicine and not be examined on it by any licensing authority. N.Y.—People v. Benham, 160 N.Y. 402, 441, 55 N.E. 11, 24 (1899). However, a person cannot become an expert in a specialized area by mere reading of the literature if he has no previous background and training in the general subject. Cal.—Hutter v. Hommel, 213 Cal. 677, 3 P.2d 554 (1931); Conn.—Stressman v. Vitiello, 114 Conn. 370, 158 A. 879 (1932). This does not mean that the court may be arbitrary, unreasonable, and/or capricious in its determination.

§ 4.10 Subjects of Testimony

The subjects of testimony of expert witnesses are not limited to the professions, but special knowledge or experience in any line of human activity not presumably shared by the average jury may authorize a conclusion to be drawn by the expert and testified to by him. D.C.—McReynolds v. National Woodworking Co., 26 F.2d 975 (D.C. Cir. 1928). It is not necessary for the skill or experience to be along desirable or even moral lines. Hence, a prostitute could be called to the stand to testify as to certain vocabulary used in her profession. It is impossible to precisely state a general rule as to subjects on which evidence may be received. However, it is generally agreed that matters of art, science, or technical training are proper subjects of testimony by experts. N.Y.—Goldstein v. Equitable Life Assurance Soc'y of U.S., 160 Misc. 364, 289 N.Y.S. 1064 (1936); Pa.—Pastelak v. Glen Alden Coal Co., 108 Pa.Super. 89, 164 A. 846 (1933).

§ 4.11 Automobile Accident

Police officers frequently are called on to testify as to how an auto accident happened, after the damage has been observed by them, even though they made no observation with respect to the actual coming together of the vehicles. Many large police departments frown on or discourage the use of their officers in civil actions between the parties because of the time lost to the department by the appearance of the officers in court. However, police administrators and officers should remember that in addition to their sworn duty to enforce the law they have the duty to see that justice is done. The officer's presence in court in civil actions is equally important with his or her appearance in the criminal court. The officer should constantly bear in mind that "There, but for the grace of God, go I" and that he or she could be a defendant or a plaintiff in a civil action and would be looking for equal justice under law.

Police officers are not alone in their ability to testify as experts in automobile accident cases. Engineers who satisfy the trial judge of their competence in the discipline they are about to give an opinion on may, in the judge's discretion, give their opinion. Such a situation arose in Tokarz v. Ford Motor Company, 8 Wash.App. 645, 508 P.2d 1370 (1973), in which the plaintiff's engineers testified that a car's drive shaft broke because of a defective weld made during its manufacture and this caused a collision with another automobile.

Usually, a police officer will not be accepted as an expert in this area unless he or she has special qualifications; for example, a patrolman who had fifteen years' experience as a highway patrolman, during which time he had investigated a considerable number of automobile accidents, and who had kept abreast of the field of automobile accident investigations by attending various refresher courses was qualified as an expert to testify as to the speed of automobiles involved in an accident. U.S.—Bonner v. Polacari, 350 F.2d 493 (10th Cir. 1965). It is proper for an expert witness to reconstruct an accident by basing his opinion on exhibits showing the physical facts as well as numerous photographs. Mo.—Edwards v. Rudowicz, 368 S.W.2d 503 (Mo.App. 1963).

§ 4.12 Airplane Crashes

Most police departments do not have qualified personnel to testify as experts in the causes of airplane accidents. Even if they had, it is usually the responsibility of federal law enforcement officers to investigate this type of occurrence. The same rules apply to this area as apply to automobile accidents, in that the mere fact that a person is a pilot and has been one for many years and has flown many miles does not necessarily qualify that person to be an expert to reconstruct the facts surrounding an airplane crash. He or she must have more knowledge and training than that to reconstruct the occurrence.

However, a witness who had flown over eleven thousand hours during twenty-two years, had visited numerous airfields, and had supervised the preparation and operation of several airfields was qualified to state an opinion as to whether a particular field was a safe place for planes to land and to draw inference from wheel tracks, although he lacked technical training and could not claim familiarity with laws relating to the maintenance of airports. U.S.—Beck v. Wings Field, 35 F.Supp. 953 (D.C.E.D.Pa. 1940), *modified on other grounds*, 122 F.2d 114 (3d Cir. 1941).

One who had many years as an assistant flight engineer with previous investigation experience in more than thirty cases of airplane engine overspeed, who made a study of numerous airplane crashes, and who was an inventor of devices concerned with propeller vibration and featherability was held to be a qualified expert witness in an action arising from an airplane accident where an overspeeding propeller was not able to be feathered. U.S.—Noel v. United Aircraft Corp., 342 F.2d 232 (3d Cir. 1964).

§ 4.13 Ballistics and Fingerprints

Many homicides have been solved by identification of the particular gun from which the bullet was fired and by the fingerprints present on the suspect gun. The problem is to get these items admitted as evidence and thus make them part of the trial record. The average layperson is not qualified to identify the markings of a bullet in order to compare them with those on a comparison bullet, nor is he or she qualified to ascertain the similarity of a suspected fingerprint pattern to a comparison fingerprint. In this area, the role of the scientific crimefighter is most important. Therefore, a ballistics expert may express an opinion as to whether a particular bullet was fired from the gun which has been placed in evidence. N.Y.—People v. Soper, 243 N.Y. 320, 153 N.E. 433 (1926). Likewise, a fingerprint expert may express his opinion as to whether or not the fingerprints in question are those of defendant. Cowdrick v. Pennsylvania R. Co., 132 N.J.L. 131, 39 A.2d 98 (1944); N.Y.—People v. Roach, 215 N.Y. 592, 109 N.E. 618 (1915).

§ 4.14 Blood Grouping Test

The problem of blood grouping to determine paternity is one that does not ordinarily concern the law enforcement officer in his or her official duties. Some states have codified this by statute. Results of blood grouping tests are admissible only to establish the impossibility of exclusion of a claimed relationship. N.Y.—J. v. J., 35 Misc.2d 243, 228 N.Y.S.2d 950 (1962); Ohio—State *ex rel.* Freeman v. Morris, 156 Ohio St. 333, 102 N.E.2d 450 (1951). However, in one case of a prosecution for rape, the defendant made a motion for a blood grouping test, and the court granted it, saying, "While it is true that in this prosecution for rape the matter of paternity of the child born to the complainant is not in issue, it nevertheless bears directly upon the question of the credibility of the complainant, for the complainant in her preliminary examination testified that she never had sexual intercourse with anyone except the defendant." N.Y.—People v. Tashman, 233 N.Y.S.2d 744, 745 (1962).

A more recent medical test known as the HLA (human leukocyte antigen) test has been said to fix paternity positively in 99.99 percent of the cases. N.J.—

State v. Whitehead, NJ. 159 Super. 433, 388 A.2d 280 (1986). Some courts are now accepting in evidence DNA tests to prove paternity. This is a more expensive procedure than the HLA test. DNA is more fully explained in Section 16.6.

§ 4.15 Forensic Science

There are many other types of experts who have been permitted to express their conclusions in the profession of forensic science. These include experts in determining the origin of blood and the part of the body that blood came from, identifying human and animal blood, identifying a particular person's blood, identifying semen, problems of broken windows, problems of attacks with firearms, identifying hair, identifying teeth, traces of vehicles, traces of teeth, footprints, questioned documents, speed detection by use of radar and Vascar, blood alcohol tests, and handwriting identification.

§ 4.16 Polygraph

The modern tendency to rely on the infallibility of machines and computers has led many people to believe that the time has come to supplant all testimony at trials and administer a lie detector test to the suspect. The results, so they think, should resolve the issue without error, and there would be no need for courthouses, judges, lawyers, court personnel, and jurors.

There was no need for the aforementioned personnel or buildings when other modes of trial were used in ancient times such as trial by ordeal, the extraction of confessions by torture, etc. Few, if any, polygraph experts would want to be the subject of a polygraph trial if they were accused of committing a heinous crime and were innocent. The natural retort to such a situation is that "It can't happen to me." However, as one lives, one realizes more and more that such things can happen. This is particularly appropriate in the profession of law enforcement, when the enforcer may be the accused. Often the enforcer is wrongfully accused because he or she has been too efficient as a police officer, or prosecutor, or judge and the malefactors in our society, who have no good reputation to lose and who are judgment-proof, point the finger at the law enforcement professional for having engaged in some nefarious activity.

Fortunately, courts have not generally admitted the results of lie detector tests on the ground that such tests are not yet sufficiently reliable and are still too much in the experimental field. Ga.—Wallace v. Moss, 121 Ga.App. 366, 174 S.E.2d 196 (1970); Pa.—Stape v. Civil Serv. Comm'n of City of Philadelphia, 404 Pa. 354, 172 A.2d 161 (1961). They are ordinarily inadmissible regardless of whether submission to the tests is by voluntary agreement, by direction of the court, or by coercion. Mich.—Stone v. Earp, 331 Mich. 606, 50 N.W.2d 172 (1951). In a civil case, it has been held admissible when it was agreed to by both parties. U.S.—Herman v. Eagle Star Ins. Co., 283 F.Supp. 33 (C.D.Cal. 1966). Where evidence was introduced to the effect that a party had submitted to a lie detector test, the court may, in its discretion, admit evidence of the result of the test, at least to the extent necessary to remove any unfair prejudice which might otherwise have ensued from the original evidence. U.S.—California Ins. Co. v. Allen, 235 F.2d 178 (5th Cir. 1956).

In an interesting lower court civil case, Walther v. O'Connell, 72 Misc.2d 316, 339 N.Y.S.2d 386 (1972), it was held that the results of a court-ordered lie detector test may be held admissible. Accordingly, when the testimony of the parties was diametrically opposed, the result of a lie detector test, administered at the direction of the court by a competent expert, was held admissible.

§ 4.17 BLOOD, URINE, BREATH

It is safe to assume that every jurisdiction has a statute that provides that a driver's blood, urine, and/or breath may be tested to ascertain whether or not a designated percentage of alcohol is present in his or her body in order to determine whether or not that driver is intoxicated when he or she is apprehended. Police departments have provided for this contingency by training certain personnel to use various instruments that are available for this purpose. After they are given the necessary training and are also trained in the field, they usually qualify to testify as experts in this area. Various jurisdictions will require a different percentage of alcohol to be present to provide prima facie evidence of the fact that the defendant was intoxicated. Federal and state courts have held that the privilege against self-incrimination of the United States Constitution offers no protection against compulsion to submit to photographing or fingerprinting, to speak, to stand, to make a particular gesture (U.S.—United States v. Wade, 388 U.S. 218, 87 S.Ct. 1926, 18 L.Ed.2d 1149 [1967]), or to submit to a blood examination, providing all possible medical safeguards have been taken to ensure that the proposed defendant is not injured in any way by the taking of the blood sample (U.S.—Schmerber v. California, 384 U.S. 757, 86 S.Ct. 1826, 16 L.Ed.2d 908 [1966]). The blood examination for intoxicated drivers requires certain corroborating factors. The demeanor of the defendant and his or her general appearance must be that of an apparently intoxicated person. Most states have enacted laws that deem that a driver has given his or her consent to be tested with respect to the alcohol content of his or her blood if there are reasonable grounds to believe that he or she is driving while intoxicated. If the driver refuses to take the test, his or her license may be suspended or revoked.

The National Safety Counsel and the American Medical Association have made recommendations to state legislatures for enactment of legislation to establish the percentages of alcohol in a person's blood that should determine, prima facie, various degrees of intoxication. These recommendations have never suggested a strict line of demarcation to be used as a sole criterion by which to judge whether an individual is intoxicated, and thus unfit to drive an automobile. The suggestion is thus made to combine the blood test with other evidence. For many years, this was done by the arresting officer testifying as to what actions he or she had observed in the defendant. Some jurisdictions are now bolstering this chemical and oral testimony with motion pictures or videotapes taken of the defendant while he or she was being examined in the place of detention.

The taking of blood from an intoxicated driver under clean, scientific conditions by qualified personnel has been held not to be contrary to the Fourth Amendment and does not offend a sense of justice. U.S.—Breithaupt v. Abram, 352 U.S. 432, 77 S.Ct. 408, 1 L.Ed.2d 448 (1957); Schmerber v. California, 384 U.S. 757, 86 S.Ct. 1826, 16 L.Ed.2d 908 (1966). Such evidence is admissible when there is corroborating evidence of intoxication. Kan.—Williams v. Hendrickson, 189 Kan. 673, 371 P.2d 188 (1962).

Breath tests, which are easier to administer, also have been held admissible. It has been held that before breath tests are admissible, the burden is on the prosecution to show

1. that the chemicals were compounded to a proper percentage for use in the machine,
2. that the operator of the machine and the machine were under periodic supervision of one who has an understanding of the scientific theory of the machine, and

3. that the witness is qualified to calculate and translate the reading of the machine into the percentage of alcohol in the blood.

Tex.—Hill v. State, 158 Tex.Crim.R. 313, 256 S.W.2d 93 (1953). See also McDonald v. Ferguson, 129 N.W.2d 348 (N.D. 1964).

Urine tests to prove intoxication have also been admissible under circumstances similar to those that apply to the blood and breath tests. D.C.—Bungardeanu v. England, 219 A.2d 104, 16 A.L.R.3d 739 (D.C. 1966). For a discussion of blood as a means of positive identification of a person, see sections 4.14 and 16.6.

§ 4.18 Handwriting Comparison

The process of examining and comparing handwriting does not precisely lend itself to conclusions solely by experts in the field. It has been held that in the absence of statute, when the authorship of a signature or writing is in dispute, other writings established as genuine may be admitted or compared (Ky.—Belcher v. Somerville, 413 S.W.2d 620 [Ky.App. 1967]; N.D.—United States Indus., Inc. v. Borr, 157 N.W.2d 708 [N.D. 1968]) and that the comparison may be made by the jury (Ind.—State *ex rel.* Winslow v. Fisher, 109 Ind.App. 644, 37 N.E.2d 280 [1941]) or by the court or referee trying the case without a jury (Conn.—Shakro v. Haddad, 149 Conn. 160, 177 A.2d 221 [1961]) or by expert witnesses (Ala.—Phillips v. Catts, 220 Ala. 332, 124 So. 884 [1929]).

The United States Supreme Court has held that submitting handwriting specimens for comparison purposes does not violate the United States Constitution. A suspect may even be compelled to give handwriting specimens without violating the Fifth Amendment protection against self-incrimination. U.S.—Gilbert v. California, 388 U.S. 263, 87 S.Ct. 1951, 18 L.Ed.2d 1178 (1967). However, some courts have held that inferences from comparisons of handwriting are far from satisfactory and should be received with great care and caution not only because of the exactness with which handwriting may be imitated, but also because of the dissimilarities to be found in different specimens of the handwriting of the same person executed at different times and under different circumstances. Mich.—Domzalski v. Jozefiak, 257 Mich. 273, 241 N.W. 259 (1932).

§ 4.19 Radar in the Detection of Speeding Vehicles

The public is aware of the widespread use of radar in detecting the speed of vehicles, yet few people are conversant with the scientific facts of radar that determine the speed of vehicles. It is not my intent to explain the Doppler effect, which uses continuous beams of microwaves sent out at fixed frequency. However, suffice it to say that the readings of a radar speed meter are now accepted in evidence, just as the courts have accepted other scientific devices. The courts take judicial notice of these items, and therefore they require no further proof. Mo.—State v. Graham, 322 S.W. 2d 188 (Mo. 1959). Defense attorneys, however, have been challenging the reliability of radar readings and are meeting with some success.

Much depends on various factors such as the competency of the person taking the reading, the causes of erroneous readings, the reliability of the device being used, variations in weather that affect the reading, a radio transmission tower in the vicinity, low-voltage conditions, and malfunction of the equipment. Many books have been published containing exhaustive treatments of the use of radar in speed measurement of motor vehicles.

§ 4.20 Vascar in the Detection of Speeding Vehicles

Vascar is of more recent vintage than radar. It is an acronym for Visual Average Speed Computer and Recorder. Many states have adopted Vascar, and courts have taken judicial notice of its reliability in detecting the speed of moving vehicles. Vascar computes the average distance between two locations, usually previously designated. Again, I do not intend to burden you with the scientific basis for an expert's conclusion, but suffice it to say that experts may come to conclusions based on their scientific knowledge.

For a more complete discussion of radar and Vascar, you are referred to *Defense of Speeding, Reckless Driving and Vehicular Homicide,* by James Farragher Campbell, P. David Fisher, and David A. Mansfield, published by Matthew Bender & Co., Inc., New York, N.Y.

§ 4.21 Spectrograph for Voiceprints

The Michigan State University Department of Audiology and Speech Sciences has been in the forefront of a study to explore the possibility of voiceprinting. Researchers have met with great success in using the spectrograph to develop voiceprints as a method of identification. Courts, however, were reluctant to recognize this technique as being valid, and therefore spectrographs were not admitted in evidence for many years.

Courts are notorious for their inability to accept new concepts and procedures quickly. Perhaps it is better this way, so that change occurs only after testing and retesting to ensure accuracy and justice.

Voiceprints are now admissible in many state and federal courts as a means of identification. U.S.—United States v. Baller, 519 F.2d 463, 17 Cr.L. 2306 (4th Cir. 1975); U.S.—State v. Reed, 18 Cr.L. 2011 (4th Cir.); Cal.—Hodo v. Superior Ct., 30 Cal.App.3d 778, 106 Cal.Rptr. 547, 548 (1973); Mass.—Commonwealth v. Lykus, 367 Mass. 191, 327 N.E.2d 671, 17 Cr.L. 2013 (1975); N.Y.—People v. Rogers, N.Y.L.J. (5/21/76).

A student who is seriously interested in the admissibility of voiceprint identification should obtain and read a report of the annual meeting of the Criminal Justice Section of the American Bar Association, held in Honolulu, August 4, 1974, on voiceprint identification. The report is available from the A.B.A. Criminal Justice Section, 1800 M Street, N.W., Washington, D.C. 20036. A comprehensive analysis also appears in the decisions of Commonwealth v. Lykus (*supra*) and People v. Rogers (*supra*).

In March of 1977, the Pennsylvania Supreme Court in Commonwealth v. Topa, 471 Pa. 223, 369 A.2d 1277 (1977), held that spectrograph techniques with respect to the identification of voices have not been generally accepted by the scientific community. This decision represented a serious setback to the technique. The court also held that the reading of spectrograms was subjective and went on to say, "Thus, as with the lie detector, there is danger that the trial judge or jury will ascribe a degree of certainty to the testimony of the expert spectrography witness which may not be deserved."

With this decision, it cannot be said that all jurisdictions are accepting voiceprints in evidence. You are cautioned to use the latest appellate decisions in your jurisdiction as a guide, inasmuch as the rule of admissibility of voiceprint identification is in such a state of indecision.

The mere fact that voiceprint identification is admissible should not, however, be considered as conclusive by the trier of the facts. Such testimony should be and is subject to the usual cross-examination procedure, and the final determination is up to the trier of the facts to make the ultimate determination of truth or falsity of the identification. Fla.—Coppolino v. State, 223 So.2d 68 (App. 1968). In Florida, Alea v. State, 265 So. 2d 96 (App. 1972), the court held that testimony of experts concerning their spectrographic voiceprint identification of defendant and voiceprints on which experts' opinions were based were admissible but the evidentiary value of the spectrographic voiceprints on which experts based their identification of defendant as person who made allegedly extraordinary telephone calls was for trier of facts. Also see United States v. Raymond, 337 F.Supp. 641 (D.D.C. 1972); United States v. Wright, 17 C.M.A. 183, 37 C.M.R. 447 (1967). This was refined further in a case that required corroboration of defendant's identification by other means. Worley v. State, 263 So.2d 613 (Fla.App. 4th D.C.A. 1972).

§ 4.22 Typewriting Comparison

It is probably apparent to everyone who drives an automobile that although your vehicle may be the same model as your friend's and you may have all the same extra equipment and you may have purchased it at the same time and place, after a short time an experienced driver will get a different feel when driving one vehicle as compared to the other. This same result occurs with typewriters. Therefore, when initially each typewriter had the same typewriting pattern, after use each typewriter assumes its own peculiarities. Accordingly, after examining a document which has been typewritten on a particular typewriter and comparing it with the document in question, a qualified expert may express his opinion as to whether the instrument in question was written on the same typewriter. N.Y.—People v. Storrs, 207 N.Y. 147, 100 N.E. 730, 45 L.R.A.(N.S.) 860 (1912); Okla.—In re Cravens Estate, 206 Okla. 174, 242 P.2d 135, 34 A.L.R.2d 615 (1952). For obvious reasons, this rule can now be applied to printers working in conjunction with computers or word processors.

§ 4.23 Physical and Mental Condition

Sometimes it becomes necessary to seek the assistance of an expert to determine if, to a reasonable medical certainty, the defendant was capable of doing the act that he or she is being charged with. This is usually accomplished by having a physician examine the defendant and report the findings to the court. A person skilled in medicine and physiology may state his inference or judgment relating to the physical condition of another person. Ga.—Gahring v. Barron, 108 Ga.App. 530, 133 S.E.2d 389 (1963); Wis.—Fehrman v. Smirl, 20 Wis.2d 1, 121 N.W.2d 255 (1963), reh'g denied, 20 Wis.2d 1, 122 NW.2d 439 (1963).

The aid of a psychiatrist is looked for if there is suspicion that a defendant does not understand the nature of the offense with which he or she is charged and is unable to assist in his or her defense. The New York Criminal Procedure Law provides for this determination in Sections 730.20 et seq., wherein the court, district attorney, or defense attorney may move for the appointment of two psychiatrists or one psychiatrist and one psychologist, at state expense, to examine the defendant with respect to his or her fitness to stand trial. If the defense attorney wants to dispute the findings of the state-appointed psychiatrist, he or she may do so, and a hearing will be scheduled to determine the issue of fitness alone. At this hearing, the state-appointed psychiatrist is permitted to testify as to his or her findings and will be subject to cross-examination by defendant's attorney. The defendant may have his or her own psychiatrist testify in his or her behalf. The defendant's psychiatrist is also subject to cross-examination. If there is a dispute as to the opinions of the psychiatrists, it is for the trier of the facts to make the proper determination. Each jurisdiction may vary slightly in this procedure, but suffice it to say that the opinions of psychiatrists and psychologists are admissible in these cases.

§ 4.24 Physician

Like the psychiatrist, who is a medical doctor with special training in psychology, the physician may be qualified as an expert to give an opinion with respect to medical diagnosis and prognosis, and this opinion is entitled to great weight. La.— Bass v. Travelers Indem. Ins. Co., 173 So.2d 399 (La.App. 1965); Mo.—Wiener v. Mutual Life Ins. Co. of N.Y., 170 S.W.2d 174 (1943), *rev'd on other grounds*, 352 Mo. 673, 179 S.W.2d 39 (1944). However, when scientific or medical theories or explanations have not become accepted medical fact, opinions based thereon are no stronger or more convincing than the theories. Wis.—Puhl v. Milwaukee Auto Ins. Co., 8 Wis.2d 343, 99 N.W.2d 163 (1959).

§ 4.25 Accountant

In white-collar crimes, the law enforcement officer is often confronted with a lack of expertise in analyzing the entries of accounts and the general bookkeeping procedures used by business. In these cases, it becomes necessary to seek the aid of an accountant. Some states have what are known as registered public accountants, who have been licensed under "grandfather" clauses in legislation. These people were accountants for many years, and by virtue of their extensive experience, they are granted licenses as registered public accountants.

Another category of accountant is the certified public accountant. These accountants, too, are licensed by the state, but they must go through rigorous academic training and pass an acknowledged difficult examination.

In any event, the opinions of registered public accountants and certified public accountants in matters pertaining to the keeping of business records are given great weight. He may state the results of his examination of books and schedules of account. Ariz.—Collison v. International Ins. Co., 58 Ariz. 156, 118 P.2d 445 (1941); Ga.—Payne v. Franklin Co., 155 Ga. 219, 116 S.E. 627 (1923).

§ 4.26 Neutron Activation Analysis

Neutron activation analysis detects the presence of traces of elements in a suspected sample of real evidence. Its adaptation to forensic science is relatively new. For example, if arsenic poisoning is suspected, the expert in neutron activation analysis may conduct tests that will reveal even minute quantities of arsenic. The process was approved and the results thereof were admitted in evidence. U.S.— United States v. Stifel, 433 F.2d 431 (6th Cir. 1970); N.Y.—People v. Pieropan, 72 Misc.2d 770, 340 N.Y.S.2d 31 (1973). For a detailed discussion of the process, you are referred to Am. Jur. Proof of Facts and Am. Jur., Proof of Facts 2d, 1 Am. Jur. Trials 481.

§ 4.27 DNA Fingerprinting

Experts are now able to positively identify a person by comparing samples of blood, semen, skin, and hair roots. This is known as DNA fingerprinting. A discussion of this procedure and reference sources for further information on the subject appear in Section 16.6.

The admissibility of DNA evidence was at first determined by the Frye test. This test was based on a decision in Frye v. United States, 54 App. D.C. 46, 293 F.

1013 (D.C.Cir. 1923). In that case, it was held that novel scientific evidence was admissible only if its proponent demonstrated that the scientific theory or technique was generally accepted in the relevant scientific community. When a novel concept arose, it was very difficult for a proponent to show that the new concept was generally accepted in the relevant scientific community. Hence, some courts accepted DNA evidence, and others refused.

In Daubert v. Merrell Dow Pharmaceuticals, Inc., 509 U.S. 579, 113 S.Ct. 2786, 125 L.Ed.2d 469 (1993), the Court noted that neither the text nor the history of Federal Rule of Evidence 702 indicated an intent to retain the Frye test. Moreover, the general acceptance test was at odds with the Rules' "general approach of relaxing the traditional barriers to 'opinion' testimony." Id. at 579, 113 S.Ct. 2786, 2794, 125 L.Ed.2d 469, 480 (1993). Nevertheless, the Court stated that judges must still admit scientific evidence only when it is reliable. The Court went further in listing a number of factors to consider in determining reliability under Rule 702:

- whether the theory or technique in question has been or can be tested,
- whether the theory or technique has been subjected to peer review and publication,
- the known or potential rate of error of the particular theory or technique and whether means exist for controlling its operation, and
- the extent to which the theory or technique has been accepted.

Once a court determines that scientific evidence is reliable, it must then satisfy itself that the evidence will assist the jury. In *Daubert,* the Court equated this inquiry with the question of relevance; i.e., is the evidence "sufficiently tied to the facts of the case" that it will assist the jury? 509 U.S. at 579, 113 S.Ct. at 2796.

Then, finally, even if a court determines that the requirements of Rule 702 have been met, Rule 403, Exclusion of Relevant Evidence on Grounds of Prejudice, Confusion, or Waste of Time, may still provide grounds for exclusion. To say this in another way, a court must be ever mindful that expert testimony possesses great potential for misleading the jury.

The *Daubert* case did not allude to the fact that in DNA evidence situations it is very important not only to show a chain of custody, but also to show efforts made to effect a continuity of condition. However, it is not required that all possibility of tampering or adulteration be eliminated. U.S.—United States v. Olson, 846 F.2d 1103, 1116 (7th Cir.), *cert. denied,* 488 U.S. 850, 109 S.Ct. 131, 102 L.Ed.2d 104 (1988). It is also necessary that the person who identifies the object testify that it appears to be in the same condition as when previously perceived by him or her. Hammett v. State, 578 S.W.2d 699, 708 (Tex.Crim.App. 1979), *cert. denied,* 448 U.S. 725, 100 S.Ct. 2905, 65 L.Ed.2d 1086 (1980).

On May 2, 1996, the National Academy of Sciences issued a report indicating that because of recent advances in knowledge and technology there is no longer reason to question the courtroom reliability of properly analyzed DNA evidence. The report further stated that the academy had developed a new combination of formulas to calculate the likelihood that a DNA match between evidence and a suspect could be explained by mere coincidence. "By using the latest information about genetic characteristics of the population as a whole, and much improved genetic profiles of racial and ethnic groups, experts have greatly improved their ability to determine whether samples come from different people."

This report was issued by the National Research Council, the academy's operating division. It supersedes a previous report on DNA evidence, issued by an academy committee in 1992, which had been used as a guide by courts and by law enforcement agencies.

The 1996 report says that every effort must be made to eliminate error in collecting DNA evidence at a crime scene and in testing it at a laboratory. All laboratories analyzing genetic evidence, says the report, should adhere to standards developed by professional organizations, such as the Technical Working Group on DNA Analysis and Methods, and should seek accreditation for DNA work by the American Society of Crime Laboratory Directors.

Dr. James Crow, professor emeritus of genetics at the University of Wisconsin, said at a news conference that "the integrity of the chain of custody is critical."

The committee suggested that forensic samples be divided into two or more parts whenever feasible in order to protect against a laboratory error. The remaining parts are then available for confirming laboratory tests.

§ 4.28 CROSS-EXAMINATION OF EXPERT WITNESSES

As indicated previously, a fundamental right guaranteed to every litigant is to have the opportunity to cross-examine a witness. If the right is denied, the direct examination is struck from the trial record. So, too, with the testimony of the expert witness. The fact that an expert may have attained certain intellectual heights does not preclude the idea that he or she might be mistaken or even that he or she might be lying. The law of evidence therefore gives the opportunity to the adverse party to cross-examine the expert concerning his or her knowledge of articles, textbooks, treatises, current publications, and other information in his or her discipline of expertise. The expert may be confronted with extracts from them and asked whether he or she is familiar with them and whether he or she agrees with them.

The reason for this rule is that such cross-examination tests the expert's credibility and reliability by inquiring as to the extent of his familiarity with authorities in his specialty and by asking whether or not he agrees with them. The abstracts with which the witness is confronted on cross-examination do not become affirmative evidence in the case. U.S.—Stottlemire v. Cawood, 215 F.Supp. 266 (D.D.C.1963).

The cross-examination should ordinarily be confined within the general scope of the direct examination. Conn.—Floyd v. Fruit Indus., Inc., 144 Conn. 659, 136 A.2d 918, 63 A.L.R.2d 1378 (1957); Ill.—Young v. Miller, 79 Ill.App.2d 463, 223 N.E.2d 854 (1967). The use of a newspaper clipping has been held to be improper. U.S.—Halsey, Stuart & Co. v. Farmers' Bank of McSherrystown, 37 F.2d 476 (3d Cir. 1930).

The cross-examiner may direct the attention of the expert to others in his or her field who have written a contrary opinion. This is permitted not to prove the contrary opinion, but merely to call into question the weight to be attached by the jury to the opinion of the witness. The cross-examiner may do this even if the writing is not relied on by the witness. He may be asked whether he has relied on or considered any authorities in formulating his opinion. Cal.—Hope v. Arrowhead & Puritas Waters, Inc., 174 Cal.App.2d 222, 344 P.2d 428 (1959). He may be asked to name the authorities on which he has based his testimony. Ill.—Wilcox v. International Harvester Co. of America, 278 Ill. 465, 116 N.E. 151 (1917).

§ 4.29 DIRECT EXAMINATION OF EXPERT WITNESSES

Expert witnesses may be examined in two basic ways:

1. through testimony of the witness based on his or her personal knowledge or observation and
2. through testimony of the witness based on a hypothetical question addressed to him or her in which the pertinent facts are assumed to be true or assumed to be so found by the jury.

The facts included in a hypothetical question must be based on evidence tending to establish them, but the facts need not be uncontroverted or clearly proved, and the court may permit the inclusion of facts as to which the party intends subsequently to offer proof. A question may be allowed even though there is a strong preponderance of evidence against the facts assumed. Cal.—Foremost Dairies, Inc. v. Industrial Accident Comm'n, 237 Cal.App.2d 560, 47 Cal.Rptr. 173 (1965); Ind.—Mounsey v. Bower, 78 Ind.App. 647, 136 N.E. 41 (1922).

In order for a witness to be allowed to compare two writings and state an inference as to whether or not they were written by the same person, it usually must be shown to the reasonable satisfaction of the court that the witness is sufficiently qualified as a skilled observer or expert to make his inference admissible as an aid to the jury. Pa.—In re Martin's Estate, 51 Dauph. 322 (Orph.Ct. 1941). However, a lay witness may compare the disputed writing with other writings proved or admitted to be genuine to refresh his memory, and if he is then able to testify from his memory, as refreshed, his statement may be received. Pa.—McNair v. Commonwealth, 26 Pa. 388 (1856). When it becomes necessary to prove handwriting, a witness acquainted with the handwriting of the supposed writer may be permitted to testify with respect to an opinion as to whether the writing in question was written or signed by him unless it appears that the writing, if made by him, was not in his usual and accustomed handwriting. Pa.—McClure v. Redman, 263 Pa. 405, 107 A.25 (1919). An opinion as to the genuineness of handwriting should be received only from one whose qualifications have been properly established by proof that he is acquainted with the writing of the writer of the document in question. In order for an ordinary witness to testify with respect to his opinion as to the genuineness of a particular writing, proof of the fact that he was acquainted with the handwriting of the supposed writer is sufficient to warrant reception of the witness's testimony, even though he is not skilled in matters of handwriting. A claim of knowledge of handwriting is prima facie sufficient to show qualification, but the fact of knowledge may appear otherwise than claimed. A witness whose knowledge of a person's handwriting was derived from having seen such person write may state an opinion as to whether a particular document was written by such person. Cal.—Armstrong v. Kline, 64 Cal.App.2d 704, 149 P.2d 445 (1944). To render a witness competent (Conn.—Phoenix State Bank & Trust Co. v. Whitcomb, 121 Conn. 32, 183 A. 5 [1936]), the ordinary witness is permitted to testify on the subject of a person's handwriting from a mental standard created by the receipt of letters or other documents from such person, even though he never had seen such person. The genuineness of the documents received by the witness must be established. N.Y.—Dunklin v. Rieglemann, 155 N.Y.S. 561 (1915); 22 C.J. 627 nn. 44, 45; 31A C.J.S. Evidence § 546(20)b.(3). A witness who in the course of official business or any other way has acquired by experience a knowledge of a person's handwriting may state as to whether a particular writing was made by such person. A witness may be deemed sufficiently qualified of the knowledge of the handwriting of the person in question by having seen writings of such person admitted by him. Pa.—Hershberger v. Hershberger, 345 Pa. 439, 29 A.2d 95 (1942). Knowledge may be acquired by paying out money on the signature of the person in question. Cal.—Gibson v. Mailhebuau, 96 Cal.App. 455, 274 P. 566 (1929). Ordinarily, the time when a witness acquired knowledge of a person's handwriting does not affect his competence, even if his knowledge of the handwriting of the person in question was not acquired until after the instrument in consideration was written. Although these matters are proffered for consideration as bearing on the weight to be accorded to his testimony. Pa.—Wilson v. Van Leer, 127 Pa. 371, 17 A. 1097 (1889). To recapitulate, in order for an ordinary witness to testify with respect to handwriting comparison, he must have general knowledge of the handwriting of the supposed writer of the document in question.

§ 4.30 OPINIONS OF LAY WITNESSES

Sometimes a lay witness must form a conclusion, for without it, it would be impossible for the witness to testify to pertinent facts that would enable the trier of the facts to form a conclusion. Accordingly, an ordinary lay witness may be called on to give his or her opinion on a question at issue whenever the facts involved cannot be so described to enable people who were not eyewitnesses to form a proper conclusion with respect to them without the conclusion of the lay witness. In such a case, there is no other way than by permitting the lay witness to express his conclusions with respect to observations made by him. N.M.—State v. Pruett, 22 N.M. 223, 160 P. 362, L.R.A.1918A 656 (1916). Usually, the qualification of an ordinary witness in this type of situation consists of just common ordinary knowledge, without other qualification. The opinions of lay witnesses have been accepted by the courts in the following situations:

1. The witness may have seen the person write, but it is not essential.
2. The witness may have received documents that created a mental image of receipt of such documents from such person.
3. The witness may have acquired experience with respect to a knowledge of the subject person's handwriting.
4. The time lapse between the acquisition of knowledge and the testimony does not affect its admissibility.

In testifying to handwriting, certainty is not essential. His statement may be allowed to go to the jury if the witness testifies to a belief, an impression, an opinion, or even a thought or states that he perceives a resemblance, although he declines to swear positively with respect to the matter. Mass.—Commonwealth v. Andrews, 143 Mass. 23, 8 N.E. 643 (1886), 22 C.J. 630, 32 C.J.S. Evidence § 546(20)c.

§ 4.31 TESTIMONY OF LAY WITNESS

§ 4.32 Handwriting Comparison

Bank tellers who cash checks and/or give out money to depositors when the depositors present signed withdrawal slips are not necessarily schooled in handwriting comparison. They are thus considered skilled laypeople with regard to the recognition of the handwriting of the people who present these articles to them for payment. Notwithstanding that fact, they, as laypeople, have to come to a conclusion in their recognition of the validity of signatures presented to them. Some banks require more than one teller to look at the signature and compare it with the signature that the bank has on file before payment is made.

You will remember that an expert witness may draw conclusions to aid the jury in its determination. The jury may accept or reject the opinion of the expert. In the area of comparison, the jury may also make its own determination as to the identity of the person from the handwriting specimens that are admitted in evidence. However, a witness who is not necessarily a professional handwriting student or expert may testify as to the genuineness of written instruments and signatures if he can reasonably satisfy the court that the witness is a skilled observer who can aid the jury in its determination. N.Y.—Daniels v. Cummins, 66 Misc.2d 575, 321 N.Y.S.2d 1009 (1971); N.Y.—Clayton v. Prudential Ins. Co. of America, 4 N.C.App. 43, 165 S.E.2d 763 (1969); R.I.—Wooddell v. Hollywood Homes, Inc., 105 R.I. 280, 252 A.2d 28 (1969).

In some cases, nonexpert witnesses were not permitted to express an opinion as to handwriting based on a comparison of the document in question. Ill.—Yelm v. Masters, 81 Ill.App.2d 186, 225 N.E.2d 152 (1967); Pa.—*In re* Martin's Estate, 51 Dauph. 322 (Orph.Ct. 1941).

As you can understand from the above, there is great disparity in the acceptance by the courts of nonexpert witness testimony in handwriting comparison. Accordingly, whether a witness may testify as to handwriting comparison is largely within the discretion of the trial court. Idaho—Lowe v. Skaggs Safeway Stores, 49 Idaho 48, 286 P. 616 (1930); N.C.—State v. Cofer, 205 N.C. 653, 172 S.E. 176 (1934).

§ 4.33 Emotion

A lay witness may testify as to the state of a person's emotions manifested by a person (e.g., whether he appeared to be angry or jesting) (N.Y.—Blake v. People, 73 N.Y. 586 [1878]); however, the motive, intention, or belief may not be the subject of testimony based on opinion, since this involves recital of someone else's state of mind. Testimony may not be allowed to the effect that the deceased person had gone to the certain street for a particular purpose. N.Y.—Bogart v. City of New York, 200 N.Y. 379, 93 N.E. 937 (1911).

A lay witness may be allowed to state that a person appeared to be agitated or upset and hostile. N.H.—Hardy v. Merrill, 56 N.H. 227, 22 Am.Rep. 441 (1875); Tenn.—Johnson Freight Lines, Inc. v. Tallent, 53 Tenn.App. 464, 384 S.W.2d 46 (1964).

§ 4.34 Sensations

An ordinary witness may testify as to his own sensory experiences, such as taste, e.g., a certain beverage which he drank appeared to be whiskey (N.Y.—People v. Marx, 128 A.D. 828, 112 N.Y.S. 1011 [1908]) or that he felt intoxicated (N.Y.—*in re* Ronny, 40 Misc.2d 194, 242 N.Y.S.2d 844 [1963]) or that he felt heat or cold.

§ 4.35 Physical Condition of a Person

A lay witness may testify as to the apparent strength, vigor, feebleness, or illness of a person. He may testify concerning physical injury or conditions susceptible to observation by an ordinary person. Cal.—Pacific Employers Ins. Co. v. Industrial Accident Comm'n, 47 Cal.App.2d 494, 118 P.2d 334 (1941).

§ 4.36 Identification by Voice

A witness who is conversing with the voice of another may testify that he knew the voice of the other person, that he had spoken with this person previously on the telephone and could positively identify the person he spoke with as being the voice of his adversary. There is sufficient identification if the witness knew the speaker and recognized his voice at the time of the telephone conversation. N.Y.—Murphy v. Jack, 142 N.Y. 215, 217, 36 N.E. 882, 883 (1894). Even if the witness was not acquainted with the speaker and did not recognize his voice at the time of the telephone conversation, the telephone conversation is admissible if the witness testifies that he met the speaker for the first time thereafter and then recognized his voice as the voice he heard over the telephone. The difference affects the weight, rather than the competency, of the evidence. Ga.—Jones v. Britt, 75 Ga.App. 142, 42 S.E.2d 648 (1947); N.Y.—People v. Strollo, 191 N.Y. 42, 83 N.E. 573 (1908).

§ 4.37 Intoxication

Under most authorities, a lay witness may testify as to whether or not another person was intoxicated at a particular time or place, provided he had a suitable opportunity for observation. N.J.—Searles v. Public Serv. R.R. Co., 100 N.J.L. 222, 126 A. 465 (1924); N.Y.—Donahue v. Meagley, 220 A.D. 469, 221 N.Y.S. 707 (1927). If a witness testifies that the person was intoxicated, he may state the extent of his intoxication (Iowa—State v. Cather, 121 Iowa 106, 96 N.W. 722 [1903]), or a witness may state whether a person had been drinking. (Md.—Cumberland & Westernport Transit Co. v. Metz, 158 Md. 424, 149 A. 4, *reargument denied*, 158 Md. 424, 149 A. 565 [1930]). On the other hand, testimony that a person was sober at a particular time has been held a mere conclusion. Ill.—Klopp v. Benevolent Protective Order of Elks, Lodge 281, 309 Ill.App. 145, 33 N.E.2d 161 (1941). A police officer's testimony with respect to observation of intoxication has been held admissible. Facts on which the opinion is based must be stated. Ga.—Hill v. Rosser, 102 Ga.App. 776, 117 S.E.2d 889 (1960).

§ 4.38 Mental Condition or Capacity of a Person

Although there is some contrary authority, as a general rule an ordinary or nonexpert witness who through acquaintance or association has had reasonably adequate opportunity to observe another person and to form a conclusion or opinion as to the mental condition of such person may, on the basis of such facts in his knowledge and observation thereof, state his opinion as to the mental condition of such person. Pa.—*In re* Owens' Estate, 167 Pa.Super. 10, 74 A.2d 705 (1950).

It has been held that opinions as to the mental condition or capacity of a person expressed by a qualified lay witness may possess substantial evidentiary value. La.—Succession of Chopin, 214 So.2d 248 (La.App. 1968). In other court cases, it was held to possess great weight where the witness was an attorney who drafted a will (Pa.—*In re* Masciantonio's Estate, 392 Pa. 362, 141 A.2d 362 [1958]; Va.—Forehand v. Sawyer, 147 Va. 105, 136 S.E. 683 [1927]) or where the witness was a subscribing witness to a will (Mich.—People v. Cole, 382 Mich. 695, 172 N.W.2d 354 [1969]; Mo.—Thompson v. Curators of University of Mo., 488 S.W.2d 617 [Mo. 1973]; W.Va.—Floyd v. Floyd, 148 W.Va. 183, 133 S.E.2d 726 [1963]).

§ 4.39 Rational or Irrational Nature of a Person's Conduct

An ordinary witness may testify as to whether a person's conduct was rational or irrational, but he may not testify that the person was of sound or unsound mind except in the case of a witness who is a subscribing witness to a will. Mich.—Henderson v. Henderson, 206 Mich. 36, 172 N.W. 623 (1919); N.Y.—Holcomb v.

Holcomb, 95 N.Y. 316 (1884); Falkides v. Falkides, 40 A.D.2d 1074, 339 N.Y.S.2d 235 (1972).

§ 4.40 Identity

An ordinary witness may, under proper circumstances where he is shown to be possessed of adequate knowledge and the capacity to apply it, be allowed to state his inference or opinion on the question of identity, whether the inquiry relates to the identity of human beings, animals, or inanimate things. The witness may also state an inference as to the correspondence of footprints. Ill.—Starkey v. Lindsey, 8 Ill.App.3d 871, 290 N.E.2d 649 (1972); N.C.—State v. Reitz, 83 N.C. 634 (1880).

§ 4.41 Speed of Moving Vehicles

An ordinary witness may testify to the rate of speed that a vehicle was moving, but he must first show some experience in observing the rate of speed of moving objects or give some other perspectory reason. N.Y.—Penny v. Rochester Railway Co., 7 App.Div. 595, 40 N.Y.S. 172 (1896), *aff'd* (1896), 154 N.Y. 770, 49 N.E. 1101 (1896); S.C.—Livingston v. Oakman, 251 S.C. 611, 164 S.E.2d 758 (1968).

§ 4.42 REVIEW OF OPINION EVIDENCE OF ORDINARY WITNESS

In Hardy v. Merrill, 56 N.H. 227, 22 Am.Rep. 441, 448–449 (1875), the court said the opinions of ordinary witnesses may be received as follows:

> Court and text writers all agree that upon questions of science and skill, opinions may be received from persons specially instructed by study and experience in the particular art or mystery to which the investigation relates . . . all concede the admissibility of the opinions of non-professional men upon a great variety of unscientific questions arising every day, and in every judicial inquiry. These are questions of identity, handwriting, quantity, value, weight, measure, time, distance, velocity, form size, age, strength, heat, cold, sickness and health; questions also, concerning various mental and moral aspects of humanity, such as disposition, . . . intoxication, veracity, general character, and particular phases of character, and other conditions and things, both moral and physical. . . .

From the above, you can see that there are many areas in which a lay witness may express a conclusion. The conclusions are those that ordinary people make in their daily lives and are the common experience of most people.

As with the opinions of experts, the jury or judge trying the facts may either accept or reject the conclusions of the lay witness and substitute other conclusions in the findings of fact.

§ 4.43 FEDERAL RULE

Federal Rule of Evidence 701 provides:

§ Rule 701. Opinion Testimony by Lay Witnesses

If the witness is not testifying as an expert, the witness' testimony in the form of opinions or inferences is limited to those opinions or inferences which are (a) rationally based on the perception of the witness and (b) helpful to a clear understanding of the witness' testimony or the determination of a fact in issue.

This rule gives the judge wide discretion in permitting opinions by lay witnesses. Witnesses often have difficulty expressing themselves in language that is not a conclusion or an opinion. It is thought that the adversary system of cross-examination will point up weakness if the judge overreaches his or her discretion in allowing conclusions of lay witnesses to be admitted in evidence. Similar provisions are to be found in California Evidence Code 800, Kansas Code of Civil Procedure 60–456(a), and New Jersey Evidence Rule 56(1).

Within the scope of this rule are not only experts in the strictest sense of the word (e.g., physicians, physicists, and architects), but also the large group sometimes called "skilled" witnesses, such as bankers or landowners testifying to land values or automobile mechanics testifying as to a malfunction in an automobile or the value of repairs to an automobile.

CROSS-REFERENCES

Federal Civil Judicial Procedure and Rules (West 1996) (Rules 702, 703, and 704).

Goode & Wellborn, Courtroom Handbook on Federal Evidence (West 1995) (Rules 702, 703, and 704).

McCormick, Evidence (4th ed. 1992) (Rules 702, 703, and 704).

RELATED DECISIONS
Opinion Evidence

Stafford v. Mussers Potato Chips, Inc.

Supreme Court, Appellate Division, Fourth
Department, 1972.
39 A.D.2d 831, 333 N.Y.S.2d 139.

The *Stafford* case is an example of a very frequent occurrence for police officers engaged
in motor vehicle traffic accident problems.
Most often the officer arrives at the scene after the accident has occurred. Some police departments require the officer to make a report
of the incident, wherein the officer is required
to indicate the cause of the accident and location of the point of impact. The officer will
obtain this information from witnesses or the
participants in the accident and may then indicate who was at fault. As you will learn later
in this book, this information is derived from
hearsay evidence, which is generally not admissible in court. There are, however, certain
exceptions to the hearsay exclusionary rule
that are discussed in detail in Chapters 6, 7, 8,
9, 10, 11, and 13 of this book.

In the *Stafford* case, the court writes about
what information a police officer may not be
permitted to testify to in a trial unless the officer has special training to qualify him or her
as an expert in the particular matter that is
the subject of the inquiry. The decision follows:

Before DEL VECCHIO, J. P., and WITMER,
MOULE, CARDAMONE and HENRY, JJ.
    MEMORANDUM:
    On April 17, 1966 at about 8:20 P.M. dece-
dent's pickup truck was proceeding northerly
on a two-lane macadam highway when it collided with defendant's southbound tractor
trailer at a point where there was a slight in-
cline proceeding south. Decedent and his passenger were killed. There was no eyewitness to
the accident. It was dark at the time. Skid
marks from the southbound vehicle veered
across into the northbound lane and debris
was scattered all around. Photographs showing the conditions immediately after the acci-

dent were received in evidence. Although
parts of defendant's examination before trial
were read into evidence, no explanation for
the accident was offered by defendant. At the
close of plaintiff's proof the court granted defendant's motion for a nonsuit, severed defendant's counterclaim and continued the trial
on the counterclaim. In our opinion upon all
the proof a prima facie case was made out sufficient to go to the jury to determine liability
in plaintiff's action. (Pfaffenbach v. White
Plains Express Corp., 17 N.Y.2d 132, 269
N.Y.S.2d 115, 216 N.E.2d 324 [1940]).

    The trial court based its dismissal on the
testimony of the state trooper who investigated the accident. He was permitted upon
cross-examination to fix the point of impact
in the southbound or defendant's lane of
travel. We have previously held that the receipt into evidence of such testimony is error,
since the trooper was not qualified as an expert, and even had he been, the conclusion he
drew as to the point of impact was within the
competence of the jury (Sacco v. Bodwitch,
34 A.D.2d 885, 312 N.Y.S.2d 259 [1971]).
The right to have a jury pass on questions of
fact may be taken from them only when "by
no rational process could the trier of the facts
base a finding in favor of the defendant upon
the evidence here presented" (Blum v. Fresh
Grown Preserve Corp., 292 N.Y. 241, 245, 54
N.E.2d 809, 811 [1944]). The Court should
take that view of the evidence most favorable
to the nonmoving party and from the inferences reasonably to be drawn therefrom determine whether a verdict might properly and
lawfully be found for the nonmoving party
(Wessel v. Krop, 30 A.D.2d 764, 291 N.Y.S.2d
986 [1937]). We are persuaded from a review
of the facts and exhibits in this case that a
verdict in favor of the plaintiff would not
have to be set aside as legally insufficient. We
note further that where plaintiff is dead and
there is no eyewitness, the plaintiff is not held
to as high a degree of proof of the cause of action as where an injured plaintiff can himself

describe the occurrence (Noseworthy v. City of New York, 298 N.Y. 76, 80, 80 N.E.2d 744, 745 [1948]). Finally, although plaintiff's attorney's objections were not made as timely as they should have been, the record makes clear that he did object to the trooper's conclusions and took an appropriate exception to the judge's order granting the motion of dismissal. We deem this sufficient to preserve the point of appeal, and even were it not, we should reverse in the interest of justice (Van v. Clayburn, 21 A.D.2d 144, 249 N.Y.S.2d 310 [1964]). Judgment reversed on the law and facts and a new trial granted with costs to abide the event.

* * *

Turbert v. Mather Motors, Inc.
Supreme Court of Connecticut, 1973.
165 Conn. 422, 334 A.2d 903.

This case is a follow-up of the ideas expressed in the preceding case. However, it is more specific as to what an officer may not testify to regarding the facts of an intersection motor vehicle accident and a conclusion concerning the cause of the accident to which the officer was not an eyewitness. By reading and understanding the principles of law in this case, a police officer in an administrative position is well advised as to what is a proper question on a printed accident investigation form that officers are required to complete as part of their written report of the occurrence. Carefully reading and analyzing the decision in this case are imperative to proper performance by an officer whose duties include the design of printed accident report forms.

There are also other basic legal principles in this decision. I urge you to find each of these principles in the same way that you might solve a puzzle.

COTTER, Associate Justice.

* * *

The defendant Smith had been driving his car south on Windsor Avenue at about 10 P.M. on the evening of the collision; directly after the accident the Smith car was located on the east side of the northbound lanes heading in a northeasterly direction, north of the Daley car which also came to rest in the northbound lanes partly in the driveway leading into the supermarket, facing in a northeasterly direction.

The defendant Smith had stopped at the traffic light with his left blinker on, intending to make a left-hand turn into the driveway. A car was stopped in the left-hand northbound lane, and when the light turned green for him, Smith waited for that car to move northerly, which it failed to do. Smith proceeded to make a left-hand turn and as he did so he was struck by the Daley car which was in the right-hand northbound lane.

The posted speed limit in the vicinity of the collision was thirty-five miles per hour in both directions; the portion of Windsor Avenue from 200 yards to the south of the opening in the esplanade in front of the twenty-four-foot-wide supermarket driveway to a point approximately 200 yards to the north of that opening was generally level and substantially straight.

When the vehicles stopped immediately after the collision, the right rear portion of the Daley car was approximately six and one-half feet from the east curb line of Windsor Avenue, on the traveled portion of the northbound lanes adjacent to the supermarket driveway entrance, and the rear portion of the Smith car also came to rest on the traveled portion of Windsor Avenue.

The defendant Daley claims that the trial court erred in instructing the jury under General Statutes § 14–299(b) which he argues is inapplicable to the facts of this case so that the instructions imposed inconsistent duties upon the drivers and confused the jury; and that the trial court erred in limiting the cross-examination of a police officer and excluding an exhibit offered by the defendant.

The determinative issue in this case is whether, as the defendant Daley contends, the trial court erred when it charged the jury pursuant to General Statutes § 14–299(b), which regulates the right-of-way at intersections when traffic is directed by traffic control signals exhibiting colored lights. The crux of the defendant's argument is that the rules prescribed by § 14–299(b) apply, by its specific terms, only to intersections as defined by General Statutes § 14–1(18) which states that an intersection "means the area embraced within the prolongation of the lateral curb lines of two or more highways which join one another at an angle, whether or not one such highway crosses the other." The defendant Daley claims that the area in question does not fall within the statutory definition because, as he argues, there is only one highway as defined by General Statutes § 14–1(16), despite the existence of traffic control signals suspended over the highway and at the supermarket entrance, a one-hundred-foot break in the esplanade, a five-second lead green light to allow southbound cars to turn left into the parking area, a pedestrian crosswalk enclosed by painted lines, and "trip" mechanisms at the entrance to control the light.

Section 14–299(b) of the General Statutes is the only section which governs motor vehicle operational conduct at areas controlled by signals exhibiting colored lights and which, at the time of the collision, mandated rules applicable to drivers facing green lights at intersections. There was no statute which specifically governed the conduct of drivers at traffic control signals exhibiting colored lights at areas other than "intersections." The trial court did not instruct the jury that the site of the accident was an intersection as the word is commonly used or an "intersection" within the meaning of the term as defined by § 14–1(18). Rather, the court charged that there was a statute which applied when a light changed from green to red and which defined the meaning of the green light. The court then quoted portions of the statute, including that language which required that traffic facing a green signal must yield to traffic lawfully within the intersection. The issue presented, therefore, assuming arguendo that the area controlled by the traffic light was not an intersection within the definition of § 14–1(18), is whether the trial court's statement defining the legal duties of drivers confronting a green light at an intersection was correct as applied to operators facing the green light controlling traffic on the four-lane highway, the crossover area and the supermarket drive-in.

Other jurisdictions have resolved the enigma wherein the legislature did not in statutory language specifically provide rules for particular factual situations involving traffic lights, e.g., the Supreme Court of Nebraska has held, where there was no statute relating to left turns at a traffic light, that "[i]n the absence of a statute or ordinance, the meaning to be given to a traffic control signal is that

which a reasonably prudent motorist would understand and apply." Heavican v. Holbrook, 187 Neb. 814, 818, 194 N.W.2d 208, 211 (1972); Galloway v. Hartman, 271 N.C. 372, 377, 156 S.E.2d 727 (1967); C.J.S. Motor Vehicles § 360(1), p. 536. Furthermore, some jurisdictions have held that statutes governing intersections applied to areas which appeared to be intersections but were not technically intersections because private roads were abutting public roads. Grulich v. Paine, 231 N.Y. 311, 132 N.E. 100 (1921); Perry v. Carter, 14 La. App. 102, 129 So. 388 (1930). The rationale of these cases was stated succinctly by the New York Court of Appeals in the *Grulich* case, supra, 231 N.Y. 316, 132 N.W. 102 (1921), wherein a railroad depot driveway abutted a public road:

> "The statutes are intended to promote safety, order and convenience. The same reasons why drivers of motor vehicles should observe the rules that are generally accepted and enforced in crossing streets where another street intersects or abuts, exist at the entrance of the driveway in question as if it had been dedicated to and accepted by the public."

References in a charge to the jury concerning the rights and duties of motorists in intersections have been held not erroneous in the case involving a collision which occurred when an automobile was making a left turn into a shopping center parking lot on a divided four-lane highway. The court reasoned that regardless of whether the area in question was an intersection, the trial court's charge was not prejudicial because it correctly stated the applicable law. Gilmore v. Marsh, 424 Pa. 361, 227 A.2d 881 (1967).

A driver when faced with a green light at an intersection must act as a reasonably prudent person with a knowledge that he cannot proceed in disregard of other vehicles in the intersection. General Statutes § 14–299(b); Gorman v. American Sumatra Tobacco Corporation, 146 Conn. 383, 386, 151 A.2d 341 (1959); Rose v. Campitello, 114 Conn. 637, 640, 159 A. 887 (1932). We have also said that in determining what is reasonable care under all the circumstances and what rules of the road are applicable, the conduct of the parties should be judged from the viewpoint of the reasonably prudent person. Although an area may not fall within the prescribed definition of an intersection, we have held that a pedestrian was justified in assuming that a driver was subject to the usual intersection rules and, therefore, that he would keep to the right of the center of the highway in turning to his left into a private entrance. McInerney v. New England Transportation Co., 131 Conn. 633, 635, 41 A.2d 764 (1945); Heavican v. Holbrook, supra. In the *McInerney* case, supra, the plaintiff was struck by a bus at an area where a private way intersected a public street. The defendant maintained that there was no requirement, as in the case of public street intersections, to keep to the right of center of such an intersection. This court rejected this contention and stated (131 Conn. pp. 634–635, 41 A.2d p. 764): "The jury were bound to consider the conduct of the plaintiff from the viewpoint of the reasonably prudent person and might well have found that to such a person the private way would have appeared to have been part of the city highway system subject to the rules of the road relating to public ways."

Automatic traffic control systems are intended to minimize the dangers inherent at the locations where they are installed and it is the duty of motor vehicle operators to obey and observe traffic signals. Drivers, passengers and pedestrians, for instance, have a right to assume that an apparently legal traffic light was placed by legal authority, which is not disputed in the case before us, that the parties act accordingly as reasonably prudent persons under the circumstances, and that the signal is still effective to control the question of negligence of one who disregards it, at least to the extent that such disregard may be taken into consideration as one of the circumstances to be passed upon. Geisking v. Sheimo, 252 Iowa 37, 41, 105 N.W.2d 599 (1960); note, 164 A.L.R. 8, 216; Blashfield, Automobile Law & Practice (Perm.Ed.) §§ 686.5, 998, 1040.

Regardless of whether the area in question be considered an intersection within the meaning of General Statutes § 14–1(18), the trial court did not erroneously impose legal burdens upon the drivers at the area in question which reasonably prudent drivers should not have assumed. Application of different standards to drivers facing green lights at divided highways with enclosed cross-walks and cross-vehicular traffic but not a statutory "intersection" would be contrary to the interests of safety and good order by contravening the normal expectations of reasonably prudent drivers, and a statutory definition is not always applicable to a complicated traffic pattern. Baird v. Gaer Bros., Inc., 152 Conn. 219, 223, 205 A.2d 490 (1965); Mathis v. Bzdula, 122 Conn. 202, 206, 188 A. 264 (1937). Statutory rules of the road are to be interpreted in light of their purpose to prevent collisions, "and, if their meaning is not definitely settled by the language used, they are to be interpreted in the light of their application to traffic moving over the highways." Mathis v. Bzdula, supra, 205, 188 A. 265 (1937). Constructions are to be avoided which are impractical and undesirably rigid. Baird v. Baer Bros., Inc., supra, 152 Conn. 223, 205 A.2d 490 (1965).

Not to utilize the statute, § 14–299(b), in instructing the jury under the circumstances of this case would lead to absurd consequences or to "possible bizarre results"; Bridgeport v. Stratford, 142 Conn. 634, 641, 642, 116 A.2d 508 (1955); since operators of motor vehicles might otherwise justifiably disregard such traffic control signals with impunity.

The defendant Daley claims not only that § 14–299(b) was inapplicable but also that it prescribed a different right-of-way than the statute under which he requested the trial court to charge, General Statutes § 14–242(a). The court instructed the jury pursuant to both statutes paraphrasing § 14–242(a). Immediately following this recitation, the court specifically told the jury, clearly applying § 14–242(a) to the southbound defendant that unless the jury found that the defendant Smith made a left turn to enter the supermarket parking lot at a time when it could not be done with reasonable safety, the jury must find that defendant negligent.

Although § 14–242(a) does embody a standard for vehicles turning left into a private alleyway, it has often been applied to left turns at intersections. Ramonas v. Zucker, 163 Conn. 142, 147, 302 A.2d 242 (1973); Michaud v. Gagne, 155 Conn. 406, 409, 232 A.2d 326 (1967); Kronish v. Provasoli, 149 Conn. 368, 371, 179 A.2d 823 (1962). The legislature has recognized that a standard of reasonable safety applies both to left turns into private alleys and left turns within intersections with its recent repeal of § 14–246 (Public Acts 1971, No. 66) and enactment of § 14–242(e), which in specific terms imposes the same duties upon drivers intending to turn left in either case. This duty is the same upon a driver facing a green light, intending to turn left; § 14–299(b); except to the degree that it may impose a higher standard of care in requiring the driver to yield not only to vehicles within the intersection or extended lateral lines but also to those so close as to constitute an imminent hazard. Yet a driver facing a green light must operate his vehicle with reasonable safety and cannot disregard the presence of other vehicles which might be approaching the intersection. Pinto v. Spigner, 163 Conn. 191, 196, 302 A.2d 266 (1973); Rose v. Campitello, 114 Conn. 637, 640, 159 A. 887 (1932).

The evidence at the trial was in sharp conflict as to the relevant and material facts surrounding the collision and the jury could properly conclude that the negligence of either Daley or Smith or of both caused the collision and the resultant injuries to the plaintiff. The question was one of fact and was resolved by the verdict.

* * *

Finally, the defendant Daley contends that the trial court improperly rejected cross-examination of a police officer, not an eyewitness, which attempted to elicit from the officer his understanding of what the defendant Daley meant when Daley told the officer that the southbound car turned "behind" the third unidentified vehicle in the left northbound lane. The court also rejected the officer's report because it contained the officer's conclusion as to the cause of the accident. The officer was allowed to read portions of his report and testify from it concerning what the defendant told him. Both defendant and plaintiff testified and submitted to cross-examination.

The admissibility of lay opinions is within the trial court's discretion and its decision will not be reversed unless that discretion is abused. State v. Orsini, 155 Conn. 367, 372, 232 A.2d 907 (1967). The trial court could reasonably conclude that a police officer, not a witness to the accident, was being asked to give his opinion as to what in fact happened at the time of the collision. When questioned concerning his intent in writing a certain paragraph of his report, he stated: "I drew a conclusion what caused the accident." The court did not abuse its discretion in refusing to admit the testimony or the report. As we said in Mucci v. LeMonte, 157 Conn. 566, 569, 254 A.2d 879, 881 (1969): "Moreover, a police officer's conclusion about the cause of or responsibility for an injury is merely an opinion which the officer would not be permitted to give if he was on the witness stand. Giamattei v. DiCerbo, 135 Conn. 159, 163, 62 A.2d 519 (1949)." See McCormick, Law of Evidence § 56.

There is no error.

In this opinion the other judges concurred.

RELATED DECISIONS
Expert Witnesses

Daubert v. Merrell Dow Pharmaceuticals, Inc.

Supreme Court of the United States, 1993. 509 U.S. 579, 113 S.Ct. 2786, 125 L.Ed.2d 469.

In the following case, infants and their guardians ad litem brought a civil action against the defendant for birth defects allegedly caused by the use of Bendectin, a prescription antinausea drug marketed by the respondent pharmaceutical corporation. A guardian ad litem is appointed by the court to protect the infant in a case before the court and may bring an action or defend an action in behalf of an infant.

Previous to this case, scientific expert opinion was permitted in evidence based on a celebrated test that became generally known as the Frye "general acceptance" test. This test evolved from the decision in Frye v. United

States, 54 App. D.C. 46, 47, 293 F. 1013, 1014 (D.C. Cir. 1923).

While there was constant improvement in scientific knowledge, it became very difficult, almost impossible, to get this new scientific knowledge admitted in evidence because the Frye test imposed a rigid "general acceptance" requirement for admission of scientific evidence.

The Federal Rules of Evidence have established a "'liberal thrust'" and a "'general approach of relaxing the traditional barriers to "opinion" evidence.'" This case discusses this evolution in interpreting the meaning of Federal Rule 702, 38 U.S.C.A. It also describes the new approach to admitting scientific evidence where the "general acceptance" test is not used to determine its admissibility. The new interpretation has been very useful in getting DNA evidence admitted.

Justice BLACKMUN delivered the opinion of the Court.

In this case we are called upon to determine the standard for admitting expert scientific testimony in a federal trial.

I

Petitioners Jason Daubert and Eric Schuller are minor children born with serious birth defects. They and their parents sued respondent in California state court, alleging that the birth defects had been caused by the mothers' ingestion of Bendectin, a prescription anti-nausea drug marketed by respondent. Respondent removed the suits to federal court on diversity grounds.

After extensive discovery, respondent moved for summary judgment, contending that Bendectin does not cause birth defects in humans and that petitioners would be unable to come forward with any admissible evidence that it does. In support of its motion, respondent submitted an affidavit of Steven H. Lamm, physician and epidemiologist, who is a well-credentialed expert on the risks from exposure to various chemical substances. Doctor Lamm stated that he had reviewed all the literature on Bendectin and human birth defects—more than 30 published studies involving over 130,000 patients. No study had found

Bendectin to be a human teratogen (*i.e.*, a substance capable of causing malformations in fetuses). On the basis of this review, Doctor Lamm concluded that maternal use of Bendectin during the first trimester of pregnancy has not been shown to be a risk factor for human birth defects.

Petitioners did not (and do not) contest this characterization of the published record regarding Bendectin. Instead, they responded to respondent's motion with the testimony of eight experts of their own, each of whom also possessed impressive credentials. These experts had concluded that Bendectin can cause birth defects. Their conclusions were based upon "in vitro" (test tube) and "in vivo" (live) animal studies that found a link between Bendectin and malformations; pharmacological studies of the chemical structure of Bendectin that purported to show similarities between the structure of the drug and that of other substances known to cause birth defects; and the "reanalysis" of previously published epidemiological (human statistical) studies.

The District Court granted respondent's motion for summary judgment. The court stated that scientific evidence is admissible only if the principle upon which it is based is "'sufficiently established to have general acceptance in the field to which it belongs.'" 727 F.Supp. 570, 572 (S.D.Cal. 1989), quoting United States v. Kilgus, 571 F.2d 508, 510 (CA9 1978). The court concluded that petitioners' evidence did not meet this standard. Given the vast body of epidemiological data concerning Bendectin, the court held, expert opinion which is not based on epidemiological evidence is not admissible to establish causation. 727 F.Supp., at 575. Thus, the animal-cell studies, live-animal studies, and chemical-structure analyses on which petitioners had relied could not raise by themselves a reasonably disputable jury issue regarding causation. *Ibid.* Petitioners' epidemiological analyses, based as they were on recalculations of data in previously published studies that had found no causal link between the drug and birth defects, were ruled to be inadmissible because they had not been published or subjected to peer review. *Ibid.*

The United States Court of Appeals for the Ninth Circuit affirmed. 951 F.2d 1128

(1991). Citing Frye v. United States, 54 App.D.C. 46, 47, 293 F. 1013, 1014 (1923), the court stated that expert opinion based on a scientific technique is inadmissible unless the technique is "generally accepted" as reliable in the relevant scientific community. 951 F.2d, at 1129–1130. The court declared that expert opinion based on a methodology that diverges "significantly from the procedures accepted by recognized authorities in the field . . . cannot be shown to be 'generally accepted as a reliable technique.'" *Id.*, at 1130, quoting United States v. Solomon, 753 F.2d 1522, 1526 (CA9 1985).

The court emphasized that other Courts of Appeals considering the risks of Bendectin had refused to admit reanalyses of epidemiological studies that had been neither published nor subjected to peer review. 951 F.2d , at 1130–1131. Those courts had found unpublished reanalyses "particularly problematic in light of the massive weight of the original published studies supporting [respondent's] position, all of which had undergone full scrutiny from the scientific community." *Id.* at 1130. Contending that reanalysis is generally accepted by the scientific community only when it is subjected to verification and scrutiny by others in the field, the Court of Appeals rejected petitioners' reanalyses as "unpublished, not subjected to the normal peer review process and generated solely for use in litigation." *Id.*, at 1131. The court concluded that petitioners' evidence provided an insufficient foundation to allow admission of expert testimony that Bendectin caused their injuries and, accordingly, that petitioners could not satisfy their burden of proving causation at trial.

We granted certiorari, ____U.S.____, 113 S.Ct. 320, 121 L.Ed.2d 240 (1992), in light of sharp divisions among the courts regarding the proper standard for the admission of expert testimony. Compare, *e.g.*, United States v. Shorter, 257 U.S.App.D.C. 358, 363–364, 809 F.2d 54, 59–60 (applying the "general acceptance" standard), cert. denied, 484 U.S. 817, 108 S.Ct. 71, 98 L.Ed.2d 35 (1987), with DeLuca v. Merrell Dow Pharmaceuticals, Inc., 911 F.2d 941, 955 (CA3 1990) (rejecting the "general acceptance" standard).

II

A

In the 70 years since its formulation in the *Frye* case, the "general acceptance" test has been the dominant standard for determining the admissibility of novel scientific evidence at trial. See E. Green & C. Nessen, Problems, Cases, and Materials on Evidence 649 (1983). Although under increasing attack of late, the rule continues to be followed by a majority of courts, including the Ninth Circuit.

The *Frye* test has its origin in a short and citation-free 1923 decision concerning the admissibility of evidence derived from a systolic blood pressure deception test, a crude precursor to the polygraph machine. In what has become a famous (perhaps infamous) passage, the then Court of Appeals for the District of Columbia described the device and its operation and declared:

> "Just when a scientific principle or discovery crosses the line between the experimental and demonstrable stages is difficult to define. Somewhere in this twilight zone the evidential force of the principle must be recognized, and while courts will go a long way in admitting expert testimony deduced from a well-recognized scientific principle or discovery, *the thing from which the deduction is made must be sufficiently established to have gained general acceptance in the particular field in which it belongs.*" 54 App.D.C., at 47, 293 F., at 1014 (emphasis added).

Because the deception test had "not yet gained such standing and scientific recognition among physiological and psychological authorities as would justify the courts in admitting expert testimony deduced from the discovery, development, and experiments thus far made," evidence of its results was ruled inadmissible. *Ibid.*

The merits of the *Frye* test have been much debated, and scholarship on its proper scope and application is legion. Petitioners' primary attack, however, is not on the content but on the continuing authority of the rule. They contend that the *Frye* test was superseded by the adoption of the Federal Rules of Evidence. We agree.

We interpret the legislatively-enacted Federal Rules of Evidence as we would any statute. Beech Aircraft Corp. v. Rainey, 488 U.S. 153, 163, 109 S.Ct. 439, 446, 102 L.Ed.2d 445 (1988). Rule 402 provides the baseline:

> "All relevant evidence is admissible, except as otherwise provided by the Constitution of the United States, by Act of Congress, by these rules, or by other rules prescribed by the Supreme Court pursuant to statutory authority. Evidence which is not relevant is not admissible."

"Relevant evidence" is defined as that which has "any tendency to make the existence of any fact that is of consequence to the determination of the action more probable or less probable than it would be without the evidence." Rule 401. The Rule's basic standard of relevance thus is a liberal one.

Frye, of course, predated the Rules by half a century. In United States v. Abel, 469 U.S. 45, 105 S.Ct. 465, 83 L.Ed.2d 450 (1984), we considered the pertinence of background common law in interpreting the Rules of Evidence. We noted that the Rules occupy the field, *id.,* at 49, 105 S.Ct., at 467, but, quoting Professor Cleary, the Reporter, explained that the common law nevertheless could serve as an aid to their application:

> "In principle, under the Federal Rules no common law of evidence remains. 'All relevant evidence is admissible, except as otherwise provided. . . .' In reality, of course, the body of common law knowledge continues to exist, though in the somewhat altered form of a source of guidance in the exercise of delegated powers." *Id.,* at 51–52, 105 S.Ct., at 469.

We found the common-law precept at issue in the *Abel* case entirely consistent with Rule 402's general requirement of admissibility, and considered it unlikely that the drafters had intended to change the rule. *Id.,* at 50–51, 105 S.Ct., at 468–469. In Bourjaily v. United States, 483 U.S. 171, 107 S.Ct. 2775, 97 L.Ed.2d 144 (1987), on the other hand, the Court was unable to find a particular common-law doctrine in the Rules, and so held it superseded.

Here there is a specific Rule that speaks to the contested issue. Rule 702, governing expert testimony, provides:

> "If scientific, technical, or other specialized knowledge will assist the trier of fact to understand the evidence or to determine a fact in issue, a witness qualified as an expert by knowledge, skill, experience, training, or education, may testify thereto in the form of an opinion or otherwise."

Nothing in the text of this Rule establishes "general acceptance" as an absolute prerequisite to admissibility. Nor does respondent present any clear indication that Rule 702 or the Rules as a whole were intended to incorporate a "general acceptance" standard. The drafting history makes no mention of *Frye,* and a rigid "general acceptance" requirement would be at odds with the "liberal thrust" of the Federal Rules and their "general approach of relaxing the traditional barriers to 'opinion' testimony." Beech Aircraft Corp. v. Rainey, 488 U.S., at 169, 109 S.Ct., at 450 (citing Rules 701 to 705). See also Weinstein, Rule 702 of the Federal Rules of Evidence is Sound; It Should Not Be Amended, 138 F.R.D. 631, 631 (1991) ("The Rules were designed to depend primarily upon lawyer-adversaries and sensible triers of fact to evaluate conflicts"). Given the Rules' permissive backdrop and their inclusion of a specific rule on expert testimony that does not mention "general acceptance," the assertion that the Rules somehow assimilated *Frye* is unconvincing. *Frye* made "general acceptance" the exclusive test for admitting expert scientific testimony. That austere standard, absent from and incompatible with the Federal Rules of Evidence, should not be applied in federal trials.

B

That the *Frye* test was displaced by the Rules of Evidence does not mean, however, that the Rules themselves place no limits on the admissibility of purportedly scientific evidence. Nor is the trial judge disabled from screening such evidence. To the contrary, under the Rules the trial judge must ensure that any and all scientific testimony or evidence admitted is not only relevant, but reliable.

The primary locus of this obligation is Rule 702, which clearly contemplates some degree of regulation of the subjects and theories about which an expert may testify. "*If scientific*, technical, or other specialized *knowledge will assist the trier of fact* to understand the evidence or to determine a fact in issue" an expert "may testify *thereto*." The subject of an expert's testimony must be "scientific . . . knowledge." The adjective "scientific" implies a grounding in the methods and procedures of science. Similarly, the word "knowledge" connotes more than subjective belief or unsupported speculation. The term "applies to any body of known facts or to any body of ideas inferred from such facts or accepted as truths on good grounds." Webster's Third New International Dictionary 1252 (1986). Of course, it would be unreasonable to conclude that the subject of scientific testimony must be "known" to a certainty; arguably, there are no certainties in science. See, *e.g.*, Brief for Nicolaas Bloembergen et al. as *Amici Curiae* 9 ("Indeed, scientists do not assert that they know what is immutably 'true'—they are committed to searching for new, temporary theories to explain, as best they can, phenomena"); Brief for American Association for the Advancement of Science and the National Academy of Sciences as *Amici Curiae* 7–8 ("Science is not an encyclopedic body of knowledge about the universe. Instead, it represents a *process* for proposing and refining theoretical explanations about the world that are subject to further testing and refinement") (emphasis in original). But, in order to qualify as "scientific knowledge," an inference or assertion must be derived by the scientific method. Proposed testimony must be supported by appropriate validation—*i.e.*, "good grounds," based on what is known. In short, the requirement that an expert's testimony pertain to "scientific knowledge" establishes a standard of evidentiary reliability.

Rule 702 further requires that the evidence or testimony "assist the trier of fact to understand the evidence or to determine a fact in issue." This condition goes primarily to relevance. "Expert testimony which does not relate to any issue in the case is not relevant and, ergo, nonhelpful." 3 Weinstein & Berger ¶ 702[02], p. 702–18. See also United States v. Downing, 753 F.2d 1224, 1242 (CA3 1985) ("An additional consideration under Rule 702—and another aspect of relevancy—is

whether expert testimony proffered in the case is sufficiently tied to the facts of the case that it will aid the jury in resolving a factual dispute"). The consideration has been aptly described by Judge Becker as one of "fit." *Ibid.* "Fit" is not always obvious, and scientific validity for one purpose is not necessarily scientific validity for other, unrelated purposes. See Starrs, *Frye v. United States* Restructured and Revitalized: A Proposal to Amend Federal Evidence Rule 702, and 26 Jurimetrics J. 249, 258 (1986). The study of the phases of the moon, for example, may provide valid scientific "knowledge" about whether a certain night was dark, and if darkness is a fact in issue, the knowledge will assist the trier of fact. However (absent creditable grounds supporting such a link), evidence that the moon was full on a certain night will not assist the trier of fact in determining whether an individual was unusually likely to have behaved irrationally on that night. Rule 702's "helpfulness" standard requires a valid scientific connection to the pertinent inquiry as a precondition to admissibility.

That these requirements are embodied in Rule 702 is not surprising. Unlike an ordinary witness, see Rule 701, an expert is permitted wide latitude to offer opinions, including those that are not based on first-hand knowledge or observation. See Rules 702 and 703. Presumably, this relaxation of the usual requirement of first-hand knowledge—a rule which represents "a 'most pervasive manifestation' of the common law insistence upon 'the most reliable sources of information,'" Advisory Committee's Notes on Fed.Rule Evid. 602 (citation omitted)—is premised on an assumption that the expert's opinion will have a reliable basis in the knowledge and experience of his discipline.

C

Faced with a proffer of expert scientific testimony, then, the trial judge must determine at the outset, pursuant to Rule 104(a), whether the expert is proposing to testify to (1) scientific knowledge that (2) will assist the trier of fact to understand or determine a fact in issue. This entails a preliminary assessment of whether the reasoning or methodology underlying the testimony is scientifically valid and of whether that reasoning or methodology properly can be applied to the facts in issue. We are confident that federal judges possess the capacity to undertake this review. Many factors will bear on the inquiry, and we do not presume to set out a definitive checklist or test. But some general observations are appropriate.

Ordinarily, a key question to be answered in determining whether a theory or technique is scientific knowledge that will assist the trier of fact will be whether it can be (and has been) tested. "Scientific methodology today is based on generating hypotheses and testing them to see if they can be falsified; indeed, this methodology is what distinguishes science from other fields of human inquiry." Green, at 645. See also C. Hempel, Philosophy of Natural Science 49 (1966) ("[T]he statements constituting a scientific explanation must be capable of empirical test"); K. Popper, Conjectures and Refutations: The Growth of Scientific Knowledge 37 (5th ed. 1989) ("[T]he criterion of the scientific status of a theory is its falsifiability, or refutability, or testability").

Another pertinent consideration is whether the theory or technique has been subjected to peer review and publication. Publication (which is but one element of peer review) is not a *sine qua non* of admissibility; it does not necessarily correlate with reliability, see S. Jasanoff, The Fifth Branch: Science Advisors as Policymakers 61–76 (1990), and in some instances well-grounded but innovative theories will not have been published, see Horrobin, The Philosophical Basis of Peer Review and the Suppression of Innovation, 263 J.Am. Med.Assn. 1438 (1990). Some propositions, moreover, are too particular, too new, or of too limited interest to be published. But submission to the scrutiny of the scientific community is a component of "good science," in part because it increases the likelihood that substantive flaws in methodology will be detected. See J. Ziman, Reliable Knowledge: An Exploration of the Grounds for Belief in Science 130–133 (1978); Relman and Angell, How Good Is Peer Review?, 321 New Eng.J.Med. 827 (1989). The fact of publication (or lack thereof) in a peer-reviewed journal thus will be a relevant, though not dispositive, consideration in assessing the scientific validity of a particular technique or methodology on which an opinion is premised.

Additionally, in the case of a particular scientific technique, the court ordinarily should consider the known or potential rate of error, see, *e.g.*, United States v. Smith, 869 F.2d 348, 353–354 (CA7 1989) (surveying studies of the error rate of spectrographic voice identification technique), and the existence and maintenance of standards controlling the technique's operation. See United States v. Williams, 583 F.2d 1194, 1198 (CA2 1978) (noting professional organization's standard governing spectrographic analysis), cert. denied, 439 U.S. 1117, 99 S.Ct. 1025, 59 L.Ed.2d 77 (1979).

Finally, "general acceptance" can yet have a bearing on the inquiry. A "reliability assessment does not require, although it does permit, explicit identification of a relevant scientific community and an express determination of a particular degree of acceptance within that community." United States v. Downing, 753 F.2d, at 1238. See also 3 Weinstein & Berger ¶ 702[03], pp. 702–41 to 702–42. Widespread acceptance can be an important factor in ruling particular evidence admissible, and "a known technique that has been able to attract only minimal support within the community," *Downing, supra*, at 1238, may properly be viewed with skepticism.

The inquiry envisioned by Rule 702 is, we emphasize, a flexible one. Its overarching subject is the scientific validity—and thus the evidentiary relevance and reliability—of the principles that underlie a proposed submission. The focus, of course, must be solely on principles and methodology, not on the conclusions that they generate.

Throughout, a judge assessing a proffer of expert scientific testimony under Rule 702 should also be mindful of other applicable rules. Rule 703 provides that expert opinions based on otherwise inadmissible hearsay are to be admitted only if the facts or data are "of a type reasonably relied upon by experts in the particular field in forming opinions or inferences upon the subject." Rule 706 allows the court at its discretion to procure the assistance of an expert of its own choosing. Finally, Rule

403 permits the exclusion of relevant evidence "if its probative value is substantially outweighed by the danger of unfair prejudice, confusion of the issues, or misleading the jury. . . ." Judge Weinstein has explained: "Expert evidence can be both powerful and quite misleading because of the difficulty in evaluating it. Because of this risk, the judge in weighing possible prejudice against probative force under Rule 403 of the present rules exercises more control over experts than over lay witnesses." Weinstein, 138 F.R.D., at 632.

III

We conclude by briefly addressing what appear to be two underlying concerns of the parties and *amici* in the case. Respondent expresses apprehension that abandonment of "general acceptance" as the exclusive requirement for admission will result in a "free-for-all" in which befuddled juries are confounded by absurd and irrational pseudoscientific assertions. In this regard respondent seems to us to be overly pessimistic about the capabilities of the jury, and of the adversary system generally. Vigorous cross-examination, presentation of contrary evidence, and careful instruction on the burden of proof are the traditional and appropriate means of attacking shaky but admissible evidence. See Rock v. Arkansas, 483 U.S. 44, 61, 107 S.Ct. 2704, 2714, 97 L.Ed.2d 37 (1987). Additionally, in the event the trial court concludes that the scintilla of evidence presented supporting a position is insufficient to allow a reasonable juror to conclude that the position more likely than not is true, the court remains free to direct a judgment, Fed.Rule Civ.Proc. 50(a), and likewise to grant summary judgment, Fed.Rule Civ.Proc. 56. Cf., *e.g.*, Turpin v. Merrell Dow Pharmaceuticals, Inc., 959 F.2d 1349 (CA6) (holding that scientific evidence that provided foundation for expert testimony, viewed in the light most favorable to plaintiffs, was not sufficient to allow a jury to find it more probable than not that defendant caused plaintiff's injury), cert. denied, 506 U.S. ___, 113 S.Ct. 84, 121 L.Ed.2d 47 (1992); Brock v. Merrell Dow Pharmaceuticals, Inc., 874 F.2d 307 (CA5 1989). (reversing judgment entered on jury verdict for plaintiffs because evidence regard-

ing causation was insufficient), modified, 884 F.2d 166 (CA5 1989), cert. denied, 494 U.S. 1046, 110 S.Ct. 1511, 108 L.Ed.2d 646 (1990); Green 680–681. These conventional devices, rather than wholesale exclusion under an uncompromising "general acceptance" test, are the appropriate safeguards where the basis of scientific testimony meets the standards of Rule 702.

Petitioners and, to a greater extent, their *amici* exhibit a different concern. They suggest that recognition of a screening role for the judge that allows for the exclusion of "invalid" evidence will sanction a stifling and repressive scientific orthodoxy and will be inimical to the search for truth. See, *e.g.*, Brief for Ronald Bayer et al. as *Amici Curiae*. It is true that open debate is an essential part of both legal and scientific analyses. Yet there are important differences between the quest for truth in the courtroom and the quest for truth in the laboratory. Scientific conclusions are subject to perpetual revision. Law, on the other hand, must resolve disputes finally and quickly. The scientific project is advanced by broad and wide-ranging consideration of a multitude of hypotheses, for those that are incorrect will eventually be shown to be so, and that in itself is an advance. Conjectures that are probably wrong are of little use, however, in the project of reaching a quick, final, and binding legal judgment—often of great consequence—about a particular set of events in the past. We recognize that in practice, a gatekeeping role for the judge, no matter how flexible, inevitably on occasion will prevent the jury from learning of authentic insights and innovations. That, nevertheless, is the balance that is struck by Rules of Evidence designed not for the exhaustive search for cosmic understanding but for the particularized resolution of legal disputes.

IV

To summarize: "general acceptance" is not a necessary precondition to the admissibility of scientific evidence under the Federal Rules of Evidence, but the Rules of Evidence—especially Rule 702—do assign to the trial judge the task of ensuring that an expert's testimony both rests on a reliable foundation and is relevant to the task at hand. Pertinent evidence based on scientifically valid principles will satisfy those demands.

The inquiries of the District Court and the Court of Appeals focused almost exclusively on "general acceptance," as gauged by publication and the decisions of other courts. Accordingly, the judgment of the Court of Appeals is vacated and the case is remanded for further proceedings consistent with this opinion.

It is so ordered.

Chief Justice REHNQUIST, with whom Justice STEVENS joins, concurring in part and dissenting in part.

* * *

Roberts v. State of Florida
Supreme Court of Florida, 1964.
164 So.2d 817.

The following decision concerns various legal principles. The reason that it was placed at this point in the book is that it describes the admissibility of testimony of a ballistics expert in identifying a comparison test bullet fired from a gun that was thus identified as a murder weapon. The decision also describes what happens to this testimony if the jury is not permitted to view the bullet in question and the bullet is not even placed in evidence.

THORNAL, Justice. John Henry Roberts and John Alfred Adderley seek reversal of verdicts and judgments convicting them of first degree murder without recommendation of mercy.

We have for consideration numerous alleged errors in the trial proceeding.

At approximately 11:30 A.M., Friday, May 12, 1961, Benjamin Franklin Campbell, Jr., was shot while tending his grocery store. A customer, standing across the store, heard one shot and also heard a voice announce "You shot me." The customer ran to an adjoining kitchen area where Mrs. Campbell was preparing her husband's dinner. Mrs. Campbell also heard a statement, "I am shot." Upon entering the store proper, she found her husband lying on the floor mortally wounded. The drawer of the cash register was open and she noted that certain ten and twenty dollar bills which were previously in the drawer had dis-

appeared. Before entering the store from the kitchen Mrs. Campbell dialed the telephone operator to call for an ambulance and the police. While on the phone she saw the heads of two people as they were leaving the front of the store. At about 6:00 P.M., May 12, 1961, John Henry Roberts was taken into custody. He was arrested initially for "investigation of the homicide." At about 11:30 P.M., May 12, 1961, John Alfred Adderley was similarly arrested. From about 6:30 P.M. until about 1:30 A.M., Roberts was interrogated by law enforcement officers. He denied any connection with the crime. Shortly after midnight May 13, and within approximately one hour after his arrest, Adderley made a full confession of his participation in the robbery and murder. He implicated Roberts. At about 11:45 A.M., May 13, 1961, Adderley was brought face to face with Roberts. Adderley stated, "It was a terrible thing we did. They have caught us . . . the only thing . . . to do . . . (is) . . . to tell the truth." Thereupon, around noon on Saturday, May 13, Roberts likewise gave a full confession, the essential aspects of which were factually corroborative of the confession made by Adderley. At the trial the defendants repudiated their confessions and undertook to establish alibis. They were found guilty of first degree murder by separate verdicts. There were no mercy recommendations. The death sentences ensued. The appellants have filed separate briefs. They seek reversal on numerous grounds which we shall discuss.

Roberts assaults the validity of his confession with the claim that it was obtained by prolonged and excessive interrogation which overcame his capacity to resist. It will be recalled that he was arrested at approximately 6:00 P.M., May 12. The interrogation started at about 6:30 P.M. and continued intermittently until 1:30 A.M. the next morning. The interrogation was not constant. There were periodic breaks. The significant fact is that at the end of this period of questioning Roberts continued to maintain his innocence. No confession was obtained during this initial interrogation. He went to bed around 1:30 A.M. He was not questioned again until after 9:30 A.M. on Saturday, May 13. In the meantime, Adderley had confessed. It is clear from the record that Roberts showed no inclination to confess until he was confronted by his accomplice. In fact, Adderley does not question the voluntariness of his confession by his brief in this Court. This, of course, does not affect Roberts.

We have held that a confession freely and voluntarily given while one is in custody for investigation of a crime is admissible at his subsequent trial. Williams v. State, 143 Fla. 826, 197 So. 562 (1941). The test of admissibility is whether the confession was voluntary. It must be shown that it was given without fear, hope of reward, or some other illegal influence or inordinate mental or physical pressures. It is true that Roberts was arrested at 6:00 P.M., Friday, May 12, and before being presented to a magistrate, his confession was obtained approximately sixteen hours later. This fact, however, would not destroy the validity of the confession if it was otherwise freely and voluntarily given. Dawson v. State, 139 So.2d 408 (Fla. 1962); Singer v. State, Fla., 109 So.2d 7 (Fla. 1959). There is no evidence to indicate either mental or physical abuse of the accused. Out of the presence of the jury, the trial judge correctly investigated the voluntariness of the confessions as a condition to their admissibility. In the presence of the jury, the defendants were permitted to offer evidence to support their view that the confessions were not freely given. This evidence went to their credibility. The jury evidently accepted the confessions. We find no basis for reversal on this point.

The state placed in evidence a .25 caliber pistol which was shown to have belonged to Roberts. Also in evidence was a shell case found at the scene of the crime and a slug removed from the body of the victim. The state then called Ed Bigler, a ballistics expert, who testified that he had test-fired the pistol and had compared the markings on the test bullet with those from the evidence bullet removed from the victim. This he did under a comparison microscope. On the basis of this experiment he submitted the opinion that the bullet which resulted in Campbell's death had been fired from the gun belonging to Roberts. The test bullet was not placed in evidence. Both Adderley and Roberts contend that the test bullet should also have been filed in evidence so that the jury could compare it with the evidence bullet which had caused the death. It is clear that the markings on the bullet could not be identified with the naked eye. Additionally, they could be interpreted only by one trained in the science or experience of ballistics.

Thompson v. Freeman, 111 Fla. 433, 149 So. 740 (1933), cited by appellants, does not support their position. It involved the authenticity of a document and was governed by a statute. We have no such situation in the instant case.

It is now well established that a witness, who qualifies as an expert in the science of ballistics, may identify a gun from which a particular bullet was fired by comparing the markings on that bullet with those on a test bullet fired by the witness through the suspect gun. An expert will be permitted to submit his opinion based on such an experiment conducted by him. The details of the experiment should be described to the jury. Riner v. State, 128 Fla. 848, 176 So. 38 (1937), rehearing denied 131 Fla. 243, 179 So. 404; State v. Vuckovich, 61 Mont. 480, 203 Pac. 491 (1922); Edwards v. State, 198 Md. 132, 81 A.2d 631, 83 A.2d 578, 26 A.L.R.2d 874 (1951).

In McKenna v. People, 124 Colo. 112, 235 P.2d 351 (1951), it was held that the opinion of an expert based on the test firing of a gun could be offered in evidence without the necessity of submitting a corroborating microphotograph for inspection by the jurors. In McKenna the expert relied upon a comparison of the test bullet with the evidence bullet under a comparison microscope. This was the identical procedure followed in the case at bar. In State v. Wojculewicz, 140 Conn. 487, 101 A.2d 495 (1954), the Court held that it was unnecessary to place the test bullet in evidence to sustain the admissibility of the expert's opinion based upon an experiment in which the test bullet was fired.

In cases such as these the opinion of the witness is allowed under the rules which govern other forms of expert testimony. He will be permitted to submit his conclusions where it is shown that by training and experience he is qualified to give an expert opinion on the basis of the ballistic tests which he himself conducted. It is not necessary that the test be conducted in the presence of the jury nor is it required that the expert submit to the jury the actual test materials. It was not error to refuse to compel the state to produce the test bullet.

When the jury was being qualified on voir dire the trial judge explained to them that it would be their function to determine the facts on the basis of the evidence. He told them that it was his duty to explain the law and their duty to apply the law to the facts. He informed them that even though they disagree with him on some statement of law, nevertheless, it was their responsibility to accept the law as he announced it. In the course of these remarks the judge stated, "If the court is mistaken as to what the law is it is not the duty of the jury to correct him, but there is a way that it can be corrected through appellate procedure." Both appellants contend that this statement constituted reversible error. They base their contention on Pait v. State, 112 So.2d 380 (Fla. 1959) and Blackwell v. State, 76 Fla. 124, 79 So. 731, 1 A.L.R. 502 (1918). In the cited cases the state attorney argued to the jury that if they committed any error it could be corrected in the Supreme Court. We held that in effect these remarks merely suggest to the jury that they need not be too greatly concerned about the results of their deliberations because there would be an appellate court to review them. Such was not the effect of the statement of the trial judge in the instant case. He impressed the jurors with the importance of their responsibility regarding factual determinations. He correctly informed them that they had no responsibility in deciding the law of the case. The power of an appellate court to review his decisions on the law did not in any particular relieve the jurors of any aspect of their vital responsibility in settling the facts. Overstreet v. State, 143 Fla. 794, 197 So. 516 (1940).

The state produced a witness, Boswell, who testified that on Monday, May 8, 1961, he accompanied Roberts to the establishment of one Livingston for the purpose of pawning Roberts' pistol. Boswell handled the negotiations with Livingston. Other testimony revealed that Roberts had redeemed his pistol from Livingston on the morning of the homicide. This was the pistol which was identified as the murder weapon. Cross-examination of Boswell indicated that he too had been taken into custody on the day the murder was committed. He was then asked "Were you a suspect?" The state's objection to the question was sustained. The defendants then made a proffer to show that if they were permitted to continue this line of questioning they could prove that Boswell had spent some five hours in jail under "suspicion" for the same crime and that "by virtue of being accused of this crime himself that he was likely to have given evidence in favor of the City [Sic] in order to get himself off the hook. . . ." The judge refused the proffer.

A defendant is permitted wide latitude in the cross-examination of a state witness to show the motive of the witness in giving testimony for the state. It is permissible to interrogate the witness on the subject of any agreement to grant him leniency or immunity from prosecution in exchange for his testimony. Henderson v. State, 135 Fla. 548, 185 So. 625, 120 A.L.R. 742 (1939); Spaeth v. United States, 232 F.2d 776, 62 A.L.R.2d 606 (6th Cir. 1956).

The proffer in the instant case did not include a showing that the witness was still suspected of the crime nor did it include a tender of proof that the state had made any concessions to him in exchange for his testimony. The proffer merely submitted a conclusion that the witness "was likely to have given evidence" in favor of the state's position. Moreover, if Boswell had been completely discredited, there was other reliable testimony regarding the pawning of the pistol. In fact, Roberts himself testified to the pawning of the pistol on May 8 and its redemption on May 12. There was no question but that the gun belonged to Roberts, that he pawned it on May 8th and retrieved it on May 12. The ruling of the trial judge on the attempted cross-examination of Boswell was not reversible error.

Prior to and during the trial Adderley repeatedly sought a severance. We have held that the allowance of a severance rests within the sound discretion of the trial judge. His decision will not be disturbed absent a showing of abuse of discretion or some significant resultant damage to the defendant who seeks a separate trial. Sawyer v. State, 100 Fla. 1603, 132 So. 188 (1931); Manson v. State, 88 So.2d 272 (Fla. 1956); Samuels v. State, 123

Fla. 280, 166 So. 743 (1936). In the instant case, there was no antagonism between the defenses of the two defendants. They both sought to establish alibis. Their attorneys collaborated constantly during the trial. In those instances where evidence was admissible against one but not against the other, the trial judge carefully instructed the jury to this effect. We do not find that the judge abused his discretion in denying the motion for severance.

Adderley further contends that the indictment against him should have been quashed because of a claimed systematic exclusion of Negroes from the grand jury. The record is devoid of any evidence to support this claim. The mere fact that in this instance only one Negro was called to serve on the petit jury does not support the claim of systematic exclusion from the grand jury. Porter v. State, 160 So.2d 104 (Fla. 1964). Adderley also contends that the grand jury which indicted him consisted of only 18 persons, rather than 23 as provided by Chapter 25554, Laws of 1949. Without exploring the constitutionality of the cited statute, it appears from the record that the 18-man grand jury was properly constituted as of the time the indictment was presented.

It is further pointed out that the indictment charged an unlawful homicide with a premeditated design. By its evidence, the state undertook to prove a homicide committed in the perpetration of a robbery. We are requested to recede from our previous holdings to the effect that an indictment generally charged an unlawful homicide with a premeditated design can be proven by evidence of a homicide committed in the perpetration of a robbery. Section 782.04, Florida Statutes, F.S.A. We see no reason to recede from our prior decisions on this point. Blake v. State, 156 So.2d 511 (Fla. 1963).

We have examined the several other points assigned for reversal. We find them to be without merit and insufficient to justify an extensive discussion.

In addition to the contentions made by the appellants, we have reviewed the evidence in detail as required by Section 924.32, Florida Statutes, F.S.A. On the basis of this examination we fail to find that the interests of justice require a new trial.

The judgments are affirmed.

It is so ordered.

Tokarz v. Ford Motor Company
Court of Appeals of Washington, Division 2, 1973.
8 Wash.App. 645, 508 P.2d 1370.

This case presents a complicated factual pattern and attempts to place the responsibility for a serious multicar accident on an alleged defect in the manufacture of a Ford Motor Company vehicle. It is suggested that you try to understand the factual pattern of this case by drawing a diagram of the traffic patterns of all the vehicles, of what happened to these vehicles during the crash, and of the locations of the vehicles as they came to a stop after the crash. You should also note the appearance of the floor of the subject vehicle and try to understand how each expert witness arrived at the conclusion reached by that expert.

In effect, I am asking you to place yourself in the jury box to try to determine what you believe the facts in this case were. Usually, however, you will want to rely on expert testimony that is admitted that you believe explains the cause of the accident. One of the reasons that this case is presented at this point is to demonstrate what a court will and will not accept in evidence with respect to the opinions of experts on ultimate facts as long as the inference drawn is not misleading or a matter of common knowledge.

PEARSON, Chief Judge.

Two actions for personal injuries and damages were commenced as a result of a three-car collision on Interstate Highway 5, approximately 5 miles south of Kalama, Washington. In the first action, Ronald and Susan Tokarz sought recovery against Ford Motor Company on a products liability theory for severe injuries Mrs. Tokarz received as the aftermath of losing control of the Tokarz 1968 Ford stationwagon. Occupants of another vehicle, Jerome and Nancy Larson and children, also brought a damage action against Ford Motor Company, Ronald and Susan Tokarz, and against Robert and Ruthann Murphy, who occupied the third involved vehicle. The Murphys cross-claimed for their injuries and damages against Ford and Tokarz.

The two actions were consolidated for trial, which the court limited to three issues: (1) the liability, if any, of Ford, the manufacturer; (2) the negligence of Susan Tokarz, if any; and (3) the damages sustained by the Tokarzes.

The jury determined the liability of Ford and fixed the Tokarzes' damages at $249,000. The effect of the verdict was to exonerate Mrs. Tokarz from fault and impose liability upon Ford for the injuries and damages to occupants of all three vehicles.

The thrust of Ford's appeal is to challenge the sufficiency of the evidence to establish its liability. In particular, Ford challenges the factual basis of expert testimony offered to establish the cause of the accident. This necessitates a detailed review of the evidence.

The accident occurred at approximately 1 P.M. on January 2, 1970. The day was bright, visibility was unlimited, and the pavement was dry. Mrs. Tokarz, a 26-year-old school teacher, was alone in her 1968 Ford stationwagon, driving south on I–5 in the extreme right-hand (outside) lane. The Ford was just over 1 year old, had 17,000 miles, and had never been serviced except for warranty maintenance. On this stretch of road, I–5 was straight and level, with two lanes going south and two lanes north. Some 150 to 200 feet directly behind Mrs. Tokarz, in the same lane, was a car driven by Jean Davis, whose husband was in the front seat. Each car was traveling about 65 miles per hour (speed limit 70) and the distance between the cars had not changed in the 10 to 15 minutes before the accident.

On the inside lane, Mr. and Mrs. Murphy were slowly overtaking the other two cars. As the Murphys moved past Mrs. Tokarz, the Ford suddenly swerved left towards the Murphy Cadillac, then right until it went onto the shoulder of the highway, and then left again, striking the right rear quarter of the Murphy car. The Cadillac's gas tank exploded, but Mr. Murphy was able to keep his car under control and bring it to a stop on the left shoulder of the highway, next to the median strip.

The Ford, however, spun out of control, passed behind the Cadillac, and eventually went backwards across the median strip onto the inside northbound lane. The Larson family, to their great misfortune, was traveling in that lane. The driver violently applied his brakes, but his Plymouth "broadsided" the Tokarz Ford, the front of the Plymouth impacting the left side of the Ford, just in front of the driver. Both cars erupted into flames, and the Ford was completely consumed.

Mr. Davis and a passing truck driver extricated Mrs. Tokarz from her stationwagon. She was severely and permanently injured. Although Mrs. Tokarz was not unconscious long, if at all, she remembers nothing from the time she left home that day until recollecting the hospital room in which she lay several days later.

Mrs. Jean Davis, the driver of the following car, observed most of the accident. Mr. Davis, a minister, was seated in the front passenger seat, but had his eyes diverted to the floorboard because the sun was shining brightly in the upper right corner of the windshield. Mr. and Mrs. Murphy observed the front hood portion of the Ford until it collided with their Cadillac. There were no other eye witnesses to the causative stages of the accident.

Mrs. Davis testified that she observed nothing unusual about the Ford or its driver during the period she followed it. The driver's head did not bob or jerk immediately before the accident. Neither did she observe sparks or dust emanate from underneath the Ford before the first collision. The Ford, however, "quickly leaped into the side of the Cadillac" and she described the movement as a "sudden jerk." On cross-examination, Mrs. Davis agreed that the movement was similar to a sudden jerk on the steering wheel. The testimony of Mr. and Mrs. Murphy essentially corroborates that of Mrs. Davis. They testified that the Ford swerved toward, away, and then toward their Cadillac. Mr. Murphy stated that the interval between swerves was "very short." Mrs. Murphy summed up the Ford's action: "suddenly it seemed to go out of control."

Following the accident, the tow truck operator, Mr. Johnson, discovered that the drive shaft of the Ford was broken and that a piece of the drive shaft was missing. He searched the area of the accident for about an hour, but did not find the missing piece. He also discovered an unusual hole under the driver's seat, directly above the drive shaft in the "hump" of the floorboard. The floor in that area is metal and the hole was produced by a force from outside the car. The ragged edges were also peculiar in that the metal on one side of the hole was doubled over the parent metal, rather than sticking up in the air. The car was eventually taken to an auto wrecking yard owned by Mr. Langley, who had been in the business for more than 20 years. In the course of his usual inspection of every car he received, Mr. Langley also noticed the hole. He remembered it well, he said, because he had never before seen a similar one in that location.

The accident scene was initially investigated by state highway troopers. Two of the officers, each with many years' experience, testified at trial. Neither officer noticed any gouges or scrapes in the concrete southbound lanes within 500 feet of the Ford that they would associate with the accident. The only marks on the road associated with the Ford that they observed were tire marks, the farthest being 234 feet from the Ford's final resting place. This tire mark was on the white center dividing line and indicated that the car was veering to the right, toward the shoulder. A private investigator, formerly with the Seattle police, and with 20 years of accident investigation experience, examined the roadway about 2 weeks later and testified that he found a significant gouge mark about 110 feet from the Ford's final position, that he definitely attributed to the broken drive shaft. The mark was straight, roughly parallel with the center line of the lane, and 9 to 11 inches long. A representative of the Tokarz insurer was present when this gouge was discovered. The two men testified that this was not the only mark in the pavement, but because of its size and configuration it was the most important.

The broken drive shaft was examined by several engineering experts. Plaintiff's experts testified that the drive shaft broke because of a defective weld, caused by automatic welding equipment at the factory.

Professor Kieling, one of the experts called by plaintiff, testified that 15 percent of the weld was brittle. The brittle portion was located just behind a flywheel-type balance weight attached to the drive line to eliminate noise. This weight was quite massive compared to the rest of the drive shaft. The defective weld, under stress created by bending due to a severe vibration induced by a rough road, caused the drive shaft to suddenly fail. He was clear and specific that the failure was sudden and not a "fatigue"-type failure. Professor Kieling and one of the police officers, each of whom had personal knowledge, testified that the outside, southbound lane of I–5 was "rough." Professor Kieling concluded that the drive shaft failed before any collision occurred and was the cause of the Ford's jerky loss of control. In his opinion, this conclusion was compelled because (1) the Cadillac-Ford collision was not severe enough to fracture a properly welded drive line; and (2) the Plymouth-Ford impact, while it could explain a broken drive shaft, could not explain the hole under the seat. In his opinion, the hole "had the imprint of the balance weight." The balance weight would only have the kinetic energy sufficient to rupture the floorboard if it were rotating at highway speeds.

Another of plaintiff's experts, Mr. C. V. Smith, while not disagreeing with Professor Kieling, offered another explanation. He agreed that the weld was brittle and the drive line failure was the cause of the loss of control. In his opinion, however, there was a defect in the missing piece. Under the influence of the rough road, this piece of the drive shaft bent, actually became deformed, and caused the defective weld to separate. The bent portion of the drive shaft, rotating at 3500 revolutions per minute and flopping about under the car, could account for the peculiar configuration of the hole in the floorboard.

Both Professor Kieling and Mr. Smith agreed that the missing piece of the fractured drive shaft was thrown clear of the car, as the shaft revolved at high speed. Both experts testified that a broken drive shaft would explain the erratic, jerky movement of the Ford before the first collision in any or all of three ways. First, the sudden severance of the drive shaft, which would disconnect the engine (the source of power) from the wheels, coupled with the tearing of the hole in the floor, could startle the driver sufficiently to cause loss of control. Second, the broken drive shaft would flop about and swing right to left under the car, bending and binding as it came into contact with the car body and the pavement; such action would tend to stop its rotation, with a result similar to intermittent application of the hand brake. Finally, the broken shaft could gouge into the pavement and actually catapult the car into an erratic movement.

Defendant's experts completely disagreed. In their opinion, the weld was neither brittle nor defective in any way. Microphotographs taken by a metallurgist were introduced to support their contention. From their examination, the fractures to the drive line were completely consistent with the severe impacts between the three vehicles. They also disagreed that the hole was caused either by the balance weight or a bent drive shaft. They testified that neither the balance weight nor the edges of the hole exhibited the abrasion or scratch markings necessary to explain a rotating injury to the floorboard. Moreover, one of Ford's experts opined that the hole exhibited the characteristics of a puncture and theorized that the missing piece of the drive shaft, broken during the impact, may have been caught between the car and the pavement and pierced the metal. The other defense expert, who did not fully subscribe to this impaling theory, testified that the hole had the characteristics of a single, sudden impact, and definitely was not from the rapidly rotating shaft or balance weight.

The defendant's experts placed great emphasis on their failure to find any evidence of the shaft's beating on the underside of the car, the absence of gouge marks in the highway reported by the police, and the testimony of Mrs. Davis that she saw no sparks or dust emanate from under the car prior to the first collision. In their opinion, these facts completely excluded the conclusions of plaintiff's experts. A Ford engineer testified that had the drive shaft broken at 65 miles per hour, the underside of the Ford would have looked "like the Fourth of July" from the sparks of metal on metal and metal on concrete. In his opinion,

the following driver in Mrs. Davis' position could not help observing what would amount to a pyrotechnic display.

All the experts agreed that the failure of the drive shaft at the so-called brittle weld was not a fatigue failure, but instead was a sudden failure. While there was some disagreement, all the experts substantially agreed that this fracture was the result of a bending of the drive shaft. Plaintiff's experts found some, albeit very slight, indications of rotational forces at work on the fracture, while defendant's experts found none at all. Thus, the critical factual question presented to the jury was "what caused the bending." Was the car's bouncing up and down on the rough roadway sufficient to induce so severe a vibration in the drive shaft that it bent and caused a defective weld to fracture, as Professor Kieling thought? Was the missing piece so defective that it bent and became deformed, due to the rough road, as Mr. Smith concluded? Or was the weld defective at all, and the best explanation of the trauma to the shaft and floorboard to be found in the violent collisions suffered by the Ford, as defendant's experts propounded? Clearly, the jury found the drive shaft to be defective and the cause of the Ford's loss of control.

Three of Ford's assignments of error are directed to the admission of opinion evidence of three experts called by plaintiff to establish the ultimate fact in issue, namely, the cause of the accident. It is contended generally that the opinions were not supported by sufficient facts and consequently were conjectural. Were those opinions excluded, Ford contends, there was insufficient evidence to support a jury verdict against it, and the causes of action should have been dismissed.

At the outset, we note that the purpose of permitting expert opinion testimony is to assist the trier of fact in understanding matters not within the common experience of mankind. Weber v. Biddle, 4 Wash.App. 519, 483 P.2d 155 (1971). It is well established that the qualification of an expert is within the discretion of the trial court, and, absent abuse, will not be disturbed on appeal. In re Estate of Hastings, 4 Wash.App. 649, 484 P.2d 442 (1971). Once basic qualifications are shown, deficiencies in the qualifications go to weight, rather than admissibility. Palmer v. Massey-Ferguson, Inc., 3 Wash.App. 508, 476 P.2d 713 (1970). Similarly, the thoroughness of an expert's examination of the real evidence is a matter of weight for the jury. Ulmer v. Ford Motor Co., 75 Wash.2d 522, 452 P.2d 729 (1969).

The limitations on expert opinion testimony are also well settled. The opinion must be founded on facts in evidence, whether disputed or undisputed, and all material facts necessary to the formulation of a sound opinion must be considered. Vaupell Indus. Plastics, Inc. v. Department of Labor & Indus., 4 Wash.App. 430, 481 P.2d 577 (1971). If the expert's opinion assumes the existence of conditions or circumstances not of record, its validity dissolves and the answer must be stricken. Hansel v. Ford Motor Co., 3 Wash.App. 151, 473 P.2d 219 (1970). So long as the answer is fairly based on material facts, supported by substantial evidence under the examiner's theory of the case, however, the opinion testimony is proper. The trial court has wide discretion to determine whether expert testimony falls within the above rules. Myers v. Harter, 76 Wash.2d 772, 459 P.2d 25 (1969); Helman v. Sacred Heart Hospital, 62 Wash.2d 136, 381 P.2d 605 (1963).

An expert may testify in terms of inference if, under the circumstances, resort to inferences is necessary to convey to the jury the full import of the factual testimony. The guiding principle is whether resort to inferences is necessary to assist the jury in understanding matters outside the common ken. Palmer v. Massey-Ferguson, Inc., *supra*. Moreover, the expert may express an opinion on the ultimate fact to be determined by the jury, so long as the inference drawn is not misleading or a matter of common knowledge. Parris v. Johnson, 3 Wash.App. 853, 479 P.2d 91 (1970).

We do not see Ford's attack on the admission of the opinions as an attack on the qualifications of plaintiff's experts, nor does Ford contend that the subject matter of the evidence is within the general knowledge of laymen. Rather, Ford invites us to clarify the limits and boundaries of what is essential to support an expert opinion on an ultimate fact, with the view of determining as a matter of law the insufficiency of the foundational facts.

We have thoroughly reviewed the record in light of the authorities and find no clarification necessary. This case falls squarely within the ambit of established precedent. Quite clearly, if the plaintiff's expert testimony is conjectural and the jury rendered its verdict on the basis of such speculation, the judgment on the verdict must fall. In Lamphiear v. Skagit Corp., 6 Wash.App. 350, 356, 493 P.2d 1018, 1023 (1972), however, we said, "A verdict does not rest on speculation or conjecture when founded on reasonable inferences drawn from circumstantial facts. . . . As we stated in Martin v. Insurance Co. of North America, 1 Wash.App. 218, 221, 460 P.2d 682, 685 (1969): 'An inference is a logical conclusion or deduction from an established fact.'"

In *Lamphiear,* plaintiff's experts propounded two inconsistent factual theories to support products liability and defendant asserted a third contradictory theory to support its defense of negligent use. We said at page 357, 493 P.2d at page 1023:

> While it is obvious plaintiffs' theories are inconsistent with each other to the extent that if one theory was correct the other could not be correct, they are not inconsistent with the main fact to be established. It is only necessary that the circumstances proved be consistent with each other and lead with reasonable certainty to the fact asserted.

In this case, the material undisputed circumstantial facts are (1) the Ford's loss of control was sudden and erratic; (2) the drive shaft was broken; (3) the break in the drive shaft was due to bending with little or no torsional stress evident; (4) a substantial piece of the drive shaft was missing and unaccounted for after a diligent search was conducted; (5) there was a peculiarly configured hole in the floorboard directly above the drive shaft; (6) the driver of a following car within 200 feet of the Ford at the time of loss of control did not see sparks emanating from under the car; (7) at the time of the accident, the Ford had 17,000 miles and had never been serviced except for warranty maintenance;

and (8) the pavement was dry and the sun was bright and glaring in the face of southbound drivers.

In addition, there was substantial evidence from which the jury could find on disputed testimony (1) that there were several marks on the highway in the path that the Ford traveled, one of which was quite peculiar in length and configuration; (2) that the pavement was rough in the outside southbound lane; and (3) that the weld on the drive shaft was brittle and left the manufacturer's control in that defective condition. We must view these facts favorably to plaintiff.

From these facts, we think plaintiff's experts were well within bounds when they gave their opinions concerning the sequence of events that established the cause of the accident as a defective drive shaft. Their "theories" were legitimate inferences deduced from the material physical facts in evidence.

Ford complains specifically that Mr. Smith's testimony of a defect in the missing piece is pure guesswork. We disagree. All the experts agreed that a properly constructed drive shaft would not fracture under the stresses induced by the rough outside southbound lane. The undisputed evidence was that the drive line was broken and a piece was missing. Moreover, it is virtually undisputed that the break was due to bending. Another undisputed fact is the hole in the floorboard.

Although disputed, the jury was entitled to find a defective weld and gouge marks in the highway, facts which are inconsistent with Ford's theory of the accident. Mr. Smith's deduction that the bending forces necessary to fracture the drive line could have been generated by a defective drive shaft is a legitimate inference. This inference follows directly from the material physical facts in evidence and explains those facts to a jury composed of laymen. Of course, his opinion is simply an inference and the jury was not required to reach his conclusion. But so far as appellate review is concerned, it was an inference based on the material facts in evidence and reached after a consideration of all material facts.

We have thoroughly reviewed the record and conclude that there is substantial evidence to support a set of circumstantial facts from which Ford's liability can be logically and reasonably inferred, which facts are inconsistent with any reasonable theory that the drive shaft broke during the collision. *Lamphiear v. Skagit Corp., supra.* The brittle weld, the gouge marks on the pavement, and the rough roadway, together with the unusual characteristics of the hole in the floor of the car, were circumstances which justified the jury in accepting the conclusions of plaintiff's expert and rejecting conclusions of defendant's expert on the cause of the accident.

We now turn to Ford's remaining contentions. Ford assigns error to the plaintiff's use of its discovery deposition of Professor Kieling. The use of discovery depositions is authorized by CR 26(d)(3), if the witness "resides out of the county and more than 20 miles from the place of trial, unless it appears that the absence of the witness was procured by the party offering the deposition; . . ." At the time of trial, it is undisputed that Professor Kieling's residence satisfied the requirements of the rule. *See* Aircraft Radio Indus., Inc. v. M. V. Palmer, Inc., 45 Wash.2d 737, 277 P.2d 737 (1954). Moreover, at the time the discovery deposition was taken, Ford was notified by plaintiff's counsel that it might be used for "other purposes, including perpetuation." The trial court did not err in admitting Professor Kieling's deposition into evidence.

Ford also assigns error for the failure of the trial court to instruct the jury to find in Ford's favor if there is nothing more tangible to proceed upon than two or more conjectural theories under one or more of which Ford would be liable and under one or more of which there would be no liability. What we said in *Raybell v. State,* 6 Wash.App. 795, 804, 496 P.2d 559 (1972) is applicable here. The theories were "substantial and not conjectural. . . ." The outcome depended upon which circumstantial evidence the jury chose to believe. Consequently, that rule was not applicable.

Finally, Ford assigns error for the trial court's giving an instruction on circumstantial evidence. That instruction was properly given, since both parties were relying upon circumstantial facts.

Judgment affirmed.

ARMSTRONG and PETRIE, JJ., concur.

Thompson v. Curators of University of Missouri

Supreme Court of Missouri, Division 2, 1973.
488 S.W.2d 617.

Very often it becomes necessary to evaluate whether a person is competent mentally to either testify or execute a will. Many times expert witnesses are not available to make this determination unless specific instances of irrational conduct can be introduced into evidence by witnesses who can testify as to what specific conduct the subject person engaged in. If that conduct is testified to by one or more lay witnesses, then a hypothetical question that requires a conclusion may be submitted to an expert in this area. However, in some situations, a lay witness may testify as to the subject's behavior and may be permitted to testify as to a conclusion on the mental competence of the subject person. This case presents such a situation, where lay witnesses were permitted to testify as to the mental competence of a person based on factual statements relating to what the subject person did and said.

MORGAN, Presiding Judge.

Joe H. Hume, a bachelor and resident of Saline County, Missouri, died on December 27, 1967. Thereafter, a document dated March 27, 1967, was admitted to probate as his last will and testament. His nearest relatives, three nephews, filed this will contest suit. The sole and only issue raised for trial was decedent's testamentary capacity on the date the purported will was executed. The jury sustained contestant's position and found that the questioned document was not the will of the decedent. Two residuary legatees, the University of Missouri and the Salter Methodist church, have appealed. We affirm.

The record reflects that the case does not involve an unusual set of facts nor any novel questions of law. On appeal, appellants submit that the judgment entered on the verdict returned should be reversed, because: (1) the contestants failed to make a submissible case, (2) lay witnesses were allowed to express opinions relative to the mental state of decedent absent a factual basis for such conclusions, and (3) the trial court unduly restricted cross-examination by appellants-proponents of the witnesses for contestants.

The objective and extent of our review is well fixed. As said in Sturm v. Routh, Mo., 373 S.W.2d 922, 928[2]: "In our consideration of this appeal we must bear in mind that the question is not what conclusion this court would reach upon a review of the evidence in the transcript, nor the result we may think the jury should have reached, but only whether there is *some substantial evidence* in the record from which a jury could reasonably have found that testator did not have sufficient testamentary capacity at the time he purportedly executed . . . [the will on March 27, 1967.]" Also appropriate, and consistent therewith, is the observation made in Machens v. Machens, Mo., 263 S.W.2d 724, 734[16], that: "Nothing in our jurisprudence is more firmly established than the rule that a jury's verdict is final (and not reviewable) on the fact issues, if its findings are supported by substantial evidence, and that our review of that question is limited to determining whether the evidence, considered most favorably to the result reached by the jury, is substantial evidence from which the jury could reasonably reach the result it did. See West's Missouri Digest, Appeal and Error, 930, 989, 999, 1001, 1002 and 1003. Of course, in this case, the jury could have taken a different view (and there was much evidence to support a different view) but, since there was substantial evidence to support the verdict, conflicting evidence is wholly immaterial on the issues (submissibility of mental incapacity . . .) presented for our decision on this appeal." In this light, after noting that the proponents did present prima facie proof of testamentary capacity, we consider whether or not contestants produced substantial evidence that the decedent was incapable of making his will at the time he attempted to do so. In this case, such a task is not difficult.

Witnesses offered by contestants included three doctors and five lay persons. Each expressed the opinion that decedent was mentally incompetent on the dates of interest. In answer to the hypothetical question posed, each doctor gave as his expert opinion the conclusion that decedent on March 27, 1967, lacked the required capacity to meet the standard of mental competency called for by the law of this state. Hall v. Mercantile Trust Co., 332 Mo. 802, 59 S.W.2d 664, 669[2–4]; Rex v. Masonic Home of Missouri, 341 Mo. 589, 108 S.W.2d 72, 84[4]; Callaway v. Blankenbaker, 346 Mo. 383, 141 S.W.2d 810, 814[4]. One indicated that decedent was "a portrait of insanity." Such testimony was not premised solely on the facts outlined in the hypothetical question. Each doctor had either known decedent for years or had examined or observed him at times near the date of the execution of the document. One such date was as close as March 17, 1967.

As to the lay witnesses, " . . . the rule is that the opinion of a lay witness as to the soundness of mind of a person whose mental condition is under investigation has no weight or value unless such opinion is based upon a knowledge of facts inconsistent with sanity . . ." Lewis v. McCullough, Mo., 413 S.W.2d 499, 504; Barnes v. Marshall, Mo., 467 S.W.2d 70, 77. In view of appellants' argument that such a foundation was missing, we have considered the same, but to avoid repetition we summarize a part of such testimony as follows: decedent imagined that his chimney had fallen down and needed a bricklayer but could not recall making the statement; imagined that people were in his yard yelling at him and raking boards up and down the side of his house; was unable to discuss whether or not his bills had been paid; never washed his eating utensils; after defendant's neighbor fed decedent's stock decedent would refeed them two or three times a day; soiled himself, his bedding and his car with bowel movements and did not seem to object to it; would not sign checks to pay outstanding bills; would arise at 2:00 to 3:00 A.M., dress with one sock on and one shoe on the other foot; thought he was married and needed to go to St. Louis to get his wife; while at his nephew's in Madison, Missouri, thought his own farm was just over the hill; was obsessed with counting his cattle and constantly wanted to recount them; would not know acquaintances in whose homes he had visited and had meals; on the evening of March 26, 1967, imagined someone was outside his nephew's home flashing a light into the window at him; accused his friend Howard Page of stealing his log chain; was found under his kitchen table confused and mixed up; got lost in his own field and wandered around in circles and could not get his bearings and did not know where his house was; did not know relatives and friends at Fitzgibbon Hospital; would come to visit his neighbor but would talk and mumble to himself and was unable to answer questions; that he would attempt to go home but would go the wrong way and have to turn around; would sit and talk to himself but could not answer a question; did not always remember when his nephew Joe had been to see him; mistook his neighbor's wife for either or both of his nephews' wives and confused his neighbor with his nephew Jim; on March 29 did not know what he was signing at the Home in Concordia; early morning of March 31 was up, cursing attendants, unmanageable, threatened attendants when they tried to give him a hypo to calm him; tried to leave the rest home repeatedly and left one night in a pouring rain walking with the help of a walker, was attempting to find his cattle to feed them and was found two and one-half blocks away; made threats to the nurses that he'd hit them if necessary; another early morning left the home going out to feed his cattle, fell outside, grabbed the nurse's ankle and tore her uniform; had to be discharged because he was unmanageable and a danger to the personnel and residents; while at the rest home in Concordia thought the adjacent cornfield was his own and that Joe Thompson had let "them" tear down his home and remove his stove.

As said in Barnes v. Marshall, supra, 467 S.W.2d 1. c. 78: "We think it is obvious that each witness detailed sufficient facts upon which to base the opinion stated. Those facts went far beyond a mere showing of peculiarities and eccentricities. They were clearly inconsistent with the conclusion that testator was of sound mind." The evidence before and after execution of the document was sufficient to raise a reasonable inference as to his mental condition on the date of execution of the same. It is not required that proof of testamentary incapacity at the very moment be made by eyewitnesses. Walter v. Alt, 348 Mo. 53, 152 S.W.2d 135. On the record before us, points one and two are ruled against appellants.

Lastly, we consider the individual complaint of the university that its right to cross-examination was unduly restricted by the trial court. At the start of the trial, counsel for appellants asked for separate cross-examination of respondents' witnesses. The trial court suggested that: "As indicated earlier in our conversations, I'm going to permit you both to ask questions on voir dire; but I still feel that in view of the fact there is just one ultimate issue and both defendants are interested in that same one issue that cross-examination should be confined to one lawyer or the other; of course the court will allow you plenty of time to confer, but as I also suggested earlier, if something arises that has some special significance to one defendant or the other, if you will request the court at that time I'll make a ruling whether or not I'll allow both of you to cross-examine the same witness."

Section 491.070, RSMo 1969, V.A. M.S., provides that a party against whom a witness has testified shall be entitled to cross-examine such witness. 58 Am.Jur., Witnesses, § 611, p. 340. Such a right and the limitations thereon have been considered often by this court. For instance, in Pettus v. Casey, Mo., 358 S.W.2d 41, 1. c. 44, it was said: "The right to cross-examine a witness who has testified for the adverse party is absolute and not a mere privilege. . . . A trial court may properly exercise its discretion as to the scope and extent of cross-examination, but it is not within the court's discretion to prevent cross-examination entirely." More specifically, as expressed in Krez v. Mickel, Mo., 431 S.W.2d 213, 1. c. 215; "The extent and scope of cross-examination in a civil proceeding is discretionary with the trial court and its rulings with respect thereto will not be disturbed unless an abuse of discretion is clearly shown." In connection with a case involving multiple defendants, the general rule, as stated in 98 C.J.S. Witnesses § 368, p. 116, is: "Where there are several codefendants, counsel of each may cross-examine plaintiff's witnesses, and in a consolidated action any party may cross-examine the witnesses of any other party; but it is undesirable for more than one attorney to cross-examine the same witnesses, and the right may be denied where the interests of the codefendants are identical."

It is obvious that an area is involved that does not lend itself to the establishment of a rigid rule. The university and the church had a mutuality of purpose with the one goal of proving that decedent had a testamentary capacity. Their interests were one and the same, and they would either profit or not together. What if each of the other named legatees had employed counsel? Would fairness, or even the statute itself, demand that the testimony of each adverse witness be subjected to cross-examination by each and every participant even where repetition would become unbearable? We think not. An orderly and fair trial does not dictate such an absurd result. From the record presented, it appears that the trial court acted properly within the rules of law noted. It was a discretionary ruling which not only allowed for an orderly trial but was conditioned to avoid prejudice to either appellant. In this connection, it is of interest that throughout the trial counsel for neither party requested a separate or additional examination of any witness. On appeal, no suggestion is made that some matter favorable to either was not brought out; and, absent a claim of prejudice or abuse of discretion by the trial court, the point is without merit.

Finding no error, the judgment is affirmed.

HENLEY and DONNELLY, JJ., and O'LEARY, Special Judge, concur.

✔ PRACTICE QUESTIONS

Select the most correct answer to complete each statement.

1. The reason that the results of a polygraph test are generally not admissible in the trial is that
   (a) their use is a violation of a person's Fifth Amendment protection against self-incrimination.
   (b) these results are not yet sufficiently reliable and are still too much in the experimental field.
   (c) a habitual liar can alter the results.
   (d) if the subject is constantly hypertensive, the results are not valid.

2. A police officer was called on to testify as to the cause of an auto accident although he did not witness the collision. His conclusions with respect to the speed of the vehicles immediately prior to impact were admissible because
   (a) he had been a police officer for more than ten years.
   (b) he had reported on many accidents while on duty.
   (c) he had been a police officer for more than fifteen years.
   (d) he was a police officer who had investigated many automobile accidents and had kept abreast of the field of automobile accident investigation.

3. In the area of opinion evidence, the following statement is true:
   (a) Many old decisions have held that an inference opinion or conclusion of a skilled or expert witness ordinarily is accepted by the court.
   (b) In most recent cases, it has been held that where the matter under inquiry is properly the subject of expert testimony, it is no objection that the opinion sought to be elicited is on the issue to be decided.
   (c) In spite of being an aid to the jury, opinion evidence may not be admitted notwithstanding its bearing directly on the main issue.
   (d) Witnesses may testify as to the conclusions they reached as a result of using any one of the endowed five senses.

4. In criminal law, an expert opinion is often needed. Which of the following statements adheres to that notion?
   (a) The testimony by the expert witness need not intend to aid the jury in its search for the truth.
   (b) The qualifications of the expert witness are not that relevant if the individual is well known in the community.
   (c) The necessary requirements before an expert may testify in a criminal case are stricter than those in a civil case.
   (d) The knowledge acquired by certain individuals in the study of criminology, police science, forensic science, and related disciplines has necessitated the use of expert opinions in criminal cases.

5. A teller in a bank who regularly cashes checks on accounts of the bank where he or she is employed is
   (a) not competent to testify as to the genuineness of a signature of a depositor who has frequently cashed bank checks with that teller, based on the depositor's account with that bank.
   (b) competent to testify as to the genuineness of a signature of a depositor who has frequently cashed bank checks with that teller, based on the depositor's account with that bank.

(c) an expert witness with respect to the genuineness of that depositor's signature.

(d) none of the above.

Indicate whether each statement is true or false.

6. An ordinary witness may not testify as to whether a person appeared to be angry.

7. An expert witness may be permitted to testify as to a conclusion with respect to the expertise of that witness, even though the trier of the facts could come to a conclusion without the expert's opinion.

CHAPTER 5

The Best Evidence Rule

§ 5.1 INTRODUCTION

The rule of evidence commonly known as the best evidence rule is that the highest degree of proof of which a case from its nature is susceptible must, if accessible, be produced; in other words, no evidence shall be received when there is an apparent possibility that the party who offers it can obtain better evidence. This elementary principle of the law of evidence embraces every issue which may be in controversy, but it applies almost exclusively to documentary evidence. Pa.—Perry v. Ryback, 302 Pa. 559, 153 A. 700 (1931). It is for the court to determine. The best evidence rule goes only to the competency of the evidence, not to its materiality, relevancy, or weight. Me.—Morgan v. Paine, 312 A.2d 178 (Me. 1973); Minn.—Stevens v. Minneapolis Fire Dep't Relief Ass'n, 219 Minn. 276, 17 N.W.2d 642 (1945); Buffalo Ins. Co. v. United Parking Stations, Inc., 277 Minn. 134, 152 N.W.2d 81 (1967).

§ 5.2 REASON FOR RULE

The reason for the best evidence rule is that it prevents fraud that might be attempted if the parties were able to prove the contents of a writing by all evidence that is referred to in the law of evidence of parol evidence. It also prevents inaccuracies in the copying of the original writing and mistakes in reading it, and when the writing itself is presented in the trial, these dangers are averted. The best evidence rule is aimed at only excluding evidence concerning the contents of the testimony, but questions as to its existence or identity may be admissible. Best evidence must always be equated to what one is trying to prove; it has a strong relation to reliability. U.S.—N.L.R.B. v. International Union of Operating Eng'rs, Local 12, 243 F.2d 134 (9th Cir. 1957).

§ 5.3 ADMISSIBILITY OF BEST EVIDENCE OBTAINABLE

When the evidence offered, although not of the highest degree or of the most satisfactory kind, is otherwise competent and the best that can be produced under the circumstances, and there is no evidence of a higher degree or more conclusive character available to the party seeking to prove the fact in issue, it is admissible. However, it still must be competent to the fact in issue. If, for any reason, it is incompetent, it may not be admissible. Thus, an affidavit of a justice of peace who tried a case as to the bases of action would not be competent as secondary evidence of the contents of the last records of justice courts. N.C.—

Higgs-Taft Furniture Co. v. Clark, 191 N.C. 369, 131 S.E. 731 (1926). Letters or documents written in duplicate are written by the same mechanical act if a carbon copy is produced. Accordingly, the carbon copy is known as a duplicate original. Ky.—Davis v. William Bros. Constr. Co., 207 Ky. 404, 269 S.W. 289 (1925); Minn.—International Harvester Co. v. Elfstrom, 101 Minn. 263, 112 N.W. 252, 12 L.R.A. (N.S.) 243 (1907). Printing press copies and all reproductions from the same setting of type are considered as originals. Ga.—Ennis v. Atlas Fin. Co., 120 Ga.App. 849, 172 S.E.2d 482 (1969); La.—Joseph Durst Corp. v. Coastal Dev. Co., 248 La. 420, 179 So.2d 17 (1965); N.Y.—Huff v. Bennett, 6 N.Y. (2 Seld.) 337 (1852); Utah—James Mfg. Co. v. Wilson, 15 Utah 2d 210, 390 P.2d 127 (1964).

§ 5.4 PHOTOCOPY

Modern offices have discontinued the use of carbon copies as wasteful. It is far less expensive to have a secretary prepare an original and then photocopy the original for file records. This presents a problem in the law of evidence, since photocopies are not considered the best evidence because they are not made by the same mechanical act. You must constantly bear in mind that the rules of evidence are designed to bring forth the truth according to the best knowledge and experience available. It is a simple matter to change the contents of the original in printing a photocopy, and accordingly common law courts will not accept these in evidence. 142 A.L.R. 1270, 76 A.L.R.2d 1356.

However, because this practice of photocopying is so widespread today, it is considered to be done in the regular course of business, and many states have enacted statutes that are in derogation of the common law and recognize this practice and consider the photocopies to be sufficiently trustworthy to be treated as originals for the purpose of the best evidence rule. N.Y.—CPLR 4539, Hospital and medical records; CPLR 2306—A. Books or papers of a library department or bureau of a municipal corporation or of the state; CPLR 2307–B; Public Officers Law 64–a; General Municipal Law 51–a.

The usual-course-of-business method of admitting photocopies is not without some obstacles. United States v. Alexander, 849 F.2d 1293, 1301 (10th Cir. 1988). In United States v. Haddock, 956 F.2d 1534, 1545 (10th Cir. 1992), the court held, inter alia, "that '[a] duplicate is admissible to the same extent as an original unless (1) a genuine question is raised as to the authenticity of the original or (2) in the circumstances it would be unfair to admit the duplicate in lieu of the original.'" Federal Rule of Evidence 1003. However, despite our age of technology, a trial court must still be wary of admitting duplicates "where the circumstances surrounding the execution of the writing presents a substantial possibility of fraud." 5 Jack B. Weinstein and Margaret A. Berger, Weinstein's Evidence § 1003[2], at 1003–9 (1991). See Chapter 10 (business records exception).

§ 5.5 Examined or Sworn Copies

A judicial record may be copied or photocopied and compared with the original on file in the court. If a witness compares the copy with the original, the copy is usually held admissible without proof that the original cannot be produced. Ark.—Moss v. State, 208 Ark. 137, 185 S.W.2d 92, 94 (1945). Usually, a statute provides that the clerk of the court may certify or authenticate the copy. See Chapters 10 (business records exception) and Chapter 15 (public records).

§ 5.6 PRIMARY AND SECONDARY EVIDENCE

If an original document is placed in evidence, it is considered to be primary evidence of its contents. However, a copy of the document or the oral statements of a witness regarding its contents are designated as secondary evidence. This usually occurs when the original has been lost or destroyed. The foundation must show that a reasonable search has been made for the original in the place where it is most likely to be (the last place that it was seen), and inquiry should be made of people who are most likely to have some knowledge of its whereabouts. Naturally, it must be shown that the original was neither destroyed with fraudulent intent nor intentionally destroyed. The court may permit a party to follow any order of proof to establish

1. that the writing had been in existence;
2. its genuineness if its authenticity is in question; and
3. a proper excuse for its not being produced:
   (a) unavailable without fault of the party desiring to prove the fact;
   (b) lost or destroyed by the party against whom the evidence is offered;
   (c) inaccessible to the party seeking to prove the fact;
   (d) held by a court in the same jurisdiction and primary evidence cannot be secured for trial;
   (e) held by a third party not within the jurisdiction of the court; or
   (f) unavailable due to failure of the adverse party to produce primary evidence on notice. 32A C.J.S. Evidence §§ 813 et seq.

§ 5.7 INADMISSIBILITY OF PRIMARY EVIDENCE

Secondary evidence of the contents of a writing cannot be introduced when it appears that, for any reason, the writing would not be admissible. For example, if the original writing constituted a privileged communication, it could not be admitted against the party to whom the privilege ran. Ill.—Krumin v. Bruknes, 255 Ill.App. 503 (1930). A fortiori, after a writing itself has been offered in evidence and rejected, parol evidence of its contents cannot be received. Ga.—Crider v. Woodward, 162 Ga. 743, 135 S.E. 95 (1926).

§ 5.8 FAILURE OF ADVERSE PARTY TO PRODUCE PRIMARY EVIDENCE ON NOTICE

Secondary evidence is admissible where the primary evidence of a fact which a party desires to prove is in the possession or control of his adversary, who fails or refuses to produce it after being notified or requested to do so (Mass.—Bresky v. Rosenberg, 256 Mass. 66, 152 N.E. 347 [1926]; N.J.—North Jersey Discount Co. v. Aetna Ins. Co., 125 N.J.L. 7, 13 A.2d 226 [1940]; N.Y.—Harmon v. Matthews, 27 N.Y.S.2d 656 [1941]) or who, after such notification or request, fails to explain why he did not produce the primary evidence. Me.—Norton v. Heywood, 20 Me. 359 (1841).

§ 5.9 EFFECT OF PRODUCTION OF ORIGINAL MATERIAL

Secondary evidence is not admissible where primary evidence is produced, but the introduction of secondary evidence on failure to produce the primary evidence is not rendered erroneous by the subsequent production of the primary evidence. Ind.—Phenix Ins. Co. v. Jacobs, 23 Ind.App. 509, 55 N.E. 778 (1899).

§ 5.10 DEGREES AND KINDS OF SECONDARY EVIDENCE

Secondary evidence of the contents of a writing may be furnished by the testimony of witnesses (U.S.—Conkling v. New York Life Ins. & Trust Co., 262 Fed. 620 [D.C.Cir. 1919]) or by the production of a copy. There is much conflict with respect to whether there are degrees of secondary evidence. It is universally accepted, however, that when a proper case can be made for the introduction of secondary evidence, any kind of secondary evidence is competent that is admissible by other rules of law unless it is shown by the nature of this evidence itself or is made to appear by the objecting party that other or more satisfactory evidence is known to the producing party and can be produced by him or her. However, courts have rejected the argument of counsel against the introduction of oral testimony of the contents of the original writing when a proper foundation was laid for the nonproduction of the original and a copy was available. In rejecting this argument, the court said, "Although the argument is plausible, it is apparent on a moment's reflection that proof of an instrument by proving a copy is merely one form of parol testimony as to its contents, and I am not aware of any rule of law that makes a distinction of grade in secondary evidence." N.Y.—Rosenbaum v. Podolsky, 97 Misc. 614, 162 N.Y.S. 227, 229 (1917).

§ 5.11 RECORDS AND JUDICIAL DOCUMENTS

Where the fact to be proved is one that the law requires to appear of record, the general rule is that the record itself or a properly authenticated copy is the best evidence and parol evidence cannot be received to prove the fact except where the record is lost or destroyed or is, for other reasons, inaccessible and a properly authenticated copy cannot be obtained. Conn.—State ex rel. Capurso v. Flis, 144 Conn. 473, 133 A.2d 901 (1957): Fla.—Milk Comm'n v. Dade County Dairies, 145 Fla. 579, 200 So. 83 (1940). The judgments and decrees of courts of record cannot be proved by parol evidence unless the record is lost or destroyed or is otherwise inaccessible and a properly authenticated copy or transcript thereof cannot be obtained. Cal.—Sills v. Forbes, 33 Cal.App.2d 219, 91 P.2d 246 (1939); Conn.—Beers v. Bridgeport Hydraulic Co., 100 Conn. 459, 124 A. 23 (1924); N.Y.—In re Diaz-Albertini's Will, 2 A.D.2d 671, 154 N.Y.S.2d 422 (1956).

However, it sometimes happens that incompetent people take minutes of a meeting of a government body and they omit some information as to what took place that is found to be a critical issue in a court proceeding or action that has been instituted as a result of what transpired at the meeting. In Adams v. Sims, 238 Ark. 696, 385 S.W.2d 13 (1964), it was held that the fact that the records of a city failed to disclose actions by its city council is not conclusive that the council did not take the same. Parol evidence is admissible to establish the real facts of corporate acts in the absence of records where the record which it kept is so meager or where the particular transaction, act, or vote is not disclosed. U.S.—Handley v. Stutz, 139 U.S. 417, 422, 11 S.Ct. 530, 532, 35 L.Ed. 227, 232 (1891); Ark.—Smith v. Ford, 203 Ark. 265, 157 S.W.2d 199 (1941); McGee v. Mainard, 208 Ark. 1001, 188 S.W.2d 635 (1945).

When a witness, while testifying, denies that he or she has ever been convicted of a crime and the prosecution knows that the witness has been previously convicted of a crime, the prosecutor may ask for a continuance to allow sufficient time to bring into court a certified copy of the transcript of judgment. This question may only be asked in a limited type of situation by U.S. attorneys and by many state prosecutors pursuant to statute. See Federal Rule of Evidence 609.

§ 5.12   RULES AND REGULATIONS OF A POLICE DEPARTMENT

The rules and regulations of a police department are usually promulgated by the chief of police, police commission, board of police commissions, or other similar entity. The authority to promulgate these rules is usually given to the person or board so designated by a legislative act. The rules and regulations thus have the force and effect of law. They prescribe the authority and limitation of authority as well as the responsibilities of the various uniform force ranks in the department and the detective or investigation units or bureaus. The nomenclature of the various positions and parts of the department varies from one department to another. If the department is large, the positions are generally known as police officer, sergeant, lieutenant, captain, inspector, chief inspector, and commissioner.

Frequently, it becomes necessary to charge a member of the police department with a violation of the rules and regulations. If this is done, the charge is usually instituted by a member of the department who has a rank higher than the officer being charged with the violation. The person charged is usually designated as the respondent, and a full trial may take place before a trial commissioner or other administrative trial judge. The legal rules of evidence that are practiced in a court of law are not implemented in such a trial, but the legal residuum rule applies, whereby in order to sustain a finding of guilt some legal evidence must have been introduced. An example of this legal theory occurred in Ginn v. City of Atlanta, 73 Ga.App. 162, 35 S.E.2d 777 (1945), where the chief of police was permitted to testify regarding a police captain's duties, although the captain's duties were provided in writing by authority of written rules of the police department. The rules should have been read into evidence, or they should have been physically offered into evidence, but in Ginn v. City of Atlanta, supra, the appellate court found no substantial error in permitting the chief to testify what the captain's duties are.

§ 5.13   VOLUMINOUS WRITINGS

Sometimes it is necessary to establish the result of voluminous writings or entries. In this case, a qualified person, such as an accountant, may testify to a summary of the documents on the condition that these documents have been made available to the other side in sufficient time for him or her to adequately inspect them. Ariz.—Collison v. International Ins. Co., 58 Ariz. 156, 118 P.2d 445 (1941); N.Y.—Public Operating Corp. v. Weingart, 257 A.D. 379, 13 N.Y.S.2d 182 (1939).

§ 5.14   LEARNED TREATISES

When an expert testifies, he or she is subject to cross-examination. When the expert's testimony is at variance with what is written in a learned treatise on the subject, it becomes necessary to impeach the expert's conclusions by the use of that learned treatise.

Let us suppose that a police scientist is testifying as to the direction a bullet shot from a revolver took as it pierced a window glass of an automobile. Let us further assume that the scientist testifies that when a bullet pierces such a window, the side from which the bullet enters the window appears like a crater of a volcano, with numerous small flakes of glass missing, while the side where it exits the window contains a round hole with the approximate circumference of the bullet.

On cross-examination, the expert may be asked whether he or she has done experiments to substantiate these conclusions. On an affirmative answer, the expert may be asked if he or she is familiar with a recognized book or treatise in forensic science such as *Introduction to Criminal Investigation*, by Richard H. Ward. If the expert denies familiarity with the named book or treatise, he or she may be asked about others. If the expert denies familiarity with all of those named, he or she may be asked what book or treatise on the subject he or she is familiar with. It is hoped that the trial counsel has the book or treatise available. If counsel does not immediately have it, he or she may ask for a continuance or ask the court to recall the witness at a subsequent date.

When the trial counsel has the book or treatise the witness claims familiarity with, he or she may ask that it be marked for identification and then ask the witness to read the contradictory material silently, or he or she may ask the court for permission to read it into evidence.

If, as in the hypothetical case indicated above, the book reads that the cone-shaped opening of the window is on the side from which the bullet exits, the trial counsel will ask the witness if he or she would like to change his or her testimony. If the witness persists in his or her testimony, counsel may ask the court for permission to read the contradictory material into evidence.

Notwithstanding the fact that such information is hearsay, courts have permitted the introduction of such evidence on the issue of the existence of the statement itself and not the truth of the statement. Miss.—Catholic Diocese of Natchez-Jackson v. Jaquith, 224 So.2d 216 (Miss. 1969). However, if a witness can be produced to vouch for the general authenticity of a publication, it may be introduced as admissible hearsay. Wash.—Most Worshipful Prince Hall Grand Lodge of Wash. v. Most Worshipful Grand Lodge, A.F. & A.M., 62 Wash.2d 28, 381 P.2d 130 (1963), *cert. denied*, 375 U.S. 945, 84 S.Ct. 352, 11 L.Ed.2d 275 (1963).

This theory of admitting learned treatises as an exception to the hearsay exclusionary rule has been codified in Federal Rule of Evidence 803 (18).

§ 5.15 RULE IN CRIMINAL CASES

In a criminal case, the rule with respect to a demand to produce is different because of the constitutional protections.

The defendant's silence or refusal would cause serious injurious inferences against him or her. Therefore, when an incriminating document appears prima facie to be in the possession of the defendant, the people may submit secondary evidence of its contents sans the necessity of just asking the defendant to produce the original. For example, a person who is in possession of lottery numbers in some states is in violation of the gambling statute. If a person is found to be in possession of a blank paper and this paper contains impressions of lottery numbers that resulted from writing on another paper in pencil or ballpoint pen, the original of which has been placed on top of the impressioned paper when the writing had been done, the impressioned paper could be admitted in evidence. Photographs of the paper done with oblique lighting could then be introduced to explain the primary (impressioned paper) evidence. In this case, the photographs would be considered as secondary evidence. The defendant could not be required to produce the original paper containing the lottery numbers.

§ 5.16 FEDERAL RULE

The Federal Rules of Evidence treat the best evidence rule in Rules 1002, 1003, and 1004:

§ **Rule 1002. Requirement of original**

To prove the content of a writing, recording, or photograph, the original writing, recording, or photograph is required, except as otherwise provided in these rules or by law.

§ **Rule 1003. Admissibility of duplicates**

A duplicate is admissible to the same extent as an original unless (1) a genuine question is raised as to the authenticity of the original or (2) in the circumstances it would be unfair to admit the duplicate in lieu of the original.

§ **Rule 1004. Admissibility of other evidence of contents**

The original is not required, and other evidence of the contents of a writing, recording, or photograph is admissible if—

(1) Originals lost or destroyed. All originals are lost or have been destroyed, unless the proponent lost or destroyed them in bad faith; or

(2) Original not obtainable. No original can be obtained by any available judicial process or procedure; or

(3) Original in possession of opponent. At a time when an original was under the control of the party against whom offered, he was put on notice, by the pleadings or otherwise, that the contents would be a subject of proof at the hearing, and he does not produce the original at the hearing; or

(4) Collateral matters. The writing, recording, or photograph is not closely related to a controlling issue.

CROSS-REFERENCES

Federal Civil Judicial Procedure and Rules (West 1996) (Rules 1002, 1003, and 1004).

Goode & Wellborn, Courtroom Handbook on Federal Evidence (West 1995) (Rules 1002, 1003, and 1004).

McCormick, Evidence §§ 229–231, 233 (4th ed. 1992) (Rules 1002, 1003, and 1004).

RELATED   DECISIONS
Best Evidence Rule

Perry v. Ryback
Supreme Court of Pennsylvania, 1931.
302 Pa. 559, 153 A. 770.

The following case involves a traffic accident wherein the widow of a person who died as a result of the accident brought a wrongful death action against the driver of the vehicle in which the decedent was a passenger. A close reading of the decision will reveal that the judge and/or the reporter made an error in stating that the decedent was willing to join Perry in the hazard or to take a chance on the result of fast driving. I have taken the liberty to correct two of these errors by placing the name of the driver, Ryback, in brackets following the name Perry, where it is appropriate, to make the meaning clear. There are several principles of law in this case relating to the best evidence rule. I urge you to see if you can find them.

*   *   *

Appeal from Court of Common Pleas, Erie County; J. W. Bouton, President Judge, specially presiding.

Action by Eugenia C. Perry against Bernie Ryback. Judgment for plaintiff, and defendant appeals.

*   *   *

KEPHART, J. Lytle Perry, Bernie Ryback, and another, members of a hunting party, were driving along the Roosevelt Highway in Ryback's car shortly after noon on November 30, 1927. Ryback, who was driving from fifty to sixty miles an hour in a very hard rain, attempted to go around an "S" curve. The car slid off the road, broke a telephone pole in half, turned over and killed Perry. Deceased's widow brought this action, for herself, and children, against Ryback, and recovered a verdict. On judgment in her favor, this appeal followed.

Appellant contends that his negligence should be imputed to Perry, since they were engaged in a joint enterprise. Whether or not the journey was a joint enterprise is immate-rial to the determination of this case. That doctrine is applicable only where one of the parties to the enterprise sues a third party. "Where the action is brought against a third party, the rule is that the negligence of one member of the joint enterprise within the scope of that enterprise will be imputed to the other. . . . When the action is brought by one member of the enterprise against another, there is no place to apply the doctrine of imputed negligence. . . . The situation when the action is brought by one member of the enterprise against the other is entirely different from that when recovery is sought against a third person." Johnson v. Hetrick, 300 Pa. 225, 233, 150 A. 477, 479 (1930).

Where the action between parties to a joint enterprise is for injuries from a negligent act, it will be treated as an ordinary action for injuries as a result of negligence. The general rule may be stated as follows: When two or more persons are engaged in any pursuit, whether it be pleasure, business, mutual convenience, or fellowship, each owes to the other the duty to exercise due care in their relation that no injury shall happen through a neglect of that duty. The care required in such relation is what men of ordinary prudence would use in similar circumstances. The fact that the mutual safety of the persons in the relation depends on the exercise of care by all does not enlarge or emphasize the duty. It is ordinary care under the circumstances. Where one in that relation fails to perform that duty, he is responsible for the resultant injury. The rights of the parties as to each other, with regard to the duty enjoined, are separate and distinct, even though one of the parties in the relation is dependent. What constitutes a failure of duty is a relative term, and must depend on the facts of each case. The owner of an automobile is liable to his guest or passenger if he negligently operates his car to the injury of his guest or passenger. We do not here determine liability if the car is driven other than by the owner.

While this liability is thus fixed on one of the parties of the enterprise through his negligent acts, there is a duty imposed on the other party, the deceased in this case. It has been stated in many of our cases that, where the action is against third persons, the duty thus resting on the other party is to caution, warn, remonstrate, or protest to the driver as to his fast or careless driving. Curran v. Lehigh Valley R. R., 299 Pa. 584, 591, 149 A. 885 (1930). See Kilpatrick v. P.R.T. Co., 290 Pa. 288, 294, pars. 2, 3, and page 295, 138 A. 830 (1927). Also Campagna v. Lyles, 298 Pa. 352, 357, 148 A. 527 (1930), and cases there cited. The same rule applies where the action is between the parties of a mutual venture. It was the duty of the deceased, when he noticed Perry [Ryback] driving at the rate of speed as here testified, to protest or warn him against it. If he failed to perform this duty, he was guilty of contributory negligence; the law would assume under such circumstances that he was satisfied with the operation of the car, and that he was willing to join Perry [Ryback] in the hazard or in taking a chance on the result of fast driving.

But, as appellee's husband is dead, the law presumes that he used due care, that is, that he did protest or remonstrate with Perry [Ryback] as to his driving. Johnson v. Hetrick, supra. The presumption of due care on the part of the deceased may be rebutted , in appellee's case, by incontrovertible, physical facts, that is, such facts as a court will take judicial notice of (Patterson v. Pittsburgh, etc., Ry. Co., 210 Pa. 47, 59 A. 318 [1904]; Unger v. P., B. & W. R. Co., 217 Pa. 106, 66 A. 235 [1907]; Hartig v. American Ice Co., 290 Pa. 21, 30, 31, 137 A. 867 [1927]), or by evidence as indicated in Hartig v. American Ice Co., supra. Where any such facts are present, or such evidence is presented, and plaintiff's case depends solely on the presumption, it must fail for want of sufficient evidence. Where the effort to rebut the presumption is by other evidence, the credibility of the witnesses is necessarily for the jury. Where there is an uncertainty as to the facts or the inferences to be drawn from them the case is necessarily for the jury. Hartig v. American Ice Co., et al., supra.

There are neither admitted nor incontrovertible physical facts or uncontroverted oral and written testimony of disinterested witnesses here to rebut the presumption. There may be some inferences, but these are not sufficient, as a matter of law, to overcome the presumption. What evidence there was on the subject, and it was all negative, was properly submitted to the jury.

Appellant contends that there are a number of alleged trial errors sufficient to cause a reversal. They are as follows: (1) The court below permitted evidence to be introduced showing deceased's habits and ability as a lawyer. (2) The stenographer was erroneously allowed to refresh her recollection of his earnings from the income tax return and ledger which she had kept. (3) That it was impossible to distinguish from plaintiff's testimony between the personal earnings of the deceased and the return from capital invested. (4) The court did not charge fully on contributory negligence.

As the question stated in 1 and 3, the rule as to the measure of damages is fully stated in Gaydos et al. v. Domabyl (Pa.) 152 A. 549, 552, an opinion handed down November 24, 1930. We there said that the jury may take into consideration deceased's "age, ability and disposition to labor, and his habits of living and expenditure." Pennsylvania R. Co. v. Butler, 57 Pa. 335, 338 (1868); Mansfield Coal & Coke Co. v. McEnery, 91 Pa. 185, 189, 36 Am.Rep. 662 (1879); McHugh v. Schlosser, 159 Pa. 480, 486, 28 A. 291, 23 L.R.A. 574, 39 Am.St.Rep. 699 (1894); Burns v. P. R. Co., 219 Pa. 225, 228, 68 A. 704 (1908). Appellant argues that evidence of character and reputation was offered and admitted. Neither the assignments of error nor the record disclose any such condition. There was no effort to prove character or reputation. It is common knowledge that a lawyer of outstanding ability or of average capacity and good habits will possess a larger clientele and will receive a greater remuneration than the lawyer of limited ability.

Where it is impossible to distinguish between personal earnings of the individual and the return from capital invested in the labor of others the net income or net results from such business should not be considered in determining the amount of damages to which the claimant is entitled. Baxter v. Phila. & R.

Ry. Co., 264 Pa. 467, 107 A. 881, 9 A.L.R. 504 (1919). But there is no such impossibility in the evidence in this case. Appellee's husband was a lawyer, and also published the Erie County Law Journal. The net income from the law practice and the journal were given, and there was testimony that more than half the income came from the law practice. Appellant had every opportunity to check the reliability of this testimony. The books, with these charges entered, were in court. The witness testified from them, and, when appellant was asked if he wished to have the items read, he specifically declined to have this done. The evidence was only important to show that his earnings were sufficient each year to give to his wife and children what, as was testified to, they received before his death. Such contributions are the basis for the measure of damages, as will be seen later. They did not comprise all his earnings and were a few hundred dollars over one-half of his net income. The verdict of $8,000 shows that the jury was very considerate in its conclusion. The charge of the court was full and explicit on the question of damages, following closely the opinion of Mr. Justice Walling in Glasco v. Green, 273 Pa. 353, 117 A. 79 (1922), and the charge was fully supported by the evidence.

While defendant's assignments of error do not cover the second question, we will consider the use of the ledger by the witness to refresh her recollection; she having made the entries of charges and being familiar with the facts. It is argued that such evidence was insufficient for the court to base any charge as to the measure of damages, relying on Muncey v. Pull. Taxi Serv. Co., 269 Pa. 97, 112 A. 30 (1921), since the evidence was not the best evidence to prove the fact at issue.

There is no general rule that the best evidence must be introduced or that better evidence must be introduced before inferior evidence. Wigmore on Evidence, vol. 2 §§ 1173, 1174. The application of the best evidence rule is ordinarily confined to primary and secondary evidence, and relates largely to the production of documents, as where one desires to prove the terms of a writing. Production of the original or an exact duplicate, must be made, unless its absence is satisfactorily explained. Here there is no attempt to prove the contents of a writing but to show the amounts of deceased's earnings. For this purpose, written or oral testimony is clearly admissible. Books of original entry are not necessarily the only evidence nor the best evidence of a given state of facts, but a party may make out his case as to such facts by the testimony of a witness. See Wigmore on Evidence, supra; also Henry's Pa. Trial Evidence, § 97, and authorities cited. Books of account are always competent to refresh the memory of a witness who had personal knowledge of a transaction. Nichols v. Haynes, 78 Pa. 174, 176 (1875); Hottle v. Weaver, 206 Pa. 87, 89, 55 A. 838 (1903). See Croushore's Estate, 79 Pa.Super.Ct. 286, 289. The fact that the latter may be more accurate is a matter for the jury.

Defendant relies on Muncey v. Pull. Taxi Serv. Co., supra, but the case does not control the instant one. Plaintiff there, who conducted a detective agency, merely stated he made $10,000 a year. This was an approximation of his earnings. We held that, as no effort was made to give any detailed account or description of his business or gross receipts and expenses, or in any manner to depict what he was doing, the evidence was not sufficient; it was merely a guess at earnings, insufficient on which to base a claim for damages. The court distinctly held that it was not always necessary to produce books to prove damages in a personal injury case.

The stenographer, testifying from the ledger, stated that she took the accounts she received from each person and kept them in the ledger and added them up. There were receipts from deceased's law and publishing business. With the book before her, she stated his net income per year was $5,700. All the evidence was admitted without objection. She stated that the receipts from the legal journal was nearly half of the net receipts. The evidence was sufficient for the jury to find deceased's earning power as it related to the contribution made to his family. Even if an objection had been made, we would not regard it as serious.

The learned trial judge endeavored to charge the jury on the question of contributory negligence as fully as it was possible for him to do, requesting appellant to point out in what respect his charge was insufficient. As we read the charge, it more than protected appellant's rights. The verdict was reasonable; the case was free from error.

The judgment of the court below is affirmed.

Chagnon Lumber Co., Inc. v. Patenaude
Supreme Court of New Hampshire, 1961.
103 N.H. 448, 174 A.2d 415.

The facts of this case may be unbelievable to many readers who have no experience in the methods of doing business in many rural communities. It is not uncommon in these communities, where people have known each other for many years, to do business by word of mouth rather than by written and signed contracts. Nevertheless, when a dispute arises, the litigation that follows is adjudicated according to the law. One of the factors here involved is known as the statute of frauds. This principle in the law of contracts provides, inter alia, that whenever there is a sale or contract to sell personal property, either goods or choses in action, and its value is a certain amount (the amount varies in different states), the statute of frauds becomes operative. While it is not the intention of this book to delve deeply into the statute, which may be found in the commercial code of your state, I believe that you should be made aware that certain types of agreements are required to be in writing in order to be enforceable in court.

In this case, you will note that the "contract" for the sale of the lumber was never signed by the parties and the original contract was not produced or its nonproduction accounted for.

BLANDIN, Justice. The plaintiff's claim, in brief, is that the defendant as an independent contractor signed a contract with a John R. Contrell to build a house for him in Lexington, Massachusetts, and that the plaintiff sold the defendant lumber and materials for the house, for which the defendant is liable.

The defendant denied these allegations and testified that he was an employee carpenter working by the day for Contrell, that he never bought the supplies himself, but told the plaintiff to charge them to Contrell.

An examination of the entire record convinces us that the sharply conflicting claims of the parties were for the jury to resolve. Hiltz v. Gould, 99 N.H. 85, 87, 105 A.2d 48 (1954). If the jury believed the defendant's evidence that the plaintiff agreed to charge the supplies to Contrell, the defendant would not be liable. Restatement, Second, Agency, § 320. It follows that the plaintiff's exception to the denial of its motion to set aside the verdict must be overruled.

In regard to the alleged contract between Contrell and the defendant, it appears that the original was never produced and that the Court in excluding the copy offered by the plaintiff found that no satisfactory excuse was given for the nonproduction. It has long been the established law that a copy of a private document (containing here merely the typed signatures of the parties) is inadmissible unless the absence of the original is satisfactorily accounted for. Wallace v. Goodall, 18 N.H. 439, 451, 455 (1846); C.J.S. Evidence §§ 813, 823, 826; see Skaling v. Remick, 97 N.H. 106, 108, 82 A.2d 81 (1951). The principle upon which the rule rests is that the original is the best evidence of the facts to be proved and that "it is to be procured and offered *if it can be had.*" IV Wigmore on Evidence (3d Ed.) § 1192(1).

Each case must rest upon its own facts and it was for the Trial Court to determine, within its discretion, whether the plaintiff had made reasonable efforts to procure the original of the alleged contract. IV Wigmore, supra, § 1194, pp. 339–340. The record convinces us that there was no abuse of discretion in the Court's finding that the absence of the original was not properly accounted for (cf. Skaling v. Remick, supra) and that the exclusion of the copy is sustainable. The order is

Judgment on the verdict.

All concurred.

State of Ohio v. James
Court of Appeals of Ohio, 1974.
41 Ohio App.2d 248, 325 N.E.2d 267.

In State of Ohio v. James, there was a question as to the admissibility of a tape recording of a conversation and other sounds accompanying the commission of a murder. The conversation and sounds were received by a police dispatcher. The dispatcher also testified regarding the incident. By reading this case, you will discover whether the tape recording or the testimony of the police dispatcher is the best evidence, or whether both can be admitted in the trial.

CRAWFORD, Presiding Judge. The defendant, Frank James, and the decedent, Lula Frey, lived at 713 Westwood Avenue in Dayton. They had an argument there on April 15, 1969. Lula Frey then called the police, who arrived at about 12:45 A.M., and left with them.

The next day, April 16, 1969, decedent was in the house at 713 Westwood talking on the telephone to the police dispatcher and, while she was holding the telephone, defendant, the appellant, came into the house and fired four shots into her and her death ensued.

Defendant claimed self-defense on the basis that he believed deceased was bringing a gun out of her bra. Such gun was never found. During this episode, the telephone was still open and connected with the police department, where the sounds transmitted by the telephone were recorded on tape. This tape recorded the shots and conversation. Defendant was convicted of the second-degree murder of Lula Frey. The tape was introduced in evidence at defendant's trial as part of the *res gestae*.

On defendant's present appeal from that conviction, his single assignment of error is the introduction into evidence of the tape recording of the conversation and other sounds received over the telephone in the office of the police dispatcher. He contended that the tape is not the best evidence, but that the best evidence would be the testimony of the police dispatcher.

Janet Welz, the police dispatcher, was called by the state to testify. She verified the accuracy of a typewritten transcript of the conversation taken from the tape. The transcript was introduced in evidence. She was not asked either on direct or cross-examination about hearing the shots recorded on the tape, which were not reflected on the typewritten transcript.

Defendant's argument that the testimony of the dispatcher would be the best evidence,

so as to render the tape inadmissible is not supported by his citations.

In People v. Kulwin, 102 Cal.App.2d 104, 226 P.2d 672 (1951), the defendant objected to the testimony of a witness to a conversation which had been recorded, contending that the recordings were the best evidence. The court held that the testimony of a witness testifying from memory is not rendered inadmissible by the existence of a record of what was heard.

Both mechanical recordings and the testimony of a witness whose memory was refreshed thereby were held properly admitted in Kilpatrick v. Kilpatrick, 123 Conn. 218, 193 A. 765 (1937). Both mechanical recording and personal testimony were held admissible in Thompson v. State, 298 P.2d 464 (Okl.Cr. 1956).

None of these cases holds that the taped record is inadmissible. On the contrary, as set forth in 29 American Jurisprudence 2d 496, Evidence, Section 436, both the tape and the oral testimony are admissible.

> "Where proof of a conversation has been of two different kinds, namely, a recording thereof and testimony by witnesses who overheard it, it has been argued that both the recording and the testimony were the best evidence; however, the courts have not relegated either to a secondary position, but have held that both types of evidence are equally competent primary evidence, and that one is not to be excluded because of the existence of the other."

Also, see annotation, 10 L.Ed.2d 1169, at 1175, entitled "Admissibility of sound recordings as evidence in Federal criminal trial." More than one witness may testify to the same facts or conversation, and the same fact may be proved by different types of proof as, for example, direct and circumstantial evidence. Where both are introduced, the one may corroborate the other, or, if they are contradictory, a question is presented for the jury.

Counsel for the state make the valid comparison between a photograph and the photographer's description of the thing or scene photographed. The photograph, if properly authenticated, as the tape was here, is clearly admissible. In fact, the photograph and the recorded tape here are much more likely to be free from error than the words of a witness testifying from memory.

The rules of evidence regarding admission and exclusion, including the rule requiring the production of the best evidence, are founded basically upon considerations of truth and reliability. A mechanical record, if audible or legible, and not tampered with, is likely to be much more accurate and dependable than oral testimony. The taped record was properly admitted and the judgment will be affirmed.

Judgment affirmed.

KERNS and SHERER, JJ., concur.

Baitcher v. Louis R. Clerico Associates, Inc.

Court of Appeals of Georgia, 1974.
132 Ga.App. 219, 207 S.E.2d 698.

This case involves the use of carbon impressions on paper. Carbon copies are not used today as often as they were in the past. However, the best evidence rules applicable to their use are appropriate today when carbonless paper is used and impressions are made on other copies with one stroke of a pen, typewriter, or similar instrument.

PANNELL, Judge. Plaintiff sued for the balance due on a contract entered March 26, 1969 for the interior design of a restaurant and the furnishing of lighting fixtures and furniture for it. Defendant denied any indebtedness existed and raised the defense of accord and satisfaction. The defendant also claimed that he had to employ others to repair work improperly performed by plaintiff and to complete certain other work not performed as agreed.

* * *

4. Appellant complains that the court erroneously admitted certain of plaintiff's exhibits in violation of the best evidence rule. The exhibits were carbon copies of documents purportedly mailed to defendant, who denied having received the originals. Assuming, arguendo, that proper objections to these exhibits were made at proffer the enumeration is without merit. "[A]ll papers executed by the same stroke upon a typewriter—those written by carbon impressions, as well as the sheet which receives the stroke of the letter from the typewriter—are alike originals. . . ." Carmichael Tile Co. v. McClelland et al., 213 Ga. 656, 659, 100 S.E.2d 902, 905 (1958). "[D]uplicate or triplicate originals, made with the same stroke of pen or typewriter as the original are admissible as primary evidence." Campbell v. Pure Oil Co. et al., 92 Ga.App. 523, 524, 88 S.E.2d 630, 631 (1955).

5. The remaining enumerations of error have been considered and are found to lack merit.

Judgment affirmed.

BELL, C.J., EBERHARDT, P.J., and DEEN, QUILLIAN, CLARK, STOLZ and WEBB, JJ., concur.

EVANS, J., dissents.

Ginn v. City of Atlanta

Court of Appeals of Georgia, Division No. 1, 1945.
73 Ga.App. 162, 35 S.E.2d 777.

This case was selected for inclusion for two reasons. First, it announces a principle of the best evidence rule wherein a chief of police was permitted to testify about a police captain's duties, even though the captain's duties were provided in writing by authority of the written rules of the police department. Neither of these means of evidence is the best evidence to the exclusion of the other.

The second reason is that it represents a caveat to all police officers who may be tempted to protect an alcoholic member of the force from departmental charges; the sanction for this practice may be very severe.

Syllabus by the Court

The court did not err in overruling, and denying the certiorari for any of the reasons assigned, as set forth in the body of the opinion.

———

Error from Superior Court, Fulton County; Edgar E. Pomeroy, Judge.

Certiorari proceeding by E. W. Ginn against the City of Atlanta and others to review action of police committee of the general council reducing plaintiff from rank of captain to rank of patrolman. To review an adverse judgment, the plaintiff brings error.

Affirmed.

See also, Ga.App., 33 S.E.2d 19.

The plaintiff in error, hereinafter called the plaintiff, was charged by M. A. Hornsby, Chief of Police of the City of Atlanta, with conduct unbecoming an officer—the plaintiff at the time being a captain in the police forces of the City of Atlanta. The specific charges are:

"Georgia. Fulton County.

"To E. W. Ginn.

"You are hereby charged with conduct unbecoming an officer of the Police Department of the City of Atlanta, with failure to perform and neglect of your duty as a Captain of said Department, and with the violation of the rules of said Department in the following particulars:

"1. On the night of December 21st, 1942, you were the Captain in charge of the evening watch, your tour of duty beginning at 4 P.M. and ending at 12 P.M. that night. At about 11 o'clock you received a call to go to the third floor of the Station House from Lt. E. S. Elliott, who reported to you that Turnkey Barge was under the influence of intoxicating liquors. Upon arrival on the third floor you found Officer D. T. Barge to be under the influence of intoxicating liquors . . . you found him to be under the influence of intoxicating liquors, and neglecting your duty you failed then and there to relieve him of duty and to take his equipment from him, but on the contrary and in violation of your clear duty as a Captain in said Department you permitted the said D. T. Barge to remain on duty at his post as a turnkey on the third floor of said Police Station.

"2. Upon arrival on the third floor of the Police Station on that night you found W. G. Scott, a turnkey from the fourth floor, on the third floor. Notwithstanding the fact that you knew that the said Scott was required on the fourth floor by the order of the Chief of Police and in order to fully protect the prisoners on the fourth floor you permitted him to remain there until relieved, thereby leaving the fourth floor without adequate turnkey protection in neglect of your duty and in violation of the rules of said Department.

"3. You improperly influenced an officer under your direction namely, Lt. E. S. Elliott, to incorrectly report the facts concerning Barge's condition, in that you directed that he submit the following in his report, which was not true in that said Barge should have been relieved from duty: 'Although I could smell the odor of alcohol on Officer Barge's breath he was not intoxicated to the extent to be relieved from his duty. Captain Ginn ordered Officer Scott to stay on the third floor with Barge, for the remainder of his tour of duty.' Lieutenant E. S. Elliott knew that the said Barge was sufficiently under the influence of intoxicating liquors to be relieved from his duty, which you knew or should have known.

"You are notified that the foregoing charges will be heard by the Police Committee of General Council at Police Station at 7:30 P.M., Thursday, January 28th, 1943. M. A. Hornsby, Chief of Police."

The plaintiff demurred to the charges ore tenus, to the general effect that they were insufficient as a matter of law. The demurrers were overruled by the Police Committee of the General Council of the City of Atlanta, the tribunal designated to pass upon the charges. To this judgment the plaintiff filed exceptions pendente lite. The case proceeded to trial and testimony was introduced by both parties. There were five of the six members of the Committee who conducted the trial, including the Mayor of the City of Atlanta. It appears from the minutes of the Committee that the five members who tried the plaintiff voted unanimously on roll call to find the plaintiff guilty of the charges against him, and on roll call the Committee voted to reduce the plaintiff from the rank of Captain to the rank of patrolman. The plaintiff obtained the writ of certiorari to the decision of the Committee. The Committee filed its answer thereto. To the answer thus filed certain exceptions were made by the plaintiff. The gist of the exceptions were that the defendants in the answer failed to point out any rule requiring the plaintiff to have removed patrolman Barge and that it failed to set forth any rules whatever governing the Police Department upon which the plaintiff could have been lawfully and legally convicted of a failure to perform his duty and that the answer did not mention any rule which is claimed to have been violated by the plaintiff. A judge of the superior court passed an order requiring the defendants to certify and file copies of any applicable rule. All other exceptions were overruled. In response to this order the defendants filed in the office of the clerk of the superior court a copy of the Rules and Regulations of the Atlanta Police Department adopted by the Police Committee of Council February 4, 1938. There appears in the said rules so filed rule No. 276, as follows: "Any member of the Police Department who has been known to be under the influence of any intoxicating drink, such as beer, wine, gin, rum, whiskey, any type of alcoholic drink, or any type of mixed alcoholic drink either while on or off duty, will be dismissed from the Force after a due trial, and proven guilty by the Police Committee of Council." And Rule No. 545 (which has fifty sub-sections), and the sub-sections applicable to this case are:

> "Any member of the Police Force may be punished by the Police Committee of Council in its discretion, either by reprimand, suspension for not longer than 90 days, or by being reduced in rank, or by dismissal from the Force, upon conviction of any one of the following offenses: 1. Drinking any kind of intoxicating alcoholic beverage, either on or off duty. . . . 4. Neglect of duty or disobedience to orders. 5. Violations of any of the Rules and Regulations. . . . 9. Conduct unbecoming an Officer. . . . 19. Any act contrary to the good order and discipline, or constituting neglect of duty, or a violation of the rules of the Department. . . . 25. The making of false Official report. . . . 36. Neglect to report any member of the Department known to be guilty of violation of any rule, regulation or order issued for the guidance of the Department. . . . 47. Untruthfulness. . . . 50. Any act of omission or commission contrary to good order and discipline, or constituting a violation of any of the provisions of the Rules and Regulations of the Department, or any of the General or Special Orders of the Department."

The case proceeded to trial and both sides introduced testimony. Lt. Elliott, testifying for the defendants, stated that he discovered that policeman Barge was intoxicated from the use of alcoholic liquors while they were both on duty, and that he reported Barge to the plaintiff, who was his superior officer, and called the plaintiff to the scene of the duties of policeman Barge and the witness Elliott; that the witness then reported to the plaintiff the conduct of the policeman Barge and the plaintiff admitted then and there that he, the plaintiff, smelled some kind of alcoholic liquor on the breath of policeman Barge. The

plaintiff called a turnkey (Scott), from the fourth floor, to stay with Barge on account of the condition of Barge; and further that when the witness Elliott came to make his report to the plaintiff, his superior officer, the plaintiff influenced him and required of him, as a superior officer, to make a false report as to the condition of Barge, and this the witness did at the instance of the plaintiff because the plaintiff was the superior officer of the witness Elliott.

The plaintiff, being sworn in his own behalf, testified in part that he was called by Lt. Elliott and that he did smell alcoholic liquors on the breath of policeman Barge; and further testified that he did leave turnkey Scott with Barge as a matter of precaution, since Barge did have the odor of alcoholic liquors on his breath, but that he, the plaintiff, did so in the exercise of the discretion with which he was clothed as captain. The plaintiff also denied that he induced Lt. Elliott to make a false report. The good character of the plaintiff was established beyond question. We do not purport to set forth all of the testimony, but we have set forth certain material portions of it and will discuss these and other phases of the evidence in the opinion.

The plaintiff has fifteen assignments of error which he urges here, including his assignment of error on the overruling of his demurrer. We will discuss them.

* * *

GARDNER, Judge.

1. (a) The court did not err in overruling the demurrer as contained in special ground 8. The specifications of the charges were sufficient in law.

(b) Special ground 1 is to the general effect that the judgment rendered by the Committee was not legally sufficient under rule No. 544. So much of that rule as is here pertinent reads: "All judgments of the Police Committee of Council shall be in writing and duly entered upon the records." In our opinion the verdict and judgment rendered by the Committee was a substantial compliance with the provisions of this rule. It appears that the substance of the verdict and judgment was unanimously reached and that it does appear on the record of the Police Committee. This assignment is without merit.

(c) The second and third assignment of error is to the general effect that there was no evidence to support the finding of the Committee. While on certain issues during the trial the evidence was in conflict, but still there was sufficient legal testimony to sustain the finding. This ground does not demand a reversal.

(d) The fourth and fifth assignments of error are to the effect that the plaintiff had violated no rule of the Police Department which had been previously adopted. This ground is based on the contention that the attaching to the amendment to the answer of the defendants was not a compliance with the order of the court in that it contained all of the rules and regulations and that it did not point out and produce any rule applicable to the charges and that neither the charges themselves nor the proof mentioned any rule which it was claimed that the plaintiff violated. The response of the defendants to the order of the court was a substantial compliance with the court's order. The judge of the superior court who required the amendment accepted the amendment as a compliance with his order and proceeded with the trial. This assignment does not require a reversal.

(e) The sixth assignment of error is to the effect that when the plaintiff had a police officer to remain with Barge it left the fourth floor of the jail unguarded and that the positive evidence was that the fourth floor was fully guarded at all times and that this charge was without any evidence to support it. We think the evidence sustains the position that there was a rule that two officers should at all times be on the fourth floor, but it is not clear that the plaintiff knew of such rule. There is some evidence to the effect that being a captain he did know or should have known of this requirement of the Chief of Police. We do not think that this assignment sets forth a reason for reversal.

(f) Special assignment seven assigns error under specification number 3 of the charges to the effect that the plaintiff improperly influenced an officer to incorrectly report the facts concerning Barge's conduct. This assignment is based on the allegation that Elliott should not have been believed by the Committee because Elliott admitted, under oath, that he had falsified his report. This was a question addressed solely to the Committee on the ground of the credibility of the witnesses, and is therefore without merit.

(g) Special ground 9 is to the effect that, over objections of the plaintiff, all of the witnesses were excluded from hearing the proceedings of the trial. It is the general and common practice in this State to exclude witnesses from the rooms during a trial, and no reason is urged here why this rule should not have been followed in the instant case nor is there any reason shown why the exclusion of the witnesses worked prejudice to the plaintiff. This assignment shows no reason for reversal.

(h) Special ground 10 is to the effect that Chief Hornsby, over objection, was permitted to testify or read from matters occurring in a written report even though it was admitted that Chief Hornsby was not present at the tower on the night in question. It was objected that the testimony was hearsay and irrelevant. These reports were reports made by the officers of the Police Department to the Chief of Police and were in court and read by the Committee. The Chief also read from the report of the plaintiff. It is our opinion that this assignment sets forth no substantial error.

(i) Assignment eleven complains that the Mayor asked Chief Hornsby what the plaintiff's duties were when it was admitted that the plaintiff's duties were provided in writing by the authority of the written law and rules of the Police Department. The rules and regulations of the Police Department on which the plaintiff was being tried were in the record in response to the plaintiff's exceptions to the Committee's answer to the certiorari. While technically it would perhaps have been more formal for the Mayor to have required the writing itself rather than the interpretation or statement from the Chief of Police, still we cannot see any substantial error in this assignment.

(j) Special grounds 12, 13, and 15 assign error because of the admission, over objections of the plaintiff, of a transcript of the evidence in the trial of policeman Barge. In our opinion this record was improperly admitted for the reason that the plaintiff was not then on trial and the record further shows that he was not present at the Barge trial. However, the Committee sitting as an administrative judicial tribunal or a quasi-judicial tribunal passing on the facts as well as the law, they are presumed to be capable of segregating the competent testimony from the incompetent testimony. The transcript of the record in the Barge case does not appear in the record in the instant case and the oral reference made by the witnesses concerning it, although illegal, do not require a reversal. Conceding that the record in the instant case does not show the admission of incompetent testimony. Aside from the incompetent testimony which was admitted, there was ample competent and legal testimony to sustain the finding of the Committee. This court dealt fully with this question in the case of Heath v. City of Atlanta, 67 Ga.App. 85, 19 S.E.2d 746, in the fourth division. See also Scott v. Hester et al., Ga.App., 35 S.E.2d 389.

(k) Special assignment 14 is based on the contention that one of the city attorneys was present and conferring and advising the Committee over objections of the plaintiff's attorney. It is contended that an ordinance of the City of Atlanta prohibits the city attorney from prosecuting police officers before the Police Committee without permission of the General Council of the City of Atlanta. It does not appear from the record that the attorney did more than consult with and advise the Committee. He asked no questions of the witnesses and took no other part in the prosecution save to confer with and advise the Committee. We are of the opinion that this ground does not show any sufficient prejudice to the plaintiff requiring a new trial. We again refer to the case of Heath v. City of Atlanta, supra, particularly to the effect that error during the progress of a trial such as the instant case does not necessarily require a reversal unless such error is prejudicial to the extent of demanding a reversal.

From the whole record which consists of over 200 pages, it is our view that the judge of the superior court did not err in overruling and denying the certiorari for any of the reasons assigned.

Judgment affirmed.

BROYLES, C.J., and MacINTYRE, J., concur.

United States v. Haddock
United States Court of Appeals, Tenth Circuit, 1992.
956 F.2d 1534.

This case involves the limitations on the admissibility of photocopies that are usually admitted into evidence under the business records exception more particularly described in Chapter 10.

Before ANDERSON and TACHA, Circuit Judges, and CHRISTENSEN, District Judge.

TACHA, Circuit Judge.

Defendant-appellant Kenneth E. Haddock appeals a jury verdict convicting him on two counts of misapplication of bank funds in violation of 18 U.S.C. § 656, six counts of bank fraud in violation of 18 U.S.C. § 1344, one count of false statement to a federally insured bank under 18 U.S.C. § 1014, and one count of making false statements to the Federal Deposit Insurance Corporation (FDIC) under 18 U.S.C. § 1007. Haddock raises the following issues on appeal: . . . (4) whether the district court abused its discretion in excluding certain documents from evidence. . . . We exercise jurisdiction under 28 U.S.C. § 1291, and we affirm in part, reverse in part and remand for resentencing and for a new trial on two counts.

BACKGROUND

This case revolves around the defendant, Kenneth E. Haddock, and his involvement with two banks—the Bank of White City and the Bank of Herington—and with another entity, First Finance, Inc. Both banks were owned by Herington Bancshares, a bank holding company of which Haddock owned fifty-five percent of the stock. During the period at issue in this case, Haddock was chairman of the board and chief executive officer of both banks. He also served as president of both banks until July, 1987. Haddock established First Finance, Inc. in 1986 for the purpose of acquiring loans from the FDIC and other lending institutions. He was president and sole shareholder of First Finance. The charges in this case involve several separate transactions.

III. Exclusion of Documents from Evidence

At trial and outside the jury's presence, counsel for Haddock proffered photocopies of six documents as evidence supporting Haddock's defense. The district court denied admission of these photocopies into evidence on the basis that "they did not have enough indication of reliability at this time that the court felt that [it] could allow them under the Rules of Evidence." In a memorandum reexamining that order, the court concluded that "the government had raised a genuine issue as to the authenticity of the originals." Defendant contends that these documents were admissible under the Federal Rules of Evidence and that the exclusion of these documents violated his Fifth Amendment and Sixth Amendment right to present evidence in his defense. The trial court is afforded broad discretion in making evidentiary rulings, and we reverse only upon a showing of abuse of that discretion. United States v. Alexander, 849 F.2d 1293, 1301 (10th Cir. 1988).

Under Rule 1001(4) of the Federal Rules of Evidence, Photocopies are considered duplicates. Rule 1003 provides that "[a] duplicate is admissible to the same extent as an original unless (1) a genuine question is raised as to the authenticity of the original or (2) in the circumstances it would be unfair to admit the duplicate in lieu of the original." Fed.R.Evid. 1003. Rule 1003 is part of a broadened set of evidentiary rules that reflect the fact that, due to modern and accurate reproduction techniques, duplicates and originals should normally be treated interchangeably. However, despite our age of technology, a trial court must still be wary of admitting duplicates "where the circumstances surrounding the execution of the writing present a substantial possibility of fraud." 5 Jack B. Weinstein & Margaret A. Berger, *Weinstein's Evidence* ¶ 1003[02], at 1003–9 (1991).

With regard to each of these photocopies, evidence presented at trial indicates that only Haddock could recall ever seeing either the original or a copy of these documents. Except for Haddock, no one—including in some cases persons who allegedly typed the document and persons to whom the original allegedly was sent—was familiar with the contents of the photocopies. In addition, witnesses testified that several of the documents bore markings and included statements that did not comport with similar documents prepared in the ordinary course of business at the Bank of White City and at the Bank of Herington. Under these circumstances, we hold that the district court did not abuse its discretion by excluding these photocopied documents from evidence. . . .

✔ PRACTICE QUESTIONS

Select the most correct answer to complete each statement.

1. The rule of evidence commonly known as the best evidence rule
   (a) does not apply to documentary evidence.
   (b) may contribute to fraud attempted by either party.
   (c) may cause inaccuracies in the copying of the original writing.
   (d) is always equated to what one is trying to prove, and it has a strong relation to reliability and usually refers to documents.

2. Which of the following is a true statement?
   (a) Photocopies are not considered the best evidence because they are not made by the same mechanical act.
   (b) According to court rules, a witness can compare a copy with the original and testify that the copy is an exact duplicate of the original.
   (c) Usually, statutes prohibit the clerk of the court from certifying the authenticity of a copy.
   (d) It is difficult to change the contents of the original in printing a photocopy.

3. Choose the most correct statement:
   (a) Secondary evidence may not be admitted if primary evidence is not available.
   (b) Oral testimony is primary evidence and should be admitted before a tape recording of the event is admitted.
   (c) If an adverse party is duly notified to produce evidence at a trial and fails to do so, secondary evidence may be admissible if the court is told that the adverse party failed to comply with the notice to produce.
   (d) All of the above are true.

4. Choose the most correct statement:
   (a) The rules and regulations of a police department do not have the force of law.
   (b) The legal rules of evidence apply to administrative disciplinary trials of a police department.
   (c) In a police disciplinary trial, the rules and regulations of the department that apply to the charges and specifications against a member of the department should be read into evidence at the trial.
   (d) In a departmental police disciplinary trial, the prosecuting officer should never be a person of higher rank than the respondent.

5. Choose the most correct statement:
   (a) Where judicial records are required as evidence in a trial, the side that is offering them into evidence is required to arrange to bring the original records into the court in order to offer them into evidence.
   (b) Where judicial records are required as evidence, the person who desires this may request the trier of the facts to visit the record room of the clerk of the court to view the subject records in that room so that they cannot easily be lost.
   (c) Where judicial records are required as evidence, the person who desires this may secure properly authenticated copies of the records and offer them as the best evidence.
   (d) All of the above are true.

Indicate whether each statement is true or false.

6. An original writing, containing a privileged communication, is the best evidence of the contents and can be admitted against the party to whom the privilege ran without a waiver of the privilege.

7. A carbon copy of an original document is admissible in evidence.

CHAPTER 6

Hearsay and Character Evidence

§ 6.1 INTRODUCTION

I doubt that there is a reader of this book who has not heard that there is a rule of evidence that excludes hearsay evidence from the trial record. The problem is, first, to recognize hearsay when you hear it and, second, to be certain that the hearsay you hear does not come within the scope of the various exceptions to the hearsay exclusionary rule.

Always keep in mind that the rules of evidence have as their object the revelation of the truth. We can therefore easily understand that when a person testifies to something that another person is alleged to have said, there is a great possibility for the unintentional distortion of the original statement. How many of us have been the recipients of half-truths from the gossiping tongues of acquaintances only to find that by the time the facts are passed from one person to another, the final statement has no resemblance to the original statement?

To guard against this type of situation, the rules of evidence have precluded the introduction of hearsay evidence with certain exceptions. These exceptions are predicated in each instance on the following:

1. the necessity for its introduction
2. the great probability of reliability

§ 6.2 HEARSAY DEFINED

To precisely define hearsay is extremely difficult. We may say that "hearsay is a statement, other than one made by the declarant while testifying at a trial or hearing, offered in evidence to prove the truth of the matter asserted" (Rule 801[c], Federal Rules of Evidence). Another definition of hearsay might be a statement made out of court that is not made in the course of the trial or hearing in which it is offered and that is offered for the truth of the fact asserted in the statement where there is no opportunity for cross-examination.

It is important to note that sometimes a statement may appear to be hearsay, but if the counsel's intention is not to offer it as proof of the fact that the statement is true and it is offered only for the fact that the statement was made, it is not hearsay. For example, upon trial for the purpose of showing that "A" had acted in the heat of passion with no intent to kill, "A" was permitted to testify that, just before the killing of his wife, she had told him that she was pregnant by reason of her relations with another man. N.Y.—People v. Harris, 209 N.Y. 70, 102 N.E. 546 (1913). The case was reversed because the court of appeals held that probative value was outweighed by danger that its admission would unreasonably prolong the trial, confuse the jury, unfairly surprise a party, and create substantial danger of prejudice.

§ 6.3 REASON FOR THE RULE

When a person testifies in open court, the adversary has an opportunity for cross-examination. The purpose of the cross-examination is to inquire into

1. the witness's ability to recall past events correctly,
2. the accuracy of his or her perception, and
3. his or her veracity.

When a statement is made out of court and is offered at trial for the truth of the assertion contained therein, there is no opportunity for cross-examination and thus no opportunity to probe the full truth from the witness. Hence, it is the deprivation of the right of cross-examination that is the primary reason for the existence of the hearsay exclusionary rule. Some cases give as an additional reason that the declarant was not under oath. However, even if the hearsay statement is made under oath, it is still not admissible. Conn.—Henry v. Kopf, 104 Conn. 73, 131 A. 412 (1925); Fla.—Smith v. Frisch's Big Boy, Inc., 208 So.2d 310 (Fla.App.1968); N.Y.—Bookman v. Stegman, 105 N.Y. 621, 11 N.E. 376 (1887).

§ 6.4 EXCEPTIONS TO HEARSAY RULE

The hearsay exclusionary rule is not absolute in that exceptions to the rule have always existed and are recognized. Many times these exceptions to the rule are allowed by authority of a state or federal statute. At other times, the common law has provided these exceptions because of necessity and the great probability of reliability, public policy, and the trustworthiness that experience has taught, or the circumstances indicate, and the probability of veracity. However, necessity alone has never been considered as a sufficient reason of itself to open the door to hearsay evidence. N.M.—Brown v. Gen. Ins. Co. of America, 70 N.M. 46, 369 P.2d 968 (1962). The burden rests on a person seeking to base hearsay evidence admitted under an exception to the hearsay rule to show clearly that the evidence falls within such exception. Pa.—Carney v. Pennsylvania R.R. Co., 428 Pa. 489, 240 A.2d 71 (1968). Many exceptions to the hearsay exclusionary rule will be discussed in detail later in this book. Federal Rules of Evidence 803 and 804(b) list exceptions to the hearsay exclusionary rule.

§ 6.5 UNAVAILABILITY OF WITNESS

We have just determined that there are recognized exceptions to the hearsay exclusionary rule. Some of the exceptions are based on the unavailability of the person who made the statement. They are former testimony, statement under belief of impending death, statement against interest, and statement of personal or family history.

Rule 804(a) of the Federal Rules of Evidence defines "unavailability as a witness" to include situations in which the declarant

(1) is exempted by ruling of the court on the ground of privilege from testifying concerning the subject matter of the declarant's statement; or

(2) persists in refusing to testify concerning the subject matter of the declarant's statement despite an order of the court to do so; or

(3) testifies to a lack of memory of the subject matter of the declarant's statement; or

(4) is unable to be present or to testify at the hearing because of death or then existing physical or mental illness or infirmity; or

(5) is absent from the hearing and the proponent of a statement has been unable to procure the declarant's attendance (or in the case of a hearsay exception under subdivision (b)(2), (3), or (4), the declarant's attendance or testimony) by process or other reasonable means.

A declarant is not unavailable as a witness if exemption, refusal, claim of lack of memory, inability, or absence is due to the procurement or wrongdoing of the proponent of a statement for the purpose of preventing the witness from attending or testifying.

The last situation might occur if the proponent of the statement did not want the witness to be present and be subject to cross-examination.

§ 6.6 NEGATIVE HEARSAY

A negative form of hearsay has been recognized, as when testimony of a court clerk to the effect that no cases of a particular type, other than the instant one, had been filed (Colo.—Hadden v. Gateway West Pub. Co., 130 Colo. 73, 273 P.2d 733 [1954]) or testimony of a party that the records do not show a divorce of particular persons (Ala.—Jordan v. Copeland, 272 Ala. 336, 131 So.2d 696 [1961]).

§ 6.7 WRITTEN OR PRINTED HEARSAY

Hearsay is not limited to oral testimony or statements; the rule applies to written as well as oral statements. Cal.—Weaver v. Bay, 216 Cal.App.2d 559, 31 Cal.Rptr. 211 (1963); Conn.—General Motors Acceptance Corp. v. Capitol Garage, Inc., 154 Conn. 593, 227 A.2d 548 (1967); N.Y.—Kaplan v. City of New York, 10 A.D.2d 319, 200 N.Y.S.2d 261 (1960).

§ 6.8 WRITTEN STATEMENTS IN JUDICIAL MATTERS—HEARSAY

Written statements have been held inadmissible under the rule excluding hearsay evidence when the form is judicial or relates to judicial matters, such as affidavits. N.J.—Union Co. Sav. Bank v. Kolpenitsky, 125 N.J.Eq. 125, 4 A.2d 413 (1939).

§ 6.9 OTHER WRITINGS—HEARSAY

Letters have been held inadmissible as hearsay. Cal.—Stoneking v. Briggs, 254 Cal.App.2d 563, 62 Cal.Rptr. 249 (1967); Conn.—Purcell v. Purcell, 101 Conn. 422, 126 A. 353 (1924); Ill.—Kane v. City of Chicago, 392 Ill. 172, 64 N.E.2d 506 (1945); N.Y.—Lindt v. Henshel, 25 N.Y.2d 357, 254 N.E.2d 746, 306 N.Y.S.2d 436 (1969). Postal cards, telegrams, match covers, memoranda, bulletins, diaries, notices, and surveyor's field notes have been held to be hearsay and inadmissible.

§ 6.10 FEDERAL RULE RELATING TO HEARSAY EVIDENCE

Rule 802. Hearsay Rule

Hearsay is not admissible except as provided by these rules or by other rules prescribed by the Supreme Court pursuant to statutory authority or by Act of Congress.

§ 6.11 REPUTATION EVIDENCE—EXCEPTION TO HEARSAY RULE—PUBLIC OR GENERAL RIGHT

Reputation evidence consists of the general statements of members of the community with relation to a particular fact and hence may be regarded as a species of composite hearsay. N.C.—*In re* Nelson's Will, 210 N.C. 398, 186 S.E. 480, 105 A.L.R. 1441 (1936). A sort of distinction is allowed between hearsay and reputation. Yet reputation is nothing more than hearsay derived from those who had the means of knowing the fact and may exist when those best acquainted with the fact are dead. Me.—Scott v. Blood, 16 Me. 192, 196 (1839).

The reputation which is admissible, however, must refer to a public or general right and not a particular exercise of it. Mass.—Enfield, Inhabitants of v. Woods, 212 Mass. 547, 99 N.E. 331 (1912). Evidence as to common reputation of ownership is admissible when claims to public lands and to water on such lands are involved, but the reputation must be that of a past generation. When evidence of ancient common reputation as to ownership of water rights was admissible, the most that could be shown by a witness was that there was an ancient common reputation in the community relative to the division and use of water for some beneficial purpose. Asking the witness what that reputation was and who was reputed to be the owner of "springs" could only mislead, since there can only be ownership of a right to take and use water and not to the corpus of the water.

Facts of genealogy stand in a peculiar position as a matter of quasi-public concern, and where the race to which a person belongs is in issue, proof of general reputation is competent. Tex.—Stewart v. Profit, 146 S.W. 563 (Tex.Civ.App. 1912). Reputation evidence cannot ordinarily be received where the fact involved is of only special or limited interest. Such facts within this rule include the individual's position in the community and his or her financial, mental, or physical condition. Cal.—Simons v. Inyo Cerro Gordo Minery & Power Co., 48 Cal.App. 524, 192 P. 144 (1920). General reputation cannot establish the existence of moral qualities, such as loyalty (Tenn.—Hart v. Reynolds, 48 Tenn. [1 Heisk.] 208 [1870], except where proof of character is permitted in case of a party.

§ 6.12 THE DIFFERENCE BETWEEN CHARACTER AND REPUTATION

Character and reputation are not synonymous. Character is what a person is morally, while reputation is what a person is reputed to be. A person may be a scoundrel, but if few people know of this fact, his reputation may be that of a good man. A person's general character has always been proved by general reputation. N.Y.—People v. Van Gaasbeck, 189 N.Y. 408, 82 N.E. 718, 22 L.R.A. (N.S.) 650 (1907). Another way of explaining the difference is by stating that character is what a person is, whereas reputation is what others believe the person to be.

§ 6.13 CHARACTER OF A WITNESS

A defendant's character may not be attacked until the defendant has brought up the issue of character in his or her own case. This is usually done by the testimony of a witness, not a party to the action, who will testify with respect to the good character of the defendant for the trait at issue in the case.

If a defendant has taken the stand in his or her own defense in a criminal case, he or she necessarily places his or her own veracity at issue. He or she may, under this situation, have another witness testify that the defendant has an excellent reputation in the community for truth and veracity in all of his or her dealings.

The prosecutor, when faced with this situation, may attempt to impeach the character of the witness who is designated as a character witness, or he or she may impeach the standards on which the witness relies in assessing the character of the defendant. In federal trials, the prosecutor may attack the character of a witness by showing a prior conviction of a crime that was punishable by death or imprisonment in excess of one year or that involved dishonesty or a false statement regardless of the punishment. This is limited, however, by a time factor. It is not admissible if more than ten years have elapsed since the date of the conviction or the release of the witness from confinement imposed for the conviction, whichever is the later date, unless the court determines that in the interests of justice the probative value of the conviction supported by specific facts and circumstances substantially outweighs its prejudicial effect. See Federal Rule of Evidence 609 for further amplification of this thought.

Many state courts do not limit the impeachment device of eliciting prior crimes from the mouth of the witness. Hence, in some states once a person is convicted as a felon, he or she cannot be believed and is adjudged an infamous person. In other states, such a person is permitted to testify, but the testimony is subject to impeachment by the introduction into evidence of the fact that the witness was convicted of a crime. The theory is that if he or she did not admit to the previous conviction and the conviction was proved, he or she is therefore more likely to be testifying to falsehoods in other testimony. The courts were careful to point out that this was an attack not on the character of the witness, but on the witness's credibility. With the adoption of Federal Rule 609, this practice is limited in federal courts, and many states are falling into line in adopting the same procedure.

A prosecutor may impeach the standards on which the character witness relies by bringing to the attention of the witness the fact that the defendant had been implicated in some prior wrongdoing and ask the witness whether he knew of this fact. He must be very careful in doing this. It may not be introduced merely for the purpose of showing the accused to be a person of bad character, likely to commit the crime charged. U.S.—United States v. Brettholz, 485 F.2d 483 (2d Cir. 1973).

In Michelson v. United States, 335 U.S. 469, 69 S.Ct. 213, 93 L.Ed. 168 (1948), the United States Supreme Court said:

> Wide discretion is accompanied by heavy responsibility on trial courts to protect the practice from any misuse. The trial judge was scrupulous to so guard in the case before us. He took pains to ascertain, out of the presence of the jury that the target of the question was an actual event, which would probably result in some comment among acquaintances if not injury to defendant's reputation. He satisfied himself that counsel was not merely taking a random shot at a reputation imprudently exposed or asking a groundless question to waft an unwarranted innuendo into the jury box.

Many scholars believe that the Michelson rule should be reinterpreted in the light of Federal Rules 405 and 608; that is, that the Federal Rules now permit inquiry only into the subjects indicated below and do not encompass all prior bad acts. Most states still permit inquiry into all prior bad acts. An old case in New York held that a witness may be interrogated upon cross-examination with respect to any immoral, vicious, or criminal act of his or her life which may affect his character and show him to be unworthy of belief. N.Y.—People v. Webster, 139 N.Y. 73, 34 N.E. 730 (1893). This is no longer the New York law.

In most state courts, however, when a witness is called to the stand to testify on behalf of a side of the controversy, the litigant who calls that witness to the stand is in effect vouching for the credibility of that witness. Accordingly, if that witness gives some unexpected response during testimony, the litigant who has called the witness to the stand may not impeach his or her own witness. This situation has been changed by Federal Rule of Evidence 607, and at this writing, a few states are now permitting impeachment of one's own witness.

Since the prevailing rule in state courts is that one cannot impeach one's own witness, it is of paramount importance to ascertain the background and character of the witness before he or she takes the stand because if the witness's personal history is bad, it might influence the trier of the facts against the side who called the witness to testify. The ultimate objective of a trial conducted in conformity with the rules of evidence is to seek out the truth. Therefore, if a witness once pleaded guilty to stealing an automobile, this fact should not affect his or her credibility as a witness. Nevertheless, states have allowed inquiry along these lines by statute (N.Y.—CPLR 4513) when the fact of the commission of the crime may affect the weight of the testimony of the witness. There is a movement away from this theory. The Federal Rules of Evidence support this view in Rule 608.

§ 6.14 FEDERAL RULE RELATING TO CHARACTER EVIDENCE

Rule 608. Evidence of character and conduct of witness

(a) **Opinion and reputation evidence of character.**—The credibility of a witness may be attacked or supported by evidence in the form of opinion or reputation, but subject to these limitations: (1) the evidence may refer only to character for truthfulness or untruthfulness, and (2) evidence of truthful character is admissible only after the character of the witness for truthfulness has been attacked by opinion or reputation evidence or otherwise.

(b) **Specific instances of conduct.**—Specific instances of conduct of a witness, for the purpose of attacking or supporting his credibility, other than conviction of crime as provided in rule 609, may not be proved by extrinsic evidence. They may, however, in the discretion of the court, if probative of truthfulness or untruthfulness, be inquired into on cross-examination of the witness (1) concerning his character for truthfulness or untruthfulness, or (2) concerning the character for truthfulness or untruthfulness of another witness as to which character the witness being cross-examined has testified.

The giving of testimony, whether by an accused or by any other witness, does not operate as a waiver of his privilege against self-incrimination when examined with respect to matters which relate only to credibility.

For the time being, it is safe to say that most state courts will permit cross-examination of a witness regarding previous commissions of crime and regarding character with respect to truthfulness or untruthfulness for the purpose of impeaching his or her credibility.

§ 6.15 REPUTATION OF A PARTY IN A CIVIL ACTION— EXCEPTION TO HEARSAY RULE

Ordinarily, in a civil action the character of a party is deemed by the law to be irrelevant in determining the merits of the controversy. Character may be a relevant fact apart, and when this is the case, evidence of the character of the person in question is admissible. For example, in a contest for custody of a minor child the character of contesting parents becomes a matter in issue and is a proper subject of proof. Iowa—Herr v. Lazor, 238 Iowa 518, 28 N.W.2d 11 (1947). Character evidence is admissible in a civil case if it is relevant for some purpose other than to raise an inference that the party did or did not do the act in issue. An apparent exception to that rule has occurred in a civil action for assault and battery, where evidence may be admitted to show that the defendant acted in self-defense and then evidence as to the violent and dangerous character of the deceased is admitted (Ark.—York v. Hampton, 229 Ark. 301, 314 S.W.2d 480 [1958]) or the person charged to have been assaulted (Cal.—Northrup v. Baker, 202 Cal.App.2d 347, 20 Cal.Rptr. 797 [1962]) is admissible. Other civil cases in which character evidence has been held admissible are (a) libel, (b) slander, and (c) malicious prosecution. However, in recent years, courts have expanded the use of character evidence in civil cases when the character of the party or the witness has been attacked. In that case, the one attacked may introduce evidence to negate the attack. Ill.—Werdell v. Turzynski, 128 Ill.App.2d 139, 262 N.E.2d 833 (1970); Federal Rule 608.

§ 6.16 CHARACTER OF DEFENDANT IN A CRIMINAL TRIAL—EXCEPTION TO HEARSAY RULE

It is well settled in a criminal prosecution that the defendant may introduce reputation evidence as to his own good character for the purpose of raising an inference that he would not be likely to commit the offense charged. N.Y.—People v. Van Gaasbeck, *supra.* Each defendant is assumed to have started his or her life afresh at the bar of justice, and if the defendant chooses, by refraining from introducing character witnesses in his or her own behalf, or if the defendant fails to exercise his or her right to take the stand in his or her own defense, the prosecution is precluded from introducing evidence relating to the bad character of the defendant. On the other hand, once the defendant opens the door by calling a character witness in his or her behalf or by taking the stand, the prosecution may introduce testimony relating to the defendant's infamous past. The rule is based on the possibility of introducing evidence that will be unduly prejudicial to the defendant. If the defendant committed a rape heretofore, he may still be innocent of the rape charge in the instant case. However, if he is a previous rapist and he introduces evidence in a rape case that he has a reputation in the community as being a moral, home-loving father and husband, the prosecution is justified in introducing his previous conviction, for if the defendant's character is relevant to prove his innocence, it is also relevant to prove his guilt. Character evidence, if believed, may, when considered with all the other evidence in a case, create a reasonable doubt when without it none would exist. U.S.—Edgington v. United States, 164 U.S. 361, 17 S.Ct. 72, 41 L.Ed. 467 (1896); N.Y.—People v. McDowell, 9 N.Y.2d 12, 172 N.E.2d 279, 210 N.Y.S.2d 514 (1961).

Evidence of other bad acts is admissible to prove predisposition when entrapment is an issue. United States v. Emenogha, 1 F.3d 473 (7th Cir. 1993). Other crimes evidence is admissible if directed toward establishing matter other than defendant's propensity to commit crime, evidence was sufficient to support jury finding that defendant committed similar act. . . . United States v. Emenogha, *supra.*

§ 6.17 CHARACTER EVIDENCE—MODE OF PROOF

Evidence of general reputation as proof of character may be probatively weak, but it makes a comparatively simple issue and one which the person affected may be supposed to be able to meet without surprise. N.C.—Nixon v. McKinney, 105 N.C. 23, 11 S.E. 154 (1890).

The accepted method of proving character is by establishing the general reputation as to the particular trait involved. Nev.—Davis v. Davis, 54 Nev. 267, 13 P.2d 1109 (1932), 22 C.J. 480 n.76. 32 C.J.S. Evidence § 434.

The reputation which is admissible is the common report which others make concerning the person in question (i.e., the talk about him which shows the opinion which is held in his community). Ky.—Asher v. Beckner, 19 Ky.L.R. 521, 41 S.W. 35 (1898). The general reputation of a person cannot be proved by a statement of one or two persons, but it must be such as is generally current in the community. Iowa—State ex rel. Seeburger v. Pickett, 202 Iowa 1321, 210 N.W. 782 (1926).

As a general rule, the character of a person cannot be proven from the personal knowledge of the witness (Ohio—Lakes v. Buckeye State Mut. Ins. Ass'n, 110 Ohio App. 115, 168 N.E.2d 895 [1959], 22 C.J. 485 n.65, C.J.S. Evidence § 433), and the personal or individual opinion of the witness is not admissible (Tex.—Tarwater v. Donley County State Bank, 277 S.W. 176 [Tex.Civ.App. 1925], 22 C.J. 484 n.65, C.J.S. Evidence § 433[b]; Vt.—In re Carleton N. Monaghan, 126 Vt. 53, 222 A.2d 665 [1966]). Usually, the reputation must be confined to the defendant's reputation in the community in which he resides (N.Y.—People v. Van Gaasbeck, supra), or where he has resided (Ky.—Louisville Times Co. v. Emrich, 252 Ky. 210, 66 S.W.2d 73 [1933], 22 C.J. 480 n.93, 32 C.J.S. Evidence § 434).

The rules of evidence have had to accommodate to present-day situations. In this exception to the hearsay rule, the courts have taken into consideration that the increase in population and the decrease in communal living in small towns have resulted in a slight change with respect to the area from which a party may draw his or her character witnesses. In large cities, it is not uncommon for a person to live in an apartment for years and not know the neighbor in the adjoining apartment. In such a case, a person may not be known in the community in which he lives, and his opportunity to create a reputation, "good or bad, is among his associates in his particular activities, or in the personal contacts of his life where he actually lives it." N.Y.—People v. Gitlow, 234 N.Y. 132, 138, 136 N.E. 317, 319 (1922).

Character evidence may also be shown by negative evidence. A witness may testify that he has lived for a considerable length of time in the same neighborhood as the defendant and has never heard anything against him in respect to peaceableness or honesty or whatever other trait might be relevant. N.Y.—People v. Van Gaasbeck, supra; Pa.—In re Horton's Estate, 347 Pa. 30, 52 A.2d 895 (1947).

When a person of previous good reputation is indicted and the news is disseminated through the community, his reputation suffers. Therefore, because of this type of situation, the rules of evidence preclude the use of character testimony for the period after the event for which the defendant is presently on trial. Ind.—In re Darrow, 175 Ind. 44, 92 N.E. 369 (1910), 22 C.J. 480 n.90, C.J.S. Evidence § 434.

There has been a movement toward deleting the use of an opinion by the character witness and in its stead substituting actual knowledge, wherein a witness would be expected to say that he or she knows that the party has an excellent character based on his or her own dealings with the subject. This concept was debated thoroughly by the House of Representatives Committee on the Judiciary and in the Congress of the United States. Notwithstanding the fact that the Committee on the Judiciary deleted the provision for making proof by testimony in the form of an opinion, it was defeated on the floor of the House of Representatives, and the old rule—that character is to be proved by the opinion of the witness—prevails.

However, when character is an essential element of the charge, claim, or defense, the defense may prove specific instances of conduct. For example, if a defendant is charged with forceful rape, the defense may introduce specific instances in which the complainant has engaged in illicit sexual intercourse with the defendant. The defense here is that a woman of previous chaste character is more likely to resist a rape than one who is known to be of loose sexual morality. See 140 A.L.R. 364 for an extensive discussion of this problem.

§ 6.18 CHARACTER OF VICTIM IN A CRIMINAL TRIAL

As a general rule, the victim's character is relevant only as to his or her reputation for veracity. The veracity of the testimony of a witness is always subject to impeachment, and the reputation of the witness in the community for telling falsehoods is certainly relevant. Sometimes the issue is presented where the victim is dead at the time of the trial as a result of the wrongful act of the defendant. In this case, evidence of the character of the victim is admissible under limited conditions, more fully explained in Sec. 6.22. In rape cases, the character of the victim is sometimes relevant and admissible. This, too, is explained more fully in Sec. 6.23.

§ 6.19 CHARACTER AS AN AID TO PROVE INNOCENCE

Sometimes a defendant is faced with an accusation that he or she committed a crime, and those who knew the defendant would say that in their view it is absolutely impossible that the defendant was the perpetrator because his or her personality and character all point to his or her innocence. The law has provided for this contingency wherein it is stated that character evidence, if believed, may, when considered with all the other evidence in the case, create a reasonable doubt when without it none would exist. U.S.—Edgington v. United States, 164 U.S. 361, 17 S.Ct. 72, 41 L.Ed. 467 (1896); N.Y.—People v. Helmbrecht, 297 N.Y. 789, 77 N.E.2d 798 (1948). An accused has the right to offer evidence of his good character, inferred from reputation testimony, to show that he was unlikely to have acted in the manner and with the intent charged in the indictment. U.S.—United States v. Lewin, 467 F.2d 1132 (7th Cir. 1972).

In a prosecution for conspiracy to violate narcotics laws, instruction by the court that jury could consider evidence of good character and reputation and determine its weight together with all other evidence in case in arriving at their verdict as to defendant's innocence or guilt is proper. Poliafico v. United States, 237 F.2d 97 (6th Cir. 1956), *cert. denied*, 352 U.S. 1025, 77 S.Ct. 590, 1 L.Ed.2d 597 (1957).

§ 6.20 ADDITIONAL FEDERAL RULE RELATING TO CHARACTER EVIDENCE

Rule 404 reads as follows:

> **Rule 404. Character evidence not admissible to prove conduct; exceptions; other crimes**
>
> (a) **Character evidence generally.**—Evidence of a person's character or a trait of his character is not admissible for the purpose of proving that he acted in conformity therewith on a particular occasion, except:
> (1) Character of accused.—Evidence of a pertinent trait of his character offered by an accused, or by the prosecution to rebut the same;

(2) Character of victim.—Evidence of a pertinent trait of character of the victim of the crime offered by an accused, or by the prosecution to rebut the same, or evidence of a character trait of peacefulness of the victim offered by the prosecution in a homicide case to rebut evidence that the victim was the first aggressor;

(3) Character of witness.—Evidence of the character of a witness, as provided in rules 607, 608, and 609.

(b) **Other crimes, wrongs, or acts.**—Evidence of other crimes, wrongs, or acts is not admissible to prove the character of a person in order to show that he acted in conformity therewith. It may, however, be admissible for other purposes, such as proof of motive, opportunity, intent, preparation, plan, knowledge, identity, or absence of mistake or accident.

§ 6.21 IMPEACHMENT OF CHARACTER WITNESS

A character witness for defendant may be asked whether he or she had ever heard that the defendant had a reputation in the past for being so brazen that he or she would steal a red-hot stove (assuming the current charge is shoplifting or a similar offense). If the witness's answer is "Yes, but that was a long time ago," it is a means of impeaching the credibility of the witness. It would materially affect the weight of the direct testimony wherein the witness testified that the defendant is well known in the community as an honest, law-abiding citizen. The witness may be asked whether he or she has heard rumors or reports in the community that may be derogatory to the defendant's reputation. The witness may also be impeached by showing his bad reputation for veracity by another witness who is qualified by reason of residence or other qualifying circumstance. N.Y.—People v. Colantone, 243 N.Y. 134, 152 N.E. 700 (1926). The personal opinion of the witness is not admissible for this purpose. N.Y.—Brill v. Muller Bros., Inc., 13 N.Y.2d 776, 192 N.E.2d 34, 242 N.Y.S.2d 69 (1963).

The witness, on cross-examination, may also be asked whether he has heard of particular instances of conduct pertinent to the trait in question. Michelson v. United States, 335 U.S. 469, 69 S.Ct. 213, 93 L.Ed. 168 (1948). It is quite obvious that such questions must be asked by the prosecutor in good faith. If, for example, the prosecutor, in an attempt to impeach a character witness who, on direct examination, had testified that the defendant had an excellent reputation in the community for honesty, questioned the witness as to a nonexistent larceny that the defendant had committed, it would be prejudicial to the defendant in a very substantial way and might justify a reversal.

§ 6.22 CHARACTER OF DECEASED IN HOMICIDE

The defense of a homicide case is often that the defendant did the act but was justified in doing this act by reason of the fact that he or she acted in self-defense of his or her own life or the life of someone in his or her company at the time. In such a case, it has been held to be perfectly proper to introduce the character of the decedent if that character was that of a quarrelsome, vindictive, or violent man and that reputation had come to the knowledge of the defendant prior to the homicide. N.Y.—People v. Druse, 103 N.Y. 655, 8 N.E. 733 (1886).

Evidence of this type is admissible to show not that decedent was the aggressor, but only that the defendant acted on the reasonable and honest belief that his life or the life of someone in his company at the time was in peril. N.Y.—People v. Rodawald, 177 N.Y. 408, 70 N.E. 1 (1904). Always bear in mind that the reputation of the decedent must have been known by the defendant before the event because it is introduced to show the state of mind of the defendant and the inference that the decedent was the aggressor. N.Y.—Stokes v. People, 53 N.Y. 164 (1873).

§ 6.23 CHARACTER OF VICTIM OF RAPE

The character of a victim in a forcible rape prosecution is very material and relevant, for the presumption is that a victim of a forcible rape who is a person of unchaste character is less likely to fight her assailant than one of previous chaste character. Nonconsent being an element of the crime, the defendant is permitted to show that the plaintiff was a common prostitute or that her reputation for chastity was bad. Previous acts between the complainant and the defendant which were acts of immorality can also be shown to give rise to the inference that she did not resist. N.Y.—Woods v. People, 55 N.Y. 515, 14 Am.Rep. 309 (1874).

This does not stand for the premise that a prostitute, or one whose reputation for chastity is bad, cannot be the subject of a rape. This is still a matter to be evaluated by the trier of the facts, be it a jury or a judge in the absence of a jury based on a waiver of a jury trial.

§ 6.24 HABIT—ROUTINE PRACTICE

Certain actions of people are routine. They are done without much thought. A person may comb his or her hair every morning using his or her right hand and not think very much about it until he or she injures that hand and realizes what he or she had been doing with it for years. There is a good argument made that when a person develops a habit of doing something in a particular manner, testimony as to this behavior should be admissible in a trial because it is most likely that the behavior at the time in question was done in the routine manner.

There is much confusion in the court decisions with respect to the admissibility of habit. Particularly when direct evidence can be produced regarding the incident, the court will reject the admission of habit. N.D.—Glatt v. Feist, 156 N.W.2d 819, 28 A.L.R.3d 1278 (N.D. 1968).

On the other hand, it has been felt that the existence of a habit, causing a more or less settled or automatic reaction to physical or mental stimulus, presents a stronger relevancy as to what happened on a particular occasion than would the mere doing of an isolated act of a similar nature at another time. Mo.—Meller v. State, 438 S.W.2d 187 (Mo. 1969); Wash.—Breimon v. General Motors Corp., 8 Wash.App. 747, 509 P.2d 398 (1973). Therefore, in some circumstances, proof of habit may be received. Cal.—Webb v. Van Noort, 239 Cal.App.2d 472, 48 Cal.Rptr. 823, 29 A.L.R.3d 781 (1966); Tex.—Allstate Ins. Co. v. Smith, 471 S.W.2d 620 (Tex.Civ.App. 1971).

§ 6.25 OFFERS TO PLEAD AND WITHDRAWAL

State courts have attempted to deal with overcrowded court calendars by offering a defendant an opportunity to plead to a lesser, included offense in satisfaction of the larger offense. The federal courts modify this by permitting the defendant to plead to one of the counts of an indictment and having the prosecutor withdraw the prosecution of the other pending counts of the indictment. Prosecutors have wide latitude in what crimes they will prosecute. This mechanism is known as plea bargaining.

Many times a defendant pleads guilty to the offense, and after the court orders an investigation and report thereof through the probation services, the court will not agree to sentence the defendant in accordance with the previously arranged disposition of the case. When this occurs, most jurists will permit the defendant to withdraw his or her plea of guilty and stand trial, but it is a discretionary act of the judge. Federal Rules of Criminal Procedure, 18 U.S.C.A. Rule 11(e)(4); U.S.—United States v. Gonzalez-Hernandez, 481 F.2d 648 (5th Cir. 1973). This is not an absolute right of defendant. It is within the sound discretion of the trial court. Federal Rules of Criminal Procedure, i.e., 18 U.S.C.A. Rule 32(d); U.S.—United States v. Presley, 478 F.2d 163 (5th Cir. 1973).

When a defendant withdraws his plea of guilty and is later tried, the fact that he had originally pled guilty is not admissible before the trier of the facts in the trial. U.S.—Harris v. Anderson, 364 F.Supp. 465 (N.C. 1973). Evidence of a plea bargain is not admissible in a civil or criminal proceeding against a person who made a plea or offer if the bargain was subsequently rejected by the judge. U.S.—United States v. Gallington, 488 F.2d 637 (8th Cir. 1973), *cert. denied,* 416 U.S. 907, 94 S.Ct. 1613, 40 L.Ed.2d 112 (1974).

§ 6.26 FEDERAL RULE RELATING TO HABIT EVIDENCE

Rule 406 of the Federal Rules of Evidence provides as follows:

Rule 406. Habit; routine practice

Evidence of the habit of a person or of the routine practice of an organization, whether corroborated or not and regardless of the presence of eyewitnesses, is relevant to prove that the conduct of the person or organization on a particular occasion was in conformity with the habit or routine practice.

CROSS-REFERENCES

Federal Civil Judicial Procedure and Rules (West 1996) (Rules 404, 803, and 804).
Goode & Wellborn, Courtroom Handbook on Federal Evidence (West 1995) (Rules 404, 803, and 804).
McCormick, Evidence §§ 245–246, 252–253 (4th ed. 1992).

RELATED DECISIONS
Hearsay

Jordan v. Copeland
Supreme Court of Alabama, 1961.
272 Ala. 336, 131 So.2d 696.

The case of Jordan v. Copeland is included at this point in the book to demonstrate that the factual patterns of some cases are difficult, but not impossible, to understand. As a further reason, this case involves the validity of a hearsay objection when a witness testifies that someone else who is not testifying searched for a record of a divorce and found no such record. The attempt to get this admitted is known as an attempt to prove a negative. The case also includes an example of the best evidence rule, discussed in a previous chapter of the book.

To understand the facts of this case, you should read the decision very quickly to grasp what is at issue. The prime contest of the litigants is over control of the estate and assets of the testatrix, Armina Jordan. The daughter of Armina Jordan is Monette Copeland. She applied for letters testamentary as the executrix of the estate of her mother. Armina Jordan's will had been admitted to probate in the probate court, and Fred Jordan, her alleged husband from 1944 to 1958 (the time of death of Armina Jordan), wanted to remove the case to the circuit court in equity and to be named executor of his "wife's" estate.

The main question to be resolved was whether the testatrix, Armina Jordan, had ever been divorced from her first husband, Arthur Stevens. If she was not divorced from Arthur Stevens, Fred Jordan would have no status in that he could not be the husband of a woman who was still married to another person. To make the fact pattern clear, I suggest you refer to the ninth paragraph from the end of the decision, which begins, "We will summarize the pertinent facts appearing from the record." Then you can prepare a synopsis of this many-times-married testatrix like the one that follows:

Testatrix & Arthur Stevens (1916–1931/1932)

3 deceased children—3 living children
(1 of the living children is Monette Copeland [appellee])

Testatrix & Arthur Wright (1936–Divorced?)

Testatrix & Fred Jordan (1944–1958, when testatrix died) (appellant)

Arthur Stevens & Callie Guynn (1948–present)

I believe a chart like this can help you better understand the facts. I therefore suggest that when you have a difficult fact pattern in a decision, creating a chart is always appropriate to assist you in understanding the issues.

The court below held that Fred Jordan, appellant, was not the husband of the testatrix and denied his petition to remove the case from the probate court to the circuit court in equity.

The Supreme Court of Alabama, after discussing the various rules of evidence, some of which I have alluded to above, concluded "that appellee [Monette Copeland] has failed to support the burden that rested on her to prove that the prior marriage had not been dissolved, and that the decree finding to the contrary is in error, for which it must be reversed and the cause remanded in order that the parties may present further proof as they may be advised."

I challenge students and faculty, as well as practitioners, to read this case carefully and contact me if they believe I have misconstrued the facts and/or ultimate decision in this case. It should be an interesting challenge to a serious student of the law.

COLEMAN, Justice. This is an appeal from a decree denying a petition to remove the administration of an estate from the probate court to the circuit court in equity.

The petitioner for removal, Fred Jordan, the appellant, asserts that he is the husband of Armina Jordan, deceased; that her will has been admitted to probate; and that appellee,

Monette Copeland, has applied for letters testamentary as executrix of the will.

The appellee asserts that testatrix was the wife of Arthur Stevens at the time of her purported marriage to appellant and that the prior marriage of Stevens to testatrix had not been dissolved at the time of her death. Appellee concludes, therefore, that appellant was not the husband of testatrix and has no such interest in her estate as would entitle him to remove the administration to the circuit court under § 139, Title 13, Code 1940.

After hearing testimony ore tenus, the court found that appellant was not the husband of testatrix, because her marriage to Stevens had not been dissolved, and denied the removal petition.

Appellant insists that the court erred in finding from the evidence that appellee had sustained the burden of proof that rested on her to show that the marriage of testatrix to Arthur Stevens had not been dissolved.

The evidence shows a ceremonial marriage of testatrix to appellant in Washington County on May 24, 1944. This is the last marriage of testatrix shown by the evidence. The evidence also showed a prior marriage of testatrix to Arthur Stevens and that he was living after the death of testatrix. He testified as a witness. The appellee asserts the invalidity of the last marriage of testatrix, that is, her marriage to appellant. The presumption is that the prior marriage has been dissolved by divorce, and the burden to show that it has not been dissolved rests upon the person seeking to impeach the last marriage, notwithstanding he is thereby required to prove a negative. Ex parte Young, 211 Ala. 508, 101 So. 51 (1924); Sloss-Sheffield Steel & Iron Co. v. Alexander, 241 Ala. 476, 3 So.2d 46 (1941); Freed v. Sallade, 245 Ala. 505, 17 So.2d 868 (1944); Jordan v. Courtney, 248 Ala. 390, 27 So.2d 783 (1946). So, the question presented on this appeal is whether or not the evidence is sufficient to support the finding that the marriage of testatrix and Arthur Stevens had not been dissolved by divorce.

The presumption of an innocent second marriage is overcome when the circumstances require a reasonable inference to the contrary. Freed v. Sallade, supra.

The circumstances shown by the evidence are as follows: Arthur Stevens testified that he married testatrix in Waynesboro, Mississippi, but had forgotten the date. A marriage certificate purporting to have been executed by the clerk of the Circuit Court of Wayne County, Mississippi, was admitted in evidence over appellant's objection. The certificate states that Stevens and "Miss Areminer Phillips" were married March 26, 1916. Stevens testified that he and testatrix had three children; that they separated in 1931 or 1932; that they were never divorced; that in 1936 he, Stevens, filed suit in Memphis, Tennessee, for a divorce but "left it" with his lawyer, "Charlie," who sent Stevens "an affidavit" when he "came back to Mississippi"; and that he never got a divorce in that proceeding and never filed any other proceeding for divorce. Stevens further said the contents of the affidavit were "The same as a divorce as I understand it," and that he lost the affidavit when he left it in Vicksburg in 1938. Stevens said also that he had not lived with testatrix since 1936, and that he now has a wife in Florida, where he was living at the time of the trial. A certificate by the ordinary of Lowndes County, Georgia, showing the marriage of "Arthur Stevens" to Callie Guynn on March 7, 1948, was received in evidence without objection. Stevens further said he did not know whether testatrix had ever obtained a divorce from him or not, that he did not know where she had lived, and that he "would hear from her along with the children." Stevens testified that he was served with process in a divorce proceeding instituted by testatrix in Waynesboro, Mississippi. It is not clear whether he was served with that process in Waynesboro or elsewhere. He said he was living in Alabama at that time and that he did not know the disposition of that case. Stevens said he did not know whether testatrix had ever obtained a divorce from him or not, and that when he married Callie Guynn "I believed I was free to marry, yes, or I would not have married."

A certificate, by the Judge of Probate of Washington County, stating that the records of his office show that Walter Wright and "Armenta" Phillips were married May 30, 1936, was introduced in evidence. A showing was admitted that Walter Wright would testify that he was married to testatrix, that he knew nothing of any divorce that she got from Stevens, and that as far as Wright knew she never had a divorce from Stevens. It was stipulated that Walter Wright was married to testatrix and divorced from her by decree of the Circuit Court of Washington County, but the validity of the marriage was not admitted.

Fred Jordan, the appellant, testified that he married testatrix in Washington County on May 24, 1944, and certificate to that effect is in evidence. He testified that after their marriage they lived together until the death of testatrix in 1958; that they had lived in Chickasaw; Chatom; Palestine, Texas; Chatom; Mizell, Mississippi; near Wagarville, Alabama; and then in Chatom until death of testatrix; that he had seen Arthur Stevens one time since 1944; that appellee, daughter of testatrix, had been in the home of appellant and testatrix "Lots of times"; and that he, appellant, had first heard the accusation that he and testatrix were not married on the day the will was supposed to be probated. With reference to records of a divorce of testatrix and Stevens, appellant testified as follows:

"**Q.** Have you ever seen a divorce decree between Armina Stevens and Arthur Stevens?
"**A.** No, sir.
"**Q.** Have you made diligent search for one?
"**A.** No, I didn't. I have since this trial started.
"**Q.** You have investigated in almost all the counties in which Armina has lived?
"**A.** Yes. Since I knew her, yes.
"**Q.** And you do not find in any of these counties a divorce proceeding between Armina and Arthur Stevens; a decree of divorce divorcing them?
"**A.** No, sir.
"Redirect examination by Mr. Turner:
"**Q.** Mr. Hurst is putting words in your mouth, isn't he?
"**Judge Pelham:** I strike that remark.
"**Q.** Did you make these investigations yourself?
"**A.** No, I didn't.
"**Q.** You are not trained in searching the records to determine whether or not there have been any divorce proceedings, is that right?
"**A.** I looked for some in different places.
"**Q.** Do you know how to search the records for a divorce?
"**A.** No, sir, I had to get somebody at the courthouses to do it for me.
"**Q.** You have done none of it yourself?
"**A.** No, sir."

Monette Copeland, appellee, testified that she was born in 1925, that her parents, Arthur Stevens and the testatrix, separated when appellee was nine or ten years old; that she, the appellee, until her own marriage in 1941, lived with the testatrix, and thereafter visited her "every three or four weeks"; that appellee had no knowledge of her mother's ever getting a divorce from Stevens, but "knew all along that she wasn't divorced from him." Appellee admitted that she filed a sworn petition to probate the will of testatrix. The petition is dated July 28, 1958, and recites in pertinent part as follows:

> "Your petitioner herewith propounds said will in which she believes that she is named as legatee and devisee and as executrix. Your petitioner further represents that the names, ages, and residences of the next of kin are as follows:
> "1. Fred J. Jordan, husband of deceased, over the age of 21 years, and a resident of Washington County, Alabama."

In answer to a question whether or not testatrix could have gotten a divorce from Stevens without appellee's knowing about it, appellee replied:

"**A.** While ago I explained to you I don't know. She could have or she could not."

This court has refused to accept the uncorroborated testimony of one of the parties of the prior marriage, to the effect that the prior marriage had never been dissolved by divorce, as being sufficient proof to establish the dissolution of the prior marriage when the evidence did not show an examination of the records of the divorce courts of the counties in which the parties had lived. Freed v. Sallade, supra; Dorsey v. Dorsey, 256 Ala. 137, 53 So.2d 601 (1951). On the second appeal in Dorsey v. Dorsey, 259 Ala. 220, 66 So.2d 135 (1953), however, the court held that the corroborating evidence was sufficient where the other party to the undissolved marriage refused to testify and the evidence showed that the divorce records in the counties where the parties had lived disclosed no divorce. In Bell v. Tennessee Coal, Iron & R. Co., 220 Ala. 422, 199 So. 813 (1941), the testimony of the wife in the prior marriage was corroborated by evidence that the records in Jefferson County, where the husband had lived, showed no divorce, and this was held to be sufficient to support a finding that the prior marriage had not been dissolved by divorce. In Sloss-Sheffield Steel & Iron Co. v. Watford, 245 Ala. 425, 17 So.2d 166 (1944), the testimony of the prior wife that the prior marriage had never been dissolved by divorce was corroborated by evidence that the records of four counties where the husband had lived did not show a divorce, and this evidence was held sufficient to rebut the presumption in favor of the subsequent marriage.

The law casts a strict burden on appellee to prove a negative, that is, that testatrix and Arthur Stevens had not been divorced. Dorsey v. Dorsey, 259 Ala. 220, 66 So.2d 135 (1953), supra; Vinson v. Vinson, 260 Ala. 254, 258, 69 So.2d 431 (1954). The testimony of the parties, not properly supported by evidence as to the divorce records in the various jurisdictions in which a decree could be rendered, is usually treated as not sufficient to overcome the presumption. Ashley v. Ashley, 255 Ala. 313, 319, 51 So.2d 239 (1951). However, such record evidence of nondivorce has not been regarded as an indispensable element of such proof in every case. Jones v. Case, 266 Ala. 498, 97 So.2d 816 (1957). The situation in Whitman v. Whitman, 253 Ala. 643, 46 So.2d 422 (1950), was like the situation here. The wife of the prior marriage, like Arthur Stevens here, testified that she knew of no divorce proceedings, but there was no evidence offered as to the statutes of the divorce records in Jefferson, one of the counties where the husband had lived, and the offered evidence as to the other county, Dallas, was held inadmissible. This court held there was no error in the decree denying relief to the first wife. Denial of relief was based on insufficiency of the evidence to overcome the presumption that the last marriage was valid. As to the testimony of the first wife that the prior marriage had not been dissolved this court said:

> ". . . . Her own testimony to that effect must be supported by legal evidence that the divorce courts of all the counties in the State, which would have jurisdiction of such a suit, did not have a record of a decree of divorce. . . ." 253 Ala. 643, 645, 46 So.2d 422, 424.

Appellee argues that the testimony of four witnesses (Arthur Stevens, Walter Wright, and appellee and appellant) is sufficient to sustain the finding that the marriage of testatrix and Stevens had never been dissolved by divorce. We do not agree.

Arthur Stevens' testimony is to the effect that he never obtained a divorce and does not know whether testatrix obtained one or not. Even if the testimony of Stevens be considered as positive that no divorce was obtained by either himself or testatrix, it would not, standing alone, be sufficient under Freed v. Sallade, supra, and the first appeal in Dorsey v. Dorsey, supra. Moreover, the action of Arthur Stevens in marrying his present wife, Callie Guynn, is not consistent with his testimony that he had never been divorced from testatrix. By his subsequent marriage, he solemnly declared that he was then free to marry again. Freed v. Sallade, 245 Ala. at page 508, 17 So.2d 868.

At best, the testimony of appellee and Walter Wright shows merely that these witnesses had no knowledge of a divorce. As appellee admitted, testatrix could have gotten a divorce without appellee knowing about it. After the death of testatrix, appellee had stated under oath in the petition to probate the will that appellant was the surviving husband of testatrix. After Stevens and testatrix separated, Walter Wright married her and later obtained a divorce in the court of Washington County. The actions of appellee and Wright are based on the proposition that Stevens and testatrix had been divorced and are diametrically opposed to the contrary inference which appellee draws from their testimony.

The testimony of appellant concerning his investigation of records falls short of establishing the fact that no divorce is shown by the records of the several counties in which testatrix and Stevens are shown to have lived after they separated. Appellant admitted he did not in his own person make the search and that he was not qualified to do so. We are of opinion that the testimony of appellant is not sufficient to establish as a fact that the records in all the counties where the parties had lived do not show a divorce of testatrix from Stevens. The testimony of appellant is that he had to get someone else at the courthouse to make the search and did none of it himself. All his testimony that the records do not show a divorce is hearsay and is not competent to show the absence of a divorce decree. Smith v. Smith, 268 Ala. 348, 106 So.2d 260 (1958). Act No. 101, General Acts 1943, page 105; Pocket Parts, Code 1940, Title 7, § 372(1). Moreover, the testimony is that he investigated "almost all," and not all, the counties involved.

We do not wish to be misunderstood on the holding that appellant's testimony with respect to his investigation is hearsay. This testimony is hearsay because he is repeating the statement of someone else who had told him that the records contained no divorce decree. His testimony is not hearsay for the reason that it is an attempt to prove the contents of a decree by parol. Hereafter in this opinion we express the view that appellant cannot, by parol, prove the existence or contents of a decree until proper predicate for secondary evidence has been laid. Parol testimony of the existence or contents of a decree is not the best evidence of its existence or contents. The fact that a decree does not exist is a different matter. Parol testimony to the effect that a decree does not appear in a record is not parol evidence of something a record contains. Such parol testimony is evidence that a record does not contain something, to wit, a divorce decree. In a strict sense, the record is the best evidence of what it does not contain, but it is manifestly impractical to require a party to introduce in evidence all the records of a court, or certified copies thereof. Competent, legal testimony given in answer to interrogatories by the register, custodian of the records of Barbour County, that a certain divorce decree did not appear in his records, was admitted to prove that fact on the second trial in Dorsey v. Dorsey, supra, 259 Ala. at page 223, 66 So.2d 135. The reason for allowing parol testimony to prove that records do not contain a divorce decree has been stated as follows:

> " . . . 'The law requires the best proof the case is susceptible of. It does not require impossibilities, and therefore did not require the production in our courts of the records of the courts of a sister state. Where there is a mass of records to examine, the law does not require the production of certified copies of all of them to prove the negative fact that a certain decree cannot be found.

Such proof may rest in parol ex necessitate rei. But there should and could have been furnished the testimony of the custodian of those records, or of other persons who qualified as familiar with them and all of them, in order that the negative fact might be clearly shown. . . .'" Note in 34 A.L.R. 495, quoting from Nelson v. Jones, 245 Mo. 579, 151 S.W. 80.

The testimony relating to the suits begun by appellant in Memphis and by testatrix in Waynesboro certainly fails to establish the fact that a divorce was granted, but it strongly supports an inference that divorce proceedings were instituted. A satisfactory conclusion as to whether those suits were actually instituted and, if so, as to their result, can hardly be reached on the record before us. We are clear to the conclusion that appellee has not proved that a divorce was not granted in either suit.

We will summarize the pertinent facts appearing from the record. Testatrix and Stevens married each other in 1916; they had six children of whom three were still living; they lived together until 1931 or 1932 when they permanently separated. Stevens made some move to initiate a suit for divorce in Memphis and testatrix did the same thing in Waynesboro, but the result of neither suit is shown. In 1936 testatrix married Arthur Wright and they were later divorced. In 1944 testatrix married appellant and lived with him until her death in 1958. Arthur Stevens married Callie Guynn in 1948 and was living with her in Florida at the time of the trial. Stevens, Wright, and appellee testified that they did not know of any divorce between Stevens and testatrix, and appellee emphatically states that she knows they were not divorced.

If their testimony be taken as positive to the effect there was no such divorce, it is nevertheless contradicted by their several actions, i.e., by Stevens in marrying Guynn, by Wright in marrying and divorcing testatrix, and by appellee in swearing that appellant was the surviving husband.

It may be that the records of all the counties concerned do not show a divorce of testatrix from Stevens, but we are of opinion that the evidence now before us is insufficient to establish that fact. Consequently, we are of opinion that appellee has failed to support the burden that rested on her to prove that the prior marriage had not been dissolved, and that the decree finding to the contrary is in error, for which it must be reversed and the cause remanded in order that the parties may present further proof as they may be advised.

Appellee cites Darrow v. Darrow, 201 Ala. 477, 78 So. 383 (1918), which appears to hold that evidence of a prior marriage and testimony by a party thereto that no notice of divorce had been served on such party prima facie, negates a dissolution of the prior marriage; and, further casts on the opposite party seeking to sustain the later marriage the burden to show a record of a decree dissolving the prior marriage. We have not found where this holding in the Darrow case has been cited or followed. It appears to be in conflict with Freed v. Sallade, Ashley v. Ashley, the first appeal in Dorsey v. Dorsey, and Vinson v. Vinson, all supra; and to the extent that it is in conflict with the later cases, the Darrow case is overruled.

As we understand appellee's brief, she concedes that appellant's objection to introduction in evidence of the Mississippi certificate of the marriage of testatrix to Stevens is well taken, but says it is error without injury. Because it thus appears that on another trial appellee will remove the grounds of this objection we forego its further consideration.

Appellant offered to prove by himself that testatrix, in her lifetime, had told appellant that she had a divorce from Stevens. The court sustained objection to this evidence and that ruling is assigned as error.

A party who is to prove a fact must do it by the highest evidence of which the nature of the thing is capable, and which it is within his power to produce. Although the court of a justice of the peace is not a court of record, our court has held that a party could not prove by the justice himself the result of a suit in his court, where the proceedings had been reduced to writing, without first laying a predicate for the introduction of secondary evidence; Bullock v. Ogburn, 13 Ala. 346 (1848). Even a judgment certificate made by the clerk for registration in the office of the judge of probate cannot be substituted for the judgment itself where the issues call for proof of the fact of an existing judgment; Boasberg

v. Cooke, 223 Ala. 389, 136 So. 797 (1931). In the absence of a predicate for secondary evidence, as was the case here, testimony of testatrix herself would not have been admissible to prove a decree dissolving her marriage to Stevens. See Cotton v. Cotton, 213 Ala. 336, 104 So. 650 (1925). Therefore, the court did not err in refusing to allow appellant to testify that testatrix had said she had a divorce from Stevens. For cases supporting this view, see McDonald v. McDonald, 180 Ga. 771, 180 S.E. 815 (1935); Trimble v. Wells, 314 Ky. 206, 234 S.W.2d 683 (1951); Weaver v. Patterson, 92 N.J.Eq. 170, 111 A. 506 (1920); Moore v. Follett, Tex.Civ.App., 11 S.W.2d 662 (Tex.Civ.App. 1929); Hupp v. Hupp, 235 S.W.2d 753. Two California cases, In re Smith's Estate, 193 P.2d 90 (Cal.App. 1920), and 33 Cal.2d 279, 201 P.2d 539 (1949), appear to be contrary to our conclusion here, but we are persuaded that the California rule is not the better one.

Reversed and remanded.

All the Justices concur.

Kaplan v. City of New York

Supreme Court, Appellate Division,
First Department, 1960.
10 A.D.2d 319, 200 N.Y.S.2d 261.

In Kaplan v. City of New York, the plaintiff sued the City of New York and a driver of a private taxicab for negligence. Kaplan won in the trial court against both defendants, but the City of New York alone appealed.

The basis of the action against the City of New York was that the city knew, or should have known, of a dangerous condition in the street at the location of the accident and failed to correct the condition. In situations such as this, the governmental authority that has control over the street owes a duty to persons using the street to correct dangerous conditions over which it has control. The party suing the government has to prove in court that the government had proper notice and reasonable time to correct the condition. This case explains the method that should be used to prove that the government had due notice and did nothing to correct the condition. If the evidence of notice is presented improperly, it is hearsay and not admissible. After reading the decision, you will know the proper method to use.

STEVENS, Justice. The plaintiffs were passengers in a private taxicab owned and operated by one Lomio. The taxicab collided with a pillar supporting an elevated transit railroad overpass on Baychester Avenue in The Bronx, causing certain injuries to the plaintiffs. Suit was instituted against Lomio, the driver of the cab, and the City. Judgment was rendered against both defendants. Lomio did not appeal. The City appealed, and the matter was reversed as to it (Kaplan v. City of New York, 6 A.D.2d 489, 179 N.Y.S.2d 885 [1920]), because of the receipt of improper testimony of prior accidents. The court said "[i]t is not proper, however, to offer such testimony unless it is first shown that the circumstances attending the earlier accidents were sufficiently similar to the relevant conditions prevailing at the time of the later accident." 6 A.D.2d at page 491, 179 N.Y.S.2d 888. On the retrial, judgment was rendered against the City, and it is from that judgment that the defendant now appeals.

The defendant contends that the plaintiffs failed to prove the existence of a dangerous condition, and that the trial court committed error by (a) admitting evidence concerning unrelated dissimilar accidents which happened at the scene; (b) permitting the reading of testimony of a witness at the first trial; and (c) permitting into evidence a notice of claim, a complaint and a bill of particulars in totally unrelated actions. It contends also that the verdicts are excessive.

* * *

The plaintiffs then introduced and were permitted to read into evidence, portions of a notice of claim and complaint of one Anna E. Wagner, dated May 21, 1951, on the theory of notice to the City of an alleged dangerous and hazardous condition. The fact that a notice of claim had been sent and received and that a complaint was served, might well be relevant and properly admissible, but only after the dangerous condition to which it relates has been shown. However, the plaintiffs were permitted to read the descriptive and conclusory allegations contained therein that the area "is in an unsafe, dangerous, obstructive and impassable condition. The most westerly post

pillar and supporting column of the superstructure then and there present is in such a manner and position that it constituted a nuisance of vehicular traffic; that this is an improperly lighted elevator pillar, and it constitutes a dangerous, unsafe, unlighted and unguarded position—it occupies a dangerous, unsafe, and unguarded position in said public highway; that it constitutes a menace to vehicular traffic"; was not properly marked, roadway unsafe, etc.

A like ruling was made as to certain papers in a prior accident, the Moore case, and a portion of the documents read to the jury. No attempt was made in either case to offer independent proof of what caused the accidents, whether human frailty, mechanical defect, or physical obstructions. (In fact an offer of proof by the defendant that 3-plus alcohol was found in the brain of Moore was excluded.) Nor were Wagner or Moore produced to testify or be subjected to cross-examination. The contents of the documents beyond title, proof of service, etc., in such circumstances were hearsay evidence, and the admission thereof was clearly prejudicial. Its effect, despite disclaimer, was to go far beyond proof of notice and tended to establish the existence of a claimed dangerous condition. The mere happening of an accident is not in and of itself proof of negligence, nor proof of freedom from contributory negligence. Proof of similar dangerous conditions attending or proximately causing prior accidents upon which plaintiff seeks to rely may be by testimonial or documentary means or a combination of both. But when testimonial in the sense that descriptive allegations of the parties are relied upon, or the natural result of their introduction in evidence is to prove both a dangerous condition and proximate cause, the parties claimant in such cases should be produced and available for cross-examination. There was no preliminary proof of similar circumstances attending the Wagner and Moore accidents.

In our view the admission into evidence of the contents of the papers, as distinguished from proof of the fact of filing and service thereof, constituted prejudicial error requiring reversal and a new trial. Again we point out that even the proof of notice would be immaterial unless it first had been established by competent evidence that a dangerous condition existed.

In Parks v. City of New York, 111 App.Div. 836, 98 N.Y.S. 94 (1906), on a retrial additional evidence of notice to the City of a defective sidewalk condition was offered by a policeman, Baxter, who testified from his personal observation of the shaky condition of the bridge or temporary sidewalk. He testified also that one Hess called his attention to the condition and that he made an oral report and a written report. Hess testified that he called Baxter's attention to the condition. The court held "[n]otice to Baxter—a police officer— was notice to the city" (111 App.Div. at page 839, 98 N.Y.S. at page 95), and that the verdict was not against the weight of the evi-

dence, either as to the defective condition or as to notice. It appeared from a former trial (Coolidge v. City of New York, 99 App.Div. 175, 90 N.Y.S. 1078 (1905)), that a city inspector, Hamel, had made several inspections of the bridge and knew its condition. There was no question but that the collapse of the bridge caused the death of plaintiff's intestate.

* * *

The judgment appealed from should be reversed, on the law and in the exercise of discretion, and a new trial ordered, with costs to abide the event.

Judgment unanimously reversed upon the law and in the exercise of discretion and a new trial ordered, with costs to abide the event. All concur.

RELATED DECISIONS
Character Evidence

People v. Mallard
Supreme Court, Criminal Term, Queens County, Part III, 1974.
78 Misc.2d 858, 358 N.Y.S.2d 913.

The role of a criminal court is to give a defendant a fair trial. The defendant who has a prior criminal record will have a disadvantage if his or her prior criminal record is made known during the trial to the trier of the facts of the instant case before the court. This is particularly true if the defendant is being tried by a jury of laypersons, who may be influenced by the defendant's prior criminal record, even though they may have said when they were being selected in the voir dire that they would decide the guilt or innocence of the defendant based only on the evidence that is admitted by the judge.

People have to be reminded that even when a defendant has such a criminal record, that defendant may, in truth, not be guilty of the crime with which he or she is now charged.

Therefore, to give the defendant a fair trial, the rules of evidence limit the types of crime that may be made known to the trier of the

facts by the presiding judge. This is explained in this case by a very knowledgeable jurist, who decided this case before equally knowledgeable attorneys. The decision is quite clear and will explain the types of crimes that may be admitted.

The determination of what evidence will be admissible in the current trial is made by the judge when the defense attorney makes a motion (an application) to the judge to make a decision on this matter. This is what was done in this case as a pretrial motion. Based on what the judge decides, the defendant, as well as the prosecutor, is in a better position to decide whether or not to enter into a plea bargain.

Abraham Werfel, Jamaica, for defendant.

Nicholas Ferraro, Dist. Atty. (Robert Cox McGann, Maspeth, of counsel), for plaintiff.

LEONARD L. FINZ, Justice. On this motion, the defendant seeks a prospective ruling to limit the District Attorney in utilizing the prior conviction record of the defendant for impeachment purposes during the trial. The troublesome and pressing issue that emerges is the extent to which the past criminal transgressions of a defendant can be revived and presented to a jury should the defendant elect to defend himself against the current charges by testifying on his own behalf.

The procedure, inspired by the recent pronouncement of the Court of Appeals in People v. Sandoval, 34 N.Y.2d 371, 357 N.Y.S.2d 849, 314 N.E.2d 413 (1974), must, therefore, be analyzed to determine the ultimate decision to be reached—what prior crimes, if any, could properly be surfaced to attack the credibility of the defendant.

As a pretrial procedure designed to protect the constitutional rights of a defendant, the name of a *Sandoval* Hearing, it would appear, can now be added to the illustrious list of constitutional safeguards joining such company as *Miranda*, *Wade*, *Huntley* and others.

In the instant matter, the defendant faces trial for robbery in the first degree, a Class B felony, conviction of which would subject him to a mandatory term of imprisonment with a possible maximum of 25 years. He has nine prior convictions, four of which are drug convictions and three gambling convictions included in that total.

What then is the special formula to be employed by a trial judge in resolving an issue that has plagued and is continuing to plague judicial discretion in order to determine its proper direction?

An examination of some of the major cases on the subject is necessary toward an ultimate decision that would be consistent with justice.

In *Sandoval* the Court of Appeals, after much discussion of the cases on the subject, concluded that the resolution of this issue must rest with the trial judge preferably for a determination in a pretrial procedure such as the one before this Court. In attempting to set forth criteria and guidelines for the proper exercise of discretion in such instances, the Court stated the following:

"From the standpoint of the prosecution, then, the evidence *should be admitted if it will have material probative value on the issue of defendant's credibility, veracity or honesty* on the witness stand. From the standpoint of the defendant it should not be admitted unless it will have such probative worth, or, even though it has such worth, if to lay it before the jury or court would otherwise be so highly prejudicial as

to call for its exclusion. The standard—whether the prejudicial effect of impeachment testimony far outweighs the probative worth of the evidence on the issue of credibility—is easy of articulation but troublesome in many cases of application." (Emphasis supplied.)

Hence, two countervailing forces, each exerting its influence on the conscience of the Court, come forward in its quest for a sound base in determining the exercise of proper discretion. On one side is the desirability of admitting prior convictions so that the jury will be able to assess the degree of credence to be given to the testimony of the defendant, and on the other, the firm recognition by the Court that to permit the impeachment of the credibility of the defendant by such device is to invite undesirable prejudice in the minds of the jury.

An uncomfortable ambivalence is created, as the Court well recognized in its succeeding statement:

"At the threshold it must be recognized as inevitable, and thus not determinative, that evidence of prior criminal, vicious or immoral conduct will always be detrimental to the defendant. . . . Will the testimony to be elicited *in cross-examination have a disproportionate and improper impact on the triers of fact? Will the apprehension of its introduction undesirably deter the defendant from taking the stand and thereby deny the jury or court significant material evidence?* (Emphasis supplied.)

One of the most significant aspects of *Sandoval* is eloquently expressed in the "recognition of the principles underlying broadened discovery in criminal procedure and a growing awareness that there may be undue prejudice to a defendant from unnecessary and immaterial development of previous misconduct."

"Trial Court discretion" becomes the common thread joining all cases on the subject of the instant application. In this regard, it is interesting to observe how attitudes in this area have changed through the years. In an early case decided in 1893, dealing with the introduction of evidence that the defendant was guilty of adulterous conduct, the Court pronounced the exercise of discretion thusly:

"It is urged that this evidence should have been excluded because it tended to implicate the defendant's wife, who was a witness for him, and thus to impeach her, in an unauthorized way, before the jury. But any apprehended misuse of this species of evidence may always be avoided by asking and obtaining an instruction to the jury that it is only to be considered in determining the credibility of the witness who makes the confession." (People v. Webster, 139 N.Y. 73, 84, 34 N.E. 730, 733.)

In view of the anticipated caveat to the jury, the impeachment evidence was held to be admissible. It is interesting to note that at the turn of the century adultery was considered so heinous as to bear on the credibility of the defendant while he was on trial for murder. Today, such conduct, although still considered immoral, would scarcely cause the lifting of an eyebrow.

Realistically, however, to suggest that an instruction to a jury, despite its articulate quality, would result, without risk, in a juror drawing a mental curtain on the fine line segregating impeachment testimony from the possible prejudice it could produce, is a nuance of human nature that eludes this Court.

This theme of avoidance of undue prejudice is not novel. The subject was, indeed, treated at length in Luck v. United States, 348 F.2d 763 (D.C.Cir. 1965). There, Circuit Judge McGowan, writing for the majority, stated (p. 769):

"In exercising discretion in this respect, a number of factors might be relevant. . . . above all, the extent to which it is more important to the search for truth in a particular case for the jury to hear the defendant's story than to know of a prior conviction. The goal of a criminal trial is the disposition of the charge in accordance with the truth. The possibility of a rehearsal of the defendant's criminal record in a given case, especially if it means that the jury will be left without one version of the truth, may or may not contribute to that objective."

Continuing in this vein in Gordon v. United States, 383 F.2d 936, 939 (D.C. Cir. 1967), Circuit Judge, and now Chief Justice, Warren Burger stated:

"The standard to be applied by the District Judge was stated in terms of whether he 'believes the prejudicial effect of impeachment far outweighs the probative relevance of the prior conviction to the issue of credibility.' The impact of criminal convictions will often be damaging to an accused and it is admittedly difficult to restrict its impact, by cautionary instructions, to the issue of credibility. The test of Luck, however, is that to bar them as impeachment the court must find that the prejudice must 'far outweigh' [emphasis supplied] the probative relevance to credibility, or that even if relevant the 'cause of truth would be helped more by letting the jury hear the defendant's story than by the defendant's foregoing that opportunity because of the fear of prejudice founded upon a prior conviction.'"

Further in the same case (p. 940):

"Even though a judge might find that the prior convictions are relevant to credibility and the risk of prejudice to the defendant does not warrant their exclusion, he may nevertheless conclude *that it is more important that the jury have the benefit of the defendant's version of the case than to have the defendant remain silent out of fear of impeachment.*" [Emphasis supplied.]

The concern of the Court (p. 941) in the foregoing cases is the same as that of the Court of Appeals in Sandoval:

"We are well aware that these are not firm guidelines which can be applied readily as though they were part of the structure of the Federal Rules of Criminal Procedure; the very nature of judicial discretion precludes rigid standards for its exercise; we seek to give some assistance to the trial judge to whom we have assigned the extremely difficult task of weighing and balancing these elusive concepts. Surely, it would be much simpler if prior convictions of an accused were *totally admissible* or *totally excludable* as impeachment; but in the face of an *explicit, unambiguous statute* allowing use of prior convictions and the holding in Luck we have little choice. The lesser step has been taken in Luck saying that the statute is to be read as permitting a discretion in the trial judge." (Emphasis supplied.)

Having in mind the list of cases issuing out of the Supreme Court of the United States, some under Chief Justice Burger, expressing a philosophy greatly protective of the rights of defendants in this regard, can it be said that there are no signposts indicating the direction in which the Court should move on this issue?

Since there appears to be reluctance to part with this rule of evidence, the Courts have sought to find a rationale which will permit its continuance where directly relevant, namely, on the issue of credibility. In United States v. Palumbo, 401 F.2d 270, 274 (2 Cir. 1968), it was said: "More recently, *Luck* has been construed to allow impeachment of a defendant by convictions involving fraud or stealing, which 'are universally regarded as conduct which reflects adversely on a man's honesty and integrity.' Gordon v. United States, 127 U.S.App.D.C. 343, 383 F.2d 936, 940 (1967)."

It is noteworthy and significant that Palumbo never took the stand. Is it too much to speculate that the Court's decision to permit cross-examination at least as to some of Palumbo's past record may have inhibited his appearance as a witness in his own behalf, thereby depriving him *de facto* of the constitutional right to relate to the jury exculpatory conduct on his part?

Following in the track of *Luck* and *Gordon* is United States v. Puco, 453 F.2d 539, 542, 543 (2 Cir. 1971), where the Court stated:

> "Reference to a defendant's criminal record *is always highly prejudicial. The average jury is unable, despite curative instructions, to limit the influence of a defendant's criminal record to the issue of credibility.* . . . While there is considerable uncertainty as to what crimes, by reason of their nature, may be considered to be highly probative of lack of veracity, we believe that a narcotics conviction has little necessary bearing on the veracity of the accused as a witness." (But see United States v. McIntosh, 138 U.S.App. D.C. 237, 426 F.2d 1231.) (Emphasis supplied.)

The scarcity of cases on the Appellate level in New York was pointed out by Mr. Justice Shapiro in People v. Duffy, 44 A.D.2d 298, 354 N.Y.S.2d 672 (1974), a case of very recent origin, although it predates *Sandoval* by several months. In *Duffy* the Court makes a scholarly review of the cases on this subject, pointing first of all to the statute (CPL 60.40, subd. 1), which allows a prosecutor to ask, if he does so "properly" if he, the defendant, has been convicted of a "specific offense." On reviewing the cases and quoting from them at length, mainly from the *Luck* and *Gordon* opinions, the Appellate Division stated the following (p. 305, 354 N.Y.S.2d p. 678):

> "On appropriate application, made either at or prior to trial, and in the exercise of a sound discretion, the trial court should determine whether an applying defendant has sustained the burden, which should be his, of demonstrating that the prejudice involved in permitting into evidence proof of prior convictions or criminal acts so far outweighs the probative value of such proof for impeachment purposes that the proof should not be received. *Hence, we today announce that to be the applicable law.*" (Emphasis supplied.)

And again, we are left with the dilemma created by a statute that permits the use of prior convictions for cross-examination against the backdrop of lofty decisional law highly suggestive of proceeding to its application with measured caution—all in the stricture of "judicial discretion." Unfortunately, however, little relief is provided the trial judge, to whom the application is addressed and who must weigh in the two pans of the scale the pressures exerted by credibility on the one hand and prejudice on the other. If one were to construct such a scale, with the lowliest offense on the one end and murder most foul on the other, where would one place the fulcrum, the point of balance, which is the present alleged crime of the defendant? And how does one, in truth, assess the weight to be placed on each side of the scale?

Once again, we observe that the "balance" issue is the overriding theme in determining the proper application of judicial discretion. So, too, in People v. Schwartzman, 24 N.Y.2d 241, 299 N.Y.S.2d 817, 247 N.E.2d 642 (1969), does the Court of Appeals proclaim its "balance" position:

> "The rules governing the admissibility of evidence of other crimes represent a balance between the probative value of such proof and the danger of prejudice which it presents to an accused. When evidence of other crimes has no purpose other than to show that a defendant is of a *criminal bent or character* and thus likely to have committed the crime charged, it should be excluded." (Emphasis supplied.)

Again, we must return to *Sandoval*, and its pronouncement of "undue prejudice to a defendant from unnecessary and immaterial development of previous misconduct."

As such, we now focus upon this defendant, whose prior criminal record consists for the most part of narcotics and gambling convictions. Would not the knowledge gained by a jury that the defendant has trafficked in narcotics be sufficient to create in the mind of a juror a prejudice, or even a fury which would eliminate for him any possibility of fair consideration—or a fair trial? In a time when such a crime is considered so serious as to be punishable by a sentence of life imprisonment, how can a judge instruct a jury, with any degree of assurance that his direction will be adhered to, that the evidence that this man was formerly convicted of selling narcotics or gambling is only to be considered as bearing on his credibility?

This, it appears to this Court, is the threshold theme, especially in the light of all constitutional safeguards that have evolved toward the protection of the basic rights of all defendants. It is in furtherance of a conscious effort on the part of those whose duty it is to administer justice to weigh the factors involved in the protection of society and the preservation of the rights of the individual, knowing full well that society as a whole can survive the impact of many calamities but that the individual is, at best, but a frail mortal, easily destroyed and impossible of resurrection, that energizes this thrust toward justice.

This Court, in its search for fairness, reaches the conclusion that only those prior convictions that bear *directly* upon the issue of the defendant's credibility be admitted into evidence. The prior crimes fitting this narrow description should be limited to perjury, fraud and deceit, larceny by misrepresentation and other closely related crimes which have at their very core *the prior dishonest or untruthful quality of the defendant*. The danger of prejudice and the fear by the defendant that he might have to remain silent in his own defense are so great as to warrant no other just determination than the total and absolute exclusion of his prior criminal record short of that which focuses precisely upon his credibility, veracity or honesty.

The gravamen of this decision rests with the resolving of all doubts in favor of the individual defendant. As such, should the trial court's decision to exclude prior convictions

be incorrect, the defendant, at best, receives but a small measure of assistance in resisting the present charges against him. Conversely, however, should the decision to admit prior convictions be an improvident one, the damage wrought could be crushing and irreversible in the minds of a jury. The alternatives leave but one conclusion—that is, that society can better withstand the result of a "close" decision against it than can the "frail mortal" defendant.

Justice, in this context, can neither be computerized, nor punched out by some mechanical brain in calibrating the exact balance which could be determined solely on the basis of raw data derived from general guidelines. This being so, and recognizing candidly the impossibility of any specific judicial criteria that could chart wisely the proper path in the pursuit of judicial discretion, the offered alternative, while not the panacea, more closely parallels the spirit of justice than its present counterpart. To this extent, *Sandoval* meets this issue brilliantly when it states that prior convictions "should not be admitted unless it will have . . . probative worth" (on the issue of defendant's credibility, veracity, or honesty).

In *Sandoval* the theme of weighing and balancing is constant. In that atmosphere, the instant decision falls squarely upon the *Sandoval* scales and is consistent with the sound tone and humane philosophy expounded therein.

Additionally, the major constitutional issue raised by the gagging of the defendant, who otherwise would speak out in his own defense, but for fear of prosecutorial cross-examination of prior crimes, is so offensive to our basic sensitivity for fairness as to warrant immediate redress and correction.

In an evolutionary sense, the former harsh common law doctrine, now codified, is eroding through judicial interpretation, approaching its inevitable demise, and leaving in its wake a residue of fairness. Stated another way: *Luck* has turned the key. *Duffy* has opened the door. *Sandoval* has invited you in, and *Mallard*, in the light of the foregoing, may permit you to stay.

Accordingly, it is the judgment of this Court, in the posture of this opinion, that the entire prior conviction record of the defendant is suppressed for purposes of cross-examination should he choose to speak out in defense of the crime for which he is *now* charged.

United States v. Emenogha
United States Court of Appeals, Seventh Circuit, 1992.
1 F.3d 473 (7th Cir. 1993).

This case is an interesting one. I believe plaintiff/appellee Vincent Nwafor was desperate, had a lot of ill-gotten gains, and was grasping at straws to save himself from drowning. He argued that the other crimes he committed should not have been introduced in evidence as through a magazine article indicating he was a person involved in drug trafficking; that he was entrapped into committing the instant crime; that the prosecution was sarcastic in disparaging defense counsel in his rebuttal so as to inflame the jury; and that other arguments he could have set forth to make his case were foreclosed because the trial court violated many principles of evidence law. I have included this case at this point in the book because it is an excellent example of an instance when evidence of other crimes, standing alone, may not be used to prove the character of a person in order to show conformity therewith. It may, however, be admissible for other purposes such as proof of motive, opportunity, intent, preparation, plan, knowledge, identity, or absence of mistake.

Before CUDAHY, RIPPLE, and KANNE, Circuit Judges.

RIPPLE, Circuit Judge.

On March 26, 1991, the appellants[1] were convicted of various drug offenses. Charles Emenogha was found guilty of one count of importing heroin and one count of possessing heroin with intent to distribute in violation of 21 U.S.C. §§ 841 (a)(1) and 952(a); Vincent Nwafor was found guilty of one count of possessing heroin with intent to distribute and five counts of distributing heroin in violation of 21 U.S.C. § 841(a)(1); and Gibson Nwafor was found guilty of ten counts of structuring financial transactions to avoid Internal Revenue reporting requirements in violation of 31 U.S.C. §§ 5324 and 5322(a).

All defendants were also convicted of conspiracy to import and distribute heroin in violation of 21 U.S.C. § 846. Mr. Emenogha was sentenced to 132 months' incarceration, Gibson Nwafor to 160 months, and Vincent Nwafor to 396 months. They now appeal various aspects of their convictions and sentences. We affirm.

I

BACKGROUND

This trio of Nigerian citizens was convicted of conspiring to import heroin from Africa for distribution in Chicago. They joined forces to smuggle the drug into this country by financing couriers to purchase heroin in Lagos, Nigeria, and to convey it to Chicago where the other conspiracy members would divide it for distribution. Vincent Nwafor, the prime mover in the enterprise, organized the purchases and the subsequent distributions. Gibson Nwafor, Vincent's brother, handled the financial arrangements. Gibson Nwafor held the profits at his own apartment, converted the proceeds to larger bills for easier handling at various Chicago banks, and wire-transferred money out of the country on Vincent Nwafor's behalf. Mr. Emenogha, who is the Nwafors' cousin, acted as a courier and brought heroin to Chicago from Nigeria on at least three occasions.

The operation was assisted by Ebenezer Dikeocha, who smuggled heroin into the United States and distributed it at least once in conjunction with Vincent Nwafor. Additional distributors were Andy Uwazoke and Ike Agu. Larry Palmer, a/k/a Lawrence Ofuokwu (hereinafter "Palmer"), an uncharged member of the conspiracy, travelled to Nigeria to purchase heroin; he pled guilty to a drug charge in Maryland and agreed to cooperate with the United States in investigating other members of the conspiracy. Other couriers for the conspiracy were Tracy Ousley, Beverly (last name not known), and Darlene Sumpter, Vincent Nwafor's girlfriend, who contacted the Drug Enforcement Administration (DEA) in 1989 and agreed to cooperate in arranging an undercover purchase of heroin between Vincent Nwafor and Chicago police officer Regina Joanes.

Palmer testified at length about the structure and activities of the conspiracy. He was privy to, and a major player in, a number of smuggling operations, including a December 1988 episode when he was involved with Vincent Nwafor and Dikeocha in importing 500 grams of heroin from Nigeria. In July 1989, Palmer met with Vincent Nwafor, Dikeocha, and Uwazoke to discuss a plan to use Tracy Ousley and Beverly to smuggle heroin from Kenya, a plan that produced 1.7 kilograms of the drug. Another plan was made that summer for Palmer to purchase drugs in Nigeria and for Tracy Ousley to bring them to the United States. Palmer made the purchase in Nigeria in October and returned to the United States, but a courier was not sent to Nigeria to pick up the drugs.

After Palmer was arrested in November 1989, he telephoned Vincent Nwafor and learned that Mr. Emenogha had returned from Nigeria with some of the drugs that Palmer had left behind. When Palmer asked about his share of the profits from these drugs, Vincent Nwafor told him that he was entitled to none because Palmer's brother in Nigeria would not relinquish a portion of the drugs that Palmer had left in his care.

The DEA arranged a number of undercover purchases with the aid of the Chicago police and Darlene Sumpter. Between January 27, 1989, and September 10, 1990, five purchases were made from Vincent Nwafor and one from Dikeocha. The purchases from Vincent Nwafor totalled over 200 grams of heroin. During the course of several of the purchases, Vincent Nwafor talked to Officer Joanes about her acting as courier and suggested that she travel to Africa via Jamaica or the Bahamas and return with the drugs in a specially built suitcase.

Gibson Nwafor's role in the conspiracy was to handle the profits efficiently. He stored the cash at his apartment, exchanged small bills for $100 bills for easy transport, and wire-transferred thousands of dollars out of the country to banks in Belgium and Germany. From February 23, 1989, to August 3, 1990, he wire-transferred $142,619 in twenty-three separate transactions. Between July 5, 1990, and September 10, 1990, he exchanged a total of $139,400 for larger bills on ten different oc-

casions. Palmer testified that he was with Gibson Nwafor when he processed large sums of drug money through various banks in such a way that he could avoid IRS reporting requirements.

Darlene Sumpter was arrested at O'Hare Airport on March 31, 1990, prior to boarding an international flight with $103,940 in $100 bills. The money was in several envelopes, some of them marked with the names Ike, MacDonald (a/k/a Emenogha), and Vin. In subsequent telephone calls, Vincent Nwafor told her that the money had been put into her luggage by other members of the conspiracy. On July 25, 1990, Mr. Emenogha was arrested on arrival at O'Hare Airport with 997 grams of heroin secreted in his suitcases. Finally, the Nwafors were arrested on September 10, 1990. Vincent Nwafor signed a consent form for a search of his apartment and storage locker. In the locker, agents found a digital scale and four plastic bags containing a substance resembling heroin. Tests later revealed that the substances amounted to approximately 400 grams of heroin in purity ranging from 2.6 percent to 35 percent. Gibson Nwafor consented to a search of his apartment where agents found $21,900 in $100 bills hidden in various places. Agents also found documents evidencing a Brussels bank account, some wire transfer receipts, and an address book with telephone numbers for Agu, Dikeocha, and Mr. Emenogha.

Following their convictions, the three appellants challenge a number of evidentiary and sentencing matters. The Nwafors also challenge their convictions on the basis of a single conspiracy.

II

DISCUSSION

A. *Standards of Review*

We review evidentiary matters for abuse of discretion. United States v. Garcia, 986 F.2d 1135, 1139 (7th Cir. 1993); United States v. Briscoe, 896 F.2d 1476, 1490 (7th Cir.), *cert. denied sub nom.* Usman v. United States, 498 U.S. 863, 111 S.Ct. 173, 112 L.Ed.2d 137 (1990). "Appellants who challenge evidentiary rulings of the district court are like rich men who wish to enter the Kingdom: their prospects compare with those of camels who wish to pass through the eye of the needle." United States v. Glecier, 923 F.2d 496, 503 (7th Cir.), *cert. denied*, — U.S. —, 112 S.Ct. 54, 116 L.Ed.2d 31 (1991). "Once a defendant has been found guilty of the crime charged, the factfinder's role as weigher of the evidence is preserved through a legal conclusion that upon judicial review *all of the evidence* is to be considered in the light most favorable to the prosecution." Jackson v. Virginia, 443 U.S. 307, 319, 99 S.Ct. 2781, 2789, 61 L.Ed.2d 560 (1979). When reviewing a challenge to the sufficiency of the evidence, we review the evidence and reasonable inferences therefrom in a light most favorable to the government, and "[i]f any rational jury could have found the defendant guilty beyond a reasonable doubt, the conviction will be affirmed." United States v. Curry, 977 F.2d 1042, 1053 (7th Cir. 1992), *cert. denied sub nom.* Holland v. United States, — U.S. —, 113 S.Ct. 1357, 122 L.Ed.2d 737 (1993). We review findings of fact in sentencing matters for clear error. United States v. Tolson, 988 F.2d 1494, 1497 (7th Cir. 1993); United States v. Davis, 938 F.2d 744, 746 (7th Cir. 1991); United States v. Feekes, 929 F.2d 334, 338 (7th Cir. 1991).

B. *Vincent Nwafor*

1. Other crimes evidence under Federal Rule of Evidence 404(b).[2] We review evidentiary rulings for abuse of discretion. United States v. Smith, 995 F.2d 662, 671 (7th Cir. 1993). Vincent Nwafor's defense theory was that he was entrapped by his girlfriend, a government informant, who induced him with the promise of sexual favors to make drug deliveries to the undercover agents. In order to counter such a defense, a government is obliged to prove beyond a reasonable doubt either the absence of government inducement or the defendant's predisposition to commit the crime. United States v. Simpson, 995 F.2d 109, 111 (7th Cir. 1993); United States v. Blackman, 950 F.2d 420, 423 (7th Cir. 1991).

As the Supreme Court has recently noted: [when] the defense of entrapment is at issue, as it was in this case, the prosecution must prove beyond reasonable doubt that the defendant was disposed to commit the criminal act prior to first being approached by Government agents.

Jacobson v. United States, — U.S. —, —, 112 S.Ct. 1535, 1540, 118 L.Ed.2d 174 (1992). Criminal disposition is "the principal element in the defense of entrapment." Mathews v. United States, 485 U.S. 58, 63, 108 S.Ct. 883, 886, 99 L.Ed.2d 54 (1988) (quoting United States v. Russell, 411 U.S. 423, 433, 93 S.Ct. 1637, 1643, 36 L.Ed.2d 366 (1973)); United States v. Sanchez, 984 F.2d 769, 773 (7th Cir. 1993). Evidence of other bad acts is admissible to prove predisposition when entrapment is at issue. United States v. Goodapple, 958 F.2d 1402, 1406 (7th Cir. 1992). Accordingly, the government sought to introduce evidence of Vincent Nwafor's 1986 conviction for his involvement in an undercover heroin buy. The evidence was admitted over Vincent Nwafor's objection.

This court has said that such evidence is subject to a four-prong test; it is admissible if (1) it is directed toward establishing a matter other than the defendant's propensity to commit the crime, (2) the evidence was sufficient to support a jury finding that the defendant committed the similar act,[3] (3) the other act is similar enough and close enough in time to be relevant to the matter in issue, and (4) the probative value is not substantially outweighed by the danger of unfair prejudice. United States v. Khorrami, 895 F.2d 1186, 1194 (7th Cir.), *cert. denied*, 498 U.S. 986, 111 S.Ct. 522, 112 L.Ed.2d 533 (1990); United States v. Zapata, 871 F.2d 616, 620–21 (7th Cir. 1989) (citing United States v. Shackleford, 738 F.2d 776 (7th Cir. 1984)). In applying this analysis, the district court is afforded a considerable amount of discretion, and we shall reverse only for abuse of that discretion. *Zapata*, 871 F.2d at 621.

Vincent Nwafor argues first that the evidence was introduced improperly to show his propensity to commit the crime, rather than merely his predisposition. We cannot accept this argument. The introduction of a prior drug conviction speaks directly to Vincent Nwafor's predisposition to engage in such illegal drug activity.

Second, Vincent Nwafor argues that the evidence is neither similar enough nor close enough in time to be relevant. Here he is charged with being the leader and organizer, but in the 1986 conviction he was merely a broker for the heroin. We cannot find this dissimilar, given his defense that he did not have a predisposition to engage in drug deals. Vincent Nwafor concedes that this court has held that five years is sufficiently close in time for purposes of Rule 404(b). *See* United States v. Zeidman, 540 F.2d 314, 319 (7th Cir. 1976). However, he maintains that the government fell afoul of the prejudice prong when it went beyond the mere introduction of the prior conviction by putting on testimony of the purchasing agent and introducing the narcotics (14.05 grams) from the 1986 case.

The only prong of the analysis that requires our attention is the final one, a Rule 403–type balancing of probative value with the risk of undue prejudice. *See Goodapple*, 958 F.2d at 1407 (the fourth prong of the Rule 404(b) analysis covers Rule 403). As a reviewing court, we cannot re-assess "the relative impact of the legitimate and illegitimate inferences supported by evidence . . . [therefore we defer to the] contemporaneous assessment of the presentation, credibility, and impact of the challenged evidence. We therefore accord great deference to the district judge's decision to admit or exclude evidence under Rule 403." United States v. York, 933 F.2d 1343, 1352 (7th Cir.), *cert. denied,* — U.S. —, 112 S.Ct. 321, 116 L.Ed.2d 262 (1991). "This type of evidence is always prejudicial to the defendant, but when . . . it is balanced against its legitimate uses, and limited to the court's instructions, the prejudice is outweighed by its probative value." United States v. Powers, 978 F.2d 354, 361 (7th Cir. 1992) (discussing 404(b) evidence), *cert. denied,* — U.S. —, 113 S.Ct. 1323, 122 L.Ed.2d 708 (1993). The probative value of this evidence is high, centered as it is on Vincent Nwafor's prior illegal drug activities. The government submits that it did not put on a mini-trial on the matter and that the testimony only involved some fifteen pages (exclusive of defense objections) of a very long transcript. The district court was the best judge of whether the time expenditure put undue emphasis on the prior act. The actual production of the baggie containing the heroin may not have been necessary.

However, the district court took great care to give repeated warnings to the jury to consider the testimony only insofar as it bears on Vincent Nwafor's predisposition to deal in drugs. *See* Tr. at 1029, 1041, 1049. These instructions served to compensate for any potential prejudice. *See* United States v. Maholias, 985 F.2d 869, 880 (7th Cir. 1993); United States v. Koen, 982 F.2d 1101, 1117 (7th Cir. 1992). Indeed, immediately after the heroin was presented, the court hastened to instruct the jury once again about the testimony's limited usefulness. Tr. at 1041. Consequently, there was no error in the admission of 404(b) evidence to show Vincent Nwafor's predisposition for involvement in illicit drug transactions.

* * *

2. Admission of magazine article for impeachment. The government sought introduction of a photocopy of a page from a magazine article dealing with the drug connection between America and Nigeria and mentioning Vincent Nwafor, among others, as one who has been named by a Chicago Grand Jury for his involvement. The article was found with other drug-related items in Vincent Nwafor's locker. Initially, the district court denied admission because of its concern that the probative value of the article was "substantially outweighed by the danger of unfair prejudice." Fed.R.Evid. 403. In light of Vincent Nwafor's denial of his intent and predisposition to distribute heroin, as well as his ownership of the heroin and scales found in the locker, the judge, sua sponte, reconsidered his earlier ruling and permitted the government to use the article for impeachment purposes only. *See* United States v. Taylor, 728 F.2d 864, 870 (7th Cir. 1984) (permitting evidence of other weapons at the defendant's residence after defendant had denied knowledge of presence of a machine gun). It is clear that reserving judgment gave the trial court an opportunity to consider the risks and to weigh them against the probative value in light of the witness's denial. Defense counsel objected to the reference in the article to a previous arrest of Vincent Nwafor, but the court correctly overruled the objection because the arrest had resulted in a conviction that was properly before the court in the form of 404(b) evidence. Tr. at 15 1223–24. In addition, further safeguards were implemented when the article was neither published to the jury nor admitted into evidence. The cross-examination was limited to questions about Vincent Nwafor's familiarity with the article and about where he kept the clipping. Tr. at 1261–64. The admission of this material, even on such a limited basis, was obviously a close call. However, the district court recognized it as such and weighed its decision. Under these circumstances, we cannot say, given the deferential standard, that reversible error was committed.[4]

* * *

Conclusion

For the foregoing reasons, we affirm the district court's judgment in all respects.

Affirmed.

[1] At the time of trial defendant Ebenezer Dikeocha was a fugitive and does not join in this appeal.

[2] Federal Rule of Evidence 404(b) provides in pertinent part:

Evidence of other crimes, wrongs, or acts is not admissible to prove the character of a person in order to show action in conformity therewith. It may, however, be admissible for other purposes, such as proof of motive, opportunity, intent, preparation, plan, knowledge, identity, or absence of mistake or accident. . . .

[3] The Supreme Court in Huddleston v. United States, 485 U.S. 681, 689, 108 S.Ct. 1496, 1501. 99 L.Ed.2d 771 (1988), clarified this prong: originally the Seventh Circuit standard was "clear and convincing evidence."

[4] Vincent Nwafor argues in the reply brief that the article was improperly sent back with the jury. But Vincent Nwafor's attorney was unable to convince this court, either in the brief or at oral argument, that there is any basis in fact and on the record for this rather rash assertion.

✔ PRACTICE QUESTIONS

Select the most correct answer to complete each statement.

1. The most acceptable definition of the concept known as hearsay would be
   (a) a statement made in the course of the trial or hearing.
   (b) a statement made out of court that is later subject to cross-examination.
   (c) a statement, other than one made by the declarant while testifying at a trial or hearing, offered in evidence to prove the truth of the matter asserted.
   (d) a statement made by a highly credible individual that is not made in the course of the trial or hearing and is not subject to cross-examination.

2. The Federal Rules of Evidence include the following definition of "unavailability as a witness":
   (a) the declarant persists in refusing to testify concerning the subject matter of his or her statement despite an order of the court to do so.
   (b) the declarant claims to be seriously ill, but no proof has been provided to the court.
   (c) the declarant has agreed with the proponent of the statement not to appear in court.
   (d) the declarant claims that his presence in court is impossible due to personal commitments.

3. Exceptions to the hearsay exclusionary rule are based on
   (a) the necessity for introducing the evidence.
   (b) the great probability of reliability.
   (c) the whim of the presiding judge.
   (d) a and b.

Indicate whether each statement is true or false.

4. Physician affidavits are not hearsay because a physician enjoys great prestige in our society and the courts will not question what a doctor swears to.

5. "W," a witness, is asked whether he has ever heard anything in the community with respect to defendant's reputation for honesty. Defendant is being tried for grand larceny. "W" testifies that he has. He is then asked where he heard it and from whom he heard it. The witness begins to answer that he heard about it from many persons in the community. The prosecutor objects to any conversations with third persons in that they are hearsay and inadmissible. The court should sustain the prosecutor's objection.

6. In a trial for murder where the defendant raises an affirmative defense of justification (self-defense), evidence of the deceased's reputation for being a violent and dangerous person is relevant and is admissible.

7. A character witness may be asked on cross-examination whether he or she had ever heard that the defendant had a reputation in the past that he or she would "steal a red-hot stove" (assuming that the instant charge is shoplifting).

CHAPTER 7

Admission Exception to Hearsay Exclusionary Rule

§ 7.1 INTRODUCTION

An admission is a statement made or an act done by a party or his or her agent within the scope of the party's or agent's authority, said statement or act being inconsistent with the party's or agent's current position at trial. For example, if a defendant, after being given proper warnings by a law enforcement officer, said that he or she was with a deceased on the night of the homicide, and if at the trial the defendant testified that he or she was not with the deceased on the night of the homicide, the prior statement to the law enforcement officer is an admission. As you can observe, the prior statement to the law enforcement officer was inconsistent with the defendant's position at trial.

This is distinguished from a confession in that a confession is a direct acknowledgment of guilt, that is, the defendant says, "Yes, I killed John Doe, and I am guilty of murder." Mo.—State v. Thompson, 396 S.W.2d 697 (Mo. 1965).

An admission is an exception to the hearsay exclusionary rule because it is a statement made or an act done by a party who is not currently on the witness stand and may, in fact, never take the witness stand; it is offered for the truth of the assertion. Naturally, if the party does not take the stand, the party making the admission may not be subject to cross-examination, except that the person testifying to the admission is subject to cross-examination. It is admissible, but the weight to be given to the admission is not as great as testimony coming from the mouth of a witness. All admissions must be scanned with care, and verbal admissions should be received with great caution. Ga.—Howard v. Hall, 112 Ga.App. 247, 145 S.E.2d 70 (1965).

Admissions are admissible as an exception to the hearsay exclusionary rule because of the great probability of reliability. An admission is evidence which tends to prove the truth of the matter admitted, which the jury or court may believe as against other evidence, and in no sense are admissions to be considered conclusive. Cal.—Frankenheimer v. Frankenheimer, 231 Cal.App.2d 101, 41 Cal.Rptr. 636 (1964). Admissions are words or acts of a party opponent offered as evidence against her. Ill.—McNealey v. Illinois Cent. R.R. Co., 43 Ill.App.2d 460, 193 N.E.2d 879 (1963). Thus, the court has held that acts, too, may be held to be admissions.

Let us assume that a police officer is on routine patrol when he suddenly hears a bell from a fire alarm box ringing. He looks toward the source of the ringing and sees a youth, the only person in the vicinity, running away from the fire alarm box.

When the youth is apprehended, he states that he was running to catch a train. Is the act of running away from the fire alarm box at the time the bell began to ring an admission? Yes, because courts have held that acts as well as words may constitute admissions (McNealey v. Illinois, *supra*), but evidence of flight or concealment is relevant and admissible only if there are facts pointing to the crime charged as the motive which prompted it. N.Y.—People v. Reddy, 261 N.Y. 479, 185 N.E. 705 (1933). Showing consciousness of guilt may be used to strengthen "other and more tangible evidence" of guilt; it is not alone sufficient to sustain a conviction. N.Y.—People v. Troche, 14 A.D.2d 361, 221 N.Y.S.2d 228 (1961).

§ 7.2 TYPES OF ADMISSIONS

There are two general types of admissions: one is a judicial admission, and the other is an extrajudicial admission. A judicial admission is made directly in connection with a judicial proceeding. It need not be in the transcript of a trial, but it may be made in the pleadings. There is some authority for the position that pretrial statements, whether in the form of statements given to police or answers to interrogatories, do not assume the status of judicial admissions, but constitute evidentiary admissions, and a party is not precluded from presenting evidence which is at variance with pretrial statements, but he does run the risk of being impeached by so doing. Cal.—Weiss v. Baba, 218 Cal.App.2d 45, 32 Cal.Rptr. 137 (1963). All admissions not on the court record or connected with the court procedure are designated as extrajudicial admissions.

§ 7.3 Formal Judicial Admissions

A formal judicial admission is a formal act done in the course of the prosecution of a judicial proceeding that obviates the necessity of producing certain evidence by conceding for the purpose of the litigation that a fact alleged by the adverse party is true. Police officers frequently experience this when they are participants in a case involving unauthorized use of a motor vehicle. The officer may hear the prosecutor ask defense counsel to stipulate, for the purpose of the hearing, or even for the trial, that the defendant did not have authority from the true owner of the vehicle to use the vehicle. The defense attorney will usually stipulate to this and hence makes a formal judicial admission on behalf of his or her client. The fact that the true owner did not give the defendant permission to use the car therefore need not be proved. The defendant may have affirmative defenses, such as the fact that he or she purchased the vehicle from someone he or she thought was the true owner or that he or she was riding as a passenger with a person he or she thought was the true owner. Formal judicial admissions are conclusive of the facts admitted in the action in which they are made. N.Y.—Coffin v. President, etc., Grand Rapids Hydraulic Co., 136 N.Y. 655, 32 N.E. 1076 (1893).

§ 7.4 Informal Judicial Admissions

An informal admission includes facts incidentally admitted in the course of a trial or judicial proceeding, for example, statements made by a party who is testifying as a witness and statements made in an affidavit[1] by a party, or statements made in a

---

[1] Iowa—Davenport v. Cummings, 15 Iowa 219 (1863); N.Y.—Morrell v. Cawley, 17 Abb.Pr. 76 (N.Y. 1863).

deposition[2] by a party that may be received in evidence as admissions in the same or any subsequent litigation.

A formal judicial admission in one action may become an admission in another action and should be classified as an informal judicial admission.[3]

A police officer may give out a traffic summons to a participant in an auto accident. The fine is usually minimal, and the person summoned may plead guilty to the traffic infraction just to get rid of the problem. Later, this person may be sued civilly for money damages by another participant in the accident. The fact that the person had pled guilty to the traffic infraction is admissible in the civil trial. In the first trial, it is an admission or, more correctly stated, a confession. In the second trial, it is called an informal judicial admission and may be used against the person. Evidence of a plea of guilty is not admissible where the issues in the criminal and civil actions are not the same. Cal.—Skelton v. Fekete, 120 Cal.App.2d 401, 261 P.2d 339 (1953).

An informal judicial admission is not conclusive; it is merely evidence of the facts admitted. Thus, in the situation of the driver who pleaded guilty to the traffic infraction, the fact that he or she pleaded guilty is admissible in the subsequent civil action merely because he or she went into traffic court and pleaded guilty. It is not conclusive of the fact that he or she was guilty. N.Y.—Ando v. Woodberry, 8 N.Y.2d 165, 203 N.Y.S.2d 74,168 N.E.2d 520 (1960).

§ 7.5 Extrajudicial Admissions

All admissions not made in the course of a judicial proceeding are extrajudicial admissions. Therefore, any oral or written statement or conduct of a party or his or her agent that is contrary to his or her position at trial and is not made in the course of a judicial proceeding is an extrajudicial admission. Iowa—Anderson v. Halverson, 126 Iowa 125, 101 N.W. 781 (1904). Oral admissions of a party are competent evidence against him or her. Cal.—California Home Extension Ass'n v. Hilborn, 37 Cal.2d 459, 235 P.2d 369 (1951); Del.—Conner v. Brown, 9 Harr. 529, 3 A.2d 64 (Del. 1938). In order to be admissible, however, an admission must be voluntary. Pa.—Logue v. Gallagher, 133 Pa.Super. 570, 3 A.2d 191 (1938). An admission may be contained in a writing made by a party or his or her authorized agent or adopted by him or her. N.Y.—Prout v. Chisolm, 21 A.D. 54, 47 N.Y.S. 376 (1897).

§ 7.6 ADMISSION BY CONDUCT

A defendant's flight from the scene of an accident is tantamount to an admission of responsibility. Conn.—Kotler v. Lalley, 112 Conn. 86, 151 A. 433 (1930). This, of course, could also be applied to flight from the scene of a crime. The principle of admission by conduct simply means that any act or conduct on the part of a party that may fairly be interpreted as an admission against interest on a material issue may be shown in evidence against him or her. N.Y.—People v. Mendel, 10 A.D.2d 767, 197 N.Y.S.2d 484 (1960), *appeal denied,* 11 A.D.2d 605, 204 N.Y.S.2d 110, *reargument and appeal denied,* 11 A.D.2d 962, 207 N.Y.S.2d 250 (1960).

---

[2] Cal.—Mayhood v. La Rosa, 58 Cal.2d 498, 374 P.2d 805, 24 Cal.Rptr. 837 (1962); N.H.—Cote v. Sears, Roebuck & Co., 86 N.H. 238, 166 A. 279 (1933).

[3] N.Y.—Ando v. Woodberry, 8 N.Y.2d 165, 168 N.E.2d 520, 203 N.Y.S.2d 74 (1960).

§ 7.7 ATTEMPTS TO SUBORN PERJURY OR SUPPRESS EVIDENCE

A person who willfully procures or induces another to commit perjury is guilty of subornation of perjury. Evidence of attempts to suborn perjury is evidence that the cause of the party by whom such attempt was made or to whom it is attributable is unjust. Mo.—Pennington v. Kansas City Rys. Co., 201 Mo.App. 483, 213 S.W. 137 (1919); Pa.—McHugh v. McHugh, 186 Pa. 197, 40 A. 410, 65 Am.St.Rep. 849, 41 L.R.A. 805 (1898). The suppression[4] or destruction[5] of documents is in the nature of an admission that they are unfavorable to the party having control of them.

§ 7.8 ADMISSION BY SILENCE

A party who is under arrest need not deny an accusation made against him and the fact that he failed to deny the accusation is not admissible as an admission. N.Y.— People v. Rutigliano, 261 N.Y. 103, 184 N.E. 689 (1933). However, silence when one would naturally be expected to speak in nonarrest situations is significant as an express admission, but the party must have had knowledge and an opportunity to reply. Ga.—Swaim v. Barton, 210 Ga. 24, 77 S.E.2d 507 (1953). When no opportunity is available to reply to a statement, silence is not evidence of an admission of the truth of the statement. N.J.—Ollert v. Ziebell, 96 N.J.L. 210, 114 A. 356 (1921); N.Y.—People v. Pollock, 226 A.D. 406, 235 N.Y.S. 553 (1929). Whether the situation is one in which the jury may reasonably find a party's conduct relevant to a fact in issue is a preliminary question for the court's discretion. 31A C.J.S. Evidence § 296.

§ 7.9 ADMISSION BY AGENTS OR SERVANTS

An agent is a person who represents a principal and who is possessed of discretionary powers within the scope of the agency, whereas a servant represents a master, having no discretionary authority but merely performing ministerial services. With this definition in mind, one can easily see that an admission within the scope of an agent's authority might tend to bind the principal; likewise, the admission of a servant within the scope of his or her services would bind the master. You will remember that an admission may be created by an act as well as by the spoken word.

To establish the responsibility to the principal, the fact of the agency must first be introduced into evidence. To accomplish this, it must be sufficiently proved, directly or inferentially, by evidence other than the statements of the declarant that he was the agent of the party to be charged with the admission and that he was acting within the scope of his authority. Idaho—Callahan v. Wolfe, 88 Idaho 444, 400 P.2d 938 (1965); La.—Bobo v. Sears, Roebuck & Co., 308 So.2d 907 (La.App. 1975); Pa.—Geesey v. Albee Pa. Homes, Inc., 211 Pa.Super. 215, 235 A.2d 175 (1967). However, the court, in its discretion, may permit the admission to be introduced before the proof of the agency. Mo.—Fielder v. Prod. Credit Ass'n, 429 S.W.2d 307 (Mo.App. 1968). The agency need not be conclusive, but it must justify a finding that the relation existed. Fla.—Lan-Chile Airlines, Inc. v. Rodriguez, 296 So.2d 498 (Fla.App. 1974); La.—Bobo v. Sears, Roebuck & Co., *supra*.

---

[4] Cal.—Ross v. San Francisco-Oakland Term. Rys. Co., 47 Cal.App. 753, 191 P. 703 (1920).

[5] Ala.—Powell v. Smith, 209 Ala. 254, 96 So. 135 (1923).

The rules with respect to servants are similar to those of agents, except that one must keep in mind that a servant never has any discretionary authority to bind his or her master, but may make admissions through acts or statements, oral or written, nevertheless. For example, a servant may make admissions binding his master by the preparation of an accident report. Ky.—City of Louisville v. Padgett, 457 S.W.2d 485 (Ky. 1970).

§ 7.10 ADMISSION BY STATEMENT AGAINST INTEREST

An agent in some cases, as well as a principal, may make a statement that will be against the principal's interest. This refers to a statement that at the time of its making is so far contrary to the declarant's pecuniary or proprietary interest, or so far tends to subject the declarant to civil or criminal liability or to render invalid a claim by the declarant against another person or entity, that a reasonable person in the declarant's position would not have made the statement unless he or she believed it to be true. A statement tending to expose the declarant to criminal liability and offered to exculpate the accused is not admissible unless corroborating circumstances clearly indicate the trustworthiness of the statement. Federal Rule of Evidence 804(b)(3). Such a statement is admissible if the declarant is not available as a witness. See also United States v. Costa, 31 F.3d 1073 (11th Cir. 1994). Let us hypothecate that previous to his death a person made a statement that the real estate that is registered in his name is really not his property, but that he is holding it in his name for his brother, who is the true owner of the real estate. The reason he gave to a listener was that his brother does not want his wife to know that he owns the real estate. If there is litigation in which the surviving brother, or the heirs of his brother, wants to reclaim the real estate, someone who heard the decedent brother make the statement, and who has no financial or other interest in the real estate, may testify as to what the deceased brother had told him.

§ 7.11 UNANSWERED WRITTEN COMMUNICATIONS— NOT AN ADMISSION

There is no rule of law that forces the recipient of a written communication to reply to this communication. A failure to answer adverse assertions in the absence of further circumstances making an answer requisite or natural has no effect as an admission. U.S.—A.B. Leach & Co. v. Peirson, 275 U.S. 120, 48 S.Ct. 57, 72 L.Ed. 194 (1927).

§ 7.12 ADMISSION AS TO INTOXICATION

A police officer on patrol may frequently be required to arrest and testify against a person who is driving a motor vehicle while under the influence of an intoxicant or narcotic. If the arrested person, without being questioned by the officer, makes a statement such as "I guess I had one too many," this statement may be testified to in court by the officer. Particular attention is drawn to the fact that the officer did not question the defendant before the admission of intoxication and/or narcotic involvement was made. If the officer had questioned the defendant without giving Miranda warnings, there is a possibility that this evidence would not be admissible at trial, particularly if the officer was going to arrest the defendant based on the officer's or another's observation of intoxication or narcotic influence. See Felker v. Bartelme, 124 Ill.App.2d 43, 260 N.E.2d 74 (1970); Hallett v. Rimer, 329 Mass. 61, 106 N.E.2d 427 (1952).

§ 7.13 OFFERS OF COMPROMISE—NOT AN ADMISSION

A compromise has often been described by lawyers as a situation in which no one is completely happy with the result, yet no one loses the case and no one wins the case, and everyone goes away from the bargaining table thinking that maybe they could have done better by trying the case to a conclusion. The law, however, encourages compromise of litigation because it speeds the wheels of justice, and most often there is a little bit of right and a little bit of wrong attached to both sides of the controversy. In order to facilitate compromises, any efforts to compromise the litigation are never admissible as evidence against any of the parties. If the contrary situation was permitted, no litigant would make an offer of compromise for fear of having this fact used against him or her as an admission. In some situations, however, parts of an offer to compromise may be considered an admission. Such a situation might occur when an admission of fact is made in the course of a negotiating session. This applies more to civil law compromises and is not relevant to the purpose of this book; it is mentioned only in passing, for example, where a defendant's liability is so clear that he or she makes an offer to liquidate damages without even discussing liability, thus tacitly admitting it. N.Y.—Brice v. Bauer, 108 N.Y. 428, 15 N.E. 695 (1888). The fact that a party admits that he made an offer of compromise does not render such offer admissible in evidence. N.C.—Stein v. Levins, 205 N.C. 302, 171 S.E. 96 (1933).

§ 7.14 WEIGHT OF ADMISSIONS

Evidence may be considered as admissible and may be entered on the trial record, but different types of evidence may have different weight with respect to the outcome of the litigation. It has been stated that oral admissions are evidence of the weakest and least satisfactory character. Mich.—Tincknell v. Ward, 285 Mich. 47, 280 N.W. 104 (1938); Mo.—Scherffius v. Orr, 442 S.W.2d 120 (Mo.App. 1969); N.Y.—Wheeler v. Lewis, 203 A.D. 222, 196 N.Y.S. 817 (1922). Verbal admissions should be received with caution and be subjected to careful scrutiny, as no class of evidence is more subject to error or abuse. Witnesses having the best motives are generally unable to state the exact language of an admission and are liable, by omission or change of words, to convey a false impression of the language used. Furthermore, no other class of testimony affords such temptations or opportunities for unscrupulous witnesses to distort the facts, or to commit open perjury, as it is often impossible to contradict their testimony at all, or at least by any other witness than the party himself. Mont.—Sylvain v. Page, 84 Mont. 424, 276 P. 16, 63 A.L.R. 528 (1929).

Admissions are to be considered like all other evidence, with the ultimate determination as to value, effect, or weight thereof being for the trier of the facts. Cal.—Kohlhauer v. Bronstein, 21 Cal.App.2d 4, 67 P.2d 1078 (1937); Conn.—Russo v. Metropolitan Life Ins. Co., 125 Conn. 132, 3 A.2d 844 (1939).

§ 7.15 SUBSEQUENT REMEDIAL MEASURES

In order to remedy a potentially hazardous condition after someone has been injured or killed, subsequent remedial measures may need to be taken. If these measures could be introduced into evidence as an admission against the person implementing these remedial measures in a trial for negligence wherein the defendant is being sued for money damages for injury and death, the likelihood is that the repair would not be made and that perhaps others would be injured or killed because of the same defect. Accordingly, public policy dictates that evidence of subsequent remedial repairs is not admissible to prove negligence or culpable conduct in connection with the event involving the instant action. However, if there is a question as to who owned or controlled the item that caused the injury or death and the defendant made the subsequent remedial measures, then the measures are admissible in evidence. Powers v. J.B. Michael & Co., 329 F.2d 674 (6th Cir. 1964).

Furthermore, if there is a question as to whether it is feasible to take remedial measures that would have avoided the injury or death and the defendant argues that remedial measures are impossible, then the fact that the subsequent remedial measures were implemented is admissible in evidence. Another instance in which subsequent remedial measures are admissible might occur when the defendant might introduce evidence that no remedial measures could be taken. In such a case, the subsequent remedial measures may be introduced as an impeachment device. See Federal Rule of Evidence 407 for a codification of this concept.

§ 7.16 FEDERAL RULE—ADMISSIONS

Federal Rule of Evidence 803 prescribes twenty-four exceptions to the hearsay exclusionary rule. Although the word "admission" is not specifically referred to, it is included in exceptions numbered 1 through 24, inclusive, where the statement or record is inconsistent with the party's or agent's current position at trial.

> **Rule 803. Hearsay Exceptions; Availability of Declarant Immaterial**
>
> The following are not excluded by the hearsay rule, even though the declarant is available as a witness:
>
> (1) **Present Sense Impression.** A statement describing or explaining an event or condition made while the declarant was perceiving the event or condition, or immediately thereafter.
>
> (2) **Excited Utterance.** A statement relating to a startling event or condition made while the declarant was under the stress of excitement caused by the event or condition.
>
> (3) **Then Existing Mental, Emotional, or Physical Condition.** A statement of the declarant's then existing state of mind, emotion, sensation, or physical condition (such as intent, plan, motive, design, mental feeling, pain, and bodily health), but not including a statement of memory or belief to prove the fact remembered or believed unless it relates to the execution, revocation, identification, or terms of declarant's will.
>
> (4) **Statements for Purposes of Medical Diagnosis or Treatment.** Statements made for purposes of medical diagnosis or treatment and describing medical history, or past or present symptoms, pain, or sensations, or the inception or general character of the cause or external source thereof insofar as reasonably pertinent to diagnosis or treatment.
>
> (5) **Recorded Recollection.** A memorandum or record concerning a matter about which a witness once had knowledge but now has insufficient recollection to enable the witness to testify fully and accurately, shown to have been made or adopted by the witness when the matter was fresh in the witness' memory and to reflect that knowledge correctly. If admitted, the memorandum or record may be read into evidence but may not itself be received as an exhibit unless offered by an adverse party.
>
> (6) **Records of Regularly Conducted Activity.** A memorandum, report, record, or data compilation, in any form, of acts, events, conditions, opinions, or diagnoses, made at or near the time by, or from information transmitted by, a person with knowledge, if kept in the course of a regularly conducted business activity,

and if it was the regular practice of that business activity to make the memorandum, report, record, or data compilation, all as shown by the testimony of the custodian or other qualified witness, unless the source of information or the method or circumstances of preparation indicate lack of trustworthiness. The term "business" as used in this paragraph includes business, institution, association, profession, occupation, and calling of every kind, whether or not conducted for profit.

(7) Absence of Entry in Records Kept in Accordance with the Provisions of Paragraph (6). Evidence that a matter is not included in the memoranda reports, records, or data compilations, in any form, kept in accordance with the provisions of paragraph (6), to prove the nonoccurrence or nonexistence of the matter, if the matter was of a kind of which a memorandum, report, record, or data compilation was regularly made and preserved, unless the sources of information or other circumstances indicate lack of trustworthiness.

(8) Public Records and Reports. Records, reports, statements, or data compilations, in any form, of public offices or agencies, setting forth (A) the activities of the office or agency, or (B) matters observed pursuant to duty imposed by law as to which matters there was a duty to report, excluding, however, in criminal cases matters observed by police officers and other law enforcement personnel, or (C) in civil actions and proceedings and against the Government in criminal cases, factual findings resulting from an investigation made pursuant to authority granted by law, unless the sources of information or other circumstances indicate lack of trustworthiness.

(9) Records of Vital Statistics. Records or data compilations, in any form, of births, fetal deaths, deaths, or marriages, if the report thereof was made to a public office pursuant to requirements of law.

(10) Absence of Public Record or Entry. To prove the absence of a record, report, statement, or data compilation, in any form, or the nonoccurrence or nonexistence of a matter of which a record, report, statement, or data compilation, in any form, was regularly made and preserved by a public office or agency, evidence in the form of a certification in accordance with rule 902, or testimony, that diligent search failed to disclose the record, report, statement, or data compilation, or entry.

(11) Records of Religious Organizations. Statements of births, marriages, divorces, deaths, legitimacy, ancestry, relationship by blood or marriage, or other similar facts of personal or family history, contained in a regularly kept record of a religious organization.

(12) Marriage, Baptismal, and Similar Certificates. Statements of fact contained in a certificate that the maker performed a marriage or other ceremony or administered a sacrament, made by a clergyman, public official, or other person authorized by the rules or practices of a religious organization or by law to perform the act certified, and purporting to have been issued at the time of the act or within a reasonable time thereafter.

(13) Family Records. Statements of fact concerning personal or family history contained in family Bibles, genealogies, charts, engravings on rings, inscriptions on family portraits, engravings on urns, crypts, or tombstones, or the like.

(14) Records of Documents Affecting an Interest in Property. The record of a document purporting to establish or affect an interest in property, as proof of the content of the original recorded document and its execution and delivery by each person by whom it purports to have been executed, if the record is a record of a public office and an applicable statute authorizes the recording of documents of that kind in that office.

(15) Statements in Documents Affecting an Interest in Property. A statement contained in a document purporting to establish or affect an interest in property if the matter stated was relevant to the purpose of the document, unless dealings with the property since the document was made have been inconsistent with the truth of the statement or the purport of the document.

(16) **Statements in Ancient Documents.** Statements in a document in existence twenty years or more the authenticity of which is established.

(17) **Market Reports, Commercial Publications.** Market quotations, tabulations, lists, directories, or other published compilations, generally used and relied upon by the public or by persons in particular occupations.

(18) **Learned Treatises.** To the extent called to the attention of an expert witness upon cross-examination or relied upon by the expert witness in direct examination, statements contained in published treatises, periodicals, or pamphlets on a subject of history, medicine, or other science or art, established as a reliable authority by the testimony or admission of the witness or by other expert testimony or by judicial notice. If admitted, the statements may be read into evidence but may not be received as exhibits.

(19) **Reputation Concerning Personal or Family History.** Reputation among members of a person's family by blood, adoption, or marriage, or among a person's associates, or in the community, concerning a person's birth, adoption, marriage, divorce, death, legitimacy, relationship by blood, adoption, or marriage, ancestry, or other similar fact of personal or family history.

(20) **Reputation Concerning Boundaries or General History.** Reputation in a community, arising before the controversy, as to boundaries of or customs affecting lands in the community, and reputation as to events of general history important to the community or State or nation in which located.

(21) **Reputation as to Character.** Reputation of a person's character among associates or in the community.

(22) **Judgment of Previous Conviction.** Evidence of a final judgment, entered after a trial or upon a plea of guilty (but not upon a plea of nolo contendere), adjudging a person guilty of a crime punishable by death or imprisonment in excess of one year, to prove any fact essential to sustain the judgment, but not including, when offered by the Government in a criminal prosecution for purposes other than impeachment, judgments against persons other than the accused. The pendency of an appeal may be shown but does not affect admissibility.

(23) **Judgment as to Personal, Family, or General History, or Boundaries.** Judgments as proof of matters of personal, family or general history, or boundaries, essential to the judgment, if the same would be provable by evidence of reputation.

(24) **Other Exceptions.** A statement not specifically covered by any of the foregoing exceptions but having equivalent circumstantial guarantees of trustworthiness, if the court determines that (A) the statement is offered as evidence of a material fact; (B) the statement is more probative on the point for which it is offered than any other evidence which the proponent can procure through reasonable efforts; and (C) the general purposes of these rules and the interests of justice will best be served by admission of the statement into evidence. However, a statement may not be admitted under this exception unless the proponent of it makes known to the adverse party sufficiently in advance of the trial or hearing to provide the adverse party with a fair opportunity to prepare to meet it, the proponent's intention to offer the statement and the particulars of it, including the name and address of the declarant.

CROSS-REFERENCES

Federal Civil Judicial Procedure and Rules (West 1996) (Rule 803).
Goode & Wellborn, Courtroom Handbook on Federal Evidence (West 1995) (Rule 803).
McCormick, Evidence (4th ed. 1992) (Rule 803).

Mayhood v. La Rosa

Supreme Court of California, 1962.
58 Cal.2d 498, 374 P.2d 805, 24 Cal.Rptr. 837.

This case involves an action to quiet title. This means that it relates to the ownership of land where the title to the property may have some impediment attached to it that may limit the ability of the alleged landowner to convey (sell) the land to another person. The other person ordinarily would not want to buy this land with the impediment on it because the buyer might have a problem when he or she wants to sell it to a new prospective buyer. A devisee is a person who is a designated beneficiary named in a last will and testament of a deceased person where the will is probated in a court. In some states, it only refers to a person named to receive real property.

One of the issues that arose in the trial of this action to quiet title was whether a party's admission contained in a deposition should have been admitted into evidence. By reading this case, you will discover the way the Supreme Court of California answered that question.

Action by husband to quiet title to land against devisee of wife and personal representative of wife's estate. The Superior Court, Solano Country, Harlow V. Greenwood, J., rendered judgment for husband and defendants appealed.

* * *

TRAYNOR, Justice. Plaintiff brought this action to quiet title to 47 acres of land against Nanette La Rosa, the granddaughter and sole devisee of Hattie Mayhood, and against the personal representative of Mrs. Mayhood's estate. Plaintiff acquired the land before his marriage to Mrs. Mayhood in 1915. Mrs. Mayhood died in 1959. During the 44 years of the marriage, the land was used to grow fruit trees and grape vines. Until he became incapacitated by illness in 1957, plaintiff devoted most of his working time and energy to managing and cultivating the orchard and vineyard. All receipts therefrom were placed in a single bank account, and all expenditures were made from this account. One such expenditure, in the amount of $12,000, was for a residence constructed on the land in 1928. Defendants offered but were not allowed to introduce evidence that another expenditure of $14,300 was made in 1939 to replant the land with trees and grape vines. The trial court, sitting without a jury, entered judgment quieting plaintiff's title and denying the relief sought in defendants' cross-complaint. Defendants appeal.

Defendants contend that the land was community property to the extent that plaintiff's efforts increased its value and funds used to improve it are attributable to his efforts and that half of such community property therefore passed to Mrs. La Rosa under the will. The trial court rejected this contention on the authority of Estate of Pepper, 158 Cal. 619, 623–624, 112 Pac. 62, 31 L.R.A., N.S., 1092 (1911).

In Estate of Neilson, 57 Cal.2d 733, 22 Cal.Rptr. 1, 371 P.2d 745 (1962), we overruled the Pepper case and held that the part of the profits of a separate property enterprise attributable to the husband's efforts are community property, whether the enterprise be classified as "commercial" or "agricultural." The funds in plaintiff's bank account were derived primarily from profits of the enterprise. These funds, which were used to pay for the improvements in 1928 and 1939, must therefore be apportioned between plaintiff's separate property and the community property. Any increase in the value of the land attributable to plaintiff's efforts was also community property. Estate of Neilson, supra, 57 Cal.2d 733 at pp. 737, 738, 22 Cal.Rptr. 1, 371 P.2d 745 (1962).

Defendants also contend that the trial court erred in ruling that they could not introduce into evidence plaintiff's deposition and certain answers he gave to interrogatories except to impeach his testimony. Code of Civil

Procedure Section 2030, subdivision (b), provides that answers to interrogatories "may be used to the same extent as provided in subdivision (d) of Section 2016 of this code for the use of the deposition of a party." Section 2016, subdivision (d), paragraph (2), provides that, "so far as admissible under the rules of evidence," any part or all of the deposition of a party "may be used by an adverse party for any purpose." Thus, insofar as plaintiff's deposition and answers to interrogatories contained admissions, they should have been admitted in evidence. (Dini v. Dini, 188 Cal.App.2d 506, 512, 10 Cal.Rptr. 570, 574 [1961]; Murray v. Manley, 170 Cal.App.2d 364, 367, 338 P.2d 976, 978 [1959].) As stated in the two cited cases, an adverse party's deposition "may be used to establish any material fact, a prima facie case, or even to prove the whole case." Consequently, a party is not limited to using an adverse party's deposition or answers to interrogatories for the purpose of impeaching his testimony.

The judgment is reversed.

GIBSON, C.J., and SCHAUER, McCOMB, PETERS, WHITE and TOBRINER, JJ., concur.

Ando v. Woodberry

Court of Appeals of New York, 1960.
8 N.Y.2d 165, 203 N.Y.S.2d 74, 168 N.E.2d 520.

This case concerns an automobile accident involving a police officer on a motorcycle and a hapless motorist who collided with each other. The motorist was given a summons for a traffic violation arising out of this incident, decided not to contest the summons, and pleaded guilty in the magistrate court.

Little did he know that by so doing he would expose himself to a possible admission of negligence in a subsequent civil action brought against the motorist by the police officer, where the officer was seeking money damages. This case arrived in the Court of Appeals of New York, which is the highest court in that state. At that time, the judge writing the decision called it a case of first impression as to whether a civil defendant's prior plea of guilty to a traffic offense may be introduced into evidence against him in a civil ac-

tion for damages arising out of the same incident. A case of first impression means that the issue had never before been decided in the New York State Court of Appeals. I suggest that you read the case and find out how the court handled this issue.

Action by motorcycle policeman for injuries sustained in collision of motorcycle and an automobile. The Supreme Court, Trial Term, Bronx County, James E. Mulcahy, J., 15 Misc.2d 774, 181 N.Y.S.2d 905, rendered judgment on verdict for defendant, and plaintiff appealed. The Supreme Court, Appellate Division, First Judicial Department, 9 A.D.2d 125, 192 N.Y.S.2d 414, entered a judgment December 4, 1959 as resettled by an order entered December 16, 1959, affirming the judgment by a divided court. Plaintiff appealed.

* * *

FULD, Judge. This appeal calls upon us to decide a question of first impression in this court: May a defendant's prior plea of guilt to a traffic offense be introduced as evidence of his carelessness in a civil action for damages?

The relevant facts are simple and undisputed. Robert Ando, a police officer, driving a motorcycle, and Edward Nichols, driving an automobile owned by Essie Woodberry, were both proceeding north on Fifth Avenue, New York City, on the afternoon of December 28, 1955. Car and motorcycle collided when Mr. Nichols attempted to make a left turn at 110th Street, and Officer Ando was injured as a result of the collision. Mr. Nichols was given a summons which charged him with failing to make a proper turn and failing to signal before turning, and he subsequently appeared in the Manhattan Traffic Division of Magistrates' Court and pleaded guilty to both charges.

Upon the negligence trial, held in the Supreme Court, the only witnesses to the occurrence of the accident were the plaintiff and the defendant Nichols, who drove the car. According to the plaintiff, Mr. Nichols, after first pulling over to the right, made a left turn without prior warning or signal and struck his motorcycle. Mr. Nichols not only denied that he had moved to the right, but asserted that he had given a signal upon making the turn. In order to strengthen his case, the plaintiff attempted to prove Mr. Nichols' plea of guilt in Traffic Court on the theory that it constituted an admission, but, upon the defendants' objection, the trial court excluded the proffered evidence. The jury returned a verdict in favor of the defendants and the Appellate Division, two Justices dissenting, affirmed the judgment subsequently rendered.

In deciding whether proof of a plea of guilty to a traffic violation should be received as evidence in chief in a subsequent civil action, it is well to recall the principle, basic to our law of evidence, that "All facts having rational probative value are admissible" unless there is sound reason to exclude them, unless, that is, "some specific rule forbids" (1 Wigmore, Evidence [3d ed., 1940], p. 293). It is this general principle which gives rationality, coherence and justification to our system of evidence and we may neglect it only at the risk of turning that system into a trackless morass of arbitrary and artificial rules.

In view of the fact that Mr. Nichols' plea of guilty to the charges leveled against him—failing to signal and making an improper turn—is relevant to the issue of his negligence in turning off Fifth Avenue, we must simply decide whether there is any justification for excluding it. Two possible grounds of exclusion suggest themselves; the first, that such testimony is hearsay and, the second, that its introduction violates public policy.

Since a prior plea of guilt represents an admission, it is not obnoxious to the hearsay rule. See 4 Wigmore, op. cit., §§ 1048, 1049, pp. 2–7. Accordingly, the courts of this State, as well as of other jurisdictions, have generally sanctioned the receipt in evidence in a negligence action of a prior plea of guilty to a traffic violation. See People v. Formato, 286 App.Div. 357, 363–364, 143 N.Y.S.2d 205, 211–212, 64 A.L.R.2d 812 (1955); Walther v. News Syndicate Co., 276 App.Div. 169, 176, 93 N.Y.S.2d 537, 544 (1950); Stanton v. Major, 274 App.Div. 864, 82 N.Y.S.2d 134 (1948); Same v. Davison, 253 App.Div. 123, 124, 1 N.Y.S.2d 374, 375 (1937); Barnum v. Morresey, 245 App.Div. 798, 280 N.Y.S. 899 (1935); Rednall v. Thompson, 108 Cal.App.2d 662, 666, 239 P.2d 693 (1952); Koch v. Elkins, 71 Idaho 50, 54, 225 P.2d 457 (1924); Dimmick v. Follis, 123 Ind.App. 701, 703, 111 N.E.2d 486 (1953); Race v. Chappell, 304 Ky. 788,

792, 202 S.W.2d 626 (1947); Morrissey v. Powell, 304 Mass. 268, 271, 23 N.E.2d 411, 124 A.L.R. 1522 (1939); Remmenga v. Selk, 150 Neb. 401, 415, 34 N.W.2d 757 (1949); Public Serv. Co. of New Hampshire v. Chancey, 94 N.H. 259, 261, 51 A.2d 845 (1947); Freas v. Sullivan, 130 Ohio St. 486, 491, 200 N.E. 639 (1936); Olk v. Marquardt, 203 Wis. 479, 485, 234 N.W. 723 (1931). Thus, when Mr. Nichols pleaded guilty to the traffic infractions charged against him, his plea of guilty amounted to a statement or admission by him that he did the act charged. As such, it should be treated like any other admission or confession, and subject to the same rules relating to its weight and effect.

The defendants insist, however, that there is a public policy which requires us to treat the admission implicit in pleading guilty to a traffic offense differently from others. It is the policy of this State, they urge, that a traffic infraction be distinguished from a crime and that it be recognized that a plea of guilt is entered in traffic court for numerous reasons unrelated to actual guilt. To support their contention, they point to subdivision 29 of Section 2 of the Vehicle and Traffic Law, Consol.Laws, c. 40, Hart v. Mealey, 287 N.Y. 39, 38 N.E.2d 121 (1942) and Walther v. News Syndicate Co., 276 App.Div. 169, 93 N.Y.S.2d 537 (1950), supra.

The portion of the Vehicle and Traffic Law relied upon provides that "a traffic infraction is not a crime, and the penalty or punishment imposed therefore . . . shall not affect or impair the credibility as a witness, or otherwise, of any person convicted thereof." (Vehicle and Traffic Law § 2, subd. 29; see, also, Civil Practice Act, § 355). Whatever else this provision may mean, it is clear that it is directed solely against the use of a conviction of a traffic infraction to "affect or impair . . . credibility as a witness" of the person convicted and not against the use of a plea as evidence in chief. The statute does no more than restate the rule of the common law that a prior conviction may be shown to attack the credibility of a witness only if it was a conviction of a *crime*. See People v. Joyce, 233 N.Y. 61, 71, 134 N.E. 836, 840 (1922); People v. Brown, 2 A.D.2d 202, 203, 153 N.Y.S.2d 744, 746 (1956); see also, Civ.Prac.Act, § 350.

Since a traffic infraction was declared not to be a crime, it was but natural for the Legislature to, in effect, codify the settled rule prohibiting the use of a conviction of such an offense to impeach the offender when called to testify as a witness. Had more than this been intended, had it been the legislative design to render evidence of a traffic infraction unavailable for *any* purpose in a subsequent civil action, it could easily have so provided. See, e.g., Minn.Stats.Ann. § 169.94, subd. 1; Colo.Rev.Stat., 13-4-140.[1] The Legislature of this State having written a clearly limited rule of exclusion, we may not apply it beyond its terms to exclude the use of a guilty plea as evidence in chief.

Nor may legislative policy be taken to justify its exclusion. Certain violations of the Vehicle and Traffic Law were denominated traffic infractions and distinguished from crimes in order to establish a new type of offense, one "with the stigma of criminality removed." Squadrito v. Griebsch, 1 N.Y.2d 471, 476, 154 N.Y.S.2d 37, 41 (1956). The legislation simply represented a recognition of the fact that most traffic violations do not involve the degree of moral turpitude associated with crime.

Our case law, likewise, offers no support for the defendants' position. It is quite true that in Hart v. Mealey, 287 N.Y. 39, 38 N.E.2d 121 (1942), supra, where the issue was whether there was sufficient evidence to justify a determination by the Commissioner of Motor Vehicles that a driver's license be revoked on account of reckless driving, this court remarked on the "weakness" of evidence of a conviction after trial—not of a plea guilt, as was inadvertently assumed by the Appellate Division—as proof of the facts involved. The Hart case, however, did not involve any issue of admissibility and, therefore, has no bearing on the issues before us. The case of Walther v. News Syndicate Co., 276 App.Div. 169, 93 N.Y.S.2d 537 (1950), supra, did not hold that a judgment of conviction of a traffic infraction after trial was inadmissible in a subsequent civil action, but it recognized that its decision represented a limited exception to the general rule announced by this court in Schindler v. Royal Ins. Co., 258 N.Y. 310, 179 N.E. 711, 80 A.L.R. 1142 (1932); see, also, Matter of Rechtschaffen's Estate, 278 N.Y. 336, 16

N.E.2d 357 (1938), and, even more significant, it expressly distinguished the case before it from those in which a plea of guilty is involved. "In such cases," wrote the court, "the record or proof of the defendant's guilty plea is received . . . as a declaration or admission against interest." Walther v. News Syndicate Co., 276 App.Div. 169, 176, 93 N.Y.S.2d 537, 544 (1950), supra. Consequently, even if we were to assume that the Appellate Division was correct in its conclusion in the Walther case—and we observe that we have never had occasion to consider the question there presented—the opinion supports, rather than detracts from, the conclusion that a guilty plea deliberately recorded by the defendant is admissible against him on the issue of his negligence in a subsequent civil action.

In addition to their reliance on policy and precedent, the defendants also offer an argument based on what they label "experience." They contend that one charged with a traffic violation pleads guilty, even though he believes himself innocent, in order to avoid the expenditure of time and money which would be involved if guilt were denied and the charge contested. Based on this assumption, they suggest that the plea of guilt must be looked upon as one of *nolo contendere*. The contention has no merit. In the first place, the plea of *nolo contendere* has long been abolished in this State (see People v. Daiboch, 265 N.Y. 125, 128, 191 N.E. 859, 860 (1934)) and may not be resurrected without legislative sanction. In the second place, while we are willing to assume that pleas to traffic charges are not infrequently prompted by considerations of expediency, we have no reliable means of judging how significant a portion of all guilty pleas to traffic charges are of this character. But, quite apart from this, there is no basis for the defendants' unverified generalization or "hunch" in cases where, as here, the alleged violation was attended with injury to the person or property of a third party and the plea carries with it serious consequences to the offender's future status as a motor vehicle operator (Vehicle and Traffic Law § 71).[2]

What the defendant Nichols is actually arguing is that, when he pleaded guilty, he "really didn't mean what he said." This claim, however, goes to the weight of evidence and entitles the defendant not to exclusion of the plea, but to an "opportunity to explain" it. Chamberlain v. Iba, 181 N.Y. 486, 490, 74 N.E. 481, 482 (1905); see, also, Wachtel v. Equitable Life Assur. Soc., 266 N.Y. 345, 351, 194 N.E. 850, 852 (1935); Gangi v. Fradus, 227 N.Y. 452, 125 N.E. 677 (1920); Hirsch v. New York Life Ins. Co., 267 App.Div. 404, 406, 45 N.Y.S.2d 892, 894 (1944); 4 Wigmore, op. cit., pp. 23–24. After the defendant has given his explanation, his reasons for pleading guilty, it is for the jurors to evaluate his testimony and decide whether the plea is entitled to any weight. As this court wrote some years ago with respect to extra-judicial admissions, it is for the jury, noting "the conditions and circumstances under which [such admissions] were made," to determine their "effect . . . and their probative weight and value, which may range from the lowest, or none at all, to conclusiveness." Gangi v. Fradus, 227 N.Y. 452, 457, 125 N.E. 677, 679 (1920), supra. The traditional treatment accorded to admissions by our courts takes account of the very claim here made, namely, that the defendant's guilty plea was not an admission that he committed the acts charged against him.

To claim that the jury will be unduly prejudiced by the introduction of a plea of guilt despite the opportunity to explain it away, we content ourselves with the statement that he underestimates the intelligence of jurors and overlooks their awareness of those very circumstances said to destroy the meaning and significance of the plea. If voluntarily and deliberately made, the plea was a statement of guilt, an admission by the defendant that he committed the acts charged, and it should be accorded no less force or effect than if made outside of court to a stranger.

The judgment of the Appellate Division should be reversed and a new trial granted, with costs to abide the event.

VAN VOORHIS, Judge (dissenting).

The law of evidence has its roots in experience, and in common experience men and women charged with minor traffic violations plead guilty to avoid inconvenience whether they are innocent or guilty. In the Federal courts it is possible for a defendant in a criminal action to plead *nolo contendere*, the ac-cepted meaning of which is that the defendant chooses not to contest and takes the consequences of conviction but without admitting the truth of the charge against him. Such a plea could not be received in evidence as a voluntary admission against interest under the reasoning of the opinion by Judge FULD in this case. The State procedure does not give opportunity to plead *nolo contendere* but that is exactly what persons accused of minor traffic violations generally mean to do and are understood to have done when they enter guilty pleas in such instances. They are subject to the punishment provided by law for the offenses to which they have pleaded guilty, but the criminal statutes do not impose the additional burden of having the conviction used in a civil action as a factual admission by the person charged that he or she did or omitted the act on which the traffic infraction depends. It is irrelevant that *nolo contendere* is not a form of plea that is used in the State courts, inasmuch as we are not confronted in this case with any of the consequences of conviction under the criminal law. We have before us merely the collateral effect of such a plea as bearing upon the civil rights of the party in an action for damages. It is contrary to ordinary experience to give that effect to this plea of guilty in the Magistrates' Court, as the Appellate Division has correctly held. When Mr. Nichols pleaded guilty in the Manhattan Traffic Division of Magistrates' Court to failure to make a proper turn or to signal, he rendered himself liable to whatever penalties were involved but in my view it cannot be said with justice or a sense of reality that he conceded whatever facts he was accused of by the arresting officer. I think that it was not intended that the first steps in the enforcement or defense of damage claims in automobile negligence accident cases should be taken in traffic courts or police courts, nor does it aid their most effective functioning if that is so (contrast Walther v. News Syndicate Co., 276 App.Div. 169, 93 N.Y.S.2d 537 [1905], with Schindler v. Royal Ins. Co., 258 N.Y. 310, 179 N.E. 711, 80 A.L.R. 1142 [1932]).

DESMOND, C.J., and DYE, FROESSEL, BURKE and FOSTER, JJ., concur with FULD, J.

VAN VOORHIS, J., dissents in an opinion. Judgment reversed, etc.

---

[1] The Minnesota statute declares that "No record of the conviction of any person for any violation of [the Highway Traffic Regulation Act] shall be admissible as evidence in any court in any civil action" (Minn.Stats.Ann. § 169.94, subd. 1).

[2] Under the so-called "point system," in effect in New York, a plea of guilt, for instance, to the charge of failing to signal or of making an improper turn, is taken into account in determining whether the offender's license should be suspended or revoked. (See pamphlet issued by the Commissioner of Motor Vehicles, entitled, "What You Need to Know About New York State's Point System for Persistent Traffic Law Violators".)

City of Louisville v. Padgett
Court of Appeals of Kentucky, 1970.
457 S.W.2d 485.

It is common practice for a governmental entity, such as a city or a county or sometimes a state, that has jurisdiction over roadways, sidewalks, buildings, etc., to require that a person who has been injured, or a person's estate if the person has been killed, as a result of the alleged negligence of the government give the government formal written notice that it is going to be sued because of the damages suffered. No action in negligence may be entertained by the court in this type of situation unless this notice has been given and the government has an opportunity to investigate and decide whether it will pay the claim without an action being instituted in court.

The time limitations for the notification of the government, the procedures involved, and the time that the government has to act on the claim are set forth in the local or state statute. Furthermore, the time within which suit is to begin is also established in the statute. This concept is derived from the common law, where the monarch cannot be sued unless the monarch gives permission to be sued.

This is the situation in the instant case, where Marsha L. Padgett sued the City of Louisville for negligence and did not include in her notice to the city, any reference to the alleged negligence of the driver of the auto in which she was riding as a passenger. The city contended that the failure of Padgett to admit the negligence on the part of the driver was a judicial admission that the driver was solely negligent and that if this was the situation, the city should have no liability.

Read the decision to see how the court handled the claim.

EDWARD P. HILL, JR., Chief Justice.

In her original and amended complaints, Marsha L. Padgett sued the City of Louisville (the City), Ruby Construction Company (Ruby), Louisville and Jefferson County Metropolitan Sewer District (Metropolitan), and Perry M. Adams for damages for injuries sustained when the automobile in which she was riding as a passenger and which was being operated by Perry M. Adams ran into a pool of water on River Road and wrecked. She alleged negligence on the part of the City, Ruby, and Metropolitan in the construction and maintenance of the drainage system of the road in question.

The City filed cross-claim against Ruby for indemnity. It also filed cross-claim against Adams for indemnity or contribution.

The City also filed cross-claim for indemnity against Metropolitan, claiming that under KRS Chapter 76 Metropolitan had the sole responsibility for the drainage of the streets of the City, including River Road at the place of the accident, and that if there was liability anywhere it was on Metropolitan. In the alternative the City asked for contribution against Metropolitan.

Metropolitan filed cross-claim against the City, Ruby, and Adams.

At the conclusion of the plaintiff's case, the circuit court sustained Ruby's motion for a directed verdict.

At the close of the entire case, the circuit court sustained Metropolitan's motion for a directed verdict and overruled plaintiff's motion for a directed verdict as to the City and Adams.

The jury returned a joint verdict against the City and Adams for $28,357.86. Later a separate judgment was entered in favor of the City against Adams for $14,178.93. Adams and his insurance carrier paid into court $10,000 (its limit of liability). This amount was accepted by plaintiff in full satisfaction of her claim against Adams under a previous agreement that Adams, then in Korea, would not demand a continuance providing plaintiff would not claim from Adams a greater amount than the limit of liability under his insurance policy. All of this was with court approval.

The City has appealed. Plaintiff filed cross-appeal against Ruby and Metropolitan. Metropolitan cross-appeals from that part of the judgment which dismissed its cross-claim against Ruby.

The facts are as follows. On November 5, 1966, at about 7:14 p.m., the car in which appellee Marsha L. Padgett was a passenger and which was being driven eastwardly on River Road in the City of Louisville by Perry Morrison Adams, after rounding a slight curve, ran into a pond or accumulation of water. The splashing water covered the windshield blinding the driver, causing him to lose control of the car. The car left the road and struck a utility pole causing serious injuries to appellee Marsha L. Padgett. The pond of water was about 200 feet long and ranged in depth up to six inches next to the curb. It was dark at the time.

Four or five days prior to the accident, an officer of the Louisville Police Department observed the accumulation of water at the place of the accident and telephoned a report thereof to police headquarters. He told the "complaint desk" something should be done to the puddle, that it was in the lane of traffic.

During or prior to 1965, Ruby contracted with the State Highway Department to construct a portion of I-64, known as Riverside Expressway, from east of the interchange at the North-South Expressway to near Washington Street.

On November 3, 1966, a city policeman notified Metropolitan of the flooding on River Road. Metropolitan placed barricades about the place and pumped the water off. On November 7, 1966, Metropolitan notified the State Highway Department of the flooding of the road, but this was after the accident. Ruby used a backhoe to dig a temporary ditch which stopped the flooding. Only one or two hours was required to do this.

On this appeal the City presents these three arguments: "(1) The negligence of the appellant, City of Louisville, if any there was, was not the proximate cause of appellee Padgett's injuries, but the independent intervening negligence of the defendant, Perry Adams, was the sole proximate cause of appellee's injuries as a matter of law; (2) appellant was, as a matter of law, entitled to judgment for indemnity on its cross-claim against Ruby, or at least a jury issue was raised on said cross-claim"; and "(3) appellant was, as a matter of law, entitled to judgment for indemnity, or in the alternative, contribution, on its cross-claim against Metropolitan Sewer District, or at least a jury issue was raised on said cross-claim."

Turning to the City's first argument, the City contends that appellee Padgett is bound under rules pertaining to judicial admissions by her notice of the accident given to the City under KRS 411.110. The City reasons that Adams, the driver, had from 321 to 375 feet after discovering the water in which to "attempt to stop the auto," apply his brakes, or turn on his windshield wipers. By all the evidence, Adams was not traveling at an excessive speed. He stated he was traveling at about 30 miles per hour. There was no evidence of drinking. Street lighting in the vicinity of the water was not good. At least two of the investigating officers used flashlights at the scene of the wreck. We have some reservations as to whether Adams was guilty of negligence, but the jury found that he was. He or his insurance carrier has satisfied the judgment, and neither has cross-appealed. So that question is not before us unless it can be said that Adams' negligence was the sole cause of the accident, and that we certainly cannot say. The City had notice of the condition from observations of two of its police officials and actually caused Metropolitan to pump the water off the road once before the accident. We think, as did the jury, that the City was guilty of negligence by failing to keep the water from accumulating or by failing to place barricades up to notify the public of the obvious hazard.

Taking Padgett's notice to the City as true, it does not admit negligence on the part of Adams and did not amount to a judicial admission.

We agree with the jury that Adams' negligence was not the sole or primary cause of the accident.

The negligence of Adams must have been the "primary and active" cause of the accident in order for the City to be entitled to indemnity. See Ambrosius Industries v. Adams, 293 S.W.2d 230 (Ky. 1956); Mackey v. Allen, 396 S.W.2d 55 (Ky. 1966); and Seelbach v. Cadick, 405 S.W.2d 745 (Ky. 1966).

* * *

The judgment is affirmed on both the direct and cross-appeals.

All concur.

Felker v. Bartelme

Appellate Court of Illinois, First District, Second Division, 1970.
124 Ill.App.2d 43, 260 N.E.2d 74.

This case introduces you to the liability of a person or firm who either sells or gives away intoxicating beverages that cause the receiver to become intoxicated and, as a result of this intoxication, to cause another person to be injured or to suffer pecuniary damage. One must show that the alleged intoxicant consumed alcohol and must present independent evidence showing that he or she was, in fact, intoxicated. This is known as a dram shop action. In addition, the decision explains the admission against interest exception to the hearsay rule and the conditions under which a codefendant's admission may or may not be admissible against the other defendant.

McCORMICK, Presiding Justice.

A suit was brought by Marilyn Felker, as administrator of the estate of her husband, Frank S. Felker, deceased. The suit grew out of a collision of an automobile driven by Warthen L.K. Hobbs and the Felker vehicle on February 8, 1963, at about 8:45 p.m. As a result of the collision Felker was killed, and his wife, as administrator of his estate, brought an action against Hobbs under the Wrongful Death Act, and against C. M. Bartelme, d/b/a Bartelme's Tavern, and Harold Feigenholtz, trustee, the fee owner of the tavern property, under the Dram Shop Act. At the close of plaintiff's case the defendants' motion for a directed verdict was granted. This appeal questions the propriety of that action of the trial court.

The collision occurred near an unregulated "T" intersection at Dundee and Landwehr Roads in Cook County. Hobbs' westbound car

was turning south when the Felker automobile, traveling east, struck it. Hobbs said he had been in the tavern about half an hour during which time he had purchased and consumed two shots of whisky and had shared a 12-ounce bottle of beer with his wife. According to Police Officer Arlie Page, Hobbs said he drank his wife's drink when she went into the washroom, but Hobbs denied having taken the drink and denied having told Officer Page he did.

Hobbs testified that the road on which the accident occurred was a two-lane road, with one lane going in each direction, and that it was dry on the evening in question. The speed limit on Dundee Road was 55 miles per hour. Hobbs testified that he put on his left turn signal as he approached Landwehr Road and "saw a car coming from the West, perhaps half a mile away. I was watching that car all the time until the collision. Two seconds before I got hit I saw a second car in the eastbound lane." This "second car" was Felker's, which collided with Hobbs'.

Officer Page arrived at the scene of the accident within minutes. In his testimony he said, "Hobbs told me he turned into a driveway instead of Landwehr Road and that he saw no oncoming headlights when he started to turn." He also testified that Hobbs had told him he "believed" he had his left turn signal on as he approached Landwehr Road.

Another police officer, J. D. Mills, testified he had a conversation with Hobbs at the hospital the morning after the accident, at which time Hobbs had admitted that while at home he had half a pint of whisky and a quart of beer, both of which he shared with his wife. The court informed the jury that that statement was binding only on the defendant who made it, and was not admissible against the tavern owner or operator. Later, the judge indicated he was not considering that testimony in his ruling on the motion for a directed verdict.

Kyle Simpson testified that he and his wife were traveling east on Dundee Road on the night in question and saw the collision. He stated: "Immediately before the collision an eastbound car passed us approximately 500 feet west of Landwehr Road. I was going about 30 miles per hour at that time. There was also a westbound car in the center of Dundee

Road. The eastbound car was going at a very high excessive rate of speed. I did not notice any directional signals being given by the westbound-car." Simpson later said he had told a police officer he had no idea how fast the car was traveling when it passed him; that before the eastbound [Felker] car reached the intersection at Landwehr it was back in the eastbound lane; and that the speed of the Felker car could have been "55 miles an hour and could have been 80 miles an hour. I would have no idea of what the speed of that car was. . . . The speed limit was 55 miles an hour. The speed of the Chevrolet [Felker car] could have been 53 miles an hour."

The question before this court is whether there existed an issue of fact which should have been submitted to the jury. In their brief the defendants assert: "No evidence was introduced with regard to the condition of sobriety of Warthen L. K. Hobbs at/or prior to the accident at 8:45 p.m. Mr. Hobbs was not asked on cross-examination about his condition nor was anyone else asked to testify who had observed it." We cannot agree that there was "no evidence" regarding the issue of Hobbs' sobriety at the time of the accident. There was evidence that he had consumed alcoholic beverages at the tavern, but such testimony would not raise a jury question as to the issue of intoxication, since the single fact that one has drunk alcohol does not permit the conclusion that he was drunk.

We do not agree with the plaintiff when he says that Illinois cases have held that the mere drinking of alcohol raises a jury question as to intoxication. The plaintiff has cited Nystrom v. Bub, 36 Ill.App.2d 333, 184 N.E.2d 273; Osborn v. Leuffgen, 381 Ill. 295, 45 N.E.2d 622; Davis v. Oettle, 43 Ill.App.2d 149, 193 N.E.2d 111; and Matkins v. Fenorsky, 348 Ill.App. 125, 108 N.E.2d 373, as supporting the proposition that the issue of intoxication is made out simply by showing that the alleged intoxicant drank alcohol, but in fact, none of those cases stands for that proposition. In each of them there was evidence that the alleged intoxicant had drunk alcohol, plus evidence of unusual behavior, or opinion evidence that defendant was drunk. Under those circumstances a jury would be entitled to conclude that the defendant was drunk.

In *Fenorsky* the defendant said he had felt "groggy" after leaving the tavern; he moved slowly and felt heavy, conditions he had not experienced before drinking. In *Oettle* the court noted at page 151, 193 N.E.2d at page 112: "A number of witnesses testified that immediately following the accident they observed Frank Emery and he was apparently intoxicated. These witnesses included a Doctor who treated Emery for his injuries at the hospital. There was not evidence to the effect that Emery was not intoxicated." In *Leuffgen* the alleged intoxicant had been sitting at a bar for some time with glasses and bottles in front of him; the bartender was partially intoxicated; and two games of dice broke up with angry quarreling followed by the alleged intoxicant's vicious assault on the decedent. The court found these facts as circumstances tending to prove intoxication.

In *Bub* a witness to the accident testified as to the condition of the alleged intoxicant by saying: . . . I have an opinion as to whether he was intoxicated or not. My opinion is I think he was drinking quite heavily and was drunk." [At page 341, 184 N.E.2d at page 276.] A registered nurse who appeared at the scene of the accident expressed the opinion that the defendant was intoxicated. These statements, together with the proof that the defendant had consumed some alcoholic beverages prior to the accident were considered sufficient to warrant a finding that the defendant was intoxicated at the time of the accident.

There are at least two elements involved in a Dram Shop action as to proof of intoxication; one must show that the alleged intoxicant consumed alcohol, and must present independent evidence showing that he was in fact intoxicated. It is not sufficient, as plaintiff suggests, to simply introduce evidence that the defendant consumed alcohol. A jury verdict under such circumstances would be based on pure conjecture since each individual's capacity for alcoholic intake varies; therefore, a jury question as to intoxication is not made out by merely proving that one had consumed alcohol.

Upon reviewing the record in the case before us we have found independent evidence tending to support the allegation that the defendant, Hobbs, was intoxicated at the time of the occurrence, and we feel there was sufficient evidence presented to justify giving the case to the jury. First, there was testimony that the defendant had consumed alcohol at the dram shop, and although there is dispute as to exactly how much he drank there, it is undisputed that he did consume alcohol at the tavern. Then, there is a contradiction as to whether or not Hobbs had his directional signal on as he attempted to turn left off Dundee Road. There is a further contradiction between Hobbs' testimony that he saw a car approaching half a mile away, and the testimony of Officer Page that Hobbs had told him he had not seen any oncoming headlights. Hobbs had mistakenly turned into a driveway, thinking it was Landwehr Road, although, by his own admission, he had made that turn at least fifty times before. There was testimony that the Felker car had passed another one, but was back in the proper lane at the time of the collision.

With this set of circumstances before us we cannot agree with the defendants that there was "no evidence" regarding Hobbs' sobriety prior to the accident. The trial court's ruling was to the effect that a verdict for the plaintiff based upon the evidence presented would not have been allowed to stand. Pedrick v. Peoria & Eastern R. R. Co., 37 Ill.2d 494, 229 N.E.2d 504. For the reasons stated above, we do not reach such a conclusion, and therefore hold that the trial court committed reversible error in directing a verdict for the defendants.

Since the case is being remanded we must discuss the issue as to whether Hobbs' alleged admission to Officer Mills concerning his consumption of whisky and beer at home was admissible against the dram shop owner and operator. The trial court had ruled that that statement was admissible only against Hobbs and not against the owner or operator. It would appear that the trial court's ruling was based on a well-established principle. The admission of a codefendant is inadmissible as against others, absent proof that the person making the admission and the codefendant had been parties to a preconceived plan or conspiracy to which the admission was relevant. When the admission is made out of the presence of and without the consent of the co-party it is inadmissible against such co-

party unless there is a showing that some form of agency relationship existed between the parties. The plaintiff sought to have the officer's version of Hobbs' admission presented to the jury in support of her contention that Hobbs was intoxicated at the time of the accident, and that it should be considered not only against Hobbs but against the persons interested in the ownership of the dram shop.

It would appear that Hobbs' admission was admissible against himself because it fell within an exception to the general rule regarding hearsay declarations. It was admissible because it was the purported statement of Hobbs himself and because it was against his interest to have made the statement since it contained inculpatory aspects. The question is one of reliability of the offered assertion. The "admission against interest" exception is based on the notion that one does not admit to facts which are against his own interest, and if he does admit them it would be fair to presume that the statement is true. Since the statement with which we are concerned falls within this category, it properly should have been admitted against Hobbs, but not against any other party absent the above required showing regarding agency. We hold that the trial court properly ruled that the statement was admissible only as against Hobbs.

The statement was against Hobbs' interest, but was self-serving at the same time. The potential self-serving aspect could have been Hobbs' reason for fabricating his own state of intoxication, since he may have assumed the plaintiff would be more likely, for practical reasons, to seek relief from the dram shop rather than from himself. Of course, we do not know of any conversation Hobbs had in the meantime. The accident occurred at 8:45 p.m., and the alleged conversation took place at 1:00 a.m. the following morning.

We cannot agree that the objection made to the admissibility of the proffered testimony was a general objection and hence raised only the issue of whether the evidence was material and relevant. The following colloquy appears in the record as having occurred during the time the objection was raised:

The Court: Was he conscious?
The Witness: Yes, sir.

Mr. Feigenholtz: I object to any conversation—

Mr. Griffith: Q. Was there any—

Mr. Feigenholtz: Just a minute, please.

The Court: It won't be binding on your clients, but—

Mr. Feigenholtz: That is the basis of my objection, your Honor.

The Court: It would be binding upon the person with whom the conversation was had, subject to rebuttal.

Mr. Griffith: I will make my same objections to that ruling that I made yesterday.

The Court: What is your objection?

Mr. Griffith: That this is admissible as to all defendants.

Court: It can't be under the rules of evidence.

We feel that the objection cannot fairly be called general. The trial court had said the conversation would not be binding as to Mr. Feigenholtz's clients [the tavern and Mr. Feigenholtz as trustee], at which point Mr. Feigenholtz indicated that such was the basis of his objection. Under the circumstances, we think the parties concerned clearly recognized that the hearsay problem was being discussed and that counsel's objection was that Hobbs' admissions were inadmissible against the dram shop defendants since the statement was hearsay as to them. The evidence was hearsay as to the dram shop defendants, and the trial court properly ruled it inadmissible as to those defendants other than Hobbs.

Since we have concluded that the case should have been submitted to a jury for its determination as to whether Hobbs was intoxicated at the time of the accident, the judgment of the Circuit Court of Cook County is reversed and the cause remanded for a new trial.

Reversed and remanded.

LYONS, J., concurs.

BURKE, Justice (dissenting):

In my opinion there was no evidence of intoxication. Therefore, the judgment should be affirmed.

United States v. Costa

United States Court of Appeals, Eleventh Circuit, 1994.
31 F.3d 1073.

This case involves, inter alia, an interpretation of Federal Rule of Evidence 804(b)(3), whereby a hearsay statement that inculpates the accused is admissible as a statement against penal interest only if (1) the declarant is not available, (2) the statement so far tends to subject the declarant to criminal liability that a reasonable person in his or her position would not have made the statement unless he or she believed it to be true, and (3) the statement is corroborated by circumstances clearly indicating its trustworthiness. The facts of this case relate an interesting short story.

Appeals from the United States District Court for the Southern District of Alabama.

Before ANDERSON and DUBINA, Circuit Judges, and ESCHBACH, Senior Circuit Judge.

DUBINA, Circuit Judge:

Appellants Jose Barros-Zao ("Barros-Zao"), Carlos Bicho ("Bicho"), and Luis Costa ("Costa") appeal their convictions of one count of conspiracy to possess with intent to distribute more than five kilograms of cocaine, in violation of 21 U.S.C. § 846 and 18 U.S.C. § 2, and one count of possession with intent to distribute more than five kilograms of cocaine, in violation of 21 U.S.C. § 841(a)(1) and 18 U.S.C. § 2. Because we hold that the district court improperly admitted certain hearsay evidence at the defendants' trial, we reverse the judgments of conviction and remand for a new trial.

I. FACTUAL BACKGROUND

On July 3, 1992, defendants Barros-Zao, Bicho, and Costa, along with Mario DaCosta, were arrested near Montgomery, Alabama. All three defendants were originally from Portugal, but at the time of their arrest they were residents of Canada. Both Barros-Zao and Costa were employed as delivery truck drivers for a fish supply company owned by Manuel DaCosta, the brother of Mario DaCosta. Bicho operated a fish market in Montreal. Mario DaCosta worked for his brother Manuel.

Previously, on June 27, 1992, Mario DaCosta and other co-conspirators, who are not involved in the present case, met with undercover agents for the United States Customs Service in New York City to negotiate the delivery of 110 kilograms of cocaine. At this meeting, an initial payment of $300,000 was made, and it was agreed that delivery would take place several days later in the Montgomery, Alabama area. On June 29, 1992, in a tape recorded telephone conversation between Manuel DaCosta and undercover customs agent Blas, Manuel DaCosta stated that Mario DaCosta would pick up the cocaine on July 3, 1992.

On July 1, 1992, Mario DaCosta and the three defendants travelled to Atlanta, Georgia. The following day, Bicho rented a Cadillac, listing Mario DaCosta as a second driver, and Barros-Zao rented a van, listing Costa as a second driver. Later that day, the group drove to Montgomery, Alabama, where they spent the night in a hotel. Both that evening and the next day, Mario DaCosta made several telephone calls to agent Blas, coordinating the delivery of the cocaine.

On July 3, 1992, Mario DaCosta and the defendants drove to the Owassa Truck Stop where they met undercover customs agents Blas and Mixon. Although these agents had dealt with Mario DaCosta previously, this was their first and only contact with the defendants. Mario DaCosta and Costa then followed the agents to a nearby interstate rest area where Blas handed Mario DaCosta the keys to a rented Lincoln Towncar. The cocaine was in the trunk of the Lincoln, but Costa never opened the trunk to confirm this. Mario DaCosta and agent Blas discussed arrangements for payment of the balance of the purchase price. Surveillance photographs were taken of Mario DaCosta and Costa at the rest area. Mario DaCosta and Costa then returned to the truck stop, with Costa driving the Lincoln. After a brief discussion, Mario DaCosta and the defendants set off for Atlanta. Costa drove the Lincoln. Bicho drove the van, and Mario DaCosta drove the Cadillac; Barros-Zao rode with Mario DaCosta.

As the group was getting on the interstate, a secret kill switch installed in the Lincoln caused it to stall. The other two vehicles then pulled off the interstate ahead of the Lincoln. Bicho waited in the van, while Mario DaCosta doubled back to check on the Lincoln. Meanwhile, Alabama state troopers arrived at the Lincoln to give assistance. After Costa consented to a search, the troopers discovered the cocaine and arrested Costa. Seeing the troopers, Mario DaCosta fled the area, but was apprehended shortly thereafter along with

Barros-Zao. Bicho, who was found still waiting on the side of the interstate, was also arrested. At that time, it was discovered that some of the screws holding the van's interior molding in place were removed and that the interior molding panels were loosened.

Once in custody, Mario DaCosta was interrogated by a customs agent and a DEA agent. One of the interrogators, Agent Barnette, informed Mario DaCosta that he was in serious trouble and facing life in prison. Agent Barnette also informed DaCosta that if he provided a truthful statement that qualified as substantial cooperation with the government, Barnette would make DaCosta's cooperation known to the United States Attorney. DaCosta then made a lengthy statement in which he changed his story three times. The final version of DaCosta's confession also implicated the three defendants. In particular, Mario DaCosta stated that the defendants knew that the purpose of the trip was to pick up cocaine. Mario DaCosta's custodial confession is the only direct evidence that the defendants were knowing members of a conspiracy. While in custody, Costa also gave a statement that was subsequently used against him at trial.

Barros-Zao and Costa claim that Mario DaCosta had asked them to make the journey to Montgomery in order to pick up and deliver a "shipment" for Manuel DaCosta. They claim they did not know that the "shipment" was cocaine. Bicho claims that Mario DaCosta invited him to come on the trip in order to check out seafood suppliers along the gulf coast after seeing the two drivers off with a "shipment." Bicho also denies knowing that the real purpose of the trip was to pick up cocaine.

II. PROCEDURAL HISTORY

Although the defendants were initially to be tried jointly with their codefendant Mario DaCosta, the district court granted a motion pursuant to Bruton v. United States, 391 U.S. 123, 88 S.Ct. 1620, 20 L.Ed.2d 476 (1968), to sever the trial of Mario DaCosta from that of the defendants. Under Bruton, severance is necessary where the government seeks to introduce at trial a custodial confession of a non-testifying defendant that incriminates both the defendant and his codefendants and where a limiting instruction would be ineffective to prevent a violation of the codefendants' constitutional rights of confrontation and cross-examination.

Mario DaCosta was tried first. Although Mario DaCosta took the stand at his own trial and recanted his custodial confession, he was convicted of both counts. Subsequently, at the trial of the defendants, Mario DaCosta invoked his Fifth Amendment right against self-incrimination and refused to testify. Despite a grant of use immunity by the government, Mario DaCosta persisted in his refusal and was held in contempt by the district court. Given the self-imposed unavailability of Mario DaCosta, the government proposed having Agent Barnette testify to Mario DaCosta's custodial confession. The defendants objected on the grounds that Mario DaCosta's confession was inadmissible hearsay and would violate their constitutional right of confrontation. The district court, relying on United States v. Garcia, 897 F.2d 1413 (7th Cir. 1990), ruled that the confession was admissible as a statement against penal interest under Rule 804(b)(3).

In addition, the district court ruled that the custodial statement of Luis Costa was admissible, but gave a limiting instruction that the jury consider the statement only with regard to Costa. The district court allowed other hearsay evidence against the defendants under the coconspirator exception to the hearsay rule. Fed.R.Evid. 801(d)(2)(E).

Ultimately, the defendants were convicted on both counts and sentenced accordingly. They then perfected this appeal. On appeal, the defendants present the following issues: (1) whether the district court erred in admitting the custodial confession of Mario DaCosta; (2) whether the district court erred in admitting the custodial statement of Luis Costa; (3) whether the district court erred in admitting other hearsay evidence under the coconspirator exception to the hearsay rule; (4) whether the defendants' convictions are supported by substantial evidence; and (5) whether the defendants' rights to a speedy trial were violated.

We hold that the custodial confession of Mario DaCosta is not genuinely against his penal interest to the extent that it directly inculpates the defendants and therefore is inadmissible under Rule 804(b)(3). Because this error is not harmless, we reverse the defendants' convictions and remand for a new trial. We further hold that the custodial statement of Luis Costa is not hearsay and that its admission at trial did not violate the defendants' confrontation rights. We also hold that the defendant's speedy trial claim is meritless and thus do not address it further. Because we remand for a new trial, we need not decide the remaining issues presented in this appeal.

III. DISCUSSION

The district court held that the custodial confession of Mario DaCosta was admissible under Rule 804(b)(3). In this circuit, a hearsay statement that inculpates the accused is admissible under Rule 804(b)(3) as a statement against penal interest only if (1) the declarant is unavailable; (2) the statement so far tends to subject the declarant to criminal liability that a reasonable person in his position would not have made the statement unless he believed it to be true; and (3) the statement is corroborated by circumstances clearly indicating its trustworthiness. United States v. Alvarez, 584 F.2d 694, 699–701 (5th Cir. 1978);[1] United States v. Sarmiento-Perez, 633 F.2d 1092, 1101 (5th Cir. Unit A Jan. 1981). With regard to the second prong of this test, whether a statement is genuinely against interest is purely a question of law and we review the district court's determination on this issue de novo. Alvarez 584 F.2d at 701. Because we hold that the custodial confession of Mario DaCosta was not genuinely against his penal interest to the extent that it directly implicated the defendants in a conspiracy, we will restrict our analysis to this prong of the against penal interest exception.

In the recent case of Williamson v. United States, —U.S.—, —, 114 S.Ct. 2431, 2437, 129 L.Ed.2d 476 (1994), the United States Supreme Court reiterated that "[t]he question under 804(b)(3) is always whether the statement was sufficiently against the declarant's penal interest 'that a reasonable person in the declarant's position would not have made the statement unless believing it to be true,' and this question can only be answered in light of all the surrounding circumstances." Whether or not a statement is truly against interest depends on a fact-intensive inquiry of the surrounding circumstances. *Id.* at —, 114 S.Ct. at 2437. In the present case, the district court ruled that the portion of Mario DaCosta's custodial confession that inculpated the defendants was against his penal interest without conducting such an inquiry.

Instead, the district court based its ruling on the Seventh Circuit's decision in the case of United States v. Garcia, 897 F.2d 1413 (7th Cir. 1990), in which that court held that a custodial confession of a non-testifying defendant inculpating a codefendant was admissible under Rule 804(b)(3). In *Garcia,* the court held that the confession implicating both defendants was against the penal interest of the declarant because it was probative of the declarant's guilt. *Id.* at 1420. In our view, the *Garcia* court's analysis of whether a custodial confession implicating a codefendant is genuinely against the penal interest of the declarant does not adequately take into account the circumstance that the confession was made while in custody.

"As [the Supreme Court] has consistently recognized, a codefendant's confession is presumptively unreliable as to the passages detailing the defendant's conduct or culpability because those passages may well be the product of the codefendant's desire to shift or spread blame, curry favor, avenge himself, or divert attention to another." Lee v. Illinois, 476 U.S. 530, 545, 106 S.Ct. 2056, 2064, 90 L.Ed.2d 514 (1986). "The unreliability of such evidence is intolerably compounded when the alleged accomplice, as here, does not testify and cannot be tested by cross-examination." *Bruton,* 391 U.S. at 136, 88 S.Ct. at 1628. The view that custodial confessions that implicate other codefendants often are not genuinely against the penal interest of the declarant is also reflected in the Advisory Committee Notes to Rule 804(b)(3), which state:

> Whether a statement is in fact against interest must be determined from the circumstances of each case. Thus a statement admitting guilt and implicating another person, made while in cus-

tody, may well be motivated by a desire to curry favor with the authorities and hence fail to qualify as against interest. . . . On the other hand, the same words spoken under different circumstances, e.g., to an acquaintance, would have no difficulty in qualifying.

Fed.R.Evid. 804 advisory committee's note.

In the case of United States v. Sarmiento-Perez, 633 F.2d 1092 (5th Cir. Unit A Jan. 1981), this circuit's predecessor considered the precise issue before us today and held that the custodial confession of a nontestifying, separately tried coconspirator/codefendant is not genuinely against penal interest insofar as it directly implicates the accused in the crime charged. In that case, the court drew a distinction between statements against penal interest that are offered to exculpate the accused and those that are offered to inculpate him. *Id.* at 1100. The distinction is made necessary by the fact that inculpatory statements implicate the confrontation rights of the accused whereas exculpatory statements do not. *Id.* Because the Supreme Court has chosen to ground confrontation values on the same bedrock of "reliability" that traditionally has been the grounding rationale for virtually all the exceptions to the hearsay rule, it is in practice difficult to discern the precise line of demarcation between the indicia of reliability that are sufficient to overcome confrontation problems and those that are sufficient to place an extrajudicial statement within the scope of a recognized exception to the hearsay rule. *Id.* at 1099–1100. Thus, the court stated, evidence that seems to fall afoul of the confrontation clause will most often fail to qualify for admission under any recognized hearsay exception. *Id.* at 1100.

Because the admission of a custodial confession of a non-testifying codefendant that inculpates the accused implicates the confrontation rights of the accused, this circuit subjects the reliability of such confessions—i.e., whether they are genuinely against the penal interest of the declarant—to a more exacting scrutiny than that applied by the Seventh Circuit in *Garcia.* As the court stated in *Sarmiento-Perez:*

> Given the advantages readily to be perceived in
> the incrimination of another for a crime in

which the declarant himself is implicated, the circumstance that the inculpatory-against-the-accused statement would have probative value against the *declarant* does not necessarily indicate that, insofar as it implicates the *accused*, it is sufficiently against the declarant's interest so as to be reliable.

Id. at 1101–02. Thus, even though such statements may appear on their face to violate the penal interest of the declarant, more evidence of reliability is required before they will be admitted under 804(b)(3).

We now turn to an analysis of the reliability of Mario DaCosta's custodial confession. At trial, Agent Barnette was allowed to testify at length as to the content of the confession. The portion of the confession that is at issue is that which directly attributes to the defendants' knowledge that the purpose of the trip to Alabama was to receive cocaine, the only direct evidence that the defendants were knowing members of a conspiracy. Particularly damning was Agent Barnette's testimony that:

> Mario said that Luis, when he picked up the car, that he knew he was going to pick up a hundred ten kilos of cocaine and that all four of the subjects; Luis Costa, Carlos Bicho, Jose Zao, Mario DaCosta discussed a hundred and ten kilos of cocaine from the time they left Newark, New Jersey until the time that they were arrested.

The first part of the quoted passage, the one specifically addressing the knowledge of Luis Costa, is not even facially against the interest of Mario DaCosta and thus should not have been admitted. The remainder of the passage is facially against the interest of Mario DaCosta in that it implicates him in a conspiracy. As in *Sarmiento-Perez,* however, our analysis cannot end here, but must continue with a close examination of all the circumstances surrounding the making of the statement to determine whether it so contravenes DaCosta's penal interest that a reasonable person in his position would not have made the statement unless he believed it to be true.

"This was not a spontaneous declaration made to friends and confederates, but a custodial confession, given under potentially coercive circumstances that could not at trial—and cannot now—be adequately examined."

Sarmiento-Perez, 633 F.2d at 1102. Not only was DaCosta in custody, but his interrogators had just told him that he was facing life in prison and that the United States Attorney would help him only if he provided substantial assistance. Thus, DaCosta had an obvious incentive to spread blame and curry favor with the authorities by implicating the defendants. In addition, anger resulting from the failure of his crime may have prompted DaCosta to implicate the defendants. Although DaCosta's interrogators claim they did not divulge to DaCosta any of their evidence against him, the fact that they knew when he was lying and the incredible chain of events that culminated in the defendants' arrest— i.e., the peculiar coincidences that the Lincoln just happened to stall and that the state patrol just happened to arrive immediately to provide assistance—certainly could have indicated to DaCosta that the government had a strong case against him already and that his best strategy would be to cut his own losses by implicating the defendants. Moreover, the interrogators' questions indicated to DaCosta that they suspected coconspirators other than the defendants. Thus, DaCosta had less to lose by naming the defendants as coconspirators as well. From these circumstances, which are not counterbalanced by circumstances indicating the reliability of the statement, it is reasonable to suppose that Mario DaCosta, and indeed a reasonable person in his position, might well have been motivated to misrepresent the role of others in the criminal enterprise, and might well have viewed the statement inculpating the defendants to be *in* his interest rather than against it.

Thus, we hold, as a matter of law, that Mario DaCosta's custodial confession is not genuinely against his interest to the extent that it directly inculpates the defendants in a conspiracy, and thus is not admissible under 804(b)(3). However, his confession would be admissible to the extent that it only implicates the defendants indirectly by, for example, allowing the jury to infer from DaCosta's knowledge of the cocaine and the defendants' presence in Alabama with DaCosta, that the defendants also knew of the cocaine.

Because DaCosta's confession was the only direct evidence against the defendants, it is highly probable that it contributed significantly to the jury's verdict. Accordingly we cannot say that its erroneous admission was harmless error. We need not find error of a constitutional proportion in order to find it reversible. *Sarmiento-Perez*, 633 F.2d at 1104. Because we are persuaded that the erroneous admission of DaCosta's confession, as the only direct evidence against the defendants, affected their substantial rights, substantial justice requires that we reverse the judgments of conviction and remand for a new trial pursuant to Fed.R.Civ.P. 61. *See Id.*

Given that we have now deemed the only direct evidence that the defendants were knowing members of a conspiracy inadmissible, upon remand, the district court will need to determine whether the remaining circumstantial evidence sufficiently links the defendants to a conspiracy to admit the hearsay statements of alleged coconspirators under Rule 801(d)(2)(E).

Finally, to assist the district court on remand, we address the defendants' claim that the district court erroneously admitted the custodial statement of Luis Costa. The basis of the defendants' objection is that Costa's statement is inadmissible hearsay and violates the confrontation rights of defendants Bicho and Barros-Zao. In the statement at issue, Costa stated that he met a certain "Tony" in a Newark, Portuguese bar, and that "Tony" asked him to travel with him to Alabama and to drive a car back to Newark. Costa denied being accompanied by anyone else on this trip and denied any knowledge that the car contained cocaine.

"'Hearsay'" is a statement, other than one made by the declarant while testifying at the trial or hearing, offered in evidence to prove the truth of the matter asserted. Fed.R.Evid. 801(c). Costa's statement is an obvious attempt to exculpate himself. The government offered the statement not for its truth, which would be absurd since the statement exculpates Costa and the government sought to inculpate him, but rather to show its falsity. By showing, through the introduction of other evidence, that Costa lied to his interrogators, the government sought to create an inference of Costa's guilt. Thus, Costa's statement is not hearsay.

The defendants also claim that Costa's statement violated the constitutional rights of Bicho and Barros-Zao to confront witnesses against them. Costa's statement, however, does not directly implicate the defendants. Rather, it implicates an unknown person referred to as "Tony." Costa's statement implicates Bicho and Barros-Zao only if the jury draws an inference that one of them is the mysterious "Tony," an inference that we note is not supported by any other evidence introduced at trial. Thus, Costa's statement implicates his codefendants only indirectly if at all. This circuit holds that "[o]nly those statements by a non-testifying defendant which directly inculpate a co-defendant give rise to the constitutional violation." United States v. Veltmann, 6 F.3d 1483, 1500 (11th Cir. 1993). Accordingly, we hold that Costa's statement does not violate the defendants' confrontation rights. We find further support for this conclusion in the fact that the district court also gave a limiting instruction that the jury consider Costa's statement only with regard to his own liability and not that of his codefendants.

IV. CONCLUSION

In sum, we hold that Mario DaCosta's custodial confession was not genuinely against his penal interest to the extent that it directly inculpated the defendants, and thus, we hold that the district court committed reversible error in that DaCosta's confession was the only direct evidence of the defendants' knowing participation in a conspiracy. In addition, we hold that the custodial statement of Luis Costa is not hearsay and that its admission by the district court did not violate the confrontation rights of defendants Bicho and Barros-Zao. We reverse the judgments of conviction and remand this action for a new trial consistent with this opinion.

REVERSED and REMANDED.

---

[1] The decisions of the United States Court of Appeals for the Fifth Circuit (the "former Fifth" or the "old Fifth"), as that court existed on September 30, 1981, handed down by that court prior to the close of business on that date, are binding as precedent in the Eleventh Circuit. Bonner v. City of Prichard, 661 F.2d 1206, 1207 (11th Cir. 1981).

✔ PRACTICE QUESTIONS

Select the most correct answer to complete each statement.

1. An admission is distinguished from a confession in that
   (a) an admission is an exception to the hearsay exclusionary rule, while the confession is not.
   (b) a party who has made an admission may not be subject to cross-examination, while the party who has made a confession is.
   (c) an admission is not considered conclusive, while a confession is.
   (d) an admission is a statement made or an act done by a party or his or her agent within the scope of the party's or agent's authority, while a confession is a direct acknowledgment of guilt.

2. A formal judicial admission
   (a) is a formal act done in the course of the prosecution of a judicial proceeding that obviates the necessity of producing certain evidence by conceding for the purpose of litigation that a fact alleged by the adverse party is true.
   (b) includes facts incidentally admitted in the course of a trial or judicial proceeding.
   (c) is a statement made by a party who is testifying as a witness, a statement made in an affidavit by a party, or a statement made in a deposition by a party that may be received in evidence as an admission in the same or any subsequent litigation.
   (d) is a judicial admission that is not conclusive; it is merely evidence of the facts admitted.

3. The Federal Rules of Evidence provide the following exception to the hearsay exclusionary rule in Rule 803:
   (a) an excited utterance relating to a startling event or condition made while a declarant was under the stress of excitement caused by the event or condition may not be admissible in evidence.
   (b) a present sense impression describing or explaining an event or condition made while the declarant was perceiving an event or condition, or immediately thereafter, is admissible in evidence.
   (c) a defendant's actions in repairing a defective sidewalk are always admissible in evidence to show that there was a defect in the sidewalk and that attempts were made to prevent injuries to other persons.
   (d) a and b.

4. (a) An offer of compromise is admissible in the subsequent trial where the offer was not accepted by one or more of the litigants.
   (b) An offer of compromise is generally not admissible in evidence at a subsequent trial of the case arising out of the same facts.
   (c) One is always required to answer a written communication regarding a complaint of wrongdoing against the receiver of the communication.
   (d) none of the above.

5. (a) A party who is under arrest need not deny an accusation made against that party, and the fact that there was no denial of the accusation is not admissible in evidence.
   (b) There is no difference between the admissibility of statements or writings made by servants or agents on behalf of their masters or principals.
   (c) In a compromise made in the course of litigation, there is always one person who has lost the case and another person who has won.

(d) All of the above statements are true.

Indicate whether each statement is true or false.

6. A confession and an admission mean the same thing.

7. There are three general types of admissions: judicial admission, extrajudicial admission, and admission made out of court to a police officer after the defendant was given a Miranda warning.

CHAPTER 8

Res Gestae Exception to Hearsay Exclusionary Rule

§ 8.1 INTRODUCTION

A layperson on the witness stand is permitted to testify as to what he or she heard, saw, smelled, tasted, or touched but usually is not permitted to testify to what he or she heard or saw someone else, other than a party to the action, say or do. This type of evidence we previously called hearsay, and it is generally not admissible in evidence except under well-defined and long-used exceptions based on necessity and a great probability of reliability. We have previously discussed admissions of a party as an exception to the hearsay exclusionary rule. The concept of res gestae is another such exception. Literally translated from the Latin, it means "the thing done."

The courts have used the theory of res gestae in many types of situations, and hence it is not possible to formulate a comprehensive definition of the term. The most practical method for you to use to understand the idea of res gestae is to become acquainted with situations in which the courts have admitted evidence that is clearly hearsay but that is customarily admissible under the res gestae exception to the hearsay exclusionary rule.

§ 8.2 HEARSAY DEFINED

The general rule excluding hearsay evidence cannot be fully understood without a clear understanding of what hearsay is. For that reason, we repeat that hearsay is

1. a statement made outside of court (this particular trial)
2. that is offered in the trial to prove the facts that are contained in it.

If the evidence is offered for the mere fact that the statement was made without regard for the truth of the assertion, it is not hearsay.

Let us assume that "W" is testifying on the witness stand in the courtroom. Let us further assume that the trial is a murder trial wherein "V" was killed and "D" is the defendant. "W" would not be permitted to testify that he hears "A" say that she ("A") had seen "D" pick up a gun from a table and shoot "V" through the chest with this gun. This is clearly a hearsay situation because "W" did not see, hear, smell, or touch anything directly connected with the commission of the crime. "W" only heard about it from someone else, and the probability of reliability in such a situation is poor. It is common knowledge that as a description is told orally by one person to another, each person carrying the description on to another is likely to change it slightly, so that when the final person hears the account, it may, and more than likely does, not even slightly resemble the original account of the occurrence. Anyone who has seen *Fiddler on the Roof* will remember how the gossiping women in the small town in Russia changed the account of what was happening as it went from one to the other and the final version had no resemblance to the original.

Another method of getting the "feel" of hearsay is to remember that "if you can't cross-examine the original person making the statement and it is offered for the truth of the assertion, it is hearsay."

The statement was made in a preceding paragraph that if the statement is offered not for the truth of the assertion, but merely to show that it was made, it should be admitted, even though it is an out-of-court statement not subject to cross-examination. Let us assume that "D," a half hour before shooting "V," was heard to have said, "I am the king of England and the great British Empire and I demand that all who come before me bow down and pay homage to me." This statement is relative in the trial on the issue of insanity. The statement was not true, for "D" did not possess such a stature in life, but it would be admissible for the fact that it was said by him and relevant on the issue of insanity to assist the jury to come to a determination of that issue. This is not hearsay.

Let us take the same statement and change the timing of it. Let us assume that it was said immediately before the shooting and "V" declined to bow down and pay homage to "D." Here, too, it would be admissible not for the truth of the statement, but because it would be part of the transaction evidencing a state of mind. This is one of the situations in which res gestae is used to permit the statements of others who are not necessarily subject to cross-examination. Always remember at this juncture that a defendant in a criminal action need not take the stand in his or her own defense and this fact shall not be interpreted against his or her presumption of innocence.

§ 8.3 REASON FOR HEARSAY RULE, REITERATED

The reason for the rule excluding hearsay is to afford an opportunity to cross-examine the witness with respect to

1. the witness's veracity,
2. the accuracy of his or her perception, and
3. his or her ability to correctly recall past events.

§ 8.4 RES GESTAE DEFINED

There is probably no term used in the law of evidence that defies a strict definition more than the term "res gestae." The literal definition in translation from the Latin language is "the thing done." In practice, its use has little relevance to its literal translation.

Some courts have defined res gestae as those circumstances which are the underlying incidents of a particular litigated act and which are admissible when illustrative of that fact. Ill.—Perzovsky v. Chicago Transit Auth., 23 Ill.App.3d 896, 320 N.E.2d 433 (1974). The same court in the same case defined it as meaning the circumstances, facts, and declarations which grow out of the main fact and serve to illustrate its character and which are so spontaneous and contemporaneous with the main fact as to exclude the idea of deliberation or fabrication *a fortiori*. Okla.—Gulf Oil Corp. v. Harris, 425 P.2d 957 (Okla. 1967); Pa.—Eller v. Work, 233 Pa.Super. 186, 336 A.2d 645 (1975).

In examining most cases, the statement or declaration concerning which testimony is offered must, in order to be admissible as part of the res gestae, possess at least the following essential elements:

1. The statement or declaration must relate to the main event and must explain, elucidate, or in some manner characterize that event.
2. It must be a natural declaration or statement growing out of the event and not a mere narrative of a past completed affair.
3. It must be a statement of fact and not the mere expression of an opinion.
4. It must be a spontaneous or instinctive utterance of thought dominated or evoked by the transaction or occurrence itself and not the product of premeditation, reflection, or design.
5. While the declaration or statement need not be coincident or contemporaneous with the occurrence of the event, it must be made at such time and under such circumstances as will exclude the presumption that it is the result of deliberation.
6. It must appear that the declaration or statement was made by one who either participated in the transaction or witnessed the act or fact concerning which the declaration, or statement, was made. 31A C.J.S. Evidence 403(1).

Res gestae declarations may be admitted only where the circumstances under which the declarations were made afford assurance of sufficient probability of their truth warranting their being received by the jury. Kan.—Pacific Indem. Co. v. Berge, 205 Kan. 755, 473 P.2d 48 (1970); Md.—Cluster v. Cole, 21 Md.App. 242, 319 A.2d 320 (1974).

I like to think of res gestae statements as being hearsay statements that have a presumption against admissibility, but if it can be shown that there is little likelihood of prefabrication or deliberation and they are relevant to the main issue, they should be admitted.

§ 8.5 RES GESTAE STATEMENTS

§ 8.6 Time of Act or Statement

An act or declaration must be substantially contemporaneous with the act of which it is alleged to be a part. If it is otherwise, it is nothing more than a narrative of what has been. Ohio—Dugan v. Industrial Comm'n of Ohio, 135 Ohio St. 652, 22 N.E.2d 132 (1939). The modern tendency seems to treat spontaneity as a substitute for contemporaneousness (i.e., the speaker should not have sufficient time to fabricate an act or a statement). N.J.—Atamanik v. Real Estate Mgmt., 21 N.J.Super. 357, 91 A.2d 268 (1952). The lapse of time between the event and the utterance is important only as it bears on the question of spontaneity. In Washington (Britton v. Washington Water Power Co., 59 Wash. 440, 110 P. 20, 33 L.R.A. [N.S.] 109 [1910]), an injured person who had been unconscious for eight days made a declaration immediately upon regaining consciousness and before he had any opportunity to reflect. The declaration was held admissible.

However, in New York (Greener v. General Elec. Co., 209 N.Y. 135, 102 N.E. 527, 46 L.R.A. [N.S.] 975 [1913], a workman stepped on a ladder that bent under his weight and threw him to the ground, causing injuries that later caused his death. The witness testified that when he saw the workman fall, he ran over to where the workman lay and asked him what happened. The injured workman replied, "My feet is broke; the ladder bent over." The court held this inadmissible and said, "The distinction to be made is in the character of the declaration, whether it be so spontaneous, or natural, an utterance as to exclude the idea of fabrication, or whether it be in the nature of a narrative of what had occurred. In the current case, the declaration of the deceased was not spontaneous; it was called forth by the inquiry as to 'what had happened' and was distinctly narrative." Other cases have admitted res gestae in response to inquiry. N.Y.—People v. Del Vermo, 192 N.Y. 470, 85 N.E. 690 (1908). Later cases have indicated that the fact that the statement was in response to an inquiry should be regarded merely as a circumstance in determining spontaneity. N.Y.—People v. Marks, 6 N.Y.2d 67, 160 N.E.2d 26, 188 N.Y.S.2d 465 (1959).

§ 8.7 Who May Be Declarant

As a general rule, res gestae statements may not be based on hearsay. Tex.—Moore v. Drummet, 478 S.W.2d 177 (Tex.Civ.App. 1972). In order for a declaration or statement to be admissible as part of the res gestae, it must appear that it was made by one who either participated in the transaction or witnessed the act or fact concerning which the declaration or statement was made. N.J.—Lieberman v. Saley, 94 N.J.Super. 156, 227 A.2d 339 (1967). For example, in an action for damages by a woman who fell while getting off a train, testimony of the conductor concerning a statement by a bystander to the effect that plaintiff fainted was not admissible as part of the res gestae when there was no showing that the bystander saw plaintiff faint or that he was present at the time of the occurrence, since he may have received the information that she fainted from others. Ark.—Hines v. Patterson, 146 Ark. 367, 225 S.W. 642 (1920).

Declarations of a deceased person may be admissible when they are part of the res gestae. Pa.—Curran v. James Regulator Co., 10 Sch.Reg. 62 (Comm.Pl.), *aff'd*, 157 Pa.Super. 44, 41 A.2d 443 (1945).

The fact that a person was dazed or shocked brought on by injury at the time he made the statement does not render his statement inadmissible, but bears on the weight and credibility thereof. S.C.—Magill v. Southern Ry. Co., 95 S.C. 306, 78 S.E. 1033 (1913).

The statement need not have been made by one of the litigants. Del.—Garrod v. Good, 7 Storey 556, 203 A.2d 112 (1964). A res gestae declaration made during the life of a person who is dead at the time of trial is admissible. Ind.—Moster v. Bower, 153 Ind.App. 158, 286 N.E.2d 418 (1972).

It follows naturally that a declarant of a res gestae statement whose statement is to be admissible must possess sufficient mental condition at the time of making the statement so as to indicate that it has probative value. Minn.—Ammundson v. Tinholt, 228 Minn. 115, 36 N.W.2d 521, 7 A.L.R.2d 1318 (1949). A person need not necessarily be competent to testify in order to have his or her res gestae statement admitted so long as the party making it had the capacity to recollect and narrate the facts to which his or her utterance relates. Wash.—Johnston v. Ohls, 76 Wash.2d 398, 457 P.2d 194 (1969) (infant).

§ 8.8 Primary Applications

The primary applications of the res gestae exception involve

1. declarations evidencing a state of mind

2. declarations by agents, servants, or employees
3. declarations by rape victims
4. spontaneous declarations
5. declarations of pain and suffering
6. declarations accompanying and explaining a relevant act
7. complaints of coerced confession
8. declarations of intention
9. startled utterances
10. declarations elucidating an act
11. declarations of testators

§ 8.9 Declarations Evidencing a State of Mind

Declarations, spontaneously made, that reflect the state of mind of the declarant are admissible under the res gestae exception. This is closely related to declarations of intention, treated later. An example of the state of mind res gestae exception took place in Braatelien v. United States, 147 F.2d 888 (8th Cir. 1945), wherein after a conspiracy was established prima facie, everything said or done by any of the conspirators in execution or furtherance of the common purpose is deemed to have been said or done by every one of them and is admissible against each of them. The declaration of each of the parties was part of the res gestae.

§ 8.10 Declarations by Agents, Servants, or Employees

A spontaneous utterance, arising from the principal fact, made by an agent or employee is admissible the same as that of any other observer. Conn.—Perry v. Haritos, 100 Conn. 476, 124 A. 44 (1924); N.J.—Kelley v. Hicks, 9 N.J.Super. 266, 76 A.2d 23 (1950); N.Y.—Golden v. Horn & Hardart Co., 244 A.D. 92, 278 N.Y.S. 385 (1935), *aff'd*, 270 N.Y. 544, 200 N.E. 309 (1936). However, an agent's declaration is receivable even though it is made outside the scope of his or her authority if, under another rule of evidence, its admissibility is not made dependent on the fact of agency. Thus, a spontaneous declaration made by an agent may be admissible as if it were made by a person, not an agent. Let us assume that a driver of a vehicle was not the owner of the vehicle, but an agent of the owner. Assume further that this driver was involved in a collision with another vehicle and, before he or she had time to think, made the statement "Oh my God. If I had not been looking in back of me, this accident would not have taken place." This statement would be admissible in evidence if heard by someone who would testify that the driver made this statement. It could be admitted as an admission and also as part of the res gestae as a spontaneous declaration. It could be admitted in the criminal action, if there is one, for criminally negligent homicide if death resulted to someone because of the action of this driver. It could also be admitted in an action against the owner of the vehicle, who gave the driver permission to use the automobile. This could be admitted against the owner of the vehicle as a spontaneous utterance of an agent or as an admission by an agent.

§ 8.11 Declarations by Rape Victims

In a forcible rape case, the timely complaint of a victim is admissible if it is made promptly or at the first suitable opportunity after the commission of the crime. It may be testified to by the victim herself or by any witness who heard her make the complaint. The testimony must be confined to the fact that the victim made such timely complaint and may not contain any of the particular facts which she stated because this would be hearsay without the probability of reliability so necessary to entitle it to the category of an exception to the hearsay exclusionary rule. N.Y.—Baccio v. People, 41 N.Y. 265 (1869).

If the complainant did not make timely complaint, it is not part of the res gestae (the part of the transaction wherein she had no time to fabricate), and hence her complaint is completely excluded from the trial record.

The later complaint might also be excluded on the theory that it was a self-serving declaration.

§ 8.12 Spontaneous Declarations

In order for a res gestae statement to be admissible under the spontaneous declaration exception to the hearsay exclusionary rule, the statement must be so spontaneous as to exclude the possibility of fabrication. Okla.—Gulf Oil Co. v. Harris, *supra*; Pa.—Eller v. Work, 233 Pa.Super. 186, 336 A.2d 645 (1975). The primary concern in cases dealing with spontaneous declarations is whether there is any likelihood that the declarant has fabricated his or her statement or that the declarant's recollection has become clouded prior to the time the statement was made. U.S.—Government of Virgin Islands v. Dyches, 507 F.2d 106 (3d Cir. 1975), *cert. denied*, 421 U.S. 917, 95 S.Ct. 1579, 43 L.Ed.2d 783. The judge who presides has wide latitude in determining what constitutes a spontaneous utterance, but this discretion must be exercised soundly based on the facts of each case. This discretion must not be disturbed on appeal unless clearly erroneous. U.S.—Pietrzak v. United States, 188 F.2d 418 (5th Cir. 1951), *cert. denied*, 342 U.S. 824, 72 S.Ct. 44, 96 L.Ed. 623; Baber v. United States, 324 F.2d 390 (D.C.Cir. 1963), *cert. denied*, 376 U.S. 972, 84 S.Ct. 1139, 12 L.Ed.2d 86.

§ 8.13 Declarations of Pain and Suffering

There can be no definite and fixed limit of time within which statements must be made to become part of the res gestae, but every case will depend on its own facts; the burden is on the party offering the evidence to show such connection as will make it admissible. Pa.—Curry v. Riggles, 302 Pa. 156, 153 A. 325 (1931). Therefore, acts or statements although subsequent to the time of the infliction of the personal injury but which follow immediately thereafter and serve to explain the event or which are done or made under such circumstances as to exclude the possibility of premeditation or design and which are so close to the injury as to be part of the occurrence are admissible as part of the res gestae. N.J.—Demeter v. Rosenberg, 114 N.J.L. 55, 175 A. 621 (1934). Statements such as exclamations and complaints of present pain and suffering are admissible. Tex.—Texas Employers' Ins. Ass'n v. Davidson, 288 S.W. 471 (Tex.Civ.App. 1926), *reh'g denied*, 290 S.W. 871. Generally, one can say that involuntary expressions of pain, such as groans, screams, or moans, are always admissible; however, declarations of current pain and suffering are not admissible except

1. when the declarant is dead at the time of trial,
2. when the statement is made to a physician in order to aid the physician in his or her attempt to treat the injured party, or
3. when the statement may be classified as a spontaneous declaration.

Statements of current pain are not admissible under this hearsay exception when made to a physician who is examining the patient not for the purpose of treating the patient, but only for the purpose of preparing the physician so that he or she may testify regarding the injuries.

§ 8.14 Declarations Accompanying and Explaining a Relevant Act

The declarations accompanying and explaining a relevant act, most often found in civil law situations, such as a statement made by a testator simultaneously with the tearing of a will that "from now on my son will have to work for a living," are admissible under this exception. Such a statement may be relevant to whether the tearing of the will was intentional or unintentional. N.Y.—Waterman v. Whitney, 11 N.Y. (1 Kern) 157 (1854). A criminal law example of the use of this exception might be a situation in which a tractor-trailer truck driver says to his helper seated next to him in the cab of the tractor, "I'll teach that guy in the Chevrolet never to cut off a truck driver again," whereupon he rams the rear of the Chevrolet, killing the driver. This example is close to the declaration of intention discussed below, except that we cannot say that the truck driver intended to kill the person in the Chevrolet, but we can say that he intended to teach that person a lesson by ramming the rear of the Chevrolet; therefore, the act was intentional, and hence the truck driver's statement is a declaration accompanying and explaining a relevant act.

§ 8.15 Complaints of Coerced Confession

Where a defendant claims that a confession offered against him had been extorted from him, it is error to exclude evidence showing that, at the first suitable opportunity, the defendant had complained of his mistreatment. N.Y.—People v. Alex, 260 N.Y. 425, 183 N.E. 906, 85 A.L.R. 939 (1933); People v. Tuomey, 17 A.D.2d 247, 234 N.Y.S.2d 318 (1962).

§ 8.16 Declarations of Intention

Certain crimes require an element showing that the defendant intended to do the proscribed act. For example, in the crime of murder, in some jurisdictions it is necessary to show that the defendant intended to do the act. Hence, a declaration of intention whereby the defendant is alleged to have stated to a third person, "When I see John [the victim], I am going to kill him," is admissible to show that the defendant had the intention to do the act and that it was premeditated. Such a statement may also be used by John (the intended victim) if, instead of being killed by the declarant, he kills the declarant in self-defense or justifiable homicide. Even if this declaration was not communicated to the intended victim, he may have someone who heard it testify that the victim had made the statement, and this would tend to prove that the intended victim killed the declarant in defense of his own life. N.Y.—Stokes v. People, 53 N.Y. 164 (1873).

§ 8.17 Startled Utterances

Sometimes a statement is made by a person while the person is under the stress of excitement produced by a startling event and before the person has had time or opportunity to reflect or contrive. U.S.—United States v. Lehman, 468 F.2d 93 (7th Cir. 1972), *cert. denied*, 409 U.S. 967, 93 S.Ct. 273, 34 L.Ed.2d 232. There is a shadow of a difference between the startled utterance and the spontaneous utterance types of exception. The startled utterance is a subdivision of the spontaneous utterance. It therefore would be safe to say that a spontaneous utterance may not be a startled utterance, whereas a startled utterance is always a spontaneous utterance. This might be a brain teaser for you to think about and understand.

§ 8.18 Declarations Elucidating an Act

Sometimes statements are made that explain an act. Let us suppose that there was a question as to the cause of death in an action on an insurance policy on the life of a deceased. If the insured took his own life, according to the terms of the policy, his estate would not collect on the accidental death benefit coverage. Let us further assume that the insured lost his life by means of a discharge of a firearm. If the insured said to his wife immediately after the shot was discharged, "The gun went off accidentally," this statement may, in the court's discretion, be admitted as part of the res gestae of the event to elucidate an act. See Falkinburg v. Prudential Ins. Co. of America, 132 Neb. 831, 273 N.W. 478 (1937); Grebe v. Vacek & Co., 103 Ill.App.2d 79, 243 N.E.2d 438 (1968); and State *ex rel.* 807, Inc. v. Saitz, 425 S.W.2d 96 (1968), for other examples of this principle.

§ 8.19 Declarations of Testators

A testator is a male person, while a testatrix is a female person, either of whom executes a last will and testament in conformity with the statutory requirements of the state in which he or she is executing the document. He or she need not be a domiciliary of that jurisdiction to make a valid and enforceable will. However, all states require that a colloquy take place between the testator and the witnesses to the last will and testament before the signature of the testator and the witnesses are affixed thereto. This is done to ascertain whether the testator is competent and whether he or she is aware that he or she is signing a will. Declarations made at that time by the decedent which are part of the transaction of executing the document come under the same exception to the hearsay exclusionary rule as indicated earlier in the chapter. For use of such a statement, see In re Walton's Estate, 206 Misc. 908, 135 N.Y.S.2d 690 (1954).

§ 8.20 COMPETENCY OF DECLARANT AS A WITNESS

It may surprise some readers that the admissibility of a res gestae statement is not dependent on whether the person who made the statement would be competent to testify if called to the witness stand. Thus, in State v. Lasecki, 90 Ohio St. 10, 106 N.E. 660, L.R.A.1915E 202 (1914), the spontaneous exclamation of a child of four years of age that "the bums killed Pa with a broomstick," made a few seconds after his father had been killed by the assault, was held admissible over the objection that the boy was not old enough to be a witness.

§ 8.21 FEDERAL RULE

The Federal Rules of Evidence do not use the words res gestae as one of the exceptions to the hearsay exclusionary rule. However, Rule 803(2) reads as follows:

Rule 803

(2) **Excited utterance.** A statement relating to a startling event or condition made while the declarant was under the stress of excitement caused by the event or condition.

CROSS-REFERENCES

Federal Civil Judicial Procedure and Rules (West 1996) (Rule 803[2]).
Goode & Wellborn, Courtroom Handbook on Federal Evidence (West 1995) (Rule 803[2]).
McCormick, Evidence (4th ed. 1992) (Rule 803[2]).

Greener v. General Electric Co.

Court of Appeals of New York, 1913.
209 N.Y. 135, 102 N.E. 527.

This case, as well as some other cases of a like nature, has been selected for inclusion in this book for two purposes. The first is to introduce you to civil law situations in order to increase your mental horizon—in this case, a wrongful death action. The second purpose is to acquaint you with the requirements of the res gestae rule that must be met in order to get a statement admitted. The judge writes about the necessity of a statement being made at or near the time of the event. If there is time for the declarant to think and/or fabricate before making the statement, it would not be admissible under the res gestae exception to the hearsay exclusionary rule.

* * *

Action by Mary Greener, as administratrix, against the General Electric Company. A judgment for plaintiff and an order denying a new trial were affirmed by the Appellate Division, Third Department (153 App.Div. 439, 138 N.Y.Supp. 273 (1912), and defendant appeals.

GRAY, J. This action was brought to recover damages of the defendant for being the cause of the death of the plaintiff's intestate, an employee. In substance, the alleged negligence was that the defendant had provided for the use of its workmen a defective and insecure ladder, in connection with an overhead crane erected in its works, from which the deceased fell, or was thrown, to the floor of the building. The facts disclosed by the evidence were such as to warrant the jurors in finding that the deceased, who was employed as a "rigger," upon the day in question was standing on top of the carriage of the crane, when he was called to by the crane repairman, from the floor, to come down and to assist in hoisting up a piece of machinery; that, in attempting to comply with the order and to descend from his position, he stepped upon an iron ladder, extending from a crane cage, which descended from the cross-girders on which the crane carriage moved, for the purpose of reaching the lateral girders and of thus using another ladder to get to the floor; that this mode of ascending, or descending, from floor to crane was not prohibited, nor unusual; that the crane ladder, which was bolted to the floor and to the top of the crane carriage, and extended some three or four feet above it, unattached, was inadequate to the strain of the weight of the deceased, when subjected to it on this occasion; that it had bent under him, throwing him to the floor; and that, as the result of injuries then received, he had subsequently died.

Without otherwise referring to the evidence, we think that the judgment appealed from might stand, were it not for a serious error committed by the trial court in the reception in evidence of a declaration of the deceased, made to a fellow workman after his fall, and which may have influenced the decision by the jurors of the question of fact. Whatever we may consider to have been the sufficiency of the other evidence, we could, and should, not assume that a declaration, made under such circumstances, may not have had its effect upon the jurors' minds. A witness, also employed as a "rigger," and who was standing a few feet away from where the deceased had fallen, went over to him, and, as he lay there, "asked him what had happened." Over the objection of the defendant, he was then allowed to state what the deceased said, and an exception was taken to the ruling. The witness testified: "When I asked him what had happened, he said: 'my feet is broke; the ladder bent over.'" The admission in evidence of the declarations of an injured person constitutes an exception to the general rule that excludes hearsay evidence, and is only justified when the declarations are spontaneous utterances, or exclamations. There is no confusion in the decisions of this court upon this question. Waldele v. N.Y.C. & H.R.R.R. Co., 95

N.Y. 274, 47 Am.Rep. 41 (1884); Martin v. N.Y., N.H. & H.R.R. Co., 103 N.Y. 626, 9 N.E. 505 (1887); People v. Del Vermo, 192 N.Y. 470, 85 N.E. 690 (1908). In Waldele v. N.Y.C. & H.R.R.R. Co., the question was carefully considered, and the authorities were reviewed. There, the testimony of a witness as to what the injured person had declared, a few minutes after the accident, as to how it happened, was admitted, and, for the error in the admission, the plaintiff's judgment was reversed. The vice of the evidence was held to be in the declaration being narrative of the past transaction, and thus depending for its truth upon the reliability of the statements of the deceased and the veracity of the witness. The decision was followed in Martin v. N.Y., N.H. & H.R.R. Co. In People v. Del Vermo, the witness was walking with the deceased and the defendant, when the former fell upon the sidewalk. The witness asked him "What is the matter?" and the deceased answered, "Del Vermo stabbed me with a knife." The admission of the witness' evidence as to this declaration was held proper "as a part of the res gestae, in the broadest sense of the term." Judge Willard Bartlett again considered the question with much care, in the light of our and of other decisions, and held that the testimony was properly received. The declaration so accompanied the occurrence of the assault as to come within the exception to the general rule.

The distinction to be made is in the character of the declaration, whether it be so spontaneous, or natural, an utterance as to exclude the idea of fabrication, or whether it be in the nature of a narrative of what had occurred. In the present case, the declaration of the deceased was not spontaneous; it was called forth by the inquiry as to "what had happened" and was distinctly narrative. As it was observed in the dissenting opinion below, "it was, in effect, a statement that the falling was not accidental, nor due to the negligence of the plaintiff's intestate, but was due to an occurrence upon which might be predicated negligence upon the part of the defendant."

For the error pointed out, the judgment must be reversed and a new trial had; costs to abide the event.

CULLEN, C.J., and WERNER, HISCOCK, COLLIN, CUDDEBACK AND MILLER, JJ., concur.

Judgment reversed, etc.

Gulf Oil Corporation v. Harris
Supreme Court of Oklahoma, 1967
425 P.2d 957.

This is another type of wrongful death case, but here the action was founded not on the common law of negligence, but on statutory law, namely, the state's workman's compensation law. The legislation involved is now generally known as worker's compensation. Although this case is similar in nature to Greener v. General Electric Co., *supra*, the court here reasoned that the statements in question, even though not made at or near the time of the event, were admissible in evidence. A reading of this case will explain the disparity in the results between the two cases and the reasons that the court held these statements admissible.

WILLIAMS, Justice. Under review in this original action is the State Industrial Court's award of death benefits to the widow of a deceased workman.

The record shows that decedent, a pumper serving employer near Meeker, had under his charge approximately twenty-seven oil wells; that he worked five days a week, approximately eight hours a day; a co-pumper had an additional 30 or so wells to pump; that when his co-pumper would have a day off decedent took charge of the additional thirty wells regularly assigned to that co-worker; that on Saturday, December 13, 1958, because of the co-pumper having his customary day off duty, decedent was responsible for all fifty-seven wells; that such day was very cold; that there was an appreciable accumulation of ice and snow; that about 8:00 or 8:30 A.M. decedent left his home in his pick-up truck to service the wells; that he took his lunch this day; that such truck was equipped with an engine-starter operated by car battery which was used to start the engines of the several wells; that he returned home about 12:30 P.M. complaining of severe pain in his chest; and that he died a few minutes later as a result of a coronary occlusion.

The cause of decedent's cardiac episode formed the principal issue before the trial tribunal. Claimant, decedent's widow, sought to attribute the fatal attack to strain and physical exertion from cranking an engine by hand on the morning in question at one of employer's well sites. She testified that decedent returned to their home on the day here involved after being away at work for four and one-half hours and further testified as follows: [That at that time]

"**A:** He was cold, and he was blue around the eyes, and around the mouth.
"**Q:** Did you learn from him there that there was anything wrong with him?
"**A:** Yes.
"**Q:** Did he make gestures or demonstrate to you anything?
"**A:** He said he had a sharp pain in his chest.
"**Q:** Did he inform you anything about where he had had this trouble?
"**A:** Yes, he said while he was working."

* * *

"**Q:** Did you call the doctor?
"**A:** Yes."

* * *

"**Q:** And by the time he [doctor] got there, was Mr. Harris dead?
"**A:** Yes, sir, I think he was."

* * *

"**Q:** Mrs. Harris, you testified a little bit ago that Mr. Harris came, and you testified that he was purple, blue around the mouth. Did he make any statement right then to you as to what he had been doing?

* * *

"**A:** Yes.
"**Q:** What did he say he had been doing?
"**A:** He said he had been cranking on this motor. First, he said he had been working. I said, 'What do you mean working?' He said 'I have been cranking this motor.' I said, 'How come you didn't use the starter?' He said, 'They were all frozen up and the starter would not do any good.'
"**Q:** Mrs. Harris, did he tell you how long?
"**A:** He said forty-five minutes. It would have been more or it could have been less. He said forty-five minutes. I don't know if he meant he cranked forty-five minutes, or he cranked and worked altogether forty-five minutes."

This testimony was admitted over the employer's objection.

Mr. Cooke, employer's production foreman, testified that he visited Mrs. Harris within two or three hours of the death of her husband and discussed the matter with her. His testimony continued, as follows, to-wit:

"**Q:** And did she give you any narrative relation, such as she has recited here, about what he had related to her about the well?
"**A:** Yes, uh-huh."

* * *

"**Q:** Why do you provide a starter?
"**A:** Too many back injuries and hernias and things you get with starting engines, they claim.
"**Q:** Do you think that is because of the unusual exertion that is required [by cranking] to start them?
"**A:** That's possibly true."

Dr. B testified of effect that Mr. Harris had reported that he had cranked one of the motors and that a sacroiliac lesion the doctor found was by Mr. Harris ascribed as to causation thereof to such activity.

Mr. Polk, decedent's co-worker, testified that after decedent's death he checked the wells he and decedent serviced; that two or three of the wells were not operating; that "There was two wells in particular. One of them was the Henthorne Estate No. 1, and there was a lot of tracks in the snow there, and there was also on the Calvin Hill, I don't remember that well number, it was either 1 or 2, but there was a lot of tracks and snow was all tracked down around the well, the engine, and both wells was down and I started them both." In answer to the question, "But if you can't start them with your starter or your starter doesn't work, then it is necessary to use the crank?" he stated, "Yeah, in some occasions." He further testified that:

". . . It was down and I started it and went on and made my rounds and also started that Henthorne well and made my rounds, and came back and the Calvin Hill was down again and I started it again."

* * *

"**Q:** And do you know that you saw evidence of where Mr. Harris had been attempting to start some of the motors there that morning?
"**A:** That's right.

"**Q:** Now whether he started them or not, you don't know?

"**A:** I do not know.

"**Q:** But you are positive about the fact that he is the only one that was out there that day?

"**A:** That's right.

"**Q:** And the tracks and the evidence that you saw around those motors were indicative to you that he had had some kind of trouble at least at one of the wells?

"**A:** That's right."

* * *

"**Q:** And all of you have, even though the company didn't want you to do that, you do have a crank there for the purpose of starting it if your starter won't work or when you are unable to start it with the self-starter, isn't that correct?

"**A:** Yes. Well, the cranks come with the engines before we got the starters, electric starters."

Mr. Harris's son testified that on occasion he had seen the deceased crank different ones of the various motors.

As shown in the foregoing recitation and from other facts in evidence, we have the following facts and circumstances in this case, to-wit: (1), According to claimant, the deceased, over a period of 1 1/2 or 2 years, had been going to doctors with chest pains; (2), on the day in question the decedent ostensibly had more than twice as much work to do (some 57 wells to get and/or keep going as against his usual 27), and that, without any help from other workmen; (3), he had to work outside in the accumulated ice and snow, where it was very cold; (4), decedent was the only person who had been out on the lease that day (working and making tracks around) until Polk, after decedent's death was reported, was sent to finish decedent's assignment for the day; (5), the deceased apparently had made a lot of tracks around at least two, possibly three, of the stationary engines; (6), these facts indicated considerable physical activity and movement around the wells by decedent; (7), the employer thought it better for the workmen to use battery-operated starters, than to crank them by hand; (8), according to its production foreman, the employer furnishes battery-operated starters to the men who start and tend its pump-engines to save them from the unusual exertion that is required to crank them and to prevent the

men having back injuries, hernias "and things you get with starting engines"; (9), decedent had been provided with such a starter; (10), the gasoline motors were more difficult to start on a cold day; Mr. Sowers, a former Seminole County Sheriff, being a graduate engineer with many years oil field experience and then Assistant State Labor Commissioner, employer's Superintendent Cooke, Dr. B, Mr. Harris's son and his co-worker, Polk, all testified of effect that cranking such a pump-engine, more especially on a cold day, was strenuous work; (11), even after being started, the engines on occasion would quit and have to be started again (e.g., the Calvin Hill well 1 or 2, that being one of the very wells around which witness Polk found decedent evidently had worked and made a lot of tracks); (12), when the pump-engines could not be started with a battery-operated starter, a workman would have to crank them by hand; (13), that, when he deemed it necessary, deceased would not refrain from cranking the motors out of deference to his condition of health; (14), the cranks were inserted into the motors at about elbow height; (15), this cranking process included removing the spark-plug from the motor, pouring some gasoline into the firing-chamber, replacing the sparkplug, inserting the crank and quickly turning the full weight of the motor by hand with the crank; (16), this would entail having to move and twist and strain and struggle, about, (giving one explanation for all the tracks Polk found when he went on duty); (17), the concern which supplied the employer with the pump-engines furnished cranks with the individual motors, which cranks were stored for use "next time" underneath the respective motors; (18), the decedent experienced the beginning of his cardiac episode between the time he left for work and his return, some 4 hours later; (19), he came home some 5 hours earlier than usual, (under circumstances warranting the State Industrial Court in determining a recognition on his part of some abnormality in his physical condition); (20), decedent's wife found decedent, upon his early arrival home, to be cold, blue and purple around the eyes and around the mouth, complaining of a sharp pain in his chest; (21), acting as a normal wife, concerned for her husband's welfare and based upon her observation of him and his statements, the wife called a physician; (22), Mr. Harris died before the physician arrived; (23), based upon his assumption that decedent had strained himself out in the cold by cranking pump-engines, the physician gave his opinion in evidence that the workman died as a result of his cardiac episode, induced by strain and exertion caused by his unusual activity in conjunction with the elements (severe weather).

The question is, (1), whether the wife in her proof showed enough circumstantial evidence by way of facts and circumstances together with the physician's opinion to demonstrate reasonably to the Industrial Court that claimant's decedent had his coronary attack as a result of his strenuous work, or, if not, (2), whether the wife may lawfully be heard to report to the trial court as a part of the res gestae that her husband, soon after his cardiac episode had commenced but also shortly before his death, then said he had this pain (which he had already reported to her that he had) "while he was working" and, by way of accounting for his blue and purple appearance about the mouth and eyes, further said that "they [the motors] were all frozen up and the starter wouldn't do any good," and that he had "been cranking on this motor," "forty-five minutes," all as a basis for the expression of medical opinion as to cause of deceased's death, or (3), whether based upon all the foregoing facts and circumstances and alleged "res gestae" evidence claimant may be permitted to recover.

We here note that in our opinion in Young v. Neely, 353 P.2d 111, 113 (Okl.1960), wherein was involved the situation of a workman being discovered lying dead, across the lower wire of a fence located on the lease where he had worked and between an operating motor he apparently had just started and one not operating but toward which he apparently had turned, this Court in sustaining an award in favor of decedent's widow, stated:

"Strain and exertion rising out of and in the course of employment constitutes ipso facto an accidental injury. Choctaw County v. Bateman, supra [208 Okl. 16, 252 P.2d 465]. It may be

proved either by direct or circumstantial evidence alone. In Marby Construction Co. v. Mitchell, Okl., 288 P.2d 1108, 1110, it is stated:

"'In a workmen's compensation case, it is not required that the claimant shall establish his right to an award by direct evidence alone, or that he produce an eyewitness to the accident. Circumstantial evidence may be used to establish the claim, and it is not necessary that the circumstantial evidence should rise to that degree of certainty as to exclude every reasonable conclusion other than that found by the trial court.'"

From a consideration of all of the facts and circumstances in this case, including but not limited to those heretofore enumerated, we are of the opinion that the award made to the claimant has been reasonably established by direct and circumstantial evidence.

An issue presented by the argument of the parties is whether there was competent evidence that decedent had tried to start a pump engine by hand-cranking which could form the basis for the hypothetical question presented to claimant's expert medical witness that assumed that decedent had made such effort. The employer contends that the activity so described and included in the hypothetical question did not stand established as a fact by competent evidence, direct or circumstantial. The claimant contends that the statements made to her by decedent immediately prior to his death from a coronary occlusion which related the circumstances surrounding the onset of his pain were properly admitted as a part of the res gestae and therefore competent evidence. We agree with the claimant's contention.

In Sand Springs Ry. Co. v. Piggee, 196 Okl. 136, 163 P.2d 545, 547 (1945), we stated:

"It is sometimes difficult to determine as to whether certain statements which would be otherwise inadmissible under the hearsay rule are admissible as part of res gestae. It may be said generally that in order for such statements to be admissible they must be made at or near the time of the occurrence of the accident, they must have been spontaneously made, they must have been provoked or influenced by the happening of the accident itself so as to become a part thereof; if made in relating a past occurrence or event they are inadmissible. Missouri O. & G.R. Co. v. Adams, 52 Okl. 557, 153 P.

200; Chicago, R.I., & P. R. Co. v. Foltz, 54 Okl. 556, 154 P. 519; Schaff v. Coyle, 121 Okl. 228, 249 P. 947; Sears, Roebuck & Co. v. Robinson, 183 Okl. 253, 80 P.2d 938."

In Henry Chevrolet Co. v. Taylor, 188 Okl. 380, 108 P.2d 1024, 1027 (1941), this Court, in discussing res gestae, stated:

". . . It seems clear that the statement was admitted upon the theory that it is a part of the res gestae, and we will confine our discussion to the question of whether the statement was properly admitted under the res gestae rule. This rule has been the subject of much discussion by this and other courts. In some jurisdictions the rule has been given a most strict construction, while in others, of which Oklahoma is one, a more liberal view is taken with regard to the application of the rule. In Margay Oil Corp. v. Jamison, supra [177 Okl. 433, 59 P.2d 790], it was said: 'The question of the admissibility of statements as part of the res gestae is largely determined by the facts and circumstances of each case, and should in a great measure be left to the determination of the trial court.'

"In view of our numerous decisions upon the question, it is not deemed necessary to enter upon a lengthy discussion of the rule. It is sufficient to say that admission of such statements is justified by the spontaneous nature of the statement, which is in itself a sufficient guarantee of the trustworthiness of such declarations to render them admissible, if they are made under the immediate influence of the occurrence to which they relate, and it is not necessary that the declarations be so strictly contemporaneous with the occurrence to which they relate as to be admissible under the so-called 'verbal act' doctrine, the element of time being important only for the purpose of determining whether the declaration was made when the speaker was under the stress of nervous excitement as a result of the occurrence to the extent that the reflective faculties were stilled and the utterance therefore a sincere expression of his actual impressions and belief. See Wigmore on Evidence (2d Ed.) § 1750. This has been the tenor of numerous Oklahoma decisions upon the question. See Gibson Oil Co., et al. v. Westbrooke, 160 Okl. 26, 16 P.2d 127, 129; . . .

*   *   *

It is clear from the above cited reasoning that this Court through a period of years has approved the admission of statements sought to be introduced as part of the res gestae

though not occurring contemporaneously with the main or principal fact. In following this reasoning, we have held that a statement made as much as 1 hour after the act it referred to was admissible as long as the evidence indicated the statement "was provoked and influenced by the happening of the event itself and therefore a part thereof." Huffman v. Gaylor, 267 P.2d 564, 567 (Okl.1954).

*   *   *

We are of the opinion that the reasoning of the above cited decisions is correct and is controlling in the instant case. Considering the circumstances under which decedent uttered the statements related by claimant concerning the difficulty he experienced in attempting to start an engine at one of the wells and the onset of his pain, we determine that such statements were admissible in evidence. These statements appear to have been made spontaneously in that they were provoked by pain and suffering and made while decedent was in a state of shock immediately prior to his death.

When the claimant saw her husband, who had taken his lunch with him, come home from work at noon, being about five hours before the time he usually returned home, and obviously ill and in pain, her natural reaction would be to inquire as to what was the matter with her husband and what had precipitated such an outwardly manifested condition. The statements of decedent in response thereto appear to have been the usual and natural expressions and exclamations of such person and spontaneous manifestations of his bodily condition naturally flowing from such condition as opposed to being deliberate, narrative descriptions of past events. Such statements were seemingly induced by the occurrence of the events surrounding the occasion and spoken while decedent was under the influence of pain, shock and excitement and at the point of death.

In view of the above cited decisions, we hold that the testimony of the claimant was properly received.

As this testimony was the basis of the hypothetical question propounded to Dr. B, the employer's contention that such question was based on facts not properly in evidence cannot be sustained. Further, as above intimated, it is clear that claimant's evidence was sufficient to sustain the award of the Industrial Court. . . .

Award sustained.

People of the State of New York v. Marks

Court of Appeals of New York, 1959.
6 N.Y.2d 67, 160 N.E.2d 26, 188 N.Y.S.2d 465.

This case distinguishes between verbal acts and spontaneous declarations. Citing Professor Wigmore, who was a respected professor and writer on evidence law, the court said that a spontaneous declaration is a true exception to the hearsay rule. It is a narrative of a past transaction, although usually of a transaction occurring immediately before.

A res gestae statement, on the other hand, refers to verbal acts that form part of the transaction itself.

This is a difficult concept to understand, and for that reason, in this case, although I believe you should read the whole case, I will attempt to make it more understandable by presenting examples of the concept as I understand it to be.

Wigmore says that there can be no definite or fixed limit of time within which the declaration shall have been made; that each case must depend on its own circumstances. Wigmore, Evidence § 1750.

With this statement in mind, let us look at this hypothetical situation. A person is walking on a street and is struck down by an automobile. Another person rushes to the injured person and arrives seconds after the injured person was hurled through the air and struck the pavement. Without being asked what happened, the injured person calls out, "Help me, my legs are numb." Under this situation, he would not be likely to be fabricating a false statement, but, in effect, I would consider this a res gestae statement as a verbal act forming part of the transaction itself. He was unable to get up on his legs.

On the other hand, if the injured person were to make a statement without having time to fabricate a lie, and not in response to a question, by saying, "Why did that idiot go through the red light?" I would consider this a

spontaneous declaration—i.e., a narrative of a past transaction, although usually of a transaction occurring immediately before—and a true exception to the hearsay rule.

In either event, the statements should be admitted into evidence.

The court also discusses who should make a determination in New York and many other states as to the admissibility of preliminary questions of fact. To understand this, I urge you to read the decision.

VAN VOORHIS, Judge. Appellant has been convicted of murder in the second degree of having shot and killed one Pickens on June 16, 1955, in the basement of 254–256 West 146th Street, New York City. The Appellate Division has affirmed. The verdict of the jury is supported by evidence. Appellant advances two points (1) that the trial court erroneously excluded evidence of a declaration by the victim exculpating appellant, and (2) that the prosecutor made prejudicial statements in his summary to the jury. These points are discussed in the order named.

Patrolman Muldoon testified that at 10:30 A.M. on the day of the homicide he was directed by radio to drive his patrol car immediately to 260 West 146th Street, where the wounded man had been seen by a person who notified the police. On his way to that address, Muldoon observed that a crowd had gathered around 2742 Eighth Avenue, where he stopped his car and found Pickens lying in the vestibule. He was suffering from a gunshot wound in his left chest which was bleeding. Muldoon had a conversation with Pickens and then took him to the Harlem Hospital where they arrived at 10:40 A.M. There is evidence that the shooting occurred at 10:25 A.M. which was five minutes before the notification of Muldoon, who testified that he talked to Pickens within a minute afterward. According to this evidence, Pickens' statement to Officer Muldoon was made six minutes after he had been shot. Muldoon testified that he asked Pickens by whom he had been shot, and wrote the answer on a card which became part of the records of the Police Department. He was interrogated upon the witness stand by defense counsel: "Q. Did you write on that aided card that the deceased was shot by one Edward Small?" An objection to this question was sustained. The officer testified that Pickens gave no indication that he was in fear of death at the time. Defense counsel offered the card in evidence, which was deemed marked for identification. This offer was made as a business record of the Police Department under Section 374–a of the Civil Practice Act, but objections to the offer and to oral testimony of Pickens' declaration were sustained. No question has been raised concerning the form of the proof and the ruling of the court was based on the inadmissibility of any statement by Pickens under these circumstances. It is assumed that Pickens told Officer Muldoon that he had been shot by Edward Small.

Appellant's first point is that this declaration by the deceased apparently exculpating defendant should have been received in evidence as a spontaneous declaration under People v. Del Vermo, 192 N.Y. 470, 85 N.E. 690, 692 (1908). There the defendant was charged with having fatally stabbed one Tony Page in the abdomen. According to the testimony of the principal witness, they were walking on Dominick Street in Rome, New York, three abreast, Tony Page being between defendant and the witness. Defendant told Tony Page, according to this witness, that he had had connection with Page's wife and was going to have connection again. "If you want to come and see," said the defendant, "I will go just right now." Tony Page responded with an epithet at which the defendant laughed, they walked together a further distance of about two blocks, when the witness saw defendant run and exclaimed: "What is the matter with that fellow?" Page walked forward four or five steps and dropped to the sidewalk. The witness inquired, "What is the matter?" and Page answered, "Del Vermo stabbed me with a knife." The witness helped him to his home where Page's wife met him, and there Page repeated in response to her inquiry: "Del Vermo stabbed me with a knife," stating that he had been killed. Page died as the result of the wound within several hours. The witness had not seen him stabbed. At the trial the first declaration made to the witness immediately after the stabbing, when Page dropped to the sidewalk, was admitted into evidence as a spontaneous declaration. The later declaration made in the presence of his wife in the house, accompanied by the exclamation "Oh! my poor children! I am going to die. What are my children going to do after this?" was admitted as a dying declaration. Later, statements to others were admitted as dying declarations.

It is not contended that appellant's exculpation by the victim was admissible as a dying declaration. Officer Muldoon testified that Pickens did not indicate that he thought that he was going to die. The holding in the Del Vermo case, supra, about spontaneous declarations is addressed to our attention.

Professor Wigmore has analyzed this subject with his usual clarity, distinguishing spontaneous declarations from the doctrine of res gestae. The latter refers to verbal acts, forming part of the transaction itself. A spontaneous declaration, upon the other hand, is a true exception to the hearsay rule (Wigmore, Evidence, § 1745). It is a narrative of a past transaction, although usually of a transaction occurring immediately before. The basis of this exception to the hearsay rule is that the spontaneity of declarations of this kind gives more assurance of veracity than is true of the usual hearsay declaration. Wigmore says (§ 1747, subd. [I]): "This general principle is based on the experience that, under certain circumstances of physical shock, a stress of nervous excitement may be produced which stills the reflective faculties and removes their control. . . . Since this utterance is made under the immediate and uncontrolled domination of the senses, and during the brief period when considerations of self-interest could not have been brought fully to bear by reasoned reflection, the utterance may be taken as particularly trustworthy (or, at least, as lacking the usual grounds of untrustworthiness), and thus as expressing the real tenor of the speaker's belief as to the facts just observed by him; and may therefore be received as testimony to those facts. The ordinary situation presenting these conditions is an affray or a railroad accident. But the principle itself is a broad one."

It was tersely stated by Bleckley, C. J., in Travelers' Ins. Co. v. Sheppard, 85 Ga. 751, 775–776, 12 S.E. 18, 26 (1890), that "What the law altogether distrusts is not after-speech, but after-thought . . . That [the declarations] shall be or appear to be spontaneous is indispensable, and it is for this reason alone that they are required to be speedy."

Wigmore says that there can be no definite or fixed limit of time within which the declaration shall have been made, that each case must depend upon its own circumstances (§ 1750), adding that the utterance must have been before there has been time to contrive and misrepresent, i.e., while the nervous excitement may be supposed still to dominate and the reflective powers to be yet in abeyance. In this context, it may be appropriate to cite the often repeated language of Judge Vann, speaking for the unanimous court in People v. Gilbert, 199 N.Y. 10, 24, 92 N.E. 85, 89 (1910), concerning what constitutes premeditation and deliberation: "While the time for reflection is not measured in minutes or seconds, it is measured by facts. The time must be long enough to make a choice, as the result of thought and reflection, and to act upon the choice thus made. It is obviously impossible to measure this period by the ordinary method of measuring time and, hence, it is necessary to measure it by what must be done." Many cases are cited by Wigmore, in some of which the time interval is shorter and in others longer than in the case at bar. The passage which has been quoted from Wigmore is important not only on account of his authority and clarity, but also for the reason that it was followed in People v. Del Vermo, supra. Wigmore's distinction is recognized in Del Vermo between spontaneous declarations and the narrower meaning of res gestae, and the first declaration by Page but not the later ones was held to have been properly admitted on account of its spontaneity, immediately after Page fell to the sidewalk.

* * *

The Court of General Sessions gave this reason for excluding the declaration by Pickens in the instant case:

"As I understand the theory, a declaration of a decedent, even if made in response to an inquiry, would be admissible, provided the element of spontaneity was present; that the statement is made so impulsively as to exclude the element of reflected fabrication. On the present state of the record, however, there has necessarily been such a lapse of time as to permit, on the part of the now deceased, a period within which he had an opportunity to reflect and to contrive, and this necessarily destroys the basic ground upon which such a statement might be conceivably introduced under the theory of the Del Vermo case, and I want the record clearly to show the grounds for the Court's rulings with respect to these alleged statements by the deceased."

According to appellant, Pickens was still subject to the nervous excitement and physical shock of having been shot, which is claimed to have stilled his reflective faculties and removed their control. In support of this view is evidence that Pickens was interrogated by Officer Muldoon six minutes after he had been shot. Assuming the time interval to have been as brief as this, a number of events occurred before decedent's conversation with Officer Muldoon. After having been shot in the basement of 254–256 West 146th Street, he was seen in the hallway of the adjacent building, 260 West 146th Street; to have reached there he must have climbed down a 3-foot ledge, mounted a flight of 15 steps, and walked, in all, about 100 feet. In the hallway, he spoke to a woman, but what he said was stricken from the record on motion of counsel for defendant. He was later seen lying in the vestibule of 2742 Eighth Avenue, where he was interrogated by Officer Muldoon. To have arrived at that location, he must have walked down the steps at 260 West 146th Street, about 45 feet westward on 146th Street, and then gone 50 feet southward on Eighth Avenue. There he was able to talk to the officer.

The People argue that his statement to Officer Muldoon implicating another man than defendant was the product of reflection. The decedent had reason to fabricate a story. He was a narcotic addict recently released from prison. Several days before the shooting he had robbed defendant of several packages of heroin. It is quite possible that in view of defendant's pugnacity, his possession of a gun and his well-merited grievance, Pickens may have feared future violence at defendant's hands. Pickens was not then anticipating death as a result of his wounds, and may have been wary of what defendant might do to him afterward if he were publicly to have charged him with armed assault.

Appellant's brief appears to concede that the circumstances under which this declaration was made are open to different interpretations concerning its spontaneity. It is urged that the declaration should have been received in evidence in any event, and the question of its spontaneity submitted to the jury like the voluntariness of a confession under Section 395 of the Code of Criminal Procedure (People v. Kennedy, 159 N.Y. 346, 54 N.E. 51 [1899]; People v. Cassidy, 133 N.Y. 612, 30 N.E. 1003 [1892]; People v. Fernandez, 301 N.Y. 302, 93 N.E.2d 859 [1950]). A decision is cited in the intermediate appellate court in California (People v. Keelin, 136 Cal.App.2d 860, 289 P.2d 520 [1972]; Annotation 56 A.L.R.2d 372) where the spontaneity of a declaration was held to have been correctly submitted to a jury, under instructions that they were to disregard it if found not to have been spontaneous.

That California decision is contrary to the practice in New York State, where the established rule is that it is for the court and not the jury to decide questions of fact preliminary to determining the admissibility of evidence (Harris v. Wilson, 7 Wend. 57 [1831]; Jones v. Hurlburt, 39 Barb. 403, 410 [1863]; Roberge v. Winne, 144 N.Y. 709, 715, 39 N.E. 631, 633 [1895]; Richardson, Evidence, § 195). In Roberge v. Winne, this court was confronted with conflicting testimony concerning whether a document offered in evidence was proper to be received. The opinion of the General Term is printed in the Court of Appeals Reports, where the affirmance was without majority opinion, stating: "It is apparent, therefore, that, before the paper offered could have been admitted the court had to decide a preliminary question of fact whether the plaintiff had such knowledge of the contents of the unsigned paper as to make it binding upon him as evidence; and, in deciding this question against the defendant, we cannot say, as matter of law, that the learned judge was in error."

* * *

This New York rule is not only well grounded in practice but is also sound in prin-

ciple. The admissibility of evidence may depend upon complicated, collateral fact issues, which would be confusing in jury trials. If, in addition to the questions of fact which are directly involved, any number of collateral issues must be tried in order to determine the admissibility of evidence upon the principal issue, it would obstruct rather than facilitate the administration of justice.

Submission to juries of the voluntariness of confessions by defendants in criminal cases is an exception to this general rule. The reason for making the exception is apparent. In such instances the confession or admission relates to the subject matter of the criminal action being tried, and the only collateral question is whether it was coerced by force or fear. That, in itself, has a bearing on the guilt or innocence of a defendant. An alleged confession or admission represents an endeavor to prove the charge at issue out of a defendant's mouth. It is advanced to prove recognition by the person charged with the crime that he himself did all or some of the things which constitute the crime charged. The voluntariness of such an admission or confession by a defendant is so intimately related to the merits of the controversy that it has become natural to submit to juries, along with the other issues on trial, whether defendants actually did say or write the damaging material which is ascribed to them. That is different from submitting to juries collateral issues of fact on which depend the admissibility of declarations by third parties.

In the case of dying declarations, it is held that "Whether the declarations were made in apprehension of death, and after the declarant had lost all hope of recovery, is to be determined by the judge" (Follett, J., People v. Kraft, 91 Hun 474, 475, 36 N.Y.S. 1034, 1035 [1896], affirmed 148 N.Y. 631, 43 N.E. 80). "The trial judge must determine, not only from the conversation of the declarant, but from the surrounding circumstances, that there is clear proof showing the certainty of speedy death and that the declarant had no hope of recovery. People v. Ludkowitz, 266 N.Y. 233, 239, 194 N.E. 688, [690] (1935)." (People v. Smith, 245 App.Div. 69, 71, 281 N.Y.S. 294, 299 [1935]). In Ludkowitz this court said (266 N.Y. 239, 194 N.E. 690

[1935]): "Whether the preliminary proof advanced is sufficient to admit the receipt in evidence of a dying declaration presents in each case a question which must be determined by the trial judge." Kraft and Del Vermo, supra, are cited as authority for this conclusion, along with People v. Smith, 104 N.Y. 491, 10 N.E. 873 (1887), in which it was held on the principal point of law in the case that it is the function of the court, and not of the jury, to rule upon preliminary questions of fact affecting the admissibility of dying declarations.

Although we are not here dealing with a dying declaration, the same principle applies that it is in the province of the court and not of the jury (as contended by appellant) to decide preliminary questions of fact on which the admissibility of the declaration depends. That applies in the case of alleged spontaneous declarations as it does to dying declarations. The law would be inconsistent if in the one kind of declaration preliminary fact questions were to be decided by the judge and in the other by the jury. On the record in this case it cannot be held that the Trial Judge erred as matter of law in finding the prelimi-

nary fact to be that the declaration of this homicidal victim lacked spontaneity, and that sufficient time had elapsed under the circumstances so that it could have been a reflective fabrication. The Trial Judge found that Pickens had opportunity to reflect and to contrive, which destroys the foundation upon which such declaration could be introduced under the Del Vermo decision.

It is argued for respondent that the evidence establishes as matter of law that Pickens had opportunity to reflect and to contrive before making this declaration, so that no preliminary question of fact was presented for the trial court to decide in ruling on the People's objection to the introduction of this declaration. We do not need to decide on that aspect, inasmuch as even if a preliminary question of fact was presented, it was resolved against appellant by the trial court.

* * *

The judgment of conviction should be affirmed.

* * *

Judgment affirmed.

RELATED DECISIONS
Complaints of Coerced Confession

People v. Tuomey
Supreme Court, Appellate Division,
Second Department, 1962.
17 A.D.2d 247, 234 N.Y.S.2d 318.

This case involves the involuntary nature of a confession to the police in that the prisoner alleges he was severely beaten and then confessed to the crime. Without my going further to explain this case, I think it appropriate to make some comments with respect to the situation in this case. You will note that the decision was from an appellate court and the incident occurred in 1960. It was not uncommon at that time for the police to "rough up" a prisoner who they thought was withholding information from them. The cliché at that time was that the prisoner slipped and fell on the

way to the station house. Fortunately, I do not believe that this is standard operating procedure in any law enforcement agency in the United States at this time. I advise all practitioners to avoid this type of behavior for three basic reasons:

1. It is against the law.
2. If the court believes the complaint of the defendant, the defendant may be acquitted of a crime that he or she actually committed when he or she might be convicted if other means were used to prove guilt beyond a reasonable doubt.
3. You never know what will happen to you in your lifetime, and you may be the subject of this treatment and be forced to confess to a crime that you did not commit.

I ask you to read this case because if I explain this case further, I will not be helping you learn how to read the law.

HILL, Justice.

Defendant was charged with breaking and entering a delicatessen store in Nassau County late Friday night, December 30, 1960, or during the early hours of the next morning, by breaking the front glass door and stealing five dollars from the cash register.

On that morning defendant was apprehended by the police and was taken to the First Precinct Station House in Baldwin. There he remained from about 12:55 P.M. until 3:27 P.M., during which time he made both an oral and a written confession. At the trial defendant claimed that the confession had been extracted from him as the result of a severe beating administered to him by the police.

Defendant claims that a number of errors during the trial deprived him of a fair trial. Only two of his contentions require extended consideration: (1) that, before reception in evidence of the confession, the trial court refused to allow defendant's counsel to show that it had been obtained from defendant as the result of severe beatings and that therefore it was not a voluntary confession; and (2) that the opportunity was denied him to prove through his parents that he (the defendant) had complained to them of such police brutality and that he had done so at the first opportunity he had had to complain to someone other than the police or other than those in apparent authority.

There can be little doubt that it is the law of this State that, where it is claimed that a confession is not voluntary, the defendant's counsel has the right to make a most searching examination before the confession may be submitted to the jury for its consideration. Here the defendant, a youth of 18 years, while he was in the custody of the police, was injured sufficiently to require treatment at a hospital. The police maintained that his injuries were caused by his falling down a flight of stairs. On the trial, before the oral confession was offered in evidence, the court denied to defendant a *voir dire* examination concerning the confession. The court ruled

that the right to such a preliminary examination applied to a written confession, but not to an oral one.

In our judgment, such ruling was error and deprived the defendant of a fair trial (People v. Doran, 246 N.Y. 409, 159 N.E. 379; People v. Fox, 121 N.Y. 449, 24 N.E. 923). In the Fox case, Judge O'Brien, speaking for the court, said (121 N.Y. 453, 454, 24 N.E. 923, 924):

"It frequently happens that the testimony is of such a character as to require the court to submit the question to the jury, to be rejected by them altogether, or given such weight as, under all the circumstances, the jury may deem proper to give to the alleged confession. But when, as in this case, a written confession of guilt is offered against a person on trial for a criminal offense, and he objects to the same, and offers to prove to the court that it was procured from him by threats or promises, or under such circumstances as would render it incompetent as evidence, it is error to receive the paper without first hearing the proof offered, and deciding upon the competency of the confession as evidence against the party making it. Com. v. Culver, 126 Mass. 464.

"When the paper in question was read to the jury, under the sanction of the court, without first hearing what the defendant had to allege against its competency, he was to that extent denied a fair trial, though the paper was received conditionally, with the understanding that it should be stricken out of the case if it afterwards was shown to be incompetent."

It is also our opinion that the Trial Court committed reversible error by excluding testimony that defendant, at the first opportunity, had complained to his parents of the alleged beatings by the police. The gravity of such error was emphasized by the fact that the examining doctor, although admitting that the defendant had complained to him that he had been beaten by the police, nevertheless in his report he (the doctor) failed to make any reference to such complaint about the police brutality. As stated in a similar case (People v. Alex, 260 N.Y. 425, 428–429, 183 N.E. 906, 907, 85 A.L.R. 939):

"The trial judge charged that the jury could consider the written confession only in the event that they found that it was not made under the influence of fear produced by threats. That was a vital issue in the case. When that issue is involved, the question of whether a defendant made complaint of mistreatment at the first opportunity or within a reasonable time is material and relevant. It is of great assistance to the jury in determining whether a defendant's claim that a confession was induced by threats and fear is the truth or an afterthought, a concocted story to escape the effect of the confession. If complaint is not timely made, when it is made suspicion is aroused that it is a subterfuge. . . .

"This refusal by the trial court to receive such testimony was highly prejudicial to the defendant, and constitutes reversible error."

It follows, therefore, that the judgment of conviction should be reversed on the law and on the facts and a new trial ordered.

Judgment reversed on the law and on the facts, and a new trial ordered.

KLEINFELD, CHRIST and HOPKINS, JJ., concur with HILL, J.

BELDOCK, P. J., dissents and votes to affirm the judgment.

RELATED DECISIONS
Startled Utterances

United States v. Sherlock
United States Court of Appeals, Ninth Circuit, 1988.
865 F.2d 1069.

In this case, excited utterances by two alleged rape victims were not admissible under Federal Rule of Evidence 803(2) because they did not qualify as excited utterances. These statements were made approximately one hour after the event as well as even later. The alleged victims had spoken to many persons after the event and did not complain of the event, and they had time to fabricate an excuse for their lateness.

Before: WRIGHT and POOLE, Circuit Judges, and WILLIAMS, District Judge.
EUGENE A. WRIGHT, Circuit Judge:

After a troublesome joint trial, a jury convicted Arnold Sherlock and Ronald Charley of assault with intent to commit rape on an Indian Reservation. This week-long trial involved the contradictory testimony of witnesses, the temporary exclusion of family members from the courtroom, prosecutorial misconduct, and several motions for severance and mistrial.

Sherlock and Charley raise many errors. They contend that excessive preindictment delay denied them due process; the court failed to afford them a public trial; its failure

to sever the trials, as well as prosecutorial misconduct, denied them a fair trial; and it erred in admitting hearsay testimony and in rejecting suggested jury instructions.

We reverse Sherlock's conviction and remand for a new trial. The court committed reversible error in denying his motions for mistrial and severance primarily based on the prosecutor's misuse of Charley's extrajudicial statement implicating Sherlock. Although the joint trial may have prejudiced Charley, we conclude that it did not deny him a fair trial. We affirm his conviction.

GENERAL FACTS

The alleged rapes of Marie Rose Bennally and Thomascita Billie occurred several miles from their school on a Navajo Indian Reservation in Arizona. On March 9, 1984, the girls accompanied four Navajo Indians, including Sherlock and Charley, in a truck off the school grounds. They stopped near a windmill in the countryside where two other Indian males joined them. All drank beer except M. Sherlock, who left before the alleged crimes. At trial both girls testified that the boys forced them to drink beer. Other witnesses contradicted that testimony.

Later, the group drove further from the school and stopped in an open area. Billie testified that while in the truck with Sherlock, he locked the doors and raped her. Bennally testified that she had left the truck to go to the bathroom when Charley tripped her and forced her to have sexual intercourse.

After the alleged rapes, both girls walked to the nearby Clitso residence. Robert Clitso gave them a ride back to the dorm, where they arrived after curfew. Later that night, both girls were interviewed by Navajo investigators and examined by a physician. At trial, many questions arose as to statements made to the Clitsos, persons at the dorm, and investigators.

PROCEDURAL BACKGROUND

The original indictment charged Sherlock, Charley, M. Sherlock, and E. White, Jr. in five counts with rape and related sexual offenses. Because of the common counts, crimes and evidence, the government intended to try all four defendants together. Before trial, however, the government dropped all charges against M. Sherlock and the several assault charges. On the first day of trial it dismissed with prejudice the charges against White. The final indictment consisted of only three counts. It charged Sherlock with rape of Thomascita Billie and charged Charley with rape of Marie Rose Bennally and carnal knowledge of her.

Sherlock and Charley moved to dismiss based on excessive preindictment delay and loss of physical evidence obtained from the alleged victims. Sherlock also moved to sever the trials on grounds that the likely admission of a statement by Charley implicating him would violate his Fifth and Sixth Amendment rights. The court denied those motions, which were renewed at trial.

The week-long trial involved inconsistent testimony from the alleged victims and other witnesses. During Bennally's testimony, the judge temporarily excluded defendants' families after he determined that closure was necessary to protect her from disruptive spectators. Neither defendant testified and only Charley put on additional witnesses in his defense. Each based his defense on the government's failure to prove guilt.

A jury convicted both defendants of assault with intent to commit rape on an Indian Reservation. 18 U.S.C. §§ 113(a), 1153. The court imposed a sentence of three years on Sherlock and five years on Charley. Both moved for a new trial, which the court denied.

Because defendants' arguments must be considered in the context of their unusual trial, we provide more detailed facts as required by our analysis of several issues.

* * *

B. Hearsay Testimony from Nez

Charley objected to admission of testimony by Nez, who was the roommate of Billie and Bennally at the time of the alleged crimes. The testimony included statements that the girls had informed Nez that they had been raped. The court admitted that hearsay under the excited utterance exception. Fed.R.Evid. 803(2). We review for abuse of discretion. United States v. Cowley, 720 F.2d 1037, 1040 (9th Cir. 1983), cert. denied, 465 U.S. 1029, 104 S.Ct. 1290, 79 L.Ed.2d 692 (1984).

Billie made her statement approximately one hour after the assault. Bennally made her statement even later. Both had spoken to several persons before telling Nez they had been raped. They had time to think about their actions and to invent an excuse about their late arrival at the dorm with alcohol on their breath. The hearsay statements do not fall under the scope of the excited utterance exception. See United States v. McLennan, 563 F.2d 943, 948 (9th Cir. 1977) (declarant must be so excited or distraught that he did not reflect on what he was saying), cert. denied, 435 U.S. 969, 98 S.Ct. 1607, 56 L.Ed.2d 60 (1978).

Even if the statements do not come within a hearsay exception, their admission was harmless. At least two other witnesses testified that the girls had told them they had been raped. We conclude that even if admission of Nez's testimony was erroneous, it is not ground for reversal.

C. Jury Instruction on Credibility

Finally, defendants claim that the court erred in refusing their instruction on the credibility of witnesses. They argue that this denied them their theory of defense, which was that the victims' stories were lies. See United States v. Ibarra-Alcarez, 830 F.2d 968, 973 (9th Cir. 1987) (defendant entitled to an instruction covering the defense theory with a legal basis and some evidentiary support); United States v. Escobar de Bright, 742 F.2d 1196, 1201 (9th Cir. 1984) (failure to instruct jury on a defense theory that is legally sound and supported by the evidence is *per se* reversible).

They offered an instruction that the jury might discredit all of a witness's testimony if it found the witness had lied on a material issue. The court instead gave this circuit's pattern instruction dealing with witness credibility. It instructed the jury that they could "disbelieve all or any part of any witness's testimony." That instruction allowed the jury to adopt the defendants' theory of the case. "It is not error to refuse a proposed instruction if the other instructions, when viewed in their entirety, cover that theory." Ibarra-Alcarez, 830 F.2d at 973; United States v. Hayes, 794 F.2d 1348, 1351 (9th Cir. 1986), *cert. denied*, 479 U.S. 1086, 107 S.Ct. 1289, 94 L.Ed.2d 146 (1987). The court did not abuse its discretion in refusing defendants' proposed instruction and in giving this circuit's model instruction.

CONCLUSION

We REVERSE Sherlock's conviction and remand for a new trial. WE AFFIRM Charley's conviction.

The mandate will issue now.

* * *

✔ PRACTICE QUESTIONS

Select the most correct answer to complete each statement.

1. The statement of an injured person is admissible into evidence for the truth of the assertion under the res gestae exception if
   (a) it is made within ten minutes of the occurrence.
   (b) the injured person is asked what happened and that person makes the statement immediately after being asked.
   (c) the injured person makes the statement immediately after he or she is injured.
   (d) the statement is reduced to writing and the injured person signs the statement under oath.

2. A spontaneous utterance, arising from a principal fact, made by an agent or employee is
   (a) not admissible because the person may be fearful of losing the employment.
   (b) admissible because the person should know the policy of the principal or employer.
   (c) not admissible because it would bind the principal or employer.
   (d) admissible because it is treated the same as a spontaneous utterance of any other observer.

3. The following circumstance may result in the admission of the statement under the res gestae exception to the hearsay exclusionary rule:
   (a) a hearsay statement that is presumed not admissible, but one that should be admitted, if it can be shown that it was made contemporaneously with the event, and that there is little likelihood of prefabrication, or deliberation.
   (b) a statement made outside of court that is offered in the trial to prove the facts that are contained in it.
   (c) a statement that relates to the main event and that explains, elucidates, or in some manner characterizes the event.
   (d) not a statement of fact, but the mere expression of an opinion.

4. In examining most cases, the statement or declaration concerning which testimony is offered must, in order to be admissible as part of the res gestae, possess at least the following essential element:
   (a) it must be a mere narrative of the past completed affair.
   (b) it must be the product of premeditation, reflection, or design.
   (c) it must be made by one who neither participated in the act nor witnessed the act or fact concerning which the declaration, or statement, was made.
   (d) it must be a spontaneous or instinctive utterance of thought dominated or evoked by the transaction or occurrence itself.

Indicate whether each statement is true or false.

5. "V" was the victim in a homicide in which a gun was used. He was heard to have said immediately after the shooting, "Mary, you bitch of a wife, why did you have to shoot me?" "W" was present during the whole episode and attempted to testify as to what "V" had said. This statement was not admitted in evidence at the trial of Mary for manslaughter. The action of the judge in excluding this evidence was proper because it was hearsay.

6. "W," a witness, heard another person, "B," say that he had heard "V," the victim, cry out immediately after he had been stabbed, "I missed the first draw this time, but I'll get you the next time." At the trial of "D," the accused, "W" was not permitted to testify as to what "B" had said. This was a proper ruling of the presiding judge.

7. "V," a victim of rape, was thrown out of a moving vehicle at 10:00 in the evening and was moderately injured. She had been held captive by her assailant for three days before she was freed in this manner. She managed to get up and walk to the first house that had illumination. She rang the bell and told the woman answering the door that she had been raped repeatedly and had been held captive for three days. The alleged assailant was later brought to trial. At the trial, the woman to whom the victim had complained was permitted to testify as to what "V" had said to her when "V" appeared at the door. This was properly received in evidence.

CHAPTER 9

Dying Declaration Exception to Hearsay Exclusionary Rule

§ 9.1 INTRODUCTION

In the discipline of criminal justice, it frequently becomes necessary for a police officer or a prosecuting official to gather admissible evidence on short notice and with little time for reflection or preparation. The dying declaration is an example of this type of situation. Theoretically, there are certain requirements in the law that must be recited to the dying declarant. It appears on the surface to be a matter of fact inquiry easily accomplished.

However, if one experiences this situation, one normally has to have nerves of steel to carry it through to a successful conclusion. The elements necessary for the admissibility of a dying declaration are as follows:

1. The declarant must be in extremis.
2. The declarant must be under a sense of impending death without any hope of recovery.
3. The declarant, if living, would be a competent witness.
4. The declaration must relate to facts and circumstances surrounding the death of the declarant and not to the declarant's opinion or conclusion.

§ 9.2 REASON FOR EXCEPTION

You will remember that if the statement is offered for the truth of the assertion and the declarant is not available for cross-examination, it is a hearsay statement. You will also remember that any exception to the hearsay exclusionary rule is based on the probability of reliability. In the case of the dying declaration, the presumption is made that the declarant who is certain of impending death wants to make peace with God and will speak the truth; hence, the probability of reliability. I have conducted polls of my classes during the past several years with respect to the probability of reliability of a dying declaration, and without exception, the students have voted against the acceptance of a dying declaration because they contend that the religious influence that gave rise to this exception is not as prevalent as it was in yesteryear. Perhaps an additional element should be added to those indicated above—that the declarant had a reputation in the community of being a religious or God-fearing person.

Nevertheless, courts still accept the dying declaration as an exception to the hearsay exclusionary rule. The principle on which dying declarations are received in evidence is that the mind, impressed with the awful idea of approaching dissolution, acts under a sanction equally powerful with that which it is presumed to feel by a solemn appeal to God upon an oath. N.Y.—People v. Sarzano, 212 N.Y. 231, 234, 106 N.E. 87, 88 (1914).

§ 9.3 ADMISSIBILITY OF DYING DECLARATIONS

§ 9.4 Specified Cases

It has been generally held that dying declarations are not admissible in civil cases. Miss.—Phillips v. Dow Chem. Co., 247 Miss. 293, 151 So.2d 199 (1963). The exception to this is where the declaration is part of the res gestae. Some jurisdictions permit dying declarations in civil actions by statute. Cal.Evid. Code § 1242; Colo.—Barsch v. Hammond, 110 Colo. 441, 135 P.2d 519 (1943). The dying declaration is usually admitted in homicide cases, and the declaration that is admitted is how the deceased's injuries resulting in his or her impending death occurred and who the person was that brought about this mortal injury. Certain jurisdictions permit the use of a dying declaration in the case of a criminal abortion where the victim dies before trial. This is not universally accepted. It is, however, safe to say that it is applicable in homicide cases when the victim is not available for the trial. Naturally, where the victim believes he is about to die and later recovers, any statement made by him as a dying declaration is not admissible as a dying declaration. However, it might be admissible as a prior inconsistent statement and may be used for impeachment purposes. In any event, the declaration must relate to the facts and circumstances pertaining to the injury or death. U.S.—Henry H. Cross Co. v. Simmons, 96 F.2d 482 (8th Cir. 1938).

Where the cause or circumstances of declarant's death are not relevant to the issues in the case, any statement allegedly made by the decedent regarding his or her impending death is not admissible as a dying declaration. Tex.—Thompson v. Mays, 707 S.W.2d 951 (Tex. 1986). Some states permit the use of dying declarations in physician license revocation proceedings. Neb.—State *ex rel*. Sorensen v. Lake, 121 Neb. 331, 236 N.W. 762 (1931).

§ 9.5 Requirements

§ 9.5(a) Declarant in extremis   In order for a dying declaration to be admissible, the declarant must be in extremis; that is, he or she must be imminently dying from the injury he or she has received and must have little time to live. In some cases, the declarant's statement was not admissible because this element of the exception to the hearsay exclusionary rule was absent. For example, where a deceased made statements relating to how he received his injury and these statements were made while he was a patient in a hospital following an operation for a hernia where it appeared, from medical testimony, that at no time while he was in the hospital was he considered to be a dying man, nor was his condition considered critical, except that a blood clot in his leg might dislodge, his statements were held to be inadmissible. Or.—Mercep v. State Indus. Accident Commission, 167 Or. 460, 118 P.2d 1061 (1941).

§ 9.5(b) Declarant under a sense of impending death   The declarant must be conscious of impending death and without any hope of recovery or expectation of recovery. Kan.—Ritchie v. Metropolitan Life Ins. Co., 145 Kan. 525, 66 P.2d 622 (1937).

In Barnard v. Keathley, 249 Ark. 346, 459 S.W.2d 121 (1970), it was held that where decedent was more anxious to consult with a lawyer than a physician on the date of his death, the trial court's refusal to admit his wife's proffered declaration, which decedent allegedly made to her to show that decedent was conscious of impending death, was not error. Let us assume that the following questions are being asked of the victim. "Mr. V, I am Officer Law, and this is Doctor Medicine. I understand that Doctor Medicine has told you that you are about to die from the injuries you have just received. Is that true?" After an affirmative answer, the officer continues. "Mr. V, do you have any hope of recovery?" After a negative answer, the officer again continues. "Do you wish to tell us who caused your injury and the facts relating to this injury?" After an affirmative answer, the decedent proceeds to identify the assailant and the circumstances of the infliction of the injury. As Officer Law and Doctor Medicine are about to leave the room, the victim turns to Dr. Medicine and says, "Doc, please save me." The last statement indicates that despite what the victim said earlier, he still has a hope of recovery, and hence his dying declaration should not be admitted.

§ 9.5(c) Competency of declarant   The declarant must be competent to testify to the facts which he declares. He must be as competent to testify to these facts as though he were present on the witness stand at the time of trial. Colo.—Barsch v. Hammond, *supra*. Accordingly, he should know the seriousness of an oath, have knowledge of the facts declared (U.S.—Henry H. Cross Co. v. Simmons, *supra*), and be of sound mind. He may not testify as to an opinion or conclusion unless he was able to do so had he lived (i.e., an expert in the particular discipline of the question). If the declaration is a suspicion or surmise, it is not admissible. N.Y.—People v. Shaw, 63 N.Y. 36 (1875).

§ 9.5(d) Declaration relative to facts surrounding declarant's death   A dying declaration must consist of facts and circumstances which led to the declarant's death. When a declarant's statement consists of opinions where the declarant had no knowledge or opportunity for knowledge of the facts included in the alleged dying declaration, the statement may not be admitted. Henry H. Cross Co. v. Simmons, *supra*.

§ 9.6 FORM OF DECLARATION

A dying declaration may be oral or in writing. There is no precise form, and it is discretionary with the trial court as to whether or not it should be admitted. N.Y.—People v. Smith, 104 N.Y. 491, 10 N.E. 873 (1887).

§ 9.7 WEIGHT OF DECLARATION

The weight of the evidence which is to be attributed to a dying declaration is determined by the jury. N.Y.—People v. Ludkowitz, 266 N.Y. 233, 194 N.E. 688 (1935). Upon request, the trial court is required to instruct the injury that a dying declaration is not to be regarded as having the same value and weight as the sworn testimony of a witness in open court. N.Y.—People v. Mleczko, 298 N.Y. 153, 81 N.E.2d 65 (1948).

§ 9.8 DYING DECLARATION—NOT A VIOLATION OF CONSTITUTIONAL PROTECTION

Under the United States Constitution and the constitutions of most states, the defendant is in a criminal prosecution entitled to confront witnesses against him or her by means of cross-examination. Many cases have attacked the constitutionality of the admission of testimony from a declarant who cannot be cross-examined. The courts have unanimously held that this objection is not tenable on the ground that such a declarant is not a witness within the meaning of such a provision, the concept being that the right accrues to a defendant against any living witness, not a dead one. N.Y.—People v. Corey, 157 N.Y. 332, 51 N.E. 1024 (1898); Pa.—Brown v. Commonwealth, 73 Pa. 321, 13 Am.Rep. 740 (1873). The defendant may still exercise his or her right of cross-examination by cross-examining the living witness who is testifying about the statement made by the dying declarant.

§ 9.9 FEDERAL RULE

Rule 804. Hearsay Exceptions: Declarant Unavailability

(b) Hearsay Exceptions. . . .

(2) *Statement Under Belief of Impending Death.* In a prosecution for homicide or in a civil action or proceeding, a statement made by a declarant while believing that the declarant's death was imminent, concerning the cause or circumstances of what the declarant believed to be impending death.

CROSS-REFERENCES

Federal Civil Judicial Procedure and Rules (West 1996) (Rule 804[b][2]).
Goode & Wellborn, Courtroom Handbook on Federal Evidence (West 1995) (Rule 804[b][2]).
McCormick, Evidence (4th ed. 1992) (Rule 804[b][2]).

```
R E L A T E D   D E C I S I O N S
Hearsay—Dying Declaration
```

People v. Sarzano

Court of Appeals of New York, 1914.
212 N.Y. 231, 106 N.E. 87.

This case explains the requirements of the dying declaration, discussed above. More particularly, it explains that a decedent must be certain that he or she is about to die and has absolutely no hope of recovery. This could be shown by the actions of the decedent, in addition to his or her statement. The approved actions that could have been manifested are mentioned by the court and should be itemized by you.

PER CURIAM. The appellant was convicted of the crime of murder in the first degree in Erie county, on February 28, 1913. He shot Saverio Gragnanello November 17, 1912, at Buffalo. Gragnanello died January 22, 1913, as the result of the shooting, as the jury found.

The trial court erred in receiving in evidence as a dying declaration the statement made by the deceased on November 17, 1912, after he had been taken to the hospital. The statement was made to Dr. George B. Stocker, who was the deputy medical examiner for Erie county. Dr. Stocker told the deceased "that his condition was critical, and we expected he would die from the way he was, and we wanted his statement for use later." "I talked to him and told him the condition he was in and that he was going to die, and I wanted an ante mortem statement for purposes that might arise later." The deceased said, "All right," he would give it, and made statements, which were written down and read to him by Dr. Stocker. The written statement was:

"Dying declaration of Salvita Greniera made on the 17th day of November, 1912, at Emergency Hospital in the city of Buffalo, county of Erie, to Geo. B. Stocker, deputy medical examiner of said county.

"He says: I consider my condition critical, and am under the influence of an impression that I am about to die, and have no hopes of my recovery from the effects of my wound. I make this statement under that impression.

"I live at 164–8 Erie street and am a saloon-keeper by occupation. My wife was in the back room of saloon and this man Mike by name and I do not know his last name went back to this room and I went back there and asked him what he wanted and told him to go out. He drew a gun and said he would shoot me. I asked him what he wanted to shoot for and again told him to go out. He immediately shot me five times. Then he ran out of the back door. I never had any trouble with him before. He was not drunk. This was between seven and eight o'clock tonight.

his
"Salvitas X Greniera."
mark

The objection to its admission "on the ground there is nothing in evidence except the statement which the doctor wrote that showed he thought he was going to die, and that his death was to be speedy," was overruled with an exception.

The learned district attorney seems confident that the statement was admissible. He points out the three wounds; that the deceased was about to undergo an operation; that a doctor told him he was in a critical condition, and they did not expect him to live; and that he stated he was under the influence of an impression or under an impression that he was about to die. The statements of the district attorney must, however, be modified in these particulars: There is no proof that the deceased knew that he was about to undergo an operation, or that the person talking to him was a doctor, or that he stated that he was under the impression that he was about to die. The statement was upon a printed blank, and the only affirmative statements of the deceased it contains are those including and following the words "I live at 164–8 Erie Street." Above those the blanks of the printed form were properly filled, and the entire statement read to him, and he said it was true.

The principle upon which dying declarations are received in evidence is that the mind, impressed with the awful idea of approaching dissolution, acts under a sanction equally powerful with that which it is presumed to feel by a solemn appeal to God upon an oath. The declarations, therefore, of a person dying under such circumstances are considered as equivalent to the evidence of the living witness upon oath. Commonwealth v. Roberts, 108 Mass. 296 (1871). Safety in receiving such declarations lies only in the fact that the declarant is so controlled by a belief that his death is certain and imminent that malice, hatred, passion, and other feelings of like nature are overwhelmed and banished by it. The evidence should be clear that the declarations were made under a sense of impending death without any hope of recovery. People v. Conklin, 175 N.Y. 333, 67 N.E. 624 (1903). Statements made by a doctor to and accepted by a declarant that there was no chance of his recovering are admissible. Commonwealth v. Brewer, 164 Mass. 577, 42 N.E. 92 (1895); Brotherton v. People, 75 N.Y. 159 (1878). If the declarant thinks there is a slight chance of living, the declarations are inadmissible. Commonwealth v. Roberts, 108 Mass. 296 (1871); Commonwealth v. Haney, 127 Mass. 455 (1879). The mere fact that the doctor told declarant that recovery was impossible is insufficient. There must be proof that the declarant believed it and had no hope of recovery. Peak v. State, 50 N.J.Law. 179, 12 Atl. 701 (1888); People v. Chase, 79 Hun, 296, 29 N.Y.Supp. 376 (1894), affirmed 143 N.Y. 669, 39 N.E. 21; People v. Evans, 40 Hun. 492 (1886). Declarant's certainty that he is about to die and lack of all hope of recovery may be proven by his express language or conduct, or inferred from his physical condition and obvious danger, or evidence of his acquiescence in the opinions of doctors or others stated to him, or other adequate circumstances. Williams v. State, 168 Ind. 87, 79 N.E. 1079 (1907); State v. Sullivan, 20 R.I. 114, 37 Atl. 673 (1897).

In the present case the preliminary proof was too slight and indefinite to justify the admission of the statement. The transaction, apart from the wounds, was this: A strange man said to the deceased when received at the hospital that his condition was critical and he was going to die, and they wanted an ante mortem statement for purposes that might arise later, and the deceased said "All right," he would give it, and the statement that he made the statement under "the influence of an impression that I am about to die, and have no hopes of my recovery from the effects of my wounds. I make this statement under that impression"—was read over to him with the other parts of the statement, and said by him to be true. The declarant did not ask for wife, children, friends, or priest or by word or act indicate that he believed his death certain and imminent. He did not say or show that he believed he would not recover and was without any hope whatsoever of living. It would be extending the rule beyond the decision in any case we have read or found, and we think beyond safety, to approve the reception in evidence of the statement. But we do not think we should reverse the judgment because of its reception. The guilt of the defendant was fully proven without it. It, in fact, added nothing to the case. The facts stated in it were proven aliunde and with great fullness and detail. It is inconceivable that the verdict of the jury would have been different had it been rejected.

The judgment of conviction should be affirmed.

* * *

Judgment of conviction affirmed.

Brown v. Commonwealth
Supreme Court of Pennsylvania, 1873.
73 Pa. 321, 13 Am.Rep. 740.

This is an old case that is primarily based on the common law concept of stare decisis. This concept still survives today in most of the states of the United States that rely on common law combined with statutory law. Statutory law is that law that is promulgated and passed by a legislative body, such as the House of Representatives and the Senate of the United States, and then signed by the chief executive officer, such as the president of the United States. Of course, the president has veto power, which may be overridden in the House of Representatives and the Senate.

It is not the intention of this text to delve into constitutional law, but from time to time, I may point out certain aspects of constitutional law, as I have done here, to make the decision more understandable.

You will note that this decision refers to the case as having arrived in the appellate court on a writ of error. To my knowledge, this means of bringing a case to an appellate court has been replaced in all jurisdictions either by an appeal or a writ of certiorari or by a certified question of law. I will leave the definition of these terms to a course in constitutional law.

You may observe that the word "offense" is spelled as "offence." This is not an error; it was spelled in that way in the United States and is still spelled that way in many countries in the British Empire and in other countries using the English language.

This case explains the various applications of the dying declaration under the hearsay exclusionary rule. State and federal statutes now usually admit testimony in evidence at a subsequent trial when that testimony originally occurred at an earlier trial between the same parties or at a hearing touching on the same subject matter. The notes of a witness to the statements are also admissible where the opposing side has an opportunity to cross-examine the witness. However, admission of these notes may be dependent on whether the witness is dead or unavailable at the time of the trial.

March 7th 1873. Before READ, C. J., AGNEW, SHARSWOOD and MERCUR, JJ. WILLIAMS, J., at Nisi Prius.

Error to the Criminal Court of Schuylkill County: No. 78, to January Term 1873.

* * *

The opinion of the court was delivered April 5th 1873.

READ, C. J. This is a writ of error to the Criminal Court of Schuylkill county, sued out under the Act of the 15th February 1870, upon the oath of the defendant, and brings up the whole record.

The constitutionality and jurisdiction of this court have been finally settled in Commonwealth v. Green, 8 P. F. Smith 226, and in Commonwealth v. Hipple, 19 Id. 9, and its concurrent jurisdiction with the Courts of

Quarter Sessions of the Peace and Oyer and Terminer and General Jail Delivery of the County of Schuylkill, is fully recognized and established by the Act of 22d April 1870 (Pamph. L. 1254), and the court below were therefore right on overruling the plea to the jurisdiction, entered by the defendant.

On the preliminary hearing before the committing magistrate, the defendant and his counsel being present, a witness was examined whose testimony was taken down by defendant's counsel, and the witness having died before the trial, the notes of his evidence proved by the counsel under oath, were offered in evidence, objected to and admitted. It was objected that by the Constitution of the state, the defendant was entitled to meet the witnesses face to face.

The doctrine on this subject is thus laid down in the 3d volume of Russell on Crimes, by Greaves, 4th edition, 1865, page 249. "If there has been a previous criminal prosecution between the same parties, and the point in issue was the same, the testimony of a deceased witness, given upon oath at the former trial, is admissible on the subsequent trial, and may be proved by any one who heard him give evidence," and the same is repeated at page 424, in the note. We find the same rule in 1 Phillips & Arnold's Evidence, pp. 306–7, and in 1 Pitt Taylor on Evidence, 4th edition, 1864, pp. 445, 447. Dr. Wharton in his valuable Treatise on Criminal Law in the United States, vol. 1, p. 667, says:

> "The testimony of a deceased witness given at a former trial or examination may be proved at a subsequent trial by persons who heard him testify. Even the notes of counsel of the testimony of such witness on a former trial between the same parties, touching the same subject-matter, are evidence when proved to be correct in substance, although the counsel does not recollect the testimony independently of his notes. The better opinion seems to be that it is sufficient to prove the substance of what the deceased witness said, provided the material particulars are stated, though it has been sometimes held, that unless the precise words could be given, the testimony would be rejected."

In The Commonwealth v. Richards, 18 Pick. 434 (1836), it was held that the 12th article of the Declaration of Rights, which provides that in criminal cases the accused shall have the right "to meet the witnesses against him face to face," is not violated by the admission of testimony in a criminal trial before a jury to prove what a deceased witness testified at the preliminary examination of the accused before a justice of the peace."

This case was affirmed seven years afterwards in Warren v. Nichols, in 6 Metc. 261 (1843), and the further ruling in that case "that the whole of the testimony of the deceased witness upon the point in question, and the *precise words used by him* must be proved," was substantially affirmed. Hubbard, Justice, dissented from this ruling and assigned very cogent reasons against it. "As the decision now stands," says this able judge, "it prescribes a rule for the admission of testimony, which the imperfection of our nature, in the construction of our memories, will not warrant. It in truth excludes the thing it proposes to admit, and at the same time opens a door for knaves to enter, where honest men cannot approach." "Other learned judges have maintained, that a rule so rigid was unwise, and I confess, I prefer the reasoning of Gibson, J., in the case of Cornell v. Green, 10 S. & R. 16, to that to the learned judge in Commonwealth v. Richards, and with him agrees also the learned author of the Treatise on the Law of Evidence." 1 Greenl. § 165.

Upon this subject the ablest discussion of the whole question is to be found in the opinion of Judge Drummond, in the United States v. Macomb, 5 McLane's Rep. 286, delivered in the Circuit Court of the United States for the District of Illinois, at July Term 1851. At the preliminary examination, a witness, since deceased, testified in relation to the offence, which was robbing the mail. The accused was present and his counsel cross-examined the witness. Witnesses were permitted on a trial before a jury, under an indictment found for the same offence, to prove what the deceased witness testified to at the preliminary examination. It is sufficient in such case to prove substantially, all that the deceased witness testified upon the particular subject of inquiry. A decision upon the same point is to be found in United States v. White, 5 Cranch's Circuit Court Rep. 460.

The 6th article of the amendments to the Constitution of the United States provides that in all criminal prosecutions the accused shall enjoy the right "to be confronted with the witnesses against him."

The Constitution of Pennsylvania of 1776, provided "that in all prosecutions for criminal offences, a man hath a right to be confronted with the witnesses." The Declaration of Rights, in the Constitution of 1790, changed the phraseology from confronting, to "to meet the witnesses face to face."

The doctrine enunciated by Judge Drummond in 1851, was followed by the Supreme Court of Missouri, after a very exhaustive argument on the constitutional question, in The State v. McO'Blenis, in 24 Missouri (3 Jones) 402, and The State v. Baker, Id. 437, in 1857, and in The State v. Houser, 26 Missouri (5 Jones 431), in 1858, and by the Supreme Court of Ohio in Summons v. The State, in 5 Ohio (N.S.) 325, in 1856.

In this state the most liberal rule has been adopted, in relation to the evidence of what was testified to by a deceased witness on a former trial or examination, as will be seen by referring to Cornell v. Green, 10 S. & R. 14; Chess v. Chess, 17 Id. 409; Moore v. Pearson, 6 W. & S. 50, and Rhine v. Robinson, 3 Casey 30, in which case Chief Justice Lewis said: "The notes of counsel, showing what a deceased witness testified to on a former trial between the same parties touching the same subject-matter, are evidence when proved to be correct in substance, although the counsel did not recollect the testimony independent of his notes, and although he did not recollect the cross-examination." To which may be added the decision in Phila. & Reading R. R. v. Spearen, 11 Wright 306 (1849), the opinion being delivered by my brother Agnew.

There was, therefore, no error in the court admitting the notes of Mr. McCool of the testimony of Ewing, a deceased witness, in the examination before the committing magistrate, or the notes of any other counsel, or those of the committing magistrate himself.

"Upon the trial of any indictment for murder, or voluntary manslaughter, it shall and may be lawful for the defendant or defendants to except to any decision of the court, upon any point of evidence or law, which exception shall be noted by the court, and filed of record as in civil cases, and a writ of error to the Supreme Court may be taken by the defendant or defendants after conviction and sentence." "If, during the trial upon any indictment for murder or voluntary manslaughter, the court shall be required by the defendant or defendants to give an opinion upon any point submitted and stated in writing, it shall be the duty of the court to answer the same fully and file the point and answer, with the records of the case." Criminal Procedure Act of 31st March 1860, §§ 57, 58, Pamph.L. 444.

Under this head is ranged the reception under objection of the dying declarations of Mrs. Kraemer, the wife of the murdered man. "The dying declarations of a person who expects to die, respecting the circumstances under which he received a mortal injury, are constantly admitted in criminal prosecutions, where the death is the subject of criminal inquiry, though the prosecution be for manslaughter; though the accused was not present when they were made, and had no opportunity for cross-examination, and against or in favor of the party charged with the death." "When every hope of this world is gone, when every motive to falsehood is silenced, and the mind is induced by the most powerful considerations to speak the truth, a situation so solemn and awful is considered by the law as creating the most impressive of sanctions." 1 Wharton's Criminal Law, § 669; 3 Russel by Greaves 250; 1 Greenleaf, §§ 156, 162, 346; 1 Taylor on Evidence 616.

"The constitutional provision," says Dr. Wharton, "that the accused shall be confronted by the witnesses against him does not *abrogate* the common law principle, that the declarations *in extremis* of the murdered person in such cases are admissible in evidence." Id.

In Woodsides v. The State, 2 Howard 655 (Miss. 1837), the court, at p. 665, in answer to the constitutional objection that the prisoner had a right to be confronted with the witness against him, say: "But it is upon the ground alone, that the murdered individual is not a witness, that his declarations made in *extremis* can be offered in evidence upon the trial of the accused. If he were or could be a witness,

his declaration upon the clearest principle would be inadmissible. His declarations are regarded as facts or circumstances connected with the murder, which, when they are established by oral testimony, the law has declared to be evidence. It is the individual who swears to the statements of the deceased that is the witness, not the deceased." In Anthony v. The State of Tennessee, 1 Meigs 277 (1838), the court says, upon the first ground of objection, "We are all of opinion that the Bill of Rights cannot be construed to prevent declarations properly made *in articulo mortis* from being given in evidence against defendants in cases of homicide."

The same doctrine is to be found in The State of Iowa v. Nash, 7 Iowa 347 (1859), and in Robbins v. State of Ohio, 8 Ohio St.R. (N.S.) 131 (1857); Com. v. Casey, 11 Cushing 417 (1853), and very directly in Com. v. Carey, 12 Id. 246. There are also various statements to the same effect in most of the decisions cited above in relation to the admission of evidence of the testimony of a deceased witness.

All these cases are confined to the dying declarations of the murdered person upon the trial of the individual accused of the murder. At the York assizes on the 17th July 1837, in Rex v. Baker, 2 Moo. & Rob. 53, it was held, on an indictment against a prisoner for the murder of A. by poison, which was also taken by B., who died in consequence, that B.'s dying declarations were admissible. Coltman, J., after consulting Parke, B., expressed himself of opinion that as it was all one transaction, the declarations were admissible, and accordingly allowed them to go to the jury, but he said he would reserve the point for the opinion of the judges. The prisoner was acquitted. This case is entitled to greater weight, as Baron Parke, the year before, in Stobart v. Dryden, 1 Mees. & Welsby 615, had been considering the question of dying declarations, after full argument, and delivered the opinion of the court. This case is mentioned in 1 Phillips and Arnold 243, in 3 Russell 268; 1 Taylor on Evidence 618.

In The State v. Terrell, 12 Richardson 321 (S.C. 1866), it was held upon the trial of an indictment for the murder of A. by poison, which was taken at the same time by B. and C., both of whom as well as A. died from its effects, the dying declarations of B. are admissible against the prisoner, although the general rule seems to be, that dying declarations are admissible only, where the indictment is for the murder of the party making the declarations. The murder was effected by putting strychnine in a bottle of whiskey, administered by the defendant, at the same time, to three persons, and caused the deaths of the grandfather and uncle of the prisoner, and of a third person, whose dying declarations were received in evidence upon the trial of the accused for the murder of his grandfather.

Upon the authority of these cases the learned judge admitted the dying declarations of the wife, upon the trial of the defendant for the murder of her husband. In this there was error, for the husband was found dead on Monday morning 26th Feb. 1872, three hundred yards from his dwelling, and his wife was discovered on the same morning lying across her bed in the house in an insensible condition and with her face and head terribly beaten and disfigured. Kraemer and his wife were both advanced in years and there was no doubt that robbery of gold and silver which was known to be in the house led to their murder, but we do not see any facts that would bring these dying declarations of Mrs. Kraemer within those two authorities, supposing them to be good law.

If the prisoner had been tried upon the indictment for the murder of Mrs. Kraemer, her dying declarations would have been strictly legal evidence against him.

* * *

The judgment is reversed and the record remanded, with this opinion, setting forth the causes of reversal to the court below for further proceeding.

Barsch v. Hammond
Supreme Court of Colorado, 1943.
110 Colo. 441, 135 P.2d 519.

In this case, the court allows a dying declaration that resulted from a conversation that the decedent had with his wife although no person had told the deceased that his death was imminent. This is not the usual situation wherein a physician explains to the dying person that he or she is about to die and that nothing can be done to help him or her.

BAKKE, Justice. This is an automobile accident case in which plaintiff in error seeks to reverse a judgment for $2,500 and costs entered in accordance with the verdict of a jury in favor of Louise B. Hammond, to whom we hereinafter refer to as Mrs. Hammond, defendant in error, whose husband died as a result of injuries sustained in the accident. A default judgment for $5,000 had been entered prior to this one, but due to a deficiency in the service of process, counsel for Mrs. Hammond confessed error; the default judgment was set aside and a trial had on the merits. Plaintiff in error, Barsch, was the owner of the truck which was being driven by his brother, his admitted agent, at the time of the accident.

The accident occurred about 3:45 A.M., October 18, 1937, near a filling station in the little town of Pinon about thirty miles south of Colorado Springs on U.S. Highway 85, where a family by the name of Holcomb operates a restaurant and service station. The place served as a "truck stop" for a number of truck drivers using the highway. The highway—an eighteen foot wide cement road—at this point is fairly level for quite a distance in each direction, although there is a curve to the left in the road towards Colorado Springs about fifteen hundred feet from the scene of the accident. There was a driveway leading off the highway to the Holcomb buildings on the west side of the road. The morning of the accident Hammond was driving south alone in a 1937 Ford sedan on this road from Colorado Springs to Pueblo, and Barsch was driving north in a thirty-two foot long tractor-trailer. Upon reaching the driveway to the filling station, Barsch turned his truck to the left without making a left hand signal, and the Hammond car crashed into it with such force that the front of his car was smashed in pinning him, Hammond, under the steering wheel, and causing injuries from which he died the next day. Since there were no eyewitnesses to the accident, other than Barsch, it is difficult to ascertain from the testimony the relative speed of each vehicle as it approached the point of collision, although Barsch admits seeing the Hammond car when it came around the curve on the north, about a quarter of a mile north of Pinon. Barsch apparently thought he had enough time to make the turn into the driveway ahead of the Hammond car.

The night was clear and the Holcomb buildings were well lighted. That Hammond saw the truck making the turn is a fair surmise because there were tire skid marks for about thirty feet ahead of the point of impact, indicating that Hammmond tried to stop his car, although Barsch testified that he did not hear any screeching of brakes; that when he saw that a crash was imminent, he stopped his truck just off the pavement at an angle to it, facing into the Holcomb driveway. From the tire marks of Hammond's car, it was apparent that he had driven off the pavement on his right in an attempt to avoid a collision. Follow the accident, most of the Hammond car was on the pavement, crosswise thereof, with the front part of it against the right front part of the tractor.

Hammond was taken to a hospital in Pueblo. His wife and children arrived there about 7:45 A.M. Mrs. Hammond testified: "As we came up to him, the children and I, he put his arm around the children, kissed each one of us, and said:

> "Mother dear, I won't ever be home with you and the babies again; I am done for. . . . He said he saw this other car coming, and it made no indication of turning, and he supposed it was going to continue on its course north, or in the direction in which it was going. . . . But all of a sudden, quite suddenly, this man turned directly in front of him, which would have been to his left, got directly in front of him, giving no intimation he was turning or going into this place. . . . When he struck the car that he was yet on the highway, partly in the highway when he struck it."

(1) This statement was admitted in evidence as a dying declaration, and its admission as such is the principal ground for reversal in this case. Other matters urged are: (2) That Hammond was intoxicated. (3) That the court should have directed a verdict for defendant. (4) That the court erred in giving instruction No. 4. (5) That there was a variance between pleading and proof. (6) That

the court erred in denying motion for a new trial.

1. Counsel for plaintiff in error objected to the introduction of the above testimony upon the ground that it was hearsay, but when opposing counsel called attention to Chapter 145, Session Laws 1937, which permits such declarations to be introduced, objection was that no proper foundation had been laid, which objection was cured by a proper foundation being laid. This statute reads, in part: "To render the declarations of the deceased competent evidence, it must be satisfactorily proved: 1, that at the time of the making of such declaration he was conscious of approaching death and believed there was no hope of recovery; 2, that such declaration was voluntarily made, and not through the persuasion of any person; 3, that such declaration was not made in answer to interrogatories calculated to lead the deceased to make any particular statement; 4, that he was of sound mind at the time of making the declaration." All of these elements were positively established by Mrs. Hammond on both direct and cross examination, and several defense witnesses corroborated Hammond's rationality.

* * *

We think there is no prejudicial error in this record.

The judgment is affirmed.

BURKE, HILLIARD and JACKSON, JJ., concur.

Barnard v. Keathley

Supreme Court of Arkansas, 1970.
249 Ark. 346, 459 S.W.2d 121.

This decision indicates that the admissibility of a dying declaration is to be determined by the trial judge based on substantial evidence. You will remember that we treated the doctrine of substantial evidence in Chapter 2 of this book, wherein we differentiated it as a standard of proof between a preponderance of the evidence and evidence beyond a reasonable doubt.

You will also notice that the court uses double negatives to express a point. This is permissible as legalese language, which I discussed in Section 1.2. The language that I am referring to is as follows:

. . . we cannot say that the trial court's holding that the requisite consciousness of impending death had not been shown was incorrect.

We would usually say this:

The trial court was correct in holding that the decedent did not have the required consciousness of impending death.

The decision speaks about an offer of proof that was not made with respect to the testimony of Mrs. Bernard, relating to the alleged dying declaration made to Mrs. Bernard by her husband, when the trial court refused to permit the statement of her husband in the trial record. An offer of proof in a jury trial is usually made in a side bar statement, outside the hearing of the jury, wherein the attorney representing the litigant whose testimony was not admitted states before a court stenographer and the judge that if the testimony is admitted, he or she will prove whatever the purpose was of getting it admitted. This procedure may be used in open court in a non-jury trial where a judge refuses to permit a question, or to permit a witness to answer a question, because the question is not proper, or admissible. In this way, the attorney preserves the right to ask the question or to have the question answered when, and if, an appellate court reviews the case.

FOGELMAN, Justice.

Appellant questions the propriety of the circuit judge's refusal to admit her testimony as to certain statements of her decedent made prior to his death, as dying declarations. She brought the action as personal representative of her late husband, Alva Leroy Barnard. She alleged that his death in his lawyer's office on February 13, 1968, resulted from an assault by appellees on the day before. She offered the testimony of the coroner. It was to the effect that, believing the death to have been from unnatural causes, he caused an autopsy to be performed. This autopsy revealed no brain damage, no abrasions about the face and head of the deceased nor any indication that trauma caused or contributed to the death of appellant's decedent. While the preliminary autopsy report showed no anatomical cause of death, the final report showed that this death

resulted from massive myocardial infarction—a heart attack. The death certificate introduced by appellant reflected the results of both autopsies.

When the trial court's ruling was made Gladys Mary Barnard had testified substantially as follows:

Her husband had been operating a taxi for almost two years; he had always enjoyed good health; he had never had any symptoms of heart trouble. Between 6:30 and 7:00 P.M. on February 12 he received a telephone call at their home in Jacksonville. She took it to be of a threatening nature and believed that he reported it to the Jacksonville Police. She left their home at 7:30 to go to a bingo party at St. Jude's Church, leaving her husband and her son Eddy and returned around 9:30. Mr. Barnard was driving into their driveway. She had never seen him in such condition. He had blood on the side of his head and bruises on his face and was shaking and afraid. She had to help him in the house. Knowing that he would be unable to drive his taxi that night, she told him to contact Lonnie Cater, his substitute driver. Barnard left and returned with Cater after almost an hour. He spent the rest of the night at home. He was up and down all night, complaining with his head. Neither of them got any sleep. She thought he was dying.

In an in camera hearing, Mrs. Barnard answered affirmatively an inquiry whether her husband stated, after she came home about 9:30 P.M., that he was going to die. In response to the question asking how many times he mentioned the fact that he thought he was going to die she answered "Several times." During the one-hour interval he was away, he had gone to the police station. Even though she suggested that he seek medical help, he did not do so. The next morning he got up about 6:00 A.M., but said he did not want to eat. He returned to bed where he remained until 8 o'clock. About 8:30 he had a driver take him to his lawyer's office in order that he might detail the events of the previous evening to the lawyer. He did not seek medical attention at this time either. As he left home, he told his wife he was going down to the lawyer's office to see what could be done and hoped he would be back, but wasn't sure whether he would or not.

The court held this testimony inadmissible because it was not adequately shown that Barnard's expressions of fear of death were made under a consciousness of impending death without hope or expectation of recovery. We do not find error in the trial court's holding.

Appellant contends that she made a prima facie showing that her decedent had a consciousness of impending death, and that the trial court should have submitted the question to the jury. In our latest expression on this subject we said that the trial judge must determine whether a proffered dying declaration was made under such circumstances as to be competent evidence before admitting it. Miller v. Goodwin & Beavers, (April 7, 1969), 439 S.W.2d 308. We also said that we review the trial court's decision on admissibility by the test of substantial evidence. To say the least, we find substantial evidence to support the trial court's holding in this case.

In order for a statement to be admissible as a dying declaration it must satisfactorily appear from the declarant's express language or from inferences fairly drawn from his condition, any evident danger and other circumstances that his sense of impending death was so certain that he was without hope or expectation of recovery. Rhea v. State, 104 Ark. 162, 147 S.W. 463; Sutton v. State, 187 Ark. 870, 63 S.W.2d 278; Comer v. State, 212 Ark. 66, 204 S.W.2d 875. There must be an abandonment of hope of survival by the declarant and a definite expectation that life is a matter of but short duration. Pinson v. State, 210 Ark. 56, 194 S.W.2d 190. In view of Barnard's greater concern for obtaining a substitute taxi driver and for reporting his alleged beating to the police than for obtaining medical attention as advised by his wife and his anxiousness to consult a lawyer rather than a physician on the day of his death, we cannot say that the trial court's holding that the requisite consciousness of impending death had not been shown was incorrect.

Appellant also argues that her testimony should have been admitted because the court later admitted the testimony of substitute taxi driver Lonnie Cater, including an alleged dying declaration of Barnard. Appellant says that her testimony as to Barnard's sense of im-

pending death was stronger than that of Cater and that Cater's testimony supplemented that of Mrs. Barnard in that respect. The correctness of the court's holding the Cater testimony admissible is not before us, so a comparison of the relative weight of their respective testimony would serve no useful purpose. The sufficiency of Cater's testimony to supply any deficiencies in Mrs. Barnard's is a question which is not presented to us, because appellant has not pointed out to us any attempt to offer her testimony after Cater testified. We can only determine the correctness of action that a trial court took or declined to take upon proper request. When a court rules on the admissibility of evidence, we can only evaluate its ruling in the light of matters which have been brought to the court's attention at the time of the ruling. In passing we note that appellant made no offer of proof to show just what Barnard's declarations to her were. It could well be that Mrs. Barnard's testimony would have been only cumulative to that of Cater.

We have found no error in the court's action, so the judgment is affirmed.

Thomson v. Mayes
Court of Appeals of Texas, Eastland, 1986. 707 S.W.2d 951.

This case involves a constructive trust. An adequate and simple definition of a constructive trust appears in the decision, and I believe a repetition of it in this introduction is superfluous.

The court also uses another term that you may not know: motion for a judgment non obstante veredicto. This is a motion (application) made by the litigant in a jury trial when the jury has arrived at a verdict that is contrary to the position that the moving party had desired at the trial. To place this motion in layperson's language, it is an application to the court to reverse the jury's verdict because the weight of the evidence is contrary to that verdict. It is a motion that is rarely granted, but I have seen it granted one time in my career.

The doctrine of unclean hands may be invoked in an equity action when the plaintiff in that action has committed some improper act. In this action, the plaintiff, who wanted to impose the constructive trust, entered into an agreement as to finality of judgment in a prior suit to probate the will of her father.

The decision includes many other legal principles drawn from the law of evidence, but because we have not studied these rules at this point in the text, I have omitted much of that material and have noted the omission by an ellipsis.

McCLOUD, Chief Justice.

This is an appeal from a suit to impose a constructive trust on the assets which passed to Donald Marshall Thompson (Don Thompson) under the will of his father, Jo B. Thompson. The other devisee under Jo B. Thompson's will is his sister, Leonette Mayes. On December 19, 1984, Mrs. Mayes brought this suit alleging that a constructive trust should be imposed upon the assets that Don Thompson received under his father's will. Don Thompson committed suicide on January 16, 1985, and Nancy Thompson (Don Thompson's mother and the former wife of Jo B. Thompson) was substituted as defendant both individually and as independent executrix under her son's will. The jury found that on or about November 12, 1982, Don Thompson "intentionally and wrongfully caused the death of Jo B. Thompson by shooting him with a gun." A judgment imposing the constructive trust was rendered for plaintiff. Defendant appeals. We affirm.

Defendant, Mrs. Thompson, argues in her first point of error that the trial court erred in overruling her motion for judgment non obstante veredicto because this suit was barred by limitations. We disagree.

Defendant contends that the two-year limitation period prescribed in Article 5526(5) applies in this case. The applicable portions of this statute provide:

There shall be commenced and prosecuted within two years after the cause of action shall have accrued, and not afterward, all actions or suits in court of the following description:

* * *

5. Action for injury done to the person of another where death ensued from such injury; and the cause of action shall be considered as having accrued at the death of the party injured.

A suit to impose a constructive trust is not an "[a]ction for injury done to the person of another"; rather, it is an action in equity to prevent unjust enrichment of a person who has wrongfully acquired property. Bounds v. Caudle, 560 S.W.2d 925 (Tex. 1977); Pope v. Garrett, 147 Tex. 18, 211 S.W.2d 559 (1948). When the proven circumstances show that the holder of the legal title may not in good conscience retain the beneficial interest, then equity converts him into a trustee. Pope v. Garrett, supra; Parks v. Dumas, 321 S.W.2d 653 (Tex.Civ.App.—Fort Worth 1959, no writ).

In her second and third points of error, defendant contends that plaintiff's suit was barred because: (1) as a matter of law, plaintiff waived her right to file this suit for constructive trust by entering into an "Agreement as to Finality of Judgment" in a prior suit to probate the will of Jo B. Thompson; and (2) as a result of her entering into the aforementioned agreement, plaintiff had unclean hands which was a bar to her suit in equity.

The "Agreement as to Finality of Judgment" was signed by Don Thompson and plaintiff. The agreement was made a part of the record in Cause No. 16,230, which was a suit to probate Jo B. Thompson's will by bill of review in the 266th District Court of Erath County. The judgment probating the will and the agreement as to its finality were signed December 19, 1984. The instant case was filed later that same day.

Nowhere in the aforementioned agreement is there a reference to either party's right to file a subsequent lawsuit involving matters not related to the probate of Jo B. Thompson's will. The agreement contains no language waiving the right to seek the establishment of a constructive trust on the assets received under the will. The agreement waives the right to appeal and makes the probate judgment final. Defendant's second point of error is overruled.

With regard to the unclean hands contention, the legal title of the assets passed to Don Thompson by virtue of his father's will. Plaintiff agreed that the judgment probating the will would become final and that she would not seek to disturb the judgment probating the will by appeal or otherwise. She has not sought to do so. Plaintiff has employed an equitable proceeding against the holder of the legal title for the wrong done and has impressed "a trust on the property in favor of the one who was in good conscience entitled to it." Pope v. Garrett, supra. It has not been shown that plaintiff's hands were unclean. Defendant's third point of error is overruled.

In her fourth point of error, defendant argues that plaintiff was not entitled to have a constructive trust imposed under the facts and circumstances of this case. Defendant contends that the provisions of TEX.CONST. art. I, sec. 21 and TEX.PROB. CODE ANN. sec 41(d) (Vernon 1980) provide that not even murder or suicide would have caused Don Thompson to forfeit his share of his father's estate. Therefore, since Don Thompson was not indicted for his father's murder and since the evidence linking him to his father's death is circumstantial, the imposition of a constructive trust in this case would be an inappropriate expansion of this doctrine. We disagree.

The jury found that Don Thompson intentionally and wrongfully caused the death of his father. There is no challenge to the sufficiency of the evidence to support that finding. Therefore, the fact that the jury's verdict was based on circumstantial evidence is not relevant to the propriety of imposition of the constructive trust.

Application of the settled law in this State to this set of facts permits the imposition of a constructive trust. As stated by the court in Bounds v. Caudle, supra at 928:

> Texas courts have taken the position that the law will impose a constructive trust upon the property of a deceased which passed either by inheritance or by will if the beneficiary willfully and wrongfully caused the death of the deceased.

Defendant's fourth point of error is overruled.

In Point of Error No. 5, defendant contends that plaintiff's case is barred by res judicata and by the doctrine of merger and bar. She argues that the constructive trust cause of action should have been included in the bill of review suit to probate Jo B. Thompson's

will and that the judgment probating the will distributed the estate to Don Thompson and plaintiff; therefore, the prior suit was a final disposition of the assets, and it barred any subsequent suits concerning those assets.

The Texas Probate Code expressly provides that district courts have jurisdiction over suits to apply constructive trusts. TEX.PROB. CODE ANN. sec 5A(b) (Vernon 1980). Defendant cites the case of Abbott Laboratories v. Gravis, 470 S.W.2d 639 (Tex. 1971), as support for her argument that any action which could have been brought in the proceeding to probate the will should have been litigated in that proceeding. Abbott is clearly distinguishable. In Abbott, the plaintiff's original suit was based on negligence in preparing and furnishing a drug to the plaintiff. In a subsequent suit, which the court held was barred by res judicata, the plaintiff pled products liability as the theory of recovery for the same alleged injuries arising from the same incident involving the drug. The court stated at page 642 that:

> [A] party cannot relitigate matters which he might have interposed, but failed to do so, in an action between the same parties or their privies in reference to *the same subject matter.* [Emphasis added.]

A suit to probate a will does not involve the "same subject matter" as a suit to impose a constructive trust.

The bill of review suit to probate the will dealt with the authenticity of the will and proof that the testator was dead. The instant suit involves the question of whether Don Thompson intentionally and wrongfully caused his father's death. The theory of recovery, the operative facts, and the measure of recovery are all different in this case. Therefore, this suit is not barred by res judicata. Griffin v. Holiday Inns of America, 496 S.W.2d 535 (Tex. 1973); Abbott Laboratories v. Gravis, supra; Ogletree v. Crates, 363 S.W.2d 431 (Tex. 1963); Moore v. Snowball, 98 Tex. 16, 81 S.W. 5 (Tex. 1904); Dobbs v. Navarro, 506 S.W.2d 671 (Tex.Civ.App.—Houston [1st Dist.] 1974, no writ).

In Point of Error No. 6, defendant contends that the trial court abused its discretion in excluding the testimony of a psychologist,

Dr. Frank Wichern, regarding his opinion as to Don Thompson's non-involvement in his father's disappearance. We disagree.

Defendant's attorney revealed to the court that he intended to ask Dr. Wichern his opinion concerning whether or not Don Thompson "may have" killed his father. Plaintiff's attorney took Dr. Wichern on voir dire to determine the basis of any opinion proffered by the doctor. Dr. Wichern testified that he had no personal knowledge of or contact with either Jo B. Thompson or Don Thompson. After Don Thompson's suicide, Dr. Wichern talked to six people for less than one hour each concerning their relationships with Don Thompson. Some of these people did not have a relationship with Don Thompson at the time of his father's disappearance. One person had neither known nor had any personal contact with Don Thompson. Dr. Wichern reviewed both Don Thompson's high school transcript and a summary prepared by his mother, the defendant, of his growth and development. Dr. Wichern listened to the tapes made by Don Thompson before he shot himself. The only other knowledge that Dr. Wichern had of Jo B. Thompson's disappearance was what he had read in *The Dallas Morning News*. Dr. Wichern testified that he compiled all of this information into a "psychological autopsy" in an effort to determine Don Thompson's state of mind at the time of his father's disappearance.

Jo B. Thompson was last seen more than two years prior to this trial. Defendant's attorney revealed to the court that he intended to ask Dr. Wichern his opinion as to Don Thompson's state of mind on the day his father disappeared. This opinion was based on information gathered after Don Thompson's suicide. Dr. Wichern testified that psychological autopsies have been used by psychologists in forming opinions as to the state of mind of alleged suicide victims at the time of their death. In those cases, the issue was whether the person committed suicide, not whether the decedent may have killed another person two years earlier.

Plaintiff's attorney inquired about the purpose, acceptance, and reliability of an opinion based on a psychological autopsy when used to determine a person's state of mind at a prior time. Pertinent portions of Dr. Wichern's testimony are:

Q. Has [a psychological autopsy] ever been used to hypothesize what the state of mind was at a prior time?

A. I have no personal knowledge of that, I suspect it could be.

Q. That's what you're attempting to do in this case; is that not correct?

A. Yes, that's right.

Q. You're not aware that it has ever been attempted before, though?

A. Not to my knowledge—personal knowledge.

At the conclusion of the voir dire, plaintiff's attorney objected to the admission of Dr. Wichern's testimony on the grounds that "there is not an underlying technical or scientific principle that it is sufficiently reliable for his testimony to be of assistance to the jury" and the testimony was not permitted by Rule 702 of the Texas Rules of Evidence. Under TEX.R.EVID. 702, an expert's testimony should not be admitted if it would be more likely to prejudice or confuse than to assist the jury. Therefore, an expert's opinion should be based on an existing body of scientific, technical, or other specialized knowledge that is pertinent to the facts in issue. The underlying technical or scientific principle should be sufficiently reliable for the testimony of the witness to be of assistance to the jury. Sutton, *Article VII: Opinions and Expert Testimony*, 20 HOUS.L.REV. 445, 459 (1983 TEX.R.EVID HANDBOOK).

The trial judge has broad discretion in determining issues concerning the general admissibility of evidence. TEX.R.EVID. 104(a). This rule is consistent with prior Texas law regarding the trial court's preliminary determination of fact as to the admissibility of expert testimony; therefore, the trial court's decision will not be overruled unless an abuse of discretion is shown. Bolstad v. Egleson, 326 S.W.2d 506 (Tex.Civ.App.—Houston 1959, writ ref'd n.r.e.); United States v. Schmidt, 711 F.2d 595 (5th Cir. 1983). The trial court did not abuse its discretion in refusing to admit this testimony, especially after the expert conceded that he did not know of any other instance where a psychological autopsy had been used in this manner.

Moreover, the issue to be decided in this case is whether Don Thompson intentionally and wrongfully caused the death of his father. Under the facts of this case, the jury did not need the assistance of scientific, technical, or specialized knowledge to decide this question. The admission of this testimony would not have assisted the jury in making inferences regarding the fact issues more effectively than the jury could do so unaided. Holloway v. State, 613 S.W.2d 497, 501 (Tex.Cr.App. 1981); Sutton, *Article VII: Opinions and Expert Testimony;* 20 HOUS.L.REV. 445, 451–461 (1983 TEX.R.EVID. HANDBOOK). Defendant's sixth point of error is overruled.

Defendant argues in Point of Error No. 7 that the trial court erred in excluding Don Thompson's alleged suicide tapes. She argues that the tapes were admissible under either TEX.R.EVID. 803(3), 804(b)(2), or 804(b)(3)(B), or under all three.

Rule 803(3) is an exception to the hearsay rule which permits the admission of a "statement of the declarant's then existing state of mind." Don Thompson's state of mind more than two years after the date his father disappeared is not material to any issue involved in this case. Therefore, even if the tapes technically fall within an exception to the hearsay rule, they still are not admissible because they are not relevant. TEX.R.EVID. 401, 402; Wellborn, *Article VIII: Hearsay,* 20 HOUS.L.REV. 477, 514 (1983 TEX.R.EVID. HANDBOOK).

These tapes were also not admissible as a dying declaration under Rule 804(b)(2). Under this rule, dying declarations which concern the cause or the circumstances of what the declarant believed to be his impending death are admissible as exceptions to the hearsay rule. The cause or circumstances of Don Thompson's death were not relevant to this case, and the tapes were properly excluded. TEX.R.EVID. 401, 402.

Defendant also contends that the tapes were admissible under TEX.R.EVID. 804(b)(3). This rule concerns statements of personal or family history and excepts certain of these statements from the hearsay prohibition. Defendant contends that the tapes are admissible because the statements on the tapes concern the death of a person to whom Don Thompson was related by blood, i.e., his father. We disagree.

On the portions of the tapes quoted in defendant's brief, Don Thompson denies any involvement in or knowledge of his father's disappearance. Consequently, the proffered statements do not concern the "death" of Jo B. Thompson and were properly excluded.

Defendant next contends that Don Thompson's responses to questions propounded to him by the examiner during a polygraph examination were improperly excluded from evidence. Defendant again relies on Rule 804(b)(3) as basis for the admission of this testimony.

The answers to the questions asked by the polygraph examiner indicate that Don Thompson did not know any of the details about his father's disappearance or did not even know if his father was dead. Therefore, these statements do not concern the "death" of his father and, in fact, tend to show that Don Thompson could not make any statement about his father's death because he did not know anything about it. Therefore, the statements were properly excluded.

In her final point of error, defendant urges that the trial court abused its discretion in refusing to grant her motion to transfer venue under TEX.R.CIV.P. 257 and 258. She contends that under Rule 258 and the controverting affidavit submitted by plaintiff is insufficient to attack the affidavit that she filed previously in support of her motion. We disagree.

Plaintiff's affiant, Mr. Oxford, swore in his affidavit that:

> I do not believe the means of knowledge whereby JOHN B. FOUTS, HOSEA WARREN, MARY A. WESTBROOK and NANCY J. THOMPSON have formed their opinions concerning a prejudice against DONALD MARSHALL THOMPSON is accurate. In my opinion his estate and its beneficiaries can obtain a fair and impartial trial on the matters in controversy in Erath County, Texas.

These statements are sufficient to raise and frame the issue of whether or not an impartial trial could be had in Erath County. Governing Board v. Pannill, 659 S.W.2d 670, 688–689 (Tex.App.—Beaumont 1983, writ ref'd n.r.e.).

Therefore, the question now becomes whether or not the trial judge, after considering the evidence produced at the hearing, abused his discretion in refusing to transfer venue. The evidence produced by defendant at the hearing was controverted by plaintiff's evidence. Both sides produced competent testimony to support their position. We find no abuse of discretion in refusing to transfer the case. Governing Board v. Pannill, supra. All points of error are overruled.

The judgment of the trial court is affirmed.

✔ PRACTICE QUESTIONS

Select the most correct answer to complete each statement.

1. The dying declaration is an example of a situation in which a police officer needs to gather admissible evidence on short notice. Which one of the following is a necessary element for the admissibility of a dying declaration?
   (a) The declarant may have hope of recovery.
   (b) The declarant must have had a reputation in the community of being a religious person.
   (c) The declarant, if living, would be a competent witness.
   (d) The declaration must relate to the declarant's opinion or conclusion on a matter requiring expert opinion, and the declarant is not so qualified.

2. The dying declaration is
   (a) an exception to the hearsay exclusionary rule.
   (b) generally admissible in civil cases.
   (c) not applicable to homicide cases.
   (d) unrelated to circumstances pertaining to the injury or death.

Indicate whether each statement is true or false.

3. "W," a witness to an alleged properly founded dying declaration, testified at the trial of an alleged perpetrator of the homicide. Upon cross-examination, he was asked whether he had heard the deceased say anything after he had identified the defendant as his assailant. "W" replied that the deceased had made one last plea to save his life to the attending physicians as they all were about to leave the room. The defense attorney moved to strike all testimony dealing with the dying declaration from the record. The judge granted his motion. This was proper.

4. There is no precise form for a dying declaration, and it is discretionary with the trial court as to whether or not it should be admitted.

5. The trial court is required to instruct the jury that a dying declaration is not to be regarded as having the same value and weight as the sworn testimony of a witness in open court even though no request is made for this charge.

6. A dying declarant stated that he was poisoned by "D." The proper foundation for the dying declaration was laid, and the declarant died. At the trial of "D," "W," a witness to the dying declaration, testified that the deceased stated that "D" had poisoned him. A motion to strike the statement was granted. This was a proper procedure.

7. The admission of a dying declaration does not violate a person's constitutional right to confront the witnesses against him or her.

CHAPTER 10

Business Records Exception to Hearsay Exclusionary Rule

§ 10.1 INTRODUCTION

Almost without exception, police officers who have testified in court are asked by astute defense counsel as to the contents of their memorandum book entries. Such entries are a form of documentary evidence that often changes the outcome of a case. It is therefore necessary that the entries in a police officer's memorandum book be accurate and made according to the precise rules of his or her department. The officer should always remember that the entries concerning the incident are, in most jurisdictions, available for inspection by defense counsel. N.Y.—People v. Gezzo, 307 N.Y. 385, 121 N.E.2d 380 (1954). Some defense counsel are very cognizant of police department procedure with respect to these entries, and a variation from these procedures might be inferred to be at variance with the truth. Improper entries might change the outcome of a case. For example, if a police department requires that an entry describing an event be written in longhand, in English, and consecutively on a line-after-line basis and that the officer sign his or her name and shield number at the end of the day's entries, an officer's account of the occurrence that includes a witness's name and address on the back of the preceding page is highly suspect. It might rightfully be inferred in the defense counsel's summation that the witness appeared after the officer's tour of duty had been completed.

§ 10.2 DOCUMENTARY EVIDENCE

Documentary evidence is evidence in the form of writing. It is that furnished by written instruments, inscriptions, and documents of all kinds. N.Y.—Ticknor v. Ticknor, 23 Misc.2d 257, 200 N.Y.S.2d 661 (1960). The admissibility of documentary evidence is subject to the same rules of evidence with respect to relevancy, competency, and materiality as is that of oral testimony. Ind.—State v. Schaller, 111 Ind.App. 128, 40 N.E.2d 976 (1942). The admissibility of documentary evidence rests in the sound discretion of the trial court. 32 C.J.S. Evidence § 624; Or.—Wynn v. Sundquist, 259 Or. 125, 485 P.2d 1085 (1971).

Photocopies come under this category. A more extensive discussion of the admissibility of photocopies is found in Section 5.4.

§ 10.3 AUTHENTICATION

In order for documentary evidence to be admissible, it must be authenticated. This may be done by sworn testimony of a witness as to the genuineness of the writing, its authenticity or identity of the document, proof of its execution, and of the correctness. Ga.—Weaver v. Georgia Power Co., 134 Ga.App. 696, 215 S.E. 2d 503 (1975). The party offering it is only required to make out a prima facie case to render it admissible. Cal.—Fakhoury v. Magner, 25 Cal.App.3d 58, 101 Cal.Rptr. 473 (1972). The foundation for such a writing might be laid in the following manner.

Let us assume that a bank teller is presented with a request by a customer to cash a check on the customer's account. The bank procedure is that the customer is required to endorse the check on the reverse side in the presence of the teller. This is done, and the teller compares the signature with the depositor's signature on file in the bank. The teller asks the head cashier to compare the signatures, and both agree that it is a valid signature. The check is cashed. After the customer receives the monthly statement of his or her account and sees this check, he or she claims that he or she had not drawn or cashed the check. When the customer receives no satisfaction from the bank, he sues the bank for the amount of the check. Before the trial, the bank serves a notice to produce the original check on the customer, who is the plaintiff. At the trial, the check is produced, and the bank places the first teller on the stand to testify that on a particular day the plaintiff presented a check for payment to the witness for "x" number of dollars, that on request the check was endorsed on the reverse side by the plaintiff, and that the witness compared the signature with that on file in the bank and enlisted the aid of the chief cashier to compare the signatures. The foundation then is being laid for the next statement by the bank's attorney: "I offer exhibit A for defendant, for identification." After the exhibit is marked by the court stenographer, the bank's attorney says, "I show you defendant's exhibit A for identification. What is this, if you know?" The witness says that it is a bank check. The attorney says, "When, if ever, have you seen this bank check before?" The witness testifies that this is the check the plaintiff endorsed in the teller's presence and on which a payment was made by the witness. The check is then offered into evidence as defendant's exhibit A in evidence.

Note that the foundation was laid by first placing the events that led to the execution of the document in proper focus, to show its relevancy; then the document was placed into evidence to let the trier of the facts draw its own conclusion. Naturally, the bank signature card would also have to be placed in evidence for a comparison.

Some documents are self-authenticating by statute in that they prove themselves. In that category are deeds which have been acknowledged before a notary public. Ind.—Patterson v. Churchman, 122 Ind. 379, 22 N.E. 662 (1889), *reh'g*, 23 N.E. 1082 [1890]. Public documents like birth, baptism, marriage, and death certificates properly sealed with an official pressure seal or certified by an official authorized to certify the documents are self-authenticated. N.Y.—Woltin v. Metropolitan Life Ins. Co., 167 Misc. 382, 4 N.Y.S.2d 296 (1938).

§ 10.4 ANCIENT DOCUMENTS

Ancient documents are also self-proving. An ancient document is one that is purported to be thirty or more years old, which is found in proper custody, and which is unblemished by alterations and is otherwise free from suspicion. It is admissible without direct proof of its execution on the theory that under such circumstances the instrument proves itself or that its due execution is presumed. Mass.—Puffer v. City of Beverly, 345 Mass. 396, 187 N.E.2d 840 (1963). Federal Rule 901(b)(8) drops the requirement to twenty years.

§ 10.5 NEWS PUBLICATIONS

Newspaper accounts are generally not admissible as documentary evidence because of their general unreliability of trustworthiness. However, some cases have admitted newspaper accounts of facts when the account was very old. U.S.—Montana Power Co. v. Federal Power Commission, 185 F.2d 491 (D.C.Cir. 1950).

§ 10.6 PRIVATE WRITINGS

Wills, deeds, and agreements reduced to writing are admissible under the documentary evidence concept. 32 C.J.S. Evidence § 623. Such a document must be proved by a person who saw its execution.

§ 10.7 DEATH CERTIFICATES

There is a difference of opinion as to the admissibility of death certificates. Generally, however, where they are made according to statutory authority and under conditions assuring the accuracy of the information contained therein, they may be admitted under the public records and documents rule. Mass.—Wadsworth v. Boston Gas Co., 352 Mass. 86, 223 N.E.2d 807 (1967); Wash.—Hayden v. Insurance Co. of N.A., 5 Wash.App. 710, 490 P.2d 454 (1971).

§ 10.8 AUTOPSY REPORTS

A report of an autopsy conducted by a duly authorized physician on behalf of the governmental authority empowered to conduct autopsies in the locality where the deceased died is admissible in evidence when relevant and when properly authenticated. Such reports are considered public records, and such records are admissible in evidence. Colo.—Michael v. John Hancock Mut. Life Ins. Co., 138 Colo. 450, 334 P.2d 1090 (1959); N.Y.—Rocco v. Travelers Ins. Co., 38 Misc.2d 311, 238 N.Y.S.2d 43 (1963).

§ 10.9 PRIVATE DOCUMENTS

Records of deeds or other private writings have been held admissible for certain purposes. For example, a mechanic's lien claim, sufficiently signed to entitle it to be filed and then filed is admissible in evidence as a "public record" under the rule allowing certain private writings to become public records by recording under a statute. Cal.—D.I. Nofsizer Lumber Co. v. Solomon, 13 Cal.App. 621, 110 P. 474 (1910). A deed would also fall within this category. Tex.—Woodson Oil Co. v. Pruett, 281 S.W.2d 159 (Tex.Civ.App. 1955); Wis.—Blaha v. Borgman, 142 Wis. 43, 124 N.W. 1047 (1910).

§ 10.10 MEMORANDUM USED BY WITNESS

A witness who is frequently called to the witness stand or even one who seldom makes such an appearance may make an entry in a book or on a piece of paper or in cement or clay or on a blackboard with chalk or in any written form so that when the time comes for the witness to testify in a trial or hearing, he or she may use this writing to revive a recollection. Sometimes a memorandum such as this fails to stimulate the witness's recollection. In such a case, the memorandum itself may be accepted into evidence as a past recollection recorded. In New York, the court of appeals stated in Howard v. McDonough, 77 N.Y. 592, 593, 8 Daly 365 (1879):

> "1. A witness may, for the purpose of refreshing his memory, use any memorandum, whether made by himself or another, written or printed, and when his memory has thus been refreshed, he must testify to facts of his own knowledge, the memorandum itself not being evidence.
>
> 2. When a witness has so far forgotten the facts that he cannot recall them, even after looking at a memorandum of them, and he testifies that he once knew them and made a memorandum of them at the time or soon after they transpired, which he intended to make correctly, and which he believes to be correct, such memorandum, in his own handwriting, may be received as evidence of the facts therein contained, although the witness has no present recollection of them.
>
> 3. Memorandum may be used in other cases which do not precisely come under either of the foregoing heads."

From a reading of the Howard v. McDonough case, it is quite apparent that the court, in its discretion, may permit past recollections recorded into evidence. The rule has been enlarged, perhaps under the instructions of paragraph 3 above: to include that it need not be in the handwriting of the witness as long as the witness saw the memorandum soon after it was made and recognized it at that time as containing a true statement of facts within his own knowledge. N.Y.—Clark v. National Shoe & Leather Bank, 164 N.Y. 498, 58 N.E. 659 (1900). This is the foundation required before a past recollection recorded may be admissible. Like all evidence, it is subject to cross-examination. Mich.—People v. Hobson, 369 Mich. 189, 119 N.W.2d 581 (1963).

§ 10.11 MEMORANDUM USED BY WITNESS—PROOF OF DUE EXECUTION

You have just learned that if a memorandum of an event was made by either the witness or another at or soon after the event and if the witness fails to refresh his or her recollection of the event after receiving the writing, the writing itself may be placed in evidence. Remember that the one placing evidence into the record of the trial has the burden of proof with respect to the credibility of the evidence. In the case of a past recollection recorded, he has the additional burden to establish the genuineness, authenticity, or identity of the document. Minn.—Walker v. Larson, 284 Minn. 99, 169 N.W.2d 737 (1969). This must be done by laying a proper foundation before the document is offered as evidence. This simply means that testimony must be elicited stating that the memorandum was written at or shortly after the event, that it was written either by the witness or by someone with whom the witness was acquainted, that it was seen at or shortly after the event, that it was the purpose and intent of the writer to make a full and accurate account of the event, that the witness believes that the writing is a true and accurate account of the event, and that the witness currently has no independent recollection of the event. After these facts are established, the written memorandum may be offered in evidence and is received in the discretion of the court, provided all nonrelevant information is covered by tape so that the jury cannot read it.

§ 10.12 BOOK ENTRIES—THE SHOP BOOK RULE

A general rule sometimes referred to as the shop book rule is that books of account of a party, or entries therein, are admissible in his or her favor to show the recorded transactions when a proper foundation is laid and the entries are relevant and material to the main issue of the case. These records are received as an exception to the hearsay exclusionary rule because of necessity and because of their probability of reliability. Del.—Edsall v. Rockland Paper Co., 38 Del. 495, 8 W.W.Harr. 495, 194 A. 115 (1937).

The common law originally precluded a party from testifying in his or her own behalf. Accordingly, tradespeople were not able to testify in their own claims.

In order to prevent a miscarriage of justice, the common law permitted a tradesman to offer into evidence his own record of the transaction in issue. In New York, a foundation had to be laid before the evidence was admissible. The plaintiff had to show

1. that the party kept no clerk;
2. that some of the articles charged had been delivered, or that some of the services charged had been rendered;
3. that the books produced were the account books of the party; and
4. that the party kept fair and honest books (this was required to be proved by those who dealt and settled with him on the basis of the books). N.Y.— Vosburgh v. Thayer, 12 Johns. 461 (N.Y. 1815).

The shop book rule still exists, but it has been replaced by statute in most jurisdictions. Many states have adopted the Uniform Business Records as Evidence Act, which abrogates many of the technical common law rules with respect to the admission of business records in evidence. This statute has expanded the operation of the common law rule that admits such records as an exception to the hearsay exclusionary rule. The Uniform Business Records as Evidence Act relating to business records applies to criminal as well as civil procedures. Ohio—State v. Phillips, 90 Ohio App. 44, 103 N.E.2d 14 (1951). See also Haskell v. United States Department of Agriculture, 930 F.2d 816 (10th Cir. 1991), regarding an investigator's report of food stamps fraud. This decision is reprinted at the end of this chapter.

In New York, Civil Practice Law and Rules § 4518 provides:

(a) *Generally.* Any writing or record, whether in the form of an entry in a book or otherwise, made as a memorandum or record of any act, transaction, occurrence or event, shall be admissible in evidence in proof of that act, transaction, occurrence or event, if the judge finds that it was made in the regular course of any business and that it was the regular course of such business to make it, at the time of the act, transaction, occurrence or event, or within a reasonable time thereafter. All other circumstances of the making of the memorandum or record, including lack of personal knowledge by the maker, may be proved to affect its weight, but they shall not affect its admissibility. The term business includes a business profession, occupation and calling of every kind.

(b) *Hospital Bills.* A hospital bill is admissible in evidence under this rule and is prima facie evidence of the facts contained provided it bears a certification by the head of the hospital or by a responsible employee in the controller's or accounting office that the bill is correct, that each of the items was necessarily supplied and that the amount charged is reasonable. This subdivision shall not apply to any proceeding in a surrogate's court nor in any action instituted by or on behalf of a hospital to recover payment for accommodations or supplies furnished or for services rendered by or in such hospital, except that in a proceeding pursuant to section one hundred eighty-nine of the lien law to determine the validity and extent of the lien of a hospital, such certified hospital bills are prima facie evidence of the fact of services and of the reasonableness of any charges which do not exceed the comparable charges made by the hospital in the care of workmen's compensation patients.

(c) *Other Records.* All records, writings and other things referred to in sections 2306 and 2307 are admissible in evidence under this rule and are prima facie evidence of the facts contained, provided they bear a certification or authentication by the head of the hospital, library, department or bureau of a municipal corporation or of the state, or by an employee delegated for that purpose.

§ 10.13 POLICE RECORDS

One of the most often subpoenaed records of a police department is the report of the facts of an accident that may evolve into a civil law dispute involving money damages. In most jurisdictions, if one person wrongs another, the wrongdoer is punished. This concept of law has been highly successful over the years in preventing willful wrongs.

There are police records other than accident reports, however, that may be admissible in evidence. For example, a police report of a stolen vehicle is not admissible to show that the car had been stolen, but it is admissible to show that it had been reported stolen. Missouri and some other states admit police reports under the Uniform Business Records as Evidence Act.

§ 10.14 ACCIDENT REPORTS

When called on to investigate the scene of an auto accident, it is a police officer's sworn duty to report the facts as he or she sees them to the best of his or her ability. Once this record is made, is it not expected that it could be used in a subsequent civil suit? Some people expect it to be used in a civil suit, but it is seldom actually admitted into evidence. Florida Statute § 316.066(4) indicates that accident reports are not admissible as evidence in any trial, civil or criminal, nor are any statements made by the participants in the accident to the police officer investigating the accident. The exact language of the statute follows:

> . . . each accident report made by a person involved in an accident and any statement made by such person to a law enforcement officer for the purpose of completing an accident report required by this section shall be without prejudice to the individual so reporting. No such report or statement shall be used as evidence in any trial, civil or criminal.
>
> The result of breath, urine, and blood tests administered as provided in [§] 316.1932 or [§] 316.1933 are not confidential and shall be admissible into evidence in accordance with the provisions of [§] 316.1934.

The accident report privilege includes all statements made to and by police officers with regard to the investigation of the accident. McTevia v. Schraq, 446 So.2d 1183 (Fla.App. 1984). The purpose of the accident report privilege is to promote truthfulness in reporting accidents to the police. This helps in the determination of who is truly at fault for the accident. It also assists the state of Florida in making highway safety a priority for all. Department of Motor Vehicles v. Corbin, 527 So.2d 868 (Fla.App. 1988), *review denied*, 534 So.2d 399. (10/7/88).

The privilege is intended to benefit the person making the statement and the person involved in the accident so as to allow them to speak truthfully without any prejudice to them in any subsequent civil trial. Department of Motor Vehicles v. Corbin, *supra*. Additionally, the privilege is intended to benefit the public by enabling the Department of Motor Vehicles to collect relevant information and statistics on persons involved in accidents. Hoctor v. Tucker, 432 So.2d 1352 (Fla.App. 1983). Because other states may have similar statutes, it is recommended that you research your state statutes for a similar law.

Most accident reports consist of information given to the officer by others after the officer arrives on the scene. If you keep in mind that the law of evidence is based on a search for truth, you can easily understand why you must ask yourself this question: "Can the person who gave the statement to the officer be cross-examined?" You will remember that it was previously said in this book that if you cannot cross-examine the person who made the statement and it is offered for the truth of the assertion, the statement is hearsay and subject to an exclusionary rule unless there is some compelling reason for its admission.

An accident record made by a police officer who did not see the facts that he or she reported on this record is not admissible in evidence (N.Y.—Johnson v. Lutz, 253 N.Y. 124, 170 N.E. 517 [1930]) unless certain conditions occur at the trial (Mich.—Galli v. Reutter, 148 Mich.App. 313, 384 N.W.2d 43 [1985]).

There are, however, exceptions to the famous Johnson v. Lutz rule:

1. Where an officer's testimony is assailed as a recent fabrication, the police blotter[1] report, as well as the memorandum book, may be admitted into the evidence to bolster his or her testimony. N.Y.—Yeargans v. Yeargans, 24 A.D.2d 280, 265 N.Y.S.2d 562, 565 (1965). For more information, refer to Section 12.9.
2. Those portions of a police report which contain admissions against interest made by a party are admissible as an exception to the hearsay rule. N.Y.— Yeargans v. Yeargans, *supra*; not now applicable in Florida and some other states.

Many lawyers, judges, and police officers misinterpret the Johnson v. Lutz decision to mean that no police accident reports are admissible in evidence. This is not the case. As has been shown in the previous list, even if someone else not under a duty to report the accident gave the information to the police officer, that information may, nevertheless, be admitted under the circumstances described above. However, there are other situations where a police accident report has been admitted. For example:

1. The observations made by the police officer of the physical circumstances existing at the time of his arrival at the scene of the accident are admissible. N.Y.—Yeargans v. Yeargans, *supra*.
2. As to those portions of the report which are based on the officer's observations, these may be admitted to impeach that portion of his testimony which is inconsistent with the report. Yeargans v. Yeargans, *supra*.
3. The contents of such reports which reflect the observations of the officer while carrying out his duty are admissible. Yeargans v. Yeargans, *supra*.

The New York decisions have been codified in CPLR 4518(a) and further clarified in Toll v. State, 32 A.D.2d 47, 299 N.Y.S.2d 589 (1969), in which the court of appeals said CPLR 4518(a) permits a police report to be admitted if

---

[1] "Police blotter" is a term used in legal decisions that means all official police records; it is not restricted to the police blotter sometimes kept at a police station house, which is a chronological record of specified police business occurring in that command. It sometimes does not include all of the police business occurring in that command, some of which is recorded in form reports and filed separately in the ordinary course of police business.

1. the entrant of those facts was the witness or
2. the person giving the entrant the information was under a business duty to relate the facts to the entrant.

If neither of the above conditions is apparent, the report may still be admitted under Kelly v. Wasserman, 5 N.Y.2d 425, 185 N.Y.S.2d 538, 158 N.E.2d 241 (1959), if

3. counsel is attempting to prove that the statement recorded therein was made by an outsider; then the facts recited in the statement may be proven by the business record if the statement qualifies as a hearsay exception, e.g., admission.

§ 10.15 TORTS

The law of civil wrong or private wrong may be referred to as tort law. A tort suit may be in the nature of an action in negligence, an action in trespass, an action in assault and battery, an action in defamation, an action in slander or libel, or one of the many other private wrong actions.

It is the intent of this book not to familiarize you with the law of tort, but just to acquaint you with the fact that it exists.

It is the duty of every police officer to enforce the law. This is often thought to be the enforcement only of the criminal law. However, this is not entirely true. The officer is responsible for the orderly administration of justice, and this responsibility includes the administration of civil justice.

§ 10.16 NO-FAULT CONCEPT OF LIABILITY

There is a movement away from this theory in the area of automobile negligence liability. The movement is called "no-fault insurance." A few states have legislated the no-fault insurance concept into law. I feel that an extensive examination of the advantages and disadvantages of the no-fault concept should not be included in this book. Nevertheless, you should be made aware of the idea that, in "no-fault," damages are paid to any injured party whether he or she was the cause of the injury or not, but the amount received may be substantially less than what the injured person would have received if he or she had not been at fault and if the other person had been negligent under the tort system of law.

There is usually a threshold amount, which varies in different states. When this amount is reached or exceeded, the wronged party is entitled to institute a suit in negligence. The threshold amount is that sum of money that the injured party expended or owes as a result of services he or she received in the treatment of the injury, plus the loss of earnings occasioned by his or her incapacity caused by the injury.

§ 10.17 COMPARATIVE NEGLIGENCE

Again, it is not my intention to include a comprehensive analysis of negligence law. That is a subject unto itself. Nevertheless, a book such as this, which deals with proof at a trial, should include a reference to negligence actions. In many states, a party who fails to exercise due care and injures another is liable to the other person for money damages, providing the other person was free from all contributory negligence. This rule created harsh and sometimes inequitable results such that even when a defendant in such an action was shown to have been greatly negligent, he or she would not get a judgment against him or her if he or she could show that the plaintiff had contributed to the accident in the slightest degree. Many states and the federal government have changed this concept by statute to apportion the damages among the parties, depending on the degree of negligence proved to the satisfaction of the trier of the facts. This is known as comparative negligence.

§ 10.18 SELF-SERVING DECLARATIONS

A self-serving declaration is an oral or written statement made, or an act done, by a party to an action, or by one in privity with him, on some prior occasion, which supports a claim of that party at the time of trial. N.Y.—Latimer v. Burrows, 163 N.Y. 7, 57 N.E. 95 (1900). As a general rule, the self-serving declarations or acts of a party are inadmissible in his or her favor, and the death of the declarant does not render his or her self-serving declarations admissible unless they are admissible by reason of a statute. 31A C.J.S. Evidence § 216. However, when a self-serving declaration is part of the res gestae, it may be admitted. Ga.—Tifton Brick & Block Co. v. Meadow, 92 Ga.App. 328, 88 S.E.2d 569 (1955); Md.—Shirks Motor Express v. Oxenham, 204 Md. 626, 106 A.2d 46 (1954).

§ 10.19 HOSPITAL RECORDS

You should now be able to understand why hospital records are admissible in evidence. You should understand that entries made in a hospital record relevant to diagnosis, prognosis, and/or treatment qualify for admission under the statutory business records exception because it is the business of the hospital to diagnose and treat people who come to the hospital for assistance.

Very often, however, a hospital record of a patient contains entries that are not necessary to diagnosis, prognosis, and/or treatment, and these entries may not be admissible under other exclusionary rules.

Self-serving declarations may appear in a hospital record. An example of this is as follows:

> Patient states that she was standing on the sidewalk of 27th Street and Park Avenue South, talking with May Jones when she was struck from behind by vehicle bearing New York registration J.D. 44 for the current year.

It is quite apparent that the only part of this statement that might reasonably be necessary for diagnosis, prognosis, and/or treatment is the fact that the patient was struck down by a vehicle. The remainder of the statement is superfluous and indeed may be described as self-serving. Perhaps the patient was crossing the street against the traffic light pattern. There would then be an issue of contributory negligence, and in that event, the patient would not be entitled to recover any money in many jurisdictions.

Accordingly, the practice is to cover over those portions of the hospital record not relevant to diagnosis, prognosis, and/or treatment before the trier of the facts may see the hospital record.

This is usually accomplished by the attorney who is offering the record in evidence at the trial. He or she does this by affixing narrow tape over the portions of the record that are not admissible in evidence and offering the remainder of the record under either the common law or the statutory business records exception.

§ 10.20 MEDICAL OFFICE RECORDS OF ACCIDENT REPORTS OF PATIENTS

One court has found that a physician's spiral notebook, which is kept by employees of the physician and contains columns on each page listing the dates on which accident patients first visited the office, and a chart summarizing relevant entries in the notebook to establish patient bills are hearsay because these entries are written, out-of-court statements offered to prove the date when the accident victim first visited the physician's office. However, they may be admitted under the business records exception to the hearsay exclusionary rule, Federal Rule of Evidence 803(6), when a witness testifies that

1. the declarant in the records had the knowledge necessary to make accurate statements,
2. the declarant recorded the statements contemporaneously with the actions which were the subject of the reports,
3. the declarant made the records in the regular course of the business activity, and
4. such records were regularly kept by the business. U.S.—United States v. Furst, 886 F.2d 558, 571 (3d Cir. 1989); United States v. Console, 13 F.3d 641, 657 (3d Cir. 1993).

§ 10.21 EMPLOYEES' TIME CARDS

Shop or time cards showing the time worked by employees during a particular day may be received in evidence. Cal.—Katz v. T.I. Butler Co., 81 Cal.App. 747, 254 P. 679 (1927); Pa.—Johnson v. Kusminsky, 287 Pa. 425, 135 A. 220 (1926); Wash.—Willett v. Davis, 30 Wash. 2d 622, 193 P.2d 321 (1948).

§ 10.22 AIRLINE TICKETS

Airline tickets are admissible under the business records exception. U.S.—Rotolo v. United States, 404 F.2d 316 (5th Cir. 1968).

§ 10.23 MAGNETIC TAPE RECORDS

There is hardly a large business conducted today that does not rely on electronic data processing. With the computer have come the familiar magnetic tape and the printout sheets. These sheets are a necessary ingredient to the functioning of the business and are now accepted under the business records exception to the hearsay exclusionary rule. Miss.—King v. State ex rel. Murdock Accept. Corp., 222 So.2d 393 (Miss. 1969). Among the more recent methods of data storage are microfiche, compact disks, magnetic disks, and CD-ROM. These may be admitted under the business entries exception providing the contents do not require interpretation or analysis. Kelly v. Wasserman, *supra*.

§ 10.24 SURVEYS

A certified copy of a survey or a map on file in the land office is usually held admissible in evidence. Me.—Jackson v. Burnham, 129 Me. 344, 152 A. 56 (1930); U.S.—Zippo Mfg. Co. v. Rogers Imports, Inc., 216 F.Supp. 670 (S.D.N.Y. 1963).

§ 10.25 LEARNED TREATISES

Opinion diverges with respect to the admissibility of learned treatises. There is a line of cases that permit standard works of recognized authority to be introduced in evidence (Ala.—Berry v. Robertson, 285 Ala. 623, 235 So.2d 657 [1970]; Nev.—Foreman v. Ver Brugghen, 81 Nev. 86, 398 P.2d 993 [1965]), but in Florida (City of St. Petersburg v. Ferguson, 193 So.2d 648 [Fla.App. 1966]), it was held that medical or other works of science or learning are inadmissible as independent evidence of the theories and opinions expressed therein or as evidence for any purpose except to some extent in connection with the examination of an expert.

§ 10.26 MARKET REPORTS

The general rule is that standard price lists and market reports which are shown to be in general circulation and relied on by those engaged in the trade may be received as evidence of market value. Iowa—Wilbur v. Buckingham, 153 Iowa 194, 132 N.W. 960 (1911). The value of automobiles, which is so necessary in prosecuting larceny cases involving automobiles, may be proven by introducing in evidence *The National Automobile Dealer's Association Blue Book* or *Guide Book.* N.M.—Curtis v. Schwartzman Packing Co., 61 N.M. 305, 299 P.2d 776 (1956); Wyo.—O'Brien v. G.M.A.C., 362 P.2d 455 (Wyo. 1961). However, it is not conclusive evidence. N.M.—O'Meara v. Commercial Ins. Co., 71 N.M. 145, 376 P.2d 486 (1962).

§ 10.27 MARRIAGE AND BAPTISMAL CERTIFICATES

Marriage and baptismal certificates are competent evidence of the facts which they recite. Ind.—Blasche v. Himelick, 140 Ind.App. 255, 210 N.E.2d 378 (1965); La.—State *ex rel.* Lytell v. Louisiana St. Bd. of Health through Rein, 153 So.2d 498 (La.App. 1963).

§ 10.28 VITAL STATISTICS

Information gathered and recorded for the preservation of health and the prevention of disease which is not always open to public inspection is not admissible as a public document or official statement. Pa.—In re Marks, 121 Pa.Super. 181, 183 A. 432 (1936). But data and records of vital statistics, such as birth, marriage, and death, may be admissible as public documents. Pa.—In re Marks, *supra.* Most jurisdictions require these documents to be certified by the clerk of the office that stores these records in order to make them admissible in evidence.

§ 10.29 FAMILY RECORDS

A record in a family Bible is considered inferior or secondary evidence where the testimony of the party who made the entry is available, and thus the record is not admissible as independent evidence. Tex.—Jaffe v. Deckard, 261 S.W. 390 (Tex.Civ.App. 1924). If no one is able to testify as to the facts related in the family Bible, that record of the date of a person's birth or death may be competent evidence. Tex.—Jaffe v. Deckard, *supra.*

§ 10.30 TRIAL COURT'S WIDE DISCRETION

A trial court has wide discretion in the admission of evidence, and such discretionary actions will not be reversed on appeal unless it can be shown that the trial court was arbitrary and abused its discretion. In Wildwood Contractors v. Thompson-Holloway Real Estate Agency, 17 Ark.App. 169, 705 S.W.2d 897 (1986), it was held that the trial judge had wide discretion to determine that a business record is so lacking in trustworthiness that it is inadmissible under the business records exception to the hearsay rule.

§ 10.31 ABSENCE OF BUSINESS RECORDS

Sometimes records that are ordinarily kept in the regular course of a business, where it was the regular practice of that business activity to make the memorandum, report, record, or data compilation, are suddenly not available when an adverse party seeks to inspect these records for the purpose of using them later at the trial. The custodian may be concealing these records or destroying or altering them. Such a situation could occur in a hospital malpractice action or in a police brutality case, where the hospital or police department has intentionally "lost" the record of the suing patient or victim because the hospital or police department employees had done something wrong in the treatment of the patient or victim, respectively.

The fact that the hospital or police department has been unable to produce this record is admissible in evidence. This works to the advantage of the suing litigant because the trier of the facts might presume that the hospital or police department intentionally did not want to have this record in evidence.

New York, as well as other states, has a provision that if such a record is not produced after a motion to produce has been granted by the court, a further motion could be made and granted for an order that the issues to which the information is relevant shall be deemed resolved for purposes of the action in accordance with the claims of the party obtaining the order. N.Y.—CPLR 3126(1).

§ 10.32 VOLUMINOUS WRITINGS

Sometimes it is impractical to attempt to offer into evidence voluminous writings, recordings, or photographs, even though the contents thereof are material to the issues in the trial. The Federal Rules of Evidence and many state rules have overcome this problem by permitting a summary of these writings, recordings, or photographs to be entered into evidence in the form of a chart, summary, or calculation. The originals, or duplicates, must be made available for examination or copying, or both, by other parties to the action at a reasonable time and place. The court may also order that they be produced in court. See Federal Rule of Evidence 1007.

§ 10.33 COMPUTER PRINTOUTS

Ordinarily, computer printouts are admissible under the business records exception to the hearsay exclusionary rule. U.S.—United States v. Miller, 771 F.2d 1219 (9th Cir. 1985); Miss.—King v. State, 222 So.2d 393 (Miss. 1969); Wash.—State v. Bradley, 17 Wash.App. 916, 567 P.2d 650 (1977). However, when the computer printout consists of an analysis or interpretative summation, it makes the computer the declarant of hearsay evidence. This part of the printout report does not qualify under the business records exception. Kan.—West v. Martin, 11 Kan.App.2d 55, 713 P.2d 957 (1986).

§ 10.34 FEDERAL RULE

The hearsay exceptions covered in this chapter are treated extensively in Federal Rule of Evidence 803 (5), (8), (9), (12), (13), (14), (15), (17), (18), and (19). The limitation on the necessity for authentication of certain documents is treated in Rule 902. You are referred to those sections in the appendix of this book so as to avoid extensive repetition.

CROSS-REFERENCES

Federal Civil Judicial Procedure and Rules (West 1996) (Rule 803[6]).
Goode & Wellborn, Courtroom Handbook on Federal Evidence (West 1995) (Rule 803[6]).
McCormick, Evidence (4th ed. 1992) (Rule 803[6]).

Howard v. McDonough

Court of Appeals of New York, 1879.
77 N.Y. 592.

You may wonder why I selected a case decided in 1879 as an example of the use of a memorandum to refresh the recollection of a witness. The reason is that this is still the law and the decision provides a succinct explanation of the rule. I also want to explain that the word "conversion" in this case refers to the civil counterpart of the crime of larceny. The civil converter unlawfully takes the property of another person, the true owner of the property, and appropriates the said property to the use of the taker of that property. In this case, the alleged unlawful taker was a city marshal. (Argued March 27, 1879; decided April 8, 1979.)

This action was brought to recover for the alleged unlawful taking of the materials and fixtures of a job printing office, which were seized by defendant McDonough as city marshal, under an execution against a third person.

Upon the trial a witness for plaintiff testified that shortly after the seizure he made a list or schedule of the articles which he knew to have been taken and of their values, which he testified he knew; the articles were very numerous. The witness was allowed over objection and exception to use the list in testifying to the articles and their value, and after he had gone through the list it was offered and received in evidence over objection and exception. *Held,* no error.

The court laid down the rule as to the use of memoranda as follows:

"The law as to the use of memoranda by witnesses while testifying is quite well settled in this State. 1. A witness may, for the purpose of refreshing his memory, use any memorandum, whether made by himself or another, written or printed, and when his memory has thus been refreshed, he must testify to facts of his own knowledge, the memorandum itself not being evidence. 2. When a witness has so far forgotten the facts that he can not recall them, even after looking at a memorandum of them, and he testifies that he once knew them and made a memorandum of them at the time or soon after they transpired, which he intended to make correctly, and which he believes to be correct, such memorandum, in his own handwriting, may be received as evidence of the facts therein contained, although the witness has no present recollection of them. 3. Memoranda may be used in other cases which do not precisely come under either of the foregoing heads. A store of goods is wrongfully seized, and an action is brought to recover for the conversion. There are thousands of items. No witness could carry in his mind all the items and the values to be attached to them. In such a case, a witness may make a list of all the items and their values, and he may aid his memory while testifying by such list. He must be able to state that all the articles named in the list were seized, and that they were of the values therein stated, and he may use the list to enable him to state the items. After the witness has testified, the memorandum which he has used may be put in evidence, not as proving anything of itself, but as a detailed statement of the items testified to by the witness. The manner in which the memorandum, in such a case, may be used is very much in the discretion of the trial judge. He may require the witness to testify to each item separately and have his evidence recorded in the minutes of the trial, and then the introduction of the memorandum will not be important; or he may allow the witness to testify quite generally, to the items and their values; and receive the memorandum as the detailed result of his examination, leaving to the adverse party a more minute cross-examination. Without the use of a memorandum in such cases, it would be difficult, if not impossible, to conduct a trial involving the examination of a large number of items. (Driggs v. Smith, 36 N.Y.Superior Ct. 283, affirmed in this court; McCormick v. Penn. Central R. R. Co., 49 N.Y. 303.)"

* * *

EARL, J., reads for affirmance.
All concur.
Judgment affirmed.

RELATED DECISIONS
Police Reports

Johnson v. Lutz
Court of Appeals of New York, 1930.
253 N.Y. 124, 170 N.E. 517.

This is a landmark case from the Court of Appeals of New York. In New York, the court of appeals is similar to courts in other states named the "supreme court" of the state in which it is located. Most states follow the principle of law in this: that a memorandum of a motor vehicle accident prepared by a police officer from hearsay statements by persons not under a duty to make informational statements about the accident cannot be received in evidence in a civil trial under the guise of a memorandum made in the regular course of business. This is so because it was not made in the regular course of any business, profession, occupation, or calling. The court would not construe this exception to the hearsay exclusionary rule to include a private memorandum that was not made in pursuance of any duty owing by the person making it or, when made upon information, that was derived from another who made the communication casually and voluntarily and not under a sanction or duty or other obligation.

Action by Irene Johnson, as administratrix of the good, chattels, and credits of John S. Johnson, deceased, against Frederick Lutz and another, copartners doing business as Chas. Lutz & Sons. From a judgment of the Appellate Division (226 App.Div. 772, 234 N.Y.S. 328 (1929)), affirming a judgment entered upon the verdict of a jury in favor of plaintiff, defendants appeal by permission.

Affirmed.

HUBBS, J. This action is to recover damages for the wrongful death of the plaintiff's intestate, who was killed when his motorcycle came into collision with the defendants' truck at a street intersection. There was a sharp conflict in the testimony in regard to the circumstances under which the collision took place. A policeman's report of the accident filed by him in the station house was offered in evidence by the defendants under Section 374-a of the Civil Practice Act, and was excluded. The sole ground for reversal urged by the appellants is that said report was erroneously excluded. That section reads:

"Any writing or record, whether in the form of an entry in a book or otherwise, made as a memorandum or record of any act, transaction, occurrence or event, shall be admissible in evidence in proof of said act, transaction, occurrence or event, if the trial judge shall find that it was made in the regular course of any business, and that it was the regular course of such business to make such memorandum or record at the time of such act, transaction, occurrence or event, or within a reasonable time thereafter. All other circumstances of the making of such writing or record, including lack of personal knowledge by the entrant or maker, may be shown to affect its weight, but they shall not affect its admissibility. The term business shall include business, profession, occupation and calling of every kind."

Prior to the decision in the well-known case of Vosburgh v. Thayer, 12 Johns. 461, decided in 1815, shopbooks could not be introduced in evidence to prove an account. The decision in that case established that they were admissible where preliminary proof could be made that there were regular dealings between the parties; that the plaintiff kept honest and fair books; that some of the articles charged had been delivered; and that the plaintiff kept no clerk. At that time it might not have been a hardship to require a shopkeeper who sued to recover an account to furnish the preliminary proof required by that decision. Business was transacted in a comparatively small way, with few, if any, clerks. Since the decision in that case, it has remained the substantial basis of all decisions upon the question in this jurisdiction prior to the enactment in 1928 of Section 374-a, Civil Practice Act.

Under modern conditions, the limitations upon the right to use books of account, memoranda, or records, made in the regular course of business, often resulted in a denial of justice, and usually in annoyance, expense, and waste of time and energy. A rule of evidence that was practical a century ago had become obsolete. The situation was appreciated, and attention was called to it by the courts and text-writers. Woods Practice Evidence (2d Ed.) 377; 3 Wigmore on Evidence (1923) § 1530.

The report of the Legal Research Committee of the Commonwealth Fund, published in 1927, by the Yale University Press, under the title "The Law of Evidence—Some Proposals for Its Reform," dealt with the question in chapter 5, under the heading "Proof of Business Transactions to Harmonize with Current Business Practice." That report, based upon extensive research, pointed out the confusion existing in decisions in different jurisdictions. It explained and illustrated the great need of a more practical, workable, and uniform rule, adapted to modern business conditions and practices. The chapter is devoted to a discussion of the pressing need of a rule of evidence which would "give evidential credit to the books upon which the mercantile and industrial world relies in the conduct of business." At the close of the chapter, the committee proposed a statute to be enacted in all jurisdictions. In compliance with such proposal, the Legislature enacted Section 374-a of the Civil Practice Act in the very words used by the committee.

It is apparent that the Legislature enacted Section 374-a to carry out the purpose announced in the report of the committee. That purpose was to secure the enactment of a statute which would afford a more workable rule of evidence in the proof of business transactions under existing business conditions.

In view of the history of Section 374-a and the purpose for which it was enacted, it is apparent that it was never intended to apply to a situation like that in the case at bar. The memorandum in question was not made in the regular course of any business, profession, occupation, or calling. The policeman who made it was not present at the time of the accident. The memorandum was made from hearsay statements of third persons who happened to be present at the scene of the accident when he arrived. It does not appear whether they saw the accident and stated to him what they knew, or stated what some other persons had told them.

The purpose of the Legislature in enacting Section 374-a was to permit a writing or record, made in the regular course of business, to be received in evidence, without the necessity of calling as witnesses all of the persons who had any part in making it provided the record was made as a part of the duty of the person making it, or on information imparted by persons who were under a duty to impart such information. The amendment permits the introduction of shopbooks without the necessity of calling all clerks who may have sold different items of account. It was not intended to permit the receipt in evidence of entries based upon voluntary hearsay statements made by third parties not engaged in the business or under any duty in relation thereto. It was said, in Mayor, etc., of New York City v. Second Ave. R. Co., 102 N.Y. 572, at page 581, 7 N.E. 905, 909, 55 Am.Rep. 839 (1886): "It is a proper qualification of the rule admitting such evidence that the account must have been made in the ordinary course of business, and that it should not be extended so as to admit a mere private memorandum, not made in pursuance of any duty owing by the person making it, or when made upon information derived from another who made the communication casually and voluntarily, and not under the sanction of duty or other obligation."

An important consideration leading to the amendment was the fact that in the business world credit is given to records made in the course of business by persons who are engaged in the business upon information given by others engaged in the same business as part of their duty.

"Such entries are dealt with in that way in the most important undertakings of mercantile and industrial life. They are the ultimate basis of calculation, investment, and general confidence in every business enterprise. Nor does the practical impossibility of obtaining constantly and permanently the verification of every employee affect the trust that is given to such books. It would seem that expedients which the entire commercial world recognizes as safe could be sanctioned, and not discredited, by courts of justice. When it is a mere question of whether provisional confidence can be placed in a certain class of statements, there cannot profitably and sensibly be one rule for the business world and another for the court-room. The merchant and the manufacturer must not be turned away remediless because the methods in which the entire community places a just confidence are a little difficult to reconcile with technical judicial scruples on the part of the same persons who as attorneys have already employed and relied upon the same methods. In short, courts must here cease to be pedantic and endeavor to be practical." 3 Wigmore on Evidence (1923) § 1530, p. 278.

The Legislature has sought by the amendment to make the courts practical. It would be unfortunate not to give the amendment a construction which will enable it to cure the evil complained of and accomplish the purpose for which it was enacted. In construing it, we should not, however, permit it to be applied in a case for which it was never intended.

The judgment should be affirmed, with costs.

CARDOZO, C.J., and POUND, CRANE, LEHMAN, KELLOGG, and O'BRIEN, JJ., concur.

Judgment affirmed.

Yeargans v. Yeargans

Supreme Court of New York, Appellate Division, First Department, 1965.
24 A.D.2d 280, 265 N.Y.S.2d 562.

This case construes a New York statute relevant to the admission of police reports in evidence under the business records exception to the hearsay exclusionary rule.

In Johnson v. Lutz, *supra*, the court did not accept the statements in a police report under the business records exception because the entries were made by a police officer but the information in these entries was given to the officer by witnesses who were not under any business obligation to do so. In Yeargans v. Yeargans, the court explained that statements made by a police officer recounting what he or she had actually observed of the situation

were made in the course of police business and were thus admissible under the business records exception.

You will note that the court refers to the statute in question as § 374-a of the Civil Practice Act. On September 1, 1963, this statute ceased to exist, and the section was substantially incorporated into a new statute called the Civil Practice Law and Rules. The section of the applicable statute was changed at that time to 4518. Thus, you can understand that the court is following the principle of stare decisis if the wording in an old statute is similar to that which is found in a new statute when the old statute is discontinued by the legislature.

* * *

Before BOTEIN, P.J., and RABIN, MC-NALLY, STEVENS and STEUER, JJ.

PER CURIAM: In this action for damages for personal injuries received August 12, 1961 by plaintiff, a passenger, when a car owned and operated by the defendant ran off the road and struck a tree, reversal is directed and a new trial ordered. The charge presented to the jury a theory contrary to that advanced by plaintiff in his bill of particulars and similarly advanced at the trial, in addition to the one so advanced. That was error. The verdict being a general one, it is impossible to determine upon what theory recovery was actually allowed. Clark v. Board of Education, 304 N.Y. 488, 490, 109 N.E.2d 73 (1953); Fein v. Board of Education, 305 N.Y. 611, 613, 11 N.E.2d 732 (1938). It was also prejudicial error to exclude the motor vehicle report offered by the defendant when the report tended to contradict the version of the accident given by the defendant in a deposition before trial. CPLR 3117(d) specifically provides "[a]t the trial, any party may rebut any relevant evidence contained in a deposition, whether introduced by him or by any other party." It may be noted that the deposition was first used by the plaintiff in his case in chief and was not used to contradict or impeach the defendant-deponent who had not yet testified. See CPLR 3117(d). The motor vehicle report filed August 14, 1961 by defendant contained a version as to the cause of the accident which differed from that given by defendant in her examination before trial. When injuries are suffered in an automobile accident in the State of New York, or the property damage exceeds a specified amount, a report is required to be filed with the Motor Vehicle Commissioner (Vehicle & Traffic Law, § 605). This report becomes a public document (Public Officers Law, § 66-a). Under certain circumstances it could be received in evidence as a public document and used to impeach the witness. While the Motor Vehicle report offered was one filed in Vermont, there was no evidence to indicate that it should be regarded other than as a public document. Moreover, the trial court was empowered to take judicial notice of applicable Vermont law (CPLR 4511).

It was also prejudicial error under the circumstances of this case to receive the police report in evidence. The police officer, John J. Ryan, a member of the Bennington, Vermont Police Department, was never called to testify and there is no indication in the report save by possible inference as to his source or sources for the information recorded. Moreover, the report was admitted before that portion of defendant's deposition was read, in which defendant stated she had given the information appearing in such report.

Of course reports of police officers made upon their own observation and while carrying out their police duties are generally admissible in evidence. Trbovich v. Burke, 234 App.Div. 384, 255 N.Y.S. 100 (1932). In that case the police blotter was admitted in evidence, the court finding proof that the entries were made on the basis of the officer's communications. The court also pointed out, however, that the jury should have been instructed that the only value of the entries "was in showing what officer Ciulis reported shortly after the accident, and that, if the entries were not found to have been based on officer Ciulis' communication, the entries were pure hearsay and entitled to no weight" (p. 385, 255 N.Y.S. p.102). Police reports have consistently been held inadmissible to establish the main fact where the information contained in the police blotter came from witnesses not engaged in the police business in the course of which the memorandum was made (Johnson v. Lutz, 226 App.Div. 772, 234

N.Y.S. 328, aff'd 253 N.Y. 124, 170 N.E. 517 [1930]), or where the employee giving the information (in addition to the bystander witnesses) "had every reason to give a biased and false report" (Needle v. New York Railways Corporation, 227 App.Div. 276, at 278, 237 N.Y.S. 547, at 549). In that case the information had been obtained from the defendant motorman. In Zaulich v. Thompkins Square Co., 10 A.D.2d 492, 200 N.Y.S.2d 550 (1930), the officer testified to what the plaintiff had told him and also to his own physical observations made upon arrival at the scene. He testified also that he had made an entry in the memorandum book which he was required by the rules of the police department to carry on his person, thereafter telephoning such information to the station house and at the end of his tour of duty examined and signed the report made from the information given. Both the report and the memorandum were excluded. This court in reversing said "it seems clear that the police report was admissible as a record made in the regular course of business pursuant to Section 374-a of the Civil Practice Act" (p. 496, 200 N.Y.S.2d p. 555). (Now CPLR 4518.) The court also observed that since the record supported an inference that the testimony was assailed as a possible recent fabrication the exclusion from evidence of the police officer's report and memorandum book to bolster the officer's testimony constituted prejudicial error (p. 497, 200 N.Y.S. p. 555). In this case the officer did not testify, nor did he witness the accident. For a discussion as to the purpose of Section 374-a of the Civil Practice Act see Williams v. Alexander, 309 N.Y. 283 at 286–287, 129 N.E.2d 417 at 419 (Fuld, J.); see also Mtr. of City of N.Y. (5thAve. Coach), 42 Misc.2d 319, 247 N.Y.S.2d 933 (1931), discussing CPLR 4518 as a restatement, in substance, of 374-a Civil Practice Act. (Cf. Kelly v. Wasserman, 5 N.Y.2d 425, 185 N.Y.S.2d 538, 158 N.E.2d 241 [1959], where Department of Welfare records consisting of a memorandum of conversations with the defendant were admissible to impeach the defendant even though he was the plaintiff's witness. Cf. Coppola v. Melvin, 241 App.Div. 611, at 612, 268 N.Y.S. 736 [1934]; Matter of Roge v. Valentine, 280 N.Y.

268, at 278, 20 N.E.2d 751, at 756 [1939]. See generally, 5 Wigmore on Evidence, 3d ed., § 1530 et seq., 5 Bender's New York Evidence, § 375. But in Wilson v. Bungalow Bar Corp. of America, 285 App.Div. 1191, 141 N.Y.S.2d 106 [1955], where the report was not based upon the police officer's own knowledge but upon information obtained from the driver of the truck involved in the accident, there was a limitation on the use of the police report to impeach the officer's testimony.) In the case before us the plaintiff simply offered a certified copy of the police report of an officer of a foreign state and the court received it. The court put no limitations in its charge upon the use or purpose for which the report was received. No exception was taken to the charge by the defendant except as to a portion referring to contributory negligence of the plaintiff.

On this record and in the interest of justice, the judgment appealed from should be reversed on the law and a new trial ordered, with costs to abide the event.

Judgment reversed on the law, and a new trial ordered, with $50 costs to abide the event. All concur except BOTEIN, P. J., who votes to affirm and RABIN, J., who concurs in the result.

Toll v. State of New York

Supreme Court, Appellate Division, Third Department, 1969.
32 A.D.2d 47, 299 N.Y.S.2d 589.

This case was decided after Johnson v. Lutz, *supra;* Yeargans v. Yeargans, *supra;* and Kelly v. Wassermann, mentioned in the text portion of this chapter. It contains many principles of law with respect to N.Y.—CPLR 4518. The one I would most like you to remember is that the conclusions of a police officer making an accident report are not admissible in evidence for the truth of the assertions because the officer is not usually an expert in the cause and effect of an automobile accident and thus is not qualified to testify as to a conclusion with respect to these issues.

The student who is concerned with the laws of states other than New York may believe that this type of case does not have any relevance for him or her. However, many states copy their statutes from other states, and that student probably has a similar statute in his or her state. Also, the courts of a state will often find the common law of another state to be persuasive reasoning and adopt it as the law of their state when there are no court decisions deciding that principle of law.

COOKE, Justice. This is an appeal from a judgment entered May 13, 1968, upon a decision of the Court of Claims, dismissing appellant's claim for personal injuries, following a trial on the issue of liability.

While it was snowing heavily and when visibility was poor, claimant, operating his automobile in the third or inside lane of the westbound portion of the six-lane Cross-Westchester Expressssway, came in contact with the State's truck, in the same lane and on a snow plowing mission, shortly after midnight on March 7, 1967. Sharp issues arose on trial, claimant testifying that the truck was stationary and without lights when hit, with the State's driver swearing it was moving at 20–25 miles per hour with two headlights, a revolving amber dome light, two regular taillights and two red flashers all operating.

The report of the State trooper, who investigated but did not witness the accident, and the accident report of the snow plow operator, made 15 days after the event and filed with the Department of Public Works, were admitted over objections. Appellant contends that the former was improperly received because of its conclusional content and its authorship by an officer who did not witness the accident, and the latter because of not being prepared within a reasonable time after the occurrence.

Subdivision (a) of CPLR 4518 provides for the introduction into evidence of a record made in the regular course of any business, where it was the regular course of such business to make it, and it was made at the time of the act, transaction, occurrence or event, or within a reasonable time thereafter. In Johnson v. Lutz, 253 N.Y. 124, 170 N.E. 517 (1930), the exclusion of a police report was upheld and the Court of Appeals read into the then existing statute a requirement, not expressly found in it, that, to be admissible, the person making the police report be the witness or that the person supplying the information to the entrant be under a business duty to do so (p. 128). (Cf. Cox v. State of New York 3 N.Y.2d 693, 699, 171 N.Y.S.2d 818, 822, 148 N.E.2d 879, 882 [1958]; Trbovich v. Burke, 234 App.Div. 384, 255 N.Y.S. 100 [1932].) Then, in Kelly v. Wasserman, 5 N.Y.2d 425, 185 N.Y.S.2d 538, 158 N.E.2d 241 (1959), in allowing the receipt of a record of the Welfare Department reciting statements of defendant, it appeared that the requirement that the informant be under a business duty to impart the information was abandoned. (Cf. Gutin v. Frank Mascali & Sons, 11 N.Y.2d, 97, 99, 226 N.Y.S.2d 434, 435, 181 N.E.2d 449, 450 [1962].) In Zaulich v. Thompkins Sq. Holding Co., 10 A.D. 2d 492, 200 N.Y.S.2d 550 (1st Dept. 1960), where plaintiff's at trial version of an accident was at variance with that given by him at the scene to a policeman and then recorded in the police report, the report was held to be admissible as a record made in the regular course of business and that it was, in any event, competent evidence to rebut the inference by plaintiff's counsel that the patrolman's testimony was a recent fabrication. In Chemical Leaman Tank Lines v. Stevens, 21 A.D.2d 556, 251 N.Y.S.2d 240 (3d Dept. 1964), a Deputy Sheriff's report containing defendant's description of an accident, which was at variance with that related by her on trial, was received, it being held that the report was admissible as a business record and that the statements to the Deputy were admissible as admissions of a party.

It is important that these decisions be reconciled and we adopt the following as a workable guide regarding the admission of police officer reports in accident cases. CPLR 4518(a) permits a police report to be admitted as proof of the facts recorded therein if (1) the entrant of those facts was the witness, or (2) the person giving the entrant the information was under a business duty to relate the facts to the entrant (Johnson v. Lutz, supra). If neither of these two requisites is satisfied but the report recites a statement of an outsider, the record may be admitted (under Kelly v. Wasserman, supra), to prove that the state-

ment recorded therein was made by the outsider (even though the main facts set forth in the business record are hearsay and excludable pursuant to Johnson) and, then, the facts recited in the statement may be proven by the business record if the statement qualifies as a hearsay exception, e.g., an admission, as in Kelly and Chemical Leaman. (Barker, Admissibility of Investigational Reports Under Business Records Statutes, 33 Albany L.Rev. 251; Prince, Evidence, 16 Syracuse L.Rev. 459–460; Prince, The Hearsay Rule, Practising Law Institute, Litigation Series, Trial Evidence, pp. 18-7 to 18-11; Supplementary Practice Commentary by Joseph M. McLaughlin, McKinney's Cons.Laws of N.Y., Book 7B, CPLR 4518, Supp., pp. 87–89; cf. Mahon v. Giordano, 30 A.D.2d 792, 291 N.Y.S.2d 854 (1968); Yeargans v. Yeargans, 24 A.D.2d 280, 265 N.Y.S.2d 562 (1966). Here, the collision not having been witnessed by the State trooper and there being no proof that whoever gave him the facts had a business duty to do so, the report is not admissible to prove the main facts; and, since no other hearsay exception applies to the information from outsiders to the trooper, Kelly does not apply and the admission of the report was error.

The police report having contained the conclusion of the officer as to the factors contributing to the impact and it being impermissible for the officer to testify to his conclusions, his written conclusions should have been excluded, if the report had been otherwise acceptable (Albert v. Stumpf, 30 A.D.2d 686, 291 N.Y.S.2d 887 [1968]; Bothner v. Keegan, 275 App.Div. 470, 472, 89 N.Y.S.2d 288, 289 [1949]). The business entry statute lifts the barrier of the hearsay objection; it does not overcome any other exclusionary rule which might properly be invoked (Richardson, Evidence [9th ed.], § 235; 5 Weinstein-Korn-Miller, N.Y.Civ.Prac., par. 4518.18).

The statutory requirement that the business record be prepared within a reasonable time after the occurrence, i.e., while the memory of the event was still fresh enough to be fairly reliable, should not be too rigidly applied and did not prevent the introduction of the accident report of the truck driver (5 Weinstein-Korn-Miller, N.Y.Civ. Prac., pars.

4518.02, 4518.17; McCormick, Evidence, p. 601). The self-serving aspect of this report did not preclude its admissibility under the statute, it being merely a consideration affecting its weight (Bromberg v. City of New York, 25 A.D.2d 885, 270 N.Y.S.2d 425 [1966]; Bishin v. New York Cent. R.R. Co., 20 A.D.2d 921, 249 N.Y.S.2d 778 [1964]).

The trial court's decision states that the Cross-Westchester Expressway contains a center mall dividing "two-lane pavements" on each side of the mall and that claimant "was not observing the posted regulation requiring travel in the right or driving lane but was driving in the mall or passing lane." Respondent's brief, however, concedes that each pavement consisted of three lanes and that there was no proof of "posted regulations."

The consideration of an inapplicable statute and regulation on such a vital facet of the issue of liability also requires reversal (cf. Morse v. Buffalo Tank Corp., 280 N.Y. 110, 119, 19 N.E.2d 981, 985 [1939]; Sarconi v. 122 West 26th St. Corp., 241 N.Y. 340, 150 N.E. 137 [1926]; Uliaszek v. Buczkowski, 259 App.Div. 967, 19 N.Y.S.2d 912 [1940]; Flaherty v. Metro Stations, 202 App.Div. 583, 587, 196 N.Y.S. 2, 6 affirmed 235 N.Y. 605, 139 N.E. 753 [1923]).

The judgment should be reversed, on the law and the facts, and a new trial ordered, with costs.

Judgment reversed, on the law and the facts, and a new trial ordered, with costs.

GIBSON, P.J., and REYNOLDS, AULISI and STALEY, JJ., concur.

RELATED DECISIONS
Audits and Computer Printouts

Wildwood Contractors v. Thompson-Holloway Real Estate Agency
Court of Appeals of Arkansas, Division 1, 1986.
17 Ark.App. 169, 705 S.W.2d 897.

This is a classic use of the business records exception to the hearsay exclusionary rule, but the decision refers to a new issue, i.e., the weight of the evidence, as opposed to its admissibility. The court means that an item of evidence may be admissible, but the trier of the facts of the case may not give it much weight in making its decision in favor of one side or the other in a trial. In the instant case, it refers to a decision on the facts and the law because the case was tried by a judge without a jury. If a jury had tried the case, we would say that the jury reached a verdict, rather than making a decision. In most jurisdictions, each party has the right to demand that the case be tried by a jury. This results in a more expensive and time-consuming trial, but some attorneys believe that their cases will get a fairer hearing or come to a more successful conclusion for their clients if the jury decides the questions of fact.

GLAZE, Judge.

Appellant, Wildwood Contractors, appeals a judgment from the Union County Circuit Court against it in favor of appellee, Thompson-Holloway Real Estate Agency, for $982.00, which represents additional insurance premiums for coverage written by appellee for appellant through the Hartford Insurance Company. The amount was determined as a result of an audit of actual business activity of appellant for a one-year period in order to "true up" premiums with actual risk incurred by the insurance company during the audit year. The audit was conducted not by appellee or its employees, but rather by the Hartford Insurance Company, which wrote appellant's insurance through appellee. The case was tried to the court without a jury, and the only witness was Robert H. Archer, a partner in the appellee insurance agency, who presented an exhibit consisting of the disputed audit. The audit was admitted into evidence over appellant's objection. Based upon the audit, the trial court found for appellee and entered judgment, finding that the audit constituted a record of regularly conducted business activity which fell within the hearsay exception provided in Unif.R.Evid. 803(6).

For reversal, appellant contends that the trial court erred in admitting the results of the audit as a business record within the hearsay exception provided in Unif.R.Evid. 803(6). The rule provides that records of a regularly conducted business activity are not excluded by the hearsay rule from evidence "unless the source of information or the method or circumstances of preparation indicate lack of trustworthiness."

Rule 803(6) articulates, *inter alia*, the types of records falling within the business records exception. As stated in Cates v. State, 267 Ark. 726, 589 S.W.2d 598 (Ark.App. 1979), there are seven factors which must be present in order for a business record to be admissible under the rule: the evidence must be (1) a record or other compilation, (2) of acts or events, (3) made at or near the time the act occurred, (4) by a person with knowledge, or from information transmitted by such a person, (5) kept in the course of a regularly conducted business, (6) which has a regular practice of recording such information, (7) all as shown by the testimony of the custodian or other qualified witness. *Id.* at 728, 589 S.W.2d at 598–599.

While this case presents several close questions as to whether the audit in question falls within the "business records" exception to the hearsay rule, we cannot say from our review of the evidence that the trial court abused its discretion in admitting the audit into evidence. The audit in question certainly qualifies as a "record" of "acts or events" consisting of business activity during a specific calendar year. In order to be admissible under Rule 803(6), the audit report must be made at or near the time of the examination of the records upon which it is based, and not necessarily when the activity shown in the audited records was performed. Pfeffer v. S. Texas Laborers' Pension Trust Fund, 679 S.W.2d 691, 694 (Tex.App. 1 Dist. 1984). Here, the audit was conducted within a reasonable time.

Archer testified that the record was compiled from information transmitted by some person with knowledge who worked for appellant. Finally, audits such as the one here, according to the evidence, are a regularly conducted business activity and are utilized as a regular practice by the insurance underwriter to square actual risk incurred with anticipated risk, and the audits are relied upon to adjust premiums.

It is the fact that regularly kept business records are relied upon for business decisions that makes them trustworthy enough to be admissible as an exception to the hearsay rule. *See* E. Cleary, *McCormick On Evidence*, Section 306 (3d Ed. 1984). A trial judge has wide discretion to determine whether a business record lacks trustworthiness. *See* United States v. Page, 544 F.2d 982, 987 (8th Cir. 1976).

Finally, appellant strongly contends that Archer was not qualified to sponsor the audit because he could not of his own personal knowledge vouch for the results of the audit or even as to the manner in which it was conducted. However, the business records exception does not mandate that the custodian be able to explain the record-keeping procedures in question. United States v. Henneberry, 719 F.2d 941, 948 (8th Cir. 1983). It is not necessary that the sponsoring witness have knowledge of the actual creation of the document in question; the personal knowledge of the sponsoring witness regarding preparation of the business record goes to the weight rather than the admissibility of the evidence. *See Page supra.* The trial judge has the discretion to determine the qualifications of witnesses and the admissibility of evidence. Smith v. Chicot-Lipe Insurance Agency, 11 Ark.App. 49, 51, 665 S.W.2d 907, 908 (1984). *See also Cates, supra.*

Based upon our review of the evidence, we cannot say that the trial court abused its discretion in finding that the audit in question fell within the requirements of Unif.R.Evid. 803(6) as a business record exception to the hearsay rule and was therefore admissible. The decision of the trial court is affirmed.

AFFIRMED.

COOPER and CLONINGER, JJ., agree.

United States v. Console

United States Court of Appeals, Third Circuit, 1993.
13 F.3d 641.

This case presents an example where the business records exception to the hearsay exclusionary rule is used in a criminal case to assist the prosecution in convicting the defendants of a federal mail fraud violation. It also presents other principles of law relevant to the contents of this book but not relevant to the principle of law being studied in this chapter.

* * *

D. ADMISSIBILITY OF THE ACCIDENT BOOK

The "Accident Book" is a spiral notebook which was kept by employees of Markoff's practice. Console App. at 76–221. One of the columns on each page listed the date of an accident patient's first visit to Markoff's office. *Id.* The government used the Accident Book, *id.*, and a chart summarizing relevant entries in the book, *id.* at 222–31, to establish that patient bills predating the date recorded in the Accident Book as the patient's first visit were fraudulent.

Rule 801 of the Federal Rule of Evidence defines hearsay as a "statement, other than one made by a declarant while testifying at the trial or hearing, offered in evidence to prove the truth of the matter asserted." Rule 801 prohibits the admission of an out-of-court statement offered to prove the truth of the matter asserted because

> the statement is inherently untrustworthy: the declarant may not have been under oath at the time of the statement, his or her credibility cannot be evaluated at trial, and he or she cannot be cross-examined.

Pelullo, 964 F.2d 193, 203 (3d Cir. 1992). The Accident Book is hearsay because the entries are written out-of-court statements offered to prove the date when accident patients first visited the Markoff office.

Console and Curcio argue that the district court in the second trial erred by admitting the Accident Book under the business record exception to the hearsay rule. Fed.R.Evid. 803(6).[11] This exception for "Records of Regularly Conducted Activity" authorizes the admission of:

> [a] memorandum, report, record, or data compilation, in any form, of acts, events, conditions, opinions, or diagnoses, made at or near the time by, or from information transmitted by, a person with knowledge, if kept in the course of a regularly conducted business activity, and if it was the regular practice of that business activity to make the memorandum, report, record, or data compilation, all as shown by the testimony of the custodian or other qualified witness, unless the source of information or the method or circumstances of preparation indicate lack of trustworthiness.

The appellants argue that the Accident Book was inadmissible hearsay because the government did not produce a witness "qualified" to give the foundation testimony required by Rule 803(6) and thus failed to introduce the foundation evidence required for the admission of the Accident Book as a business record. Console Br. at 18–27; Curcio Br. at 34–39, 43. They also argue that even if the Accident Book qualified as a business record, it was inadmissible under Rule 803(6) because "the method or circumstances of [its] preparation indicate lack of trustworthiness." *Id.* at 27–31. We exercise plenary review over the district court's interpretation of the Federal Rules of Evidence, but review a ruling based on a permissible interpretation of a rule for abuse of discretion. United States v. Furst, 886 F.2d 558, 571 (3d Cir. 1989) (citing In re Japanese Elec. Prods. Antitrust Litig., 723 F.2d 238, 265 (1983), *rev'd on other grounds sub nom.* Matsushita Elec. Indus. Co. v. Zenith Radio Corp., 475 U.S. 574, 106 S.Ct. 1348, 89 L.Ed.2d 538 (1986)), *cert. denied,* 493 U.S. 1062, 110 S.Ct. 878, 107 L.Ed.2d 961 (1990). *See also* Petruzzi's IGA v. Darling-Delaware

Co., 998 F.2d 1224, 1237 (3d Cir.), *cert. denied,* — U.S. —, 114 S.Ct. 554, 126 L.Ed.2d 455 (1993).

Rule 803(6) does not require the foundation evidence for the admission of a business record to be provided by the record's custodian. Instead, the rule authorizes parties to elicit the evidence from any "other qualified witness." Fed.R.Evid. 803(6). We have recognized that the term "other qualified witness" should be construed broadly, and that a qualified witness "'need not be an employee of the [record-keeping] entity so long as he understands the system.'" *Pelullo,* 964 F.2d at 201 (quoting 4 Jack B. Weinstein & Margaret A. Berger, *Weinstein's Evidence* ¶ 803(6)[02], at 803-178). Thus, a qualified witness only need "have familiarity with the record-keeping system" and the ability to attest to the foundational requirements of Rule 803(6). *Id.* at 201–02. The foundation requirements to which a qualified witness must attest are:

> (1) [that] the declarant in the records had knowledge to make accurate statements; (2) that the declarant recorded statements contemporaneously with the actions which were the subject of the reports; (3) that the declarant made the record in the regular course of the business activity; and (4) that such records were regularly kept by the business.

Furst, 886 F.2d at 571 (citing Rule 803(6)).

The district court did not abuse its discretion by admitting the Accident Book and the summary chart derived from it. Sharon Campbell, the witness through whom the Accident Book was introduced into evidence, was a "qualified witness." Markoff employed her for seven years as a file clerk, a therapist, a receptionist, and a clerk in the "legal department." Govt.App. at 971–72. Her testimony indicates that through her work, she became familiar with the office record-keeping system and the various forms and documents regularly kept by the office. Govt.App. at 972–80, 990–95; Console App. at 237–53, 272–75, 306–12. Campbell's familiarity with the office record-keeping system enabled her to attest to each of the four foundation requirements for the admission of the Accident Book as a business record.

Campbell testified that her mother, who also was a Markoff employee, first created the book in 1980 to organize the "legal department" by providing a record of certain key dates including: the date of the patient's accident; the date of the patient's first visit to Markoff's office; and the dates on which the legal department sent certain documents to the patient's attorney. Console App. at 238–44; 306–08. Campbell also testified that the office receptionist generally entered the date of a patient's first visit when the patient came in or at the end of the receptionist's shift. She then identified the Accident Book entries that she had made and those that her mother had made. *Id.* at 245–47. Finally, Campbell testified that while she was employed in the "legal department" of the Markoff practice, she relied on the Accident Book and inserted information in the book when "something was overlooked." *Id.* at 249–53, 310–12. Based on this experience, she concluded that the Accident Book was "85 to 95 percent" accurate. *Id.* at 310.

Campbell's testimony satisfied the foundation requirements of Rule 803(6) because it "demonstrate[d] that the records [in the Accident Book] were made contemporaneously with the act the documents purport[ed] to record by someone with knowledge of the subject matter, that they were made in the regular course of business, and that such records were regularly kept by the business." *Pelullo,* 964 F.2d at 201. The government also called three other employees of the Markoff office who had made entries in the Accident Book, and their testimony regarding the book corroborated Campbell's Console App. at 324–33, 349–55, 369–75. Furthermore, although the evidence indicates that the Accident Book was not completely accurate, the circumstances of its production indicate that it was sufficiently reliable to constitute a business record.

Finally, the appellants' argument that the Accident Book was inadmissible under Rule 803(6) because the employees who made entries in the Accident Book and in other business records used to fill in omissions in the Accident Book relied on information provided by patients lacks merit. Rule 803(6) does not require that the person transmitting the recorded information "be under a business duty to provide accurate information." United States v. Patrick, 959 F.2d 991, 1001 (D.C.Cir. 1992). Instead, "it is sufficient if it is shown that . . . [the] standard practice was to verify the information provided," *id.*,[12] or that the information transmitted met the requirements of another hearsay exception, Fed.R.Evid. 805. *See* Michael H. Graham, Federal Practice and Procedure: Federal Rules of Evidence § 6757, at 643 (1992).

In this case, there was testimony indicating that the existing file of someone who was not a new patient was retrieved and forwarded to Markoff, and no new medical history chart was prepared. Console App. at 327, 373. This procedure indicates that when the receptionist did not have personal knowledge of whether a patient's visit was his or her first, there was a process for ascertaining this information. Moreover, a patient's statement that he or she is visiting a doctor for the first time satisfies the requirements of another hearsay exception, Rule 803(4), which provides that "[s]tatements made for purposes of medical diagnosis or treatment and describing medical history" are not excluded by the hearsay rule. *See* Wilson v. Zapata Off-Shore Co., 939 F.2d 260, 271–72 (5th Cir. 1991). During oral argument, Console argued at length that the information obtained from the patients for the Accident Book was only significant for billing purposes, and thus was in itself hearsay, which in view of Fed.R.Evid. 805 was inadmissible. The record indicates, however, that the information taken from the patient for the Accident Book was given to Markoff for use when he saw the patient. Console App. at 324–25. Indeed, at the trial Console did not even cite Fed.R.Evid. 805 to object to the Accident Book on the ground that it contained "[h]earsay included within hearsay" so that the included hearsay itself was required to conform to an exception to the hearsay rule. Rather, his objection was general.[13] Overall we are satisfied that the circumstances of the Accident Book's creation and the source of its contents, *i.e.,* patients and business records created based on the personal knowledge of Markoff's employees and patients, provide suf-

ficient indicia of trustworthiness to satisfy the business record exception.[14]

The appellants analogize this case to *Pelullo* and *Furst*, Console Br. at 19–21, Curcio Br. at 35–36, 38–39, two cases in which we held that the foundation requirements of Rule 803(6) had not been satisfied. But this case is distinguishable from *Pelullo* because in *Pelullo* the government sought to introduce bank-generated records of wire transfers through an FBI agent who "did not purport to have familiarity with the record-keeping system of the banks, nor . . . attest to any of the other requirements of Rule 803(6)." *Pelullo*, 964 F.2d at 201–02. *Furst* is also distinguishable because in *Furst* "neither witness called by the government [to lay a foundation for the purported business records] had any knowledge as to the accuracy of the information on which the . . . documents were based or as to the knowledge of the persons who prepared the records," *Furst*, 886 F.2d at 572, and "the government did not call a single employee to explain the origin of the data reflected in the documents," *id.* at 572 n. 18. Consequently it cannot be contended successfully on the basis of either *Pelullo* or *Furst* that the district court abused its discretion in the admission of the Accident Book and the summary chart based on it.[15]

*   *   *

---

[11] They also argue that the Accident Book was not authenticated properly. Console Br. at 18 n. 62 (3d Cir. 1976), *cert. denied*, 429 U.S. 1038, 97 S.Ct. 732, 50 L.Ed.2d 748 (1977).

[12] *See also* United States v. Zapata, 871 F.2d 616, 625 (7th Cir. 1989); United States v. Lieberman, 637 F.2d 95, 100–01 (2d Cir. 1980).

[13] Even on appeal Console did not cite Rule 805 in his brief.

[14] Console also argues that the district court's admission of the Accident Book violated the Confrontation Clause of the Constitution. Console Br. at 29–31. This argument lacks merit inasmuch as the Accident Book qualified as a business record under Rule 803(6), a well-established exception to the hearsay rule. White v. Illinois, — U.S. —, 112 S.Ct. 736, 742 n. 8, 116 L.Ed.2d 848 (1992).

[15] "Summaries of voluminous business records are admissible in evidence where the records are already in evidence, permitting independent verification of the summaries." Meister v. Commissioner of Internal Revenue, 504 F.2d 505, 513 (3d Cir. 1974) (citations omitted), *cert. denied*, 421 U.S. 964, 95 S.Ct. 1951, 44 L.Ed.2d 450 (1975).

Haskell v. United States Department of Agriculture

United States Court of Appeals, Tenth Circuit, 1991.

930 F.2d 816.

This case is another example of the use of the business records exception to the hearsay exclusionary rule. In this case, the court holds that the exception is applicable to the business of a United States government agency. It discusses the admissibility of evidence under Federal Rule of Evidence 803(6) and also mentions the possible public records exception of Federal Rule of Evidence 803(8). The court declines, however, to rule on the district court's acceptance of the evidence under the public records exception because it finds that evidence admissible under the business records exception.

* * *

Before LOGAN, MOORE and BALDOCK, Circuit Judges.

LOGAN, Circuit Judge.

Appellant William C. Haskell, Jr. (Haskell) sought review of an administrative decision of the appellee United States Department of Agriculture (Secretary) permanently disqualifying his store, Haskell Brothers Grocery, from participation in the food stamp program. 7 C.F.R. § 278.6(a).[1] Haskell's store was charged with thirteen separate violations of Food and Nutrition Service (FNS) regulations including trafficking in food stamps for cash and marijuana and exchanging food stamps for ineligible items.[2]

At the time of this appeal, Haskell was the sole owner of the Haskell Brothers Grocery. The record indicates, however, that the various other members of the Haskell family, cited in the violations, have been involved in the ownership and operation of the business in the past, including Haskell's father, two sisters, and two brothers. The investigation also revealed the involvement of Richard Clark, whose relationship, if any, to the Haskell family is unknown.

The store originally was approved for participation in the food stamp program in 1978. Due to a history of excessive food stamp redemptions, the store was investigated for possible violations of FNS regulations in April 1980. In 1981, the store was penalized for exchanging food stamps for cash and marijuana. Thereafter, the FNS made yearly educational visits to the store until January 1986, when a second investigation for possible violations was initiated. At the time of this investigation, Muriel Haskell, sister of William Haskell, Jr., was a co-owner of the store. Between October 1986 and January 1987, the co-owners and other store employees engaged in transactions with an investigative aide in which food stamps were exchanged for cash, marijuana, and other noneligible items. These violations resulted in a decision by the Secretary to disqualify the store permanently from participation in the food stamp program.

Upon review of the Secretary's decision, the district court granted the Secretary's motion for summary judgment and denied Haskell's cross motion for summary judgment and motion to suppress. *Haskell v. United States Dep't of Agriculture,* 743 F.Supp. 765 (D.Kan. 1990). We consider three issues on appeal: (1) whether the transaction reports prepared during the FNS investigation should have been excluded by the district court because they were hearsay; (2) whether Haskell was denied due process during the administrative proceedings; and (3) whether the district court appropriately affirmed sanctions imposed by the Secretary upon Haskell.[3]

This court reviews an award of summary judgment de novo, viewing the record in the light most favorable to the nonmoving party. *See* Ewing v. Amoco Oil Co., 823 F.2d 1432, 1437 (10th Cir. 1987). We review a district court's evidentiary rulings using an abuse of discretion standard. United States v. Alexander, 849 F.2d 1293, 1301 (10th Cir. 1988).

Under this standard, a trial court's rulings "will not be disturbed unless the appellate court has a definite and firm conviction that the lower court made a clear error of judgment or exceeded the bounds of permissible choice in the circumstances." United States v. Ortiz, 804 F.2d 1161, 1164 n. 2 (10th Cir. 1986).

I

We first address the question whether the Secretary's transaction reports would be admissible at trial. We affirm the district court's conclusion that such reports, though hearsay, would be admissible.

An investigative aide visited Haskell's grocery store on several occasions. Immediately following each visit to Haskell's store a transaction report was completed and signed by the investigative aide and by the special agent assigned to the investigation. Each report stated the nature of the transaction, a description of the store employee involved in the transaction, and whether ineligible items were exchanged for food stamps. A report was completed following each contact, whether or not a violation took place. I R. tab 20, ex. B. Following completion of the investigation, but before a final administrative determination, the investigative aide involved in these transactions was killed in an automobile accident. Nonetheless, the transaction reports were considered by the FNS in making its disqualification determination and by the district court in granting the Secretary's motion for summary judgment.

Haskell now challenges the district court's determination that the transaction reports would be admissible at trial under two exceptions to the hearsay rule: Fed.R.Evid. 803(6) (the business records exception) and 803(8) (the public records exception). Because we agree that the reports would be admissible under Rule 803(6), we do not reach the court's Rule 803(8) ruling.

Rule 803(6) allows hearsay statements to be admitted as evidence when they are contained in a writing or record "of acts, events, conditions, opinions, or diagnoses, made at or near the time by, or from information transmitted by, a person with knowledge, if kept in the course of a regularly conducted business

activity. . . ." In Abdel v. United States, 670 F.2d 73 (7th Cir. 1982), the Seventh Circuit addressed whether transaction reports prepared in the course of an FNS investigation are admissible under Rule 803(6). The FNS procedures employed in preparing those reports were virtually identical to the procedures employed in preparing the reports at issue in the instant case. An investigative aide, working with a compliance specialist, visited Abdel's store eight times. The aide, who was given food stamps supplied by the compliance specialist, would enter the store and shop for eligible as well as ineligible food items. The aide then would report to the compliance specialist who would record all items purchased and the amount of food stamps exchanged. A transaction report would be prepared immediately and signed by both the compliance specialist and the aide. The procedure was the same after each of the eight contacts by the aide. The transaction reports then were submitted to the investigating authority according to Department of Agriculture procedures. Id. at 75.

In holding the transaction reports admissible under Rule 803(6), the Abdel court determined the reports "were prepared pursuant to the [Secretary's] mandate to effectuate the purpose of the Food Stamp Program, which is to: 'permit low-income households to obtain a more nutritious diet through normal channels of trade by increasing food purchasing power for all eligible households who apply for participation.'" 670 F.2d at 76 (quoting 7 U.S.C. § 2011) (footnote omitted).

This conclusion is consistent with numerous cases holding that records and reports, prepared in the regular course of federal agency law enforcement investigations, are admissible under hearsay exceptions. See, e.g., Bell v. Birmingham Linen Serv., 715 F.2d 1552, 1554 n. 4 (11th Cir. 1983) (EEOC determination held admissible evidence), cert. denied, 467 U.S. 1204, 104 S.Ct. 2385, 81 L.Ed.2d 344 (1984); Local Union No. 59, Int'l Bhd of Elec. Workers v. Namco Elec., Inc. 653 F.2d 143, 145 (5th Cir. 1981) (results of NLRB investigation held admissible); Falcon v. General Tel. Co. of S.W., 626 F.2d 369, 382 (5th Cir. 1980) (GSA reports admissible if "made pursuant to duties derived from authority granted by law"), *vacated on other grounds*, 450 U.S. 1036, 101 S.Ct. 1752, 68 L.Ed.2d 234 (1981); Smith v. Universal Servs., Inc., 454 F.2d 154, 158 (5th Cir. 1972) (EEOC investigation report held admissible). Accordingly, we hold that the district court properly considered the transaction reports in granting summary judgment.

II

Haskell next argues that the district court erred in concluding that he was afforded adequate procedural due process during the administrative proceedings. The district court, assuming that Haskell possessed a property interest in the privilege of continued participation in the food stamp program, determined that he had received adequate notice, opportunity to be heard via the submission of information to the review officer, and opportunity to reply to the charge letter. Haskell v. United States Dep't of Agriculture, 743 F.Supp. at 771. Also, Haskell, upon request, was granted a review of the disqualification determination with additional opportunity to submit information in support of his position.[4] Although Haskell was not afforded an evidentiary hearing at the administrative level, he sought and received de novo review of the administrative decision from the district court.[5] When such an opportunity for judicial review exists, the lack of an evidentiary hearing at the administrative level is not a denial of due process. Mc-Glory v. United States, 763 F.2d 309, 311–12 (7th Cir. 1985); Cross v. United States, 512 F.2d 1212, 1217 (4th Cir. 1975). "[O]nce a participant seeks review de novo, the adequacy of the administrative process as an abstract matter is no longer important. . . . The adequacy of the prior process is no more important than the 'process' that precedes an agency's decision to commence a proceeding or suit. . . ." McGlory v. United States, 763 F.2d at 312.

Haskell further argues that admission of the transaction reports at trial would violate his due process rights because he could not confront and cross-examine the investigating aide who helped prepare them. We disagree. We already have determined that the transac-

tion reports are admissible under Rule 803(6). Thus, even if due process entitles Haskell to cross-examine adverse witnesses, Haskell's inability to cross-examine the aide is not fatal to the admission of the transaction reports. *See, e.g.,* Ohio v. Roberts, 448 U.S. 56, 63, 100 S.Ct. 2531, 2537, 65 L.Ed. 2d 597 (1980) (Noting in criminal case that if literally applied, "the [confrontation] Clause would abrogate virtually every hearsay exception, a result long rejected as unintended and too extreme.").

III

Finally, we conclude that the district court appropriately upheld the sanctions imposed by the Secretary. "[T]he Secretary's imposition of sanctions, such as . . . disqualification . . . or penalties should be upheld upon trial de novo unless the court finds that the Secretary's choice of sanction is unwarranted in law or without justification in fact." Joudeh v. United States, 783 F.2d 176, 178 (10th Cir. 1986) (citing Kulkin v. Bergland, 626 F.2d 181 (1st Cir. 1980)); *see also* Wolf v. United States, 662 F.2d 676, 678 (10th Cir. 1981) (arbitrary and capricious standard is the most favorable standard of review possible for plaintiff seeking review of sanctions imposed by Secretary). In light of the admissible evidence of violations contained in the transaction reports and Haskell's failure to offer any specific facts refuting the violations, we concur with the district court that no material issue of fact exists and that defendant is entitled to judgment as a matter of law. *See Kulkin*, 626 F.2d at 183–84.

Appellant's motions to appoint an attorney to orally argue and for oral argument are DE-NIED. The judgment of the United States District Court for the District of Kansas is AF-FIRMED.

---

[1] The regulation authorizes disqualification of

"any authorized retail food store . . . from further participation in the program if the firm fails to comply with the Food Stamp Act. . . . [D]isqualification shall be permanent for a firm's third sanction or a disqualification based on trafficking in coupons or ATP cards."

7 C.F.R. § 278.6(a).

2   Trafficking is defined as "the buying or selling of coupons or ATP [authorization to participate] cards for cash." 7 C.F.R. § 271.2.
3   After examining the briefs and appellate record, this panel has determined unanimously that oral argument would not materially assist the determination of this appeal. *See* Fed.R. App.P. 34(a); 10th Cir.R. 34.1.9. The case is therefore ordered submitted without oral argument.
4   The only additional information submitted by Haskell was affidavits of other Haskell family members involved in the violations, stating that they were not involved in the operation of the business at the time the violations occurred.
5   A store owner who disagrees with the Secretary's decision to impose penalties for food stamp violations may seek de novo review in the United States District Court. 7 U.S.C. § 2023, 7 C.F.R. § 279.10.

✔ PRACTICE QUESTIONS

Select the most correct answer to complete each statement. Your answers should be based upon information included in Chapter 10.

1. (a) Courts allow business records to be introduced in evidence because they like to learn how a business is conducted and this may be done when business records are placed in evidence.
   (b) Business records are primarily documents, i.e., anything written that is capable of being read. Every record that is recorded by a business is admissible under the business records exception to the hearsay exclusionary rule.
   (c) A police report may be admitted into evidence under the business records exception if the observations made by the police officer of the physical circumstances existing at the time of the arrival of the officer are included in the report and other relevant but excludible information is taped over before the trier of the facts sees the report.
   (d) If a bystander witnesses an automobile accident and volunteers facts to the police officer relating to how the accident occurred, the report is admissible.

2. (a) Airline tickets are not admissible under the business records exception.
   (b) Hospital records are fully admissible under the business records exception in all cases so that the work of the hospital can continue while a case is being tried in court.
   (c) A report of an autopsy conducted by a duly authorized physician on behalf of the governmental authority empowered to conduct autopsies in the locality where the deceased died is admissible in evidence when relevant and when properly authenticated.
   (d) Newspaper accounts are always admissible as documentary evidence.

3. (a) A trial court does not have wide discretion in allowing or denying the admission of evidence.
   (b) Vital statistics, such as records of birth, marriage, and death, may be admissible in evidence. The clerk where these records are kept is usually required to certify them, or the court will not admit them in evidence.
   (c) Hospital records are never admissible in evidence.
   (d) Accident reports by police officers are entirely inadmissible in evidence.

4. (a) A tort is a private or civil wrong.
   (b) A police blotter is a soft piece of absorbent paper that was used by the police when they used to write their police reports in ink. It absorbed any excess ink so that it would not spread on the page.
   (c) A police officer is usually required to keep a book, most often characterized as a memorandum book. If the officer is conversant with shorthand

writing, he or she is usually permitted to use that style of writing in this book to speed up the process of recording information.

(d) All of the above.

5. (a) Newspaper accounts are generally held admissible in evidence because they are generally reliable.

(b) Employee time cards showing the time of the day worked by employees during a particular day may not be received in evidence as an exception to the hearsay exclusionary rule.

(c) An ancient document is self-proving, provided it is more than thirty years old, is unembellished by alterations, is found in proper custody, and is otherwise free from suspicion.

(d) All of the above.

Indicate whether each statement is true or false.

6. "P," a police officer, observes an auto accident. He makes a report to his department of the facts of the accident and indicates on the report that he was a witness. At a subsequent trial, one of the parties attempts to introduce the report into evidence after laying the proper foundation. The judge grants the motion to keep the report out of the record of the trial. This is improper.

7. Certified hospital records are admissible in evidence by the injured party when the records contain information on diagnosis, prognosis, and/or treatment and specifically exclude a history portion not relevant to diagnosis, prognosis, and/or treatment.

CHAPTER 11

Personal or Family History Exception to Hearsay Exclusionary Rule

§ 11.1 INTRODUCTION

With every exception to the hearsay exclusionary rule, we must ask ourselves whether there is a necessity for the exception and whether there is great probability of reliability. Personal or family records appear to meet these requirements. It is highly improbable that a record of a birth; death; marriage; adoption; divorce; legitimacy; relationship by blood, adoption, or marriage; ancestry; or other similar fact of personal or family history found in family Bibles; genealogies; charts; engravings on rings; inscriptions on family portraits; engravings on urns, crypts, or tombstones; or the like would be unreliable. Accordingly, these items are admissible as an exception to the hearsay exclusionary rule when certain criteria are met. A form of this type of evidence is referred to as pedigree evidence. The Federal Rules of Evidence permit this hearsay evidence in the trial record even though the declarant is available as a witness. Federal Rule of Evidence 803(19).

§ 11.2 ELEMENTS

Most states require that

1. the declarant was competent at the time of making the statement,
2. the declarant be dead;
3. the declarant was related by blood or affinity to the family about which he or she speaks,
4. the declarations were made ante litem motam, and
5. matters of pedigree be in issue.

Some states permit this information into the trial record even though the declarant is available as a witness. W.Va.—State v. Adkins, 106 W.Va. 658, 146 S.E. 732 (1929). The Federal Rules of Evidence also admit this evidence even though the declarant is available as a witness. Federal Rule of Evidence 803(19). I believe that the better rule, which still exists among many states, is that if the declarant is available as a witness, he or she is thus available for cross-examination, and his or her credibility may be tested. The pedigree exception to the hearsay exclusionary rule is a well-established exception. Fla.—Cone v. Benjamin, 157 Fla.

800, 27 So.2d 90 (1946); N.Y.—*In re* Dowd's Estate, 18 A.D.2d 715, 236 N.Y.S.2d 147 (1962).

§ 11.3 DEATH OF DECLARANT

Declarations of pedigree will ordinarily not be received as an exception to the hearsay exclusionary rule when better evidence is available. Va.—Rawles v. Bazel, 141 Va. 734, 126 S.E. 690 (1925). As a general rule, declarations as to pedigree are not admissible unless declarant is dead. Tex.—Simpson v. Simpson, 380 S.W.2d 855 (Tex.Civ.App. 1964). However, the rule is sometimes relaxed when declarant is beyond the jurisdiction of the court (Or.—Garvin v. Western Cooperage Co., 94 Or. 487, 184 P. 555 [1919]) or is incapable of testifying (Ala.—Perolio v. Doe, 197 Ala. 560, 73 So. 197 [1916]).

§ 11.4 RELATIONSHIP OF DECLARANT

As a general rule for a declaration of pedigree to be admissible, it must have been made by someone related to the family concerned. Del.—Pote v. Farren, 3 W.W.Harr. 1, 129 A. 238 (1925); Tenn.—*In re* McElroy's Adoption, 522 S.W.2d 345 (Tenn.App. 1975).

§ 11.5 STATEMENT MADE ANTE LITEM MOTAM

In order to get a pedigree declaration admitted, it is necessary that the declarant be disinterested to the extent of having no motive which would induce him to state the fact otherwise than as he understood it. It must therefore be shown that the statement was made ante litem motam. Cal.—Peterson v. Peterson, 121 Cal.App.2d 1, 262 P.2d 613 (1953); Haw.—*In re* Cunha's Estate, 49 Haw. 273, 414 P.2d 925 (1966).

§ 11.6 MATTERS OF PEDIGREE MUST BE IN ISSUE

In order to bring a case within the pedigree exception to the hearsay exclusionary rule, the issue must be genealogical in that pedigree must be directly in issue and not merely incidental. In a prosecution for rape in the second degree, the declarations of the deceased mother of the complainant are inadmissible to establish the complainant's age. N.Y.—People v. Lammes, 208 A.D. 533, 203 N.Y.S. 736 (1924). Mo.—Bailey v. Metropolitan Life Ins. Co., 115 S.W.2d 151, *cert. quashed*, 343 Mo. 435, 121 S.W.2d 789 (1938).

§ 11.7 DECLARATION—FORM

A pedigree declaration is not required to be in a precise form. It is admissible if in any form capable of conveying thought, provided the authenticity of the vehicle conveying the statement is established to the satisfaction of the court. Ariz.—*In re* Wallin's Estate, 16 Ariz.App. 34, 490 P.2d 863 (1971); N.J.—*In re* Blau's Estate, 4 N.J.Super. 343, 67 A.2d 316 (1949). However, it must be a statement of fact and not of opinion of the members of the family. Tex.—Keith v. Keith, 39 Tex.Civ.App. 363, 87 S.W. 384 (1905). The declaration may be oral (Mo.—Fedina's Estate v. Fedina, 491 S.W.2d 552 [Mo. 1973]) or in writing (Mich.—Matter of Egbert's Estate, 105 Mich.App. 395, 306 N.W.2d 525 [1981]).

§ 11.8 DECLARANT'S LACK OF PERSONAL KNOWLEDGE

There is a conflict of authority with respect to whether declarant is required to have actual knowledge of the contents of the pedigree declaration. In Idaho, a case held that a witness may testify to facts of family history if his or her knowledge of the subject is derived from intimate acquaintance with the family or families (albeit hearsay upon hearsay). Idaho—*In re* Stone's Estate, 77 Idaho 63, 286 P.2d 329 (1955). However, another case holds that as to matters of family history, reputation or tradition the declarations concerning such matters or one connected with the family are admissible notwithstanding declarant did not disclose the source or an authoritive source for such knowledge. Mo.—Gordon v. Metropolitan Life Ins. Co., 238 Mo.App. 46, 176 S.W.2d 506 (1943).

§ 11.9 FEDERAL RULE

Rule 803: Hearsay exceptions; availability of declarant immaterial

The following are not excluded by the hearsay rule, even though the declarant is available as a witness:

*   *   *

(19) **Reputation concerning person or family history.** Reputation among members of a person's family by blood, adoption, or marriage, or among a person's associates, or in the community, concerning a person's birth, adoption, marriage, divorce, death, legitimacy, relationship by blood, adoption, or marriage, ancestry, or other similar fact of personal or family history.

CROSS-REFERENCES

Federal Civil Judicial Procedure and Rules (West 1996) (Rule 803[19]).
Goode & Wellborn, Courtroom Handbook on Federal Evidence (West 1995) (Rule 803[19]).
McCormick, Evidence (4th ed. 1992) (Rule 803[19]).

Cone v. Benjamin

**Supreme Court of Florida, Division B, 1946.
157 Fla. 800, 27 So.2d 90.**

This decision refers to a person designated by the court as administrator with the will annexed. This means that the person who is charged with the administration of the estate of the deceased person was not named to administer the estate in the last will and testament of the deceased person, but that the court named that person to perform that function: i.e., to gather the assets of the estate, to pay the expenses of the decedent, to pay the creditors of the decedent, to pay the accrued taxes of the deceased, to take out his or her fee for services rendered (subject to court approval), to pay assets or money to those named as beneficiaries in the will, and finally to pay over the remainder in order of preference according to the closeness of the family relationship as provided by the applicable statute of the state where the deceased person resided prior to his or her demise. This person is designated by the court if the person named in the will to perform this function is dead, is incompetent, or renounces the designation.

In some states, the person named is called an executor if that person is a male and an executrix if female. In other jurisdictions, such as the state of Florida, the person is called a personal representative regardless of the gender of that person. In the instant case, apparently the person named as personal representative in the will had died.

The abbreviation c.t.a. refers to the Latin phrase *cum testamento annexo*, i.e., with the will annexed.

In this case, the administrator c.t.a., Roy L. Benjamin, was required, inter alia, to find the proper heirs and beneficiaries to receive the assets of the estates of a husband and wife who had died childless. Both died as a result of a single accident wherein the wife died a little later than the husband. The administrator invoked the aid of the pedigree exception to the hearsay exclusionary rule to prove certain persons were entitled to the residuary estate. It is an interesting puzzle that the court decided. It makes for good reading and teaches you how best to provide for the preparation of a last will and testament so that one's assets go to the proper persons after death.

Appeal from Circuit Court, Pinellas County; T. Frank Hobson, Judge.

* * *

BROWN, Justice. On January 28, 1931, Harrison J. Stewart and Ada Cone Stewart, his wife, an aged and childless couple, who had been residents of St. Petersburg, Florida, for some twenty years, lost their lives in that city as a result of a collision between an automobile in which they were riding and a train. Both died on the day of the collision, but the husband died about an hour prior to the death of his wife. Each of them left a will giving to the other all of his or her estate. Both wills were duly probated.

Soon thereafter the County Judge of Pinellas County appointed Roy L. Benjamin as administrator with the will annexed of the estates of each of the deceased persons, and he duly qualified as such. The estate of Harrison J. Stewart consisted mostly of personal property, stocks, bonds, mortgages, etc., which the administrator's inventory showed amounted to $47,803.13, and some real estate of the value of $10,000, or more. The inventory of Ada Cone Stewart's estate showed no assets discovered. Notice to creditors, legatees, distributees, etc., was duly published for eight weeks, and proof of publication filed, as required by Sections 5597, 5598, C.G.L. of 1927.

On February 15, 1932, Roy L. Benjamin, as administrator c. t. a. of the estate of Harrison J. Stewart, filed a bill of complaint in the Circuit Court of Pinellas County, entitled "A bill for instructions to administrator," against himself, as administrator of Ada Cone Stewart's estate, the New England Life Insurance Company, and unknown heirs of Ada Cone

Stewart. The purpose of the bill was to determine which of the decedents died first, and who were the proper heirs and beneficiaries to receive the assets of the two estates. . . .

* * *

We come now to the evidence relied on by appellants to prove heirship. None of the twenty-two persons, whom the appellants' bill alleged to be the heirs of Ada Cone Stewart, appeared in court or testified in this case. Nine of them declined to join as plaintiffs in the suit, and were made defendants. Counsel for appellants sought to prove such heirship by offering in evidence a book, written and published by one William Whitney Cone of Brandsville, Mo., in 1903, which purported to give a history of the Cone family in America, wherein the names of Ada Cone Stewart, and some 6,567 other persons, appears, and by offering the testimony of several witnesses in an effort to prove that Mrs. Stewart was a cousin of, or related to, the author, the theory being that this rendered the book admissible in evidence as a written declaration made by "a member of the family."

"The rule is that declarations of deceased persons who were de jure related by blood or marriage to the family in question may be given in evidence in matters of pedigree. (Citing authorities.) A qualification of the rule is that before a declaration can be admitted in evidence the relationship of the declarant with the family must be established by some proof independent of the declaration itself." Fulkerson v. Holmes, 117 U.S. 389, 6 S.Ct. 780, 784, 29 L.Ed. 915 (1886). The opinion in this leading case also says: "This exception (to the rule against hearsay) has been recognized on the ground of necessity; for as in inquires respecting relationship or descent facts must often be proved which occurred many years before the trial, and were known to but few persons, it is obvious that the strict enforcement in such cases of the rules against hearsay evidence would frequently occasion a failure of justice. Tayl.Ev. § 635. Traditional evidence is therefore admissible."

"The rule of admission is accordingly restricted to the declarations of deceased persons who were related by blood or marriage to the person whose pedigree is in issue and therefore to the declarations of declarants interested in the succession in question. . . . The declaration of friends, servants and neighbors might not be received, but the rule is now declared by nearly all the authorities that the declarations are confined to those made by legal relatives. So far as blood relatives are concerned, the law does not seem to have limited the inquiry within any particular degree of relationship, although the declarations of very remote relatives might be entitled to very little weight." Jones on Evidence, 2d Ed., Section 1132.

* * *μ

Generally speaking, the theory underlying the acceptance of the declaration as to pedigree made by deceased persons who were members of or intimately connected with the family is based upon the theory that such persons were familiar with those matters of family history, tradition and repute with which the members of most families are familiar, although based upon hearsay within the family, and that, having been made before any controversy had arisen, there was no motive to speak other than the truth. As was said by Justice Paxson in the old case of Sitler v. Gehr, supra:

"Indeed we scarcely realize how little we actually know from our own observation and investigation. We learn the truths of history, the secrets of science and our knowledge of the world generally, from what we have read, or from what others have told us. What does a man know of his own deceased ancestors but what he has learned from his immediate relatives? How was the plaintiff, who had never seen Balser Behr, of Berks County, to know that the latter was his uncle except from his mother? It is in just such cases that the strict rules of evidence are relaxed as regards hearsay. If it were otherwise pedigree could not be proved at all in many cases, and in one sense it is primary not secondary evidence. The law upon this point is clearly stated in 1 Wharton's Evidence, Sec. 201: 'Pedigree, from the nature of things, is open to proof by hearsay in respect to all family incidents, as to which no living witness can be found. If what has been handed down in families cannot be in this way proved, pedigree could not, in most cases, be proved at all.'"

See also C.J.S., Evidence, § 226, p. 970 et seq.; 1 Greenleaf on Evidence, 3rd Ed., Sec. 114 et seq.; 20 Am.Jur. 409 et seq., and other authorities already cited.

It is also well settled that entries as to births, deaths, and marriages shown by family Bibles, Church registers and certificates and inscriptions on monuments; hospital records and hotel registers (under certain circumstances and for certain purposes); letters of deceased relatives containing statements as to family matters, although entitled to different degrees of credibility; recitals in wills, deeds of conveyance, and in marriage settlements and certificates; inscriptions on family portraits, rings, and other family memorials; school censuses and other books and public records which mention births, marriages and deaths, are admissible under certain circumstances. All these, and other matters, are treated in the books.

The book here in question, entitled "Some Account of the Cone Family in America," was written over a period of years by William Whitney Cone and published by him in 1903. This was abundantly proven by his daughter, Mrs. Isabelle C. Harvey, a resident of Topeka, Kansas. The book is more than a mere declaration by a member of a family of matters of family history and repute which would ordinarily be known by any member of any particular family. It is a history and genealogy of the Cone family in America, replete with personal sketches of the careers of many members of that family. It deals primarily with the descendants of Daniel Cone, progenitor in America of the most numerous branch of the Cone family, who settled in Haddam, Connecticut, in 1662, when he appears as one of twenty-eight persons who received from the Connecticut Colony a grant of a considerable body of land situated on both sides of the Connecticut River. The first mention of Daniel Cone, which the author was able to find, was a requisition, signed by Governor John Winthrop, of the Connecticut Colony, to Peter Stuyvesant, Governor of New Netherlands, dated March 2, 1657, and contained in the Massachusetts Historical Collection. The requisition, in the form of a letter, begins: "Honored Sir: Complaint being made to me by Daniel Cone that one James Parker," etc.

In C.J.S., Evidence § 717, p. 626, it is said:

"As a general rule a book or other publication printed by a private person and not shown to be approved by any public authority is not competent evidence of the facts therein stated, at least if it does not appear to be in general use among the class of persons interested in the matters of which it treats, and if on account of the recent occurrence of the facts or for other reasons they may be proved by living witnesses or other better evidence. Books and other printed publications shown to be in general use among the class of persons interested in the matters which they contain have, however, been held admissible."

This is indeed a remarkable book; handsomely published and skillfully arranged. The evidence shows that the author carried on an enormous correspondence and also made a trip East, especially to Connecticut, to check over the records and to obtain information. He was born in Monroe County, N.Y., December 18, 1836. He moved from New York to Kansas in 1869, where he engaged in newspaper work and was also clerk in the State Historical Society. He moved to Brandsville, Missouri, in 1896 and lived there until his death, in 1924. He was interested in historical matters and wrote a History of Shawnee County, and contributed to historical magazines. This we get from the book itself and from the testimony of his daughter, Mrs. Harvey. The book is a combination of genealogy and history, and consists of 547 pages including the index. Five hundred copies were published and all but about six volumes, which the author and his family retained, were distributed mostly among the numerous members of the Cone family in thirty-one states. Several copies were deposited in public libraries. Former Governor of Florida, Hon. Frederick P. Cone, obtained a copy. These books were sold at $5 per volume, which was very small compensation indeed to the author for his many years of painstaking work and investigation. Independently of the book, the relationship of the author to the Cone family, whose history he gives, is established by the testimony of his daughter, his grandson, Randal C. Harvey, and to some extent by George A. Root, coworker with the author of another genealogy, "The Bishop Family."

There was ample evidence that this book was well received and regarded as authoritative by many members of the Cone family, including Florida's recent Governor, Frederick P.

Cone, whose name is included in the book, Serial No. 6522, and his ancestorship shown. It is true that Governor Cone belonged to a different branch of the family from that of these appellants, but his testimony was that from information he had received from his father and uncles he was quite familiar with his family history for several generations back, and said that he had checked the book with his own knowledge of the history of his branch of the Cone family, and found that it was correct with the exception of a few immaterial errors as to dates and initials. Otherwise the book was correct for four generations back, which was as far as his information went. That he had discussed the book with some of his own family at Statesboro, Georgia, where his great-grandfather lived during the Revolutionary War, and that they stated practically the same facts as those set forth in the book and he considered it an authentic history of the Cone family. He also said that he had met many members of the Cone family from Ohio and practically all of the northeastern states and some of the western states and had discussed the Cone family book with some two dozen of them. He had no interest in this litigation and knew nothing about it until shortly before he was called to testify. The author of the book, who was at that time State Librarian of Missouri, wrote him about it when he was getting it up and later wrote to Governor Cone's brother, who gave the author some information about his immediate family and their ancestors.

The author expresses his appreciation to a long list of persons who have assisted him in assembling available data, and in furnishing family records. He makes no claims to infallibility. But the modesty of his preface tends to increase one's confidence in the author and compiler.

Appellees contend that the book referred to is a mere private writing of William Whitney Cone, and nothing more than a written declaration by him printed in book form. And there being no proof aliunde that the writer was related to Ada Cone Stewart, it was not admissible evidence.

If appellees' premises were correct, we could readily agree, but for the reasons above stated we think that the book is more than a mere declaration of the author, and it having been proven by several witnesses who were members of the Cone family that they had found it to be authentic, we have reached the conclusion that the book constituted at least prima facie evidence of the genealogy of the Cone family and that the chancellor below was not in error when he admitted it in evidence. We find no precedent directly in point which sustains our conclusion, but we are convinced of its soundness. The chancellor did not pass directly upon its evidentiary value, however, as he decided the case against these appellants on other grounds. We have examined this book sufficiently to find that it shows prima facie that Ada Cone Stewart was a fifth cousin of the author of the book, both being direct descendants of the progenitor of the main branch of the Cone family in America, Daniel Cone. Appellants contend that this book clearly shows that all the plaintiffs and nine defendants are relations and heirs of Ada C. Stewart, most of them being second cousins.

* * *

The decree is reversed and the cause remanded, with directions to enter a decree for appellants and such of appellees as are found to be heirs of Ada Cone Stewart. If the chancellor becomes convinced that it is necessary to take further testimony on the issues of this relationship, then nothing in this opinion shall be construed as restricting his power to do that.

Reversed and remanded.

CHAPMAN, C. J., and THOMAS and SEBRING, JJ., concur.

Peterson v. Peterson
District Court of Appeal, First District, Division 1, California, 1953.
121 Cal.App.2d 1, 262 P.2d 613.

This case involves a paternity action where a female tried unsuccessfully to prove that a male friend was the father of her child. The case would be tried differently today because DNA can be used to ascertain the identity of the father. Prior to the use of DNA, blood tests could determine that a male could not have been the father of the child, but could not prove with certainty that he was the father. To put it another way, it could have been determined that he may have been the father. Today DNA tests, more specifically described in Sections 4.14, 4.27, and 16.6 of this book, can determine almost positively whether a paternity suspect is the father of the child.

However, in this case, the mother of the child tried to use the pedigree exception to the hearsay exclusionary rule. When you read this case, you will find an interesting scenario and learn why the pedigree exception was not applicable.

Paternity proceeding. The Superior Court, County of Marin, Jordan L. Martinelli, J., entered judgment on verdict for alleged father and child appealed.

PETERS, Presiding Justice. This action was instituted by a child through his mother, Anne Kinney, against defendant to have it determined that defendant is the father of plaintiff, and to secure support, counsel fees and costs. At the trial the only witnesses produced were defendant and plaintiff's mother. The jury brought in a verdict for defendant. From the judgment entered on that verdict plaintiff appeals.

The child was born July 26, 1948. The complaint was not filed until July 10, 1951. The cause was tried in March, 1952. The evidence was directly conflicting. Anne testified to meeting respondent on an army transport upon her return to this country from Germany; that upon his promise to get a divorce and to marry her she spent two nights, October 17 and 18, 1947, in two designated hotels in New York City with respondent; that she had sexual intercourse with him on those occasions; that she was then 32 years of age; that prior and subsequent to those two nights she had never had intercourse with any other man; that just before embarking on the transport she had her regular menstrual period.

Respondent, who had been married for ten years at the time of trial, denied these accusations. He admitted meeting Anne on the transport; denied any romantic overtures while on shipboard; admitted that he took Anne to dinner twice in New York but differed from Anne as to the dates, he claiming the two dates were October 16, and 17, 1947. He admitted that, on October 17th, after both

had had considerable to drink, he propositioned Anne to spend the night with him at a hotel, and she agreed, but claimed that they were unable to find a hotel that was not full, and so he returned her to her hotel, where men were not admitted, without having accomplished his purpose, and returned to the ship where he was employed. He denied that then, or at any other time, he had had intercourse with Anne.

Anne testified that defendant had registered the first night at Hotel Walcott, and the second night she, at defendant's suggestion, had registered as "Mr. and Mrs. A. Kinney" at the Breslin Hotel. Letters from both hotels were admitted in evidence. The Breslin's records failed to show that a Kinney or a Peterson had registered there on any of the critical nights. The Walcott's records showed a "Mr. and Mrs. A. Peterson and party" had registered on October 15, 1947, and had checked out on October 17, 1947. No other record was found of a Kinney or Peterson registration for the nights in question.

It is not necessary to recount the evidence on these matters in further detail. It is obvious that on the critical issue of whether respondent had intercourse with Anne in October of 1947 there was a direct conflict. The burden rested on appellant to prove his [her] case by a preponderance of the evidence. It was the jury's function to pass on the credibility of the two witnesses. It obviously was not convinced by Anne's story. Moreover, no contention is made that the evidence does not support the verdict and judgment.

The major contention of appellant is that error of a most prejudicial nature was committed on the cross-examination of Anne, in that respondent was then permitted to bring out her general relationships with other men over a period of about six years, and long prior to the period of possible conception. This, it is contended, was prejudicial error even though appellant's counsel at the trial (new counsel have been secured to handle this appeal) made no objection of any kind to the testimony in question.

On this issue the record shows the following: On direct examination by counsel for plaintiff Anne testified that she had been in the Women's Army Corps for three years, and had worked overseas as a civilian for about two years; that she was in Europe, either in the military service or as a civilian, from 1945 to September or October, 1947; that she met respondent on shipboard, and that it was upon their arrival in New York that the events above mentioned occurred. She also, on direct, testified that the events above mentioned occurred. She also, on direct, testified that she never had had intercourse with any other man before or subsequent to October of 1947.

On the cross-examination of Anne respondent elaborated on these matters first brought out on direct. Not one objection was made to this cross-examination. Thus, Anne testified that she was 32 in October of 1947; that she had been born in a small town in Alabama; that after the death of her father she lived for about a year in Birmingham, Alabama, with her sister; that both joined the service in 1941, her sister as a nurse, and she as a WAC; that she spent three years in the WACs, mostly in this country, but a short time in France and Germany. Respondent's counsel had her describe the various military establishments where she had been stationed. She testified that she had spent 2 1/2 years at Mitchell Field, New York, as an aircraft dispatcher; that in these various camps she frequently saw and came in contact with many men, and was under the command of male personnel. It was brought out that Mitchell Field was close to New York City, but she denied making frequent visits to the metropolitan area. She then testified that she was sent overseas and spent several months in France and Germany; that in August of 1945 her enlistment expired, and she elected to stay in Germany on a civilian job; that she lived at Hertz, Germany, near Frankfurt; that she was so employed until September of 1947, when she returned to the United States; that during her stay at Hertz she first lived in an apartment and later in a commandeered house. She admitted that during this period she was in constant contact with male civilian and military personnel. It was brought out that Anne frequently ate and danced with military and civilian personnel, but she denied any steady romances with any particular individual.

In his argument to the jury counsel for respondent, without objection, was permitted to refer to the above evidence and to argue that it indicated Anne's lack of moral home ties during the five plus years she was in government service, and that this background rendered it highly unlikely that she would suddenly surrender her virtue at age 32, but rather indicated that she had lived a life where many men had the opportunity of being the father of the child.

It is urged that this line of questioning and argument was undertaken for the sole purpose of besmirching Anne's reputation and prejudicing her before the jury, and constituted serious and prejudicial error. It is undoubtedly the law that, in such actions, evidence of immorality of the mother prior to the period of possible conception, or questions designed to bring out or imply acts of immorality for the purpose of showing bad character, or for impeachment, are inadmissible, and that it is error to even ask such questions. People v. Crandall, 125 Cal. 129, 57 Pac. 785 (1899). . . . But there are authorities which hold that the trial court may permit questions about general background which, while incidentally or inferentially degrading, may serve to test the credibility and memory of a witness. People v. Le Baron, 92 Cal.App. 550, 268 P. 651, 269 Pac. 476 (1928). . . .

* * *

The last contention that need be mentioned is that the trial court improperly excluded evidence claimed to be admissible under the pedigree exception to the hearsay rule. This contention is predicated upon the fact that on the direct examination of Anne she was prevented from testifying that at birth she had the appellant christened "Clifford Anthony Peterson." Later on cross-examination she testified that she had not told respondent that she intended to name the child after him until some time after the child had been so christened.

It is of course true that declarations of pedigree by those in the family group are generally admissible to prove facts of family history. But there are limitations on this exception to the hearsay rule. If a controversy or a motive to deceive exists when such declarations are made they are then inadmissible. They are then self-serving hearsay. Wigmore, Evidence, Vol. V, pp. 298–302, §§ 1483 and 1484; see, generally, In re Estate of Walden, 166 Cal. 446, 137 Pac. 35 (1914); In re Jessup, 81 Cal. 408, 21 P. 976, 22 Pac. 742, 1028, 6 L.R.A. 594 (1890).

We do not find it necessary to pass on the question as to whether this evidence was admissible or inadmissible. Even if admissible it would only have tended to show that when the child was born his mother claimed or believed that respondent was the father. That fact was already before the jury, particularly by the testimony of Anne that she never had intercourse during her life with any one but respondent. It is also obvious that the jury knew that the child was named Clifford Anthony Peterson because the complaint so names the appellant, and also names Clifford A. Peterson as defendant. Thus, even if such evidence should have been admitted, its exclusion could not have been prejudicial.

The judgment appealed from is affirmed.

People v. Lammes
Supreme Court, Appellate Division,
Fourth Department, 1924.
208 A.D. 533, 203 N.Y.S. 736.

This case involves a conviction for statutory rape wherein the age of the victim was a question of fact. Evidence of her age was received at trial under the pedigree exception to the hearsay exclusionary rule. The appellate court majority held that it was an error to admit this evidence. The decision explains why it should not have been admitted.

CLARK, J. The defendant was convicted in Monroe county of the crime of rape in the second degree. Defendant formerly resided with his wife in the village of Spencerport, N.Y., where he conducted a bakery. In the year 1922 the complainant, Gertrude Scharn, went to work for defendant in his bakery, and they became intimate friends; she resided with defendant and his wife while she worked for them.

In the fall of 1922 complainant went to Ogden, Utah, to live with her father, and in December, 1922, defendant went to Utah and

saw the complaining witness. He returned to Spencerport in January or February, 1923, and continued to live with his wife in that village. The complaining witness, Miss Scharn, returned to Rochester April 30, 1923; defendant having furnished her money to defray her traveling expenses. When she arrived in Rochester, in response to her request over the telephone, defendant went to the New York Central station and met her, and they went to a room on Chatham street, and it is claimed by the people that on the morning of May 1, 1923, at said room, defendant had sexual intercourse with the complainant, Gertrude Scharn.

On the trial she testified that said intercourse took place at that time, and there was sufficient evidence corroborating the prosecutrix as to the act of sexual intercourse with defendant, but she was not sufficiently corroborated as to her age. She testified that she became 18 years of age on the 17th day of May, 1923, and that the act of sexual intercourse charged against defendant was committed on the 1st day of May 1923, only 16 days before she became 18 years of age, according to her own testimony.

The law requires that, in a case of this character, the prosecutrix must be corroborated, and that such corroboration must extend to every material fact essential to constitute the crime charged, and in this case that rule would apply to the fact of the age of the prosecutrix, as well as to each of the material facts essential to constitute the crime. People v. Plath, 100 N.Y. 590, 3 N.E. 790, 53 Am.Rep. 236 (1886); People v. Page, 162 N.Y. 272, 56 N.E. 750 (1900).

The only corroboration of the prosecutrix on the question of her age is an affidavit made by her mother (deceased) on a school census blank, and sworn to before a police officer of the city of Rochester as a commissioner of deeds. According to that affidavit, the prosecutrix was under the age of 18 years at the time she claimed to have had intercourse with the defendant. I think the admission of this affidavit of the mother, purporting to state the date of birth of the prosecutrix, was improper, and that it constituted such a substantial error as to require the reversal of the judgment.

This affidavit was hearsay evidence pure and simple. It was received on the theory that it established the pedigree of the complainant. It could not be properly received for any such purpose for age is not essential to establish pedigree, and the question of pedigree was not necessarily involved in this case. Bowen v. Preferred Accident Ins. Co., 68 App.Div. 342, 74 N.Y.Supp. 101 (1902); Bowen v. Preferred Accident Ins. Co., 82 App.Div. 458, 81 N.Y.Supp. 840 (1903). . . .

One of the facts that the people were obliged to establish in order to convict this defendant was that the complainant was under the age of 18 years at the time he had intercourse with her. Penal Law, § 2010. No conviction could properly be had upon the testimony of the prosecutrix, unsupported by other evidence. Penal Law, § 2013. The only other evidence in this case on the question of the age of the prosecutrix was the affidavit of her mother above referred to.

Under the circumstances as disclosed by the evidence, an inspection of the complaining witness would not aid the jury in determining her age at the time she alleges the crime was committed. People v. Todoro, 160 N.Y.Supp. 352 (Sup. 1916); People v. Marks, 146 App. Div. 11, 13, 130 N.Y.Supp. 524 (1911). The judgment of conviction should be reversed, and a new trial granted.

Judgment of conviction reversed, upon questions of law and fact, and new trial granted. All concur, except DAVIS and CROUCH, JJ., who dissent, and vote for affirmance, in an opinion by DAVIS, J.

DAVIS, J. (dissenting). The crime is alleged to have occurred on May 1, 1923. The main facts are well established. Gertrude Scharn, the complaining witness, testified that she became 18 years of age on May 17, 1923. This evidence must be corroborated, because it constitutes one of the material facts essential for a legal conviction. Penal Law, § 2013; People v. Todoro, 224 N.Y. 129, 120 N.E. 135 (1918); People v. Harrison, 63 Misc.Rep. 18, 117 N.Y.Supp. 477 (1909).

There was no direct testimony corroborating Gertrude as to her age. She was born in Holland. Her father and mother came with her to this country in 1916, and resided in Rochester. Evidently the parents separated for some reason. The father went to live in Utah. The mother and daughter remained in Rochester, residing on Berkley street, and Gertrude went to school. Testimony of witnesses called by defendant, who knew them both, together with complainant's evidence, established the fact of such residence.

To this home on November 8, 1920, came one Carroll, a policeman, taking the school census. This was apparently shortly before the mother's death, for Gertrude's testimony is that her mother died during that month. The usual school census blank was made out, and Alida Scharn, the mother, signed it and made oath as to the truth of the statements therein contained before the police officer, who was also a commissioner of deeds. The father was not within the jurisdiction of the court at the time of the trial. That sworn statement of the deceased mother was produced, identified, and received in evidence over the objection of the defendant's counsel. It stated that Gertrude Scharn was born in Holland on May 17, 1905.

I think this evidence competent on the question of complainant's age. It is, of course, hearsay. So, also, was the testimony of Gertrude herself on that subject. Declarations in regard to pedigree, though hearsay, are admissible, where made before a controversy arose or action brought and the declarant is a deceased relative. . . . Aalholm v. People, 211 N.Y. 406, 416, 105 N.E. 647, L.R.A. 1915D, 215, Ann.Cas.1915C, 1039 (1914). It is admitted on the theory that it is the best evidence that can be then obtained. People v. Koerner, 154 N.Y. 355, 370, 48 N.E. 730 (1897). Matters of pedigree include such facts as those concerning birth (Eisenlord v. Clum, 126 N.Y. 552, 27 N.E. 1024, 12 L.R.A. 836) (1891), and the time when such event happened (Washington v. Bank for Savings in City of New York, 171 N.Y. 166, 173, 63 N.E. 831, 89 Am.St.Rep. 800) (1902). Age may not of itself be an element of pedigree (People v. Sheppard, 44 Hun, 565 [1887]; Bowen v. Preferred Accident Ins. Co., 68 App.Div. 342, 344, 74 N.Y.Supp. 101 [1902]); but, if the date of birth may be proved, the question of the person's age is merely a matter of computation. There is no sound reason why age, when an issue, may not be proved in the same manner as any question of pedigree. I do not regard the rule fixed in this state that declarations of such a genealogical fact as the date of birth are inadmissible. Certainly the weight of modern authority supports the rule favoring admission, when better evidence may not be obtained, whether the issue is strictly one of pedigree or otherwise. Chamberlayne's Modern Law of Evidence, §§ 2923, 2929; Wigmore on Evidence (2d Ed.) § 1503.

The number of persons having actual knowledge of the date of birth is always limited—generally, at the most, to the mother, father, physician, and midwife or nurse. There are times when such witnesses cannot be called to make proof of this essential fact, so the law of necessity accepts records or declarations made by such persons when there was no object to deceive rather than concede that proof of a patent fact is impossible. Washington v. Bank for Savings, supra, page 175 (63 N.E. 834 [1902]); Griffin v. Train, 90 App.Div. 16, 20, 85 N.Y.S. 686; 22 C.J. 216, 234 (1904). So a record made in the family Bible may be admitted to prove the date of birth, and thereby the age of a person (Penal Law, § 817; People v. Slater, 119 Cal. 620, 51 Pac. 957 [1898]; 33 Cyc. 1473) no matter by whom the entry is made (Union Central Life Ins. Co. v. Pollard, 94 Va. 146, 26 S.E. 421, 36 L.R.A. 271, 64 Am.St.Rep. 715 [1897]; Jones v. Jones, 45 Md. 144, 160 [1876]; Wigmore on Evidence [2d Ed.] § 1496); and direct testimony may be given by a physician, based on a record he made at the time of the birth of a child, or by the father concerning an entry in the family Bible, as showing the age of a prosecutrix in such an action as this (James v. State, 125 Ark. 269, 188 S.W. 806 [1916]).

Records of such facts as the age of a person must have recognized reliability and authenticity, or they will be excluded. Penal Law, § 817; . . . Buffalo Loan, Trust & Safe-Deposit Co. v. Knights Templar & Masonic Ass'n, 126 N.Y. 450, 27 N.E. 942, 22 Am.St.Rep. 839 (1891). The evidence offered in this case may not be so impeached. The record offered was made pursuant to a provision of law. Education Law, § 650, and section 651, as amended by Laws 1917, c. 567. It was intended to secure accuracy. Id. § 653. Very likely the records made in its books by the census board would have been competent under the circumstances. Richards v. Robin, 178 App.Div. 535, 165 N.Y.Supp. 780 (1917); Swift & Co. v. Rennard, 119 Ill.App. 173; Armstrong v. Modern Woodmen, 93 Wash. 352, 160 Pac. 946, Ann.Cas.1918E, 263 (1916). But we do not need to determine that question. The original affidavit of the mother was produced. That sworn statement would seem to be as reliable as would be her unverified entry in a family Bible. Russell v. Jackson, 22 Wend. 277, 280 (1839). While not made admissible by statute, as are records of birth and baptism, or entries in the family Bible, if the evidence was admissible in the civil case, it was admissible here. Code Cr.Proc. § 392. The mother possessed peculiar knowledge on the subject. To her the birth of her daughter must always have been a significant event. When she made the affidavit, there was no reason for making the false statement. The mother cannot now give testimony, and the law must be content with the best available evidence. If the jury were convinced of its truth and reliability, it constituted the necessary corroboration.

In such cases, the appearance of the complaining witness on the stand may be considered by the jury in reaching a conclusion as to her age. Penal Law, § 817; . . . State v. Davis, 237 Mo. 237, 140 S.W. 902 (1911); Wigmore on Evidence, §§ 222, 1154 (subd. 3). In this case such evidence might be of slight value, because the complainant lacked but 16 days of being 18 years of age when the act was perpetrated, and she was 14 days past 18 when the trial began. It would obviously be difficult by ordinary observation to make such fine discriminations. People v. Marks, 146 App. Div. 11, 130 N.Y.S. 524 (1911); People v. Todoro, 160 N.Y.S. 352 (1916). But I think we may not hold as a matter of law that the jury could not have taken her appearance into consideration. People v. Justices of Court of Special Sessions of County of New York, 10 Hun. 224, 226 (1877).

I vote for affirmance of the judgment of conviction.

CROUCH, J., concurs.

In the Matter of the Estate of Wallin v. State of Arizona Ex Rel. Swift
Court of Appeals of Arizona, 1971.
16 Ariz.App. 34, 490 P.2d 863.

In this case, the appellate court held that pedigree evidence of a person's lineage should have been admitted. Some new legal terms are used that will require explanation in order to fully understand what transpired in this case.

The decision uses the term "escheat." This means that property is turned over to the state. This occurs when there are no claimants to the property who are legally entitled to receive it. It also occurs in some states when a bank account does not have any activity, i.e., deposits or withdrawals, for a number of years. Some states fix the number of years as three years without activity.

"Ex rel." refers to the Latin phrase "ex relatione," which means a legal proceeding that is instituted by the attorney general, or other proper person, in the name of and in behalf of the state but on the information and at the instigation of an individual who has a private interest in the matter.

This case is an excellent example of a situation where the pedigree exception to the hearsay exclusionary rule allows admission of such evidence.

HOWARD, Judge. Hugo A. Wallin died intestate in 1968 and Letters of Administration were issued to one Forest V. Bender. In December, 1969, the appellant filed a petition to determine heirship. The petition alleged that the appellant's ward, Beda Wallin, an incompetent, was the decedent's sister and his only surviving heir at law.

An answer was filed by the administrator denying Beda Wallin's relationship to the decedent and the State of Arizona filed a notice of appearance and concurred in the administrator's answer. Subsequently, the State filed a complaint seeking an order of escheat. Both matters were consolidated for trial which resulted in the court denying appellant's petition to have Beda Wallin declared an heir of the decedent. The court found that the decedent died intestate and without heirs and ordered his estate escheated to the State of Arizona. This appeal followed attacking the correctness of both determinations.

Since reversal of the ruling in the heirship proceeding is dispositive of this appeal, we address ourselves to that aspect of the appeal.

The burden of establishing a claim of heirship is on the alleged heir. Edgar v. Dickens, 230 Ark. 7, 320 S.W.2d 761 (1959); In re Hobart's Estate, 82 Cal. App.2d 502, 187 P.2d 105 (1947). On the other hand escheats are not favored and it is presumed that a decedent left heirs or next of kin capable of inheriting property. Risbry v. Swan, 124 Colo. 567, 239 P.2d 600 (1951); In re Holmlund's Estate, 232 Or. 49, 374 P.2d 393 (1962).

The thrust of appellant's attack on appeal is the exclusion of certain documentary evidence offered to prove the relationship between the decedent and Beda Wallin. These documents consisted of the following:

1. A certified copy of the marriage record of one Carl A. Wallen and Matilda Nordien showing that their marriage took place in LaMoure County, North Dakota, on June 16, 1900, indicating that both were of LaMoure County and their ages were 38 and 28 respectively.

2. A "registration of death record" showing Karl August Wallen died on January 14, 1916 in the province of Saskatchewan, Canada, at the age of 53 years 5 months and 2 days. It indicated that he was a widower at the time of death.

3. A "registration of death" showing that Matilda Wallen[1] died on October 12, 1910 in the province of Saskatchewan, Canada, at the age of 41. It indicated that she was married at the time of death.

4. Letters of guardianship issued to Grace J. Daugherty by the county court of LaMoure County, North Dakota, evidencing her appointment as guardian of the person and estate of Beda Wallin, an incompetent person.

5. A copy of a petition for letters of administration for the Estate of Peter Nordin filed in LaMoure County, North Dakota, county court. The petition, filed by Carrie Nordin and verified by her, dated October 3, 1934 contains the following caption:

"In the Matter of the Estate of Peter Nordin, deceased
Carrie Nordin,

Petitioner,

v.

Charles Nordin, Emma Johanson, Mathilda Wallin (deceased), Beda Wallin a nd Hugo Wallin, Children of Mathilda Wallin, deceased,
Respondents."

The petition alleged that the decedent Peter Nordin died intestate and that the next of kin and the heirs at law under the law of succession were: Carrie Nordin, widow of decedent, residence being Gladstone Township, Marion, North Dakota, age 69; Charles Nordin, brother of decedent, age 62, address Litchville, North Dakota; Emma Johanson, sister, age 60, address Angelstad, Sweden; Beda Wallin, niece, address Marion, N.D., age 30; Hugo Wallin, nephew, age 33, address Washington, Mo., both children of Mathilda Wallin, deceased, sister of said decedent; and Lina Magnuson, Hallarp, Annerstad, Sweden. It further alleged:

"That your petitioner is the widow of said deceased, and therefore, as your petitioner is advised and believes, is entitled to a letter of administration of the estate of said deceased but request [sic] that her niece Beda Wallin be appointed as the administratrix of the estate of said decedent."

6. A copy of a final decree of distribution in the Estate of Peter Nordin (LaMoure County, North Dakota). The caption of this document reads as follows:

"Beda Wallin,

Petitioner,

v.

Charles Nordin, Emma Johanson, Lina Magnuson, Hugo Wallin and Carrie Nordin,
Respondents."

It directed distribution of the decedent's estate to his surviving widow, Carrie Nordin, and that Beda Wallin, administratrix, upon filing satisfactory evidence of distribution, would be finally discharged from her trust as administratrix. This decree was dated July 26, 1935.

Admitted into evidence was the death certificate of Hugo August Wallin indicating that he died on February 16, 1968 in Tucson, Arizona, at the age of 66 and that he was born in North Dakota.

Various objections were made to the introduction of the excluded documents, primarily on the grounds that they were hearsay and lacked relevance. The trial court, in sustaining the objections, was of the opinion that there was no showing of relevancy and that there was a great deal of hearsay in the documents.

A well-recognized exception to the hearsay rules exists in respect of proof of matters of family history, relationships and pedigree and subject to certain limitations and restrictions, hearsay evidence is admissible to prove such matters. 29 Am.Jur.2d, Evidence § 508. As stated in the foregoing text:

"Such evidence is held admissible not only because of the extreme difficulty of producing any better evidence—that is, because it is the best evidence of which the nature of the matter admits—but also because of its general reliability. Indeed, it has been held that evidence in respect of pedigree, or ancestral lineage, does not stand upon the footing of secondary evidence, to be excluded if some other witness can be produced who speaks upon the subject from his own knowledge."

No particular form of statement is required to render a declaration as to pedigree admissible in evidence. It may be oral or written, such as a letter, descriptions in wills and in Bibles—these are admitted upon the principle that they are the natural effusions of a person who must know the truth and who speaks upon an occasion when his mind stands in an even position, without any temptation to exceed or fall short of the truth.

Examination of the petition for letters of administration filed in North Dakota in 1934 reveals that it contains a recitation concerning Beda Wallin and Hugo Wallin as to their relationship inter se and to the decedent. It refers to the age of Hugo Wallin at that time which ties in with his age at the date of his death.

Although an allegation with respect to heirship in one proceeding may not be conclusive in a subsequent one, Behan v. Treasurer & Receiver General, 276 Mass. 502, 177

N.E. 654 (1931), a statement as to pedigree in a foreign probate petition and the proceedings thereon is competent evidence as to relationship. In re Weis' Estate, 224 Cal.App.2d 19, 36 Cal.Rptr. 266 (1964); Melton v. Anderson, 32 Tenn.App. 335, 222 S.W.2d 666 (1948); Burrell v. Westbrook, 163 S.W.2d 695 (Tex.Civ.App. 1942); See C.J.S. Evidence § 232.

Generally speaking, written declarations are admissible when it appears the declarant is dead or unavailable and is a member of the family. In re Weis' Estate, supra; 2 Jones on Evidence § 286. The 1934 petition for letters of administration reflects that the petitioner, Carrie Nordin, was then 69 years of age. Under these circumstances, it would not be inappropriate to indulge in the presumption that she was unavailable to testify. We may also presume from the fact that letters issued to Beda Wallin pursuant to Carrie Nordin's request, that the probate court found that they were related. Since written declarations made by a member of the family concerning pedigree are admissible, we believe that it was improper to exclude the documents pertaining to the North Dakota probate.

In the case of In re Weis' Estate, supra, the probate court found that the putative heir was the decedent's half sister. This finding was challenged on the ground that the evidence was insufficient to support it. The claimant, just as in the case at bench, because of her incompetency, was unable to offer any testimony or evidence bearing upon her relationship to the decedent. In attempting to prove family relationship between the decedent and the claimant, certified copies of various documents such as death certificates, a marriage certificate, divorce complaints and copies of documents relating to the insanity proceedings of the claimant were introduced. Also, certified copies of documents relating to the administration of the estate of a sister in law of the decedent were introduced. On appeal, it was contended that these documents were all hearsay, hence inadmissible. The California Appellate Court did not pass upon the admissibility of documents other than those relating to the probate proceedings and held that the assertions made therein as to relationships, although hearsay, were admissible

within the "family history" exception to the hearsay rule and were sufficient to support the finding that the claimant was the decedent's half sister.

As to the other documents which were refused admission, it would appear that they became relevant once the record in the North Dakota probate proceeding is admitted into evidence. The certified copies of the marriage certificate and death certificate are admissible as prima facie evidence of the facts therein stated, A.R.S. §§ 12-2264 and 2265; Ranger Insurance Co. v. Industrial Commission, 15 Ariz.App. 45, 485 P.2d 869 (1971). Examination of the various documents reveal that LaMoure County, North Dakota, was where the Nordin probate took place, where Carl A. Wallen and Mathilda Nordien were married, and where a guardian was appointed for Beda Wallin. Also, the ages set forth in the various documents are corroborative of identity, as are the similarity of names. It is not inappropriate, in determining a claim of heirship, to consider these circumstances. In re Lipovsky's Estate, 238 Cal.App.2d 604, 48 Cal.Rptr. 41 (1966); In re Hooper's Estate, 53 Wash.2d 262, 332 P.2d 1077 (1958).

We hold that the trial court erroneously excluded the documentary exhibits in the heirship proceeding. As a consequence thereof, the judgment of escheat must be reversed and the cause remanded for a new trial.

KRUCKER, C. J., and HATHAWAY, J., concur.

---

[1] The decedent's name is handwritten and it is difficult to determine whether the surname is Wallen or Waleen. However the signature of the informant contains two l's. (Karl Wallen or Karl Wallin.)

Matter of Egbert's Estate
Court of Appeals of Michigan, 1981.
105 Mich.App. 395, 306 N.W.2d 525.

This case is a perfect example of the application of the pedigree exception to the hearsay exclusionary rule to resolve a dispute between litigants. It is also an example of the court righting a wrong committed by an attorney. The appellate court specifically mentions MRE 103d (Michigan Rule of Evidence 103d), which allows a court to take notice of plain errors affecting substantial rights although they were not brought to the attention of the court. Another way of stating this is that the appellate court in the interest of justice may rectify plain errors of counsel or the court when substantial rights were abrogated by such errors in the trial.

Before BEALSEY, P. J., and R. B. BURNS and HOEHN,* JJ.

PER CURIAM.

Charles Ernest Egbert died intestate on June 26, 1978, at the age of 91. On October 5, 1978, following uncontested testimony two days earlier, Beatrice Bedenbaugh and Ernest D. Egbert were determined to be first cousins of the decedent and his sole heirs-at-law. On October 20, 1978, Renee Alice Unseld, hereinafter plaintiff, filed a petition claiming to be the niece and sole heir-at-law of the deceased and asking that all prior proceedings in the estate be quashed and held for nought on the grounds that they were instituted and carried forward by persons with no pecuniary interest in the estate. After a hearing on the petition held on November 20, 1978, the probate court held that plaintiff had failed to convince the court by a preponderance of the evidence that she was, in fact, decedent's niece. Following an unsuccessful appeal to the circuit court, plaintiff appeals to this Court by leave granted.

Plaintiff first contends that the probate court erred in denying her request to admit into evidence two proposed exhibits to prove her relationship to decedent. The first proposed exhibit, a memorial card, was voluntarily withdrawn by plaintiff's counsel and, therefore, the question of its admissibility is not properly before this Court.

The second proposed exhibit was a picture postcard. On the front of the postcard is a photograph of a young girl, who plaintiff alleges is herself. On the back is the alleged handwriting of the deceased stating: "Ren Robinson, My Sister, Daughter, Age About 3, /s/Ernest Egbert."

When plaintiff sought to admit the exhibit, defendants objected that it was not admissible because it was hearsay. After plaintiff's counsel could not cite an exception to the hearsay rule, the trial judge ruled that the exhibit was inadmissible.

This photograph is admissible under MRE 804(b)(4) which provides:

"(b) Hearsay exceptions. The following are not excluded by the hearsay rule if the declarant is unavailable as a witness:

*   *   *

"(4) Statement of personal or family history. (A) A statement concerning the declarant's own birth, adoption, marriage, divorce, legitimacy, relationship by blood, adoption, or marriage, ancestry, or other similar fact of personal or family history, even though declarant had no means of acquiring personal knowledge of the matter stated; or (B) a statement concerning the foregoing matters, and death also, of another person, if the declarant was related to the other by blood, adoption, or marriage or was so intimately associated with the other's family as to be likely to have accurate information concerning the matter declared."

Defendants maintain that the photograph is inadmissible, citing Lamoreaux v. Attorney General, where the Michigan Supreme Court held that the alleged relationship must be shown by other evidence in addition to the statement of the alleged relative. *Lamoreaux* is no longer valid authority in light of the statement in MRE 101 that "[t]hese rules govern proceedings in the courts of this state to the extent and with the exceptions stated in Rule 1101," which are not pertinent here.

Moreover, *Lamoreaux* is distinguishable, as the court there was not concerned with hearsay statements of a deceased person as to his family ties, but, rather, as to the citizenship of a relative.

The photograph could also be admissible under MRE 803(16) as an ancient document in existence 20 years or more, or under MRE 803(13), which provides that the following are not excluded by the hearsay rule:

"(13) Family records. Statements of fact concerning personal or family history contained in family Bibles, genealogies, charts, engravings on rings, *inscriptions on family portraits*, engravings on urns, crypts, or tombstones, or the like." (Emphasis added.)

Having determined that the photograph was admissible, the question remains whether error may be predicated on the probate court's sustaining of defendant's objection to admissibility where plaintiff's counsel failed to argue appropriate grounds for admissibility. MRE 102 provides:

> "These rules are intended to secure fairness in administration, elimination of unjustifiable expense and delay, and promotion of growth and development of the law of evidence to the end that the truth may be ascertained and proceedings justly determined."

More to the point, MRE 103(d) states:

> "(d) Plain error. Nothing in this rule precludes taking notice of plain errors affecting substantial rights although they were not brought to the attention of the court."

Although, generally, error requiring reversal will not be found where admissible evidence was excluded but the proper grounds for admissibility were not presented to the trial court, where, as here, the excluded evidence, if given any weight at all, would be crucial and, perhaps, determinative of the lawsuit, the better rule is that the trial court is bound to follow the law, whether or not it has been cited to the court.

Therefore, we set aside the probate court's determination of heirs and remand for a hearing on the merits with full opportunity to offer all evidence relevant to a determination of heirs.

Plaintiff's second claim is that the probate judge in this case is clearly prejudiced against plaintiff and her counsel and, therefore, should be disqualified from hearing the matter in the event the case is remanded. This claim is not supported by the record.

REVERSED and REMANDED.

✔ PRACTICE QUESTIONS

Select the most correct answer to complete each statement. Your answer should be based upon information included in Chapter 11.

1. (a) Pedigree evidence is admissible to show the date of birth and the father's name of a person.
   (b) As a general rule, for a declaration of pedigree to be admissible, it must have been made by someone not related to the family concerned.
   (c) Declarations of pedigree as an exception to the hearsay exclusionary rule will ordinarily not be received when better evidence is available.
   (d) Declarations of pedigree are required to be in a precise form in order for the declaration to be admissible in evidence.

2. (a) In order to get a pedigree declaration admitted, it is necessary that the declarant be disinterested to the extent of having no motive that would induce him or her to state the facts otherwise than as he or she understood them and that the declaration be made ante litem motam.
   (b) Pedigree statements to be admissible should be made after there is a motive to deceive.
   (c) The following elements are necessary in most states for a pedigree (personal or family history) to be declared admissible:
      1. The declarant was competent at the time of making the statement.
      2. The declarant shall be alive at the time of the trial.
      3. The declarant was not related by blood or affinity to the family about which he or she speaks.
      4. The declarations were made post litem motam.
      5. Matters of pedigree must be in issue.
   (d) Federal Rule of Evidence 803(19) does not permit the introduction of pedigree evidence if the declarant is available as a witness.

Indicate whether each statement is true or false.

3. A duly authenticated photograph of the inscription on a tombstone is admissible in evidence to show the truth of the statements engraved thereon.

4. Where matters of pedigree are in issue, a statement or writing that was made by a person who is dead at the time of trial, whose declarations were made ante litem motam, and who had no other qualifications necessary for a pedigree exception is admissible in evidence.

5. The declaration of pedigree need not be in a precise form in order to be admissible.

6. In a rape case, the declarations of the deceased mother of the alleged rape victim with respect to the age of the victim are admissible under the pedigree exception.

7. A Bible containing handwritten statements concerning the genealogy of persons is admissible in a probate (surrogate) proceeding to determine who should be entitled to an inheritance from a deceased person mentioned in the statements contained in the subject Bible.

CHAPTER 12

Privileged Communications

§ 12.1 INTRODUCTION

If you have watched a television performance of a courtroom trial, you have probably heard the phrase "privileged communication." If you substitute the word "confidential" for the word "privileged," you have a better understanding of the concept of privileged communication. When one speaks to another in confidence, he or she usually does so with the thought that the contents of the communication will not be divulged by the listener. In certain situations, the law has contended that the best interests of society will be served by prohibiting the listener from divulging the information he or she has received unless the informer has expressly released the listener from this prohibition. The idea of privileged communication, which originated in the common law, is based on a code of honor under which certain categories of people could not divulge information given to them in confidence. Later, it was enacted into the statutory law to include communications involving ministers, priests, rabbis, attorneys, physicians, and psychologists; certain conversations between husband and wife; and compromise offers. The statutes do not give blanket coverage to these people but do include them in controlled situations.

§ 12.2 FAILURE TO WAIVE PRIVILEGED COMMUNICATION—INFERENCE

There is a conflict of authority with respect to whether or not an unfavorable inference may be drawn from the refusal of a party to waive the privilege of a confidential communication. The prevailing view appears to be that no unfavorable inference shall be drawn from the failure of a party to waive the privilege. In Meyer v. Russell, 55 N.D. 546, 214 N.W. 857 (1927), it was held that failure to call as witnesses physicians who first attended the injured plaintiff does not permit a presumption that their testimony would have been unfavorable.

§ 12.3 CLERGY

It is well recognized that there was no common-law privilege in the case of confidential communications with or confessions made to a member of the clergy. The legislatures of most jurisdictions, however, have found it to be in the best interest of the public to enact statutes granting such a privilege to a member of the clergy of any religion. The New York Civil Practice Law and Rules provides in § 4505: "Unless the person confessing or confiding waives the privilege, a clergyman or other minister of any religion or duly accredited Christian Science practitioner shall not be allowed to disclose a confession or confidence made to him in his professional character as spiritual advisor." You should take particular note of the words "in his professional character as spiritual advisor." If the penitent or confessor made an inculpatory statement to such a clergyperson, not knowing that the listener was a clergyperson, it would appear that the clergyperson would not be bound by the privilege. On the other hand, it has been held that it is not essential that the penitent be a member of the same church as the clergyman. Minn.—Matter of Swenson, 183 Minn. 602, 237 N.W. 589 (1931). Statutes in different jurisdictions vary with respect to how this privilege is waived. Some require that the waiver only be at the trial, except that a waiver between the attorneys representing adverse interests is also acceptable even though done before the trial.

§ 12.4 HOSPITAL RECORDS

It has been indicated in Chapter 10 that hospital records are admissible when the entries were necessary for diagnosis, prognosis, and/or treatment. This was allowed by the common law business records rule and by the statutory rules enacted by most states authorizing the use of hospital records in trials. We now have the problem of a head-on collision between rules of law. On the one hand, the statute permits introduction of the records into evidence, and on the other hand, a privileged communication exists between physician and patient. The courts, in some cases, have excluded hospital records where they involve a communication between a doctor and a patient and the patient does not waive his or her privilege. N.Y.—Vanderhule v. Berinstein, 285 A.D. 290, 136 N.Y.S.2d 95 (1954).

However, a patient waives the doctor-patient privilege by bringing an action that places his or her physical condition in issue. N.Y.—Burgos v. Flower & Fifth Ave. Hosp. 108 Misc.2d 225, 437 N.Y.S.2d 218 (1980).

§ 12.5 PHYSICIAN

No privilege existed at common law between physician and patient. In 1828, New York State became the first state to pass a law creating this privilege. The current statute that specifies this privilege is found in N.Y.—CPLR 4504.

> § 4504. Physician, dentist and nurse
>
> (a) **Confidential information privileged.** Unless the patient waives the privilege, a person authorized to practice medicine, registered professional nursing, licensed practical nursing or dentistry shall not be allowed to disclose any information which he acquired in attending a patient in a professional capacity, and which was necessary to enable him to act in that capacity. The relationship of a physician and patient shall exist between a medical corporation, as defined in article forty-four of the public health law, a professional service corporation organized under article fifteen of the business corporation law to practice medicine, and the patients to whom they respectively render professional medical services. . . .

An analysis of CPLR 4504 reveals that four elements must exist in order for this rule to operate:

1. There must be a relationship of physician and patient, or dentist and patient, or registered nurse or licensed practical nurse and patient.
2. The persons named must be duly authorized under the law to practice their respective professions.

3. The information must be acquired while attending the patient.
4. The information must be necessary to enable the professional to act in that capacity.

When you analyze the preceding elements, you can easily imagine many situations in which a physician-patient relationship may exist and confidences may be expressed by the patient to the physician, said confidences not coming within the scope of the privilege. It is for this reason that I previously indicated a caveat that the statutes include certain categories of people in controlled situations only. For example, there is no privilege where the patient has a relationship with a chiropractor, a midwife, or an unregistered practical nurse; where the information given by the patient is not necessary for diagnosis and/or treatment (N.Y.—People v. Decina, 2 N.Y.2d 133, 138 N.E.2d 799, 157 N.Y.S.2d 558 [1956]); and where a physician is required by law to report a wound inflicted by a deadly weapon (Ohio—State v. Antill, 26 Ohio Op. 366, 197 N.E.2d 548 [1964]).

§ 12.6 PSYCHOTHERAPIST

A psychotherapist is a person who is particularly qualified to treat mental and emotional conditions. In this capacity, sometimes it becomes necessary to gain knowledge of the innermost feelings and thoughts of the patient in order to arrive at a method of treatment. The psychotherapist therefore must, of necessity, be one who keeps secret and privileged everything that is said by the patient unless the patient waives this privilege. Therefore, the statutes guardedly cover this relationship.

On June 13, 1996, the United States Supreme Court in a 7–2 decision held that the confidential communication privilege also extends to such communications that are made to licensed social workers in the course of psychotherapy. Carrie Jaffee, Special Administrator for Ricky Allen, Sr., deceased, petitioner v. Mary Lu Redmond, et al., __U.S.__, 116 S.Ct. 1923, 135 L.Ed.2d 337, 59 Cr. L. 2143 (1996). The Court decided this case by interpreting Federal Rule of Evidence 501, which permits the federal courts to define new privileges by interpreting common law principles. In this case a licensed social worker counseled a police officer after she had killed a person in the line of duty. The Court held that neither the police officer nor the licensed social worker were obligated to produce the notes of their sessions to the estate of the decedent who was suing for money damages, in that the notes were privileged.

§ 12.7 HUSBAND AND WIFE

Before women's liberation, the common law considered a woman little more than a chattel in many circumstances. For example, in common law, the husband or wife of a party to an action was disqualified as a witness. Eng.—Davis v. Dinwoody, 4 T.R. 678, 100 Eng.Rep. 1241 (5/14/1792). There were some exceptions to this blanket rule, but the statutory law of most jurisdictions has removed most uncertainties in this area of privileged communications. New York State has enacted one statute covering this area: CPLR 4512.

In summary, CPLR 4512 states that in an action found on adultery as a ground for divorce neither spouse is competent to testify against the other except

1. to prove the marriage,
2. to disprove the adultery, or
3. to disprove a defense after evidence has been introduced tending to prove such defense.

Note that the prohibition applies only to divorce actions founded on adultery and not to other grounds of actions wherein husband and wife might be adversaries such as one for separation or a divorce based on cruel and inhuman treatment or other statutory reasons.

CPLR 4502 also provides that neither spouse may be required or, without the consent of the other if living, allowed to disclose a confidential communication made by one to the other during marriage.

At common law, in a prosecution of one spouse for an injury inflicted on the other, the injured spouse was a competent witness. The 1909 Penal Law of New York, §2445, prohibited the revelation of a confidential communication between husband and wife. The 1967 Penal Law of New York omitted this section with the apparent result of a return to the common law.

The reason for invoking the privilege is to protect and strengthen the marital bond. If the spouses are not living together but are married in name only, the privilege does not exist unless the communication was made as part of an attempted reconciliation. N.Y.—People v. Oyola, 6 N.Y.2d 259, 160 N.E.2d 494, 189 N.Y.S.2d 203 (1959).

The privilege is continued after divorce and even after the death of one of the parties. U.S.—Pereira v. United States, 347 U.S. 1, 74 S.Ct. 358, 98 L.Ed. 435 (1954).

§ 12.8 POLICE INFORMANT

The work quality of a detective is no better than his or her information. In order to operate efficiently, a police department needs the information supplied to it by police informants. If the names of informants were divulged, fewer people would volunteer information or be in the business of supplying information to police authorities. It is apparent that if these people were identified, they would either bear the scars of their profession or have a much shortened life span. Accordingly, it becomes necessary, in the public interest, to protect informants.

Frequently, defense attorneys will, in the course of pretrial motions or even at the trial itself, request that the identity of the police informant be revealed. There has been some confusion with respect to the discretion of the judge to reveal the identity of the confidential informant of the police. It appears that for the most part the state does not have to disclose the name of the informant who gave information to the police in order to establish probable cause for the issuance of a search warrant. In United States v. Ventresca, 380 U.S. 102, 85 S.Ct. 741, 13 L.Ed.2d 684 (1965), the Court held that "an affidavit may be based upon hearsay information and need not reflect the direct personal observation of the affiant so long as the magistrate is informed of some of the underlying circumstances supporting the affiant's conclusions and his belief that any informant whose identity need not be disclosed . . . was credible and his information reliable."

It therefore can be said that an officer who gets information from an informant who has previously proved reliable will not be required to divulge the identity of the informant for the purpose of establishing the probable cause necessary for the issuance of a search warrant. It might also be further stated that the identity of informants will not be revealed if the information leads to the discovery of the crime.

This privilege, however, is not without exception. In Roviaro v. United States, 353 U.S. 53, 77 S.Ct. 623, 1 L.Ed.2d 639 (1957), a prosecutor was required to divulge the identity of an informant where the informant had a direct involvement as the sole participant with an accused in the offense for which the accused was being tried.

The privilege runs to the favor of the government in the interest of the public. It does not run to the informant. Hence, if the government wants to identify the informant, it may do so by waiving the privilege without first getting the permission of the informant.

In a New York case, the prosecution refused to divulge the name of an informer and went one step further in not offering any evidence of his reliability, thereby failing to establish the existence of probable cause to make the arrest; the indictment was dismissed by the New York Court of Appeals. N.Y.—People v. Malinsky, 19 N.Y.2d 262, 225 N.E.2d 748, 279 N.Y.S.2d 20 (1967).

However, when observations of two defendants by a police officer were sufficient, quite apart from the informer's communication, to establish that probable cause existed to support issuance of a warrant for the search of an apartment for policy violations, or indeed to arrest without a warrant, the prosecution did not have to disclose the identity of the informer or produce him upon the motion of those two defendants to set aside the search warrant and suppress evidence seized on the search conducted pursuant thereto. N.Y.—People v. Smith, 21 N.Y.2d 698, 234 N.E.2d 460, 287 N.Y.S.2d 425 (1967).

There is a need to protect the government's privilege of nondisclosure of the identity of informants so as to encourage citizens to communicate their knowledge of crime to law enforcement officials.

Government's privilege of nondisclosure of the identity of informers of violations of law is limited by the fundamental requirements of fairness and must give way when its assertion would seriously prejudice the defendant by making a fair hearing impossible. Denial of disclosure of the identity of an informant did not deprive defendant of a fair trial when the informant's communication was not essential to the establishment of probable cause for issuance of a search warrant, since the informer's information that defendant was selling narcotics was independently verified and corroborated by the observations of detectives during their stakeout of defendant's apartment and building. N.Y.—People v. Cerrato, 24 N.Y.2d 1, 246 N.E.2d 501, 298 N.Y.S.2d 688 (1969), *cert. denied*, 397 U.S. 940, 90 S.Ct. 951, 25 L.Ed.2d 120 (1970).

It would therefore appear that the courts are reluctant to order the prosecutor to divulge the identity of an informer. But if a fair defense requires the identity of the informer and there is no other evidence that the prosecution can rely on to substantiate probable cause for the arrest, the court will dismiss the indictment unless the prosecution reveals the identity of the informer to the defendant.

The better practice for police officers to follow is to obtain the initial information from informants and then make observations by themselves that may lead them to conclude, by virtue of their training and experience, that criminal activity is occurring, describing the type of criminal activity that they believe is taking place. Suspicion alone will not produce probable cause to obtain a warrant.

§ 12.9   STATEMENTS MADE TO POLICE OFFICERS INVESTIGATING MOTOR VEHICLE ACCIDENTS

The Florida legislature has enacted § 316.066(4), which establishes a privilege running in favor of the participants in an accident to deny the admissibility in evidence in any trial, civil or criminal, of accident reports or statements made by the participants in the accident to the police officer investigating the accident. The privilege does not apply in criminal trials unless it is a Fifth Amendment violation. State v. Riley, 617 So.2d 340 (Fla.App.1993).

However, a motorist who was following the vehicles that were involved in the accident may testify as to what he or she observed, providing that the person was not involved in the accident in any way. McTevia v. Schrag, 446 So.2d 1183, 1184 (Fla.App. 1984). Also, the privilege does not apply to protect findings and statements made in criminal or homicide investigators' reports. Standely v. White, 326 So.2d 68 (Fla.App. 1976).

Some localities in Florida are now employing public service aides to investigate and report accidents. They are being used allegedly as an economy measure because they are paid less than sworn officers and free sworn officers for other law enforcement activities. I know of no cases that have determined that §316.066(4) applies to them as well as to police officers, but I assume it will apply to them as well.

If you want to determine whether your jurisdiction has a similar statute, look up any of the aforementioned cases in So.2d and ascertain the West Key Number attributed to that case. Then check the West digest for your state, if it has one, using the West Key Number assigned, and you may find a case dealing with the same topic. The decision probably identifies the number of the statute in your state. You can then read it to see if it conforms to the Florida statute.

For more information on this privilege, refer to Section 10.14.

§ 12.10 ATTORNEY

When a client visits the office of an attorney to ask the attorney's assistance with some difficulty the client is involved in, the client must, of necessity, reveal certain facts that he or she might not want the whole world to know. In order for the attorney to fully and competently advise the client as to a course of action to be taken, the attorney must know all of the relevant facts about the situation. The law presumes this and protects the client by a privilege. In effect, when the client is talking to the attorney, the client is talking to himself or herself. A different result obtains when a third person is present during the conversation. The common law permitted an eavesdropper to a confidential communication to disclose the contents of the communication. Today that would be a violation of the constitutional right of counsel. However, if a communication is made in the presence of a third party who is not the agent of the attorney or the client, the privilege does not apply because it is apparent that the communication was not intended to be confidential. Baumann v. Steingester, 213 N.Y. 328, 107 N.E. 578 (1915).

Assume that a client consults with a person whom the client reasonably believes to be an attorney, but that person is not, in fact, an attorney. If the client gives the "attorney" confidential information, this information is not admissible in evidence. There are stringent requirements the client must meet when claiming to have mistakenly believed that the imposter was an attorney. They are precisely indicated in United States v. Tyler, 745 F.Supp. 423 (W.D.Mich. 1990), which is included at the end of this chapter.

§ 12.11 OVERHEARD BY THIRD PERSONS

Ordinarily, privileged communications overhead by third persons lose their status as privileged communications. This may occur in attorney-client relationships (U.S.—Wolfle v. United States, 291 U.S. 7, 54 S.Ct. 279, 78 L.Ed. 617 [1934]), husband-wife situations (N.Y.—People v. McCormack, 278 A.D. 191, 104 N.Y.S.2d 139 [1951]), or any like situations, the reasoning being that if it was really a confidential communication, the relator would not have wanted to have a third person share in the secret.

§ 12.12 WAIVER

The privileged communication may be waived by the oral or written consent of the person to whom the privilege runs. If it is done orally, it may be by the failure on the part of the person to whom the privilege runs to object to its admissibility at the time of trial.

A patient waives his privilege when he calls his attending physician to testify in behalf of the patient with respect to the patient's physical or mental condition. N.Y.—Steinberg, v. New York Life Ins. Co., 263 N.Y. 45, 188 N.E. 152, 90 A.L.R. 642 (1933).

A peculiar result occurs when the representative of one who has been killed by the negligent act of another sues the other person in what is known as a wrongful death action. In this type of action, it is necessary for the decedent's representative to tender proof of the decedent's pecuniary worth (i.e., his or her health and earning capacity) to his or her next of kin. The representative must therefore produce evidence of the decedent's good health. When the representative does this, courts have held that he or she waives the doctor-patient privilege and the defendant may then validly expect the physician who treated the decedent to testify as to what he or she found with respect to the quality of decedent's health. N.Y.—Eder v. Cashin, 281 A.D. 456, 120 N.Y.S.2d 165 (1953).

Once a person waives his or her privilege in a trial, either by affirmative action or by failing to object to its admission by the other side, the cases have held that the privilege is waived for all time. N.Y.—People v. Bloom, 193 N.Y. 1, 85 N.E. 824, 18 L.R.A.(N.S.). 898 (1908). Testimony elicited on cross-examination, however, does not waive the privilege. N.Y.—Vilardi v. Vilardi, 200 Misc. 1043, 107 N.Y.S.2d 342 (1951).

§ 12.13 STATE SECRETS

You are reminded that the rules of evidence have as their basis the ascertainment of the truth according to the best ability and the conscience and mind. In the area of the state secrets privilege, it is easy to understand that great injustice could be done to a defendant if the prosecution were to rely unscrupulously on the right to refrain from furnishing certain information on the ground that to do so would reveal state secrets. In most cases involving this point, it has been held that the judge ought to have some facts presented to him or her on which to base a decision unless there is clear evidence that the disclosure would be dangerous to the government.

In the interest of justice, where the refusal might seriously prevent the defense from presenting its case, the prosecutor may be required to move for a dismissal of charges. U.S.—United States v. Reynolds, 345 U.S. 1, 73 S.Ct. 528, 97 L.Ed. 727 (1953).

Proposed Federal Rule 509 was a codification of the exclusion from evidence of state secrets. Congress failed to enact it, however, and the common law rule still prevails.

§ 12.14 EXECUTIVE PRIVILEGE

Little was known about the term "executive privilege" before it was invoked by President Nixon during the Watergate controversy of 1974.

The concept is that in the running of the government the president has the implied right to keep secret all of the conversations he or she has with others with respect to the administration of the office. The United States Supreme Court, in an 8–0 decision, rejected such claims, and this was probably the major reason for Nixon's resignation on August 9, 1974. U.S.—United States v. Nixon, 418 U.S. 683, 94 S.Ct. 3090, 41 L.Ed.2d 1039 (1974). However, in Wood v. Breier, 66 F.R.D. 8 (E.D.Wis. 1975), *appeal dismissed*, 534 F.2d 330 (U.S.Ct.App. 7th Cir. 1976), the court held that the applicability of executive privilege must be determined by a case-by-case ad hoc balancing of public policies and the material that is sought to be discovered.

§ 12.15 NEWSPAPER REPORTER

Great influence has been brought on state and national legislatures to extend the concept of privileged communications to the sources of information given to newspaper reporters. Frequently, reporters have gone to jail because they have refused to divulge the source of their information after being directed to do so by a judge. This area of the law may change, but as of this writing a newspaper reporter called as a witness before a grand jury cannot, under the common law, lawfully refuse to answer pertinent questions relating to communications made to him or her on the ground that such communications are privileged. N.Y.—People *ex rel.* Mooney v. Sheriff of New York County, 269 N.Y. 291, 199 N.E. 415, 102 A.L.R. 769 (1936).

The reason given by the courts and legislatures for not granting this privilege is that the interest of the public in the due administration of the law is superior to any private considerations that may exist between journalists and their informants.

There is a conflict of constitutional law in this area with respect to the protections of the First Amendment (freedom of the press) and the Fifth Amendment (self-incrimination). It is not completely within the scope of this text to delve deeply into constitutional law problems, but suffice it to say that in most jurisdictions a journalist does not enjoy the privilege unless it is expressly provided for by statute. New York and New Jersey are among the jurisdictions that have legislation protecting the sources of information of journalists, but these statutes are being interpreted by the courts, and erosions of the privilege have already taken place.

In June of 1972, the Supreme Court of the United States handed down a decision in the case of United States v. Earl Caldwell, 408 U.S. 665, 92 S.Ct. 2646, 33 L.Ed.2d 626, involving Earl Caldwell of the *New York Times* and two other newsmen. There, the Court held that the First Amendment did not give newspaper reporters an automatic right or privilege to refuse to testify before grand juries about their work. However, it did not require the jailing of all newspaper reporters who refuse to testify. It left open the concept that in determining whether to uphold subpoenas of newspaper reporters the courts must balance the interests of a free press against the interests of the grand jury investigation to which the reporter is being asked to contribute. It also said that Congress was free to create whatever "newsman's privilege" it sees fit—including an "absolute privilege."

In New Jersey, where a statutory privilege for newspaper reporters exists, a re-porter, Peter J. Bridge, was confined to jail for attempting to exercise the privilege. The state courts of New Jersey, 120 N.J.Super. 460, 295 A.2d 3(1972), held that Bridge waived the privilege when he named one person as having given him infor-mation. You are referred to your own state laws for a more detailed analysis of the law in your jurisdiction.

A later case, in which the United States Supreme Court denied certiorari, thereby making the holding of the United States Court of Appeals the law of the land, held that "the journalists' federal common law qualified privilege is not lim-ited solely to protection of confidential sources; the compelled production of a re-porter's resource materials can constitute a significant intrusion into the news gathering and editorial processes and, like compelled disclosure of sources, can substantially undercut the public policy favoring the free flow of information to the public that is the foundation for the privilege." United States v. Cuthbertson, 630 F.2d 139 (3d Cir. 1980), *cert. denied,* 449 U.S. 1126, 101 S.Ct. 945, 67 L.Ed.2d 113 (1981).

§ 12.16 STATUTORY IMMUNITY

When fishing, many times people catch a small fish but throw it back into the wa-ter or use it as bait to get a larger fish. So, too, in the law enforcement profession. Sometimes it becomes necessary to let a small-time "punk" go free in order to get at the higher-echelon criminal. The legislatures understand this phenomenon and have enacted statutes giving law enforcement officials, particularly prosecutors, the authority to grant immunity to those who would claim the protection of the Fifth Amendment self-incrimination clause. The theory is that if immunity is granted, there is no reason for the witness to ask for the privilege. In this manner, much information can be secured by the government that probably would not have become known but for the granting of the immunity privilege.

§ 12.17 PRIVILEGE BETWEEN PAROLEE AND PAROLE OFFICER, AND PROBATIONER AND PROBATION OFFICER

The United States Court of Appeals for the Eighth Circuit held that there is no privilege between a parolee and a probation (parole) officer in United States v. Simmons, 964 F.2d 763, 768–769 (8th Cir.), *cert. denied,* 506 U.S. 1011, 113 S.Ct. 632, 121 L.Ed.2d 563 (1992).

§ 12.18 FEDERAL RULE

Rule 501. General rule

Except as otherwise required by the Constitution of the United States or provided by Act of Congress or in rules prescribed by the Supreme Court pursuant to statutory au-thority, the privilege of a witness, person, government, State, or political subdivision thereof shall be governed by the principles of the common law as they may be inter-preted by the courts of the United States in the light of reason and experience. How-ever, in civil actions and proceedings, with respect to an element of a claim or defense as to which State law supplies the rule of decision, the privilege of a witness, person, government, State, or political subdivision thereof shall be determined in accordance with State law.

The United States Supreme Court prescribed twelve additional rules with respect to privilege, but Congress failed to enact them. In essence, the Advisory Committees Note to the Federal Rules of Evidence explained that the grand design of these provisions does not readily lend itself to codification.

CROSS-REFERENCES

Federal Civil Judicial Procedure and Rules (West 1996) (Rule 501).
Goode & Wellborn, Courtroom Handbook on Federal Evidence (West 1995) (Rule 501).
McCormick, Evidence (4th ed. 1992) (Rule 501).

Vanderhule v. Berinstein

Supreme Court, Appellate Division, Third
Department, 1954.
285 A.D., 290, 136 N.Y.S.2d 95.

This case presents an example of a privileged
communication in which a person made statements to an employee of a state hospital as to
his prior history in order to be properly diagnosed and treated. In New York, a state hospital is usually the equivalent of a psychiatric
hospital, formerly known as an insane asylum.
To better understand the facts in this case, I
thought it best to explain this fact. Although
this is a civil action in negligence, it is useful
for a person educated in criminal justice to be
aware of other legal subjects. Criminal law is a
small part of the study of law.

HALPERN, Justice. The plaintiffs appeal from
an order setting aside a verdict in their favor
and dismissing the complaint in an action to
recover damages for an assault committed by
an employee of the defendants, and from the
judgment entered pursuant to the order.

The first four defendants named in the title
are copartners owning and operating a bowling alley in the City of Binghamton, New
York, known as the State Bowling Center.
The defendant Randall is the general manager
of the Bowling Center. The Bowling Center
has twenty bowling alleys at which 200 people
bowl in an evening in two shifts. Immediately
adjacent to the alleys, there are benches upon
which the bowlers sit between games. Behind
the benches are several rows of seats for spectators. In an adjoining room, there is a lun-
cheonette where food and beer are served.

Overlooking the bowling alleys is a desk at
which a supervisory employee known as a
"desk man" is stationed. He collects the
money from the team captains and designates
the alleys at which the teams are to bowl. He
also makes announcements over the public
address system, and generally is in charge of
the Bowling Center when the manager is not
present. The desk man serves as the assistant

manager and is sometimes referred to by that
title.

On September 2, 1952, three weeks before
the occurrence of the assault which gave rise
to this action, a man named Finkle applied to
the defendant Randall for a job. He had just
come to the city and had no permanent place
of residence and he had no funds. Randall admitted that Finkle had all the characteristics
of a "floater" except that he was a "little bit
better dressed than a floater."

Finkle did not have any letter of reference
from any former employer; in fact, he evaded
the question and did not give the name of any
former employer when Randall asked him
about it. Randall made no other inquiries except a request for Finkle's social security number. Finkle was hired as a pin setter. After being so employed for a week, he was promoted
to desk man and assistant manager, next in
command to Randall, the general manager.
No inquiry was made as to his history or background prior to his promotion to desk man
and assistant manager. There was some evidence that during the period of his employment, Finkle had told a fellow employee that
he had "had trouble with the police agencies
in Albany" and that this information had
been reported to the general manager.

Randall had rented a room in his own
apartment to Finkle and, on October 12,
1952, while they were riding home together,
Finkle made some statements, which were obviously irrational or confused, to the effect
that "the Democrat organization" was "holding his wife in Albany" and "wouldn't let him
get to see her." Randall heard this statement
but "took it as a joke"; he did not pursue the
matter with Finkle and he made no further inquiry of anyone.

The next evening, October 13, 1952, the
plaintiffs, Mr. and Mrs. Vanderhule, went to
the Bowling Center shortly before nine
o'clock for a game in a league in which Mr.
Vanderhule was a member. Upon their arrival,
Finkle was acting as the desk man, during the

first series of games. During the second series, he was replaced by another man at the desk and Finkle temporarily served as a pin setter, because of an emergency which had arisen due to the absence of one of the pin boys. About half past ten o'clock, while Mrs. Vanderhule was keeping score for her husband's team, Finkle approached her and struck her in the face, without any provocation and without any apparent reason. She had seen Finkle the week before when she had been at the Bowling Center, bowling on a girls' team, but there was no evidence of the occurrence of any altercation that night or of any other incident which might account for the assault. When Mr. Vanderhule observed the assault upon his wife, he engaged in a tussle with Finkle and in the course of it, he fell and fractured his knee.

The defendant Randall was in his office at the time. When he was told of the assault, his immediate response was that Finkle "must have gone off his rocker."

Subsequently, Finkle was confined to the Binghamton State Hospital and was not available upon the trial as a witness for either side.

An action was brought for the assault upon the wife and for the injury suffered by the husband. The complaint alleged several causes of action, two principal grounds of recovery being advanced. One was that the defendants knew or, in the exercise of care, should have known of Finkle's "paranoid and psychopathic tendencies" and that the defendants were negligent in employing and retaining him. The other ground of recovery was that the defendants, in consideration of a fee paid them, "promised and agreed to treat plaintiffs properly and carefully and to protect them at all times while they were at said State Bowling Center," and that the defendants had breached the agreement.

The Trial Court dismissed the so-called contract cause of action at the close of the case but submitted the negligence cause of action to the jury. The jury reported a verdict in favor of the plaintiffs. The court thereafter set the verdict aside and granted the motion made by the defendants at the close of the case to dismiss the complaint. The dismissal was based upon the ground that the plaintiffs had failed to establish that the negligence of the defendants was the proximate cause of the plaintiffs' injuries. The court reasoned that the defendants were under a duty to make inquiry before hiring an employee and that they had breached that duty in employing Finkle without any "inquiry or investigation as to his character or past," but that this negligence was not the proximate cause of the injury because there was no proof of "any fact concerning Finkle or his past, which any inquiry, however extensive and thorough, would have disclosed that his employment would be a potential danger to others."

A more conventional way of expressing the trial court's conclusion would be to say that the defendants had not been guilty of any negligence. The trial court conceived of the defendants' duty as a duty in the abstract to make inquiry but that is not a duty for the breach of which an action could be maintained. "'Proof of negligence in the air, so to speak, will not do.'" Palsgraf v. Long Island R. Co., 248 N.Y. 339, 341, 162 N.E. 99, 59 A.L.R. 1253 (1928). The ultimate duty of the defendants, for a breach of which the defendants could be held liable, was the duty to refrain from hiring or retaining anyone whom they knew or, in the exercise of reasonable care, they should have known was potentially dangerous. If, as the court concluded, there was no evidence which warranted the inference that the defendants knew or should have known that Finkle was potentially dangerous, there was no negligence on their part in selecting and retaining Finkle as an employee. The question of proximate cause would arise only if it were found that the defendants had been guilty of negligence in retaining Finkle and the question would then be whether the negligence was causally connected with the assault. On that issue there could be little doubt. The risk of assault upon a patron was well within the range of the foreseeable consequences of retaining a potentially dangerous employee.

The troublesome question here is not the question of proximate cause but of negligence. Partly because of the reliance of the plaintiffs' counsel upon incompetent methods of proving the character and prior conduct of Finkle, to which reference is made below, evidence of negligence at the conclusion of the case was very thin. However for the purpose of determining whether a sufficient case had been made out for submission to the jury, the plaintiffs were entitled, under the elementary rule, to that view of the evidence which was most favorable to their claim.

"The question of negligence is for a jury when there is a conflict in the evidence or when, though there is no such conflict, fair-minded men can draw more than one inference from the undisputed facts. Mead v. Parker, 111 N.Y. 259, 262, 18 N.E. 727, 728; Salt Springs Nat. Bank v. Sloan, 135 N.Y. 371, 384, 32 N.E. 231, 235. In our judgment, fair-minded jurors could here reasonably have inferred from the undisputed facts a failure of the defendant to exercise . . . the due care and caution that were required." Veihelmann v. Manufacturers Safe Deposit Co., 303 N.Y. 526, 530, 104 N.E.2d 888, 890.

Looking at the evidence, which we have summarized above, in the light most favorable to the plaintiffs, we think there was sufficient evidence to make the question of the defendants' negligence a question of fact for the jury. The irrational remarks by Finkle the evening before the assault, coupled with the peculiar circumstances under which he had been employed and promoted, permitted a finding by fair-minded jurors that the general manager should have realized that Finkle was mentally unstable and that it was dangerous to retain him. Furthermore, even if the circumstances were not sufficient of themselves to charge the defendants with notice of Finkle's condition, they were sufficient, when combined with the further fact that Finkle was confined to a mental institution shortly after the assault, to warrant a finding by a jury that, if diligent inquiry had been made before the assault, a history of prior mental instability would have been uncovered.

We therefore cannot accept the trial court's conclusion that the defendants were free from negligence as a matter of law. Cf. McCrink v. City of New York, 296 N.Y. 99, 71 N.E.2d 419 (1950); Fleming v. Bronfin, 80 A.2d 915 (D.C.Mun.App. 1951).

However, we are of the opinion that the verdict in favor of the plaintiffs was against the weight of the evidence. The distinction between a case insufficient in law and a case not supported by the weight of the evidence is a well-settled one and we believe that this is an appropriate case in which to apply the distinction, see §457-a, Civil Practice Act; Fifteenth Annual Report of the N.Y. Judicial Council, 1949, p.241. We therefore sustain so much of the order as sets the verdict aside but we modify the order by granting a new trial instead of dismissing the complaint.

As has been noted above, the plaintiffs sought to prove prior assaults by Finkle by introducing into evidence a memorandum made by a police officer purporting to contain an admission by Finkle that "he had been arrested in Albany in 1950 for the same thing." Any admission by Finkle, even if proved by the testimony of the police officer to whom he had made it, was not admissible in evidence against the defendants. In any event, the memorandum of the alleged conversation was not admissible under Section 374-a of the Civil Practice Act as a record made in the regular course of business. Johnson v. Lutz, 253 N.Y. 124, 170 N.E. 517 (1930). The trial court correctly excluded this proof. It also correctly excluded the records of the Binghamton State Hospital containing statements by Finkle as to his prior history, which the plaintiffs offered to show prior irrational conduct. This proof was inadmissible both upon the ground that the statements were privileged communications and upon the ground that they were not made in the regular course of business. Civil Practice Act, §§352, 374-a; Matter of Warrington, 303 N.Y. 129, 100 N.E.2d 170 (1951); Matter of Coddington's Will, 307 N.Y. 181, 120 N.E.2d 777 (1954).

As we have indicated, even without this proof, we believe that there was sufficient evidence to warrant submission of the case to the jury but we point out that the case is so thin that a resubmission of the cases upon the same proof may well result in requiring the court again to set aside any verdict in favor of the plaintiffs. The lines of inquiry suggested by the excluded proof should therefore be fully explored prior to the new trial.

* * *

Judgment appealed from reversed, on the law and the facts, and the order setting aside the verdict of the jury is modified by eliminating the provision for the dismissal of the complaint and by substituting therefor a direction that a new trial be ordered, and, as so modified, the order is affirmed, on the law and facts, with costs to abide the event.

BERGAN, J. P. and COON, IMRIE and ZELLER, JJ., concur.

State of Ohio v. Antill

Supreme Court of Ohio, 1964.
176 Ohio St. 61, 197 N.E.2d 548.

This case explains exceptions to the exclusion of privileged information between spouses, as well as the privileged information exclusion of the physician-patient relationship. It balances the need of the public to enforce the peace of the community with the need to have these privileges in place for the common welfare of society.

MATTHIAS, Judge. This case presents two questions for determination by the court:

1. Is a wife a competent witness and can she be compelled to testify against her husband under an indictment charging that he "did unlawfully assault . . . [his wife] with a dangerous weapon or instrument likely to produce great bodily harm," where a personal injury to the wife resulted therefrom?
2. Is the physician who treats a person who has suffered a wound inflicted by a deadly weapon permitted to testify as to the condition of the victim, in a criminal prosecution therefor?

At common law, there are certain exceptions to the general rule excluding a husband and wife from testifying for or against each other. In actions involving a personal injury of one committed by the other, the injured spouse is permitted to testify. This exception was said to be based on "necessity." As a general rule, no outsider is present when a person injures his spouse. If the injured person were not permitted to testify, the law would be powerless to redress the wrong. The guilty party would be able to injure his spouse in the privacy of their home with complete immunity. An exception was therefore necessary in order to prevent injustice. 8 Wigmore, Evidence (1961), 242, Section 2239.

This court in Whipp v. State, 34 Ohio St. 87 (1877), permitted a husband to testify against his wife. The wife had been indicted for assault with intent to kill her husband. The court recognized the general exclusionary rule but held that the husband was a competent witness since his wife had inflicted a personal injury on him.

The Whipp case was cited and approved in State v. Orth, 79 Ohio St. 130, 86 N.E. 476, 222 L.R.A.,N.S.,240 (1908).

The exception in case of personal injury by the husband or wife to the other was codified in Ohio. 86 Ohio Laws, p. 161 (1889). Section 2945.42, Revised Code, authorizes a husband and wife to testify against each other in a prosecution for personal injury of either by the other. In the instant case, the husband was indicted for assault with a dangerous weapon. He allegedly struck his wife and stabbed her with a butcher knife. To hold that the wife is not a competent witness under such circumstances places a strained interpretation on the language of Section 2945.42, Revised Code, and ignores its common-law background.

The injured spouse is permitted to testify in order that he or she will not be exposed to personal injury without having a remedy. However, where, as here, the facts constitute a crime, his or her right to testify also ensures that the public will not suffer an offense without a remedy. The wrongdoer not only injures his spouse but he also injures the public, and it is for his offense against the public that he is subject to criminal prosecution. When the injured spouse is a witness for the state his competency cannot be affected by his desires or fears. He must testify to protect the public. Turner v. State, 60 Miss. 351, 45 Am.Rep. 412 (1882).

The demand for the testimony of the injured spouse comes not from him alone but from the community as a whole. Every member of the community has a duty to give whatever testimony he is capable of giving. The truth must be known, as far as possible, to enable the law to provide justice in each case. See 8 Wigmore, Evidence (1961), 70, Section 2192; and In re Story, 159 Ohio St. 144, 148, 149, 111 N.E.2d 385, 36 A.L.R.2d 1312 (1953).

In some instances, the law feels that another interest is sufficiently important to warrant an exception to this duty to give testimony. Thus, to promote marital peace there is a privilege not to disclose in court confidential communications between husband and wife. However, the basis for this privilege is lacking where a person is tried for assaulting his spouse.

"... it is an overgenerous assumption that the wife who has been beaten, poisoned or deserted is still on such terms of delicate good feeling with her spouse that her testimony must not be enforced lest the iridescent halo of peace be dispelled by the breath of disparaging testimony. And if there were, conceivably, any such peace, would it be a peace such as the law could desire to protect? Could it be any other peace than that which the tyrant secures for himself by oppression?" 8 Wigmore, Evidence (1961), 242, 243, Section 2239.

Under the circumstances involved in the instant case, the wife is competent and like any other witness can be compelled to testify. If she refuses she can be found in contempt and imprisoned until she agrees to testify. See Sections 2705.02(C) and 2705.06, Revised Code.

No violation of the physician-patient privilege (Section 2317.02, Revised Code) occurred in allowing the physician who treated the victim to testify. The purpose of this privilege is to encourage patients to make a full disclosure of their symptoms and condition to their physicians without fear that such matters will later become public. Against the interest of the patient in having his condition remain confidential must be balanced the interest of the public in detecting crimes in order to protect society.

To accomplish this end, the General Assembly, in 1961, enacted Section 2917.44, Revised Code (129 Ohio Laws, p. 1034), which reads, in part, as follows:

"... any physician who treats, or is called upon to treat, any such wound [gunshot wound or wound inflicted by a deadly weapon] shall make a report setting forth a description of the wounded person, his name and address, if known, and a description of the nature and location of such wound.

"No person who makes a report in good faith with a view of complying with the requirements of this section shall, by reason thereof, have violated any confidential relationship. . . ."

It is, therefore, proper for the physician who treats a person wounded by a deadly weapon to testify in court as to the nature of the wound. The publicity against which the privilege is supposed to protect has already taken place. The details of the wound must have been reported by the physician to a law-enforcement officer. The only purpose that sustaining the privilege can now serve is to obstruct the course of justice.

The function of this court in reviewing a conviction is limited to the question of whether there was sufficient evidence to warrant the submission of the case to the jury and to support the verdict returned. State v. Sheppard (1956), 165 Ohio St. 293, paragraph five of the syllabus, 135 N.E.2d 340.

If there is evidence from which reasonable minds can reach different conclusions on the issue of whether the defendant is guilty beyond a reasonable doubt, the case should be submitted to the jury for its determination.

* * *

Dr. Christman, who was called to treat Mrs. Antill's wounds, testified as follows:

"**Q.** Did he [the defendant] make any statements to you while Esther was there or you and he when he came?

". . .

"**A.** He stated *he would not use a squad car* [to send Mrs. Antill to a hospital] *and he said he would see her fall off the chair and bleed to death without calling an ambulance.*

". . .

"**Q.** I will ask you also, Doctor, whether or not it could have happened—that wound you examined—whether that could have happened by a person just walking, say, into a sharp instrument?

". . .

"**A.** I would expect a person [to] *recoil* as quickly as possible." (Emphasis added.)

Mrs. Antill testified as follows:

"**Q.** How did you receive that wound?
"**A.** Well, I was very much irritated at him and I pushed the chair toward him and he whirled around and *he had a dish and knife in his hand, so I came against it.*"

* * *

The jury is the sole judge of the weight of the evidence and the credibility of witnesses. It may believe or disbelieve any witness or accept part of what a witness says and reject the rest. In reaching its verdict, the jury should consider the demeanor of the witness and the manner in which he testifies, his connection or relationship with the prosecution or the defendant, and his interest, if any, in the outcome. The jury may also consider the failure of the defendant to take the stand in his own behalf.

We, therefore, find that there was sufficient evidence in this cause to warrant its submission to the jury and to support the verdict rendered.

Judgment affirmed.

* * *

RELATED DECISIONS
Overheard Communications

Baumann v. Steingester
Court of Appeals of New York, 1915.
213 N.Y. 328, 107 N.E. 578.

This case is an easy one to read and comprehend. It involves an attorney-client communication that was found not to be privileged. It is a common practice for third parties to be present when one party is discussing a legal matter with an attorney. One can see that there is a caveat to be given to the client if he or she does not want to waive this privilege.

Appeal from Supreme Court, Appellate Division, Second Department.

Action by Lena Baumann against Henry C. Steingester, Magdalena Fuhge, and others, to construe a will. A judgment in favor of the plaintiff was affirmed by the Appellate Division (159 App.Div. 923, 144 N.Y.Supp. 1105), and the defendant Magdalena Fuhge appeals. . . .

SEABURY, J. This action was commenced to obtain a construction of the last will of Maria Schadrack, deceased, and to have it adjudged that the plaintiff is the legatee described in subdivision 1 of paragraph "third" of said will, and that she is one of the three residuary legatees referred to in paragraph "sixth" of said will. The appellant, Magdalena Fuhge, answered, and asked to have it adjudged that she is the legatee described in the two paragraphs of the will referred to above.

The question at issue upon the trial related to the identity of the legatee referred to as "Lena Baumann" in the following paragraphs of the will. Subdivision 1 of paragraph third provides that the testatrix gives "the sum of $1,000 to my niece Lena Baumann of Richmond Hill in the county and borough of Queens," paragraph sixth provides that the testatrix gives "all the rest and residue of my estate to my three nieces, Helene Bang, Katherine Hainer, and Lena Baumann, to be divided among them share and share alike." The plaintiff is a grandniece of the testatrix, and at the time the will was made resided at Richmond Hill. The appellant is a niece of the testatrix, and her maiden name was Magdalena Baumann. There was evidence received upon the trial to show that the testatrix was accustomed to speak of her as "Lena Baumann," and that while she resided at the time the will was made at a place about one mile from Richmond Hill, the testatrix was also accustomed to refer to this place as "Richmond Hill." It thus appears that the language used in these two paragraphs of the will does not accurately designate either the plaintiff or the appellant. It does not accurately designate the plaintiff because the reference in the will is to a niece of the testatrix, and the plaintiff is a grandniece. It does not accurately designate the appellant because while her maiden name was Magdalena Baumann her name at the time the will was made was Magdalena Fuhge, and she did not reside at Richmond Hill. These facts appearing by extrinsic evidence, there was a latent ambiguity in the will. Parol evidence was properly receivable in the effort to dissolve this ambiguity. Lefevre v. Lefevre, 59 N.Y. 434 (1875); Matter of Taylor, Cloak v. Hammond, L.R. 34 Ch. Div. 255; Henderson v. Henderson, 1 Ir.Rep. 353 [1905].

In view of the unanimous affirmance by the Appellate Division of the judgment appealed from, the single question which survives for consideration in this court relates to the rulings of the Special Term excluding the evidence of the witness Kellar. Mr. Kellar was the attorney for the testatrix, and was the draftsman of and a subscribing witness to her will. The testatrix, a woman about 70 years of age called upon Mr. Kellar and gave him instructions as to the drawing of her will. With her on this occasion and present at the office of Mr. Kellar at the time was Mrs. Stiefhold. Mrs. Stiefhold lived with the testatrix and acted as companion and housekeeper. The instructions as to her will were given to Mr. Kellar in the presence of Mrs. Stiefhold, who, while within hearing, testified that she "did not pay very much attention." When Mr. Kellar was called as a witness he was asked as to the instructions he had received from the testatrix as to the legacies and the provisions for the residuary estate. The question was excluded under objection of the plaintiff and subject to the exception of the appellant. It thus becomes necessary to determine whether Mr. Kellar, the attorney, should have been permitted to testify to communications which took place between himself and his client, the testatrix, in the presence of Mrs. Stiefhold. This evidence should have been received and considered by the court below. Doheny v. Lacy, 168 N.Y. 213, 223, 61 N.E. 255 (1901).... Mrs. Stiefhold was not present and acting in the character of a confidential agent of the testatrix, nor was her presence necessary to enable the parties to communicate with each other. No attempt was made by the testatrix to prevent her hearing the communication which she made to her attorney. The fact that Mrs. Stiefhold did "not pay very much attention" to what was said does not alter the situation. She was within hearing and, so far as the testatrix knew, heard all that was said. If the testatrix had desired her communication with her attorney to be confidential, she could have asked Mrs. Stiefhold to withdraw from the room or have communicated with her attorney when Mrs. Stiefhold was not present. She did not do either of these things, but on the contrary, gave her instructions to her attorney as to the manner in which she wished to have her will drawn, in the presence of Mrs. Stiefhold. The fact that these instructions were given in the presence and in the hearing of Mrs. Stiefhold is a circumstance indicative of the fact that the communication was not made in confidence. A third person even though a mere stranger or bystander, in whose hearing communications are made by a client to an attorney, may testify to such communications. Jackson v. French, 3 Wend. 337, 20 Am.Dec. 699 (1829); People v. Buchanan, supra. To allow a stranger or bystander who overhears such a conversation to testify to what he heard and at the same time preclude the attorney of the client from giving his testimony as to what occurred might often result unfairly to the client for whose protection the privilege is designed. The communication not being confidential the attorney is not privileged from disclosing it. Where there is no confidence reposed, no privilege can be asserted. In such cases the attorney is permitted to testify not because the privilege has been waived, but because the communication, not having been made in confidence, was not privileged. The privilege which exempts one from giving testimony, except in so far as it is embodied in statutory provisions, cannot be extended to cover cases not within the reason upon which the privilege rests.

* * *

The judgment should be reversed and a new trial granted, with costs to abide the event.

RELATED DECISIONS
Government Secrets

United States v. Reynolds
Supreme Court of the United States, 1953.
345 U.S. 1, 73 S.Ct. 528, 97 L.Ed. 727.

This case is an example of the use of a claim of privilege by the United States in order to prevent disclosure of government secrets in civil litigation. The defendant in the initial action was the United States, and both the United States District Court and the United States Court of Appeals held that the government should produce the required documents and that if it failed to do so, the court would enter an order that the facts on the issue of negligence would be taken as established in the plaintiff's favor, pursuant to Rule 37 (b)(2)(i) of the Federal Rules of Civil Procedure.

The United States Supreme Court reviewed the history of this privilege and made a determination as to the right of the government under the facts of this case. You are encouraged to ascertain how the Court decided the issue.

Three separate actions under Federal Tort Claims Act by widows of civilians killed in crash of an Air Force plane. The United States District Court for the Eastern District of Pennsylvania, 10 F.R.D. 468, rendered judgments for plaintiffs, and the United States appealed. The Court of Appeals, 192 F.2d 987, affirmed, and the Supreme Court granted certiorari.   .   .   .

Mr. Chief Justice VINSON delivered the opinion of the Court.

These suits under the Tort Claims Act arise from the death of three civilians in the crash of a B-29 aircraft at Waycross, Georgia, on October 6, 1948. Because an important question of the Government's privilege to resist discovery is involved, we granted certiorari. 343 U.S. 918, 72 S.Ct. 678, 96 L.Ed. 1332 (1952).

The aircraft had taken flight for the purpose of testing secret electronic equipment, with four civilian observers aboard. While aloft, fire broke out in one of the bomber's engines. Six of the nine crew members, and three of the four civilian observers were killed in the crash.

The widows of the three deceased civilian observers brought consolidated suits against the United States. In the pre-trial stages the plaintiffs moved, under Rule 34 of the Federal Rules of Civil Procedure, for production of the Air Force's official accident investigation report and the statements of the three surviving crew members, taken in connection with the official investigation. The Government moved to quash the motion, claiming that these matters were privileged against disclosure pursuant to Air Force regulations promulgated under R.S. § 161. The District Judge sustained plaintiffs' motion, holding that good cause for production had been shown. The claim of privilege under R.S. § 161 was rejected on the premise that the Tort Claims Act, in making the Government liable "in the same manner" as a private individual had waived any privilege based upon executive control over governmental documents.

Shortly after this decision, the District Court received a letter from the Secretary of the Air Force, stating that "it has been determined that it would not be in the public interest to furnish this report. . . ." The court allowed a rehearing on its earlier order, and at the rehearing the Secretary of the Air Force filed a formal "Claim of Privilege." This document repeated the prior claim based generally on R.S. § 161, and then stated that the Government further objected to production of the documents "for the reason that the aircraft in question, together with the personnel on board, were engaged in a highly secret mission of the Air Force." An affidavit of the Judge Advocate General, United States Air Force, was also filed with the court, which asserted that the demanded material could not be furnished "without seriously hampering national security, flying safety and the development of highly technical and secret military equipment." The same affidavit offered to produce the three surviving crew members, without cost, for examination by the plaintiffs. The witnesses would be allowed to refresh their memories from any statement made by them to the Air Force, and authorized to testify as to all matters except those of a "classified nature."

The District Court ordered the Government to produce the documents in order that the court might determine whether they contained privileged matter. The Government declined, so the court entered an order, under Rule 37(b)(2)(i), that the facts on the issue of negligence would be taken as established in plaintiffs' favor. After a hearing to determine damages, final judgment was entered for the plaintiffs. The Court of Appeals affirmed, both as to the showing of good cause for production of the documents, and as to the ultimate disposition of the case as a consequence of the Government's refusal to produce the documents.

We have had broad propositions pressed upon us for decision. On behalf of the Government it has been urged that the executive department heads have power to withhold any documents in their custody from judicial view if they deem it to be in the public interest. Respondents have asserted that the executive's power to withhold documents was waived by the Torts Claims Act. Both positions have constitutional overtones which we find it unnecessary to pass upon there being a narrower ground for decision. Touhy v. Ragen, 340 U.S. 462, 71 S.Ct. 416, 95 L.Ed. 417 (1951); Rescue Army v. Municipal Court of Los Angeles, 331 U.S. 549, 574–585, 67 S.Ct. 1409, 1422–1427, 91 L.Ed. 1666 (1947).

The Tort Claims Act expressly makes the Federal Rules of Civil Procedure applicable to suits against the United States. The judgment in this case imposed liability upon the Government by operation of Rule 37, for refusal to produce documents under Rule 34. Since Rule 34 compels production only of matters "not privileged," the essential question is whether there was a valid claim of privilege under the Rule. We hold that there was, and that, therefore, the judgment below subjected the United States to liability on terms to which Congress did not consent by the Tort Claims Act.

We think it should be clear that the term "not privileged" as used in Rule 34, refers to "privileges" as that term is understood in the law of evidence. When the Secretary of the Air Force lodged his formal "Claim of Privilege," he attempted therein to invoke the privilege against revealing military secrets, a privilege which is well established in the law of evidence. The existence of the privilege is conceded by the court below, and, indeed, by the most outspoken critics of governmental claims to privilege.

Judicial experience with the privilege which protects military and state secrets has been limited in this country. English experience has been more extensive, but still relatively slight compared with other evidentiary privileges. Nevertheless, the principles which control the application of the privilege emerge quite clearly from the available precedents. The privilege belongs to the Government and must be asserted by it; it can neither be claimed nor waived by a private party. It is not to be lightly invoked. There must be a formal claim of privilege, lodged by the head of the department which has control over the matter, after actual personal consideration by that officer. The court itself must determine whether the circumstances are appropriate for the claim of privilege, and yet do so without forcing a disclosure of the very thing the privilege is designed to protect. The latter requirement is the only one which presents real difficulty. As to it, we find it helpful to draw upon judicial experience in dealing with an analogous privilege, the privilege against self-incrimination.

The privilege against self-incrimination presented the courts with a similar sort of problem. Too much judicial inquiry into the claim of privilege would force disclosure of the thing the privilege was meant to protect, while a complete abandonment of judicial control would lead to intolerable abuses. Indeed, in the earlier stages of judicial experience with the problem, both extremes were advocated, some saying that the bare assertion by the witness must be taken as conclusive, and others saying that the witness should be required to reveal the matter behind his claim of privilege to the judge for verification. Neither extreme prevailed, and a sound formula of compromise was developed. This formula received authoritative expression in this country as early as the Burr trial. There are differences in phraseology, but in substance it is agreed that the court must be satisfied from all the evidence and circumstances, and "from the implications of the question, in the setting in which it is asked, that a responsive answer to the question or an explanation of why it cannot be answered might be dangerous because injurious exposure could result." Hoffman v. United States, 341 U.S. 479, 486–487, 71 S.Ct. 814, 818, 95 L.Ed. 1118 (1951). If the court is so satisfied, the claim of the privilege will be accepted without requiring further disclosure.

Regardless of how it is articulated, some like formula of compromise must be applied here. Judicial control over the evidence in a case cannot be abdicated to the caprice of executive officers. Yet we will not go so far as to say that the court may automatically require a complete disclosure to the judge before the claim of privilege will be accepted in any case. It may be possible to satisfy the court, from all the circumstances of the case, that there is a reasonable danger that compulsion of the evidence will expose military matters which, in the interest of national security, should not be divulged. When this is the case, the occasion for the privilege is appropriate, and the court should not jeopardize the security which the privilege is meant to protect by insisting upon an examination of the evidence, even by the judge alone, in chambers.

In the instant case we cannot escape judicial notice that this is a time of vigorous preparation for national defense. Experience in the past war has made it common knowledge that air power is one of the most potent weapons in our scheme of defense, and that newly developing electronic devices have greatly enhanced the effective use of air power. It is equally apparent that these electronic devices must be kept secret if their full military advantage is to be exploited in the national interests. On the record before the trial court it appeared that this accident occurred to a military plane which had gone aloft to test secret electronic equipment. Certainly there was a reasonable danger that the accident investigation report would contain references to the secret electronic equipment which was the primary concern of the mission.

Of course, even with this information before him, the trial judge was in no position to decide that the report was privileged until there had been a formal claim of privilege. Thus it was entirely proper to rule initially that petitioner had shown probable cause for discovery of the documents. Thereafter, when the formal claim of privilege was filed by the Secretary of the Air Force, under circumstances indicating a reasonable possibility that military secrets were involved, there was certainly a sufficient showing of privilege to cut off further demand for the document on the showing of necessity for its compulsion that had then been made.

In each case, the showing of necessity which was made will determine how far the court should probe in satisfying itself that the occasion for invoking the privilege is appropriate. Where there is a strong showing of necessity, the claim of privilege should not be lightly accepted, but even the most compelling necessity cannot overcome the claim of privilege if the court is ultimately satisfied that military secrets are at stake. A fortiori, where necessity is dubious, a formal claim of privilege, made under the circumstances of this case, will have to prevail. Here, necessity was greatly minimized by an available alternative, which might have given respondents the evidence to make out their case without forcing a showdown on the claim of privilege. By their failure to pursue that alternative, respondents have posed the privilege question for decision with the formal claim of privilege set against a dubious showing of necessity.

There is nothing to suggest that the electronic equipment, in this case, had any causal connection with the accident. Therefore, it should be possible for respondents to adduce the essential facts as to causation without resort to material touching upon military secrets. Respondents were given a reasonable opportunity to do just that, when petitioner formally offered to make the surviving crew members available for examination. We think the offer should have been accepted.

* * *

The decision of the Court of Appeals is reversed and the case will be remanded to the

District Court for further proceedings consistent with the views expressed in this opinion.

Reversed and remanded.

Mr. Justice BLACK, Mr. Justice FRANKFURTER, and Mr. Justice JACKSON dissent substantially for the reasons set forth in the opinion of Judge Maris below. 192 F.2d 987.

Jencks v. United States

Supreme Court of the United States, 1957.
353 U.S. 657, 77 S.Ct. 1007, 1 L.Ed.2d 1103.

A United States Supreme Court decision is customarily lengthy because it may reflect the combined opinions of the Chief Justice and eight Associate Justices of the Court. Most often it represents a splitting of opinions, with the majority of the justices representing the holding of the Court. In this decision, Justice Whittaker did not take part. He might have recused himself because he had a possible conflict of interest, he might not have been on the bench at any time that the case came before the Court, or he might have been ill. The decision does not include an explanation for his not taking part.

Because of this decision, Congress passed a law covering what is generally known as 3500 material. This refers to §3500 of Title 18 of the United States Code, wherein it states the following:

(b) After a witness called by the United States has testified on direct examination, the court shall, on motion of the defendant, order the United States to produce any statement (as hereinafter defined) of the witness in possession of the United States which relates to the subject matter as to which the witness has testified. If the entire contents of any such statement relates to the subject matter of the testimony of the witness, the court shall order it to be delivered directly to the defendant for his examination and use. . . .

A reasonable time is then given to the defendant and his or her counsel to read and make notes from the statement so that it may be used on cross-examination.

Mr. Justice BRENNAN delivered the opinion of the Court.

On April 28, 1950, the petitioner, as president of Amalgamated Bayard District Union, Local 890, International Union of Mine, Mill & Smelter Workers, filed an "Affidavit of Non-Communist Union Officer" with the National Labor Relations Board, pursuant to §9(h) of the National Labor Relations Act.[1] He has been convicted under a two-count indictment charging that he violated 18 U.S.C. §1001, 18 U.S.C.A. §1001[2] by falsely swearing in that affidavit that he was not on April 28, 1950, a member of the Communist party or affiliated with such Party. The Court of Appeals for the Fifth Circuit affirmed the conviction,[3] and also an order of the District Court denying the petitioner's motion for a new trial.[4] This Court granted certiorari.[5]

Two alleged trial errors are presented for our review. Harvey F. Matusow and J. W. Ford, the Government's principal witnesses, were Communist Party members paid by the Federal Bureau of Investigation contemporaneously to make oral or written reports of Communist Party activities in which they participated. They made such reports to the F.B.I. of activities allegedly participated in by the petitioner, about which they testified at the trial. Error is asserted in the denial by the trial judge of the petitioners' motions to direct the Government to produce these reports for inspection and use in cross-examining Matusow and Ford. Error is also alleged in the instructions given to the jury on membership, affiliation, and the credibility of informers.[6]

Former Party members testified that they and the petitioner, as members of the Communist Party of New Mexico, had been expressly instructed to conceal their membership and not to carry membership cards. They also testified that the Party kept no membership records or minutes of membership meetings, and that such meetings were secretly arranged and clandestinely held. One of the witnesses said that special care was taken to conceal the Party membership of members, like the petitioner, "occupying strategic and important positions in labor unions and other organizations where public knowledge of their membership to non-Communists would jeopardize their position in the organization." Accordingly, the Government did not attempt to prove the petitioner's alleged membership in the Communist Party on April 28, 1950, with any direct admissions by the petitioner of membership, by proof of his compliance with Party membership requirements, or that his name appeared upon a membership roster, or that he carried a membership card.

The evidence relied upon by the Government was entirely circumstantial. It consisted of testimony of conduct of the petitioner from early 1946 through October 15, 1949, and of Matusow's testimony concerning alleged conversations between him and the petitioner at a vacation ranch in July or August 1950, and concerning a lecture delivered by the petitioner at the ranch. The Government also attached probative weight to the action of the petitioner in executing and filing an Affidavit of Non-Communist Union Officer on October 15, 1949, because of the events surrounding the filing of that affidavit. The Government bridged the gap between October 15, 1949, and July or August 1950 with the testimony of Ford that, during that period, the Party took no disciplinary action against the petitioner for defection or deviation, and did not replace the petitioner in the Party office which Ford testified the petitioner held as a member of the Party State Board.

The first alleged Party activity of the petitioner preceded his union employment. A witness, who was a Party member in the spring of 1946, testified that, at that time, he and the petitioner were present at a closed Party meeting at the home of the Party chairman for Colorado, where the petitioner, a veteran of World War II, led in urging that veterans who were Party members spread out into several veterans' organizations and not all join the same one, the better to further Party work.

Later in 1946 the petitioner was employed by the International Union of Mine, Mill & Smelter Workers as business agent for several local unions in the Silver City–Bayard, New Mexico, area. It was testified that one of the petitioner's first acts was to meet with the International Union's then Regional Director for the Southwest, a Communist Party member, and with the Communist Party organizer for the area, to develop plans for organizing a Party group within each of those locals, which later merged to form Amalgamated Local 890 under the petitioner's presidency.

J. W. Ford was a member of the Communist Party of New Mexico from 1946 to September 1950 and, from 1948, was a member of the State Board and a Party security officer. He said that in 1948 he became a paid undercover agent for the F.B.I.[7] and reported regularly upon Party activities and meetings. He testified that the petitioner was also a Party and a State Board member, and he related in detail occurrences at five closed Party meetings which he said the petitioner attended.

At the first meeting, in August 1948, Ford said the Party members worked out a plan to support the petitioner's candidacy for Congress on the ticket of the Progressive Party. At the second meeting, in February 1949, Ford said that the petitioner and other Communist Party members were appointed delegates to a meeting of the Mexican-American Association in Phoenix, Arizona, to further a Party plan to infiltrate that organization and to use it for the Party's purposes. At the third meeting, in April 1949, Ford said that the Party's state organization was completed, and the petitioner was appointed to the State Board and the Party leader in the southern half of the State. At the fourth meeting, in May 1949, Ford said that the petitioner gave a progress report upon his success in recruiting Party members among labor groups, and offered to use Local 890's newspaper, "The Union Worker," which he edited, to support issues of Party interest. At the fifth meeting, in August 1949, Ford said that preparations were made for another meeting later in that month of the Mexican-American Association in Albuquerque, and that the delegates, including the petitioner, were instructed to give vigorous support to the meeting but to take care not to make themselves conspicuous in the proceedings.

Ford's duties as a Party security officer were to keep watch on all Party members and to report "any particular defections from the Communist philosophy or any peculiar actions, statements or associations, which would endanger the security of the Communist Party of the state." If any defection reported by a security officer were considered important, the member "would be called in and would be either severely reprimanded or criticized, or disciplined. If he refused to accept such discipline he would either be suspended or expelled." Ford testified that, between August 1949 and September 1950, when Ford ceased his activities with the New Mexico party, there was no disciplinary action taken against the petitioner and, to his knowledge, the petitioner was not replaced in his position on the State Board of the Communist Party.

The events leading up to the petitioner's execution and filing, on October 15, 1949, of an Affidavit of Non-Communist Union Officer were testified to by a former International Union representative, a Communist Party member during 1947 to 1949. He said that, about 17 months before, in May or June 1948, a meeting of Party members, holding offices in locals of the International Union of Mine, Mill & Smelter Workers, was held in Denver to formulate plans for combatting a movement, led by non-Communists, to secede from the International Union. He said that the Party members, including the petitioner, were informed of Party policy not to sign affidavits required by §9(h) of the then recently enacted Taft-Hartley Act. There was no testimony that that policy changed before October 15, 1949.

The affidavit was filed shortly before a C.I.O. convention was scheduled to expel the Mine-Mill International and other unions from its membership. After filing the affidavit, the petitioner and other Local 890 officers published an article in "The Union Worker" charging that the contemplated C.I.O. action was part of a program of "right-wing unions . . . gobbling up chunks of militant unions. . . . Our International Union and its officers have swallowed a lot of guff, a lot of insults. But that is not the point. . . . Now that our Union has signed the phony affidavits we can defend ourselves . . . in case of raids. We do not fear attack from that quarter any longer."

Matusow was a member of the Communist Party of New York and was a paid undercover agent for the F.B.I. before he went to New Mexico.[8] In July or August 1950, he spent a 10-day vacation on a ranch near Taos, New Mexico, with the petitioner and a number of other people. He testified to several conversations with the petitioner there. He said he twice told the petitioner of his desire to transfer his membership from the New York to the New Mexico Party, and that on both occasions the petitioner applauded the idea and told him, "we can use you out here, we need more active Party members." On one of these occasions, Matusow said, the petitioner asked him for suggestions for a lecture the petitioner was preparing for delivery at the ranch, particularly as to what the New York Communists were doing about the Stockholm Peace Appeal. Matusow described to the petitioner a "do-day" program adopted in New York when the Party members were doers, not talkers, and performed some activity, such as painting signs around a baseball stadium urging support for the Peace Appeal. He testified that the petitioner showed great interest in the idea and said he might bring it back to his fellow Party members in Silver City.

Matusow testified that the petitioner delivered his planned lecture, informed his audience of the "do-day" idea, praised the Soviet Union's disarmament plan, referred to the United States as the aggressor in Korea, and urged all to read the "Daily People's World," identified by Matusow as the "West Coast Communist Party newspaper." Another witness, an expelled member of Amalgamated Local 890, testified that petitioner, during 1950, 1951 and 1952, repeatedly urged at union meetings that the union members read that paper.

Matusow also testified that, in one of their conversations, the petitioner told him of a program he was developing with leaders of the Mexican Miners Union to negotiate simultaneous expiration dates of collective bargaining agreements, to further a joint action of Mexican and American workers to cut off production to slow down the Korean War effort. Matusow also testified that when he told the petitioner that he had joined the Taos Chapter of the Mexican-American Association, the petitioner told him that this was proper Communist work because the Association was a key organization, controlled by the Party, for Communist activities in new Mexico and that he, the petitioner, was active in the Association in the Silver City area.[9]

Ford and Matusow were subjected to vigorous cross-examination about their employment as informers for the F.B.I. Ford testified that in 1948 he went to the F.B.I. and offered his services, which were accepted. He thereafter regularly submitted reports to the F.B.I., "sometimes once a week, sometimes twice a month, and at various other times; maybe three or four times a week, depending on the number of meetings . . . [he] attended and the distance between the meetings." He said that his reports were made immediately following each meeting, while the events were still fresh in his memory. He could not recall, however, which reports were oral and which in writing.

The petitioner moved "for an order directing an inspection of reports of the witness Ford to the Federal Bureau of Investigation dealing with each of the meetings which he said that he attended with the defendant Jencks in the years 1948 and 1949." The trial judge, without stating reasons, denied the motion.

Matusow, on his cross-examination, testified that he made both oral and written reports to the F.B.I. on events at the ranch, including his conversations with the petitioner. The trial judge, again without reasons, denied the motion to require "the prosecution to produce in Court the reports submitted to the F.B.I. by this witness [Matusow] concerning matters which he saw or heard at the . . . Ranch during the period that he was a guest there. . . . [10]

The Government opposed petitioner's motions at the trial upon the sole ground that a preliminary foundation was not laid of inconsistency between the contents of the reports and the testimony of Matusow and Ford. The Court of Appeals rested the affirmance primarily upon that ground.[11]

Both the trial court and the Court of Appeals erred. We hold that the petitioner was not required to lay a preliminary foundation of inconsistency, because a sufficient foundation was established by the testimony of Matusow and Ford that their reports were of the events and activities related in their testimony.

The reliance of the Court of Appeals upon Gordon v. United States, 344 U.S. 414, 73 S.Ct. 369, 97 L.Ed. 447 (1953), is misplaced. It is true that one fact mentioned in this Court's opinion was that the witness admitted that the documents involved contradicted his testimony. However, to say that Gordon held

a preliminary showing of inconsistency a prerequisite to an accused's right to the production for inspection of documents in the Government's possession, is to misinterpret the Court's opinion. The necessary essentials of a foundation, emphasized in that opinion, and present here, are that "[t]he demand was for production of . . . *specific documents and did not propose any broad or blind fishing expedition* among documents possessed by the Government on the chance that something impeaching might turn up. Nor was this a demand for statements taken from persons or informants not offered as witnesses." (Emphasis added.) 344 U.S. at page 419, 73 S.Ct. at page 373. We reaffirm and re-emphasize these essentials. "For production purposes, it need only appear that the evidence is relevant, competent, and outside of any exclusionary rule. . . ." 344 U.S. at page 420, 73 S.Ct. at page 373.

The crucial nature of the testimony of Ford and Matusow to the Government's case is conspicuously apparent. The impeachment of that testimony was singularly important to the petitioner. The value of the reports for impeachment purposes was highlighted by the admissions of both witnesses that they could not remember what reports were oral and what written, and by Matusow's admission: "I don't recall what I put in my reports two or three years ago, written or oral, I don't know what they were."

Every experienced trial judge and trial lawyer knows the value for impeaching purposes of statements of the witness recording the events before time dulls treacherous memory. Flat contradiction between the witness' testimony and the version of the events given in his reports is not the only test of inconsistency. The omission from the reports of facts related at the trial, or a contrast in emphasis upon the same facts, even a different order of treatment, are also relevant to the cross-examining process of testing the credibility of a witness' trial testimony.

Requiring the accused first to show conflict between the reports and the testimony is actually to deny the accused evidence relevant and material to his defense. The occasion for determining a conflict cannot arise until after the witness has testified and unless he admits conflict, as in Gordon, the accused is helpless to know or discover conflict without inspecting the reports.[12] A requirement of a showing of conflict would be clearly incompatible with our standards for the administration of criminal justice in the federal courts and must therefore be rejected. For the interest of the United States in a criminal prosecution ". . . is not that it shall win a case, but that justice shall be done. . . ." Berger v. United States, 295 U.S. 78, 88, 55 S.Ct. 629, 633, 79 L.Ed. 1314 (1935).[13]

This Court held in Goldman v. United States, 316 U.S. 129, 132, 62 S.Ct. 993, 995, 86 L.Ed. 1322 (1942), that the trial judge had discretion to deny inspection when the witness ". . . does not use his notes or memoranda [relating to his testimony] in court. . . ." We now hold that the petitioner was entitled to an order directing the Government to produce for inspection all reports of Matusow and Ford in its possession, written and, when orally made, as recorded by the F.B.I., touching the events and activities as to which they testified at the trial. We hold, further, that the petitioner is entitled to inspect the reports to decide whether to use them in his defense. Because only the defense is adequately equipped to determine the effective use for purpose of discrediting the Government's witness and thereby furthering the accused's defense, the defense must initially be entitled to see them to determine what use may be made of them. Justice requires no less.[14]

The practice of producing government documents to the trial judge for his determination of relevancy and materiality, without hearing the accused, is disapproved.[15] Relevancy and materiality for the purposes of production and inspection, with a view to use on cross-examination, are established when the reports are shown to relate to the testimony of the witness. Only after inspection of the reports by the accused, must the trial judge determine admissibility—e.g., evidentiary questions of inconsistency, materiality, and relevancy—of the contents and the method to be employed for the elimination of parts immaterial or irrelevant. See Gordon v. United States, 344 U.S. at page 418, 73 S.Ct. at page 372.

In the courts below the Government did not assert that the reports were privileged against disclosure on grounds of national security, confidential character of the reports, public interest or otherwise. In its brief in this Court, however, the Government argues that, absent a showing of contradiction, "[t]he rule urged by petitioner . . . disregards the legitimate interest that each party—including the Government—has in safe-guarding the privacy of its files, particularly where the documents in question were obtained in confidence. Production of such documents, even to a court, should not be compelled in the absence of a preliminary showing by the party making the request." The petitioner's counsel, believing that Court of Appeals' decisions imposed such a qualification, restricted his motions to a request for production of the reports to the trial judge for the judge's inspection and determination whether and to what extent the reports should be made available to the petitioner.

It is unquestionably true that the protection of vital national interests may militate against public disclosure of documents in the Government's possession. This has been recognized in decisions of this Court in civil causes where the Court has considered the statutory authority conferred upon the departments of government to adopt regulations "not inconsistent with law, for . . . use . . . of the records, papers . . . appertaining" to his department.[16] The Attorney General has adopted regulations pursuant to this authority declaring all Justice Department records confidential and that no disclosure, including disclosure in response to subpoena, may be made without his permission.[17]

But this Court has noticed, in United States v. Reynolds, 345 U.S. 1, 73 S.Ct. 528, 97 L.Ed. 727 (1953), the holdings of the Court of Appeals for the Second Circuit[18] that, in criminal causes ". . . the Government can invoke its evidentiary privileges only at the price of letting the defendant go free. The rationale of the criminal cases is that, since the Government which prosecutes an accused also has the duty to see that justice is done, it is unconscionable to allow it to undertake prosecution and then invoke its governmental privileges to deprive the accused of anything which might be material to his defense. . . ." 345 U.S. at page 12, 73 S.Ct. at page 534.

In United States v. Andolschek, 142 F.2d 503, 506 (2d Cir. 1944), Judge Learned Hand said:

". . . While we must accept it as lawful for a department to suppress documents, even when they will help determine controversies between third persons, we cannot agree that this should include their suppression in a criminal prosecution, founded upon those very dealings to which the documents relate, and whose criminality they will, or may, tend to exculpate. So far as they directly touch the criminal dealings, the prosecution necessarily ends any confidential character the documents may possess; it must be conducted in the open, and will lay bare their subject matter. The government must choose; either it must leave the transactions in the obscurity from which a trial will draw them, or it must expose them fully. Nor does it seem to us possible to draw any line between documents whose contents bear directly upon the criminal transactions, and those which may be only indirectly relevant. Not only would such a distinction be extremely difficult to apply in practice, but the same reasons which forbid suppression in one case forbid it in the other, though not, perhaps, quite so imperatively. . . ."

We hold that the criminal action must be dismissed when the Government, on the ground of privilege, elects not to comply with an order to produce, for the accused's inspection and for admission in evidence, relevant statements or reports in its possession of government witnesses touching the subject matter of their testimony at the trial. Accord, Roviaro v. United States, 353 U.S. 53, 60–61, 77 S.Ct. 623, 627–628, 1 L.Ed.2d 639 (1957). The burden is the Government's, not to be shifted to the trial judge, to decide whether the public prejudice of allowing the crime to go unpunished is greater than that attendant upon the possible disclosure of state secrets and other confidential information in the Government's possession.

Reversed.

Mr. Justice FRANKFURTER joins the opinion of the Court, but deeming that the questions relating to the instructions to the jury should be dealt with, since a new trial has been directed, he agrees with the respects in which, and the reasons for which, Mr. Justice BURTON finds them erroneous.

Mr. Justice WHITTAKER took no part in the consideration or decision of this case.

Mr. Justice BURTON, whom Mr. Justice HARLAN joins, concurring in the result.

Separate concurring decision of Mr. Justice BURTON and Mr. Justice HARLAN, deleted. Dissent of Mr. Justice CLARK, omitted.

---

[1] 61 Stat. 143, 146, as amended, 65 Stat. 602, 29 U.S.C. §159(h), 29 U.S.C.A. §159(h). Section 9(h) provides that processes of the National Labor Relations Board will be unavailable to a labor organization ". . . unless there is on file with the Board an affidavit executed . . . by each officer of such labor organization . . . that he is not a member of the Communist Party or affiliated with such party, and that he does not believe in, and is not a member of or supports any organization that believes in or teaches, the overthrow of the United States Government by force or by any illegal or unconstitutional methods. . . ."

[2] 62 Stat. 749.

[3] 226 F.2d 540 (5th Cir. 1955).

[4] 226 F.2d 553 (5th Cir. 1955).

[5] 350 U.S. 980, 76 S.Ct. 467, 100 L.Ed. 849 (1956).

[6] Because of our disposition of this case, it is unnecessary to consider the alleged errors in these instructions.

[7] From 1948 through 1953, Ford was paid $7,025 for his services. Of that sum, approximately $3,325 covered the period to which his testimony related.

[8] Other activities of Matusow are described in Communist Party of the United States v. Subversive Activities Control Board, 351 U.S. 115, 76 S.Ct. 663, 100 L.Ed. 1003 (1956), and United States v. Flynn, 130 F.Supp. 412 (S.D.N.Y. 1955).

[9] Matusow recanted as deliberately false the testimony given by him at the trial. On the basis of this recantation, the petitioner moved for a new trial, while his appeal from the conviction was pending, on grounds of newly discovered evidence. After extended hearings, the District Court denied the motion.

[10] During the hearings on the motion for a new trial, the petitioner made several requests for the production of documents in the possession of the Government, relating to the testimony given. Those motions were denied. Because of our disposition of this case, it was unnecessary to consider these rulings.

[11] In upholding the refusal to require the production of the reports, the Court of Appeals said: ". . . Upon a proper showing that the Government has possession of such inconsistent statements and the presence of the other requisite conditions, a person charged with crime would be permitted to examine and use them. But no such showing was made here. . . ." 226 F.2d at page 552.

[12] Cf. United States v. Burr, 25 Fed.Cas. page 187, No. 14,694, wherein Chief Justice Marshall, when confronted with a request for the inspection of a letter addressed to the President and in the possession of the attorney for the United States, stated: "Now, if a paper be in possession of the opposite party, what statement of its contents or applicability can be expected from the person who claims its production, he not precisely knowing its contents? . . .

". . . It is objected that the particular passages of the letter which are required are not pointed out. But how can this be done while the letter itself is with-held? . . ." 25 Fed.Cas. at page 191.

[13] United States v. Schneiderman, 106 F.Supp. 731 (S.D.Cal. 1952); People v. Dellabonda, 265 Mich. 486, 251 N.W. 594 (1934); see Canon 5, American Bar Association, Canons of Professional Ethics (1947).

[14] Chief Justice Marshall also said in United States v. Burr, 25 Fed.Cas. page 187, No. 14,694: "Let it be sup-posed that the letter may not contain anything re-specting the person now before the court. Still it may respect a witness material in the case, and become im-portant by bearing on his testimony. Different repre-sentations may have been made by that witness, or his conduct may have been such as to affect his testimony. In various modes a paper may bear upon the case, al-though before the case be opened its particular appli-cation cannot be perceived by the judge. . . ." 25 Fed.Cas. at page 191.

What is true before the case is opened is equally true as the case unfolds. The trial judge cannot perceive or determine the relevancy and materiality of the docu-ments to the defense without hearing defense argu-ment, after inspection, as to its bearing upon the case.

[15] See, e.g., United States v. Grayson, 166 F.2d 863, 869 (2d Cir. 1948); United States v. Beekman, 155 F.2d 580, 584 (2d Cir. 1946); United States v. Ebeling, 146 F.2d 254, 256 (2d Cir. 1945); United States v. Cohen, 145 F.2d 82, 92 (2d Cir. 1944); United States v. Krule-witch, 145 F.2d 76, 78, 156 A.L.R. 337 (2d Cir. 1944).

[16] R.S. §161, 5 U.S.C. §22, 5 U.S.C.A. §22; United States v. Reynolds, 345 U.S. 1, 73 S.Ct. 528, 97 L.Ed. 727 (1953); cf. Totten v. United States, 92 U.S. 105, 23 L.Ed. 605 (1875).

[17] Atty.Gen.Order No. 3229, 28 CFR, 1946 Supp. §51.71 (1939); Atty.Gen.Order No. 3229, Supp. 2, Pike & Fischer Admin.Law (2d), Dept. of Justice 1 (1947); Atty.Gen.Order No. 3229, Rev., 18 Fed.Reg. 1368 (1953).

[18] United States v. Beekman, 155 F.2d 580 (2d Cir. 1946); United States v. Andolschek, 142 F.2d 503 (2d Cir. 1944).

RELATED DECISIONS
Newsgathering Privilege

United States v. Cuthbertson

United States Court of Appeals, Third Circuit, 1980.
630 F.2d 139.

This decision involves the delicate right of a journalist not to divulge sources that were used by the journalist to draw conclusions about the criminal activity of a defendant, which may be in conflict with the criminal defendant's right to inspect the source mate-rial to determine if it might be of assistance in preparing a defense against the government's accusations in the criminal trial. The journal-ists rely on the First Amendment to the United States Constitution to protect the re-quested material from disclosure. The court treats this material in great detail. Much of the decision that I believe is not crucial to an understanding of the problem has been de-leted in the interest of brevity.

Before SEITZ, Chief Judge, and GIBBONS and ROSENN, Circuit Judges.

OPINION OF THE COURT

SEITZ, Chief Judge.

CBS Inc. (CBS) appeals from an order of the district court adjudging it in civil con-tempt for failure to comply with a court or-der directing it to submit certain materials to the court prior to trial for in camera in-spection.

I.

On December 3, 1978, CBS broadcast an investigative report on its news program 60 MINUTES concerning the business of fast-food franchising. Entitled "From Burgers to Bankruptcy," the report focused on the activi-ties of Wild Bill's Family Restaurants (Wild Bill's) and concluded with a statement by Mike Wallace that the FBI and the United States Attorney in Newark, New Jersey, had been investigating Wild Bill's and expected to present evidence to a grand jury in the near future.

On September 5, 1979, a grand jury in Newark returned an indictment against sev-eral principals of Wild Bill's (the defendants). The indictment charged the defendants with one count of conspiracy and nineteen counts of fraud arising out of the Wild Bill's franchis-ing operation.

Approximately five months later, and less than one month before their trial was scheduled to begin, the defendants served CBS with a subpoena duces tecum asking CBS to produce before trial:

[I]nvestigator's notes regarding interviews with franchisees and employees of Wild Bill's, filmed interviews of such individuals which were not aired, which are called "out-takes" and notes pertaining to franchisees and employees who refused to be interviewed by your investigators, and, also all video tapes, audio tapes, notes, memoranda, reports and documents of any nature pertaining to the preparation of the program aired in December, 1978 entitled "From Burgers to Bankruptcy."

CBS moved to quash the subpoena, asserting a first amendment privilege for newsgathering that protected the requested materials.

The district court held a hearing on March 4, 1980, to consider the motion to quash. In an oral opinion issued at the end of this hearing, the district court ruled that the subpoena as written was overbroad and not enforceable under Fed.R.Crim.P. 17(c). However, because the defendants' trial was set to begin in one week, the court decided to confront CBS's privilege claim immediately instead of waiting for the trial. It based this decision on several factors, including a desire to avoid disrupting the trial and needlessly increasing its expense, and to afford an opportunity to obtain appellate review of the court's privilege decision before the start of the trial.

The district court relied on our recent decision in Riley v. City of Chester, 612 F.2d 708 (3d Cir. 1979), to find a qualified privilege protecting journalists in their newsgathering function. Because the privilege was not absolute, the court concluded that it must determine whether the privilege should yield to the defendants' need for the information sought. It also concluded that it could not make this determination without first seeing the information in CBS's possession. Therefore, the court directed the government to furnish CBS with a list of the witnesses it intended to call at trial. Instead of quashing the defendants' subpoena entirely on the basis of Fed.R.Crim.P. 17(c), the court modified it and ordered CBS to produce to the court for in camera inspec-

tion prior to trial all verbatim or substantially verbatim statements in CBS's possession made by persons named in the witness list.

The court's order did not provide for the release of any of these statements to the defendants before the trial. Rather, the court stated that it would entertain a motion by the defendants for disclosure of such statements after each witness in question testified on direct examination at trial. Only then would the court balance the defendants' need for the statements against the interests underlying the privilege. After so ruling, the court gave CBS until March 6 to decide whether to comply with the subpoena as modified.

After the March 4 hearing, the defendants served CBS with a second subpoena. This subpoena sought production directly to the defendants of all verbatim or substantially verbatim statements relating or referring to Wild Bill's made by roughly 100 named persons. The great majority of these persons were franchisees or potential franchisees of Wild Bill's and former employees of Wild Bill's. Although it appears that there is some overlap between the persons included in this subpoena and in the government's witness list, we cannot determine from the record the extent of the overlap.

At a hearing held on March 6, the district court also denied enforcement of this subpoena. Because it previously had held that a qualified journalist's privilege protected the type of material sought by this subpoena, the court concluded that direct production of these statements to the defendants was improper. It modified this subpoena to conform to its March 4 ruling and directed CBS to produce to the court for in camera review prior to trial all verbatim and substantially verbatim statements made by the franchisees and potential franchisees listed in the second subpoena. The court did not order production of the statements of Wild Bill's employees or the other persons named in the subpoena and did not specify a procedure for production of the franchisees' statements to the defendants at trial.

The court incorporated this ruling into its March 4 order. The result required CBS to give to the court for in camera inspection all film and audio tapes or written transcripts that reproduced any verbatim or substantially verbatim statements made by: 1) any individuals named in the witness list, and 2) the franchisees or potential franchisees named in the second subpoena.

CBS, however, informed the court that it would not comply with this production order. Therefore, the court held CBS in civil contempt and imposed a fine of $1 per day for every day that CBS remained in contempt. This court thereafter granted a stay pending disposition of this appeal.

CBS attacks the contempt citation on two grounds. First, it argues that the defendants' subpoenas, even as modified by the district court, did not satisfy the requirements of Fed.R.Crim.P. 17(c). Second, it asserts that the material the district court ordered it to produce is protected by a qualified first amendment privilege not to disclose unpublished information and that the district court did not give proper weight to this privilege when it ordered production for in camera review.

II.

Fed.R.Crim.P. 17 governs the use of subpoenas in criminal cases. Subsection (c) of that rule covers subpoenas of documentary evidence and provides that:

> A subpoena may also command the person to whom it is directed to produce the books, papers, documents or other objects designated therein. The court on motion made promptly may quash or modify the subpoena if compliance would be unreasonable or oppressive. The court may direct that books, papers, documents or objects designated in the subpoena be produced before the court at a time prior to the trial or prior to the time when they are to be offered in evidence and may upon their production permit [them] to be inspected by the parties and their attorneys.

We will assume for purposes of this appeal that the rule permits the district court to require production of material to the court prior to trial without also allowing the party seeking production to inspect the material pretrial. CBS does not argue otherwise. In analyzing CBS's rule 17(c) argument, it is helpful to consider the two subpoenas involved in this case separately.

* * *

III.

CBS contests its contempt citation on a second ground. It argues that the material the district court ordered it to produce is protected by the first amendment, qualified privilege not to disclose unpublished information and that the defendants have not shown sufficient need for this material to justify even production for in camera review as ordered by the district court. Given our rule 17(c) holdings, we need consider CBS's privilege contentions only as they relate to that part of the contempt citation based on CBS's failure to produce statements of witnesses the government intends to call at trial.

A.

The defendants initially assert that the privilege relied on by CBS does not exist. However, in our recent decision in Riley v. City of Chester, 612 F.2d 708 (3d Cir. 1979), we held that journalists have a federal common-law qualified privilege arising under Fed.R.Evid. 501 to refuse to divulge their confidential sources. This holding was based, in part, on the strong public policy supporting the unfettered communication to the public of information and opinion, a policy we found to be grounded in the first amendment. We also found support for this privilege in Branzburg v. Hayes, 408 U.S. 665, 92 S.Ct. 2646, 33 L.Ed.2d 626 (1972), where the Supreme Court acknowledged the existence of first amendment protection for newsgathering. *See* 612 F.2d at 714–15.

Riley was a civil action brought under 42 U.S.C. §1983 (1976). The defendants argue that the privilege recognized in *Riley* is inapplicable in a criminal case because of the criminal defendant's sixth amendment rights to compulsory process and to confront witnesses against him and his due process right to a fair trial. We disagree. Although *Riley* did not consider the existence of a qualified privilege in a criminal case, *see* 612 F.2d at 617, we find it to be persuasive authority in this case.

First, the interests of the press that form the foundation for the privilege are not diminished because the nature of the underlying proceeding out of which the request for the information arises is a criminal trial. CBS's interest in protecting confidential sources, preventing intrusion into the editorial process, and avoiding the possibility of self-censorship created by compelled disclosure of sources and unpublished notes does not change because a case is civil or criminal.

Moreover, acceptance of defendants' views that their constitutional interests in a criminal trial preclude the existence of a journalists' privilege in criminal cases would amount to a finding that these interests always prevail over the first amendment interests underlying that privilege. However, in Nebraska Press Association v. Stuart, 427 U.S. 539, 561, 96 S.Ct. 2791, 2803, 49 L.Ed.2d 683 (1976), the Supreme Court stated that:

> The authors of the Bill of Rights did not undertake to assign priorities as between First Amendment and Sixth Amendment rights, ranking one as superior to the other. . . . [I]f the authors of these guarantees, fully aware of the potential conflicts between them, were unwilling or unable to resolve the issue by assigning to one priority over the other, it is not for us to rewrite the Constitution by undertaking what they declined to do.

A defendant's sixth amendment and due process rights certainly are not irrelevant when a journalists' privilege is asserted. But rather than affecting the existence of the qualified privilege, we think that these rights are important factors that must be considered in deciding whether, in the circumstances of an individual case, the privilege must yield to the defendant's need for the information.

The privilege recognized in *Riley* involved only protection of confidential sources. In this case, the government has obtained waivers from all of its witnesses permitting disclosure of their statements held by CBS. CBS asserts, however, that the privilege also protects unpublished material held by it regardless of the confidentiality of the source.

We do not think that the privilege can be limited solely to protection of sources. The compelled production of a reporter's resource materials can constitute a significant intrusion into the newsgathering and editorial processes. *See* Loadholtz v. Fields, 389 F.Supp.

1299, 1303 (M.D.Fla. 1975). Like the compelled disclosure of confidential sources, it may substantially undercut the public policy favoring the free flow of information to the public that is the foundation for the privilege. *See* Riley v. City of Chester, *supra*. Therefore, we hold that the privilege extends to unpublished materials in the possession of CBS. *See* Altemore Construction Co. v. Building & Construction Trades Council, 443 F.Supp. 489, 491 (E.D.Pa. 1977) ("this qualified privilege can even apply when the news source and, perhaps, a portion of the withheld writing are not confidential"). Of course, the lack of a confidential source may be an important element in balancing the defendant's need for the material sought against the interest of the journalist in preventing production in a particular case.

Nor does the fact that the government has obtained waivers from its witnesses waive the privilege. The privilege belongs to CBS, not the potential witnesses, and it may be waived only by its holder. *Cf.* Republic Gear Co. v. Borg-Warner Corp., 381 F.2d 551 (2d Cir. 1967) (attorney-client privilege may be waived only by the client, the holder of the privilege); Perrignon v. Berger Brunswig Corp., 77 F.R.D. 455 (N.D.Cal. 1978) (same).

In summary, we hold that journalists possess a qualified privilege not to divulge confidential sources and not to disclose unpublished information in their possession in criminal cases. We note that this holding is consistent with many cases that have recognized such a privilege in criminal cases. *See e.g.,* Farr v. Pitchess, 522 F.2d 464 (9th Cir. 1975), *cert. denied,* 427 U.S. 912, 96 S.Ct. 3200, 49 L.Ed.2d 1203 (1976); United States v. Hubbard, 493 F.Supp. 202 (D.D.C. 1979); Commonwealth v. Brown, 214 Va. 755, 204 S.E.2d 429, *cert. denied,* 419 U.S. 966, 95 S.Ct. 229, 42 L.Ed.2d 182 (1974). *But see* United States v. Liddy, 354 F.Supp. 208 (D.D.C. 1972).

B.

Because the privilege is qualified, there may be countervailing interests that will require it to yield in a particular case, Riley v.

City of Chester, 612 F.2d 703, 715 (3d Cir. 1979), and the district court must balance the defendant's need for the material against the interests underlying the privilege to make this determination. The district court has not yet made this balancing decision in the present case, and we need not determine the precise factors the district court should consider and how it should weigh them in making its decision. The only issue confronting us is whether the district court properly ordered production for in camera review to facilitate this balancing process at trial.

On appeal, CBS does not contend that in camera review is an improper method for the district court to use in making this privilege decision. However, it argues that even in camera review inhibits the journalist's exercise of rights protected by the first amendment and that the privilege prohibits such review absent a preliminary showing of need by the defendants. *See* New York Times Co. v. Jascalevich, 439 U.S. 1331, 99 S.Ct. 11, 58 L.Ed.2d 38 (1978) (Marshall, J., in chambers). In particular, CBS contends that the court may not order production of privileged material for in camera review unless the defendants have shown both that they cannot obtain the material from another source without implicating first amendment values and that the material is "centrally relevant" to preparation of their defense.

We agree with CBS that an order for production of privileged materials for in camera review may not be based solely on the defendants' request for the material. If the material is available from a nonjournalistic source, the defendants can obtain the information they seek without intruding on the first amendment interests of CBS. In this situation, both the defendants' need for the information and CBS's first amendment interests are satisfied. Therefore, the district court should not be required to make the delicate balance of interests required by the privilege unless the defendant first shows that he is unable to acquire the information from another source that does not enjoy the protection of the privilege.

Given our rule 17(c) holding, the only material we are concerned with in this case is the verbatim and substantially verbatim state-

ments held by CBS of witnesses that the government intends to call at trial. By their very nature, these statements are not obtainable from any other source. They are unique bits of evidence that are frozen at a particular place and time. Even if the defendants attempted to interview all of the government witnesses and the witnesses cooperated with them, the defendants would not obtain the particular statements that may be useful for impeachment purposes at trial. Thus, we think that the defendants have met their burden of establishing that the information that the district court ordered produced for in camera review is not available from another, unprivileged source.

CBS also suggests that in camera production is improper unless the defendants show that the witnesses' statements are "centrally relevant" to their defense. We already have held that the modification of defendants' first subpoena satisfied rule 17(c), which limits subpoenas duces tecum in criminal cases to relevant evidentiary material. We think that a defendant has made a sufficient showing to justify production of privileged material to the court for in camera review if his subpoena complies with rule 17(c) and if he establishes that the information sought is not available from another source. Because both conditions are satisfied for the modification of the first subpoena in this case, we conclude that the part of the district court's production order requiring CBS to produce the witnesses' statements for in camera review was consistent with the privilege. We need not decide, however, whether any additional showing must be made by the defendants to overcome the privilege and to compel production of these statements to them at trial.

IV

We will affirm CBS's contempt citation to the extent that it is based on CBS's failure to produce for in camera review by the court statements in its possession made by persons on the government's witness list. Insofar as the contempt order is predicated on production of statements of nonwitnesses, it will be reversed.

Each party shall bear its own costs.

R E L A T E D   D E C I S I O N S
Attorney-Client Privilege

United States v. Tyler

**United States District Court, W.D.Mich., 1990.
745 F.Supp. 423.**

This case is, in my opinion, one in which justice prevails. It involves the protection of an attorney-client privileged communication when the attorney was an impostor who claimed that he was an attorney and was, in fact, not an attorney.

Please read the case and see if you agree with the court's and my opinion.

AMENDED OPINION[1]

ENSLEN, District Judge.

This matter is before the Court on defendant Tyler's motion in limine to preclude admission at trial of correspondence between defendant Tyler and "attorney" Melvin Deutsch. Defendant Tyler requests an order precluding the government from introducing at trial, either directly or indirectly, correspondence between himself and Melvin Deutsch, or evidence of the contents of the correspondence. Defendant Tyler asserts that the correspondence is inadmissible at trial because it is protected by attorney-client privilege. At a hearing in this matter on July 23, 1990, defendant Tyler testified that he met Melvin P. Deutsch while they were in federal prison in Oxford, Wisconsin. Mr. Tyler testified that he believed that Mr. Deutsch was an attorney, that Mr. Deutsch had diplomas, including a law school diploma, on the wall of his cell and that Mr. Tyler, along with other inmates, addressed Mr. Deutsch as "counselor." Mr. Tyler testified that he shared a cell with Mr. Deutsch for a period of time, and that he gave Mr. Deutsch $50.00 to represent him on a legal matter involving the parole board. Mr. Tyler testified that this parole matter was connected to the instant case, but he was unable to explain how it was related.

Affidavits have now been submitted from counsel for the government and defendant indicating that Melvin P. Deutsch is not currently a member of the bar in California, Illinois, or New York (government's affidavit at 2-3). Further, the affidavit of defendant's counsel states that he contacted a Mrs. Loray Olan, of the Attorney Registration Office of New York, and she indicated that as far back as 1926, there has not been a Melvin P. Deutsch registered or admitted to practice law in the State of New York. Defendant's counsel also contacted Linda Kim of the Membership Records Department of the California Bar Examiners, who indicated that Melvin P. Deutsch was not now nor in the past licensed to practice law in the state of California. Defendant's counsel also states that he spoke with Tom Hocking of the Law Society of Upper Canada, Ontario, who also indicated that as of July 26, 1990, Melvin P. Deutsch had never been registered to practice law in the Province of Ontario. This last information is particularly interesting in light of the affidavit of government's counsel which states that Melvin P. Deutsch stated, in a conversation with government counsel, that he graduated from the York School of Law in Toronto, Canada in 1956 and that he practiced law in Canada until 1987 when he was convicted of wire fraud. However, the Court contacted York School of Law and learned that it did not exist in 1956.

Discussion

The issue in this matter concerns the common law rule that an attorney cannot disclose confidences entrusted by a client without the client's permission. The attorney-client privilege has long been one of the testimonial privileges recognized by common law. Klitzman, Klitzman & Gallagher v. Krut, 744 F.2d 955 (3rd Cir. 1984). The privilege arises whenever legal service, assistance, advice or opinion is sought from an attorney in his or her capacity as an attorney, and under circumstances that support a finding of an attorney-client relationship. United States v. Demuaro, 581 F.2d 50 (2d Cir. 1978), *citing* United States v. Kovel, 296 F.2d 918 (2d Cir. 1961). There are many cases, including those cited by defendant in support of his motion,[2] which discuss when an attorney client relationship arises between a client and someone who is licensed to practice law; surprisingly, however, there is scant case law on the question of whether an attorney-client privilege applies when the defendant erroneously believes that he or she is consulting with an attorney, but the person who is being consulted is not licensed to practice law.

The only case which this Court has discovered which directly addresses the issue at hand is United States v. Boffa, 513 F.Supp. 517 (D.Del. 1981).[3] In *Boffa*, defendants filed a motion to suppress evidence claimed to have been received by the prosecution from a man named Morgan who the defendants claimed had fraudulently represented himself as an attorney. The court noted:

> [T]he rationale behind the privilege equally supports the theory that the privilege should be extended to those who make confidential communications to an individual in the genuine, but mistaken, belief that he is an attorney. (cites omitted). Prudence dictates that such a belief should be reasonable in order to lay claim to the protection of the privilege and that a 'respectable degree of precaution' in engaging the services of the 'attorney' must be demonstrated. (cite omitted). Where such a belief is proved, however, the client should not be compelled to bear the risk of his 'attorney's' deception and he should be entitled to the benefits of the privilege as long as his bona fide belief in his counsel's status is maintained.

Boffa, 513 F.Supp. at 523. The court went on to outline the following criteria which the defendants were required to prove in order to qualify for the relief sought.

> (1) [T]hat Morgan fraudulently held himself out to the defendant as an attorney; (2) that the defendant genuinely and reasonably believed that Morgan was an attorney; (3) that pursuant to this belief, the defendant made confidential communications to Morgan . . . ; (4) that Morgan disclosed to the government the confidential communications he received from the defendants; and (5) that the government used these disclosures as a source for obtaining other evidence that it intends to use at the trial. . . .

Boffa, 513 F.Supp. at 523. In *Boffa* the court found that these criteria had not been met, and thus denied defendants' motion to suppress.

In the case at hand, the government urges this Court to find that the above criteria have not been met, asserting that Mr. Deutsch denies that he "held himself out to be the defendant's attorney" and that "it stretches imaginations to the limits to accept Mr. Tyler's claim that he is so ingenuous as to believe that a person convicted of a felony will be in a position to legally represent him upon his release from the prison cell they shared." Brief at 4. I disagree. First, it is not necessary that Mr. Deutsch "held himself out to be the defendant's attorney," rather, all that is called for is that Mr. Deutsch held himself out as an attorney, and that Mr. Tyler reasonably believed this representation. I believe this standard has been met. Mr. Deutsch admits that he posted a legal diploma on his cell wall, Affidavit of David Scheiber, Government Counsel, at 1, and Mr. Tyler testified that Mr. Deutsch assisted prisoners on all types of legal matters and that he was addressed as "counselor" by fellow prisoners. The government has introduced no evidence to refute this testimony. Mr. Tyler's belief that Mr. Deutsch was an attorney was reasonable under the circumstances. Further, this court does not find the fact that Mr. Tyler did not know that a person convicted of a felony would not usually be allowed to practice law to be "ingenuous." To expect a layperson to be familiar with the internal discipline procedures of the Bar is unreasonable.

I am convinced that the criteria outlined in *Boffa* impose a reasonable standard upon which to decide this question. Further, I am persuaded that defendant has met those criteria. Mr. Deutsch held himself out as an attorney to Mr. Tyler and others, and Mr. Tyler genuinely and reasonably believed that Mr. Deutsch was an attorney. Pursuant to his belief, Mr. Deutsch made confidential communications to Mr. Tyler seeking legal advice and opinions.[4] Further, both the government and defendant Tyler admit that Mr. Deutsch provided copies of these letters to the government and the government plans to use these letters as evidence during the upcoming trial.

The attorney-client privilege should be applied to the correspondence in question. Accordingly, I will enter an order granting defendant's motion to suppress and prohibiting the government from introducing evidence either directly or indirectly of the communications between Defendant Tyler and Melvin P. Deutsch.

Defendant Yepez has filed a motion for severance under Bruton v. United States, 391 U.S. 123, 88 S.Ct. 1620, 20 L.Ed.2d 476 (1968) and the government has also filed a motion under *Bruton*. Because both of those motions turn on evidence contained in the letters discussed above, they need no longer be considered and are dismissed as moot.

---

[1] An earlier, substantially similar, version of this opinion was issued by the Court on August 2, 1990.

[2] *See e.g.,* Kearns v. Fred Lavery Porsche Audi Company, 745 F.2d 600 (Fed.Cir. 1984) and Westinghouse Electric Corp. v. Kerr-McGee Corp., 580 F.2d 1311 (7th Cir. 1978).

[3] In Dabney v. Investment Corp. of America, 82 F.R.D. 464 (E.D.Pa. 1979), the court noted that an exception exists to the general requirement that an attorney-confidant be a member of the bar in cases where the client is genuinely mistaken as to the attorney's credentials, citing to 8 Wigmore, Evidence § 2302. However, the court found that the exception was inapplicable to the facts before it, as it was known by all that the person in question was a law student and had not, at the time in question, been admitted to the bar.

[4] The government notes correctly that Mr. Tyler has been represented by Attorney Daniel Fagan throughout this entire matter, and suggests that this fact means that Mr. Tyler could not have been seeking legal advice from Mr. Deutsch. When questioned on this fact during his testimony Mr. Tyler explained that he was attempting to garner a "second opinion" from Mr. Deutsch, an explanation which this Court finds to be reasonable and believable. The fact that at one time Mr. Tyler was unsure of Attorney Fagan is further evidenced by a letter from Mr. Tyler to this Court dated July 1, 1990, in which Mr. Tyler indicated a "major breakdown in this attorney-client relationship" and requested that this Court appoint different counsel to represent him. Letter of July 1, 1990. This matter was settled before trial with Mr. Tyler withdrawing his request and agreeing to be represented by Mr. Fagan.

✔ PRACTICE QUESTIONS

Indicate whether each statement is true or false.

1. "W," a wife, heard her husband, "D," confess to the commission of a crime for which "D" was brought to trial. "W" and "D" were living together as man and wife at the time of his confession to her. "W" explained the circumstances of the confession to the prosecutor. The prosecutor refused to put "W" on the stand as a witness. The action of the prosecutor was correct.

2. Usually, the government need not reveal the identity of an undercover agent for the purpose of obtaining the issuance of a search warrant.

3. The government need not disclose the identity of an undercover agent in a trial for the sale of narcotics in violation of the law. If such an agent makes a "buy," he need not testify at the trial, and the defendant may still be found guilty.

4. An attorney interviewed a client, and a friend of the client was present during the interview. The attorney asked his client whether or not he would like the friend to leave because what the client might say could be confidential. The client indicated that he wanted the friend to remain. The client then confessed to the commission of a serious crime. The attorney was retained, and he revealed the confession to the police without the client's approval. The attorney's actions were not a violation of a privileged communication.

5. The United States government has granted a statutory privilege to newspaper reporters not to reveal the identity of their sources of information.

Select the most correct answer to complete each statement. Your selection should be based upon material that is included in Chapter 11 of this book.

6. (a) "Statutory immunity" is a term applied to the statutory authority given to prosecutors to grant immunity from prosecution for a person's criminal acts in return for that person's cooperation in solving and convicting other persons of crimes.

   (b) "Statutory immunity" is a term applied to a statute that is enacted to make something legal that has been illegal up to the time of the effective date of the statute.

   (c) "Executive privilege" is a term applied to the executive department of a government that permits a leader of a foreign government to commit acts that would be criminal if committed in the United States.

   (d) A waiver of a privilege must always be in writing and signed by the person making the waiver.

7. (a) The state may seek to keep state secrets out of a trial, but if it does so, the defendant in a criminal case is entitled to the granting of a motion for dismissal by the prosecutor.

   (b) A plaintiff in a civil action for damages does not waive his or her privilege of confidential communications between physician and patient when he calls his or her physician to testify in the trial relating to the injuries received.

   (c) Once a person waives his or her privilege in a trial, in any way, the cases have held that the privilege is waived for this trial alone.

   (d) A spouse injured by his or her spouse has a privilege of confidential communications with the injured spouse in order to prevent the injured spouse from testifying about how the injury was received.

CHAPTER 13

Declaration Against Interest Exception to Hearsay Exclusionary Rule

§ 13.1 INTRODUCTION

Generally, declarations made by a litigant that are against his or her interest, even though they may be hearsay, are admissible as an exception to the hearsay exclusionary rule under certain conditions and may be admissible as proof both of facts directly asserted and of facts incidental thereto and within the scope of the declaration. As with other exceptions to the hearsay exclusionary rule, there must be necessity and a great probability of reliability.

§ 13.2 ELEMENTS OF THE EXCEPTION

A declaration against interest, in order to be admissible, must contain the following elements:

1. The declaration when made is against the pecuniary or proprietary interest and, in New York and some other states, the penal interest of the declarant.
2. The declarant is dead at the time of trial (in some states, the declarant may be unavailable).
3. The declarant had competent knowledge of the facts.
4. There was no probable motive to misrepresent the facts.

§ 13.3 Declaration Against Pecuniary or Proprietary Interest

To bring a statement within the exception, a money or property interest of the declarant must prejudice his or her present contention. Let us assume that a complainant in a criminal action testifies at a hearing in a lower court before the case is presented to the grand jury. He then testifies before the grand jury, and an indictment is brought against the defendant for grand larceny of $16,000. The defendant is arraigned before the trial court on the grand larceny charge, he pleads not guilty, and a date is set for trial. Before the date for trial, the complainant makes a statement to a third party that he never had $16,000 in his possession and he is only making the complaint against the defendant because the defendant had taken away the complainant's lady friend. Before the trial, the complainant dies, and the district attorney attempts to prove the case by reading the testimony of the complainant before the hearing court. Conceivably, the statement made by the complainant relating to the fact that he never had $16,000 in his possession and that he was making the complaint against the defendant because the defendant had taken away the deceased's lady friend, although hearsay, may be admitted under the declaration against interest exception because

1. the statement was against the declarant's interest, since he could be sued for false arrest, and also he would not have a right of recovery in the civil action for conversion;
2. he was dead at the time of trial;
3. he had competent knowledge of the facts; and
4. there was no probable motive to misrepresent the facts.

Another example in which incidental and collateral facts and circumstances were admitted in a declaration against interest occurred in a leading English case, Higham v. Ridway, 10 East. 109, 103 Eng.Rep. 717 (6/30/1808). In this case, a midwife made an entry of the delivery of a child on a certain day, and this entry referred to a ledger in which the midwife had entered a charge for services and a notation of payment at a later date. The entry of birth was held admissible as evidence of the child's age after the midwife had died.

It has been held that declarations against pecuniary interest are exceptions and therefore admissible, even when made by a person not a party to the litigation. La.—Campbell v. American Home Assurance Co., 260 La. 1047, 258 So.2d 81 (1972). In that case, the plaintiffs sued their own insurance carrier for damages arising out of a motor vehicle collision under an uninsured motorist provision of their policy. The attorney for the owners of the other vehicle (not a party to the instant action) had written a letter to plaintiffs' attorney, indicating that his client did not carry liability insurance on the vehicle. The attorney's letter was admissible as evidence, even though he was not a party to the instant action.

Another example of this rule occurred in Texas (Cornell & Co. v. Pace, 703 S.W.2d 398 [Tex.App. 1986]), where it was held that statements of a former partner, now deceased, that were against his pecuniary interest were admissible against the administratrix in a suit for a partnership accounting within the exception to the hearsay rule.

§ 13.4 Declaration Against Penal Interest

There is movement afoot to make a declaration against penal interest a declaration against interest that is admissible. However, the prevailing rule is that a declaration against penal interest is not admissible. U.S.—Donnelly v. United States, 228 U.S. 243, 33 S.Ct. 449, 57 L.Ed. 820 (1913). Some states permit declarations against penal interest to be received. Md.—Brennan v. State, 151 Md. 265, 134 A. 148, 48 A.L.R. 342 (1926); Minn.—State v. Voges, 197 Minn. 85, 266 N.W. 265 (1936); N.Y.—People v. Brown, 26 N.Y.2d 88, 257 N.E.2d 16, 308 N.Y.S.2d 825 (1970). However, a plea of guilty to a motor vehicle violation was held not to be within the rule. Okla.—Dover v. Smith, 385 P.2d 287 (Okla. 1963).

Federal Rule of Evidence 804(b)(3) has further qualified this concept by holding: "A statement tending to expose the declarants to criminal liability and offered to exculpate the accused is not admissible unless corroborating circumstances clearly indicate the trustworthiness of the statement." Therefore, according to the federal rule, if "D," a defendant in the murder trial of "V," is able to get "W," a witness, to testify that "A" had confessed to the murder of "V," the confession might be admissible if there is some corroboration of "A's" statement. Fingerprints of "A" on the murder weapon might satisfy this requirement.

A later federal case declined to admit an inmate's statement about where he had hidden a knife in that it was held not to be a statement against interest and could not be admitted as an exception to the hearsay rule under Federal Rule of Evidence 804(b)(3). Goff v. Nix, 626 F.Supp. 736 (S.D.Iowa 1984), reversed 803 F.2d 358 (8th Cir. 1986).

The Model Code of Evidence would make a declaration admissible where the fact asserted subjects the declarant to civil or criminal liability or even to social disapproval.

If the declaration is contrary to both penal and pecuniary interests, there is no question in any jurisdiction but that the statement would be admissible if all other requirements are satisfied.

§ 13.5 Unavailability of Declarant

Declarations against interest are admissible only when the declarant is unavailable as a witness. Some authorities contend that the declarant must be dead. Others contend that if the declarant cannot be compelled to testify because he is absent from the jurisdiction of the court, the declaration may be received. Pa.—Alter v. Berghaus, 8 Watts 77 (1839). In another case, absence from the jurisdiction was not sufficient. N.Y.—Bunge Corp. v. Manufacturers Hanover Trust Co., 65 Misc.2d 829, 318 N.Y.S.2d 819 (1971). The law is not consistent in the declaration against interest exception, and you are referred to your own state legal digest to ascertain the law applicable to your jurisdiction. However, in all jurisdictions where the declarant is dead and all other necessary elements are present, the exception is admissible. Ala.—Taylor v. First Nat'l Bank of Tuskaloosa [sic], 279 Ala. 624, 189 So.2d 141 (1966); Tenn.—Tom Love Grocery Co. v. Maryland Casualty Co., 166 Tenn. 275, 61 S.W.2d 672 (1933).

§ 13.6 Declarant's Knowledge That Declaration Is Against His or Her Interest

The fact that the declarant is aware at the time of making a statement that it was against his or her pecuniary or proprietary interest is a necessary component because this fact furnishes the circumstantial probability of the statement's trustworthiness. However, most of the cases I have read on this subject do not list the declarant's awareness as a separate element of this exception. Rule 509 of the Model Code of Evidence adopts the reasonable person test, wherein a reasonable person must have known that the declaration was against his or her interest. In a New York case (Ellwanger v. Whiteford, 15 A.D.2d 898, 225 N.Y.S.2d 734 [1962]), the court held that the declarant's awareness was an essential requirement of the declaration against interest exception.

§ 13.7 No Probable Motive to Misrepresent

In order to render a declaration against interest admissible, there must be a great probability of reliability, and therefore there should be a great probability of the trustworthiness of the declaration. But if a declaration is actually against the interest of the declarant, it is immaterial that the declarant may have had a motive to misrepresent the matter. N.H.—Rau v. First Nat'l Stores, 97 N.H. 490, 92 A.2d 921 (1952). Where there exists both a self-serving and a self-disserving interest, the latter must preponderate over the self-serving interest. La.—Demasi v. Whitney Trust & Sav. Bank, 176 So. 703 (La.App. 1937).

§ 13.8   DECLARATION AGAINST PRINCIPAL'S INTEREST BY AGENT

The material statements of an agent who is acting for a principal are admissible as an exception to the hearsay rule when offered by a party opponent. La.—Pennington v. F. G. Sullivan, Jr., Contractors, Inc. 416 So.2d 192 (La.App.), *writ denied,* 421 So.2d 248 (La. 1982); Dykes v. Peabody Shoreline Geophysical, 482 So.2d 662 (La.App. 1985).

In Nekolny v. Painter, 653 F.2d 1164 (7th Cir. 1981), an agent of a civil defendant made statements as to why plaintiffs were terminated from their employment by Lyons Township, saying it was because they supported a defeated candidate for town supervisor. These statements were held to be nonhearsay statements that were made on behalf of the successful candidate and that were contrary to the pecuniary interest of the successful candidate if the employees were determined not to be policymakers. If they were not policymakers, the statements would be admissible under Federal Rule of Evidence 801 (d) (2) (c), (d) as admissions against a party opponent.

§ 13.9   FEDERAL RULE

Rule 804. Hearsay exceptions: declarant unavailable

(3) **Statement Against Interest.** A statement which was at the time of its making so far contrary to the declarant's pecuniary or proprietary interest, or so far tended to subject the declarant to civil or criminal liability, or to render invalid a claim by the declarant against another, that a reasonable person in the declarant's position would not have made the statement unless believing it to be true. A statement tending to expose the declarant to criminal liability and offered to exculpate the accused is not admissible unless corroborating circumstances clearly indicate the trustworthiness of the statement.

CROSS-REFERENCES

Federal Civil Judicial Procedure and Rules (West 1996) (Rule 804[b][3]).
Goode & Wellborn, Courtroom Handbook on Federal Evidence (West 1995) (Rule 804[b][3]).
McCormick, Evidence (4th ed. 1992) (Rule 804[b][3]).

Tom Love Grocery Co. v. Maryland Casualty Co.

Supreme Court of Tennessee, 1933.
166 Tenn. 275, 61 S.W.2d 672.

When you read the decision in this case, the first reaction you may have is to ask yourself why the court is making such an important issue out of a dispute involving $63. To answer that question, I refer you to the date of the decision, i.e., 1933. At this time, $63 was probably more than the average person who was lucky enough to be employed earned in two or three weeks. At that time, the United States was in the midst of the Great Depression. I selected this case to enlarge your mental horizon as to the purchasing power of the dollar at that time, as well as to provide an opportunity for you to read an excellent decision on the unavailability of a person to testify if that person had been convicted of a crime that was labeled an infamous crime. Infamy is defined as a qualification of a person's legal status produced by his or her conviction of an infamous crime, and the consequent loss of honor and credit, which at common law and by statute in some jurisdictions renders that person incompetent to be a witness.

* * *

Appeal from Chancery Court, Shelby County; M. C. Ketchum, Chancellor.

Suit by the Tom Love Grocery Company against the Maryland Casualty Company. From a judgment of the Court of Appeals affirming a judgment for plaintiff, the defendant appeals.

* * *

COOK, Justice. The complainant sued to recover upon a policy of indemnity against burglary of merchandise. The sharply controverted question of fact was whether the goods were taken by entry through force and violence evidenced by visible marks on the premises. The issues, submitted to the jury, were whether or not complainant's warehouse was burglarized, and, if so, what goods were taken.

Under the charge, in which we find no prejudicial error, the jury found that the house was burglarized through forcible entry evidenced by visible marks of violence, and goods of the value of $63 carried away. The chancellor rendered a decree upon the verdict, which the Court of Appeals affirmed.

Before the trial, Fred M. Stubblefield was arrested for the burglary and made a written confession to Inspector Griffin, and an oral statement to Mr. Tom Love, disclosing with particularity all the facts attending the burglary. He was convicted of burglary, and as a result was disqualified as a witness by the judgment of infamy. The chancellor admitted Stubblefield's extrajudicial statement to Inspector Griffin and Mr. Tom Love disclosing the facts of the burglary over the objection of the defendant. The Court of Appeals held the statements admissible as a declaration against interest because they subjected Stubblefield to both civil and criminal liability by statute (Code, §§ 10913–11795) and the common-law (Scruggs v. Davis, 5 Sneed 261), and because Stubblefield was unavailable as a witness by reason of the judgment of infamy.

No rule is more familiar than that which requires the exclusion of unsworn statements or hearsay offered as evidence. Such statements are excluded, because they have not borne the test of cross-examination and are given without the sanction of an oath. There is no opportunity of inquiry into the character of the declarant and his motives for making the statement. Those who repeat such declarations to the court stand upon the simple assertion that the statements were made, and are not obliged to enter into particulars or explain ambiguities in the declarant's statement. If called upon to do so, they could satisfy the inquiry by repeating what they heard.

There are, however, exceptions to the hearsay rule which authorize the reception of admissions and declarations against interest. Declarations, to be distinguished from admissions, as to facts relevant to the matter of inquiry, are admissible in evidence when it appears that the declarant is dead, that the declaration was against his pecuniary or proprietary interest, and that he had no probable motive to falsify the fact declared.

Text-writers, asserting that a litigant has a substantive right to prove his case whether he has one or not, criticize the courts for excluding certain declarations, and insist that administrative necessity requires the admission of extrajudicial assertion of an unavailable witness when the case is absolutely dependent upon his unsworn statement, regardless of the cause of his unavailability. In a few cases, appellate courts, apparently wincing under the prod of criticism, have relaxed the rule and extended the exception beyond declarants whose evidence became unavailable by death. For instance, in Weber v. Railway Co., 175 Iowa 368, 151 N.W. 852, 864, L.R.A.1918A, 626 (1915), a divided court held insanity, calling it mental death, a ground of unavailability, and admitted the declaration. But the majority said: "We do not want to be understood here as extending the rule, in the exception to hearsay evidence, heretofore referred to, beyond the record in this case."

In Griffith v. Sauls, 77 Tex. 630, 14 S.W. 230 (1892), the declaration of a witness unavailable because of his physical condition was held admissible.

Beyond these we find no cases directly in point, and find no authority for extending the rule beyond unavailability by death.

Cases involving the admissibility of declarations by parties and others identified in interest with them are not in point. In our case of Overton v. Hardin, 6 Cold. 375 (1869), the inclusion rested upon the rule that the declaration of parties identified in interest is admissible as primary evidence.

In Harton v. Lyons, 97 Tenn. 180, 36 S.W. 851 (1896), and Brooks v. Lowenstein, 95 Tenn. 262, 35 S.W. 89 (1896), the statements attending the transaction were admissible as part of the res gestae.

Another class of cases hold declarations against title by an owner in possession against those claiming under him admissible as primary evidence. For the distinction, see 22 C.J. 232, 2 Jones on Evidence, § 327, and 4 Chamberlayne, § 2770. Neither are cases in point

that involve the reception of secondary proof of evidence given at a former trial, for that character of evidence is beyond the scope of the hearsay rule, being unaffected by the mischiefs against which the rule is directed.

The distinction between the reception of admissions, the reception of evidence given upon a former trial, and the reception of declarations by parties and their privies or agents, and the reception of declarations against interest, cannot be fused by any sort of intellectual metabolism as is attempted in some instances, so as to interchangeably see the several rules to let in hearsay.

The weight of authority is against the unreasonable extension of the exceptions to the rule, and most of the cases held that it is only when the declarant is dead that his declaration against interest will be received. Reasoning and authority support the conclusion that the exception should not be extended to include infamy along with insanity and death as another ground of unavailability authorizing the reception as evidence of the statement of a witness subsequently adjudged infamous.

The parties to this litigation are the insured and the insurer. Stubblefield, the burglar, was not a party to the contract of insurance nor a representative of the parties. It was error to admit his unsworn statement as evidence. For a discussion of the principles underlying the rule applied, in addition to the authorities already mentioned, we refer to 4 Chamberlayne, § 2780; Smith v. Hanson, 34 Utah 171, 96 Pac. 1087, 18 L.R.A. (N.S.) 520 (1908); Penner v. Cooper, 4 Munf. (18 Va.) 458 (1815); Ibbitson v. Brown, 5 Iowa 532 (1858); Mahaska County v. Ingalls, 16 Iowa 81 (1864); United States v. Mulholland, 50 F. 413, 419 (D.C. 1892), and our own cases of Peck v. State, 86 Tenn. 267, 6 S.W. 389 (1888); Rhea v. State, 10 Yerg. 258 (1837); Draper v. Stanley, 1 Heisk. 432 (1870); Middle Tennessee Railroad Co. v. McMillan, 134 Tenn. 490, 184 S.W. 20 (1916); Adcock v. Simon, 2 Tenn.App. 617 (1926); Brier Hill Collieries v. Pile, 4 Tenn.App. 468 (1926); Harton v. Lyons, 97 Tenn. 180, 36 S.W. 851 (1896); Nichol v. Ridley, 5 Yerg. 63, 26 Am.Dec. 254 (1833); Wright v. State, 9 Yerg. 342 (1836); Cox v. State, 160 Tenn. 221, 22 S.W.2d 225 (1893).

Other assignments of error directed to the charge and to the refusal of the court to direct a verdict are without merit. For error in admitting the confession and statement of Stubblefield as evidence in the cause, the judgment of the Court of Appeals is reversed, and the cause remanded to the chancery court of Shelby county for another trial.

People of the State of New York v. Brown

Court of Appeals of New York, 1970.
26 N.Y.2d 88, 257 N.E.2d 16, 308 N.Y.S.2d 825.

The decision in this case involves the issue of whether a person's alleged statement against interest should be admitted in evidence if the person refuses to testify as to this statement on the grounds of the Fifth Amendment right not to be forced to incriminate oneself. The decision traces the history of the rule and decides whether the refusal to testify should satisfy the requirement that the person who allegedly made the statement be absent, dead, or beyond the jurisdiction of the court.

Defendant was convicted before the Onondaga County Court, Albert Orenstein, J., of murder in the second degree and of carrying a dangerous weapon and he appealed. The Supreme Court, Appellate Division, 28 A.D.2d 646, 282 N.Y.S.2d 215, affirmed and permission to appeal was granted.

* * *

BERGAN, Judge. The main issue in this case, where appellant has been convicted of murder in the second degree, is whether he acted in self-defense. In turn this depends on the proof of appellant's contention that the deceased had a pistol drawn when appellant shot him.

One witness for appellant testified to this effect; but several prosecution witnesses testified decedent did not have a pistol in hand when defendant shot him and the police found no pistol on decedent's clothes or on the floor of the premises where the shooting occurred.

This brings into focus the importance of an admission made both to the police and to appellant's lawyer by one Shelton Seals, who at the time of trial was being held in jail on a charge of robbery, that he had "picked up the gun" apparently which he used in the robbery "immediately after the shooting" for which appellant has been convicted. This admission was made in a conversation at the jail with appellant's counsel; another and similar admission was made by Seals in a confession to the police.

If it had been true that Seals picked up a gun from the floor of the premises immediately after the shooting for which defendant has been convicted, this could have a significant bearing on defendant's contention that decedent was armed and that defendant acted in his own defense.

Seals was called as a defense witness. He refused to answer questions on constitutional grounds. Appellant then offered proof of his admissions. The court sustained objections to them. The ruling was clearly proper upon settled authority in this State. Thus the important question presented by this appeal is whether the existing rule should be continued or abandoned in favor of a more rational view of admissibility of declarations against interest.

In discussing the admissibility of such declarations against interest as an exception to the hearsay rule, Richardson makes the categorical statement that "The fact that the declaration alleged to have been made would subject the declarant to criminal liability is held not to be sufficient to bring it within the declaration against interest exception to the rule against hearsay evidence" (Richardson, Evidence [9th ed.], § 241, pp. 232, 233).

This, as it has been noted, has undoubtedly been the rule in New York (Kittridge v. Grannis, 244 N.Y. 168, 175, 176, 155 N.E. 88, 90 [1927]; Ellwanger v. Whiteford, 15 A.D.2d 898, 225 N.Y.S.2d 734 [1962], affirmed 12 N.Y.2d 1037, 239 N.Y.S.2d 680, 190 N.E.2d 24); in the Federal Courts (Donnelly v. United States, 228 U.S. 243, 33 S.Ct. 449, 57 L.Ed. 820 [1913]); and in a majority of the States (C.J.S.Evidence § 219, pp. 608–609).

Yet the distinction which would authorize a court to receive proof that a man admitted he never had title to an Elgin watch, but not to receive proof that he had admitted striking Jones over the head with a club, assuming equal relevancy of both statements, does not readily withstand analysis.

Holmes attacked the distinction in his notable dissent in *Donnelly* (supra, 228 U.S. pp. 277–278, 33 S.Ct. p. 461) in which, among other things, he said:

> "The rules of evidence in the main are based on experience, logic, and common sense, less hampered by history than some parts of the substantive law. There is no decision by this court against the admissibility of such a confession; the English cases since the separation of the two countries do not bind us; the exception to the hearsay rule in the case of declarations against interest is well known; no other statement is so much against interest as a confession of murder; it is far more calculated to convince than dying declarations, which would be let in to hang a man (Mattox v. United States, 146 U.S. 140, 13 S.Ct. 50, 36 L.Ed. 917 [1892]); and when we surround the accused with so many safeguards, some of which seem to me excessive; I think we ought to give him the benefit of a fact that, if proved, commonly would have such weight. The history of the law and the arguments against the English doctrine are so well and fully stated by Mr. Wigmore that there is no need to set them forth at greater length. 2 Wigmore, Ev. §§ 1476, 1477."

Wigmore, as Holmes notes, developed the argument against the distinction, not only on the basis of sheer logic, but on the historical ground that the English cases which created the distinction, particularly the Sussex Peerage Case (11 Cl. & Fin. 85, 109) were a departure from the basic rule of long standing that admissions against interest generally were received, where relevant, and the declarant dead. The *Peerage* decision was regarded by Wigmore as "not strongly argued and not considered by the judges in the light of the precedents" (5 Wigmore, Evidence, [3d ed.], § 1476, p. 283). Wigmore concludes his comprehensive analysis of the problem with the statement: "It is therefore not too late to retrace our steps, and to discard this barbarous doctrine" (op.cit., p. 290).

There seems to be developing in this country a gradual change of viewpoint which would abolish the distinction. In 1964 the Supreme Court of California decided People v. Spriggs, 60 Cal.2d 868, 36 Cal.Rptr. 841, 389

P.2d 377, opn. per Traynor, J. This held that proof defendant's companion admitted to the police that the heroin found on the ground was hers was admissible.

Justice Traynor, discussing the usual rule that admission against pecuniary interest was admissible, said: "A declaration against penal interest is no less trustworthy. As we pointed out in People v. One 1948 Chevrolet Conv. Coupe, 45 Cal.2d 613, 622, 290 P.2d 538, 55 A.L.R.2d 1272 (1956), a person's interest against being criminally implicated gives reasonable assurance of the veracity of his statement made against that interest. Moreover, since the conviction of a crime ordinarily entails economic loss, the traditional concept of a 'pecuniary interest' could logically include one's 'penal interest'" (60 Cal.2d pp. 874–875, 36 Cal.Rptr. p. 845, 389 P.2d p. 381 [1964]).

In the same direction in Missouri, see Moore v. Metropolitan Life Ins. Co., 237 S.W.2d 210 (Mo.App. 1951), and Sutter v. Easterly (354 Mo. 282, 189 S.W.2d 284 [1945]) where there is a good discussion of Wigmore's analysis; and in Arizona, Deike v. Great Atlantic & Pacific Tea Co., 3 Ariz.App. 430, 415 P.2d 145 (1966).

If, as it is argued, Seals picked up a gun on the floor after the shooting (a gun with which he subsequently committed a robbery) it would be a matter of importance in reaching the truth as to whether or not decedent was armed and it would tend to substantiate defendant's self-defense argument. This kind of admission might well be more important and reliable than the testimony of defendant's witness that decedent had a gun in hand.

There is another facet. The rule on admissions against interest was based on the absence of the witness; and usually this meant that he was dead. But whether the person is dead, or beyond the jurisdiction, or will not testify, and cannot be compelled to testify because of a constitutional privilege, all equally spell out unavailability of trial testimony. If the rule is to be changed to include penal admissions against interest, it ought to embrace unavailability because of the assertion of constitutional right which might be fairly common in the area of penal admissions.

This is the way the St. Louis Court of Appeals approached the question in Moore v. Metropolitan Life Ins. Co., 237 S.W.2d 210, 212 (Mo.App. 1951), supra: "In other words, having regard for the principle of necessity which justifies resort to secondary evidence, a witness who stands upon his constitutional rights is, as a practical proposition, just as fully unavailable as though he were insane or dead or prevented from testifying because of some other acceptable reason. Sutter v. Easterly, 354 Mo. 282, 189 S.W.2d 284, 162 A.L.R. 437."

In People v. Spriggs, 60 Cal.2d 868, 36 Cal.Rptr. 841, 389 P.2d 377 (1964), supra, the California Supreme Court held the admission against penal interest admissible without reaching, on that record, the kind of lack of availability which would become a basis for taking the admission. The record of that trial did not show whether she was available.

But Judge Traynor's footnote 3 (p. 875, 36 Cal.Rptr. p. 845, 389 P.2d p. 381) was to the effect that "If Mrs. Roland had taken the witness stand, but refused to testify regarding possession of narcotics, invoking her constitutional right not to incriminate herself, she would not have been available as a witness."

The rule in New York should be modernized to hold that an admission against penal interest will be received where material and where the person making the admission is dead, beyond the jurisdiction and thus not available; or where he is in court and refuses to testify as to the fact of the admission on the ground of self incrimination.

Since there is to be a new trial two other points raised by appellant require discussion. The first is that the People were permitted excessive cross-examination of defendant when he took the stand as a witness in his own behalf. One line of questions related to his participation in a fight in which the victim was cut with a knife. Another concerned his paternity of a child, and his relationship with Pamela Sargent, one of the prosecution witnesses. This included inquiry concerning a paternity action in the Family Court.

The District Attorney contends that the questions relating to the assault and other matters were in good faith which is supported by files in his office. Some of this cross-examination was improper, especially the references to the paternity proceedings and perhaps also the incidents of relationships. But if the questions about the assault were asked in good faith they would be proper (see, e.g., People v. Alamo, 23 N.Y.2d 630, 298 N.Y.S.2d 681, 246 N.E.2d 496 [1969]); People v. Van Gaasbeck, 189 N.Y. 408, 82 N.E. 718, 22 L.R.A.,N.S., 650 [1907]).

Appellant also argues he should have been allowed to examine a witness who testified for the defense concerning an attempt by that witness' wife to influence his testimony and to influence him not to testify. The witness' wife, who was a sister of decedent, had been an important prosecution witness. One of the questions excluded was her conversation with her husband (the defense witness) on "whether or not you should testify in this lawsuit."

The sister was, as it has been noted, an important prosecution witness, and her interest or bias would have been relevant. And it would not have been necessary to ask her about the conversation to lay a foundation for showing her bias or interest (People v. Brooks, 131 N.Y. 321, 30 N.E. 189 [1892]; People v. Lustig, 206 N.Y. 162, 99 N.E. 183 [1912]); People v. Michalow, 229 N.Y. 325, 128 N.E. 228 [1920]). The inquiry should have been allowed.

The judgment should be reversed and a new trial ordered.

FULD, C. J., and BURKE, SCILEPPI, BREITEL, JASEN and GIBSON, JJ., concur.

Judgment reversed, etc.

Goff v. Nix

United States District Court, Southern District, Iowa, 1984.
626 F.Supp. 736.

This is an interesting case, particularly to those readers who are employed in a correctional institution. While the discussion in this decision relates primarily to unreasonable searches and seizures in the context of visual body cavity searches of inmates at a prison and to constitutional rights of prisoners, it also refers to declarations against interest as an exception to the hearsay exclusionary rule. The question is whether this exception applies to an inmate making a statement as to how a knife may be kept hidden in the rectal cavity.

DONALD E. O'BRIEN, Chief Judge.

This case was tried to the Court on the grounds of the Iowa State Penitentiary (ISP) at Fort Madison, Iowa. Previously, the Court granted Plaintiff Goff part of his requested preliminary injunction which enjoined certain visual body cavity (vbc) searches at ISP. After trial, the Court permanently enjoins the defendants in substantially the same way as set out in the preliminary injunction order with some modifications.

I. FINDINGS OF FACT

At the beginning of the preliminary injunction evidentiary hearing, the parties stipulated to certain facts. Transcript, March 15, 1984 Hearing pp. 9–12 (hereinafter Tr. —). The Court summarized the stipulated facts in the preliminary injunction order. Goff v. Nix, Civil No. 84-129 E, slip op. 4–9 (S.D.Iowa March 22, 1984). The Court incorporates the summary of stipulated facts by reference with two clarifications.

First, the paragraph enumerated 2 should read as follows:

2. When an inmate from cellhouse 20 is to be taken to the exercise area, he hands his clothes to an officer standing outside his cell. The clothes are then shaken down and handed back. The inmate is then taken to a shower and strip searched.

The testimony at trial shows that strip searches conducted prior to exercise did not include a vbc search.

Second, the paragraph enumerated 12 should read as follows:

12. One tower, Tower 7, has responsibility for viewing the four 319 exercise pens as well as other areas.

The Court will not restate all of the Findings of Fact which it made in the preliminary injunction order. In that Order, the Court reserved the right to make additional findings; thus, the Court supplements those findings as follows:

Plaintiffs do challenge the visual anal cavity search which is set forth in Policy No. 84-3-2-567, Procedure B., 10. This procedure provides that the inmate is to be searched by a member of the same sex in an area as private as is possible, without jeopardizing the safety of the searcher or the effectiveness of the search. The inmate's anal cavity is not to be physically probed nor is the inmate touched by the searcher during the search.

The Court further finds that a visual body cavity search which requires the inmate to bend over and spread his buttocks so that the anus is visible to the searcher is intrusive, degrading, humiliating, embarrassing, and greatly increases an inmate's feelings of vulnerability. The Court further finds that these feelings of humiliation, degradation, and vulnerability are increased when a vbc search is accompanied by verbal harassment from the correctional officer(s) conducting the search. Such verbal harassment during a vbc search, including comments with homosexual references or allusion, does not further or promote any institutional security concern and is totally without legitimate purpose. Indeed, verbal harassment during a vbc search has a negative impact upon the security of ISP in that it causes some inmates to become more resentful, more hostile, and more likely to rebel against other assertions of authority. Thus, verbal harassment causes an increase in the tensions at ISP. The evidence and the reasonable inferences therefrom show that many of the correctional officers at ISP perform the vbc searches in an orderly manner without verbal harassment. However, the Court finds that some correctional officers, in some situations, conduct vbc searches in less than an appropriate manner. In other words, the evidence showed that some vbc searches are accompanied by teasing, rude and offensive comments, and other verbal harassment.

In the preliminary injunction Order, the Court granted authority to ISP officials of the status of Security Director or above to conduct a vbc search of an inmate upon "a reasonably clear indication that an inmate is actually concealing something in a body cavity." To date, the Court has received no notice that this authority has been used despite the injunction.

The Court finds that the vbc searches are ineffective in revealing contraband except in cases where a string or part of the item hidden is protruding from the anus or where signs such as excess lubricant, blood or feces are present. Where such signs are observable during a strip search, further inspection including the use of a vbc search would be permitted after approval by the Security Director or higher official. A vbc search will not reveal contraband completely hidden in the rectal cavity.

Security Director John Emmett testified that segregated inmates are vbc searched after, but not before, their exercise. At times during the exercise period, sixteen inmates are in the exercise pens and are watched by two guards, one of whom is in the tower. This occurs when four other guards are escorting inmates to or from the exercise pen. Otherwise, these four guards are observing the exercise pens.

The Court and the parties inspected the penitentiary premises; for an inmate to escape from the new visiting room at ISP, he would have to get by four locked doors, two sliding type and two with guard controlled locks. Four locked doors also protect the infirmary. Inmates taken to the infirmary are under constant supervision and are in restraints unless the treatment requires otherwise. Additionally, segregated inmates are prevented from having access to general population inmates while in the infirmary. The claimed justification for requiring a vbc search after an infirmary visit is that the administration does not have total control over who provides health care because these services are rendered under contract. Defendants are concerned that the company providing health care services may bring in a new doctor or a specialist who does not fully appreciate the security rules. In view of the other security measure [sic] surrounding infirmary visits, the Court finds that this security concern is exaggerated and does not justify use of the vbc search before or after such visits.

The justification for vbc searching an inmate before he goes to the visiting room is that he may take a weapon into the visiting room and use the weapon to take a hostage or attack someone. The Court enjoined vbc searches before contact visits with attorneys, legal interns, clergy, the prison chaplain, and the ombudsman. Vbc searches before other contact visits were not enjoined. The Court finds that the chance that an inmate would wish to attack an attorney, chaplain, clergyman or ombudsman is exceedingly remote and the evidence showed no history of any such attack. Second, because of the security measures which are readily apparent to the inmates, the possibility that an inmate would try to take a hostage as a way to escape from the visiting room is also remote. The Court finds the use of a vbc search prior to these visits is an exaggerated response to these security concerns.

The defendants' justification for searching an inmate after one of these five types of contact visits is that the visitor might give the inmate contraband which the inmate could hide in his rectal cavity and take back into the prison. There is no indication that these types of visitors have attempted smuggling in the past. For this concern to actually happen, the visitor would have to get the contraband into the institution without being detected, the item would have to be removed for [from] its hiding place and then passed to the inmate, and the inmate would have to then conceal it in his rectal cavity. The chances of this sequence of events happening and going undetected is quite remote. First, attorneys, clergy, chaplains, legal interns, and the ombudsman are not the type of people who smuggle contraband to inmates. Second, the surveillance makes it nearly impossible for an item to be hidden by the inmate in his rectal cavity. Inmates do not wear their own prison garb on a visit; they are given "visiting clothing" after the strip search which is conducted prior to the visit. Thus, the clothes worn for a visit will not be split or torn to give the inmate easy access to his rectal cavity. After the visit is over, the prisoners are taken back to a private area, the "visiting clothing" is removed, and they are again strip searched.

Finally, the squat-and-cough search procedure is no longer condoned by the administration of ISP. The Court finds that the squat-

and-cough search procedure is an ineffective type of anal body cavity search which accomplishes nothing other than to degrade and humiliate the inmate recipient. See Tr. 210.

II. CONCLUSIONS OF LAW

The Fourth Amendment provides in pertinent part:

> The right of the people to be secure in their persons . . . against unreasonable searches and seizures, shall not be violated. . . .

The Fourth Amendment protects people, not places. Katz v. United States, 389 U.S. 347, 351, 88 S.Ct. 507, 511, 19 L.Ed.2d 576 (1967). Thus, individuals retain the right to be free from "unreasonable government intrusions into their legitimate expectations of privacy." United States v. Chadwick, 433 U.S. 1, 7, 97 S.Ct. 2476, 2481, 53 L.Ed.2d 538 (1977). To pass muster under the Fourth Amendment, a search must be reasonable. "Reasonableness" is determined by balancing the intrusiveness of the search on the individual's Fourth Amendment interest against the search's promotion of legitimate government interests. Delaware v. Prouse, 440 U.S. 648, 654, 99 S.Ct. 1391, 1396, 59 L.Ed.2d 660 (1979). In the context of visual body cavity searches, the Supreme Court has stated:

> The test of reasonableness under the Fourth Amendment is not capable of precise definition or mechanical application. In each case it requires a balancing of the need for the particular search against the invasion of personal rights that the search entails. Courts must consider the scope of the particular intrusion, the manner in which it is conducted, the justification for initiating it, and the place in which it is conducted.

Bell v. Wolfish, 441 U.S. 520, 559, 99 S.Ct. 1861, 1884, 60 L.Ed.2d 447 (1979).

The Court adopts the following method of analyzing "reasonableness" under the Fourth Amendment.

1. Does the inmate have a legitimate expectation of privacy?
   (a) Have the inmates exhibited an actual (subjective) expectation of privacy?

(b) Is that expectation one which society is prepared to recognize as "reasonable"?
2. Do the challenged searches promote legitimate governmental interests?

See Katz, 389 U.S. at 361, 88 S.Ct. at 516 (Harlan, J., concurring).

Defendants urge this Court to extend the holding in Hudson v. Palmer, 468 U.S. 517, 104 S.Ct. 3194, 82 L.Ed.2d 393 (1984), relating to a prisoner's cell to a prisoner's body. In that case the Supreme Court held

> that society is not prepared to recognize as legitimate any subjective expectation of privacy that a prisoner might have in his prison cell and that accordingly, the Fourth Amendment proscription against unreasonable searches does not apply within the confines of the prison cell.

Id. at —, 104 S.Ct. at 3200. Defendants argue that an inmate retains no reasonable expectation of privacy in his body. The Court disagrees. The Court finds that the inmates have an actual expectation of privacy but that their subjective expectations are significantly diminished by the fact that they are incarcerated. Next, the Court concludes that society recognizes a legitimate expectation of inmates that they are free from excessive and unwarranted searches of a highly intrusive nature. The Supreme Court has set for the the general principal that

> convicted prisoners do not forfeit all constitutional protections by reason of their conviction and confinement in prison.

Bell v. Wolfish, 441 U.S. at 545, 99 S.Ct., at 1877. Thus, this Court concludes that inmates do retain some of the Fourth Amendment's protections while incarcerated.

Having concluded that the Fourth Amendment is applicable to protect the integrity of an inmate's body, the next step is to consider the justifications asserted for the vbc searches. At this point, the Court turns to the amount of deference which the judiciary should accord those officials responsible for the day-to-day operation of a penal institution. In Bell v. Wolfish, *supra,* the Supreme Court stated:

> Prison administrators therefore should be accorded wide-ranging deference in the adoption and execution of policies and practices that in

their judgment are needed to preserve internal order and discipline and to maintain institutional security. (Cites and footnote omitted). "Such considerations are peculiarly within the province and professional expertise of correction officials and, in the absence of substantial evidence in the record to indicate that the officials have exaggerated their response to these considerations, courts should ordinarily defer to their expert judgment in such matters." Pell v. Procunier, 417 U.S. 817, 827, 94 S.Ct. 2800, 2806, 41 L.Ed.2d 495.

This idea of judicial deference does not, however, mean that the authority of prison administrators is unchecked by the United States Constitution. Indeed, in Bell v. Wolfish, 441 U.S. at 546, 99 S.Ct., at 1878, Justice Rehnquist stated:

There must be a "mutual accommodation between institutional needs and objectives and the provisions of the Constitution that are of general application." Wolff v. McDonnell, *supra*, 418 U.S. 539 at 556, 94 S.Ct. 2963, 2975, 41 L.Ed.2d 935.

While this Court appreciates the policy concerns justifying the idea of judicial deference, the Court also recognizes that the purpose of the Bill of Rights is to enshrine certain fundamental principles beyond the reach of governmental officials or legislative majorities. Hudson v. Palmer, 468 U.S. at —, 104 S.Ct. at 3215 (Stevens, J., dissenting). Furthermore, this Court shares the views of Justice Blackmun when he stated:

I am concerned about the [Supreme] Court's apparent willingness to substitute the rhetoric of judicial deference for meaningful scrutiny of constitutional claims in the prison setting. *See* Rhodes v. Chapman, 452 U.S. 337, 369 [101 S.Ct. 2392, 2410, 69 L.Ed.2d 59] (1981) (opinion concurring in the judgment). Courts unquestionably should be reluctant to second-guess prison administrators' opinions about the need for security measures; when constitutional standards look in whole or in part to the effectiveness of administrative practices, good-faith administrative judgments are entitled to substantial weight. The fact that particular measures advance prison security, however, does not make them *ipso-facto* constitutional. Cf. Bell v. Wolfish, 441 U.S., at 539, n. 20 [99 S.Ct. at 1874 n. 20]. I recognize that constitutional challenges to prison conditions, like similarly expansive challenges to the workings of other institutions, pose a danger of excessive judicial intervention. At the same time, however, careless invocations of "deference" run the risk of returning us to the passivity of several decades ago, when the then-prevailing barbarism and squalor of many prisons were met with a judicial blind eye and a "hands off" approach. As we recognized in Bell v. Wolfish, the fact that initial responsibility for the Nation's prisons is vested in prison administrators "does not mean that constitutional rights are not to be scrupulously observed." *Id.*, at 562 [99 S.Ct., at 1886]

Block v. Rutherford, — U.S. —, —, 104 S.Ct. 3227, 3236, 82 L.Ed.2d 438 (1984) (Blackmun, J., concurring in judgment). In short, there is a constitutional line which constrains the discretion of prison administrators.

The Court concludes that consideration of the promotion of legitimate governmental interests should be analyzed in the context of when and where the vbc search is used. In Bell v. Wolfish, the Supreme Court set forth four factors which a court must consider in performing the Fourth Amendment balancing test. The four factors are:

(1) The scope of the particular intrusion,
(2) The manner in which it is conducted,
(3) The justification for initiating it, and
(4) The place in which it is conducted.

These factors indicate that the reasonableness of a given search is dependent upon the facts and circumstances surrounding that search. Thus, the Court concludes that the justifications or governmental interests promoted by a given search must also be considered in their factual context. As a result, the Court rejects defendants' argument that all situations involving contact visits with individuals from outside the institution should be held to be a categorically reasonable situation permitting a vbc search. Rather, the Court will consider the propriety of the vbc search in a number of separate settings.

1. *Attorneys.* The use of vbc searches before and after attorney visits is troubling in that an inmate's fundamental constitutional right of access to the courts is involved in addition to his Fourth Amendment rights. *See* Simms v. Brierton, 500 F.Supp. 813 (N.D.Ill.

1980). In view of recent Eighth Circuit precedent, Hahn v. McLey, 737 F.2d 771 (8th Cir. 1984); Nelson v. Redfield Lithograph Printing, 728 F.2d 1003 (8th Cir. 1984), inmate-attorney visits will play an important role in the process for vindicating prisoners' constitutional rights. As previously found, the use of the vbc searches before and after attorney visits will have a chilling effect on the assertion of inmates' legal rights. In balancing the degree to which these searches promote security against the prisoners' privacy and due process interests, the Court concludes that these searches are unconstitutional unless there is some independent clear reason to suspect an individual lawyer or intern by reason of his or her past actions or statements.

2. *Legal interns.* The situation presented by legal intern visitors is similar to attorney visitors. Because of the burden the vbc search places on the right to access to the courts, the Court concludes that vbc searched [sic] before and after such visits shall be enjoined.

3. *Clergy.* Clergy, like attorneys, must produce their credentials before they will be allowed to visit an inmate at ISP. Iowa Administrative Code Chapter 291-21.-3(4). The Court concludes that these searches are unreasonable and, thus, unconstitutional.

4. *Prison chaplain.* The prison chaplain is hired by the Department of Corrections and is part of the ISP staff. Requiring an inmate to submit to a vbc search before and/or after such a visit is unreasonable and shall be enjoined.

5. *Ombudsman.* Similarly, the ombudsman is a state employee who presents no real danger of passing or receiving contraband from an inmate. Thus, vbc searches before and after such visits are unreasonable and shall be enjoined.

6. *Infirmary.* The Court finds the use of vbc searches before and after an inmate visit to the new infirmary area is an exaggerated response to the security needs presented by the situation. Furthermore, the use of the vbc searches has the effect of keeping inmates with legitimate medical needs from visiting the infirmary. A prisoner should not have to choose between getting medical relief and submitting to a vbc search. The Court concludes that these searches are unreasonable and shall be enjoined.

7. *University of Iowa Hospital.* In trips to the University Hospital, the inmates are in the same areas that are open to the general public. In crowded hallways, there may be physical touching between the inmate and someone the guard does not know. Furthermore, the computerized records of the Hospital make it possible for Hospital employees to find out when an inmate will be visiting the Hospital. This information can be passed to friends of the inmate. Some physical examinations of inmates are done outside the presence of a guard. In view of the many variables which may occur during a Hospital visit, the Court will modify the preliminary injunction so that the searches can be conducted at the Hospital both on arrival and upon leaving the Hospital. However, the use of the vbc search before leaving the prison on such a trip is unreasonable and shall continue to be enjoined. The Court has distinguished between vbc searches conducted before leaving the prison and those conducted upon arrival at the Hospital to lessen the burden on the right to medical treatment, i.e., to reduce the number of incidences where the records show an inmate refused to submit to a vbc search at the prison before leaving for the Hospital and thus was not allowed to make the trip to the Hospital.

8. *Court (on prison grounds).* Two trailer houses inside the ISP fences but outside the prison walls serve as court facilities for certain legal proceedings which involve prisoners. This Court conducts its hearings and trials in many civil rights actions in those facilities. While in court, the inmates are always under the observation of at least one—and usually several more—correctional officers. In court the inmates' handcuffs and belly chains are removed. Leg restraints, if the inmate is in a status which requires them, are left secured. While in the witness room in the trailer house which is adjacent to the court room, the inmates are always under the supervision of one or more correctional officers and they remain in their restraints. In view of the restraints and supervision by correctional officers, the Court is persuaded that, in the context of vbc searches before and after court visits on the prison grounds, the security interests of ISP are not promoted by the use of the vbc search to a degree significant enough to outweigh the

privacy interest of the inmates and vbc searches will not be conducted in these situations.

9. *Court outside Prison.* Inmates on court visits are always in the close presence of at least two security guards and usually several more except when conferring with their attorney and sometimes when the security guard allows them privacy inside a restroom stall. The possibility that an attorney would allow an inmate to place or retrieve an item from his anal cavity is exceedingly remote. Also, the chance that an attorney would give an inmate contraband which he could hide during a later trip to the restroom is minimal and remote. During court visits, the guards are much more in control of what happens with the inmate. This distinguishes court visits from Hospital visits. The Court concludes that vbc searches before and after court visits outside the prison are unreasonable.

10. *Exercise.* The Court appreciates the frankness of the defendants' statement that:

> Candidly, the Penitentiary policy of giving visual body cavity searches before and after segregated inmate's exercise is not as obviously constitutional as is the policy of requiring such searches in the cases previously described since infirmary visits and exercise do not require the inmate to leave the prison and do not bring him into contact with people from outside the institution.

Defendant's Trial Brief, p. 19. Also, the testimony of Dr. Mintzes, formerly the warden at State Prison in Jackson, Michigan, and Warden Armontrout supports the conclusion that these searches do not advance the security of ISP to any significant degree. Given the surveillance of the exercise pens by correctional officers, the use of restraints to and from the exercise pens, the number of guards performing the escort, and the physical make up of the pens, the Court finds the use of vbc searches upon return from exercise is an exaggerated response to the perceived security needs of ISP. Consequently, these searches are unreasonable.

With respect to verbal harassment during those vbc searches not prohibited by this Court's injunction, the Court concludes that verbal abuse and harassment can render an

otherwise constitutional vbc search unconstitutional. In Bell v. Wolfish, 441 U.S., at 560, 99 S.Ct., at 1885, the Court stated:

> Nor do we doubt, as the District Court noted, that on occasion a security guard may conduct the search in an abusive fashion. [Wolfish v. Levi,] 439 F.Supp. [114], at 147 [(1977)]. Such abuse cannot be condoned. The searches must be conducted in a reasonable manner. Schmerber v. California, *supra* [384 U.S. 575], at 771–772 [86 S.Ct. 1826, 1836, 16 L.Ed. 908 (1966)]. But we deal here with the question whether visual body cavity inspections as contemplated by the MCC rules can *ever* be conducted on less than probable cause. [Emphasis in original].

In light of this language and the second of the four factors set forth on page 12 above, it appears that conduct by guards which increases the humiliation and degradation inherent in a vbc search and which does not promote institutional security cannot be tolerated. Consequently, this Court will enjoin correctional officers and other officials of ISP from teasing, making abusive or rude comments, or otherwise verbally harassing inmates during a vbc search.

III.

A. Evidence and Procedure. On July 20, 1984, the plaintiffs filed a motion for leave to file amended and supplemented complaints. During the course of the trial, defendants made various motions to dismiss and strike evidence based on the assertion that the matters presented were not raised by the pleadings. The Court reserved ruling on defendants' motions to strike and motions to dismiss subject to the plaintiffs filing a motion for leave to amend. Under Fed.R.Civ.P. 15 and the Eighth Circuit precedent interpreting that rule, *E.g.* Asay v. Hallmark Cards, Inc., 594 F.2d 692 (8th Cir. 1979), leave to amend shall be freely given. The Court will grant plaintiffs leave to amend. The Court finds the defendants were not prejudiced by the amendment because this Court's preliminary injunction order entered well before trial clearly defined the various categories of vbc searches which were to be considered. The defendants were, at the time of trial, clearly prepared to address the various categories of vbc searches which were enjoined by the preliminary injunction. During the trial, the defendants moved to strike the testimony of Inmate Derl Sharp and moved to strike the testimony of Plaintiff Heaton. The Court reserved ruling on those motions and gave the defendants the opportunity to reassert their motions to strike after plaintiffs had amended their complaint. The defendants have not reasserted these motions to strike although given ample opportunity to do so. The Court will overrule the motions to strike and the testimony of Inmate Sharp and Plaintiff Heaton will be received as relevant evidence.

Defendants called as a witness Warden Bill Armontrout of the Missouri State Penitentiary which is located in Jefferson City, Missouri. Warden Armontrout testified, over the objections of the plaintiffs, about what two inmates had told him regarding knives which they kept hidden in their rectal cavities. The plaintiffs assert that this testimony should be excluded because, first, defendants failed to comply with requests for discovery regarding experts and, thus, said testimony should be excluded under Fed.R.Civ.P. 37(b)(2)(B) as a sanction for such failure and, second, the testimony of Warden Armontrout was hearsay that did not fall within one of the recognized exceptions to the hearsay rule.

The Court is not persuaded that it should exclude this testimony on the basis of discovery rule violations even though the rule was violated.

As to the hearsay objection, despite defendants' contention, the Court concludes that the testimony was offered for the truth of the matter asserted. The Notes of Advisory Committee to Rule 801 state:

> If the significance of an offered statement lies solely in the fact it was made, no issue is raised as to the truth of anything asserted, and the statement is not hearsay.

The practical thrust of Warden Armontrout's testimony was not that inmates say they hide knives in their anal cavity, but that inmates actually do hide knives in such a fashion.

Next, the Court concludes that the statement by the inmate about where he hid the knife is not a statement against interest as that phrase is used in Fed.R.Evid. 804(b)(3).

The evidence does not show that the exact *hiding place* of the weapon is something which could subject the declarant to greater criminal or penal sanctions. Furthermore, the inmate declarants could easily have had a motive to deceive Warden Armontrout in an effort to preserve the secrecy of what the inmate regarded as a better hiding place. Consequently, the Court concludes that the statements by the two inmates to Warden Armontrout do not fall within the hearsay exceptions set forth in Fed.R.Evid. 804(b)(3), 804(b)(5), or 803(24). Thus, plaintiffs' objections to the testimony by Warden Armontrout about statements made to him by inmates shall be sustained and that testimony shall be stricken from the record.

The practical effect of this hearsay ruling upon the defendants' case is minimal because the Court recognizes that it is possible for an inmate to conceal a properly wrapped weapon in his anal cavity. In addition, the plaintiffs do not contend that it is impossible to conceal a dangerous weapon in the anal cavity.

B. Standing. The defendants contend that none of the three named plaintiffs have standing to challenge the visual body cavity searches before or after visits to the University of Iowa Hospital, or before or after visits from an attorney, clergyman, or the prison ombudsman. Defendants' contention is premised upon the argument that the plaintiffs must have been subjected to a vbc search in making that particular type of visit before the plaintiffs would be entitled to a permanent injunction which prevents a vbc search before or after that type of visit.

Plaintiff Goff has standing to challenge the vbc searches before or after visits with an attorney. Plaintiff Goff's suit was initiated because he was required to submit to an anal body cavity search before being allowed to see his attorney. Plaintiff Goff refused to submit to the search procedures which were used at that time and, thus, was not allowed to see his attorney. Furthermore, the Court finds that the challenged vbc searches, if not enjoined, pose a threat of injury which is both real and immediate, as opposed to merely conjectural or hypothetical. The test for an actual "case or controversy" which the United States Supreme Court has adopted is that there be a threat of injury which is real and immediate, and not merely speculative. *See* City of Los Angeles v. Lyons, 461 U.S. 95, 102, 103, S.Ct. 1660, 1665, 75 L.Ed.2d 675, 684 (1983). Defendants argue that plaintiffs' claim is based on "the speculative assertion that at some time in the future they *may* wish to engage in some of the activities covered by the visual body cavity search policy and upon that occurrence *may* be subject to a visual body cavity search." Defendants Post-Trial Brief, p. 18. First, part of the reasoning behind the present vbc search policy is that it is mandatory in certain situations and therefore does not give the prison guards the opportunity to exercise their discretion in an arbitrary or discriminatory manner. Second, plaintiffs cannot control when they will need the services of the University of Iowa Hospital. Also, plaintiffs are unable to control all the situations in which it would be desirable to speak directly with an attorney. Finally, and most importantly, plaintiffs should not be forced to choose between having their Fourth Amendment rights violated by an unconstitutional vbc search and foregoing a visit with an attorney (Due Process—access to the courts), a clergyman (First Amendment—freedom of religion), or the prison ombudsman (while access to the ombudsman may not implicate a fundamental constitutional right, it is important to inmates as a way to bring problems inside ISP to the attention of someone who is outside the institution).

C. Report. At the close of the evidence presented on July 16, 1984, the Court directed counsel for the defendants to report to the Court on the effect that the issuance of the preliminary injunction had on inmates who had been disciplined for refusing to submit to the squat and cough procedure. In part, the Court was concerned with whether the sanctions for refusing to submit to that anal body cavity search were suspended or eliminated by the administration after the injunction was issued. In a letter dated December 11, 1984, the Court was informed by defense counsel that the disciplinary segregation being served by Goff and Schertz was not suspended. Heaton was reported to not have received a disciplinary report as a result of the refusal to squat and cough.

D. Damages. The issue of damages was entertained at the trial. The Court requests the input of counsel regarding the manner in which that question should be handled; specifically, is there a need for a further hearing on damages?

IT IS THEREFORE ORDERED that defendants are hereby permanently enjoined from conducting visual and body cavity searches in the following situations:

1. Before or after contact visits with attorneys, legal interns with a notarized letter of introduction from a licensed attorney, clergy, the prison chaplain, or representatives of the prison ombudsman's office.

2. Before going to or after coming from the prison infirmary.

3. Before leaving the prison on a trip to University of Iowa Hospitals. However, as a modification of the preliminary injunction, vbc searches can be conducted upon arrival at the Hospital and before leaving the Hospital.

4. Before or after attendance by inmates at court dates, whether on the prison grounds or in any other location, unless the inmate is out of restraints and actually beyond the visual supervision of ISP correctional officers. Private visits with attorneys shall not be considered as being outside the visual supervision or out of restraints.

5. Before going to or after coming from the exercise areas.

IT IS FURTHER ORDERED that the practice known as "squat-and-cough" shall be permanently enjoined from being used under any circumstances at ISP.

IT IS FURTHER ORDERED that correctional officers and other ISP officials shall be enjoined from teasing, making abusive or rude comments, or otherwise verbally harassing inmates during a vbc search.

IT IS FURTHER ORDERED that this Order does NOT prevent the defendants from conducting visual body cavity searches in the following situations:

(a) Before or after "contact" visits with any visitors coming to the prison except as set out above.

(b) Upon initial admission to the prison or before or after being outside the prison on furlough, transfer or work release.

(c) Before or after a segregated prisoner has mixed with the "general population" without supervision or restraints.

(d) Before or after an inmate, in any set of circumstances, had demonstrated activity which would give an official of the penitentiary of the status of Security Director or above a reasonably clear indication than an inmate is actually concealing something in his anal cavity. In any such situations, the burden will be on the Warden to show that the use of this exception was reasonable.

IT IS FURTHER ORDERED that this Order shall apply to all inmates at the Iowa State Penitentiary, not only to cellhouse 20 and 319 inmates.

IT IS FURTHER ORDERED that plaintiffs shall submit their pleadings setting out their position on damages within twelve days from the date this Order is filed. Defendants shall respond in six days.

Dykes v. Peabody Shoreline Geophysical

Supreme Court of Louisiana, 1985.
482 So.2d 662.

This short decision demonstrates that an agent of a principal may make a statement against the interest of the principal and it will be admissible in evidence.

Before EDWARDS, SHORTESS and SAVOIE, JJ.

EDWARDS, Judge.

The plaintiffs in these consolidated cases sued to recover property damages and general damages for inconvenience, mental anguish and invasion of privacy, the damages having been caused by seismic blasting operations conducted by defendant, Peabody Shoreline Geophysical (Peabody). The suits were tried together before a jury which awarded plaintiffs a total of $180,000. Peabody and its insurer, Transportation Insurance Company, have suspensively appealed the judgment.

Peabody raises five basic issues. First, Peabody contends that plaintiffs failed to prove that its activities caused the damages. The second contention is that the jury's awards were excessive. Third, that the trial court erred in denying Peabody's exception of prescription on the claims brought by the two minor children of Bryan Dykes. The fourth issue raised is that the trial court erroneously taxed as costs the fees for certain discovery depositions never introduced or admitted at trial, and fees for supposedly expert witnesses who were never qualified as experts or accepted by the trial court. Finally, Peabody assigns error to the admission of certain hearsay testimony.

Defendant was conducting seismic operations in and around Montpelier, Louisiana, in December of 1980. The particular explosion complained of occurred at about noon at a drill site located on Mrs. Campbell's property approximately 700 feet from her home. Five one-pound charges of explosives, spaced five feet apart on a line and lowered 100 feet below ground, were to be detonated in sequence at intervals of thirty seconds. For some reason unknown, the entire load went off at the same time. Plaintiffs testified that they were quite startled and that the earth shook and windows and walls rattled.

Four of the five plaintiffs were at home when the blast occurred. Bryan Dykes had come home for lunch. He testified that he heard a single blast that "felt like an earthquake" and "shook the whole house." He then saw a crack in the fireplace in the mortar of the brick above the mantel. Gloria Dykes, his wife, was in the kitchen cooking. She said that she heard a loud noise, felt a tremor, and then saw a crack in the kitchen floor.

Maxine Ard, who had been working in her garden and had just stepped inside, also testified that the explosion felt like an earthquake and that it shook the whole house. Mrs. Campbell testified that she had just lain down after lunch and was lying upon her bed when she felt the house and the bed shake.

Later that day, Bryan Dykes drove over to the blasting site. He was the mayor of Montpelier at the time and was aware that seismic operations had been in progress for a couple of weeks. He testified that he met a man who was sitting in a Peabody company truck who told him that they had made a mistake and had accidently set off all five charges at once. The man agreed to accompany Dykes to his home to inspect the damages. The man also contacted Joseph Faulk, Peabody's permit agent, who arrived about an hour later. Dykes testified that Faulk admitted Peabody's responsibility for all damages caused by the explosion and that Faulk agreed to bring in insurance adjusters to settle the damage claims in a couple of weeks. Ultimately, Dykes testified, Faulk apparently changed his mind and did nothing.

Immediately after the explosion, Maxine Ard telephoned Bryan Dykes to find out what had happened. She then went to the blast site herself. She testified that she, too, met a man there who said Peabody had had an accident.

All of the plaintiffs testified that prior to the explosion their homes were in generally good condition but that immediately after it, and in the weeks that followed, there appeared various damages which they attributed to the blast and which, in the case of the Ard and Dykes homes, progressively worsened during the three years before trial.

Dykes testified that he and his family had to move out of their house for three or four days while he located and repaired a break in the sewer line to the septic tank. In addition, he said there was a crack which ran the length of the slab upon which the house was built, indicating structural damage.

Eddie and Maxine Ard testified to similar damages, including problems with the waterline to their commode and cracks in the slab and in the mortar on both sides of the house.

Mrs. Campbell testified that the explosion knocked some plates off her kitchen wall and that several weeks later about half of her kitchen ceiling collapsed, ruining the carpet. She found it particularly stressful, she said, since at that particular moment she was fixing lunch for her husband who was recovering from a heart attack. Mrs. Campbell, like the other plaintiffs, suffered plumbing problems, having to replace some broken galvanized pipes under her house.

In addition, Mrs. Campbell testified that Peabody trespassed on her property. She said that she had signed a permit, which she introduced into evidence, authorizing Peabody to lay cable across her property but giving no permission for seismic activity. Several weeks after the explosion, accompanied by Bryan Dykes, she found drill holes on a corner of her property where the blasting had been done.

HEARSAY—CAUSALITY

Defendants contend that plaintiffs failed to prove a causal connection between the seismic activities and the damages. At trial, plaintiffs offered testimony concerning statements made by the unidentified truck driver and Joe Faulk in support of causality. Defendants allege error by the trial court in admitting this hearsay testimony. We hold that while it is hearsay, it is also admissible. Plainly, material statements of an agent who is acting for a principal are admissible as an exception to the hearsay rule when offered by a party opponent. Pennington v. F. G. Sullivan, Jr., Contractors, Inc., 416 So.2d 192 (La.App. 1st Cir. 1982), *writ denied*, 421 So.2d 248 (La. 1982). Furthermore, declarations against pecuniary interests are an admissible exception, even when made by a person not a party to the litigation. Campbell v. American Home Assurance Company, 260 La. 1047, 258 So.2d 81 (1972).

Peabody was less than staunch in defending this point. Counsel made no objection to the admission into evidence of Joe Faulk's business card. This card on its face clearly confirmed that Joe Faulk was Peabody's agent. Moreover, defendants raised no objection to the testimony by Bryan Dykes that the unidentified Peabody employee in the truck telephoned Joe Faulk and asked him to come discuss with plaintiffs the damages they had sustained.

We hold, therefore, that plaintiffs adequately carried their burden of proving a causal connection between the explosion and the damages.

In rebuttal, Peabody offered the argument of "scientific impossibility." This consisted of testimony by an expert in explosives and stress analysis who holds degrees in mathematics and physics. The witness purported to show, by mathematical and scientific calculations, that it was a *total impossibility* for the explosion to have caused the damage. This defense has been used before in blasting cases, with minimal success. Given the choice between an obvious fact and a technical, scientific denial of that fact, our courts have refused to accept the denial. In Fontenot v. Magnolia Petroleum Co., 227 La. 866, 80 So.2d 845 (1955), the Supreme Court said at page 848:

> Impressed as we are with the unchallenged and unrebutted proof by plaintiffs, we necessarily conclude that the evidence clearly establishes the claim of plaintiffs in that the general and extensive damages to their homes were nonexistent prior to, and were the causal result of, the geophysical operations conducted by defendants. The fact that plaintiffs did not discover these substantial injuries until two days after defendants' operations, or that the homes were of frail or cheap construction (with no substantive proof to support this conclusion) does not in any wise relieve defendants of liability.

Similarly, in Pate v. Western Geophysical Co. of America, 91 So.2d 431, 433 (La.App. 2d Cir. 1956), dismissing the defendant's argument of scientific impossibility, the Second Circuit observed,

> Again, while it may be said that such testimony establishes the so-called scientific impossibility of the damage resulting from the explosive operations, the fact is that the only reasonable conclusion is that such damage was caused by and is attributable to defendant's operations.

In Roshong v. Travelers Insurance Company, 281 So.2d 785, 788 (La.App. 3d Cir. 1973), the Third Circuit went so far as to establish a rule of evidence:

> [W]e find that the expert testimony . . . that the injury sustained under the circumstances could not possibly have been caused by the seismic explosions . . . *legally insufficient* to rebut the prima facie case established by Roshong. Five witnesses testified that damage to the structure was nonexistent at the time of the blasts and became apparent within two days of the explosions. The evidence supports a conclusion that all damage found by the experts is related to the seismic explorations, and that these explorations were a cause in fact of all of the damage. [Emphasis added.]

See also Peak v. Cantey, 302 So.2d 335 (La.App. 1st Cir. 1974); Greer v. State Department of Transportation and Development, 437 So.2d 1170 (La.App. 2d Cir. 1983); Wright v. Superior Oil Co., 138 So.2d 688 (La.App. 3d Cir. 1962).

Nekolny v. Painter
United States Court of Appeals, Seventh Circuit, 1981.
653 F.2d 1164.

This case involves the termination of employment of town employees. When they were terminated, they received a letter of termination signed by the successful candidate for the position of town supervisor. These letters were delivered to them by another town employee, who allegedly stated orally to them that they were being dismissed because they had supported the defeated candidate in the election.

The issue arose as to whether these statements were hearsay and, if they were not, whether they should be admitted into evidence under Federal Rule of Evidence 801(d)(2)(c), (d), wherein they are admissions by a party opponent as to the reasons for the termination of employment.

The court makes a determination as to whether these statements should be admitted into evidence, as well as deciding other matters of damages.

Before SWYGERT,* Senior Circuit Judge, and WOOD and CUDAHY, Circuit Judges.

SWYGERT, Senior Circuit Judge.

This appeal involves the First Amendment rights of three Lyons Township employees who were found by a jury to have lost their jobs because they had campaigned for the Township Supervisor's opponent in an election. The defendant-appellant Supervisor alleges as error the district court's allocation of the burden and standard of proof; the directed verdict finding that the Senior Citizens' Coordinator was not a policymaker; the denial of immunity to the defendant in her individual capacity and the denial of qualified immunity; the admission of testimony as to statements made by the defendant's "liaison"; and the award of damages for mental and emotional distress. It is also contended that the verdicts were against the manifest weight of the evidence.

We affirm the judgments of the district court as regard plaintiffs Nekolny and Dahms, except for the damages awarded for mental and emotional distress to all three plaintiffs which are reversed for lack of a sufficient foundation in the record. We also hold that the directed verdict finding plaintiff Dumas not to be a policymaker was error. Accordingly we remand for a determination by the trier of fact according to the standards we have set forth in this opinion.

I

Ann Painter, a Republican and the defendant in this lawsuit, took office as Supervisor of Lyons Township on April 18, 1977. All three plaintiffs were at that time employed by Lyons Township, each having been hired during the term of the previous Supervisor. Plaintiff Edward Nekolny was a bus driver for the Senior Citizens' Bus Service; plaintiff Patrick Dumas was the Senior Citizens' Coordinator, and plaintiff Maria Dahms was a Secretary-Dispatcher. Within six weeks of Painter's incumbency, all three had lost their jobs, although the defendant asserted that Dahms had resigned voluntarily. Each plaintiff had campaigned vigorously for the defendant's opponent, a member of the Bipartisan Party, and against the defendant in the election for Supervisor.

Plaintiffs brought their action under 42 U.S.C. § 1983, alleging that defendant Painter had violated their constitutional rights to freedom of speech and association under the First and Fourteenth Amendments of the United States Constitution by terminating them or forcing them to resign from their positions with Lyons Township because of their campaign activity on behalf of her political opponent. Defendant took the position that Nekolny was dismissed because of health problems and concern for the safe transporting of senior citizens, that Dumas' position was abolished in keeping with defendant's campaign promises to eliminate the four top-paying appointed positions within the Township government, and that Dahms had voluntarily resigned on being informed that due to a reassessment of program needs, her work load and pay would be decreased. Nekolny and Dahms testified that James Hickey, then defendant's liaison to the Senior Citizens' Bus Service, told them that the defendant wanted to terminate them because they had campaigned against her. Hickey denied making those statements. Although it was not disputed that Painter had made a campaign pledge to abolish four positions including that held by Dumas, it was also clear that after terminating Dumas, Painter named Hickey the new Senior Citizens' Coordinator, albeit at a reduced salary.

A jury trial on the issue of liability resulted in a verdict for the plaintiffs. Damages were assessed by the jury as follows: for Nekolny, $40,000 in lost earnings and fringe benefits, $5,000 for mental and emotional stress and $5,000 for punitive damages; for Dumas, $12,000 in lost earnings and fringe benefits, $13,000 for additional expenses, $2,500 for mental and emotional distress and $5,000 for punitive damages; for Dahms, $17,000 in lost earnings and fringe benefits, $2,500 for emotional and mental distress and $5,000 for punitive damages. This appeal followed.

II

The defendant argues that the trial judge incorrectly allocated the burden of proof when he instructed the jury on the issue of Painter's motive for terminating Nekolny, reducing Dahms' salary, and abolishing Dumas' position. The special interrogatory submitted to the jury was in two parts. It first required a finding that

> a motivating factor [in the termination of the respective plaintiff's employment] was the work the plaintiff performed in the campaign of the defendant's opponent and against the defendant. (On *this* question, the *Plaintiff* has the burden of proof.)

(emphasis in original.)
The form continued:

> If your answer to question No. 1 is "Yes" then answer question No. 2.

The second question asked whether the defendant would have taken the same action

> even if [the plaintiff] had not worked in McCullom's campaign: (On *this* question, the *Defendant* has the burden of proof).

(emphasis in original.)
The special interrogatory thus assigned each plaintiff the burden of proving that his or her campaign activities were a motivating

factor in Painter's action. If the plaintiff succeeded, the burden of proof shifted to the defendant to prove that the defendant would have taken the same action with regard to the plaintiff's employment though he or she had not campaigned against the defendant.

According to the defendant, the proper allocation would have required proof that the sole reason for the defendant's unfavorable action was the campaign activities on behalf of Painter's opponent. Moreover, in the defendant's view the burden of proof should have rested entirely on the plaintiffs. It is argued that such an allocation was made in Elrod v. Burns, 427 U.S. 347, 96 S.Ct. 2673, 49 L.Ed.2d 547 (1976), in which the Supreme Court held that employees of the Cook County Sheriff's office could not be discharged solely because of their partisan political affiliation. In *Elrod*, however, unlike the instant case, the issue of the motive for the firings was not disputed. There the defendant conceded that the employees were terminated because they were not Democrats. Thus the Court did not confront the issue of allocating the burden of proof on the motivation issue. Instead the question was whether a complaint alleging firings solely for partisan political reasons stated a First Amendment claim, and the Court held that it did. The similarity between our case and *Elrod* is that in both cases the plaintiffs alleged termination of their employment for political reasons in the context of an election. In our case, however, the defendant hotly contested plaintiffs' allegations that the terminations were political.

Because we are in this case faced with a dispute as to the motive for a termination of employment allegedly for conduct protected by the First Amendment, our case is similar to Mount Healthy City School District Board of Education v. Doyle, 429 U.S. 274, 97 S.Ct. 568, 50 L.Ed.2d 471 (1977). There a nontenured teacher was not rehired allegedly for exercising his First Amendment rights. In *Mount Healthy*, the defendant School Board had stated that one of the two reasons for not rehiring the plaintiff was conduct found by the district court to be "clearly protected by the First Amendment." The district court held that because that reason had played a "substantial part" in the Board's decision, the

plaintiff was entitled to reinstatement with back pay. The Court of Appeals affirmed. The Supreme Court vacated the judgment and remanded for a determination made according to what it held to be the proper allocation of the burden of proof:

> Initially in this case, the burden was properly placed upon respondent to show that his conduct was constitutionally protected and that this conduct was a "substantial factor"—or, to put it in other words, that it was a "motivating factor" in the Board's decision not to rehire him. Respondent having carried that burden, however, the District Court should have gone on to determine whether the Board had shown by a preponderance of the evidence that it would have reached the same decision as to respondent's reemployment even in the absence of the protected conduct.

429 U.S. at 287, 97 S.Ct. at 576 (footnote omitted).

The *Mount Healthy* test was used by the trial judge in the instant case. Each plaintiff had the burden of proving that the protected conduct was a "motivating factor" in the action taken against him before the burden shifted to the defendant to prove that the termination would have occurred even if that plaintiff had not worked for the election of the defendant's opponent. In our view, that allocation was proper.

We must reject the defendant's suggestion that we adopt a "sole motive" test in the case of terminations of employment after a change of administration following an election. To require that the plaintiff prove that the protected conduct was the "sole motive" for his termination would in our view run the risk of not adequately protecting victims of First Amendment violations. One can scarcely imagine an employee about whom an employer could not find some other dissatisfaction apart from that employee's protected conduct. The claim of a public employee who was terminated in fact for protected conduct could too easily be defeated because his employer asserted a convincing but nonmotivating reason for the discharge. The *Mount Healthy* test allows a defendant to terminate an employee for any legitimate reason, even where, as in *Mount Healthy* itself, a reason violative of the First Amendment was also a substantial or motivating factor in the decision. It should also be noted that the plaintiff has the initial burden of proving by a preponderance of the evidence[1] that the protected conduct was a "substantial" or "motivating" factor. That burden is not insignificant. A disgruntled employee fired for legitimate reasons would not be able to satisfy his burden merely by showing that he carried the political card of the opposition party or that he favored the defendant's opponent in the election.

In this case, the evidence showed that James Hickey, the defendant's liasan [sic] to the Senior Citizens' Bus Service and later the Senior Citizens' Coordinator, told Nekolny and Dahms that Painter wanted to terminate their employment because they had worked against her election. Plaintiff Dahms testified that Hickey said Dumas was out of a job for the same reason. It was not disputed that Painter had pledged in her campaign to abolish Dumas' job if she was elected. Nevertheless Dumas did not concede that his job was ultimately abolished but argued that it was resurrected in a somewhat altered form for Hickey who had worked in Painter's campaign. Although Hickey's reduced salary is evidence tending to support the defendant's position that Dumas was terminated for reasons having to do with the goals of the new administration, there was sufficient evidence that Dumas was terminated because he campaigned against Painter to allow that issue to go to the jury. We cannot say as a matter of law that there was no violation of Dumas' First Amendment rights.[2]

III

The defendant also challenges the directed verdict entered in favor of plaintiff Dumas on the issue of whether Dumas was a policymaker and thus excepted from the prohibitions of Elrod v. Burns. Here we agree with the defendant and conclude that the trial judge erred in deciding as a matter of law that Dumas did not occupy a policymaking position.

The policymaking exception was discussed by this court in Illinois State Employees Union v. Lewis, 473 F.2d 561 (7th Cir. 1972), *cert. denied*, 410 U.S. 928, 93 S.Ct. 1364, 35

L.Ed.2d 590 (1973). Then-Judge Stevens stated:

> Plaintiffs properly do not challenge the public executive's right to use political philosophy or affiliation as one criterion in the selection of policy-making (sic) officials. Moreover, considerations of personal loyalty, or other factors besides determination of policy, may justify the employment of political associates in certain positions. . . . [J]ustification is a matter of proof or at least argument, directed at particular kinds of jobs.

473 F.2d at 574.

In Elrod v. Burns, 427 U.S. 347, 96 S.Ct. 2673, 49 L.Ed.2d 547 (1976), Justice Brennan writing for a plurality of the Court, agreed with the *Lewis* distinction between policymaking and non-policymaking employees:

> A second interest advanced in support of patronage is the need for political loyalty of employees, not to the end that effectiveness and efficiency be insured, but to the end that representative government not be undercut by tactics obstructing the implementation of policies of the new administration, policies presumably sanctioned by the electorate. . . . Limiting patronage dismissals to policymaking positions is sufficient to achieve this governmental end. An employee with responsibilities that are not well defined or are of broad scope more likely functions in a policymaking position. . . . [C]onsideration should also be given to whether the employee acts as an adviser or formulates plans for the implementation of broad goals. Thus, the political loyalty "justification is a matter of proof, or at least argument, directed at particular kinds of jobs." Illinois State Employees Union v. Lewis, 473 F.2d at 574. Since, as we have noted, it is the government's burden to demonstrate an overriding interest in order to validate an encroachment on protected interests, the burden of establishing this justification as to any particular respondent will rest on the petitioners on remand, cases of doubt being resolved in favor of the particular respondent.

427 U.S. at 367–68, 96 S.Ct. at 2687.

Recently the Supreme Court, in upholding a determination that assistant public defenders were not policymakers and thus could not be fired for their political beliefs, noted:

> [T]he ultimate inquiry is not whether the label "policymaker" or "confidential" fits a particular

position; rather, the question is whether the hiring authority can demonstrate that party affiliation is an appropriate requirement for the effective performance of the public office involved.

Branti v. Finkel, 445 U.S. 507, 518, 100 S.Ct. 1287, 1295, 63 L.Ed.2d 574 (1980).

The determination of status as a policymaker in many cases presents a difficult factual question. Rosenthal v. Rizzo, 555 F.2d 390 (3d Cir.), *cert denied,* 434 U.S. 892, 98 S.Ct. 268, 54 L.Ed.2d 178 (1977). We are persuaded that the defendant has here presented sufficient evidence from which a reasonable juror could conclude that Dumas' position was within the policymaking exception. A narrow definition of who is a policymaker necessarily increases the chances of "undercut[ting] . . . the implementation of the policies of the new administration, policies presumably sanctioned by the electorate." *Elrod,* 427 U.S. at 367, 96 S.Ct. at 2687. That ability of the government to implement the will of the people is fundamental to our system of representative democracy. We recognize that policymaking and policy implementation may occur at many levels, even within a particular office whose sphere of authority is narrowly circumscribed. The test is whether the position held by the individual authorizes, either directly or indirectly, meaningful input into government decisionmaking on issues where there is room for principled disagreement on goals or their implementation.

That standard must be applied to Dumas, the ex-Senior Citizens' Coordinator of Lyons Township. His functions included conducting feasibility studies and other research concerning the nature and extent of programs for senior citizens. His proposals were directed to the Township Supervisor and the Board of Auditors. One program to help temporarily handicapped senior citizens was implemented by the prior administration at Dumas' recommendation and was abolished when Painter was elected Supervisor. Dumas was one of the four highest paid employees in the Township, tending to signify a position of some influence. That he did not have final decisionmaking authority is not determinative. *See* Indiana State Employers Assoc., Inc. v. Negley, 365 F.Supp. 225 (S.D.Ind. 1973), *aff'd,* 501 F.2d 1239 (7th Cir. 1974). There was, in short, evidence from which a reasonable juror could conclude that the Senior Citizens' Coordinator had meaningful input into decisionmaking concerning the nature and scope of a major township program. Therefore it was for the trier of fact to determine whether Dumas was a policymaker. The district court erred in directing a verdict on that issue.

IV

The defendant next argues that she is immune from liability individually and is liable, if at all, only in her official capacity. The plaintiffs sued Painter both individually and as Supervisor of Lyons Township. Officialcapacity suits, the Supreme Court has stated, "generally represent only another way of pleading an action against an entity of which an officer is an agent. . . ." Monell v. New York City Dept. of Social Services, 436 U.S. 658, 690 n.55, 98 S.Ct. 2018, 2035 n.55, 56 L.Ed.2d 611 (1978). In *Monell* the Court, overruling Monroe v. Pape, 365 U.S. 167, 151 S.Ct. 473, 5 L.Ed.2d 492 (1961), held that local governments were "persons" and thus suable under § 1983. Damages sought from government officers in their official capacity had before *Monell* often been barred as "subterfuges that contravene the exemption from § 1983 announced in *Monroe* [for municipalities]." Muzquiz v. City of San Antonio, 528 F.2d 499 (5th Cir. 1976) (en banc) (adopting in pertinent part 520 F.2d 1002, 1009 (Godbold, J., dissenting)); *see generally* Nahmod, Civil Rights & Civil Liberties Litigation at § 6.04.

Here plaintiffs sued Painter individually in order to be able to collect damages from Painter herself and thus establish that Township funds were not their only source of relief. Now that *Monell* allows municipalities to be sued in their own name, recovery from the public treasury is possible in cases of government officials being sued in their official capacity. Defendant incorrectly leaps to the conclusion, however, that therefore only an official capacity and not an individual suit is appropriate here. We see no reason to assume on the basis of *Monell* that the law of individual liability has changed. We are unpersuaded that the district court should have immunized Painter from individual liability in this action.

Painter also contends that the trial judge erroneously failed to grant her qualified immunity. We do not agree. To be entitled to the special exemption from § 1983 liability provided by the doctrine of qualified immunity, Painter

> must be held to a standard of conduct based not only on permissible intentions, but also on knowledge of the basic, unquestioned constitutional rights of [her employees].

Wood v. Strickland, 420 U.S. 308, 322, 95 S.Ct. 992, 1001, 43 L.Ed.2d 214 (1975).

> She is not immune from liability if she knew or reasonably should have known that the action [she] took within [her] sphere of official responsibility would violate the constitutional rights of [those] affected, or if [she] took the action with the malicious intention to cause a deprivation of constitutional rights or other injury to the [plaintiff].

Id.

Without reaching the issue of her subjective intent we conclude that the trial judge properly determined that Painter knew or should have known that her actions were constitutionally infirm. The jury found that the termination of each plaintiff's employment was politically motivated, in violation of that plaintiff's First Amendment rights. It is clear that the law was not unsettled on this point. In Elrod v. Burns, 427 U.S. 347, 96 S.Ct. 2673, 49 L.Ed.2d 547 (1976), the Supreme Court had expressly forbidden political firings following an election, and in Mount Healthy City School District Board of Education v. Doyle, 429 U.S. 274, 97 S.Ct. 568, 50 L.Ed.2d 471 (1977), the Court held that the presence of both permissible and impermissible motives did not legalize a termination that would not have occurred but for the existence of conduct protected by the First Amendment. Qualified immunity was not available to the defendant here.

V

The defendant alleges that the trial court erred in admitting testimony as to statements allegedly made by James Hickey concerning the defendant's state of mind.[3] Testimony as to Hickey's statements was allowed as admissions against the defendant by her agent. Painter argues that those statements should not have been admitted because Hickey did not have authority to say either what he did or anything else concerning the plaintiffs' employment.

Admissibility in this instance is controlled by Rule 801(d)(2)(D) of the Federal Rules of Evidence, which provides:

> A statement is not hearsay if . . . [it] is offered against a party and is . . . a statement by his agent or servant concerning a matter within the scope of his agency or employment, made during the existence of the relationship. . . .

We cannot say that the trial judge erred in concluding that Hickey was Painter's agent and that his statements concerned "a matter within the scope of his agency or employment." Rule 801(d)(2)(C), unlike 801(d)(2)(D), requires that a statement be "by a person authorized by him to make a statement concerning the subject." Rule 801(d)(2)(D), however, says nothing about an agent having authority to make a statement on a particular subject. After the fact of the agency is established, Rule 801(d)(2)(D) requires only that the statement "concern a matter within the scope of [the] agency or employment." Northern Oil Co., Inc. v. Socony Motor Oil Co., Inc., 347 F.2d 81 (2d Cir. 1965), cited by the defendant for the proposition that the agent must have authority to make statements in a given area, was decided before the enactment of Rule 801(d)(2)(D). In fact, *Northern Oil* was referred to in the Advisory Committee Notes to Rule 801(d)(2)(D) as an example of the older and more narrow view not favored by the Committee. Notes of Advisory Committee on Proposed Rules (*reprinted in* Fed.Rules Evid. Rule 801, 28 U.S.C.A.). Rule 801(d)(2)(D) takes the broader view that an agent or servant who speaks on any matter within the scope of his agency or employment during the existence of that relationship, is unlikely to make statements damaging to his principal or employer unless those statements are true.

Here Painter herself testified that Hickey was her "liaison" and "advisor" to the senior citizens program, in which all three plaintiffs were employed. Painter acknowledged that she met with Hickey "almost every day." Painter stated that she and Hickey had interviewed Dahms for the job, that she and Hickey had discussed Dahms' work, that Hickey had recommended to her that Dahms' work load be reduced, and that she had directed Hickey to communicate news of the reduction to Dahms. Hickey, who had previously investigated and reported to Painter on Nekolny's health and job performance, was charged by Painter with delivery of the letter terminating his employment as well. Painter also conceded that she herself had had almost no contact with any of the plaintiffs. In her brief, Painter argues that an agency cannot be established by the statements of the agent alone. In this case, however, the principal's own testimony establishes the fact and the scope of the agency relationship sufficiently to make the disputed statements admissible.[4]

It is clear to us, as it was to the plaintiffs, that Hickey was speaking of a matter within the scope of his agency or employment when he discussed with Dahms and Nekolny the reasons for the decisions concerning their employment.

VI

Finally, the defendant argues for reversal on the damages awarded for emotional and mental distress. We agree that there was insufficient evidence of injury to support the award.

Although mental and emotional distress caused by the denial of First Amendment rights is compensable, an award of damages for such injury will not stand without proof that such injury actually was caused. *See* Carey v. Piphus, 435 U.S. 247, 264, 98 S.Ct. 1042, 1052, 55 L.Ed.2d 252 (1978); Gertz v. Robert Welch, Inc., 418 U.S. 323, 350, 94 S.Ct. 2997, 3012, 41 L.Ed.2d 789 (1974). The only evidence of injury contained in this record was Nekolny's testimony that on learning he was terminated he was "very depressed," Dahms' statement that she was at one point subsequent to leaving her job "a little despondent and [lacking] motivation," and Dumas' testimony, on being asked whether he looked for employment after losing his job, "Well, I

didn't work for six weeks, I was completely humiliated, and I stayed close to home."

That evidence is insufficient to constitute proof of compensable mental or emotional injury.

> Although essentially subjective, genuine injury in this respect may be evidenced by one's conduct and observed by others. Juries must be guided by appropriate instructions, and an award of damages must be supported by competent evidence concerning the injury.

Carey v. Piphus, 435 U.S. at 264 n.20, 98 S.Ct. at 1052 n.20 (citation omitted).

A single statement by a party that he was "depressed," "a little despondent," or even "completely humiliated" (the latter in the context of explaining why other employment was not sought), is not enough to establish injury even when the statement is considered along with the facts of this case. The circumstances here do not approach the egregiousness of those found in Seaton v. Sky Realty Company, Inc., 491 F.2d 634 (7th Cir. 1974).

Although at one point the trial judge decided that he would not permit evidence on the issue of emotional injury, plaintiffs' counsel did not make an offer of proof according to Federal Rule of Evidence 103(a)(2). Moreover, counsel did not offer to present further evidence when the judge later reversed his position and decided to allow the jury to award damages on this issue. According to the record presented here, plaintiffs were not entitled to damages for emotional injury and the award of those damages must be reversed.

VII

The judgments in favor of Nekolny and Dahms are affirmed except for that portion of the damage award attributable to mental and emotional distress. Because a directed verdict was erroneously entered on the issue of whether plaintiff Dumas was a policymaker, we vacate the judgment and remand for a determination on that issue by the trier of fact. In the event Dumas is found not to be a policymaker, he is entitled to all damages except those attributable to mental and emotional distress.

CUDAHY, Circuit Judge, concurring:

I agree that *Mount Healthy* compels us to shift the burden of persuasion to the defendant once the plaintiffs have made a prima facie showing that political activity was a "motivating factor" in the discharges. As a matter of good policy, however, it is unclear to me why the analysis of Texas Department of Community Affairs v. Burdine, 450 U.S. 248, 101 S.Ct. 1089, 67 L.Ed.2d 207 (1981) should not be equally appropriate here. In *Burdine*, a Title VII case, the Court held that the ultimate burden of persuasion "remains at all time with the plaintiff," although once the plaintiff has proved a prima facie case of discrimination, the defendant bears the intermediate burden of "producing evidence that the plaintiff was rejected, or someone else was preferred, for a legitimate, nondiscriminatory reason." *Id.* 450 U.S. at 254, 101 S.Ct. at 1094.

Although it is a leading decision involving the First Amendment rights of government employees, *Mount Healthy* did not address allegedly partisan political terminations in the framework of an election, where the reasonable prerogatives of the candidates returned by the voters must be weighed in the balance. In addition, successful candidates may be assigned the ultimate burden of proving the propriety of wholly meritorious firings. While the result in the case before us does not seem inappropriate, I am concerned that, in the context of allegedly partisan discharges of defeated campaigners, the broad sweep of the *Mount Healthy* analysis may create undesirable pitfalls for successful candidates.

---

* At the time of oral argument, Judge Swygert was a circuit judge in active service; he assumed senior status on July 1, 1981.
[1] The defendant contends that the trial court erred when it instructed the jury that plaintiffs' burden was to prove their case by a preponderance of the evidence. Painter relies on Judge Campbell's concurrence in Illinois State Employees Union v. Lewis, 473 F.2d 561, 579 (7th Cir. 1972), *cert. denied* 410 U.S. 928, 93 S.Ct. 1364, 35 L.Ed.2d 590 (1973) in which he stated his view that in political discharge cases the burden should remain on the discharged employee to "demonstrate by the clear and convincing weight of the evidence that his dismissal resulted solely because of his political associations."

The *Mount Healthy* decision does not require the plaintiff to prove illegal motivation by clear and convincing evidence, and we have already noted that the test there established does not require that the illegal

reason be the sole motive. The defendant argues, however, that a proper concern that government officials not be harassed by vexatious lawsuits brought in the context of changes in administration mandates a heavier burden than in other First Amendment discharge cases. We decline to adopt the defendant's suggestion. Rather we agree with then-Judge Stevens who addressed that concern in *Lewis*:

> If a government department is, in fact, managed on a nonpolitical basis, there is little likelihood that litigation alleging that dismissals were politically motivated would seriously hamper the administration of government. . . . The price which a government must pay to protect the constitutional liberties of its employees is some loss of the efficiency enjoyed by private employers; the Supreme Court has repeatedly decided that the value of those individual liberties is well worth the cost.
>
> That cost will loom large only if it is assumed that political considerations will motivate a large number of employment decisions. . . . But to the extent employment decisions are based on political considerations, they involve a factor not normally present in the private sector; the tendency of that factor quite clearly is in the direction of less, rather than more, efficiency.

473 F.2d at 575.
[2] There is no merit to the defendant's contention that the verdicts were against the manifest weight of the evidence. Our review of the record reveals sufficient evidence on which the jury could base its findings. Although much of plaintiffs' evidence was controverted by the defendant, issues of credibility are for the jury to decide. Hampton v. Hanrahan, 600 F.2d 600, 625 (7th Cir. 1979).
[3] Plaintiff Nekolny testified that Hickey told him, "You know I tried to talk to Ann Painter. I tried to save your job for you, but the way you and your wife worked in the campaign I can't do anything with Ann Painter. You are being fired." Plaintiff Dahms also testified to hearing Hickey make those statements. Moreover, in a separate meeting with Hickey, Dahms testified that Hickey said "Mrs. Painter was very upset with all of us. She was a very vindictive person and was set on cleaning house and getting rid of everyone that campaigned against her." Dahms also testified that Hickey said he was Painter's "personal hatchet man," that Hickey suggested Dahms was also "going" for campaigning against Painter, and stated that Painter had not "figured out how she was going to get rid of me yet."
[4] Although we need not rely on Hickey's testimony, we note that the

> broadly stated proposition that the authority of an agent cannot be proved "out of the mouth of the agent" is true only if it is considered with its numerous exceptions. . . . For example, when made in court under oath, subject to the tests of cross examination and penalties of perjury, those circumstances are regarded as making the statement sufficiently trustworthy to be received.

Murphy Auto Parts Co. v. Ball, 249 F.2d 508, 510 (D.C.Cir. 1957), *cert. denied,* 355 U.S. 932, 78 S.Ct. 413, 2 L.Ed.2d 415 (1958). Hickey's testimony about his job responsibilities and the testimony of the plaintiffs reinforce our conclusion.

✔ PRACTICE QUESTIONS

Indicate whether each statement is true or false.

1. "A" brought charges against "D" for grand larceny. A hearing occurred where the judge held the charges for consideration of the grand jury. "A" was the only witness at the hearing and was subject to cross-examination. "A" later told "W" that he brought the charges against "D" because "D" had taken away "A's" lady friend and that in truth "D" never took anything of value from "A." "A" had no motive to misrepresent this fact to "W." "A" died before the trial but after the grand jury indicted "D" based on "A's" testimony before that body. The prosecutor attempted to prove his case by reading a transcript of "A's" testimony at the hearing. "W" was called as a witness for the defense and was permitted to testify as to what "A" had told him with respect to "D's" innocence. This was properly admitted.

2. "D" admitted to "W" that he committed a crime that "A" was to go on trial for within a few days. "W" told "A's" lawyer about what he had heard, and the lawyer confronted "D" and asked him to testify at the trial of "A." "D" was in jail serving a term of 30 days, and he had already served 15 days. He told the lawyer that he would confess to the crime from the witness stand. When "D" was brought to the courtroom and was enjoying his holiday away from jail, he had a change of mind. He took the stand, and when questioned on direct examination by the defense attorney, he refused to testify on the grounds of constitutional privilege against self-incrimination. The defense attorney called "W" to the stand, and "W" was permitted to testify what "D" had told him regarding his confession. This was proper.

3. "A" was the owner of Blackacre. He devised Blackacre to "B." "A" lived many years after executing his will and told "C" that he once executed a will devising Blackacre to "B" but that he really did not own the property that he devised because it was really owned by "D," who was the brother of "A." "A" had no motive to misrepresent this fact when he spoke with "C." There was no recorded deed in either "A's" or "D's" name, but they had lived on this land together for over 35 years. They had paid no taxes on the land, but the land had never been sold at a tax sale because of an error in the recorder's office of the town in which Blackacre was situated. "A" died, and his will was probated. There was a contest in that "D" claimed title to the land. At the trial, "C" was not permitted to testify as to what "A" had told him regarding "D's" interest in the land. This was proper (Blackacre was held under the doctrine of adverse possession).

4. Only the following conditions are necessary in order for a declaration against interest to be admissible in evidence:
   (a) the declaration when made must be against the pecuniary or proprietary interest and, more recently, the penal interest of the declarant;
   (b) the declarant is dead or, in some states, unavailable at the time of trial or exercises his or her constitutional privilege against self-incrimination; and
   (c) the declarant had competent knowledge of the facts.

5. "A" had an auto accident in which "P" was severely injured. At the scene of the accident, "A" said to "P," "Don't worry. It was all my fault. My insurance company will pay for your damages." There was a civil action arising out of this collision. "A" died before the trial. "A's" representatives defended the action. Unknown to "A," the insurance company policy had not been paid by "A's"

wife, and the policy had lapsed. "P" was not permitted to testify as to what "A" had said to him. This was proper.

Select the most correct answer to complete each statement based on material included in chapter 13 of this book.

6. (a) A declaration against interest may be admitted into evidence if the declaration is against the moral interest of the declarant.
    (b) A declaration against interest may be admitted into evidence in all states if the declaration is against the declarant's penal interest.
    (c) The declaration against interest rule does not require that the declarant know that the declaration was against his or her interest.
    (d) A material statement of an agent who is acting for a principal that is against the interest of the principal is admissible when offered by a party opponent.

7. (a) To be admissible, a declaration against interest must contain the following elements:
        1. The declaration when made is against the pecuniary or proprietary interest and, in New York and some other states, the penal interest of the declarant.
        2. The declarant is dead at the time of trial (in some states, the declarant may be unavailable).
        3. The declarant had competent knowledge of the facts.
        4. There was no probable motive to misrepresent the facts.
    (b) In New York State, a declaration against penal interest may not be introduced in evidence.
    (c) In a declaration against interest situation, where there is a self-serving and a self-disserving interest, the former must preponderate over the self-disserving interest.
    (d) None of the above.

CHAPTER 14

Self-Serving Declaration

§ 14.1 INTRODUCTION

Generally, a declaration that is characterized as a self-serving declaration or act of a party, whether written or oral, is not admissible in evidence in his favor. Mich.—Kobmann v. Ross, 374 Mich. 678, 133 N.W.2d 195 (1965). Even when the declarant is dead or not available at the time of trial, his or her previous self-serving declaration or act is not admissible.

To understand the idea of a self-serving declaration, it is best to explain it by an example. Let us assume that you are in an automobile accident and a subsequent suit is brought for money damages. Let us further assume that immediately after the collision you jump out of your vehicle and shout at the driver of the other vehicle, "Why did you pass that red traffic light?"

These words uttered by you, if believed by the trier of the facts, would imply that the other driver was at fault and you were not at fault. Now assume that you are later testifying at the trial where you are the plaintiff and you are asked, "Immediately after the collision of the vehicles, what, if anything, did you say to the defendant, and what, if anything, did he say to you?" You reply, "I jumped out of my auto and I shouted at the defendant and asked him why he passed the red traffic light." This statement should be objected to by opposing counsel in that it implies that the defendant passed the red traffic light. On the other hand, you may testify that when you arrived at the intersection, the traffic light was green for you. You are then testifying to a fact seen and perceived, not to a statement in your own favor that you previously made.

The self-serving declaration has been defined as a statement made by a party in his own interest at some time and place out of court; and it does not include testimony which he gives as a witness at the trial. Cal.—Weber v. Leuschner, 240 Cal.App.2d 829, 50 Cal.Rptr. 86 (1966); Conn.—Dawson v. Davis, 125 Conn. 330, 5 A.2d 703 (1939); Ga.—Childers v. Ackerman Constr. Co., 211 Ga. 350, 86 S.E.2d 227 (1955).

§ 14.2 EFFECT OF ADMISSION OF DECLARATION OVER OBJECTION

If there is direct evidence admitted relating to the same matters which a party had been permitted to testify to over objection, even though it was self-serving, it has been held that it should not be considered prejudicial error. Pa.—*In re* O'Keefe's Estate, 27 Leh.L.J. 17 (Orph.Ct.); Tex.—Johnson v. Tunstall, 25 S.W.2d 828 (Tex.Com.App. 1930).

§ 14.3　EFFECT OF FAILURE TO OBJECT

If a self-serving declaration is admitted and the opposing counsel fails to object, the evidence cannot later be objected to as being incompetent and therefore inadmissible. N.Y.—Thyll v. New York and L.B.R. Co., 92 A.D. 513, 87 N.Y.S. 345 (1904).

§ 14.4　ACTS AS SELF-SERVING DECLARATIONS

Acts which are self-serving are a different form of a declaration. They are not admissible. Thus, checks which were endorsed by defendant after the trial in a lower court, which were offered to show his customary method of endorsing checks, were properly excluded as being self-serving acts. Mass.—Benuliewicz v. Berger, 245 Mass. 137, 139 N.E. 784 (1923).

§ 14.5　EXCEPTIONS TO SELF-SERVING DECLARATION EXCLUSIONARY RULE

The following are exceptions to the self-serving declaration exclusionary rule:

1. part of the res gestae,
2. state of mind,
3. charts or drawings, and
4. declarations of pain.

§ 14.6　Part of Res Gestae

When considering the general rules of nonadmissibility of self-serving declarations, if we compare it with the hearsay exclusionary rule, we will find great similarities. You will no doubt remember that we said that hearsay evidence is generally not admissible, but there are exceptions to the hearsay exclusionary rule, so that when there is necessity and a great probability of reliability, we permit this type of evidence into the trial record.

For example, you may recall that res gestae statements are admissible as an exception to the hearsay exclusionary rule. Similarly, res gestae self-serving declarations are admissible as an exception to the self-serving declaration exclusionary rule. Ill.—Werdell v. Turzynski, 128 Ill.App.2d 139, 262 N.E.2d 833 (1970); N.J.—Schloss v. Trounstine, 135 N.J.L. 11, 49 A.2d 677 (1946). However, it must be noted with great emphasis that a party may not bolster his case by testifying to his own self-serving declaration, even if it is part of the res gestae. Minn.—Perkins v. Great N. Ry. Co., 152 Minn. 226, 188 N.W. 564 (1922).

For example, a defendant in a homicide trial could not testify that, simultaneously with the defendant shooting the fatal bullet, the defendant said to the deceased, "Don't throw that knife at me." However, another who heard the statement might testify to it on the grounds that it was a res gestae statement, even though it might be self-serving on the issue of justification.

§ 14.7　State of Mind

Self-serving declarations have been admitted to show the state of mind or intention of the declarant and not for the truth of the contents of the statement. Cal.—Alocco v. Fouche, 190 Cal.App.2d 244, 11 Cal.Rptr. 818 (1961); Ensher, Alexander & Barsoom, Inc. v. Ensher, 210 Cal.App.2d 184, 26 Cal.Rptr. 381 (1962); Conn.—McDermott v. McDermott, 97 Conn. 31, 115 A. 638 (1921).

§ 14.8 Charts or Drawings

Charts or drawings made by a party are admissible to clarify testimony, even though they may be self-serving; so, too, are motion pictures. Tex.—Richardson v. Missouri–K–T.R. Co. of Tex., 205 S.W.2d 819 (Tex.Civ.App. 1947).

§ 14.9 Declarations of Pain

Often a physician requires a statement from the patient as to what is hurting the patient. This is necessary for the physician to properly diagnose and treat the illness or injury. It is assumed that the patient is telling the physician the truth because if the patient were lying, he or she might receive treatment that might be injurious. Accordingly, statements of pain made by a patient to a physician for the purpose of diagnosis and treatment are admissible, even though they may later be self-serving in a trial. U.S.—Hartford Accident & Indem. Co. v. Baugh, 87 F.2d 240 (5th Cir. 1936), *cert. denied*, 300 U.S. 679, 57 S.Ct. 670, 81 L.Ed. 883 (1937). If the statement is made to a physician for a purpose other than treatment, it is hearsay and not an exception to the hearsay exclusionary rule; it may be self-serving and therefore not admissible. Mich.—Jones v. President, Village of Portland, 88 Mich. 598, 50 N.W. 731 (1891); Kobmann v. Ross, 374 Mich. 678, 133 N.W.2d 195 (1965); Ohio—Toledo Rys. & Light Co. v. Prus, 7 Ohio App. 412; Tex.—Gaines v. Stewart, 57 S.W.2d 207 (Tex.Civ.App. 1933).

Declarations of groans and screams made by a person to another, not an attending physician, however, were found to be admissible on the ground that it is better and clearer and a more vigorous description of the then existing physical condition of the party by the eyewitness than could be given in any other way. N.Y.—Roche v. Brooklyn City and Newtown R.R. Co., 105 N.Y. 294, 11 N.E. 630 (1887).

To summarize the area of self-serving declarations that courts have held admissible when pain and suffering are the issue before the court, we can say the following:

1. If the person makes an involuntary expression of pain, such as an involuntary scream or a groan or a moan, it is admissible.
2. Declarations of pain that the person makes regarding his or her current condition are not admissible except when a statement is made admissible by some other exception to the hearsay rule, when the declarant is dead, or when the statement is made to a physician for the purpose of treatment.

CROSS-REFERENCES

Richardson on Evidence (9th ed.), Prince ch. 21.

RELATED DECISIONS
Self-Serving Declaration

McDermott v. McDermott
**Supreme Court of Errors of Connecticut, 1921.
97 Conn. 31, 115 A. 638.**

This case introduces you to the economic consequences of marital discord where a husband apparently signed a deed of real property over to his wife, placed the deed in a bureau drawer, and locked the drawer. Apparently, his wife was able to get into the drawer and recorded the deed. In real estate conveyance law, the actual delivery of a deed by the grantor to the grantee is a necessary component in the transfer of ownership of real property. It appears that the husband had no intention of transferring ownership of the property to his wife but executed the document to cause her to do or not do some unknown act. To place this in the vernacular, we might say he did it "to shut her up."

In addition to this behavior, he made some damaging statements to other people with regard to the ownership of the premises. I suggest that you read this case to see how the court decides whether the damaging statements that he made were or were not admissible into evidence. The case may also be a caveat on how to deal with one's spouse in situations such as those indicated in this dispute.

Appeal from Superior Court, New Haven County; Isaac Wolfe, Judge.

Suit by Michael McDermott against Mary McDermott to compel defendant to cause an alleged undelivered deed of real estate owned by the plaintiff to be erased from the land records, and requiring the premises to be conveyed to the plaintiff. Judgment for the plaintiff, with appeal by defendant.

* * *

WHEELER, C.J. The defendant submits her appeal upon the single point as to whether or not the plaintiff, by his acts and conduct, ratified the act of the defendant in placing the deed on record of the premises which the plaintiff seeks, by this action, to have conveyed to him. The defendant's counsel rightly says that the corrections of the finding are not indispensable to the success of her claim of ratification, except the correction of paragraph 43, and all of the motion to correct may well be disregarded, as either not well taken or as immaterial, except as to this paragraph, and this we propose considering at a later stage of the case.

The finding relates that the plaintiff executed a deed of certain premises, made to the defendant as grantee, but never delivered the same, and placed it among his private papers in a bureau drawer and locked the drawer. Afterward, in September, 1919, plaintiff learned that the defendant had taken the deed and placed it on the land records, without the knowledge or consent of the plaintiff. Immediately upon learning of this, the plaintiff made demand upon the defendant for the return of the deed, but defendant said she purposed holding this property. Prior to this time the plaintiff and defendant had been living together in these premises, and, upon defendant's refusal of plaintiff's demand, he moved from these premises, and has not since lived with the defendant. On October 3, 1919, the plaintiff caused a lis pendens to be placed on the land records, giving notice that he claimed title to the property. On October 23, 1919, he caused the present action to be instituted. In December, 1919, he filed his application in the superior court for the appointment of a receiver of the rents of the premises; but, at the suggestion of the court, a bond in lieu thereof was given by the defendant. On March 30, 1921, the plaintiff again brought his application for the appointment of a receiver for the rents, and on March 31, 1921, the court passed an order appointing such receiver. Since its institution the plaintiff has duly pressed this action clear up to the trial.

The defendant relies for her conclusion of ratification upon the acts and statements of the plaintiff in telling a painter who had presented a bill for work done prior to the taking of this deed by the defendant that he should collect it of the defendant as she was the owner of this property; in telling the savings bank, about October 29, 1919, to send its bill for interest which it had sent to the plaintiff, to the defendant; and in telling the water company, and an insurance firm, to send their bills to the defendant. The defendant subsequently paid each of these bills. The trial court also found, in paragraph 43, that—

> "All of said statements aforesaid concerning the sending of the bills to defendant and the ownership of the property were made by plaintiff because defendant had recorded said deed and the premises stood in her name upon the record, and as she was in possession of said property and was receiving the full benefit thereof, the charges against the property should be paid by her. Plaintiff in making such statements did not intend to and did not in fact ratify, confirm, or adopt the act of defendant in taking said deed into her possession and recording the same, nor intend that title to said premises should be and remain in defendant."

The defendant assigns as error this finding that the plaintiff did not intend to, and did not in fact, ratify the taking of the deed in making these statements to the painter, the water company, the savings bank, and the insurance firm; and the defendant insists that the finding, thus corrected, will present a clear case of ratification of the possession by the defendant of this deed and of these premises.

Whether a grantor intended to make delivery of a deed is a question of fact; intention is a mental process, and of necessity it must be proved by the statement or acts of the person whose act is being scrutinized. When the question at issue was whether one had turned over his salary to his wife as a gift, we said:

> "The question, then, is whether, in a situation where the intent of the witness is material, he may testify directly as to his intent at the time of the transaction under investigation. We think he may, since intent is a mental fact requisite to create a gift." Fox v. Shanley, 94 Conn. 350, 362, 109 A. 249, 254 (1920).

And in Meriden Trust & Safe Deposit Co. v. Miller, 88 Conn. 157, 162, 90 A. 228, 229 (1914), we said:

> "We think the finding of the intent to make present gifts was an inference of fact open to the trial court to draw. . . . A question of intent is a question of fact, the determination of which is not reviewable unless the conclusion drawn by the trier is one which cannot reasonably be made."

And in Humiston v. Preston, 66 Conn. 579, 34 A. 544 (1896), we held—where the question of the delivery of a deed depended upon the intent with which an act was performed—that the question was one of fact, and the decision of the trial court thereon was not subject to review on appeal. Wiley v. London & Lancashire Fire Ins. Co., 89 Conn. 35, 39, 92 A. 678 (1915); Kronfield v. Missal, 87 Conn. 491, 493, 494, 89 A. 95 (1914); Saltzsieder v. Saltzsieder, 219 N.Y. 523, 530, 114 N.E. 856 (1917).

The intention with which these statements were made by the plaintiff, whether intending to ratify the conveyance to the defendant or not, was a question of fact, and the evidence amply justified the trial court in finding that the plaintiff did not intend to ratify this conveyance.

If the case were to be disposed of without the further finding of that part of paragraph 43 which recites that in these statements the plaintiff did not in fact ratify the conveyance to defendant, the facts found would lead to the conclusion that the plaintiff did not ratify, whether the conclusion be regarded as one of law or fact, or of mixed law and fact. If ratification be regarded as a question of fact, as our decisions hold, the finding that plaintiff did not intend to ratify of necessity would compel the inference that no ratification then occurred. But if ratification be regarded as a question of law, where the facts are undisputed, the only conclusion which these facts permit is that no ratification took place when these statements were made. Whether there has been a delivery of a deed, or a ratification of a deed, are questions alike in character. Some authorities say the question of delivery is one of law upon the facts. Lee v. Parker, 171 N.C. 144, 151, 88 S.E. 217 (1916); Saltzsieder v. Saltzsieder, 219 N.Y. 523, 530, 114 N.E. 856 (1917); Earle v. Earle, 20 N.J.Law. 347. Others say it is one of law and fact, upon a given set of facts. Johnston v. Kramer Bros. & Co.,

203 F. 733, 736 (D.C. 1913); Midkiff v. Colton, 155 C.C.A. 149, 242 F. 373, 379 (1917). Others hold it to be a question of fact. Bishop v. Burke, 207 Mass. 133, 140, 93 N.E. 254 (1911); Cook v. Lee, 72 N.H. 569, 572, 58 A. 511 (1904). And a few hold it to be ordinarily a question of fact, or a mixed question of law and fact. Wood v. Montpelier, 85 Vt. 467, 82 A. 671, 677, Ann.Cas. 1914D, 500 (1912).

In Humiston v. Preston, 66 Conn. 579, 34 A. 544 (1896), we said that, where the delivery depends upon the intent with which a certain act is performed, the question is one of fact; and similarly we held the question of waiver and abandonment one of fact, Chatfield Co. v. O'Neill, 89 Conn. 172, 175, 93 A. 133 (1915); also acceptance and acquiescence, Evarts v. Johnson, 88 Conn. 683, 686, 92 A. 434 (1914); and whether a contract had been repudiated, McLaughlin v. Thomas, 86 Conn. 252, 258, 85 A. 370 (1913). In Home Banking & Realty Co. v. Baum, 85 Conn. 383, 389, 82 A. 970 (1912), and Curnane v. Scheidel, 70 Conn. 13, 17, 38 A. 875 (1897), the trial court found the ratification as a question of fact. While in Gallup v. Fox, 64 Conn. 491, 495, 30 A. 756 (1895), the charge of the trial court, that ratification was a fact for the jury to find from the evidence, was not held to be error. Devlin on Deeds, vol. 1, (3d Ed.) p. 411, § 268, states the rule to be:

> "The question whether the grantor ratified the delivery, as against a mortgagee from the grantee relying upon the deed, is one that may be submitted to a jury."

Since ratification in a given case depends ultimately upon the intention with which the act or acts, from which ratification is claimed, were done, and since intention is a mental fact, and its finding clearly one of fact, the finding in a given case of ratification is one of fact, and not reviewable, unless the conclusion of ratification, drawn from the facts, is plainly erroneous. Nolan v. New York, N.H. & H.R. Co., 70 Conn. 159, 174, 39 A. 115, 43 L.R.A. 305 (1898). In other words, unless the conclusion drawn be one which men reasoning in a reasonable way would not draw, the finding of ratification must stand, and, except for this limited purpose it is not reviewable.

The exception to a single ruling on evidence is assigned as error. The plaintiff testified in his own behalf, and on cross-examination was asked if he had not gone to the savings bank, the water company, the insurance firm, and the painter, and told them to send their bills to defendant, as she owned the property, and, having answered these questions in the affirmative on redirect he testified that he had, upon learning of the recording of the deed, consulted a lawyer, and caused to be drawn and recorded a lis pendens or caveat. This instrument contained a declaration of ownership of these premises by the plaintiff. The defendant objected to the offer in evidence of this lis pendens, upon the ground that it was a self-serving declaration, made after the fact. It was claimed in explanation of plaintiff's conduct and of his claim that he never intended to convey these premises to defendant. The court admitted the offer, and we think properly. The recording of this instrument was an act indicative of plaintiff's intention, and the fact that it contained declarations in support of plaintiff's claim did not make the act and the instrument inadmissible. Both were inseparable, and unless admitted the truth would have been shut out. We repeat what we said of the rule against the admission of hearsay evidence in Engel v. Conti, 78 Conn. 351, 354, 62 A. 210, 211:

> "It is not one that can be safely strained beyond its established limits."

Other assignments of error we find no occasion to consider.

There is no error.

The other Judges concurred.

Gaines v. Stewart
Court of Civil Appeals of Texas, 1933.
57 S.W.2d 207.

This case was selected to illustrate that not all statements made to a physician regarding pain and suffering are admissible as an exception to the rule against the admissibility of self-serving declarations. It will further enlighten you on insurance coverage. If a defendant in any civil action has insurance coverage that will pay any money damages that might be awarded against the defendant, this fact of insurance coverage should never be made known to the trier of the facts. If it is made known to the trier of the facts before or during the trial, the court should order a mistrial if a motion is made for that relief. This does not mean that one or the other party has won or lost the case, but it might require a new trial from the beginning with a new trier of the facts, whether it be a jury or a judge.

Appeal from District Court, Tom Green County; John F. Sutton, Judge.

Suit by J. C. Stewart against C. I. Gaines. Judgment for plaintiff, and defendant appeals.

* * *

BAUGH, Justice. Suit by Stewart against Gaines for damages to his car and for personal injuries resulting from a collision between his car and a truck owned by Gaines and being operated over a public highway in Tom Green county. Upon the jury's answers to special issues, judgment was rendered in favor of Stewart for $3,604; hence this appeal.

Appellant's first proposition is that it was error to permit Dr. Nibling, who treated Stewart in May, 1929, for his injuries at the time same were received, to testify as to what Stewart told him in May, 1930, approximately one year thereafter, about pains he was then suffering in his knees and legs; because such examination and statements so made in 1930 were not for purposes of treatment, but for the purpose of enabling Dr. Nibling to testify in this suit concerning the injuries theretofore received, the continuing nature of same, and the probable future disability of Stewart resulting therefrom.

We think this contention should be sustained. Dr. Nibling testified that he did not examine Stewart in May, 1930, for purposes of treatment, but to enable him to testify as a witness; and that he had discharged Stewart from treatment for his injuries nearly a year before. It does not appear that Dr. Nibling attempted to discover whether such pains existed in Stewart's legs other than by Stewart's own statements to that effect. These facts and circumstances we think bring such testimony under condemnation of the rule against hearsay and self-serving declarations. T. & N. O. Ry. v. Stephens, 198 S.W. 396 (Tex.Civ. App. 1917) (writ dismissed) is a case directly in point. In Wheeler v. Ry. Co., 91 Tex. 356, 43

S.W. 876 (1898), the same issue was raised, and though the Supreme Court declined to pass upon it because not properly presented, the court did intimate that such testimony was inadmissible. And in M., K. & T. Ry. Co. v. Johnson, 95 Tex. 411, 67 S.W. 768 (1902), a state of facts substantially identical with the instant case, the writ was granted upon the exact question here presented. While the court held in that case that the issue was not properly raised, it clearly committed itself to the view that such declarations under such circumstances are not admissible. A very complete and exhaustive set of annotations from numerous state and federal decisions on this question is to be found in 67 A.L.R. 10. See, also, 17 Tex.Jur., §§ 245 and 272, pp. 589 and 649.

The test in such case appears to be whether the motive and opportunity to fabricate without detection the symptoms complained of is presented. Undoubtedly a qualified physician can testify as to symptoms and conditions of injury or disease made known to or discovered by him in his treatment of his patient. Or to such conditions as he finds in the patient from his own independent examination of him. But where an injured party, for the express purpose of qualifying a physician to testify in his behalf about matters on which such party seeks a recovery, makes statements as to subjective matters of pain, suffering, etc., not disclosed to the physician by other and independent means, there exists both motive and opportunity for the patient to magnify or feign injuries. Under such circumstances his statements become clearly self-serving and hearsay, and should not be admitted.

The next proposition complains that it was error to render judgment against appellant because the issue of ownership of the truck was not submitted to the jury. There was no error in this. It was not a disputed issue. The evidence is uncontradicted that appellant owned the truck in question and that Stayton, the driver at the time of the collision, was his servant acting within the scope of his employment. It was not necessary, therefore, to submit such issue to the jury. Livezey v. Putnam Supply Co., 30 S.W.2d 902 (Tex.Civ.App. 1930) (writ ref); Emergency Clinic v. Continental Inv. Co., 41 S.W.2d 640, 641 (Tex.Civ.App. 1931); Berryman v. Norfleet,

41 S.W.2d 722 (Tex.Civ.App. 1931); Stedman Fruit Co. v. Smith, 45 S.W.2d 804 (Tex.Civ.App. 1932); Article 2190, Rev.St. 1925, as amended by chapter 78, p. 120, Acts Reg.Sess. 42d Leg. (1931), Vernon's Ann.Civ.St. art. 2190. This was not an independent ground of recovery, but merely one of the elements in plaintiff's cause of action. No request was made that it be submitted. See Ormsby v. Ratcliffe, 117 Tex. 242, 1 S.W.2d 1084 (1928); I. T. A. v. Bettis, 52 S.W.2d 1059, 1061 (Tex.Civ.App. 1932) (writ ref.).

Appellant's next proposition raises the issue of misconduct of the jury, in that one juror informed the others that under the law Gaines had to carry insurance on his truck, and that the insurance company, and not Gaines, would have to pay whatever judgment Stewart recovered. This statement was also reaffirmed as true by another juror. Three jurors testified on motion for rehearing that the matter of Gaines having insurance was discussed in the jury room. Two of these jurors, Rice and Key, denied that it in any manner influenced their verdict. The juror Schrum, while he testified on cross-examination that he would not render a larger verdict against an insurance company than he would against an individual, also testified, among other things, with reference to the matter of insurance discussed in the jury room, as follows:

"Q. Is it not a fact you were influenced in how you would answer those questions by considering whether or not Mr. Gaines had insurance?
A. To be plain, I hung the jury for awhile on account they were giving him more than I thought we had evidence to justify.
"Q. Why did you agree to the sum you did agree to?
A. The main thing was, they were all against me on it.
"Q. What other reason?
A. I thought, and knowing they always carried insurance—I knew according to law he had to carry insurance—and at the start nobody seemed to know whether they did or not, and I had in my mind that they did."

And on cross-examination further:

"Q. You gave in because there were eleven against you?
A. I gave in to that and what I had in mind too.

"Q. You would not go into the jury box and willingly render judgment against one party more than you would another?
A. No, sir.
"Q. In agreeing to the sum you did agree upon, were you or not influenced by your belief that Mr. Gaines had insurance?
A. I knew it was the law for them to have it.
"Q. In agreeing to that sum did you or not consider that fact?
A. I cannot say positively, but it is bound to have had a little influence on me."

It has been repeatedly held that injection into the jury's deliberations of extraneous matters not in evidence and prejudicial in character is ground for reversal, unless it appears that no injury to the losing party resulted. And this is particularly true where the jury is informed that some insurance company, and not the defendant named, is to bear the loss, and such information, not in evidence, influenced the jury's verdict. See D. & H. Truck Line v. Lavallee, 7 S.W.2d 661, 663 (Tex.Civ.App. 1928), and cases there cited and discussed; Moore v. Ivey, 277 S.W. 106 (Tex.Com.App. 1926); Great West Mill & El. Co. v. Hess, 281 S.W. 234 (Tex.Civ.App. 1926); Red Star Coaches v. Lamb, 41 S.W.2d 523 (Tex.Civ.App. 1897); S. H. Kress & Co. v. Dyer, 49 S.W.2d 986, 989 (Tex.Civ.App. 1899).

Injection of such extraneous matters, prejudicial in nature, by one or more of the jurors, clearly constitutes misconduct; and where there is any reasonable doubt as to its injurious effect the verdict should be set aside. Casstevens v. T. & P. Ry. Co., 119 Tex. 456, 32 S.W.2d 637, 73 A.L.R. 89 (1930); Moore v. Ivey, supra; Small v. Taylor, 54 S.W.2d 151, 153 (Tex.Civ.App. 1932). Not only was a doubt raised as to other jurors, but we think it clearly appears from the above-quoted testimony of the juror Schrum that his verdict was influenced by the purported information that insurance protected the defendant against liability.

Appellee contends that, since the evidence showed that appellant operated three trucks under a permit, he was required by law to carry liability insurance under Acts 42d Leg. (1931) p. 480, c. 277, § 13 of amendments to article 911b, Vernon's Ann.Civ.St.; that the jurors were presumed to know the law; and that, therefore, no misconduct should result from their discussion of what the law requires. Numerous cases are cited holding that in such cases, where insurance is carried, the insurance company is a proper party to the suit.

However, the record does not sustain appellee's contention. The act cited applies to "motor carriers" and "contract carriers" for hire over the public highways. The evidence in this case shows that Gaines was in the produce business, owned the trucks in question, and hauled his own produce over the highways. There was no evidence that he hauled anything for others for hire. If not, then the requirement of the statute cited that he carry insurance did not apply to him. Under such circumstances and the settled line of decisions, we think the trial court abused his discretion in overruling appellant's motion for a rehearing.

For the errors pointed out, the judgment must be reversed and the cause remanded. The other error complained of by appellant need not occur upon another trial.

Reversed and remanded.

Perkins v. Great Northern Railway Co.

Supreme Court of Minnesota, 1922.
152 Minn. 226, 188 N.W. 564.

This case relates to an accident suffered by a railroad employee, who then made a statement to two people as to how he received his injury. This statement was made about one and a half hours after the occurrence and was held to be inadmissible because it was a self-serving declaration.

Appeal from District Court, Douglas County; Carroll A. Nye, Judge.

Action by J. F. Perkins against the Great Northern Railway Company. Judgment for plaintiff, and motion for new trial was granted, unless plaintiff consent to a reduction in the verdict, which he did, and the defendant appeals from an order denying a new trial. . . .

LEES, C. Plaintiff was head brakeman on one of defendant's freight trains. On September 16, 1920, he was injured when he fell from the train while it was running between Cokato and Smith Lake in this state. He brought this action under the federal Employers' Liability Act (U.S.Comp.St. §§ 8657–8665), charging defendant with negligence in the following particulars: (1) In permitting the handhold on top of a refrigerator car next to the engine to become so insecure that it pulled out as plaintiff was descending from the car to the tender; (2) in operating the engine with a "Johnson bar" or reverse lever, which was so defective that the engineer was unable to control the movements of the train, and, as a consequence, the train was jerked and the refrigerator car suddenly and violently thrown against the engine.

The jury were instructed not to consider the evidence relating to the alleged defective condition of the reverse lever, but that plaintiff was entitled to a verdict if the handhold was defective or if the motion of the train was suddenly and violently checked without warning to plaintiff, and his injury resulted proximately from either cause. A verdict was returned in plaintiff's favor for $31,000. Defendant moved for judgment notwithstanding or for a new trial. The motion for judgment was denied. The motion for a new trial was granted, unless plaintiff consented to accepted a reduction of the verdict to $24,000. He consented to the reduction, and defendant appealed.

1. There was evidence tending to show that the handle of the hatch cover on the refrigerator car next to the engine was missing. It was attached to a block of wood fastened by screws to the roof of the car near the handhold alleged to have been defective. The federal Safety Appliance Act (U.S.Comp.St. § 8605 et seq.) does not extend to hatch handles on refrigerator cars. The accident happened at about 1 o'clock in the morning. Seven or eight hours later, a section man found a hatch handle on the ground beside the track at the place where plaintiff fell from the train. The screws were still in the block of wood, and showed that they had been pulled out of the roof of the car. Defendant's inspectors who examined the car soon after the accident testified that they found the handhold firmly bolted to the roof of the car; that there

was rust on the thread of the bolts, indicating that they had not been recently disturbed; and that the hatch handle was not to be found. Defendant contends that it was conclusively shown that plaintiff grasped the hatch handle instead of the handhold when he attempted to descend from the car; that it gave way and as a result he fell. Plaintiff testified that as he started to go over the end of the car the "grab-iron fell loose," and he lost his balance; that he knew it gave way because he felt it pull through his hand; that he did not know whether it broke away from the car, but did know that the end next to the running board pulled loose. He also testified that he went down the ladder at the end of the car next to the engine earlier in the night, and noticed nothing wrong with the handhold at that time. All the physical facts tend to show that plaintiff was mistaken, and that in fact he grasped the hatch handle instead of the handhold when he started to go down the car, but it is unnecessary to decide whether a verdict based on the charge that the handhold was defective should be allowed to stand, for there must be a new trial for another reason.

* * *

3. When plaintiff was missed, George A. Coppersmith, one of defendant's conductors, took an engine and caboose and went back to look for him. He arrived at the place of the accident at the same time as a farmer named Preus. When plaintiff was giving his testimony in chief, and after he had stated how he was hurt, he was asked this question:

"Q. Was there any talk between you and him [Coppersmith] in regard to the happening of the accident?
A. Yes, sir.
"Q. This talk . . . was about an hour and a half after you were hurt, was it?
A. Yes, sir; something like that.
"Q. Now I wish you would tell the jury what you said to Mr. Coppersmith regarding how the accident happened and what he said to you."

Objection was made on the ground that the question called for hearsay testimony and a self-serving declaration, and that there was no foundation for the admission of a res gestae statement. The objection was overruled, and plaintiff answered:

"He says, 'How did it happen, Buddy?' and I said, 'The engineer jerked the cars, the handhold gave way, and I fell.'"

Subsequently and without objection testimony to the same effect was given by Mr. Preus. In view of this, if it was error to receive plaintiff's testimony, it is doubtful whether the error was prejudicial. But since there is to be a new trial, it is proper to indicate our views respecting the admissibility of the testimony objected to. In harmony with the decided weight of authority, this court has adopted the rule that in general the testimony of a party may not be confirmed by proving previous declarations in his own favor consonant with his testimony. Fredin v. Richards, 66 Minn. 46, 68 N.W. 402 (1896); State v. La Bar, 131 Minn. 432, 155 N.W. 211 (1916); Barrett v. Van Duzee, 139 Minn. 351, 166 N.W. 407 (1918). The exception to the rule mentioned in State v. La Bar was elaborately considered in Lyke v. Lehigh Valley Rd. Co., 236 Pa. 38, 84 A. 595 (1912). See also, 2 Wigmore, Evid. §1124; Jones, Evid. §870. It is clear that the general rule and not the exception is applicable to the testimony in question.

It is suggested that plaintiff's declaration, though self-serving, was so closely connected with the accident that it must be regarded as a spontaneous utterance, and hence was properly received in evidence as part of the res gestae. To say the least, this is doubtful. A considerable period of time intervened between the accident and the declaration—enough to permit of afterthought, which the law distrusts. There was a longer interval of time than in any case where the admission of declarations has been sustained. . . . Lambrecht v. Schreyer, 129 Minn. 271, 152 N.W. 645, L.R.A.1915E, 812 (1915); . . . State v. Rothi, 188 N.W. 50 (Minn. 1922). Conceding for the purpose of this discussion that, in the exercise of the broad discretion possessed by the trial court, it was not required to reject the testimony for this reason, another difficulty is encountered. Plaintiff had testified fully to the circumstances under which he was injured. The jury had his sworn statement. He was not impeached by proof of contrary statements out of court. In effect he was permitted to give in evidence his unsworn self-serving declaration otherwise clearly inadmissible on the theory that because the declaration was part of the res gestae he might testify that he had made it, and that, if made, it tended to prove that the facts were as he had related them from the witness stand. In support of this theory, it may be argued that the law permits one who heard the spontaneous utterance of a party to testify to it and hence there is no good reason why the party himself may not testify to his own exclamations. In Lambrecht v. Schreyer, supra, it was said that the testimony might come from the person who made the declaration, but this was said with reference to testimony given by a witness for the plaintiff, and not by the plaintiff himself. So far as we have discovered, it has never been held that a party may bolster up his case by testimony that he made a self-serving declaration so closely connected with an injury he received as to be part of the res gestae, and a court should be reluctant to adopt a rule of evidence which would tempt a party accidently injured to make evidence for himself. Plaintiff's testimony was not made competent because Preus and Coppersmith heard his statement. It would have been just as competent if heard by someone he did not know and could not procure as a witness. In no state has the res gestae doctrine been extended farther than in Minnesota. The extension now proposed would not serve the purpose of getting at the truth, which is the sole end towards which all rules of evidence should be directed. For these reasons we are of the opinion that plaintiff should not have been allowed to give the testimony in question.

The other denying a new trial is reversed, and a new trial granted.

Alocco v. Fouche
District Court of Appeal of California, 1961.
190 Cal.App.2d 244, 11 Cal.Rptr. 818.

This case was selected to reveal how a self-serving declaration may be admitted only for the purpose of showing the state of mind of the person who made the statement. It was also selected to demonstrate what the legal significance of mutual wills is and how a person should be particularly careful when entering into such an agreement.

KAUFMAN, Presiding Justice.

This is an appeal from a judgment quieting respondent's title to an undivided one-half interest in certain real property held under a deed of gift by the appellant. On appeal, it is argued that the evidence does not support the findings and that the trial court erred in the admission of certain evidence and in its rulings on appellant's affirmative defenses. There is no merit in any of these arguments.

The record reveals the following: The appellant, Ann Fouche, and the respondent, Noel Alocco, are brother and sister and the heirs at law of their parents, Maria and Camillo Alocco. In 1948, Maria and Camillo made and executed a joint and mutual will which contained the following provision: "We, Camillo Alocco and Maria Alocco, husband and wife . . . do each mutually, in consideration of the other making his will, and of the provisions made herein, in each other's behalf, make this our joint and mutual Will and Testament and agree that the same cannot be changed or varied by either, without the consent in writing of the other. . . ."

The will further provided that upon the death of either spouse, all property owned by them at the time of their death was to go to the survivor, and upon the death of the survivor, the property was to be divided equally between the two children. Camillo died on March 27, 1952. The joint and mutual will was duly admitted to probate and Maria appointed as executrix thereof. On April 24, 1952, the court in the probate proceedings terminated the interest of Camillo Alocco, deceased, in and to the real property standing in the name of Maria and Camillo as joint tenants [Parcel 2]; on December 2, 1952, the court made and entered its decree of distribution, whereby the remaining portion of the real property of Maria and Camillo [Parcel 1], together with the balance of the estate, was distributed to Maria Alocco, pursuant to the terms and provisions of the joint and mutual will.

At the time of her father's death, the appellant and her family lived with Maria at the family home. In December, 1952, Maria asked the respondent to live there also. Maria got along very well with him. The appellant and Maria quarreled often and bitterly. In August,

1953, Maria asked the appellant to leave the premises and hired a lawyer to evict her as she would not go voluntarily. Maria also filed a complaint against the appellant, accusing her of taking things from the premises. Thereafter, in violation of the provision of the joint will, Maria on August 24, 1953, executed a will leaving all of her property to the respondent, and a power of attorney authorizing the respondent to borrow money on her property. Maria made certain improvements on the property; she obtained a personal loan for $750, and then increased it to $2,000 and secured it by a promissory note and deed of trust on the property. Maria had a stroke and was bedridden for several months thereafter. The respondent employed extra help to take care of her.

In the early part of 1954, Maria wanted to visit her brother, Mr. Musso, in Connecticut, to urge him to come and live with her on her property. She bought a car and the respondent under the above mentioned power of attorney increased the mortgages on the property to $4,000 in order to pay for the trip. Maria made the trip with the respondent and his family. In June, 1954, the appellant went to the office of attorney Block to demand an accounting from the respondent and received one which was satisfactory except for items of $1,000 for the trip to Connecticut, $750 which he had borrowed from Maria and a further sum of $300 for Maria's clothes and food.

In the latter part of June, apparently at the urging of her sister-in-law, Beatrice Caristi, Maria went to attorney Block, for the purpose of making a new will. Mr. Block drew a new will leaving the property to the appellant and respondent, share and share alike. Beatrice explained the will to Maria in Italian and Maria executed it on July 1, 1954. After this time, Maria went to live with Beatrice who charged her $100 a month to take care of her. Thereafter, the appellant told Maria that she would charge her only $50 a month and promised to be good to her. Maria went to live with the appellant on these terms. The appellant testified that Maria wanted her to take care of the property and use the income to take care of her for the rest of her life. The value of the property was about $40,000 and the income approximately $290 per month.

Thereafter, on October 18, 1954, the appellant went to a lawyer's office with Maria, and Maria executed a deed of gift, conveying all of her property to the appellant. No gift tax return was filed at this time nor delivery of the deed made, and the appellant testified that she considered the property as still belonging to Maria until Maria's death when it would become her own absolutely.

In October, 1956, Beatrice visited Maria at the appellant's home. Maria indicated that she was not happy and wanted to live on her own property with her brother, and asked Beatrice to write to him. Mr. Musso arrived in November, 1956, and went to the appellant's home with Beatrice, who began to discuss the arrangements for carrying out Maria's wishes. A heated argument started during which the appellant claimed to be the owner of the property in question under the deed of gift. Maria repeatedly denied the appellant's ownership and stated that the property was still her own. The dispute raged for several days and all attempts to settle it were unsuccessful. Maria became ill and was hospitalized. Appellant removed her from the hospital after a few days, and would not permit Beatrice or anyone to see or talk to Maria. At one time, the appellant told Beatrice that Maria had gone to Italy, and would not let Beatrice's husband into the house.

Thereafter, on November 9, 1956, Beatrice instituted an action [No. 277634] to set aside the deed on grounds of fraud and undue influence and also filed a petition for guardianship of Maria. The sheriff was unable to find Maria to serve the papers on her and a subsequent attempt at service was also unsuccessful. Finally, the papers were served on appellant's attorneys and a conference was arranged for December 17, 1956, at the Alameda County Courthouse. Beatrice's attorney was allowed to talk to Maria, but Beatrice was not permitted to do so.

While this matter was pending, Maria died on July 9, 1957. Thereafter, the respondent was substituted as plaintiff in Beatrice's action [No. 277634], and filed an action [No. 287432], on the contract in the joint and mutual will for quasi-specific performance for his half of the real property. The appellant set up the affirmative defenses of unclean hands and estoppel due to the probate court's distribution of the estate of Camillo to Maria without restrictions. The two actions were consolidated for trial.

The trial court found the material facts as stated above, and further found that the appellant occupied a confidential and fiduciary relationship to Maria; that the appellant took advantage of this relationship and obtained a deed of gift by the exercise of undue influence over Maria; that at the time of the execution of the deed of gift, Maria did not intend to convey the said real property to the appellant nor to divest herself of her interest therein; that Maria did not comprehend the nature of the document she was signing and did not know whether it was a will or a deed because the legal effect of signing such a document was apparently not explained to her and she did not have the mental ability to comprehend the nature or legal effect of her act; likewise, the appellant understood that Maria did not intend to convey the title to said real property to her but understood that it was in the nature of an attempted testamentary disposition of her property to the appellant.

The court further found that the effect of the said joint and mutual will was both testamentary and contractual, and that the said contract and agreement in the joint and mutual will was fair and reasonable and adequately supported by good and sufficient consideration; that all of the real property acquired by Maria and Camillo was community property; that under the joint and mutual will, the balance of the estate of Camillo was devised and bequeathed to Maria outright to be used by her for her support and maintenance during her life under the terms of the contract in the joint and mutual will, and upon her death the remainder was to be divided equally between the respondent and the appellant, share and share alike; that Maria was in good faith required not to alienate or make a testamentary disposition of the property in violation of the terms of the contract contained in the said joint and mutual will, which she attempted to do by making the said deed of gift of the said real property to appellant; that under said agreement the respondent was entitled to an undivided one-half interest in the real property and that the

appellant by reason of the deed of gift held an undivided one-half interest in the real property as trustee for the respondent and must account to him for one-half of the rents, issues and profits thereof from the date of the death of Maria, and that the respondent's title should be quieted.

The court also found against the appellant on both of her affirmative defenses, and that in order to settle the dispute between the parties, the property should be sold and the proceeds divided between them, and entered judgment accordingly.

The first argument on appeal is that the evidence does not support the findings. We cannot agree. When a finding of fact is attacked on the ground of insufficiency of the evidence, the power of an appellate court begins and ends with the determination as to whether there is any substantial evidence, contradicted or uncontradicted, which will support the finding. Grainger v. Antoyan, 48 Cal. 2d 805, 807, 313 P.2d 848. The evidence is uncontroverted that Maria was severely ill, had only a second grade education in Italy, knew nothing of business affairs, was forgetful, and generally was not very bright; after her stroke in 1953, she was much worse and even more forgetful; she had the mentality of a nine-year-old child. She was also possessed of a violent temper which caused her to alternate in her affections toward her children and fed the flames of various family disputes mentioned above. Her deceased husband was apparently aware of her shortcomings and the joint and mutual will was executed to eliminate any incentive for quarreling. There was also uncontroverted evidence that at the time of the execution of the deed of gift, Maria reposed trust and confidence in the appellant who collected the rents from the real property and had access to Maria's bank account; that the appellant was active in the preparation, execution and recording of the deed of gift and paid no consideration for it. Under these circumstances, appellant had the burden of overcoming the presumption of undue influence. Rieger v. Rich, 163 Cal.App.2d 651, 329 P.2d 770; Faulkner v. Beatty, 161 Cal.App.2d 547, 327 P.2d 41; Sparks v. Sparks, 101 Cal.App.2d 129, 225 P.2d 238; Campbell v. Genshlea, 180 Cal. 213, 224, 180 P. 336. This she has not done. There is no question that the evidence amply sustains the finding that the deed of gift was obtained by the appellant by the exercise of undue influence over Maria and in violation of the contract contained in the joint and mutual will, and that there was no valid and effective delivery of the deed to the appellant.

Appellant next argues that there is no evidence to support the trial court's finding of an alleged agreement between Maria and Camillo that their property was to be divided between the appellant and the respondent. The agreement was in the joint and mutual will, and the authorities in this state are quite definite that the effect of such a document is both testamentary and contractual; that the testamentary provisions may be revoked by either party prior to the death of the other, but after the death of the other and the acceptance of benefits under the provisions thereof by the survivor, the survivor may not make a valid testamentary disposition of the property in violation of the contract. Lich v. Carlin, 184 Cal.App.2d —, 7 Cal.Rptr. 555; Van Houten v. Whitaker, 169 Cal.App.2d 510, 337 P.2d 900; Scherb v. Nelson, 155 Cal.App.2d 184, 317 P.2d 164; Brown v. Superior Court, 34 Cal.2d 559, 212 P.2d 878; Notten v. Mensing, 3 Cal.2d 469, 45 P.2d 198; Sonnicksen v. Sonnicksen, 45 Cal.App.2d 46, 113 P.2d 495; Rolls v. Allen, 204 Cal. 604, 269 P. 450; Estate of Rolls, 193 Cal. 594, 226 P. 608.

Appellant next argues that there is no evidence to indicate the Parcel 2 was community property of Maria and Camillo as this parcel was acquired in 1924 and title taken in joint tenancy. When Beatrice testified that this parcel was acquired during the marriage, appellant's counsel objected. The court in ruling on the objection indicated that there was no question that it was community property. Appellant's counsel made no further objection. There is no question that the court's ruling was proper. While the general rule is that the taking of title as joint tenants is tantamount to a binding agreement that the same should not be held as community property (Schindler v. Schindler, 126 Cal.App.2d 597, 272 P.2d 566), it has long been established that the character of property thus held may be changed by an executed oral agreement between the parties. Woods v. Security-First Nat. Bank, 46 Cal.2d 697, 299 P.2d 657. The agreement may be express or implied (Long v. Long, 88 Cal.App.2d 544, 199 P.2d 47), and the change in status may be shown by the nature of the transaction or appear from the surrounding circumstances (James v. Pawsey, 162 Cal.App.2d 740, 328 P.2d 1023.) Here, the record adequately supports the finding that the property was community. Whatever may have been the form of the title to Parcel 2, the property was acquired with community funds and the presumption of section 164 of the Civil Code applies. Furthermore, the subsequent mutual will evidenced that they would treat the whole as community property (Brewer v. Simpson, 53 Cal.2d 567, 584–585, 2 Cal.Rptr. 609; Lich v. Carlin, supra; Van Houten v. Whitaker, supra).

Appellant next argues that the evidence does not sustain the trial court's finding on her special defense of unclean hands as she is entitled to an accounting from the respondent for the period of time from August, 1953, to July 1, 1954, when he was handling Maria's affairs. The evidence indicates that this matter was instigated by the appellant and Beatrice and subsequently dropped by Maria. The trial court properly ruled that apparently an accounting had been had and the matter was not gone into any further.

Appellant further argues that the court erroneously admitted the testimony of witnesses about their conversations with Maria before and after the execution of the deed to her. The court clearly indicated that the testimony was admissible for the limited purpose of showing Maria's mental capacity and condition was being admitted subject to a motion to strike and that counsel would have ample opportunity to argue the point and file briefs.

Such self-serving declarations are admissible to show the state of mind of the grantor, or donor, or testator at the time of execution of an instrument, his susceptibility to influence and relation to those around him and the beneficiaries. American Trust Co. v. Fitzmaurice, 131 Cal.App.2d 382, 280 P.2d 545; Cox v. Schnerr, 172 Cal. 371, 156 P. 509; Kelly v. Bank of America, 112 Cal.App.2d 388, 246 P.2d 92, 34 A.L.R.2d 578; Pailhe v. Pailhe, 113 Cal.App.2d 53, 247 P.2d 838;

Piercy v. Piercy, 18 Cal.App. 751, 124 P. 561. """... when the intention or state of mind of the alleged donor is involved, evidence of declarations made by him before or after the transaction is admissible though the declarations were not made in the presence of the adverse party. [Citing cases.]""" Pailhe v. Pailhe, supra, 113 Cal.App.2d at page 63, 247 P.2d at page 844.

Appellant's counsel did not ask for a ruling on his motion. The failure of a court to formally rule on evidence received subject to objection is without prejudice if the objections were untenable and the court finds in accordance with the evidence. Clopton v. Clopton, 162 Cal. 27, 121 P. 720; Witkin, Calif.Evid., §718, p. 748.

The final argument on appeal is that the trial court erroneously ruled on her affirmative defense of estoppel. Appellant argues that the probate decree distributing the property to Maria free from any restrictions is conclusive of respondent's rights. It is well settled, however, that jurisdiction over contracts to make a particular disposition of property by will rests in equity and not in probate (Brown v. Superior Court, 34 Cal.2d 559, 560, 212 P.2d 878).

No prejudicial error appearing, the judgment is hereby affirmed.

DRAPER and SHOEMAKER, JJ., concur.

✔ PRACTICE QUESTIONS

Indicate whether each statement is true or false.

1. "A" and "B" had an altercation. When the police officer arrived at the scene, "A" said to the officer, "'B' hit me first." Both "A" and "B" were arrested on cross-complaints, and the police officer was not permitted to testify as to what "A" had said respecting who hit whom first. This was proper.

2. "D," a defendant in a tort action in negligence for pain and suffering, took action pictures of the plaintiff playing tennis after the plaintiff had received his injuries. The plaintiff at the trial testified that he walks with great difficulty since receiving his injury and has been in that condition continuously since the occurrence. "D" was permitted to project the motion pictures after a proper foundation had been laid. This was proper.

3. "P," a plaintiff in a tort action in negligence, told M.D., his physician, about what hurt him. He did this to enable M.D. to properly treat him. Later, at the trial, M.D. attempted to testify as to what complaints of pain "P" had made to him when "P" had visited M.D.'s office for treatment. An objection to this testimony on the basis of self-serving declaration was sustained by the trial judge. This was proper.

4. A defendant in a homicide case was heard to say to the deceased, simultaneously with the shooting of the fatal bullet, "Don't throw that knife at me." The defendant testified that he made the statement. This was improperly received.

5. A self-serving declaration by a prosecution witness was admitted at a trial, and the defendant was found guilty. Another attorney represented the defendant on the appeal. When the second attorney read the transcript of the trial, he noticed that the trial attorney had failed to object to the introduction of the self-serving declaration. In his brief on appeal, he based his main argument on the damage done to his client by the inclusion of the self-serving declaration. The appeals court refused to overturn the conviction on this ground. This was proper.

The following questions are to be answered by indicating the letter that precedes the most correct answer. Questions 6 and 7 are to be answered based upon information given in the introduction to this chapter and in the discussion of the effect of self-serving declarations.

6. (a) A self-serving declaration is a statement made by a litigant, out of court, that reflects a fact to be proved at trial that would be against the interest of the declarant if admitted into evidence at the trial.
   (b) A self-serving declaration is not generally admissible in evidence if its contents are in favor of the declarant.
   (c) It is prejudicial error to admit a self-serving declaration over the objections of another party to litigation.
   (d) Res gestae self-serving declarations are not admissible in evidence at a trial.

7. (a) Acts may be considered to be self-serving declarations.
   (b) In a homicide case, a defendant who is raising the defense of justification can testify that he (the defendant) said to the decedent immediately before he shot and killed him, "Throw that gun on the floor."
   (c) A self-serving declaration cannot be admitted to show the state of mind of the declarant or the truth of the assertion.
   (d) Motion pictures and/or charts are not admissible in evidence to clarify testimony because these items might be considered to be self-serving.

CHAPTER 15

Public Records Exception to Hearsay Exclusionary Rule

§ 15.1 INTRODUCTION

It is often necessary for the contents of a public record to be offered in evidence for the truth of the assertion contained therein. As indicated earlier, a document (record) may be considered as hearsay just as much as an oral statement by one not actually testifying at the time. However, because of the great probability of reliability and, further, because of the necessity of introducing the contents of public records into evidence, the courts have permitted properly authenticated records to be admitted into evidence. It is quite evident that because the public official who has custody of the records has no motive to distort the truth and they were made in the discharge of his or her duty, such records are considered to be received as an exception to the hearsay exclusionary rule.

If the public official were required to be called in every case in which a public record is subpoenaed, it would put a strain on the efficient operation of the office. Hence, the courts have permitted public records that are kept in the ordinary course of business to be admissible in evidence.

Each jurisdiction may have its own rules with respect to the admission of public records as an exception to the hearsay exclusionary rule. In New York, CPLR 4520 reads:

> Where a public officer is required as authorized, by special provision of law, to make a certificate or an affidavit to a fact ascertained, or an act performed, by him in the course of his official duty, and to file or deposit it in a public office of the state, the certificate or affidavit so filed or deposited is prima facie evidence of the facts stated.

§ 15.2 RELEVANCY AND COMPETENCY

Naturally, a public record cannot be admitted unless the facts contained therein are relevant, competent, and material to the issue before the court. Conn.—City of New London v. Pequot Point Beach Co., 112 Conn. 340, 152 A. 136 (1930). The records which are admissible under this exception to the hearsay exclusionary rule are those to which the public officer would be able to testify were he called as a witness. They must deal with observed facts. U.S.—Vanadium Corp. of Am. v. Fidelity & Deposit Co. of Md., 159 F.2d 105 (2d Cir. 1947); N.C.—Hutton v. Willowbrook Care Center, Inc., 79 N.C.App. 134, 338 S.E.2d 801 (1986).

§ 15.3 PUBLIC CHARACTER

Public records must be essentially public in nature. If they are really private records, they may not be admitted into evidence. For example, an entry in the books of a poor persons' asylum, made by an unknown person not in the regular course of the entrant's business, with respect to the date of a child's birth and the name of the mother was held to be inadmissible to prove pedigree. R.I.—Budlong v. Budlong, 48 R.I. 144, 136 A. 308 (1927).

However, records which a private person is required to make and file with the government may be admissible as public records. 32 C.J.S. Evidence §626 (1964); Pa.—Harrison v. Metropolitan Life Ins. Co., 168 Pa.Super. 474, 79 A.2d 115 (1951).

A statement recorded in a death certificate that a decedent committed suicide, where there was no witness to the occurrence, is a mere opinion and is not admissible in a trial of a case where the issue was the fact of the suicide. See Carson v. Metropolitan Life Ins. Co., 156 Ohio St. 104, 100 N.E.2d 197 (1951), for a discussion of this rule.

§ 15.4 BIRTH, DEATH, AND MARRIAGE CERTIFICATES

In all of the states, birth, death, and marriage certificates are required to be filed with the official who has custody of vital statistics. Ordinarily, a physician, a clerk, or a member of the clergy who may not be a public official is the person who prepares these documents. Authorities, however, differ as to the extent to which birth, death, and marriage certificates are admissible to prove matters other than the fact of the event and the date thereof. There is authority that these records are not to be used in litigation between private parties of the facts recorded because they are only kept to assist officials in the conduct of the affairs of their office. Neb.—Sovereign Camp W. W. v. Grandon, 64 Neb. 39, 89 N.W. 448 (1902).

The more modern view is that a certified copy of a death certificate is admissible in all actions, private or public, as prima facie evidence of all facts contained therein. Cal.—Pilcher v. New York Life Ins. Co., 25 Cal.App.3d 717, 102 Cal.Rptr. 82 (1972). However, a different view was adopted in Florida (Charleston Nat'l Bank v. Hennessy, 404 F.2d 539 [5th Cir. 1968]), where the court held that the opinion of a coroner, a layman without medical training, that decedent "apparently had heart attack," based in part on information given him by others at the scene of accident, plus his own observation of the exterior condition of the body, was an inadmissible part of an official death certificate. It is simple to understand that the statement made by the coroner would not have been admitted if the coroner were testifying in person because it would have been hearsay and not an exception to the exclusionary rule.

§ 15.5 PUBLIC RECORDS OF A SISTER STATE

Public records of sister states may be admissible in courts of your state, but they must be properly authenticated. Even though copies of records of other states are sworn to, they may not be received in evidence until it is demonstrated that these records were kept in accordance with law. Ohio—Richmond v. Patterson, 3 Ohio 368 (1828). For example, it has been held that in order to permit the introduction in evidence of a certified copy of the record of the incorporation of a corporation in another state, the laws of such state must authorize its incorporation. Mont.—Harvey E. Mack Co. v. Ryan, 80 Mont. 524, 261 P. 283 (1927).

The record of a sister state must be authenticated by the custodian of the record. The custodian affixes to the document a certification with his or her signature and seal of office. In the legal profession, this is commonly referred to as an authentication flag. It has also been held that a copy of a record which is attested to by a clerk and which did not have a certificate of the secretary of state, judge, or other designated official stating that the attestation of the clerk is in proper form and that he has proper authority, was not received in evidence. Mass.—Bay State Wholesale Drug Co. v. Whitman, 280 Mass. 188, 182 N.E. 361 (1932).

The purpose of the authentication requirements is to guarantee that the original record really exists, as exemplified. This is accomplished by showing

1. that the person certifying the record has the authority to do so,
2. that the person certifying is the current incumbent and keeper of the record,
3. that the signature of the person certifying is genuine, and
4. that the seal is genuine.

The same general rules apply to public records of foreign countries, as well as to state records in federal courts.

§ 15.6 AUTOPSY REPORTS

As the knowledge of medicine and forensic science increases, it becomes increasingly important to the criminal justice community to have the reports of autopsies included in the trial record to "wrap up" a case against a defendant. These autopsy reports are admissible in evidence under the public documents exception to the hearsay exclusionary rule. They could also find their way into the trial record through the business records exception to the hearsay exclusionary rule. The results of an autopsy have been permitted into evidence. Ala.—Simon v. State, 108 Ala. 27, 18 So. 731 (1896); Tex.—McClelland v. Great S. Life Ins. Co., 220 S.W.2d 515 (Tex.Civ.App. 1949).

§ 15.7 JUDICIAL RECORDS

A witness may be asked by the prosecuting officer whether he or she has ever been convicted of a crime. If the witness answers in the negative, the prosecuting officer has the obligation to produce evidence to the contrary if the officer is aware of it. The question is asked of the witness for the purpose of determining the credibility of the witness, not his or her character. In New York, the offering into evidence of a certificate issued by a criminal court, or the clerk thereof, certifying that a judgment of conviction against a designated defendant has been entered in such court constitutes presumptive evidence of the facts stated in such certificate. N.Y.—CPL § 60.60(1).

§ 15.8 FINGERPRINT RECORDS

It is not uncommon for fingerprint records to be introduced into evidence in a criminal trial. These are public records, even though they are not generally open to the inspection of the public without court order. In New York, the legislature has provided that a report of a public servant charged with the custody of official fingerprint records which contains a certification that the fingerprints of a designated person who has previously been convicted of an offense are identical with those of a defendant in a criminal action constitutes presumptive evidence of the fact that such defendant has previously been convicted of such offense. N.Y.—CPL §60.60(2).

§ 15.9 PROOF OF THE EXISTENCE OF A PUBLIC RECORD

Whenever a public record is taken from the office of its custodian, there is great danger that it will be lost, misplaced, or destroyed. Accordingly, the laws of most jurisdictions provide for proof of the existence of the public record by means of duly authenticated copies. Colo.—Landauer v. Huey, 143 Colo. 76, 352 P.2d 302 (1960); N.Y.—CPLR 4540, 4542, and 4543 (incorporating the rules of common law.)

§ 15.10 EXEMPLIFIED COPIES

An exemplified copy of a public record is a copy that is made in the name of the sovereign power. In order for a public record to be admissible in evidence, it is necessary that it should be exemplified by the certificate of the proper officer or otherwise authenticated (Ill.—*In re* Ersch's Estate, 29 Ill.2d 572, 195 N.E.2d 149 [1963]) unless any objection based on lack of such authentication is waived (Vt.—Davenport v. Davenport, 80 Vt. 400, 68 A. 49 [1907]). Copies of public records or documents purporting to be exemplifications or certified copies must be in the proper form and in compliance with statutory requirements as to authentication enacted by Congress or the various state legislatures. N.C.—Neff v. Queen City Coach Co., 16 N.C.App. 466, 192 S.E.2d 587 (1972).

§ 15.11 CERTIFIED COPIES

A certified copy is a copy of an official document certified as correct by the person who has legal custody of the record or by any other official who is authorized by a statute to certify said document. This implies that the officer has compared the copy with the original and that it is a correct transcript therefrom and of the whole of the original. In some states, the authorizing statute requires these words to be spelled out. Particular procedural practices vary in each jurisdiction, but usually the authorizing statute requires a certificate to be attached to the document signed by the legal custodian or duly authorized representative with his or her official seal affixed. In New York, when a certification is made by a county clerk, the county seal must be affixed. N.Y.—CPLR 4540(b).

§ 15.12 EXAMINED OR SWORN COPIES

An examined or sworn copy must be proved by testimony of a person who is on the stand as a witness. The witness testifies that he or she has compared the copy with the original record, word for word, or has examined the copy word for word while another person read the original aloud to him or her. An examined copy can be authenticated only by proof of comparison with the original and not by proof of comparison with some other copy. 32 C.J.S. Evidence §650 (1964); Tex.—Grimes v. Bastrop, 26 Tex. 310 (1862).

§ 15.13 METHODS TO PROVE A PUBLIC RECORD

At common law, public documents could always be proved by the simple manner of examined or sworn copies indicated in the preceding paragraph. If the party wanted to be more effective before the trier of the facts, he or she would use, as an alternative, an exemplified copy or a certified copy. As indicated above, New York is among the many states that have simplified the method of proving public records by providing particular methods of proof by statute (N.Y.—CPLR 4540, 4541, 4542, and finally 4543, which permits proof of a fact or a writing by any other method authorized by any applicable statute or by the rules of evidence at common law). Parol evidence is usually not admissible to prove the contents of a public record, but it is generally admissible to prove that the record does not exist or the record is silent as to particular acts or proceedings. Conn.—Mower v. State Dep't of Health, 108 Conn. 74, 142 A. 473 (1928); Fla.—Kent v. Knowles, 101 Fla. 1375, 133 So. 315 (1931).

§ 15.14 PRIVATE WRITINGS—REVISITED

We previously discussed private writings in connection with the business records exception to the hearsay exclusionary rule. Private writings can also be considered when discussing the public records exception because many writings, although private, may become public. Private writings that might be public or quasi-public may consist of such things as corporate instruments, checks drawn on banks, church registers, baptismal registers, and the like.

Writings such as those enumerated must be proved to be genuine before they are admissible in evidence. The authenticity of the writing may be proved by testimony of anyone who was present when the writing was executed and saw the paper signed by the necessary parties. The proof can also be adduced by circumstantial evidence. Ga.—Cotton States Mut. Ins. Co. v. Clark, 114 Ga.App. 439, 151 S.E.2d 780 (1966); Mich.—Champion v. Champion, 368 Mich. 84, 117 N.W.2d 107 (1962).

§ 15.15 PUBLIC RECORDS (DOCUMENTS) MAY BE BUSINESS RECORDS

Sometimes the terms "public records" and "public documents" are used interchangeably. Furthermore, these records/documents may be admissible under the business records exception to the hearsay exclusionary rule, as described in Chapter 10 and the preceding section, if all requisites of both exceptions are complied with. U.S.—Haskell v. United States Dept. of Agriculture, 930 F.2d 816 (10th Cir. 1991). An example of a public record being held inadmissible occurred in Minnesota (Kelzer v. Wachholz, 381 N.W.2d 852 [Minn.App. 1986]), wherein the defendant in a tort action attempted to introduce into evidence a report of the Bureau of Criminal Apprehension concerning the match of a boot belonging to him and a bootprint found at the scene. The court held that there was a lack of proper foundation because the defendant attempted to introduce the report through the testimony of the property owner, who had no knowledge of or relationship to the report's preparation.

Federal Rule of Evidence 803(8) through (15) describes the hearsay exceptions regarding public records.

§ 15.16 FEDERAL RULE—HEARSAY EXCEPTIONS

Rule 803. Hearsay exceptions; availability of declarant immaterial . . .

(8) **Public records and reports.** Records, reports, statements, or data compilations, in any form, of public offices or agencies, setting forth (A) the activities of the office or agency, or (B) matters observed pursuant to duty imposed by law as to which matters there was a duty to report, excluding, however, in criminal cases matters observed by police officers and other law enforcement personnel, or (C) in civil actions and proceedings and against the Government in criminal cases, factual findings resulting from an investigation made pursuant to authority granted by law, unless the sources of information or other circumstances indicate lack of trustworthiness.

(9) **Records of vital statistics.** Record or data compilations, in any form, of births, fetal deaths, deaths, or marriages, if the report thereof was made to a public office pursuant to requirements of law.

(10) **Absence of public record or entry.** To prove the absence of a record, report, statement, or data compilation, in any form, or the nonoccurrence or nonexistence of a matter of which a record, report, statement, or data compilation, in any form, was regularly made and preserved by a public office or agency, evidence in the form of a certification in accordance with rule 902, or testimony, that diligent search failed to disclose the record, report, statement, or data compilation, or entry.

(11) **Records of religious organizations.** Statements of births, marriages, divorces, deaths, legitimacy, ancestry, relationship by blood or marriage, or other similar facts of personal or family history, contained in a regularly kept record of a religious organization.

(12) **Marriage, baptismal, and similar certificates.** Statements of fact contained in a certificate that the maker performed a marriage or other ceremony or administered a sacrament, made by a clergyman, public official, or other person authorized by the rules or practices of a religious organization or by law to perform the act certified, and purporting to have been issued at the time of the act or within a reasonable time thereafter.

(13) **Family records.** Statements of fact concerning personal or family history contained in family Bibles, genealogies, charts, engravings on rings, inscriptions on family portraits, engravings on urns, crypts, or tombstones, or the like.

(14) **Records of documents affecting an interest in property.** The record of a document purporting to establish or affect an interest in property, as proof of the content of the original recorded document and its execution and delivery by each person by whom it purports to have been executed, if the record is a record of a public office and an applicable statute authorizes the recording of documents of that kind in that office.

(15) **Statements in documents affecting an interest in property.** A statement contained in a document purporting to establish or affect an interest in property if the matter stated was relevant to the purpose of the document, unless dealings with the property since the document was made have been inconsistent with the truth of the statement or the purport of the document.

§ 15.17 FEDERAL RULE—PUBLIC RECORDS

Rule 1005 addresses the admissibility of public records.

Rule 1005. Public records.

The contents of an official record, or of a document authorized to be recorded or filed and actually recorded or filed, including data compilations in any form, if otherwise admissible, may be proved by copy, certified as correct in accordance with rule 902 or testified to be correct by a witness who has compared it with the original. If a copy which complies with the foregoing cannot be obtained by the exercise of reasonable diligence, then other evidence of the contents may be given.

CROSS-REFERENCES

Federal Civil Judicial Procedure and Rules (West 1996) (Rules 803[8], [9], [10], [12], [14]; 901; 902; 1001; and 1005).

Goode & Wellborn, Courtroom Handbook on Federal Evidence (West 1995) (Rules 803[8], [9], [10], [12], [14]; 901; 902; 1001; and 1005).

McCormick, Evidence (4th ed. 1992) (Rules 803[8], [9], [10], [12], [14]; 901; 902; 1001; and 1005).

RELATED DECISIONS
Public Documents

People of the State of New York v. Franklin

Supreme Court of New York, Appellate Division,
Fourth Department, 1961.
14 A.D.2d 985, 222 N.Y.S.2d 173.

This case involves the production of evidence during the punishment phase of a trial after the defendant has been found guilty. A trial that has two phases is usually referred to as a bifurcated trial. In this case, it was important to ascertain whether the defendant had been convicted of his fourth felony. If he had been, he would, under New York law, be subject to a sentence of life imprisonment. In the legal and police parlance, that person is a "four-time loser." In this case, the method of proving prior convictions is set forth in New York Code of Criminal Procedure §482-a, now known as Criminal Procedures Law §60.60(1), and if the convictions were in a foreign state, they had to comply with §395 of the Civil Practice Act, now codified in Rule 4542b of the Civil Practice Law and Rules, which took effect in 1963.

If you are residing and/or studying in a state other than New York, you may have no interest in knowing the New York statutes. However, legislators of each state are accustomed to copying laws from other states, and I encourage you to research your state statutes to ascertain if the requirements for proving a record in your state's courts are the same as those required by the New York statutes in order to prove prior convictions for felonies.

* * *

Before WILLIAMS, P. J., and GOLDMAN, McCLUSKY and HENRY, JJ.

MEMORANDUM. Defendant appeals from his conviction of grand larceny, second degree and from the determination that he was a fourth felony offender. The record amply supports his larceny conviction and this is affirmed. Upon arraignment on the information charging him with having been convicted of prior felonies defendant stood mute. Upon the prior felonies hearing the trial court received in evidence certain exhibits purporting to show convictions of felonies in North Carolina. These documents do not conform to the requisites of Sec. 482-a of the Code of Criminal Procedure. There was no certification of the clerk that the records of conviction had been signed or filed. Furthermore, these exhibits were improperly received for they did not comply with Section 395 of the Civil Practice Act (proof of foreign court records, and proceedings) and section 398-b (authentication of copy). See Martens v. Martens, 284 N.Y. 363, 365, 31 N.E.2d 489 (1941). The County Court did not properly have all the facts before it and could not determine under established rules of question of recognition or nonrecognition when the statutory mandate for qualifying the records of the judgments of conviction was disregarded and where there was admittedly no formal common-law proof to support the introduction of these documents into evidence. The district attorney's contention that a court may take judicial notice of any official seal or signature does not cure the error in the receipt of these exhibits. The limitations upon the availability of judicial notice in such circumstances are pointed out by Judge Cardozo in People v. Reese, 258 N.Y. 89, at p. 98, 179 N.E. 305, at p. 307, 79 A.L.R. 1329 (1932). The prior convictions must be proved beyond a reasonable doubt. (2 Wharton's Criminal Evidence, Sec. 645, p. 539.) The conviction on the prior felonies hearing must be reversed and a new trial had.

Judgment of conviction of grand larceny second degree unanimously affirmed and judgment of conviction of prior felonies unanimously reversed on the law and facts and new trial granted as to prior felonies.

Kelzer v. Wachholz
Court of Appeals of Minnesota,
381 N.W.2d 852 (1986).

This case was selected to demonstrate that the appellate court considered it to be error for the trial court to exclude a report of the Minnesota Bureau of Criminal Apprehension, referred to as BCA in the decision. The trial court excluded the report for lack of foundation. This means that the trial court did not find that any evidence was submitted providing the basis for the BCA report, which concluded that a plaster cast taken of a footprint had insufficient characteristics for any conclusion to be drawn from a comparison with the wet and muddy boot found in the home of the defendant. The plaster casts were not entered into evidence, nor was there a witness who could explain how the casts were made and the negative results demonstrated. Naturally, such a witness would have been subject to cross-examination. This might have satisfied the trial judge's requirement for a proper foundation for the BCA report to be placed in evidence.

However, the appellate court stated that the trial court's decision did not affect the outcome of the trial, and therefore even if the trial court made an error, it would be considered harmless error.

This brings us to another point of law that requires an explanation. There is seldom a lengthy trial that does not contain some errors as to the admittance or nonadmittance of evidence or some statements that the judge or attorneys make during the trial that are improper. We then come to the issue of substantial errors and harmless errors. Substantial errors are those that the appellate court concludes affected the results of the trial. Harmless errors are those that the appellate court believes had no effect on the results of the trial. In this case, you will note that the appellate court stated that errors, if there were errors, were harmless errors and did not change the result of the trial.

A reference is made to comparative negligence in this decision. This is a concept employed in some jurisdictions in negligence actions where a plaintiff and a defendant were both negligent and the trier of the fact may apply a proportion of the negligence to each side. Thus, if the plaintiff was 40 percent negligent and the defendant was 60 percent negligent and $100,000.00 was determined to be the total amount of damages, then the $100,000.00 that the plaintiff would have been entitled to had the defendant been totally negligent would be reduced to $60,000.00.

Negligence is defined as an omission or failure to do an act or perform a duty or an omission or failure due to want of due care or attention.

The court indicates that comparative negligence does not apply in an intentional tort. A tort is a wrong or wrongful act for which a plaintiff can file an action (lawsuit) to recover money to pay for the damages he or she has sustained.

Considered and decided by LESLIE, P. J., and PARKER and CRIPPEN, JJ.

OPINION

CRIPPEN, Judge.

Respondent Leon Kelzer sued appellant Wayne Wachholz to recover damages to his property and punitive damages, alleging that Wachholz committed intentional torts of trespass and damage to property. Ardis Kelzer, Leon Kelzer's daughter, sued Wachholz for personal injuries resulting from the same conduct. The jury found liability and awarded $2500 compensatory damages and $12,500 punitive damages to Leon Kelzer, and $43,540 in compensatory damages to his daughter. Wachholz appeals from the judgment and from the order denying his motions for judgment notwithstanding the verdict and for a new trial. We affirm.

FACTS

Ardis Kelzer lives and works on her family's farm in rural Carver County. As she was returning home at about 12:30 A.M. one night in late September 1983, she found an abandoned pickup truck sitting on the road near a field road that leads into the Kelzer property. The truck was not off on the shoulder of the road but was sitting right in the driving lane, creating a hazard. Ardis noticed that the truck was marked "Wachholz Trucking."

Ardis continued on to the house where she called the sheriff about the truck. After making the call, she went to the barn, where she discovered that two animals had been released from their pen. Ardis confined the animals and left the barn.

Outside, Ardis noticed a light by a machine shed. At first she thought the police had arrived to check on the abandoned truck. Then she realized the light was actually a fire in the machine shed. She went back to the house, awakened her parents, and then ran towards the barn to get some buckets for water. As she ran she slipped, fell, and cut her thumb on a piece of broken glass that was lying on the ground.

The fire had been started in the rock box of a tractor parked in the machine shed. The rock box is a metal, square box on the front end of a tractor, where weights can be placed to balance the machine. At trial, Leon Kelzer testified that over two dozen empty seed sacks were also in the rock box, left over from a previous planting day. Burned pieces of paper were strewn on the floor of the shed, and the remains of burned matches were found nearby. After first using a fire extinguisher on the burning tractor, Leon Kelzer succeeded in driving the tractor out of the shed and over to a water hydrant, where the fire was completely extinguished.

In addition to the damage to the tractor, part of the Kelzer's fence had been torn down, a motorcycle seat had been slashed, and a pickup truck in the shed had dirt in its oil filler pipe, a cut radiator hose, and a broken battery post. Another piece of machinery had a slashed generator belt, a slashed tire, and a missing distributor cap. Tools were also missing from the shed.

Because of Ardis Kelzer's report about the Wachholz truck, the police went to appellant's house about 2:00 A.M. They found the truck there, and discovered that the hood was still warm. They also observed fresh wet mud

on the floor of the truck. When Wachholz's wife let the police into the house, they found appellant asleep in the living room. The police awakened Wachholz and questioned him about his activities that night. He stated that he had no recollection about the last two hours, saying only that he had been at a bar with a friend. He said that he was too intoxicated to remember anything.

The police found a pair of wet, muddy boots and a pair of wet, muddy blue jeans inside the front door of Wachholz's house. Leon Kelzer and one of the police officers testified that the prints found in the mud around the shed and on the field road matched the shape and contour of the boots. The police officer testified that after returning with the boots to the scene and putting them into a print, he formed an opinion that these were the boots that made the prints. Leon Kelzer agreed.

Wachholz, who proceeded pro se, attempted to have a Minnesota Bureau of Criminal Apprehension (BCA) laboratory report admitted into evidence, but the trial court excluded it for lack of foundation. The report concludes that a plaster cast taken of the footprint had insufficient characteristics for any conclusions to be drawn from a comparison with the boot. The boots themselves were admitted into evidence.

Leon Kelzer testified that he was a supervisor on the town board of Waconia from 1979 until 1984 and that his position put Wachholz on the "opposite side of the fence" from him several times. He testified that at a zoning hearing about a month before the September incident, Wachholz and his father had applied for a zoning variance and were in attendance at the meeting, seated behind Kelzer. Kelzer testified that when he made some comments about the inappropriateness of the variance, appellant's father said: "Well, there he goes again, that s.o.b. Everytime he speaks up he's trouble." Wachholz replied: "Well, he'll get his trouble one of these days too." The clerk for the city of Waconia, who was sitting with Kelzer at the zoning hearing, also testified that the appellant and his father made these remarks.

ISSUES

1. Was it error to omit a jury instruction on comparative negligence?
2. Was it error to exclude the BCA report?

ANALYSIS

The Minnesota Rules of Civil Procedure state that:

> No party may assign as error *** omissions in the charge [to the jury], unless he objects thereto before the jury retires to consider its verdict, stating distinctly the matter to which he objects and the grounds of his objections. An error in the instructions with respect to fundamental law or controlling principle may be assigned in a motion for a new trial though it was not otherwise called to the attention of the court.

Minn.R.Civ.P. 51 (1985). Because appellant made no objection to the jury instructions at trial, he may subsequently question the instructions only if there was an error with respect to a fundamental law or controlling principle.

Wachholz alleges that it was error not to give a jury instruction on comparative fault when fault of the plaintiff is obvious. He claims that this instruction should be given without demand when a party proceeds pro se.

Because the case was tried purely as an intentional tort case, appellant's arguments must fail. Intentional tort actions are not subject to the comparative fault statute. *See* Minn.Stat. §604.01 (1984). Fault of Ardis Kelzer, whether obvious or not, is irrelevant to her cause of action.

2. Evidentiary rulings on foundation are committed to the sound discretion of the trial judge and are not the basis for reversal unless that discretion has been clearly abused. Jenson v. Touche Ross & Co., 335 N.W.2d 720, 725 (Minn. 1983). Further, before an error in the exclusion of evidence may be grounds for a new trial, it must appear the evidence might reasonably have changed the result of the trial if it had been admitted. *Id.* The court in *Jenson* was construing Minnesota's harmless error rule. *See* Minn.R.Civ.P. 61. Rule 61 provides:

> No error in either the admission or the exclusion of evidence and no error or defect in any ruling or order or in anything done or omitted by the court or by any of the parties is ground for granting a new trial or for setting aside a verdict or for vacating, modifying or otherwise disturbing a judgment or order, unless refusal to take such action appears to the court inconsistent with substantial justice. The court at every stage of the proceeding must disregard any error or defect in the proceeding which does not affect the substantial rights of the parties.

Minn.R.Civ.P. 61.

Wachholz attempted to admit the BCA report through the testimony of Leon Kelzer, who had no knowledge of or relationship to the preparation of the report. The exclusion of the report was within the judge's discretion because there was lack of foundation.

Relying again on his pro se status, Wachholz nevertheless argues that the trial court erred in excluding the BCA report. He contends that an attorney would have easily established the necessary foundation for the admission of the report. He points out that, had he obtained a certified copy of the report, it would have been inadmissible even without a foundation witness. *See* Minn.R.Evid. 902(4). On the other hand, the trial judge advised Wachholz more than once that he should obtain counsel. The judge also took the time to explain each of respondent's objections and every ruling from the bench. There was no error.

Even if we were to accept appellant's argument, the trial court's decision was harmless. The BCA report merely states that a comparison of the plaster cast with the boot was inconclusive, not that the cast was not of the boot's track.

Even more importantly, if the BCA report had been admitted, and if its admission might have weakened the testimony of Leon Kelzer and the police officer about the match between the prints and the boots, the jury had ample additional evidence upon which to base a verdict for respondent. Wachholz had previously expressed animosity towards respondent. Wachholz never denied doing the damage; he only denied responsibility for it and claimed not to remember where he was or what he was doing from midnight until 2:00 A.M. that night. His truck was parked on the main road where it intersects with the Kelzer field road. His boots and jeans were wet and muddy, and his truck had fresh, wet mud on it. He told the police where he was and with whom, but at trial he did not produce any alibi witnesses on his behalf.

DECISION

The trial court did not err in choosing not to instruct the jury on the law of comparative negligence. It was within the trial court's discretion to exclude the BCA report. Even if error could be found in the exclusion of the report, the decision was harmless.

Affirmed.

✔ PRACTICE QUESTIONS

Indicate whether each statement is true or false.

1. "D" is convicted of driving while intoxicated. The jurisdiction where "D" was convicted makes driving while intoxicated a misdemeanor except where the defendant had previously been convicted of driving while intoxicated. The instant conviction is a felony. Upon sentencing, the prosecutor tells the judge that "D" has been previously convicted of driving while intoxicated in another state. "D" denies this, and a hearing of this issue takes place. The prosecutor presents in evidence, over objection, an abstract of a criminal justice department record of the foreign state with a form signature affixed thereto. It was proper to admit this abstract.

2. "A" is the alleged daughter of "B." "B" died intestate, having great wealth. "A" made claim to her share of the inheritance in a probate (surrogate) court. A trial ensued, and "A" introduced into evidence a certified copy of a birth certificate filed in the same county as the court was located. The certificate was admitted to show the date of birth of "A" and her mother's name. This is proper procedure in all jurisdictions.

3. "A" was married in Cooke County of "X" state. He was previously married in "Y" County of Nebraska without ever obtaining a divorce from his first wife. His second wife did not learn about the former marriage until a month after her marriage to "A." She brought an action for annulment based on a prior marriage that was not dissolved. Her attorney attempted to place an exemplified copy of the record of the prior marriage into evidence. This was not permitted. The action of the judge was proper.

4. "A" had an accident with her motor vehicle. The jurisdiction where the accident occurred requires each motorist to file an accident report with the commissioner of motor vehicles of the state when a person is injured. "B" was injured in this collision. At a trial for damages, "B" submitted into evidence a certified copy of the motor vehicle accident report of "A." This was received and was proper.

5. "A," a clerk of a county, duly authorized by law to certify public records in his possession, certifies that he has compared a purported marriage certificate with a copy of the original, which is kept in his custody. At a trial for criminal bigamy, the prosecutor places in evidence, over objection, the above-indicated certified copy of the copy of the marriage certificate. This is proper.

Select the most correct answer to complete each statement.

6. (a) A public record may be admitted into evidence even though it is not relevant, competent, and material to the issue before the court.
   (b) Public records are considered as hearsay. However, because of the great probability of reliability and, further, because of the necessity of introducing the contents of public records into evidence, courts have permitted properly authenticated public records to be admitted into evidence where the content was relevant, material, and competent to the issues at trial.
   (c) Autopsy reports of pathologists or medical examiners are never admitted into evidence under the public record exception because they are gruesome.
   (d) There is authority that birth records may be admitted in paternity cases to show that the alleged father is named as the father in the child's birth certificate.

7. (a) Public records are admitted into evidence as an exception to the hearsay exclusionary rule in certain circumstances as provided for in the Federal Rules of Evidence.
   (b) Parol evidence is usually admissible to prove the contents of a public record.
   (c) A public record need not be made into an exemplified copy in order to be admissible in evidence.
   (d) Public records may usually be removed to the courtroom in order to be placed in evidence at a trial.

CHAPTER 16

Real Evidence

§ 16.1 INTRODUCTION

You should differentiate among real evidence, circumstantial evidence, rule of evidence, positive and negative evidence, legal evidence, extrinsic evidence, direct evidence, and the like. Not all of these terms are treated in this text so that it might be kept to a reasonable and practical size. However, the terms most often encountered by a law enforcement officer are included. For definitions of the terms above that are not discussed in this book, you are referred to *Black's Law Dictionary*.

You should be particularly familiar with the term "real evidence." This is evidence that can be presented to the trier of the facts to see, touch, or smell or that is generally perceptible to the senses. A book, a bloodstained knife, a revolver, an inscription on a gravestone presented to the court by means of a photograph, and a photograph of a mutilated person are examples of real evidence. The judge has wide discretion in the admission of evidence generally, and particularly in cases in which the display of an actual person or the photograph of a person or a scene may be so gruesome as to be prejudicial to any of the litigants. In such cases, the judge may require the witness to testify from his or her own mouth instead of exhibiting the gruesome subject to the trier of the facts.

§ 16.2 FOUNDATION FOR INTRODUCTION

It is of paramount importance to show the relevance of every item of evidence before it can be considered for admissibility. To satisfy this requirement, the object must be properly identified; it may also be necessary to show that the object exhibited to the jury is in substantially the same condition as it was at the time of the event in issue. N.Y.—People v. Flanigan, 174 N.Y. 356, 66 N.E. 988 (1903).

With regard to establishing the chain of custody of an exhibit, the ultimate question is whether authentication is sufficiently complete so as to convince the court of the improbability that the original item has been exchanged or otherwise tampered with. U.S.—United States v. Mendel, 746 F.2d 155 (2d Cir. 1984), *cert. denied*, 469 U.S. 1213, 105 S.Ct. 1184, 84 L.Ed.2d 331 (1985). In Indiana (Rust v. Guinn, 429 N.E.2d 299 [Ind.App. 1981]), the trial court's admission into evidence of a jar containing chicken manure was upheld.

The admission or exclusion of evidence rests largely within the discretion of the trial court. Ariz.—Arnold v. Frigid Food Exp. Co., 9 Ariz.App. 472, 453 P.2d 983 (1969); N.Y.—Riddle v. Memorial Hosp., 43 A.D.2d 750, 349 N.Y.S.2d 855 (1973); R.I.—Martin v. Estrella, 107 R.I. 247, 266 A.2d 41 (1970). Thus, it is part of the trial judge's function to decide necessary preliminary questions of fact, such as the identity of articles offered in evidence (U.S.—Meadows & Walker Drilling Co. v. Phillips Petroleum Co., 417 F.2d 378 [5th Cir. 1969]; Wyo.—Friesen v.

Schmelzel, 78 Wyo. 1, 318 P.2d 368 [1957]), and having reached the conclusion that the information to be gained by inspection is relevant, the court decides whether the jury will be granted or refused a view of real or personal property (Ill.—Tudor Iron-Works v. Weber, 129 Ill. 538, 21 N.E. 1078 [1889]).

§ 16.3 CRIME SCENE

Most law enforcement agencies have prescribed procedures to guide its personnel when a member of the force comes on the scene of a crime. It is of paramount importance for the solution of the crime and for its ultimate legal prosecution to ensure that there is no interference with any real evidence found on the scene that may destroy its usefulness as evidence in a subsequent criminal action. Articles used in the commission of a crime or connected with it are admissible in evidence, but the prosecution must show a connection between the article and the accused to show relevance.

Where a defendant was charged with conspiracy to commit a robbery that gave the appearance of involving a weapon, evidence of defendant's relation to guns found inside his automobile and of the fact that guns that could be used in the commission of such a crime were available to him was relevant and admissible. U.S.—United States v. Vosper, 493 F.2d 433 (5th Cir. 1974). In a United States Court of Appeals in Kansas, it was held that proof of possession of means or instruments to commit the offense charged is probative. U.S.—United States v. Leaphart, 513 F.2d 747 (10th Cir. 1975).

§ 16.4 EXHIBITION OF PERSONS AND OBJECTS

There is frequently an attempt in paternity proceedings to exhibit the child to the tribunal to show the resemblance between the respondent male and the child. This is an extremely prejudicial practice because if the infant and the father are of the same race, there is usually some similar characteristics that an advocate can point out to prove his or her case. Some jurisdictions still permit the introduction of this evidence, but the better view, which prevails in New York and most other states, is to exclude this type of evidence because the subject of human resemblance is deemed largely a matter of fancy and guesswork; this is especially true concerning very young children. Department of Public Welfare of the City of New York v. Hamilton, 282 A.D. 1025, 126 N.Y.S.2d 240 (1953).

On the other hand, objects that are relevant to the issues of the trial and are in the same condition as at the time of the occurrence are admissible in evidence. When a tangible object is offered into evidence to prove its quality, character, or condition at the time of an earlier occurrence in issue, the article is relevant and competent only if its condition is substantially unchanged, so that its current condition fairly represents the past condition, but changes in condition that do not destroy the evidentiary value of the object do not prevent its reception. U.S.—United States v. Skelley, 501 F.2d 447 (7th Cir. 1974), *cert. denied*, 419 U.S. 1051, 95 S. Ct. 629, 42 L.Ed.2d 647 (1974).

When an object possesses unique characteristics and any material alteration would be readily apparent, a simple in-court identification is sufficient to warrant admission of the object into evidence. N.Y.—People v. Basciano, 109 A.D.2d 945, 486 N.Y.S.2d 434 (1985).

§ 16.5 BLOODSTAINS

Forensic scientists have developed tests to identify bloodstains, indicating the likelihood that the blood was the blood of a particular individual. Scotland Yard has been in the forefront of this investigation with respect to dried bloodstains, and further work was done by Professors Alexander Joseph and Jerome Metzner of John Jay College of Criminal Justice in cooperation with Bryan J. Culliford of the London Metropolitan Police. The resulting publication, entitled *Examination and Typing of Blood Stains in the Crime Laboratory*, is available from the Superintendent of Documents, United States Government Printing Office, Washington, D.C., Stock Number 2700–0083.

Sometimes the question is raised as to whether or not a specimen of blood is from a human or from some other animal. This can be determined, and courts have accepted expert opinions with respect to this finding. Del.—State v. Miller, 14 Del. 564, 32 A. 137 (1895); Pa.—Commonwealth v. Crossmire, 156 Pa. 304, 27 A. 40 (1893).

Experts can determine by the shape of the bloodstain the circumstances of a murder. If the distance the blood falls is short, the stain appears as a round spot. If the blood falls from a greater height, the stain has jagged edges. The greater the height, the more jagged the blood drops will be. If the blood drops are not at right angles to the surface, forensic scientists can determine the movement of the person who was bleeding. These and other facts about bloodstains are known by the experts in this discipline. For the purpose of this text, however, it is sufficient to know that bloodstains are admissible in evidence, and experts can then be called to testify as to the probable significance and origin of these bloodstains. See Dinsmore v. State, 61 Neb. 418, 85 N.W. 445 (1901), for a discussion relating to expert opinion on the flow of blood.

§ 16.6 DNA FINGERPRINTING

Dr. A.J. Jeffries of Leicester University in Great Britain, along with his colleagues, invented a technique that has become known as DNA fingerprinting. The name is derived from deoxyribonucleic acid, the material that makes up the genes. The appellation "fingerprint" has been added because the results obtained from the process are thought to be similar in certainty to the science of fingerprint analysis and classification.

DNA fingerprinting is a multifaceted process that determines the identity of an individual by means of a comparison of complex genetic traits found in such items as blood, semen, skin, and hair roots. Former tests of these items only identified a fraction of the genetic variations. As of the time of this writing, many criminal convictions have been obtained and many paternity proceedings have been conclusively determined as a result of the admission in evidence of expert opinion predicated on DNA fingerprinting.

In Andrews v. State, an Orlando, Florida, case tried in 1988, 533 So.2d 841 (Fla.App.), *review denied*, 542 So.2d 1332 (Fla. 1989), the DNA fingerprint pattern of the defendant was admitted in evidence and found to the satisfaction of the jury to be specific to the defendant. It was alleged by the expert that in the case of this defendant the ratio of certainty was one in ten billion persons (except for identical twins).

DNA fingerprints can be recorded in bar codes similar to those being used on various products at present. The use of DNA fingerprints is a dramatic new weapon for law enforcement. It has been used in Great Britain to exculpate a defendant who had been incarcerated for approximately three months. The perpetrator of the crime was subsequently identified and convicted by his DNA fingerprint.

The concept is gradually being accepted in many jurisdictions in the United States and the United Kingdom. Although the science of DNA fingerprinting is new, many trial courts have admitted the patterns in evidence along with expert testimony.

Any person who is interested in more detailed information on this subject is referred to the following sources:

- Dr. Lawrence Kobilinsky, Professor of Forensic Science, John Jay College of Criminal Justice, New York, N.Y. 10019.
- R. M. White and J. J. Greenwood, "DNA Fingerprinting and the Law," *Modern Law Review* 51 (March 1988): 145–155.
- D. C. Moss, "The New Fingerprints," *American Bar Association Journal* 74 (May 1988): 66–70.

§ 16.7 GARMENTS

Garments worn by a party to the court action that are logically relevant to the issues are admissible in evidence. A landmark case, Warden v. Hayden, 387 U.S. 294, 87 S.Ct. 1642, 18 L.Ed.2d 782 (1967), is best illustrative of this point. In this case, a suspected robber went into his house after being pursued, disrobed, and placed his outermost garments in a washing machine in the cellar of the premises. A constitutional search and seizure issue was also present in this case, but this is not germane to the point illustrated at this juncture in this text. The garments were introduced in evidence after a proper foundation for their relevance was established.

§ 16.8 WEAPONS

If a defendant is accused of a crime of violence in which a weapon was used and he or she is found to possess a weapon at the time of arrest, the weapon is not necessarily admissible in evidence for proof that the defendant committed the crime with which he or she is charged. For example, if the victim had a fatal stab wound, the fact that the alleged perpetrator was found to have a .38 caliber revolver on his person at the time of his arrest would not be relevant to prove that the defendant had stabbed the decedent to death.

Wounds may be examined by experts, who may testify to the kind of gun by which the wound was inflicted. Ky.—Franklin v. Commonwealth, 20 Ky.L. 1137, 105 Ky. 237, 48 S.W. 986 (1899). It follows naturally that if the expert can determine that a particular gun was the cause of the injury, the gun found on the accused that matches the description of the expert would therefore be admissible in evidence because its relevancy is established.

§ 16.9 PHOTOGRAPHS

One picture is worth a thousand words. The admissibility of photographs, however, must be very limited, or the thousand words may convey incorrect conclusions to the trier of the facts.

A photograph must be properly authenticated before it is admissible. Authentication must be made by testimony of a witness who is well acquainted with the subject of the photograph to the effect that the photograph is a substantially true and faithful representation of the place, object, or person sought to be described as it existed at the time pertinent to the inquiry. Mo.—State *ex rel.* State Highway Comm'n v. Cone, 338 S.W.2d 22 (Mo. 1960); N.Y.—Gerzel v. City of New York, 117 A.D.2d 549, 499 N.Y.S.2d 60 (1986); N.C.—State v. Strickland, 276 N.C. 253, 173 S.E.2d 129 (1970); Wyo.—Metcalfe v. Winchester, 72 Wyo. 142, 262 P.2d 404 (1953).

Posed photographs may also be admissible if they are properly authenticated. A person who sustains injuries to his or her body may take photographs of the injured portions of his or her body to show to the trier of the facts how that portion of the body looked after the injury. The complainant or someone in his or her behalf would be required to testify as to when, where, and how the photographs were taken to establish the relevancy. If the pictures are too gruesome, the judge may not permit their introduction, but if the photographs are gruesome, this will not, of itself, render them inadmissible. It is subject to judicial discretion. U.S.—Halk v. Hollins, 629 F.Supp. 1134 (E.D. Mo.1986); Fla.—Breeding's Dania Drug Co. v. Runyon, 147 Fla. 123, 2 So.2d 376 (1941).

The admissibility of photographs is to be determined preliminarily by the trial court in the exercise of sound discretion, but the credibility of testimony that the photograph is a fair representation is a matter for the jury. S.D.—Johnson v. Chicago & N.W. Ry. Co., 71 S.D. 132, 22 N.W.2d 725 (1946). Enlargements of photographs are admissible where there is testimony that the conditions are fairly represented. Mo.—Carver v. Missouri-Kansas-Texas Ry. Co., 362 Mo. 897, 245 S.W.2d 96 (1952).

§ 16.10 X-RAYS

An x-ray that is properly authenticated in a manner similar to the way in which a photograph is authenticated and shown to be accurate may be admitted when it may aid the jury in understanding the nature and extent of injuries sustained by the party to the action. Cal.—Wilburn v. United States Gypsum Co., 16 Cal.App.2d 111, 60 P.2d 188 (1936); Ill.—Cooney v. Hughes, 310 Ill.App. 371, 34 N.E.2d 566 (1941).

§ 16.11 MOTION PICTURES

How many times have we heard that motion pictures are taken of riot scenes, funerals of leaders of organized crime, and plaintiffs in personal injury cases who claim total incapacity although they are photographed playing tennis?

Some states are videotaping trials to speed up the judicial process. Testimony is taken outside of the presence of the judge and jury. When objections are made to the testimony, the judge rules on the objections after a private viewing. The objectionable matter is deleted, and the motion picture of the trial is shown to the jury minus the deleted material. The jury then reaches its conclusions of fact. Florida, among other states, is accepting videotapes of the testimony of expert witnesses taken in their own offices.

All of these motion pictures, unknown at the common law, are admissible in evidence today. There is a great danger, however, that cutting out relevant material will affect the conclusion reached by the trier of the facts, and this has to be closely monitored. U.S.—Millers' Nat'l Ins. Co., Chicago, Ill. v. Wichita Flour Mills Co., 257 F.2d 93 (10th Cir. 1958). However, the admissibility of motion pictures is largely left to the discretion of the trial judge. Md.—State v. United R. & Elec. Co., 162 Md. 404, 159 A. 916, 83 A.L.R. 1307 (1932).

In Tennessee (Clark v. St. Thomas Hosp., 676 S.W.2d 347 [1984]), the court held that a videotape reenactment of a hospital patient's fall, which resulted in injuries to the patient, was properly admitted when the tape depicted events as testified to by the laboratory technician. The decision in this case includes a succinct review of the admissibility of photographic evidence.

Videotapes and photographs are admissible if their probative value is not outweighed by their inflammatory effect. Ill.—Barenbrugge v. Rich, 141 Ill.App.3d 1046, 96 Ill. Dec. 163, 490 N.E.2d 1368 (1986).

Aerial photographs by law enforcement officers have taken on a new importance since the United States Supreme Court decided California v. Ciraolo, 476 U.S. 207, 106 S.Ct. 1809, 90 L.Ed.2d 210, 39 Cr.L. 3106 (1986), in which the Court permitted a search from a low-flying airplane, even though the police officers in the airplane had no warrant.

§ 16.12 ENLARGEMENTS

Sometimes enlargements of photographs become a practical necessity for the proper presentation of evidence. In this way, an enlarged photograph may be placed on an easel in the courtroom, and an advocate can, by means of a pointer, call the attention of the jury to certain aspects of the enlarged photograph. This can also be accomplished by projection of a negative of the photograph on a screen in the courtroom.

There can be no objection to the admissibility of an enlarged photograph, providing it does not have a tendency to mislead. Ga.—Western & A.R.R. v. Reed, 35 Ga.App. 538, 134 S.E. 134 (1926); N.Y.—Jarvis v. Long Island R.R. Co., 50 Misc.2d 769, 271 N.Y.S.2d 799 (1965), *aff'd*, 25 A.D.2d 617, 268 N.Y.S.2d 963 (1966). However, when the party who produced the enlargements was not present when the enlargements were made and there were variations not visible in the original, the enlargements were excluded. Pa.—Poelcher v. Zink, 375 Pa. 539, 101 A.2d 628 (1954).

The same rules prevail with respect to other enlargements, such as handwriting exemplars, fingerprint pictures, and x-ray negative enlargements.

§ 16.13 AERIAL PHOTOGRAPHS

The judge has discretion as to the admissibility of many items of evidence. This discretion, however, must not be abused so as to become arbitrary, unreasonable, and capricious. Great discretion is given to the jurist, particularly in determining the admissibility of aerial photographs. If other evidence provides the trier of the facts with a sufficiently accurate comprehension of the subject matter, aerial photographs will be excluded. Conn.—Trombly v. New York, N.H. & H. Ry. Co., 137 Conn. 465, 78 A.2d 689 (1951); La.—Airway Homes, Inc. v. Boe, 140 So.2d 264 (La.App. 1962).

§ 16.14 DOCUMENTS

Documents are characterized as real evidence and are admissible when relevant and authenticated. For a thorough discussion of the admissibility of documents and case authorities, see Chapter 10.

§ 16.15 WRITINGS

Writings, like documents, are characterized as real evidence, and their admissibility is treated in Chapter 10. You are likewise referred to the discussion of private and public writings contained in that chapter.

§ 16.16 GRUESOME OR PREJUDICIAL

As previously stated, if pictures are too gruesome, the judge may not permit their introduction, but if the photograph is gruesome, this will not, of itself, render it inadmissible. It is subject to judicial discretion. Fla.—Breeding's Dania Drug Co. v. Runyan, 147 Fla. 123, 2 So.2d 376 (1941). It could occur that a gruesome photograph, the subject of which was capable of testamentary exposition, is offered into evidence and the judge, over objection, permits its introduction. If it is so prejudicial to the party against whom it is offered, some argue that it is sufficiently prejudicial error to result in a reversal. However, the overwhelming weight of authority is to affirm the discretion of the trial judge as to the admission of gruesome photographs. Minn.—Hoffman v. Naslund, 274 Minn. 521, 144 N.W.2d 580 (1966); N.H.—Zielinski v. Cornwell, 100 N.H. 34, 118 A.2d 734 (1955); Wash.—Gephart v. Stout, 11 Wash.2d 184 118 P.2d 801 (1941).

Videotapes and photographs are admissible if their probative value is not outweighed by their inflammatory effect. Barenbrugge v. Rich, 141 Ill.App. 3d 1046, 96 Ill. Dec. 163, 490 N.E.2d 1368 (1986).

§ 16.17 NONVISUAL

Real evidence has been defined as meaning a fact, the existence of which is perceptible to the senses. Vt.—McGrath v. Haines, 125 Vt. 49, 209 A.2d 479 (1965). If we then are referring to the senses, we are referring to perception as a result of outside stimuli, commonly referred to as the five senses of touching, hearing, seeing, smelling, and tasting. If real evidence that is relevant is admissible in evidence, it therefore logically follows that such stimuli that will make a person perceive without the intervention of oral testimony that something was hot to the touch, or smelled like rotten eggs, or was a screeching sound, or felt like a sponge, or tasted sour are the results of conclusions of perception and should, upon proper foundation, be admitted in evidence. Thus, phonograph records which were played in the presence of a jury in a criminal prosecution were held to be admissible. N.Y.—Riddle v. Memorial Hosp., 43 A.D.2d 750, 349 N.Y.S.2d 855 (1973); Pa.—Commonwealth v. Clark, 123 Pa.Super. 277, 187 A. 237 (1936).

§ 16.18 MODELS, DIAGRAMS, AND MAPS

Models, diagrams, and maps, all of which are real evidence, may also be further subdivided to be defined as demonstrative evidence. Real evidence involves the production in court of some object which has a direct part in the incident and includes the exhibition of injured parts of the body. Demonstrative evidence involves the production in court of such things as models, maps, photographs, or x-ray pictures which have no probative value in themselves but serve merely as visual aids to the trier of the facts in comprehending the verbal testimony of the witness. Tex.—Mapco, Inc. v. Holt, 476 S.W.2d 64 (Tex.Civ.App. 1971).

§ 16.19 HANDWRITING EXEMPLARS

Examples of the handwriting of a suspect offered for comparison with the handwriting of another document in evidence are another form of demonstrative evidence. The genuineness of a standard of comparison must be preliminarily and satisfactorily established, and the discretionary action of the trial court in admitting or rejecting the standard will not ordinarily be disturbed. Pa.—Shannon v. Castner, 21 Pa.Super. 294 (1906). There is no violation of Fifth Amendment protection against self-incrimination in requiring a suspect to give handwriting specimens. U.S.—United States v. Mara, 410 U.S. 19, 93 S.Ct. 774, 35 L.Ed.2d 99 (1973).

§ 16.20 PAINT CHIPS OR STAINS

Sometimes it becomes of crucial importance to show that a suspect was at the scene of a crime in the face of denial that he or she was present. If paint chips or stains are detected in his or her clothing or in his or her hair or other parts of his or her person, these specimens may lead to identification of the paint as being similar to that found at the scene of the crime. This can be done by microscopic spectrographic diagnosis and microchemical analysis, even with minute quantities of paint. The paint chip or stain is admissible in evidence subject to the connection of the testimony of the expert witness who will explain its relevance to the issues of the case. For a discussion of this, see Cardwell v. Lewis, 417 U.S. 583, 94 S.Ct. 2464, 41 L.Ed.2d 325 (1974).

§ 16.21 DUST

It may come as somewhat of a shock to the student that even dust could, in a proper case, be real or demonstrative evidence. Such was the case when, in an action against an employer for illness resulting from poisoning, jars of dust collected from the room in which the employee worked were admitted into evidence. N.J.—Davis v. New Jersey Zinc Co., 116 N.J.L. 103, 182 A. 850 (1936).

§ 16.22 BLACKBOARD

Blackboards may be used in the presentation of evidence but under strict restrictions. For example, a witness may not write a copy of a disputed signature on a blackboard and then by alleged copies of authentic writings institute a comparison between them and the copy of the alleged forged signature. Pa.—Groff v. Groff, 209 Pa. 603, 59 A. 65 (1904).

§ 16.23 ARTICLES USED IN CRIME

An article used in the commission of a crime might be a weapon, an automobile, a boat, an airplane, a disguise, or any number of items of personal property that directly or indirectly aided the perpetrator in the implementation of the crime. If these articles have a direct part in the incident, they are admitted as real evidence. If they have no probative value in themselves but serve merely as visual aids to help the trier of the facts comprehend the verbal testimony of a witness, they may also be admitted if it is important for the jury to understand the significance of it and their display is explanatory. Ill.—Smith v. Ohio Oil Co., 10 Ill.App.2d 67, 134 N.E.2d 526, 58 A.L.R.2d 680 (1956).

§ 16.24 INTOXICATION TEST APPARATUS

A defense attorney in an intoxicated driver case may question the results of a drunkometer and may require the prosecution witness to reenact the test in court, subject to the discretion of the judge. However, when there is evidence of scientific tests, such as a drunkometer test, regarding the amount of alcohol in the breath of a suspected intoxicated person, it is essential that the reliability of the tests and the results thereof be generally recognized and accepted before evidence thereof is admissible. Ala.—Rivers v. Black, 259 Ala. 528, 68 So.2d 2 (1953).

§ 16.25 EXPERIMENTS

There is the mythical story of a defense attorney who was defending a client accused of poisoning another. The lawyer showed the jury a bottle of the alleged suspected poison, and in his attempt to prove that the solution could not kill a human being, he drank the solution in front of the jury, to the utter astonishment of all. A recess was immediately called, and the attorney is alleged to have repaired to the men's room, where his aide was waiting with an emetic to induce vomiting. Whether this ever happened is highly improbable, but it is worth remembering in order to show that experiments may be conducted in the courtroom, but the situation must be substantially similar to the factual situation of the issue of the trial.

Generally, the result of an experiment or test is admissible at trial to show the nature, quality, or tendency of an object, provided the conditions under which the experiment or test was conducted were sufficiently similar to those existing at the time in question. N.Y.—Washington v. Long Island R.R. Co., 13 A.D.2d 710, 214 N.Y.S.2d 115 (1961).

§ 16.26 CONTINUITY OF EVIDENCE

In police science, we know that there must be continuity of evidence or the evidence will not be admitted at trial. There is continuity of evidence if the law enforcement authority can demonstrate that the evidence is in the same condition at the trial as it was at the time the property came into the possession of the police authority. Department regulations usually mandate that small articles be scratched with some identification mark, such as the number of the officer's shield, or that they be placed in sealed envelopes and the officer write his or her signature and shield number over the flap so that if it is opened, it will be visible to the eye. The officer is also required to testify what hands the evidence passed through. All of this is done to reasonably assure the trier of the facts that the evidence has not been altered in any way. This is referred to as a chain of custody. Conn.—State v. Brown, 163 Conn. 52, 301 A.2d 547 (1972).

It can be generally said that the unbroken chain of possession must be demonstrated by calling each person who has had access to or possession of the evidence for the purpose of establishing identity and unchanged conditions, and such is particularly required if the sole proof of guilt rests on chemical analysis of a blood specimen or drug and if such proof is available. If circumstances provide reasonable assurances of identity and unchanged conditions and it would be an impossible requirement to produce each physical custodian as a witness, there can be a relaxation of such general rule. N.Y.—People v. Porter, 46 A.D.2d 307, 362 N.Y.S.2d 249 (1974).

§ 16.27 FEDERAL RULES—GENERAL

The Federal Rules of Evidence do not mention the term "real evidence" by name, but in Rule 401, there is a definition of "relevant evidence" as being evidence "having any tendency to make the existence of any fact that is of consequence to the determination of the action more probable or less probable than it would be without the evidence." In Rule 402, it is mandated that "all relevant evidence is admissible, except as otherwise provided by the Constitution of the United States, by Act of Congress, by these rules, or by other rules prescribed by the Supreme Court pursuant to statutory authority. Evidence which is not relevant is not admissible."

Records, documents, and process or system are specifically referred to in Federal Rules of Evidence 901 and 902, and recordings and photographs are covered in Rule 1001. Public records are found in Rule 1005.

Therefore, although the Federal Rules of Evidence do not specifically include all of the items discussed in this chapter, each item is included by inference after reference is made to Rules 401 and 402.

§ 16.28 FEDERAL RULE—EXCLUSION OF RELEVANT EVIDENCE

Rule 403. Exclusion of relevant evidence on grounds of prejudice, confusion, or waste of time

Although relevant, evidence may be excluded if its probative value is substantially outweighed by the danger of unfair prejudice, confusion of the issues, or misleading the jury, or by considerations of undue delay, waste of time, or needless presentation of cumulative evidence.

NOTES OF ADVISORY COMMITTEE ON 1972 PROPOSED RULES

The case law recognizes that certain circumstances call for the exclusion of evidence which is of unquestioned relevance. These circumstances entail risks which range all the way from inducing decision on a purely emotional basis, at one extreme, to nothing more harmful than merely wasting time, at the other extreme. Situations in this area call for balancing the probative value of and need for the evidence against the harm likely to result from its admission. Slough, Relevancy Unraveled, 5 Kan.L.Rev. 1, 12–15 (1956); Trautman, Logical or Legal Relevancy—A Conflict in Theory, 5 Van.L.Rev. 385, 392 (1952); McCormick § 152, pp. 319–321. The rules which follow in this Article are concrete applications evolved for particular situations. However, they reflect the policies underlying the present rule, which is designed as a guide for the handling of situations for which no specific rules have been formulated.

Exclusion for risk of unfair prejudice, confusion of issues, misleading the jury, or waste of time, all find ample support in the authorities. "Unfair prejudice" within its context means an undue tendency to suggest decision on an improper basis, commonly, though not necessarily, an emotional one.

The rule does not enumerate surprise as a ground for exclusion, in this respect following Wigmore's view of the common law. 6 Wigmore § 1849. Cf. McCormick § 152, p. 320, n. 29, listing unfair surprise as a ground for exclusion but stating that it is usually "coupled with the danger of prejudice and confusion of issues." While Uniform Rule 45 incorporates surprise as a ground and is followed in Kansas Code of Civil Procedure § 60–445, surprise is not included in California Evidence Code § 352 or New Jersey Rule 4, though both the latter otherwise substantially embody Uniform Rule 45. While it can scarcely be doubted that claims of unfair surprise may still be justified despite procedural requirements of notice and instrumentalities of discovery, the granting of a continuance is a more appropriate remedy than exclusion of the evidence.

Tentative Recommendation and a Study Relating to the Uniform Rules of Evidence (Art. VI. Extrinsic Policies Affecting Admissibility), Cal. Law Revision Comm'n, Rep., Rec. & Studies, 612 (1964). Moreover, the impact of a rule excluding evidence on the ground of surprise would be difficult to estimate.

In reaching a decision whether to exclude on grounds of unfair prejudice, consideration should be given to the probable effectiveness or lack of effectiveness of a limiting instruction. See Rule 106 [now 105] and Advisory Committee's Note thereunder. The availability of other means of proof may also be an appropriate factor.

CROSS-REFERENCES

Federal Civil Judicial Procedure and Rules (West 1966) (Rules 401 and 402).

Goode & Wellborn, Courtroom Handbook on Federal Evidence (West 1995) (Rules 401 and 402).

McCormick, Evidence (4th ed. 1992) (Rules 401 and 402).

RELATED DECISIONS
Real Evidence

United States v. Skelley

United States Court of Appeals, Seventh Circuit,
1974.
501 F.2d 447.

This case represents a situation where a defendant is "drowning" but attempts to reverse his conviction by "grasping at straws." He assigns many claims of error in his trial that the appellate court summarily dismisses. However, one claim of error the court discusses in great length. He was found in possession of counterfeit American bills. The apparent basic color of the bills had changed from the usual green color to blue at the time of trial, and the jury might have considered this peculiar color as evidence that the defendant must have known that the bills were not genuine and thus had the requisite guilty knowledge to make his possession a crime. He urged that the evidence was improperly admitted and prejudicial in the absence of a foundation showing that the bills were not the same color as when they were seized.

The decision is not too difficult to read and understand, and thus I ask you to read and analyze the court's opinion with respect to this claim of error.

JULIUS J. HOFFMAN, Senior District Judge.

Defendant appeals from a judgment of conviction for unlawful possession of counterfeit obligations of the United States, 18 U.S.C.A. §472. Finding no prejudicial error, we affirm.

Through his court-appointed counsel, defendant relies upon six asserted errors of the district court: (1) a 72-day delay between issuance of the federal warrant for defendant's arrest and his subsequent arrest and arraignment, during which period he was jailed on a related state charge; (2) the admission into evidence of the counterfeit money, allegedly without a proper foundation that the bills were in the same condition—and of the same color—as when seized from defendant; (3) a claimed variance caused by the transposition of two digits in the serial numbers of the counterfeit bills; (4) allegedly prejudicial argument by the United States attorney inviting the jury, without a foundation in expert testimony, to appraise the probability of obtaining fingerprints from a leather wallet; (5) additional allegedly prejudicial argument by the prosecutor, urging the credibility of a witness' prior inconsistent statement which had been admitted to impeach his current testimony and not to prove the truth of the matter asserted; and (6) allegedly improper comment in the prosecutor's summation upon defendant's refusal to answer certain questions without consulting his attorney.

Delay in Arraignment. Defendant's argument concerning the alleged delay in "arraignment" does not involve the familiar principle that a confession is inadmissible if obtained during detention for an unreasonable period of time between the arrest and the prisoner's appearance before a magistrate. See Mallory v. United States, 354 U.S. 449, 77 S.Ct. 1356, 1 L.Ed.2d 1479 (1957); McNabb v. United States, 318 U.S. 332, 63 S.Ct. 608, 87 L.Ed. 819 (1943); 18 U.S.C.A. §3501 (1968). Here no confession was made.

Nor does the case present the question of what remedy, if any, beyond exclusion of confessions, might be appropriate for unreasonable federal detention prior to appearance before a magistrate, in violation of the command of Rule 5(a), Fed.R.Crim.Pro., directing the arresting officer to "take the arrested person without unnecessary delay" before a magistrate. The detention here was by the state, upon charges arising wholly under state law, for driving while under the influence of drugs, unlawful possession of drugs, and possession of hypodermic syringes. After hearing, the district judge found nothing to suggest that this imprisonment was in any way attributable to federal authority, through collusion or otherwise. See United States v. Romano, 482 F.2d 1183, 1190–1191 (5th Cir. 1973); United States v. Moriarty, 375 F.2d 901 (7th Cir.

1967), certiorari denied 388 U.S. 911, 87 S.Ct. 2116, 18 L.Ed.2d 1350 (1967). The defendant would not have gained his liberty by being admitted to bail by a magistrate upon the federal charge, and the supposed delay did nothing to prolong his detention.

The arrest on state charges was made by state officers on January 21, 1973 (a Sunday), and defendant was arraigned the next day on those state charges before the Circuit Court of Effingham County, Illinois, and was detained for want of bail in the county jail. The counterfeit Federal Reserve notes found in defendant's car were delivered to an agent of the United States Secret Service, who swore out a federal complaint on January 29, 1973. The warrant for defendant's arrest on this charge was issued the same day, and a federal detainer was lodged with the state officials. When defendant was released from state custody on April 11, 1973, upon dismissal or imminent dismissal of the state charges, he was immediately arrested on the outstanding federal warrant and taken before a federal magistrate who appointed counsel to represent him.

Nothing in this course of events violates either of the objectives of the prohibition against unreasonable delay between the arrest and the appearance before a magistrate. No confession was elicited during a period of coercive detention, and the detention itself was a result of pending state charges. Even if the detention were somehow attributable to the pendency of federal charges, on a supposition finding no support in the facts, defendant does not argue that he was thereby unlawfully deprived of his liberty in view of his inability to make bail, or that the necessary remedy for prolonged pre-hearing detention is dismissal of the substantive charge even though no prejudice appears. His argument is rather that he was prejudiced because the delay in arresting him under the federal warrant operated to delay the appointment of counsel to defend against the federal charge, and allowed the federal authorities to complete their investigation before defendant's counsel could begin. In this interim, the federal officers obtained a statement, incriminating defendant, from one of his associates.

On analysis, defendant is complaining not about any delay between arrest and the magis-

trate appearance, but about delay in the arrest itself, which would have set the wheels in motion to provide him with defense counsel for the federal charge. A similar claim was rejected by the Supreme Court in United States v. Hoffa, 385 U.S. 293, 310, 87 S.Ct. 408, 17 L.Ed.2d 374 (1966). There defendant complained that the federal authorities' delay in arresting him impaired his right to counsel under the Fifth Amendment, since it permitted the officers to interrogate the defendant without the presence of his lawyer, and that the defendant's statements thus procured were inadmissible. The Court declared: "There is no constitutional right to be arrested. . . . Law enforcement officers are under no constitutional duty to call a halt to a criminal investigation the moment they have the minimum evidence to establish probable cause, a quantum of evidence which may fall far short of the amount necessary to support a criminal conviction." 385 U.S. 310. For the same reasons, in this case the government had no duty to arrest defendant, and provide him with counsel, before continuing its investigation. See United States v. Palazzo, 488 F.2d 942, 948 (5th Cir. 1974); Koran v. United States, 469 F.2d 1071 (5th Cir. 1972). The fact that he was otherwise in custody did not curtail the investigatory power. "When an individual is in custody on probable cause, the police may, of course, seek out evidence in the field to be used at trial against him." Miranda v. Arizona, 384 U.S. 436, 477, 86 S.Ct. 1602, 1929, 16 L.Ed.2d 694 (1966).

Condition of the $20 Bills. In his second assignment of error, defendant claims that the twenty-seven counterfeit $20 bills were improperly admitted into evidence over his objection that no proper foundation had been laid in the absence of evidence that the bills were in substantially the same condition when offered as when they were first seized. Of course, when a tangible object is offered into evidence to prove its quality, character, or condition at the time of an earlier occurrence in issue, the article is relevant and competent only if its condition is substantially unchanged, so that its present condition fairly represents the past condition. See McCormick, Evidence §212 (2d ed. 1972); 7 Wigmore, Evidence §2129 (3d ed. 1940). But changes in condition which "do not destroy the evidentiary value of the object" do not prevent its reception. Comment, Preconditions for Admission of Demonstrative Evidence, 61 Nw.U.L. Rev. 472, 484 (1966). Here the $20 bills partook of the nature of written documents, since their written content was itself evidence of their counterfeit character: the fact that multiple bills bore identical serial numbers established their lack of genuineness. They were adequately identified by government witnesses as the bills found in defendant's automobile. When a written document is properly identified as the same document previously examined, it is implicit in the identification that the content is the same, and nothing would be added by a direct negative answer to the question where its written contents have been altered or changed.

Apart from their written content, defendant asserts that the bills when offered were blue in color, unlike genuine green currency, and argues that the jury might have considered this peculiar color as evidence that the defendant must have known that the bills were not genuine, and thus had the requisite guilty knowledge to make his possession a crime. For this purpose, he urges, the evidence was improper and prejudicial in the absence of a foundation showing that the bills were the same color as when they were seized. While a possible change in color would affect the probative value of the bills on this issue of intent, no change in color could destroy the relevance of the bills to show their counterfeit character from the identity of serial numbers, and their competence as evidence for this purpose is unimpaired by the unexcluded possibility of a change in color. In such a situation, when offered evidence bears on two issues, and a proper foundation has been laid as to one of those issues, the evidence is admissible over a general objection. See McCormick, Evidence, §59 (2d ed. 1972). Here the evidence disclosed that the bills had been subjected to tests and analysis in the process of examining them for fingerprints. Upon appropriate and specific request, the trial judge might have given the jury a cautionary and limiting instruction to forestall any prejudicial inference that the color of the bills remained un-

changed through these tests. No such request was made, and the general objection that no proper foundation had been laid was correctly overruled.

Variance in Serial Numbers. Over defendant's objection, twenty-seven counterfeit $20 Federal Reserve notes were admitted into evidence. Except for serial numbers, the bills were identical. All purported to be notes drawn on the Federal Reserve Bank of Philadelphia, Series of 1969, Check Letter H., Face Plate No. 88, and Back Plate No. 120. Ten fictitious serial numbers were also identical except that two digits were transposed, so that some of the bills bore No. C20309642A while the remainder were numbered C 203 06942A. The indictment alleged that twenty-five of the bills bore the first number, and two the second. When they were offered into evidence, however, it appeared that the indictment's description was erroneous, reversing the quantities. Actually, twenty-five of the bills bore the serial number alleged to be the number appearing on the group of two, and only two contained the serial number described in the indictment as the number on the group of twenty-five. Upon defendant's objection to this variance, the district court granted the government's motion to strike the serial numbers from the indictment, and the numbers were physically obliterated by interlineation. Defendant's objections were overruled.

At the outset, it is clear and conceded that there was no necessity to set forth the fictitious serial numbers in the indictment, and that the indictment would have been legally sufficient without this descriptive surplusage. It is enough that the indictment sets forth "a plain, concise and definite written statement of the essential facts constituting the offense charged," Rule 7(c)(1), Fed.R.Crim.Pro., meeting "the requirement that the accused be informed of the charges against him, so that he can prepare his defense and so that he may be protected against a second prosecution for the same offense." United States v. Cassell, 452 F.2d 533, 536 (7th Cir. 1971). "Setting out the counterfeit bills or describing them by their fictitious serial numbers or otherwise would have afforded no real protection against a second prosecution for the same offense, because the number of identical facsimiles which might possibly be printed are limitless." Neville v. United States, 272 F.2d 414, 416 (5th Cir. 1959), certiorari denied 362 U.S. 924, 80 S.Ct. 678, 4 L.Ed.2d 743 (1960).

In several early cases decided a century ago, it was nonetheless held that if the indictment does set forth the serial numbers by way of description, they must be proved, although surplusage, according to the letter of the charge. See United States v. Hall, 26 Fed.Cas.No. 15,283, p. 82 (Cir.Ct.Dist.Col. 1832); United States v. Mason, 26 Fed.Cas.No. 15,736, p. 1192 (S.D.N.Y. 1875). But see United States v. Howard, 26 Fed.Cas.No. 15,403, p. 388 (C.C.Mass. 1837) (Story, J.). This strict view was explained as merely an application of the prevailing rules against variance between pleading and proof, derived by analogy from the rules applicable in civil proceedings. United States v. Hardyman, 38 U.S. 176, 179, 10 L.Ed. 113 (1839). Today, such a requirement "may well be classed with what the late Justice Holmes designated as 'technicalities that were deemed vital a hundred or perhaps even fifty years ago.'" Simon v. United States, 78 F.2d 454, 455 (6th Cir. 1935). There the Sixth Circuit found no material or fatal variance when the indictment described the counterfeit bill as bearing Face Plate No. 1245 and the number on the bill offered into evidence was I-245. In Heisler v. United States, 394 F.2d 692 (9th Cir. 1968), the Ninth Circuit concluded the variance was not fatal in a bench trial when the indictment described the counterfeit note as a $20 bill and the evidence showed it to be a $10 bill. And in United States v. Taylor, 464 F.2d 240, 241–242 (2d Cir. 1972), the Second Circuit relegated to a footnote its rejection of the claim of variance when the indictment described the counterfeit bills as Treasury notes when the proof revealed them to be Federal Reserve notes. See also United States v. Cassell, 452 F.2d 533, 536 (7th Cir. 1971) (no variance when no proof was offered to show stolen Treasury checks were "genuine" as alleged in indictment). Cf. Graffi v. United States, 22 F.2d 593 (7th Cir. 1927).

Thus the deletion of the serial numbers did not impair the sufficiency of the indictment, and the clerical discrepancy between pleading and proof of the serial numbers did not amount to a fatal variance. Although the numbers were surplusage, unnecessary to plead or prove, defendant argues that it was error to implement these conclusions by the physical act of deleting the serial numbers from the indictment, marking them out. The argument builds upon the base of the constitutional guarantee of indictment by grand jury, as declared by the Fifth Amendment. To allow the prosecutor and court to amend the indictment, to change the nature or character of the crime charged by the grand jury, would be inconsistent with this guarantee. Ex parte Bain, 121 U.S. 1, 7 S.Ct. 781, 30 L.Ed. 849 (1887). Extending the rule, courts have held that an indictment cannot be amended even with the consent of the defendant. See, e.g., Carney v. United States, 163 F.2d 784 (9th Cir. 1947), certiorari denied 332 U.S. 824, 68 S.Ct. 165, 92 L.Ed. 400 (1948). In deference to this principle, the Federal Rules of Criminal Procedure, while generally authorizing amendment of an information (Rule 7[c]), provide only that "on motion of the defendant" the court may "strike surplusage from the indictment." Rule 7(d). The absence of specific authority for deletion of surplusage without defendant's consent has not been construed, however, to forbid the judge from instructing the jury to disregard descriptive surplusage in the indictment which varies from the proof when the written indictment itself remains untouched. United States v. Edwards, 465 F.2d 943, 950 (9th Cir. 1972). Nor does the rule prohibit correction of obvious clerical or typographical errors in the indictment, to change the initial letter of defendant's patronymic from K (Kenny) to D (Denny). United States v. Denny, 165 F.2d 668 (7th Cir. 1947), certiorari denied 333 U.S. 844, 68 S.Ct. 662, 92 L.Ed. 1127 (1948).

While the exceptions do not completely engulf the rule, we are not prepared to make a fetish of the prohibition against amendment of an indictment by holding that it is reversible error to interlineate fictitious serial numbers which are inaccurate solely because of the transposition of two digits in a ten digit string, which could have been omitted entirely from the indictment with no consequence, which need not be proved even if alleged, which the jury could have been instructed to ignore, which might have been corrected as typographical errors which correctly describe some of the bills in evidence, and which are incorrect only with respect to whether the quantity of bills bearing one number or the other is twenty-five or two. Neither the nature nor the gravity of the offense is affected by the discrepancy. Under the circumstances, any technical error that might have been committed by touching pen to paper to alter the indictment itself, is wholly without substance, and could not have prejudiced defendant's rights. In United States v. Buble, 440 F.2d 405 (9th Cir. 1971), the trial court had not merely stricken inaccurate numbers from the indictment, but had permitted the substitution of different numbers, to correct an obvious error in the dates on which allegedly false tax returns had been filed. The Ninth Circuit found no prejudicial error, observing that the "indictment did not require amendments, so amendments did not prejudice the defendant. The variance in the proof from the original indictment still could not have permitted the case to go to the jury." 440 F.2d 406.

* * *

Affirmed.

RELATED DECISIONS
Photographs and Motion Pictures

Breeding's Dania Drug Co. v. Runyon
Supreme Court of Florida, 1941.
147 Fla. 123, 2 So.2d 376.

This case presents an overview of tort law where several parties are named as defendants. In cases such as this, the tendency is for each defendant to say, "I am not responsible; the other party or parties are responsible." The question of the admissibility of photographs into the trial record is discussed. In some cases, the trial judge refused to admit such photographs because the defendant argued that they are too gruesome and might unfairly influence the jury. The defendant also argued that the objects depicted or injuries sustained by a person can be adequately explained by oral testimony.

The trial judge usually has discretion in this matter, but that discretion may not be abused. By reading this case, you can see how the trial judge handled this objection and how the Supreme Court of Florida treated the judge's decision.

Error to Circuit Court, Dade County; Arthur Gomez, Judge.

* * *

ADAMS Justice. Plaintiff recovered a $20,000 judgment against the defendants as joint tort feasors.

The plaintiff, a refrigeration man, was summoned by defendant, Breeding, to make certain repairs on some electrical refrigeration equipment in his drug store. Upon arriving plaintiff pulled the switch to disconnect the current from the compressor. Apparently the current was off, however, the pulling of the switch cut off only 110 of the 220 volts. In the course of the work the plaintiff's body came in contact with the compressor carrying 110 volts, resulting in his injury.

Negligence is charged by Lyon Electric Company for improper wiring. Jersey Ice Cream Company is charged with installing the refrigeration equipment and leaving it to be operated after having knowledge that the wiring was defective and dangerous. Liability is charged to Breeding and Breeding Dania Drug Company for using the aforesaid equipment without inspection as required by city ordinance.

The record convinces us that the equipment was defectively wired. We are also satisfied that the defective wiring was the proximate cause of plaintiff's injury. Did the plaintiff produce sufficient evidence to show the concurring negligence of all the defendants caused the injury? Louisville & N. R. R. Co. v. Allen, 67 Fla. 257, 65 So. 8, 12 L.R.A. 1915C, 20 (1914):

"If their acts of negligence, however separate and distinct in themselves, are concurrent in producing the injury, their liability is joint as well as several. . . . Each becomes liable because of his neglect of duty, and they are jointly liable for the single injury inflicted because the acts or omissions of both have contributed to it."

There was sufficient evidence before the jury that the electrical work was done by defendant, Lyon Electric Company. There was sufficient evidence before the jury that the refrigerating equipment was installed by defendant, Jersey Ice Cream Company, and that its agent knew of the dangerous condition.

The other defendants used the equipment approximately one year without an inspection as required by city ordinance. The occupant of premises is liable for latent defects which proximately cause injury to his invitees. The law fixes the duty of the occupant to exercise a reasonable degree of care commensurate with the surrounding circumstances. King v. Cooney-Eckstein Co., 66 Fla. 246, 63 So. 659, Ann.Cas. 1916C, 163 (1914). The evidence is legally sufficient to submit the case to the jury. The probative weight of the testimony is for the jury. The verdict should not [be] set aside in the absence of a clear showing that it is contrary to the great weight of the evidence.

The defendant, Jersey Ice Cream Company, disclaims liability because the refrigerating equipment was installed by an independent contractor. With this we do not agree. The Ice Cream Company insists it did not make the electric connection and is for that reason not liable. The Ice Cream Company, having undertaken to install the equipment, is obligated to install same in a reasonably safe manner. Its servant gained knowledge, within the scope of his employment, that the equipment was dangerous. This notice was imputed to the Ice Cream Company. 2 Am.Jur., Agency §368. Neglecting to remove the danger contributing to plaintiff's injury makes a case against the Ice Cream Company.

We now consider whether the verdict is excessive. The burden is with him who assails the amount of the verdict to show that it is wholly unsupported by the evidence, or that the jury was influenced by passion, prejudice or other improper motive. Tampa Electric Company v. Bazemore, 85 Fla. 164, 96 So. 297 (1923).

The plaintiff's burn was described by the attending physician as a third degree burn, meaning a total destruction. Portions of the skull were burned so badly as to require removal. The plaintiff was 32 years of age and earning $27 per week at the time of injury. At the time of trial he had undergone four operations and required more. He will never be able to engage in normal work. His pain has obviously been great. Hospitalization and medical attention has been continuous and will continue for some time. The plaintiff will suffer ailments, loss of earnings, loss of personal appearance and inconvenience the remainder of his life. Our conclusion is that the verdict is not excessive. Courts are reluctant to substitute their judgment for that of the jury as to damages.

We now consider the propriety of exhibiting pictures of plaintiff's injury to the jury. In this we find no error. There was evidence that the pictures reflected the true condition of plaintiff.

The defendants had ample opportunity to cross examine the photographer; to explain or refute their genuineness. The fact that they might have been gruesome did not render them inadmissible. The purpose of all testimony is to reveal the truth to the end that courts and juries may be persuaded by it to a just decision.

Error is asserted for the refusal to give certain requested charges. We have examined them in the light of the charge given by the court and find no error.

Finding no reversible error in the record, the judgment is affirmed.

State of North Carolina v. Strickland
Supreme Court of North Carolina, 1970.
287 N.C. 253, 173 S.E.2d 129.

This case explains when motion pictures are admissible in evidence and distinguishes between sound motion pictures and silent motion pictures. It makes this distinction in affirming the constitutional right of a defendant not to incriminate himself by oral testimony unless he waives his privilege.

* * *

BRANCH, Justice. The question presented for decision by this appeal is whether the North Carolina Court of Appeals erred in holding that sound motion pictures, taken of defendant approximately two hours after he was alleged to have operated an automobile upon the public highways of North Carolina while under the influence of intoxicating liquor, were properly admitted into evidence.

Defendant contends that the use of the sound moving pictures violated his Fifth Amendment privilege guaranteeing that a person cannot be "compelled in a criminal case to be a witness against himself" and the guarantee of Article I, Section 11 of the North Carolina Constitution that a person shall "not be compelled to give self-incriminating evidence."

The Federal courts have recognized that the Fifth Amendment privilege against self-incrimination relates only to testimonial or communicative acts of the person seeking to exercise the privilege and does not apply to acts not communicative in nature. Schmerber v. California, 384 U.S. 757, 86 S.Ct. 1826, 16 L.Ed.2d 908 (1966); Holt v. United States, 218 U.S. 245, 31 S.Ct. 2, 54 L.Ed. 1021 (1910).

In the case of Schmerber v. California, supra, a physician withdrew blood from the defendant at the direction of a State officer, over objection of the accused, and in a State prosecution for driving an automobile while under the influence of intoxicating liquor offered in evidence an analysis of the blood so taken for the purpose of showing intoxication of accused. The defendant objected to the introduction of this evidence, contending that this violated his Fifth Amendment privilege against self-incrimination. Holding the blood test evidence competent because it was not his testimony or his communicative act, the United States Supreme Court stated:

> "(B)oth federal and state courts have usually held that it (Fifth Amendment) offers no protection against compulsion to submit to fingerprinting, photographing, or measurements, to write or speak for identification, to appear in court, or stand, to assume a stance, to walk, or to make a particular gesture. The distinction which has emerged, often expressed in different ways, is that the privilege is a bar against compelling 'communications' or 'testimony,' but that compulsion which makes a suspect or accused the source of 'real or physical evidence' does not violate it."

Another leading case in the federal court structure is Holt v. United States, supra, in which there was evidence that prior to the trial the accused, over his objection, was compelled to put on a blouse that "fitted" him. Mr. Justice Holmes, speaking for the Court, rejected the argument that this was a violation as "based upon an extravagant extension of the 5th Amendment," and went on to say:

> "(T)he prohibition of compelling a man in a criminal court to be a witness against himself is a prohibition of the use of physical or moral compulsion to extort communications from him, not an exclusion of his body as evidence when it may be material. The objection in principle would forbid a jury to look at a prisoner and compare his features with a photograph in proof." 218 U.S. at 252–253, 31 S.Ct. at 6, 54 L.Ed. at 1030.

Generally, the basic principles which govern the admissibility of photographs apply to motion pictures, and where they are relevant and have been properly authenticated, they are admissible in evidence. They have been used in both criminal and civil trials for many purposes, e.g., civil cases: Lehmuth v. Long Beach Unified School Dist., 53 Cal.2d 544, 2 Cal.Rptr. 279, 348 P.2d 887 (1960) (motion picture depicting condition of personal injury victim); McGoorty v. Benhart, 305 Ill.App. 458, 27 N.E.2d 289 (1940) (motion pictures admissible to discredit the testimony of a personal injury claimant by showing activity inconsistent with alleged injury); Sparks v. Employers Mut. Liab. Ins. Co. of Wis., 83 So.2d 453 (La.Ct.App. 1955) (motion picture admissible to show condition of a person, place, object, or activity). E.g., Criminal cases: People v. Hayes, 21 Cal.App.2d 320, 71 P.2d 321 (1937) (sound motion picture of confession held admissible); People v. Dabb, 32 Cal.2d 491, 197 P.2d 1 (1948) (sound pictures of re-enactment by defendants of a crime). 41

Notre Dame Lawyer, 1009, 1010, n. 6 (1965–66); Scott, Photographic Evidence, §624; 62 A.L.R.2d 686. However, there is very little authority on the precise question of using moving pictures in cases in which a person is charged with driving on the public highways while under the influence of intoxicating liquor and asserts his constitutional right against self-incrimination. According to our research only one jurisdiction, Oklahoma, has adopted the view supporting defendant's position.

* * *

North Carolina has long recognized the distinction between compulsory testimonial evidence and compulsory physical disclosure. The North Carolina view is summarized in State v. Paschal, 253 N.C. 795, 117 S.E.2d 749 (1961), by Bobbitt, J. (now C. J.) as follows:

> "The established rule in this jurisdiction is that '(t)he scope of the privilege against self-incrimination, in history and in principle, includes only the process of testifying by word of mouth or in writing, i.e., the process of disclosure by utterance. It has no application to such physical, evidential circumstances as may exist on the accused's body or about his person.' State v. Rogers, 233 N.C. 390, 399, 64 S.E.2d 572, where Ervin, J., reviews prior decisions of this Court. See also State v. Grayson, 239 N.C. 453, 458, 80 S.E.2d 387, opinion by Parker, J., and cases cited.
>
> "Where this rule applies, it is held that the admission of evidence of a defendant's *refusal to submit* to a chemical test designed to measure the alcoholic content of his blood does not violate his constitutional right against self-incrimination."

See also Branch v. State, 269 N.C. 642, 153 S.E.2d 343; State v. Gaskill, 256 N.C. 652, 142 S.E.2d 873.

Both better reasoning and the prevailing weight of authority lead us to follow the views adopted by Colorado, Texas and Ohio.

Brock, J., speaking for the Court of Appeals, correctly and concisely stated:

> "Talking motion pictures of an accused in a criminal action are not per se testimonial in nature, and, where they are properly used to illustrate competent and relevant testimony of a witness, their use does not violate accused's privilege against self-incrimination."

However, the State cannot introduce substantive evidence or add to the testimony of a witness under the guise of using a moving picture to illustrate the testimony of the witness. Nevertheless, if the testimony of a witness is generally consistent with the illustrative evidence, a slight variation only affects the credibility of the evidence. State v. Brooks, 260 N.C. 186, 132 S.E.2d 354 (1963).

The burden here was upon the State to prove that defendant operated his motor vehicle upon the public highways or streets while he was under the influence of intoxicating liquor. Defendant admitted that he had been drinking, but denied that he was operating his automobile when it was wrecked. He also defended upon the ground that even if the jury should find that he was the operator of the motor vehicle, his intoxication resulted from consuming alcoholic beverages in the two-hour period which elapsed between the wreck and the time when the sound moving pictures were made.

In the instant case the moving picture not only depicted defendant's physical condition and his ability (or inability) to coordinate his movements; its sound track recorded the following incriminating statement—"communicated by the accused from his knowledge of the offense": "Q. Have you had anything to drink since they stopped you? A. No, sir."

This question and answer presented testimony from defendant which tended to show not only that he was driving the motor vehicle but that he was under the influence of intoxicating liquor at the time. It placed him at the scene of the wreck and completely destroyed his contention that his intoxication resulted from drinking subsequent to the wreck. The statement was clearly substantive evidence, competent as an admission if competent at all. It certainly did not illustrate the testimony of any other witness.

It is the law in this state "that in-custody statements attributed to a defendant, when offered by the State and objected to by the defendant, 'are inadmissible *for any purpose* unless, after a voir dire hearing in the absence of the jury, the court, based upon sufficient evidence' makes factual findings that such statements were voluntarily and understandingly made by the defendant after he had been fully advised as to his constitutional rights." State v. Catrett, 276 N.C. 86, 171 S.E.2d 398, . . . This statement from *Catrett* was made with reference to the defendant's in-custody statements which were offered for *impeachment* purposes. A *fortiori,* it is applicable to the statement which defendant made in consequence of the interrogation quoted above.

The Oklahoma case of Stewart v. State, supra, cited as being contrary to the view adopted by this Court, is in partial accord with this decision, in that it holds that sound motion pictures taken of a defendant are inadmissible in evidence without a showing that prior to the taking he was advised of his right to counsel and given the admonitions required by Miranda v. State of Arizona, 384 U.S. 436, 86 S.Ct. 1602, 16 L.Ed.2d 694 (1966), and Escobedo v. State of Illinois, 378 U.S. 478, 84 S.Ct. 1758, 12 L.Ed.2d 977 (1964).

In the instant case, since no *voir dire* was held, there must be a new trial.

Aside from the constitutional and procedural questions here presented, we think it appropriate to observe that the use of properly authenticated moving pictures to illustrate a witness' testimony may be of invaluable aid in the jury's search for a verdict that speaks the truth. However, the powerful impact of this type of evidence requires the trial judge to examine carefully into its authenticity, relevancy, and competency, and—if he finds it to be competent—to give the jury proper limiting instructions at the time it is introduced. When a moving picture is offered into evidence, upon defendant's request the trial judge should allow the defendant's counsel to preview it so that he can intelligently enter objections to those portions which he may deem uncorroborative or otherwise objectionable. Furthermore, when the sound motion picture contains incriminating statements by the defendant—made "from his knowledge of the offense"—upon defendant's objection, the judge must conduct a *voir dire* to determine the admissibility of the in-custody statements or admissions contained in the sound picture.

We find no fallacy in the reasoning of the North Carolina Court of Appeals to the effect that G.S. § 114-19 did not create a new rule of evidence. Even a cursory reading of this statute in connection with the chapter and article in which it is found leads to the conclusion that the statute is concerned with the compilation and preservation of statistics and records rather than the creation of a new rule of evidence.

For reasons stated, the decision of the Court of Appeals is reversed and the cause is remanded to that Court with direction to award a new trial, to be conducted in accordance with the principles herein set forth.

Reversed and remanded.

Gerzel v. City of New York
Supreme Court, Appellate Division, First Department, 1986.
117 A.D.2d 549, 499 N.Y.S.2d 60.

This case demonstrates the admissibility of a photograph of the city-owned premises where a person was injured as a result of defective stairs at the entrance. This photograph was taken the day of the injury. Most governments that I am familiar with have a statute requiring prompt notification to the government of a pending cause of action against that government. Failing to give this notice within a specified time period prevents a person from suing that government for any injuries or property damage sustained. This requirement was originally based in common law, where the king could not be sued until the king gave permission to the aggrieved person to institute a suit against him. Thus, the government requires that notice be given of the possibility that injuries or damages have been sustained as a result of action by the government or by agents or servants of the government. The government then has the right within the prescribed time to settle the claim. If the government does not settle the claim, then the aggrieved person is given permission to institute the civil suit against the government. The times designed by statute may vary from one government to the other.

Before SANDLER, J.P., and SULLIVAN, LYNCH and ROSENBERGER, JJ.

MEMORANDUM DECISION

Order, Supreme Court, New York County, (Blyn, J.) entered December 11, 1984, which denied petitioner's motion for leave to file a late notice of claim, reversed, on the law, the facts, and in the exercise of discretion, and the motion is granted, without costs.

On November 4, 1983, at approximately 4:25 P.M., the seventy-four year old petitioner Andrew Gerzel fell while descending the steps of the City owned premises at 19 Fulton Street in Manhattan by reason of an alleged discrepancy in the height of the risers of the steps. He sustained a fracture of his left lower arm. Petitioner reported the accident to an unnamed employee of the premises. A Sergeant Howell took two photographs of the steps, as witnessed by one Willie Williams, and an unidentified individual took Gerzel's statement and completed a report the same day. Apparently, the report was thereafter kept on file by the manager of the premises. On July 3, 1983, seven months after the accident, petitioner, by his attorney, served a verified notice of claim upon the office of the Comptroller. Upon disallowance of the claim, petitioner moved for leave to file a late notice of claim pursuant to Section 50-e of the General Municipal Law. Difficulty in ascertaining ownership of the premises; which had various shops, a restaurant, a cafe, and the South Street Seaport Museum, was the primary reason given for failure timely to file the notice of claim. Special Term denied the motion, holding that the City lacked actual notice of the essential facts constituting the claim. The court noted that the accident report relied upon to establish actual notice lacked any reference to a claimed defect or marked discrepancy in the height of the risers of the steps.

Our evaluation of the facts and circumstances in this personal injury action leads us to conclude that Special Term improvidently exercised its discretion in denying petitioner an opportunity to have his claim adjudicated on the merits. We reverse to grant the motion. General Municipal Law § 50-e empowers the courts to evaluate requests for relief from the ninety-day filing requirement by striking an "equitable balance . . . between a public corporation's reasonable need for prompt notification of claims against it and an injured party's interest in just compensation." Heiman v. City of N.Y., 85 A.D.2d 25, 28, 447 N.Y.S.2d 158 (1st Dept. 1982), quoting Camarella v. East Irondequoit Cent. School Bd., 34 N.Y.2d 139, 142–143, 356 N.Y.S.2d 553, 313 N.E.2d 29 (1974). The statute, General Municipal Law § 50-e(5), directs the courts to consider "in particular, whether the public corporation . . . acquired actual knowledge of the essential facts constituting the claim" within the ninety-day filing period or a reasonable time thereafter. Other relevant factors include the reason for the delay and whether the delay substantially prejudiced the public corporation's ability to defend on the merits. The only legitimate purpose served by Section 50-e is to protect the public corporation against spurious claims and to assure it "an adequate opportunity to explore the merits of the claim while information is still readily available." Teresta v. City of N.Y., 304 N.Y. 440, 443, 108 N.E.2d 397 (1952). *See also* Matter of Beary v. City of Rye, 44 N.Y.2d 398, 412, 406 N.Y.S.2d 9, 377 N.E.2d 453 (1978).

It is manifest on the record that the City acquired actual knowledge of the essential facts constituting the claim by reason of the accident report and photographs. Innes v. County of Genesee, 99 A.D.2d 642, 643, 472 N.Y.S.2d, 223 (4th Dept., 1984); Flynn v. City of Long Beach, 94 A.D.2d 713, 714, 462 N.Y.S.2d 243 (2d Dept., 1983), see also Caselli v. City of New York, 105 A.D.2d 251, 256; 483 N.Y.S.2d 401 (2d Dept., 1984). The report sets for the date, time, and place of the alleged accident, the manner in which the injuries occurred and the nature of the injury. It reflects petitioner's statement that he "did not see the (2) step." The photographs clearly sufficed to apprise the City of the alleged negligence involved, a defective and dangerous condition of the steps. They may be used to prove constructive notice of an alleged defect since they were taken reasonably close to the time of the accident. See Karten v. City of New York, 109 A.D.2d 126, 127, 490

N.Y.S.2d 503 (1st Dept., 1985). The accident report and the photographs taken sufficiently connected the accident and the alleged defective condition in the steps. *Compare* Fox v. City of New York, 91 A.D.2d 624, 456 N.Y.S.2d 806 (2d Dept., 1982). The fact that the report was apparently filed on the premises where the accident occurred, rather than with the Police Department is, in the circumstances, not significant.

Another relevant factor is the excuse for the delay in giving notice. Petitioner's affidavit and his attorney's affirmation allege that they mistakenly assumed the Rouse Corporation owned the premises, given its commercial appearance. Four months after petitioner retained him in January 1984, petitioner's attorney attempted to ascertain the true owner and immediately served a notice of claim when the Record Abstract report came to his attention. While petitioner's explanation for the seven-month delay involved here is troublesome, the presence or absence of any one factor under Section 50-e, is not necessarily determinative. Rather, all facts and circumstances should be considered. Matter of Cicio v. New York, 98 A.D.2d 38, 39, 469 N.Y.S.2d 467 (2d Dept., 1983).

Counsel's failure to present a more reasonable explanation is without significance given the existence of actual notice and the City's failure to show substantial prejudice by the late notice. Rechenberger v. Nassau County Medical Center, 112 A.D.2d 150, 153, 490 N.Y.S.2d 838 (2d Dept., 1985). The record reveals that petitioner, upon returning to inspect the steps within the ninety-day filing period, discovered that the risers were repaired. Indeed, on January 12, 1984, two months after the accident, petitioner photographed the steps as repaired. Respondent fails to demonstrate substantial prejudice from the delay in filing the notice of claim in light of these repairs. Even a timely filed notice, on the usual form, served after the repairs, but well within the ninety-day period, would not have enabled the City to perform an inspection of the steps in their original condition. The information available now is substantially the same as it would have been had a timely notice of claim been filed. Rechenberger v. Nassau

County Medical Center, *supra.* In any event, we believe respondent will encounter little difficulty in reconstructing the events of November 4th. There is a complete record of the facts underlying petitioner's tort claim.

All concur except LYNCH, J.

Barenbrugge v. Rich
Appellate Court of Illinois, 1986.
141 Ill.App.3d 1046, 96 Ill.Dec. 163, 490 N.E.2d 1368.

This case is on a medical malpractice action wherein a 28-year-old female was allegedly misdiagnosed and mistreated medically. A videotape and photographs depicting plaintiff's condition and circumstances that occurred because of the actions of the defendant were offered in evidence. Defendant contended that the video and photographs were inflammatory to the jury and would prejudice the jury against the defendant. The appellate court makes an interesting observation with respect to this argument.

Justice HARTMAN delivered the opinion of the court:

Defendant doctor appeals the judgment entered against her after a jury trial in a medical malpractice suit which alleged that she and another physician, not involved in this appeal, negligently failed to diagnose breast cancer while it was still treatable. On appeal we are asked to decide whether: (1) the circuit court erred in refusing to transfer venue; and (2) a new trial should be ordered because: (a) the circuit court failed to issue instructions on contributory negligence; (b) contrary to indications at trial, two of plaintiff's expert witnesses received compensation for their testimony; (c) the arousal of the jury's passion and prejudice was evident from its verdict.

Decedent, Renee Barenbrugge, age 28, died during the trial and her husband, Craig, was appointed special administrator of her estate. For purposes of simplicity, we shall apply the term "plaintiff" to Renee.

Evidence in the record as to the onset and history of plaintiff's disease is conflicting; however, there is evidence upon which the jury could have based its verdict that in November 1978, the then 22-year old plaintiff visited defendant, Dr. Nancy Rich, an obstetrician-gynecologist, for the first time for a routine premarital examination. Plaintiff then had no complaints with respect to her breasts. Her examination was normal. She returned to defendant on February 27, 1979 and complained of pain and a lump in her left breast. Dr. Rich testified both that she ". . . felt a lump of breast tissue . . ." and that "[i]t was normal breast tissue." And again, "I did not feel a mass. I felt a lump of breast tissue." Still further, ". . . I decided it was absolutely normal in every way." She described this condition as normal thickening of tissue, although at trial two experts asserted that thickening is not normal. Plaintiff complained that she was experiencing breast pain at this time. Dr. Rich's records did not contain this complaint. Dr. Lawrence Gunn, a surgeon to whom Dr. Rich later referred plaintiff, recorded on January 31, 1980 that plaintiff experienced breast pain for one year, which would encompass the February 27, 1979 visit with Dr. Rich.

On July 16, 1979, plaintiff returned to Dr. Rich for a regular examination and for birth control pills. She asserted that she complained of a lump in her left breast and pain on this visit; Dr. Rich's record indicates no such complaint. Plaintiff's next visit was again six months later on January 17, 1980. Plaintiff expressed concern about her breast at this time. The records of Dr. Rich for that visit contain no description of plaintiff's complaints, except that she was "very worried." The record does show an entry "probable fibrocystic." Dr. Rich then referred plaintiff to Dr. Gunn for a second opinion regarding plaintiff's breasts. Plaintiff saw Dr. Gunn on January 31, 1980 and complained of breast pain. There is a question as to whether she complained of other irregularities. Dr. Gunn observed that plaintiff's left breast, including the areola, was 25% larger than the right, and that the veins in the left breast were prominent. No mammogram was ever performed on or ordered for plaintiff by either defendant or Dr. Gunn.

On May 31, 1980, plaintiff called defendant complaining of severe abdominal pain.

They met at Hinsdale Hospital and since plaintiff was also complaining of the lump and breast pain, defendant performed a breast exam. Dr. Rich found irregularities which led her to believe that plaintiff's breast was malignant. Two days later, on June 2, 1980, plaintiff saw Dr. Gunn who performed a needle biopsy in the area of the lump, which detected cancer.

Plaintiff was admitted to the hospital and on June 3, 1980, Dr. Gunn performed a surgical biopsy to determine the extent of the disease. A tissue sample taken from the supraclavicular area was sent to pathologists for analysis. Later that date a report on frozen tissue was sent to Dr. Gunn indicating no malignancy. He reported to plaintiff that the node he had felt was not cancerous and that a mastectomy would be performed. The next day Dr. Gunn performed a radical mastectomy on plaintiff, a decision made without the benefit of the pathologists' report on a permanent section of tissue which did indicate the advance of cancer. After the mastectomy plaintiff underwent radiation and chemotherapy. She later underwent further surgery performed by other physicians at other institutions.

On April 20, 1981, plaintiff filed a medical malpractice action against Drs. Rich and Gunn in Cook County circuit court, alleging negligent failure to diagnose her cancer. Numerous amendments were made to her complaint. Other defendants were joined, including certain individual pathologists and their professional corporation, DuPage Pathology Associates ("DPA").

The cause ultimately went to trial on September 26, 1984. Plaintiff's expert testified that her cancer could have been detected by mammography 1 1/2 years before it was removed and, if it had been detected in February 1979, her chances of cure would have been 95%, but with the passage of time, survival chances decreased until, by the time of actual diagnosis, her prognosis was very grave. Plaintiff died while the trial was in progress on October 13, 1984. A settlement was reached with Dr. Gunn in the amount of $900,000 and with DPA for $500. The settlement with DPA was assertedly based upon "either a $50,000 loan agreement or, if a settlement or verdict in excess of this amount was achieved against any defendant then a payment of $500." The jury found Dr. Rich liable and the circuit court entered judgment in the amount of $2,099,500, from which this appeal proceeds.

* * *

IV

In her final argument, defendant contends that the verdict was a result of sympathy, passion and prejudice stemming from plaintiff's death during the trial, the admission of a videotape depicting a day in the life of plaintiff after her operation and other photographic evidence, and the volume of testimony detailing plaintiff's suffering, the cumulative effect of which is claimed to have tainted the jury's verdict and requires a new trial. This contention is not persuasive.

In the course of *voir dire,* numerous and repeated questions were asked of prospective jurors as to possible sympathy created by plaintiff's condition and impending death. The jury was thereafter accepted by defendant. Also, during the opening statement by counsel for the pathologists, plaintiff's impending death was mentioned. In light of such juror qualification and its preparation for plaintiff's condition at trial and her death, the jury's verdict cannot be said to have been tainted.

Videotape and photographs are admissible if their probative value is not outweighed by their inflammatory effect. (Bullard v. Barnes (1984), 102 Ill.2d 505, 519–20, 82 Ill.Dec. 448, 468 N.E.2d 1228.) No assertion is made here that the evidence was not an accurate portrayal of plaintiff's condition and circumstances; its probative value is not seriously questioned. The insistence that such evidence is merely cumulative is not persuasive. (Sparling v. Peabody Coal Co (1974), 59 Ill.2d 491, 500–01, 322 N.E.2d 5.) Videotapes similar to the tape admitted in the present case have been found admissible in other states. (Pisal v. Stamford Hospital [1980], 180 Conn. 314, 430 A.2d 1, 8; Caprara v. Chrysler Corp. [1979], 71 A.D.2d 515, 423 N.Y.S.2d 694, 698–99, *aff'd* [1981], 52 N.Y.S.2d 114, 436 N.Y.S.2d 251, 417 N.E.2d 545; Air Shields, Inc. v. Spears [Tex.Civ.App. 1979], 590 S.W.2d 574, 580.) The appearance of plaintiff's son in this evidence was proper in that it was established that caring for him was part of plaintiff's daily routine. (Pisel v. Stamford Hospital.) Therefore, the introduction of this evidence was not error.

For the foregoing reasons, we find no basis upon which to reverse the jury's verdict or the judgment of the circuit court. Accordingly, we affirm.

Affirmed.

BILANDIC, P.J., and SCARIANO, J., concur.

RELATED DECISIONS
Chain of Custody for Evidence

People v. Basciano
Supreme Court Appellate Division, Third Department, 1985.
109 A.D.2d 945, 486 N.Y.S.2d 434.

Burglary is a crime that is usually defined as the breaking and entering of a building of another with intent to commit a crime therein. Some jurisdictions limit the crime to include only felonies. There is no requirement, known to me, that the intended crime actually be committed. Some jurisdictions have omitted the requirement of a break, leaving the unlawful entry as the required element of the crime.

For a precise definition of the crime of burglary, I refer you to the criminal statutes of your jurisdiction, which will include that jurisdiction's definition of the word "burglary."

In the instant case, a fingerprint found at the crime scene was matched with a print of the defendant on file with the local police department. He was convicted, and he appealed his conviction based on the facts that wholly circumstantial evidence was insufficient to establish his guilt and that the prosecution failed to establish a chain of custody with respect to the fingerprints that were on file at the police department. The court discusses both of these arguments in the decision.

LEVINE, Justice.

Appeal from a judgment of the County Court of Ulster County, rendered December 5, 1983, upon a verdict convicting defendant of the crime of burglary in the third degree.

On the morning of January 6, 1983, the maintenance manager of the Skateland Roller Rink in the Village of New Paltz arrived at work to find that the front window of the rink had been broken and the arcade games located inside had been tipped over, with their coin boxes removed and emptied. In the course of the subsequent police investigation, a police officer was able to "lift" a clear fingerprint impression from a box inside one of the game machines which had encased its coin box. It was readily inferable that the print was fresh, since it had no dust on it, while the rest of the box was thickly covered with dust. It was subsequently found that this print was identical to defendant's fingerprint on file at the New Paltz Police Department. Defendant was charged with the crime and was ultimately convicted of third degree burglary.

On this appeal, defendant argues that the evidence adduced at trial, being wholly circumstantial, was insufficient to establish his guilt. We disagree. The standard of proof in criminal cases where the sole evidence of guilt is circumstantial is that "the facts from which the inference of defendant's guilt is drawn must be 'inconsistent with his innocence and must exclude to a moral certainty every other reasonable hypothesis'" (People v. Way, 59 N.Y.2d 361, 365, 465 N.Y.S.2d 853, 452 N.E.2d 1181, *quoting* People v. Bearden, 290 N.Y. 478, 480, 49 N.E.2d 785; *accord* People v. Gates, 24 N.Y.2d 666, 669, 301 N.Y.S.2d 597, 249 N.E.2d 450). Here, the trial testimony clearly established that the burglary which led to the opening of the arcade games had to have occurred sometime after the rink closed at 10:45 P.M. on January 5, 1983 and before the custodian entered the rink at 9:45 A.M. on the next day. Defendant had no permission to be on the premises during this time period. Further, the fresh fingerprint (identified by an expert witness as that of defendant's right-hand middle finger) was discovered *inside* one

of the machines, on the box encasing a jimmied coin box. Additional testimony disclosed that the inside of the machine was kept locked and that no one had a key to it except six employees of Mid-Hudson Amusement, Inc., the company which owned and serviced the machines. Defendant had never been an employee of Mid-Hudson nor of any other vending company. Since defendant thus had no lawful access to the interior of the machine, the only reasonable inference to be drawn from the presence of his fresh fingerprint inside the machine was that he had forcibly opened it for the purpose of extracting its cash contents. This was sufficient to sustain each and every element of the crime of burglary without establishing that a larceny had actually also been committed (*see* People v. Mackey, 49 N.Y.2d 274, 425 N.Y.S.2d 288, 401 N.E.2d 398).

Finally, we reject defendant's contention that the fingerprint evidence should not have been admitted on the ground that the prosecution failed to establish a chain of custody with respect to the earlier set of defendant's fingerprints which were on file at the New Paltz Police Department and by which defendant was identified as the person whose fingerprint was found inside the arcade game. Strict proof of the chain of custody of a nonfungible piece of evidence, such as a police fingerprint file card, is not required (People v. Anderson, 99 A.D.2d 560, 561, 470 N.Y.S.2d 946; People v. Washington, 96 A.D.2d 996, 997, 467 N.Y.S.2d 87). When an object possesses unique characteristics and any material alteration would be readily apparent, a simple in-court identification is sufficient to warrant admission (People v. Julian, 41 N.Y.2d 340, 343, 392 N.Y.S.2d 610, 360 N.E.2d 1310). Accordingly, the trial court was correct in admitting the fingerprint card in question upon the testimony of the police fingerprint expert who stated that the card had been delivered to him by another police officer who had obtained it directly from the files of the police department, and who further testified that the prints on the card had neither been tampered with nor altered.

Judgment affirmed.

MAHONEY, P.J., and KANE, CASEY and WEISS, JJ., concur.

RELATED DECISIONS
Olfactory Real Evidence

Rust v. Guinn
Court of Appeals of Indiana, 1981.
429 N.E.2d 299.

This case involves the presentation of real evidence to a jury in order to properly enlighten them as to the facts in dispute. It is a rather lengthy case, for an evidence law case, but it reads very quickly and is quite humorous, but not so funny to the litigants. Read it; you will enjoy it.

NEAL, Presiding Judge.

STATEMENT OF THE CASE

This is an action for abatement of a nuisance and damages brought by Hubert Guinn, Jr. and Margaret Suzanne Guinn (Guinns) against David Rust, Rose Acre Farms, Inc., Lookacres, Inc., and Eggacres, Inc. (hereinafter collectively referred to as Eggacres when appropriate). Upon Eggacres' motion, the trial was bifurcated. Following a bench trial, the trial court ruled that a private nuisance existed and that such was abatable. Upon trial to a jury on the issue of damages, such were assessed against Eggacres in the amount of $9,500. Costs of the action were charged to Eggacres as well. From the judgment entered upon the jury's award, Eggacres brings this appeal. Eggacres does not appeal the initial judgment of the trial court in which the existence of the private nuisance was determined.

We affirm.

STATEMENT OF THE FACTS

The Guinns have resided on an 80-acre farm in Jackson County since 1965. Lookacres, Inc. and Eggacres, Inc. have operated facilities for the production of chicken eggs on property adjacent to the Guinns since 1969. The combined operations employ some 495,000 for the purpose. Prior to 1969 the Guinns, who are presumably persons possessed of ordinary olfactory sensibilities, enjoyed their rural home with its attendant aroma, and suffered the normal amount of flies generally encountered in farm living.

Until 1976, Eggacres employed a system of lagoons for the purpose of storing accumulated chicken manure, two of which lagoons are located within 300 yards of the Guinns' farmhouse. At times the lagoons were suffered to attain a state of overflow. The redolence emanating from the lagoons achieved such a state of odoriferocity at times as to compel the Guinns to maintain their residence in a sealed state, to curtail their regular outdoor activities, and on occasion to vacate their residence in favor of more savory environs. Mrs. Guinn testified that as a result of the foul odor, which was characterized as "a urine-like, a gas, ammonia smell," she sometimes vomited, gagged, and was otherwise nauseated, and experienced a burning sensation in her eyes. Devotion of the lagoons as a means of primary waste disposal was begun to be phased out in 1976; they are now used for the purpose of storing egg wash water and also for emergency purposes. Since 1977, the lagoons have been treated bacterially to diminish the odor and to purify the water.

After the Eggacres facilities commenced operations, a significantly larger number of flies began to visit the Guinns' property at intermittent times than had previously been the case, and these were found to have generated from Eggacres. A program of fly control involving the use of sprays and insecticides undertaken by Eggacres during the years 1969 through 1974 proved ineffective, and the odor of the sprays and insecticides themselves compounded the Guinns' discomfort. In 1974, a successful method of fly control exploiting the flies' natural predators was launched, and by 1975 the fly problem subsided.

The method of waste disposal employed by Eggacres since 1976 utilizes wet manure pits maintained beneath the chicken houses to catch and temporarily hold the droppings. When these pits are filled, the contents are removed and hauled away by trucks. Eventually the material is spread over nearby fields for the purpose of fertilization. Although the change in the means of disposal proved effective in eliminating the effluvium attributable to the lagoons, the new scheme has caused additional problems for the Guinns. The trucks hauling their fresh cargo frequently pass the Guinns' property and on occasion spill portions of the guanic substance in front of the residence, resulting in odor problems.

Based upon the foregoing facts, the trial court concluded the following:

"1. That Defendants, Lookacres, Inc., and Eggacres, Inc., by their method of operation of their lawful business, did create offensive odors, as to Plaintiffs, in excess of those normally associated with farm living from 1969 through 1977, which said odors were, during said period, unreasonable to a person of ordinary sensibilities.

2. That Defendants, Lookacres, Inc., and Eggacres, Inc., by their method of operation of their lawful business, as to Plaintiffs, in excess of those normally associated with farm living from 1969 through 1975, which said populations of flies were, during said period, unreasonable to a person of ordinary sensibilities.

3. That Defendants, Lookacres, Inc., and Eggacres, Inc., by their negligence have created, and continue to create, offensive odors, as to Plaintiffs, by spilling chicken waste in front of Plaintiffs' property, which odors are in excess of those normally associated with farm living and are, therefore, unreasonable to a person of ordinary sensibilities.

4. That Defendants, Lookacres, Inc., and Eggacres, Inc., have, thereby, since 1969 maintained a private nuisance, as defined by IC 1971, 34-1-52-1, which has been and is currently offensive to the senses and an interference with Plaintiffs' use and enjoyment of their property.

5. That said nuisance is abatable.

6. That the lawful and important social and economic nature of Defendants' businesses do not preclude Plaintiffs from being compensated for the burden placed upon the free use and enjoyment of their property resulting from said nuisance."

Trial was later had before a jury wherein damages in the amount of $9,500 were assessed against Eggacres. From the latter judgment, Eggacres appeals.

ISSUES

We have consolidated the three errors assigned by Eggacres into two issues and restate them as follows:

I. Whether the trial court erroneously instructed the jury on the measure of damages for an abatable private nuisance; and

II. Whether the trial court erroneously admitted into evidence at the trial on the issue of damages a jar of chicken manure.

DISCUSSION AND DECISION

Issue I. Measure of damages

Eggacres contends the trial court erroneously instructed the jury as to the damages recoverable for the nuisance found to have existed, alleging the jury was permitted to consider improper factors in making their determination. Eggacres tendered the following instruction, which was refused by the trial court:

"It has previously been determined that the facilities of the defendants known as Eggacres and Lookacres did during the period of 1969 through 1975 constitute a nuisance as to the plaintiffs with respect to causing excessive amounts of flies and did during the period 1969 through 1977 constitute a nuisance as to the plaintiffs with respect to causing excessive unpleasant odors, and did during the period of 1976 to the present constitute a nuisance as to the plaintiffs with respect to the occasional spillage of chicken waste upon the public road in front of plaintiffs' residence. If you find from the evidence that the plaintiffs' use and enjoyment of their property was unreasonably interfered with by such conditions, you should award them damages to compensate them for the interference with and loss of the use and enjoyment of their property caused by such conditions during such period. The measure of damages which you must apply to determine the plaintiffs' damages for the interference with and loss of use and enjoyment of their property is the reduction in the fair rental value of plaintiffs' real estate caused by the nuisance conditions. In other words, the difference between what you find would have been the fair rental value of plaintiffs' real estate without such nuisance conditions and what you find was the fair rental value with such nuisance conditions is the damage sustained by plaintiffs by reason of the interference with and loss of use and enjoyment of their real estate."

The trial court gave the following final instruction concerning damages:

"In determining the amount of damages sustained by the plaintiffs as a result of the nuisance maintained by the defendants, you may consider:

(1) Damages for interference with the plaintiffs' use and enjoyment of their property which damages are measured by the reduction in the fair rental value of the property during the period of existence of the nuisance proximately caused by the nuisance;

(2) Damages for actual expenses incurred by plaintiff in attempting to mitigate the effects proximately caused by the nuisance conditions found to have existed; and

(3) Damages for injury to health proximately caused by the nuisance.

Damages are not to be presumed. The burden is on the plaintiffs to prove by a preponderance of the evidence the damages proximately caused in the nuisance maintained by the defendants."

Eggacres contends the jury was erroneously instructed as to the proper measure of damages for an abatable private nuisance because the instruction allowed for consideration to be given to losses in addition to the diminution in rental value proximately caused by the nuisance. These losses, enumerated (2) and (3) in the instruction respectively, include actual expenses incurred by the Guinns in attempting to mitigate the effects of the nuisance, and injury to health proximately caused by the nuisance.

The essence of Eggacres' tendered instruction is that the extent of damages recoverable is limited to the diminution in rental value of the Guinns' property caused by the nuisance. The substance of the tendered instruction was clearly stated in the given instruction, paragraph (1). In the recent case of State v. Bouras, (1981) Ind.App., 423 N.E.2d 741, 744 (transfer pending) the court stated the following concerning refusal of instructions:

"Giving instructions is entrusted to the trial court's discretion, and its refusal to give a tendered instruction is grounds for reversal only if

the substance of the instruction was required to be given and was not adequately covered by other instructions given by the court. Smith v. Insurance Company of North America, (1980) Ind.App., 411 N.E.2d 638; Piwowar v. Washington Lumber and Coal Company, (1980) Ind.App., 405 N.E.2d 576. A tendered instruction is required to be given only if it covers an essential element of the case supported by evidence, correctly states the law material to the case and when no other instruction covers that area of the law. Dahlberg v. Ogle, (1978) 268 Ind. 30, 373 N.E.2d 159; Davis v. State, (1976) 265 Ind. 476, 355 N.E.2d 836; School City of Gary v. Claudio, (1980) Ind.App., 413 N.E.2d 628; Burkett v. Crulo Trucking Co., (1976) 171 Ind.App. 166, 355 N.E.2d 253; Jackman v. Montgomery; (1974) 162 Ind.App. 558, 320 N.E.2d 770."

Because the measure of damages sought by Eggacres was included in the given instruction, there was no error in refusing the tendered instruction.

We must now consider whether the instruction given by the court was a correct statement of the law, since error is assigned to the giving of that instruction.

Recent Indiana cases have held that the general measure of damages for an abatable private nuisance is the loss of use of the land, as measured by the diminution in rental value, proximately caused by the nuisance. Friendship Farms Camps, Inc. v. Parson, (1977) 172 Ind.App. 73, 79, 359 N.E.2d 280; Yeager and Sullivan, Inc. v. O'Neill, (1975) 163 Ind.App. 466, 480, 324 N.E.2d 846; Davoust v. Mitchell, (1970) 146 Ind.App. 536, 543, 257 N.E.2d 332; Cleveland, Cincinnati, Chicago & St. Louis Railway Company v. King, (1900) 23 Ind.App. 573, 55 N.E. 875. *See also,* Cox v. Schlachter, (1970) 147 Ind.App. 530, 537, 262 N.E.2d 550; Harrison v. Indiana Auto Shredders Co., (7th Cir. 1976) 528 F.2d 1107. Eggacres contends that the holdings of these cases support the proposition that the damages are to be thus *limited.* We have been directed to no cases, and our own efforts have discovered none, expressly *excluding* the damages elements at issue here.

We first note that our nuisance statutes are silent on the issue of damages recoverable. Ind. Code 34-1-52-1 defines a nuisance as follows:

> "Whatever is injurious to health, or indecent, or offensive to the senses, or an obstruction to the free use of property, so as essentially to interfere with the comfortable enjoyment of life or property, is a nuisance, and the subject of an action."

Ind. Code 34-1-52-2 states:

> "Such action may be brought by any persons whose property is injuriously affected, or whose personal enjoyment is lessened by the nuisance."

And in Ind. Code 34-1-52-3, the remedies section, we find the following language:

> "Where a proper case is made, the nuisance may be enjoined or abated, and damages recovered therefor."

Eggacres argues that while evidence pertaining to injury to health, indecency, and offensiveness to the senses is relevant to the issue of determining the existence of a nuisance, recovery in damages for these matters is not permitted under the Indiana statutes or cases.

We discern the issue to be essentially this: While the damages *for the loss of use of property* attributable to an abatable private nuisance are properly limited to the dimunition in the fair market rental value, may those persons harmed by the nuisance recover damages for losses distinct from those losses occasioned by the interference with the use of their property? We answer this question in the affirmative. In so doing, we are in accordance with a number of our sister jurisdictions as well as other eminent authorities.

We think that dicta found in an early Indiana case is supportive of our conclusion. In Weston Paper Company v. Pope, (1900) 155 Ind. 394, 57 N.E. 719, the plaintiffs were landowners who maintained a farm three miles downstream from the defendant corporation's paper mill. Discharge of effluents from the mill into the stream produced a condition found to "constitute a nuisance," and an award of damages to the plaintiffs was sustained. The court stated:

> "We cannot agree that there was no legal evidence to sustain the assessment of damages. There was direct evidence that a much larger amount of damages than that assessed by the court was sustained from impairment of rental value. *Besides, the court was not restricted to mere depreciation of property but might also have properly considered the inconvenience and discomfort caused [plaintiffs] and their families even though there be no arithmetical rule for the estimate of such damages.* Baltimore, etc., Co. v. Fifth Baptist Church, 108 U.S. 317, 335, 2 S.Ct. 719 [731], 27 L.Ed. 739." (Our emphasis.)

115 Ind. at 402–03, 57 N.E. 719.

In Restatement (Second) of Torts §929(1) (1977) it is stated:

> "Harm to Land from Past Invasions
> (1) If one is entitled to a judgment for harm to land resulting from a past invasion and not amounting to a total destruction of value, the damages include compensation for
> (a) the difference between the value of the land before the harm and the value after the harm, or at his election in an appropriate case, the cost of restoration that has been or may be reasonably incurred,
> (b) the loss of use of the land, and
> (c) discomfort and annoyance to him as an occupant."

And, Dean Prosser would not restrict the Guinns to the diminution in rental value occasioned by the nuisance as their sole remedy:

> "As in the case of any other tort, the plaintiff may recover his damages in an action at law. In such an action the principal elements of damages are the value attached to the use or enjoyment of which he has been deprived, or—which often amounts to a measure of the same thing—the loss of the rental or use value of the property for the duration of a temporary nuisance . . . and in addition the value of any personal discomfort or inconvenience which the plaintiff has suffered, or of any injury to health or other personal injury sustained by the plaintiff, or by members of his family so far as they affect his own enjoyment of the premises, as well as any reasonable expenses which he has incurred on account of the nuisance."

Prosser, The Law of Torts §90 (4th ed. 1971) pp. 602–03 (footnotes omitted). *See also,* 66 C.J.S. Nuisances §82 (1950).

In their excellent brief the Guinns cite many cases from other jurisdictions that indeed recognize damages for an abatable private nuisance are not restricted to the reduction in rental value. *See*, City of San Jose v. Superior Court of Santa Clara County, (1974) 12 Cal.3d 447, 525 P.2d 701, 115 Cal.Rptr. 797; Miller v. Carnation Co., (1977) 39 Colo.App. 1, 564 P.2d 127; Nair v. Thow; (1968) 156 Conn. 445, 242 A.2d 757; Nitram Chemicals, Inc. v. Parker, (1967) Fla.App., 200 So.2d 220; Pollard v. Land West, Inc., (1974) 96 Idaho 274, 526 P.2d 1110; Earl v. Clark, (1974) Iowa, 219 N.W.2d 487; Holmberg v. Bergin, (1969) 285 Minn. 250, 172 N.W.2d 739; Nevada Cement Co. v. Lemler, (1973) 89 Nev. 447, 514 P.2d 1180; Spencer Creek Pollution Control Ass'n v. Organic Fertilizer Co., (1973) 264 Or. 557, 505 P.2d 919; Hendrix v. City of Maryville, (1968) 58 Tenn.App. 457, 431 S.W.2d 292; Lacy Feed Co. v. Parrish, (1974) Tex.Civ.App., 517 S.W.2d 845.

Eggacres further contends that an award of damages over and above the diminution in rental value amounts to a double recovery, presumably because these elements of damages would be reflected in the diminution of rental value. We disagree. This argument was faced squarely in Miller v. Carnation Company, (1977) 39 Colo.App. 1, 564 P.2d 127, and rejected. The Colorado court therein distinguished between the plaintiff's proprietary loss, i.e. loss of use and enjoyment of land, and his personal losses, i.e. annoyance, discomfort, and inconvenience, and held that an occupant-owner may recover both, citing Restatement (Second) of Torts §929, comment e. We agree that personal losses suffered by a plaintiff in a nuisance action, as distinct from loss of use of the property as measured in the reduction in rental value, are compensable.

Eggacres complains that the instruction given was erroneous insofar as it permitted the jury to consider "injury to health" in assessing the damages, contending that there was no competent evidence to support such award. We disagree. Mrs. Guinn testified that the pervasive order emanating from Eggacres' operations caused her to vomit, gag, feel otherwise nauseated and sick, and experience a burning sensation in her eyes. Eggacres maintains that such lay testimony is not competent to prove a causal connection between the odors and Mrs. Guinns' physical reaction thereto. In Davoust v. Mitchell, *supra*, Judge Lowdermilk stated:

"This court has heretofore said that the trial court could consider the ordinary affairs in the lives of men and women and although this court cannot and does not weigh the evidence, we are of the opinion that in deciding whether the evidence is sufficient to sustain the judgment, that we, too, may consider things that happen in the ordinary affairs of life and men."

146 Ind.App. at 542, 257 N.E.2d 332.

Thus we may reflect upon our experience and in so doing find that it does not require expert medical opinion to establish a causal nexus between the exposure to extremely foul odor and the resultant physical responses to which Mrs. Guinn testified. Eggacres' interpretation that, "Parenthetically, these three cases (*Yeager & Sullivan, Davoust,* and *Cox*) also establish that isolated incidents of nausea and vomiting do not amount to an 'injury to health' under clause 3 of Final Instruction Number 4, *even assuming* Final Instruction Number 4, to be correct," is not borne out by our reading of those cases. There was competent evidence to support the giving of the instruction.

We conclude the jury was properly instructed on the measure of damages. Additionally, we note that amount of damages awarded as well within the evidence presented at trial. *See Friendship Farms, supra,* 359 N.E.2d at 285.

Issue II. The Jar

Eggacres contends the trial court erred in admitting into evidence, over strenuous objection, a jar of chicken manure. This evidence was presented to Mr. Guinn during his direct examination. He opened the jar, smelled the contents, and testified that the odor was similar to that which he experienced on his property, and which had been previously described as a "urine-like, gas, ammonia smell." The jar was then passed among the jury for their olfactory examination. Later, during the direct examination of Mrs. Guinn, she also testified that the odors were similar.

Eggacres claims the exhibit was erroneously admitted for the reasons that it was not relevant to a material issue of fact, that it was likely to have a prejudicial impact on the jury, and that it could only have been introduced in order to arouse the empathy of the jury.

The admissibility of evidence is within the sound discretion of the trial court. Tapp v. State, (1980) Ind.App., 406 N.E.2d 296. This court will reverse a trial court for abuse of that discretion only when the trial court's action is clearly erroneous and against the facts and circumstances before the trial court or reasonable inferences to be drawn therefrom. Dunbar v. Dunbar, (1969) 145 Ind.App. 479, 251 N.E.2d 468.

The general standard regarding the relevancy of evidence is whether the evidence has the logical tendency to prove a material fact. In re Marriage of Gray, (1981) Ind.App., 422 N.E.2d 696. The issue in the trial before the jury was the amount of damages to be awarded, and we concluded in Issue I, *supra*, that damages for injury to health are available to a plaintiff in an action of this kind. This evidence was given to the members of the jury to help them understand the Guinns' verbal testimony, given without objection, concerning the nature of the odors to which they were subjected, which odors, according to Mrs. Guinn, caused her to become ill on several occasions. We cannot presume that all the jurors, or any one of them, were familiar with the aromatic characteristics of chicken manure. Evidence tending to illustrate the nature of the odors involved in this nuisance action is, therefore, relevant. Evidence may be found to be relevant even though its ability to persuade is extremely light. Smith v. Crouse-Hinds Co., (1978) Ind.App., 373 N.E.2d 923.

Eggacres complains that this particular jar of chicken manure was not relevant for two reasons: (1) the concentration of manure in the jar was not representative of manure in an "open environment," and (2) the manure gathered from the fields, some two years after the trial court found the odoriferous aspect of the nuisance to have abated, was not reflective of conditions during the time the nuisance existed.

The jar of manure at issue here was demonstrative evidence. For demonstrative evidence to be admissible, that is, relevant to a material issue, the party proffering the evidence must establish a proper foundation. Stath v. Williams, (1977) Ind.App., 367 N.E.2d 1120. The trial court is vested with discretion to determine whether an adequate foundation has been laid. Whitaker v. St. Joseph's Hospital, (1981) Ind.App., 415 N.E.2d 737. Here, Mr. Guinn testified as to the manner of the manure's collection and to the place at which the manure was obtained. Mr. Guinn and Mrs. Guinn each testified that the odor of the manure in the jar was representative of the odors to which they were subjected. We cannot say the trial court abused its discretion determining that a proper foundation was established.

Eggacres next contends the jar of manure was likely to have a prejudicial impact on the jury, and could have only been proffered for the purpose of arousing the empathy of the jury.

It is true that evidence that is found to be relevant may nonetheless be inadmissible if its prejudicial impact is found to outweigh its probative value. Smith v. Crouse-Hinds Company, *supra*. The task of making this assessment is assigned to the trial court and is reviewable only for an abuse of discretion. The prejudice alleged to have been manifest upon the admission of the evidence is that once the members of the jury examined the jar and its contents, they would not likely ignore what they had smelled, and Eggacres was prevented from "fighting back." We see no abuse of discretion. The Guinns were subject to cross-examination at which time Eggacres could pursue the issue of whether the contents of the jar was representative of the odors experienced by them. We think that this evidence was neither prejudicial nor highly inflammatory. Consequently, we hold there was no error in its admission.

Having examined the issues assigned by Eggacres and finding no reversible error, we affirm this cause in all respects.

Affirmed.

RATLIFF and YOUNG (participating by designation), JJ., concur.

✔ PRACTICE QUESTIONS

Indicate whether each statement is true or false.

1. If a person dies as a result of a fatal stab wound, the fact that the alleged perpetrator had a .38 caliber revolver on his person at the time of his arrest would be treated as relevant to prove that he stabbed the decedent to death.

2. An x-ray that is properly authenticated in a manner similar to the way in which a photograph is authenticated and shown to be accurate may be admitted when it may aid the jury in understanding the nature and extent of injuries sustained by a party to the action.

Select the most correct answer to complete each statement.

3. A defendant was found in possession of a gun that, according to ballistics analysis, had ejected a bullet that caused the illegal death of a person. The gun was admitted in evidence at the trial of the defendant for the homicide of the person who had received the mortal injury from the gun. The evidence was properly admitted, assuming that a motion to suppress the evidence was denied, because
   (a) it proved beyond a reasonable doubt that the defendant shot the deceased.
   (b) it was incompetent and therefore relevant.
   (c) it was admissible as relevant and circumstantial evidence.
   (d) it was admissible not as evidence directly related to the trial issues but as circumstantial evidence.

4. A specimen of dried blood _____ be identified as human or animal blood.
   (a) can never
   (b) can

5. A handwriting specimen was demanded of a witness. The witness refused on the ground that he was being deprived of his constitutional right to avoid self-incrimination. He was so advised by his counsel. His claim was correct because
   (a) he was deprived of his right to counsel.
   (b) his handwriting exemplar was his own property and could not be taken without a warrant.
   (c) if his handwriting were taken and admitted in evidence, it would be a denial of his Fifth Amendment Rights.
   (d) none of the above.

Indicate whether the following statements in questions 6 and 7 are true or false.

6. A photograph need not be properly authenticated before it is admissible.

7. A trial judge has no discretion to determine whether or not objects are too gruesome to be admitted in evidence as real evidence.

CHAPTER 17

Presumptions

§ 17.1 INTRODUCTION

Anyone reading this page has probably heard the much quoted phrase, "A defendant in a criminal action is presumed to be innocent and his guilt must be established beyond any reasonable doubt." To state it another way, there is an inference that a defendant is innocent, and it is now up to the prosecution to rebut that inference and convince the trier of the facts beyond a reasonable doubt that this inference is not correct. It has been said that a presumption is a rule of evidence, but it is also a rule of law as to which party will first proceed and go forward with the evidence. It is an inference of the existence or nonexistence of some fact which courts or juries are required or permitted to draw from the proof of other facts. Fla.—Nationwide Mut. Ins. Co. v. Griffin, 222 So.2d 754 (Fla.App. 1969); Ill.— Flynn v. Vancil, 41 Ill.2d 236, 242 N.E.2d 237 (1968). Presumptions have been created in the law from motives of public policy and for the sake of greater certainty. Del.—Bailey v. Blodgett, 49 Del. (10 Terry) 485, 119 A.2d 756 (1955). The inference is mandatory once the "basic fact," the fact which gives rise to the presumption, is established on the trial. Model Code of Evidence Rule 701. This inference (presumed fact) continues until it is overcome by sufficient evidence to the contrary. N.Y.—St. Andrassy v. Mooney, 262 N.Y. 368, 186 N.E. 867 (1933). Where the evidence rebutting a presumption presents an issue of credibility, it is for the jury to determine whether the rebuttal evidence is to be believed and consequently for the jury to determine whether the presumption has been destroyed. N.Y.—Bornhurst v. Massachusetts Bonding & Ins. Co., 21 N.Y.2d 581, 289 N.Y.S.2d 937, 237 N.E.2d 201 (1968).

Sometimes there is a little confusion as to the difference between a presumption and an inference. The difference was explained clearly in Larmay v. VanEtten, 129 Vt. 368, 278 A.2d 736 (1971), where the court said, "A 'presumption' is a deduction which the law requires a trier to make; an 'inference' is a deduction which the trier may or may not make according to his own conclusions." It was defined more cryptically in Cross v. Passumpsic Fiber Leather Co., 90 Vt. 397, 98 A. 1010, where the court said, "A presumption is mandatory; an inference, permissible." A fortiori, Hinds v. John Hancock Mut. Life Ins. Co., *infra*.

§ 17.2 CONSTITUTIONALITY OF PRESUMPTIONS

Many of the liberties we enjoy have been brought about by lawyers who have argued vehemently in favor of their clients. Often their cause seemed to be doomed at the outset, but in spite of criticism from the populace at large and from many of their colleagues at the bar, they continued in their persistence for what they believed was right. Many times this has been done at great financial and physical cost to themselves and their families. These are the unsung heroes of our democracy. They were not always successful.

Sometimes statutes create presumptions unknown to the common law. For example, 18 U.S.C.A. §545 makes possession of unlawfully imported goods sufficient for conviction of smuggling, unless explained. In New York Penal Law §165.15(5), we find that the possession by any person of a defaced machine gun or firearm is presumptive evidence that such person defaced the same.

At first impression, you may think that statutes such as those indicated above are unconstitutional because they force the defendant to come forth with an explanation and hence might be a violation of the privilege against incrimination and due process of law prescribed in the Fifth and Fourteenth Amendments of the United States Constitution. The courts have ruled otherwise. Congress has power to provide in a criminal statute that proof of one fact shall constitute presumptive evidence of another fact. U.S.—United States v. Di Mario, 473 F.2d 1046 (6th Cir. 1973), *cert. denied,* 412 U.S. 907, 93 S.Ct. 2298, 36 L.Ed.2d 972 (1973). The test of the validity of a presumption created by statute is that there must be a rational connection between the facts proved and the facts presumed. U.S.—United States *ex rel.* Rogalski v. Jackson, 58 F.Supp. 218 (D.C.N.D.N.Y. 1944), *aff'd,* 146 F.2d 251, *cert denied,* 324 U.S. 873, 65 S.Ct. 1011, 89 L.Ed. 1427 (1945).

The New York statute quoted was tested in People v. Russo, 278 A.D. 98, 103 N.Y.S.2d 603 (1951), *aff'd,* 303 N.Y. 673, 102 N.E.2d 834 (1951), and it was found that the presumption in the statute was rebuttable and thus the statute was constitutional. Some later cases hold that statutory presumptions that presume a defendant guilty by unexplained behavior are unconstitutional as a violation of the Fourteenth Amendment due process clause. See United States v. Gainey, 380 U.S. 63, 85 S.Ct. 754, 13 L.Ed.2d 658 (1965); United States v. Romano, 382 U.S. 136, 86 S.Ct. 279, 15 L.Ed.2d 210 (1965).

§ 17.3 CLASSES OF PRESUMPTIONS

Presumptions have been divided into the following five classes:

1. Presumptions of law
2. Presumptions of fact
3. Mixed presumptions
4. Rebuttable presumptions
5. Conclusive presumptions

§17.4 Presumptions of Law

A presumption of law is an inference which, in the absence of direct evidence on the subject, the law requires to be drawn from the existence of certain established facts. 31A C.J.S. Evidence 210 (1964). Generally, the effect of the presumption is to place the burden on the adversary to come forward with evidence to rebut the presumption. A presumption of law has been said to be the only true presumption. Utah—Wyatt v. Baughman, 121 Utah 98, 239 P.2d 193 (1951). A presumption of law derives its force from the law of the jurisdiction, not from logic or probability, whereas a presumption of fact is a mere inference. Tenn.—Berretta v. American Cas. Co. of Reading, Pa. 181 Tenn. 118, 178 S.W.2d 753 (1944). The rule that a mere presumption disappears in the face of rebutting evidence has no application where the legislature has directed that the establishment of one fact is prima facie evidence of another fact. Ariz.—Mitchell v. Emblade, 81 Ariz. 121, 301 P.2d 1032 (1956). A presumption of law may be created by statute if there is some justification of public policy. Mo.—Kellogg v. Murphy, 349 Mo. 1165, 164 S.W.2d 285 (1942). For example, New York Penal Law §265.15 reads as follows: "(1) the presence in any room, dwelling, structure or vehicle of any machine-gun is presumptive evidence of its unlawful possession by all persons occupying the place where such machine-gun is found." Other examples of presumptions of law in New York are the presumption of disqualification under Education Law §3022(2) and the presumption of regularity. N.Y.—People v. Langan, 303 N.Y. 474, 104 N.E.2d 861 (1952). We can thus observe that presumptions of law may be presumptions created by statutory law and presumptions created by case law (common law). The presumption is overcome when the adversary produces "substantial" evidence to the contrary. N.Y.—People v. Langan, *supra*. However, some presumptions require a higher degree of rebuttal evidence, for example, the presumption of legitimacy, the presumption of innocence, the presumption against suicide, and the presumption of validity of marriage.

§17.5 Presumptions of Fact

A presumption of fact is that mental process by which the existence of one fact is inferred from proof of some other fact or facts with which experience shows it is usually associated by succession or coexistence. N.C.—*In re* Wall's Will, 223 N.C. 591, 27 S.E.2d 728 (1943). In one New York case, it was held that a presumption of fact is no presumption at all. The court said that it is a term used to describe a logical inference which the trier of the facts is authorized, but not required, to draw from the evidence in the case. Justice v. Lang, 52 N.Y. 323 (1873). The ruling in Justice v. Lang, *supra*, is at variance with the distinction enunciated in Larmey v. Vanetten, *supra*. You will note that Justice v. Lang was decided in 1873, whereas Larmey v. Vanetten was decided in 1971. I urge you to accept the distinction adapted in the Larmey v. Vanetten case. Disputable presumptions are "rules about evidence" in that an inference is permissible, whereas a "presumption" is mandatory and compels the finding of a presumed fact in the absence of evidence to the contrary. Me.—Hinds v. John Hancock Mut. Life Ins. Co., 155 Me. 349, 155 A.2d 721 (1959). A presumption of fact must be drawn from premises which are uncertain. Conn.—Savin Exp. Co. v. Hanover Fire Ins. Co., 132 Conn. 181, 43 A.2d 69 (1945); Fla.—Atlantic Coast Line R. Co. v. McIntosh, 144 Fla. 356, 198 So. 92 (1940).

An example in this area is a case in which the defendant was being sued for conversion of property. A suit such as this is the civil law equivalent of a larceny of property found in the criminal law. The distinction between these actions is that in the civil action the plaintiff is looking for a money judgment against the defendant, whereas in the criminal action the government is looking for penal sanctions against the defendant. Armed with this knowledge, you will understand the decision in Williams v. Sinclair Refining Co., 39 N.M. 388, 47 P.2d 910 (1935). In this action for conversion of personalty contained in a gasoline filling station, wherein there was no direct testimony showing what personalty was in the station when the defendant took possession thereof and wherein the trial court found that the defendant converted personalty, the presumption that the property that the plaintiff had left locked in the station remained and continued in the same condition in which he left it is strong enough to warrant accepting as true a presumed fact that the defendant had possession of the property.

§17.6 Mixed Presumptions

Sometimes it becomes difficult to characterize a presumption as one solely of fact or solely of law. This occurs when a presumption of fact, from its strength, importance, or frequent occurrence, becomes a quasi–presumption of law. Scholars have called this a mixed presumption of law and fact because the court lays down the law and the jury acts on it. N.C.—Lee v. Pearce, 68 N.C. 76 (1873).

§17.7 Rebuttable Presumptions

A rebuttable presumption is a type of evidence that may be accepted and acted on when there is no other evidence to uphold the contention for which it stands but one which may be overcome by other evidence. Iowa—*In re* Weems' Estate, 258 Iowa 711, 139 N.W.2d 922 (1966). The jury may determine if the presumption has been destroyed. N.Y.—Bornhurst v. Massachusetts Bonding & Ins. Co., 21 N.Y.2d 581, 289 N.Y.S.2d 937, 237 N.E.2d 201 (1968).

Later in this chapter, you will read about the presumption of regularity. Such a presumption, however, is rebuttable, as are so many other presumptions. An example of such a presumption being rebuttable occurred in Louisiana (Houston v. Administrator of Div. of Employment Sec., 191 So.2d 167 [La.App. 1966]). In that case, a claimant said he did not receive notice of a hearing (allegedly sent to him), and therefore he should have been permitted to introduce additional evidence before a board of review, and this board should then have decided whether the claimant had received the notice. The Court of Appeal of Louisiana agreed with the claimant.

§17.8 Conclusive Presumptions

A conclusive presumption, on the other hand, is one which is really a rule of substantive law rather than an evidentiary rule. Cal.—Hagny v. Flournoy, 19 Cal.App.3d 496, 96 Cal.Rptr. 786 (1971). Conclusive presumptions are those that rest on a ground of policy so compelling in character that they override the generally fundamental requirement of law that fact questions be resolved according to proof. U.S.—United States v. Provident Trust Co., 291 U.S. 272, 54 S.Ct. 389, 78 L.Ed. 793 (1934). A conclusive presumption cannot be rebutted by other evidence. It is an inference which the law makes so peremptorily that it cannot be overturned by contrary proof, however strong. N.Y.—Brandt v. Morning Journal Ass'n, 81 A.D. 183, 80 N.Y.S. 1002 (1903), *aff'd,* 177 N.Y. 544, 69 N.E. 1120 (1904).

§ 17.9 PRESUMED FACTS

§17.10 Legitimacy

The presumption that every person is born in wedlock from parents who were legally married to each other at the time of conception is a strong presumption of law. The presumption of legitimacy is now rebuttable, although in early common law it was not.

The presumption may now be rebutted by "clear and convincing" evidence which establishes illegitimacy. N.Y.—Committee of Public Welfare v. Ryan, 238 A.D. 607, 265 N.Y.S. 286 (1933). Proof of a husband's impotency or of his lack of access and a negative result of a reliable blood grouping test which is properly conducted which excludes the husband as the father are types of proof which have been held to be clear and convincing. N.Y.—Foglio v. Foglio, 13 Misc.2d 767, 176 N.Y.S.2d 43 (1958).

§17.11 Favoring Love of Life

There is a presumption that a person wants to live unless there is evidence to the contrary. It is therefore presumed that no one will voluntarily do an act which will endanger his own life or the life of others. Iowa—Schofield v. White, 250 Iowa 571, 95 N.W.2d 40 (1959). Even in civil cases where a person had been found dead, even with marks of violence, nothing else appearing, the presumption is that decedent was not murdered. Tenn.—Nichols v. Mutual Life Ins. of N.Y., 178 Tenn. 209, 156 S.W.2d 436 (1941). In another case, murder was held not to be presumed from the mere fact of killing by a gunshot wound. U.S.—McClure v. New York Life Ins. Co., 50 F.2d 972 (D.C.W.D. La. Shreveport Div. 1931). We can therefore say that there is a presumption against a person committing suicide and a presumption against a person willfully taking the life of another. These presumptions are rebuttable in the same way as other presumptions can be negated.

§17.12 Sanity

Sanity is considered the normal condition of man. Every man is presumed to be sane until the contrary is proved. N.Y.—Jones v. Jones, 137 N.Y. 610, 33 N.E. 479 (1893). If a person is found to have committed suicide, the presumption of sanity is not overcome because the cases have held that sane men have taken their own lives. N.Y.—Weed v. Mutual Benefit Life Ins. Co., 70 N.Y. 561 (1877). Formerly, in criminal cases, the presumption of sanity should disappear when substantial evidence to the contrary is introduced by the defendant. The burden of coming forward with evidence of insanity is on the defendant. N.Y.—People v. Egnor, 175 N.Y. 419, 67 N.E. 906 (1903). New York codified this burden of going forward by making insanity a defense. N.Y.—Penal Law §30.05 (now repealed).

In 1984, the New York law was changed. Section 30.05 of the Penal Law was repealed, and in its place §40.15, titled "Mental disease or defect," was passed. The new section reenacted the former definition without substantive change (see People v. Adams, 26 N.Y.2d 129, 309 N.Y.S.2d 145, 257 N.E.2d 610 [1970], for an explanation of the definition). The new statute declared the condition to be an "affirmative defense" instead of a "defense." The difference between these terms is basically as follows. An affirmative defense requires the party who alleges it to prove it by a preponderance of the evidence, whereas a defense requires the prosecutor to disprove the defense beyond a reasonable doubt.

From the discussion of quantum of proof in Chapter 2, you will remember that the proof beyond a reasonable doubt concept requires that the scale of justice have a heavy weight on the side of guilt in order to prove a case beyond a reasonable doubt, as opposed to the preponderance of evidence scale that is usually found in civil cases. The burden on the prosecutor to disprove the insanity defense was so great that it was difficult to disprove the defendant's allegation that he was insane at the time of the commission of the crime. The new statute recognizes that insanity is an excuse but eases the burden on the prosecutor. The defendant, in order to be able to take advantage of this statute, must introduce evidence of such convincing quality as to outweigh any proof to the contrary. These are all issues of fact for the jury to decide on all of the proof in the case from whatever source it comes.

This statute has been successfully used to obtain an acquittal when intent is a necessary element of the crime where the defendant could not have had the intent required because of a mental defect. N.Y.—People v. Colavecchio, 11 A.D.2d 161, 202 N.Y.S.2d 119 (1960).

The United States Supreme Court has upheld the constitutionality of placing the burden of proving insanity on the defendant. Rivera v. Delaware, 429 U.S. 877, 97 S.Ct. 226, 50 L.Ed.2d 160 (1976).

Similar changes in the insanity defense have taken place in many states and in the federal law. For a more detailed explanation of the federal changes that began to take place in 1984, after the assassination attempt on President Reagan, see Rule 12.2, Federal Rules of Criminal Procedure, and 18 U.S.C.A. §§4241 et seq. However, once insanity has been established, it will be presumed to have continued. Fla.—Stanley v. Campbell, 157 Fla. 891, 27 So.2d 411 (1946); Mass.—Parry v. Parry, 316 Mass. 692, 56 N.E.2d 875 (1944); N.Y.—Rosario v. State, 42 Misc.2d 699, 248 N.Y.S.2d 734 (1964).

§17.13 Marriage

When a marriage ceremony is performed, it is presumed that it was properly and legally performed (N.Y.—Fisher v. Fisher, 250 N.Y. 313, 165 N.E. 460 [1929]) and that the marriage is continuing (Ky.—Kentucky Stave Co. v. Page, 125 S.W. 170 [Ky.App. 1910]). A stricter rule is apparent in criminal prosecutions than in civil actions. Accordingly, in a prosecution for bigamy, there had to be direct proof of the marriage. N.Y.—Hayes v. People, 25 N.Y. 390 (1862). In New York, a marriage certificate is prima facie evidence of the marriage. N.Y.—CPLR 4526.

§17.14 Chastity

There is a presumption that people are moral and that they are chaste and virtuous, notwithstanding the modern concept of many people of reverse marriage—the honeymoon first, the living together second, and the wedding third. The presumption of chastity, however, may be rebutted by evidence to the contrary. Cal.—People ex rel. Bradford v. Laine, 41 Cal.App. 345, 182 P. 986 (1919). For example, Missouri Statute §559.300 provides: "If any person over the age of seventeen years shall have carnal knowledge of any unmarried female, of previously chaste character, between the age of sixteen and eighteen years of age, he shall be guilty of felony. . . ." The prosecutor, relying on the presumption of chastity, does not have to prove the female as being chaste. This is a rebuttable presumption that may be rebutted by the defendant.

§17.15 Regularity

There is a presumption in favor of the regularity and validity of a private transaction. For example, in the absence of evidence to the contrary, the foreclosure of a mortgage, being shown, is presumed to be regular and valid. Ala.—Williams v. Oates, 212 Ala. 396, 102 So. 712 (1924). There is also a presumption of regularity in favor of blood tests in the absence of evidence that such tests call for unusual medical skill. U.S.—Wong Fuey Ying v. Dulles, 137 F.Supp. 470 (U.S.D.C.D. Mass. 1956). However, see the section on rebuttable presumptions, *supra*.

§17.16 Validity of Judicial Acts and Duties

Where a court is one of general jurisdiction, there is a presumption that the proceedings are regular and valid. Cal.—In re Newman's Estate, 75 Cal. 213, 16 P. 887, 7 Am.St.Rep. 146 (1888); N.Y.—Hiser v. Davis, 234 N.Y. 300, 137 N.E. 596 (1922). This presumption is conclusive unless it is impeached by the record itself; it does not fall within the rule that presumptions are dissipated by contrary evidence, and hence it is not affected by constrictive admission by demurrer of a change in the bill to the contrary. Tenn.—McCartney v. Gamble, 184 Tenn. 243, 198 S.W.2d 552 (1946). No presumptions are permitted against the validity of a judgment of a court of record. Tex.—*Ex parte* Kuehne, 111 Tex.Crim. 363, 12 S.W.2d 790 (1927). It is presumed that a judgment is valid and subsisting and was rendered only after a hearing according to law. Mont.—State v. Broadwater County Fourteenth Judicial Dist. Ct., 51 Mont. 310, 152 P. 753 (1915). There is a presumption that a judgment roll was actually filed in the clerk's office and that it contained the judgment appearing in the judgment book. N.Y.—Burke v. Kaltenbach, 125 A.D. 261, 109 N.Y.S. 225 (1908).

§17.17 Death After Absence

Under the common law, if a person is absent for more than seven years and has not been heard from in his or her usual places of contact, the person is presumed to have died. This is important to establish civil rights of survivors. For example, an action may then be instituted to have the absentee declared dead so that a spouse may remarry or so that the person's assets may be distributed to beneficiaries or devisees (if the absentee has executed a last will and testament) or to distributees (if the absentee has never executed a last will and testament). Some jurisdictions have shortened the period of absence to five years, or to a shorter period if the person's life has been imperiled. N.Y.—Estates, Powers and Trusts Law §2–1.7. The presumption may be negated by proof showing that the alleged decedent is still alive. In People v. Niccoli, 102 Cal.App.2d 814, 228 P.2d 827 (1951), a surety on a defendant's bond attempted to avoid forfeiture of bail and to have the alleged decedent declared judicially dead. The petitioner introduced evidence that defendant had disappeared after leaving his auto at an airport and that an extensive search had failed to locate him. Other evidence indicated that defendant had been indicted, was a member of a group who had been the subject of a murderous assault, and had good reason to flee. The court upheld the forfeiture on the ground that where a motive or doubt as to the reason for the absence exists, the presumption of continued life remains.

The decision above raises new considerations: first, the fact that the presumption of death is not conclusive and, second, the fact that some situations place one presumption against another. In such a situation, the law of evidence maintains that one presumption is stronger than the other. In the *Niccoli* case, we see that the court held that the presumption of continuance is stronger than the presumption of death after unexplained absence.

§17.18 Conflicting Presumption—First Impression

We have just seen that the presumption of the continuance of life is a stronger presumption than that of death after a period of years of unexplained absence. Rule 301(b) of the Uniform Rules of Evidence provides: "If presumptions are inconsistent, the presumption applies that is founded upon weightier considerations of policy. If considerations of policy are of equal weight neither presumption applies." Conflicting presumptions are explained more fully later in the chapter.

§17.19 Continuance

You have been exposed to several situations wherein the presumption of continuance has been indicated to be a strong presumption. To this point, we have not defined what a presumption of continuance is. It is really an inference or a presumption of fact. Proof of the existence at a particular time of a fact of a continuous nature gives rise to an inference within logical limits that it exists at a subsequent time. Mass.—Malden Trust Co. v. George, 303 Mass. 528, 22 N.E.2d 74 (1939).

Let us assume that four police officers are trailing a suspect and they find that the suspect enters a residential house that is unattached and has four sides to it with two doors leading to the outside. The police officers station themselves so that between the four of them they have unobstructed view of all sides of the house. The suspect does not come out of the house until one and half hours have passed. He then comes out the front door and is followed again by all the police officers. The hour and a half between the time that he entered the house and the time that he exited from the house might be inferred as the time he remained in the house. The officers observed a known fact—that he entered the house and they did not see him come out until an hour and a half later. Based on the presumption of continuance, it would be logical to infer that he remained in the house during that time. However, this is a rebuttable presumption of fact because if a later and recent inspection of the house reveals a subterranean tunnel in the basement of the house, which leads to a location out of the sight of the officers, the presumption of continuance of a fact is negated.

§17.20 Ownership from Possession

When an officer sees a person wearing an overcoat in a cold climate and there is nothing to make the officer suspicious of the person, the officer presumes that the wearer has ownership of the coat. However, this type of presumption has been held to be "the lowest species of evidence," in Rawley v. Brown, 71 N.Y. 85 (1877). It is merely presumptive and liable to be overcome by any evidence showing that the character of the possession is not necessarily as owner. If the custody and possession are shown to be as equally consistent with an outstanding ownership in a third person as with a title in the one having the possession, no presumption of ownership arises solely from such possession.

§17.21 Innocence

In every criminal trial, the defendant is presumed to be innocent of the offense with which he or she is charged. This is based on the common law but is reinforced by statute in most jurisdictions. This presumption means that the burden is on the people to establish the guilt of the defendant beyond all reasonable doubt. This does not mean beyond all doubt, for if this were so, it would be highly unlikely that any defendant would ever be convicted.

In Dodson v. United States, 23 F.2d 401 (4th Cir. 1928), the court held "that a presumption of innocence is not a mere belief at the beginning of the trial that the accused is probably innocent. It is not a will-o-the-wisp, which appears and disappears as the trial progresses. It is a legal presumption which the jurors must consider along with the evidence and the inferences arising from the evidence, when they come finally to pass upon the case. In this sense, the presumption of innocence does accompany the accused through every stage of the trial."

In some jurisdictions, the presumption of innocence is regarded as a matter of evidence in the case. (See 34 A.L.R. 938, 47 A.L.R. 968, 94 A.L.R. 1042, 152 A.L.R. 626.) It is customary to charge the jury concerning the burden of proof, that the defendant is presumed to be innocent.

This presumption of innocence applies to civil as well as criminal cases. Ariz.—State v. Miranda, 3 Ariz.App. 550, 416 P.2d 444 (1966); Cal.—Guidera v. Lapiana, 52 Cal.App. 460, 199 P. 557 (1921); N.J.—Michaels v. Michaels, 91

N.J.Eq. 408, 110 A. 573 (1920). The presumption of innocence is not a presumption of law in some jurisdictions but is evidentiary. It regulates the burden of the evidence. Cal.—Alford v. Bello, 130 Cal.App.2d 291, 278 P.2d 962 (1955). It therefore is considered to be a mixed presumption of law and fact. However, many jurisdictions have made this a presumption of law. N.Y.—CPL § 300.10(2). The presumption means that the burden is always on the prosecution to establish the guilt of the accused beyond a reasonable doubt.

The defendant is entitled to rest upon the presumption of innocence in his favor until this presumption is so far outweighed by the evidence offered by the prosecution that the jury is convinced of his guilt beyond a reasonable doubt. He need not take the stand in his own defense and no inference is to be drawn by his failure to take the stand if so requested by the defendant. N.Y.—CPL § 300.10(2).

§ 17.22   Receipt by Addressee of Mail Deposited in Post Office

There is a presumption that mail, properly addressed and placed in a post office collection box with postage prepaid, is presumed to have been received by the addressee. There must be satisfactory proof that it was duly mailed. N.Y.—James E. Cashman, Inc. v. Spellman, 233 A.D. 45, 251 N.Y.S. 240 (1931). This presumption is rebuttable by evidence that it was not, in fact, delivered or received. Pa.—Teitelbaum v. Board of Revision of Taxes, 65 Pa.D&C. 619 (1949). The proof of due mailing need not consist of direct and positive testimony to the fact of mailing. Proof of the existence of an office practice or custom in the mailing of letters, together with proof that the custom was followed in the particular instance, may constitute sufficient evidence of mailing to support a presumption of due receipt. 31A C.J.S. Evidence § 136 (1964). See the earlier section on rebuttable presumptions.

§ 17.23 Guilt from Possession of Fruits of Crime

The recent and exclusive possession of the fruits of a crime, if unexplained, justifies the inference of guilt. This rule is applicable to all crimes. N.Y.—Knickerbocker v. People, 43 N.Y. 177 (1870); People v. Roman, 12 N.Y.2d 220, 238 N.Y.S.2d 665, 188 N.E.2d 904 (1963). This is a presumption of fact and not of law because the jury is permitted to draw the inference. Let us suppose that an automobile is wanted on a stolen vehicle alarm. The police officer on patrol is alerted, and he sees an automobile meeting the description of the wanted car. He also observes two young men in the car, and it is being operated by one of them. The alarm has been transmitted within 24 hours prior to the officer's viewing the vehicle. There is a strong presumption that the occupants of the vehicle stole the automobile. After being apprehended and brought to court, the defendant who was driving the vehicle takes the stand and testifies that he rented the vehicle from a car rental agency and that he was of the opinion that he could keep it an additional week without notifying the car rental agency. He also testified that the extra week had not yet passed when he was arrested. He then had no intention of stealing the vehicle, and this negates larcenous intent. He did, however, breach a contractual relationship, and in New York State, as well as in some others, he would be guilty of an offense of unauthorized use of a motor vehicle, a class A misdemeanor punishable, upon conviction, by up to a $1,000 fine and/or up to one year in prison. His passenger might testify that he had no knowledge of the unauthorized use but did know that the vehicle was a rented vehicle. The jury might determine that the passenger was not guilty of any crime.

The preceding case probably would never come to trial in a practical situation because after hearing the facts, and if believing them, the district attorney or state attorney would probably ask the court to dismiss the charges against the passenger on the condition that the defendant release civilly all persons who might be responsible for his incarceration. The prosecutor would probably then recommend the acceptance of a plea to a class B misdemeanor (in New York), for which there might be criminal sanctions of up to three months in jail and/or a fine of $500, as well as other sanctions, with a recommendation to the court that the driver be fined. The complainant would still have a civil remedy available for breach of contract. This dual remedy is contrary to the common law in that in common law the complainant must select either a civil remedy or a criminal remedy, not both. In New York, as well as in many other jurisdictions, the legislature has passed statutes in derogation of the common law that make both civil and criminal remedies available to the person aggrieved. N.Y.—Penal Law §5.10(3); CPLR 106.

§17.24 Flight

When an officer arrives at the scene of a reported crime and observes people running from the scene, the officer's first impression is that the running people have committed the crime and are running from the scene. After further reflection, one may understand that there may be other reasons for the flight. Perhaps the person who is running is trying to save his or her life, or perhaps the person is trying to save his or her marital life (he or she might have been in the wrong place at the wrong time) or his or her political life (for the preceding reasons). The person might have run instinctively without realizing why.

All of the circumstances above tend to explain why most states do not consider flight of the accused as a legal presumption of guilt, although it may be introduced as evidence of guilt. N.M.—State v. Rodriguez, 23 N.M. 156, 167 P. 426 (1917). Some states consider flight or concealment an admission of guilt, but such evidence is very weak and has no weight whatever unless there are facts pointing to the motive which prompted it. N.Y.—People v. Reddy, 261 N.Y. 479, 185 N.E. 705, 87 A.L.R. 763 (1933).

§17.25 Constitutionality of Legislative Acts

When a legislative body, be it the Congress of the United States, a state legislature, a city council, or a board of selectmen, enacts a statute, the courts have held that there is a presumption that the statute is constitutional. This, of course, is a rebuttable presumption. It therefore becomes the burden of a person or group of persons who may test the constitutionality of the statute to overcome the presumption by clearly overcoming the evidence sustaining its constitutionality. N.Y.—Wasmuth v. Allen, 14 N.Y.2d 391, 252 N.Y.S.2d 65, 200 N.E.2d 756 (1964).

It is the duty of the Supreme Court to uphold statutes unless it is satisfied beyond a reasonable doubt that the legislature went outside the Constitution in enacting the challenged legislation. N.M.—State v. Ball, 104 N.M. 176, 718 P.2d 686 (1986).

§17.26 Regularity of Official Acts

Let us assume that a hypothetical law requires that a legislative bill be considered for "x" days before it is enacted and then sent to the governor of the state and signed by the governor within "y" days. Once this bill is signed into law and is entered on the laws of the state, there is a presumption that all of the requirements of proper enactment were adhered to. This, again, is a rebuttable presumption. Another way of saying this is that it is presumed that a public official properly and regularly discharges his or her duties or performs acts required by law in accordance with the law and the authority conferred on him or her. Vt.—*In re* Waterhouse, 125 Vt. 202, 212 A.2d 696 (1965); W.Va.—State *ex rel* Smith v. Boles, 150 W.Va. 1, 146 S.E.2d 585 (1965). This presumption is a very strong one and prevails until overcome by clear and convincing evidence to the contrary. U.S.—United States v. Chemical Foundation, Inc., 272 U.S. 1, 47 S.Ct. 1, 71 L.Ed. 131 (1926).

§17.27 Failure to Call a Witness

If a material witness is available to be called to testify on behalf of a litigant and this witness is not called, the fact might be called to the attention of the trier of the facts. The trier of the facts might be persuaded that the reason that this witness was not called is that if he or she did testify, his or her testimony would not support the position of the party who failed to call him or her. This is a dangerous assumption, however, because there might have been other reasons to prevent the calling of this witness. The witness might not be articulate; he or she might be mentally unsound; under a legal prohibition, he or she might be extremely nervous; or he or she might be suffering from some disease or impediment that would, when the totality of the circumstances are considered, preclude calling this witness to the stand. Nevertheless, there is a general presumption that in the absence of explanation the failure to call a witness may create an inference against such party where the witness is available. Conn.—Raia v. Topehius, 165 Conn. 231, 332 A.2d 93 (1973); R.I.—Benevides v. Canario, 111 R.I. 204, 301 A.2d 75 (1973); Wash.—Rognrust v. Seto, 2 Wash.App. 215, 467 P.2d 204 (1970).

§17.28 Withholding Evidence

If material evidence is peculiarly in the control of a litigant and that litigant fails to introduce it at trial or, at the very least, fails to attempt its introduction at trial, it is natural for the trier of the facts to conclude that he or she must be hiding something that would cause the trier of the facts to decide the case against the person who acts in this manner. In the absence of an explanation, the failure or refusal of a party to produce evidence may create an adverse inference where such evidence is within his or her knowledge. Cal.—Am-Cal. Inv. Co. v. Sharlyn Estates, Inc., 255 Cal.App.2d 526, 63 Cal.Rptr. 518 (1967); La.—Arnone v. Anzalone, 481 So.2d 1047 (La.App. 1985); Nev.—Ewing v. Sargent, 87 Nev. 74, 482 P.2d 819 (1971). However, the application of the so-called silent evidence presumption against defendants was improper where there was no showing that defendants had missing witnesses available and failed to call them. La.—Brossette v. Clofort, 481 So.2d 637 (La.App. 1985).

§17.29 Identity of Person by Identity of Name

In the United States, composed as it is of so many ethnic, religious, and racial groups, it is not an unreasonable presumption that a person who has the same name as you and the same middle initial as you is, in fact, you. This is a rebuttable presumption but, nevertheless, is a reasonable presumption in this country. I hasten to limit this presumption to this country; many other countries have problems with this because so many people who have the same name are residing there.

In the telephone directories of some European countries, the employment of the individual follows the name so as to differentiate the identity of the person. However, if we carried this concept a little further, we could have a name like Johannes Schmitt, the baker, and we could presume that a certain Johannes Schmitt who is a baker and resides in that town is the person we think he is.

This presumption is stronger in civil cases than in criminal actions. Identity of name is not always sufficient in criminal prosecutions to show the identity of a person, but it may be accepted as sufficient if fortified by circumstances. N.Y.—People v. Reese, 258 N.Y. 89, 179 N.E. 305, 79 A.L.R. 1329 (1932).

§ 17.30 Knowledge of the Law

As a practical matter, if there was no presumption that everyone knew the law, malefactors might violate the law with impunity if they merely indicated that they did not know their behavior was a breach of the law. Admittedly, I am hard-pressed to explain why the United States Supreme Court, in Miranda v. Arizona, 384 U.S. 436, 86 S.Ct. 1602, 16 L.Ed.2d 694 (1966), made it mandatory for law enforcement officers to advise every prisoner, immediately upon initiating custodial interrogation, about his or her rights to retain a lawyer, to remain silent, etc., if we all are presumed to know the law. Nevertheless, in other areas, the courts have held that as a general rule, subject to qualifications, all people are presumed to know, and are bound to take notice of, the general public laws of the country or state in which they have residence or do business. Ga.—Grady County v. Banker, 81 Ga.App. 701, 59 S.E.2d 732 (1950); Minn.—City of Bloomington v. Munson, 300 Minn. 195, 221 N.W.2d 787 (1974); Mo.—Thies v. St. Louis County, 402 S.W.2d 376 (1966).

As a matter of public policy, all persons are charged with knowledge of the law pertaining to their transactions. Ala.—Turner v. State Employees' Retirement Sys., 485 So.2d 765 (Ala.Civ.App. 1986). A testator is presumed to have known the law at the time of execution of his will. Wash.—Matter of Estate of Mell, 105 Wash.2d 518, 716 P.2d 836 (1986). Likewise, a police officer is imputed with knowledge of the law, including the fact that warrantless searches are per se unconstitutional unless a specific exception to the rule exists. Idaho—State v. Johnson, 110 Idaho 516, 716 P.2d 1288 (1986).

§ 17.31 Regularity of Acts Done in the Course of Business

Like the presumption explained previously with reference to the regularity of official acts, so, too, there is a presumption of regularity of acts done in the regular course of business. Therefore, if a clerk usually completes a sales slip and includes the name of a purchaser on that sales slip and if the name is given to that clerk by the vendee, there is a presumption that the clerk placed the correct name on that sales slip. In the absence of a showing to the contrary, it is presumed that the ordinary course of business or conduct was followed in a particular case. Ark.—Les-Bil, Inc. v. General Waterworks Corp., 256 Ark. 905, 511 S.W.2d 166 (1974); Del.—David J. Greene & Co. v. Dunhill Int'l, Inc., 249 A.2d 427 (Del.Ch. 1968); Fla.—In re Sackett's Estate, 171 So.2d 906 (Fla.App. 1965).

§ 17.32 Res Ipsa Loquitur

"Res ipsa loquitur" is a Latin term that may be defined literally as "the thing speaks for itself." It is applied in the negligence aspect of civil law to be a rule of evidence whereby negligence of the alleged wrongdoer may be inferred from the mere fact that the accident happened, that the instrumentality of the accident was under the exclusive control or management of the alleged wrongdoer, and that one could reasonably believe that in the absence of negligence the injury would not have occurred. In effect, then, the doctrine creates a presumption that the alleged wrongdoer was at fault, and he has to come forward with evidence to show that he was not at fault. Cal.—Bauhofer v. Crawford, 16 Cal.App. 676, 117 P. 931 (1911).

§ 17.33 CONFLICTING PRESUMPTIONS

No general rule can be laid down as to the effect of a particular presumption in the actual trial of a case, since this depends on the rule in the particular jurisdiction and the purpose the presumption is designed to serve. Conn.—O'Dea v. Amodeo, 118 Conn. 58, 170 A. 486 (1934). Where a presumption is a matter of public policy promulgated by a legislature, it disappears when substantial evidence of facts which rebut the presumption is introduced, but where the presumption is founded on the laws of nature, it will not be brushed aside by a mere contradiction. Ark.— Union Cent. Life Ins. Co. v. Sims, 208 Ark. 1069, 189 S.W.2d 193 (1945). Where presumptions are of unequal weight, the stronger will prevail. For example, we have already discussed the presumption of continuance. Let us assume that a man and woman were validly married; there is, then, a presumption that the marriage has continued. Let us further assume that one of the parties to the first marriage entered into a second marriage with a third person. There is a presumption of validity attaching to the second marriage. We thus have two presumptions in direct conflict with each other. In Apelbaum v. Apelbaum, 7 A.D.2d 911, 183 N.Y.S.2d 54 (1959), it was held that the presumption of the validity of the later marriage is considered so strong as to place on the party asserting the invalidity of the second marriage the burden of proving that the first marriage had not ended before the second marriage.

The example above only considered two contradictory presumptions. You can well understand that many presumptions might come into conflict with each other, and a general rule that will cover all situations is difficult to arrive at.

§ 17.34 EFFECT OF PRESUMPTIONS AS A SUBSTITUTE FOR EVIDENCE

It is quite simple to understand that when one party has a presumption favoring his or her position, he or she does not have to introduce evidence to substantiate his or her position. If there are two persons in an automobile and a gun illegally possessed is found on the floor of this automobile by a police officer, in most states there is a statutory presumption that all people in the automobile illegally possessed that gun. The prosecutor is not charged with the responsibility of introducing proof at the trial that each of the occupants possessed the gun, knowing that it was illegally possessed. In this hypothetical case, we also call on the common law presumption of knowledge of the law of the state or county by all people residing or doing business in that place.

We then use presumptions as a substitute for evidence. This shifts the burden of going forward with the evidence to the other litigant. Note, however, that in a criminal trial the burden of proving the defendant guilty beyond any reasonable doubt always remains on the prosecution, but the burden of going forward with the evidence may shift to the defendant because of the use of presumptions by the prosecutor. The burden of proof is not affected by a presumption. Fla.—Leonetti v. Boone, 74 So.2d 551 (Fla.1954); Ill.—Lucas v. Bowman Dairy Co., 50 Ill.App.2d

413, 200 N.E.2d 374 (1964). The Federal Rules of Evidence provide in Rule 301 that in civil cases a presumption imposes on the other party the burden of going forward.

The burden of going forward with the evidence in simple possession of controlled substances cases shall be on the person claiming the benefit of an exception, e.g., immunity of federal, state, local, and other officials in possession of a controlled substance. See 21 U.S.C.A. §§ 885 et seq. Generally, the presumptions of the common law are applicable to federal criminal procedure.

§ 17.35 FEDERAL RULE

The Federal Rules of Evidence have included sections on presumptions:

Rule 301. Presumptions in general in civil actions and proceedings.

In all civil actions and proceedings not otherwise provided for by Act of Congress or by these rules, a presumption imposes on the party against whom it is directed the burden of going forward with evidence to rebut or meet the presumption, but does not shift to such party the burden of proof in the sense of the risk of nonpersuasion, which remains throughout the trial upon the party on whom it was originally cast.

Rule 302. Applicability of state law in civil actions and proceedings.

In civil actions and proceedings, the effect of a presumption respecting a fact which is an element of a claim or defense as to which State law supplies the rule of decision is determined in accordance with State law.

Originally, a proposed Rule 303 was to be adopted to include presumptions in criminal cases. This was not adopted by Congress, and the Advisory Committee's notes indicate that there are presumptions spelled out in specific criminal statutes and that differences between the permissible operation of presumptions against the accused in criminal cases and in other situations prevent the formulation of a comprehensive definition of the term "presumption" and none is attempted, so common law presumptions continue.

CROSS-REFERENCES

Federal Civil Judicial Procedure and Rules (West 1996) (Rules 301 and 302).
Goode & Wellborn, Courtroom Handbook on Federal Evidence (West 1995) (Rules 301 and 302).
McCormick, Evidence (4th ed. 1992) (Rules 301 and 302).

RELATED DECISIONS
Presumptions

Neely v. Provident Life & Accident Insurance Co. of Chattanooga, Tennessee

Supreme Court of Pennsylvania, 1936.
322 Pa. 417, 185 A. 784.

At the outset, permit me to explain what a judgment n.o.v. is. At the end of a jury trial, the party who has lost the case may make a motion for a judgment non obstante veredicto. This is a Latin phrase meaning "notwithstanding the verdict." The word "notwithstanding" may further be defined as "in spite of." Therefore, a losing party in a jury matter may ask the court to give judgment in favor of that party in spite of the fact that the jury has given a verdict against the party who is making this application. The reason that is given in such motions is that the weight of the evidence presented in the trial was so contrary to the verdict of the jury that justice requires the judge to overrule the verdict of the jury. The verdict of the court, overruling the jury's verdict, is commonly referred to as a judgment n.o.v.

This decision presents a comprehensive treatment of the concepts of presumption and inference and determines from whom the proof must come.

* * *

MAXEY, Justice. Plaintiffs are beneficiaries in certain policies of accident insurance issued by the defendant to Dr. Edgar C. Neely, now deceased. One policy insured "against the effects of bodily injuries sustained directly, solely and exclusively through accidental means," in the principal sum of $15,000 and weekly benefits. The other policy insured in the principal sum of $1,500 and weekly sickness and accident benefits "against loss of life, limb, limbs, sight of time, resulting without other contributing cause from bodily injury . . . which is effected solely by the happening of a purely accidental event." Since the plaintiffs in the two cases claimed under the same policies, a stipulation was filed to try both cases together, and, in the event of a verdict for the plaintiffs, the latter by stipulation agreed as to how the proceeds should be divided.

The insured died on October 3, 1932. Plaintiffs' averment was that "on or about August 20, 1932, while Dr. Neely was treating a patient, a piece of glass from an ampoule accidently became inbedded in the forefinger of his right hand and that as a result the finger [later amputated] became infested with septic poisoning," which proved fatal.

Defendant denied these averments, and declared "that leukemia and diabetes fundamentally predisposed to the gangrene of the right forefinger, requiring amputation thereof." Defendant set forth that the insured did not die as a result of septic poisoning, but "from broncho-pneumonia, with leukemia as a secondary underlying cause." Webster's New International Dictionary (2d Ed.) defines "leukemia" as "a morbid state due to derangement of the blood-making organs and characterized by an excessive number of leucocytes [white corpuscles] in the blood."

After trial, the jury returned a verdict for plaintiffs in the sum of $18,975. Defendant made a motion for judgment n. o. v., having at the trial presented a point for binding instructions in its favor. The motion for judgment n. o. v. was later overruled. This appeal followed.

On August 21, 1932, Dr. Neely showed his right index finger to Miss Hancock, who was a registered, trained nurse attached to his office and who was in his employ for five years. Upon examining his finger, she found a small puncture about the size of a pinhead between the first joint and tip of his finger. Around this puncture there was an area of inflamed flesh about half the size of a dime. It was brought out on cross-examination of this witness that Dr. Neely had told her that he had loosened the flesh with a knife around the puncture. Miss Hancock sterilized a surgical knife, probed the wound, and therein felt a gritty substance of some kind which she was able to move backward and forward. She treated the wound with lysol and mercurochrome. She saw the wound the next day, at which time the inflammation had increased. She and Dr. Neely then probed it. She treated the wound on August 29th, when Dr. Neely consulted a physician. Dr. Neely was confined to his bed on September 3d, and on September 5th was taken to the hospital, where the wound in his finger was incised. Upon returning to his home, he was confined to his bed and left it only when he went to his physician's office, until September 9th, when the inflammation had progressed just beyond the third finger and a few red streaks appeared beyond the joint. On September 16th he was taken to the hospital; the inflammation had increased and red streaks appeared upon his arm. On this day his finger was amputated. He returned to his home on September 17th, and he was thereafter confined to his bed, and died on October 3d.

Dr. Lenker testified that, when Dr. Neely came to him as a patient, he found him suffering intensely with pain. The witness gave as his opinion that the puncture that he described was caused by "external violence of some kind." After describing his patient's condition, he testified that the center "of infection was the site of the injury, the opening in his finger." He said the patient "was suffering from an infected hand, which later on developed into an infection which extended up his arm, which resulted in blood poisoning or what we call septicemia." He was asked: "How did the infection get in his finger," and he answered: "Through the opening in his finger."

Dr. Smith testified that, after the incision was made on the 5th of September, Dr. Neely showed signs of improvement, "then the infection seemed to progress until the 16th." He described Dr. Neely as suffering from "an infected wound of the finger." When asked his opinion as to what caused Dr. Neely's death, he answered: "Infection of the finger, followed by a blood stream infection."

The jury was justified in coming to the conclusion from the evidence presented to it that the insured died of blood poisoning which was caused by an infection in his right forefinger. As to the further and fundamental question of whether or not this infection of the forefinger was caused by an accident, plaintiffs had to rely upon circumstantial evidence. As to that the learned trial judge said in his charge to the jury: "The several circumstances relied upon to support the fact [in issue] cannot be presumed, but must be established by proof of the same weight and force as if each were itself the main fact in issue, which here is: 'Was there an accident?'" The court then called attention to the fact that the evidence as to the accident was largely that of Miss Hancock, the nurse who probed the puncture she saw in the doctor's right forefinger and who felt therein a moveable gritty substance. In view of the fact that a moveable, gritty substance was not ordinarily found in a person's right forefinger, the jury were permitted to infer that this substance entered the finger by accidental means. In Watkins v. Prudential Ins. Co., 315 Pa. 497, 173 A. 644, 651, 95 A.L.R. 869 (1934), we said: "The operative facts of the insurance policy sued upon were 'external, violent and accidental means' causing the insured's death, and any evidence, whether direct or circumstantial, that tends to prove the operative facts, is admissible. . . . Causes of action are always set forth affirmatively and if they are to prevail they must be supported either (1) by facts tending to prove directly the cause of action pleaded or (2) by legitimate inferences from circumstances which have met the tests of admissibility." In Hill v. Central Accident Ins. Co., 209 Pa. 632, 59 A. 262 (1904), whether or not the gunshot wound which caused the death of the insured was caused by a pistol accidentally or intentionally discharged was left to the jury to decide from the attendant circumstances. Greenleaf on Evidence (15th ed.) §13, was quoted as follows: "In civil cases it is sufficient, if the evidence on the whole agrees with and supports the hypothesis which it is adduced to prove. . . . In both cases [civil and criminal] the verdict may well be founded on circumstances alone, and these often lead to a conclusion more satisfactory than direct evidence." In Urban v. Equitable Life Assur. Soc., 310 Pa. 342, 165 A. 388 (1933), the jury were permitted to infer from circumstances whether the inhalation of the gas which caused the death of the insured was accidental or intentional. In Pomorskie v. Prudential Life Ins. Co., 318 Pa. 185, 177 A 783 (1935), an accident policy case, this court held that the issue was for the jury on evidence that the body of deceased was found with signs of head injuries apparently caused by a fall, and an autopsy revealed no indications of death from disease. In Mars v. Philadelphia Rapid T. Co., 303 Pa. 80, 154 A. 290, 292 (1931), we stated that, where a fact is deducible as a reasonable inference from the facts and conditions directly proved, it cannot be classed as a mere conjecture or surmise or guess, and that "in both the civil and criminal law, circumstantial evidence is competent evidence."

In Com. v. Harman, 4 Pa. 269, 273 (1846), Chief Justice Gibson declared: "All evidence is more or less circumstantial, the difference being only in the degree." He used an illustration in which the cause of death was inferred, because, as he said, "we cannot account for the death on any other supposition." Chief Justice Bigelow, in Com. v. Jeffries, 7 Allen (Mass.) 548, 563, 83 Am.Dec. 712 (1863), said: "The process of ascertaining one fact from the existence of another is essential to the investigation of truth, and prevails in courts of law as well as in the ordinary affairs of life." In Gray v. Com., 101 Pa. 380, 47 Am.Rep. 733 (1882), in which a defendant was on trial for his life, Mr. Justice Paxson said:

> "We are not jurors, and are not called upon to weigh the evidence . . . further than to say . . . whether there is sufficient evidence to submit to the jury upon a particular question of fact." We also declared that absolute certainty is not required. Wigmore says in the second edition of his Evidence, vol. 1, § 27, p. 232: "The conclusions and tests of every day experience must constantly control the standards of legal logic."

Appellant in its paper book quotes from page 208 of Thayer's Preliminary Treatise on Evidence at the Common Law, that "the jury's verdict . . . must be defensible in point of sense; it must not be absurd or whimsical." The next sentence on the same page of Professor Thayer's book is not quoted by appellant. It reads as follows: "This, of course, is a different thing from imposing upon the jury the judge's own private standard of what is reasonable. . . . The judges are not an appellate jury." On pages 194 and 195, Thayer says in respect to inferences: "The right inference or conclusion, in point of fact, is itself matter of fact, and to be ascertained by the jury. As regards reasoning, the judges have no exclusive office; the jury also must perform it at every step. . . . Courts might always have done their own reasoning, after a fashion, if they had been in possession of a full supply of primary fact; but they were not; and when once juries were called in, at no period of their history could they discharge their special function of ascertaining and reporting facts, without going through a process of reasoning."

Defendant contends that, although the injury to the finger may have been accidental, the probing of the wound by Dr. Neely was an intentional and injurious act. The answer is that, if an accident to the finger started the sequence of events which terminated fatally, the company would be liable under these policies, even though the treatment invited by the trauma contributed to the fatal result. If the insured met with an accident to his finger, the probing of the wound, done admittedly by him, was a natural and probable result, and this probing, though a concurring cause of death, would not bar plaintiffs' recovery, for the accident was the proximate cause. In Jones v. Commonwealth Casualty Co., 255 Pa. 566, 571, 100 S. 450, 451 (1917), the insured's death through accidental means was the fact in issue, and this court held that, though peritonitis is the immediate cause of death and this was due to an operation, "the operation was made necessary by the injury, and defendant cannot escape liability so long as the operation was skillfully performed, as to which no question is raised." In 1 C.J. § 180, p. 470, the following is given as a definition of "proximate cause" as applied to accident policies, "that cause which directly produces the effect, as distinguished from the remote cause, the cause which sets in motion a train of events which brings about a result without the intervention of any force operating and working actively from a new and independent source." In Continental Casualty Co. v. Colvin, 77 Kan. 561, 95 Pac. 565 (1908), it was held that the requirement of an accident policy that death must have resulted "necessarily and solely" from accidental injury is satisfied where the injury was the predominating and efficient cause of the death, and that "other conditions were set in motion by the injury, which may have contributed to [the death], is immaterial." In Gardner v. United Surety Co., 110 Minn. 291, 125 N.W. 264, 266, 26 L.R.A. (N.S.) 1004 (1910), it was held that, when injury is caused by means insured against, and medical treatment administered is rendered necessary by the nature of the injury, the death of the insured, if caused by the injury and the medical treatment, was accidental, within a policy insuring against death caused by "external, violent, and accidental means." In Isitt et al., Exrs., v. The Railway Passengers Assurance Co. (1889) 22 Q.B.Div. 504, the question was whether or not the deceased had died from the effects of an injury caused by accident. The assured had fallen down and dislocated his shoulder. He was taken home and put to bed, where he died twenty-one days later from pneumonia. The court held: "The deceased would not have died as and when he did if it had not been for the accident. . . . He was reduced by the accident to a state of debility in which he was more susceptible of cold than he would have been but for the accident, and was also less able to resist the effects of any illness which might come to him. . . . These facts constitute a chain of circumstances leading naturally from the injury to the death. . . . The circumstances leading up to the death, including the cold which caused pneumonia, were the reasonable and natural consequences of the injury." In French v. Fidelity, etc., Co. of New York, 135 Wis. 259, 115 N.W. 869, 17 L.R.A.(N.S.) 1011 (1908), it was held that, where death results from disease which follows as a natural, although not as a necessary, consequence of an accidental physical injury, the death is within the terms of an accident policy insuring one against bodily injuries sustained through external means, independently of all other causes, the death being the proximate result of the injury, and not of the disease as an independent cause.

In the argument of appellant's counsel, the greatest stress is placed upon the proposition that "inferences cannot be based upon inferences." In other part of their paper book they express what they consider to be the identical proposition by saying that "presumptions cannot be based upon presumptions." While counsel treat these two quoted statements as meaning precisely the same thing, they are in fact two distinct propositions, respectively untenable and sound. As we pointed out in Watkins v. Prudential Ins. Co., supra, there is "a welter of loose language . . . concerning presumptions." We there attempted to make plain the distinction between a presumption and an inference. We said: "They [presumptions] are not evidence and should not be substituted for evidence. . . . Presumptions are not fact suppliers; they are guideposts indicating whence proof must come." We quoted from Professor Thayer in his Storrs Lectures in 1896 as follows: "A presumption itself contributes no evidence, and has no probative quality. . . . A presumption may be called 'an instrument of proof,' in the sense that it determines from whom evidence shall come. . . . The moment these conceptions give way to the perfectly distinct notion of evidence proper—i.e., probative matter, which may be a basis of inference something capable of being weighed in the scales of reason and compared and estimated with other matter of the probative sort—so that we get to treating the presumption of innocence or any other presumption, as being evidence in this its true sense, then we have wandered into the region of shadows and phantoms." Wigmore on Evidence (2d Ed.) vol. 5 §2491 (also cited by us in the Watkins case), says: "The distinction between presumptions 'of law' and presumptions 'of fact' is in truth the difference between things that are in reality presumptions and things that are not presumptions at all. . . . The presumption is not the fact itself, nor the inference itself, but the legal consequence attached to it. . . . A 'presumption of fact,' in the loose sense, is merely an improper term for the rational potency, or probative value, of the evidentiary fact, regarded as not having this necessary legal consequence. . . . There is but one kind of presumption, and the term 'presumption of fact' should be discarded as useless and confusing."

With the distinction clearly in mind between presumptions and inferences, it is obvious that no presumption can be founded on a presumption; and it is equally obvious that inferences may be founded on inferences, as they are in the investigations carried on by scientific men and in the everyday affairs of life. As to the proposition that inferences cannot be based on inferences, Wigmore on Evidence (2d Ed.) vol. 1 §41, says: "There is no such rule; nor can be. If there were, hardly a single trial could be adequately prosecuted. For example, on a charge of murder, the defendant's gun is found discharged; from this we infer that he discharged it; and from this we infer that it was his bullet which struck and killed the deceased. Or, the defendant is shown to have been sharpening a knife; from this we argue that he had a design to use it upon the deceased; and from this we argue that the fatal stab was the result of this design. In these and innumerable daily instances we build up inference upon inference, and yet no court ever thought of forbidding it. All departments of reasoning, all scientific work, every day's trials, proceed upon such data. The judicial utterances that sanction the fallacious and impracticable limitation, originally put forward without authority, must be taken as valid only for the particular evidentiary facts therein ruled upon." Dean William Tricket in an article published in The Forum of the Dickinson School of Law for March, 1906, vol. 10, p. 123, characterizes the postulate that, "when facts are to be inferred from other facts the latter must be established by direct evidence" as "error," and suggests that as a doctrine occasionally recognized as a principle of proof it ought to be "extirpated."

Both in the activities of laymen and in the administration of justice there are many examples of the permissible drawing of more than one inference from a primary established fact. When jurors in their deliberations arrive by a process of reasoning at an acceptable inference of fact, they have a right to add such fact to any previous facts found by them and proceed by ratiocination from such fact or facts to additional inferences of fact and then proceed still further by like process until they arrive at the ultimate conclusion on the issue trying.

In the instant case, the jury, starting with the primary fact testified to, namely, that a "foreign substance" was located in the insured's right forefinger on August 20, 1932, had a right to infer that this substance got in there accidentally; that it or the probe inserted therein as part of a treatment reasonably necessitated by its troublesome presence, caused an infection; that this infection reached the blood stream and caused septicemia; and that this led directly to the insured's death. This was all a legally permissible process of reasoning leading directly to the conclusion which found formal expression in the verdict.

The judgments are affirmed.

People v. Reddy
Court of Appeals of New York, 1933.
261 N.Y. 479, 185 N.E. 705.

This decision provides an example of how corroboration is necessary in some cases and of what effect evidence of flight may have on the final result of a trial. It is interesting to note that when an appellate decision refers to a judge in a lower court as a learned trial judge, the trial judge is being ridiculed, and the judgment of the trial judge is usually reversed.

* * *

CROUCH, Judge. On the night of August 6, 1931, two robbers held up a cider stube, so called, on West Forty-fourth street in the city of New York. In the course of the robbery, one of the victims was shot and killed. The robber who fired the shots was pursued and captured. His name was Baumann. The other one escaped. Baumann and his companion, designed as John Doe, were indicted for murder in the first degree. Baumann was tried and convicted as charged. The judgment of conviction was affirmed by this court. People v. Baumann, 259 N.Y. 600, 182 N.E. 198 (1932). Subsequently the defendant here was arrested and brought to trial as being Baumann's companion and the person named as John Doe in the indictment. His appeal is from a judgment of conviction for murder in the first degree. That conviction was had upon the testimony of Baumann. Unless Baumann be corroborated by other evidence tending to connect the defendant with the commission of the crime, the conviction must be set aside. Code Cr.Proc. §399.

Baumann testified that he was twenty-one years of age and had known the defendant Reddy, who was commonly called "Howie," for five or six years, although he had seen little of him during the year preceding the murder; that on the afternoon of the murder he had driven with Reddy from Keansburg, N.J., where they had both been staying for several days; that after they reached New York, Reddy suggested that they join in a holdup, to which Baumann agreed; that they separated with an understanding that they would meet at Tenth avenue and Forty-ninth street at 7 o'clock in the evening, Reddy in the meantime to get pistols and arrange for the use of a taxicab; that they met at the time and place stated, boarded a taxicab and drove off; that Reddy gave witness a pistol and some extra cartridges; that the taxicab stopped at Forty-fourth street about six doors from Ninth avenue; that Reddy alighted from the taxicab, followed by the witness, the motor being kept running; that the witness took out his pistol, opened the door, and went into the cider stube, followed by Reddy; that they ordered the people in the place to put up their hands and go to the rear of the store; that Reddy did most of the searching while the witness kept the victims covered with his pistol; that when the cash register had been rifled and the pockets of the victims searched, Reddy stepped past the witness saying, "Come on, let's go," and proceeded rapidly toward the front door; that as witness turned to follow, Munich, one of the victims, grappled with him; that at that time Reddy was close to the front door; that witness shouted out, "Wait a minute, Howie, this guy has got me," but Reddy proceeded out; that the struggle between witness and Munich ended after a short time with the firing of three shots, after which Munich fell away from the witness, whereupon the witness ran out and saw the taxicab turning into Ninth avenue; that the witness never saw Reddy again until the trial.

It further appears that when Baumann was searched, following his capture, there was found on him a small photograph of Reddy. He repeatedly denied that that was a photograph of the man who was with him; on the contrary, he asserted that his companion was an "Italian fellow." Baumann's conviction was affirmed by this court on June 1, 1932, and his execution was set for July 14, 1932. Within a few hours of the time set for execution, Baumann made a statement which for the first time implicated Reddy. A reprieve of twenty-four hours resulted, during which the district attorney took a statement from Baumann. A second reprieve put off execution until the night of August 18th. The statements which Baumann had made were not wholly true, and it was not until almost the moment of execution on the night of August 18th that Baumann sent for the district attorney and made still another statement which apparently satisfied that official. A further reprieve was thereupon granted to cover the time of Reddy's trial. After that trial, Baumann's sentence was commuted to life imprisonment. Baumann on this trial asserted that his testimony on his own trial and all statements made by him relating to the identity of his companion had been intentional and deliberate lies for the purpose of shielding Reddy. He frankly admitted that he finally implicated Reddy and became a witness for the people solely to save his own life, and to that end he would not hesitate to lie. The defendant did not take the stand.

* * *

The law of corroboration under section 399 of the Code of Criminal Procedure was concisely but comprehensively stated in People v. Dixon, 231 N.Y. 111, 116, 131 N.E. 752, 754 (1921). "The corroborative evidence," said the opinion, "need not show the commission of the crime; it need not show that defendant was connected with the commission of the crime. (People v. Mayhew, 150 N.Y. 34, 353 [44 N.E. 971]; People v. Cohen, 223 N.Y. 406, 426 [119 N.E. 886]). It is enough if it tends to connect the defendant with the commission of the crime in such a way as may reasonably satisfy the jury that the accomplice is telling the truth." Since the web of proof in every case is unique, corroboration "may vary in its nature according to the circumstances of the particular case." Id. When the trial judge finds that there is some corroborative evidence, it is his duty to submit it "to the jury for them to say first, whether it was worthy of belief, and secondly, whether if true it tended to connect defendant with the commission of the crime." Id., 231 N.Y. 117, 131 N.E. 752, 754 (1921).

The learned trial judge found the possibility of corroboration in evidence related to two matters. One was the alleged flight of defendant following the crime; the other was Baumann's stronger motive for implicating as his companion the man actually guilty, rather than one who was innocent. Accordingly, he submitted to the jury the evidence relating to each of these matters, to say whether it was true, and, if so, whether it tended to connect the defendant with the commission of the crime.

In respect to the matter of the stronger motive, the argument was that Baumann would naturally feel resentment against the man who, instead of responding to his appeal for help, had deserted him and fled in the taxicab with all the loot, leaving him to be hunted through the streets and captured; and hence that his testimony incriminating the defendant was credible in spite of the admitted character and interest of Baumann. So the trial judge charged the jury as follows: "If you find that that contention has merit, you may consider whether that is corroborated by the evidence of the other witnesses. . . . You have heard the testimony of several of the witnesses who were in the place, and of the officers. It is for you to say whether they establish, apart from Baumann, that the other man did escape, did get away in a taxicab, and that Baumann, in consequence of having no taxicab to get into, was captured. If you find that their testimony corroborates Baumann on the question that his accomplice abandoned him, thereby furnishing Baumann with a motive to testify truthfully against the accomplice, you may consider whether that is evidence that tends to connect this defendant with the crime; that is, to show that this defendant is that unknown man that escaped, and that the unknown man was not some other man, some guilty man whom Baumann is shielding."

* * *

In respect to the matter of flight, the general rule is well settled. Evidence of flight, concealment, or analogous conduct is always admissible. From of old, when unexplained, it has been deemed indicative of a consciousness of guilt, and hence of guilt itself. Proverbs, XXVIII, 1; People v. Ogle, 104 N.Y. 511, 514,

11 N.E. 53 (1887); People v. Fiorentino, 197 N.Y. 560, 567, 91 N.E. 195, 198 (1910); Hictory v. United States, 160 U.S. 408, 16 S.Ct. 327, 40 L.Ed. 474 (1896). But "ordinarily it is of slight value, and of none whatever unless there are facts pointing to the motive which prompted it." People v. Fiorentino, supra; People v. Stilwell, 244 N.Y. 196, 199, 155 N.E. 98 (1927). Its consideration, as pointed out long ago, should not be pressed too far. Commonwealth v. Webster, 5 Cush. (Mass.) 295, 52 Am.Dec. 711 (1850). To the extent that it is evidence of guilt itself, it must be taken as corroborative of an accomplice's incriminating testimony.

* * *

The judgment of conviction should be reversed and a new trial ordered.

Simpson v. Simpson
Court of Civil Appeals of Texas, 1964.
380 S.W.2d 855.

This case involves a dispute as to who is entitled to the estate of a decedent who apparently was married more than once to different spouses. The term "putative wife" is used in the decision. The person named as the putative wife is the one who was commonly referred to as being the wife of the decedent. The terms "laches," "estoppel," and "res judicata" are defined in the glossary included in this book.

A motion for summary judgment in favor of the moving party may never be granted if there is even a slight issue of fact between the parties. Therefore, if there is a question as to the truth of factual assertions between litigants, this question (issue) must be decided by the trier of the facts, either a jury or a judge, after a trial has occurred. In this case, the appellate court rules on the admissibility of an affidavit relating to pedigree and on the relative weight of presumptions of the validity of first and second marriages.

* * *

CLAUDE WILLIAMS, Justice. Letha Bethel Simpson brought this suit to establish and recover her undivided interest in the estate of Charles J. Simpson, deceased. She alleged that she was lawfully married to Charles J. Simpson (hereinafter referred to as defendant) on March 5, 1913 and remained his lawful wife until he died in December 1960. Plaintiff named Eloise Simpson as defendant, alleging that she was a putative wife of Charles J. Simpson at the time of his death, and was in physical possession of the property sought to be recovered by plaintiff. Defendant answered, asserting a general denial as well as affirmative defenses of laches, estoppel, *res judicata,* and limitations. Defendant then filed her motion for summary judgment which plaintiff opposed. The court, based upon supporting affidavits and depositions, sustained defendant's motion for summary judgment and plaintiff brings this appeal.

FACTS

Marriage, a status said to be of divine origin, is the pedestal around which the facts of this case revolve. The historical background of this case covers almost a half century (1913–1960). Affidavits and depositions reveal the following as a chronological history of relevant events relating to appellant.

Appellant married decedent on March 5, 1913 in the State of Arkansas. To this union there was born on August 26, 1914, a male child, Floyd Charles Simpson. In February 1917 decedent left her saying that he was going away to work and would send for her. She never saw him since that time. The first she heard from him was thirty years later, in 1947. Appellant attempted to locate decedent during World War I by communicating with the "War Board" who told her they would try to find decedent but such efforts were apparently fruitless. Appellant was never served with legal papers of any nature with regard to the decedent and appellant did not obtain a divorce or annulment from the decedent at any time prior to decedent's death in 1960. In 1920, having concluded that decedent was dead, appellant married one O'Donnell and lived with him until 1930 when they separated. O'Donnell died in 1941. On December 14, 1941, still under the impression she was a feme sole, appellant entered into a ceremonial marriage with Morrill Adams and continued to live with him, as husband and wife, in the State of Kansas, until this marriage was dissolved by court decree in 1954. In 1947, appellant was advised by her son that decedent was alive, living in Dallas, Texas, and married and had children by said marriage. Appellant, upon learning this information, continued to live with Morrill Adams for a period of seven years at which time she obtained a divorce from him in 1954. Charles J. Simpson died on December 21, 1960 in Dallas, Texas. This action was instituted on August 31, 1961.

Affidavits and depositions reveal the following chronological history of relevant events as to decedent and appellee Eloise Simpson. In 1924, approximately seven years after separating from appellant, decedent married Verda Mae Burton in Los Angeles, California. In applying for this marriage license, decedent certified that this marriage was his first marriage and that he was single, not divorced. Decedent and Verda Mae remained married until July 5, 1950 when she obtained a divorce from decedent. Three children were born to this union. In 1947 decedent located his son, Floyd Charles Simpson, in the State of Kansas, and visited with him in Dallas and elsewhere on several occasions. After the reunion of decedent and his son, Floyd Charles Simpson advised his mother concerning decedent's residence in Dallas, as well as his present marital status. On one occasion during a visit between decedent and his son, decedent stated to Floyd Charles Simpson that he, decedent, had never secured a divorce from appellant. In 1950 Verda Mae obtained a divorce from decedent in Dallas County. In 1950 decedent married appellee and such marriage continued until the date of decedent's death in December 1960. No children were born of this union. The official records of Los Angeles County, California, Denver County, Colorado, Tarrant County, Texas, and Dallas County, Texas, the only places in which decedent lived from 1924 until the date of his death in 1960, reflected the decedent never procured an annulment or divorce from appellant.

OPINION

By her first point on appeal appellant contends that the trial court erred in granting appellee's motion for summary judgment for the reason that the record conclusively shows the existence of a genuine fact issue as to whether the appellant was lawfully married to decedent from 1913 until the date of decedent's death in 1960. By her counter points, appellee contends that the summary judgment was proper because the evidence presented does not overcome the presumption of the validity of the marriage between decedent and appellee. She also contends that the statement of Floyd Charles Simpson in his affidavit that his father told him in 1948 that he had never secured a divorce from his mother, appellant, is not a statement of a fact that would be admissible as evidence as required by Rule 166-A(e), Texas Rules of Civil Procedure.

The institution of marriage is a status, more than a mere contract, and has been defined as the voluntary union for life of one man and one woman as husband and wife, to the exclusion of all others. 38 Tex.Jur.2d, pp. 28–29, Sec. 1; Grigsby v. Reib, 105 Tex. 597, 153 S.W. 1124 (1913). It has long been the established law of Texas that a ceremonial marriage entered into in accordance with legal forms will raise the presumption, or inference of its legality. One of the strongest presumptions of law is that a marriage, once being shown, is valid. However, as here, on proof of a second marriage by a party to a prior marriage, the question is presented as to whether a presumption of validity will attach to the second marriage. The generally accepted view is that a second marriage will be presumed to be valid and that such presumption is stronger than and overcomes the presumption of continuance of the prior marriage. 38 Tex.Jur.2d, pp. 89–91, Sec. 44; 14 A.L.R.2d 10–11; . . .

However, such a presumption, strong though it may be, is a rebuttable one. Nixon, et al. v. Wichita Land & Cattle Co., 84 Tex. 408, 19 S.W. 560; . . . While it has been held that the presumption of validity of a subsequent marriage may be rebutted only by evidence that negatives every possible method by which the prior marriage could have been dissolved (Texas Employers Ins. Ass'n v. Gomez, 313 S.W.2d 956 (Tex.Civ.App. 1958)) it has been ruled, with equal force, that in order to rebut the presumption of legality of the second marriage such need not be established absolutely or to a moral certainty, the plaintiff

only being required to introduce sufficient evidence, standing alone, to negative such facts, in which case the weight of the evidence would be for the jury. Hudspeth v. Hudspeth, Tex.Civ.App., 206 S.W.2d 863.

* * *

Appellee argues forcefully that the language of the Supreme Court in Texas Employers Ins. Ass'n v. Elder, 155 Tex. 27, 282 S.W.2d 371 (1955), to the effect that the presumption is one of the strongest known to law, and is, in itself, evidence, and may even outweigh positive evidence to the contrary, is controlling in this case. With full recognition of the forcefulness of the language utilized by our Supreme Court we must not blind ourselves to the pertinent fact that we are here dealing with a motion for summary judgment and not a trial on the merits, as was the Elder case, supra. The familiar rule has been announced repeatedly that in determining the question of whether or not material issues of fact were raised by the evidence, the court, on review, must review all the evidence in the light most favorable to the petitioners; disregard the conflicts in the testimony; and indulge, in favor of the petitioners, every intendment reasonably deducible from the evidence. Any doubt that exists in the mind of the reviewing court must be resolved in favor of the party against whom the motion was granted. Gulbenkian v. Penn, 151 Tex. 412, 252 S.W.2d 929 (1953).

Applying these rules to the factual situation here presented, we find that while appellant probably did not prove the continued existence of her marital relationship with decedent between 1917 and 1960 to a moral certainty, or beyond any doubt, yet she did introduce some evidence of probative force to negative the fact that her marriage to decedent had not been dissolved by divorce or annulment. While it is true that a jury weighing this evidence might be influenced greatly by the presumption of law relating to the validity of the second marriage, yet that is not the question for our decision. We must decide whether there are *any facts in evidence* in this record which would support appellant's contention and thereby which should have been submitted to a jury or a court, as triers of fact. In our opinion appellant has satisfied the law by producing sufficient evidence in the form of affidavits and depositions to create an issue of fact as to the dissolution of the prior marriage. As to appellee's counter point relating to the inadmissibility of the affidavit of appellant's son in which he relates that in 1948 his father told him that he, decedent, had never divorced appellant, we believe that such affidavit was admissible evidence. We think it was within the exception to the hearsay rule which permits testimony concerning declarations about pedigree and family history. Texas Law of Evidence, McCormick & Ray, Vol. 2, Sections 1341–1348, pp. 184–194, and cases there cited. Should we be mistaken in this regard, we feel that even without such affidavit appellant has met the burden imposed upon her to present sufficient evidence of probative force to create an issue of fact that should have been submitted to a jury. Appellant's first point is sustained.

* * *

The judgment of the trial court is reversed and remanded.

Reversed and remanded.

Larmay v. Vanetten

Supreme Court of Vermont, 1971.
129 Vt. 368, 278 A.2d 736.

This decision distinguishes a presumption and an inference. It also further explains the procedure of directed verdict.

Before HOLDEN, C. J., SHANGRAW, BARNEY, SMITH AND KEYSER, JJ.

KEYSER, Justice.

This is an automobile passenger case brought to recover damages for injuries suffered by the plaintiff. The defendant denied liability and asserted the affirmative defenses of contributory negligence and assumptions of the risk by the plaintiff.

Trial was by jury. At the close of all of the evidence plaintiff moved for a directed verdict as to liability. The court granted the motion and submitted the case on the question of damages. The jury returned a verdict for the plaintiff to recover the sum of $5500.00. The defendant appealed and claims (1) that the trial court erred in directing a verdict for the plaintiff and (2) that the verdict was excessive.

In considering the defendant's first ground for appeal we must take the evidence in the light most favorable to the defendant, she being the party against whom the motion was directed. The evidence thus viewed discloses the following factual situation relative to the defendant's liability.

The plaintiff was returning from work at about 7:30 P.M. on December 22, 1967 as a passenger in a Cadillac car owned and operated by a Mr. Goodrich northerly on Route 7 just south of Shelburne Village. The defendant was operating her Volvo automobile southerly at the same time and place. She was travelling behind a hay truck and in front of an automobile driven by a Mr. Pond. It was nearly dark and the cars had their lights on. Each vehicle was being operated at approximately 40–45 miles per hour.

As the cars approached each other on the brow of a hill, the cars were in a near head-on collision which, according to the testimony, was caused by the defendant's car moving into the north-bound lane in which the Goodrich car was travelling. The defendant concedes in her brief that her car travelled to her left into the northbound lane of traffic although she testified that she had no recollection of the facts surrounding the accident. The defendant was returning home from work after an office party and the last thing she recalled was that she was following behind a truck or tractor trailer through the village of Shelburne. The defendant's vehicle came to rest mostly in the northbound lane.

Mr. Pond testified that he pulled out in back of a Volvo on Route 7 in South Burlington and was following it and that the defendant's car was right behind a truck or tractor trailer. He said he "noticed it (the Volvo) tended to dart from one side of the road to the other, from the shoulder past the yellow line or center line and back to the shoulder again . . . and it went like this all the way to Shelburne, at which point the accident took place." This evidence was uncontradicted.

The defendant contends that the mere presence of her vehicle in the opposite lane of traffic or the passage of her vehicle over the center line of the highway does not establish negligence on her part as a matter of law.

By granting plaintiff's motion for a directed verdict, the court ruled that on the evidence the defendant was guilty of negligence as a matter of law in the operation of her automobile. Beaucage v. Russell, 127 Vt. 58, 60, 238 A.2d 6311. The burden of showing that the defendant was guilty of some negligent act or omission that proximately caused the accident was, of course, on the plaintiff. Burleson v. Caledonia Sand & Gravel Co., 127 Vt. 594, 596, 255 A.2d 680.

Under the rules of the road governing the conduct and operation of vehicles upon a public highway, 23 V.S.A. § 1032, it is provided:

> "Operators of vehicles proceeding in opposite directions shall exercise due care and shall each keep to the right of the center of the highway so as to pass without interference."

Other applicable rules of the road are found in 23 V.S.A. §§ 1035 and 1037. The pertinent part of Section 1035 requires that "(a)n operator of a vehicle overtaking another vehicle proceeding in the same direction shall not pass . . . to the left of the center of the highway unless the way ahead is clear of approaching traffic." Section 1037 provides that "(a) vehicle shall not pass another from the rear at the top of a hill or on a curve where the view ahead is in anywise obstructed, ..." So too, the defendant was under the duty to have her car under reasonable control. Williamson v. Clark, 103 Vt. 288, 291, 153 A. 448.

The rules of the road are safety statutes and proof of their violation, on the part of one charged with negligence, makes out a prima facie case of negligence against the offending operator. Heath v. Orlandi, 127 Vt. 204, 206, 243 A.2d 792. But this presumption of negligence is, of course, open to rebuttal. *Ibid.* See also Gilbert v. Churchill, 127 Vt. 457, 461, 252 A.2d 528. A true legal presumption is in the nature of evidence, and is to be weighed as such. Sheldon v. Wright, 80 Vt. 298, 319, 67 A. 807. Being a disputable presumption, it shifts to the party against whom it operates the burden of evidence. And the prima facie case would become the established case, if nothing further appears. Hammonds, Inc. v. Flanders, 109 Vt. 78, 82, 191 A. 925. The presumption points out to the party on whom it lies the duty of going forward with evidence on the fact presumed. And when that party has produced evidence fairly and reasonably tending to show that the real fact is not as presumed, the office of the presumption is performed and disappears from the arena. Tyrrell v. Prudential Ins. Co. of America, 109 Vt. 6, 23–24, 192 A. 184. We are not unmindful that safety rules are not hard and fast, nor absolute in application to all circumstances. Smith v. Blow & Cote, Inc., 124 Vt. 64, 69, 196 A.2d 489.

Thus, if the defendant desired to overcome the effect of the presumption it was her duty to present evidence to rebut it. She was accorded this opportunity but failed to exercise it. A diligent search of the record fails to disclose any evidence introduced by her in this respect. Her own testimony, of course, does not touch on the question of how and why the accident happened as it did. The defendant offered no countervailing evidence to the presumption or to explain her manner of operating her vehicle "darting from one side of the road to the other." If there was any such evidence it was not forthcoming and this left the presumption of negligence standing unchallenged.

The defendant claims the plaintiff, before he can have the benefit of prima facie negligence doctrine, is required "to establish, through evidence, that it was an act of the defendant-operator which caused defendant's vehicle to cross the center line." This is not the law and, furthermore, the unchallenged testimony of Mr. Pond demonstrates with definite clarity that it was the act of the defendant which caused her car to be on the wrong side of the road.

The appellant calls attention to the testimony of Mr. Pond where he testified:

> "Well, we were heading—I was directly in back of the Volvo. We were heading up the hill out of Shelburne, and the Volvo was very close to the hay truck. It seemed it was almost under the hay truck, and then I just remember the Volvo darting out into the northbound lane as if the car went out of control or it was a last minute decision to pass the hay truck, and at that time the Cadillac was right there and they just hit head-on."

Later, he said: "I couldn't determine whether the Volvo was passing the hay truck. It was such a sudden move, it looked like it got out of control."

The defendant contends that Mr. Pond's "testimony clearly justifies a permissible inference that, for some reason, the defendant's vehicle became out of control before it ever left its proper lane of travel." A permissible inference must rest upon a logical deduction from established facts in order to provide a conclusion which the triers of fact may or may not find along with the other evidence in a case.

The defendant argues that since there was evidence allowing a reasonable inference of mechanical failure or dangerous road conditions, the court erred in granting plaintiff's motion for a directed verdict as to liability. First, there was no evidence of the existence of dangerous road condition but there was evidence that the weather was fair. Secondly, the testimony of Mr. Pond neither supports the argument nor the rationalization claimed for it. The evidence fails to establish the basic fact or facts which rise up to meet and counter the presumption of negligence.

Although we find no evidence in the record on which such an inference could be based, we must bear in mind that a presumption and an inference are not the same thing. A "presumption" is a deduction which the law requires a trier to make; an "inference" is a deduction which the trier may or may not make according to his own conclusions. A presumption is mandatory; an inference, permissible. Cross v. Passumpsic Fiber Leather Co., 90 Vt. 397, 407, 98 A. 1010.

At the close of all of the evidence, the plaintiff, having established a violation of the safety statutes, made out a prima facie case of negligence against which no rebuttal evidence was produced fairly and reasonably tending to show the real fact was not as presumed. Thus confronted, the trial court properly granted plaintiff's motion on the question of liability. Scrizzi v. Baraw, 127 Vt. 315, 320, 248 A.2d 725.

The defendant cites cases relating to the doctrine of *res ipsa loquitur* which she claims is applicable because this case she asserts involves an unexplained accident. Concerning this claim we need only to point out that

there are no basic facts in the record establishing the application of the doctrine. See Marsigli v. C. W. Averill Co., 123 Vt. 234, 236, 185 A.2d 732.

The defendant claims the court erred in denying her motion to set aside the verdict of $5500.00 as excessive. The defendant's argument is primarily based on the fact that the medical bills incurred by plaintiff amount to only about $200 and no permanent injuries were shown.

That ground of the motion which asserted the verdict was against the weight of, and not sustained by, the evidence was directed to the discretion of the trial court. Scrizzi v. Baraw, supra, at page 322, 248 A.2d 725. The right to set aside a verdict is based, ultimately on the proposition that an injustice would result from permitting the verdict to stand. Verdicts are not to be lightly disregarded, for it is the proper province of the jury to settle questions of fact. *Ibid.* In considering the motion, the court takes the evidence in the light most favorable to the plaintiff and excludes the effect of modifying evidence.

The defendant's principal argument is that the verdict was grossly excessive under the circumstances shown by the evidence. The evidence in the light most favorable to the plaintiff shows that the plaintiff had facial and spinal injuries, had a post-traumatic syndrome, suffered pain for sometime, was under medical treatment and medication at the time of trial, had lost income for lack of ability to perform his usual duties as salesman, further pain and medication would continue for a time, and that he was treated by a surgeon and neurologist. His medical expenses were $241.90.

General verdicts should be construed to give them effect, if that can reasonably be done. And, ordinarily, the court will not interfere with the jury's province to determine the amount of damages where the evidence as to damages is conflicting. Brunelle v. Coffey, 128 Vt. —, 264 A.2d 782, 786. This court will not interfere unless it appears that the jury's determination is so small or large that it plainly indicates the award was the product of prejudice or other misguidance which undermines its validity as a verdict. Quesnel v. Raleigh, 128 Vt. —, 258 A.2d 840, 843. See also Gustin v. Asskov, 129 Me. 494, 151 A. 443, 444.

Our search of the record does not indicate that the jury acted as a result of passion, prejudice, or other improper motive. The court's refusal to set the verdict aside as to damages is sustained since no abuse of discretion has been established. Quesnel v. Raleigh, supra, at p. 845. We are satisfied that the motion was properly denied.

Judgment affirmed.

Houston v. Administrator of Division of Employment Security

Court of Appeals of Louisiana, 1966.
191 So.2d 167.

This short decision explains that presumptions of regularity in office procedure may be rebuttable.

Before CULPEPPER, TATE and HOOD, JJ. CULPEPPER, Judge.

This is an appeal by the Administrator of the Division of Employment Security from a judgment of the district court, pursuant to LSA-R.S. 23:1634.

Ernest Houston filed a claim for unemployment compensation benefits. (See LSA-R.S. 23:1621–1635 for the procedure for filing and determining these claims.) The agency made an initial determination that the claimant was not entitled to benefits because he voluntarily quit his job (as a cook in a cafe) without good cause connected with his employment. On being notified of his disqualification, claimant appealed to the Appeals Referee. The issue in this case arises from the fact that the claimant did not appear at the hearing called by the referee. The claimant contends he received no notice of the hearing.

A copy of the notice, in the records of the division, shows that on June 14, 1965 notice was mailed to the claimant, at the address shown on his claim, "General Delivery, Marksville, Louisiana," advising him that a hearing before the Appeals Referee would be held in the Employment Office, 805 Murray Street, Alexandria, Louisiana on Monday, June 21, 1965, at 10:30 A.M. At the appointed time and place the referee called for the claimant. When he did not answer, the referee waited for an additional 15 minutes, after which time he again called for the claimant, all in accordance with Rule No. 7 of the Louisiana Board of Review. Receiving no answer the second time, the Appeals Referee dismissed the claimant's appeal "with prejudice for lack of prosecution."

The claimant then appealed to the Louisiana Board of Review, asserting that he did not receive notice of the hearing before the Appeals Referee. The Board took no new evidence. It simply found the referee correctly dismissed the appeal "because of non-appearance in accordance with Rule No. 7."

The claimant then petitioned the district court for judicial review. In the district court the claimant was apparently allowed to testify that he did not receive the notice. Although the record does not contain this testimony, the district judge's written opinion states:

> "The Court questioned this claimant considerably, was impressed with his sincerity and apparent truthfulness. He positively maintains that he never received the notice of the hearing; he had been waiting for it; if he had received it, he intended to be present."

Judgment was rendered remanding the case to the Board, with directions that proper notice be given and the case reopened to provide claimant an opportunity to present his evidence. From this judgment, the administrator has appealed.

The administrator relies on Sweet v. Brown, La.App., 125 So.2d 261 (3rd Cir. 1960), which was followed in Austin v. Administrator, Division of Emp. Sec., La.App., 158 So.2d 74 (1st Cir. 1963). In the Sweet case the Department's record of the claim contained a notation by office personnel that a notice was mailed to the claimant on a certain date. It was argued that this mere notation in the record was not sufficient proof of the date or the mailing; and that the Department should, in addition, be required to show by registered mail receipts, postmarks or testimony of office personnel that the notice was properly mailed on the date indicated. We held that this notation in the record was sufficient proof to establish a presumption that the notice was mailed on the date shown, because public employees are presumed to perform properly the duties required of them and official records are presumed to be correct. But, we expressly stated there was absolutely no evidence to rebut this presumption.

The administrator apparently contends that under the holdings in these cases there is a conclusive presumption that the information appearing on the face of the notice is correct, i.e., (1) that the notice was mailed on the date shown, and (2) that the claimant received it. We do not so interpret the cited cases. We think these presumptions are not conclusive; but, instead, are rebuttable.

For a general discussion of the classes of presumptions and distinctions between them see 31A C.J.S. Verbo Evidence §115, pp. 196–199. As a general rule, the presumption of proper performance of official duties and correctness of official records is rebuttable. Coen v. Toups, La.App., 168 So.2d 893 (2nd Cir. 1964) and authorities cites therein. Likewise, several Louisiana cases state that the presumption of receipt of a letter properly addressed and mailed is rebuttable. Paz v. Implement Dealers Mutual Insurance Co., 89 So.2d 514 (Orl.App. 1956).

With this understanding of the law, it is apparent the Board of Review should have allowed the claimant to introduce additional evidence at its hearing, or on remand to the appeals tribunal, to rebut the presumption that claimant received the notice. LSA-R.S. 23:1630 expressly allows the board to hear additional evidence. After receiving such additional evidence, the board should decide whether claimant received the notice. This is a question of fact for the board, not the courts.

The district judge is expressly forbidden to receive additional evidence. LSA.-R.S. 23:1634 provides:

> "No additional evidence shall be received by the court, but the court may order additional evidence to be taken before the board of review, and the board of review may, after hearing such additional evidence, modify its findings of fact or conclusions, and file such additional or modified findings and conclusions, together with a transcript of the additional record, with the court."

For the reasons assigned, the judgment of the district court is amended to read as follows: The decision of the Board of Review is reversed and set aside. This case is remanded to the Board of Review for the taking of additional evidence in accordance with the views expressed herein; and for further proceedings in accordance with law.

Amended and affirmed.

✔ PRACTICE QUESTIONS

Indicate whether each statement is true or false.

1. "D" was brought to trial for murder. At the trial, "D" stood mute. The judge charged the jury that "D" is entitled to a presumption of innocence and that the fact that he did not take the stand to testify should not influence its decision. He further charged that the prosecutor had the burden of proving "D" guilty beyond any reasonable doubt. The judge's instructions were correct.

2. Police officers are trailing a suspect, and they find that he has entered a house. The officers surround the house on all sides and keep it under constant observation. The suspect is seen coming out of the house one and a half hours after he had gone in. There is a presumption that the suspect continued to remain in this house during that time.

3. Your instructor is seen to be in possession of a valuable pen. It is presumed that he rightfully owns the pen.

4. "W" was the wife of "H." "H" went on a fishing trip and never returned. "W" kept hoping that "H" would return until after seven years had passed. She then started to keep company with "D," who married her the following year. "W"

told the marriage license clerk that her former husband had been missing for eight years, and he issued the marriage license. His action was proper.

5. "D" was out on bail on a charge of extortion. His auto was found at an airport, and an extensive search failed to locate him. He was a member of a group that had been the subject of a murderous assault, and he had good reason to flee. The state has a five-year presumption of death statute. The bondsman attempted to get his bond back from the court based on the presumption that "D" was dead because he had absented himself for more than five years. The court upheld the forfeiture because where a motive or doubt as to the reason for the absence exists, the presumption of continued life remains. The court's action was proper.

Select the most correct answer to complete each statement.

6. "D" was seated alone in the front passenger seat of a vehicle. "P," a police officer with a sixth sense, did not like the looks of "D" and checked out the license plate number of the vehicle, only to find that the vehicle was stolen. After obtaining assistance from a fellow officer, he arrested "D" for unauthorized use of a stolen vehicle and grand larceny (grand theft). "D" claimed that he did not know that the vehicle was stolen.
    (a) Since "D" was not in the driver's seat, the prosecutor could not use the presumption of guilt from possession of the fruits of the crime in the trial.
    (b) Since "D" was in possession of the vehicle when seen by "P," the presumption would lie. However, it is a rebuttable presumption, and "D" would have the burden of going forward with the evidence to be found not guilty.
    (c) Since "D" claimed that he did not know it was stolen, he cannot be held liable.
    (d) None of the above.

7. (a) A "presumption" is a deduction that the law requires a trier of the facts to make, whereas an "inference" is a deduction that the trier may or may not make according to the trier's own conclusions.
    (b) Presumptions have been divided into the following four classes:
        (1) presumptions of law
        (2) presumptions of fact
        (3) rebuttable presumptions
        (4) conclusive presumptions
    (c) There is no presumption of sanity.
    (d) When a marriage ceremony is performed, it is presumed that it was not conducted properly.

CHAPTER 18

Admissions in Pretrial Pleadings, Agreements by Stipulation Admissions in Open Court, and Judicial Notice

§ 18.1 INTRODUCTION

In every trial, one of the parties has the burden of proof. In a criminal trial, the burden is on the prosecution to prove the defendant's guilt beyond a reasonable doubt. Sometimes the burden shifts to a slight degree. For example, in some jurisdictions, if the defendant raises a defense that he or she is an infant and therefore incapable of committing the crime, the prosecution must disprove this defense beyond a reasonable doubt. On the other hand, it is an affirmative defense in any prosecution for coercion committed by instilling in the victim a fear that he or she or another person would be charged with a crime to assert that the defendant reasonably believed the threatened charge to be true and his or her sole purpose was to compel or induce the victim to take reasonable action to make good the wrong that was the subject of such threatened charge. N.Y.—Penal Law § 135.75. In this case, the defendant in New York, and in many other jurisdictions, would merely have to go forward with the evidence to establish his or her affirmative defense by a preponderance of the evidence. N.Y.—Penal Law § 25.00.

Let us assume that a homeowner looks at his front door and finds drawings in crayon on it. He believes that a certain neighborhood boy did this as a prank. He finds the boy, accuses him of drawing with crayons, forces him bodily to the scene of the alleged crime, and compels him to scrub the door until the crayon marks are removed. The boy returns to his home and tells his parents. The parents cause criminal charges to be brought against the homeowner. One of the charges is coercion (i.e., compelling the boy to engage in conduct that he has a legal right to abstain from doing). Later investigation by the authorities reveals that another boy committed the act. The homeowner can raise the affirmative defense of the fact that he reasonably believed that the boy he coerced had committed the act of defacing his property. He need only establish this by a preponderance of the evidence.

However, it is basic in a criminal case that the rule that the defendant is entitled to the benefit of a reasonable doubt applies not only to the case as made by the prosecution, but also to any defense interposed. N.Y.—People v. Downs, 123 N.Y. 558, 564, 25 N.E. 988, 989 (1890). It therefore seems to be that the true rule is that if the defendant interposes an affirmative defense in some jurisdictions, the burden of coming forward with the evidence is on the defendant, but the burden still remains with the prosecution to prove the defendant guilty beyond any reasonable doubt.

Certain items of fact that need not be proved may be introduced at trial. The reason these items need not be proved is that it would needlessly prolong the trial and insult the intelligence of all concerned. The following need not be proved:

1. that which is admitted in pretrial pleadings
2. that which is agreed to by pretrial pleadings by means of stipulation
3. that which is admitted by lawyer adversaries or their parties in open court
4. that which is judicially noticed

§18.2 That Which Is Admitted in Pretrial Pleadings

Before a court case comes to trial, there may be exchanges between the lawyer adversaries of what are termed pretrial pleadings. These are more prevalent in a civil case than in a criminal case. However, even in a criminal case, there may be some pretrial pleadings. The pleadings consist of writings that are prepared by the attorneys and submitted to the court. For example, in the usual criminal case, an affidavit is prepared, sometimes known as a complaint or an accusatory instrument, charging the defendant with the commission of an offense or crime or other type of infraction of the law. The terms "offense," "crime," "felony," "traffic infraction," and "violation" may have different definitions in different jurisdictions, and you are advised to consult your state's criminal laws for precise definitions of these terms in the involved jurisdiction. However, basically all jurisdictions have formal written accusatory instruments. They may also be termed "informations" or "indictments," depending again on the jurisdiction and the severity of the legal infraction.

Sometimes the accusatory instrument is a general statement alleging misconduct by the defendant and indicating that the misconduct was a violation of the designated section of a statute. The defendant's attorney will then serve on the prosecution what is known as a demand for a bill of particulars. Let us assume that an indictment charges a defendant with the unlawful possession of a firearm on a designated date at a designated place in violation of a section of a state statute. The defendant's attorney may serve on the prosecutor and the court clerk a motion for a bill of particulars returnable at a future session of the court in which he or she demands to know more about the allegation of misconduct in order to properly defend the defendant. The defendant's attorney may ask such questions as the following:

1. What is the exact location and time of the day that the defendant is alleged to have possessed the firearm?
2. Was the defendant alone or with others at the time of the apprehension?
3. If the defendant was with others, what are the names and addresses of the others?
4. Was the defendant in an auto or on foot or in a building at the time of apprehension?

5. If the defendant was in an auto, what seat was he in immediately before the apprehension?
6. Was the weapon found on the person of the defendant or in some other place?
7. If the weapon was found in some other place, in what place was it found?
8. If the weapon was found in an automobile, was this a vehicle designed to carry merchandise as a public livery, or was this a taxicab or other type of vehicle?
9. Was the defendant operating this vehicle for hire, or was he operating it not for hire, or was he a passenger?

It is quite evident that the list of questions could be carried on much further.

The court determines what it feels is necessary for the defendant to know to provide a defense and what is evidentiary and can only be brought out at the trial. The court will then direct the prosecutor to answer certain of the demands for a bill of particulars. Let us assume that the court directs the district attorney to answer questions 4, 5, 6, 7, and 9 and the prosecutor, in writing, answers that the defendant was in an automobile in the driver's seat, that the weapon was found in the rear section of a taxicab where others were seated, and that the defendant was operating the vehicle for hire. If the prosecutor did not answer with these facts, it would have been necessary for defense counsel to introduce testimony in order to inform the trier of the facts that the defendant was a taxi or public livery driver who was hired to transport passengers and/or cargo and had no knowledge of the contents of the cargo or was transporting the cargo lawfully.

In civil actions, as has been said, the use of admissions in pretrial pleadings is much more widespread. In some jurisdictions, the case is begun by the service of a summons on the defendant, followed by a notice of appearance and demand for a complaint from the defendant's counsel to plaintiff's counsel. This is followed by service of a complaint on the defendant's counsel, which, in turn, is followed by an answer to the complaint. Here, too, there may be a demand for a bill of particulars, which, if not honored by the adversary, is followed by a notice of motion for a bill of particulars returnable in court, much the same as in the criminal case. This may be followed by an examination before trial, or a deposition of the plaintiff. These are all characterized as pretrial pleadings, and certain admissions made in these papers need not be proved at the trial by witnesses. This shortens the trial without any injustice being done to either party.

§18.3 That Which Is Agreed to by Pretrial Pleadings by Means of Stipulation

Let us return to our taxi or livery driver. It might be possible for the defense counsel to ask the prosecutor to stipulate (agree to a fact situation) that the defendant was operating a taxi as a taxi driver for hire at the time of the alleged wrongful possession of the weapon, that others were in the vehicle with him at the time, and that the weapon was found in the rear of the vehicle. If the prosecutor agrees to these facts, the defense attorney may have this stipulation typed, and both the defendant's attorney and the prosecutor will subscribe their names to the document. At the time of trial, it may be read into evidence so that the trier of the facts will understand that these facts were agreed to and need not be proved by testimony of witnesses. You may wonder why a prosecutor would agree to such a stipulation. This is done because the prosecutor does not believe it is material to prove that the taxi driver was actually in a conspiracy with the passengers. This will be accomplished by the introduction of other evidence.

§18.4 That Which Is Admitted by Lawyer Adversaries or Their Parties in Open Court

Let us once again return to our taxi driver. The defendant's attorney may in open court, immediately before the trial, address the prosecutor thus: "Will the people stipulate that defendant John Doe at the time of the alleged commission of this offense was a driver of the ABC Taxi Corp.; that he was operating an auto owned by the said corporation, which was a public taxi cab bearing license plate or tag number 034567 for this state and that he was on duty as a public hack; and that other people were in the rear compartment of the vehicle?" When the prosecutor answers, "So stipulated," the result is that there has been a stipulation in open court of facts that need not be proved by the lengthy testimony of witnesses. Sometimes the defendant might stipulate that he or she was at a particular place at a particular time, and this, too, might shorten the trial without any harm being done to the litigants.

§18.5 That Which Is Judicially Noticed

When something is judicially noticed, it is the same as a judicial shortcut or a doing away with evidence because there is no necessity for it. Cal.—Varcoe v. Lee, 180 Cal. 338, 181 P. 223 (1919). It is the cognizance of certain facts that judges and jurors may properly take and act on without proof because they already know them. 31A C.J.S. Evidence §6 (1964). Judicial notice has been termed judicial knowledge (Wash.—State v. Brooks, 58 Wash. 648, 109 P. 211 [1910]) or judicial cognizance (Ala.—Teat v. C.D. Chapman & Co., 1 Ala.App. 491, 56 So. 267 [1911]). Generally speaking, judicial knowledge is limited to facts evidenced by public records and facts of general notoriety. N.J.—Mancuso v. Rothenberg, 67 N.J.Super. 248, 170 A.2d 482 (1961). The jury has the power to consider as proven any matter that is of common knowledge in the community. Tex.—P.T. & E. Co. v. Beasley, 698 S.W.2d 190 (Tex.Ct.App. 1985).

§ 18.6 MATTERS OF JUDICIAL NOTICE

§18.7 Statutory Directions

Statutes often delineate matters of which courts may take judicial notice or shall take judicial notice. A close reading of the previous sentence will demonstrate that those statutes that use the word "may" leave the taking of judicial notice to the discretion of the court, whereas those that use the word "shall" make it mandatory for the courts to take judicial notice. There is some divergence of opinion, however, in this area. Some courts have held that although a statute controls as to the matters of which a court will take judicial notice, its purport is merely that when a court may take judicial notice of those matters and things therein enumerated, it will do so only when requested and when they are relevant to some matter in issue. N.D.—*In re* McKee's Estate, 67 N.D. 504, 274 N.W. 601 (1937).

§18.8 Common Knowledge

Courts may properly take judicial notice of facts that may be regarded as forming part of the common knowledge of every person of ordinary understanding and intelligence. Conn.—Muse v. Page, 125 Conn. 219, 4 A.2d 329 (1939); Fla.—State v. Sarasota County, 118 Fla. 629, 159 So. 797 (1935). For example, there is no person of ordinary understanding and intelligence who does not know that the Statue of Liberty is located in New York City's harbor and is a mecca for tourists visiting

New York City. A court could therefore take judicial notice of this. It should be borne in mind that what might be a proper subject of judicial notice at one time may not be at another. Mo.—Calvin F. Feutz Funeral Home, Inc. v. Werner's Estate, 417 S.W.2d 25 (Mo.App. 1967).

§18.9 Method of Ascertaining Facts

Judicial notice of facts may extend to areas that are beyond the actual knowledge of the judge, when he may ascertain these facts by resorting to any source which he feels would be helpful. He may require the assistance of the party to ask him to take judicial notice, or he may investigate the matter himself or may use both methods. Ill.—Village of Catlin v. Tilton, 281 Ill. 601, 117 N.E. 999 (1917). To express it another way, one of the parties to the trial may ask the judge to take judicial notice of certain facts, or the judge may judicially notice the matter on his or her own initiative. In the latter case, the judge is said to act sua sponte. In Apostolic Church v. American Honda Motor Co. Inc., 833 S.W.2d 553 (Tex.Ct.App. 1992), the court was permitted to take judicial notice of the fact that a local highway was known by two names without a formal request for judicial notice being made by a party.

In the process of judicial notice, a judge may seek sources of information to assist him and in such process counsel of either side are entitled to offer materials containing the information, even though the judge may or may not rely on them or use them. The judge may request assistance from counsel and, for lack of such assistance, may decline to notice the desired fact. Nev.—Choate v. Ransom, 74 Nev. 100, 323 P.2d 700 (1958).

For the court to be required to take judicial notice upon request of a party, the court must, of necessity, be supplied with specific information that is the subject of the request; otherwise, it is discretionary whether the court takes judicial notice. Federal Rule of Evidence 201(c), (d); Colo.—Durbin v. Bonanza, 716 P.2d 1124 (App. 1986).

The judge may refer to properly authenticated public official documents or records of all kinds, to dictionaries or publications or encyclopedias, or to other books. N.Y.—Auerbach v. Mr. and Mrs. Foster's Place, 128 Misc. 875, 220 N.Y.S. 281 (1927).

§18.10 Court's Discretion

The power to take judicial notice is to be exercised by courts with caution. Care must be taken that the requisite notoriety exists, and any reasonable doubt on the subject should be promptly resolved by the court not taking judicial notice. Fla.—Makos v. Prince, 64 So.2d 670 (Fla. 1953); N.Y.—Berg v. Oriental Consol. Min. Co., 70 N.Y.S.2d 19 (1947). However, when the matter of judicial recognizance is one of law, the court is bound to take judicial notice of it. Fla.—Atlantic Coast Line R. Co. v. Holliday, 73 Fla. 269, 74 So. 479 (1917).

§18.11 Facts Agreed—Admitted or Uncontroverted

Even if the respective adversaries agree or admit, or if one party fails to controvert a fact in a pleading, the court may find the fact to be otherwise by resorting to its judicial knowledge. Wash.—Gottstein v. Lister, 88 Wash. 462, 153 P. 595 (1915). However, judicial knowledge has been taken of the truth of matters admitted by counsel in his or her oral arguments. U.S.—Benesch v. Underwood, 132 F.2d 430 (6th Cir. 1942).

§18.12 Statutes or Other Law

In general, a court will take judicial notice and apply the law of its own jurisdiction without pleading and proof thereof. Cal.—People by Mosk v. Lynam, 253 Cal.App.2d 959, 61 Cal.Rptr. 800 (1967); N.Y.—Souveran Fabrics Corp. v. Virginia Fibre Corp., 32 A.D.2d 753, 301 N.Y.S.2d 273 (1969). Accordingly, judicial notice is taken of the rules of common law (N.Y.—Stokes v. Macken, 62 Barb. Ch. 145 [1861]) and the principles of equity (Tex.—Nimmo v. Davis, 7 Tex. 26 [1851]). Doctrines established in England since the Declaration of Independence of the United States are not judicially noticed where their existence as constituting the law of England is in question. U.S.—Liverpool & G.W. Steam Co. v. Insurance Co. of N.Am., 129 U.S. 464, 9 S.Ct. 480, 32 L.Ed. 800 (1889). All laws of every state and territory of the United States and the District of Columbia have been judicially noticed. U.S.—Flanigan v. Security-First Nat'l Bank of Los Angeles, 41 F.Supp. 77 (S.D. Cal. 1941).

Judicial notice of a statute includes the history of its introduction to the legislature (N.Y.—Dale Eng'g Co. v. State, 114 Misc. 233, 186 N.Y.S. 490 [1921]), when it was passed and approved (Ind.—State *ex rel.* Rabb v. Holmes, 196 Ind. 157, 147 N.E. 622 [1925]), and when it went into effect (Fla.—Gaulden v. Kirk, 47 So.2d 567 [Fla. 1950]). Judicial notice cannot be taken of a law before the date on which it is to take effect. Mo.—State *ex rel.* Brunjes v. Bockelman, 240 S.W. 209 (Mo. 1922).

Courts of equity will judicially notice the doctrines of equity jurisprudence and practice. Tex.—Nimmo v. State, 7 Tex. 26 (1851). Opinions of the attorney general have been judicially noticed. La.—Coco v. Jones, 154 La. 124, 97 So. 337 (1923).

§18.13 Public Law of Sister States and Territories of the United States

In the absence of a statute to the contrary, courts will not take judicial notice of the laws of other states. Most states, however, provide by statute or court rule that judicial notice will be taken of the public law of sister states, territories, and the United States. N.Y.—CPLR 4511(a). In the New York rule, the court is required, without request, to take judicial notice of the public laws of the aforementioned governments. A *fortiori*—Tex.—Ossorio v. Leon, 705 S.W.2d 219 (Tex.App. 1985).

§18.14 Laws of Foreign Countries

The problem of judicial notice of the laws of foreign countries is similar to that of the states in that, unless otherwise provided by statute, the courts do not take judicial notice of the laws of foreign countries. Again, this situation can be altered, however, by the states themselves. For example, New York State, by virtue of Rule 4511(b) of the CPLR, directs that courts may take judicial notice of the laws of foreign countries or their political subdivisions. In effect, this statute gives the court discretion, even though another part of the same rule seemingly makes it mandatory for a court to take judicial notice of the laws of a foreign country or its political subdivision when a party requests such notice, "furnishes the court sufficient information to enable it to comply with the request and has given each adverse party notice of his intention to request it." There are other requirements that are not pertinent to the purposes of this book, but the word "sufficient" in the rule is so nebulous as to leave it to the discretion of the court.

§ 18.15 Private Statutes

Sometimes laws are passed by legislatures that are specifically for the benefit of designated people. These are not necessarily preferential laws, but are usually passed to correct some injustice. For example, if a person is improperly convicted of a crime and incarcerated for a long period, the legislature may pass a specific private law that will in some measure indemnify the person for the injustice perpetrated on him or her. Such a law will be voted on, naming the subject person. Sometimes such a law is appended to some other bill currently before the legislature. These laws are called private statutes. It is, however, difficult to distinguish between a private and a public statute. It may generally be said that a statute that affects the public at large is a public statute, and this is true even when the statute is limited in its operation to a particular locality.

There is a general rule that the court may not judicially notice a private statute in the absence of a constitutional or statutory provision to the contrary. Fla.—Trustees of Internal Imp. Fund v. Claughton, 86 So.2d 775 (Fla. 1956). This general rule is modified by statute in many states. New York State has modified it by CPLR 4511(b), which provides, in part, that the New York court may "take judicial notice without request of private acts and resolutions of the Congress of the United States and of the legislature" of New York.

§ 18.16 County, Town, and Municipal Laws, Ordinances, or By-Laws

Generally, judicial notice of county, town, and municipal laws, ordinances, or by-laws will not be taken by the courts except where there is official sanction from the government (N.Y.—CPLR 4511[a]), or where there is an admission of the existence thereof by counsel (Ill.—Weber Co. v. Stevenson Grocery Co., 194 Ill.App. 432 [1895]), or where the existence of the ordinance is so generally known that the court may notice it as a matter of common knowledge (R.I.—Town of Lincoln v. Cournoyer, 95 R.I. 280, 186 A.2d 728 [1962]). Each jurisdiction may be different in this, but you must begin with the premise that judicial notice of county, town, and municipal laws is not taken, in accordance with common law principles, while keeping in mind that this concept may be to the contrary if a statute is passed in derogation of the common law. In the case of municipal courts, trying municipal violations, generally judicial notice may be taken of municipal ordinances. Traffic courts will take judicial notice of municipal traffic regulations. Cal.—People v. Cowles, 142 Cal.App.2d Supp. 865, 298 P.2d 732 (1956).

However, a court is permitted to take judicial notice of village ordinances. N.Y.—People v. Goldsmith, 110 Misc.2d 528, 442 N.Y.S.2d 760 (1981).

§ 18.17 Fact

The principles involving the judicial notice of matters of fact are not unlike those of judicial notice of matters of law in that they are judicial shortcuts to the proper administration of justice. Courts have been known to take judicial notice of the principal offices in their own state (31 C.J.S. Evidence § 37 [1964]); or official signatures or seals of a foreign state (Conn.—Creer v. Active Auto. Exch., 99 Conn. 266, 121 A. 888 [1923]); geographical facts, such as the fact that the general distance between two cities would permit the accused to be at the scene of both the crime and the alibi on the same day (Ill.—People ex rel. Lejcar v. Meyering, 345 Ill. 449, 178 N.E. 80 [1931]); and scientific facts, such as the general reliability of the radar speed meter as a mechanism for measuring the speed of a moving vehicle, thereby eliminating the need in each case of testimony of an expert to explain the function or scientific principles on which the radar instrument relies for its calculation; or the course and laws of nature, such as the alternation of day and night; or the course of the seasons (Ark.—Floyd v. Ricks, 14 Ark. 286, 58 Am.Dec. 374 [1853]); or the fact that another court had a finding in a decision that "seat belts save lives" (N.Y.—Wells v. State, 130 Misc.2d 113, 495 N.Y.S.2d 591 [1985]).

§18.18 Time of the Rising and Setting of the Sun

Many times the main issue in a case is whether or not the sun had risen or fallen at a particular time. Statutes that require a vehicle to be illuminated frequently refer to the terms "sunrise" and "sunset." Courts will, however, admit, not strictly as evidence but merely for the ostensible purpose of refreshing the court's recollection, any reputable almanac containing tables giving the periods of the rising and setting of the sun and moon on each day of the year. N.Y.—Montenes v. Metropolitan St. Ry. Co., 77 A.D. 493, 78 N.Y.S. 1059 (1902). Weather reports issued by the United States Weather Bureau, however, are in themselves admissible in evidence. N.Y.—CPLR 4528. These reports contain other information besides precipitation and temperature reports. They also include the times of sunrise and sunset and other pertinent information.

§18.19 Ordinary and Generally Accepted Meaning of English Words

You will recall from the introduction of this chapter that certain items of evidence that need not be proved may be introduced into a trial. It was also explained that the reason these items need not be proved is that it would needlessly prolong the trial and insult the intelligence of all concerned. Can you imagine to what lengths a trial might go if every word that was used in the testimony required a dictionary definition to cause the trier of the facts to better understand the issues? Naturally, it would be ridiculous to permit this sort of thing in the conduct of a trial. Accordingly, it has been held that courts may take judicial notice of the meaning of words and phrases. N.Y.—Turner-Looker Co. v. Aprile, 195 A.D. 706, 187 N.Y.S. 367 (1921), *aff'd*, 234 N.Y. 517, 138 N.E. 429 (1922). When a witness testifies that he or she saw a railroad train coming along the track at a fast rate of speed, everyone knows that it consisted of a vehicle or vehicles operating on steel tracks restricted to the use of a railroad. Another case presenting this concept is Pearis v. Goldschmidt, 37 A.D.2d 1001, 325 N.Y.S.2d 506 (1971), in which the court held that it would take judicial cognizance of the words "sale of whisky in bond" to mean sale in bonded warehouses.

§18.20 Delivery of Mail Without Zip Code Address

The requirements that an address on mail include a zip code designation is not a requirement of the New York Election Law. Hence, judicial notice was taken that mail addressed to a given street name along with city and state would be delivered to a resident at that address, as would mail precisely addressed with a zip code included. N.Y.—Kemp v. Monroe County Bd. of Elections, 129 Misc.2d 491, 493 N.Y.S.2d 529 (1985).

§ 18.21 JUDICIAL NOTICE OF OTHER FACTS

There are innumerable other facts that courts will take judicial notice of, but it is the function of this text to present a general treatment of the subject of the law of evidence, not to be exhaustive.

§ 18.22 CHANGES IN THE LAW OF JUDICIAL NOTICE

The law of judicial notice is constantly changing. Changing conditions of human life, and the boundless variety of facts presented to the courts, cause new applications of the doctrine to take place. A court in 1900 would not be able to take judicial notice that it is possible for a person to be placed on the moon, nor could it take judicial notice that an airplane could fly across the Atlantic Ocean in less than four hours. Yet, today, a court would take judicial notice of these facts. You can easily comprehend various other changes in the conditions of human life that were unthought of in former years and that are common knowledge today.

§ 18.23 CONCLUSIVENESS OF JUDICIAL NOTICE

Usually, what is judicially noticed is not a matter concerning which there is any controversy. If there is a possibility of controversy, the court should not judicially notice the law or the fact. However, there is some disagreement among the authorities as to the effect that should be given to a fact that is judicially noticed. Some courts have held that once the court admits a fact as judicially noticed, the fact should be indisputable and evidence to the contrary should be rejected. N.J.— State v. Cromwell, 6 N.J.Misc. 221, 140 A. 429 (1928). Other courts have held that a fact judicially noticed is only a rule of evidence, and if the question is disputable, contrary evidence is competent and should be admitted. Mo.—Timson v. Manufacturers' Coal & Coke Co., 220 Mo. 580, 119 S.W. 565 (1909).

§ 18.24 FEDERAL RULE

In Thayer's Preliminary Treatise on Evidence (279–280) (1898), we find that he wrote:

> In conducting a process of judicial reasoning, as of other reasoning, not a step can be taken without assuming something which has not been proved; and the capacity to do this with competent judgment and efficiency, is imputed to judges and juries as part of their necessary mental outfit.

With this definition in mind, the Advisory Committee was instrumental in causing the enactment of Rule 201 of the Federal Rules of Evidence, which reads as follows:

Rule 201. Judicial notice of adjudicative facts

(a) **Scope of rule.**—This rule governs only judicial notice of adjudicative facts.
(b) **Kinds of facts.**—A judicially noticed fact must be one not subject to reasonable dispute in that it is either (1) generally known within the territorial jurisdiction of the trial court or (2) capable of accurate and ready determination by resort to sources whose accuracy cannot reasonably be questioned.
(c) **When discretionary.**—A court may take judicial notice, whether requested or not.
(d) **When mandatory.**—A court shall take judicial notice if requested by a party and supplied with the necessary information.

(e) **Opportunity to be heard.**—A party is entitled upon timely request to an opportunity to be heard as to the propriety of taking judicial notice and the tenor of the matter noticed. In the absence of prior notification, the request may be made after judicial notice has been taken.

(f) **Time of taking notice.**—Judicial notice may be taken at any stage of the proceeding.

(g) **Instructing jury.**—In a civil action or proceeding, the court shall instruct the jury to accept as conclusive any fact judicially noticed. In a criminal case the court shall instruct the jury that it may, but is not required to, accept as conclusive any fact judicially noticed.

Adjudicative facts have been defined as those facts which normally go to a jury in a jury case (U.S.—Ikerd v. Lapworth, 435 F.2d 197 [7th Cir. 1970], where the distance between two locations was judicially noticed).

Those adjudicative facts that a court might take judicial notice of must be facts that are beyond controversy, such as the fact that the City of Miami, Florida, is in Dade County, Florida, and that it has a higher mean average weather temperature than New York City.

The Federal Rules of Evidence omitted a rule regarding judicial notice of legislative facts because, according to the note by the Advisory Committee, these matters have traditionally been treated as requiring pleading and proof and are left to the Rules of Civil Procedure and the Rules of Criminal Procedure. The Advisory Committee further added that judicial notice of a rule of law is a proper concern not of the rules of evidence, but rather of the rules of procedure. Rule 44.1, Federal Rules of Civil Practice; Rule 26.1, Federal Rules of Criminal Practice.

No federal rule deals with judicial notice of "legislative" facts because of fundamental differences between "adjudicative" facts and "legislative" facts. Adjudicative facts are the facts of a particular case, whereas legislative facts are those that have relevance to legal reasoning and the lawmaking process, whether in the formulation of a legal principle or ruling by a judge or court or in the enactment of a legislative body. The terminology was coined by Professor Kenneth Davis in his article "An Approach to Problems of Evidence in the Administrative Process," 55 Harv. L. Rev., 364, 404–407 (1942).

The usual method of establishing adjudicative facts is through the introduction of evidence, ordinarily consisting of the testimony of witnesses. If particular facts are outside of reasonable controversy, the testimony is dispensed with. A high degree of indisputability is the essential prerequisite.

According to Professor Davis, legislative facts are different. Facts most needed in thinking about difficult problems of law and policy are not clearly indisputable. Therefore, one should not take judicial notice of these legislative facts.

Rule 44.1, Federal Rules of Civil Procedure, and Rule 26.1, Federal Rules of Criminal Procedure, treat judicial notice of foreign law.

CROSS-REFERENCES

Federal Civil Judicial Procedure and Rules (West 1996) (Rule 201).
Goode & Wellborn, Courtroom Handbook on Federal Evidence (West 1995) (Rule 201).
McCormick, Evidence (4th ed. 1992) (Rule 201).

Mancuso v. Rothenberg

**Supreme Court of New Jersey, Appellate
Division, 1961.**
67 N.J.Super. 248, 170 A.2d 482.

You may need to read this decision several times before you understand the facts. However, I am certain that with a little perseverance, accompanied by the motto "Never give up," you will understand who is suing whom, the reasons for the suit, and the coverage and exclusions contained in the insurance policy of Motors Insurance Corporation, the company covering the defendant, Rothenberg. This is another of those cases where everyone wants to make the other party liable for the loss.

As I have previously indicated in this book, it is my intention not only to make you knowledgeable of the rules of evidence, but also to increase your mental horizon with respect to other aspects of human experience. In this case, I believe that you will be made aware of situations where judicial notice may or may not be invoked, as well as realizing that you always need to carefully read contracts, insurance policies, etc., including the fine print, to inform yourself of the pitfalls in commercial dealings that should be avoided.

To help you understand this case with a little less effort, I am presenting below some facts in concise fashion:

1. The plaintiffs, the Mancusos, owned the damaged auto.
2. They were insured by Emmco Insurance Company.
3. Rothenberg was driving the subject vehicle while on a pleasure trip.
4. Rothenberg had an accident with the Mancusos' vehicle, striking a vehicle that was operated by Louis Bender and owned by Alfred Bender.
5. At the time of the accident, Rothenberg owned another vehicle insured by Motors Insurance Corporation, who insured Rothenberg for operation of his own vehicle and any other vehicle he was driving.

6. The Benders, defendants in this case, collected the full amount of their damages less the $50.00 deductible from Emmco (the insurer of the Mancusos' car).

Many insurance companies have a clause in their policies that gives them the right to sue someone else in the name of their insured in order to try to recover the money that the insurance company paid out and also to sue on behalf of their insured to recover the deductible amount (in this case, $50.00) for their client (in this case, the Mancusos).

In the instant case, Emmco, having been given the right to sue in the name of the Mancusos because it was a subrogee (it was substituted in place of the Mancusos with respect to rights, claims, etc.), brought what is known as third-party action (an action against a party who was not originally part of the litigation). The third party in this case was Motors Insurance Corporation (the insurer of the vehicle that Rothenberg owned but was not operating at the time of the accident).

At the trial stage of this case, Motors Insurance Corporation lost its case, and it is now appealing to try to reverse the judgment.

In the appeal, Motors attempted to have the court take judicial notice of the practice of insurance companies of including in their automobile insurance policies an "omnibus clause," which insures the named insured, plus those who operate the insured vehicle with the named insured's permission. Motors argued that this is so common and widespread a practice that this court may take judicial notice thereof.

The instant court dealt with this question, and I ask you to ascertain what the court said of the argument.

Action wherein defendant, who was driving plaintiffs' automobile at time of damage to it, impleaded his collision insurer as a third-party defendant. The trial court rendered judgment for this defendant against his insurer, and the insurer appealed. . . .

LEWIS, J.A.D. Plaintiffs Salvatore Mancuso and Ruby Mancuso, co-owners of a Fiat automobile, were insured against damages thereto, less $50 deductible, by Emmco Insurance Company (hereinafter referred to as Emmco).

On August 5, 1959 at 3:45 A.M., defendant Leonard Rothenberg, with the permission of the plaintiffs, was driving the Fiat, on a mission for his own benefit, when he became involved in a collision with another car owned by the defendant Alfred Bender and operated by his agent, defendant Louis Bender. The Fiat car was damaged. At the time of the accident, defendant Rothenberg owned a Plymouth automobile (not involved in the accident). He was at that time insured by Motors Insurance Corporation (hereinafter referred to as Motors) against damage from collision, less $50 deductible. This coverage extended to his Plymouth automobile and to any non-owned vehicle which he might have the occasion to operate.

The plaintiffs collected their loss (less $50) from Emmco, and instituted suit against Rothenberg for the full amount thereof, for the benefit of their carrier Emmco, as subrogee, and for themselves as to the $50 deducted. Defendant Rothenberg, pursuant to order for leave to file third-party complaint impleaded his insurance carrier, Motors, as a third-party defendant. Motors denied liability, maintaining that its policy did not afford coverage to the defendant Rothenberg relative to the matters set forth in the third-party complaint, that collision insurance covering the Fiat was issued and loss thereunder paid by Emmco (less $50), and that, under the circumstances, its coverage was excess insurance. The limits of the Emmco policy had not been exceeded.

The damages to the Fiat car were stipulated by the plaintiffs and the defendant Rothenberg to be $552.73. Motors agreed that such figure represented a fair and reasonable value of the repairs to the car. There was an additional towing charge of $25 covered by the policy of Motors. The case was tried without a jury, and the court found that there was no negligence on the part of the defendants Benders and, on their motion, without objection, judgment was entered in their favor. The court further found that the sole negligence and proximate cause of the accident rested

with Rothenberg, and, accordingly, found for the plaintiffs and entered judgment against the defendant Rothenberg in the amount of $552.73. The court also found that the insurance policy of Motors "was issued for the protection of Rothenberg, not on a Fiat," and entered judgment for Rothenberg on the third-party complaint against Motors for $527.73, representing damages of $552.73 plus $25 towing charges less $50 which was deductible.

The contract of insurance contained a statement in bold red print: "This Policy DOES NOT PROVIDE bodily injury and property damage liability insurance or any other coverage for which a specific premium charge is not made, and does not comply with any Financial Responsibility Law." The declaration page of the policy indicates that premiums were paid for coverages including "E Collision or Upset (actual cash value less $50 deductible)" and "F Towing and Labor Costs." Under that portion of the policy relating to "Insuring Agreements," there is a provision as to "Coverage E-Collision" by which the insurance company agreed:

> "To pay for loss caused by collision to the owned automobile or to a non-owned automobile but only for the amount of each such loss in excess of the deductible amount stated in the declarations as applicable hereto."

Specific exclusions are enumerated, and item (c) is invoked. It reads: "to loss to a non-owned automobile arising out of its use by the insured in the automobile business." The recited conditions of the policy include, *inter alia*, a paragraph captioned "13. Other Insurance," which provides:

> "If the insured has other insurance against a loss covered by this policy, the company shall not be liable under this policy for a greater proportion of such loss than the applicable limit of liability of this policy bears to the total applicable limit of liability of all valid and collectible insurance against such loss; provided, however, the insurance with respect to a temporary substitute automobile or non-owned automobile shall be excess insurance over any other valid and collectible insurance."

It is uncontroverted that Rothenberg did not have any other collision insurance and that he was operating a non-owner's vehicle when the accident occurred. The court found as a matter of fact, supported by ample evidence, that he was engaged in a pleasure trip at the time of the accident, and that the loss sustained did not arise under circumstances that could be construed within the policy exclusion "use by the insured in the automobile business." Accordingly, the primary liability of Motors under the quoted provision of "Coverage E-Collision" is beyond question.

On the other hand, quoted condition 13 presents disputed language for construction. Motors maintains: (1) this provision is not limited to insurance by and for the insured; (2) the words "other insurance" as therein used should be liberally interpreted; and (3) the clause "provided, however, the insurance with respect to a temporary substitute automobile or non-owned automobile shall be excess insurance over any other valid and collectible insurance" is a lawful limitation which should be construed to mean "irrespective of whether other such insurance was procured by persons other than the named insured." In support of its contentions, reliance is placed upon Woodrich Construction Co. v. Indemnity Ins. Co., 252 Minn. 86, 89 N.W.2d 412 (Sup.Ct. 1958). That case, however, is distinguishable in that it dealt with comprehensive liability and not collision insurance. Moreover, four employers' comprehensive general liability policies were before the court for analysis, comparison, and construction, and each of the four policies contained an "other insurance" clause.

The theory of Motors' defense at the trial level was that exclusion "C" of its policy relieved it of liability, and that, in any event, under condition 13 Motors could only be liable for excess insurance as the Fiat car was covered by an Emmco policy allegedly valid and collectible.

* * *

It is urged that the practice of insurance companies to include in their automobile insurance policies an "omnibus clause" insuring (in addition to the named insured) those who operate the insured vehicle, with the named insured's permission, is so common and widespread that this court may take judicial notice thereof. Insurance policies, and special clauses therein, are matters of contractual relationship between the parties, and their rights thereunder are ordinarily settled by the specific terms and conditions of their agreement. Judge (now Justice) Francis in the case of Mau v. Union Labor Life Ins. Co., 31 N.J.Super. 362, 106 A.2d 748 (App.Div. 1954), refused to notice judicially that an inscription "WT-18 Ctf. No. 57," inserted under the designation "Number" on a policy of life insurance, indicated the existence of an employer's group insurance contract. *A fortiori*, this court should not take judicial notice of the existence of an "omnibus clause," or the terms and conditions of such a clause, or any part of an insurance contract which is not in evidence. Judicial notice is generally limited to facts of record and facts of general knowledge. "It is said that the term 'judicial notice' means no more than that the court will bring to its aid and consider, without proof of the facts, its knowledge of those matters of public concern which are known by all well-informed persons." C.J.S. Evidence §6, p. 509. . . . The Emmco policy is not a matter of record or within common knowledge.

Motors advanced defenses at the trial level; interrogatories were propounded; and the Emmco policy was within reach of Motors by *subpoena duces tecum*. A review of the entire record does not reveal elements of surprise or injustice that would impel the exercise of our original jurisdiction under R.R. 1:5-4(a) and 2:5, as urged by Motors, or to invoke R.R. 1:27A and relax the rules that limit judicial review to matters presented to the trial court.

Judgment affirmed.

Berg v. Oriental Consolidated Mining Co.

Supreme Court, Trial Term, New York County, 1947.
70 N.Y.S.2d 19.

This case resulted in a well-reasoned decision with respect to the application of judicial notice to foreign law.

* * *

BOTEIN, Justice. Plaintiff seeks in this action to recover from defendant, as paying agent of the Oriental Consolidated Mining Company, the sum of $23,016 allegedly due to him as liquidating dividends in dissolution upon certain shares of stock of that mining company.

These shares of stock were originally owned by plaintiff's aunt, to whom certificates were issued in October 1906. She was a resident of Switzerland; the certificates of stock were deposited in Switzerland. Plaintiff testified at the trial that in Switzerland in 1923 he acquired legal title to the shares from his aunt in consideration of his promise to support her for the rest of her life. He has bulwarked his testimony by proof that in December 1923 his aunt wrote the mining company a letter in which she stated that plaintiff "is now the owner of all my shares in your company." In addition he has had delivered to defendant the stock certificates, bearing an assignment in his favor dated May 8, 1933.

Defendant contends that plaintiff has failed to prove his title to the shares, arguing that the evidence fails to establish delivery of the certificates and of the assignment to plaintiff prior to his aunt's death in 1943. Defendant has established that on August 7, 1925 and again on September 14, 1932 plaintiff's aunt executed codicils to her will confirming a bequest of the shares to plaintiff, in the later of which codicils she stated that the certificates had been endorsed by her *in blank*. Defendant has submitted in evidence a document executed by plaintiff's aunt on August 1, 1939 in which she referred to plaintiff as her "heir presumptive" and in which she stated that he "has to dispose of *the income of my* Consolidated Mining Company Shares." It appears further that the certificates of stock were deposited by plaintiff's aunt in the Depositocasse of the City of Berne, Switzerland, some time prior to July 12, 1920 and remained there until 1945, when plaintiff arranged for their delivery to defendant. These facts, contends defendant, negate plaintiff's ownership as he has claimed it in this action and requires him to secure title to the shares by probate of his aunt's will. They at least raise an issue which can only be resolved by recourse to the laws of Switzerland.

It is well established that transfers of securities, checks and bills of exchange and shares of stock are governed by the laws of the country where the property is situated at the time of the transfer. 2 Beale, Treatise on the Conflict of Laws §262.1; Weissman v. Banque de Bruxelles, 254 N.Y. 488, 494, 173 N.E. 835,

837 (1931); Hutchinson v. Ross, 262 N.Y. 381, 187 N.E. 65, 89 A.L.R. 1007 (1933); Direction der Disconto-Gesellschaft v. United States Steel Co., 267 U.S. 22, 28, 45 S.Ct. 207, 69 L.Ed. 495 (1925). Since the certificates of stock were physically present in Switzerland and the transfer to plaintiff is claimed to have been accomplished there, the law of that country must be applied to determine the validity of the transfer.

The plaintiff has claimed ownership and title to the stock under a contract made or transaction which took place in Switzerland, relating to certificates there situated. Considerations of justice and convenience require that plaintiff bear the burden of proving, in this case, that he acquired ownership and title in accordance with the laws of Switzerland and not that the defendant carry the burden of proving to the contrary. Arams v. Arams, 182 Misc. 328, 45 N.Y.S.2d 251 (1944). The plaintiff's proof of the law of Switzerland is incomplete, is vigorously challenged by the defendant, and falls short of establishing his ownership and title under the facts which he has proved. While Section 344-a, Civil Practice Act, authorizes the court to take judicial notice of foreign law and to discover the same by independent research, nevertheless this right is to be exercised with caution in the discretion of the court. The section does not give "a judge the right to decide cases, not merely upon his own private discoveries of foreign law, but, also, upon his own translation of foreign languages . . ." and "must be applied with discriminating care and with due regard for all the 'legal niceties' of fair dealing and due process of law." Arams v. Arams, 182 Misc. 336, 45 N.Y.S.2d 251, 258 (1944).

Judgment is therefore directed for the defendant, and the complaint is dismissed, without prejudice.

People of the State of New York v. Payne
District Court of New York, Suffolk County, Fifth District, 1969.
60 Misc.2d 830, 305 N.Y.S.2d 23.

This case presents an example of where a court can recognize the existence of the public policy of the United States. In the case, the policy was expressed in a statement of the secretary of the interior of the United States with respect to the unrestricted use of motor vehicles at a designated location that affects the preservation of the relatively unspoiled and undeveloped beaches, dunes, and other natural features. The location that is written about is Fire Island, New York, a summer recreation area that is very well known in the New York, Connecticut, and New Jersey area.

* * *

DECISION

ANGELO MAUCERI, Judge. The defendant herein was charged with a violation of Section Six of the Vehicular Uses Great South Beach Ordinance of the Town of Islip, in particular "Vehicles for which a permit shall not have been issued are prohibited from being operated from May 15th to October 1st between the hours of 9 A.M. and 6 P.M. Between October 1st and May 15th, vehicles for which a permit shall have been issued are permitted to operate on the beach at any hour."

The definition of beach in the ordinance is "the beach shall encompass all real property at Fire Island and should include all of that area in the Town of Islip along the shore of the Atlantic Ocean lying between low water marks as a southerly boundary and the crest of the dunes as a northerly boundary."

The contention of the defendant in this matter is that the statute is unconstitutional, unreasonable, arbitrary and capricious and his argument in this regard is that the definition of the word beach is beyond any definitive scope, that the word has ever attained before in the English language and that this definition is arbitrary and unreasonable in that it has no foundation in fact or science that all the land on Fire Island is a beach.

The defendant further contends that the statute is arbitrary since there are no modes of transportation on Fire Island other than by vehicular travel and it is unreasonable to prohibit the residents of the island from said travel during the hours in the ordinance.

They further contend that since the ordinance doesn't prohibit all traffic during all hours, that the ordinance is not directed to its original purpose to prevent erosion of the dunes and of the sand areas on Fire Island.

The Town of Islip is opposed to all of these contentions and feels that they have the right to declare as public policy the protection of a vital seashore area which can be eroded by extra heavy vehicular traffic. The Court has taken all of the arguments into consideration of both counsel and in considering the arguments of the defense counsel with regard to the validity of the instant statute, let it be said that it is the duty of the Court to sustain the police powers of the Legislature unless they are clearly, plainly and palpably in violation of the Constitution. (People v. Schweinler Press, 214 N.Y. 395, 108 N.E. 639, L.R.A. 1918A, 1124 [1915]). Such enactment under the police power will not be invalidated merely because there is an earnest conflict of serious opinion as to its validity. Judicial review can only be limited to an inquiry as to whether there was a reasonable basis for the Legislature's determination. (People v. Ryan, 230 App.Div. 252, 243 N.Y.S.2d 644 [1963]). In order to invalidate the instant Legislation enacted under the police power of the Town of Islip, it must be shown as a matter of law, that the ordinance is not justifiable under any permissible or intelligent interpretation of all of the facts and is not a reasonable exercise of the police powers. (Wiggins v. Somers, 4 N.Y.2d 215, 173 N.Y.S.2d 579, 149 N.E.2d 869 [1958]). Reasonableness of necessity must be considered in the light of each problem as it is presented. (Town of Somers v. Camarco, 308 N.Y. 537, 127 N.E.2d 327 [1955]). And so, in this case the Court must consider the reasonableness of the exercise of the police powers of the Town of Islip in the Vehicular Ordinance in light of the problem presented. In L. I. Beach Buggy Association et al. v. Town of Islip et al., 58 Misc.2d 295, 300, 295 N.Y.S.2d 268, 275–276 (1969), the Supreme Court of Suffolk County, Special Term, Justice Geiler presiding, the Court took judicial notice of the public policy of the United States with regard to the statement of the Secretary of the Interior who, on the 21st of July, 1967, stated the following:

"The unrestricted use of motor vehicles in the Fire Island National Seashore, conflicts with the purposes of the Act of September 11th, 1964, authorizing the establishment of this Seashore, to conserve and preserve for the use of future generations certain relatively unspoiled and undeveloped beaches, dunes and other natural features within Suffolk County, N.Y., which possess high values to the Nation as examples of unspoiled areas of great natural beauty in close proximity to large concentrations of urban population; conflicts with the administration of the Seashore to be established with the primary aim of conserving the natural resources located there; is inconsistent with statutory limitations on access to that section of the Seashore lying between the easterly boundary of the Brookhaven Town Park at Davis Park and the westerly boundary of the Smith Point County Park; and is incompatible with the preservation therein of the flora and fauna and the physiographic conditions now prevailing and conflicts with the preservation of such section and of the Sunken Forest Preserve in as nearly their present state and condition as possible."

This Court would be remiss if it did not extend that same judicial notice to the public policy of the United States and, it is clear to this Court that the Town of Islip has the police power to regulate vehicular traffic on Fire Island in order to protect the area from erosion, the municipality is justified in guarding against vehicles which, during the peak travel hours of the summer months, would contribute to erosion by continual travel over the sand area with distinct probability that the vehicles would traverse the dunes indiscriminately.

This ordinance is reasonably formulated to prevent as much as humanly possible in this regard. If the statute had prohibited vehicular traffic completely at all times, this certainly would be an arbitrary, unreasonable and capricious act.

The motions of the defendant to dismiss this information on the grounds of its unconstitutionality are denied. On the facts and on the law, after trial, the Court finds the defendant guilty as charged and sets the sentencing down before the Court on September 29th, 1969.

Wells v. State

Supreme Court, Steuben County, 1985.
130 Misc.2d 113, 495 N.Y.S.2d 591.

This decision is a comprehensive study of the power of the state to require an occupant of an automobile to wear a seat belt while operating said vehicle. The plaintiff is seeking a declaratory judgment as to the constitutionality of the state's requirement to wear a seat belt.

A declaratory judgment is a judgment handed down by a court that declares the rights of the parties or expresses the opinion of the court on a question of law, without ordering anything to be done.

I am certain that many people have entertained the idea that they can do whatever they wish with their bodies and that this right is given to them pursuant to the United States Constitution, as well as state constitutions. The decision discusses this conflict and arrives at an answer. I am also certain that you will be interested in knowing the answer and the reasons on which this answer is based.

MYRON E. TILLMAN, Justice.

The Court has before it a motion made by the Attorney General for summary judgment in this declaratory judgment action.

The Plaintiff herein was issued a traffic citation in the City of Corning, New York, for failure to wear his seat belt while operating his motor vehicle in violation of Section 1229-c of the Vehicle and Traffic Law, commonly known as the "Seat Belt Law." Upon appearance in Corning City Court, the Plaintiff asked for and received a stay of prosecution in order to pursue this declaratory judgment action.

Plaintiff's complaint alleges that the "Seat Belt Law" exceeds constitutional limitations. Specifically, that his right to privacy and those rights guaranteed by the IV, IX, X and XIV Amendments of the United States Constitution have been violated. In addition, the complaint alleges that the law "is beyond the power granted the legislature by Article III, Section I of the Constitution of the State of New York."

Plaintiff, in his affidavit in opposition to this motion, and his counsel, in oral argument, submitted that there are triable issues of fact. They argue that this Court must explore the intent of the legislature by ordering a hearing. Their argument contends that this Court cannot assume that the generally articulated intent of the legislature was to promote the health, safety and welfare of the people.

Plaintiff's counsel questioned the "hidden intent" or the "political intent" of individual lawmakers in passing this bill (i.e., reference to the number of times similar legislation had been introduced, but failed to pass).

It is well established in the law that the granting of a summary judgment motion constitutes a drastic remedy. The cases stating this concept are so well known and so numerous as to make their citation unnecessary. This concept, however, does not preclude the granting of summary judgment where there is no triable issue of fact. In order to defeat a motion for summary judgment, the Plaintiff herein must do more than submit arguments based upon surmise, conjecture and suspicion. Gray Mfg. Co. v. Pathe Industries, Inc., 1969, 33 A.D.2d 739, 305 N.Y.S.2d 794, aff'd. 26 N.Y.2d 1045, 312 N.Y.S.2d 200, 260 N.E.2d 821; Dabney v. Ayre, 1982, 87 A.D.2d 957, 451 N.Y.S.2d 218. An affidavit of an attorney lacking personal knowledge of the facts is without probative value and should be disregarded. Starbo v. Ruddy, 1978, 66 A.D.2d 950, 411 N.Y.S.2d 707.

Plaintiff, by means of his own affidavit, uses conjecture and surmise to pose questions as to the individual intents of the lawmakers. A Court may not inquire into the motives of the State Legislature. There is a well established presumption in favor of the constitutionality of a legislative enactment. People v. Pace, 1981, 111 Misc.2d 488, 444 N.Y.S.2d 529. Every legislative enactment carries with it a presumption that there existed the necessary factual support for its provisions. Betty-June School, Inc. v. Young, 1959, 195 N.Y.S.2d 16, mod. on other grounds, 10 A.D.2d 648, 197 N.Y.S.2d 760; Gail Turner Nurses Agency, Inc. v. State, 1959, 17 Misc.2d 273, 190 N.Y.S.2d 720. The presumption that the determination of the legislature is supported by facts known to it obtains unless facts judicially known or proved preclude that possibility. Mid-States Freight Lines, Inc. v. Bates, 1952, 200 Misc. 885, 111 N.Y.S.2d 568, aff'd. 279 App.Div. 451, 111 N.Y.S.2d 578, aff'd 304 N.Y. 700, 107 N.E.2d 603, reh. den. 304 N.Y. 788, 109 N.E.2d 82 and cert. den. 345 U.S. 908, 73 S.Ct. 648, 97 L.Ed. 1344. The fact that legislation of a similar nature has been introduced but failed to pass on many occasions is not one that persuades the Court that

it may explore the area of legislative intent. There is little question that what motivates one legislator to propose or make a speech urging the passage of a statute is not necessarily what motivates scores of others to enact it. United States v. O'Brien, 391 U.S. 367, 383–384, 88 S.Ct. 1673, 20 L.Ed.2d 672. If under any possible state of facts an act would be constitutional, the Courts will not make a separate investigation of the facts or attempt to decide whether the legislature has reached a correct conclusion with respect to them. The legislature is presumed to have investigated and found the necessary facts. Judicial restraint in this regard is an important recognition of the separate powers of our three governmental branches.

Judicial inquiry into legislative intent is only appropriate as an aid to statutory interpretation, and then only when the statute in question is so ambiguous that the Court must consult the legislative purpose in order to determine whether the statute applies to the particular case. Roosevelt Raceway, Inc. v. Monaghan, 1961, 9 N.Y.2d 293, 304, 213 N.Y.S.2d 729, 174 N.E.2d 71; Mosley v. Gorfinkel, 1975, 81 Misc.2d 999, 1001, 367 N.Y.S.2d 155.

Plaintiff relies on Consumer-Farmer Milk Co-op, Inc. v. Wickham, 25 A.D.2d 413, 270 N.Y.S.2d 184, for his contention that summary judgment is precluded where the issue of the constitutionality of a statute is involved. This reliance is misplaced. *Wickham*, supra, raised the question of whether or not appellant's activities involved transactions in interstate commerce, the Commerce Clause (U.S. Const., Art. 1, Section 8, cl. 3), which would, if proved, inhibit the power of the State to regulate those activities. This was clearly a factual issue which precluded summary judgment.

In the case at bar there is no factual issue before this Court which would preclude the Court from entertaining the motion before it.

Plaintiff, in his complaint, claims that enactment of the "Seat Belt Law" is beyond the power of the legislature. In oral argument before the Court, Plaintiff was emphatic in his view that the limits of the police power should be restricted and jealously guarded.

The sovereign power, which rests in all of the States of the Union, is that legislative function which has not been limited by the

Federal or State Constitutions. The legislative function is unlimited and practically absolute. This inherent sovereign power is commonly referred to as the police power. The definition of the police power has proved elusive, but the approach to individual cases has been pragmatic, making this a gradual growing body of the law in the best tradition of the common law. In spite of the breadth of the police power and the total uncertainty of limitations from any standpoint of firm definition or established rigidity, it is undeniably subject to both specific and general constitutional provisions.

The complaint herein expands the concept that the "Seat Belt Law" is beyond the power of the legislature to enact by declaring that the law "deprives Plaintiff of his right to make an intelligent decision which pertains solely to his person and his personal safety."

The amicus curiae brief before the Court took the view that Plaintiff relied on the constitutional and philosophical limitation of governmental power (the philosophy enunciated by the nineteenth century British philosopher, John Stuart Mill). The amicus brief attempts to demonstrate how this philosophy (the concept that the individual is not accountable to society for this [his] actions insofar as these acts affect no person but himself) has been rejected by authoritative judicial precedents. The United States Supreme Court has rejected Mill's maxim as a measure of State legislative power. Specifically, they point out that it would prevent prosecutions for obscenity, suicide, self-mutilation, adultery, and gambling, among other offenses (See Paris Adult Theatre v. Slaton, 1973, 413 U.S. 49, 68 and n. 14 and 15, 93 S.Ct. 2628, 2641 and n. 14 and 15, 37 L.Ed.2d 446.

Counsel for Plaintiff, in oral argument, discussed the concept of individual liberty and relied upon the maxims of Thomas Jefferson, in particular that the liberty of the individual should be jealously guarded. He declared that the "Seat Belt Law" set a dangerous precedent infringing basic individual liberty and personal freedom. Counsel gave the Court examples of the extremes to which this governmental act by way of precedent could take us if this "Seat Belt Law" was not found unconstitutional (example: legislative prohibition of smoking).

Ultimately, all social legislation affects someone's "freedom"; competing interests have to be carefully weighed and a reasonable and rational relationship to the purpose for which the police power has been exercised must be demonstrated. Plaintiff views this statute as a confrontation between the right of the individual to determine his own fate and the power of the State to interfere with this determination. This argument ignores the democratic concept of the consent of the people. In a democracy the government governs with the consent of the governed. The State's police power is ill defined and often vulnerable to abuse. In a representative government the people must be vigilant and exercise their power. They must change their elected representatives if they disagree with their collective legislative acts. If the liberty of the individual is the only criteria one has, then the logical extension of that concept, in the extreme, is anarchy. As Winston Churchill said, "Many forms of government have been tried and will be tried in this world of sin and woe. No one pretends that democracy is perfect or all wise. Indeed, it has been said that democracy is the worst form of government, except all those other forms that have been tried from time to time." (Winston S. Churchill, November 11, 1947, in the House of Commons).

Plaintiff submitted that Roe v. Wade, 410 U.S. 113, 93 S.Ct. 705, 35 L.Ed.2d 147, stands for the concept of "my body, my integrity." However, *Roe*, supra, does say that the State might invade that sanctuary under certain circumstances based upon the theory that the individual does not have an unlimited right to abuse or invade his or her own body. More importantly, however, the issue of one's right to control one's own body, and the government's attempt to interfere with what takes place inside that body, can hardly be compared with the State's interference with the liberty of the individual inside his or her automobile.

Plaintiff submits that in People v. Onofre, 51 N.Y.2d 476, 494, 434 N.Y.S.2d 947, 415 N.E.2d 936, the Court of Appeals recognized the protection afforded the individual of his personal integrity and autonomy. This interpretation of *Onofre*, supra, ignores the fact that the majority were at pains to distinguish *Onofre*, supra, from their decision in People v. Shepard, 50 N.Y.2d 640, 431 N.Y.S.2d 363, 409 N.E.2d 840. *Shepard*, supra, was a decision based on the legislative finding that the drug, marijuana, was sufficiently harmful to warrant punishing its possession. *Onofre*, supra, by contrast, was based on the fact that neither the People nor the dissent had cited any authority or evidence that the practice of consensual sodomy in private is harmful.

Clearly, the majority felt that the showing of harm to the individual was a basis upon which the protection to personal autonomy might be infringed.

This Court must determine whether a law compelling motorists to use a seat belt advances the State's interest in protecting the health, safety and welfare of its citizens. Legislation tending to promote this interest is a proper exercise of the State's police power. An appropriate test, then, for any legislation which mandates public conduct and restricts individual choice should measure a statute in light of its reasonable and rational relationship to the purpose for which the law was enacted.

Numerous studies, both here and abroad, have demonstrated that the use of seat belts does significantly lower, not only mortality rates, but the severity of injuries in automobile crashes. The manual lap and shoulder belt has been standard equipment in all cars built in the United States since 1967, and a comprehensive analysis conducted by the University of Michigan in 1980 of thousands of accidents postulated that such restraints are 40 to 50 percent effective in reducing fatalities and even more effective in reducing moderate to critical injuries. The Governor's message, in approving the "Seat Belt Law," indicated those recommending approval of the legislation. Among, but by no means least, of these recommendations the New York Public Interest Research Group, Inc. pointed out that "requiring seat belt use for public safety reasons is in no way related to the bleak, soul-killing totalitarianism of Orwell's novel." (Chapter Law Memoranda, Governor's Approval Memorandum, Appendix 23). The New York State Automobile Association informed the Governor that in a poll taken in May, 1984, members of the Automobile Club of New York favored

mandatory seat belt use by 70 percent of more than 5,000 members (Governor's Approval Memorandum, Supra, Exhibit 36).

The State has a compelling interest in saving lives (the ultimate goal in the promotion of health and safety), but in addition to this, the State has an interest in promoting the welfare of its citizens. The cost to society of the results of death or severe injuries is enormous. The long-term care, often extending to lifetime care, of paraplegics, quadraplegics and patients on life-support systems devolves on the State. Each year over 700,000 persons are hospitalized with head injuries; over 100,000 of those persons will die, another 30,000 to 50,000 will sustain brain damage severe enough to cause prolonged hospitalization and rehabilitation for intellectual, physical or behavioral impairment. A very large percentage of those persons will never return to a normal life or be able to work, and the cost to this Nation is over $15 billion annually. (Governor's Approval Memorandum, supra, Exhibit 38).

This aspect of highway safety was discussed and approved as a proper State interest in a United States District Court in Massachusetts, responding to a claim that the mandating of protection headgear for motorcyclists deprived them of freedom of choice and that such choice did not affect the public welfare, when the Court stated society's interest in minimizing highway accidents. Simon v. Sargent, 1972, 346 F.Supp. 277; and see also Love v. Bell, 1970, 171 Colo. 27, 465 P.2d 118.

Plaintiff submits that wearing a seat belt is within the realm of personal autonomy and that his decision to wear a seat belt should be his alone. This issue has also been addressed in a case involving a State motorcyclist helmet requirement when the Court said:

"Death on the highway can no longer be considered as a personal and individual tragedy alone. The mounting carnage has long since reached proportions of a public disaster. Legislation reasonably designed to reduce the toll may for that reason alone be sufficiently imbued with the public interest to meet the constitutional test required for a valid exercise of the State's police power." State v. Anderson, 1968, 3 N.C.App. 124, 126, 164 S.E.2d 48, 50, aff'd. 276 N.C. 168, 166 S.E.2d 49.

The thesis that the mandatory "Seat Belt Law" reduces the carnage on our roads from automobile accidents has been supported by experience in New York State. The State has experienced an 18 percent decrease in occupant fatalities during the first six months that the law has been enforced. Ninety-seven less lives have been lost in 1985 when compared to 1984. Measuring the first five months of 1984 and 1985, national fatalities were up 4.1 percent. New York fatalities were down 9 percent in the same period (all categories of fatals). In addition, the miles traveled in the period January–June were up by nearly one billion miles (2.5 percent). In the period January–April, the number of injured occupants was down by 8.4 percent over 1984, and this despite an increase in occupants of 1–3 percent. Moreover, restraint use has gone from 16 percent before the law to 69 percent after January 1, 1985 (the effective date), and recent surveys show a 57 percent usage. With greater compliance the figures would no doubt be even more impressive. Other factors may have impact on these statistics, but the mandatory "Seat Belt Law" is the most significant change during this time of enactment in New York.

The Plaintiff, personally in oral argument, raised the issue of the danger of the seat belt. He contended that its use had been known to cause severe injury and death. No probative evidence was submitted to the Court to support this contention, nor did the complaint plead that use of the seat belt is not reasonably related to a valid exercise of the police power. This issue as to whether the seat belt is the perfect remedy or whether, on balance, its benefits outweigh its disadvantages is a policy question, not a justifiable consideration. However, even had the complaint raised the issue of the effectiveness of the seat belt, the point was dealt with by the Court of Appeals in Spier v. Barker, 1974, 35 N.Y.2d 444, 445, 363 N.Y.S.2d 916, 323 N.E.2d 164. The Court gave recognition to the fact that seat belts save lives. This court may take judicial notice of this decision and its finding. Slater v. Slater, 208 App.Div. 567, 204 N.Y.S. 112, aff'd 240 N.Y. 557, 148 N.E. 703, People v. Herkimer, 4 Cow (N.Y.) 345, Kane v. Walsh, 295 N.Y. 198, 66 N.E.2d 53. Where a matter can be established by judicial notice, it need not be inquired into by evidentiary trial. People v. French Bottling Works, 259 N.Y. 4, 7, 180 N.E. 537. Judicial notice is appropriate on pretrial motions that seek the dismissal of Plaintiff's case. Pfleuger v. Pfleuger, 304 N.Y. 148, 106 N.E.2d 495.

Plaintiff's complaint appears to raise an equal protection issue by reference to the 14th Amendment, although this is not specifically pled.

In Vehicle and Traffic Law, Section 1229-c(9), there are exemptions not only for rear seat passengers over a certain age in privately owned vehicles, but for "taxis, liveries, tractors, trucks with a maximum gross weight of eighteen thousand pounds or over, and buses other than school buses."

The classifications created by the statute are not based on race, alienage, age or nationality and, therefore, the strict scrutiny test to determine whether the challenged law is "necessary to promote a *compelling* government interest" is not indicated. Shapiro v. Thompson, 394 U.S. 618, 634, 89 S.Ct. 1322, 1331, 22 L.Ed.2d 600. Needed is a "rational basis" test to determine whether the varied treatment of separate classifications of citizens "rests on grounds wholly irrelevant to the achievement of the State's objective." McGowan v. Maryland, 366 U.S. 420, 425, 81 S.Ct. 1101, 1104, 6 L.Ed.2d 393. When a State regulates a problem it is not under any obligation to regulate all phases of it or every class of acts or actors involved in it. Williamson v. Lee Optical, 1955, 348 U.S. 483, 489, 75 S.Ct. 461, 465, 99 L.Ed. 563; on the contrary, the State may regulate partially or one step at a time without violating the 14th Amendment's equal protection clause. Williamson v. Lee Optical, supra.

This Court, upon hearing the Plaintiff personally in oral argument before the Court, is aware and respectful of Plaintiff's sincere and strongly held views. The Court, too, is an admirer of Thomas Jefferson and those framers of our Constitution, who so persuasively espoused ideas which would protect the individual from governmental tyranny over the minds, bodies and lives of its citizens. At issue in all legislative action involving personal freedom is the application of those principles. The Court acknowledges probable disagreement with this Court's judicially applied determination in this case, under these facts. We can only defer to that best and most basic concept of our founding fathers which allowed differing beliefs and defended at all costs their fellow citizens' right to their disagreement.

In addition, every Court who reflects on these most fundamental concepts cannot forego a respectful restraint when considering the powers and rights of another constitutionally established branch of government.

The Plaintiff, subsequent to the hearing, submitted a letter to the Court, together with a letter from Paul Cozad of the Human Factors Consultants, which dealt with the interpretation of statistics. This Court cannot consider this submission over the objection of the Attorney General. The letter does not address the legal issues, but sets forth Mr. Wells' political philosophy and views. Despite this, even if the Court did consider this submission, the interpretation of data is not a function of the Courts. Under the separation of powers doctrine, one of the most fundamental principles of the American Constitutional system, governmental powers are divided among the three departments of government—legislative, executive and judicial—and each of these is separate from, and may not infringe on the independence of the others. Clearly, it is a function of the legislature to interpret data; the function of the Court is to see that the legislation subsequently passed bears a rational relationship to the goals to be achieved.

The Court finds that the New York State mandatory "Seat Belt Law" is a valid constitutional exercise of legislative power and, therefore, grants the motion for summary judgment.

Apostolic Church v. American Honda Motor Company, Inc.
Court of Appeals of Texas, 1992.
833 S.W.2d 553.

This case will show you an example of a party trying desperately to prevent the loss of property, caused here by a judgment of foreclosure entered against the Apostolic Church. The church is the appellant here, and it raised many questions of law in the appeal.

All issues presented by the church were decided against it. The appellee, American Honda, made a counterclaim for damages that it sustained for legal services and other claims arising out of this action. It claimed that all of the claims made by the appellant were frivolous. The appellee stated that it was making this counterclaim under the authority of Texas Rule of Appeal 84. The court refused to agree with American Honda on this point because the court could not say that the appeal was taken solely to delay the foreclosure.

Among the points of law considered was whether it was necessary for a proponent to get the court to take judicial notice of a local geographical fact. The question involved is, was it necessary that the proponent produce background information to persuade the court to take judicial notice of this fact?

Other questions raised were whether Highway 96 North links with the city of Center, Texas, and the neighboring community of Tenaha and whether the court may take judicial notice of this fact without other evidence of background information. Read the decision to decide if the court may do this.

* * *

RAMEY, Chief Justice.

This appeal involves the validity of two judicial liens. In a bench trial, the trial court rendered judgment in favor of the Appellee judgment creditor, American Honda Motor Company, Inc., ruling that it owned valid judgment liens upon two tracts of land which had been conveyed by gift deeds from the judgment debtor, Bill G. Hayden and wife ("Haydens"), to Appellant, the Apostolic Church. Appellant contends that the trial court erred, because the judgment liens had not been properly perfected, and also because the liens had been canceled by the Haydens' subsequent discharge in bankruptcy. We do not agree; we will affirm the trial court's judgment, but deny Appellee's counterpoint.

The Haydens had owned three separate tracts of land in Shelby county. Appellee secured a money judgment against Hayden in 1985. Appellee sought to create judgment liens against the Haydens' property by recording and indexing an abstract of the judgment in Shelby county in March of 1985. In subsequent transactions, the Haydens conveyed two of the tracts to Appellant. In 1987, the Haydens petitioned for and were, later that year, discharged from their debts in bankruptcy proceedings. Some eight months thereafter, Appellee instituted the suit underlying this appeal to foreclose the judgment liens upon the two tracts of land. Judgment foreclosing these liens was signed by the trial court on December 14, 1989.

Appellant presents twelve points of error. Appellant considers together its first nine points of error; we will likewise address them as a group.

Judgment liens are statutorily created; without substantial compliance with the statutes, no lien attaches. Citicorp Real Estate, Inc. v. Banque Arabe Internationale D'Investissement, 747 S.W.2d 926, 929 (Tex.App.—Dallas 1988, writ denied). Appellant contends that Appellee's abstract of judgment did not substantially comply with the statutory requirements of section 52.003 of the Texas Property Code,[1] thereby failing to create valid judgment liens. According to §52.003 of the property code, an abstract of judgment must contain the following seven elements:

(1) the names of the plaintiff and defendant;
(2) the birthdate and driver's license number of the defendant if available to the clerk or justice;
(3) the number of the suit in which the judgment was rendered;
(4) the defendant's address, or if the address is not shown in the suit, the nature of citation and the date and place of service of citation;
(5) the date on which the judgment was rendered;
(6) the amount for which the judgment was rendered and the balance due; and
(7) the rate of interest specified in the judgment.

Appellant asserts that the judgment liens were deficient in five respects, four in the abstract of judgment itself: it allegedly failed to 1) state correctly the balance due thereon, 2) state the amount of any credits already paid, 3) state the defendant's address, or, alternatively, 4) state the nature and the date and place of the service of citation upon the judgment debtor. Fifth, Appellant contends that

the abstract of judgment was not properly indexed.

Concerning the indexing of the abstract, Appellant alleges that there is no evidence "that Appellee's abstract of judgment was indexed in the reverse indexes of the abstract of judgment records under the defendant's name." The record shows otherwise. The names of the plaintiff and defendant in the prior judgment appear alphabetically in both the direct and the indirect indexes in the Shelby County Clerk's office. Appellant's points of error attacking the indexing of the judgment are overruled.

As to the alleged deficiency stemming from the abstract's failure to state the sum of money due the judgment creditor, the abstract of judgment shows the date and amount of the original judgment. The amount of costs and rate of interest are also stated. These entries are identical to those recited in the 1985 judgment.

The abstract is silent concerning the amount of credits paid, but Hayden acknowledged at trial that he had paid nothing on the judgment. This failure of the abstract to affirmatively reflect that no credits had been paid on the judgment does not invalidate the lien, because an abstract of judgment need not affirmatively contain an entry that no payments have been made. Willis v. Pegues, 218 S.W. 96 (Tex.Civ.App.—Beaumont 1920, no writ).

Appellant has cited a number of cases in support of its contention that the abstract of judgment was defective, because there was no amount-due shown. These cases involved actual misstatements of the sums due the judgment creditor or, in some instances, the omission of parties to the underlying judgment. In none of them did the abstract of judgment furnish the requisite facts from which the sum owed could be correctly calculated.

It has been held that an abstract of judgment substantially complies with the statute when the abstract shows the amount and date of the original judgment, the interest rate, and any applicable costs or credits, even if the judgment fails to expressly state the amount due thereon. Kingman Texas Implement Co. v. Borders, 156 S.W. 614, 615 (Tex.Civ.App.—San Antonio 1913, no writ). If determination of the balance due requires merely a mathematical calculation, the abstract will not be found to be defective in not expressly stating the balance due. *Id.; see* American Petroleum Exchange, Inc. et al. v. Lord, 399 S.W.2d 213, 216 (Tex.Civ.App.—Amarillo 1966, writ ref'd n.r.e.). Here, the amount-due can be determined by a mathematical calculation utilizing the information in the abstract. We overrule Appellant's points of error based upon the omission from the abstract of judgment of the amount-due the judgment creditor.

Appellant also attacks the trial court's conclusion of law that the abstract of judgment substantially complied with Texas Property Code §52.003, in that the undisputed evidence shows that the abstract did not state Hayden's address *or* the nature of the citation and date and place of service of the citation. The issue here is Hayden's address; the alternative data pertaining to the nature and service of the citation was omitted.

If no address for Hayden was shown in the abstract of judgment, no lien would attach. *Citicorp Real Estate, Inc.*, 747 S.W.2d at 929; Texas American Bank/Fort Worth, N.A. v. Southern Union Exploration Co., 714 S.W.2d 105, 107 (Tex.App.—Eastland 1986, writ ref'd n.r.e.). Such is not the case here. The abstract of judgment shows the debtor's address to be "Tenaha Hwy, Center, TX". Thus, the remaining question is whether the stated address is accurate and sufficiently descriptive.

Hayden testified that he resided on Highway 96 North, which is also designated as Route 3, Box 498. Highway nomenclature and designations within the trial court's jurisdiction are matters of common knowledge and proper subjects for judicial notice. Fairall v. Sutphen, 296 S.W.2d 309, 311 (Tex.Civ.App.—Fort Worth 1956, no writ); Tex.R.Evid. 201. Here, Appellee did ask the court to take judicial notice that Highway 96 North was also known as the Tenaha Highway from Center, Texas. In matters involving geographical knowledge, it is not necessary that a formal request for judicial notice be made by a party. Harper v. Killion, 162 Tex. 481, 348 S.W.2d 521, 523 (1961). It is, therefore, not required that the court formally announce that he was taking judicial notice of such fact.

It is likewise a matter of judicial knowledge that Center and Tenaha are situated in Shelby County. Southwestern Investment Co. v. Shipley, 400 S.W.2d 304, 306 (Tex. 1966). They are within the trial court's jurisdiction. There was no proof, nor is it argued here, that the address stated in the abstract was incorrect. Whether Highway 96 North links Center and the neighboring Shelby county community of Tenaha is a fact of such notoriety that there is no necessity of accompanying the request for judicial notice with additional background information, in order for it to be mandatorily judicially noticed. Tex.R.Civ.Evid. 201(d); Wellborn, *Judicial Notice Under Article II of the Texas Rules of Evidence*, 19 St. Mary's Law Journal 17 (1987). Therefore, formal proof that Highway 69 North is the Tenaha Highway from Center, Texas is not required. Under this record we cannot overrule the trial court's conclusion of law of substantial compliance with Texas Property Code §52.003 because the abstract of judgment failed to show Hayden's address.

Furthermore, an attack upon a conclusion of law may only be reviewed to determine its correctness as a matter of law. Mercer v. Bludworth, 715 S.W.2d 693, 697 (Tex.App.—Houston [1st Dist.] 1986, writ ref'd n.r.e.); First Nat'l Bank in Dallas v. Kinabrew, 589 S.W.2d 137, 146 (Tex.Civ.App.—Tyler 1979, writ ref'd n.r.e.). Appellant has failed to demonstrate that this conclusion of law was not correct; therefore, it will not be disturbed. For these reasons, Appellant's point of error pertaining to defects in the judgment debtor's address is overruled. Thus, all of Appellant's points of error claiming defects in the abstract of judgment are overruled.

Appellant's final three points of error assert that the court erred because the Haydens' personal discharge in bankruptcy canceled the liens upon the two tracts. These two prepetition liens were valid and were not avoided during the bankruptcy proceedings. The Supreme Court of the United States has recently held that liens on real estate survive bankruptcy. Farrey v. Sanderfoot, — U.S. —, 111 S.Ct. 1825, 1829, 114 LEd.2d 337 (1991). "Rather, a bankruptcy discharge extinguishes only one mode of enforcing a claim—namely, an action against the debtor *in personam*—while leaving intact another—namely, an action against the debtor *in rem*." Dewsnup v.

Timm, — U.S. —, 112 S.Ct. 773, 778, 116 L.Ed.2d 903 (1992); Johnson v. Home State Bank, — U.S. —, 111 S.Ct. 2150, 2154, 115 L.Ed.2d 66 (1991). No attempt was made to cancel and discharge the liens upon the two tracts under the specific provisions of Tex.Prop.Code Ann. §52.022–.024 (Vernon 1984). We hold that the Haydens' bankruptcy discharge, without more, did not extinguish these judicial liens, and points of error ten, eleven and twelve are overruled.

Another potential issue on appeal, which was the subject of extensive proof at the trial, was whether the two tracts in question had been the Haydens' homestead. Appellant admitted in its responsive brief that homestead was not an issue on appeal. There is nothing to review on the homestead claim.

In a single counterpoint, Appellee seeks to recover damages, because several of Appellant's points of error are alleged to be frivolous and made for the purpose of delay. Such sanctions may be ordered in civil cases. Tex.R.App.P. 84. While we have held that none of Appellant's points of error should be sustained, we cannot say that the appeal was taken solely for delay and without sufficient cause. Appellee has not condemned all of Appellant's points of error as frivolous. Indeed, questions raised herein as to the statutory requirements pertaining to the judgment debtor's address and the omission of the amount due entry in the abstract of judgment have not heretofore been precisely answered in Texas.

Appellant cites Dolenz v. A____B____, 742 S.W.2d 82 (Tex.App.—Dallas, 1987) and Trinity Universal Insurance Company v. Farley, 408 S.W.2d 776 (Tex.Civ.App.—Tyler 1966, no writ) in support of his motion for sanctions. *Dolenz* is inapplicable, because in that case the appellate court found that all of the points urged by Appellant were specious. 742 S.W.2d at 86. The *Farley* case likewise is not helpful, because this Court denied sanctions in that case. 408 S.W.2d at 780. Appellee's counterpoint is overruled.

The judgment of the trial court is affirmed.

---

[1] Unless otherwise noted, all statutory references in this opinion are to Tex.Prop.Code Ann. §52.001 *et seq.* (Vernon 1984).

✔ PRACTICE QUESTIONS

Indicate whether each statement is true or false.

1. "D," a defendant in a criminal action in which he was charged with unauthorized use of a motor vehicle, stipulated that the owner of the vehicle did not give him permission to operate the vehicle. However, he pleaded not guilty to the crime. This is permitted in court.

2. At a trial of an action, the time of sunrise and the weather on a particular day were highly material. The judge sent his clerk to obtain a copy of the United States Weather Bureau report for that day, covering the area in question. The clerk returned with the report, it was read into evidence, and the court took judicial notice of the contents. This was proper.

3. A judge could take judicial notice of the facts that water freezes at 32 degrees Fahrenheit at a standard pressure and that the resultant ice takes up more space than the water.

4. "J," a judge, took judicial notice that "D," the defendant, could have been in Detroit and Miami on the same day. This was proper.

5. According to the common law, judicial notice may be taken of county, town, and municipal ordinances.

Select the most correct answer to complete each statement.

6. (a) In the absence of a statute to the contrary, courts will take judicial notice of the laws of other states.

   (b) The principles involving judicial notice of matters of fact are not unlike those for judicial notice of matters of law in that they are judicial shortcuts to the proper administration of justice.

   (c) Courts may not take judicial notice of facts that may be regarded as forming the common knowledge of every person of ordinary understanding and intelligence.

   (d) Pretrial pleadings are not exchanged by attorney adversaries before a trial because this may cause their clients to think that they are not earning their fees.

7. (a) A defendant in a criminal trial is entitled to the benefit of a reasonable doubt in the case as made by the prosecution as well as in any defense interposed on the defendant's behalf.

   (b) If one party fails to controvert a fact in a pleading, the court cannot find the fact to be otherwise by resorting to its judicial knowledge.

   (c) Mail addressed without a zip code cannot be judicially noticed as having been properly delivered, even though the remaining part of the address was correct and the mail was placed in a receptacle under the jurisdiction and care of the United States Postal Service.

   (d) If there is a controversy as to what is judicially noticed, the court may take judicial notice of a controverted fact that the court believes is most likely to have occurred.

CHAPTER 19

Unconstitutionally Obtained Evidence

§ 19.1 INTRODUCTION—THE EXCLUSIONARY RULE

It is not the function of this book to explain in detail about evidence that is subject to an exclusionary rule because of constitutional prohibitions. However, since it is a basic requirement that all law enforcement personnel be aware of certain limitations in the use of evidence garnered from constitutionally protected areas, a general discussion of this topic follows.

While the general law of evidence is constantly changing, this area of law has not undergone drastic revision in recent years, except for the enactment of the Federal Rules of Evidence, effective July 1, 1975, and several amendments that have been added from time to time. The rules dealing with the exclusion of evidence that has been seized in a manner that violates the constitutional guarantees of the inhabitants of our land, however, have experienced great changes caused by interpretations of the United States Constitution by the United States Supreme Court. This Court considers cases each term where at least four justices consider a substantial federal question is involved, whether on a certified question of law from a lower court, a petition for writ of certiorari, or on appeal.

In order to effectively control excesses by law enforcement officers, the courts have devised a procedure that has been called the exclusionary rule. If the court finds that the law enforcement officer violated a basic constitutional right of a defendant, the court orders that all evidence obtained through violation of the defendant's constitutional rights not be admitted in evidence at the trial of the defendant.

The trier of the facts therefore is never to consider this evidence in its deliberation as to the guilt or innocence of the defendant. Hence, many offenders who are clearly guilty of the crimes with which they are charged are acquitted or have the charges dropped because of insufficient evidence.

The cry of law enforcement has been that the United States Supreme Court has handcuffed them and yet they are expected to do a job.

A crisis in law enforcement has been taking place because of the stringent limitations placed on the government in the enforcement of laws. Whenever a crisis develops, whether it be in the family, in business, or in government, it is time to stop to reevaluate goals, procedures, and theories to come up with a viable solution. Most often the solution is found. Law enforcement has been responding to this crisis by professionalization and greater in-depth training.

Lawyers as legal counsel to police departments were unheard of in small departments until recently. The International Association of Chiefs of Police now has a section consisting solely of legal advisors to law enforcement agencies. There is a common need, and the law enforcement community is rising to the occasion.

On the other hand, the strict limitations on law enforcement established by the Warren Court (the Supreme Court under Chief Justice Earl Warren) were eased somewhat by the Burger Court (the Supreme Court under Chief Justice Warren Burger). The Burger Court leaned toward the primary issue of the guilt or innocence of the defendant and considered this factor in its decisions when there was no wanton abuse by law enforcement personnel.

As indicated previously, this text is not designed to treat constitutional law in detail but is meant to give you a general view of the theories so that you can deal with the problem in a better frame of mind.

§ 19.2 THE CONSTITUTION—A LIVING DOCUMENT

The Constitution of the United States has been described as a living document in that the framers of the Constitution were careful not to define with any degree of specificity many of the terms used. For example, Article I, Section 8, Paragraph 3 reads:

> To regulate Commerce with foreign Nations, and among the several States, and with the Indiana Tribes; . . .

The most ingenious minds of the framers would never think that there would be a day in the future that almost instantaneous communication could be achieved by telephone, telegraph, radio, computer, and television. Nor could they be expected to know that some day people could fly in aircraft all over the world. The vague use of the word "commerce" has been interpreted by the judiciary to include all of the above without any structural change of the wording of the basic document.

Another example of the loose use of language is found in the Fourth Amendment, where we find a prohibition against unreasonable search and seizure. The word "unreasonable" was left for future generations to define pursuant to the customs, mores, and needs of the times. Article III of the Constitution, which was interpreted by Chief Justice John Marshall in Marbury v. Madison, 5 U.S. (1 Cranch) 137, 2 L.Ed. 60 (1803), held that the Supreme Court has constitutional powers to strike down statutes, state or federal, that violate commands of the federal Constitution. In this way, as the needs of the nation change and the identities of the Associate Justices of the Supreme Court and the Chief Justice of the United States change, so do the interpretations of the Constitution, adhering, however, whenever possible, to the concept of stare decisis.

§ 19.3 THE EARLY FUNCTION OF THE UNITED STATES GOVERNMENT

We must remember that in the latter part of the eighteenth century the colonies consisted of scattered settlements with small cities. The population consisted of approximately 75 percent farmers, with the remaining 25 percent distributed among tradesmen, merchants, craftsmen, seamen, and professionals. It was generally considered that the function of government was to maintain law and order and to protect life, liberty, and property from internal and external threats. The individual followed his or her own interests in competition with other individuals without interference from the government. The elderly or sick were cared for by their families or charitable associations. There was no civil police department as we know it today until one was implemented in London, England, by Sir Robert Peel in 1829. The citizenry did not expect nor did they wish such benefits as unemployment compensation, old-age pensions, consumer protection laws, free health care, and free legal services—and their concomitant high taxes.

§ 19.4 THE OFFENDER'S RIGHTS UNDER EARLY COMMON LAW

It has taken centuries to evolve the concept of a fair trial as we know it. There was no procedural guarantee in early English history for those accused of crime. They had a system sometimes referred to as the "Hue and Cry." In this system, a victim of a crime would raise a hue and cry, and all of the inhabitants of the area would arm themselves to seek the felon. If the accused was captured, a hastily convened court would try the defendant. If he or she resisted capture, a member of the community could legally kill the person. Usually, he or she had little chance of getting an impartial jury, and the defendant could not testify as a defense witness. The subject was usually executed by being hanged or thrown off a cliff by the victim or a relative of the victim.

If an accusation was made against an alleged perpetrator who escaped, the escapee would be declared an outlaw and was thus not entitled to the protection of the law, whatever that might be. In that case, the person could be executed without a prior indictment. If an outlaw was apprehended while in the possession of stolen goods, the outlaw could be executed summarily by a member of the area.

It is easy to see how, under this system of justice, nefarious persons caused the imprisonment and/or death of others who might have been in the way of the accuser in one way or another.

§ 19.5 THE RULE OF LAW

There is a concept known as the rule of law under which Anglo-Saxon law has come to operate. It is enunciated when, in the latter part of the nineteenth century, the English constitutional scholar Albert V. Dicey wrote that the rule of law has three distinct parts. The third part does not apply to American law and is not included below. The first two are abbreviated as follows:

1. No man is punishable or can be lawfully made to suffer in body or goods except for a distinct breach of law established in the ordinary legal manner before the ordinary courts of the land. . . .
2. No man is above the law. . . . Every man . . . is subject to the ordinary law of the realm.

See Cambell v. Hall, Leef 655; K & L 487 (1774).

We have no better example of the operation of this concept than when President Richard Nixon, one of the most powerful persons in the world at that time, was caused to resign from office because of a breach of the law.

§ 19.6 PROCEDURAL SAFEGUARDS OF THE ACCUSED

Fortunately for the law-abiding person, as well as the criminal, the practices of the ancient common law with respect to the apprehension and trial of one accused of crime are no longer used. Today, in the United States, many safeguards are afforded to the accused to prevent an infringement of constitutional rights in the interest of justice. It was not uncommon, even in recent years, to force confessions from accused persons by third-degree methods. The pain and torture, both physical and mental, that was inflicted on criminal suspects often caused them to admit to the commission of crimes in which they had not been involved. Accordingly, the courts have ensured that this type of activity by law enforcement officers would be for naught and the prisoner/defendant would be free. The procedural safeguards are based on the integrity of the individual and government by law rather than by men.

§ 19.7 CONSTITUTIONAL BASIS FOR ARREST

While there was a common law basis for arrest of violators of the common law prior to the adoption of the Constitution, the Constitution authorizes arrest of malefactors but proscribes certain limitations on this power. We find these limitations outlined in the Fourth, Fifth, Sixth, and Eighth Amendments to the original document.

Statutory penal codes came later on in our history. The New York Penal Code was enacted in 1881, consisting of 727 sections, which proscribed conduct that would be considered a violation of the law.

§ 19.8 MOTOR VEHICLES—STATUTORY AUTHORITY TO STOP

The police power, i.e., control over the health, welfare, and morals, is one of the powers reserved to the states in the United States Constitution by virtue of the reserve powers clause of the Tenth Amendment of that document. Accordingly, the power to regulate the ownership and movement of motor vehicles is vested in each of the states. The states have legislated licensing statutes whereby an operator of a motor vehicle must first qualify for a license to operate and/or own a motor vehicle. In order for the state to enforce compliance, it is therefore necessary to give power and authority to law enforcement personnel charged with the responsibility of enforcing traffic laws to stop drivers of motor vehicles and ascertain whether they are properly licensed to operate the vehicle and whether the vehicle is properly registered. Each state has such a statute.

> **Fla.—322.15** (1) Every licensee shall have his operator's or chauffeur's license in his immediate possession at all times when operating a motor vehicle and shall display the same upon demand of a patrol officer, peace officer, or field deputy or inspector of the department.

An officer's motive for checking a driver's license and registration is immaterial. The fact that he was suspicious that a driver of a particular automobile may be committing a crime neither adds to nor detracts from his authority to stop the automobile and check the driver's license. Fla.—Cameron v. State, 112 So.2d 864 (Fla.App. 1959). A municipal police department could operate a "road block" or similar system for the purpose of checking automobile driver's licenses, and such practice did not amount to an illegal search and seizure contrary to state and federal constitutions, nor did it amount to an unconstitutional invasion of a motorist's right to use the public ways. Fla.—City of Miami v. Aronovitz, 114 So.2d 784 (Fla. 1959).

It follows therefore that if an officer has probable cause to check a driver's license, as statutorily authorized, any evidence the officer observes by virtue of this activity would be admissible into evidence.

§ 19.9 FINGERPRINTS—DETENTION FOR

It is common knowledge that a person may be positively identified by his or her fingerprints and that no two persons have ever been found to have identical fingerprints. The courts have taken judicial notice of this scientific fact. Fingerprint classification was reportedly first developed by the Chinese. Fingerprints were found to be commonly used for identifications purposes during the Tang Dynasty (618 to 906 A.D.). The most widely used system today is the Galton-Henry system. This science, like so many others, is now computerized, but it still requires a fingerprint expert to classify the prints being examined.

As a practical matter, it becomes necessary to keep a record of persons who have been arrested and convicted of crime to enable the law enforcement community to detect crime and also to properly charge the defendant. Many statutes carry a higher sanction if the defendant has been previously convicted. Statutes provide that in certain types of arrests the prisoner is required to be fingerprinted.

> **Conn.—Gen.Stat.Ann. § 29-11.** The bureau in the state police department known as the state bureau of identification, shall be maintained for the purpose of providing an authentic record of each person over sixteen years of age who is charged with the commission of any crime involving moral turpitude and of providing definite information relative to the identity of each person so arrested and of providing a record of the final judgment of the court resulting from such arrest. . . .

Many states now have statutes requiring the return of all fingerprints, photos, descriptions, and other identification data and all copies and duplicates thereof to the person whose fingerprints were taken, if the defendant is later acquitted or the charges are dismissed or not prosecuted. See Conn.Gen.Stat.Ann. § 29.15.

Therefore, it is incumbent upon law enforcement officers to detain arrestees for the purpose of taking their fingerprints.

§ 19.10 CLOSE PURSUIT ARRESTS

Each state has its own criminal procedure law or criminal code. In these statutes are found the grounds on which a law enforcement officer or citizen may make an arrest of a person who is believed to have committed an offense against society. The law enforcement powers of police officers are applicable within the jurisdiction in which they are appointed. It was not uncommon in the days of the Old West for the malefactor to race the sheriff to the border of the officer's jurisdiction, and if the criminal was successful in getting across the border before being apprehended, he or she might find sanctuary because the officer was not authorized to make an arrest beyond his or her jurisdiction. To avoid this miscarriage of justice, states have adopted what have been termed close pursuit, hot pursuit, or fresh pursuit laws. An example is 11 Del.Code Ann. §§ 1931 and 1932, which read as follows:

> **§ 1931. Definitions**
>
> As used in this subchapter
>
> "Fresh pursuit" includes fresh pursuit as defined by the common law, and also the pursuit of a person who has committed a felony or a misdemeanor or a violation of the Motor Vehicle Code of this State or who is reasonably suspected of having committed a felony or a misdemeanor or a violation of the Motor Vehicle Code of this State, and also includes the pursuit of a person suspected of having committed a supposed felony or misdemeanor or violation of the Motor Vehicle Code of the State though no viola-

tion of the law has actually been committed, if there is reasonable grounds for believing that a violation of the law has been committed; however, fresh pursuit as used in this subchapter does not necessarily imply instant pursuit, but pursuit without reasonable delay. (41 Del.Laws, c. 216 § 5; 11 Del.C. 1953, § 1931; 56 Del.Laws, c. 154 § 1.)

§ 1932. Arrest by out-of-state police

(a) Any member of a duly organized state, county or municipal peace unit of another state of the United States who enters this State in fresh pursuit, and continues within this State in such fresh pursuit, of a person in order to arrest him on the ground that he is believed to have committed a felony, a misdemeanor or a violation of the Motor Vehicle Code in such other state, shall have the same authority to arrest and hold such person in custody, as has any member of any duly organized state, county or municipal peace unit of this State, to arrest and hold in custody a person on the ground that he is believed to have committed a felony, a misdemeanor or a violation of the Motor Vehicle Code in this State.

(b) This section shall not be construed so as to make unlawful any arrest in this State which would otherwise be lawful. (41 Del.Laws, c. 216 §§ 1, 3; 11 Del.C. 1953, § 2.)

§ 19.11 THE FIRST, FOURTH, FIFTH, SIXTH, EIGHTH, TENTH, AND FOURTEENTH AMENDMENTS

We speak of the First, Fourth, Fifth, Sixth, Eighth, Tenth, and Fourteenth Amendments as amendments to the Constitution that everyone who has completed a high school education in the United States has read and knows, or should know, by rote memory. Experience, however, has demonstrated to the contrary. In order to help you become acquainted with the contents of these amendments, which have become so important in the administration of the criminal law, they are reproduced below. These amendments are part of the first ten amendments to the Constitution, which are known as the Bill of Rights. They were placed in the Constitution shortly after its adoption, in order to comply with the demands of certain states that made their adoption a condition of ratification.

AMENDMENT I (Freedom of religion, speech, press, assemblage, and petition)
Congress shall make no law respecting an establishment of religion, or prohibiting the free exercise thereof; or abridging the freedom of speech, or of the press, or the right of the people peaceably to assemble, and to petition the Government for a redress of grievances.

AMENDMENT IV (Searches and seizures)
The right of the people to be secure in their persons, houses, papers, and effects, against unreasonable searches and seizures, shall not be violated, and no Warrants shall issue, but upon probable cause, supported by Oath or affirmation, and particularly describing the place to be searched, and the persons or things to be seized.

AMENDMENT V (Criminal indictment, double jeopardy, self-incrimination, due process, compensation for taking private property)
No person shall be held to answer for a capital, or otherwise infamous crime, unless on a presentment or indictment of a Grand Jury, except in cases arising in the land or naval forces, or in the Militia, when in actual service in time of War or public danger; nor shall any person be subject for the same offence to be twice put in jeopardy of life or limb, nor shall be compelled in any criminal

case to be a witness against himself, nor be deprived of life, liberty, or property, without due process of law; nor shall private property be taken for public use without just compensation.

AMENDMENT VI (Rights of defendant in criminal prosecutions)

In all criminal prosecutions, the accused shall enjoy the right to a speedy and public trial, by an impartial jury of the State and district wherein the crime shall have been committed; which district shall have been previously ascertained by law, and to be informed of the nature and cause of the accusation; to be confronted with the witnesses against him; to have compulsory process for obtaining witnesses in his favor, and to have the assistance of counsel for his defence.

AMENDMENT VIII (Excessive bail, cruel and unusual punishments)

Excessive bail shall not be required, nor excessive fines imposed, nor cruel and unusual punishments inflicted.

AMENDMENT X (Powers reserved to the states)

The powers not delegated to the United States by the Constitution, nor prohibited by it to the States, are reserved to the States respectively, or to the people.

AMENDMENT XIV (§ 1. Citizens, privileges and immunities, due process, equal protection)

Section 1. All persons born or naturalized in the United States and subject to the jurisdiction thereof, are citizens of the United States and of the State wherein they reside. No State shall make or enforce any law which shall abridge the privileges or immunities of citizens of the United States; nor shall any State deprive any person of life, liberty, or property, without due process of law; nor deny to any person within its jurisdiction the equal protection of the laws.

(Sections 2, 3, 4, and 5 are not applicable to this discussion.)

§ 19.12 EVIDENCE OBTAINED BY VIOLATION OF THE FIRST AMENDMENT

You will recall that our founding fathers were interested in making certain that they did not recreate in the new world a system of government like the one they had fled from in the old world. They were particularly concerned about the right of a person to speak and publish his or her convictions whether or not those in authority concurred in them. The First Amendment to the Constitution was to guarantee this right for their contemporaries and for their posterity. The lawbooks have been replete with many cases involving a temporary restriction on a person's right to determine his or her religion, to speak, to publish, to assemble, and to petition against the government for redresses.

Fortunately, the courts have held in favor of any persons so wronged. There are many countries that have such provisions in their constitutions, but because of a lack of a system of checks and balances whereby the legislative, judicial, and executive branches of the government check and balance each other, the words in the constitutions of these other nations have become meaningless. We have had statutes that have been declared unconstitutional and hence unenforceable because they violate the First Amendment. U.S.—Shuttlesworth v. Birmingham, 394 U.S. 147, 89 S.Ct. 935, 22 L.Ed.2d 162 (1969).

§ 19.13 EVIDENCE OBTAINED BY VIOLATION OF THE FOURTH AMENDMENT IN COMBINATION WITH THE FOURTEENTH AMENDMENT

It was first thought that the proscriptions of the first ten amendments to the United States Constitution were applicable against the federal government alone in that each citizen of a state retained his or her state citizenship and was also a citizen of the United States of America. Through painstaking efforts on the part of many attorneys, most of the proscriptions were made applicable against the individual states by United States Supreme Court decisions that absorbed the Bill of Rights amendments on a case-by-case basis after the adoption of the Fourteenth Amendment. A further amplification of this concept is left to a course of study dealing exclusively with constitutional law.

§ 19.14 EVIDENCE OBTAINED BY MEANS OF UNREASONABLE SEARCH AND SEIZURE

The United States Supreme Court construes the meaning of the words used in the Constitution by deciding cases that come before the Court. Accordingly, the law changes based on the most recent decisions of the Supreme Court. You are advised to refresh your recollection as to how the common law is changed. This was explained in Chapter 1. See Figure 1.

The Fourth Amendment to the United States Constitution has been interpreted by perhaps more cases than any other constitutional amendment except perhaps the First Amendment.

The Constitution grants power to each of our divisions of government (i.e., executive, judicial, and legislative), but through a system of checks and balances it also places restraints on that power to the end that no branch of the government is too powerful to the exclusion of the other branches.

The executive power is charged with implementing court orders and the law as enacted by the legislative power. The judicial power is charged with construing the Constitution and statutory law.

The Fourth Amendment does not prohibit all searches. It only prohibits unreasonable searches. What may be considered unreasonable at one stage in our history may not be considered unreasonable at a later point in our history.

For example, during 1960, it would have been considered highly unreasonable for a prospective passenger on a commercial airliner to be searched for weapons. It is submitted that if such a search was conducted at that time and an unlawfully possessed firearm was found on a prospective passenger, the search would be held to be unconstitutional and all such evidence would not be admissible in a trial for the unlawful possession of a firearm.

By 1973, however, the courts had determined that it was not unreasonable to search a prospective passenger of a commercial airliner for weapons because of the high incidence of hijacking of airplanes. The United States Constitution prohibition against unreasonable search and seizure has been held to be a prohibition against state action in Mapp v. Ohio, 367 U.S. 643, 81 S.Ct. 1684, 6 L.Ed.2d 1081 (1961).

In order to prevent law enforcement authorities from overreaching their powers, the courts have adopted what has been called an exclusionary rule, discussed in §19.1. In essence, the courts will not admit evidence into the trial that has been obtained by means of a violation of the defendant's constitutional rights. The procedural methods employed by counsel to implement this exclusion will be discussed later in this book.

As indicated above, in Mapp v. Ohio, *supra*, the United States Supreme Court interceded in unreasonable search and seizure activities by state law enforcement personnel and applied the exclusionary rules to state action. This opened a Pandora's box and caused many state cases to find their way into the federal courts. The Burger Court began to qualify and limit some of the decisions of the Warren Court. In 1976, for example, in the case of Stone v. Powell, 428 U.S. 465, 96 S.Ct. 3037, 49 L.Ed.2d 1067 (1976), the Court held that after a defendant has been afforded an opportunity for the full and fair litigation of Fourth Amendment claims by the state, he may not thereafter obtain habeas corpus relief on the ground that illegally seized evidence was introduced at his trial. The Court emphasized that the purpose of the judicially created exclusionary rule is deterrence and that the policies behind it are not absolute, but relative to the competing public interest in the determination of truth at trial by means of highly probative evidence. Balancing the utility of the exclusionary rule against the cost of extending it to collateral review, therefore, reveals that the costs exceed the marginal benefits. Application of the rule "deflects the truth finding process and often frees the guilty." On the other hand, "[t]here is no reason to believe . . . that the overall educative effect of the exclusionary rule would be appreciably diminished if search and seizure claims could not be raised in federal habeas corpus review of state convictions."

§ 19.15 ARREST WARRANT REQUIREMENTS

We have just read the caveats of the Fourth Amendment with respect to the issuance of warrants. It has been the function of the courts to define what was meant by this direction. The word "particularly" and the phrase "probable cause" have been the subject of much litigation. U.S.—Andresen v. Maryland, 423 U.S. 822, 96 S.Ct. 36, 46 L.Ed.2d 39 (1975); N.Y.—People v. Malinsky et al., 19 N.Y.2d 262, 225 N.E.2d 748, 279 N.Y.S.2d 20 (1967).

The usual procedure is for the law enforcement officer to obtain information, either by his or her own direct observation or through a reliable informant, coupled with the officer's observation, that a crime is being committed at a particular location and/or a particular wanted person may be found at a particular address. The officer will state in affidavit form his or her request and reasons that he or she believes that a warrant will assist the officer in affecting an arrest for violation of law.

The independent judicial officer will read the affidavit and decide in his or her judgment, based on the allegations in the affidavit, whether there is probable cause for the issuance of the warrant and whether there is sufficient particularity. If so satisfied, the judicial officer will sign a warrant directing the law enforcement officer to make the search and/or arrest and bring the results of the search and/or arrest before the judicial officer. When this occurs, many states call this a "return." An inventory is made of all items seized and presented to the court. The law enforcement officer is charged with the responsibility of safeguarding the items seized until such time as they are required by the prosecution for introduction into evidence. Sometimes the officer will scratch his or her initials on the surface of the evidence for identification purposes at a later date. If the evidence is capable of being placed into an envelope or bag or container, some departments require their officers to seal the receptacle and sign their names over the seal to ensure continuity of control of the evidence.

Naturally, there will be variations of this procedure in different jurisdictions, but mainly the thought is to safeguard the evidence and to ensure its reliability when it is offered as real evidence at the trial. The judicial officer is usually a judge or justice of a court, but the United States Supreme Court has held in Shadwick v. City of Tampa, 407 U.S. 345, 92 S.Ct. 2119, 32 L.Ed.2d 783 (1972), that a clerk of a court may issue warrants in designated situations.

§ 19.16 EVIDENCE OBTAINED IN VIOLATION OF RIGHT OF PRIVACY BY MEANS OF ILLEGAL WIRETAPS OR EAVESDROPPING

The fathers of our government could not possibly envisage the electronic age of today, but because the Constitution is a living document, the Supreme Court finally included wiretapping within the protection of the Fourth Amendment. The case history of this amendment also went a full circle. In the early cases, the Court held that the proscription was limited to search and seizure of material things. Olmstead v. United States, 277 U.S. 438, 48 S.Ct. 564, 72 L.Ed. 944 (1928). Later, however, the Court held that illegal wiretaps violated the Federal Communication Act of 1934. Still later, the Supreme Court held that surveillance without trespass and without seizure of material fell within the protection of the Fourth Amendment of the United States Constitution. Katz v. United States, 389 U.S. 347, 88 S.Ct. 507, 19 L.Ed.2d 576 (1967). Title 3 of the Omnibus Crime Control Act authorizes wiretapping under specified conditions. This act has no effect on actions by state officials in this area unless a state statute is passed to supplement the federal statute. You should consult the statutory law in your state to determine the admissibility of this type of evidence in your jurisdiction.

Subsequently, statutes have been enacted reaffirming limitations on wiretapping to include state law enforcement officers.

§ 19.17 EVIDENCE OBTAINED BY VIRTUE OF A SEARCH WARRANT

Where probable cause is shown, the law enforcement officer obtains a search warrant from a judicial officer. This officer makes an independent assessment of the facts based on an affidavit signed by a law enforcement officer or others, and if he or she is convinced, based on the evidence produced, that probable cause exists for the issuance of the search warrant, the judicial officer issues and signs such a warrant, particularly describing the places to be searched and/or the persons or items to be seized. The law enforcement officer, armed with a search warrant, may conduct the search or seizure but must strictly adhere to the directions in the warrant. If the officer fails in this, all evidence that is brought to the court may later be found to be inadmissible.

There are other situations wherein the courts have held that the evidence was not obtained in an unreasonable manner. Some of these are as follows:

1. Evidence seized incidental to a lawful arrest.
2. Evidence seized by virtue of the defendant or someone in lawful control of a premises consenting to the search.
3. Evidence seized from the person of a consenting defendant.
4. Evidence obtained from a vehicle where the items seized were in open view.
5. Evidence seized from an area that is not constitutionally protected.
6. Evidence obtained by a private person who has no connection with a law enforcement agency (the constitutional protections have been construed to protect one against official action and not private acts).

7. Weapons found by a police officer as a result of a stop and frisk when necessary to protect the officer or anyone in the vicinity.
8. Evidence seized from the person of one who has been arrested for a traffic violation.
9. Probable cause arrest.
10. Automobile search (inventory search).

Not only is evidence that has been obtained by an unreasonable search not admissible in evidence, but also any information obtained as a result of the illegal search is excluded under a doctrine that has become known as the "fruit of poisonous tree" doctrine.

§ 19.18 SEARCH INCIDENTAL TO A LAWFUL ARREST

Once a lawful arrest has been made, the officer is required, in order to safeguard himself or herself, the prisoner, and others with whom the prisoner may come in contact, to make a thorough search of the prisoner. Any contraband that is surfaced as a result of this search is admissible under the doctrine that it is admissible as incidental to a lawful arrest. This principle was explained by the Court in Agnello v. United States, 269 U.S. 20, 30, 46 S.Ct. 4, 70 L.Ed. 145 (1925), where the Court said that "the right without a search warrant contemporaneously to search persons lawfully arrested while committing crime and to search the place where the arrest is made in order to find and seize things connected with the crime as well as weapons and other things to effect an escape from custody, is not to be doubted." In Chimel v. California, 395 U.S. 752, 89 S.Ct. 2034, 23 L.Ed.2d 685 (1969), the Court again gave full authority to an officer to make a search incidental to a lawful arrest and included the area into which the arrestee may reach or the area within his immediate control.

§ 19.19 CONSENT SEARCH

The Constitution prohibits unreasonable searches; it does not prohibit consent searches. When a person consents to a search, he or she is, in effect, waiving any right to contest the search as being unconstitutional. In practice, courts have looked very carefully into the credibility of an officer's testimony that the defendant consented to a search. Assuming that a wife in the absence of her husband may waive his constitutional immunity against search of his dwelling as granted by Article I, §14 of the Constitution of Ohio, such waiver cannot be said to have occurred where the testimony as to the wife's assent is conflicting and there is a probability that any assent given was by reason of the coercive influence of an officer or officers of the law. Ohio—State v. Lindway, 131 Ohio St. 166, 2 N.E.2d 490 (1936).

§ 19.20 PLAIN OR OPEN VIEW DOCTRINE

The plain or open view doctrine can best be explained by an example.

If a police officer is walking on a foot patrol beat and he observes an automobile parked on his post wherein the back seat has several decks of glassine envelopes containing white powder and two hypodermic needles, the officer has good grounds to arrest the occupant or the person who claims the vehicle.

Objects falling in plain view of an officer who has a right to be in the position to have the view are subject to seizure and may be introduced in evidence. U.S.—Harris v. United States, 390 U.S. 234, 88 S.Ct. 992, 19 L.Ed.2d 1067 (1968).

§ 19.21 NONCONSTITUTIONALLY PROTECTED AREAS

The Fourth Amendment protects persons and places from unreasonable interference with their privacy by agents of government. It does not protect persons when they may be carrying out criminal acts in areas which are public and the officer has probable cause to make the arrest. U.S.—United States v. Watson, 423 U.S. 411, 96 S.Ct. 820, 46 L.Ed.2d 598 (1976).

§ 19.22 PRIVATE PERSON'S ARREST

The individual's protection in the Bill of Rights of the United States Constitution has been construed to be effective against governmental authority and not against the acts of private persons. In Miranda v. Arizona, 384 U.S. 436, 444, 86 S.Ct. 1602, 16 L.Ed.2d 694 (1966), the Court specifically pointed out, "It was necessary in Escobedo, as here, to insure that what was proclaimed in the Constitution had not become but a 'form of words', Silverthorne Lumber Co. v. United States, 251 U.S. 385, 392, 40 S.Ct. 182, 64 L.Ed. 319 (1920), in the hands of government officials. . . . By custodial interrogation, we mean questioning initiated by law enforcement officers after a person has been taken into custody or otherwise deprived of his freedom of action in any significant way."

Therefore, it may be reasoned that a store detective employed by a private corporation who is not deputized by any governmental authority need not adhere to the constitutional mandate of *Miranda*.

§ 19.23 STOP AND FRISK SEARCH

The stop and frisk search is designed to protect a law enforcement officer or anyone in the vicinity from the harmful effects of weapons found on the person of the defendant. To effect this result, the officer is permitted to pat down the outer garments of a suspect to ascertain whether the suspect is carrying a concealed weapon, and if so, the officer is authorized to remove the weapon from the suspect and place him or her under arrest. There is a problem if the suspect is of the opposite sex to the searching officer because there is the latent complaint that the officer performed this frisk for his or her sexual gratification. This might be a cogent argument for the practice of causing men and women police officers to be assigned together either on foot patrol or in cruiser patrol.

The leading cases in this area are Terry v. Ohio, 392 U.S. 1, 88 S.Ct. 1868, 20 L.Ed.2d 889 (1968), and Peters v. New York, 392 U.S. 40, 88 S.Ct. 1889, 20 L.Ed.2d 917 (1968). In the former case, there was no statutory authorization for the stop and frisk. In the latter case, there was a statute directing such a search. In both cases, the court upheld the validity of the search.

§ 19.24 TRAFFIC VIOLATION—EVIDENCE SEIZED INCIDENTAL TO LAWFUL ARREST

A custodial arrest of a suspect based on probable cause is a reasonable intrusion under the Fourth Amendment; that intrusion being lawful, a search incident to the arrest requires no additional justification. It is the fact of the lawful arrest that establishes the authority to search. Where there is a lawful custodial arrest and a full search of the person, it is a reasonable search requiring no warrant. This principle applies to all lawful arrests including but not limited to an arrest for a traffic offense that carried a mandatory minimum prison sentence or fine, or both, where heroin was found on the person arrested and the heroin was admissible in evidence. U.S.—United States v. Willie Robinson, Jr., 414 U.S. 218, 94 S.Ct. 467, 38 L.Ed.2d 427 (1973). In Gustafson v. State of Florida, 414 U.S. 260, 94 S.Ct. 488, 38 L.Ed.2d 456 (1973), the Court held that a person arrested for the offense of driving his automobile without a valid operator's license may be taken into custody and a police officer was entitled to make a full search of the petitioner's person. All "fruits," instrumentalities or contrabands found on such person, probative of criminal conduct are admissible in evidence as incidental to a lawful arrest. It is not material that the initial offense did not carry a mandatory minimum sentence.

§ 19.25 PROBABLE CAUSE SEARCH

The Fourth Amendment to the United States Constitution provides, among other items, that no warrants are to be issued but upon probable cause. The various state criminal procedure statutes have similarly provided. Arrests and searches, however, can be made without a warrant where the officer has probable cause to effect the arrest and the search and where there is insufficient time, as a practical matter, to first obtain a search warrant from a detached magistrate. Although no search warrant has been issued, intoxicating liquor which is discovered in an automobile by an officer who has stopped and searched such automobile in good faith, and relying on bona fide information, may be offered in evidence. Ohio—Houck v. State, 106 Ohio St. 195, 140 N.E. 112 (1922).

§ 19.26 AUTOMOBILE SEARCH

The automobile is particularly vulnerable to lawful search by law enforcement officers. As has been previously noted, the state law enforcement officer has a responsibility to see that the traffic laws are complied with. This gives him or her a wedge to inspect the vehicle. States have given law enforcement officers further authority to inspect the contents of vehicles by other statutes. For example, Pennsylvania authorizes officers whose duty it is to enforce the game laws to stop and search vehicles. Failure to stop the vehicle when so ordered makes the malefactor liable to a fine. Pa.—34 Pa.Statutes § 1311.73(*o*).

When a vehicle is impounded by the police, an inventory search has been held to be a constitutionally valid search. Neb.—State v. Wallen, 185 Neb. 44, 173 N.W.2d 372 (1970).

In a 1976 case, South Dakota v. Opperman, 428 U.S. 364, 96 S.Ct. 3092, 49 L.Ed.2d 1000 (1976), a defendant's car was impounded by the police for multiple parking violations. Following the police department's standard inventory procedures, the police made an inventory of the contents of the car and discovered marijuana in a closed, unlocked glove compartment. The defendant was convicted of possession of marijuana after his motion to suppress was denied. The court affirmed his conviction, holding that the routine inventory search of the impounded automobile was not an unreasonable search and seizure. The search was primarily for the purpose of safeguarding valuables in plain view inside the car, and there was no indication that the standard procedure followed served as a pretext for a criminal investigation.

Another 1976 auto search case was Texas v. White, 423 U.S. 67, 96 S.Ct. 304, 46 L.Ed.2d 209 (1976), wherein the Court held that a warrantless search of an automobile at a police station was permissible if probable cause to search was present at the scene of the arrest.

§ 19.27 DOG SNIFFING—BLOODHOUND EVIDENCE

It is well known that dogs have been trained to track down suspects by smelling garments of the suspect and by tracing the movements of the suspect until apprehended. Such evidence is not inadmissible on the ground that the dog is the witness and cannot be cross-examined. It is the human testimony which makes the trailing done by the animal competent. Ohio—State v. Dickerson, 77 Ohio St. 34, 82 N.E. 969 (1907). Dogs have also been trained to smell narcotics or gun powder and alert law enforcement officers to the locations of these items. In order to get this evidence admitted into the trial record, the prosecutor must lay a foundation. The prosecutor is required to show by testimony of the trainer the qualifications of the trainer and the dog and the facts that no interference with the condition of suspected items found at the scene of the occurrence had been countenanced until the arrival of the dog and that, in the case of tracking, the dog had been placed on the suspected trail of the offender, no interruptions occurred in the tracking, and there was other circumstantial evidence linking the suspect with the crime. For an extended discussion of dog sniffing, or what is sometimes referred to as bloodhound evidence, see United States v. Bronstein, N.Y.L.J. (2d Cir. Aug. 13, 1975); Pedigo v. Commonwealth, 103 Ky. 41, 44 S.W. 143, 42 L.R.A. 432, 19 Ky.L.Rptr. 1723 (1898); Terrell v. State, 3 Md.App. 340, 239 A.2d 128 (1968).

§ 19.28 EVIDENCE OF CONFESSION IN VIOLATION OF THE FIFTH AMENDMENT

To understand the Fifth Amendment, one must know of the history of government prior to the adoption of the Constitution.

It was not uncommon for those in authority to seize the persons of suspected malefactors and torture them until they confessed their crimes. It was found that persons so tortured would admit to crimes even though they were not guilty of these crimes so that their torture might be stopped. There were also incidents wherein a defendant would be successively tried until he or she was found guilty. Our founding fathers, recognizing the human temperament and desiring to put an end to such practices, incorporated safeguards in the Constitution to prevent miscarriages of justice.

Accordingly, we often hear that a person "takes the Fifth." In effect, that person is exercising the right to refrain from making statements that might incriminate the speaker as having committed a crime.

In the development of American constitutional law through decisions of the United States Supreme Court, it became apparent that law enforcement officers were using various methods to extract confessions from suspected perpetrators in contravention of the constitutional rights of both the Fifth and the Sixth Amendments of the United States Constitution. The Court finally came to the conclusion in the case of Miranda v. Arizona, 384 U.S. 436, 86 S.Ct. 1602, 16 L.Ed.2d 694 (1966),

> that when an individual was held for custodial interrogation by law enforcement officers, he must be clearly informed that he has a right to consult with a lawyer and to have the lawyer with him during interrogation. That prior to investigation the person must be warned that he has a right to remain silent, that any statement he does make may be used as evidence against him, and that he has a right to the presence of an attorney either retained or appointed by the court, if he cannot afford to retain an attorney. The defendant may waive these rights provided the waiver is made voluntarily, knowingly and intelligently. If he indicates in any manner, at any stage of the process

that he wishes to consult with an attorney before speaking there can be no questioning. If the individual is alone and indicates in any manner that he does not wish to be interrogated, the police may not question him. If he may have answered some questions or volunteered some statements on his own, it does not deprive him of the right to refrain from answering any further questions until he has consulted with an attorney and thereafter consents to be questioned.

The Court used the male gender throughout the decision because it was acceptable practice at that time.

If evidence is obtained in violation of these caveats, the evidence is not admissible. However, the Supreme Court has been qualifying the *Miranda* holding by subsequent decisions. For example, if a defendant has not been given these warnings and makes an inculpatory statement, this statement may not be used in the prosecution's direct case, but if the defendant takes the stand to testify and testifies to a statement contradicting that which he made to the law enforcement officer, the defendant's statement made without prior *Miranda* warnings may be admissible for impeachment purposes. U.S.—Oregon v. Hass, 420 U.S. 714, 95 S.Ct. 1215, 43 LEd.2d 570 (1976). A further refinement of the *Miranda* decision is to be found in Commonwealth v. Simpson, 370 Mass. 119, 345 N.E.2d 899 (Mass. 1976), where a defendant was invited to come to a police station and the police questioned him without advising him of his *Miranda* rights. The Supreme Court held that this was not custodial interrogation in that the defendant was there voluntarily and could have left if he so desired. No doubt more decisions whittling away the strictures of *Miranda* are on the way.

§ 19.29 EVIDENCE OBTAINED IN VIOLATION OF THE SIXTH AMENDMENT

The Sixth Amendment to the Constitution provides:

> In all criminal prosecutions, the accused shall enjoy the right to a speedy and public trial, by an impartial jury of the State and district wherein the crime shall have been committed; which district shall have been previously ascertained by law, and to be informed of the nature and cause of the accusation; to be confronted with the witnesses against him; to have compulsory process for obtaining witnesses in his favor, and to have the assistance of counsel for his defence.

The decisional law dealing with this amendment has been very interesting and has run a full circle. For example, at one time, the states were not required to provide counsel for all defendants. Later, they were required to provide counsel for certain types of crimes. Still later, counsel was to be provided in every case where there was a possibility of incarceration. U.S.—Gideon v. Wainwright, 372 U.S. 335, 83 S.Ct. 792, 9 L.Ed.2d 799 (1963); Argersinger v. Hamlin, 407 U.S. 25, 92 S.Ct. 2006, 32 L.Ed.2d 530 (1972).

In 1976, the Burger Court handed down a decision in Geders v. United States, 425 U.S. 80, 96 S.Ct. 1330, 47 L.Ed.2d 592 (1976), wherein the Court held that a defendant was denied his right of counsel when a trial court ordered that the defendant and his counsel were not to confer during an overnight recess of the trial. Defendant had been testifying on direct examination when an overnight recess was called. Cross-examination was to be held shortly thereafter.

A 1977 case, Brewer v. Williams, 430 U.S. 387, 97 S.Ct. 1232, 51 L.Ed.2d 424, decided March 23, 1977, held that a defendant was denied his right to counsel when an officer accompanying the defendant on a long auto ride to a place of detention, in an effort to locate the body of a deceased child, inveigled the defendant to tell the officers where the body of the child was by telling the defendant that the child was entitled to a Christian burial. The officer knew that the defendant was Christian and a very religious man. The defendant had already retained counsel, and the officer had agreed with counsel that the defendant would not be questioned during the ride to the detention facility. This case went up to the Supreme Court on a writ of habeas corpus, notwithstanding the fact that in Stone v. Powell, 428 U.S. 465, 96 S.Ct. 3037, 49 L.Ed.2d 1067 (1976), the Court said that the federal courts should not be available to state prisoners for habeas corpus review of a Fourth Amendment violation where it has been fairly and fully litigated in the state courts. It appears that the Court is not precluding habeas corpus relief to state prisoners in alleged Fifth and Sixth Amendment rights questions.

In Nix v. Williams, 467 U.S. 431, 104 S.Ct. 2501, 81 L.Ed.2d 377 (1984), the Brewer v. Williams decision, *supra,* was modified where a suspect was inveigled by the police to tell them where he had buried a child whom he had killed. In that case, there were volunteers who, it was contended, were searching the area and would have discovered the body without the aid of the perpetrator. The Court held that the discovery and condition of the body were properly admitted in evidence.

§ 19.30 PROCEDURAL METHOD TO EXCLUDE EVIDENCE UNCONSTITUTIONALLY OBTAINED

It is the function of the defendant's attorney to move to suppress any evidence illegally obtained. This is usually accomplished by making a written motion based on affidavits of the defendant and the attorney explaining to the court the reasons that they believe are good grounds for the exclusion of certain evidence obtained in violation of the defendant's constitutional rights. The moving papers request a hearing before the court to determine whether the items of evidence should be excluded at the trial.

This procedure is called pretrial motion practice. Here, too, it is not the intent of this book to make trial lawyers out of you, but a general knowledge of the pretrial motion practice may be useful to the law enforcement officer to enable him or her to understand his or her position more fully.

In the ordinary course of events, the court grants a hearing. The legal profession has given names to certain of these pretrial hearings and motions as follows:

1. Huntley hearing—determines the admissibility of a confession.
2. Wade hearing—determines the legality of an identification.
3. Controvert a warrant hearing—determines whether probable cause existed for the issuance of a warrant or whether a warrant was validly executed.
4. *Miranda* hearing—determines whether the defendant was given the proper admonition with respect to his or her right of counsel.
5. Motion to inspect grand jury minutes—determines whether legal evidence sufficient to sustain a conviction was testified to in grand jury proceedings.
6. Motion to suppress.

In such hearing in New York and other states, the ordinary exclusionary rules of evidence applicable to trials of criminal actions are inapplicable to the extent that evidence tending to demonstrate that the evidence sought to be suppressed was or was not unlawfully or improperly obtained is admissible even though of a hearsay nature or otherwise incompetent by trial standards. N.Y.—CPL §375.60(4).

§ 19.31 PLEA BARGAINING

Reference has been made in §6.25 to what would happen in a practical situation. The district attorney and defense counsel enter into negotiations to permit the defendant to plead guilty to a lesser included offense. This is known as plea bargaining. There has been much discussion of late as to the desirability of accepting pleas from defendants for lesser included offenses rather than the one with which they are charged. It might be informative to explain the purpose of plea bargaining. Since there are so many safeguards on behalf of a defendant built into a criminal trial, the prosecution reasons that there is a great likelihood of a substantial error being committed that might result in a reversal of a conviction by an appellate court, with the further result that many offenders may not be properly punished. In addition to this problem, the length of time that it takes to try a case before a jury under our present system is long. If every case was tried to its conclusion and every appeal was granted a hearing, the wheels of justice would come to sudden grinding halt, and no justice would be dispensed. Admittedly, plea bargaining is not real justice either, but it is an attempt to face the realities of the situation. However, several jurisdictions have discontinued the practice, and there is a powerful movement to discontinue it in other jurisdictions. The criminal justice system in the United States leaves much to be desired, but it is attempting to cure some of its ills. Just as no one's body is perfect at all times, so, too, is our criminal justice system not perfect at all times.

The rules of evidence, however, are used when the case cannot be negotiated for one or more reasons and the trial must run its course to a full conclusion.

§ 19.32 CONCLUSION

This chapter is presented as an introduction to constitutional problems in the admission of some evidence. It is not intended to be exhaustive or up to date as to the decisions of the United States Supreme Court that are handed down each year. Most undergraduate colleges and universities present courses dealing particularly with constitutional law for criminal justice. There are many textbooks on this subject that are updated annually with changes in this area of the law. The study of this law could require a course continuing for one year. Most colleges with which I am familiar try to give students a fairly comprehensive understanding of this subject in one semester. I have included herein cross-references to treatises that, at the time of this writing, are updated annually.

You should understand that if a law enforcement officer arrests a perpetrator for a crime and the perpetrator is not given his or her constitutionally protected rights, the officer is, in effect, laying the groundwork for the subsequent dismissal of the charges against the defendant. Often the prosecutor is unable to continue with the prosecution of the case because the evidence that he or she has left after the exclusion of the tainted evidence is insufficient to convict the defendant. Special care on the part of the law enforcement officer is essential if he or she wants to see justice prevail.

CROSS-REFERENCES

Treatises

I. Klein, Constitutional Law for Criminal Justice Professionals (3rd ed., Coral Gables Publishing Co. 1992), Supplement 1996, ch. 6.

I. Klein, The Law of Arrest, Search, Seizure, and Liability Issues—Principles, Cases, and Comments (Coral Gables Publishing Co. 1994), Supplement 1996, ch. 2.

✔ PRACTICE QUESTIONS

Indicate whether each statement is true or false.

1. The Fourth Amendment to the United States Constitution prohibits unreasonable search and seizure of persons, houses, papers, and effects and specifically prohibits unlawful searches and seizures; no warrants shall issue, but upon probable cause, supported by oath or affirmation and particularly describing the place to be searched and the persons or things to be seized.

2. Evidence obtained by unreasonable search and seizure may be introduced at trial if it is illegal for the defendant to possess this evidence.

3. Fingerprint identification is thought to have been in use in China during the Tang Dynasty (618–906 A.D.).

4. All privileges and immunities, due process, and equal protection are guaranteed against state infringement by the Fourteenth Amendment of the United States Constitution. This applies to noncitizens within the state's jurisdiction.

5. The United States Constitution's prohibition of unreasonable search and seizure by state law enforcement officers was upheld in the case of Mapp v. Ohio.

6. If evidence is obtained by a state law enforcement officer using a wiretap of a telephone line and the officer did not know that a court order was necessary in order to get any information that was learned by overhearing the conversation on the wiretap, the evidence may be admitted anyway if the judge uses discretion and permits it to be received.

7. When a vehicle is impounded by police, it is obligatory that the police conduct an inventory search of the contents of the vehicle. Any unlawfully possessed articles found in that vehicle may not be admitted into evidence against the owner of that vehicle.

APPENDIX A

Federal Rules of Evidence

Including Amendments Received Through December 1, 1994

ARTICLE I. GENERAL PROVISIONS

Rule 101. Scope

These rules govern proceedings in the courts of the United States and before the United States bankruptcy judges and United States magistrate judges, to the extent and with the exceptions stated in rule 1101.

[Amended March 2, 1987, effective October 1, 1987; April 25, 1988, effective November 1, 1988; April 22, 1993, effective December 1, 1993.]

Rule 102. Purpose and Construction

These rules shall be construed to secure fairness in administration, elimination of unjustifiable expense and delay, and promotion of growth and development of the law of evidence to the end that the truth may be ascertained and proceedings justly determined.

Rule 103. Rulings on Evidence

(a) Effect of Erroneous Ruling. Error may not be predicated upon a ruling which admits or excludes evidence unless a substantial right of the party is affected, and

(1) *Objection.* In case the ruling is one admitting evidence, a timely objection or motion to strike appears of record, stating the specific ground of objection, if the specific ground was not apparent from the context; or

(2) *Offer of Proof.* In case the ruling is one excluding evidence, the substance of the evidence was made known to the court by offer or was apparent from the context within which questions were asked.

(b) Record of Offer and Ruling. The court may add any other or further statement which shows the character of the evidence, the form in which it was offered, the objection made, and the ruling thereon. It may direct the making of an offer in question and answer form.

(c) Hearing of Jury. In jury cases, proceedings shall be conducted, to the extent practicable, so as to prevent inadmissible evidence from being suggested to the jury by any means, such as making statements or offers of proof or asking questions in the hearing of the jury.

(d) Plain Error. Nothing in this rule precludes taking notice of plain errors affecting substantial rights although they were not brought to the attention of the court.

Rule 104. Preliminary Questions

(a) Questions of Admissibility Generally. Preliminary questions concerning the qualification of a person to be a witness, the existence of a privilege, or the admissibility of evidence shall be determined by the court, subject to the provisions of subdivision (b). In making its determination it is not bound by the rules of evidence except those with respect to privileges.

(b) Relevancy Conditioned on Fact. When the relevancy of evidence depends upon the fulfillment of a condition of fact, the court shall admit it upon, or subject to, the introduction of evidence sufficient to support a finding of the fulfillment of the condition.

(c) Hearing of Jury. Hearings on the admissibility of confessions shall in all cases be conducted out of the hearing of the jury. Hearings on other preliminary matters shall be so conducted when the interests of justice require, or when an accused is a witness and so requests.

(d) Testimony by Accused. The accused does not, by testifying upon a preliminary matter, become subject to cross-examination as to other issues in the case.

(e) Weight and Credibility. This rule does not limit the right of a party to introduce before the jury evidence relevant to weight or credibility.

[Amended March 2, 1987, effective October 1, 1987.]

Rule 105. Limited Admissibility

When evidence which is admissible as to one party or for one purpose but not admissible as to another party or for another purpose is admitted, the court, upon request, shall restrict the evidence to its proper scope and instruct the jury accordingly.

Rule 106. Remainder of or Related Writings or Recorded Statements

When a writing or recorded statement or part thereof is introduced by a party, an adverse party may require the introduction at that time of any other part or any other writing or recorded statement which ought in fairness to be considered contemporaneously with it.

[Amended March 2, 1987, effective October 1, 1987.]

ARTICLE II. JUDICIAL NOTICE

Rule 201. Judicial Notice of Adjudicative Facts

(a) Scope of Rule. This rule governs only judicial notice of adjudicative facts.

(b) Kinds of Facts. A judicially noticed fact must be one not subject to reasonable dispute in that it is either (1) generally known within the territorial jurisdiction of the trial court or (2) capable of accurate and ready determination by resort to sources whose accuracy cannot reasonably be questioned.

(c) When Discretionary. A court may take judicial notice, whether requested or not.

(d) **When Mandatory.** A court shall take judicial notice if requested by a party and supplied with the necessary information.

(e) **Opportunity to Be Heard.** A party is entitled upon timely request to an opportunity to be heard as to the propriety of taking judicial notice and the tenor of the matter noticed. In the absence of prior notification, the request may be made after judicial notice has been taken.

(f) **Time of Taking Notice.** Judicial notice may be taken at any stage of the proceeding.

(g) **Instructing Jury.** In a civil action or proceeding, the court shall instruct the jury to accept as conclusive any fact judicially noticed. In a criminal case, the court shall instruct the jury that it may, but is not required to, accept as conclusive any fact judicially noticed.

ARTICLE III.   PRESUMPTIONS IN CIVIL ACTIONS AND PROCEEDINGS

Rule 301. Presumptions in General in Civil Actions and Proceedings

In all civil actions and proceedings not otherwise provided for by Act of Congress or by these rules, a presumption imposes on the party against whom it is directed the burden of going forward with evidence to rebut or meet the presumption, but does not shift to such party the burden of proof in the sense of the risk of nonpersuasion, which remains throughout the trial upon the party on whom it was originally cast.

Rule 302. Applicability of State Law in Civil Actions and Proceedings

In civil actions and proceedings, the effect of a presumption respecting a fact which is an element of a claim or defense as to which State law supplies the rule of decision is determined in accordance with State law.

ARTICLE IV.   RELEVANCY AND ITS LIMITS

Rule 401. Definition of "Relevant Evidence"

"Relevant evidence" means evidence having any tendency to make the existence of any fact that is of consequence to the determination of the action more probable or less probable than it would be without the evidence.

Rule 402. Relevant Evidence Generally Admissible; Irrelevant Evidence Inadmissible

All relevant evidence is admissible, except as otherwise provided by the Constitution of the United States, by Act of Congress, by these rules, or by other rules prescribed by the Supreme Court pursuant to statutory authority. Evidence which is not relevant is not admissible.

Rule 403. Exclusion of Relevant Evidence on Grounds of Prejudice, Confusion, or Waste of Time

Although relevant, evidence may be excluded if its probative value is substantially outweighed by the danger of unfair prejudice, confusion of the issues, or misleading the jury, or by considerations of undue delay, waste of time, or needless presentation of cumulative evidence.

Rule 404. Character Evidence Not Admissible to Prove Conduct; Exceptions; Other Crimes

(a) Character Evidence Generally. Evidence of a person's character or a trait of character is not admissible for the purpose of proving action in conformity therewith on a particular occasion, except:

(1) *Character of Accused.* Evidence of a pertinent trait of character offered by an accused, or by the prosecution to rebut the same;

(2) *Character of Victim.* Evidence of a pertinent trait of character of the victim of the crime offered by an accused, or by the prosecution to rebut the same, or evidence of a character trait of peacefulness of the victim offered by the prosecution in a homicide case to rebut evidence that the victim was the first aggressor;

(3) *Character of Witness.* Evidence of the character of a witness, as provided in rules 607, 608, and 609.

(b) Other Crimes, Wrongs, or Acts. Evidence of other crimes, wrongs, or acts is not admissible to prove the character of a person in order to show action in conformity therewith. It may, however, be admissible for other purposes, such as proof of motive, opportunity, intent, preparation, plan, knowledge, identity, or absence of mistake or accident, provided that upon request by the accused, the prosecution in a criminal case shall provide reasonable notice in advance of trial, or during trial if the court excuses pretrial notice on good cause shown, of the general nature of any such evidence it intends to introduce at trial.

[Amended March 2, 1987, effective October 1, 1987; April 30, 1991, effective December 1, 1991.]

Rule 405. Methods of Proving Character

(a) Reputation or Opinion. In all cases in which evidence of character or a trait of character of a person is admissible, proof may be made by testimony as to reputation or by testimony in the form of an opinion. On cross-examination, inquiry is allowable into relevant specific instances of conduct.

(b) Specific Instances of Conduct. In cases in which character or a trait of character of a person is an essential element of a charge, claim, or defense, proof may also be made of specific instances of that person's conduct.

[Amended March 2, 1987, effective October 1, 1987.]

Rule 406. Habit; Routine Practice

Evidence of the habit of a person or of the routine practice of an organization, whether corroborated or not and regardless of the presence of eyewitnesses, is relevant to prove that the conduct of the person or organization on a particular occasion was in conformity with the habit or routine practice.

Rule 407. Subsequent Remedial Measures

When, after an event, measures are taken which, if taken previously, would have made the event less likely to occur, evidence of the subsequent measures is not admissible to prove negligence or culpable conduct in connection with the event. This rule does not require the exclusion of evidence of subsequent measures when offered for another purpose, such as proving ownership, control, or feasibility of precautionary measures, if controverted, or impeachment.

Rule 408. Compromise and Offers to Compromise

Evidence of (1) furnishing or offering or promising to furnish, or (2) accepting or offering or promising to accept, a valuable consideration in compromising or attempting to compromise a claim which was disputed as to either validity or amount, is not admissible to prove liability for or invalidity of the claim or its amount. Evidence of conduct or statements made in compromise negotiations is likewise not admissible. This rule does not require the exclusion of any evidence otherwise discoverable merely because it is presented in the course of compromise negotiations. This rule also does not require exclusion when the evidence is offered for another purpose, such as proving bias or prejudice of a witness, negativing a contention of undue delay, or proving an effort to obstruct a criminal investigation or prosecution.

Rule 409. Payment of Medical and Similar Expenses

Evidence of furnishing or offering or promising to pay medical, hospital, or similar expenses occasioned by an injury is not admissible to prove liability for the injury.

Rule 410. Inadmissibility of Pleas, Plea Discussions, and Related Statements

Except as otherwise provided in this rule, evidence of the following is not, in any civil or criminal proceeding, admissible against the defendant who made the plea or was a participant in the plea discussions:

(1) a plea of guilty which was later withdrawn;

(2) a plea of nolo contendere;

(3) any statement made in the course of any proceedings under Rule 11 of the Federal Rules of Criminal Procedure or comparable state procedure regarding either of the foregoing pleas; or

(4) any statement made in the course of plea discussions with an attorney for the prosecuting authority which do not result in a plea of guilty or which result in a plea of guilty later withdrawn.

However, such a statement is admissible (i) in any proceeding wherein another statement made in the course of the same plea or plea discussions has been introduced and the statement ought in fairness be considered contemporaneously with it, or (ii) in a criminal proceeding for perjury or false statement if the statement was made by the defendant under oath, on the record and in the presence of counsel.

[Amended by Pub.L. 94-149, §1(9), December 12, 1975, 89 Stat. 805; amended April 30, 1979, effective December 1, 1980 (effective date pursuant to Pub.L. 96-42, July 31, 1979, 93 Stat. 326).]

Rule 411. Liability Insurance

Evidence that a person was or was not insured against liability is not admissible upon the issue whether the person acted negligently or otherwise wrongfully. This rule does not require the exclusion of evidence of insurance against liability when offered for another purpose, such as proof of agency, ownership, or control, or bias or prejudice of a witness.

[Amended March 2, 1987, effective October 1, 1987.]

Rule 412. Sex Offense Cases; Relevance of Alleged Victim's Past Sexual Behavior or Alleged Sexual Predisposition

(a) Evidence Generally Inadmissible. The following evidence is not admissible in any civil or criminal proceeding involving alleged sexual misconduct except as provided in subdivisions (b) and (c):

(1) Evidence offered to prove that any alleged victim engaged in other sexual behavior.

(2) Evidence offered to prove any alleged victim's sexual predisposition.

(b) Exceptions.

(1) In a criminal case, the following evidence is admissible, if otherwise admissible under these rules:

(A) evidence of specific instances of sexual behavior by the alleged victim offered to prove that a person other than the accused was the source of semen, injury or other physical evidence;

(B) evidence of specific instances of sexual behavior by the alleged victim with respect to the person accused of the sexual misconduct offered by the accused to prove consent or by the prosecution; and

(C) evidence of the exclusion of which would violate the constitutional rights of the defendant.

(2) In a civil case, evidence offered to prove the sexual behavior or sexual predisposition of any alleged victim is admissible if it is otherwise admissible under these rules and its probative value substantially outweighs the danger of harm to any victim and of unfair prejudice to any party. Evidence of an alleged victim's reputation is admissible only if it has been placed in controversy by the alleged victim.

(c) Procedure to Determine Admissibility.

(1) A party intending to offer evidence under subdivision (b) must—

(A) file a written motion at least 14 days before trial specifically describing the evidence and stating the purpose for which it is offered unless the court, for good cause, requires a different time for filing or permits filing during trial; and

(B) serve the motion on all parties and notify the alleged victim or, when appropriate, the alleged victim's guardian or representative.

(2) Before admitting evidence under this rule the court must conduct a hearing in camera and afford the victim and parties a right to attend and be heard. The motion, related papers, and the record of the hearing must be sealed and remain under seal unless the court orders otherwise.

[Adopted by Pub.L. 95-540, §2(a), October 28, 1978, 92 Stat. 2046, applicable to trials that begin more than 30 days after October 28, 1978; amended by Pub.L. 100-690, Title VII, §7046(a), November 18, 1988, 102 Stat. 4400; amended April 29, 1994, effective December 1, 1994; amended by Pub.L. 103-322, Title IV, §40141(b), September 13, 1994, 108 Stat. 1919, effective December 1, 1994.]

Rule 413. Evidence of Similar Crimes in Sexual Assault Cases

(a) In a criminal case in which the defendant is accused of an offense of sexual assault, evidence of the defendant's commission of another offense or offenses of sexual assault is admissible, and may be considered for its bearing on any matter to which it is relevant.

(b) In a case in which the Government intends to offer evidence under this rule, the attorney for the Government shall disclose the evidence to the defendant, including statements of witnesses or a summary of the substance of any testimony that is expected to be offered, at least fifteen days before the scheduled date of trial or at such later time as the court may allow for good cause.

(c) This rule shall not be construed to limit the admission or consideration of evidence under any other rule.

(d) For purposes of this rule and Rule 415, "offense of sexual assault" means a crime under Federal law or the law of a State (as defined in section 513 of title 18, United States Code) that involved—

(1) any conduct proscribed by chapter 109A of title 18, United States Code;

(2) contact, without consent, between any part of the defendant's body or an object and the genitals or anus of another person;

(3) contact, without consent, between the genitals or anus of the defendant and any part of another person's body;

(4) deriving sexual pleasure or gratification from the infliction of death, bodily injury, or physical pain on another person; or

(5) an attempt or conspiracy to engage in conduct described in paragraphs (1)–(4).

[Added Sept. 13, 1994, Pub.L. 103-322, Title XXXII, § 320935(a), 108 Stat. 2135.]

Effective Date

Pub.L. 103-322, Title XXXII, § 320935, Sept. 13, 1994, 108 Stat. 2135, provided that:

(a) [*Amended Federal Rules of Evidence by adding new rules 413, 414, and 415)*]

(b) *Implementation.*—The amendments made by subsection (a) shall become effective pursuant to subsection (d).

(c) *Recommendations by Judicial Conference.*—Not later than 150 days after the date of enactment of this Act [Sept. 13, 1994], the Judicial Conference of the United States shall transmit to Congress a report containing recommendations for amending the Federal Rules of Evidence as they affect the admission of evidence of a defendant's prior sexual assault or child molestation crimes in cases involving sexual assault and child molestation. The Rules Enabling Act [section 2071 et seq. of Title 28, Judiciary and Judicial Procedure] shall not apply to the recommendations made by the Judicial Conference pursuant to this section.

(d) *Congressional Action.*—

(1) If the recommendations described in subsection (c) are the same as the amendment made by subsection (a), then the amendments made by subsection (a) shall become effective 30 days after the transmittal of the recommendations.

(2) If the recommendations described in subsection (c) are different than the amendments made by subsection (a), the amendments made by subsection (a) shall become effective 150 days after the transmittal of the recommendations unless otherwise provided by law.

(3) If the Judicial Conference fails to comply with subsection (c), the amendments made by subsection (a) shall become effective 150 days after the date the recommendations were due under subsection (c) unless otherwise provided by law.

(e) *Application.—The amendments made by subsection (a) shall apply to proceedings commenced on or after the effective date of such amendments.*

Rule 414. Evidence of Similar Crimes in Child Molestation Cases

(a) In a criminal case in which the defendant is accused of an offense of child molestation, evidence of the defendant's commission of another offense or offenses of child molestation is admissible, and may be considered for its bearing on any matter to which it is relevant.

(b) In a case in which the Government intends to offer evidence under this rule, the attorney for the Government shall disclose the evidence to the defendant, including statements of witnesses or a summary of the substance of any testimony that is expected to be offered, at least fifteen days before the scheduled date of trial or at such later time as the court may allow for good cause.

(c) This rule shall not be construed to limit the admission or consideration of evidence under any other rule.

(d) For purposes of this rule and Rule 415, "child" means a person below the age of fourteen, and "offense of child molestation" means a crime under Federal law or the law of a State (as defined in section 513 of title 18, United States Code) that involved—

(1) any conduct proscribed by chapter 109A of title 18, United States Code, that was committed in relation to a child;

(2) any conduct proscribed by chapter 110 of title 18, United States Code;

(3) contact between any part of the defendant's body or an object and the genitals or anus of a child;

(4) contact between the genitals or anus of the defendant and any part of the body of a child;

(5) deriving sexual pleasure or gratification from the infliction of death, bodily injury, or physical pain on a child; or

(6) an attempt or conspiracy to engage in conduct described in paragraphs (1)–(5).

[Added Sept. 13, 1994, Pub.L. 103-322, Title XXXII, §320935(a), 108 Stat. 2135.]

Effective Date

See Effective Date note set out under Rule 413.

Rule 415. Evidence of Similar Acts in Civil Cases Concerning Sexual Assault or Child Molestation

(a) In a civil case in which a claim for damages or other relief is predicated on a party's alleged commission of conduct constituting an offense of sexual assault or child molestation, evidence of that party's commission of another offense or offenses of sexual assault or child molestation is admissible and may be considered as provided in Rule 413 and Rule 414 of these rules.

(b) A party who intends to offer evidence under this rule shall disclose the evidence to the party against whom it will be offered, including statements of witnesses or a summary of the substance of any testimony that is expected to be offered, at least fifteen days before the scheduled date of trial or at such later time as the court may allow for good cause.

(c) This rule shall not be construed to limit the admission or consideration of evidence under any other rule.

[Added Sept. 13, 1994, Pub.L. 103-322, Title XXXII, §320935(a), 108 Stat. 2135.]

Effective Date

See Effective Date note set out under Rule 413.

ARTICLE V. PRIVILEGES

Rule 501. General Rule

Except as otherwise required by the Constitution of the United States or provided by Act of Congress or in rules prescribed by the Supreme Court pursuant to statutory authority, the privilege of a witness, person, government, State, or political subdivision thereof shall be governed by the principles of the common law as they may be interpreted by the courts of the United States in the light of reason and experience. However, in civil actions and proceedings, with respect to an element of a claim or defense as to which State law supplies the rule of decision, the privilege of a witness, person, government, State, or political subdivision thereof shall be determined in accordance with State law.

ARTICLE VI. WITNESSES

Rule 601. General Rule of Competency

Every person is competent to be a witness except as otherwise provided in these rules. However, in civil actions and proceedings, with respect to an element of a claim or defense as to which State law supplies the rule of decision, the competency of a witness shall be determined in accordance with State law.

Rule 602. Lack of Personal Knowledge

A witness may not testify to a matter unless evidence is introduced sufficient to support a finding that the witness has personal knowledge of the matter. Evidence to prove personal knowledge may, but need not, consist of the witness' own testimony. This rule is subject to the provisions of rule 703, relating to opinion testimony by expert witnesses.

[Amended March 2, 1987, effective October 1, 1987; April 25, 1988, effective November 1, 1988.]

Rule 603. Oath or Affirmation

Before testifying, every witness shall be required to declare that the witness will testify truthfully, by oath or affirmation administered in a form calculated to awaken the witness' conscience and impress the witness' mind with the duty to do so.

[Amended March 2, 1987, effective October 1, 1987.]

Rule 604. Interpreters

An interpreter is subject to the provisions of these rules relating to qualification as an expert and the administration of an oath or affirmation to make a true translation.

[Amended March 2, 1987, effective October 1, 1987.]

Rule 605. Competency of Judge as Witness

The judge presiding at the trial may not testify in that trial as a witness. No objection need be made in order to preserve the point.

Rule 606. Competency of Juror as Witness

(a) At the Trial. A member of the jury may not testify as a witness before that jury in the trial of the case in which the juror is sitting. If the juror is called so to testify, the opposing party shall be afforded an opportunity to object out of the presence of the jury.

(b) Inquiry Into Validity of Verdict or Indictment. Upon an inquiry into the validity of a verdict or indictment, a juror may not testify as to any matter or statement occurring during the course of the jury's deliberations or to the effect of anything upon that or any other juror's mind or emotions as influencing the juror to assent to or dissent from the verdict or indictment or concerning the juror's mental processes in connection therewith, except that a juror may testify on the question whether extraneous prejudicial information was improperly brought to the jury's attention or whether any outside influence was improperly brought to bear upon any juror. Nor may a juror's affidavit or evidence of any statement by the juror concerning a matter about which the juror would be precluded from testifying be received for these purposes.

[Amended by Pub.L. 94-149, §1(10), December 12, 1975, 89 Stat. 805; amended March 2, 1987, effective October 1, 1987.]

Rule 607. Who May Impeach

The credibility of a witness may be attacked by any party, including the party calling the witness.

[Amended March 2, 1987, effective October 1, 1987.]

Rule 608. Evidence of Character and Conduct of Witness

(a) Opinion and Reputation Evidence of Character. The credibility of a witness may be attacked or supported by evidence in the form of opinion or reputation, but subject to these limitations: (1) the evidence may refer only to character for truthfulness or untruthfulness, and (2) evidence of truthful character is admissible only after the character of the witness for truthfulness has been attacked by opinion or reputation evidence or otherwise.

(b) Specific Instances of Conduct. Specific instances of the conduct of a witness, for the purpose of attacking or supporting the witness' credibility, other than conviction of crime as provided in rule 609, may not be proved by extrinsic evidence. They may, however, in the discretion of the court, if probative of truthfulness or untruthfulness, be inquired into on cross-examination of the witness (1) concerning the witness' character for truthfulness or untruthfulness, or (2) concerning the character for truthfulness or untruthfulness of another witness as to which character the witness being cross-examined has testified.

The giving of testimony, whether by an accused or by any other witness, does not operate as a waiver of the accused's or the witness' privilege against self-incrimination when examined with respect to matters which relate only to credibility.

[Amended March 2, 1987, effective October 1, 1987; April 25, 1988, effective November 1, 1988.]

Rule 609. Impeachment by Evidence of Conviction of Crime

(a) General Rule. For the purpose of attacking the credibility of a witness,

(1) evidence that a witness other than an accused has been convicted of a crime shall be admitted, subject to Rule 403, if the crime was punishable by death or imprisonment in excess of one year under the law under which the witness was convicted, and evidence that an accused has been convicted of such a crime shall be admitted if the court determines that the probative value of admitting this evidence outweighs its prejudicial effect to the accused; and

(2) evidence that any witness has been convicted of a crime shall be admitted if it involved dishonesty or false statement, regardless of the punishment.

(b) Time Limit. Evidence of a conviction under this rule is not admissible if a period of more than ten years has elapsed since the date of the conviction or of the release of the witness from the confinement imposed for that conviction, whichever is the later date, unless the court determines, in the interests of justice, that the probative value of the conviction supported by specific facts and circumstances substantially outweighs its prejudicial effect. However, evidence of a conviction more than 10 years old as calculated herein, is not admissible unless the proponent gives to the adverse party sufficient advance written notice of intent to use such evidence to provide the adverse party with a fair opportunity to contest the use of such evidence.

(c) Effect of Pardon, Annulment, or Certificate of Rehabilitation. Evidence of a conviction is not admissible under this rule if (1) the conviction has been the subject of a pardon, annulment, certificate of rehabilitation, or other equivalent procedure based on a finding of the rehabilitation of the person convicted, and that person has not been convicted of a subsequent crime which was punishable by death or imprisonment in excess of one year, or (2) the conviction has been the subject of a pardon, annulment, or other equivalent procedure based on a finding of innocence.

(d) Juvenile Adjudications. Evidence of juvenile adjudications is generally not admissible under this rule. The court may, however, in a criminal case allow evidence of a juvenile adjudication of a witness other than the accused if conviction of the offense would be admissible to attack the credibility of an adult and the court is satisfied that admission in evidence is necessary for a fair determination of the issue of guilt or innocence.

(e) Pendency of Appeal. The pendency of an appeal therefrom does not render evidence of a conviction inadmissible. Evidence of the pendency of an appeal is admissible.

[Amended March 2, 1987, effective October 1, 1987; January 26, 1990, effective December 1, 1990.]

Rule 610. Religious Beliefs or Opinions

Evidence of the beliefs or opinions of a witness on matters of religion is not admissible for the purpose of showing that by reason of their nature the witness' credibility is impaired or enhanced.

[Amended March 2, 1987, effective October 1, 1987.]

Rule 611. Mode and Order of Interrogation and Presentation

(a) Control by Court. The court shall exercise reasonable control over the mode and order of interrogating witnesses and presenting evidence so as to (1) make the interrogation and presentation effective for the ascertainment of the truth, (2) avoid needless consumption of time, and (3) protect witnesses from harassment or undue embarrassment.

(b) Scope of Cross-Examination. Cross-examination should be limited to the subject matter of the direct examination and matters affecting the credibility of the witness. The court may, in the exercise of discretion, permit inquiry into additional matters as if on direct examination.

(c) Leading Questions. Leading questions should not be used on the direct examination of a witness except as may be necessary to develop the witness' testimony. Ordinarily leading questions should be permitted on cross-examination. When a party calls a hostile witness, an adverse party, or a witness identified with an adverse party, interrogation may be by leading questions.
[Amended March 2, 1987, effective October 1, 1987.]

Rule 612. Writing Used to Refresh Memory

Except as otherwise provided in criminal proceedings by section 3500 of title 18, United States Code, if a witness uses a writing to refresh memory for the purpose of testifying, either—

(1) while testifying, or
(2) before testifying, if the court in its discretion determines it is necessary in the interests of justice,

an adverse party is entitled to have the writing produced at the hearing, to inspect it, to cross-examine the witness thereon, and to introduce in evidence those portions which relate to the testimony of the witness. If it is claimed that the writing contains matters not related to the subject matter of the testimony the court shall examine the writing in camera, excise any portions not so related, and order delivery of the remainder to the party entitled thereto. Any portion withheld over objections shall be preserved and made available to the appellate court in the event of an appeal. If a writing is not produced or delivered pursuant to order under this rule, the court shall make any order justice requires, except that in criminal cases when the prosecution elects not to comply, the order shall be one striking the testimony or, if the court in its discretion determines that the interests of justice so require, declaring a mistrial.
[Amended March 2, 1987, effective October 1, 1987.]

Rule 613. Prior Statements of Witnesses

(a) Examining Witness Concerning Prior Statement. In examining a witness concerning a prior statement made by the witness, whether written or not, the statement need not be shown nor its contents disclosed to the witness at that time, but on request the same shall be shown or disclosed to opposing counsel.

(b) Extrinsic Evidence of Prior Inconsistent Statement of Witness. Extrinsic evidence of a prior inconsistent statement by a witness is not admissible unless the witness is afforded an opportunity to explain or deny the same and the opposite party is afforded an opportunity to interrogate the witness thereon, or the interests of justice otherwise require. This provision does not apply to admissions of a party-opponent as defined in rule 801(d)(2).
[Amended March 2, 1987, effective October 1, 1987; April 25, 1988, effective November 1, 1988.]

Rule 614. Calling and Interrogation of Witnesses by Court

(a) Calling by Court. The court may, on its own motion or at the suggestion of a party, call witnesses, and all parties are entitled to cross-examine witnesses thus called.

(b) Interrogation by Court. The court may interrogate witnesses, whether called by itself or by a party.

(c) Objections. Objections to the calling of witnesses by the court or to interrogation by it may be made at the time or at the next available opportunity when the jury is not present.

Rule 615. Exclusion of Witnesses

At the request of a party the court shall order witnesses excluded so that they cannot hear the testimony of other witnesses, and it may make the order of its own motion. This rule does not authorize exclusion of (1) a party who is a natural person, or (2) an officer or employee of a party which is not a natural person designated as its representative by its attorney, or (3) a person whose presence is shown by a party to be essential to the presentation of the party's cause.

[Amended March 2, 1987, effective October 1, 1987; April 25, 1988, effective November 1, 1988; amended by Pub.L.100-690, Title VII, §7075(a), November 18, 1988, 102 Stat. 4405 (although amendment by Pub.L. 100-690 could not be executed due to prior amendment by Court order which made the same change effective November 1, 1988).]

ARTICLE VII. OPINIONS AND EXPERT TESTIMONY

Rule 701. Opinion Testimony by Lay Witnesses

If the witness is not testifying as an expert, the witness' testimony in the form of opinions or inferences is limited to those opinions or inferences which are (a) rationally based on the perception of the witness and (b) helpful to a clear understanding of the witness' testimony or the determination of a fact in issue.

[Amended March 2, 1987, effective October 1, 1987.]

Rule 702. Testimony by Experts

If scientific, technical, or other specialized knowledge will assist the trier of fact to understand the evidence or to determine a fact in issue, a witness qualified as an expert by knowledge, skill, experience, training, or education, may testify thereto in the form of an opinion or otherwise.

Rule 703. Bases of Opinion Testimony by Experts

The facts or data in the particular case upon which an expert bases an opinion or inference may be those perceived by or made known to the expert at or before the hearing. If of a type reasonably relied upon by experts in the particular field in forming opinions or inferences upon the subject, the facts or data need not be admissible in evidence.

[Amended March 2, 1987, effective October 1, 1987.]

Rule 704. Opinion on Ultimate Issue

(a) Except as provided in subdivision (b), testimony in the form of an opinion or inference otherwise admissible is not objectionable because it embraces an ultimate issue to be decided by the trier of fact.

(b) No expert witness testifying with respect to the mental state or condition of a defendant in a criminal case may state an opinion or inference as to whether the defendant did or did not have the mental state or condition constituting an element of the crime charged or of a defense thereto. Such ultimate issues are matters for the trier of fact alone.

[Amended by Pub.L. 98-473, Title II, §406, October 12, 1984, 98 Stat. 2067.]

Rule 705. Disclosure of Facts or Data Underlying Expert Opinion

The expert may testify in terms of opinion or inference and give reasons therefor without first testifying to the underlying facts or data, unless the court requires otherwise. The expert may in any event be required to disclose the underlying facts or data on cross-examination.

[Amended March 2, 1987, effective October 1, 1987; April 22, 1993, effective December 1, 1993.]

Rule 706. Court Appointed Experts

(a) Appointment. The court may on its own motion or on the motion of any party enter an order to show cause why expert witnesses should not be appointed, and may request the parties to submit nominations. The court may appoint any expert witnesses agreed upon by the parties, and may appoint expert witnesses of its own selection. An expert witness shall not be appointed by the court unless the witness consents to act. A witness so appointed shall be informed of the witness' duties by the court in writing, a copy of which shall be filed with the clerk, or at a conference in which the parties shall have opportunity to participate. A witness so appointed shall advise the parties of the witness's findings, if any; the witness' deposition may be taken by any party; and the witness may be called to testify by the court or any party. The witness shall be subject to cross-examination by each party, including a party calling the witness.

(b) Compensation. Expert witnesses so appointed are entitled to reasonable compensation in whatever sum the court may allow. The compensation thus fixed is payable from funds which may be provided by law in criminal cases and civil actions and proceedings involving just compensation under the fifth amendment. In other civil actions and proceedings the compensation shall be paid by the parties in such proportion and at such time as the court directs, and thereafter charged in like manner as other costs.

(c) Disclosure of Appointment. In the exercise of its discretion, the court may authorize disclosure to the jury of the fact that the court appointed the expert witness.

(d) Parties' Experts of Own Selection. Nothing in this rule limits the parties in calling expert witnesses of their own selection.

[Amended March 2, 1987, effective October 1, 1987.]

ARTICLE VIII. HEARSAY

Rule 801. Definitions

The following definitions apply under this article.

(a) Statement. A "statement" is (1) an oral or written assertion or (2) non-verbal conduct of a person, if it is intended by the person as an assertion.

(b) Declarant. A "declarant" is a person who makes a statement.

(c) Hearsay. "Hearsay" is a statement, other than one made by the declarant while testifying at the trial or hearing, offered in evidence to prove the truth of the matter asserted.

(d) Statements Which Are Not Hearsay. A statement is not hearsay if—

(1) *Prior Statement by Witness.* The declarant testifies at the trial or hearing and is subject to cross-examination concerning the statement, and the statement is (A) inconsistent with the declarant's testimony, and was given under oath subject to the penalty of perjury at a trial, hearing, or other proceeding, or in a deposition, or (B) consistent with the declarant's testimony and is offered to rebut an express or implied charge against the declarant of recent fabrication or improper influence or motive, or (C) one of identification of a person made after perceiving the person; or

(2) *Admission by Party-Opponent.* The statement is offered against a party and is (A) the party's own statement in either an individual or a representative capacity or (B) a statement of which the party has manifested an adoption or belief in its truth, or (C) a statement by a person authorized by the party to make a statement concerning the subject, or (D) a statement by the party's agent or servant concerning a matter within the scope of the agency or employment, made during the existence of the relationship, or (E) a statement by a coconspirator of a party during the course and in furtherance of the conspiracy.

[Amended by Pub.L. 94-113, §1, October 16, 1975, 89 Stat. 576; amended March 2, 1987, effective October 1, 1987.]

Rule 802. Hearsay Rule

Hearsay is not admissible except as provided by these rules or by other rules prescribed by the Supreme Court pursuant to statutory authority or by Act of Congress.

Rule 803. Hearsay Exceptions; Availability of Declarant Immaterial

The following are not excluded by the hearsay rule, even though the declarant is available as a witness:

(1) Present Sense Impression. A statement describing or explaining an event or condition made while the declarant was perceiving the event or condition, or immediately thereafter.

(2) Excited Utterance. A statement relating to a startling event or condition made while the declarant was under the stress of excitement caused by the event or condition.

(3) Then Existing Mental, Emotional, or Physical Condition. A statement of the declarant's then existing state of mind, emotion, sensation, or physical condition (such as intent, plan, motive, design, mental feeling, pain, and bodily health), but not including a statement of memory or belief to prove the fact, remembered or believed unless it relates to the execution, revocation, identification, or terms of declarant's will.

(4) Statements for Purposes of Medical Diagnosis or Treatment. Statements made for purposes of medical diagnosis or treatment and describing medical history, or past or present symptoms, pain, or sensations, or the inception or general character of the cause or external source thereof insofar as reasonably pertinent to diagnosis or treatment.

(5) Recorded Recollection. A memorandum or record concerning a matter about which a witness once had knowledge but now has insufficient recollection to enable the witness to testify fully and accurately, shown to have been made or adopted by the witness when the matter was fresh in the witness' memory and to reflect that knowledge correctly. If admitted, the memorandum or record may be read into evidence but may not itself be received as an exhibit unless offered by an adverse party.

(6) Records of Regularly Conducted Activity. A memorandum, report, record, or data compilation, in any form, of acts, events, conditions, opinions, or diagnoses, made at or near the time by, or from information transmitted by, a person with knowledge, if kept in the course of a regularly conducted business activity, and if it was the regular practice of that business activity to make the memorandum, report, record, or data compilation, all as shown by the testimony of the custodian or other qualified witness, unless the source of information or the method or circumstances of preparation indicate lack of trustworthiness. The term "business" as used in this paragraph includes business, institution, association, profession, occupation, and calling of every kind, whether or not conducted for profit.

(7) Absence of Entry in Records Kept in Accordance With the Provisions of Paragraph (6). Evidence that a matter is not included in the memoranda reports, records, or data compilations, in any form, kept in accordance with the provisions of paragraph (6), to prove the nonoccurrence or nonexistence of the matter, if the matter was of a kind of which a memorandum, report, record, or data compilation was regularly made and preserved, unless the sources of information or other circumstances indicate lack of trustworthiness.

(8) Public Records and Reports. Records, reports, statements, or data compilations, in any form, of public offices or agencies, setting forth (A) the activities of the office or agency, or (B) matters observed pursuant to duty imposed by law as to which matters there was a duty to report, excluding, however, in criminal cases matters observed by police officers and other law enforcement personnel, or (C) in civil actions and proceedings and against the Government in criminal cases, factual findings resulting from an investigation made pursuant to authority granted by law, unless the sources of information or other circumstances indicate lack of trustworthiness.

(9) Records of Vital Statistics. Records or data compilations, in any form, of births, fetal deaths, deaths, or marriages, if the report thereof was made to a public office pursuant to requirements of law.

(10) Absence of Public Record or Entry. To prove the absence of a record, report, statement, or data compilation, in any form, or the nonoccurrence or nonexistence of a matter of which a record, report, statement, or data compilation, in any form, was regularly made and preserved by a public office or agency, evidence in the form of a certification in accordance with rule 902, or testimony, that diligent search failed to disclose the record, report, statement, or data compilation, or entry.

(11) Records of Religious Organizations. Statements of births, marriages, divorces, deaths, legitimacy, ancestry, relationship by blood or marriage, or other similar facts of personal or family history, contained in a regularly kept record of a religious organization.

(12) Marriage, Baptismal, and Similar Certificates. Statements of fact contained in a certificate that the maker performed a marriage or other ceremony or administered a sacrament, made by a clergyman, public official, or other person authorized by the rules or practices of a religious organization or by law to perform the act certified, and purporting to have been issued at the time of the act or within a reasonable time thereafter.

(13) Family Records. Statements of fact concerning personal or family history contained in family Bibles, genealogies, charts, engravings on rings, inscriptions on family portraits, engravings on urns, crypts, or tombstones, or the like.

(14) Records of Documents Affecting an Interest in Property. The record of a document purporting to establish or affect an interest in property, as proof of the content of the original recorded document and its execution and delivery by each person by whom it purports to have been executed, if the record is a record of a public office and an applicable statute authorizes the recording of documents of that kind in that office.

(15) Statements in Documents Affecting an Interest in Property. A statement contained in a document purporting to establish or affect an interest in property if the matter stated was relevant to the purpose of the document, unless dealings with the property since the document was made have been inconsistent with the truth of the statement or the purport of the document.

(16) Statements in Ancient Documents. Statements in a document in existence twenty years or more the authenticity of which is established.

(17) Market Reports, Commercial Publications. Market quotations, tabulations, lists, directories, or other published compilations, generally used and relied upon by the public or by persons in particular occupations.

(18) Learned Treatises. To the extent called to the attention of an expert witness upon cross-examination or relied upon by the expert witness in direct examination, statements contained in published treatises, periodicals, or pamphlets on a subject of history, medicine, or other science or art, established as a reliable authority by the testimony or admission of the witness or by other expert testimony or by judicial notice. If admitted, the statements may be read into evidence but may not be received as exhibits.

(19) Reputation Concerning Personal or Family History. Reputation among members of a person's family by blood, adoption, or marriage, or among a person's associates, or in the community, concerning a person's birth, adoption, marriage, divorce, death, legitimacy, relationship by blood, adoption, or marriage, ancestry, or other similar fact of personal or family history.

(20) Reputation Concerning Boundaries or General History. Reputation in a community, arising before the controversy, as to boundaries of or customs affecting lands in the community, and reputation as to events of general history important to the community or State or nation in which located.

(21) Reputation as to Character. Reputation of a person's character among associates or in the community.

(22) Judgment of Previous Conviction. Evidence of a final judgment, entered after a trial or upon a plea of guilty (but not upon a plea of nolo contendere), adjudging a person guilty of a crime punishable by death or imprisonment in excess of one year, to prove any fact essential to sustain the judgment, but not including, when offered by the Government in a criminal prosecution for purposes other than impeachment, judgments against persons other than the accused. The pendency of an appeal may be shown but does not affect admissibility.

(23) Judgment as to Personal, Family, or General History, or Boundaries. Judgments as proof of matters of personal, family or general history, or boundaries, essential to the judgment, if the same would be provable by evidence of reputation.

(24) Other Exceptions. A statement not specifically covered by any of the foregoing exceptions but having equivalent circumstantial guarantees of trustworthiness, if the court determines that (A) the statement is offered as evidence of a material fact; (B) the statement is more probative on the point for which it is offered than any other evidence which the proponent can procure through reasonable efforts; and (C) the general purposes of these rules and the interests of justice will best be served by admission of the statement into evidence. However, a statement may not be admitted under this exception unless the proponent of it makes known to the adverse party sufficiently in advance of the trial or hearing to provide the adverse party with a fair opportunity to prepare to meet it, the proponent's intention to offer the statement and the particulars of it, including the name and address of the declarant.

[Amended by Pub.L. 94-149, § 1(11), December 12, 1975, 89 Stat. 805; amended March 2, 1987, effective October 1, 1987.]

Rule 804. Hearsay Exceptions; Declarant Unavailable

(a) Definition of Unavailability. "Unavailability as a witness" includes situations in which the declarant—

(1) is exempted by ruling of the court on the ground of privilege from testifying concerning the subject matter of the declarant's statement; or

(2) persists in refusing to testify concerning the subject matter of the declarant's statement despite an order of the court to do so; or

(3) testifies to a lack of memory of the subject matter of the declarant's statement; or

(4) is unable to be present or to testify at the hearing because of death or then existing physical or mental illness or infirmity; or

(5) is absent from the hearing and the proponent of a statement has been unable to procure the declarant's attendance (or in the case of a hearsay exception under subdivision (b)(2), (3), or (4), the declarant's attendance or testimony) by process or other reasonable means.

A declarant is not unavailable as a witness if exemption, refusal, claim of lack of memory, inability, or absence is due to the procurement of wrongdoing of the proponent of a statement for the purpose of preventing the witness from attending or testifying.

(b) Hearsay Exceptions. The following are not excluded by the hearsay rule if the declarant is unavailable as a witness:

(1) *Former Testimony.* Testimony given as a witness at another hearing of the same or a different proceeding, or in a deposition taken in compliance with law in the course of the same or another proceeding, if the party against whom the testimony is now offered, or, in a civil action or proceeding, a predecessor in interest, had an opportunity and similar motive to develop the testimony by direct, cross, or redirect examination.

(2) *Statement Under Belief of Impending Death.* In a prosecution for homicide or in a civil action or proceeding, a statement made by a declarant while believing that the declarant's death was imminent, concerning the cause or circumstances of what the declarant believed to be impending death.

(3) *Statement Against Interest.* A statement which was at the time of its making so far contrary to the declarant's pecuniary or proprietary interest, or so far tended to subject the declarant to civil or criminal liability, or to render invalid a claim by the declarant against another, that a reasonable person in the declarant's position would not have made the statement unless believing it to be true. A statement tending to expose the declarant to criminal liability and offered to exculpate the accused is not admissible unless corroborating circumstances clearly indicate the trustworthiness of the statement.

(4) *Statement of Personal or Family History.*

(A) A statement concerning the declarant's own birth, adoption, marriage, divorce, legitimacy, relationship by blood, adoption, or marriage, ancestry, or other similar fact of personal or family history, even though declarant had no means of acquiring personal knowledge of the matter stated; or

(B) a statement concerning the foregoing matters, and death also, of another person, if the declarant was related to the other by blood, adoption, or marriage or was so intimately associated with the other's family as to be likely to have accurate information concerning the matter declared.

(5) *Other Exceptions.* A statement not specifically covered by any of the foregoing exceptions but having equivalent circumstantial guarantees of trustworthiness, if the court determines that (A) the statement is offered as evidence of a material fact; (B) the statement is more probative on the point for which it is offered than any other evidence which the proponent can procure through reasonable efforts; and (C) the general purposes of these rules and the interests of justice will best be served by admission of the statement into evidence. However, a statement may not be admitted under this exception unless the proponent of it makes known to the adverse party sufficiently in advance of the trial or hearing to provide the adverse party with a fair opportunity to prepare to meet it, the proponent's intention to offer the statement and the particulars of it, including the name and address of the declarant.

[Amended by Pub.L. 94-149, §1(12) and (13), December 12, 1975, 89 Stat. 806; amended March 2, 1987, effective October 1, 1987; amended by Pub.L. 100-690, Title VII, §7075(b), November 18, 1988, 102 Stat. 4405.]

Rule 805. Hearsay Within Hearsay

Hearsay included within hearsay is not excluded under the hearsay rule if each part of the combined statements conforms with an exception to the hearsay rule provided in these rules.

Rule 806. Attacking and Supporting Credibility of Declarant

When a hearsay statement, or a statement defined in Rule 801(d)(2), (C), (D), or (E), has been admitted in evidence, the credibility of the declarant may be attacked, and if attacked may be supported, by any evidence which would be admissible for those purposes if declarant had testified as a witness. Evidence of a statement or conduct by the declarant at any time, inconsistent with the declarant's hearsay statement, is not subject to any requirement that the declarant may have been afforded an opportunity to deny or explain. If the party against whom a hearsay statement has been admitted calls the declarant as a witness, the party is entitled to examine the declarant on the statement as if under cross-examination.

[Amended March 2, 1987, effective October 1, 1987.]

ARTICLE IX. AUTHENTICATION AND IDENTIFICATION

Rule 901. Requirement of Authentication or Identification

(a) General Provision. The requirement of authentication or identification as a condition precedent to admissibility is satisfied by evidence sufficient to support a finding that the matter in question is what its proponent claims.

(b) Illustrations. By way of illustration only, and not by way of limitation, the following are examples of authentication or identification conforming with the requirements of this rule:

(1) *Testimony of Witness With Knowledge.* Testimony that a matter is what it is claimed to be.

(2) *Nonexpert Opinion on Handwriting.* Nonexpert opinion as to the genuineness of handwriting, based upon familiarity not acquired for purposes of the litigation.

(3) *Comparison by Trier or Expert Witness.* Comparison by the trier of fact or by expert witnesses with specimens which have been authenticated.

(4) *Distinctive Characteristics and the Like.* Appearance, contents, substance, internal patterns, or other distinctive characteristics, taken in conjunction with circumstances.

(5) *Voice Identification.* Identification of a voice, whether heard firsthand or through mechanical or electronic transmission or recording, by opinion based upon hearing the voice at any time under circumstances connecting it with the alleged speaker.

(6) *Telephone Conversations.* Telephone conversations, by evidence that a call was made to the number assigned at the time by the telephone company to a particular person or business, if (A) in the case of a person, circumstances, including self-identification, show the person answering to be the one called, or (B) in the case of a business, the call was made to a place of business and the conversation related to business reasonably transacted over the telephone.

(7) *Public Records or Reports.* Evidence that a writing authorized by law to be recorded or filed and in fact recorded or filed in a public office, or a purported public record, report, statement, or data compilation, in any form, is from the public office where items of this nature are kept.

(8) *Ancient Documents or Data Compilation.* Evidence that a document or data compilation, in any form, (A) is in such condition as to create no suspicion concerning its authenticity, (B) was in a place where it, if authentic, would likely be, and (C) has been in existence 20 years or more at the time it is offered.

(9) *Process or System.* Evidence describing a process or system used to produce a result and showing that the process or system produces an accurate result.

(10) *Methods Provided by Statute or Rule.* Any method of authentication or identification provided by Act of Congress or by other rules prescribed by the Supreme Court pursuant to statutory authority.

Rule 902. Self-Authentication

Extrinsic evidence of authenticity as a condition precedent to admissibility is not required with respect to the following:

(1) Domestic Public Documents Under Seal. A document bearing a seal purporting to be that of the United States, or of any State, district, Commonwealth, territory, or insular possession thereof, or the Panama Canal Zone, or the Trust Territory of the Pacific Islands, or of a political subdivision, department, officer, or agency thereof, and a signature purporting to be an attestation or execution.

(2) Domestic Public Documents Not Under Seal. A document purporting to bear the signature in the official capacity of an officer or employee of any entity included in paragraph (1) hereof, having no seal, if a public officer having a seal and having official duties in the district or political subdivision of the officer or employee certifies under seal that the signer has the official capacity and that the signature is genuine.

(3) Foreign Public Documents. A document purporting to be executed or attested in an official capacity by a person authorized by the laws of a foreign country to make the execution or attestation, and accompanied by a final certification as to the genuineness of the signature and official position (A) of the executing or attesting person, or (B) of any foreign official whose certificate of genuineness of signature and official position relates to the execution or attestation or is in a chain of certificates of genuineness of signature and official position relating to the execution or attestation. A final certification may be made by a secretary of an embassy or legation, consul general, consul, vice consul, or consular agent of the United States, or a diplomatic or consular official of the foreign country assigned or accredited to the United States. If reasonable opportunity has been given to all parties to investigate the authenticity and accuracy of official documents, the court may, for good cause shown, order that they be treated as presumptively authentic without final certification or permit them to be evidenced by an attested summary with or without final certification.

(4) Certified Copies of Public Records. A copy of an official record or report or entry therein, or of a document authorized by law to be recorded or filed and actually recorded or filed in a public office, including data compilations in any form, certified as correct by the custodian or other person authorized to make the certification, by certificate complying with paragraph (1), (2), or (3) of this rule or complying with any Act of Congress or rule prescribed by the Supreme Court pursuant to statutory authority.

(5) Official Publications. Books, pamphlets, or other publications purporting to be issued by public authority.

(6) Newspapers and Periodicals. Printed materials purporting to be newspapers or periodicals.

(7) Trade Inscriptions and the Like. Inscriptions, signs, tags, or labels purporting to have been affixed in the course of business and indicating ownership, control, or origin.

(8) Acknowledged Documents. Documents accompanied by a certificate of acknowledgment executed in the manner provided by law by a notary public or other officer authorized by law to take acknowledgments.

(9) Commercial Paper and Related Documents. Commercial paper, signatures thereon, and documents relating thereto to the extent provided by general commercial law.

(10) Presumptions Under Acts of Congress. Any signature, document, or other matter declared by Act of Congress to be presumptively or prima facie genuine or authentic.

[Amended March 2, 1987, effective October 1, 1987; April 25, 1988, effective November 1, 1988.]

Rule 903. Subscribing Witness' Testimony Unnecessary

The testimony of a subscribing witness is not necessary to authenticate a writing unless required by the laws of the jurisdiction whose laws govern the validity of the writing.

ARTICLE X. CONTENTS OF WRITINGS, RECORDINGS, AND PHOTOGRAPHS

Rule 1001. Definitions

For purposes of this article the following definitions are applicable:

(1) Writings and Recordings. "Writings" and "recordings" consist of letters, words, or numbers, or their equivalent, set down by handwriting, typewriting, printing, photostating, photographing, magnetic impulse, mechanical or electronic recording, or other form of data compilation.

(2) Photographs. "Photographs" include still photographs, X-ray films, video tapes, and motion pictures.

(3) Original. An "original" of a writing or recording is the writing or recording itself or any counterpart intended to have the same effect by a person executing or issuing it. An "original" of a photograph includes the negative or any print therefrom. If data are stored in a computer or similar device, any printout or other output readable by sight, shown to reflect the data accurately, is an "original."

(4) Duplicate. A "duplicate" is a counterpart produced by the same impression as the original, or from the same matrix, or by means of photography, including enlargements and miniatures, or by mechanical or electronic re-recording, or by chemical reproduction, or by other equivalent techniques which accurately reproduce the original.

Rule 1002. Requirement of Original

To prove the content of a writing, recording, or photograph, the original writing, recording, or photograph is required, except as otherwise provided in these rules or by Act of Congress.

Rule 1003. Admissibility of Duplicates

A duplicate is admissible to the same extent as an original unless (1) a genuine question is raised as to the authenticity of the original or (2) in the circumstances it would be unfair to admit the duplicate in lieu of the original.

Rule 1004. Admissibility of Other Evidence of Contents

The original is not required, and other evidence of the contents of a writing, recording, or photograph is admissible if—

(1) Originals Lost or Destroyed. All originals are lost or have been destroyed, unless the proponent lost or destroyed them in bad faith; or

(2) Original Not Obtainable. No original can be obtained by any available judicial process or procedure; or

(3) Original in Possession of Opponent. At a time when an original was under the control of the party against whom offered, that party was put on notice, by the pleadings or otherwise, that the contents would be a subject of proof at the hearing, and that party does not produce the original at the hearing; or

(4) Collateral Matters. The writing, recording, or photograph is not closely related to a controlling issue.

[Amended March 2, 1987, effective October 1, 1987.]

Rule 1005. Public Records

The contents of an official record, or of a document authorized to be recorded or filed and actually recorded or filed, including data compilations in any form, if otherwise admissible, may be proved by copy, certified as correct in accordance with rule 902 or testified to be correct by a witness who has compared it with the original. If a copy which complies with the foregoing cannot be obtained by the exercise of reasonable diligence, then other evidence of the contents may be given.

Rule 1006. Summaries

The contents of voluminous writings, recordings, or photographs which cannot conveniently be examined in court may be presented in the form of a chart, summary, or calculation. The originals, or duplicates, shall be made available for examination or copying, or both, by other parties at reasonable time and place. The court may order that they be produced in court.

Rule 1007. Testimony or Written Admission of Party

Contents of writings, recordings, or photographs may be proved by the testimony or deposition of the party against whom offered or by that party's written admission, without accounting for the nonproduction of the original.
[Amended March 2, 1987, effective October 1, 1987.]

Rule 1008. Functions of Court and Jury

When the admissibility of other evidence of contents of writings, recordings, or photographs under these rules depends upon the fulfillment of a condition of fact, the question whether the condition has been fulfilled is ordinarily for the court to determine in accordance with the provisions of rule 104. However, when an issue is raised (a) whether the asserted writing ever existed, or (b) whether another writing, recording, or photograph produced at the trial is the original, or (c) whether other evidence of contents correctly reflects the contents, the issue is for the trier of fact to determine as in the case of other issues of fact.

ARTICLE XI. MISCELLANEOUS RULES

Rule 1101. Applicability of Rules

(a) **Courts and Judges.** These rules apply to the United States district courts, the District Court of Guam, the District Court of the Virgin Islands, the District Court for the Northern Mariana Islands, the United States courts of appeals, the United States Claims Court, and to United States bankruptcy judges and United States magistrate judges, in the actions, cases, and proceedings and to the extent hereinafter set forth. The terms "judge" and "court" in these rules include United States bankruptcy judges and United States magistrate judges.

(b) **Proceedings Generally.** These rules apply generally to civil actions and proceedings, including admiralty and maritime cases, to criminal cases and proceedings, to contempt proceedings except those in which the court may act summarily, and to proceedings and cases under title 11, United States Code.

(c) **Rule of Privilege.** The rule with respect to privileges applies at all stages of all actions, cases, and proceedings.

(d) Rules Inapplicable. The rules (other than with respect to privileges) do not apply in the following situations:

(1) *Preliminary Questions of Fact.* The determination of questions of fact preliminary to admissibility of evidence when the issue is to be determined by the court under rule 104.

(2) *Grand Jury.* Proceedings before grand juries.

(3) *Miscellaneous Proceedings.* Proceedings for extradition or rendition; preliminary examinations in criminal cases; sentencing, or granting or revoking probation; issuance of warrants for arrest, criminal summonses, and search warrants; and proceedings with respect to release on bail or otherwise.

(e) Rules Applicable in Part. In the following proceedings these rules apply to the extent that matters of evidence are not provided for in the statutes which govern procedure therein or in other rules prescribed by the Supreme Court pursuant to statutory authority: the trial of misdemeanors and other petty offenses before United States magistrate judges; review of agency actions when the facts are subject to trial de novo under section 706(2)(F) of title 5, United States Code; review of orders of the Secretary of Agriculture under section 2 of the Act entitled "An Act to authorize association of producers of agricultural products" approved February 18, 1922 (7 U.S.C. 292), and under sections 6 and 7(c) of the Perishable Agricultural Commodities Act, 1930 (7 U.S.C. 499f, 499g(c)); naturalization and revocation of naturalization under sections 310–318 of the Immigration and Nationality Act (8 U.S.C. 1421–1429); prize proceedings in admiralty under sections 7651–7681 of title 10, United States Code; review of orders of the Secretary of the Interior under section 2 of the Act entitled "An Act authorizing associations of producers of aquatic products" approved June 25, 1934 (15 U.S.C. 522); review of orders of petroleum control boards under section 5 of the Act entitled "An Act to regulate interstate and foreign commerce in petroleum and its products by prohibiting the shipment in such commerce of petroleum and its products produced in violation of State law, and for other purposes", approved February 22, 1935 (15 U.S.C. 715d); actions for fines, penalties, or forfeitures under part V of title IV of the Tariff Act of 1930 (19 U.S.C. 1581–1624), or under the Anti-Smuggling Act (19 U.S.C. 1701–1711); criminal libel for condemnation, exclusion of imports, or other proceedings under the Federal Food, Drug, and Cosmetic Act (21 U.S.C. 301–392); disputes between seamen under sections 4079, 4080, and 4081 of the Revised Statutes (22 U.S.C. 256–258); habeas corpus under sections 2241–2254 of title 28, United States Code; motions to vacate, set aside or correct sentence under section 2255 of title 28, United States Code; actions for penalties for refusal to transport destitute seamen under section 4578 of the Revised Statutes (46 U.S.C. 679);[1] actions against the United States under the Act entitled "An Act authorizing suits against the United States in admiralty for damage caused by and salvage service rendered to public vessels belonging to the United States, and for other purposes", approved March 3, 1925 (46 U.S.C. 781–790), as implemented by section 7730 of title 10, United States Code.

[Amended by Pub.L. 94-149, §1(14), December 12, 1975, 89 Stat. 806; Pub.L. 95-598, Title II, §251, November 6, 1978, 92 Stat. 2673, effective October 1, 1979; Pub.L. 97-164, Title I, §142, April 2, 1982, 96 Stat. 45, effective October 1, 1982; amended March 2, 1987, effective October 1, 1987; April 25, 1988, effective November 1, 1988; amended by Pub.L. 100-690, Title VII, §7075(c)(1), November 18, 1988, 102 Stat. 4405 (although amendment by Pub.L. 100-690 could not be executed due to prior amendment by Court or-

---

[1] Law Revision Counsel Note: Repealed and reenacted as 46 U.S.C. 11104(b)–(d) by Pub.L. 98-89, §§1, 2(a), 4(b), August 26, 1983, 97 Stat. 500.

der which made the same change effective November 1, 1988); amended April 22, 1993, effective December 1, 1993.]

Rule 1102. Amendments

Amendments to the Federal Rules of Evidence may be made as provided in section 2072 of title 28 of the United States Code.
[Amended April 30, 1991, effective December 1, 1991.]

Rule 1103. Title

These rules may be known and cited as the Federal Rules of Evidence.

APPENDIX B

Glossary

The following glossary of legal terms is not intended to be exhaustive. It may be used by the student as an easily available aid to a better understanding of the text portion and the edited decisions contained in the preceding pages.*

*Ab Initio: From the first; from the beginning.

*Abstention: In constitutional law this term is sometimes used by a federal court when it declines to exercise its jurisdiction over a matter, pending a final determination of it in the courts of a state.

*Abuse of Discretion: Legal name given to a court review of the actions of a trial court or administrative officer where petitioner claims that discretion exercised was arbitrary, discriminatory, and/or unreasonable.

*Abuse of Process: The use of legal papers for a purpose other than intended by law, resulting in unlawful harassment to the recipient.

*Accessory: One who aids in the commission or attempted commission of an offense or in assisting a perpetrator of an offense to avoid apprehension.

*Accomplice: A person who voluntarily acts with another to commit or attempt to commit an offense, both persons having a shared criminal purpose.

*Accusation: A charge of wrongdoing made against a person. It may include a prosecutor's information, a grand jury indictment, or a complainant's formal affidavit of complaint.

*Acquittal: A finding that a defendant is not guilty of the offense for which s/he was charged.

*Actus Reus: The guilty act as opposed to the mens rea which is the guilty mind.

*Ad Hoc: For this particular purpose.

*Adjudication: The judicial determination of a controversy between parties wherein judgment is pronounced. May also apply to administrative tribunals.

Adjudicative Facts: "Adjudicative facts," of which trial court may take notice if fact is not subject to reasonable dispute, are those to which law is applied in process of adjudication; they are facts that, in jury case, normally go to jury. Grason Elec. Co. v. Sacramento Mun. Utility Dist., D.C.Cal. 571 F.Supp. 1504, 1521. . . . Those facts that must be found beyond a reasonable doubt by trier of fact before there can be a conviction. Sundberg v. State, Alaska App., 667 P.2d 1268, 1271.

*Admissible Evidence: All means by which any alleged matter of fact is proved or disproved which is permitted into a trial record pursuant to the law of the court's jurisdiction.

*Admission: In criminal law, the voluntary statements made or an act done which is contrary to a person's position on trial. It falls short of a confession which is a direct acknowledgment of guilt.

*Adversary: An opponent in a legal controversy.

Adverse Possession: A method of acquisition of title to real property by possession for a statutory period under certain conditions. Lowery v. Garfield County, 122 Mont. 571, 208 P.2d 478, 486. . . . In order to establish title in this manner, there must be proof of nonpermissive use which is actual, open, notorious, exclusive and adverse for the statutorily prescribed period. Ryan v. Stavros, 348 Mass. 251, 203 N.E.2d 85.

*Affiant: The person who subscribes his/her signature to an affidavit.

---

*Every word preceded by an asterisk is reprinted from *Constitutional Law for Criminal Justice Professionals*, 3rd edition, with permission of Copyright holder, Coral Gables Publishing Co., Inc. All other terms are reprinted from *Black's Law Dictionary*, 6th edition, with permission of West Publishing Co.

*Affidavit: A statement in writing subscribed by a signature of a person which was affixed under oath before a notary public, a magistrate, or a commissioner of deeds.

*Affirm: To attest to the truth of a statement or the act of an appellate court indicating that the ruling or decision of the lower court was correct.

Affirmative Defense: In pleading, matter asserted by defendant which, assuming the complaint to be true, constitutes a defense to it. A response to a plaintiff's claim which attacks the plaintiff's *legal* right to bring an action, as opposed to attacking the truth of claim. . . . Affirmative defenses in criminal cases include insanity, intoxication, self-defense, automatism, coercion, alibi, and duress.

*A Fortiori: All the more; a term which is used which draws a conclusion by giving a reason; to the same effect.

Agent: A person authorized by another (principal) to act for or in place of him; one entrusted with another's business. Humphries v. Going, D.C.N.C., 59 F.R.D. 583, 587.

*Aid and Abet: To intentionally assist another to attempt to or to commit a criminal offense.

*Alibi: A provable account of a person's whereabouts at a particular time which negates that person's involvement in a criminal offense.

Allege: To state, recite, claim, assert, or charge; to make an allegation.

*Amicus Curiae: Friend of the court. Used frequently where nonlitigants submit memoranda of law to assist the court to render a decision in a pending matter.

Ancient Document (Ancient Writings): Documents bearing on their face every evidence of age and authenticity, of age of 30 [or 20] years, and coming from a natural and reasonable official custody. Hartzell v. U.S., C.C.A.Iowa, 72 F.2d 569, 579. These are presumed to be genuine without express proof, when coming from the proper custody.

Answer: The response of a defendant to the plaintiff's complaint, denying in part or in whole the allegations made by the plaintiff.

Ante Litem Motam: At time when declarant had no motive to distort truth. Before suit brought, before controversy instituted. Also, before the controversy arose.

Appeal: Resort to a superior (i.e. appellate) court to review the decision of an inferior (i.e. trial) court or administrative agency.

Appellant: The party who takes an appeal from one court or jurisdiction to another.

Appellee: The party in a cause against whom an appeal is taken; that is, the party who has an interest adverse to setting aside or reversing the judgment.

*Arraignment: A proceeding wherein the accused is informed of the nature of the charges against him/her. This is done before a judge or a magistrate. The accused is asked how s/he pleads to the charges and bail conditions are sometimes set pending a trial at a later date.

*Arrest: The initial taking into custody of a person by law enforcement authorities to answer for a criminal offense or violation of a code or ordinance.

*Assault: Any unlawful attempt to inflict bodily injury upon another, accompanied by the apparent present ability to do the act.

*Assignment of Error: An allegation made by appellant against a trial judge charging error which is the ground for reversal.

*Attainder: In common law, a mark of infamy given to a convicted felon resulting in loss of all civil rights. *See* bill of attainder.

*Attempt: An overt act, beyond mere preparation, to commit an offense.

Authentication: In the law of evidence, the act or mode of giving authority or legal authenticity to a statute, record, or other written instrument, or a certified copy thereof, so as to render it legally admissible in evidence.

*Bail: A pecuniary or other security accepted by a court or duly authorized officer to insure the appearance of a defendant at every stage of the proceedings up to final incarceration, dismissal, payment of fine, and/or sentence of probation.

*Bailiff: A court attendant or court officer.

*Bar (Attorneys): Duly licensed attorneys are designated as being admitted to the bar of courts.

*Bar (Procedure): A barrier to relitigating the same issue (position in courtroom). Defendant standing before the judge is called "prisoner at the bar" (partition in court room separating judge, court personnel and attorneys litigating the instant case from others in courtroom).

*Barrister: English practitioner of law who functions as a trial counsel.

*Battery: The touching of another person done willfully and in anger.

*Bench: The place where the judge or judges sit while in a courtroom.

*Bench Warrant: A court order directing a law enforcement officer to seize a named person and bring that person before the court.

Best Evidence: Primary evidence, as distinguished from secondary; original, as distinguished from substitutionary; the best and highest evidence of which the nature of the case is susceptible, not the highest or strongest evidence which the nature of the thing to be proved admits of. The original of a written instrument is itself always regarded as the primary or best possible evidence of its existence and contents; a copy, or the recollection of a witness, would be secondary evidence.

Bifurcated Trial: Trial of issues separately, e.g. guilt and punishment, or guilt and sanity, in criminal trial.

*Bill of Attainder: A legislative act designed to inflict punishment upon a named person or persons without the benefit of a judicial trial. A legislature however has power to quell disorder in the chamber and may punish and/or incarcerate for contempt as long as accused has opportunity to appear and respond to charges.

Bill of Particulars: A written statement or specification of the particulars of the demand for which an action at law is brought, . . . furnished by one of the parties to the other, either voluntarily or in compliance with a judge's order for that purpose. It is designed to aid the defendant in interposing the proper answer and in preparing for trial, by giving him detailed information regarding the cause of action stated in the complaint.

Bill of Rights: That portion of Constitution guaranteeing rights and privileges to the individual; i.e. first ten Amendments of U.S. Constitution.

*Brief (Court Use): A written argument presented to a judge, panel of judges, or an administrative law judge to persuade that person to decide an issue presently before the tribunal in favor of one of the litigants.

*Brief (Student Use): An epitome of a written decision which the student writes as an aid to remembering the legal history, questions of law, facts of the case, opinion and judgment of the court.

*Burden of Proof: The requirement of a litigant to persuade the trier of the facts that the allegations made against the other party to an action are true. In criminal law, the government is required to prove its case beyond any reasonable doubt. In civil cases, the party bringing the action is required to prove the allegations by a preponderance of evidence. In administrative hearings, the allegations must be proven by substantial evidence or by clear and convincing evidence.

Burglary: A person is guilty of burglary if he enters a building or occupied structure, or separately secured or occupied portion thereof, with purpose to commit a crime therein, unless the premises are at the time, open to the public or the actor is licensed or privileged to enter.

Business Record: [D]ocumentary evidence . . . admissible if identified by its entrant, or one under whose supervision it is kept and shown to be original or first permanent entry, made in routine course of business, at or near time of recorded transaction, by one having both duty to so record and personal knowledge of transaction represented by entry. Simmons v. State, 175 Ind.App. 333, 371 N.E.2d 1316, 1320. . . . Journals, books of account and other records which may be ordered produced as part of discovery in trial or preparation of case and generally given broad interpretation for such purposes.

*Caveat: A warning.

Certified Copy: A copy of a document or record, signed and certified as a true copy by the officer to whose custody the original is entrusted.

*Certiorari: A common law writ issued from a higher court to an inferior court, commanding the inferior court to certify and send the record of a particular case, previously decided by the inferior court, to the higher court for review of the inferior court's actions in the case.

Chain of Custody: In evidence, the one who offers real evidence, such as the narcotics in a trial of drug case, must account for the custody of the evidence from the moment in which it reaches his custody until the moment in which it is offered in evidence, and such evidence goes to weight not to admissibility of evidence. Com. v. White, 353 Mass. 409, 232 N.E.2d 335.

Character Evidence: Evidence of person's moral standing in community based on reputation.

*Circumstantial Evidence: Secondary facts from which a rational inference may be logically arrived at to prove a principal fact.

*Citation: A written or printed command to a person to appear before a court on the day and time indicated. Also used as a location in a publication where a legal case may be found.

Civil: Of or relating to the state or its citizenry. Relating to private rights and remedies sought by civil actions as contrasted with criminal proceedings.

Civil Law: Laws concerned with civil or private rights and remedies, as contrasted with criminal laws.

*Civil Liberties: Courses of action that a person is entitled to which are immune from governmental interference. They may be limitations of governmental action, e.g., liberty of free speech guaranteed in the First Amendment of the United States Constitution.

*Civil Rights: A course of action which a person is entitled to which is defined by positive laws enacted by government, e.g., right to bring a civil action against the government pursuant to statutory authority.

*Clear and Convincing: A standard of proof beyond a mere preponderance but not as much as beyond a reasonable doubt. Usually that quantum of proof required of a party to prevail in an administrative tribunal. Similar to substantial evidence.

*Clear and Present Danger: A limitation on the unfettered exercise of free speech such as shouting "fire" in a crowded theater when in fact there is no fire or no danger present.

*Collateral Attack: A challenge to a judgment brought about indirectly and not by direct appeal, e.g., habeas corpus petition instead of appeal of a prior rendered judgment.

*Collateral Estoppel: The determination of litigated facts is binding on those parties in all future proceedings against each other. The constitutional prohibition against double jeopardy enables a defendant to plead collateral estoppel if a primary issue was previously litigated and defendant's contention prevailed at former trial.

*Comity: A judicial courtesy wherein one court yields to another court of concomitant jurisdiction based on the concept that a court which first asserts its jurisdiction will not be interfered with by another court, e.g., judgments of courts of competent jurisdiction of foreign nations are not interfered with by other state or federal courts based on comity.

*Common Law: A system of jurisprudence which is derived from Anglo-Saxon law from principles, rather than rules, based on justice, reason, and common sense, judicially originated. The principles change with the needs of the community.

Comparative Negligence: Under comparative negligence statutes or doctrines, negligence is measured in terms of percentage, and any damages allowed shall be diminished in proportion to amount of negligence attributable to the person for whose injury, damage or death recovery is sought.

Competency: In the law of evidence, the presence of those characteristics, or the absence of those disabilities, which render a witness legally fit and qualified to give testimony in a court of justice; applied, in the same sense, to documents or other written evidence. . . . Competency differs from credibility. The former is a question which arises before considering the evidence given by the witness; the latter concerns the degree of credit to be given to his testimony.

*Competent (Court): One having proper jurisdiction.

*Competent (Person): Capacity to understand and act reasonably.

*Competent (Witness): Capacity to understand.

Competent Evidence: That which the very nature of the thing to be proven requires, as, the production of a writing where its contents are the subject of inquiry. Also, generally, admissible (i.e. relevant and material) as opposed to "incompetent" or "inadmissible" evidence. Frick v. State, Okl.Cr., 509 P.2d 135, 136.

Complainant: One who applies to the courts for legal redress by filing complaint (i.e. plaintiff). Also, one who instigates prosecution or who prefers accusation against suspected person.

Complaint: The original or initial pleading by which an action is commenced under codes or Rules of Civil Procedure. . . . In criminal law, a charge, preferred before a magistrate having jurisdiction, that a person named (or an unknown person) has committed a specified offense, with an offer to prove the fact, to the end that a prosecution may be instituted.

Conclusive Presumption: Exists when an ultimate fact is presumed to be true upon proof of another fact, and no evidence, no matter how persuasive, can rebut it. . . . McInerney v. Berman, D.C.Mass., 473 F.Supp. 187, 188.

*Confession: A direct acknowledgment of guilt.

*Conjugal Visitation (Prison): Permission to engage in sexual intercourse between the inmate and his/her spouse.

Conspiracy: A combination or confederacy between two or more persons formed for the purpose of committing, by their joint efforts, some unlawful or criminal act, or some act which is lawful in itself, but becomes unlawful when done by the concerted action of the conspirators, or for the purpose of using criminal or unlawful means to the commission of an act not in itself unlawful.

Constructive Trust: Trust created by operation of law against one who by actual or constructive fraud, by duress or by abuse of confidence, or by commission of wrong, or by any form of unconscionable conduct, or other questionable means, has obtained or holds legal right to property which he should not, in equity and good conscience, hold and enjoy. Davis v. Howard, 19 Or.App. 310, 527 P.2d 422, 424.

*Contempt of Court: An act or an omission tending to obstruct or interfere with the orderly administration of a court or to affect the dignity of a court.

Contraband: In general, any property which is unlawful to produce or possess.

Contributory Negligence: Conduct by a plaintiff which is below the standard to which he is legally required to conform for his own protection and which is a contributing cause which cooperates with the negligence of the defendant in causing the plaintiff's harm. Li v. Yellow Cab Co. of California, 13 Cal.3d 804, 119 Cal.Rptr. 858, 864, 532 P.2d 1226.

Conversion: An unauthorized assumption and exercise of the right of ownership over goods or personal chattels belonging to another, to the alteration of their condition or the exclusion of the owner's rights.

*Corporal Punishment: Pain inflicted upon a person as a means of correction or to prevent recidivism, e.g., whipping of a prisoner.

Corroborative (Corroborating) Evidence: Evidence supplementary to that already given and tending to strengthen or confirm it. Additional evidence of a different character to the same point. Edwards v. Edwards, Tenn.App., 501 S.W.2d 283, 289.

Counsel, Right to: Constitutional right of criminal defendant to court appointed attorney if he is financially unable to retain private counsel; guaranteed by Sixth and Fourteenth Amendments to U.S. Constitution, and as well by court rule (Fed.R.Crim.P. 44), and statute (18 U.S.C.A. §3006A).

Courts of Appeals, U.S.: Intermediate appellate courts created by Congress in 1891 and known until 1948 as United States Circuit Courts of Appeals, sitting in eleven numbered circuits, the District of Columbia, and the Court of Appeals for the Federal Circuit. Normally cases are heard by divisions of three judges sitting together, but on certain matters all the judges of a circuit may hear a case. Courts of Appeals have appellate jurisdiction over most cases decided by United States District Courts and review and enforce orders of many federal administrative bodies. The decisions of the courts of appeals are final except as they are subject to discretionary review on appeal by the Supreme Court. 28 U.S.C.A. 41, 43, 1291.

Credibility: Worthiness of belief; that quality in a witness which renders his evidence worthy of belief.

*Crime: Any act which the government has declared to be contrary to the public good, which is declared by statute to be a crime and which is prosecuted in a criminal proceeding. In some jurisdictions crimes only include felonies and/or misdemeanors.

*Crime Against Nature: Deviant social behavior relevant to sexual acts, e.g., sodomy; sexual intercourse with a dead body.

Criminal Law: The substantive criminal law is that law which for the purpose of preventing harm to society, (1) declares what conduct is criminal, and (b) prescribes the punishment to be imposed for such conduct.

Criminology: The study of the nature of, causes of, and means of dealing with crime.

Cross-Examination: The examination of a witness upon a trial or hearing, or upon taking a deposition, by the party opposed to the one who produced him, upon his evidence given in chief, to test its truth, to further develop it, or for other purposes.

*Cruel and Unusual Punishment: Amorphous term which cannot be defined with specificity. Punishment which is shocking to reasonable persons. United States Supreme Court interprets this phrase on an ad hoc basis.

*Custodial Interrogation: The confinement of a person by law enforcement agents/officers. The person is not free to leave and is questioned about a crime.

Declarations Against Interest: An out of court statement by a declarant who is unavailable as a witness is admissible as an exception to the rule against hearsay if the statement was against his interest at the time it was made. Under the common law the statement must have been against the pecuniary or proprietary interest of the declarant. Under Federal Rule of Evidence 804(b)(3) and the law of some states, the statement may also be admitted if it was against the penal interest of the declarant.

Declaratory Judgment: A binding adjudication of the rights and status of litigants even though no consequential relief is awarded. Brimmer v. Thomson, Wyo., 521 P.2d 574, 579.

Defamation: An intentional false communication, either published or publicly spoken, that injures another's reputation or good name.

Defendant: The person defending or denying; the party against whom relief or recovery is sought in an action or suit or the accused in a criminal case.

Defense: That which is offered and alleged by the party proceeded against in an action or suit, as a reason in law or fact why the plaintiff should not recover or establish what he seeks. . . . Evidence offered by accused to defeat criminal charge.

*De Minimus: Insignificant; of no importance; not important enough to take the time and attention of a court.

Demonstrative Evidence: Real ("thing") evidence such as the gun in a trial of homicide or the contract itself in the trial of a contract case. Evidence apart from the testimony of witnesses concerning the thing. Such evidence may include maps, diagrams, photographs, models, charts, medical illustrations, X-rays.

*Demurrer: An answer to a complaint which declares that even if all of the facts stated in the complaint are true, it does not state a cause of action. The court ruling on a demurrer may grant summary judgment for the prevailing party, thus terminating the case.

*De Novo: To start for another time from the beginning.

*Deposition: A statement of a person reduced to writing which is subscribed under oath or affirmation.

*Dictum (Obiter Dictum): A statement made by the court which is included in a judicial opinion and is not necessarily pertinent to the facts of the instant case. A dictum is not considered to be binding on future cases.

Direct Evidence: Evidence in form of testimony from a witness who actually saw, heard or touched the subject of questioning. State v. Baker, 249 Or. 549, 438 P.2d 978, 980.

Direct Examination: The first interrogation or examination of a witness, on the merits, by the party on whose behalf he is called.

Directed Verdict: In a case in which the party with the burden of proof has failed to present a prima facie case for jury consideration, the trial judge may order the entry of a verdict without allowing the jury to consider it, because, as a matter of law, there can be only one such verdict. Fed.R.Civil P. 50(a).

*Discovery Process: Pretrial procedure whereby litigants supply information to their adversary before trial, which is necessary to the other party's position at trial.

Discretion: As applied to public officers connotes action taken in light of reason as applied to all facts and with view to rights of all parties to action while having regard for what is right and equitable under all circumstances and law. State v. Whitman, R.I., 431 A.2d 1229, 1233.

*Dismiss (Appeal): To place parties in same position as if no appeal were taken.

*Dismiss (Legal): To terminate a court case without a trial.

District Courts (U.S.): Each state is comprised of one or more federal judicial districts, and in each district there is a district court. 28 U.S.C.A. §81 et seq. The United States district courts are the trial courts with general Federal jurisdiction over cases involving federal laws or offenses and actions between citizens of different states. . . . Only one judge is usually required to hear and decide a case in a district court, but in some kinds of cases it is required that three

judges be called together to comprise the court. (28 U.S.C.A. § 2284).

*Diversity of Citizenship: Where citizens of different states are litigants in an action. It may be cause for federal court jurisdiction if other requirements are met.

DNA Identification: DNA profiling or fingerprinting is an analysis of Deoxyribonucleic Acid (DNA) resulting in the identification of an individual's patterned chemical structure of genetic information. . . . A forensic technique used in criminal cases to identify, or rule out, crime suspect and in paternity cases to identify, or rule out, father of child.

Document: An instrument on which is recorded, by means of letters, figures, or marks, the original, official, or legal form of something, which may be evidentially used.

Documentary Evidence: Evidence derived from conventional symbols (such as letters) by which ideas are represented on material substances. Such evidence as is furnished by written instruments, inscriptions, documents of all kinds, and also any inanimate objects admissible for the purpose, as distinguished from "oral" evidence, or that delivered by human beings viva voce. People v. Purcell, 22 Cal.App.2d 126, 70 P.2d 706, 709.

*Domicile: A place of permanent residence where a person intends to return when absent. A person may have only one domicile but may have many residences.

*Double Jeopardy: A person who is tried again for a crime which has been litigated to an acquittal or conviction is said to be twice placed in jeopardy if tried again for the same offense. A mistrial or appeal does not prevent a second trial unless the mistrial was the result of brash behavior by the prosecution in an obvious attempt to try the defendant at another time.

Dram Shop Acts: Many states have Dram Shop or Civil Liability Acts which impose liability on the seller of intoxicating liquors (which may or may not include beer), when a third party is injured as a result of the intoxication of the buyer where the sale has caused or contributed to such intoxication.

*Due Process: A phrase without a fixed meaning. It has been interpreted by the U.S. Supreme Court as requiring a government to exercise fundamental fairness in the administration of criminal justice.

Dying Declarations: Statements made by a person who believes he is about to die in reference to the manner in which he received the injuries of which he is dying, or other immediate cause of his death, and in reference to the person who inflicted such injuries or the connection with such injuries of a person who is charged or suspected of having committed them.

Eighth Amendment: The amendment to the U.S. Constitution added in 1791 which prohibits excessive bail, excessive fines and cruel and unusual punishment.

*En Banc: By the full court.

*Enjoin: A command by a court to do or refrain from doing a specific act.

Equity: Justice administered according to fairness as contrasted with the strictly formulated rules of common law. . . . [T]he object is to render the administration of justice more complete, by affording relief when the courts of law are incompetent to give it, or to give it with effect, or by exercising certain branches of jurisdiction independently of them.

Error: A mistaken judgment or incorrect belief as to the existence or effect of matters of fact, or a false or mistaken conception or application of the law. Such a mistaken or false conception or application of the law to the facts of a cause as will furnish ground for a review of the proceedings upon a writ of error.

Escheat: A reversion of property to the state in consequence of a want of any individual competent to inherit.

Estoppel: "Estoppel" means that party is prevented by his own acts from claiming a right to detriment of other party who was entitled to rely on such conduct and has acted accordingly. Graham v. Asbury, 112 Ariz. 184, 540 P.2d 656, 658.

*Et Seq.: And the following.

*Evidence: All matter of proof offered in a trial to prove or disprove an issue of fact.

Examined Copy: A copy of a record, public book, or register, and which has been compared with the original.

Excited Utterance: In evidence, a statement relating to a startling event or condition made while the declarant was under the stress of excitement caused by the event or condition.

*Exclusionary Rule: A judicially contrived procedure which prevents evidence unconstitutionally obtained by law enforcement officers from being introduced into evidence at a criminal trial and is not to be considered by the triers of the facts of the case in arriving at a verdict.

*Exculpatory: Statements or evidence which tends to prove that a person was not the perpetrator of a criminal offense.

*Execute: The killing of a prisoner by authority of the government; the signing of a legal instrument.

Executive Privilege: This privilege, based on constitutional doctrine of separation of powers, ex-

empts the executive from disclosure requirements applicable to the ordinary citizen or organization where such exemption is necessary to the discharge of highly important executive responsibilities involved in maintaining governmental operations, and extends not only to military and diplomatic secrets but also to documents integral to an appropriate exercise of the executive's domestic decisional and policy making functions, that is, those documents reflecting the frank expression necessary in intra-governmental advisory and deliberative communications. 5 U.S.C.A. § 552(b)(1). Black v. Sheraton Corp. of America, D.C.D.C., 371 F.Supp. 97, 100.

Exemplified Copy: Copy of document which has been authenticated.

Ex Parte: On one side only; by or for one party. . . . A judicial proceeding, order, injunction, etc., is said to be ex parte when it is taken or granted at the instance and for the benefit of one party only, and without notice to, or contestation by, any person adversely interested. "Ex parte," in the heading of a reported case, signifies that the name following is that of the party upon whose application the case is heard.

Expert Witness: One who by reason of education or specialized experience possesses superior knowledge respecting a subject about which persons having no particular training are incapable of forming an accurate opinion or deducing correct conclusions. Kim Mfg., Inc. v. Superior Metal Treating, Inc., Mo.App., 537 S.W.2d 424, 428.

*Ex Post Facto Law: A law which declares designated behavior to be a crime which, when committed, was noncriminal; or increases the punishment after it was committed; or diminishes the requisite proof for conviction.

Ex Rel. (Ex Relatione): Upon relation or information. Legal proceedings which are instituted by the attorney general (or other proper person) in the name and behalf of the state, but on the information and at the instigation of an individual who has a private interest in the matter, are said to be taken "on the relation" . . . of such person. . . . Such a cause is usually entitled thus: "State *ex rel*. Doe v. Roe."

Extrajudicial Admissions: Those made outside of court.

Extrinsic Evidence: External evidence, or that which is not contained in the body of an agreement, contract, and the like. Evidence which does not appear on the face of a document, but which is available from other sources such as statements by the parties and other circumstances surrounding the transaction.

*Fair Hearing: An extrajudicial hearing usually authorized by statute to determine a controversy in an administrative tribunal. It must be conducted in a manner which includes an opportunity for all sides to present evidence, e.g., 42 U.S.C.A. Sect. 602(a)(4) requiring fair hearing prior to termination of welfare benefits.

*Felony: A crime for which a person may be imprisoned for at least a year and a day.

Fifth Amendment: Amendment to U.S. Constitution providing that no person shall be required to answer for a capital or otherwise infamous offense unless on indictment or presentment of a grand jury except in military cases; that no person will suffer double jeopardy; that no person will be compelled to be a witness against himself; that no person shall be deprived of life, liberty or property without due process of law and that private property will not be taken for public use without just compensation.

First Amendment: Amendment to U.S. Constitution guaranteeing basic freedoms of speech, religion, press, and assembly and the right to petition the government for redress of grievances.

*First Impression: The first time that a question of law has been decided by a court.

Forensic: Belonging to courts of justice.

Fourteenth Amendment: The Fourteenth Amendment of the Constitution of the United States, ratified in 1868, creates or at least recognizes for the first time a citizenship of the United States, as distinct from that of the states; forbids the making or enforcement by any state of any law abridging the privileges and immunities of citizens of the United States; and secures all "persons" against any state action which results in either deprivation of life, liberty, or property without due process of law, or, in denial of the equal protection of the laws.

Fourth Amendment: Amendment of the U.S. Constitution guaranteeing people the right to be secure in their homes and property against unreasonable searches and seizures and providing that no warrants shall issue except upon probable cause and then only as to specific places to be searched and persons and things to be seized.

Frauds, Statute of: This is the common designation of a very celebrated English statute . . . , passed in 1677, which has been adopted, in a more or less modified form, in nearly all of the United States. Its chief characteristic is the provision that no suit or action shall be maintained on certain classes of contracts or engagements unless there shall be a note or memorandum thereof in writing signed by the party to be charged or by his authorized agent. . . .

*Frisk: The patting down of the outer clothing of a person who is suspected of carrying a concealed weapon.

*Fruit of the Poisonous Tree Doctrine: If a law enforcement officer obtains information from a defendant in an unconstitutional manner, although that evidence is not used at the defendant's trial, other evidence ascertained as a result of the illegally obtained evidence is also excludable from the trial, based on the doctrine of the fruit of the poisonous tree. Such other evidence has been held to be admissible, however, for impeachment when defendant testifies.

*Full Faith and Credit: Phrase applied to the United States Constitution which requires the "public Acts, Records and Judicial Proceedings" of one state to be respected by each of the sister states, Art. 4, Sec. 1.

Fundamental Error: In appellate practice, error which goes to the merits of the plaintiff's cause of action, and which will be considered on review, whether assigned as error or not, where the justice of the case seems to require it. Error of such character as to render judgment void. Error so grave that, if not rectified, would result in denial of fundamental due process. Roberts v. State, Ind., 492 N.E.2d 310, 313.

*Grand Jury: A body of people (usually 23) who serve as part of the criminal justice system. The grand jury's function is to investigate and indict persons for crimes or render information or presentments for crimes committed in its territorial jurisdiction. It may also find that a complaint of criminal activity is not worthy of an indictment or information.

Guardian ad Litem: A guardian ad litem is a special guardian appointed by the court in which a particular litigation is pending to represent an infant, ward or unborn person in that particular litigation, and the status of guardian ad litem exists only in that specific litigation in which the appointment occurs. Bowen v. Sonnenburg, Ind.App., 411 N.E.2d 390, 396.

*Guilty (Criminal): The finding beyond a reasonable doubt, by a jury or judge presiding without a jury, after a trial, or after a judicial confession of guilt, that a defendant committed the crime charged.

*Habeas Corpus Writ: A court order requiring a person who has custody of another person to be present in court with the detainee so that the court can inquire as to the legality of the detention. Writs of Habeas Corpus may be directed to a Commissioner of Prisons and may also be used in child custody and elderly guardianship litigation.

*Harmless Error: Error conducted during a trial which an appellate court has concluded does not affect a defendant's substantial right to cause a reviewing court to reverse the judgment of the trial court.

*Head Note: Summary of facts, questions of law, decision and judgment of a case.

*Hearing: A proceeding where evidence is taken to determine issues of fact. It may be an administrative hearing, e.g., police agency disciplinary hearing; suppression hearing (to determine whether evidence was unconstitutionally seized); prima facie hearing (to determine if allegations constitute a crime). Some hearings do not require formal rules of evidence.

Hearsay: A term applied to that species of testimony given by a witness who relates, not what he knows personally, but what others have told him, or what he has heard said by others. A statement, other than one made by the declarant while testifying at the trial or hearing, offered in evidence to prove the truth of the matter asserted. Fed.R.Evid. 801(c).

*Hearsay Rule: In the law of evidence hearsay is not generally admitted into evidence unless the material offered is one or more of the recognized exceptions. It is evidence of a statement made by a witness which is restating what another person either orally said or wrote, when it is offered for the truth of the assertion.

*Hung Jury: A trial jury which cannot agree on a verdict according to the number set forth by law in its jurisdiction. Most criminal courts require a unanimous vote for conviction. Some require a substantial majority, e.g., 10–2. A retrial does not subject the defendant to double jeopardy.

*Ibid.: In the same book or on the same page. It avoids repetition of source data.

Immaterial Evidence: Evidence which lacks probative weight and is unlikely to influence the tribunal in resolving the issue before it. Such evidence is commonly objected to by opposing counsel, and disallowed by the court.

*Immunity: Usually a right of absolution from prosecution for a criminal act given to a witness to a crime in exchange for information given to a Grand Jury or prosecutor. A Grand Jury or a prosecutor has power to grant immunity.

*Impeachment: Term applied to questions directed toward a witness who is testifying under cross-examination in an attempt to obtain contradictory statements to affect the credibility of the witness.

*In Camera: In chambers of the judge. Chambers can mean the judge's office or it could mean the robing room adjacent to the court room.

Incompetency: Lack of ability, knowledge, legal qualification, or fitness to discharge the required duty or professional obligation. A relative term which may be employed as meaning disqualification, inability or incapacity and it can refer to lack of legal qualifications or fitness to discharge the required duty and to show want of physical or intellectual or moral fitness. County Bd. of Ed. of Clarke County v. Oliver, 270 Ala. 107, 116 So.2d 566, 567.

*Incriminate: To involve either one's self or another as responsible for criminal conduct.

*Inculpatory: Tending to involve one's self or another as responsible for criminal conduct; incriminating.

*Independent Source: Information acquired by a law enforcement agency which is not tainted by any violation of a constitutional right.

*Indictment: A formal written accusation drawn up by a prosecutor and presented to a Grand Jury which then investigates the charge. If a prima facie crime is found, the foreman of the Grand Jury endorses the indictment as a "True Bill." If the charges are not substantiated, "No True Bill" is found and the indictment is so endorsed. It usually applies to felony offenses only.

Infamous: Shameful or disgraceful.

Infamy: Condition of being infamous. A qualification of a man's legal status produced by his conviction of an infamous crime and the consequent loss of honor and credit, which, at common law, rendered him incompetent as a witness, and by statute in some jurisdictions entails other disabilities.

Infancy: Minority; the state of a person who is under the age of legal majority,—at common law, twenty-one years [now, eighteen years in many jurisdictions].

Inference: In the law of evidence, a truth or proposition drawn from another which is supposed or admitted to be true. . . . A logical and reasonable conclusion of a fact not presented by direct evidence but which, by process of logic and reason, a trier of fact may conclude exists from the established facts. State v. Hyde, Mo.App., 682 S.W.2d 103, 106. Computer Identics Corp. v. Southern Pacific Co., C.A.Mass., 756 F.2d 200, 204. Inferences are deductions or conclusions which with reason and common sense lead the jury to draw from facts which have been established by the evidence in the case.

*Informant: A person who supplies information to a law enforcement officer referring to the commission of a crime or to some set of facts requiring the attention of the law enforcement agency.

Information: An accusation exhibited against a person for some criminal offense, without an indictment. An accusation in the nature of an indictment, from which it differs only in being presented by a competent public officer on his oath of office, instead of a grand jury on their oath. A written accusation made by a public prosecutor, without the intervention of a grand jury. Salvail v. Sharkey, 108 R.I. 63, 271 A.2d 814, 817.

*In Loco Parentis: In the place of a parent.

Intent: A state of mind in which a person seeks to accomplish a given result through a course of action. . . . A mental attitude which can seldom be proved by direct evidence, but must ordinarily be proved by circumstances from which it may be inferred. State v. Gantt, 26 N.C.App. 554, 217 S.E.2d 3, 5.

*Interrogation: Questioning of a person to ascertain facts.

*Issue (In Courtroom Setting or Controversy): A certain point of law or fact which is in dispute.

*Judge (Trial Judge): The presiding officer in a trial whose duty it is to see that a fair, impartial, and orderly trial is conducted, adhering to the Constitution of the United States, the Constitution of the State (if state jurisdiction), the laws of the court's jurisdiction and the rules of the court. The judge is an impartial arbiter who rules on the admissibility of evidence and motions of various types and instructs the fact triers as to the law of the case. Some jurisdictions give judges the title of "Justice."

*Judgment: The final determination of the rights of parties to a lawsuit, whether civil or criminal, which determination is made by a judge or panel of judges, and which is entered in the clerk's records of the case.

Judgment Non Obstante Veredicto: See N.O.V.

Judicial Admissions: Judicial admissions are those made in court by a person's attorney for the purpose of being used as a substitute for the regular legal evidence of the facts at the trial. A formal waiver of proof that relieves opposing party from making proof of admitted fact and bars party who made admission from disputing it. E-Tex Dairy Queen, Inc. v. Adair, Tex.Civ.App., 566 S.W.2d 37, 39.

Judicial Notice: The act by which a court, in conducting a trial, or framing its decision, will, of its own motion or on request of a party, and without the production of evidence, recognize the existence and truth of certain facts, having a bearing on the controversy at bar, which, from their nature, are not properly the subject of testimony, or which are universally regarded as established by common notoriety, e.g., the laws of the state, international law, historical events, the constitution and course of nature, main geographical features, etc.

Jurisdiction: It is the power of the court to decide a matter in controversy and presupposes the existence of a duly constituted court with control over the subject matter and the parties. Pinner v. Pinner, 33 N.C.App. 204, 234 S.E.2d 633. Jurisdiction defines the powers of courts to inquire into facts, apply the law, make decisions, and declare judgment. Police Com'r of Boston v. Municipal Court of Dorchester Dist., 374 Mass. 640, 374 N.E.2d 272, 285.

Jurisprudence: The philosophy of law, or the science which treats the principles of positive law and legal relations. . . . [W]hen a new or doubtful case arises to which two different rules seem, when taken literally, to be equally applicable, it may be, and often is, the function of jurisprudence to consider the ultimate effect which would be produced if each rule were applied to an indefinite number of similar cases, and to choose that rule which, when so applied, will produce the greatest advantage to the community.

Jury: A certain number of men and women selected according to law, and sworn (jurati) to inquire of certain matters of fact, and declare the truth upon evidence to be laid before them. . . . A jury is a body of persons temporarily selected from the citizens of a particular district, and invested with power to present or indict a person for a public offense, or to try a question of fact.

*Jury Charge (Judge's Charge to Jury): At the end of the testimony of a jury trial, each side indicates that it "rests." Thereupon it is the duty of the trial judge to explain the law of the case to the jury before it goes to the deliberation room. This is called "the Judge's Charge."

Laches: "Doctrine of laches," is based upon maxim that equity aids the vigilant and not those who slumber on their rights. It is defined as neglect to assert a right or claim which, taken together with lapse of time and other circumstances causing prejudice to adverse party, operates as bar in court of equity. Wooded Shores Property Owners Ass'n, Inc. v. Mathews, 37 Ill.App. 3d 334, 345 N.E.2d 186, 189. . . . [N]eglect or omission to do what one should do as warrants presumption that one has abandoned right or claim. Eldridge v. Idaho State Penitentiary, 54 Idaho 213, 30 P.2d 781, 784. . . .

Lay Witness: Person called to give testimony who does not possess any expertise in the matters about which he testifies.

Leading Question: One which instructs witness how to answer or puts into his mouth words to be echoed back, People v. Hamilton, Gen.Sess., 30 N.Y.S.2d 155, 158. . . . Leading questions are usually deemed improper on the direct examination of a witness except as may be necessary to develop the witnesses' testimony. Ordinarily leading questions are permitted on cross-examination.

Legal Evidence: A broad general term meaning all admissible evidence, including both oral and documentary, but with a further implication that it must be of such a character as tends reasonably and substantially to prove the point, not to raise a mere suspicion or conjecture.

*Lesser Included Offense: A crime or violation of law which is part of a more serious crime. A crime having less aggravating elements than a more serious crime which carries greater sanctions (punishment), e.g., larceny is a lesser included offense of robbery.

Libel: A method of defamation expressed by print, writing, pictures, or signs. In its most general sense, any publication that is injurious to the reputation of another.

*Lineup: A procedure where law enforcement officers select a number of persons to stand or sit next to each other to be viewed by witnesses or victims of crime to ascertain whether any or all of the selected persons committed a criminal offense. This is usually done before a one-way mirror with a suspect's attorney present and the proceedings are recorded.

Litigant: A party to a lawsuit (i.e. plaintiff or defendant); one engaged in litigation. . . .

*Litigation: A controversy between parties which is brought to a court for determination of the issues.

*Magistrate: A judicial officer authorized to conduct preliminary hearings, set bail conditions, administer oaths, and issue warrants. Most jurisdictions do not authorize magistrates to conduct trials of criminal offenses. A judge may also be a magistrate.

*Malum in Se: Bad in itself; naturally evil, e.g., murder.

*Malum Prohibitum: Bad or wrong because it is made unlawful by statute, e.g., driving a vehicle on the wrong side of the street.

*Mandamus Writ: A court order wherein the court orders a designated person (governmental official or corporate officer) to perform a designated act.

Material: Important; more or less necessary; having influence or effect; going to the merits; having to do with matter, as distinguished from form.

Material Evidence: That quality of evidence which tends to influence the trier of fact because of its logical connection with the issue. Evidence which has an effective influence or bearing on question in issue. Barr v. Dolphin Holding Corp., Sup., 141 N.Y.S.2d 906, 908.

Material Fact: One which is essential to the case, defense, application, etc., and without which it could not be supported. One which tends to establish any of issues raised.

*Mens Rea: A mental state required in criminal law; intention; criminal negligence (gross); reckless and/or knowing.

***Miranda* Rule:** Prior to any custodial interrogation (that is, questioning initiated by law enforcement officers after a person is taken into custody or otherwise deprived of his freedom in any significant way) the person must be warned: 1. That he has a right to remain silent; 2. That any statement he does make may be used as evidence against him; 3. That he has a right to the presence of an attorney; 4. That if he cannot afford an attorney, one will be appointed for him prior to any questioning if he so desires.

*Misdemeanor: A class of criminal deviance which is usually punished by a maximum of $1,000 fine and/or up to one year in a county or city jail. It is less serious than a felony. Different jurisdictions classify misdemeanors and sanctions for violation thereof differently.

*Mistrial: Where a prejudicial error occurs, a judge, on motion or sua sponte, may declare a mistrial. This has the effect of declaring the trial a nullity and does not preclude another trial of the same parties on the same facts. It is not a ground for a defense of double jeopardy.

*Motion: An application to a judge or panel of judges requesting the relief desired, e.g., motion for a new trial.

Motive: Cause or reason that moves the will and induces action. . . . The circumstance tending to establish the requisite mens rea for a criminal act and is the inducement which impels or leads the mind to indulge in a criminal act. State v. Segotta, App., 100 N.M. 18, 665 P.2d 280, 287.

Negative Evidence: Testimony that an alleged fact did not exist.

Negligence: The omission to do something which a reasonable man, guided by those ordinary considerations which ordinarily regulate human affairs, would do, or the doing of something which a reasonable and prudent man would not do.

*Nisi Prius: In American law it has come to mean any court where a case is heard by a judge and jury for the first time. An appellate court is not a nisi prius court.

*Nolo Contendere: From the Latin and common law courts where a defendant tells the court that he/she does not wish to interpose a defense or plea of not guilty in a criminal action. Some state courts do not permit a defendant to answer a charge in this way. The court must find a factual basis to accept this. It is not a confession of guilt. In criminal law it has the same effect as a plea of guilty.

*N.O.V.: From the Latin—Non Obstante Veredicto. A motion for a judgment N.O.V., if granted, is one which reverses the conclusions reached by a jury because the court reasoned that based on the facts presented in the trial, the jury had no reasonable grounds to reach the conclusion indicated in its verdict.

Nuisance: That which annoys and disturbs one in possession of his property, rendering its ordinary use or occupation physically uncomfortable to him; e.g. smoke, odors, noise, or vibration. Patton v. Westwood Country Club Co., 18 Ohio App.2d 137, 247 N.E.2d 761, 763, 47 O.O.2d 247.

*Nunc pro Tunc: If a court order includes this phrase, it means that the action ordered to be taken reverts back to a specified time as if it had been taken at that time. It is frequently used to permit late filing of papers when it is in the interest of justice to permit such late filing.

Oath: An affirmation of truth of a statement, which renders one willfully asserting untrue statements punishable for perjury.

*Obiter Dicta: *See* dictum.

Objection: The act of a party who objects to some matter or proceeding in the course of a trial, or an argument or reason urged by him in support of his contention that the matter or proceeding objected to is improper or illegal. Used to call the court's attention to improper evidence or procedure.

Offer of Proof: At a trial or hearing, when an objection to a question has been sustained, the party aggrieved by the ruling may indicate for the record (out of the presence of the jury) the answer which would have been given if the question had not been excluded.

*Opening Statement: This is a speech which the adversaries in a criminal trial make to the jury before any testimony is received in evidence. It is used to acquaint the jury with the facts and issues of a case which that litigant intends to prove. In criminal cases, many jurisdictions permit a defendant to waive a right to an opening statement.

*Opinion: The reason that a judge gives for the court's conclusion. It differs from a decision which is the judgment of the court.

Opinion Evidence or Testimony: Evidence of what the witness thinks, believes, or infers in regard to facts in dispute, as distinguished from his personal knowledge of the facts themselves. The rules of evidence ordinarily do not permit witnesses to testify as to opinions or conclusions.

Overrule: To supersede; annul; reverse; make void; reject by subsequent action or decision. A judicial decision is said to be overruled when a later decision, rendered by the same court or by a superior court in the same system, expresses a judgment upon the same question of law directly opposite to that which was before given, thereby depriving the earlier opinion of all authority as a precedent.

*Oyer and Terminer: These were old English courts where the King would appoint a person to act as a judge to hear and determine a case forthwith, instead of waiting for the normal judicial procedure of the realm to prosecute, hear, and determine a criminal case.

*Pardon: A power to forgive vested in the executive of the government, i.e., President, Governor. Its effect is to restore all rights to the defendant as if the defendant had never committed the criminal act for which s/he was pardoned.

*Parole: This may be descriptive of a discretionary decision of an official or board of parole who has lawful authority to permit a prisoner to serve part of his/her sentence in the community. One who is on parole is serving part of the imposed sentence outside of confinement and in the community.

Parol Evidence: Oral or verbal evidence; that which is given by word of mouth; the ordinary kind of evidence given by witnesses in court. In a particular sense, and with reference to contracts, deeds, wills, and other writings, parol evidence is the same as extraneous evidence. . . .

Party: A "party" to an action is a person whose name is designated on record as plaintiff or defendant. M & A Elec. Power Co-op. v. True, Mo.App., 480 S.W.2d 310, 314.

Pedigree: Lineage, descent, and succession of families . . . genealogy. . . . The "pedigree exception" to hearsay rule allows consideration of hearsay evidence regarding a person's family relationship as proof of existence of the relationship. Smith v. Givens, 223 Va. 455, 290 S.E.2d 844, 846.

People: A state; as the people of the state of New York. A nation in its collective and political capacity. The aggregate or mass of the individuals who constitute the state. Loi Hoa v. Nagle, C.C.A.Cal., 13 F.2d 80, 81.

*Perjury: A criminal offense where a person makes a false statement while under oath or affirmation.

*Petition: A written request made to a court or governmental authority asking for an act to be done; sometimes referred to as a prayer for relief.

Petitioner: One who presents a petition to a court, officer, or legislative body. The one who starts an equity proceeding or the one who takes an appeal from a judgment.

Petit Jury: The ordinary jury for the trial of a civil or criminal action; so called to distinguish it from the grand jury.

Plaintiff: A person who brings an action; the party who complains or sues in a civil action and is so named on the record. . . . The prosecution (i.e. State or United States) in a criminal case.

*Plain View: This phrase is applied to items of evidence which a law enforcement officer sees without having violated a person's constitutional rights and which s/he came upon inadvertently while performing normal duties.

*Plea: This is a formal answer to a charge against a defendant for a criminal offense, e.g., guilty, not guilty.

*Plea Bargaining: This is a negotiation procedure where the criminal defendant's attorney discusses a possibility of the defendant's pleading guilty to a lesser included offense in return for the prosecutor's either not recommending a severe sanction or not proceeding to trial on the original charge.

*Police Power: The power of the government to provide for the health, welfare, safety, morals, and general welfare of those persons within its territorial jurisdiction.

Polygraph: Also known as a lie detector, it is an electro-mechanical instrument used to determine whether an examinee is truthfully answering questions. It simultaneously measures and records certain physiological changes in the human body which it is believed are involuntarily caused by an examinee's conscious attempt to deceive an interrogator. U.S. v. DeBetham, D.C.Cal., 348 F.Supp. 1377, 1384.

Positive Evidence: Direct evidence. Eye witness testimony. Direct proof of the fact or point in issues; evidence which, if believed, establishes the truth or falsehood of a fact in issue, and does not arise from any presumption.

*Preamble: A statement of purpose and intent which precedes the specific articles and sections of a constitution.

Precedent: An adjudged case or decision of a court, considered as furnishing an example or authority for an identical or similar case afterwards arising or a similar question of law. Courts attempt to decide cases on the basis of principles established in prior cases.

Prejudicial Error: One which affects or presumptively affects the final results of the trial. State v. Gilcrist, 15 Wash.App. 892, 552 P.2d 690, 693.

Such may be ground for new trial and reversal of judgment. Fed.R.Civil P. 59.

*Preliminary Hearing: Usually a hearing held before a magistrate to determine if probable cause exists to hold a defendant for a trial or indictment. Bail conditions are sometimes set at the end of this hearing.

Preponderance of Evidence: As standard of proof in civil cases, is evidence which is of greater weight or more convincing than the evidence which is offered in opposition to it; that is, evidence which as a whole shows that the fact sought to be proved is more probable than not. Braud v. Kinchen, La.App., 310 So.2d 657, 659.

*Presentment: An investigation and accusation of crime made by a Grand Jury, initiated by itself without the participation of the prosecutor. A prosecutor has the discretion not to sign a presentment and not to prosecute the accusation.

Presumption: A presumption is an assumption of fact that the law requires to be made from another fact or group of facts found or otherwise established in the action. A presumption is not evidence. A presumption is either conclusive or rebuttable.

Presumptions of Fact: Such are presumptions which do not compel a finding of the presumed fact but which warrant one when the basic fact has been proved.

Presumptions of Law: A presumption of law is one which, once the basic fact is proved and no evidence to the contrary has been introduced, compels a finding of the existence of the presumed fact. The presumption of law is rebuttable and in most cases the adversary introduces evidence designed to overcome it.

*Prima Facie: If on the facts presented, unexplained, a defendant might be found guilty of a criminal offense in that all of the elements of a crime have been shown to exist, we say that the prosecution has proved a prima facie case.

Prima Facie Evidence: Evidence good and sufficient on its face. Such evidence as, in the judgment of the law, is sufficient to establish a given fact, or the group or chain of facts constituting the party's claim or defense, and which if not rebutted or contradicted, will remain sufficient.

Primary Evidence: Primary evidence means original or first-hand evidence; the best evidence that the nature of the case admits of; the evidence which is required in the first instance, and which must fail before secondary evidence can be admitted.

Principal: The term "principal" describes one who has permitted or directed another (i.e. agent or servant) to act for his benefit and subject to his direction and control, such that the acts of the agent become binding on the principal.

*Prison: This is a place where criminal defendants of the state or federal courts are incarcerated, usually after they have been found guilty. A jail is the term applied to City or County places of incarceration, usually used for detention while awaiting trial or incarceration for less serious offenses.

Private Bill (Statute): Legislation for the special benefit of an individual or a locality.

Privileged Communications: Those statements made by certain persons within a protected relationship such as husband-wife, attorney-client, priest-penitent and the like which the law protects from forced disclosure on the witness stand at the option of the witness, client, penitent, spouse.

*Probable Cause: The reasoning process that a reasonable person uses to conclude that (a) there is a good reason to make an arrest, and (b) there is a good reason to suspect that a person has contraband or evidence of crime in the suspect's possession.

*Probation: A sanction imposed on those convicted of a crime wherein the offender is subject to conditions of behavior laid down by the judge. The defendant may be under the supervision of a probation officer to whom s/he must periodically report, or may be on a nonreporting status.

*Pro Bono Publico: When attorneys represent a client without fee it is said that the representation is pro bono publico, i.e., for the public good.

Proof: Any fact or circumstance which leads the mind to the affirmative or negative of any proposition. The conviction or persuasion of the mind of a judge or jury, by the exhibition of evidence, of the reality of a fact alleged. Ellis v. Wolfe-Shoemaker Motor Co., 227 Mo.App. 508, 55 S.W.2d 309.

*Pro Se: For himself. Refers to a person arguing his/her own case instead of retaining an attorney.

Prosecution: A criminal action; a proceeding instituted and carried on by due course of law, before a competent tribunal, for the purpose of determining the guilt or innocence of a person charged with crime. U.S. v. Reisinger, 128 U.S. 398, 9 S.Ct. 99, 32 L.Ed. 480. . . . By an extension of its meaning, "prosecution" is also used to designate the government (state or federal) as the party proceeding in a criminal action, or the prosecutor, or counsel. . . .

Proximate Cause: That which stands next in causation to the effect, not necessarily in time or space but in causal relation. The proximate cause of an injury is the primary or moving cause, or that which, in a natural and continuous sequence, unbroken by an efficient intervening cause, produces the injury and without which the accident could not have happened, if the injury be one which might be reasonably anticipated or foreseen as a natural consequence of the wrongful act.

Public Document: A state paper, or other instrument of public importance or interest, issued or published by authority of congress or a state legislature. Also any document or record, evidencing or connected with the public business or the administration of public affairs, preserved in or issued by any department of the government. . . . Broadly any document open to public inspection.

Public Record: Public records are those records which a governmental unit is required by law to keep or which it is necessary to keep in discharge of duties imposed by law; e.g. records of land transactions kept at county court house; records of court cases kept by clerk of court. Curran v. Board of Park Com'rs, Lake County Metropolitan Park Dist., Com.Pl., 22 Ohio Misc. 197, 259 N.E.2d 757, 759, 51 O.O.2d 321.

*Quasi: Almost; like; e.g., quasi-criminal proceeding which is almost like a criminal proceeding but not actually one; e.g., a parole revocation proceeding.

*Question of Fact: An issue of what actually occurred at the time of the incident which brings the parties before the court. This issue is decided by a jury if the trial is one with a jury. If no jury is present, it is decided by the judge.

*Question of Law: A dispute of what rule of law is applicable to the case at bar. The judge decides the issue of what rule of law is to determine the results in the instant case.

*Quid pro Quo: Something in exchange for something, e.g., a witness may testify in behalf of the prosecution if the state will grant immunity from prosecution to the witness.

*Quo Warranto: By what authority. This is an ancient common law writ.

Real Evidence: Evidence furnished by things themselves, on view or inspection, as distinguished from a description of them by the mouth of a witness. . . .

*Reasonable Doubt: Refers to the quantum of proof required to prove a defendant guilty in a criminal trial. The trier of the facts is required to come to the conclusion that a defendant is guilty beyond a reasonable doubt. This does not mean all doubt, but beyond the doubt that a reasonable person would have.

*Reasonable Man (Person): This is a phrase which characterizes what a normal, average person with ordinary knowledge, intelligence, and judgment might do in a given set of circumstances. It is not necessarily what the particular judge hearing or reviewing the case might do but what a hypothetical normal person's actions might be, given the same factual situation.

Rebuttable Presumption: In the law of evidence, a presumption which may be rebutted by evidence.

Record: A written account of some act, court proceeding, transaction, or instrument, drawn up, under authority of law, by a proper officer, and designed to remain as a memorial or permanent evidence of the matters to which it relates. People ex rel. Simons v. Dowling, 84 Misc. 201, 146 N.Y.S. 919, 920.

Recross Examination: An examination of a witness by a cross-examiner subsequent to a redirect examination of the witness.

Redirect Examination: An examination of a witness by the direct examiner subsequent to the cross-examination of the witness.

Relevancy: Applicability to the issue joined. That quality of evidence which renders it properly applicable in determining the truth and falsity of the matters in issue between the parties to a suit.

Relevant Evidence: Evidence tending to prove or disprove an alleged fact. Evidence having any tendency to make the existence of any fact that is of consequence to the determination of the action more probable or less probable than it would be without the evidence. Fed.Evid.R. 401.

*Remand: To send back. Sometimes refers to a case being sent back to the court which decided it previously. Also refers to a prisoner being sent back to a prison or detention facility.

Remedy: The means by which a right is enforced or the violation of a right is prevented, redressed, or compensated. Long Leaf Lumber, Inc. v. Svolos, La.App., 258 So.2d 121, 124.

Remoteness: Want of close connection between a wrong and the injury which prevents the party injured from claiming compensation from the wrongdoer.

Reputation: Estimation in which one is held; the character imputed to a person by those acquainted with him. . . . It is necessarily based upon hearsay, Stewart v. State, 148 Tex.Cr.R. 480, 188 S.W.2d 167, 170, but may be admissible if falling within the established exceptions to the hearsay rule.

Res Gestae: "Res gestae" means literally things or things happened and therefore, to be admissible as exception to hearsay rule, words spoken, thoughts expressed, and gestures made, must all be so closely connected to occurrence or event

in both time and substance as to be a part of the happening. McCandless v. Inland Northwest Film Service, Inc., 64 Wash.2d 523, 392 P.2d 613, 618. . . . A spontaneous declaration made by a person immediately after an event and before the mind has an opportunity to conjure a falsehood.

Res Ipsa Loquitur: The thing speaks for itself. Rebuttable presumption or inference that defendant was negligent, which arises upon proof that instrumentality causing injury was in defendant's exclusive control, and that the accident was one which ordinarily does not happen in the absence of negligence.

*Res Judicata (Res Adjudicata): The thing decided. The issue has previously been decided by a court of competent jurisdiction and thus is not to be relitigated.

Reverse: To overthrow, vacate, set aside, make void, annul, repeal, or revoke; as, to reverse a judgment, sentence or decree of a lower court by an appellate court, or to change to the contrary or to a former condition. Department of Water and Power of City of Los Angeles v. Inyo Chemical Co., Cal.App., 100 P.2d 822, 826.

*Reversible Error: An error committed at the trial which substantially affected the outcome of the trial, that mandates either a new trial or a reversal of the outcome. Also known as "substantial error" or "prejudicial error."

*Revocation: Term used in connection with revocation of parole. It means that the parolee is returned to prison, usually to serve the remainder of his/her original sentence of incarceration.

Ruling: A judicial or administrative interpretation of a provision of a statute, order, regulation, or ordinance. . . . May also refer to judicial determination of admissibility of evidence, allowance of motion, etc.

*Sanction: To permit one to do something. Also used to indicate punishment for violation of accepted behavior.

*Search Warrant: A court order directing a law enforcement officer to search for and return to the court particular items of personal property to be used in the prosecution of a person for violation of a statute.

Secondary Evidence: That which is inferior to primary or best evidence. Thus, a copy of an instrument, or oral evidence of its contents, is secondary evidence of the instrument and contents. It is that species of evidence which becomes admissible, when the primary or best evidence of the fact in question is lost or inaccessible. . . .

*Selective Incorporation: This term has been used to indicate that the United States Supreme Court has absorbed most of the Bill of Rights into the minimum requirements that a state must afford to inhabitants but not every one of these rights. This has been done by the authority of the Fourteenth Amendment of the United States Constitution.

Self-Incrimination: Acts or declarations either as testimony at trial or prior to trial by which one implicates himself in a crime.

Self Serving Declaration: A species of hearsay evidence consisting of an extrajudicial declaration by a party to an action, the import of which is to prove an essential element of his case. . . . Statement, oral or written, or equivalent act, by or on behalf of a party which if admitted would constitute evidence in his favor. Werdell v. Turzynski, 128 Ill.App.2d 139, 262 N.E.2d 833, 838.

Servant: An employee.

Severance: Act of severing, or state of being severed; partition; separation; e.g. a claim against a party may be severed and proceeded with separately. Fed.R.Civil P. 21. Separation of cases so that they can be tried separately.

Shop-Book Rule: An exception to the hearsay evidence rule, permitting the introduction in evidence of books of original entry made in the usual course of business, and introduced by one with custody of them, and upon general authentication. Clayton v. Metropolitan Life Ins. Co., 96 Utah 331, 85 P.2d 819, 822; Fed.Evid.R. 803(6), (7); 28 U.S.C.A. 1732.

*Show-up: This is to be distinguished from a lineup. In a show-up the suspect is exhibited singularly to a crime victim. This is usually done shortly after the crime has taken place where speed and the practicalities of the situation warrant this type of identification instead of a lineup.

Sixth Amendment: The Sixth Amendment of the U.S. Constitution includes such rights as the right to speedy and public trial by an impartial jury, right to be informed of the nature of the accusation, the right to confront witnesses, the right to assistance of counsel and compulsory process.

Slander: Oral defamation; the speaking of false and malicious words concerning another, whereby injury results to his reputation. Lloyd v. Commissioner of Internal Revenue, C.C.A.7, 55 F.2d 842, 844.

Spectrograph: Voice print analysis is a method of identification based on the comparison of graphic representations or "spectrograms" made of human voices. Such method utilizes a machine known as a "spectrograph" which separates the sound of human voices into the three component elements of time, frequency and intensity.

Spontaneous Declarations: A statement is admissible as a "spontaneous declaration" if there was an occurrence sufficiently startling to produce a spontaneous and unreflecting statement, if there was an absence of time to fabricate, and if the statement related to the circumstances of the occurrence. People v. Was, 22 Ill.App.3d 859, 318 N.E.2d 309, 313.

*Standing: A court's recognition of a party to a lawsuit that the party is properly before the court.

*Star Chamber: An ancient English court whose jurisdiction and procedure became so onerous that it was abolished. The privilege against self-incrimination in America resulted from Star Chamber abuses.

*Stare Decisis: To stand by decided cases; to decide cases based on precedent of what the courts have decided on similar issues in earlier cases.

Statutory Law: That body of law created by acts of the legislature in contrast to constitutional law and law generated by decisions of courts and administrative bodies.

Statutory Presumption: A presumption, either rebuttable or conclusive, which is created by statute in contrast to a common law presumption. . . .

*Stop and Frisk: Refers to law enforcement's authority to stops a suspected person and pat that person's outer clothing to search for a concealed weapon. The officer must have reason to believe that the suspect is armed and dangerous.

Sua Sponte: Of his or its own will or motion; voluntarily; without prompting or suggestion.

Suborn: To prepare, provide, or procure especially in a secret or underhand manner. United States v. Silverman, C.C.A.Pa., 106 F.2d 750, 751.

Subpoena: A subpoena is a command to appear at a certain time and place to give testimony upon a certain matter.

Subrogee: A person who is subrogated; one who succeeds to the rights of another by subrogation.

Substantial Evidence Rule: Such evidence that a reasonable mind might accept as adequate to support a conclusion. It is that quality of evidence necessary for a court to affirm a decision of an administrative board [or hearing officer].

Sufficiency of Evidence: Term refers to test prescribed by rule providing that grand jury ought to find an indictment when all the evidence taken together, if unexplained or uncontradicted, would warrant a conviction by the trier of the offense. State v. Parks, Alaska, 437 P.2d 642, 644.

Summary Judgment: Procedural device available for prompt and expeditious disposition of controversy without trial when there is no dispute as to either material fact or inferences to be drawn from undisputed facts, or if only question of law is involved. American State Bank of Killdeer v. Hewson, N.D., 411 N.W.2d 57, 60.

*Suppression of Evidence: When evidence is unconstitutionally obtained by law enforcement authorities, the defendant makes a motion to suppress this evidence. After a hearing before a judge, the judge will indicate that the motion is granted. This means that the prosecutor is not permitted to use the unconstitutionally obtained evidence in the trial of this defendant. Often the prosecutor is unable to proceed with the case without this evidence.

Supra: Above; upon. This word occurring by itself in a book refers the reader to a previous part of the book. . . .

Sustain: To affirm, uphold or approve, as when an appellate court sustains the decision of a lower court. To grant, as when a judge sustains an objection to testimony or evidence, he or she agrees with the objection and gives it effect.

Tenth Amendment: An amendment to the U.S. Constitution (1791) which provides that the powers not delegated to the federal government are reserved to the States or to the people.

Testator(-trix): One who makes or has made a testament or will; one who dies leaving a will.

Testimonial Evidence: Evidence elicited from a witness in contrast to documentary or real evidence.

Testimony: Evidence given by a competent witness under oath or affirmation; as distinguished from evidence derived from writings, and other sources. . . . Testimony properly means only such evidence as is delivered by a witness on the trial of a cause, either orally or in the form of affidavits or depositions.

Third Party Action: A proceeding distinct from the main action. It is in the nature of an indemnity or contribution, the purpose of which is to bring into the lawsuit a party who is or may be liable to defendant for all or part of plaintiff's claim against defendant. Howard v. Ward County, D.C.N.D., 418 F.Supp. 494, 507.

Tort: A private or civil wrong or injury, including action for bad faith breach of contract, for which the court will provide a remedy in the form of an action for damages. K Mart Corp. v. Ponsock, 103 Nev. 39, 732 P.2d 1364, 1368. . . . It may be either (1) a direct invasion of some legal right of the individual; (2) infraction of some public duty by which special damage accrues to the individual; (3) the violation of some private obligation by which like damage accrues to the individual.

*Trial: The legal proceeding where testimony is offered before a judge sitting without a jury, or a judge sitting with a jury, where issues of fact and law are determined.

Trier of fact: Term includes (a) the jury and (b) the court when the court is trying an issue of fact other than one relating to the admissibility of evidence. Calif.Evid.Code. . . . Also may refer to hearing officer or judge in administrative proceeding.

*True Bill: A Grand Jury finding that an indictment presented to it by the prosecutor is based on sufficient probable cause. The foreman then signs the indictment and it becomes a true bill.

Ultimate Facts: Facts which are necessary to determine issues in case, as distinguished from evidentiary facts supporting them. O'Shea v. Hatch, App., 97 N.M. 409, 640 P.2d 515, 520. Final facts required to establish plaintiff's cause of action of defendant's defense. Williams v. Pilot Life Ins. Co., 288 N.C. 338, 218 S.E.2d 368, 371.

Unclean Hands Doctrine: Principle that one who has unclean hands is not entitled to relief in equity. Doctrine means no more than that one who has defrauded his adversary in the subject matter of the action will not be heard to assert right in equity.

*Vacate: To make void; to set aside as though it never existed; to move out.

Verbal Acts: Situations in which legal consequences flow from the fact that words were said, e.g. the words of offer and acceptance which create a contract, or words of slander upon which an action for damages is based. The rule against hearsay does not apply to proof of relevant verbal acts because evidence of such acts is being offered to prove something other than the truth of an out of court assertion.

*Verdict: The conclusion reached by a jury or judge deciding the facts as to the issues after the completion of other parts of a trial.

Voir Dire: To speak the truth. This phrase denotes the preliminary examination which the court and attorneys make of prospective jurors to determine their qualification and suitability to serve as jurors. [Also used to question proposed expert witness as to expert's qualifications.]

*Waiver: A voluntary giving up of a known right, e.g., a waiver of jury trial wherein the defendant in a criminal action intentionally gives up his/her right to be tried by a jury.

*Warrant (Criminal Law): A court order directing a law enforcement officer to perform an indicated act, e.g., search warrant, arrest warrant.

Weight: A measure of heaviness or ponderosity; and in a metaphorical sense influence, effectiveness, or power to influence judgment or conduct.

Witness: In general, one who, being present, personally sees or perceives a thing; a beholder, spectator, or eyewitness. One who is called to testify before a court. People v. Ruiz, 100 Misc.2d 562, 419 N.Y.S.2d 864, 866.

*Writ: A court order directing a named person to perform a specifically indicated act.

Wrongful Death Action: Type of lawsuit brought on behalf of a deceased person's beneficiaries that alleges that death was attributable to the willful or negligent act of another.

APPENDIX C

Answers to Practice Questions

Chapter 1:
1. F (§1.4)
2. T (§1.5)
3. F (§1.3)
4. F (§1.4)
5. T (§1.5)
6. (c) (§1.7)
7. (b) (§1.2)

Chapter 2:
1. F (§2.1)
2. T (§2.1)
3. F (§2.6)
4. T (§2.17)
5. F (§2.17)
6. (b) (§2.15)
7. (a) (§2.19)

Chapter 3:
1. (a) (§3.6)
2. (b) (§3.3)
3. (c) (§3.12)
4. (a) (§3.27)
5. (c) (§3.1)
6. F (§3.10)
7. F (§3.8)

Chapter 4:
1. (b) (§4.16)
2. (d) (§4.11)
3. (b) (§4.3)
4. (d) (§4.4)
5. (b) (§4.32)
6. T (§4.33)
7. F (§4.3)

Chapter 5:
1. (d) (§5.2)
2. (a) (§5.4)
3. (c) (§5.8)

4. (c) (§5.12)
5. (c) (§5.11)
6. F (§5.7)
7. T (§5.3)

Chapter 6:
1. (c) (§6.1)
2. (a) (§6.5)
3. (d) (§6.1)
4. F (§6.8)
5. F (§6.17)
6. T (§§3.27, 6.22)
7. T (§6.21)

Chapter 7:
1. (d) (§7.1)
2. (a) (§7.3)
3. (b) (§7.16)
4. (b) (§§7.11, 7.13)
5. (a) (§§7.8, 7.9)
6. F (§7.1)
7. F (§7.2)

Chapter 8:
1. (c) (§8.6)
2. (d) (§8.10)
3. (a) (§8.4)
4. (d) (§8.4)
5. F (§8.7)
6. T (§8.7)
7. T (§8.11)

Chapter 9:
1. (c) (§9.5(c))
2. (a) (§9.9)
3. T (§9.1)
4. T (§9.6)
5. F (§9.7)
6. T (§9.5(c))
7. T (§9.8)

Chapter 10:
1. (c) (§§ 10.11, 10.19)
2. (c) (§ 10.8)
3. (b) (§ 10.9)
4. (a) (§ 10.15)
5. (c) (§ 10.4)
6. T (§ 10.14)
7. T (§ 10.19)

Chapter 11:
1. (c) (§ 11.3)
2. (a) (§ 11.5)
3. T (§ 11.1)
4. F (§ 11.2)
5. T (§ 11.7)
6. F (§ 11.6)
7. T (§ 11.1)

Chapter 12:
1. T (§ 12.7)
2. T (§ 12.8)
3. F (§ 12.9)
4. T (§ 12.10)
5. F (§ 12.15)
6. (a) (§ 12.16)
7. (a) (§ 12.13)

Chapter 13:
1. T (§ 13.3)
2. T (§ 13.4)
3. F (§ 13.3)
4. F (§ 13.2)
5. T (§§ 13.2, 13.6)
6. (d) (§ 13.8)
7. (a) (§ 13.2)

Chapter 14:
1. T (§ 14.1)
2. T (§ 14.8)
3. F (§ 14.9)
4. T (§ 14.6)
5. T (§ 14.3)
6. (b) (§ 14.1)
7. (a) (§§ 14.1, 14.4)

Chapter 15:
1. F (§ 15.15)
2. F (§ 15.4—not in all jurisdictions)

3. F (§ 15.5)
4. T (§ 15.3)
5. F (§ 15.11—certified copy must be compared with an original to be admissible in evidence.)
6. (b) (§ 15.1)
7. (a) (§ 15.6)

Chapter 16:
1. F (§ 16.8)
2. T (§ 16.10)
3. (c) (§ 16.3)
4. (b) (§ 16.5)
5. (d) (§ 16.19)
6. F (§ 16.9)
7. F (§ 16.16)

Chapter 17:
1. T (§ 17.21)
2. T (§ 17.19)
3. T (§ 17.20)
4. F (§ 17.17)
5. T (§ 17.17—should have a judicial determination of death)
6. (b) (§ 17.23)
7. (a) (§ 17.1)

Chapter 18:
1. T (§ 18.4—Perhaps the taxi company dispatcher gave the defendant permission, but he had no authority from the registered owner to give permission to the defendant.)
2. T (§ 18.18)
3. T (§ 18.17)
4. T (§ 18.17)
5. F (§ 18.16)
6. (b) (§ 18.13)
7. (a) (§ 18.1)

Chapter 19:
1. T (§ 19.11)
2. F (§ 19.11)
3. T (§ 19.9)
4. T (§ 19.11—Amendment XIV, Section 1)
5. T (§ 19.14)
6. F (§ 19.16)
7. F (§ 19.17—item 10)

■ TABLE OF CASES

The principal cases are in italic type. Cases cited or discussed are in roman type. References are to pages. Cases cited in principal cases and within other quoted materials are not included.

■ INDEX

ISBN 0-314-20077-0

90000